150

The Real Abraham Lincoln

Also by Reinhard H. Luthin

THE FIRST LINCOLN CAMPAIGN

AMERICAN DEMAGOGUES: TWENTIETH CENTURY

LINCOLN AND THE PATRONAGE
In Collaboration with Dean Emeritus Harry J. Carman of Columbia College, Columbia University

The Real Abraham Lincoln

A COMPLETE ONE VOLUME HISTORY OF HIS LIFE AND TIMES

REINHARD H. LUTHIN

PRENTICE-HALL, INC. ENGLEWOOD CLIFFS, NEW JERSEY

LIBRARY OF CONGRESS CATALOG CARD NUMBER 60-13048

PRINTED IN THE UNITED STATES OF AMERICA

76216-T

To the memory of my sister

CLOTILDE LUTHIN

Acknowledgments

ABOVE all I want to express my gratitude to my sisters, Mrs. Hildegard Luthin Stone, of New York, and the late Miss Clotilde Luthin, for their long and constant insistence, over the years, that I endeavor to write a comprehensive book on the man who is regarded by millions throughout the world as the greatest human ever produced by our country.

My friend and editor at Prentice-Hall, Mr. David Legerman, has provided valuable literary counsel and contributed severe but constructive criticism far beyond the call of his professional editorial duty. Mr. Legerman's labor on this manuscript, and his unwavering confidence that this book was somewhat different from other works on the Civil War President, proved a source of deep satisfaction.

My former teachers of history and erstwhile academic colleagues at Columbia University, Dean Emeritus Harry J. Carman (my co-author of *Lincoln and the Patronage*) and Professor Emeritus Allan Nevins, dean of American historians, have for more than a quarter of a century vastly contributed to my knowledge of the American past. My former colleagues and present friends at Trinity College, Hartford, Connecticut, Professor D. G. Brinton Thompson, Professor George B. Cooper, II, and Dean Robert M. Vogel, have continually inspired me to finish this lengthy volume of the life and times of Lincoln, and have also contributed rich suggestions on the form that the book should assume. Professor Ollinger Crenshaw of Washington and Lee University, Lexington, Virginia; Professor

Emeritus Charles C. Tansill of Georgetown University, Washington, D.C.; Professor Robert A. East of Brooklyn College, Brooklyn, New York,—all have given freely of their profound knowledge of bibliography and sources. The late Professor William K. Boyd, my teacher in the Graduate School of History at Duke University, Durham, North Carolina, was the first instructor to make me realize that the Civil War can not possibly be understood unless the history of three sections, the North, the border slave states, and the South, are studied in relation to each other. That realization is indispensable to any author who desires to write a serious work on the war of 1861-65.

Throughout the years my knowledge of Lincoln and the Civil War, as well as of the history of Illinois and of the Southern states, has been greatly enlarged by conversations and correspondence with certain scholars and students. Among those are Dr. Roy P. Basler of the Library of Congress, Washington, D.C., editor (with Mrs. Marion D. Pratt and Mr. Lloyd A. Dunlap) of the definitive eight-volume *Collected Works of Abraham Lincoln;* Mr. John J. Duff of New York, attorney and Lincoln scholar, author of the recently published comprehensive book, *A. Lincoln: Prairie Lawyer;* Dr. Newton C. Farr of Chicago, Civil War authority; Mr. Arnold Gates of Garden City, New York, literary editor of the *Lincoln Herald;* Professor Holman Hamilton of the University of Kentucky, authority on Lincoln's Whig Party and biographer of President Zachary Taylor; Former President Stewart W. McClelland of Lincoln Memorial University, now of Indianapolis, Indiana; Dr. R. Gerald McMurtry, Director of the Lincoln National Life Foundation, Fort Wayne, Indiana, author of significant Lincoln books and editor of *Lincoln Lore;* the late President Emeritus Robert Lee Kincaid of Lincoln Memorial University, biographer of Lincoln's most intimate friend, Joshua F. Speed; Mr. Richard F. Lufkin of Boston, Massachusetts, author of revealing contributions to the *Lincoln Herald;* Mr. Henry E. Luhrs, of Shippensburg, Pennsylvania, authority on Lincoln's Gettysburg Address; Mr. Jay Monaghan, former State Historian of Illinois, now of the Henry E. Huntington Library, San Marino, California, and author of numerous works on Lincoln and Illinois history, and scholarly compiler of the two-volume *Lincoln Bibliography;* Dr. C. Percy Powell of the Library of Congress, student and indexer of the 194-volume Robert Todd Lincoln Collection, President Lincoln's own White House file, now deposited in the nation's library; the late Dr. Harry E. Pratt, State Historian of Illinois, author of the very original volume, *The Personal Finances of Abraham Lincoln,* and contributor to countless profound articles on Lincoln to the *Journal of the Illinois State Historical Society* and the *Illinois Bar Journal,* a truly pre-eminent world authority on the Civil War President; the late Professor James G. Randall of the University of Illinois, Urbana, Illinois, greatest of all twentieth-century Lincoln scholars; Lieutenant Bert Sheldon of Washington, D.C., collector of Lincolniana and authority on Lincoln's assassination and John Wilkes Booth; the late Dr. Benjamin P. Thomas, author of the authoritative one-volume biography of Lincoln, published in 1952; Professor Wayne C. Temple of Lincoln Memorial University, Harrogate, Tennessee, author of the forthcoming volume on Lincoln's young newspaper friend, Noah Brooks, and editor-in-chief of the *Lincoln Herald;* and Dr. Louis A. Warren, Director Emeritus of the Lincoln National Life Foundation, Fort Wayne, Indiana, founder and long-time editor of *Lincoln Lore,* prolific author and learned lecturer on Lincoln, and the most eminent authority on Lincoln's earliest years in Kentucky and Indiana.

It would prove impossible to write a serious non-fiction book without the close co-operation and indispensable aid of librarians. Members of the staff of the Columbia University Libraries have graciously opened their rich collections of

Americana to me. Among those Columbia librarians I wish to thank are Dr. Richard H. Logsden, Director of Libraries; Mr. Charles W. Mixer, Associate Director of Libraries; Miss Constance M. Winchell, Reference Librarian; Mr. Miles O. Price, Law Librarian; Mr. Roland Baughman, Head of the Special Collections Department; Miss Darthula Wilcox, Librarian of the School of Library Service and curator of the microfilms of the Robert Todd Lincoln Collection and other basic sources of Americana; Mr. Paul Palmer, Librarian of Burgess History Library; and Mr. Harry Hart of the Columbia College Library. Other librarians who have aided me through the years in research are Mr. Donald Engley, Librarian of Trinity College, Hartford, Connecticut; Mr. George Adams of the Connecticut State Library, Hartford; and Mr. John Berthel, Librarian of the Johns Hopkins University Library, Baltimore, Maryland.

Countless friends have inspired me to continue this lengthy work on Lincoln at times when it seemed physically (and from the viewpoint of time) impossible to complete it. In particular I want to thank the following: Former Dean Lawrence H. Chamberlain of Columbia College, Columbia University; Mr. and Mrs. Fred Chiaventone of New York; Mr. and Mrs. Horace Coon of Montclair, New Jersey; Mrs. Isaac W. Digges of New York; Mr. Bruce M. Guthrie of Elizabeth, New Jersey; Mr. Joseph Lawler of New York; my niece, Miss Muriel Luthin of Bellmore, New York; my nephew, Lieutenant Richard B. Luthin, U.S.N., and his wife, Mrs. Nell Gentry Luthin, of Jacksonville, Florida; Mr. L. Holt Moore of New York; Mr. and Mrs. Robert Pettit of Mendham, New Jersey; Professor George B. Sargent, 2nd, of New York University, and his wife, Mrs. Dorothy Munger Sargent; my former colleague at Barnard College, Professor Raymond J. Saulnier, Chairman of the President's Council of Economic Advisers, Washington, D.C.; Mr. and Mrs. John Stroud of East Orange, New Jersey; Dr. Raymond Walters, Jr., of New York; and Miss Kimberly J. Wiss of New York.

Certain people in Pakistan have taken a deep interest in my work. Among the friends of my country in this new Asiatic nation I wish to acknowledge the encouragement of Professor A. Halim, Head of the Department of History at the University of Dacca, East Bengal, Pakistan, where I taught for one year on a Fulbright lectureship; Mr. K. Sarwar Hasan of the Pakistan Institute of International Affairs, Karachi, Pakistan; and Mr. Mohammad Salam of the United States Educational Foundation in Pakistan, Karachi, Pakistan.

New York, N.Y. R.H.L.
February, 1960

Preface

"BIOGRAPHIES, as generally written, are not only misleading, but false. The author makes a wonderful hero of his subject. He magnifies his perfections, if he has any, and suppresses his imperfections. History is not history unless it is the truth."

That critical comment on most biographies and histories was made by the man who was to have more of such books, as well as novels, poems, and plays written about him (nearly all of them excessively eulogistic), than any other American before or since—Abraham Lincoln.

It would be interesting to know how Lincoln, a modest, self-effacing man, not given to exaggerations and distortions, would have reacted to the thousands of undiscriminating, almost mystically interpretive, books about him that have cascaded from presses since his assassination a century ago—piles of idolatrous pages that have shrouded him in an unearthly maze of adoration.

Lincoln has survived through the decades as a legendary hero, nonpareil. He remains a subject erroneously romanticized in streams of printer's ink and in the verbose speeches of politicians and civic leaders on each Lincoln Day. This unrealistic image has been created by earlier biographies and histories, February

12 orations, the published evocations of novelists, poets and playwrights (all full of unproved anecdotes), by motion picture scenarists, and hordes of radio and television script writers. Only during the past three decades, beginning with the late Senator Albert J. Beveridge's superb two-volume work treating the period through the Douglas debates, has Lincoln started to receive mature historical attention. Not until the decade between 1945-1955 did the late Professor James G. Randall publish his unrivaled four volume tome, *Lincoln the President,* the last volume of which was co-authored by Professor Richard N. Current.

This present biography of America's all-time favorite son, written by a New Yorker who has studied under both Northern historians at Columbia University, and Southern historians at Duke University, represents the final product of two decades of research and writing on Lincoln, hearing about him from his family since early childhood, talking with numberless Illinois historians and compilers of Lincolniana, and a generation of teaching the history of the United States in colleges and universities. It is a book which seeks to present Lincoln in a fact-filled single volume, from his birth to his burial, keeping as free as possible from the "legendary," "anecdotal" and "folk-lorish" alloy.

However imperfectly realized, this life of Lincoln is intended for those who want a comparatively brief narrative of the sixteenth president's career and personal life, based on the latest available research and sources, as well as for those who wish to pursue the finer points of study in the life and times of this most significant American.

For readers who fall into this latter category, namely students, teachers of history and political science, Lincoln and Civil War scholars, a comprehensive list of annotated sources is provided in the back of the book.

Extensive use has been made of the large Robert Todd Lincoln Collection in the Library of Congress, President Lincoln's own White House file (first opened to investigators in 1947), the eight-volume *Collected Works of Abraham Lincoln,* edited by Roy P. Basler, Marion D. Pratt, and Lloyd A. Dunlap, published in 1953, the multi-volume *Official Records of the Union and Confederate Armies,* unpublished doctoral dissertations and masters theses treating Lincoln and the Civil War, and countless collections of private papers of Lincoln's own contemporaries which are to be found in libraries, historical societies, and other repositories throughout the United States.

Lincoln scholars among my friends and acquaintances have criticized parts of these chapters over the years, but to the author alone must be ascribed any factual errors or unsoundness of interpretation that may be presented in this book.

R.H.L.

Contents

PREFACE

INTRODUCTION

1
BACKWOODS BEGINNINGS

2
NEW SALEM LIFE

3
PRAIRIE POLITICIAN AND LEGISLATOR

4
EARLY SPRINGFIELD YEARS

5
LAW OFFICE, COURT, AND CIRCUIT

6
LINCOLN'S ROMANCES

7
THE LONE WHIG FROM ILLINOIS

8
THE PERSONAL LINCOLN

9
MR. AND MRS. A. LINCOLN

10
BACK TO THE LAW

11
LINCOLN'S CELEBRATED LAW CASES

12
ANTI-SLAVERY MODERATE

13
DUELING WITH DOUGLAS

14
PURSUING THE PRESIDENCY

15
REPUBLICAN STANDARD-BEARER

16
PRESIDENT-ELECT: *Crisis and Cabinet*

17
THE INAUGURATION

18
WAR WITH SECESSION

19
FROM FORT SUMTER TO FIRST BULL RUN

20
FROM BULL RUN TO BALL'S BLUFF

21
LINCOLN AND HIS LIEUTENANTS

22
THE LINCOLN-MCCLELLAN MUDDLE

23
FACING THE SLAVERY ORDEAL

24
POLITICAL PROBLEMS AND MILITARY MISTAKES

25
FALLING FORTUNES

26
PORTRAIT OF THE PRESIDENT

27
WHITE HOUSE FAMILY

28
UPWARD SWING: *Gettysburg and Vicksburg*

29
SUMMER STORM CLOUDS / 1863

30
BRIGHT AUTUMN / 1863

31
PLANS FOR REUNION:
Restoring the Recovered States

32
PRESIDENTIAL RIVALS AND MILITARY REVERSES

33
RENOMINATED FOR PRESIDENT

34
THE TORTUROUS SUMMER TIME

35
RUNNING FOR RE-ELECTION

36
PATRONAGE PROBLEMS AND MILITARY VICTORIES

37
SLAVERY ABOLITION AND RECONSTRUCTION

38
TRIUMPH OF THE UNION

39
ENTER BOOTH

40
FATEFUL FRIDAY

41
A NIGHT OF HORROR—AND DEATH

42
TO THE AGES

BIBLIOGRAPHY AND NOTES

Introduction

THE march of Lincolnian scholarship during the last generations has been sustained and impressive. We know much more today about the great Illinoisan than we did when in 1928 Albert J. Beveridge brought out the two volumes which covered his life down to the eve of the Civil War. Since then we have had the six richly human volumes by Carl Sandburg, full of anecdote and poetic insights, and the four keenly analytical volumes by James G. Randall on the Presidential years. The finely-written one-volume life by Lord Charnwood, distinguished by breadth of view, has been succeeded by Benjamin P. Thomas' volume, expert in fact and ripe in judgment. A long list of special studies, ranging from William E. Baringer's account of Lincoln in the early Vandalia days to Jay Monaghan's exploration of his handling of foreign affairs, have appeared. The work still goes on. Within the year John J. Duff's volume, *A. Lincoln: Prairie Lawyer,* and Louis A. Warren's *Lincoln's Youth: Seven to Twenty-one* have proved that important new facts can be discovered. Meanwhile, the history of the time, and especially of the years 1850-1860, has been largely rewritten.

In some respects the most important contribution of all to the subject has been the publication of the really definitive *Collected Works* by the Abraham Lincoln Association of Springfield under the editorship of Roy P. Basler and his associates.

The progressive accumulation of knowledge makes it important, from time to time, that its best fruits be gathered into comprehensive new biographies. Even if they are mere compendiums of facts old and new, they have a useful place. Their value is enhanced if, as in this volume, the author adds research of his own, and presents interpretations which possess novelty. The books named above attest the fact that a wide variety of attitudes may be taken toward Lincoln and the principal events of his life, and room always exists for new explanations of the chief areas of his career.

Dr. Reinhard Luthin has a variety of qualifications for the task he has set himself. An industrious and conscientious scholar, he has attained an almost unrivalled knowledge of the literature bearing on the subject. His friends in Columbia University and elsewhere have marvelled at the range and exactness of his bibliographical lore. In dealing with the thousands of titles upon Lincoln, which include both pretentiously worthless volumes and obscure publications of high merit, this acquaintance with every book, every pamphlet, every article, is of the utmost value. He has himself inquired into some of the cloudy issues of the Lincoln story, and the volume he wrote with Harry J. Carman, *Lincoln and the Patronage,* is one of the indispensable items on any Lincoln shelf.

In addition to its summarization of the best new knowledge, this book has interest in two particular elements. One is the thoroughness, at once entertaining and illuminating, with which Dr. Luthin has searched some of the odd nooks of Lincoln's life: his courtships and marriage, the opinion of him held by his Springfield neighbors, his family relationships, and so on down to the circumstances surrounding his murder. The other and more important is the completeness with which he traces Lincoln's development as a politician. That Lincoln would not have been so great a statesman—that he would have been much less effective as a national leader—had he not been given a realistic training in local and state politics, is a fact too often overlooked. Some of his friends, after he was apotheosized, never liked to have this aspect of the man emphasized. Gideon Welles, for example, angrily contradicted the statement of Charles Francis Adams that Lincoln had been an adroit political manager; he was completely above the tricks and wiles that had been the stock-in-trade of Adams's friend Seward, wrote Welles. Lincoln himself repeatedly spoke in critical terms of mere politicians, and once declared: "I have never been a contriver." In any pejorative sense of the word, he was certainly not a contriver; but happily for the country, he was most astute in contriving political means to attain great statesmanlike ends. This fact Dr. Luthin ably illustrates.

Every work on Lincoln since the great ten-volume history of the man and his times by Nicolay and Hay has had its peculiar values and peculiar shortcomings. The more thoroughly Mr. Luthin's volume is read, the greater will its virtues appear. It contains a wealth of accurate detail not to be found in any other one-volume work; its scholarship is abreast of the latest findings, and its judgments are well supported. The author is not afraid to be unconventional, and some readers may differ from certain of his views; but they will not deny his mastery of the facts. His book will repay not only reading but study and should long maintain a place all its own; a place between the very short treatments of the great President, and the very long treatments, between the more austere historical works and those which are intent solely on the human aspects of Lincoln.

ALLAN NEVINS

DeWitt Clinton Professor
Emeritus of History,
Columbia University

Henry E. Huntington Library
San Marino, California
August, 1960

"Fellow-citizens, *we* cannot escape history. We of this Congress and this administration will be remembered in spite of ourselves."

—PRESIDENT ABRAHAM LINCOLN,
ANNUAL MESSAGE TO CONGRESS,
DECEMBER 1, 1862.

BACKWOODS BEGINNINGS

1

I

KENTUCKY! That very name held magical magnetism for late eighteenth-century pioneers, despite the somber significance of its Indian title, "Dark and Bloody Ground." Kentucky conjured up visions of blue grass, Indians, frontier adventures, opportunities for the acquisition of land and fortune, and the allurement of an indefinable something excitingly new in the West. Daniel Boone had left his peaceful home on the banks of the Yadkin in North Carolina to wander westward, as he said, "in quest of the country of Kentucky."

This Kentucky country, a virgin territory of indeterminate vastness, vibrant with fresh life, growth, and challenge, invited adventure-bent men and their families from the eastern regions of the South, and fused them into a distinctively American race. Here a new frontier society was evolving, conditioned by its rich opportunities and raw environment. It was a brisk new section across the mountains from Virginia and North Carolina, where the settlers believed in a material progress, presumably manifestly destined, and were aggressively filled with faith in a full future.

Kentucky was populated with meteoric speed even in an era of snail-pace transportation facilities and trails that passed for roads. Settlers from Virginia and North Carolina, some even from Maryland, started filtering into the Kentucky country while the War for Independence still raged. This became a mass migratory movement in succeeding years, partially due to liberal land grants made by the mother state, Virginia. Soon, after becoming politically separated from Virginia, it was admitted as a state of the Union in 1792. And by 1797 Kentucky contained a population of nearly 200,000.

Most of the people of this lusty, youthful Blue Grass State were frontiersmen, and among them was a farmer and militia captain from Rockingham County, Virginia, who had settled in Kentucky about 1782. His name was one which was to become familiar to the entire world: Abraham Lincoln.

II

This Abraham Lincoln was descended from a weaver, Samuel Lincoln of Hingham, England, who had migrated to Hingham, Massachusetts, in 1637. Some of Samuel's descendants had demonstrated themselves a restless lot, who continually migrated to the westernmost outposts of American settlements. Each 20 years or so they trekked farther away from the Atlantic seaboard, from Massachusetts to New Jersey, then to Pennsylvania, and finally to backcountry Virginia, where the first Abraham Lincoln was born.

This Abraham was the paternal grandfather of the renowned sixteenth President of the U.S. Following his family traditions, he, too, migrated, this time settling his family near Hughes Station in Jefferson County, Kentucky, some twenty miles east of Louisville, where, four years later, he was killed from ambush by Indians.

The murdered man's grandson and namesake evidently knew little more than this about either his grandfather or his Northern forebears, for, when writing about them in later years, Lincoln said merely:

> My paternal grandfather, Abraham Lincoln, emigrated from Rockingham County, Virginia, to Kentucky, about 1781 or 2, where, a year or two later, he was killed by Indians, not in battle, but by stealth, when he was laboring to open a farm in the forest. His ancestors, who were Quakers, went to Virginia from Berks County, Pennsylvania. An effort to identify them with the New England family of the same name [Lincoln] ended in nothing more definite than a similarity of Christian names in both families, such as Enoch, Levi, Mordecai, Solomon, Abraham, and the like.

III

Lincoln's father, Thomas Lincoln, son of the murdered first Abraham Lincoln, led an existence substantially similar to that of his migratory forebears, wandering from county to county in Kentucky, working as odd-jobs laborer, carpenter, and farmer, usually finding himself somewhere on the border between the wilderness and the oustide world. Thomas showed scant ambition in learning to read and write. Lincoln himself was to say of his father: "Thomas . . . even in childhood was a wandering labor boy, and grew up litterally (sic) without education. He never did more in the way of writing than to bunglingly sign his own name. . . . Having reached his 28th year, he married Nancy Hanks."

In 1806 Thomas Lincoln decided to take a wife. Legend has it that he first proposed marriage to Sarah Bush, known as "Sally," but that she rejected him and wed Daniel Johnston, later Hardin County jailer. Thomas was not discouraged, for, shortly after Sally and Johnston were married, he proposed to another young lady named Nancy Hanks. This second choice accepted him. On June 10, 1806, Thomas and Nancy's cousin and guardian, Richard Berry Jr. signed a bond of his intention of marriage.

The marriage took place two days later in the Beech Fork settlement of Washington County. Nancy's cousin, Sarah Mitchell was the bridesmaid, and probably Thomas's eldest brother, Mordecai, was the "best man." The ceremony was performed by the Reverend Jesse Head, a Methodist preacher.

Kentucky frontier weddings were featured, according to Dr. Daniel Drake, who practiced medicine there, by "scenes of carousel, and of mirth and merriment of no very chastened character." The festivities following the Hanks-Lincoln nuptials were no exception. According to Christopher C. Graham, who claimed to have attended the gormandizing and frolicsome "infare" celebrating the union of Thomas and Nancy:

"We had bear meat that you can eat the grease of; and it does not rise like other fats; venison, wild turkey and ducks; eggs wild and tame (so common that you could buy them at two bits a bushel); maple sugar strung on a string to bite off for coffee and whiskey; syrup in big gourds; peach-and-honey; a sheep that the two families barbecued whole over the coals of wood burned in a pit, and covered with green boughs to keep the juices in; and a race for the whiskey bottle."

IV

Whence came the bride, Nancy Hanks Lincoln?

There is little authentic information about this woman who was to bear and bring up one of the most illustrious men in world history. It is known that she was illiterate, for she used a cross rather than a signature in marking her name. But controversy has raged for an entire century as to what she really looked like. The best authorities have disagreed on the color of her hair and eyes, her weight and height, and her tastes and disposition. Indeed, there are few contemporary documents to tell us about her. Instead we have relied on the numberless eulogies, poems, plays and novels about Lincoln to determine her influence on him as a young boy and her inspiration to him in later years.

Nancy Hanks's parentage is as obscure as other details about her. The most learned authorities, except Dr. Louis A. Warren, have insisted that she was born out of wedlock. And a statement by Lincoln's law partner, William H. Herndon supports this view. Herndon maintained that in 1850 "Mr. Lincoln . . . said, among other things, that she was the illegitimate daughter of Lucy Hanks and a well-bred Virginia farmer or planter." But Abraham Lincoln, himself, left very few written references about his mother. One of these was the bit of autobiography he furnished Jesse W. Fell in 1859, in which, after stating that his parents were born in Virginia of "undistinguished or second families," he made brief mention of his mother, declaring that she came "of a family of the name of Hanks." In his lengthier autobiographical sketch for John L. Scripps in June, 1860, Lincoln dismissed his mother with only short reference to the fact that she had been born in Virginia. During that same year, when he was standing for President, he wrote to Samuel Haycraft of Elizabethtown, Kentucky: "You are mistaken about my mother—her maiden name was Nancy Hanks."

V

Thomas and his new bride, following their marriage, set up housekeeping in crude quarters at Elizabethtown, in Hardin County. Thomas was not the shiftless, poverty-pinched ne'er-do-well usually portrayed by legend. Kentucky court records, tax-books, and other public documents, not discovered until the present century, indicate that he owned land, paid substantial taxes, and served on juries, although he did not amass any great wealth.

Toward the end of 1808, Thomas, Nancy, and their infant daughter Sarah, who had been born in February of 1807, left Elizabethtown to settle southeast of there near a town called Hodgen's mill and later Hodgenville. There Tom put down an initial payment on 300 acres by the Sinking Spring near Nolin Creek in an area known as "the Barrens," a desolate spot where the trees had been partially reduced by Indians for the purpose of making a grazing ground for buffalo and other game. And to Tom and Nancy Lincoln, in their log cabin by the Sinking Spring, their first son was born on February 12, 1809. They named him Abraham after Tom's father.

VI

When Abraham had reached two years of age, Thomas Lincoln moved his family from the cabin near Nolin Creek to one on Knob Creek, in another part of Hardin County which today is Larue County, on the road from Beardstown, Kentucky, to Nashville, Tennessee. This cabin Abraham remembered as his first home, subsequently stating: "As my parents have told me, I was born on Nolin. . . . My earliest recollection, however, is of the Knob Creek place."

The Lincolns' Knob Creek cabin had packed-down earth for a floor, while the roof was held in place by poles and stones. Through the log walls a small square opening let in dim light from outside. At the cabin's end stood a crude fireplace of stone with chimney of sticks and clay. And although the Lincolns' cabin was rather isolated, it was near the main thoroughfare between Louisville, Kentucky, and Nashville, over which people passed daily. The Indians had already disappeared, the community was somewhat settled, and county government was already established. A sufficient supply of water and timber existed. Here Abe Lincoln spent the first years of his childhood.

Very little of the information concerning Lincoln's early life in Hardin County has been authenticated. It is made up, for the most part, of his later brief references, chatty remarks by the Hanks family and old timers of the area in later years, and old court records. Over the years this small fund of fact has become so saturated with folklore that much of our knowledge of this period of Lincoln's life is unreliable.

William Herndon remarked that his law partner's reference to his earliest years in Kentucky were painfully vague and dim, and in his middle age, Lincoln grew significantly reserved about anything pertaining to his early experiences. When John L. Scripps of the Chicago *Press & Tribune* interviewed Lincoln for research for a campaign biography in 1860, he noted his strong disinclination to talk about his Kentucky life. Only on rare occasions could anyone persuade him to talk on the subject. When his White House secretaries and future biographers, John G. Nicolay and John Hay, asked him what he recalled as a boy in Kentucky about the War of 1812-15 against England, Lincoln replied: "Nothing but this. I had been fishing one day and caught a little fish which I was taking home. I met a soldier in the road, and, having been always told at home that we must be good to soldiers, I gave him my fish."

Another memory Lincoln had of his boyhood was of a big rain rushing down a gorge and soaking into the family farm. He said: "The other boys planted the corn in what we called the 'big field'—it contained seven acres—and I dropped the pumpkin seed. I dropped two seeds every other hill and every other row. The next Sunday morning there came a big rain in the hills; it did not rain a drop in the valley, but the water, coming down through the gorges, washed ground, corn, pumpkin seeds, and all clear off the field."

Lincoln started his short formal education at a log school two miles from the Lincoln cabin and farm, near the present Kentucky town of Athertonville. His remarks about this school consist of a simple statement that he and his sister, Sarah, "were sent for short periods, to A.B.C. schools, the first kept by Zachariah Riney, and the second by Caleb Hazel." In 1811 or perhaps in 1812, Nancy bore another son who died while still a baby. Abraham's only reference to his brother was when he wrote: "A brother, younger, died in infancy."

VII

It seemed natural enough that the fast peopling of Kentucky could not proceed without serious legal squabbles over ownership of its land. The original plan of acquisition, so loosely formulated and capriciously carried out, brewed numberless heated controversies over land titles throughout the State, which were partially settled by fists, rifles, or courts. Lincoln's father found himself involved in such controversies, fighting competitors who questioned his titles to acres.

The title to one farm that Tom Lincoln had purchased, that at Mill Creek, proved to be defective, for when it was surveyed it was found to contain only 200 acres instead of the 238 which he supposed that he had bought. Title to the senior Lincoln's second purchase was declared legally irregular by the Hardin County Circuit Court; that tribunal ordered that he should recover the $200 which he had paid for it. Thomas Lincoln's third and last difficulty, a suit to deprive him of his Knob Creek farm, was soon pending in the county court late in 1816. By this time, however, Tom had grown discouraged and had decided to leave Kentucky with his family and move to the neighboring state, Indiana.

Abraham Lincoln declared of his father's decision to leave the Blue Grass State and settle in Indiana: "This removal was partly on account of slavery; but chiefly on account of the difficulty in land titles in Ky."

Lincoln's father fully appreciated the more generous Indiana land laws. In the Hoosier State land was described by the rectangular system of surveys provided for in the Ordinance of 1787, rather than by the ancient method of metes and bounds which prevailed in Kentucky. Of greater allurement, most Indiana land could be bought directly from the Federal Government. Once a settler had paid for his tract, he did not have to be concerned about the validity of his title.

The Lincoln family's only possessions when they moved to Indiana in December 1816, were a few horses, bedding, clothing, some pots and pans. They had to rely on Thomas's kit of tools and the forest trees for their furniture and on his rifle and Abe's fishing tackle for their food.

Laboriously and slowly the Lincoln caravan trekked westward, by foot, ox cart, and horse, through sparsely settled Breckinridge County, Kentucky, and then to the Ohio River. Lincoln's early biographer, Joseph H. Barrett, recorded of that rugged trip from Kentucky to Indiana: "Arrived at the appointed landing on the banks of the Ohio, it only remained to embark the little caravan upon a flatboat, and to cross the stream, now swelled to fair proportions by the autumn rains. Finally after reaching the Indiana side, the adventurers landed at or near Anderson's creek . . . about one hundred and forty miles below Louisville, by the river, and sixty above Evansville [in Indiana]."

Tom Lincoln called a halt for his family at Pigeon Creek in Perry County in southwestern Indiana, not far distant from the Ohio River. The last miles proved a painful ordeal as the Lincolns cut their way through thick entanglements of trees and vines. Abraham Lincoln subsequently told one friend, Henry J. Raymond of the New York *Times*, that he "never passed through a harder experience than he did in going from Thompson's Ferry to Spencer County, Indiana." This reaction to his first experience in the Hoosier region, which would be his home, seemed natural enough. Indiana, recently admitted into the Union, was a wild, raw, and remote outpost of American civilization—a vast forest populated by people who were half hunters, half farmers.

VIII

Lincoln himself described his new home community, Pigeon Creek: "It was a wild region, with many bears and other wild animals in the woods." He observed that it was an "unbroken forest; and the clearing away of surplus wood was the great task ahead." His most vivid recollection for years thereafter would be the axe. "That most useful instrument," he wrote, was soon put into his hands and he would be "almost constantly handling it" until he had reached twenty-three years of age.

The Lincolns' first task was to build a cabin. These crude log structures were made with the help of neighbors, with incredible speed. Oliver Johnson, a pioneer who reached southern Indiana about the same time as the Lincolns, reported about the first days of a typical new settler and the building of his home: "The first thing on hand, after movin' into a new country like this, was to build a cabin to live in. . . . Most always there was a neighbor or two with their boys willin' to help a newcomer. Some would go to the woods, fell the trees, and cut the logs into the right lengths. Somebody would bring an ox team and drag up the logs. . . . Our cabin was eighteen feet wide and twenty feet long, which was about the universal size in our locality." Once Lincoln related to a fellow lawyer: "It was pretty pinching times, at first in Indiana, getting the cabin built, and the clearing for the crops; but presently we got reasonably comfortable."

Life in Gentryville, the hamlet nearest to the Lincoln cabin, differed slightly from that of any center of people on the Indiana frontier. Dwellings stood scattered far apart. Inhabitants worked hard and played even harder. They would travel long distances to a log-rolling, a cabin-raising, a wedding, or any other gathering that might turn into a fast and furious frolic. One Spencer County resident reminisced: "On such occasions the young women carried their shoes in their hands, and only put them on when about to join the company. The ladies drank whiskey-toddy, while the men took it straight; and both sexes dance the live-long night barefooted on puncheon floors."

Churches, too, played a major part in the Lincolns' Indiana community, for exhorting clergymen attracted throngs for miles around. At camp-meeting revivals these early nineteenth-century frontier Protestant Savonarolas preached a muscular, shirt-sleeve religion of fear and hope that mesmerized rough-hewn frontiersmen and their women folk. They welcomed, sometimes semi-hysterically with shrieks, groans, and bodily contortions, this spiritual spellbinding. Lincoln's father became a member of the Pigeon Creek Baptist Church.

Specific factual accounts of the Lincolns of Pigeon Creek are few. Once again historians have been forced to rely on the stories and remarks of old men and women who were once the Lincolns' neighbors in Spencer County for information about young Abe's formative years. As one historian has lamented, other than these accounts and occasional court records, "hardly any notice has been taken of the fact that he spent fourteen years in Indiana."

It is unfortunate that we must sketchily reconstruct this important quarter of Lincoln's life, for it contained many significant events. The first of these was the death of his mother in 1818 shortly after the family had settled in Pigeon Creek. She had fallen victim to the "milk sick," a fatal sickness that had become an epidemic in the southern Indiana region.

This must have been the first really painful experience of young Abe's life, for old-timers recounted, years later, that he sat in front of the Lincoln cabin lamenting that the family's poor and helpless condition made it necessary for his father to construct a crude coffin of black cherry in which to bury his mother. She was thus meanly buried on a knoll a short distance from the family cabin.

IX

Thomas Lincoln did not remain widowed for long, however. A year later, in December of 1819, he travelled back to Elizabethtown where Sarah Bush Johnston, the woman who had turned him down fifteen years before and was now widowed, was living. This time she accepted his proposal and returned with him to Pigeon Creek as the second Mrs. Thomas Lincoln.

Sarah's three children also returned to Pigeon Creek, so that in 1820, according to the Federal Census of that year, the Lincolns' small cabin was bursting at the seams with eight inhabitants. Eleven-year-old Abraham Lincoln was listed merely as a "male under 16." The others in the cabin were his father, who was then 44, his stepmother Sarah 32, Dennis F. Hanks, his late mother's cousin, 21, his sister Sarah Lincoln, 13, and his stepsisters and stepbrother, Elizabeth Johnston, 13, Matilda Johnston 9, and John Johnston, 5.

An anecdote concerning this second marriage suggests that the dry, rustic sense of humor for which Abe Lincoln was later to become famous originated with his father. According to a piece in the scrapbook of Nancy Hall, Sarah Johnston's great-granddaughter, Sarah, supposedly asked her new husband: "Thomas, you never yet told me who you like best, your first wife or me." Tom answered, "Sarah, that reminds me of old John Hardin down in Kentucky who had a fine-looking pair of horses, and a neighbor came in one day and looking at them said, 'John, which one of these horses do you like the best?' John said, 'I can't tell; one of them kicks and the other bites and I don't know which is wust.'"

Sarah, like Abe's mother Nancy, had had no formal schooling and could not write her own name, but she greatly encouraged his desire to learn. Her own son, John, shunned books and, thus, became the prime favorite of Thomas, who, neighbors later maintained, liked him for a hunting and fishing companion while castigating Abe for "fooling himself with eddication."

So in 1820, Abe's limited formal education continued at another "subscription" school which was started in the Pigeon Creek community. Its curriculum was determined by the availability of teachers, the time pupils could be spared from work on their fathers' farms, and the degree of wintry weather. So the school term usually lasted only about two months.

"There were schools, so called," declared Lincoln of his Indiana life in later years, "but no qualification was ever required of a teacher beyond *'readin,' 'writin,'* and *'cipherin,'* to the Rule of Three. If a straggler supposed to understand Latin happened to sojourn in the neighborhood, he was looked upon as a wizzard (sic). There was absolutely nothing to excite ambition for education."

Lincoln told how he "went to A.B.C. schools by littles" in Indiana, and he named three of his teachers—Andrew Crawford, one "Sweeney," and Azel W. Dorsey. Crawford acted as justice of the peace on the side and specialized in teaching etiquette, or "manners," as that subject was then called. Little is known about "Sweeney," except that his correct name was James Swaney and he was only nine years older than the boy Lincoln. Dorsey had been successively county treasurer, coroner, merchant, and then teacher. Of Tom Lincoln's boy, Dorsey merely reminisced: "He pursued his studies, came to the log cabin school house arrayed in buck skin clothes, a raccoon-skin cap, and provided with an old arithmetic."

When Abe had reached his fifteenth or sixteenth year he was finally able to do simple arithmetic. Some of his original tables, with his written calculations, have been preserved. At that same time he composed childish doggerel, one piece running:

Abraham Lincoln
his hand and pen
he will be good but
God knows When.

Another of Abe's juvenile verses was:

Abraham Lincoln is my name[e]
And with my pen I wrote the same
I wrote in both hast[e] and speed
and left it here for fools to read.

Besides brief attendance at the A.B.C. school, Abe acquired rudimentary education of sorts on his own. His mother's cousin, Dennis Hanks, who lived with the Lincolns, related: "We learned by sight, scent, and hearing. We heard all that was said, and talked over and over the questions heard; wore them slick, greasy, and threadbare."

Abe had a retentive memory, and he recalled in later years some of the books that he had read. For fiction he had little taste, and he once confided that he never read a novel through. More than three decades later, as President-elect of the United States, he was to tell the New Jersey State Senate, at Trenton, about his boyhood reading of Parson Weems's biography of George Washington: "Away back in my childhood, the earliest days of my being able to read, I got hold of a small book . . . 'Weems's

Life of Washington.' I remember all the accounts there given of the battle fields and struggles for the liberties of the country, and none fixed themselves upon my imagination so deeply as the struggle here in Trenton, New-Jersey. The crossing of the river; the contest with the Hessians; the great hardships endured at that time, all fixed themselves on my memory more than any single revolutionary event."

Lincoln insisted on learning the meaning of language that he could not comprehend on first hearing. Later he told one clergyman, Reverend J. P. Gulliver:

"I remember how, when a mere child, I used to get irritated when anybody talked to me in a way I could not understand. That always disturbed my temper. I can remember going to my little bedroom, after hearing the neighbors talk of an evening with my father, and spending no small part of the night walking up and down, and trying to make out what was the exact meaning of some of their, to me, dark sayings. I could not sleep, though I often tried to, when I got on such a hunt after an idea, until I had caught it; and when I thought I had got it, I was not satisfied until I had repeated it over and over, until I had put it in language plain, as I thought, for any boy I knew to comprehend. This was a kind of passion with me."

X

Lincoln in his teens grew fast physically, and by nineteen stood six feet, four inches. His weight would never be quite proportionate to his great height. His towering, ungainly figure, with lengthy arms, huge hands, and relatively small chest development would always make him conspicuous in any group. His muscular strength during his Indiana youth was formidable, and tales were told later of the back-breaking weight that he could lift, the crashing force of his swing of an axe. The best evidence indicates that these accounts of his physical strength were only slightly exaggerated, if at all.

The Pigeon Creek youth spent time, of necessity, in callus-making chores, helping his father on the farm and hiring himself out to neighbors. It appears, however, that he, despite his prodigious physical power, did not actually become deeply devoted to hard labor; and by no means did he turn into the industrious rail-splitter and farm-loving worker of tradition. He disliked manual jobs and did no more than was necessary. John Romine, for whom Lincoln worked at pulling fodder for a while, subsequently recalled: "Abe was awful lazy. he would laugh and talk and crack jokes and tell stores all the time. didn't love work, but dearly loved his pay. . . . Lincoln said to me one day, that his father taught him to work, but never learned him to love it."

More than a dozen years later Lincoln informed his most personal friend, Joshua F. Speeed: "As to your farm matter, I have no sympathy with you. *I* have no farm, nor ever expect to have; and, consequently, have not studied the subject enough to be much interested with it." The year before he was elected President, Lincoln told the Wisconsin State Agricultural Society that he was "in no sort a farmer."

During 1827 Lincoln worked for James Taylor as a ferry man on a flatboat near the confluence of Anderson Creek with the Ohio River. The same year he earned his first dollar for a single job by transporting two travelers out to a steamer on the Ohio aboard his flatboat. Years later, as President, he still remembered that incident and told one of his Cabinet members, Secretary of State William H. Seward, about it: "Two men came down to the shore in carriages with trunks, and looking at the different boats singled out mine. . . . 'Will you,' said one of them, 'take us and our trunks out to the steamer?' 'Certainly,' said I. I was very glad to have the chance of earning something. . . . I sculled them out to the steamboat. They got on board, and I lifted up their heavy trunks, and put them on deck . . . Each of them took from his pocket a silver half-dollar. . . . I could scarcely believe my eyes as I picked up the money. . . . I could scarcely credit that I, a poor boy, had earned a dollar in less than a day."

On one occasion in his ferrying jobs Lincoln found himself in dispute with John and Lin Dill, two brothers who operated a ferry across the Ohio River between Lincoln's Indiana region and Kentucky. Angrily they charged that Abe was interfering with their licensed ferry business by transporting passengers for hire. Before fists could fly the Dills and Lincoln brought their quarrel before Squire Samuel Pate, a Kentucky justice of the peace. The "trial" was informally conducted in Pate's home. The brothers complained that Lincoln was illegally infringing on their ferry franchise. Abe admitted taking travelers and their baggage out to passing steamboats but insisted that he had not realized that this constituted a breach of the law.

The rail-thin youthful defendant from Spencer County, clad in deerskin shirt, home-made jeans breeches dyed brown with walnut bark, his coonskin cap crumbled in his big, calloused hands, impressed Pate, who consulted Littell's *Laws of Kentucky*. He read the chapter, "An Act Respecting the Establishment of Ferries." The evidence indicated that the Pigeon Creek boatman had taken, passengers for hire out to the middle of the river. But this according to Kentucky Legislature was no offense. So Pate dismissed the case.

Tradition declares that Abe first became interested in the law from that minor litigation against the Dill brothers, and that he would attend various trials before Squire Pate on "court day."

XI

In 1828, the last year of his teens, Lincoln made his first long trip—all the way down the Ohio and Mississippi rivers to New Orleans. The merchant, James Gentry of nearby Gentryville, hired him to aid his son, Allen, in taking a cargo of produce on a flatboat down to that celebrated Southern port. The trip was marred when they were attacked by a group of Negroes along the Louisiana coast, but both youths escaped serious injury. In later reminiscences, Lincoln described this untoward incident, referring to himself in the third person.

"When he [Lincoln] was nineteen, still residing in Indiana, he made his first trip upon a flat-boat to New Orleans. He was a hired hand merely; and he and a son of the owner, without other assistance, made the trip. The nature of part of the cargo-load, as it was called—made it necessary for them to linger and trade along the Sugar coast—and one night they were attacked by seven negroes with intent to kill and rob them. They were hurt some in the melee, but succeeded in driving the negroes from the boat, and then 'cut cable,' 'weighed anchor' and left."

The sight of glamorous New Orleans attracted the two young men. There they saw strange people vastly more varied and exotic in looks and conduct than those in their home southern Indiana. That Louisiana metropolis was even then a picturesque, tough, cosmopolitan port where the French *voyageur* and the crude American hunter, who trapped beavers and other animals for pelts, met the polished Old World exiles. It was a market place and a playground where variations of French, Spanish, and English, assorted patois, and frontier American slang flowed together in the dirty, noisy streets. It was a turbulent city that thrived on lawless frolics, heavy drinking, and reckless gambling. And here, even in 1828, virtueless women practiced by the wholesale the world's oldest profession.

After several days in this unique city Lincoln and Gentry turned northward on the Gentry flatboat and returned to their frontier Indiana homes.

XII

During the year of this New Orleans trip Lincoln suffered another personal blow—the death of his sister, Sarah Lincoln Grigsby.

Sarah had married Aaron Grigsby, a young man from the Pigeon Creek community, a year and half before she died in child birth on January 20, 1828.

Lincoln, who had never liked the Grigsbys, was inclined to blame them for his sister's death. So when two of the Grigsby brothers, Reuben and Charles, married their fiancées in a joint ceremony during the spring of 1828, it was charged that Lincoln instigated a practical joke which involved maneuvering the brides into the wrong bedrooms on the wedding night. More evidence indicates that Lincoln wrote some bawdy doggerel about that nuptial mishap, entitled "The First Chronicles of Reuben." But even more indelicate than these "First Chronicles of Reuben" were some stanzas which the aged Mrs. Elizabeth Crawford recited from memory, perhaps faultily, after Lincoln's death, that she insisted he had composed. Those stanzas, as repeated by Mrs. Crawford, ran:

I will tell you a joke about Joel and Mary.
It is neither a joke nor a story,
For Reuben and Charles have married two girls,
But Billy has married a boy.
The girls he had tried on every side,
But none could he get to agree.
All was in vain, he went home again,
And since that he's married to Natty.

So Billy and Natty agreed very well,
And mama's well pleased with the match.
The egg it is laid, but Natty's afraid
The shell is so soft it never will hatch,
But Betsy, she said, "You cursed bald head,
My suitor you never can be,
Besides your ill shape proclaims you an ape,
And that never can answer for me."

These stanzas evidently also refer to the Grigsby clan that, according to ancient Spencer County residents, Lincoln never forgave.

XIII

Not long after Sarah's death, however, the Lincolns were again on the move. Some members of the Hanks family had moved to Macon County, Illinois, and they were writing Tom Lincoln glowing reports of the fertile soil in that area. Tom needed little urging to leave Spencer County, for there were renewed rumors of another epidemic of the "milk sick." So, in March of 1830, he gathered his family, his livestock, wagons, and supplies and set out for Illinois.

Abe Lincoln would remain sentimental for years over his Indiana homeland. During a speaking tour in Spencer County fourteen years later, he composed this bit of doggerel about the Pigeon Creek community:

My childhood's home I see again,
And sadden with the view.
And still, as memory crowds my brain,
There's pleasure in it too.

Abe subsequently described the journey to Illinois, again in the third person:

"March 1st. 1830—A. [Abraham] having just completed his 21st. year, his father and family, with the families of the two daughters and sons-in-law, of his step-mother, left the old homestead in Indiana, and came to Illinois. Their mode of conveyance was waggons (sic) drawn by ox-teams, or A. drove one of the teams. They reached the county of Macon, and there some time within the same month of March. His father and family settled a new place on the North side of the Sangamon river, at the junction of the timber-land and prairie, about ten miles Westerly from Decatur. Here they built a log cabin, into which they removed, and made sufficient of rails to fence ten acres of ground, fenced and broke the ground, and raised a crop of sow[n] corn upon it the same year."

Lincoln spent some time at splitting rails with another member of his late mother's family, Charles Hanks.

In May, only two months after settling in Macon County, Lincoln, with his stepbrother, John, his mother's cousin, Dennis, and others, signed a petition for a change of site of the election polling place. This is the first known political document which Lincoln ever signed. The petition (now in the possession of the Macon County Clerk's office at Decatur, Illinois), reads:

May 26 1830.

To the Hon. County Comrs. Court for the County of Macon

We the undersigned qualified voters in the Decatur Precinct earnestly request your honors to change the present place of holding Elections in said Precinct from Permenius Smallwoods to the Court house in Decatur.

In the ensuing election campaign the twenty-one-year-old Lincoln was prevailed upon to deliver the first political speech of his life. W. L. W. Ewing, future Acting Governor of Illinois and United States Senator, and one John F. Posey were running for the House of Representatives, or Assembly, of the state Legislature. Both came to Decatur in quest of votes. One Macon County resident, George Close, told about it: "As Posey did not *treat* we persuaded L. [Lincoln] to get up and abuse him—said he would if I would not laugh at him—was frightened but got warmed up and made the best speech of the day. Did not abuse Posey but spoke well of both men—pictured out the future of Illinois. When he got through Ewing said 'he was a bright one.' "

Lincoln's speech on that occasion, his baptism on the electioneering stump, is supposed to have emphasized the necessity for making the Sangamon River more navigable. At the election held in August both Ewing and Posey were elected from a field of nine candidates to the Illinois Legislature.

The twelve months during which Abe Lincoln lived near Decatur have frequently been described as the "hardest year" in Macon County's annals. During the summer an epidemic of malaria plagued the community. In the cold months following, the blizzard of 1830-31 blanketed the region for weeks. That season became known as the "winter of the deep snow." Thereafter Macon County settlers and old-timers mentioned dates in terms of "before," "during," or "after the deep snow."

XIV

One snow-banked day during that "deep snow" in February, 1831, there arrived in Macon County a short, enterprising man from Hickman Creek, Kentucky. His name was Denton Offutt.

Described as "a trader and speculator who always had his eyes open to the main chance," Offutt offered Abe Lincoln's cousin, John Hanks, a job of piloting a flatboat filled with provisions for sale, down to New Orleans as soon as the snows melted. In Hanks' words: "I hunted up Abe, and introduced him and John D. Johnston, his stepbrother, to Offutt. After some talk, we made an arrangement with Offutt at 50¢ a day and $60.00 to make the trip to New Orleans."

Lincoln, relating these circumstances destined to take him from his Macon County home permanently, subsequently wrote about it in the third person:

"During the winter of the very celebrated 'deep snow' of Illinois . . . A. [Abraham] together with his step-mother's son, John D. Johnston, and John Hanks, yet residing in Macon county, hired themselves to one Denton Offutt, to take a flat boat from Beardstown, Illinois, to New-Orleans; and for that purpose, were to join him—Offutt—at Springfield, Ills. so soon as the snow should go off. When it did go off which was about the 1st. of March 1831—the county was so flooded, as to make traveling by land impracticable; to obviate which difficulty the [they] purchased a large canoe and came down the Sangamon river in it. This is the time and the manner of A's first entrance into Sangamon County."

NEW SALEM LIFE

2

I

SANGAMON COUNTY!

Into that prairie region along the Sangamon River Abe Lincoln, his stepbrother, John D. Johnston, and his cousin, John Hanks, paddled their canoe on the way to meet their new boss, Denton Offutt. In 1821, the decade before Lincoln and his companions set out along the Sangamon, the Illinois legislature created the County of Sangamon along the banks of this river, which rises in what is now Champaign County and empties into the Illinois River. Their search for Offutt brought the three young men into the principal town of this Sangamon County—Springfield. Here they found their employer entertaining some acquaintances at the Buckhorn Tavern.

Offutt had encountered an obstacle to his plan for shipping produce to New Orleans. He could not rent a flatboat. So the erstwhile sailors became carpenters. Offutt hired them to cut timber on government land and float the logs down the river to Fitzpatrick's mill, where the lumber could be sawed to build a flatboat.

While they were cutting timber and building the boat in that April of 1831, Lincoln, Johnston, and Hanks camped in a "shanty shed," which they had hastily constructed, and ate Abe's cooking, except when they were invited to dine with friendly neighbors. One of these, Caleb Carmen, describes the young Lincoln, who was then so tall and gangling that the pants legs of his jeans were short enough to expose part of his sharp shinbone, as appearing to be a "Green horn," though after an hour's conversation with him, Carmen confessed, "I found him no Green horn."

Another man who recalled Abe Lincoln during this period was the Sangamon County assessor, Erastus Wright. He describes Lincoln in Sangamo Town helping his companions build the flatboat with his "boots off, hat, coat, and vest off, pants rolled up to his knees, shirt wet with sweat and combing his fuzzie hair with his fingers as he pounded away at the boat."

After several weeks of labor, Lincoln, Johnston, and Hanks finished the flatboat, and Offutt proceeded to fill it with barrel pork, corn, and hogs, whose eyes had been sewn shut to make it easier to drive them. About this inhumane practice Lincoln wrote: "Offutt bought thirty odd large fat live hogs, but found difficulty in driving them from where [he] purchased them to the boat, and thereupon conceived the whim that he could sew up their eyes and drive them where he pleased. No sooner thought of than decided, he put his hands, including A. [Abraham] at the job, which they completed—all but the driving. In their blind condition they could not be driven out of the lot or field they were in. This expedient failing, they were tied and hauled on carts to the boat."

The cumbersome craft, with Lincoln at the steering oar, started down the Sangamon River in late April. Trouble soon overtook it. The flood waters had receded very fast, leaving timber obstructions in the water blocking the way; the flatboat stuck fast on Rutledge's mill dam at a village on a bluff. The village was New Salem.

He later told voters about this mishap on the mill dam: "In the month of March, 1831, in company with others, I commenced the building of a flatboat on the Sangamon, and finished and took her out in the course of the spring. . . . The time at which we crossed the mill dam, being in the last days of April, the water was lower than it had been since the breaking of winter in February, or than it was for several weeks after. The principal difficulties we encountered in descending the river were from the drifted timber."

The sight of the overloaded flatboat stranded halfway over the Rutledge dam quickly brought a crowd of curious New Salem villagers to the bank of the river. While they shouted advice flavored with backwoods wit, Lincoln went ashore and borrowed an auger. He used this instrument to bore holes in the flatboat's bottom through which the water could run out. The weight of the cargo having been lifted, the craft was maneuvered over the dam. With the auger holes plugged, it proceeded along the Sangamon River, then then into the Illinois, and finally down the Mississippi to New Orleans.

During the many weeks required by this journey, Offutt discovered Lincoln's dependable qualities. In the third person Lincoln related subsequently: "During this boat enterprize acquaintance with Offutt, who was previously an entire stranger, he conceived a liking for A. [Abraham] and believing he could turn him to account, he contracted with him to act as clerk for him, on his return from New-Orleans, in charge of a store and Mill at New-Salem."

Offutt disembarked from the returning packet at St. Louis, where he was to purchase the goods for his contemplated store at New Salem and arrange for their shipment to that village. Lincoln, meanwhile, spent some weeks in Coles County, Illinois, where his father and stepmother had moved shortly before.

In late July, 1831, Lincoln arrived at New Salem to take up his job as Offutt's store clerk. In a letter to Martin S. Morris a dozen years later Lincoln referred to himself at this time of his introduction to New Salem as "a friendless, uneducated, penniless boy, working on a flat boat—at ten dollars per month."

II

What manner of place was New Salem?

Only three years before, in 1828, New Salem on the Sangamon, twenty miles from the growing town of Springfield, had been only a primeval prairie, with trees and wild animals its only life. Then Reverend John M. Camron, a preacher and millwright from Georgia, and his uncle by marriage, John M. Rutledge from South Carolina, had come along in quest of a likely location for a grist mill. These two Southern entrepeneurs, following the winding, narrow Sangamon, found a spot where the river met a bluff and was deflected to the north. Here the stream became extremely narrow, making the job of building a dam comparatively easy and cheap. In July, 1828, Camron had pre-empted more than 150 acres of government land on the river's west bank, extending half a mile from the shore. With Rutledge he petitioned the Legislature of Illinois for a charter to build a dam, and permission was granted early in the new year. With the mill dam under way they employed Reuben Harrison, a surveyor, to lay out a town, which they christened New Salem. Presumably the name was taken from "Salem," the ancient name of Jerusalem.

When Lincoln reached New Salem in July, 1831, to assume his job as Offutt's store clerk, few houses had been built and the village was dependant upon the saw and grist mill to bring in trade. During the single decade of its existence it resembled any other contemporary Western frontier community, so many of which sprang up and were soon abandoned and forgotten. New Salem itself would be unknown today if Abraham Lincoln had not happened into it and made it his home.

Although destined never to have many more than 150 inhabitants, Lincoln's new home village had a trading area of ten to fifteen miles radius that gave it an importance beyond its diminutive size. During Lincoln's residence there from late 1831 to early 1837, New Salem had at times three or four stores, a grist and saw mill, a post office, a blacksmith shop, a carding machine, a tanner, a cooper, and two doctors. The tavern received occasional passengers from the four-horse mail stage which passed through the village twice weekly, and flatboats on the Sangamon occasionally halted there.

Upon reaching New Salem Lincoln learned with dismay that Denton Offutt had not put in an appearance, and further, the merchandise for the store had not arrived. Offutt had made a trip back to his native Kentucky to settle his mother's estate. While waiting for his employer to arrive, Abe boarded at Rutledge's Inn, so tradition declares. During those first days as a New Salemite he wandered about the village and surrounding countryside, making the acquaintance of the settlers.

Lincoln had not been in New Salem more than a number of days when, on August 1, an election was held. Seeing a body of men gathered together, he wandered over to them and found that they were waiting for the polling place in a private house to open. The delay was caused by the absence of one of the duly appointed election clerks.

Since Lincoln could write legibly and spell correctly, talents not shared by everyone in the community, he was asked to act as one of the clerks. He accepted, and, although only a recent arrival in the village, he availed himself of the privilege of voting for a congressman, justices of the peace, and constables.

This, certainly, was politics on a very minor scale, but throughout his life in New Salem, Lincoln was to prepare in this small manner for the vocation that would lead him eventually to the Presidency of the United States.

Denton Offutt finally arrived in New Salem during the following month. And he opened his store, at the edge of the bluff above the mill, with Abe Lincoln as clerk.

The typical Western frontier store such as Offutt's during the early nineteenth century, was housed in a log cabin, about twenty feet square, often with a lean-to addition behind the fireplace, that served for storage space and sleeping quarters. A short counter ran parallel to one side wall. There were chairs or stools to accommodate the proprietor, his clerk, or those village hangers-on for whom the store served as a second home. It thus became the prime center for local gossip. Gunpowder, whiskey and calico were among the best-selling merchandise. Among other standard articles of trade were candle wicking, cotton thread, axes, saws and files, bar iron, sieves and riddles, shovels, candle and bullet molds, pig lead and shot, smoothing irons, cutlery and crockery, looking glasses, groceries, molasses, muslins, flannels, combs, buttons, whalebones, and "Yankee notions" this last including whatever knicknacks the wholesaler had most recently added to his stock.

Lincoln's clerk job for Offutt paid him fifteen dollars a month and the privilege of sleeping in the store. It was his first freedom from the physical labor that had always been his lot. His back-bending, muscle-straining days of manual labor were ended, except for occasional heavy work about the store and a few later odd jobs that he was compelled to take. No longer would he work as farmer's hired hand, rail splitter, or flatboat oarsman. Always attracted to the village and town, rather than the woods and the desolate prairies, he now enjoyed a more sedentary occupation in Offutt's employ. He would find time to read newspapers, meet people and talk with them.

III

Lincoln's New Salem, like most Western frontier settlements of that era, was deficient in decorum, dignity, quiet, and effete "Eastern" behavior. A newcomer to town usually endured a stern physical and mental ordeal at the hands of the rougher villagers. Sometimes he would be challenged to run a foot race, jump, pitch the maul, or wrestle. If he could not excel in these, they might pull his nose, squirt tobacco juice at his face, nail him to a hogshead by his coat, roll him down a hill, sink him momentarily in the Sangamon river, or cuff him about, and then turn him off as unfit company. Any excuse was utilized to provide a fist fight or wrestling match. Offutt's clerk was soon called upon to "prove" himself by the village's bully boys.

On the outskirts of New Salem lay a grove named after John Clary, an early settler. Clary's sons and some of their cronies, a rollicking, boisterous, disorderly, hard-drinking, two-fisted lot, were known as the "Clary's Grove Boys." Their leader, Jack Armstrong, a pugnacious giant, was reputed to be able to throw any man in town in a wrestling match. And soon Abe Lincoln found himself challenged to meet Armstrong in combat.

Tradition has the Lincoln versus Armstrong wrestling match as a celebrated one which the whole village watched; and tradition has handed down numerous accounts of how the match ended—in a draw, in Lincoln's victory, and otherwise; but no tales ever relate that Lincoln was thrown by Armstrong. The real result is still in doubt today. But it is certain that the contest terminated in Lincoln and Armstrong becoming fast friends. Offutt's clerk would henceforth be "accepted" by the Clary's Grove Boys, as well as by New Salem's less belligerent citizens.

During that winter of 1831-32 Lincoln continued to improve his education. As he declared in his later autobiography for Scripps: "What he has in the way of education, he has picked up. After he was twenty-three, and had separated from his father, he studied English grammar, imperfectly of course, but so as to speak and write as well as he now does."

Mentor Graham, New Salem schoolmaster, is traditionally credited with advising Lincoln to study Samuel Kirkham's *English Grammar in Familiar Lectures.* Some writers have even insisted that Abe sat in Graham's classroom. Graham's joint biographers have entitled their book, *Mentor Graham, The Man Who Taught Lincoln.* But that schoolmaster's role in educating Lincoln has been grossly overemphasized. Lack of contemporary evidence leaves Graham as having a negligible influence, if any, on Lincoln's learning.

Lincoln was soon drafting for villagers various kinds of legal papers, bills of sale for land or other property, and receipts for payment of a debt. Typical was such a document that the twenty-three-year-old Abe drew up for John Ferguson, dated January 25, 1832: "Know all men by these presents that I, John Ferguson, for and in considderation (sic) of the sum of thirty five dollars have given, granted, bargained, and sold all my right and title in and to the New Salem ferry in Sangamon County unto Alexander Trent."

Stories by the hundreds have come down through the decades that Lincoln, as a youth in Indiana and a young man in New Salem, acquired every book for fifty miles around, walking vast distances to borrow them, and hungrily reading them all from cover to cover. But the best evidence indicates that he did not read books as profusely as this "Lincoln legend" has stated. Often the young Lincoln glanced through a volume and then tossed it aside. Stephen T. Logan, who within a decade would become Lincoln's law partner and who knew Lincoln's New Salem fellow-townsmen well, maintained in later years about Lincoln: "I don't think he studied very much. . . . He was not much of a reader." Another of his law partners, Herndon, only two years after Lincoln's death, revealed: "Mr. Lincoln seldom bought a new book and seldom read one. Mr. Lincoln's education was almost entirely a newspaper one." And the artist Francis B. Carpenter, who spent several months at the White House during the Civil War period painting a picture of Lincoln and his Cabinet in connection with the Proclamation of Emancipation, quoted Lincoln as actually telling him: "I never read an entire novel in my life."

Herndon was correct in pointing to Lincoln's love of newspapers. In the dailies and weeklies that came to New Salem weeks late, Offutt's store clerk learned about politics and other public questions as reported and interpreted by the then grossly politically partisan press.

To the people of his community in that time, however, Lincoln appeared to ravenously devour books. They themselves read few or no books, so, it was natural for them in later decades to remember Lincoln who by then had achieved immortality, as an ardent book-lover who borrowed and seemingly absorbed every volume on which he could lay his hands. Several studies, relying on this testimony by Lincoln's New Salem neighbors, have been published over the decades listing all the titles of the books Lincoln supposedly read. But Logan, Herndon, and Carpenter's observations are more accurate and reliable, for they were much more intimate with Lincoln than any of these old-timers, whose memories tended to be clouded by the years.

Other than newspapers, Lincoln's only real literary interest was poetry. He was particularly fond of melancholy verse. One New Salemite, Jason Duncan, in 1831 found an anonymous poem, and showed it to Lincoln. It became Abe's favorite verse for the rest of his life, and he often recited it to others. He called it "Immortality", but some who heard him recite it referred to it by its introductory line, "Oh, why should the spirit of mortal be proud?" The poem follows a Biblical theme in paraphrasing the third chapter of Job and the first chapter of Ecclesiastes.

"Oh, why should the spirit of mortal be proud," later revealed to have come from the pen of the Scottish poet, William Knox, emphasizes the belief in the earthly transiency of things, repeating the idea that succeeding generations undergo the same experiences as their forefathers, only to die also. Why, then should the spirit of mortal be proud? Its stanzas impart the essence of humility and resignation.

Lincoln's high opinion of Knox's poem never wavered. Fifteen years later he sent a copy of it to a Quincy lawyer, Andrew Johnston, who was interested in verse, informing Johnston: "I am not the author. I would give all I am worth, and go in debt, to be able to write so fine a piece as I think that is. Neither do I know who is the author. I met it in a straggling form in a newspaper last summer, and I remember to have seen it once before, about fifteen years ago, and that is all I know about it."

In his later Chicago eulogy of the deceased President Zachary Taylor, during 1850, Lincoln concluded with six stanzas of Knox's poem, the last one reading:

> 'Tis the wink of an eye, 'tis the draught of a breath,
> From the blossoms of health, to the paleness of death.
> From the gilded saloon, to the bier and the shroud.
> Oh, why should the spirit of mortal be proud!

IV

Abe Lincoln proved a satisfactory store clerk. But it was as a raconteur and arguer rather than as a salesman and merchandizer that he excelled with those villagers who congregated about Offutt's store to spill and absorb local gossip, swap anecdotes, tell jokes, and argue politics. The chief topic of discussion at the time were the relative virtues and vices of the rival national candidates, President Andrew Jackson and Senator Henry Clay of Kentucky. The presidential election of 1832 was approaching, and those antagonists, would be pitted against each other on the national electoral ballot in each state in the struggle for the White House. And even in that early day Lincoln was veering toward preference for Clay.

It is evident that at this time Lincoln was thinking in terms of a political career, for he determined to improve his speaking, and he attended meetings of the New Salem Debating Society. Lincoln folklore is filled with tales of how he, first in Indiana, then in Macon County, and finally in New Salem, practiced oratory by making extemporaneous speeches to tree trunks and corn stalks. Now early in 1832 he made his first public address in New Salem. One villager, R. B. Rutledge, recalled it: "As he arose to speak, his tall form towered above the little assembly. Both hands were thrust down deep in the pockets of his pantaloons. A perceptible smile at once lit up the face of the audience, for all anticipated the relation of some humorous story. But he opened up discussion in splendid style, to the infinite astonishment of his friends."

Meanwhile, Lincoln's boss, Offutt, had paid scant attention to his store, devoting his time and ever enterprising vigor to importing Tennessee seed corn. Early in 1832, after his store, with Lincoln as clerk, had operated less than eight months, it failed. Offutt left New Salem and subsequently practiced the horse-taming occupation as "Dr. Denton Offutt," even writing a tract, *Phrenology & Physiology of Animals*. The last that Lincoln was to hear of this enterprising but restless entrepreneur was almost three decades later. Offutt in 1861 was to send a letter to his former store clerk, then President-elect of the United States, requesting a federal job—a request which President-elect Lincoln did not grant.

So in the Spring of 1832 Abe Lincoln found himself without a job.

At this point excitement gripped Springfield in particular and the whole of Sangamon County in general. The steamboat *Talisman* was going to try to make its way up the Sangamon river.

The Sangamon was a narrow and shallow stream filled with hidden tree trunks, drifting timber and debris and lined with thick underbrush. On this treacherous river twenty miles from New Salem lay Springfield, the fastest growing town in the county. If the river could be successfully navigated as far as Springfield, the town and the county would become an increasingly important center of transportation and trade with the East. Its boosters already were predicting that Springfield would soon replace Vandalia as the capital of the state. So interest in the *Talisman's* voyage ran high.

"Captain" Vincent Bogue, the skipper of the *Talisman,* had hired several young men and had equipped them with long-handled axes to cut off over-hanging limbs and to clear snags from the channel. Among these young men was Abe Lincoln.

Passing New Salem, the steamboat puffed up the river in March of 1832, finally tying up at a point seven miles from Springfield. A gala reception awaited the ship and her crew at Springfield. A dance was given at the court house, and liquid cheer was dispensed in huge quantities at a tavern, the "Indian Queen." The local rhymesters composed doggerel in anticipation of the success of the *Talisman's* navigation and in hope for a greater Springfield:

> Oh, Captain Bogue, he gave the load,
> And Captain Bogue, he showed the road,
> And he came up with a right good-will
> And tied his boat up to his mill.
>
> And we are up the Sangamaw
> And sure will have a good hurrah.
> So fill your glasses to the brim
> With whiskey, brandy, wine and gin.

The *Talisman,* however, was not to achieve its goal. Receding water forced "Captain" Bogue to start his return trip without going farther.

An experienced boatsman, J. Rowan Herndon, was engaged to pilot the craft back to Beardstown. And, again, Lincoln was among those hired to aid in that return trip. Traveling at the snail's-pace of four miles a day, the steamer barely kept afloat as the river fell. At New Salem a portion of the dam was torn down in order to enable her to pass.

Finally, the *Talisman* succeeded in reaching Beardstown, and Lincoln and the other hired hands received forty dollars each for their work.

V

Lincoln had no sooner returned to New Salem after the abortive *Talisman* trip than Illinois became engulfed with fear over the "invasion" of Black Hawk, the Sauk Indian chief, and his followers.

The Black Hawk War, which would briefly interrupt Lincoln's New Salem life, had a lengthy and complex origin. In 1804 representatives of the Sauk and Fox Indian tribes had signed a treaty with the United States Government, ceding all of their lands east of the Mississippi and a segment of their hunting grounds west of that river. That Indian delegation, then in St. Louis to surrender the murderer of a white man, had not been authorized to make such an extravagant cession. However, one article, providing that the Indians might continue to occupy the land until further notice, eased the impact of that treaty.

During the War of 1812-15 some of the tribesmen had sided with the British against the United States. Inept American diplomacy, British generosity, and resentment over the 1804 treaty had inspired an Indian faction, led by the pro-British Black Hawk, a Sauk chief, to action. Year after year, following the War of 1812-15, white American frontiersmen plowed their furrows closer to Saukenuk, the principal Sauk village at the mouth of the Rock River. As white men advanced from the south and east, the wild life, upon which the Indians depended for food and trading skins, retreated. The Sauk and Foxes were forced to go farther north and west for the peltries they traded for guns, traps, and other necessities. This carried them into the territory of the Sioux and precipitated warfare for the next generation.

By 1827 Illinoisans were demanding that the United States Government remove the Sauks and Foxes from the ceded lands. In 1828 the Secretary of War announced that, by May, 1829, the Indians would be gone from Illinois. With the expectation that the redmen would not return to Saukenuk, a party of white American squatters settled there. But some Sauks and Foxes returned in 1829, and whites and Indians passed an uneasy summer as unfriendly neighbors.

During the following year some Sauk and Foxes followed their leader, Black Hawk, back to Saukenuk. But when General Edmund Penleton Gaines moved on this band with nearly 2,000 troops, Black Hawk withdrew with his men, putting up no resistance.

General Gaines extracted a promise from the Indians not to return again. Apparently the incident was closed. Nevertheless, in the winter of 1831-32 Black Hawk's hopes revived. Rumors reached him that he would receive aid from several other tribes and the British. With these not overly substantial assurances he was able to persuade some 2,000 Sauk and Foxes to accompany him back across the Mississippi.

The return of the "British Band" of Indians, as Black Hawk's followers were called, coincided with the arrival at Rock Island of General Henry Atkinson with a small force of regular troops to prevent a threatened attack by the Menominee and Sioux tribes on their bitter enemies, the Sauks and the Foxes. When Black Hawk's men refused to retreat, General Atkinson called on Illinois for help from that State's militia.

On April 7, 1832, twelve days before Governor John Reynolds of

Illinois called for mounted volunteers to fight Black Hawk's "invasion," Abe Lincoln was elected a captain of the Thirty-first Regiment of Illinois Militia. It was another indication of how quickly he had become popular after his arrival in New Salem.

On April 21, two days after Governor Reynolds's call for volunteers reached New Salem, recruits gathered at a farm on Richland Creek, nine miles to the southwest. On the 26th, Springfield's *Sangamo Journal,* taking note of the huge number of Kentucky-descended young men among the volunteers, burst into rhyme as it wished them godspeed in their fight against Black Hawk:

> Brave Sangamon hath arm'd
> All to defend her right
> Arouse ye old Kentucky boys,
> The foremost in the fight,
> Away! Away! Away!

At Richland Creek one group formed itself into a company, and elected Offutt's former store clerk its Captain. Lincoln phrased it: "To his own surprise, he was elected captain of it." One New Salemite, Dr. John Allen, described that election subsequently: "Way Capt. was chosen was that the candidates stood out alone and the men walked to the man that they chose to be their leader. At least three out of every four went to Lincoln at once, when it was found that he was the choice they kept coming over to him until his opponent was left standing almost alone." It seemed inevitable that Lincoln would have been chosen company commander, since those who chose him were the same friends who had elected him Captain of the militia company in New Salem earlier in the month.

The Black Hawk War proved a minor conflict of short duration, with only two engagements meriting descriptions as battles. These occurred at Wisconsin Heights and Bad Axe, in neither of which Lincoln participated.

Captain Lincoln's company on April 28 drew supplies for the next day's march: soap, candles, flint, gridirons, tin buckets, coffee boilers, tin pans, tin cups, and thirty muskets and bayonets. Soon food became scarce, and some of Lincoln's men preyed on the hogs at nearby farms before the arrival of reinforcements. Marches up Rock River in May were ordered by the commanding General, ostensibly in pursuit of the Indians but actually to keep the volunteers busy so that they would not desert and return home. At a small Potawatomi village, near present-day Sycamore, a crisis developed when the troops demanded their discharge. Governor Reynolds called Lincoln and the other captains together and asked for a vote on continuing the pursuit of the enemy or going home. It resulted in a tie. That vote infuriated General Samuel Whiteside, who growlingly declared that he would no longer lead such men except to be discharged. The march south to Ottawa, the place of discharge, began, but was interrupted by a day spent in searching the men for articles of plunder stolen from two deserted villages of friendly Indians. Mustering out began at Ottawa on May 26. Captain Lincoln's company was honorably discharged from the United States Army.

Lincoln, now a former Captain, re-enlisted—as a private! Perhaps his decision to continue in service against Black Hawk and his warriors for an additional twenty days was prompted by several considerations: his recognition of the need for protection of the northern Illinois settlers, his predicament at having no job to which to return and his realization that, as an already announced candidate for the Legislature of Illinois, it was expedient, from the viewpoint of vote getting, to see the war through.

Private Lincoln for his second enlistment was mustered by Lieutenant Robert Anderson (nearly thirty years later to be commander of besieged Fort Sumter) into the mounted Independent Rangers under Captain Elijah Iles. In that contingent were several former generals, colonels, and captains. Lincoln furnished his own arms valued at $10 and a horse and equipment worth $120. Where he secured the funds is still a mystery.

Captain Iles's company, with Private Lincoln of New Salem in it, was ordered on June 5 to be prepared to take the field "on an excursion of several days." Reduced to forty-eight men, the contingent left Ottawa on a march to Dixon's Ferry with orders to report to Colonel Zachary Taylor, future Mexican War hero and President of the United States. Their equipment, besides arms, consisted of blankets, tin cups, coffee pots, and such food as bread and fat side meat, which they ate raw or broiled. Then Private Lincoln's company was ordered to Galena, their captain being instructed to collect information about the enemy. On the return march to Dixon's Ferry, they passed a camp of 170 Sioux, Menominee, and Winnebago Indians, anti-Black Hawk red warriors under command of an American colonel. Lincoln's commanding officer, Captain Iles, reported to Colonel Taylor that the small bodies of hostile Indians who had committed minor depredations seemed more anxious to obtain horses than white men's scalps.

Private Lincoln's twenty-day second enlistment ended without his encountering Black Hawk's warriors in battle. He was mustered out of service by Lieutenant Anderson at Fort Wilbourn, but he re-enlisted again, this time as a Private in the Independent Spy Company commanded by Captain Jacob M. Early. From June 20 until his term was concluded on July 10, Lincoln served under Early, during which brief period he was destined not to see battle action against the Indians. Through the swamp and sink holes up White Water River, Early's men, Lincoln among them, unsuccessfully scoured the country for two days in search of Black Hawk's marauders. When supplies were exhausted,

General Atkinson dismissed the independent commands, of which Lincoln's outfit was one.

Lincoln was called on by Captain Early to write the company's mustering out roll. On his own papers Lincoln could read that he was honorably discharged "with the special thanks of Brigadier General H. Atkinson, Commander in Chief of the Army of the Illinois Frontier . . . at Headquarters on White Water of Rock River."

Lincoln's horse and that of one of his messmates, Private George M. Harrison, were stolen the day they were mustered out. He and Harrison were forced to make most of the 250-mile journey home on foot. In Peoria the two mustered-out Black Hawk War veterans purchased a canoe in which to make the trip down the Illinois River to Havana, where, after selling their canoe, Lincoln and his companion walked the twenty-eight-mile hot, sandy trail to New Salem.

Back in New Salem, Lincoln learned that he had still some "paper" work to finish in connection with his former commission as Captain. He wrote out discharges for a few of the men who had served under him. One of these discharges, recently discovered, for a Private Nathan Drake, entirely in Lincoln's handwriting and dated July 24, 1832, reads:

> I do hereby certify that Nathan Drake volunteered and served as a private in the company I commanded, in the regiment commanded by Colonel Samuel M. Thompson, in the Brigade commanded by Brigadier General Samuel Whiteside, in an expedition against the Sac and Fox Indians—and that he was enrolled on the 29th day of April and discharged on the 8th day of June 1832—having served forty and two thirds days—given under my hand this 24th July 1832.
>
> A. Lincoln, Captain.

Lincoln, in one of his two autobiographical sketches, told of his Black Hawk service briefly: "He went through the campaign, served near three months, met the ordinary hardships of such an expedition, but was in no battle."

Sixteen years later, in 1848, Lincoln joked about his experiences in the expedition against Black Hawk and his followers in a speech to his colleagues in the House of Representatives at Washington. The purpose of the speech was purely politically partisan. He was ridiculing the record of the contemporary Democratic candidate for President in the War of 1812. He said of Senator Lewis Cass of Michigan:

"In the days of the Black Hawk War, I fought, bled, and came away. Speaking of General Cass's career, reminds me of my own. I was not at Stillman's defeat, but I was about as near it as Cass was to Hull's surrender; and, like him, I saw the place very soon afterwards. It is quite certain I did not break my sword, for I had none to break; but I bent a musket pretty badly on one occasion. If Cass broke his sword, the idea is, he broke it in desperation; I bent the musket by accident. If General Cass went in advance of me in picking whortleberries [huckleberries], I guess I surpassed him in charges upon the wild onions. If he saw any live fighting Indians, it was more than I did, but I had a good deal of bloody struggles with the mosquitoes; and although I never fainted from loss of blood, I can truly say I was often hungry."

Still later, in 1858, Lincoln in an electioneering speech referred to the conflict against Black Hawk as "a war which truly was not a very extensive one, or calculated to make great heroes of men engaged in it."

Within himself, however, Lincoln was proud of his Black Hawk War service, however devoid it was of military glory. He was pleased when bounty lands were awarded by the Federal Government to veterans of that modest conflict. He located both of his warrants for acreage in Iowa. He also referred to his election as a Captain as a success which gave him profound pleasure.

Lincoln was never to be known widely as "Captain Lincoln," although many who were with him in pursuing Black Hawk's Indians pretentiously clung to their military titles throughout life.

VI

Back at New Salem from his Black Hawk War service in July, 1832, the unemployed store clerk continued his campaign for a seat in the House of Representatives, or Assembly, of the state Legislature of Illinois. He lost the election.

In his autobiography for Scripps, Lincoln told about his predicament at this time:

"Returning from the [war] campaign, and encouraged by his great popularity among his immediate neighbors, he, the same year, ran for the Legislature and was beaten—his own precinct, however, casting its vote 277 for and 7, against him. And this while he was an avowed Clay man, and the precinct the autumn afterwards, giving a majority of 115 to Genl. Jackson over Mr. Clay [for President]. This was the only time A. [Abraham] was beaten on a direct vote of the people. He was now without means and out of business, but was anxious to remain with his friends who had treated him with so much generosity, especially as he had nothing elsewhere to go to. He studied what he should do—thought of learning the black-smith trade—thought of trying to study law—rather thought he could not succeed at that without a better education. Before long, strangely enough, a man offered to sell and did sell, to A. [Abraham] and another [William F. Berry] as poor as himself, an old stock of goods, upon credit. They opened as merchants."

Thus was opened another general store in New Salem: Berry & Lincoln.

During the following January (1833) the new store partners bought out the stock of Reuben Radford, whose goods had been scattered by a night invasion of his place by the Clary's Grove boys.

Two months later Senior Partner Berry and Junior Partner Lincoln were granted a permit to sell spiritous liquors. The Commissioner of Sangamon County "ordered that William F. Berry, in the name of Berry and Lincoln, have license to keep a tavern in New Salem," and fixed the prices to be charged for beverages, board, and bedding of a horse:

French Brandy per ½ pint			25¢	Breakfast dinner supper		25¢
Peach " " " "			18¾	Lodging for night		12½
Apple " " " "			12	Horse for night		25¢
Holland Gin " " "			18¾	Single feed		12½
Domestic Gin " " "			12½			
Wine " " "			25	Breakfast dinner or Supper for Stage passengers		37½
Rum " " "			18¾			
Whiskey " " "			12½			

This bond was signed, "Abraham Lincoln, Wm. F. Berry," with Lincoln's New Salem friend, Bowling Green, Justice of the Peace, as surety.

After Lincoln's death in 1865, a fierce controversy raged as to whether the Berry & Lincoln store at New Salem sold liquor over the counter by the drink in 1833. Some of Lincoln's staunch prohibition-oriented defenders of the late nineteenth and early twentieth centuries insisted that Lincoln was strongly opposed to the over-the-counter sale of liquor. But it is very likely that the two partners did a profitable business in retail sales of alcohol.

Corn, the basic ingredient of whiskey, was the principal crop in and about Lincoln's region of Illinois. Whiskey distilling, therefore, constituted a common household industry. The resulting alcoholic drinks were an accepted tonic, restorative, and all-purpose medicine on the frontier, and it was often served to refresh and enliven people at dances, weddings, cabin raisings, baptisms, and various social frolics; to reward volunteer workers at the corn crib and harvests; and also to console mourners at funerals. Most general stores, such as that of Berry & Lincoln, sold liquor, and little or no ignominy or social disgrace was then attached to its traffic in those years before the church-inspired temperance and prohibition movements. Whiskey was no more out of place in a small frontier store than nails, black powder, tea, or calico. One New Salem old-timer put it this way: "As was customary in those days the 'merchants,' besides the usual supply of notions, calico, groceries, tobacco, etc., kept 'always on hand' a barrel or two of Monongahela or Old Rye, 'to be sold in quantities to suit the purchaser.' "

The sale of alcoholic beverages at the Berry & Lincoln store was to be resurrected in future years by Lincoln's political opponents in efforts to alienate the church-going vote. Senator Stephen A. Douglas in 1858, with Lincoln on the same speaker's platform, alluded to Lincoln as having once been a "flourishing grocery-keeper" in New Salem; and, during Lincoln's campaign for President in 1860, one opposition campaign sheet accused him of having worked as a "grog-shop keeper" who "sold red-eye at a picayune a nip."

The Berry & Lincoln business soon closed up. In Lincoln's expressive phrase, their store "winked out"—words which inspired later writers on Lincoln to conclude that his heavy drinking partner, Berry, had become his own best customer, guzzling the profitable liquid merchandise and neglecting the store business. Still a bone of contention today is the reason for the store's failure. It has never been determined whether Berry's imbibing, Lincoln's preoccupation with politics and other activities, or both led to the collapse of their business.

VII

His store-keeping days ended, Lincoln accepted the job of Postmaster at New Salem in May, 1833. The position came from President Andrew Jackson's administration, although Lincoln was by now known as an ardent Anti-Jacksonite and a follower of Old Hickory's arch opponent, Henry Clay. Lincoln explained that the office was "too insignificant to make his politics an objection."

Lincoln's village mail-handling job, not onerous or burdensome, provided him with opportunity to read all of the newspapers that came through his office. Dr. John Allen of New Salem subsequently recalled Lincoln's happy reaction to his appointment: "Never saw a man better pleased. . . . As he said, he would then have access to all the newspapers —never yet being able to get half that he wanted before." Free from such store chores as drawing molasses and whiskey and cutting calico, the new Postmaster at New Salem now had time and opportunity to pore through out-of-state papers, particularly the Louisville *Journal,* the St. Louis *Missouri Republican,* the Cincinnati *Gazette,* and the Washington *National Intelligencer.*

The post office, too, enabled Lincoln to become better acquainted with settlers in New Salem and the surrounding country. He conducted the office in a highly informal way, using it to do favors for fellow-villagers. By now he had taken a full plunge into politics, and in 1834 he finally realized his ambition by being elected a Representative in the state Legislature. One New Salemite, Mathew S. Marsh, wrote East to a relative in 1835, telling how Lincoln carelessly left the post office open and provided free postage for his favorites. Marsh's letter to his relative read:

"The Post Master (Mr. Lincoln) is very careless about leaving his office open and unlocked during the day—half the time I go in and get my papers etc., without any one being there as was the case yesterday. The letter was only marked 25 and even if he had been there and known it was double, he would not have charged me any more—lucky he is a clever fellow and a particular friend of mine. If he is there when I carry this to the office—I will get him to 'Frank' it." Lincoln was apparently there when Marsh called, for he franked the letter for Marsh, thus making himself liable to a ten-dollar fine by Federal law. On the outside of the letter was written:

Free, A. Lincoln, P.M.
New Salem, Ill., Sept. 22.

Postmaster Lincoln the year previous had written one letter which indicated his indifference to postal regulations where his friends and political supporters were concerned. He penned these words to a fellow New Salemite: "At your request I send you a receipt for the postage on your paper. I am some what surprised at your request. I will, however, comply with it. The law requires News paper postage to be paid in advance and now that I have waited a full year you choose to wound my feelings by insinuating that unless you get a receipt I will probably make you pay it again."

Another existing letter, written as late as 1836 by Samuel D. Lockwood, before whom Lincoln was then appearing in a law case as attorney, was franked by him at Springfield. And this more than four months after the New Salem Post Office had been abolished!

Lincoln's compensation for three years' service as Postmaster amounted to a total salary of between $150 and $175. He was allowed 30 per cent of the receipts, up to $100, and 25 per cent of the next $100. He also received 50 per cent of the postage on newspapers, magazines, and pamphlets, and he was allowed two cents for every free letter delivered from his office, excepting those which were addressed to him. By virtue of his office Lincoln had the right to send and receive personal letters free and to receive one newspaper daily without charge.

VIII

More lucrative to Lincoln than the postmastership was his job as deputy county surveyor. Settlers were crowding into the community and demands arose on all sides for the establishment of boundary lines, for location of roads, and for surveys of new towns. The surveyor of Sangamon County, John Calhoun, a Jacksonite, found himself overburdened with work and offered Lincoln, an Anti-Jacksonite, a job as his assistant. Lincoln accepted, later telling how he "procured a compass and chain, studied Flint and Gibson a little, and went at it."

Lincoln was assigned to survey the northwestern part of Sangamon County, which later became Menard County. His first survey of record was made for Russell Godbey in January, 1834, a job for which he was reputed to have received two buckskins, which Mrs. Hannah Armstrong "foxed" on his pants to protect them from the briars.

Lincoln is known to have made surveys of three roads, three school sections, a dozen tracts of farm land ranging in size from 4 acres to 160 acres, and of the towns of Petersburg, New Boston, Albany, Huron, and Bath. Lincoln a generation later, in his celebrated United States Senate campaign against Stephen A. Douglas, recalled to voters of Bath that he "on this very spot, 22 years ago, had with his own hands staked out the first plat of this town of Bath."

Odd jobs supplemented Lincoln's earnings from his postmastership and surveying jobs. He worked at a still, subsequently in a debate with Douglas admitting that he "did work the latter part of one winter in a little still-house, up at the head of a hollow."

Official errands and temporary jobs—some of modest political patronage—yielded additional revenue to Lincoln. He served on juries occasionally. For clerking at elections, which he did frequently, he received one dollar per day; carrying poll sheets to the county seat, Springfield, meant a payment of $2.50.

Meanwhile, in 1834, Lincoln made another try for a seat in the Legislature of Illinois.

PRAIRIE POLITICIAN AND LEGISLATOR

3

I

ABRAHAM LINCOLN soon found Sangamon County fertile field for the practice of the profession in which he excelled: politics. For his central Illinois region, like the rest of the western frontier of his era, provided unique opportunities for men with electioneering skills and ambition for public position and power.

Politics in raw and rustic early nineteenth-century Illinois offered a turbulent political training ground for ambitious lawyers, newspaper editors, and county schoolmasters, or petty merchants and farmers, whose meager educational backgrounds were no obstacle to election in a society with an increasing number of elective offices. The western frontier gave rise to the purest form of democracy, in which the commonest of men rather than the semi-aristocratic republicans like Washington, Hamilton, and Adams controlled the state governments. And a successful candidate could rely only on his wits in the political infighting and backstage maneuvering that was central to political existence on the frontier. The professional western candidate for office was a master in the demagogic technique of exciting rather than informing his audiences, and this demagoguery was the rule rather than the exception in election campaigns in this remote region west of the Appalachians.

In the 1830's, Illinois politics had not yet come under the control of the party organizations. Rather, individual cliques vied for power by any means, foul or fair. Illustrative of the politicians' attitudes during this era is this letter to Governor Ninian Edwards from one of his lieutenants:

"We must make Wilson and Lockwood and their friends fight with us. They shall not be indifferent any longer, and hold themselves like Pope, ready to dine with our enemies whilst our slain carcasses are yet bleeding. Embroil every man of them in the contest. . . . Could you write without attacking Kane, would it not be better? If you can whip his forces by killing off his generals, is it not the safest way to whip him too? Fix it so as to force him to attack as Duncan has done. They intend to have him in the scales. Give him no excuse to say he has been *dragged* into it. They will drag him in."

In 1832, the twenty-three-year-old Lincoln plunged into this political cauldron as a candidate for the Illinois Legislature.

II

A politician to the bone, Lincoln never denied that he was otherwise. Although his eulogistic biographers later sought to make him a leader above mundane politics, Lincoln himself declared to his fellow-legislators in 1837, after talking about the machinations of politicians: "I say this with the greater freedom because, being a politician myself, none can regard it as personal." In 1858 he scribbled on some paper: "I have never professed an indifference to the honors of official station; and were I to do so now, I should only make myself ridiculous." And a year later he told a gathering of the Wisconsin State Agricultural Society at Milwaukee: "I am not quite sure that there is not cause of suspicion against you, in selecting me, in some sort a politician, and in no sort a farmer, to address you."

Lincoln, sensing his popularity in New Salem, in early March, 1832, a month before he left for the Black Hawk War, announced his candidacy for the House of Representatives (or Assembly) of the Illinois Legislature. His communication of March 9, "To the People of Sangamon County," offering himself as candidate, appeared in the *Sangamo Journal* of Springfield six days later. In it he advocated improvement of the Sangamon River to make it more navigable, abolition of exorbitant interest rates on loans, and the spread of education "as the most important subject which we as a people can be engaged in." He informed the voters in demagogic vein: "I am young and unknown to many of you. I was born and have ever remained in the most humble walks of life. I have no wealthy relations to recommend me."

After his brief Black Hawk War service Lincoln resumed his delayed campaign for state Representative. The *Sangamo Journal* had neglected to mention him as one of the Sangamon Countyites who had gone to war. At Lincoln's request that newspaper in its July 19 issue corrected the oversight: "Some weeks ago we gave a list of those candidates (eight) of this County (omitting by accident the name of Captain Lincoln, of New Salem) who were on the frontier periling their lives in the service of their country."

Candidate Lincoln stumped Sangamon County, shaking hands with farmers, lending them a hand very briefly with the pitchfork, and sometimes tossing horseshoes with them. He went from cabin to cabin, soliciting votes and acting like any Illinois office aspirant of that day. Governor Thomas Ford pointedly described that technique in his early history of the state: "As a candidate did not offer himself as the champion of any party, he usually agreed with all opinions, and promised everything demanded by the people." Lincoln utilized his talent for telling anecdotes. A. Y. Ellis, who claimed to have seen and heard Lincoln on that vote foraging campaign, stated: "He told several anecdotes, and applied them, as I thought very well. He also told the boys several stories which drew them after him." In advocating Henry Clay's favorite doctrines, a protective tariff, internal improvements, and a national bank, he told one audience: "My politics are short and sweet, like the old woman's dance."

When Sangamon Countyites voted on August 6, 1832, they defeated Lincoln. Running eighth in a field of thirteen county candidates for four legislative seats, he polled 657 votes in the county, of which 277 were given him in his own New Salem precinct.

During the following year, 1833, Lincoln accepted the New Salem postmastership. This enabled him to become better acquainted with the public, and in the 1834 election he presented himself again as a candidate for Representative.

William H. Herndon later reported about this second campaign:

"I have Lincoln's word for it that it was more of a hand-shaking campaign than anything else. Rowan Herndon relates that he came to his house during the harvest, when there were a large number of men at work in the field. He was introduced to them, but they did not hesitate to apprize him of their esteem for a man who could labor; and their admiration for a candidate for office was gauged somewhat by the amount of work he could do. Learning these facts, Lincoln took hold of a cradle, and handling it with remarkable speed, soon distanced those who undertook to follow him. The men were satisfied, and it is presumed he lost no votes in that crowd."

Although Lincoln was an admirer of Henry Clay personally and a supporter of his principles, he received strong backing in his campaign from President Jackson's supporters, arch foes of Clay. This was a tribute to Lincoln's popularity. Lincoln's second law partner, Stephen T. Logan, explained subsequently:

"In 1832 while he [Lincoln] got a very large vote in his own precinct of New Salem, they hadn't voted for him very well in other parts of the county. This made his friends down there very mad, and as they were mostly democratic, but were for Lincoln on personal grounds, in the next race [1834] they told their democratic brethren in the other parts of the county that they must help elect Lincoln, or else they wouldn't support the other democratic candidates. This they did purely out of their personal regard for him, and through that influence he was elected in 1834."

In winning, Lincoln ran second in a field of four victorious candidates, polling 1,376 votes to the biggest vote-getter's 1,390.

After the election, life for Lincoln continued as before—distributing mail, surveying, doing odd jobs, mingling with people as he awaited the meeting of the Illinois Legislature more than four months off in December.

During those weeks between August and December, 1834, the young Representative-elect of New Salem found time to begin the study of law. He started his legal career at the suggestion of John T. Stuart, Springfield attorney and Sangamon County's Whig leader, who had also been chosen a Representative at the recent election. Lincoln, in his 1860 Presidential autobiography for Scripps, narrated: "Major John T. Stuart, then in full practice of law, was also elected. During the canvass, in a private conversation he encouraged A. [Abraham] [to] study law. After the election he borrowed books of Stuart, took them home with him, and went at it in good earnest. He studied with nobody. He still mixed in the surveying to pay board and clothing bills. When the Legislature met, the books were dropped."

III

In late November, 1834, the near-twenty-six-year-old federal Postmaster of New Salem and state Representative-elect, accompanied by John T. Stuart and other Sangamon Countyites who had been elected law-makers, rode in a stage coach from Springfield to Vandalia, the state capital town, for the opening of the first session of the Ninth General Assembly of Illinois, the state legislature.

After two days and a night of bouncing over seventy-five miles of bumpy roads in the over-crowded coach, Lincoln and his colleagues reached Vandalia. The driver, on entering town, whipped up his horse and blew a blast on his horn as he drew up before the Vandalia Inn.

This State governmental seat, an overgrown village of log cabins containing eight hundred people, stood atop a bluff overlooking the Kaskaskia River, in the Fayette County semi-wilderness. Vandalia's streets in 1834 lay covered with mud or dust, depending on the weather. One visitor several years later described the place in William Oliver's *Eight Months In Illinois:* "Bilious fever prevailed here, and there were several patients in the hotel where we stayed. . . . Vandalia can not be a healthy place with this dismal swamp on one side, and some very low wet prairies on the other." Like most state capitals before and since, it was a heavy-drinking town.

Vandalia was to exert a determining influence on the legislator from New Salem. His public career is better understood by devoting more attention to his association with power-wielding politicians in behind-doors caucuses there, than to his relations with obscure folklorish New Salem pioneers whom he would forget within four years. Here Lincoln received his first real professional political education.

Lincoln and this primitive capital possessed things in common—a certain frontier uncouthness, a ramshackle appearance, and a look of incompleteness. As the State capital the town was an experiment, and the same might have been noted of the solon from New Salem. All of this despite his appearance in a new sixty-dollar tailor-made suit, which he had bought with part of the two hundred dollars he had borrowed from Coleman Smoot, a New Salemite. The loan, observed Lincoln whimsically, was a sort of penalty upon Smoot for having voted for him.

Lincoln's friend, law mentor, colleague and party leader, Representative John T. Stuart, was recognized as Sangamon County's undisputed anti-Jacksonian chieftain. He showed Lincoln around Vandalia. Stuart's wife later described Abe's appearance as: "A raw tall . . . very countrified looking man, yet who spoke with such force and vigor that he held the close attention of all."

Both Lincoln and Stuart, like most of President Jackson's opponents and Henry Clay's disciples, were soon called "Whigs." It was a name taken from the late eighteenth-century English Whig party, which had opposed the British king. In 1834 American cartoonists drew caricatures of autocratic President Jackson as "King Andrew I." And so organized opposition to Jacksonism was called "Whiggery."

Lincoln became an ardent Whig because of his adulation for Henry Clay, though he had never met the magnetic "Harry of the West." He approved of Clay's "American System," particularly the internal improvements at federal government expense. On one occasion he was to refer to the venerable Kentuckian as "my beau-ideal of a statesman." Too, Lincoln was never to be anything but a moderate, and the Whigs were the party of conservatism, at fierce odds with radical Jacksonian democracy.

Lincoln's Vandalia was a turbulent political arena, a center of "log-rolling" for passage of special legislation. Ambitious legislators and lobbyists devoted only to themselves, their personal interests, and their sections, manipulated these "deals" at the expense of the general public welfare. John Reynolds, who had just relinquished the Illinois governorship, lamented in later years: "I immediately discovered that I could effect nothing in the legislature, in the office of governor." And Thomas Ford, destined to serve as Governor from 1842 to 1844, stated in his history of Illinois, about the pioneer legislators: "Almost everything done there was done from personal motives. Special legislation for the benefit of friends occupied members."

Among the ambitious Illinois politicians that Lincoln first met at Vandalia was a round-faced, short, rotund Vermont-born Jacksonite from Morgan County, Stephen Arnold Douglas. The Democratic Party's future Little Giant, whose career was to constantly cross Lincoln's, was already a master in capturing a crowd. He had learned the entertainment-packed arts of the frontier stump, where his bombastic oratory exploded like fireworks as he savagely denounced President Jackson's foes. Demagogically Douglas would shed his coat and collar and shake his shock of dark hair as his voice boomed in defense of Old Hickory.

Representative Lincoln, measuring himself by the attainment of others and solicitous to match his talents with his rivals', later recorded about Douglas and himself: "We were both young men then; he a trifle younger than I. Even then, we were both ambitious; I, perhaps, quite as much as he."

IV

When the solon from New Salem on Monday, December 1, 1834, entered the State House for the first session of the Lower House of the General Assembly of Illinois, he found himself with his legislative colleagues, Jacksonites and Clayite Anti-Jacksonites, in a building which, although erected only ten years previous, verged on collapse. Acting Governor William L. D. Ewing, in his farewell address, noted: "The appearance of the building is not calculated to add either character or credit to the State."

The members sat at long tables, three to each table. The Speaker presided from a similar one, slightly elevated, equipped with a pewter inkstand. Sand boxes were distributed about for the use of tobacco chewers who had been designated by one critic as "statesmen of great expectorations." Most representatives were dressed in long, black, wide-lapelled coats, tight trousers, and stiff collars held high by neck pieces called "stocks" which encircled their necks with layers of black cloth. It has been commented that "the honorable representatives looked more dignified and formal than they were in fact."

Lincoln found that he and his fellow Whigs in that Ninth General Assembly were a minority in Jackson-crazed Illinois. Of eighty-one members in both houses, only ten senators and eighteen representatives were Whigs. He would almost invariably follow the anti-Jacksonian party line for more than twenty years to come, although members in 1834 were given no party labels in the House *Journal*. With few exceptions his name would be recorded always on roll calls with his friend and mentor, Stuart, who had been chosen Whig minority leader in the Assembly.

Lincoln, as a new member, was given no choice committee posts. He was placed on various minor special committees including the unimportant Committee on Public Accounts and Expenditures. Stuart, who planned to run for Congress, was grooming his young New Salem colleague and protegé as his possible successor as the Whig leader of the House. And even in those very early days Lincoln was entrusted with writing some bills which would be sponsored by other less literate members.

The session was only four days old when, on December 5, Lincoln gave notice that he would, on the Monday following or after, introduce a bill to "limit the jurisdiction of Justices of the Peace." The next Tuesday he sponsored his bill, which was read and ordered to a second reading.

This bill, Lincoln's first attempt at legislating, was inspired by his discussions with Bowling Green, who had held the office of Justice of the Peace in New Salem since its inception. Lincoln's measure provided that a justice of the peace should not have jurisdiction over any civil case unless it was in the precinct in which the defendant resided, or in which the contract on which the suit was brought was made and entered into, or made payable. But the House Committee, to which Lincoln's bill was referred, reported out a substitute measure. The House referred the substitute to a second committee, on which Lincoln served. This committee drafted a new bill, only to have the Senate table it.

Lincoln's Justice of the Peace bill had met the fate of most measures—amended or altered to death. It was the type of fate about which Governor Ford of Illinois made this quip: "The rage for amending and altering was so great, that it was said to be a good thing that the Holy Scriptures did not have to come before the Legislature; for that body would be certain to alter and amend."

Lincoln enjoyed better luck with his second sponsored bill, an act to authorize Samuel Musick to build a toll bridge across Salt Creek in Sangamon County. Musick, operator of a ferry, felt that increased travel on the Springfield-Peoria road justified the expense of constructing such an overpass. Sponsored on December 15, Lincoln's bill passed the House in amended form five days later.

The legislative session was only five weeks old when, in January, 1835, the Representative from New Salem tested his brand of humor on the House floor. One member proposed a resolution, "That the nomination of Samuel McHattan, for County Surveyor of Schuyler county . . . be vacated for the reason that said office was not vacant at the time such nomination was made." The member from New Salem held forth on that motion. The *Sangamo Journal* on January 17, 1835, reported the news from Vandalia:

"Mr. Lincoln said, that if, as appeared to be the opinion of legal gentlemen, there was no danger of the new surveyor's ousting the old one so long as he persisted not to die—he would suggest the propriety of letting matters remain as they were, so that if the old surveyor should hereafter conclude to die, there would be a new one ready made without troubling the Legislature." The resolution was tabled.

During that session Lincoln loyally supported Henry Clay's defense of the United States Bank, then in the throes of destruction by President Jackson. And when that first session of the Ninth General Assembly, by the dim light of candles, adjourned *sine die* on the evening of February 13, 1835, Lincoln could look back on invaluable training in the severe school of State-capital politics.

V

Returning to New Salem after the Legislature's adjournment, Lincoln resumed his law study which he had begun before the session convened. As he said in his autobiography, "When the Legislature met, the law books were dropped, but were taken up again at the end of the session." He visited the office of John T. Stuart and his partner, Henry E. Dummer, to borrow or return law books. In between his legal studies he resumed his Postmaster's duties and also accepted appointment as county deputy surveyor.

All this time Lincoln kept his political fences in repair, building up a personal following outside New Salem. Recognizing that the life blood of the practical political body was patronage, he was vigilant in trying to care for his supporters, even though his opposition controlled the State government. Here is a typical letter that he wrote in November,

1835, to Governor Joseph Duncan in behalf of a prospective follower: "Understanding that Mr. Levi Davis of Vandalia is an applicant for the office of Auditor of Public Accounts. I take the liberty to say to you, that his appointment to that office would be entirely satisfactory to me, and, I doubt not, to most others who are friends of qualification and merit."

Early the next December, Representative Lincoln was again in Vandalia for the special session of the Legislature. Since his legal mentor and Whig party boss, Representative Stuart, had his eye on a seat in Congress and thus played a less active role in mapping party strategy, Lincoln became more important as a Whig leader.

With re-election ever in mind, the New Salem member vigilantly watched the interests of Sangamon County and its citizens who wanted "things done" for themselves. He and the other Sangamonites in state House and Senate had plans to have the State capital moved from Vandalia, in Fayette County, to Springfield in their own county. They engaged in profuse "log-rolling," viz., uniting with legislative colleagues from other counties in the passage or defeat of laws that would help or hamper their respective countries. The Sangamon County delegations in both houses were now feverishly casting their votes in favor of appropriations for roads and other "internal improvements," in anticipation of reciprocal aid from legislators of those counties benefitted.

In January, 1836, the special legislative session ended, and Members rushed home to get their re-election campaigns rolling.

In the months following, the *Sangamo Journal* called on all candidates to "show their hands." In June, Lincoln answered the *Journal:* "Agreed. Here's mine"—and he enclosed his platform, which called for universal white adult suffrage, "by no means excluding females," and for the favorite Whig proposal of the federal government to distribute to the states the proceeds of the sale of public lands, so that states could finance canal and railroad construction and other internal improvements.

Lincoln, on June 21, 1836, penned a rebuke to a Democratic politician, Robert Allen, who had been circulating charges designed to injure his chances for re-election. He wrote:

> Last week you passed through this place and stated publicly that you were in possession of a fact or facts, which if known to the public would entirely destroy the prospects of N. W. Edwards and myself at the ensuing election, but that through favor to us you would forbear to divulge them. . . . If I have done anything, either by design or misadventure, which if known would subject me to a forfeiture of that [public] confidence, he that knows of that thing, and conceals it, is a traitor to his country's interest. . . . I am flattered with the personal regard you manifested for me; but I do hope that on mature reflection you will view the public interest as a paramount consideration and let the worst come. . . . I wish an answer to this, and you are at liberty to publish both if you choose.

Division of Lincoln's vast Sangamon County, then sixty-five miles long and fifty-five miles wide, became a prime re-election issue. The lengthy journey for some settlers to the county seat, Springfield, brewed dissatisfaction and demands that Sangamon be split up into several counties, a sentiment supported by land speculators and town promoters. Candidate Lincoln found himself in a dilemma. If he opposed county division too vigorously, he might defeat himself for a second term. If he favored it too vocally, it would take precedence over his more significant plan to persuade the Legislature to pass a law for the removal of the State capital from Vandalia to Springfield. Any hope of winning the parliamentary fight for change in the State's seat of government would require the dedicated and combined efforts of all legislators from Sangamon County. Lincoln skillfully got past his dilemma by evading the issue of county division.

And he won re-election by an impressive vote.

VI

"Our chances to [take the] seat of Government to Springfield are better than I ex[pected]. An Internal Improvement Convention was held here since we met, which recommended a loan of several milli[ions] of dollars on the faith of the State to construct Railroads."

This letter, which Lincoln sent to Mary Owens on December 13, 1836, indicated that the "Move the Capital to Springfield" crusade would be tightly intertwined with the plan to vote huge public funds for the construction of roads, canals, and other public improvements at State expense. "Log-rolling" was the theme when the Legislature convened at Vandalia that December. The spearheads of the pro-Springfield movement, militant, skilful, and trading, were the "Long Nine," led by Lincoln.

Sangamon County had elected seven representatives—one of them Lincoln—and two senators, who banded together because of their local political interests, particularly to secure the capital for Springfield. Each stood six feet or over, and they became dubbed "The Long Nine." The six-foot-four New Salemite, who called himself "the longest of the nine," was their acknowledged strategy director. The other eight were State Senators Job Fletcher and Archer G. Herndon and Representatives William E. Elkin, John Dawson, Robert L. Wilson, Andrew McCormick, Dan Stone, and Ninian W. Edwards. The highly pedigreed Edwards, son of Former Governor Ninian Edwards of Illinois, came from the Springfield social elite. Within two years his wife's half sister from

Kentucky, Mary Ann Todd, would arrive to live in the Edwards mansion.

The Lincoln-led "Long Nine," in their grim determination to have the capital removed to Springfield, in angry opposition to those who insisted that it remain in Vandalia, or be transferred to Alton or some other town, showed rare judgment in accomplishing their ends. Lincoln and his eight fellows agreed to the adoption, for other regions of the State, of extravagant appropriations for construction of internal improvements, all in return for the votes of these regions' representatives on the capital-removal bill. Sangamon County's seven votes in the House and two votes in the Senate were promised for a railroad here, a canal there, a bridge somewhere else, provided that support for Springfield as the State government seat were pledged in return. Too, those groups who clamored for the division of Sangamon County into several counties were placated by promises that their wishes would be fulfilled after the capital was transferred to Springfield.

The "Long Nine" succeeded in having both houses of the Legislature repeal the law that located the capital by popular vote. In its place the two chambers passed legislation providing that the location of the new capital would be made by the legislators of both houses on February 28, when the internal improvement issue would be out of the way. Lincoln mapped strategy and guided the pro-Springfield forces, receiving help from those law-makers who wanted only to take the capital from Vandalia and place it in Alton or some even smaller town.

On February 28 the ballot on the new location was taken. On the first roll call Springfield received 35 votes, more than twice as many as Vandalia, its nearest competitor. On the next two ballots Springfield increased its lead. Then "band wagon" statesmen went for the Sangamon County town. On the fourth, Springfield received a majority of votes. In two years Springfield was to be the Illinois capital.

Two years later the Vandalia *Free Press* angrily noted: "Mr. Lincoln admitted that *Sangamon county had received great and important benefits, at the last session of the Legislature, in return for giving support, thro' her delegation, to the system of Internal Improvements.*"

Lincoln's future law partner, Stephen T. Logan, remonstrated with him for having supported the recklessly expensive internal-improvement appropriations. Later Logan revealed: "I was in Vandalia that winter and had a talk with Lincoln there. I remember that I took him to task for voting for the Internal Improvement scheme. He seemed to acquiesce in the correctness of my views as I presented them to him. But he said he couldn't help himself—he had to vote for it in order to secure the removal here [to Springfield] of the seat of government."

On that evening of the day of their victory, February 28, the triumphant legislators celebrated at Ebenezer Capps's tavern in Vandalia. The original bill for the banquet, rendered by Capps, to John Dawson, one of Lincoln's "Long Nine," and paid by the wealthy Edwards, another of the "Long Nine," has been preserved:

Vandalia, Ill., Feb. 28, 1837.

Colonel Dawson to E. Capps, Dr.:

81 bottles of champagne at $2.00 each	$162.00
Drinks	6.00
32 pounds almonds	8.00
10 pounds raisins	10.00
Cigars	10.00
Oysters	10.00
Apples	3.00
Eatables	12.00
Breakage	2.00
Sundries	.50
TOTAL	$223.50

Rec'd payment of N. W. Edwards, March 4th.
[signed] E. Capps.

And so Lincoln, "Long Nine" leader, log-rolled the State capital into Springfield.

VII

When news reached Springfield that the legislative battle for the State capital had been won, there were eardrum-piercing demonstrations of joy. Normally sober citizens' heads ached and their stomachs rolled from surplus celebration. The "groceries" and inns did a record business. Lincoln and others of the tall Sangamon solons would soon be welcomed with public dinners and the effervescent buncombe of local orators, and Abe received the lion's share of the praise.

Less than two months after passage of the capital-removal bill Lincoln wound up his affairs in New Salem and decided to settle in Springfield. In the new State capital he would be close to future significant political operations and to his law partnership with John T. Stuart. Years later Albert S. Edwards, declared: "I never heard why Mr. Lincoln made the change of residence. I suppose it was because Springfield was the larger place with more future in it."

Representative Lincoln in April, 1837, packed his scanty belongings in saddle bags and rode on a borrowed horse to Springfield. Arriving there, he entered the store of Joshua Fry Speed, a transplanted Kentuckian, and ordered a mattress and other accessories. When Speed's price of $17 was more than the impecunious politician could afford, Speed generously invited him to share his quarters. Lincoln accepted, and thus began a close lifelong relationship with Speed, to whom he was to refer as "my most intimate friend."

Abe was now a permanent Springfield resident.

EARLY SPRINGFIELD YEARS

4

I

THE Springfield in which Abraham Lincoln settled in 1837 then comprised an unattractive, crude community of fewer than 2,000 inhabitants. The town was built around an open square subsequently occupied by the State House. Its streets were unimproved. In summer, people and horses kicked up clouds of blinding dust that coated houses and shrubbery, and in winter, horses sank over their haunches into black, sticky mud in which wagons got adhesively mired almost to their hubs.

The townspeople showed themselves eager for distinction. Now that the State capital was to be shifted, they started improving the streets and beautifying the community. It would be a desirable locality for a practicing politician and lawyer like Lincoln. It was Illinois' new political Mecca and the site of both the Sangamon County and the State courts.

The settlers of Springfield started to become pretentious. Wealth made its gaudy display and sought to attain a pre-eminence from which learning and refinement were frequently excluded. "Family" asserted itself. People who laid claim to a presumably long line of distinguished ancestors became socially superior. The Edwardses, the Todds, and the Stuarts, surrounded by servants, led graciously comfortable lives in their large houses. Ninian W. Edwards, son and heir of Former Governor Ninian Edwards, had married Elizabeth Todd of Lexington, Kentucky. And in another two years Elizabeth's sister, Mary Ann Todd, would come from Lexington to Springfield to make her home with the Edwardses and become a belle of the town's high society.

But the man who had led the successful struggle to bring the capital to Springfield found his first weeks in town depressing ones. The "great deal of flourishing about in carriages here," as he described the activities of Springfield's cultivated classes, deepened his dejection at his own poverty and caused him painful sensitivity over his social shortcomings. Less than one month after he changed his residence from New Salem he moodily summed up his feelings in a letter to a Mary Owens. "This thing of living in Springfield," he told her, "is rather a dull business after all, at least it is so to me. I am quite as lonesome here as [I] ever was anywhere in my life. I have been spoken to by but one woman since I've been here, and should not have been by her, if she could have avoided it. I've never been to church yet, nor probably shall not be soon. I stay away because I am conscious I should not know how to behave myself."

Such gloomy thoughts were partly caused by his deliberate discouragement of Miss Owen's attentions. His pessimistic mood partially passed away when he found absorbing occupation in politics and law. Too, he drew pleasure in the gab-fests at Speed's store.

Lincoln made Speed's store a sort of headquarters, even a second home, after he went to live with Mr. and Mrs. William Butler. In Speed's place politics, religion, and other controversial topics were discussed and argued. Around the fireplace gathered Lincoln, Edward D. Baker, another Whig manager, Orville H. Browning, State Senator from Quincy, an especially conservative Whig, and the brilliant Jacksonian Democrat, Stephen A. Douglas.

Some of the more intellectually gifted Springfielders, among them Milton Hay and James Matheny, formed a society for debate and literary efforts which Lincoln entertained with a few lines of rhyme. A "Young Men's Lyceum" had been also organized in Springfield. Here Lincoln was to deliver his first significant speech, "Perpetuation of Our Political Institutions," early in 1838.

A favorite diversion on the Illinois frontier of Lincoln's early Springfield years was the art of telling bawdy "stories." Lincoln, as a natural "mixer" and inbred politician, had made himself proficient in this art. The obscenity of some of his yarns probably was due to the fact that his childhood and youth had been spent among coarse people in the Indiana semi-wilderness. In later years, of course, he married Mary Todd, a proper and decorous lady from Lexington, Kentucky. In some circles of Illinois society off-color humor would continue as a passport to popularity for many years.

II

Lincoln's love for politics was not lessened by his new residence in Springfield. It was the new capital town; he held his seat in the Legislature, still meeting at Vandalia, and his law partner, mentor, and friend, John T. Stuart, reigned as Whig party overlord in the town and county.

The next year, 1838, Stuart would realize his ambition by his election to Congress over the Democrat, Douglas—a spectacular contest in which both candidates used veritable tree trunks, ox carts, barrels, and canal dumps from which to harangue the voters. In over 36,000 votes cast, Stuart defeated Douglas—by a majority of 36.

Lincoln, like his partner Stuart, revealed himself as much at home in a political caucus as in a courtroom, quite as adept in adopting Whig party pronunciamentoes as in drafting legal briefs, and as skilled in arousing stump audiences as in swaying judges and juries. Frequently the junior partner of Stuart & Lincoln left his law desk to call at the office of the *Sangamo Journal,* Whiggery's main mouthpiece. He grew friendly with its editor, Simeon Francis, and contributed political pieces, barbs at the Democrats, to that paper, appearing under such nom de plumes as "John Blubberhead," "Citizen of Sangamon," "Conservative," "Our Correspondent" and the "Sampson's Ghost" letters which demonstrated the extent to which the press was intertwined with politics, and politics with the law.

Lincoln's first public speech, 1838, the address to the "Young Men's Lyceum" of Springfield was not political partisanship. It revealed in Lincoln elements of his future statesmanship, and it showed that he possessed hidden qualities which placed him in high stature above any Illinois politician of his day.

He had grown alarmed at what he called in this address "the increasing disregard for law which pervades the country," particularly the outrages committed by mobs, as demonstrated by the horrors of lynch law in Mississippi and Missouri and the recent shooting of the abolitionist editor, Elijah P. Lovejoy, at Alton, in his own Illinois. He declared that the victims of mob rule ranged "from gamblers to Negroes, from Negroes to white citizens, and from these to strangers; till, dead men were seen literally dangling from boughs of trees." He cautioned: "Whenever the vicious portion of population shall be permitted to gather in bands of hundreds and thousands, and burn churches, ravage and rob provision stores, throw printing presses into rivers, shoot editors, and hang and burn obnoxious persons at pleasure, and with impunity; depend on it, this Government can not last." He pleaded: "Let reverence for the laws be breathed by every American mother to the lisping babe that prattles on her lap—let it be taught in schools, in seminaries, and in colleges;—let it be written in Primmers (sic), spelling books, and in Almanacs;—let it be preached from the pulpit, proclaimed in legislative halls, and enforced in courts of justice. And, in short, let it become the *political religion* of the nation; and let the old and the young, the rich and the poor, the grave and the gay, of all sexes and tongues, and colors and conditions, sacrifice unceasingly upon its altars."

Lincoln's Lyceum lecture indicated his knowledge of the alarming social conditions that prevailed in sections of the nation and was notable for the ideas which, he said, should be followed. It appealed against mob rule and sounded a clarion call to his fellow Sangamon Countyites to aid in advancing orderly processes of law and order, as befitted a self-governing nation. The address sounded refreshingly free from the usual politician-tinted superficialities of his pre-presidential period. It was to be acknowledged his first speech of distinction.

Later in 1838, he returned to the purely political platform, electioneering for a third legislative term. There loomed again the apparently never-dying issue of dividing Sangamon County into several counties.

During that year numberless meetings had been held in Sangamon, town fought town, and small-fry politicians saw chance for election to the Legislature on that issue. Working "coalitions" from various geographic areas were formed behind closed doors to carve out more counties from Lincoln's home county. In private correspondence strong animosity was expressed against the so-called "Whig Junto" in Springfield, which dictated Illinois Whiggery's destinies, and of which Lincoln was leader, now that John T. Stuart was involved with congressional duties and national politics. One Democratic candidate for the Legislature criticized "the spirit of intolerance and the hand of injustice" and the "dictatorial edicts" of the Lincoln-led coterie of Whig bosses and bosslets.

Lincoln learned in April, as he prepared his re-lection campaign, that a "deal" had been made by the Democratic overlords of Petersburg, Mt. Pulaski, and Allenton to divide Sangamon County into four equal squares, with the county seats of the proposed three new counties located in those three towns. Knowledge of this deal provoked land owners in other towns. A general feeling prevailed among Sangamon County farmers that some division should be made as a matter of convenience to them, but there existed no agreement on boundaries for the proposed new counties. Lincoln perceived that sentiment called for some splitting up of his county, and went along with the tide. He won a third term as Representative.

At the 1838-39 session of the Legislature Lincoln secured a place on the Committee on Counties. Although willing to follow public sentiment for Sangamon County division, he did not desire to see it cut into four equal squares, which would place his own town, Springfield, the State capital, in a corner of one square. Soon the Legislature received a petition against the proposed division of the county. It requested that the law-makers "make such just and reasonable division of said county, so that no line will come nearer than twelve miles of the town of Springfield." It was signed by 1,700 Whigs and Democrats, including numerous friends of Lincoln.

As a member of the House Committee on Counties Lincoln drafted a bill creating three new counties out of Sangamon, but his bill did not do any harm to Springfield. He reported his bill to the House on January 16, 1839, and the measure finally passed both houses of the Legislature without a recorded vote. The three new counties were named Menard, Logan, and Dane, and the first would contain his now extinct former home village of New Salem, which had been swallowed up by the town of Petersburg, the county seat of the new Menard County. Lincoln's bill left in Sangamon County a half dozen townships to the east of Springfield that would have been cut off if he had not succeeded in side-tracking the "four equal parts" proposal.

That 1838-39 session, the Eleventh General Assembly of the State of Illinois, was destined to be the last one to be held in Vandalia. Yet Vandalia's die-hard champions still fought to retain the capital, though the law for its removal to Springfield had been passed two years before! William L. D. Ewing, who represented Vandalia, announced his intention to introduce "An act to repeal certain laws relative to the permanent location of the Government of the State of Illinois." Alarmed, Lincoln rallied his forces to beat Ewing's action. In that debate the disgruntled Ewing demanded of the Whig members, indicating Lincoln: "Gentlemen, have you no other champion than this coarse and vulgar fellow to bring into the lists against me? Do you suppose that I will condescend to break a lance with your low and obscene colleague?"

Ewing's attempt to have the Legislature reconsider retaining the State capital in Vandalia failed, largely owing to Lincoln's leadership in its opposition. And three months following adjournment of that 1838-39 session, Governor Thomas Carlin proclaimed that, as of July 4, 1839, Springfield would become the capital of Illinois.

III

The presidential campaign of 1840 threw Illinois and the rest of the nation into a semi-delirium for months. It was a spectacle in which anti-Jacksonian Whigs, Lincoln's party, out-demagogued the demagogic Jacksonian Democrats.

Andrew Jackson, upon leaving the White House early in 1837, bequeathed to his hand-picked "Crown Prince" and successor, New York State Boss Martin Van Buren, a supremely popular Jacksonian party emphasizing the nobility of "common" men and hatred of aristocrats and cultivated classes, a party strongly appealing to the democratic western frontier.

But the effete eastern seaboarder, President Van Buren, having New York State in the palm of his hand, could not live up nationally to his nicknames, "Red Fox of Kinderhook" and "Little Magician," in holding Jacksonian mass support on the western frontier. Too, Van Buren was further bedevilled and bewitched by the fact that, no sooner had he installed himself in the presidency, than the panic of 1837 cast its grim shadow over the nation. The opposition Whigs now gleefully saw opportunity to exploit "hard times" presumably created by Van Buren and Jacksonian financial policies.

The Whigs at their national convention in Harrisburg, Pennsylvania, in December, 1839, rejected the celebrated Henry Clay and Daniel Webster, and named as their presidential standard-bearer General William Henry Harrison of Ohio. A grizzled western Indian fighter of elite Virginia ancestry, Harrison had a military record which could be resurrected and exhibited to the citizenry as a sure vote-getter. Jackson's mighty Missouri lieutenant, Senator Thomas Hart Benton, in his *Thirty Years' View,* expressed the Whigs' strategy: "The leading statesmen of the Whig party were passed by to make room for a candidate more sure of being elected. The success of General Jackson had turned the attention of those who managed the presidential nominations to military men, and an 'odor of gun powder' was considered a sufficient attraction to rally the masses." The Whigs chose John Tyler, a former Jacksonite of Virginia, who had broken with Old Hickory, as Harrison's Vice-Presidential running mate.

The Whig's decision not to adopt a national platform, on which Harrison and Tyler would run, indicated their dread of committing themselves on issues. Harrison hurrah and denunciation of Democrats who had started the economic depression were Whiggery's mob-mastering appeals all in lieu of discussion of public questions.

An unfortunate sneer in a Democratic newspaper in Baltimore gave the Whigs their campaign slogan. That Democratic journal had observed that old Harrison would be content to live out his remaining days in a log cabin, with a barrel of cider near by. Immediately Whig strategists transformed their well-born Virginia-gentry-descended candidate, Harrison, who lived prosperously in a North Bend, Ohio, mansion, into a simple living frontier farmer who threshed his own wheat, dwelled in a log cabin, and consumed the poor man's drink, cider. Their electioneering for Harrison comprised a phantasmagoria of cabins, coonskin caps, cider and songs, calculated to emphasize Harrison's "common man's" virtues, in contrast to Van Buren's life of luxury in the "Presidential Palace," drinking imported wines and dressing in silken clothing—all in lieu of the discussion of issues, except to emphasize that Van Buren had caused the depression. At times this Harrison-Van Buren national campaign appeared a contest between two styles of architecture, two varieties of alcoholic beverages, and two modes of dress. When the noted Whig editor of the Louisville *Journal,* George D. Prentice, was asked to explain how cider symbolized "Old Tippecanoe" (as Harrison was called after one of his Indian battles years before), Prentice replied with finality: "All we know is that it runs well."

Out on the Illinois prairies, where Lincoln was mixing Whig politics with his law practice for Stuart & Lincoln, feverish excitement was generated over that carnival-like "log cabin and cider" election of 1840.

The junior partner of Stuart & Lincoln and Representative in the Legislature plunged into the battle to beat President Van Buren and carry Illinois for "Old Tippecanoe and Tyler, too."

IV

Lincoln did not attend that Harrisburg conclave that nominated Harrison and Tyler. Now over thirty years old, he had not as yet traveled farther east than his native Kentucky. But he gave all his strength and took much time out from his law practice to organize Illinois for the Harrison-Tyler ticket.

By mail Lincoln kept his law partner and political associate, Congressman Stuart, informed. To Stuart in Washington he mailed this request:

> Be sure to send me as many copies of the life of Harrison, as you can spare from other uses.
>
> *Be verry* (sic) *sure* to procure and send me the Senate Journal of New York of September, 1814. I have a newspaper article which says that that document proves that Van Buren voted against raisin[g] troops in the last war.
>
> And in general, send me every thing you think will be a good *'war-club.'* The nomination of Harrison takes first rate. You know I am never sanguine, but I believe he will carry the State.

Lincoln himself had been appointed a presidential elector for Harrison, to be placed on the ballot in the national November election in Illinois. In addition, he mapped campaign strategy, as well as running for a fourth term as state Representative and aiding Stuart's re-election contest.

For the national fight the state Whig convention, meeting in Springfield, had provided for a party State Central Committee, composed of Lincoln and four of his close cronies—Speed, Edward D. Baker, his own politically crazed personal physician, Dr. Anson G. Henry, and Richard F. Barrett. This Lincoln-led committee, denounced by Democrats as the "Whig Junto," drew up a comprehensive plan of party organization down to the precinct level, which, in varied forms, has done yeoman electioneering service for all American political groups ever since.

Through this plan, mapped largely by Lincoln, according to a "confidential" circular, which he and his "Whig Junto" associates sent to key party men throughout Illinois, a complete party organization was outlined, "so that every Whig can be brought to the polls in the coming presidential contest." They admonished each of the suggested county committees to divide its county into small districts, with sub-committees, whose duty it would be to draw up a list of all the voters and to designate how each was expected to vote. Each sub-committee was instructed to "keep a constant watch on the doubtful voters." "On election days see that every Whig is brought to the polls." Lincoln and his state committee enclosed a prospectus for a campaign newspaper, which "will be published so low that everyone can afford it." To this end it was expected that every county would contribute fifty or one hundred dollars. "And the copies will be forwarded" for distribution among "our political opponents." It was cautioned: "Plan of operations will of course be *concealed from every one except our good friends,* who of right ought to know them."

That Whig campaign paper, called *The Old Soldier,* in eulogy of General Harrison, was printed at the *Sangamo Journal* office in Springfield. Lincoln and his party state committee announced that they would superintend that electioneering organ but that all good Whigs were its editors. *The Old Soldier* opened its editorial batteries of invective on Van Buren and the Democrats. Elatedly Lincoln reported to Stuart: "Subscriptions pour in without abatement." The Democrats with their own sheet, called *Old Hickory* in tribute to the retired General and Former President Andrew Jackson, answered the Whigs with verbose vituperation. *Old Hickory* was edited by Stephen A. Douglas and Lincoln's former surveyor boss, John Calhoun.

As soon as the Legislature had adjourned, Lincoln took to the hustings for Harrison, even going into his native Kentucky on one occasion.

Since stump speaking and story-telling were favorite amusements in Lincoln's Illinois, he drew huge crowds, though the state was steeped in Jacksonism. He regaled his audiences with anecdotes and satire, in an accent and vocabularly savoring of the frontier. He mimicked his opponents, and his rustic audiences yelled for more. At Springfield he imitated one Democrat, Jesse B. Thomas, in gesture and voice, even caricaturing Thomas's walk and body motion, and he exaggeratedly reproduced Thomas's more conspicuous facial expressions.

Lincoln and his friend and fellow Whig Junto colleague, the spellbinding Edward D. Baker, covered the "Wabash Country" of eastern Illinois, where, as Baker later complained, they made speeches one day and shook with the ague the next. It proved a severe physical ordeal for Lincoln, who was naturally healthy and unusually robust despite his "rail-like" form. With no railroad facilities and only a few stage lines, the speakers traveled on horseback, carrying their saddle-bags filled with "hickory" shirts and woolen socks, covering long distances over pairies and swamps. Elihu B. Washburne, subsequently a Whig congressman from the Galena district, told of Lincoln's help to Harrison: "He stumped all the middle and lower part of the State with great effect, traveling from the Wabash to the Mississippi in the hot months of July and August, shaking with the ague one day, and addressing the people the next."

In the August state election Lincoln was re-elected Representative for a fourth term. But he ran poorly. Of five Whig condidates elected representatives, his vote was the lowest.

The November election returns told a more melancholy story for the Illinois Whigs. Although Harrison was chosen President over Van Buren, Lincoln's efforts to carry the State for the old General failed. Illinois's popular vote stood: Van Buren, 47,433; Harrison, 45,576.

V

With General Harrison elected President of the United States and himself re-elected state Representative, Lincoln showed burning interest in the incoming administration's distribution of federal patronage. To Stuart, still in Washington, he wrote in mid-December, six weeks following Old Tippecanoe's triumph: "I express my preference in a few cases, as follows: For marshal, first, John Dawson; second, Dr. B. F. Edwards. For Postmaster here, Dr. Henry; Carlinville, Joseph C. Howell. There is no question of the propriety of removing the postmaster at Carlinville. I have been told by so many different persons as to preclude all doubt of its truth, that he boldly refused to deliver from his office during the canvass all documents franked by Whig members of Congress."

Lincoln showed himself especially anxious to secure from Harrison's administration the Springfield postmastership for his friend, physician, and fellow "Whig Junto" member, Dr. Anson G. Henry. So deeply did Henry immerse himself in politics that his medical practice declined. Henry had conducted a study of the St. Louis cholera epidemic and then pronounced that disease not contagious. He was probably a better politician than a doctor. The national administration refused to appoint Lincoln's doctor-politician friend Postmaster of Lincoln's home town, inferentially revealing how little value it placed on the Whig Junto leader's services in the recent campaign.

The state Legislature, which convened at Springfield in December, 1840, saw Lincoln's last service as a state law-maker.

The new State House being not quite completed, the House of Representatives convened at the First Methodist Church. On the fifth of December Lincoln, again Whig minority leader, created some stir by what came to be known in the future as his "jump" from a window for the purpose of postponing action on the resumption of specie payments in the State's tangled development of public finance.

Under a law passed at the previous session, the State Bank in Springfield was obligated to resume specie payments at the end of the "next ensuing session" of the Legislature. The Democrats intended the special session to expire on Saturday, December 5, before the opening of the regular session on the following Monday; if they could bring this about, the Bank would have to resume specie payments on December 7 or forfeit its charter and close its doors. The Whigs, under Lincoln's leadership, were determined that the special session should run continuously into the regular session without a *sine die* adjournment, thus postponing resumption until the close of the regular session about March 1.

Lincoln devised the strategy that the Whigs should prevent adjournment by the simple expedient of remaining away and preventing the necessary quorum (61 of the 91 members) from being present. Eighty-six members responded to morning roll call on December 5. More than twenty Whigs were absent when the House re-convened at three in the afternoon. Efforts of the sergeant-at-arms to bring them in were unsuccessful, and no quorum was present when evening came. The House still sat in session.

Suddenly Lincoln and two fellow Whig members, Joseph Gillespie of Edwardsville and Asahel Gridley of Bloomington, on hand to keep an eye out for their party's interests, found themselves caught napping. Several Democrats who had been ill were brought in to make a quorum. Lincoln and his two party colleagues failed to keep count. They voted "nay" on a Democratic motion to take up the Senate resolution to adjourn *sine die* (without setting a day for further consideration), and the motion passed, 48 to 13. Ignoring the fact that this roll call showed a bare quorum present, the three Whigs, Representatives Lincoln, Gillespie, and Gridley, voted "nay" again on a House concurrence in the resolution, which passed, 46 to 15. After these two votes against the Whig position—too late to do any good—Lincoln and the two other Whigs stepped out of the window of the first floor of the church, five feet down to the ground. The Legislature held its first session in the new State House the following Monday, December 7, the first day of the regular session. The State Bank resumed specie payments that same day.

Springfield's Democratic organ, the *Illinois State Register,* exaggerated the seriousness of Lincoln's "jump" and ridiculed him. Entitling its lengthy partisan account "Conspiracy of the Federal Members of the Legislature to Revolutionize the State Government," the *Register* commented with presumable alarm:

"A laughable circumstance took place while the yeas and nays were being called on the passage of the resolution. Mr. Lincoln, of Sangamon, who was present during the whole scene, and who appeared to enjoy the embarrassment of the House, suddenly looked very grave after the Speaker announced that a quorum was present. The conspiracy having failed, Mr. Lincoln came under great excitement, and having attempted and failed to get out at the door, very unceremoniously *raised the window and jumped out,* followed by one or two other members. This gymnastic performance of Mr. Lincoln and his flying brethren, did not occur until *after they had voted!* and consequently the House did not interfere with their extraordinary feat. . . . His legs reached nearly from the window to the ground." The *Register* complimented the Democrats on having saved American institutions: "Destroy the Legislature, and what is left? Anarchy! which may lead to Monarchy! In the present instance, the Legislature was saved by the firmness of the Democratic members, to whom too much praise cannot be awarded."

VI

When 1841 rolled around the following month, Lincoln had lost interest in his legislative labors. Between January 1 and 21 he attended the sessions only half a dozen times, though from late January until March 1, when the session adjourned, he attended regularly and participated in its proceedings.

During that period of frequent absence from his seat during January he had grown ill or mentally upset, for he wrote two letters to Stuart in Washington, one on the 20th and another on the 23rd, complaining of his meloncholia and expressing how miserable he felt. Part of the reason for his misery was the fact that his formal engagement to marry Mary Todd had just been broken, three weeks previously, on a day which he, in a letter of despair and depression to Speed, later called "that fatal first of Jan. '41."

After retiring from the Legislature, Lincoln sought solace by devoting more time to his law practice upon which he was now free to concentrate.

LAW OFFICE, COURT, AND CIRCUIT

5

I

TRADITION tells us that Lincoln, as an Indiana backwoods boy, read the *Revised Statutes* of that State. When he lived in New Salem he supposedly had borrowed *Statutes of Illinois* and other legal volumes from that village's justice of the peace, Bowling Green.

Finally, he acquired Blackstone's *Commentaries*. William Dean Howells told how, in 1860, Lincoln secured his first basic legal book: "He [Lincoln] bought an old copy of Blackstone, one day, at auction, in Springfield, and on his return to New Salem, attacked the work with characteristic energy."

Another version of how he acquired his Blackstone was told in 1860 by Lincoln to an artist, Alban J. Conant, who was painting his portrait. Conant declared later: "He [Lincoln] told me, too, how for half a dollar he bought a barrel of odds and ends from a migrating farmer who asked him to take it to lighten his wagon on the heavy roads. After stowing it away for some time, Lincoln came upon it, and found that the only thing of value in it was a copy of Blackstone's Commentaries. He described how much it interested him. . . . He concluded: 'I fairly devoured every sentence.' "

Lincoln, during his New Salem life, took to drafting legal documents for the villagers: bills of sale, deeds, transfers of titles to land and other property, mortgages, agreements of various kinds, and wills.

John T. Stuart had encouraged Lincoln to study law, and from 1834 to early 1837 Lincoln visited the office of Stuart & Dummer at Springfield to borrow their books. Henry E. Dummer, New England-born, was an especially erudite attorney who had attended Bowdoin College in Maine and then Harvard Law School, and who had known the mighty Justice Joseph Story of the United States Supreme Court. Lincoln in later years advised a student to read law in Dummer's office, pointing out: "Mr. Dummer is a very clever man and an excellent lawyer (much better than I, in law-learning)." Dummer subsequently described Abe Lincoln in 1837 as "the most uncouth looking" young man he had ever seen.

In between sessions of the Legislature, Representative Lincoln continued law reading by himself. As he subsequently told one student: "I did not read with any one . . . I read at New Salem;" he advised another aspiring attorney to read by himself, emphasizing, "This is precisely the way I came to the law."

Lincoln in March, 1836, went through the preliminary formality of being certified as a "person of good moral character" by the Circuit Court of Sangamon County at Springfield—the first step to qualifying as an attorney. In the following September a license to practice law was issued him by two justices of the State Supreme Court. Lincoln presented himself to the Court's clerk for enrollment as provided by statute, and swore to support the state and federal constitutions. Then on March 1, 1837, the young Representative was enrolled as an attorney and counsellor, licensed to practice in all Illinois courts. This was the time at which he decided to move from the tiny village, which had been his home for nearly six years, to Springfield.

II

In April, 1837, he forsook New Salem for Springfield. In the *Sangamo Journal* on the 15th a formal notice of the dissolution of the Stuart & Dummer law firm appeared. There was also a professional notice: "J. T. Stuart & A. Lincoln, Attorneys and Counselors at Law, will practice, conjointly, in the Courts of this Judicial Circuit. Office No. 4 Hoffman's Row, upstairs, Springfield, April 12, 1837."

The Stuart & Lincoln office, in the upper story of a building opposite the northwest corner of the present Court House Square in Springfield, over the room where the Sangamon County court held its sessions, was furnished with a table that answered for a desk, and a small lounge or bed; also a chair covered with buffalo robe, in which the junior partner sometimes sat for his reading and resting. A crude bookcase stood in one corner.

The operation of the Stuart & Lincoln firm is the story of Abraham Lincoln's start in law practice. Since Stuart spent a surplus of time and energy in Whig politics, Lincoln was left with the burden of work. He prepared briefs and pleadings, represented the firm's clients in court, and laboriously answered correspondence in long hand.

The first case in which Lincoln figured was *Hawthorne v. Wooldridge,* comprising three causes growing out of one business transaction, which Stuart had taken on—one involving a contract, another for trespass, and a third in replevin. Lincoln represented his firm when he acted for the defendant, Woodridge, who had failed to furnish the plaintiff, James P. Hawthorne, "two yoke of oxen to break up twenty acres of prairie-sod ground;" moreover, Lincoln's client refused to allow Hawthorne to have access to the ground for the raising of "corn or wheat at the option of the plaintiff." Then Lincoln's client had "beat and bruised" Hawthorne when the latter tried to enter the disputed cornfield. The case was settled out of court.

Most of Lincoln's early cases, like that concerning Hawthorne and Wooldridge, proved rather petty and uninspiring. For the most part, they were actions arising out of neighborhood quarrels, differences over livestock, disputes about a cooking-stove, litigation involving damage to crops by trespassing cattle, injuries inflicted on livestock by vicious watch dogs, replevin suits to recover possession of cattle, horses, and sheep running at large, and diverse slander and libel suits intended to vindicate the alleged honesty and integrity of aggrieved parties, cases for debt, and a few divorces.

Among the heterogeny of cases handled by the Stuart & Lincoln firm was one which attracted a surplus of notoriety because it was so tightly intertwined with the Whig and Democratic struggle for political supremacy and thus became a prime topic of controversy in the rival partisan newspapers.

In May, 1837, Mary Anderson and her son, Richard, widow and child of the late Joseph Anderson, came to Springfield to take possession of and sell ten acres of land owned at the time of his death (or so they believed) by their respective husband and father, who had resided in Fulton County. The property lay a few miles north of Springfield. But the dead man's widow and son found the land to be occupied by General James Adams, a former attorney for the deceased and also a dominant

Democrat in Sangamon County politics. Adams laid claim to the acreage upon a deed of record from Anderson. He refused to surrender possession of the land to the widow and her son, whereupon they consulted Lincoln for legal advice.

Lincoln's first move as counsel for Mary and Richard Anderson was to call in the extremely able Stephen T. Logan as associate counsel. This done, Lincoln proceeded to draw up a contract for a contingent fee, whereby the firm of Stuart & Lincoln, along with Logan, would receive one-half of the tract, conditioned upon their recovery of the same for the widow and her son. Lincoln's original draft of the contract with the Andersons reads:

> Whereas the heirs of Joseph Anderson, deceased, are about to commence an action in chancery in the Sangamon Circuit Court, for the recovery of a certain piece of ground [describing the land in controversy]; and whereas, Stephen T. Logan, John T. Stuart and A. Lincoln have engaged to prosecute the suit as attorneys for the said heirs, we, the subscribers, being the widow and one of the sons of the said Anderson deceased, agree to give to said Logan, Stuart and Lincoln one-half of the said piece of ground for their services, provided they recover the same; but are not bound to pay anything unless this piece of ground be recovered.

Lincoln, after examining the papers in the Recorder's office, convinced himself that the transfer of the land from the late Joseph Anderson to Adams was spurious. He instituted court action to have the transfer set aside.

But neither side appeared anxious to press the suit to a determination, and it dragged on until November 29, 1843, when by reason of Adams's death, an order of discontinuance was entered. The suit having been abated, the tract of land was inventoried in Adams's estate, and was sold by the executor to one Lewis. By mesne conveyances, title eventually became vested in the city of Springfield as part of Oak Ridge Cemetery, a site destined, ironically, to become Lincoln's last resting place nearly a quarter-century later.

The Adams estate received the money from the sale of the disputed land, and not a dollar ever went to the widow Anderson and her son.

Although Lincoln, Stuart, and Logan received no compensation for their legal services in behalf of Mary and Richard Anderson, Lincoln made some political capital out of the case against Adams while the litigation was pending and Adams still living.

As the case dragged on, Adams, a Democrat, ran against Lincoln's friend, physician, and Whig political ally, Dr. Anson G. Henry, for Probate Justice of the Peace of Sangamon County. Two days before the election there was circulated in the streets of Springfield a handbill, later admittedly written by Lincoln and turned out by the presses of the Whig

Sangamo Journal, charging Adams with having acquired the Anderson property by fraud.

Prior to that, someone writing under the pseudonym "Sampson's Ghost," had conducted in the *Journal* a sly campaign against Adams, in the form of six letters. Those political tracts against Adams went far beyond the legal issues of the Andersons' case against Adams for recovery of the land. It all amounted to a fierce journalistic fight between Lincoln and Adams, or an unseemly war of words between opposing Whig and Democratic party newspapers.

III

Since Stuart devoted most of his time to Whig politics, an ever greater portion of the firm's work was actually loaded on Lincoln. Entries in the preserved account books of Stuart & Lincoln indicate that most of the pleadings in their cases are in the junior partner's handwriting.

Stuart & Lincoln's account book, in Lincoln's script, indicates that the firm's practice was more extensive than lucrative; that their cases were often petty and their retainers picayunish. Among the more trivial business may be listed:

E.C. Ross	
To Stuart & Lincoln	Dr.
1837—April—To attendance at trial of right of J.F. Davis' property before Moffett	$5.00
Mather, Lamb & Co	
To Stuart & Lincoln	Dr.
1837—To attendance at trial of right of J.F. Davis' property before Moffett	$5.00
Wiley & Wood	
To Stuart & Lincoln	Dr.
1837-8 To defense of Chancery case of Ely	$50.00
Credit by coat to Stuart—	15.00
	$35.00
Peyton L. Harrison	
To Stuart & Lincoln	Dr.
1838—March—To case with Dickinson	$10.00

Lincoln proved himself not particularly methodical in his office. The firm's papers were often scattered hither and yon. He carried notes in his vest pocket or put them into a drawer. Later his usual receptacle for carrying papers would be his high stovepipe hat. Lincoln in 1838 apologized to a Vandalia lawyer for failure to reply to a letter sooner: "We received yours of the 2nd Inst. by due course of mail, and have only to offer in excuse for not answering it sooner, that we have been in a great state of confusion here ever since the receipt of your letter. . . . We beg your pardon for our neglect in this business; if it had been important to you or your client we would have done better."

Lincoln late in 1838 participated in his first major case—the defense of a murderer.

Lincoln's client, Henry B. Truett, former Register of the Land Office at Galena, went on trial for the fatal shooting in Springfield of Dr. Jacob M. Early, physician, politician and Methodist preacher, after a political argument in which "damned rascal" and other epithets were hurled. Truett, son-in-law of a Democratic congressman, William L. May, through whose influence he had received his federal job, had become convinced that Early was the guiding force in a move to have him fired from office.

Lincoln, along with his partner, Stuart, and also Stephen T. Logan and Cyrus Walker, all Whigs, were retained to defend Truett, a Democrat. Stephen A. Douglas, the future celebrated "Little Giant," was appointed by the State to prosecute Truett. The trial began on October 8, 1838. Although Logan headed defense counsel, Lincoln made the final plea for the accused murderer, which Logan called "a short but strong and sensible speech."

At the close of the fifth day the Judge instructed the jurors. They retired for deliberation upstairs to the Stuart & Lincoln office, which the partners often rented as a juror's room. The jurors brought in a verdict of not guilty for Truett.

That sort of verdict was not unusual in the Illinois of Lincoln's day. As Governor Thomas Ford explained a decade later: "In all cases of murder arising from heat of blood in a fight, it was impossible to convict."

Lincoln's acquitted client, Truett, was subsequently elected Mayor of Galena, then moved to San Francisco and engaged in the liquor business, and in 1855 wounded an opponent in a duel.

Lincoln's partner, Stuart, in that same year, 1838, won the coveted seat in Congress after the roughest of knock-down-and-drag-out contests against the Democrat, Stephen A. Douglas—by the razor-thin margin of 36 votes. When in 1839 Stuart went off to Washington to take his House seat, Lincoln signalized his departure by writing across the top of a fresh page in the firm's account book: "Commencement of Lincoln's administration. 1839, Nov. 2."

For a time Lincoln continued his entries in the account book. But he soon found such an orthodox method of bookkeeping too arduous, for he was never a methodical man. Milton Hay, at that time a student in the Stuart & Lincoln office, described the system which the junior partner used. Hay was present when Stuart returned to Springfield at the end of his first congressional term. The two partners held a lengthy conversation, Stuart describing events at Washington, and Lincoln giving an account of state and county happenings. When Stuart rose to leave, Lincoln pulled from a cherry-colored box some packages of money, giving them to Stuart. They contained Stuart's half of the firm's earnings while he was in Washington. Each package was labeled with the amount of money in it, with the name of the client from whom it was received.

Thus Lincoln, before he was thirty, had come far for a man of his limited education and backwoods beginnings, both in politics and law. He was serving his third term as state legislator and was recognized as a Whig party leader, and held a law partnership with one of the better established attorneys of downstate Illinois.

IV

The Stuart & Lincoln law partnership increased its practice in 1839, when the State offices were removed from Vandalia to Springfield.

The Supreme Court of Illinois held its first session in the new capital town. The Sangamon County Circuit Court was already there. The federal court would hold its session there also. On December 3, the junior partner was admitted to practice in the United States tribunals.

In January, 1840, Lincoln appeared in his first state Supreme Court case, *Ingram v. Gibbs,* on appeal from Pike County. His second case before that tribunal, *Thomas v. Heirs of Broadwell,* occurred the following June in a litigation arising in Morgan County. Nothing is known about these two litigations, except that both were dismissed on Lincoln's motion. Better known today is his third Supreme Court case, *Scammon v. Cline,* which he lost. Until recent years, this was erroneously believed to be his first case in that court.

Scammon v. Cline grew out of a promissory note for only $52 made out by Cornelius Cline, of Boone County, to one Whitney for "value received in goods." Whitney assigned this note to Jonathan Y. Scammon, a Chicago financier, who then brought suit to collect on it before a justice of the peace. Judgment was given in favor of the debtor, Cline, in February, 1939. The records do not show why the note was considered not binding, except perhaps that Boone Counties would not decide against their fellow Booneite, Cline, in favor of a Chicago capitalist like Scammon. It might have been the age-old conflict of creditor versus debtor that so colored American life. Scammon appealed the case to the Boone County Circuit Court, but there he lost again.

Scammon's lawyer in part of the proceedings was Norman B. Judd of Chicago, destined to be one of Lincoln's "Warwicks" who aided him so effectively in securing the Republican presidential nomination a score of years later. The hitherto victorious defendant, Cline, retained a Boone County attorney, James Loop, to represent him, and Loop hired Lincoln to argue Cline's case in the Supreme Court at Springfield, early in 1840.

Lincoln, in presenting Cline's case before the Supreme Court, according to tradition, announced that he could find no precedents for the decision which the Boone County court had given in favor of his client, but he argued from the facts of the case and expounded on what he thought should be the law.

Chief Justice John M. Wilson reversed judgment and remanded the case back to the Boone County Circuit Court. Thus Lincoln lost his case for Cline. But the locally prejudiced county tribunal then decided in favor of their citizen, Cline, once more.

Lincoln found himself not overly fond of the drudgery of legal routine. He disliked drawing declarations and pleas and inwardly disapproved of the artificialities and refinements which were even then beginning to creep into the pleadings. He disregarded forms whenever it was possible to do so. "There was," points out Frederick Trevor Hill, one of the better authorities on Lincoln's law career, "nothing mechanical, precise, or methodical about the man, and in all those housewifely virtues which characterize the careful, orderly, exact solicitor he was utterly deficient. He never knew where his papers were."

When Stuart went to Congress, Lincoln was forced to carry an even bigger burden of the firm's work. The senior partner's long absences at Washington created more confusion about the misplacing of papers. In December, 1839, Lincoln sent this message of appeal to Stuart in Washington:

"A d——d hawk billed yankee is here, besetting me at every turn I take, saying that Robert Kinzie never received the $80, to which he was entitled. Can you tell any thing about the matter?

"Again Old Mr. Wright, who lives up South Fork some where, is teasing me continually about some *deeds* which he says he left with you, but which I can find nothing of. Can you tell me where they are?"

By the beginning of 1841 Lincoln found himself in miserable physical and mental shape. His strength was taxed by legislative labors as Whig minority leader and his recent back-breaking, vitality-sapping electioneering efforts for General Harrison in distant swampy, dank regions. His nerves were frayed by his turbulent romance with Mary Todd, culminating in the breaking of his engagement on January 1. Crushed with gnawing mental torture, he, on the 23rd, confided by mail to Stuart that he was "the most miserable man living." "I must die or be better, as it appears to me," adding: "If I could be myself, I would rather remain at home with Judge Logan"—Stephen T. Logan.

He finally became his normal self again in a few months, but he did not want to continue his partnership with Stuart. When in April, Stuart returned from Washington to Springfield, they had a long discussion about their firm's future. Soon the *Sangamo Journal* printed a professional notice of the dissolution of the Lincoln & Stuart partnership.

Lincoln now was taken into partnership by Stephen T. Logan, former Judge of the Sangamon County Circuit and one of the State's leading lawyers.

V

Lincoln drew valuable experience in his new law partnership with Logan. For the new senior partner was recognized as one of the talented technicians of jurisprudence in Illinois and an abler advocate than Stuart. Too, Logan was not as interested in public office as Stuart, and he devoted more time and energy to his practice. Logan was to be the most constructive influence in moulding Lincoln as a lawyer.

Logan had from the first respected Lincoln's legal ability. As Judge of the Sangamon County Circuit Court he had made the order admitting Lincoln to the Illinois bar. He had signed the journal entry which had terminated Lincoln's first case, *Hawthorne v. Wooldridge.* In three cases in which Lincoln had opposed Logan as counsel in the Supreme Court, Lincoln had emerged as victor.

Logan was soon to learn, however, that his new junior partner was not read profoundly in general law but that he studied each individual case. Declared Logan later:

"I don't think he studied very much. I think he learned his law more in the study of cases. He would work hard and learn all there was in a case he had in hand. He got to be a pretty good lawyer, though his general knowledge of law was never very formidable. But he would study out his case and make about as much of it as anybody. . . . He would get a case and try to know all there was connected with it."

Lincoln owned few law books. But he had access to the library of the state Supreme Court, only a short distance from the Logan & Lincoln office. Whenever he had any matter in hand which required specific reading, he availed himself of that ample library. In that manner he was enabled to appear in court with his case well prepared.

Logan & Lincoln rose to the top among Illinois law firms, owing to Logan's ability, Lincoln's skill in reasoning to juries, and the fact that they were located in the State capital town and the center of the Legislature, as well as the Sangamon County Circuit, Supreme, and United

States District courts. From all over Illinois there came legal business of diverse kinds. For a time the two partners almost monopolized the litigation brought before the Supreme Court. At that Court's December, 1841, term the junior partner alone argued fourteen appeals, losing only four. During the 1842-43 terms, the Logan & Lincoln firm argued twenty-four cases and was successful in all except seven. During his partnership with Logan the rising young attorney personally participated in thirty-nine Illinois Supreme Court cases.

The partnership found bankruptcy cases an ample source of income in the thirteen months that the state Bankruptcy Law was in effect from February, 1842, to March, 1843. Between them Logan and Lincoln handled seventy-seven such cases, more than any other Springfield firm, which placed them in a fourth-place tie in the entire State for the number of such business-failure litigations handled.

The procedure which the firm followed was outlined by Lincoln in a letter during February, 1842, to an attorney in Paris, Illinois:

"Yours of the 10th is duly received. Judge Logan & myself are doing business together now and we are willing to attend to your cases as you propose. . . .

"Thinking it may aid you a little, I send you one of our blank forms of Petitions. It, you will see, is framed to be sworn to before the Federal court clerk, and, in your cases, will have [to] be so far changed, as to be sworn to before the clerk of your circuit court; and his certificate must be accompanied with his official seal. The schedules, too, must be attended to. Be sure that they contain the creditors *names,* their *residences,* the *amounts* due each, the *debtors names,* their *residences,* and the *amounts* they owe, also all *property* and *where* located.

"Also be sure that the Schedules are *signed* by the applicants as well as the Petition.

"Publication will have to be made here in one paper, and in one nearest the residence of the applicant. Write us in each case where this last advertisement is to be sent—whether to you or to what paper."

A few actions in which Lincoln was involved as counsel, such as the seduction case, *Grable v. Margrave,* became landmarks in Illinois jurisprudence.

In the Gallatin County Circuit Court Thomas Margrave sued William G. Grable to recover damages because Grable had allegedly seduced his daughter. The jury awarded Margrave $300 for the loss of his daughter's services, disgrace inflicted on the Margrave family, and the loss of the society and comfort of his daughter. The defendant, the alleged seducer Grable, appealed to the state Supreme Court.

Lincoln was hired by Margrave's Gallatin County lawyer, Samuel D. Marshall of Shawneetown, to defend Margrave in Grable's appeal to the State's highest court in September, 1841.

Lincoln, in his argument, won for Margrave. The Supreme Court upheld the Gallatin County Circuit verdict, and decreed: "The father may not only recover the damages he has sustained by the loss of service, and the payment of necessary expenses, but the jury may award him compensation for the disgrace cast upon the family, and the loss of the society and comfort of his daughter."

VI

Lincoln during 1841, along with Logan and Edward D. Baker, his Whig political partner, defended three debt-ridden brothers, William, Henry, and Archibald Trailor of Springfield for the alleged murder of the more affluent Archibald Fisher, who had disappeared. Henry Trailor confessed to the sheriff that his two brothers had killed the still missing Fisher, suggesting where Fisher's murdered body could be found. Feeling ran high, and talk of lynching the brothers was heard.

Lincoln, in a communication to his friend, Speed, in June told about it:

"We have had the highest state of excitement here for a week past that our community has ever witnessed. . . . Henry Trailor . . . said he guessed the body [of Fisher] could be found in Spring Creek between the Beardstown road bridge and Hickoxes mill. Away the People swept like a herd of buffaloes, and cut down Hickoxes mill dam *nolens volens,* to draw the water out of the pond; and then went up and down, and down and up the creek, fishing and raking, and ducking and diving for two days, and after all, no dead body found."

At the Trailor brothers' arraignment Lincoln and his defense associates, Logan and Baker, raised doubts about the veracity of Henry Trailor's confession which involved his brothers in the murder of Fisher. By doctor's testimony they brought out that the missing, presumably dead, Fisher had previously sustained an injury to the head from the bursting of a gun and ever since had not been quite mentally normal, that on occasions Fisher had wandered away in a condition of derangement for long absences. Was it possible that Fisher had gone off again by himself and was really not dead?

Further police search revealed Fisher's whereabouts. The demented man had indeed wandered off again, but he was alive, staying in another town. The two brothers, accused by a third brother of murdering Fisher, were naturally released.

Henry Trailor stuck to his story that the now very much living Fisher was dead. Also, disappointment that there would be no hanging of the Trailor brothers prevailed in some circles. Lincoln continued his narrative to Speed about this extraordinary case: "Henry still protested that no power on earth could ever show Fisher alive. Thus stands this curious affair. . . . Langford [James R. Langford, a carpenter] who had taken the lead in cutting down Hickoxes mill dam . . . looked most awfully woe-begone . . . and Hart [Ellis Hart], the little drayman that hauled Molly [Mary Todd] home once, said it was too *damned* bad to have so much trouble, and no hanging after all."

Lincoln found it difficult to collect his fee from the exonerated William Trailor. He sued to collect it after Trailor's death, in the name of Logan & Lincoln.

Lincoln and his partner also handled divorce cases, such as that of Clarissa Wren, who was sued for divorce by her husband, Aquilla Wren. Logan represented the defendant wife when the marriage was dissolved in 1844, while Lincoln handled the case when the question of alimony came up at the next term of court. For the firm's fee Lincoln drew up a note for $150, which was signed by Clarissa Wren and two sureties, and later paid by the man who married the divorced Clarissa.

Lincoln did so well financially in his professional association with Logan, from 1841 to 1844, that in 1844 he was enabled to buy a house on Eighth Street in Springfield for himself, his wife Mary, and son, Bobby. He had married Mary Todd two years earlier.

Later in 1844, the Logan & Lincoln firm was broken up. The senior partner explained that he wanted his son as his partner. Lincoln then took as a partner the younger William H. Herndon.

VII

Lincoln's third, last, and longest-term law partner, Billy Herndon, was Kentucky-born, Illinois-reared, and only twenty-six years old when he became Abe's junior partner in the new Lincoln & Herndon firm.

The son of pro-slavery Archer G. Herndon, who was the owner of the "Indian Queen," a Springfield tavern-hotel, and was one of Lincoln's fellow "Long Nine" Sangamon County legislators, William H. Herndon had attended Illinois College in Jacksonville, where he learned anti-slavery sentiments from President Edward Beecher (brother of Harriet Beecher Stowe) and an abolition-minded faculty. Billy had first seen Lincoln in 1832 when young Abe had aided in piloting the *Talisman* up the Sangamon River. He had worked, also, in Joshua F. Speed's store, where he heard Representative Lincoln and others hold forth near the stove and cracker barrel. He joined the Whig Party, but found himself more strongly opposed to slavery than the average member of Henry Clay's following. He read law and was admitted to the Illinois bar in 1844, and had then become a clerk in the Logan & Lincoln office.

Once when Herndon was asked why Lincoln took him in as partner, he answered: "I don't know and no one else does." Politics played its part in Lincoln's choice of a new law partner. He had learned much from Stuart and Logan, but he had always been the firm's junior member, having the tedious duty of keeping files and records and doing the real drudgery work of the office. Now that he was starting out for himself and, like Stuart, wanted to go to Congress, he desired a younger man under him. Herndon fit the qualifications. The young lawyer's presence in the firm would leave him free to work for his nomination for Congress. Young Herndon had no political aspirations, another significant factor. As one Illinois settler phrased it: "Lincoln had learned that a law office could not be run when all the members wanted to go to Congress." Lincoln also saw advantage from young Whigs like Herndon, those whom he described as those "shrewd, wild boys about town." Herndon had already proved himself a skilled Whig organizer around Springfield, although he never went after public office himself.

For an office the new Lincoln & Herndon firm rented a room in a brick building, across the square from the court house. It was a dreary cluttered place at the end of a dark hall on the second floor. Two grimy windows looked out over stable roofs, littered back yards and unsightly ash heaps. A long pine table, scarred from jack-knife carving, stood in the room's center, with a shorter table at the end forming a "T." A secretary, with drawers below and pigeon holes stuffed with papers above, stood in one corner. A book case containing volumes stood in another. Four or five cane-bottomed chairs, a rickety sofa alongside the wall, and, in winter, an unblackened wood-burning "Drum" stove, completed the equipment. The office floor appeared unacquainted with broom or mop, except when an uncommonly energetic law student decided to clean up.

"Lincoln's favorite position," declared one student in the office, "when unraveling some knotty law point, was to stretch both of his long legs at full length upon a chair in front of him. In this position, with books on the table nearby and in his lap, he worked up his case."

The partnership inserted its advertisement in Springfield's Whig *Illinois State Journal,* in the "Business Directory" section. Between a dentist's appeals for patients and a harness-maker's call for customers appeared this public card for clients:

> LINCOLN & HERNDON
> *Attorneys And Counsellors At Law*
> *will practice in the Courts*
> *of Law and Chancery in this State.*
> *Springfield, Illinois.*

Lincoln wrote the most important papers and did the pleading in court. Herndon performed the more routine jobs, handled correspondence, and dug up authorities and precedent cases when Lincoln prepared briefs. Albert T. Bledsoe, who practiced law in Springfield during the 1840's, vividly remembered how the work of Lincoln & Herndon was so physically unevenly divided. Bledsoe commented: "Herndon with creditable zeal and industry, would collect all sorts of cases and authorities for him. From these he [Lincoln] would make his selections, and prepare his arguments, to the great disgust often, no doubt, of Mr. Herndon, who saw so much of the materials collected by him thrown aside as useless."

Herndon brought to Lincoln's law office more order and system than ever before, although he was not a paragon of neatness. Before long papers were being misplaced, just as in the days when Lincoln had Stuart as partner. Lincoln was often absent from Springfield, on the circuit practicing law or attending to politics.

VIII

Business began slowly for the new Lincoln & Herndon partnership. Not until March, 1845, was the first Lincoln & Herndon case heard in the Sangamon County Circuit Court. But in time Lincoln's name and political associations drew clients. Soon the two attorneys had as much business as they could handle. During their first year together they had only fourteen cases in the county Circuit Court, but in the following twelve months they handled more than twice that many. By the end of 1845 Lincoln & Herndon were running legal affairs for firms as far distant as Peoria.

Since it was not uncommon in Illinois for State's attorneys to be replaced, temporarily, by outside lawyers, Lincoln on some occasions found himself a prosecutor in behalf of the People. With Josiah Lamborn, in 1846 he appeared for the People in the prosecution of two brothers, James and George Denton, indicted for the murder of Cassius Brown, whom they had hacked to death with axes.

The Dentons' trial came up in Petersburg (the town that had absorbed New Salem) in Menard County. Counsel for one brother moved for a severance, and it was ordered that the two brothers should have separate trials. A jury was empaneled in the case of James Denton. The trial, held June 11 and 12, ended in a hung jury.

Lincoln is credited with having persuaded his associate prosecutor, Lamborn, to drop further prosecution of the Denton brothers, in view of the absence of eye witnesses to the killing. Apparently Lincoln's urging was heeded, for the record shows no further proceedings against the accused Dentons.

Later that year, 1846, Lincoln was elected to Congress as a Whig. But since the Thirtieth Congress would not convene until the next year, he remained at his law practice.

In May, 1847, he was retained to defend Sigler H. Lester of Coles County, on a charge of assault with intent to commit murder. On Lincoln's petition Lester's trial was moved to Cumberland County, in a log school at Greenup. Lincoln lost that case. Lester was convicted and sentenced to one year in the State penitentiary.

Lincoln then wrote and signed a petition to the Governor for clemency, stating that "there are circumstances which in our opinion render it proper that the Executive clemency should be extended to him." That petition was signed by 353 citizens of Coles County, where his father, stepmother, stepbrother, and Hanks family members lived. Among the signers of this petition for Lester were his stepbrother, John D. Johnston, and his own cousin, Dennis Hanks. Governor French pardoned the convicted Lester after he had served three months in the Alton penitentiary.

IX

Before Lincoln, late in 1847, left Illinois with his family for Washington to take his congressional seat, he accepted as client, a Kentucky slaveholder, Robert Matson, who was endeavoring to secure legally the return of a family of his slaves whom he had originally brought to Illinois. It was a case which shocked later lovers of Lincoln, some of whom have since tried to explain away Lincoln's action in trying to have Matson's slaves returned to Kentucky, there to be sold for labor on plantations in the deep South.

Back in 1843 Matson, an unmarried Kentuckian of aristocratic background, who had served in his State's legislature, had purchased land in Coles County, Illinois, known as "Black Grove," which he worked with the aid of slaves brought from his plantation in Bourbon County, Kentucky, each spring, to be returned there after the harvest. In such manner Matson preserved their legal status as slaves, not permanently situated in the State of Illinois and thus in no danger of acquiring the status of free men.

Lincoln, as co-counsel for Matson, in order to make certain that there would be no confusion about the slaves, invariably called a witness to "his solemn declaration that the slaves were here [in Illinois] temporarily and to be returned shortly to his [Matson's] plantation in Bourbon County." But there loomed one exception among Matson's human property—Anthony Bryant, a former slave, who remained continuously in Black Grove, acting as overseer of the others and who thus became, in contemplation of law, a free man.

All went well with this arrangement by Matson until the spring of 1847, when he brought a group of slaves from Kentucky to perform the farm work at Black Grove for the season. Among them was Bryant's wife, Jane, (reputedly the illegitimate daughter of Matson's brother) accompanied by her four children.

Matson's "housekeeper" mistress, Mary Corbin, a white woman whom the bachelor Matson had brought from Kentucky, grew enraged at Jane one day and threatened to have Matson ship her and her brood back to Kentucky, from there to be sent to plantations in the far South. The erstwhile slave, Bryant, and his family, aided by a few Illinois anti-slavery men, an inn-keeper named Gideon M. Ashmore and a physician, Dr. Hiram Rutherford, were given refuge at Ashmore's inn.

When the angry Matson failed to convince his slaves to return to him, he took legal action. He retained Usher F. Linder, prominent attorney of Coles County, who had once served in the State legislature with Lincoln. Linder, acting under the provision of the Illinois "Black Laws," procured a writ from the local justice of the peace, calling for the production of Matson's Negroes, whereupon they were lodged in the jail at Charleston as runaway slaves. Appearing as counsel for the imprisoned Negroes was another of Lincoln's former legislative colleagues, Orlando B. Ficklin.

While Matson's slaves remained incarcerated, their benefactors, Ashmore and Dr. Rutherford, sued out a writ of *habeas corpus,* that legal doctrine which would inquire into the cause of a person's detention, and where the prison confinement was found unlawful, for his release therefrom. By the time the *habeas corpus* came to be heard in the Coles County Circuit Court, the case had brewed abundant public controversy. Chief Justice William Wilson of the state Supreme Court, on circuit duty, presided over the case in court, aided by Judge Samuel H. Treat, then of the Eighth Judicial Circuit.

Just before the hearing in court started, Lincoln arrived in Charleston and became associated with Linder as counsel for the slave-owner, Matson. Tradition declares that Lincoln was asked to act as co-attorney for the other side, for the slaves, but that he refused. The most profound modern scholar of Lincoln's law career, John J. Duff, concludes:

"Knowing that Lincoln (in common with Herndon and most lawyers of his day) had no qualms about injecting himself into important cases, the suspicion intrudes that he went to Charleston in order to get in on the Matson case, and for no other reason. Lincoln once characterized it [the slavery question], in a now famous passage, as the basic issue of whether one man should live by the sweat of another's brow. With his acceptance of the defense of Matson, Lincoln became the devil's own advocate, arraying himself on the side of the affirmative of that proposition."

It is, of course, impossible to learn what went on in Lincoln's mind when he accepted the defense of a Kentucky slave-holder in the legal fight to have runaway bonded black people returned to the South from Illinois. The future Emancipator's motives will naturally remain open to conjecture and doubt.

That hearing on the writ of *habeas corpus* began in the Coles County Circuit Court at Charleston on October 16, 1847. No jury would decide it; only the judges, Wilson and Treat. In that emotionally charged courtroom, Ficklin and Charles H. Constable acted for the slaves. Ficklin argued that the Ordinance of 1787 and the state Constitution of Illinois conferred freedom upon former slaves. Constable gave forth a lengthy dissertation on Anglo-Saxon concepts of freedom. Linder, co-counsel with Lincoln for Matson, argued that every citizen must be protected in the protection of his property. Then Lincoln addressed the Court.

Lincoln contended that Bryant's slave wife, Jane, had come to Illinois as a *seasonal* worker, who was to be returned to Kentucky after harvesting the crops, in accordance with her master Matson's annual custom, and that therefore she, as well as her children, never at any time had acquired the status of residents of Illinois. Lincoln's argument was good law but not elevated humanitarianism in the man who was in future to be acclaimed as the world's most illustrious emancipator of slaves. Lincoln, inconsistently enough, had only six years before, in 1841 at the Tazewell County Circuit Court, argued in one case, *Bailey v. Cromwell,* that the Ordinance of 1787 and the state Illinois Constitution had conferred freedom upon former slaves!

Lincoln and Linder lost their case for Matson. In rendering decision on the *habeas corpus* hearing, Judges Wilson and Treat found that the slaves should "be and remain free and discharged from all servitude whatever to any person or persons from henceforth and forever."

Lincoln's professional participation in behalf of a client who wanted to reclaim his slaves, continues to disturb those present-day students who elevate Lincoln to near-deistic loftiness as freer of the bonded colored people. Some have contended that his appearance as counsel for Matson was only a listless effort in which he did not exert his full energies and legal talents for his client. Such a conclusion would seem highly untenable. In the appropriate analysis of John J. Duff, who has studied Lincoln's law practice longer and more deeply than any other scholar: "The attempt to gloss over Lincoln's acceptance of the [Matson] case by having it appear that he was halfhearted in protecting the interests of a slaveholder, even though his own client, is pure hogwash—another instance of the fantastic lengths to which some authors have gone to render immune from any slight dispraise the name of Abraham Lincoln."

Before Lincoln, shortly after the Matson case decision late in 1847, left for Washington to be sworn in as a member of the national House of Representatives, the Lincoln & Herndon firm's day book for that year listed more than one hundred cases for that calendar twelve-month period.

X

Abraham Lincoln still walks the streets at midnight in Springfield—so Vachel Lindsay lyrically declared in his poem. This same spiritual Lincoln might well be walking the main streets of various county-seat towns in Illinois today. For from 1839 to the eve of his nomination for President in 1860, in the spring and fall of each year (except when he served in Congress) Lincoln followed the court sessions on the Eighth Judicial Circuit in his itinerant practice of law.

Shortly after becoming Stuart's partner in 1837, Lincoln was sent by Stuart to Bloomington to try a case in the McLean County Circuit Court for an Englishman, John W. Baddeley. When Baddeley glanced at Stuart's gangling, ill-dressed junior partner, he dispensed with the Stuart & Lincoln firm's legal services and retained another attorney. That was Lincoln's first experience "on the circuit."

Illinois was growing almost astronomically in population. New counties were formed, more courts and longer terms were necessitated, and existing judicial circuits were reorganized and new ones created. In 1839, when Lawyer Lincoln started traveling extensively from county court to county court in his legal practice, his home Sangamon County was transferred from the First to the Eighth Judicial Circuit. Thenceforth he would "ride the Eighth," although it was continually being reorganized with different counties added or detached from it. Over it he would travel on horseback, in horse-and-carriage, and later by railroad to reach the courts in these various counties.

The Eighth Judicial Circuit, originally comprising eight counties, was enlarged year by year until 1845, when those original eight were increased to seventeen in number, which, if shaded, would have darkened over one-fifth of the State's area.

In Lincoln's day the Judge of the Circuit would come to the county seat to hold a term of court. Accompanying him would be lawyers, such as Lincoln, who would find at each of the courts their cases, made ready for them by local lawyers, which the visiting circuit-riding attorney would handle in court. Usually he had time only sufficient to hold a consultation with the local lawyer who had retained him to argue the cause in court, to find out the details of the case, and present them at the trial.

Those county courts on the circuit, measured by modern standards, were primitive institutions. A courthouse was little larger than an ordinary dwelling. Law libraries were few, but litigation was simple. Often cases were susceptible to determination on principle and local custom, rather than through learned citation of parallel past cases. This condition suited Lincoln. For he would never be deeply rooted in the law from the scholarly viewpoint. He would never acquire that theoretical and profound knowledge that makes a great jurist. Lawyers then depended quite as much on their frontier oratory and their personal bearing before the jury as on their knowledge of the law and presentation of cases based on precedent.

On the circuit Lincoln showed himself only ordinarily successful in winning cases. But when he had time for reflection he demonstrated that he was a formidable advocate. His record of successes at the bar were to be vastly more impressive in the state Supreme Court at Springfield, where he had time to meditate and to use that court's amply stocked library, than on the circuit.

The farflung Eighth Judicial Circuit, over which Lincoln rode, had its rigors and uninviting aspects—long distances over bad roads, indescribably badly cooked food at the inns and taverns, uncomfortable and sometimes roach-ridden sleeping quarters. Life on the circuit nonetheless grew into an inherent and often pleasant part of the work of most attorneys who took the vows of circuit practice. The impressions and friendships of those county-to-county travels and practice were never effaced from the minds of those lawyers who rode over it during the spring and fall court terms.

The opening of the Circuit Court in any county over which Lincoln and other attorneys rode brought together throngs of people from the surrounding countryside and other towns and villages who, in an amusement-starved frontier community, went to court to see the Judge, plaintiffs, defendants, lawyers, and jurors perform.

To Lincoln, as to other advocates, this itinerant law practice for part of the year, away from Springfield, proved a pleasant way of life as well as means of livelihood. The circuit exerted quite as magnetic a hold on him as it did to other barnstorming barristers. The excitement of court week at county-seat towns, the camaraderie of fellow-traveling counselors, and even of the Judge, the sociability during the evenings at the inn, hotel, or boarding-house—all were to Lincoln's liking.

Lincoln's travels on the circuit, from 1839 onward to his presidential nomination twenty years later (except for the interval at Washington as congressman) made him an even better politician than he otherwise would have been. Not only did he meet Whig county leaders, but also he was given opportunity to learn, first hand, what was happening over other parts of Illinois. He learned about what voters were thinking. He found some answers to the perpetual dilemma of practicing politicians: What issues could stir voters into marching to the ballot-boxes?

The Eighth Judicial Circuit served as the best training ground for Lincoln's public career. It gave him an opportunity to keep in touch with influential Whig professionals and the general citizenry in a far-flung area.

Meanwhile, from 1840 to 1842, Lincoln was undergoing an ordeal in his courtship with Mary Todd.

LINCOLN'S ROMANCES

I

YEARS after Lincoln had died and risen to national and world distinction, numerous elderly women claimed, or were represented by old-timers in Indiana and Illinois and romantic-minded authors, as having many decades before "kept company" with Abe Lincoln. This plethora of Lincoln's female companions inspired one critical scholar to pen an article, "Sixteen Traditional Lincoln Sweethearts."

Yet Lincoln, by no manipulation of imagination, could be considered a "lady's man." William E. Barton, one of the better early twentieth-century Lincoln authors, even wrote one book, *Lincoln The Woman-Hater*.

The truth seems to have been, however, that Lincoln concerned himself with the world of women vastly less than the arena of politics. His intimate friend of both the Springfield and Washington years, Ward H. Lamon, has stated: "Politics were his world."

II

As a boy in Indiana Lincoln manifested some interest in girls. Spencer County old-timers told of his interest in fifteen-year-old Kate Roby, who later married Allen Gentry, Lincoln's companion on his first flat boat trip down to New Orleans. Kate in later years, like others of the "Sixteen Traditional Lincoln Sweethearts," elaborated on her friendship with the Spencer County backwoods boy. Kate told how she strolled down to the Ohio River with Abe, where they sat on the bank, watched the moon, and dangled their feet in the water.

When young Abe clerked in the New Salem store, however, his interest in the opposite sex waned, overshadowed by his absorption in making friends with everybody. One of his grocery employers recalled: "He always disliked to wait on ladies, preferring, he said, to wait on the men and boys." In 1860 Lincoln confessed his lack of comprehension regarding women, writing Mrs. M. J. Green: "The truth is I never correspond much with ladies; and hence I postpone writing letters to them, as a business which I do not understand."

While Lincoln was serving his first term in the State House of Representatives in 1835, news broke in Sand Ridge Prairie, seven miles from New Salem, that a young girl, Ann Rutledge, daughter of the tavern-keeper, had died from "brain fever."

Lincoln had boarded at the tavern of Ann's father, James Rutledge, during his early days in New Salem, and the Rutledges were his intimate friends, as was Ann's fiancee, John McNamar. When Ann died in August, 1835, Lincoln grieved, apparently like every one else who knew her.

Almost one quarter-century later, when Lincoln as President was steering the United States through civil war strife, the names of Abe and the late Ann Rutledge were first publicly linked in an almost invisible romance, from which he presumably never recovered. This mention was made in an obscure Illinois weekly, the *Menard Axis* of Petersburg, on February 15, 1862, by its editor, John Hill, a former New Salemite, under the banner headline, "A Romance of Reality." This account, which strung out an unflattering account of Abe, whom it called a "love-sick swain," did not mention Ann Rutledge by name.

After Lincoln's death his law partner, William H. Herndon, came into possession of a clipping of Hill's *Menard Axis* article of several years previous concerning Lincoln and his New Salem sweetheart. Herndon also visited some aging former New Salemites and wrote to various descendants of Ann Rutledge. The result was his lecture of November, 1866, in which Ann's name was first revealed to the nation to become another part of the Lincoln legend.

In that lecture, delivered at Springfield one year and a half following

Lincoln's death, Herndon elaborated on various subjects. It had the painfully lengthy title, "Abraham Lincoln. New Salem, Pioneering and *the* Poem." That last referred to Lincoln's favorite poem, William Knox's "Oh, why should the spirit of mortal be proud." Herndon told his audience: "Lincoln loved Ann Rutledge better than his own life." No other person beside himself, the law partner assured his hearers, understood "the many delicate wheels and hidden springs of the story of Lincoln, Miss Rutledge, the Poem, and its relation to the two, in time and place." Ann was a "beautiful, amiable, and lovely girl of nineteen," and she had been engaged to both Lincoln and John McNamar at the same time. Herndon added, "She suffered, pined, ate not and slept not," and soon died of a raging fever.

Lincoln's son, Robert Todd Lincoln, waxed furiously irate at Herndon over his lecture on his late father and Ann Rutledge. Several days after the lecture Bob Lincoln wrote Judge David Davis: "Mr. Wm. H. Herndon is making an ass of himself in his lectures. . . . If you have seen his lecture on 'Abraham Lincoln & Ann Rutledge,' I have no doubt you will feel the impropriety of such a publication even if it were, which I much doubt, all true." Later Lincoln's widow, Mary Todd Lincoln, sent these words to Judge Davis: "I shall remain firm in my conviction that Ann Rutledge is a myth—for in all his confidential communications such a romantic name was never breathed."

The nation and the world had not heard the last of the alleged Lincoln-Rutledge romance. When in 1872 Lincoln's close friend, Ward H. Lamon, published his Lincoln biography, ghost-written by another and based on Herndon's notes that he had bought, the romance between the young Representative of New Salem and the tavern-keeper's daughter appeared prominently. Seventeen years later, in 1889, Herndon himself, in collaboration with Jesse W. Weik, brought out his own life of Lincoln. Abundant space, embellished with more details, was devoted to the romance. Among such passages were: "He [Lincoln] became plunged in despair, and many of his friends feared that reason would desert [after Ann's death]. . . . He had great fits of mental depression, and wandered up and down the river and into the woods woefully abstracted. . . . To one friend he complained that the thought 'that the snows and rains fall upon her grave filled him with indescribable grief.' He was watched with especial vigilance during the damp, stormy days, under the belief that dark and gloomy weather might produce such a depression of spirits as to induce him to take his own life."

Not until well into the present twentieth century could scholars, casting skeptical eyes on the authenticity of the Lincoln-Rutledge romance, conclude that it rests on shaky historical evidence, based entirely on reminiscences of very aged people, written or dictated at Herndon's request after Lincoln's death. But the story is still elaborated on and presented to the public as true history by the literary and show-business professions.

III

Representative Lincoln in the early 1830's was introduced to a none too attractive, overweight girl from Kentucky named Mary Owens.

Mary was the sister of Mrs. Bennett Abell of New Salem, who was interested in promoting a match between Mary and Lincoln. How serious the affair grew is still matter of conjecture. But it was plain that Mary intended to wed Lincoln, and that Lincoln made some sort of promise.

When the special session of the Legislature assembled in December, 1836, Lincoln wrote Mary Owens a letter from Vandalia in which he informed her of an illness that he had contracted:

> I have been sick ever since I arrived here, or I should have written sooner. It is but little difference, however, as I have verry (sic) little to write. And more, the longer I can avoid the mortification of looking in the Post Office for your letter and not finding it, the better. You see I am mad about that *old letter* yet. I dont like verry (sic) well to risk you again. I'll try you once more any how. . . .
>
> You recollect I mentioned in the outset of this letter that I had been unwell. That is the fact, though I believe I am about well now; but that, with other things I can not account for, have conspired and have gotten my spirits so low, that I feel that I would rather be any place in the world than here. I really can not endure the thought of staying here ten weeks. Write back as soon as you get this, and if possible say something that will please me, for I have not [been] pleased since I left you. This letter is so dry and [stupid] that I am ashamed to send it, but with my prese [nt feel] ings I can not do any better.

Lincoln signed it, "Your friend, Lincoln."

Several months later Lincoln moved his residence from New Salem, where Mary Owens lived, to the new state capital town, Springfield. By that time, early in 1837, he showed scant enthusiasm for marrying her. In May he sent her another letter, a lengthy one devoid of romantic ardor:

> Springfield, May 7, 1837.
>
> Friend Mary
>
> I have commenced two letters to send you before this, both of which displeased me before I got half done, and so I tore them up. The first I thought wasn't serious enough, and the second was on the other extreme. I shall send this, turn out as it may.
>
> That thing of living in Springfield is rather a dull business after all, at least it is so to me. I am quite as lonesome here as [I] ever was anywhere in my life. . . . I am often thinking about what we said of your coming to live at Springfield. I am afraid you would not be satisfied. There is a great deal of flourishing about in carriages here, which it would be your doom

> to see without sharing it. You would have to be poor without the means of hiding your poverty. Do you believe you could bear that patiently? Whatever woman may cast her lot with mine, should any ever do so, it is my intention to do all in my power to make her happy and contented; and there is nothing I can immagine (sic), that would make me more unhappy than to fail in the effort. I know I should be much happier with you than the way I am, provided I saw no signs of discontent in you. What you have said to me may have been in jest, or I may have misunderstood it. If so, then let it be forgotten; if otherwise, I much wish you would think seriously before you decide.

Lincoln, in this unencouraging message to Mary, continued:

> For my part I have already decided. What I have said I will most positively abide by, provided you wish it. My opinion is that you had better not do it. You have not been accustomed to hardship, and it may be more severe than you now immagine (sic). I know you are capable of thinking correctly on any subject; and if you deliberate maturely upon this, before you decide, then I am willing to abide your decision.
>
> You must write me a good long letter after you get this. You have nothing else to do, and though it might not seem interesting to you, after you had written it, it would be a good deal of company to me in this 'busy wilderness.' Tell your sister I don't want to hear any more about selling out and moving. That gives me the hypo whenever I think of it.
>
> Yours, etc.,
> Lincoln.

Lincoln's letter, lacking unqualified willingness to marry the young lady, did not end his association with her yet. Three months later, in August, 1837, he rode from his Springfield home to New Salem, where he saw her again. Returning home, he sent her another long letter on August 16, informing her that she was at liberty to marry him, if that would make her happier; but he would release her from any promises if she thought otherwise. "You must know that I can not see you, or think of you, with entire indifference;" he wrote her, "and yet it may be, that you, are mistaken in regard to what my real feelings towards you are. . . . If you feel yourself in any degree bound to me, I am now willing to release you, provided you wish it; while, on the other hand, I am willing, and even anxious to bind you faster, if I can be convinced that it will, in any considerable degree, add to your happiness." Lincoln added, "If it suits you best to not answer this—farewell—a long life and a merry one attend you. But if you conclude to write back, speak as plainly as I do."

With that letter Lincoln's correspondence with Mary Owens stopped; at least, no other of his messages to her has been unearthed. Later she married another man, Jesse Vineyard of Missouri. In subsequent years she told why she had rejected Lincoln: "I thought Mr. Lincoln was deficient in those little links which make up the chain of a woman's happiness."

Lincoln, during the previous legislative session held at Vandalia, had boarded at the home of State Senator Orville H. Browning, a Whig who represented the Quincy district. Like Lincoln, Browning was a native Kentuckian, had served in the Black Hawk War, had read law, and was a Whig. There the comparison ended. Browning had attended college, was well indoctrinated with the social graces, dressed with sartorial meticulousness, and was prepossessing. Lincoln nonetheless struck up an almost lifelong friendship with Browning and his wife.

The year after his split with Mary Owens, Lincoln bared his soul about her in words confided to Mrs. Browning, without mentioning Mary's name. Lincoln told her in a letter that he had suggested to a New Salem friend that, if she brought back her sister from Kentucky, he would marry her; he had met Mary once three years before. When Mary appeared in New Salem for a second time, Lincoln wrote Mrs. Browning that he was sorely disappointed in her looks. She lacked physical charm and was altogether too fat. "I knew she was over-size, but she now appeared a fair match for Falstaff," Lincoln wrote Mrs. Browning in unchivalrous vein. "When I beheld her, I could not for my life avoid thinking of my mother; and this, not from withered features, for her skin was too full of fat, to permit its contracting in to wrinkles, but from her want of teeth, weather-beaten appearance in general, and from a kind of notion that ran in my head that *nothing* could have commenced at the size of infancy, and reached her present bulk in less than thirty-five or forty years; and, in short, I was not at all pleased with her. But what could I do? I had told her sister that I would take her for better or worse." Toward the close of his letter Lincoln told Mrs. Browning: "I have now come to the conclusion never again to think of marrying. I can never be satisfied with any one who would be block-head enough to have me."

Lincoln's letter to Eliza Browning about Mary Owens was crude; not worthy of a gentleman. Lincoln's present-day armies of admirers merely excuse it by declaring that he was "not in character" when he wrote it. The only creditable part of the letter lay in the fact that he did not mention Mary by name. After Lincoln's death Eliza's husband, Orville H. Browning, confided to another Illinois politician in a note: "Neither Mrs. Browning nor myself ever knew from him who the lady referred to in the letter was. Of course, neither of us ever asked him, nor did he ever inform us."

IV

Late in 1839, a year after his letter to Mrs. Browning, Lincoln joined three other legislative colleagues in sending a written appeal to her, begging her to bring some women with her to Springfield, indicating their lack of feminine company. This request to Mrs. Browning read: "We the undersigned, respectfully represent to your *Honoress,* that we are in great need of your society in this town of Springfield; and therefore humbly pray that your *Honoress* will repair to the Seat of Government, bringing in your train all ladies in general, who may be at your command; and all Mr. Browning's sisters in that particular. And as faithful and dutiful Petitioners we promise that if you grant this request, we will render unto your *Honoress* due attention and faithful obedience to, your orders in general & to Miss Browning's in particular."

During that year, Lincoln is quoted as having joked about his failure to attract women when he spoke of the "Long Nine" delegation from Sangamon in the Legislature. Declared he: "I have been called the longest of the nine. Now, if any woman old or young ever thought there was any particular charm in this distinguished specimen of number nine, I have, as yet, been so unfortunate as not to have discovered it."

Lincoln revealed his lack of confidence in matters concerning the opposite sex three years after that, when he wrote his friend, Joshua F. Speed, now of Louisville, Kentucky: "I should like to see that 'Sis' of yours, that was absent when I was there [in Louisville], tho' I suppose she would run away again, if she were to hear I was coming."

Unversed in the jousts of gallantry, the bachelor legislator of Springfield was unattractive to women. Although not possessed of a harsh soul, he lacked those social graces and small gallantries so admired by the feminine world.

Meanwhile, Springfield had received an influx of citizens when the state offices were moved up from Vandalia. Preparations were made to receive the legislators, including Representative Lincoln, as familiar sights for the first time in December of that year. Social life took on a new accelerated appearance. The town's society arbiters, Mr. and Mrs. Ninian W. Edwards, son and daughter-in-law of the renowned former United States Senator and Governor of the same name, both transplanted Kentuckians like so many other Springfielders, soon received as their permanent guest Mrs. Edwards' half-sister from Lexington, Kentucky. Her name was Mary Ann Todd.

V

In Mary Todd's social background and heritage was a severe contrast to Lincoln's. She had been born on December 13, 1818, at Lexington, in the rich Blue Grass country of slaveholding Kentucky. Then called the "Athens of the West," Lexington was removed from frontier primitiveness and noted for its self-constituted high society, who lived graciously, consumed fine food, drank palatable bourbon whiskey, maintained properly appointed homes, and sponsored good educational institutions, among them Transylvania University. Some of Lexington's citizens were renowned in politics, chief among them that highest priest of Whiggery, Henry Clay, who lived on his estate, "Ashland," nearby.

Mary Ann, who had come to live with her half-sister and brother-in-law, the Edwardses of Springfield, Illinois, was the daughter of Robert Smith Todd and Eliza Parker Todd, both of distinguished ancestry. Todd, Transylvania University graduate, War of 1812 veteran, lawyer, business man, slaveholder, old-school gentleman, Kentucky state legislator, and Whig Party lieutenant for Clay, wielded influence in and around Lexington. After the death of his wife, Mary's mother, Robert remarried and raised a new series of children. Mary and her sisters and brothers grew up in her father and stepmother's hospitable home in Lexington, but her association with her stepmother proved anything but happy. Mary attended Madame Victorie Mentelle's exclusive girl's school in Lexington. In 1837, when she had reached nineteen, she visited her sister, Elizabeth, and Elizabeth's husband, Ninian W. Edwards, in Springfield. She returned to Kentucky and two years later came back to Springfield to make the Edwards's home her permanent residence.

When Mary first came to live in the Illinois capital town in 1839, she was a plump young lady with clear blue eyes, good complexion, and soft brown hair. She was described as friendly and hospitable, with a "warmth of manner." She even revealed a sense of humor about her obesity to her friends, as in one letter of 1840 to Mercy Levering: "I still am the ruddy *pineknot,* only not quite so great an exuberance of flesh, as it once was my lot to contend with, although quite a sufficiency." Occasionally an intimate joked about her excess weight. When she was once given a lift home to the Edwards house in a two-wheeled cart by a drayman named Ellis Hart, Dr. Elias H. Merryman of Springfield composed a jingle:

> Up flew windows, out popped heads,
> To see this Lady gay
> In silken cloak and feathers white
> A-riding on the dray.
>
> At length arrived at Edwards' gate
> Hart backed the usual way
> And taking out the iron pin
> He rolled her off the dray.

Abraham Lincoln, in a letter to Speed two years later, referred to "Hart, the little drayman that hauled Molly home once." Lincoln was sometimes to call Mary Todd "Molly."

Mary Todd revelled in Springfield's social life. James C. Conkling, fiance of her friend Mercy Levering, in 1840 wrote to Mercy about Mary: "She is the very creature of excitement you know and never enjoys herself more than when in society and surrounded by a company of merry friends." But Mary's agreeable disposition disappeared beneath sarcastic and biting comments at times. She often betrayed her disapproval by her looks at any given moment. Her nephew, Albert S. Edwards, later commented: "She was also impulsive and made no attempt to conceal her feelings. . . . Her face was an index to every passing emotion." Those who knew her best described her as possessed of a charming personality marred only by a transient hauteur of manner and a caustic, devastating wit that cut like the sting of a hornet.

Society in Springfield, although essentially democratic, had its select groups, the most exclusive being Mary's own, the "Edwards clique." At the Edwards's mansion, where Mary lived, important people gathered, among them rising politicians, including Representative Lincoln. Since his law partner was John Todd Stuart, a distant cousin of the Kentucky Todds, Lincoln was partially "accepted" by the starchy Edwardses. But Lincoln was usually more at ease talking politics and spinning drolleries among his own group in town than in bowing, dancing, and indulging in chit-chat at the Edwards' soirées.

The rising Democrat, Stephen A. Douglas, frequented the political Whig-steeped Edwards home, despite his opposing party beliefs. The future Little Giant had recently transformed himself from a carelessly dressed bachelor into a well-groomed gentleman and attended cotillion parties. Douglas danced gracefully despite his bulky form and ever bulging belly. Sometimes he acted as Mary Todd's escort although he did not, as often supposed, solicit her hand in marriage and become Lincoln's rival in love as in politics. Mary in later years declared of Douglas: "I liked him well enough, but that was all."

Mary felt exuberantly happy as she confided to her best girl friend, Mercy Levering, about the Edwards's plans for the coming 1840-41 social season: "We expect a very gay winter, evening before my sister gave a most agreeable party, upwards of a hundred graced the festive scene." In a later decade Mary would reminisce to Mrs. Gideon Welles, wife of her husband's Secretary of the Navy: "In our little coterie in Springfield, in the days of my girlhood, we had a society of gentlemen, who have since, been distinguished. . . . My great and glorious husband comes *first*. . . . Douglas, Trumbull, Baker, Hardin, Shields, such choice spirits, were the habitues of our drawing room."

That group of men who graced the Edwards mansion and knew Mary Todd comprised indeed an aggregation of truly skilled political practitioners. Besides the future President and the nation's future most distinguished Democrat, Lincoln and Douglas, there was Lyman Trumbull, destined to be Douglas's United States Senate colleague from

Illinois and to serve in the national Upper House through the Civil War and Reconstruction; the English-born Edward D. Baker, soon to be congressman from Illinois, one of Lincoln's closest cronies, and later United States Senator from Oregon; John J. Hardin, cousin of Mary Todd, also to serve in Congress, and within several years to give his life at Buena Vista in the Mexican War leading his First Illinois Volunteers regiment; and the Irish-born mercurial James Shields, destined to be the only man ever to serve three states successively (Illinois, Minnesota, and Missouri) in the United States Senate.

Representative Lincoln, when the session of the Legislature met late in 1839, received a printed card, headed "Cotillion Party," which invited him, along with Speed, Douglas, Shields, and others to that elaborate affair in December. It is possible that Lincoln first met Mary Todd formally for the first time on that occasion. But it was not until a year later, December of 1840, that his name appears in one of her preserved letters.

Mary saw in this frontier legislator of lowly social beginnings a man of strange but attractive contradictions. He was fond of women, but awkward and tactless in their presence, subject to fits of melancholia, yet a humorous story-teller. He was a wily politician, nonetheless an individual of impeccable personal honesty, ungainly in appearance, though possessed of a magnetic manner.

VI

During the summer of 1840 Mary Todd visited her uncle, Judge David Todd of Columbia, Missouri. There she was shown attention by a grandson of the loquacious Virginia Revolutionary War patriot, Patrick Henry. Mary was excited over this scion of a proud Virginia family. "There is *one* being here," Mary wrote back home from Missouri to her friend, Mercy Levering, "who cannot brook the mention of my return [to Springfield], an agreeable lawyer & grandson of *Patrick Henry—what an honor!* I shall never survive it—I wish you could see him, the most perfect original I ever met. My beaux have *always* been *hard bargains* at any rate. Uncle and others think he surpasses his *noble ancestor* in *talents,* yet Merc I love him not, & my hand will never be given, where my heart is not."

Tradition today in Missouri declares that Abraham Lincoln journeyed to see Mary at Columbia and also participated in a rally there for the Whig presidential candidate, General Harrison. But no evidence supports this belief. But when Mary returned to Springfield in the autumn of 1840 she and Lincoln were, in the Illinois parlance, "a-courtin'."

The noisy "log cabin and cider" national election between Harrison and his Democratic opponent, President Van Buren, crowded out most subjects in the political caldron that was Springfield. Mary, like Lincoln, ardently agitated for Harrison and all other Whigs. Her father in Kentucky was still one of Clay's lieutenants, and the anti-Jacksonian prejudice dug deep into her. During an era when family, social manners, and domesticity encompassed a woman's entire world, Mary was exciting herself over the Whig Party's fortunes.

While Lincoln took to the hustings for Harrison in distant counties, Mary listened to the electioneering "Tippecanoe Singing Club" of Springfield and cheered them on. She wrote Mercy after Harrison's victory: "I suppose like the rest of us *Whigs* . . . you have been rejoicing in the recent election of Gen. Harrison. . . . This fall I became quite a *politician*, rather an unladylike profession."

Toward the end of 1840 Lincoln and Mary Todd became engaged to marry. Whether a wedding date was fixed does not appear from the record or any evidence ever unearthed.

Suddenly in December Mary lapsed into a somber mood. "Why is it," she queried Mercy Levering by mail, "that married folks always become so serious?" She told of one recently wed girl: "Her *silver tones*, the other evening were not quite so captain like as was their wont in former times." She spoke of another young lady about to be married and referred to her own approaching union with Lincoln in these words: "I am pleased she is about perpetrating the *crime of matrimony*, like some of our friends in *this place*, M & L for instance, I think she will be much happier." She told of a contemplated trip with Lincoln and other friends to Jacksonville.

When Mary pondered on the *"crime of matrimony,"* she was ironically using the word "crime," because the Todds and the Edwardses were by now opposing her marriage to Lincoln.

Mary's family felt that Lincoln had come from "nowhere." Her niece, Katherine Helm, subsequently spoke of this family disapproval of the marriage. "Nebulous" was the adjective that Miss Helm used about Lincoln's future. Mary's nephew, Albert S. Edwards, son of Mr. and Mrs. Ninian W. Edwards, also testified that his parents were convinced that Lincoln did not qualify socially. "Up to the time of the courtship," stated Albert Edwards concerning his parents, Mary's brother-in-law and half-sister, "they made Lincoln welcome and encouraged his visits. . . . When my mother saw that things were becoming serious between Lincoln and Mary, she treated him rather coldly. The invitations to call were not pressed." A gentle-born Todd lady of the Kentucky Blue Grass, sister-in-law of the town's top aristocrat, would be incongruously matched with a coarse man of Indiana backwoods origin and poor purse.

During those last months of 1840 Lincoln was afflicted with a malady which he soon called "hypochondriasm." Weeks of strength-sapping campaigning for Harrison for President under severely strenuous traveling conditions in outlandish regions during the hot months were taking their toll. His stumping ordeal had required days of hard horseback riding over parched prairies and sticky swamps. He felt unhappy, too, over his showing in his own re-election campaign in which he had polled the lowest number of the five Whig representatives chosen from Sangamon County.

Aside from his run-down physical condition, his gloom over his political future, fits of "hypochondriasm," and general ignorance in dealing with women, Lincoln felt hurt about the opposition of Mary's family. He quipped on a few occasions that while one "d" was enough to spell God, it took two "d's" for Todd.

Lincoln had his own reasons, which no biographer or historian can fathom, for concluding that marriage to Mary was not for him. Supposedly he sent a letter to her, begging off, and then showed it to Speed, whose reputation as a prairie Lothario he appreciated, but Speed threw the letter into the fire, commenting that feelings of the heart should not be committed to paper. At least, that is one familiar story around Springfield.

On New Year's Day, 1841, Lincoln visited Mary. He presumably explained to her the contents of his letter to her that Speed had destroyed, so the story runs. What really happened on that first day of the year will never be exactly or even remotely known. Lincoln himself referred to the occasion in a later letter to Speed as "that fatal first of Jany. '41." Thus with the opening of 1841, he found himself "disengaged" and a bachelor for some time to come.

VII

Lincoln, following his break with Mary, sank into deep depression.

He absented himself from the Legislature from January 13 to 19. On the 20th he sent a remarkable letter to his law-partner, Congressman John T. Stuart, then at Washington, confiding, "I have, within the last few days, been making a most discreditable exhibition of myself in the way of hypochondriasm." He requested Stuart to try to secure from the Harrison Administration the Postmaster's job at Springfield for his friend and physician, Dr. Anson G. Henry. He added: "Dr. Henry is necessary to my existence." Three days later, the 23rd, Lincoln sent another message to Stuart, in a similar melancholy vein. He told Stuart of "the deplorable state of my mind at this time," adding the unhappy thought: "I am now the most miserable man living. If what I feel were equally distributed to the whole human family, there would not be one cheerful face on the earth. Whether I shall ever be better I can not tell; I awfully forebode I shall not. To remain as I am is impossible; I must die or be better, it appears to me."

Stuart in Washington grew alarmed about his friend and law-partner. A change of scene, far from Springfield, even out of the United States in some exotic land, might, he felt, be the solution for Lincoln. Thus one day after the Harrison Adminstration took office he sent a written request to Secretary of State Daniel Webster, recommending Lincoln for the diplomatic post of *Charge d'Affaires* in Colombia. But that mission went to another.

Lincoln's condition during that unnerving January of 1841 was obvious to those who saw him. On January 22, at the time he was pouring out his woes to Stuart, one Springfield visitor wrote John J. Hardin: "We have been very much distressed, on Mr. Lincoln's account; hearing he had two Cat fits, and a Duck fit since we left." Two days later, the 24th, Mercy Levering's husband-to-be, James C. Conkling of Springfield, sent Mercy a letter telling how Lincoln looked:

"Poor L! how are the mighty fallen! He was confined about a week, but though he now appears again he is reduced and emaciated in appearance and seems scarcely to possess strength enough to speak above a whisper. His case at present is truly deplorable but what prospect there may be for ultimate relief I cannot pretend to say." Conkling added: "I doubt not but he can declare 'That loving is a painful thrill, And not to love more painful still.' "

Lincoln's plight and Mary Todd's future continued as subjects of correspondence between Conkling and Mercy Levering. Mercy replied to him, referring to Abraham Lincoln: "Poor A—I fear his is a blighted heart! perhaps if he were as persevering as Mr. W—he might finally be successful." The "Mr. W." mentioned by Mercy was Edwin B. Webb, a middle-aged widower with two children, who was now pursuing Mary Todd. Conkling replied to Mercy about Lincoln: "And L, poor hapless simple swain who loved most true but was not loved again—I suppose he will now endeavor to drown his cares among the intricacies and perplexities of the law."

By this time, with the adjournment of the Legislature in March, Lincoln's term as Representative had ended. In another month he would devote more time to the law, with Stephen T. Logan as his new partner.

Lawyer Lincoln, with the coming of spring, emerged from his depression. His friend Speed having returned to his native Kentucky to live, Lincoln now roomed at the house of Mr. and Mrs. William Butler of Springfield, where he had hitherto only taken his meals. Butler held the job of Clerk of the Circuit Court and involved himself in Whig politics.

Butler's wife kept Speed informed about Lincoln's condition, saying it was improving. And Speed happily wrote back to Butler: "I am glad to hear from Mrs. Butler that Lincoln is on the mend." That was in May, 1841.

The almost rehabilitated Lincoln perhaps paid court to Mrs. Butler's very much younger sister, Sarah Rickard, as has been mentioned. In a letter to Speed in June, Lincoln declared: "I have not seen Sarah since my long trip, and I am going out there as soon as I mail this letter." Again he informed Speed early the next year: "I have seen Sarah but once. She seemed verry (sic) cheerful, and so, I said nothing to her about what we spoke." Two months later, in March, 1842, Lincoln confided to his best friend: "One thing I can tell you which I know you will be glad to hear; and that is, that I have seen Sarah, and scrutinized her feelings as well as I could, and am fully convinced, she is far happier now, than she has been for the last fifteen months past."

Lincoln's interest in marrying Sarah Rickard remains one of those enigmas with which Lincoln's life is filled. Perhaps there had been some sort of affair between her and Speed, with Lincoln acting as a mere intermediary. Speed had married another in the previous February. But Sarah herself, like so many others of Lincoln's "traditional sweethearts," in subsequent years claimed that Lincoln wanted her for his bride. After Lincoln's death she wrote Herndon:

"Mr. Lincoln did make a proposal of marriage to me in the summer, or perhaps later, in the year 1840. He brought to my attention the accounts in the Bible of the patriarch Abraham's marriage to Sarah, and used that historical union as an argument in his own behalf. My reason for declining his proposal was the wide difference in our ages. I was only sixteen, and had given the subject of matrimony but very little, if any, thought. . . . He seemed almost like an older brother."

Meanwhile, Mary Todd remained morose and served as target of gossip among Springfield settlers, particularly about the attentions showered upon her by the widower Webb. In mid-June (1841) she confided in a note to Mercy Levering that "the last two or three months have been of *interminable* length," that she suffered "some *lingering regrets* over the past, which time can alone overshadow with its healing balm." Her name having been linked romantically with Webb, who had two children by his late wife, Mary assured Mercy, "In your friendly & confiding ears allow me to whisper that my *heart can never be his.* I have deeply regretted that his constant visits, attentions etc should have given room for remarks, which were to me unpleasant. There being a slight difference of some eighteen or twenty summers in our years, would preclude all possibility of congenealty (sic) of feeling, without which I should never feel justifiable in resigning my happiness into the safe keeping of another, even should that other be far too worthy for me, with his two *sweet little objections.*" That last referred to Webb's children.

Mary in that letter to Mercy mentioned Lincoln, whom she referred to as "Joshua's friend,"—the friend of Joshua F. Speed. "Joshua's friend," she confided to Mercy, "deems me unworthy of notice, as I have not met *him* in the gay world for months. With the usual comfort of misery, imagine that others were as seldom gladdened by his presence as my humble self, yet I would that the case were different, that he would once more resume his station in Society, that 'Richard should be himself again,' much, much happiness would it afford me."

VIII

Lincoln by that summer of 1841 was still carrying on his confidential correspondence with his friend, Speed.

In August Lincoln visited Speed at his home in Farmington, near Louisville, for several weeks. There the old friends of the store in Springfield unburdened their respective affairs of the heart to each other.

At the Speed home Lincoln happily romped with Speed's half-sister, Mary. When he returned to Springfield and rode the Eighth Judicial Circuit again in his migratory law practice, he recalled his good times at the Speeds' house. "When I remembered," he wrote Mary Speed, "that you and I were something of cronies while I was at Farmington, and that, while there, I once was under the necessity of shutting you up in a room to prevent your committing an assault and battery upon me, I instantly decided that you should be the devoted one." He inquired about her brother Joshua's latest girl, Fanny Henning. "Are you not convinced that she is one of the sweetest girls in the world?"

Speed had returned with Lincoln to Springfield for a visit. The two intimate friends confided to each other delicate details about their respective love problems. Then Speed returned to Kentucky and became engaged to Fanny Henning. Soon Speed revealed the same hesitancy about marrying Fanny as Lincoln had about Mary Todd nearly one year previous.

The letters sent by Lincoln to his marriage-wary friend, Joshua, to whom he wrote more privately than to any other person in his entire life, throw light on Lincoln's own changing emotions toward matrimony and his regret over his estrangement from Mary Todd.

In his message of February 3, 1842, to Speed, Lincoln assured him that the anxiety felt over Fanny's health and life "must and will forever banish those horid (sic) doubts" of his affection for her. Lincoln further added: "But I hope your melancholy bodings as to her early death, are not well founded. I even hope, that ere this reaches you, she will have returned with improved and still improving health; and that you will have met her, and forgotten the sorrows of the past, in the enjoyment of the present." Lincoln informed Speed about his own improved health: "I have been quite clear of hypo since you left."

Lincoln's best friend finally acquired courage and went through the marriage ceremony with Fanny, on February 15. Two days before the wedding Lincoln sent the anxious groom-to-be words of moral support:

"When this shall have reached you, you will have been Fanny's husband several days. . . . I am now fully convinced, that you love her as ardently as you are capable of loving. . . . If you went through the ceremony *calmly,* or even with sufficient composure not to excite alarm in any present, you are safe, beyond question, and in two or three months, to say the most, will be the happiest of men." When he received news that Joshua was securely bound to Fanny Henning in wedlock, Lincoln sent word back to the newly wed husband: "I tell you, Speed, our *forebodings,* for which you and I are rather peculiar, are all the worst sort of nonsense. . . . When your nerves once get steady now, the whole trouble will be over forever."

Lincoln during the next few weeks showed signs of shaking off his own "forebodings." In his next message to Joshua in March (1842) he spoke frankly of his past broken engagement to Mary Todd. After telling Joshua how thrilled he was to learn that the new husband was *"far happier than you ever expected to be"* as a married man, Lincoln penned this significant thought about his ruptured romance with Mary:

"I tell you, that the short space it took me to read your last letter, gave me more pleasure, than the total sum of all I have enjoyed since that fatal first of Jany. '41. Since then, it seems to me, I should have been entirely happy, but for the never-absent idea, that there is *one* still unhappy whom I have contributed to make so. That still kills my soul. I can not but reproach myself, for even wishing to be happy while she is otherwise. She accompanied a large party on the Rail Road cars, to Jacksonville last monday; and on her return, spoke, so that I heard of it, of having enjoyed the trip exceedingly. God be praised for that."

Lincoln continued his comforting correspondence with the now maritally acclimated Speed. In July, he was casting off some of his agnostic feeling and writing his friend in Kentucky: "God made me one of the instruments of bringing your Fanny and you together, which union, I have no doubt He has fore-ordained. Whatever He designs, He will do for *me* yet. 'Stand *still* and see the salvation of the Lord' is my text now."

IX

By that summer of 1842 Lincoln was hoping for reconciliation with Mary Todd.

Suddenly a tense political situation entangled itself in the destinies of the lowly-born lawyer-politician and the well-born Blue Grass belle. Resulting from a series of dramatic incidents which offered the socially unveneered Lincoln the opportunity to demonstrate his chivalry to the proud Kentucky lady, it revolved about the Whig-inspired "Rebecca Letters," aimed at the Democratic state auditor, James Shields, which appeared anonymously in the Whig *Sangamo Journal* of Springfield.

On August 19, 1842, the *Sangamo Journal* printed the first of the "Rebecca" political epistles, in backwoods language, lamenting the sad predicament in which Illinois people found themselves following the failure of the State Bank earlier in the year. "Rebecca" blamed the Democratic Party office-holders. When the Democrat Auditor, Shields sent out the Governor's instructions to take nothing but gold and silver in taxes, another "Rebecca" letter appeared in the *Journal* on September 2. This second letter, which Lincoln was to admit writing, made Shields the butt of ridicule. On the 9th appeared another in the *Journal,* which attacked Shields's lack of courage. On the 16th the paper printed some doggerel signed "Cathleen," ridiculing the Irish "blarney" of Shields, who had been born in Ireland.

But Mary Todd was involved in the authorship of anti-Shields pieces. Years later she recalled in a letter to a friend:

"I committed his [Shields's] *follies,* to rhyme, and very silly verses they were, only, they were said to abound in sarcasm, causing them to be very offensive to the Genl. [Shields]. A gentleman friend, carried them off. . . . One day, I saw them, strangely enough in the daily papers. Genl. Shields, called upon the Editor [Simeon Francis], and demanded the author. The Editor, requested *a day* to reflect upon it. The latter called upon Mr. Lincoln. . . . Mr. L. then replied, say to Shields, that 'I am responsible.' Mr. L. thought no more of it, when about two weeks afterwards, while he was 150 miles away from S. [Springfield] attending court, Shields followed him up & demanded satisfaction."

The infuriated Shields demanded satisfaction from Lincoln on the field of honor. "Seconds" ceremoniously arranged for a duel between Lincoln and Shields, with pistols as weapons.

On September 22, 1842, the two rivals, the Whig Lincoln and the Democratic Shields, accompanied by their seconds, crossed the Mississippi River to Missouri, since dueling was legally permitted in Illinois.

At the last moment the duel was suspended. An agreement was patched up whereby Lincoln's apology was read. Having averted the duel with Shields through the intercession of John J. Hardin and others, he then sought consolation in another letter to Joshua F. Speed. On October 5 he informed Speed: "You have heard of my duel with Shields, and I have now to inform you that the duelling business still rages in this city," and he told Speed of another duel in which Shields was involved, which also had been averted. Lincoln's main topic in this letter, however, was marriage. He wrote his Kentucky crony of "that subject which you know to be of such infinite solicitude to me." He queried Speed: " 'Are you now, in *feeling* as well as *judgement* (sic) glad you are married as you are?' From any body but me, this would be an impudent question not to be tolerated; but I know you will pardon it in me. Please answer it quickly as I feel impatient to know."

The impatience of Lincoln was evident in the following four weeks.

The "Rebecca Letters" and the resulting averted duel with Shields had the effect of aiding in a reuniting of Lincoln and Mary Todd—a reconciliation brought about by the wife of the *Sangamo Journal's* editor, Mrs. Simeon Francis, and other mutual friends of the couple.

At the Edwards mansion on November 4, 1842, Abraham Lincoln and Mary Todd were married. She was attired in a white brocaded dress. The Episcopal minister, Reverend Charles Dresser, performed the ceremony.

Mary chose Julia Jayne, her friend, as one of her bridesmaids. Within another year Julia would wed a rising young politician, Lyman Trumbull. Lincoln selected James H. Matheny as his best man.

How did Lincoln look to those who watched him going through the marriage ceremony with Mary? Not overly cheerful, according to some of those present, as they recalled in later years. "Lincoln looked and acted as if he were going to the slaughter," testified Matheny years later. While dressing for his wedding at the home of William Butler, where he boarded, Lincoln, when asked privately where he was going, allegedly replied, "To hell, I reckon," according to Butler's son, Speed Butler.

A humorous incident was said to have enlivened the ceremony. Among the guests was Justice Thomas C. Browne of the Illinois Supreme Court. That rustic and jovial frontier jurist had never seen so formal a wedding ritual as that Todd-Lincoln affair, with the dignified Reverend Dresser reading the impressive Episcopal service, garbed in his religious robes. When Dresser asked Lincoln to repeat after him that he endowed the bride with all his worldly goods, Judge Browne interrupted the speaking of the marriage lines to caution: "Lincoln, the Statute fixes all that." Even Dresser could not suppress a smile of amusement.

At the appropriate moment during the ceremony Lincoln presented to his bride a wedding ring, on the inside of which were engraved the words, "Love Is Eternal."

Shortly after the wedding Lincoln entered in his Bible: "Abraham Lincoln and Mary Todd, married, November 4—1842." And one week later he sent from Springfield a letter to another lawyer, Samuel D. Marshall of Shawneetown, Illinois: "Nothing new here, except my marrying, which to me, is matter of profound wonder."

THE LONE WHIG FROM ILLINOIS

7

I

EVER competing with the law and his family in Lincoln's affections was politics. As his intimate friend of his late Illinois and war years, Ward H. Lamon, stated: "Politics were his world—a world filled with hopeful enchantments."

Lincoln's was a spirit maneuvering for public place. For a long time he had set his sights on Congress.

In February, 1843, only three months after his marriage to Mary Todd, Lincoln took time out from his law cases to assure Whigs that he was willing to go to Washington. To one lawyer and politician he wrote: "Now if you should hear any one say that Lincoln don't want to go to Congress, I wish you as a personal friend of mine, would tell him you have reason to believe he is mistaken. The truth is, I would like to go very much."

The following month he drafted resolutions for adoption at a Whig meeting in Springfield and conferred with local leaders on strategy and formation of party committees. One address, which he composed in that month, signed by himself, his new law partner, Stephen T. Logan, and Albert T. Bledsoe, stated the issues on which Illinois Whigs would wage the national election campaign in the following year, 1844, with Henry Clay as presidential standard-bearer.

II

Lincoln, in his plans to run for Congress, found himself confronted by two human obstacles: his friend, Edward D. Baker of his own Sangamon County, and John J. Hardin of Morgan County, his real rival and, ironically, a cousin of his wife, Mary. All three were popular Whigs, excellent speakers before juries and political rallies, and veterans of the Black Hawk War—this last a prime vote-garnering asset. Each wanted to represent the Whig-voting Seventh Illinois Congressional District, then made up of eleven counties.

After backstage operations, conferences, profuse correspondence, and political "deals," Lincoln finally found a way out of the impasse. Each of the three, he, Baker, and Hardin, would have one term in Congress.

When Hardin appeared the strongest candidate, Lincoln, as the Sangamon County chairman of the District Convention in May, 1843, withdrew his friend Baker's candidacy, with Baker's consent. Hardin was nominated as Whig candidate for Congress and then elected. To appease Baker, Lincoln sponsored a resolution, declaring that "this convention, as individuals, recommend E. D. Baker as a suitable person to be voted for by the Whigs of this district, for representative in Congress, at the election of 1844." Lincoln's plan was for Baker to succeed Hardin as congressman the following year (1844), and he himself would follow Baker in 1846.

Hardin stepped aside for Baker in 1844, as agreed, and Lincoln awaited his term two years hence. He spoke for Baker's candidacy in 1844, at the same time serving as a presidential elector for Henry Clay, who had been nominated Whig national standard-bearer. He served as the guiding spirit of the Whig State Central Committee, which conducted Clay's campaign in Illinois. He aided in launching two Clay electioneering sheets, *The Olive Branch,* and a German-language paper. He stumped several Illinois counties so ardently that the observant Judge David Davis remarked: "Lincoln is the best stump speaker in the State. Shows the want of early education, but has great powers as a speaker."

Into southern Indiana, his boyhood home region, Lincoln rode on horseback, day after day pouring forth praise of his beloved Harry of the West, his "beau-ideal of a statesman." He held forth at Bruceville,

Vincennes, Washington, Boonville, Rockport and finally at Gentryville, the home of his youth. One scrap from the Rockport *Herald* of November 1, 1844, has been preserved: "Mr. Lincoln, of Springfield, Ill., addressed a large and respectable audience at the court house on Wednesday evening last, upon the Whig policy. His main argument was directed in pointing out the advantages of a Protective Tariff. He handled that subject in a manner that done (sic) honor to himself and the Whig cause. Other subjects were investigated in like manner. His speech was plain, argumentative and of an hour's duration."

Lincoln's efforts in Clay's behalf proved fruitless. The high priest of Whiggery lost to his Democratic opponent, James K. Polk, by a razor-thin margin. New York, top-heavy with electoral votes, was the deciding factor, and Clay lost it, and with it the presidential election, by a paltry 5,000 votes.

Lincoln and his wife learned through a letter from her stepmother in Lexington, Kentucky, how Clay took the grim news from New York, indicating his defeat for President. Mrs. Todd had attended a wedding reception in Lexington at which Clay was present when he received the message telling him of his defeat in the decisive Empire State, and she wrote her stepdaughter, Mary Todd Lincoln, about it:

"Mr. Clay . . . opened the paper and as he read the deathknell of his political hopes and life-long ambition, I saw a distinct blue shade begin at the roots of his hair, pass slowly over his face like a cloud and then disappear. He stood for a moment as if frozen. He laid down the paper, and turning to a table, filled a glass of wine, and raising it to his lips with a pleasant smile, said: 'I drink to the health and happiness of all assembled here.' Setting down his glass, he resumed his conversation, as if nothing had occurred and was, as usual, the life and light of the company. . . . We left the wedding party with heavy hearts. Alas! our gallant 'Harry of the West' has fought his last presidential battle."

III

All seemed set for Lincoln to take his turn in running as Whig candidate for Congress, come 1846. But both Former Congressman Hardin and Congressman Baker had tasted of Washington life, contracted "Potomac fever" and wanted more. Each threatened to oppose Lincoln for Congress, violating their unwritten gentleman's agreement.

Lincoln with some persuasion induced Baker to give up his fight for a second term. Hardin, however, showed battle.

Hardin proposed to Lincoln that the convention nominating system be discarded and a new method, less favorable to Lincoln's chances, be substituted. Lincoln refused, and grew irritated at Hardin. "To yield to Hardin under present circumstances," he protested to another Whig leader, "seems to me as nothing else than yielding to one who would sacrifice me altogether. . . . You know that my only argument is that 'turn about is fair play.' This he practically at least, denies." Among Whig politicians and editors in other counties of the Seventh Congressional District Lincoln labored as he rode the circuit in his law practice. In alarm he sent word to the *Tazewell Whig* editor: "I wish you would let nothing appear in your paper which may operate against me."

Meanwhile, certain of Hardin's friends saw the political necessity of having him step aside, as was apparently tacitly agreed three years previous. One of Hardin's best friends persuaded him: "Lincoln . . . spins a good yarn, is what we call a clever fellow, has mixed much with our citizens, and has done much in sustaining Whig principles," adding, "Our people think that it is Abraham's turn now." After more maneuvering, haggling, and letter-passing between Lincoln and Hardin, Lincoln and other Whigs, Hardin and his friends, and Baker and his friends, Hardin reluctantly withdrew from the congressional race in February, 1846, leaving the field clear for Lincoln.

The Democrats reached into the pulpit for their candidate to run against Lincoln and came up with Peter Cartwright, an itinerant preacher. Thus the circuit-riding Whig lawyer faced the circuit-riding Democratic evangelist. A militant Methodist foe of alcoholism and atheism, Cartwright accused Lincoln of having stated in a speech that drunkards were often as honest and generous as church-goers, sometimes more so. Lincoln had really made a statement to that effect four years before. Now Cartwright accused Lincoln of infidelity to Christian doctrines.

On the agnostic issue Lincoln replied to Cartwright in a public circular, dated July 31, 1846, which appeared in some Illinois Whig newspapers in August. The only time that Lincoln in his entire life had or was ever to express his religious views publicly, this statement follows:

To the Voters of the Seventh Congressional District

Fellow Citizens:

A charge having got into circulation in some of the neighborhoods of this District, in substance that I am an open scoffer of Christianity, I have by the advice of some friends concluded to notice the subject in this form. That I am not a member of any Christian Church, is true; but I have never denied the truth of the Scriptures; and I have never spoken with intentional disrespect of religion in general, or of any denomination of Christians in particular. It is true that in early life I was inclined to believe in what is called the 'Doctrine of Necessity'—that is, that the human mind is impelled to action, or held in rest by some power, over which the mind itself has no control; and I have sometimes (with one, two or three, but never publicly) tried to maintain this opinion in argument. The habit of arguing thus however, I have, entirely left off for more than five years. And I add here, I have always understood this same opinion to be held by several of the Christian denominations. The foregoing, is the whole truth, briefly stated, in relation to myself, upon this subject.

I do not think I could myself, be brought to support a man for office, whom I knew to be an open enemy of, and scoffer at, religion. Leaving the higher matter of eternal consequences, betweeen him and his Maker, I still do not think any man has the right thus to insult the feelings, and injure the morals, of the community in which he may live. If, then, I was guilty of such conduct, I should blame no man who should condemn me for it; but I do blame those, whoever they may be, who falsely put such a charge in circulation against me.

July 31, 1846. A. Lincoln.

Cartwrights's tactics proved fruitless against the persuasive Lincoln. When the ballots were counted, Lincoln's plurality over him reached more than 1,500 in some 14,000 votes cast. Lincoln would be the only one of his political party in his State's delegation to Congress—the lone Whig from Illinois.

IV

Congressman-elect Lincoln of the Seventh Illinois District felt not too supremely elated over his victory. He confided to Speed: "Being elected to Congress, though I am very grateful to our friends for having done it, has not pleased me as much as I expected."

The new Congressman elect attended the Rivers and Harbor Convention at Chicago, called for July, 1847, to protest President Pierce's opposition to federal appropriations for internal improvements. When David Dudley Field, a Democrat from New York, denounced internal improvements, Lincoln replied to him. Not much publicity was given him by the local press but an eccentric-looking Whig editor from the metropolis, Horace Greeley of the New York *Tribune,* gave him some space: "Hon. Abraham Lincoln, a tall specimen of an Illinoisan . . . was called out, and spoke briefly and happily in reply to Mr. Field."

A few days following the Rivers and Harbor Convention, a reporter for the Boston *Courier,* J. H. Buckingham, found himself a fellow-passenger with Lincoln on the stage coach between Peoria and Springfield. To his paper Buckingham reported the politicking congressman-elect: "We were now in the district represented by our Whig Congressman, and he knew, or appeared to know, every body we met. . . . Such a shaking of hands—such a how-d'ye do—such a greeting of different kinds, as we saw, was never seen before; it seemed as if he knew everything, and he had a kind word, a smile and a bow for every body on the road, even to the horses, and the cattle, and the swine."

During that sixteen-month interval between his election and the convening of the Thirtieth Congress, Lincoln was hectored by federal job hunters, although he was a Whig, and Polk's administration was Democratic. Congressman John A. McClernand, a Democrat, enlisted Lincoln's aid in saving the position of another Democrat who was about to be fired. "You can count on me under like circumstances for a similar favor," assured McClernand.

In October, 1847, Lincoln leased his house on Eighth Street for ninety dollars for the year and set out for Washington with Mrs. Lincoln and their two sons, Bob and Eddie, the latter named after Lincoln's intimate Whig friend, Edward D. Baker. En route the Lincoln family met Joshua Speed at St. Louis and then proceeded to Kentucky. They paid a prolonged visit to Mrs. Lincoln's family at Lexington. For the first time Lincoln met his in-laws, State Senator and Mrs. Robert S. Todd, his wife's father and stepmother.

Lincoln's most exhilarating experience in Lexington occurred when that town's most illustrious citizen, Henry Clay, delivered a speech to which he listened intently. As Lincoln listened, Harry of the West loquaciously and scathingly assailed President Polk for having provoked the then raging war with Mexico. That conflict could have been averted, Clay avowed in his best spellbinding appeal, if General Zachary Taylor had not been ordered by the Polk Administration to plant his cannon on the east bank of the Rio Grande River. "This is no war of defense," he charged. Of slavery the eminent Kentuckian, "Mr. Whig," himself a slaveholder, declared: "I have ever regarded slavery as a great evil."

In Lexington Lincoln could see the slave system at close range. Although the black servants in the Todd household seemed contented, he could readily have discerned that slavery had its dismal side. In town several bonded Negroes were under indictment for having poisoned their masters or mistresses, the slave auction block stood in the court yard, the whipping post was conspicuous, and the Lexington *Observer & Reporter* ran advertisements for the return of runaway slaves. From the terrace of the home of his wife's grandmother Lincoln could look over the spiked palings that separated everything from the slave jail.

The Lincolns journeyed on to Washington, D. C., for the opening of Congress, arriving there late in November, 1847.

V

Lincoln, with his wife and two sons, found temporary lodging at Brown's Indian Queen Hotel in the national capital city. A day or two later they moved to cheaper lodgings, a boarding house, patronized by

Whigs, operated by a widow, Mrs. Ann Sprigg, located on the present Library of Congress site.

On December 4, Lincoln attended a caucus of Whig congressmen which nominated the aristocratic Robert C. Winthrop, of Massachusetts, for Speaker of the House. On the 6th the Thirtieth Congress convened, and the lone Whig from Illinois took the oath administered to him. For Speaker he voted for Winthrop, who was elected over the Democrat. On the 8th, when they drew for seats, Lincoln picked Number 191.

"As you are all so anxious for me to distinguish myself," Lincoln sent home word to Herndon, "I have concluded to do so before long." Within a month he did "distinguish" himself but not to the satisfaction of voters back home. He had listened to Clay's fiery words at Lexington on the causes of the conflict with Mexico and pondered over the question of war guilt. Too, it had become the Whig party line to blame the Democratic President Polk for provoking hostilities, a view confirmed by later scholarly historians.

On December 22, 1847, Congressman Lincoln introduced into the House his so-called "Spot Resolutions," adhering to the Whig charge that the fight with Mexico had been a "Democratic" one precipitated by Polk. In these resolutions he demanded full investigation of facts which would establish whether "the particular spot" on which American troops had been fired on by Mexican soldiers was or was not on American soil. A few days later the lone Whig from Illinois denounced the President. Then he voted for the resolutions of the Whig Congressman George Ashmun of Massachusetts, declaring that the war had been "unnecessarily and unconstitutionally" begun by Polk.

Lincoln, just another first-term congressman, did not impress President Polk with his "spot" resolutions. In the bulky multi-volume diaries kept by the Chief Executive there is not a single mention of Lincoln, although the names of other Whig members of the House are frequently noted.

Although Lincoln's anti-war stand, as the conflict raged, was courageous if partisan, it proved unpopular in his Seventh Congressional District of Illinois. Inspired by the Democrats, they nicknamed their representative at Washington "Spotty" Lincoln, a congressman talking anti-war with American troops fighting Mexicans.

Lincoln did not escape the office-hunters, even though a Democrat was the President. Of the clamoring job-hunters back home, Lincoln in January, 1848, complained: "There are two great obstacles in the way which they do not seem to understand—first, the President has no such appointments to give—and secondly, if he had, he could hardly be expected to give them to Whigs, at the solicitation of a Whig member of Congress."

Lincoln led the unpretentious, inconspicuous private life of a first-term congressman, particularly when his wife, Mary, left Washington with his two sons, Bob and Eddie, to spend time at her father's home in Lexington. Balls, receptions, and elaborate dinners, given by society leaders and Cabinet officers, provided most of Washington's formal social life on an upper level, aside from the affairs tendered by the foreign Diplomatic Corps. But a new congressman in protocol-minded Washington was not invited to such top-level formal functions.

Lincoln spent some spare time in the capital city telling stories at Mrs. Sprigg's boarding house, where he still lived. Members of Congress lodging there usually formed groups, each called a "Mess." One of the boarders at Mrs. Sprigg's menage, a physician, Dr. Samuel C. Busey, subsequently told about the Whig member from Illinois. "When about to tell an anecdote during a meal," narrated Busey, "he would lay down his knife and fork, place his elbows on the table, rest his face between his hands, and begin with the words, 'that reminds me,' and proceed. Everybody prepared for the explosions sure to follow."

One of Lincoln's hang-outs during leisure hours was the post office of the House of Representatives. His favorite place there was at the left of the open fireplace, where, tilting back his head in a chair with his long arms reaching over to the chimney jamb, he would tell a repertoire of stories. Sometimes he reminisced about the Black Hawk War, conversationally reliving camp experiences with the assembled listeners, some of whom undoubtedly shared the far from glorious adventures in that unbloodiest of conflicts.

For exercise Lincoln bowled. Usually he used the alleys of James Caspari's hotel, known as the Congress Hall Refectory, on Capitol Square, the corner east of the House of Representatives.

VI

Lincoln admired several Whig congressional colleagues, particularly those from the South. He was especially impressed with Representative Alexander H. Stephens of Georgia—brilliant, diminutive in size, and tubercular in health. To his law partner, Herndon, he sent word home early in 1848:

"I just take up my pen to say, that Mr. Stephens of Georgia, a slim, pale-faced, consumptive man, with a voice like Logan's, has just concluded the very best speech, of an hour's length, I ever heard.

"My old, withered, dry eyes are full of tears yet.

"If he writes it out anything like he delivered it, our people shall see a good many copies of it."

Stephens, thirteen years later, would be chosen Vice-President of the Confederate States of America.

Lincoln, in co-operation with Congressman Stephens and other Southern Whig colleagues in the House, abandoned his erstwhile political idol, Henry Clay, as a possible Whig presidential candidate in that year, 1848, and took up General Zachary Taylor—"Old Rough and Ready," a Louisiana slaveholder and the hero of the Mexican War. Lincoln and his congressional Whig clique formed a "Taylor Club" in Congress. Some called them the "Young Indians."

To a Taylor-for-President demonstration at Philadelphia in February, 1848, Lincoln advised: "I am decidedly in favor of General Taylor as the Whig candidate for the next presidency." By mail he urged one Illinois Whig leader: "Mr. Clay's chance for an election is just no chance at all. . . . In my judgment we can elect nobody but General Taylor." To a Whig chieftain of Galena he appealed: "Send us a good Taylor delegate." In June he attended the Whig National Convention at Philadelphia, at which Harry of the West was shelved and "Old Rough and Ready" named as the party's standard-bearer.

Upon his return from Philadelphia, the Whig congressman from Illinois requested his law-partner, Herndon, by mail: "You young men get together and form a 'Rough and Ready' Club, and have regular meetings and speeches. Take in everybody you can get. . . . As you go along gather up all the shrewd, wild boys about town, whether just of age or a little under age. . . . Let everyone play the part he can best play—some speak, some sing, and all 'holler.' " In July Lincoln took the House floor to give forth a crude, partisan attack on Senator Lewis Cass of Michigan, Democratic candidate for President against Taylor. He ridiculed Cass's much-publicized record as a War of 1812 hero, declaring in mock seriousness that he, too, was a military hero of the Black Hawk War. Said he on that congressional floor: "I did not break my sword, for I had none to break; but I bent a musket pretty badly on one occasion. If Cass broke his sword, the idea is he broke it in desperation; I bent the musket by accident."

That First Session of the Thirtieth Congress lasted more than eight months, adjourning August 14, 1848. The *Congressional Globe* (predecessor of the present *Congressional Record*) contains twenty-seven references to Lincoln during that session, ranging from vote listings to extensive recordings of his several speeches. His blistering attack on Polk's pro-war policy was given two pages, as was his discussion of the old Whig doctrine of internal improvements. A third oration, ponderously entitled, "The Presidential Question and that of the Territories Ceded to the United States by Mexico," in which he poked fun at Democratic Candidate Cass's War of 1812 record, rated three pages.

VII

After adjournment of that session of Congress in mid-August, most members hurried home to set in motion their campaigns for re-election. Lincoln did not seek a second term. He would have liked to run again but he had given his word to other Whig leaders in his Seventh District that he would not. It was now the turn of his former law partner, Logan, to take the Seventh seat. Besides, his anti-war speech on the "spot" resolutions had alienated even Whigs in the counties that made up his district. "I made the declaration that I would not be a candidate again, more from a wish to deal fairly with others, to keep peace among our friends, and to keep the district from going to the enemy, than for any cause personal to myself," he confided to Herndon. He added, "But to enter myself as a competitor of others, or to authorize any one to enter me, is what my word and honor forbid."

Lincoln remained in Washington for several weeks, franking campaign documents and corresponding with Whigs seemingly everywhere in behalf of Taylor's presidential candidacy. In early September he sent a letter to an ironmaster and Whig politician of Lancaster, Pennsylvania, the cantankerous Thaddeus Stevens, asking about party prospects in the Keystone State. He wrote Stevens: "You may possibly remember seeing me at the Philadelphia Convention—introduced to you as the lone Whig star of Illinois. Since the adjournment, I have remained here, so long, in the Whig document room. . . . I desire the undisguised opinion of some experienced and sagacious Pennsylvania politician, as to how the vote of that state, for governor, and president, is likely to go."

Hearing about shaky Whig fortunes in Massachusetts, where the "third-party" Democratic "Free Soil" presidential candidacy of Former President Martin Van Buren was cutting into the anti-slavery Whig element of voters because Taylor was a slaveholder, Lincoln hastened to the Bay State later in September. He held forth for Taylor and Whiggery at Worcester, where he was so little known that he was introduced as "Abram" Lincoln. He hobnobbed with such well-born Whigs as Robert C. Winthrop, for whom he had voted for Speaker of Congress at the beginning of the past session. At Worcester Lincoln's sarcasm toward the Democrat, Cass, and Van Buren were reported in the press to be "inimitable." The crowd shouted: "Go on! Go on!" when he had finished his oratorical disrespects to the regular Democrats and "Free Soil" anti-slavery Democrats.

Lincoln continued his stumping tour through New Bedford, Boston, Lowell, Dorchester, Chelsea, Cambridge, Taunton, and back to Boston. At the then "Athens of America" Lincoln spoke before polished, urbane

Whigs at Tremont Temple. He shared the platform with the celebrated Former Governor William H. Seward of New York.

The Boston *Atlas* described Lincoln as "a capital specimen of a 'Sucker Whig,' six feet at least in his stocking feet, and every way worthy to represent that Spartan band of the only Whig district in poor benighted Illinois." Overshadowed by Seward, he was given only scant space in the Boston press. Three of the city's journals called him "Abram" Lincoln; another devoted two columns to Seward's speech and dismissed Lincoln's in less than forty words.

Lincoln's Tremont Temple speech indicated no promise of his future fame as an anti-slavery leader. Seward's oration, meaty with observations and penetrating analyses, started Lincoln reflecting, according to Seward's son. The junior Seward quoted the Illinois Whig congressman as informing his father after the meeting: "Governor Seward, I have been thinking about what you said in your speech. I reckon you are right. We have got to deal with this slavery question, and got to give much more attention to it than we have been doing."

Homeward bound from Massachusetts, Lincoln stopped at Albany and called on Thurlow Weed, Seward's political manager and boss of New York State Whiggery. He also visited with Millard Fillmore, Comptroller of the State, who had been catapulted into the Vice-Presidential spot at the national convention. But eventually the Illinois congressman left the Empire State capital city, forgotten by such big party powers.

Early in October Lincoln arrived home in Springfield. He was greeted with a sarcastic editorial of mock welcome by the local Democratic daily, the *State Register:* "We are pleased to observe that his arduous duties since the adjournment of Congress in franking and loading down the mails with Whig electioneering documents have not impaired his health."

Lincoln found a discouraging situation among the Whigs. In the August election his former law partner and fellow Whig, Stephen T. Logan, had gone down before a Democrat in the fight for Lincoln's congressional seat. And the leaders were blaming Lincoln's anti-war stand at Washington for the loss of the only consistently Whig district in the State. Whig papers had neglected to publish most of the documents that he had so laboriously franked to them. To make matters worse, the older Whigs were not giving the younger party members opportunities, complained Herndon.

Lincoln carried on in his determination to carry Illinois for General Taylor and Millard Fillmore in the national contest in November. He stumped several counties.

But all proved fruitless. When the votes were counted, although Taylor was elected President, he lost Illinois. Lincoln's prestige in party affairs plummeted to a low point.

VIII

The Second Session of the Thirtieth Congress lasted from December 4, 1848, to March 4, 1849. In those ninety days left of his congressional term Lincoln endeavored to care for the needs of his constituents and particularly of his Whig allies.

In that short session he voted on bills relating to slavery. He supported the Wilmot Proviso, which provided that any land acquired from Mexico as a result of the recent war should have in it a specific prohibition of slavery.

Lincoln was placed on a committee named to manage President-elect Taylor's inaugural ball. March 4 fell on a Sunday. On the next morning Lincoln attended the induction ceremonies and also the inaugural ball in the evening. Certainly he could not have dreamed that like honors would come to him in another dozen years.

With President Taylor's national Whig administration now in power, Lincoln was overwhelmed by the cascade of demands for patronage that poured into his office and home. Even his wife's family sent in their requests. His father-in-law, Robert S. Todd of Lexington, Kentucky, sought from Lincoln intercession for a federal job for the son-in-law of his brother. When Lincoln did not respond promptly, the applicant wrote him, tartly suggesting, "Should you have forgotten, ask Mary who I am."

To his deep regret, Lincoln learned that the administration at Washington placed a paltry price on his services in the recent campaign and gave him no credit for Taylor's victory in November. Unsuccessfully Lincoln endeavored to persuade the administration to give a Cabinet position to Edward D. Baker, who had been elected to Congress from another Illinois district.

Former Congressman Lincoln also urged the powers in Washington that he and Baker should be consulted on federal patronage allotted to Illinois. "When a citizen of Illinois is to be appointed to your Department to an office either in or out of the state," he wrote Secretary of the Treasury William M. Meredith, in behalf of himself and Baker, "we most respectfully ask to be heard." He accompanied Baker on a visit to Secretary of the Interior Thomas Ewing and followed this visit with a letter to Meredith on March 11, declaring that no Illinois appointments should be made "without consultation with us." Both Cabinet members remained unimpressed by Lincoln's requests.

Lincoln also wanted a federal job for himself—the undistinguished but lucrative and patronage-rich Commissionership of the General Land Office.

The Former Congressman of the Seventh Illinois District maneuvered, by personal interviews and massive long-distance correspondence, with influential Whigs in various states. He made a special trip to Washington in his extraordinary efforts. He wrote countless letters soliciting support for the job of Land Office Commissioner—just how many was not suspected until a century later, in 1947, when the main body of Lincoln's personal papers revealed the amount of effort he had used to be appointed. His quest after that office was the subject of more letters than anything else in the papers from the period before 1850 that he preserved for posterity.

Lincoln's chief rival for the Land Office was another Illinoisan, Justin Butterfield, whom Lincoln's supporters dubbed "Old Butternuts," a bewigged fellow with more powerful support than Lincoln. The Democratic press lampooned the Lincoln-Butterfield battle for the job with doggerel:

> Away went *Justin,* neck or naught;
> Away went hat and wig;
> He little dreamed when he set out
> Of running such a rig.
>
> Away went *Lincoln* who but he;
> His fame soon spread around;
> He carries weight! he rides a race;
> He's for an *Office* bound.

Lincoln was crestfallen when the Taylor administration gave Butterfield the job of Commissioner of the General Land Office.

In July, 1849, shortly after he returned to law practice, he complained to Secretary of State John M. Clayton about President Taylor's action in letting his Cabinet dictate appointments to federal office. Such action would be ruinous to Whigs. "It is fixing for the President," he protested to Clayton, "the unjust and ruinous character of being a mere man of straw. This must be arrested, or it will damn us all inevitably."

Secretary of the Interior Ewing tried to salve Lincoln's feelings when, in September, 1849, he offered him the post of Governor of Oregon Territory. On the 27th Lincoln telegraphed Ewing: "I respectfully decline Governorship of Oregon." Lincoln's friend and former physician, Dr. Anson G. Henry, explained to Ewing why Lincoln refused the appointment: "for reasons I presume Entirely personal to himself and *certain friends* whose claims he Early pressed upon Genl. Taylor for appointment to office." In later years back-fence gossip said that Lincoln's determination not to go to remote and distant Oregon was based on Mary Lincoln's opposition to the whole idea. He also refused the Taylor administration's offer of the Secretaryship of Oregon Territory.

Lincoln's term in Congress had not advanced his reputation and had cost him much of his old law practice. And he had not been awarded appreciable recognition for having been an original Taylor-for-President promoter. His experience as a national legislator, however brief, had nonetheless given him baptism in the national political caldron at Washington.

With a family to support and no government job and only limited savings, the former lone Whig congressman from Illinois returned to the law.

THE PERSONAL LINCOLN

I

WHAT was the Lincoln of Springfield like?

"Full of contradictions."

So Lincoln's earliest serious biographer, Reverend Josiah G. Holland, commented about him after he had interviewed scores of Springfielders shortly after the assassination in 1865.

Eight years later, in 1873, Lincoln's old-time Springfield Whig colleague and fellow-lawyer, Albert T. Bledsoe, added: "He was, take him all in all, one of the most incomprehensible personages we have ever known." Herndon said of his late law partner: "Lincoln is unknown, and possibly always will be." Still later Judge O. T. Reeves of Bloomington, Illinois, who met Lincoln frequently, summed up his personality as "complex and not easy of solution."

II

What did he look like?

Only Lincoln's blindest admirers could consider him handsome. His ungainly form, with long arms and legs, craggy brow, tousled hair, wrinkled face and forehead, large fleshy nose, heavy lips, and sunken cheeks with a wart on one of them did not enhance his outward appearance. And his dress did nothing to alleviate this appearance. His battered top hat, well-worn, ill-fitting coat, long innocent of tailor's iron, trousers too short for his lengthy legs, unpolished boots, soiled stock at neck, and shabby umbrella made a very uncomplimentary portrait.

Lincoln, seen by Carl Schurz at Quincy during that October 13, 1858 debate against Douglas, was described by Schurz:

"That swarthy face with its strong features, its deep furrows, and its benignant, melancholy eyes . . . was clean shaven, and looked even more haggard and careworn than later when it was framed by whiskers. On his head he wore a somewhat battered 'stove-pipe' hat. His neck emerged, long and sinewy, from a white collar turned down over a thin black necktie. His lank, ungainly body was clad in a rusty black dress coat with sleeves that should have been longer. . . . His black trousers permitted a very full view of his large feet. On his left arm he carried a gray woolen shawl. . . . His left hand held a cotton umbrella of the bulging kind, and also a black satchel."

Lincoln's sloppy appearance, paradoxically enough, gave him a certain attraction to some; his very uniqueness was arresting. One Southern girl, Lillian Foster, who saw and heard him at one of the debates with Douglas in 1858, noted in her daybook: "In person he is tall and awkward, in manner ungainly. His face is certainly ugly, but not repulsive; on the contrary, the good humor, generosity and intellect beaming from it, make the eye love to linger there until you almost fancy him good-looking."

The following year, 1859, one British observer, hearing Lincoln speak at Cincinnati, later described him as embodying a composite American, the embodiment of the Union—"long and lank as the traditional Yankee; lean and hungry as the 'poor white' of the South that he was born; with the arm of a Hoosier that can whip his weight in wild cats; with a backward length of skull and feeble occiput which reminds me of the Indian characters; and yet with an eye full of softness, a voice full of affection and even delicacy. . . . It was a physical necessity that this average American should have been born in the most central of the States—Kentucky."

III

Intellectually, Lincoln did not read profusely, except newspapers and reports from political precincts.

Poetry, particularly that of Shakespeare, Byron, and Burns, kept his interest to some extent, but his correspondence is filled with politics and law, not literary allusions. His favorite verse was that beginning with, "Oh, why should the spirit of mortal be proud?"

Aside from poetry, politics, law cases, and newspapers, Lincoln read less in Springfield and on the legal circuit than he had during his earlier New Salem life. Albert T. Bledsoe, who knew him so well in the earlier Springfield years, revealed: "All that is said about his having been 'a great reader' is sheer fiction. He did his reading, even in regard to his law cases, as some men do their religion, by *proxy,* by his Good-Man-Friday, William H. Herndon." But Bledsoe also pointed out: "He possessed the power of patent thought; he could distinguish, analyse, and *meditate*—and these alone made him a formidable antagonist, both at the Bar and on the hustings."

Lincoln read only limited history books and biography. He accepted both with major reservations. "He thought that history as generally written was altogether too unreliable," explained his fellow Whig legislator, Joseph Gillespie. Lincoln was also quoted by Herndon as remarking: "Biographies as written are false and misleading. The author of the life of his hero paints him as a perfect man—magnifies his perfections and suppresses his imperfections—describes the success of his hero in glowing terms, never once hinting at his failures and his blunders."

Lincoln liked the theatre, whether dramatic plays, comedies, "magic lantern" slides, or professional poetry readings, some of which played Springfield on tour. In 1858 he heard Eloise Bridges, a dramatic reader, recite "Nothing To Wear," a poem concerning a wealthy New York clotheshorse, "Flora McFlimsey," purchaser of twelve drayloads of dresses in Paris, who still complained that she had "nothing to wear." Flora's disgusted fiancee, "Harry," suggested that she was "perhaps a Hottentot."

A reporter for one Springfield newspaper closely watched Lincoln as he listened to Miss Bridges read "Nothing To Wear." The reporter wrote: "The Hon. A. Lincoln was one of the audience and had become deeply interested . . . and was leaning his head upon his hand, *a la Juliet,* his soul apparently wrapped in the story. When Miss B. [Bridges] came to that poem descriptive of the quarrel between Miss Flora McFlimsey and her love, he could hardly contain himself, and at the words, 'perhaps a Hottentot,' he could not control himself, and 'O, yes,' escaped involuntarily from his lips."

While trying a case in Chicago early in 1860, Lincoln and Henry C. Whitney attended a performance of Rumsey and Newcomb's Minstrels and heard "Dixie" sung. It was, related Whitney, "the most extravagant minstrel performance I ever saw. Lincoln was perfectly 'taken' with it; and clapped his great hands, demanding an *encore,* louder than anyone."

Lincoln's mind often wandered during his relaxations. One Springfield correspondent of a New York daily called on him in 1860, and sent word to his paper: "While playing chess, Mr. Lincoln seems to be continually thinking of something else. Those who have played with him say he plays as if it were a mechanical pastime to occupy his hands while his mind is busy with some other subject, just as one often twirls a cane, or as a pretty coquette toys her fan."

Truth was, Lincoln was frequently overtaken by melancholia.

IV

"I never saw so gloomy and melancholy a face in my life," reminisced Johua F. Speed about his first meeting with Lincoln in 1837. That summed up the consensus of most of Lincoln's intimates, who later testified to his periods of absent thought when he saw nothing around him.

His first law partner, Stuart, declared that Lincoln fell hopeless victim to melancholia, and surely his letters to Stuart during the time of his broken engagement to Mary Todd early in 1841 bears out the reliability of Stuart's judgment.

Henry C. Whitney, with whom Lincoln rode the circuit during the late 1850's, told how he and Stuart on one occasion watched Lincoln in a courtroom, sitting alone in a corner wrapped in abstraction and gloom. Whitney related: "It appeared as if he was pursuing in his mind some specific, sad object. . . . His sad face would assume, at times, deeper phases of grief, but no relief came from dark and despairing melancholy, till he was aroused by the breaking up of court, when he emerged like one awakened from sleep."

Lincoln's taste in poetry revealed his melancholic disposition. His favorite verse, beginning with "Oh, why should the spirit of mortal be proud," is anything but joyful.

After his stumping tour for Henry Clay in his boyhood Indiana region during 1844, Lincoln penned a poem, beginning with "My childhood home I see again," which ended:

I hear the loved survivors tell
   How naught from death could save,
Till every sound appears a knell,
   And every spot a grave.

I range the fields with pensive tread,
   And pace the hollow rooms,
And feel (companion of the dead)
   I'm living in the tombs.

Lincoln's tour in Indiana for Clay's candidacy also inspired him to compose another poem. This was about a youthful playmate there, Matthew Gentry, who had gone insane at only nineteen years and was still living in wretched condition. Lincoln's first two and last stanzas about the crazed Gentry read:

> But here's an object more of dread
>   Than ought the grave contains—
> A human form with reason fled,
>   While wretched life remains.
>
> Poor Matthew! Once of genius bright,
>   A fortune-favored child—
> More locked for aye, in mental night,
>   A haggard mad-man wild.
>
> O death! Thou awe-inspiring prince,
>   That keeps the world in fear;
> Why dost thou tear more blest ones hence,
>   And leave him ling'ring here.

Lincoln, in his public eulogy for the deceased President Zachary Taylor at Chicago in 1850, again sounded a morbid note by stating "The death of the late President may not be without its use, in reminding us, that *we,* too, must die," and by then reciting stanzas from "Oh, why should the spirit of mortal be proud."

Lincoln's tastes in music, which were uncultivated, suggested his escape from normal optimism. Among his favorite songs were plaintive Scotch airs. "Annie Laurie," "Mary of Argyle," and especially "Auld Robin Gray" held attraction for him.

Various causes have been suggested in past and modern times to account for Lincoln's sad mental disposition. One ascribed it to the failure of his digestive system to function normally. At Stuart's urging, Lincoln once commenced taking blue mass pills but abandoned the habit because, he complained, the pills made him peevish. Herndon attributed Lincoln's depressed hours to grief over Ann Rutledge's death—an untenable explanation. He also blamed Mary Todd Lincoln's temperament for Lincoln's forebodings. Later biographers have agreed with him about Mary's baneful effect on her husband's disposition, although in recent years Mrs. Lincoln has attracted much sympathetic support from a host of writers. One of these, a biological scientist interested in the effect of climatic elements on human conduct, has even offered another explanation, that Lincoln was a "linear" type of man—tall, thin, without reserves of fat, sugar, and vitamins. Such types run to introspection because on cold days a tall man's blood vessels constrict, thus forcing a fall of blood pressure and consequent bleak despair, according to this author, Dr. William F. Peterson.

In all probability Lincoln's melancholy spells originated hereditarily, and were unfathomable by human scrutiny.

At times he showed traces of superstition. In 1856 he admitted to one Iowa politician by letter: "I am superstitious. I have scarcely known a party, preceding an election, to call in help from the neighboring states, but they lost the state." Lincoln had grown up in an Indiana community where some settlers believed in witches, others sent for lizards to cure sick cattle, and still others insisted that the moon exerted a fearful influence for good or evil. There were those Hoosier pioneers who were certain that, if a bird flew into a window, someone in the family would shortly die. Some Indiana backwoodsmen consulted "faith doctors" who claimed to cure diseases by performing strange hocus-pocus ceremonies. A belief in the "mad" stone existed, too.

Lincoln on one occasion took his son, Robert, to such a curing rock, owned by a quack practitioner in Terre Haute, Indiana, when the child was bitten by a dog.

In 1860 Lincoln saw "visions" of himself as he looked into the mirror following his election as President.

Moody, morbid, meditative, introspective—that was Lincoln at times. After his death numberless Spiritualists claimed him as one of their cult. Books were written by professional occult mediums, each solemnly avowing that he or she had spoken to Lincoln in the spirit world. But Lincoln's intimates are unanimous, and so are later historians, in demolishing ideas that he was a Spiritualist.

V

Lincoln had another side to him beside his melancholy and moody one. His mind ran the whole gamut from abysmal dejection to rollicking gaiety. Herndon has well stated in a hitherto unpublished letter: "He was sad and cheerful by turns." Judge David Davis commented: "Lincoln's stories were merely devices to whistle down sadness." Henry Villard, who first saw Lincoln in 1858, and during 1860-61 "covered" him for the New York *Herald* in Springfield, later recalled: "A high-pitched laughter lighted up his otherwise melancholy countenance with thorough merriment."

Lincoln's fame as a story teller and humorist grew in Illinois and later in Washington. At times the pre-presidential Lincoln expressed himself in quaint phrases. In 1848 he refreshed the memory of one former Springfield lawyer then practicing in Mississippi: "Perhaps you have forgotten me. Don't you remember a long black fellow who rode on horseback with you from Tremont to Springfield nearly ten years ago, swimming your horses over the Mackinaw on the trip? Well, I am that same fellow yet."

Once when describing to Joshua Speed what his son, Eddie, looked like, he compared him to his older son, Bob: "He is very much such a child as Bob was at his age—rather of a longer order. Bob is 'short and low' . . . one of the little rare-ripe sort, that are smarter at about five than ever after."

While still in Congress, Lincoln sent to Mrs. Lincoln news about another Illinois House member's wife: "Mrs. Richardson is still here; and what is more, has a baby—so Richardson says, and he ought to know."

When his former law partner, Logan, was badly defeated in one campaign for Congress, Lincoln told the news to another: "Logan is worse beaten than any other man ever was since elections were invented."

Lincoln whimsically asked for renewal of a railroad pass from the Chicago & Alton Railroad superintendent by the term, "chalked hat," since the white check was placed in the passenger's hat band. Lincoln requested: "Says Tom to John 'Heres your old rotten wheelbarrow. I've broke it, usin' on it. I wish *you* would mend it, case I shall want to borrow it this arter-noon.' Acting on this precedent, I say, 'Heres your old 'chalked hat.' I wish you would take it, and send me a new one, case I shall want to use it the first of March.' "

Lincoln has come down through the ages as a side-splitting joker, but most of the humorous anecdotes and stories credited to him were not told while he lived. They were narrated long years after his death and therefore lack authentication. One of them, however, was taken down by Benjamin F. Shaw of Dixon, Illinois, immediately after he had heard Lincoln tell it at a dinner in Decatur on February 22, 1856. According to Shaw, Lincoln declared that he felt like the ugly man riding in the woods who encountered an old woman on horseback. "Well, for land sake, you are the homeliest man I ever saw," she told him. He answered, "Yes, madam, but I can't help it,"—to which the ancient female retorted: "No, I suppose not, but you might stay at home."

Another joke of contemporary record told by Lincoln on himself also concerned unattractive looks. According to William L. Gross of Mount Sterling, Illinois, who jotted it down in his day-book in 1858, Lincoln told how he had avowed that, if he ever met a man homelier than himself, he would shoot him, and forthwith he shouldered a gun in quest of such an unhandsome individual. When Lincoln met such an imaginary man worse looking than himself, he presumably prepared to shoot him. The man agreed to be killed, assuring Lincoln: "Sir, all that I have got to say is, if I am any worse looking than you are, for *God's sake, shoot me,* and git me out of the way."

Lincoln used humorous allusions in political debate. As a congressman he supported a proposal for federal funds, instead of tonnage duties, to finance internal improvements, and in a speech he asked the House: "How could we make any entirely new improvements [of roads, canals, and rivers] by means of tonnage duties? . . . The idea that we could, involves the same absurdity as the Irish bull about the new boots. 'I shall niver git 'em on,' says Patrick, 'till I wear 'em a day or two, and stretch 'em a little.' We shall never make a canal by tonnage duties, until it shall have been made a while, so the tonnage can get into it." In that same oration to Congress Lincoln sought to prove that President Polk, a Democrat, was mistakenly appealing to a declaration by the revered Thomas Jefferson. Charged Lincoln: "This opinion of Mr. Jefferson, in one branch at least, is, in the hands of Mr. Polk, like McFingal's gun: 'Bears wide and kicks the owner over.' "

In 1856, after the Democrats had rejected Franklin Pierce in favor of James Buchanan, Lincoln said of Pierce's eulogy on Buchanan's election as President: "Like a rejected lover, making merry at the wedding of his rival, the President felicitates hugely over the late Presidential election."

In his face-to-face debate with Douglas for Senator in 1858, Lillian Foster noted, Lincoln stood "on the stump, ready, humorous, argumentative, and [told] an anecdote with inconceivable quaintness and effect." In his Quincy duel of words with Douglas, amid the crowd's laughter and glee, he accused the Little Giant of a "specious and fantastical arrangement of words by which a man can prove a horse-chestnut to be a chestnut horse." At Quincy, too, Lincoln in ridicule compared Douglas's doctrine on slavery in the territories with "homeopathic soup." "Judge Douglas has sung paeans of praise to his 'popular sovereignty' doctrine until his Supreme Court co-operating with him has *squatted* his squatter sovereignty out. . . . Has it not got down as thin as the homeopathic soup that was made by boiling the shadow of a pigeon that had starved to death?" There followed "roars of laughter and cheering."

Most Springfielders after Lincoln's death avowed that he told no stories smacking of smut. Dr. Preston H. Bailhache has stated: "Mr. Lincoln was never given to promiscuous story telling as some times represented. . . . They were always clean. . . . I never heard a word from his lips that might not be repeated in the hearing of the most fastidious."

Lincoln nonetheless told at least one "joke" publicly, before an audience, that was out of bounds in mixed company—one of his lectures on "Discoveries and Inventions," delivered on several occasions in 1859. Indelicately he told his Adam-and-Eve "fig leaf" apron story:

"As might be expected he [Adam] seems not to have been a very observing man at first; for it appears he went about naked a considerable length of time, before he even noticed that obvious fact. But when he did observe it, the observation was not lost upon him; for it immediately led to the first of all inventions, of which we have any direct account—the *fig-leaf apron.*" The italics were Lincoln's.

Two paragraphs later in that address on discoveries and inventions Lincoln continued:

"And this reminds me of what I passed unnoticed before, that the very first invention was a joint operation, Eve having shared with Adam in the getting up of the apron. And, indeed, judging from the fact that sewing has come down to our times as 'woman's work' it is very probable that she took the leading part; he, perhaps, doing no more than to stand by and thread the needle. That proceeding may be reckoned as the mother of all 'Sewing societies.' "

Until the eve of his departure from Springfield for Washington as President-elect, Lincoln exercised his talent of amusing his listeners. On November 20, 1860, two weeks following his election as the nation's Chief Executive, Mrs. William H. Bailhache, wife of the *Illinois State Journal* owner, wrote her mother: "Mr. L. . . . amused us nearly all the evening telling funny stories and cracking jokes."

But some times his gloom would follow his gaiety. Black despondency and boisterous humor followed one another like cloud and sunshine in a day of doubtful storm.

VI

Authors have devoted as many books, brochures, and articles to Lincoln's religion, or lack of religion, as to almost any other facet of his life. Nearly all of these reams of pages are of a controversial nature.

Lincoln's earliest biographers, Josiah G. Holland and Isaac N. Arnold, portrayed him as a paragon of religious devotion.

The portrait of Lincoln as a profound believer in the Christian religion was later contradicted by men who knew him well in the early Illinois years.

While Lincoln, years later as President, was steering the nation through civil war in 1862, he was presented to a limited reading public in Illinois as an agnostic by one former New Salemite, John Hill, in the obscure Petersburg weekly, the *Menard Axis.* Hill claimed that in New Salem the Lincoln youth had prepared an anti-Christian essay, a paper which he was prevailed upon to burn. Wrote Hill: "He employed his intellectual faculties in writing a dissertion (sic) against the doctrine of the divinity of the scriptures. Of this he soon repented, and consigned his production to the flames. He had designed it for publication, but his senior friends, pointing him to [Tom] Paine and Valtaire (sic), wrought a change in his intentions, and perhaps his destiny."

Years after Lincoln's death his law partner, Herndon, who knew John Hill well (and in whose papers a copy of Hill's article was found) elaborated on this story.

Lincoln in his early years did not live in a deeply religious community. Pioneer Indiana and Illinois frontiersmen were rough and generally irreligious and were to remain that way until the revivals of the 1840's. During Lincoln's New Salem life the Sabbath there was often a day of disorder, sometimes riot. John T. Stuart subsequently stated about Lincoln as he knew him: "He was an avowed and open infidel and sometimes bordered on atheism. . . . He shocked me." Logan Hay, one-time law partner of Lincoln's second law partner, Logan, later wrote to his nephew, John Hay, one of Lincoln's later presidential secretaries: "Candor compels me to say that at this [pre-presidential] period Mr. Lincoln could hardly be termed a devout believer in the authenticity of the Bible (but this is for your ear only)."

Lincoln was wed to Mary Todd in an Episcopal ceremony, and Mary went to the Presbyterian church services in Springfield, as she was to do in future years as First Lady in Washington.

Lincoln publicly referred to his views concerning religion on only one occasion, when he ran for Congress in 1846. In that previously quoted handbill given to the voters, he admitted: "That I am not a member of any Christian Church, is true."

As long as he lived, Lincoln was never to join any denominational religion. After 1850, following the death of his son, Eddie, he went to Sunday services irregularly at the First Presbyterian Church in Springfield for a period. He formed a friendship with its minister, Rev. Dr. James Smith, and he read Dr. Smith's book designed to lead skeptics to the Christian faith by rational argument. But that Presbyterian clergyman failed to convert him.

Not until after Lincoln's death did his religion turn into an angry topic of controversy, each side endeavoring to prove its own viewpoint by prolific publication on that still raging subject. In truth, Lincoln was not a religious man to the point of subscribing to any organized denomination or faith. Rather, he was a Christian in the broadest acceptance of that term.

Lincoln, while not a member of any church himself, believed firmly in religious freedom. While co-operating with anti-Catholic, anti-immigrant Know-Nothings as allies in his political battles against the Catholic-catering Democrats, he himself would not join their "American" or Know-Nothing Party. He wrote Owen Lovejoy in 1855 about the Know-Nothings: "About us here they are mostly my old political and personal friends." In that same letter to Lovejoy he stated: "I have hoped their organization would die without the painful necessity of my taking an open stand against them. Of their principles I think little better than

I do of those of the slavery extensionists. Indeed I do not perceive how any one professing to be sensitive to the wrongs of the negroes, can join in a league to degrade a class of white men." To his friend, Speed, in that same year he sent word:

"I am not a Know-Nothing. That is certain. How could I be? . . . When the Know-Nothings get control, it [the Constitution] will read 'all men are created equal, except negroes, *and foreigners, and Catholics.*' When it comes to this, I shall prefer emigrating to some country where they make no pretence of loving liberty—to Russia, for instance, where despotism can be taken pure, and without the base alloy of hypocrisy."

Herndon, in a little known interview with a New York reporter only two years after Lincoln's death, said of him: "He had no prejudices against any class, preferring the Germans to any of the foreign element, yet tolerating—as I never could—even the Irish." Herndon expressed his own anti-Catholic opinion in the words, those "wandering roving robbing Irish" who voted Democrat by bloc. In 1858 Herndon yelled angrily: "God damn the Irish, I want it distinctly understood that we [Republicans] are willing to have war with them."

VII

What were some of Lincoln's other characteristics? He revealed himself as filled with modesty, unready to express himself on his innermost thoughts; and not indifferent to money-making. Too, he had a mechanical turn of mind, able to understand elementary engineering principles.

Lincoln's modesty and freedom from pretence were noted by almost every one who knew him well. This is obvious also in his correspondence and public speeches.

"If you collect the signatures of all persons who are no less distinguished than I," he replied to one autograph collector when he served in Congress, "you will have an undistinguished mass of names." When he compared Henry Clay's views on the Mexican War with his own, he asked: "What, then, is the difference except that he is a great man and I am a small one?"

Lincoln demonstrated his simplicity in exaggerated form in his own autobiographical sketch for the *Congressional Directory:*

> Born February 12, 1809, in Hardin County, Kentucky.
> Education—defective.
> Profession—a lawyer.
> Have been a captain of volunteers in Black Hawk War.
> Postmaster at a very small office.
> Four times a member of the Illinois legislature and
> a member of the lower house of Congress.

Following his election in 1860 Mrs. Bailhache of Springfield visited the Lincolns, and shortly after wrote: "Mr. L. has not altered one bit. . . . I could hardly realize that I was sitting in the august presence of a *real live President.*"

Early in 1861 Lincoln, as President-elect, was visited by one who sought to impress him by reciting Julius Caesar's quotations. Lincoln pointed to other visitors and answered: "My friend, I regret to say that I have to refer your classics to these gentlemen who, I presume, are better versed in Latin lore than myself."

Lincoln rarely committed himself on his innermost thoughts. He maintained a particular silence on significant subjects, like most professional politicians. During his pre-presidential period he failed to measure his words in his "House Divided" speech, but made up for that radical utterance by toning down future orations in that campaign against Douglas. Judge David Davis declared of Lincoln: "He was the most reticent, secretive man I ever saw or expect to see." Herndon has well concluded: "Mr. Lincoln was a cool, cautious, conservative and long headed man."

As a "cool, cautious, conservative and long headed man," to borrow Herndon's description, Lincoln certainly was not the money-shunning, non-materialistic person portrayed to posterity. He was well aware of the necessity for tangible resources and their decisive influence upon human conduct, as evidenced by his accumulation of vastly more of the worldly goods and money than the average man of his day.

Lincoln's first business venture, his New Salem partnership with Bill Berry in the store, had proved a failure, and he then took up the postmaster's post as well as doing surveying and sundry jobs. Then came his law partnership with John T. Stuart. The firm's fees were small, and the two made a pittance on the side by renting their office as a jury room during the court term. Lincoln's partnership with Logan brought him bigger retainers, enabling him to buy his house on Eighth Street. After his service in Congress his law practice with Herndon grew to substantial proportions and he saved enough to speculate in land and lend money at substantial interest rates on mortgages and other collateral. On one occasion he came into possession of a piece of land in his namesake town of Lincoln in Logan County, Illinois, when the borrower deeded it to him in lieu of an unpaid $200 loan at 10 per cent interest, which Lincoln had extended to him.

Lincoln demonstrated frugality in his money expenditures, although his wife, Mary, showed extravagances. He bought few new clothes for himself, did not spend money on liquor, never gambled, spent the minimum of money on food for himself while on the circuit, and contributed little money to his stepmother's support. Once in the tone of a man who had overspent, he remarked concerning the cost of his celebrated campaign for Senator against Douglas: "I do not believe I have spent a cent less than five hundred dollars in this canvass."

By the time of his election as President in 1860, Lincoln had more than $9,000 invested in interest-bearing notes and mortgages, while his real estate, principally his home, was worth $5,000. That comprised a substantial fortune for his time in Illinois.

The list of Lincoln's savings, which he drew up during his last days at Springfield in 1861, reveals that he lent money to various friends on notes totalling more than $9,300 at ten per cent interest, some of it with mortgages given as collateral in return; that he had a bank balance of $1,600; that he owned his home in Springfield (which he insured for $3,200) and his lot in the town of Lincoln in Logan County. He owned a 16-acre tract of land in Iowa which he did not include in his list. Those were not the holdings of a poverty-pinched man. He had arrived in Springfield twenty-four years before as a penniless state legislator and was taken into Speed's store for living quarters. Certainly Lincoln's assets in 1861 did not suggest a man who has so often been portrayed as one who did not like money.

Lincoln's practicability was evident in his mechanical talents which were considerable for a layman of his era. He devised an improved method for lifting vessels over shoals, and in 1849 took out a patent on it at the United States Patent Office in Washington. In cases that he handled in the federal courts he explained to the jurors the intricacies of various machines.

VIII

Lincoln enjoyed a personal, professional, and business reputation for high ethics and integrity. By 1858 he was being called "Honest Abe" by his intimates. It had started as a complimentary political nickname to match his opponent Douglas's famous sobriquet, "Little Giant." But "Honest Abe" was taken up by those who knew Lincoln personally, and has remained down to the present day.

Few, if any, ever addressed Lincoln to his face as "Abe." Those Illinoisans who knew him best noted this. "No one called Mr. Lincoln 'Abe,' " asserted James S. Ewing. "I never heard any man call Mr. Lincoln 'Abe' in his own presence," stated John W. Bunn. Henry C. Whitney observed: "Lincoln disdained ceremony, but he gave no license for being called 'Abe.' His preference was being called 'Lincoln' with no handle at all." Not even Judge Davis felt sufficiently free to address Lincoln as "Abe."

Lincoln for his part called his associates by their family names, usually using "Mr."—all except to his younger friend and sometime associate counsel, Ward Hill Lamon, whom he addressed as "Hill." Lamon in his letters to Lincoln addressed him as "Mr. Lincoln" or "Dear Sir." Lincoln always called Stephen T. Logan, "Logan;" Leonard Swett was "Swett;" and Henry Whitney, "Whitney."

Herndon has well summed up his law partner: "Lincoln was a man of great dignity and yet democratic—easy of approach. He would up to a certain point allow any approach but go beyond *that,* and his dignity soon protected itself, and wilted the man who dared go beyond the proprieties of the occasion."

Lincoln, like most dignified men, was averse to violent disagreement between people.

One Massachusetts journalist, the aforementioned Buckingham, riding in the stage-coach with Congressman-elect Lincoln toward Springfield in 1847, noted the fretfulness of the passengers, with the exception of Lincoln. Buckingham sent home word to his Boston paper: "We started in a grumbling humor, but our Whig congressman was determined to be good natured, and to keep all the rest so if he could; he told stories . . . until we all laughed, in spite of the dismal circumstances in which we were placed."

In his congressional speech on internal improvements he opened by assuring his colleagues: "I desire to do nothing which may be disagreeable to any of the members."

Lincoln's belief in conciliation between contending elements went to strong extremes, and he disdained fisticuffs on all occasions. One Peoria County farmer, Enoch Huggins, in 1858 sent word to a relative: "Lincoln sees into anything quick if a man should insult him he would laugh at him and shame him out of it sooner than fight him."

Lincoln demonstrated this trait that same year when, in his Senatorial campaign against Douglas, the belligerent Little Giant was reported to be ready to fight Lincoln with his hands. Lincoln at Havana, Illinois, declined, explaining to his audience: "A fight would *prove* nothing which is an issue in this campaign. It might establish that Judge Douglas is a more muscular man than myself, or it might demonstrate that I am a more muscular man than Judge Douglas." That was all. The idea was preposterous.

Lincoln, despite his busy days in law and politics, gave his time freely to writing to young people. To his law partner, Herndon, who complained about "old fossils" in the Whig Party constantly holding back younger men and giving them no opportunity, Lincoln, then in Congress, mailed words of encouragement. The way for a young man to rise was to improve himself in every way and not permit his mind to brood over attempted injury by the elders. "I have some the advantage of you in the world's experience merely by being older; and it is this that induces me to advise." To an aspiring attorney Lincoln suggested that litigation be discouraged, honesty be placed above professional success, and that "work, work, work is the main thing." While in Kansas during 1859 he wrote some words into the album of Mary Delahay, daughter of his friend, Mark Delahay:

"With pleasure I write my name in your Album. Ere long some younger man will be more happy to confer *his* name upon *you.*

"Dont allow it, Mary, until fully assured that he is worthy of the happiness—Dec. 7, 1859.

"Your friend
"A. Lincoln."

IX

Lincoln had his share of aversions and indifferences: farm life, food, and alcohol.

The prevailing notion that Lincoln was a rural type is a misconception spawned by his log cabin birth, backwoods boyhood, log-chopping youth, his later vote-garnering sobriquet, "Railsplitter," and the "folklore" interpretations presented by authors of Lincoln long after his assassination.

Despite the log-cabin and railsplitter legends that shroud his memory, Lincoln had left the rustic life far behind him long before he reached thirty years, and he never cared to go back to it. An attorney and not an agrarian, politically rather than pastorally minded in his adult years, he expressed his aversion to farm existence in a private letter to his friend, Speed. In hay-and-hog-hating vein, he in 1842 wrote his best of all friends, who had bought some cultivated acreage in Kentucky: "As to your farm matter, I have no sympathy with you. *I* have no farm, nor ever expect to have; and, consequently, have not studied the subject enough to be much interested in it."

Less than a year before he was nominated for President, Lincoln addressed the Wisconsin Agricultural Society in Milwaukee, speaking with un-Lincolnian frankness about farmers:

"I presume I am not expected to employ the time assigned me, in the mere flattery of farmers, as a class. My opinion of them is that, in proportion to numbers, they are neither better nor worse than other people. . . . On reflection, I am not quite sure that there is not cause of suspicion against you, in selecting me, in some sort a politician, and in no sort a farmer, to address you."

In Lincoln's list of especially intimate Illinois friends, not a single one farmed for a livelihood. Except for Speed (a merchant who moved back to Kentucky), all were either lawyers, politicians, or sometimes elected officeholders like himself. Ward H. Lamon, Orville H. Browning, Judge David Davis, Leonard Swett, Edward D. Baker, John T. Stuart, Stephen T. Logan, Joseph Gillespie, and Henry C. Whitney were attorneys plunged into politics. Dr. Anson G. Henry was a physician turned politician and one of the "Whig Junto." Lincoln's preserved papers are filled with law items and politics, with scant mention of matters agricultural.

Food, both as to quantity and quality, became a matter of comparative indifference to him. "Lincoln," related Herndon, "could sit and think without rest or food longer than any man I ever saw." As lawyer on the Eighth Judicial Circuit, the digestion-damaging meals did not bother him. "If every other fellow grumbled at the bill-of-fare which greeted us at many of the dingy taverns, Lincoln said nothing," recalled Judge Davis. Lincoln did not compensate for his refusal to drink liquor by concentrating on food, as did other teetotalers.

Lincoln remained a non-consumer of strong drink all his life. It was so in the Illinois years, too.

During his Indiana backwoods boyhood Lincoln saw liquor as a medium of exchange. In New Salem whiskey-imbibing was prevalent, and Lincoln sold it in the store he owned jointly with the liquor-loving Bill Berry. But he never drank it himself, either in New Salem, in Springfield, or on the circuit.

Lincoln believed firmly in temperance, even delivering a speech before the Washingtonians at Springfield on Washington's Birthday in 1842. That group was dedicated to temperance and sobriety and, curiously enough, had named their society after the First President, not known for his light drinking. But Lincoln did not favor prohibition legislation. "Persuasion, kind, unassuming persuasion" was the best manner of solving the liquor problem, he told the Washingtonians. Ward H. Lamon, who knew him so well, said: "Lincoln disliked sumptuary laws and would not prescribe by statute what other men should eat or drink. When the temperance men ran to the Legislature to invoke the power of the state, his voice—the most eloquent of them—was silent. He did not oppose them, but quietly withdrew from the cause and left others to manage it." When the "Maine Law" prohibition agitation injected itself into Illinois politics in the mid-1850's, Lincoln did not become a "Maine Law" man, as did so many of the Whig politicians.

Lincoln felt deep sympathy for victims of alcoholism. In his Washingtonian Society address, he described them: "Generally they are kind, generous and charitable, even beyond the example of their more staid neighbors."

Those Illinoisans who were best acquainted with Lincoln for years are agreed that he did not touch hard drink. Joshua Speed said that Lincoln never drank alcohol. Lamon, himself a constant consumer of the distilled grain and a steady frequenter of the saloon beneath his office in Danville, stated: "He had no taste for spiritous liquors." Logan, his second law partner, testified: "I never in my life saw Lincoln taste liquor. In going around the circuit with him I sometimes myself got and took a little after having got wet in a storm or swum a creek . . . but he didn't even take it then."

Lincoln, although an abstainer himself, did not rebuke his roistering friends when they indulged in the bottle. Lamon, his young friend and circuit law partner, was usually the gustiest of guzzlers. Lincoln's home town Republican newspaper, the *State Journal,* which some called "Lincoln's paper," printed this notice about a dinner held at Concert Hall in January, 1859: "Among the invited guests we observed Hon. Abraham Lincoln of this city and U. F. Linder, Esq., of Coles County. The banquet was spread by Myers and embraced all that could be desired by the greatest epicure. The company sat down at nine o'clock, and after satisfying the appetite with eatables, the 'mountain dew' was brought out, and, together with a number of mysterious looking bottles, was freely circulated during the remainder of the evening. The regular toasts were in order by Messrs. Lincoln, Linder, Matheny, Blaisdell, and others."

One of Lincoln's favorite quips was one told him by an old man to whom he playfully told that he had no vices: "It's my experience that folks who have no vices have generally very few virtues."

X

Lincoln, publicized as a "man of the people" through the decades, has been portrayed as more democratic in his views than he actually was. Many present-day citizens are shocked when they find that Lincoln sent his son, Bob, first to Phillips Exeter Academy and then to Harvard. Though in the modern era many attempts have been made to snatch Lincoln's phrases out of their contexts in order to give a labored tangency to very liberal, even "leftist" causes, Lincoln, like nearly all American lawyers and professional men, was essentially a conservative. Even his views against slavery were quite moderate.

In politics Lincoln spent most of his public life in Henry Clay's conservative Whig Party, the opposition to leveling radical Jacksonism. He reluctantly left that organization in 1856 when it disintegrated and affiliated with the more moderate wing of the Republican Party, always frowning on abolitionism and various plans to hurry along changes in the American social system. In his famed Cooper Institute Address of 1860 he stood on solidly conservative ground, criticized John Brown, and harked back to the Founding Fathers.

In his economic views Lincoln staunchly supported the capitalist concept of private property and held the most unrevolutionary views on the relations between capital and labor. He revealed himself as an unswerving believer in that institution of which he was one himself and which has been sacred to the United States: the "self-made man."

In his Kalamazoo, Michigan, address of 1856, while on the stump, he rejected the idea that American workingmen constituted a distinct class and had to remain manual laborers. He declared to his Michigan listeners: "There is no such class. The man who labored for another last year, this year labors for himself, and next year he will hire others to labor for him." In that same speech he also stated: "We stand at once the wonder and admiration of the whole world, and we must enquire what it is that has given us so much prosperity. This cause is that every man can make himself."

Three years later, in 1859, he told a Cincinnati audience: "That men who are industrious, and sober, and honest in the pursuit of their own interests should after a while accumulate capital, and after that should be allowed to enjoy it in peace, and also if they should choose when they have accumulated it to use it to save themselves from actual labor and hire other people for them, is right."

Two days later, September 19, 1859, at Indianapolis, Lincoln told his listeners, as reported by that city's daily, the *Atlas:*

"There was a certain relation between capital and labor, and it was proper that it existed. Men who were industrious and sober, and honest in the pursuit of their own interests, should after a while accumulate capital, and after that should be allowed to enjoy it in peace, and if they chose, when they had accumulated capital, to use it to save themselves from actual labor and hire other people to labor for them, it was right. They did not wrong the man they employed, for they found men who have not their own land to work upon or shops to work in, and who were benefitted by working for them as hired laborers, receiving their capital for it."

Six months later, two months before his nomination for President, Lincoln told a gathering at New Haven, Connecticut: "What is the true condition of the laborer? I take it that it is best for all to leave each man free to acquire property as fast as he can. Some will get wealthy. I don't believe in a law to prevent a man from getting rich; it would do more harm than good. So while we do not propose any war upon capital, we do wish to allow the humblest man an equal chance to get rich with everybody else." He added to those Connecticut people: "I am not ashamed to confess that twenty-five years ago I was a hired laborer, mauling rails, at work on a flat-boat—just what might happen to any poor man's son!"

Lincoln, after less than one year as President, would tell Congress in his First Annual Message: "Capital has its rights, which are as worthy of protection as any other rights." He added:

"There is not of necessity any such thing as the free hired laborer being fixed to that condition for life. Many independent men everywhere in these States a few years back in their lives were hired laborers. The prudent, penniless beginner in the world labors for wages awhile, saves a surplus with which to buy tools or land for himself, then labors on his own account another while, and at length hires another beginner to help him. This is the just and generous and prosperous system which opens the way to all, gives hope to all, and consequent energy and progress and improvement of condition to all."

Lincoln always held a horror toward popular violence, mob rule, or citizens taking the law into their own hands and deliberately destroying lives and property. His Lyceum speech at Springfield in 1838 is his most elaborate expression of his views on this disapproval of "the mob." He was inspired to speak out against this form of "vigilantism," self organized law-enforcers setting themselves up as censors, captors, judges, jurors, and even executioners. This mob spirit had recently vented itself in St. Louis, where a free mulatto, who stabbed an officer while resisting arrest, was deliberately burned by outraged citizens led on by rabble-rousers and human incendiaries; down at Vicksburg, Mississippi, where three white gamblers were strung up a tree by a crowd; and right in Alton, Illinois, where in 1837 a crowd killed the abolitionist editor, Elijah P. Lovejoy, when he attempted to protect his printing press from being thrown into the river. Lincoln in his Lyceum address mentioned all three of those instances, and emphasized: "There is no grievance that is a fit object of redress by mob law."

Lincoln was destined to make his best known expression against lawless destruction of property and the proper relation between labor and capital in March, 1864, one year before his assassination, to a committee of the New York Workingmen's Association, which had elected him an honorary member. He told them:

"The strongest bond of human sympathy, outside of the family relation, should be one uniting all working people, of all nations, and tongues, and kindreds. Nor should this lead to a war upon property, or the owners of property. Property is the fruit of labor—property is desirable—is a positive good in the world. That some should be rich, shows that others may become rich, and hence is just encouragement to industry and enterprize. Let not him who is houseless pull down the house of another; but let him labor diligently and build one for himself, thus by example assuring that his own shall be safe from violence when built."

XI

Lincoln suggested a typical mid-nineteenth-century self-made Middlewestern politician and home-grown lawyer, although his personal integrity can be measured far above the average professional party man and practitioner at the bar. His early career appeared not unusual, and his partisanship as Whig, then as Republican, gave little indication of future national or international immortality. Although not a prolific student of cultural subjects, he read extensively in political messages, law books and papers, newspapers, and election-precinct figures: he possessed an analytical and logical mind of extraordinary greatness. Preeminently he was a practical man, cautious in politics, conservative in his business views, and determined not to run too far in advance of public sentiment.

Thousands of Midwestern public men and attorneys, before and after Lincoln, led careers that parallel his to the half-century mark of their lives. Lincoln was to be near his fiftieth birthday when, in 1858, his debates against Douglas for United States Senator catapulted him to a measure of fame outside of Illinois.

Thus stood the personal Lincoln, near the threshold of his significant career as America's greatest immortal.

MR. AND MRS. A. LINCOLN

I

THE most permanent part of Lincoln's personal life, of course, comprised his joys and sorrows with his wife and sons.

"Popular" writing over the decades has produced a stereotyped portrait all too familiar—that of the henpecked husband hectored and nagged by his shrewish wife. A truer picture of Lincoln's life, though, can be reconstructed from little known records and reappraisal of old familiar facts, while taking into account Mary Todd Lincoln's mental instability.

II

Mary had a distinguished heritage. She was the great-granddaughter of General Andrew Porter, mathematician and strategist of Revolutionary War distinction, and the granddaughter of Major-General Levi Todd of the Kentucky militia. Her own life had begun amid genteel, gracious surroundings in Kentucky, sharply in contrast to her husband's. This glaring difference in the respective youthful atmospheres of Mr. and Mrs. A. Lincoln of Springfield, Illinois, was mentioned by a traveler, Elias P. Fordham, in 1818, the year when Mary was born. Fordham noted in his journal that Blue Grass Kentucky possessed a "cleanliness which strongly contrasts with the dirty Ohio houses and the Indiana and Illinois pigsties, in which men, women, and children wallow in promiscuous filth. But the Kentuckians have servants." The servants were almost exclusively slaves.

Ever since her Kentucky girlhood, however, Mary's relations with people, her family, servants, and neighbors in Lexington and Springfield, then with Lincoln, were often complicated by her minor mental disturbances. Born into a huge family in which three of her sisters and brothers were afflicted with what her later physician-biographer, Dr. W. A. Evans, called "abnormal personalities," she was, "as a child subject to temper tantrums." She was only seven years old when her mother died. Her father, Robert S. Todd, well-known business man and friend and lieutenant of Henry Clay, remarried, but Mary's associations with her stepmother, Mrs. Betsey Humphreys Todd, proved rarely harmonious. Once Mary wrote Lincoln about her stepmother: "If she thought any of us were on her hands again, I believe she would be *worse* than ever."

Leaving her Lexington, Kentucky, home, Mary came to Springfield to live in the stately mansion of her brother-in-law and half-sister, Mr. and Mrs. Ninian W. Edwards, in 1839. There she led a glamorous and exciting life in the capital town's high society. Then she met and married Lincoln after a prolonged see-sawing courtship, involving the broken engagement. Mr. and Mrs. A. Lincoln had lived at the Globe Tavern on Adams Street in Springfield, a hostelry kept by the widowed Mrs. Sarah Beck. Thus the belle turned bride passed from the well-appointed Edwards home to a plain boarding house.

Some months following his marriage, Lincoln sent word to his former Springfield friend now living in Kentucky. To Speed he reported: "We are not keeping house; but boarding at the Globe tavern, which is very well kept now by a widow lady of the name of Beck. Our room (the same Dr. [William S.] Wallace occupied there) and boarding only costs four dollars a week." In another note to Speed, in March, 1843, four months following his marriage, Lincoln wrote: "About the prospect of your having a namesake at our house cant say, exactly yet."

Actually Mary was maturely pregnant at that time. But their child, a son, would not be named for Speed. When the infant was born, at the

Globe Tavern on August 1, 1843, three days less than nine months after their marriage, he was named for Mary's father, Robert Todd.

Among the boarders at the Globe Tavern at that time were Albert T. Bledsoe, then a fellow Whig party associate and attorney, his wife, and his daughter, Sophie. Subsequently, Sophie Bledsoe gave her recollections of the humble circumstances attending those first weeks after Bob Lincoln was born: "When Robert was born, Mrs. Lincoln had no nurse for herself or the baby. Whether this was due to poverty or more probably to the great difficulty of securing domestic help, I do not know. But my mother, who never cared personally for Mrs. Lincoln, went every day to her room in the hotel, washed and dressed the baby, and made the mother comfortable and the room tidy, for several weeks, till Mrs. Lincoln was able to do these things for herself."

After the Globe Tavern, Abraham, Mary, and their infant son, Bob, lived for a time in a modest cottage. Then Lincoln in January, 1844, with money made from his law partnership with Logan, bought the story-and-a half brown house on Eighth and Jackson Streets in Springfield from Reverend Charles Dresser, the Episcopal clergyman who had performed his marriage to Mary. The price was $1,500. That house, with additions, enlargements, and improvements which Lincoln made, would remain their residence for seventeen years, until February, 1861, when he went to Washington as President-elect, except for the short interval in which he served in Congress during 1847-49.

Lincoln's prolonged absences on the Eighth Judicial Circuit in his itinerant practice of law and his journeys to other towns for political rallies made hardships for Mary Todd Lincoln. Nearly half of the year he was away on the circuit, three months in spring and three months in autumn. Of the traveling attorneys on the Eighth, he alone covered that far-flung circuit. It was a time-consuming, at times impossible task for him to visit home on week-ends and return for court cases in distant counties in time for their trial. During the 1840's travel was by horseback and horse-and-buggy, and when railroads were constructed in the fifties, the trains averaged a speed of only twenty miles an hour, with connections poor. Mary, therefore, was lonesome. On one occasion she confided to her friend: "I hope you may never feel as lonely as I sometimes do, surrounded by much that renders life desirable."

The Lincolns, more than three years following their marriage, had a second child, another son, born on March 10, 1846. They named him Edward Baker, after Lincoln's close Whig associate and friend, Congressman Edward D. Baker.

Eddie's birth occurred at the precise time when Lincoln was wrangling with both Congressman Baker and John J. Hardin over who should receive the nomination for Congress from the Seventh District.

III

Lincoln found himself wed to a very politically-minded woman. Together they were steeped in Whig Party loyalty and devotion to Henry Clay, most illustrious citizen of her home town, whom she had known since girlhood.

Mary encouraged Lincoln to pursue his political career. But little or no aid came from her own family Whig clan. Although Edwards was her brother-in-law and one of Lincoln's former "Long Nine" Whig colleagues from Sangamon County in the Legislature, and John T. Stuart was her cousin and Lincoln's own former political mentor and law partner, they did not use influence to further Lincoln's party fortunes. He would have to do it all himself, if he was to advance in public life under Whiggery's banner. Despite Lincoln's own paucity of spare time owing to his law practice, he was constantly urged ahead on political trails by his wife.

When they departed for Congress late in 1847, he and Mrs. Lincoln rented their Eighth Street home to Cornelius Ludlum and started for Washington by a circuitous route, stopping for a visit at her father's and stepmother's house in Lexington, Kentucky.

Arrived at Washington for the opening of the Thirtieth Congress in early December, 1847, Lincoln with his wife and two sons, Bob and the infant Eddie, put up at Brown's Hotel and later moved to Mrs. Ann Sprigg's boarding house, on the present site of the Library of Congress. At Mrs. Sprigg's Mary did not mix freely with the other paying guests. One of the other boarders, Dr. Samuel C. Busey, subsequently stated that Mrs. Lincoln "was so retiring that she was rarely seen except at meals." Busey noted that the older Lincoln boy, Bob, was spoiled.

Mary, after only several months with Lincoln at Mrs. Sprigg's, left Washington with her two sons and went to visit the Todd home in Lexington for a long stay.

Lincoln's letters from Washington to Mary in Lexington were those of an affectionate lonesome husband and father, and contradict stories of constant haggling between the two that have come down through legend to the present day.

In one message to "Dear Mary," penned on April 16, 1848, the Whig congressman from Illinois bemoaned the monotonous drudgery of his office and the tedious work of dispatching political documents to his constituents and party workers. "In this troublesome world," he wrote his wife, "we are never quite satisfied. When you were here, I thought you hindered me some in attending to business—no variety—it has grown exceedingly tasteless to me. I hate to sit down and direct documents, and I hate to stay in this old room by myself." He mentioned his wife's request to buy stockings for baby Eddie. He had inquired in all of the Washington stores and could discover "only one pair of any sort" that he believed would fit "Eddie's dear little feet."

In that letter, too, Lincoln expressed to Mary his concern lest she offend her father, with whom she was staying, by her attentions to persons he disliked. "I wish you to enjoy yourself in every possible way," he assured her; and he cautioned, "But is there no danger of wounding the feelings of your good father, by being so openly intimate with the Wickliffe family?" Robert Wickliffe was a bitter personal and political foe of Mary's father and the two were becoming involved in a law suit. In his letter to Mary, Lincoln referred to the guests at Mrs. Sprigg's house significantly: "All the house—or rather, all with whom you were on decided good terms—send their love. The others say nothing."

Lincoln in that letter revealed his understanding of his wife's torturing headaches, seeking to placate her by playful compliment, and expressing his concern for her health: "Are you entirely free from head-ache? That is good—good—considering it is the first spring you have been free from it since we were acquainted. I am afraid you will get so well, and fat, and young, as to be wanting to marry again. Tell Louisa I want her to watch you a little for me. Get weighed, and write me how much you weigh." He then requested his wife to remember him to Bobby and Eddie: "What did he and Eddy think of the little letters father sent them? Don't let the blessed fellows forget father."

Lincoln received equally affectionate letters from Mary. In May she sent him one, telling about how she wanted to accompany some Lexington friends East, informing him: "How much, I wish, instead of writing, we were together this evening. I feel very sad away from you." She assured him that the two boys' eyes brighten at mention of his name. She ended her letter, "My love to all, Truly yours, M. L."

Lincoln's letter to her of June 12, on her wish to come to Washington, referred to her uneven temperament: "Will you be a *good girl* in all things, if I consent? Then come along, and that as *soon* as possible. Having got the idea in my head, I shall be impatient till I see you." He ended the message: "Come on just as soon as you can. I want to see you, and our dear—*dear* boys very much. Every body here wants to see our dear Bobby. Affectionately, A. Lincoln."

When Mary delayed in leaving Lexington, Lincoln sent these words: "Father expected to see you all sooner; but let it pass; stay as long as you please, and come when you please. Kiss and love the dear rascals."

Mary Lincoln did not return to Washington, and would not see the national capital again until she went there as First Lady of the land more than a dozen years later. Lincoln, remaining in Washington, plunged into his work for Taylor for President.

IV

Lincoln, following his congressional service early in 1849, without a government job after failing to secure the Commissionership of the General Land Office, returned almost full time to the law, taking out only little time for politics until 1854. He resumed his law partnership with William H. Herndon in the Lincoln & Herndon firm.

All too unhappily Lincoln learned of the bad feeling existing between his wife and his law partner. Later, Herndon was to deliver public lectures on the unhappiness between Lincoln and Mrs. Lincoln and to perpetuate the Ann Rutledge "romance" legend. That strained relationship between Mary Lincoln and Billy Herndon had existed ever since they had met each other back in 1839.

Herndon had encountered the then Mary Todd at a reception in Springfield, waltzed with her, and, seeking to compliment and also display his peculiar humor, he had told her, after the dance, that she had waltzed with the grace of a serpent. Mary was not complimented. She had turned on him angrily and flashed back a cold answer: "Mr. Herndon, comparison to a serpent is rather severe irony, especially to a newcomer." Neither Mary nor Herndon ever forgot that incident.

Mrs. Lincoln's disapproval of Billy Herndon mounted after he became her husband's law partner. He was not her type of man, and she particularly frowned on his indulgence in strong drink. She had a brother who had fallen victim to alcoholism, and she wanted no one around her who loved liquor. Two years after Lincoln's death she wrote Judge David Davis, who then acted as administrator of Lincoln's estate, her own reason why Lincoln made Herndon his law partner: "Out of pity he took him into his office, when he was almost a hopeless inebriate." This was her purely personal explanation, filled with prejudice, and, of course, not the prime reason why her husband made Herndon a partner. Lincoln's own desire for a hardworking subordinate, who would do the real chores of law labor (as he had done for Stuart and then Logan) persuaded the future President to form the firm of Lincoln & Herndon. The junior partner had, indeed, kept up the partnership's business while Lincoln served in Congress.

Seldom, if ever, did Mrs. Lincoln invite Herndon to her home. But if she wanted no part of him socially, she had her own favorite guests, one of whom was Isaac N. Arnold of Chicago. A future member of Congress, loyal political supporter of Lincoln in the coming trying war years, and destined to be a biographer of Lincoln, Arnold always spoke in extravagant terms about Mary's hospitality when he visited Springfield. Arnold reminisced: "Mrs. Lincoln's table was famed for the excellence of many rare Kentucky dishes, and in season, it was loaded with venison, wild turkeys, prairie chickens, quail, and other game."

If Mary Lincoln served such a good and extravagant table as pictured by Arnold, it undoubtedly was none of Lincoln's doing. He remained indifferent to the taste of food and was inclined to be frugal in expenditures.

V

Herndon, while undoubtedly off base factually in his revelation about Lincoln's romance with Ann Rutledge (spoken and written after Lincoln's death), was essentially accurate in his insistence that Lincoln led a turbulent life with his wife. He failed, however, to make allowances for Mary's emotional instability that was to lead to her mental breakdown in future years.

The Todd family in Kentucky, Illinois, and elsewhere had a long established record for hot tempers and quick, angry decisions, and the many-branched clan contained proportionately more than its share of mentally unbalanced members. Mary took out her ire on Lincoln more than the average wife of that day, and he became a particularly harassed husband. Some of the Springfield neighbors called him "hen pecked." But he possessed Job-like patience both in politics and in his personal life.

Milton Hay of Springfield, even while Lincoln lived in 1862, referred to him in a letter to Mrs. Hay as "on old *poke easy* that used to walk our streets and was said to be *hen pecked.*" Once on the circuit Lincoln commented about John T. Stuart, himself a Todd, when speaking of Mrs. Stuart: "I just tell you whoever married into the Todd family gets the worst of it." Once when Mrs. Lincoln's Kentucky niece, Katherine Todd Helm, gave a provoking gentleman a tart answer, Lincoln chuckled, "The child has a tongue like the rest of the Todds."

Only several years after her marriage to Lincoln, pregnancy, childbirth, household drudgery (she could not always keep a maid), and sick headaches—her modern biographer, Ruth Painter Randall, has called them "migraine"—were beginning to take their toll on Lincoln's intensely emotional wife. She would become abnormally hysterical if her son, Bobby, would "run away" for a few hours; and she would scream, "Bobbie's lost!" When the child accidentally swallowed some lime, she yelled in terror: "Bobbie will die! Bobbie will die!" Thunder storms panicked her, she was plunged into deep forebodings by her husband's long absences on the law circuit and at political meetings. The death of her second son, Eddie, in 1850 crushed her for years.

Too, some of her husband's habits grated on her sensitivities. At times Lincoln demonstrated indifference to domestic niceties and an untidiness that irritated this proudly reared woman of Kentucky Blue Grass society. One of his former sweethearts, Mary Owens, was to comment after Lincoln's death that he was "deficient in those little links which make up the chain of a woman's happiness."

Lincoln's tardiness for meals at times annoyed her. One of her half-sisters from Kentucky, Emilie Todd Helm, told how on one occasion the chicken had already been burned to a crisp in the oven when, two hours late; "in sauntered Lincoln as innocent as a lamb of any infraction of domestic routine." Lincoln passed it all off lightly by remarking in good humor: "Bring on the cinders and see how quickly they will disappear."

Lincoln, early in 1857, specially annoyed Mary when he subscribed to a newly established Republican newspaper, called *The Republican,* in Springfield. When the paper was delivered, she snapped at him, "Now are you going to take another worthless little paper?" While Lincoln was away, Mary cancelled the subscription, with the result that a resentful little paragraph was printed in it, creating a misunderstanding which Lincoln, as a prominent Republican leader, found necessary to clear up. Tactfully Lincoln apologized for this action in an explanation, marked "Private," to the editor: "When the paper was brought to my house, my wife said to me, 'Now are you going to take another worthless little paper?' I said to her *evasively,* 'I have not directed the paper to be left.' From this, in my absence, she sent the message to the carrier. This is the whole story."

Mrs. Lincoln's irritation about her husband subscribing to that new paper was based not so much on economy as upon her feeling that she did not feel quite right about the infant Republican Party; it was too radical, too much anti-slavery for her. She grieved when her husband finally left their beloved Whig Party after almost two years of hesitation and joined the Republicans. This despite the fact that she wanted him to advance in public life and the Whigs were now, in 1857, a mere skeleton of a party. Her own conservatism and Southern heritage were too strong for her to become immediately reconciled to an anti-slavery political party such as the Republicans.

In the campaign of 1856 Mary had wanted to see Former President Millard Fillmore, third party Whig-"American" candidate for President, who was friendly to the South, elected over the Democrat, James Buchanan, and the Republican, John C. Frémont, for whom Lincoln had taken the stump both in Illinois and Michigan. On November 23, 1856, less than three weeks following that national election, she wrote her half-sister in Kentucky, telling her of her own preference for Fillmore and shielding Lincoln from the taint of Republican abolitionism just because he had supported Frémont. Mary sent these words to Emilie Todd Helm: "My weak woman's heart was too Southern in feeling to sympathize with any but Fillmore. I have always been a great admirer of his, he made so good a President & is so just a man & feels the *necessity* of keeping foreigners within bounds." She also emphasized to her half-sister: "Although Mr. L. is, or was, a Fremont man, you must not include him with so many of those who belong to that party, an *abolitionist.* In principle he is far from it. All he desires is that slavery shall not be extended, let it remain where it is."

Herndon, strongly anti-slavery himself, was essentially correct when he later insisted that Mary Lincoln was "decidedly pro-slavery in her views." Her reputation as a sympathizer of the "peculiar institution" of her native South—Kentucky was still a slave State—was such that, in 1855, one anti-slavery editor of Galena, Illinois, Charles H. Ray, wrote his congressman about Lincoln: "I must confess I am afraid of 'Abe'. . . . I have thought that he would not come squarely up to the mark in a hand to hand fight with Southern influence and dictation. His wife, you know, is a Todd—of a pro-slavery family."

VI

Mary Todd Lincoln, within the limitations of her emotional unbalance, which was to land her in a Chicago mental institution after her husband's death, proved a loyal wife to him and a devoted mother to their sons.

Lincoln had pet names for his wife. Before their marriage he called her "Molly." Sometimes he playfully addressed her as "Puss." After their sons were born, he referred to her as "Mother," and occasionally, the "little woman."

Mrs. Lincoln shopped regularly at the Yates & Smith store, one of whose partners, Clark M. Smith, was married to her youngest sister, Anna Maria Todd. The store advertised "Staple and Fancy Dry Goods, Groceries, Boots and Shoes." There Lincoln's wife bought the family groceries, silks, gaiter boots, other household goods, and clothing.

Old charge accounts of Springfield stores, still preserved, indicate that Mrs. Lincoln was busy over the stove, scrubbing brush, and needle. Although she had a whole series of maids, none of them remained in her employ for long. She either discharged them or they left with no happy memories of her. She showed irritation at her Irish domestics, and in one letter to her half-sister in 1856 she complained about what she contended with when she employed what she called the "Wild Irish."

Mary Lincoln showed good taste in decorating the house on Eighth Street. One visiting newspaperman from Utica, in upstate New York, called there in 1860 and described the Lincoln home as neatly but not extravagantly furnished, "a modest household" provided over by a "true type of American lady." Flowers were set upon the table, pictures hung on walls, ornaments were few but appropriate, everything rested in its proper place, and the Utica reporter sent word to his paper: "What a pleasant home Abe Lincoln has."

The Lincolns at the start of 1850 sustained their first common personal tragedy: the death of their son Eddie, who passed away on February 1.

Six days following Eddie's death there appeared in the *Illinois State Journal,* "by request," an anonymously written poem, "Dear Eddie," which ran:

> The silken waves of his glossy hair
> Lie still over his marble brow. . . .
> Angel boy—fare thee well, farewell
> Sweet Eddie, we bid thee adieu!
> Bright is the home to him now given,
> For "of such is the kingdom of Heaven."

Three weeks following Eddie's death, Lincoln sent one of his infrequent letters to his stepbrother, John D. Johnston of Coles County, Illinois, telling him of his son's passing: "I suppose you had not learned that we lost our little boy. He was sick fifty two days & died the morning of the first day of this month. It was not our *first,* but our second child. We miss him very much."

Less than eleven months following Eddie's death, another son was born to Mr. and Mrs. Lincoln. They named him William Wallace Lincoln, after the Springfield physician who was married to Frances Todd, still another of Mary's sisters. The new son was instantly nicknamed "Willie." Of all the Lincoln sons, Willie soon gave promise of growing into the brightest and best-looking. Born so soon after Eddie's passing, Willie became the fond object of his parents, particularly of his mother.

Two years after Willie's birth, another son came to the Lincolns on April 4, 1853. They named him Thomas, after Lincoln's father, who had died in 1851. Lincoln called him "Tad." This fourth and last of the Lincoln boys was also fourth and last in brightness and mental alertness, by all odds the most backward of them all. He was to be handicapped by a speech impediment, either a cleft palate or a tied tongue, which was to endear him the more to his father. During Lincoln's future presidential term, Tad was to be recognized as Lincoln's favorite son.

Most aloof and aristocratic of the sons was the eldest, Robert Todd Lincoln. Lincoln sent Bob to a fashionable Eastern private school—a circumstance destined to sound most un-Lincolnian to those who worshipped at the shrine of the "legendary" Lincoln of democracy and equality of man.

After placing Bob in a private school in Springfield and an institution called "Illinois State University," Mr. and Mrs. Lincoln sent him East to the exclusive Phillips Exeter Academy in New Hampshire to prepare for Harvard College. Bob Lincoln failed fifteen of his sixteen subjects in his entrance examination for Harvard. But in 1860 he was finally enrolled in the distinguished Cambridge college, destined to graduate from there in 1864.

Growing up in Springfield, Bob did not know his father too intimately, being mostly with his mother during Lincoln's long absences from home. In later years the junior Lincoln confessed in one of his few private letters: "My Father's life was of a kind which gave me but little opportunity to learn the details of his early career. During my childhood & early youth he was almost constantly away from home, attending courts or making political speeches." Bob was to favor his mother and her family and, like his father, rarely if ever spoke of the Hankses. Herndon has disapprovingly appraised Bob: "He is a Todd and not a Lincoln;" again Herndon pronounced judgment, "Bob is not his 'daddy' nor like him in any respect whatever. Bob is little, proud, aristocratic, and haughty, his mother's 'baby' all through."

After Bob left Springfield for Phillips Exeter in 1859, Mrs. Lincoln piningly confided to a neighbor: "It almost appears, as if light & mirth had departed with him." Few shared her view. Those Springfielders who knew the introvert and chilly Robert Todd Lincoln felt that he exuded little light or mirthfulness.

Lincoln remained devoted to his sons. As Dr. Preston H. Bailhache, the Springfield physician, pointed out correctly: "Mr. Lincoln was always very solicitous when his boys were sick, and a more devoted father I have never known. His sympathy was almost motherly."

VII

Lincoln's action in 1853 in naming his last son "Thomas," after his father, who had passed away more than two years previous, proved one of the few instances in which he remembered his own Lincoln family. Neither did he bother much about his late mother's people, the Hanks clan. In fact, during Lincoln's lifetime no monument was ever erected over the neglected grave of Nancy Hanks Lincoln in Indiana.

When Lincoln married Mary Todd in 1842, neither his father, his stepmother, his stepbrother John, Dennis Hanks, nor any of the Lincolns, Hankses, or Johnstons were present at the ceremony. None of them were invited. One of the Halls, of his late mother's family, subsequently stated that Lincoln's father and stepmother, Thomas and Sarah, did not even know that Abraham was wed until he told them later on a visit to

Coles County in his itinerant law practice. Dennis Hanks, after Lincoln's death, replying to a question whether Lincoln "cared for" his own family, answered: "When he was with us, he seemed to think a great deal of us; but I thought sometimes it was hypocritical, but I am not sure."

There appears no evidence that Lincoln spent much if any time associating with the Hankses. Herndon, whose opinions one takes or leaves, claimed in a private letter to T. H. Bartlett years later that Lincoln's mother, Nancy Hanks Lincoln, had been the illegitimate daughter of a Virginia planter and that he, Lincoln, inherited his mental qualities and literacy from his out-of-wedlock Old Dominion maternal grandfather. Lincoln's great mind, insisted Herndon, never came from a Hanks; declaring in uncomplimentary terms, "The Hanks are the lowest people in the world."

Most scholars are inclined to agree that, while Lincoln's mother was illegitimately born, her father (Abraham Lincoln's maternal grandfather) was not necessarily a Virginia aristocrat. Today the search for a lawfully wedded father for Nancy Hanks Lincoln still continues indefatigably among historians and genealogists.

Lincoln's father, Thomas Lincoln, fell ill at his Coles County farm in the spring of 1849. On May 25 the stepbrother, John D. Johnston, informed Lincoln of the bad news by mail:

> Dear Brother
>
> I hast to in form you that Father is yet a Live & that is all & he craves to See you all the time & he wants you to come if you as able to git hure, for you are, his own flush & blood & it is nothing more than native for him to crave to see you, he says he has all most despared of seeing you, & he wonts you to pre pare to meet him in the unknown world, or in heven, for he thinks that our saviour has a Crown of glory, prepared for *him* I wright this with a bursting heart, I came to town for the Doctor, & I won you to make an effort to come, if your ar able to get hure, & he wonts me to tell your wife that he Loves hure & wants hure to, hure prepare to meet him at ower Saviours feet, we are all well, your Brother in hast,
>
> J. D. Johnston.

Thomas Lincoln lived on for almost two more years, passing away on January 17, 1851. It is not known how often Lincoln visited him during his many months of illness. But less than one week before his father died, Lincoln sent a letter to his stepbrother, John:

> Springfield, Jany. 12, 1851.
>
> Dear Brother:
>
> On the day before yeaterday I received a letter from Harriett [Harriett Hanks Chapman], written at Greenup. She says she has just returned from your house; and that Father [is very] low, and will hardly recover. She also

s[ays] you have written me two letters; and that [although] you do not expect me to come now, yo[u wonder] that I do not write. I received both. . . . It appeared to me I could write nothing which could do any good. You already know I desire that neither Father or Mother shall be in want of any comfort either in health or sickness while they live; and I feel sure you have not failed to use my name, if necessary, to procure a doctor, or any thing else for Father in his present sickness. My business is such that I could hardly leave home now, if it were not, as it is, that my own wife is sick-abed. (It is a case of baby-sickness, and I suppose is not dangerous). I sincerely hope Father may yet recover his health; but at all events tell him to remember to call upon, and confide in, our great, and good, and merciful Maker; who will not turn away from him in any extremity. He notes the fall of a sparrow, and numbers the hairs of our heads; and He will not forget the dying man, who puts his trust in Him. Say to him [Father] that if we could meet now, it is doubtful whether it would not be more painful than pleasant; but that if it be his lot to go now, he will soon have a joyous [meeting] with many loved ones gone before; and where [the rest] of us, through the help of God, hope ere-long [to join] them.

Write me again when you receive this.

Affectionately.
A. Lincoln.

Lincoln's only preserved words to his illiterate widowed stepmother, Mrs. Sarah Bush Johnston Lincoln, written in November, 1851, less than a year after his father's death, were contained as a post-script to a letter which he sent his stepbrother, to be read to her:

"A word for Mother:

"Chapman [Augustus H. Chapman] tells me he wants you to go and live with him. If I were you I would try it awhile. If you get tired of it (as I think you will not) you can return to your own home. Chapman feels very kindly to you; and I have no doubt he will make your situation very pleasant." Chapman had married Mrs. Lincoln's granddaughter.

Lincoln continued to have as few warm affections for his stepbrother as ever. This unindustrious man, with whom Lincoln had made his second flatboat trip down to New Orleans for Denton Offutt two decades before, was usually neglecting his crops on his Coles County farm, and soon became known as the "Beau Brummel of Goosenest Prairie." Often he was in money troubles, and Lincoln sent him at least several letters severely advising him. When in 1851 John wrote Lincoln telling of his contemplated plans to sell his Coles County land and move to Missouri, Lincoln replied to him:

"What can you do in Missouri better than here? Is the land any richer? Can you there, any more than here, raise corn, & wheat & oats, without work? Will any body there, any more than here, do your work for you? If you intend to go to work, there is no better place than right where you are; if you do not intend to work, you can not get along any where. Squirming & crawling about from place to place can do no good. You have raised no crop this year. . . . You are destitute because you have *idled* away all your time."

Lincoln opposed John's plan to sell the land because it would hurt his mother; it had evidently been left by Thomas Lincoln, Abraham's father. Lincoln ended his letter to his stepbrother with stern words: "The Eastern forty acres I intend for Mother to keep while she lives—if you *will not cultivate it;* it will rent for enough to support her—at least it will rent for something. Her Dower in the other forties, she can let you have, and no thanks to [me]." Apparently Lincoln was concerned, lest John leave his mother destitute.

The following year, 1852, Lincoln's stepbrother, the "Beau Brummel of Goosenest Prairie," left Coles County and settled in Arkansas.

It was abundantly clear that Lincoln, when he settled in New Salem after his flatboat trip for Offutt back in 1831, had left his own family, the Lincolns, the Johnstons, and the Hankses, behind him. They were not of his world.

BACK TO THE LAW

10

I

FOLLOWING his retirement from Congress in 1849 and his failure to persuade President Zachary Taylor's administration to give him the federal job of Commissioner of the General Land Office, Lincoln found himself depending on his law practice to support his wife and sons.

II

Three days after the Thirtieth Congress terminated in March, 1849, the erstwhile lone Whig member from Illinois was admitted to practice in the United States Supreme Court. In all, there is record that he participated in two cases before that highest American tribunal.

His first case in the Supreme Court at Washington, *Lewis v. Lewis*, involved the construction and operation of the statutes of limitations of the

State of Illinois. Lincoln and another lawyer, Lawrence, argued the appellee's case, while one Mr. Wright appeared for the appellant. The Court's majority opinion, delivered by Chief Justice Roger B. Taney opposed Lincoln's version, but Mr. Justice John McLean, in a dissenting opinion, held in accordance with Lincoln's contentions.

Lincoln's second case in the Supreme Court at Washington was *Forsythe v. Reynolds* at the December, 1853, term. He appeared on behalf of the appellant in association with two other lawyers. Arguing on the other side, although probably Lincoln did not see him face to face, was Salmon P. Chase of Ohio, destined to be a presidential rival of Lincoln and also his Secretary of the Treasury; too, Lincoln was, within a dozen years, to elevate Chase to Taney's place as the high court's Chief Justice. This case in 1853 involved the ownership of certain lands in Peoria, Illinois, and the construction of United States statutes governing land grants to settlers.

Neither of Lincoln's federal Supreme Court cases determined any major principle of law. Nonetheless they gave him the satisfaction, dear to all American attorneys, of arguing in this most elevated of tribunals.

III

Former Congressman Lincoln had little law practice of his own left when his House term expired in 1849, but Billy Herndon had, by hard work, kept up the firm's business.

Lincoln held scant hope of resurrecting his political career, and thus one original strong reason for his partnership with Herndon—a younger man to do the legal chores while the senior partner pursued politics—was removed. Herndon, however, desired that the firm should continue.

Before resuming his professional connection with Herndon, Lincoln was offered a partnership with a successful Chicago attorney, Grant Goodrich. This sounded unattractive to Lincoln. He declined Goodrich's offer, telling Judge David Davis that, if he went to the ever growing city on Lake Michigan, he would "have to sit down and study hard, that it would kill him, that he would rather go round the circuit than to sit down and die in Chicago."

Thus the two partners, Lincoln and Herndon, practiced again under the old firm name in Springfield. Now would commence Lincoln's practice of law as a significant part of his life. In another decade, writing his autobiography in the third person, he commented: "Upon his return from Congress he went to the practice of law with greater earnestness than ever before."

The law office on the west side of the square in Springfield, outside of which swung the shingle, "Lincoln & Herndon," had remained unchanged during the senior member's congressional service at Washington. Its unscrubbed windows looked out over the monotony of a trafficless alley. Two work tables, which served the partners as desks, were arranged in the shape of a lop-sided "T;" one had its pine service indented with a jack-knife, the other was beige-covered and much shorter. A secretary of bulging drawers and overstuffed pigeon holes, four or five cane-bottomed chairs, a long rickety sofa propped against the wall, bookshelves with such worncovered titles as *Chitty, Redfield, Kent,* and *Blackstone,* and *Illinois Statutes* were other furnishings in the Lincoln & Herndon office. Usually the place remained dirty, for completely inadequate were the cleanings by law students and charwomen.

Lincoln himself remained disorderly in his paper work, and Herndon was not much better. The partners were constantly searching for mislaid papers. One huge envelope stuffed full of papers on Lincoln's desk bore the words: "When you can't find it anywhere else, look in this."

There were times when either or both partners had to confess frankly that documents sent them were "lost or destroyed and cannot be found after search among the papers of Lincoln & Herndon." That was Herndon's exact phrasing, in his handwriting, on an affidavit of September 28, 1857. Lincoln himself penned one note of apology to another lawyer for not having answered his letter sooner: "First, I have been very busy in the United States Court; second, when I received the letter, I put it in my old hat and buying a new one the next day, the old one was set aside, and so the letter was lost sight of for a time."

Nor was bookkeeping in the Lincoln & Herndon office more systematic. After the first year the partners kept no accounts against themselves, simply dividing the fees paid them. Lincoln followed a habit of setting aside one-half of the money he received for each case, marking it, "Herndon's half." Herndon would bring in fees collected on the circuit in a small gunny sack and would count out the money in equal shares. Lincoln told his fellow-lawyer on the circuit, Henry C. Whitney: "Billy and I never had the scratch of a pen between us; we just divide as we go along."

Lincoln & Herndon gave up the firm's office in the Tinsley Building sometime during the late 1840's. After short periods in several other locations they moved to the second floor of a brick building at 105 South Fifth Street. Here they remained until Lincoln's departure for Washington as President-elect in 1861.

Today Herndon is a prime target for the Lincoln lovers of indiscriminating tastes because of his post-war unchivalrous treatment of Mrs. Lincoln in his lectures and writings and his blunt biography of his immortal law partner. Yet Herndon cannot be dismissed as an undependable source of information about Lincoln's career. It is quite impossible to study Lincoln adequately in his pre-presidential years without leaning on Herndon's writings and the voluminous letters that he collected. He was one of the six Illinoisans who knew Lincoln intimately and wrote extensively about him. The other five were Ward H. Lamon (who had his biography of Lincoln "ghosted" by another and depended largely on Herndon's notes, the circuit-riding lawyer, Henry C. Whitney; the Chicago attorney and congressman Isaac N. Arnold; and Lincoln's own presidential secretaries, John G. Nicolay and John Hay.

Legend has handed down numberless stories about how Lawyer Lincoln would abandon a case because he became convinced that his client lacked "uprightness." Also tales have been circulated through the decades about his refusal to argue a case unless he was thoroughly satisfied with his client's moral attitude. This image of Lincoln as a lawyer has been repudiated by the research recently published by John J. Duff. Whatever the fastidiousness of Lincoln's conscience, he actually accepted any kind of case, sometimes for the plaintiff, on other occasions for the defendant, apparently regardless of the justice or lack of justice in the litigation or criminal pleading, as any specific and comprehensive study of his law practice will tellingly demonstrate. Once Lincoln accepted a case, he tried it to the hilt and worked tirelessly for his client, no matter how lofty or sordid the principles at issue. Few conceptions of Lincoln can be more shallow, few contain more folklore, than the one which interprets him as an advocate so lofty of principle that he was continually declining to represent people whose cases were not based on the purest ethics. Duff has correctly concluded: "If there is one indisputable fact about Lincoln's work in the courts, it is that from the moment of his retainer he played for keeps. . . . Lincoln left no stone unturned in invoking every defense available to a client." In reality he never could have handled such a huge and diversified practice on the not always virtuous Illinois frontier if he had held rigidly to such austere legal ethics. Actually the diversity of the Lincoln & Herndon practice sounds amazing. In the Illinois county and State courts at Springfield, Lincoln's itinerant practice on the Eighth Judicial Circuit, and his appearances in the United States district courts at Springfield and at Chicago, the range and variety of his professional law work are apparent. Appeals from justices' courts to the circuit court, from the circuit court to the state Supreme Court, appeals to the United States Supreme Court, actions in foreclosure, debt, replevin, trespass, partition, suretyship, actions for specific performance, suits over dower rights, slander and divorce actions, suits to compel stockholders to pay their assessments, personal injury actions, suits involving patent infringements, will contests, actions seeking injunctions; actions to impress mechanics' liens, criminal cases involving offenses from gambling to murder, nuances of maritime law—all were handled by Lincoln in that age of the general practitioner.

Lincoln was concerned with retainers, like nearly all lawyers, although he is known not to have overcharged his clients, except perhaps in a major case that he handled for the Illinois Central Railroad. He expressed his attitude in his "Notes for Law Lecture," declaring: "The matter of fees is important, far beyond the mere question of bread and butter involved. Properly attended to, fuller justice is done both lawyer and client. An exorbitant fee should never be claimed. As a general rule never take your whole fee in advance, nor more than a small retainer. Settle the amount of fee and take a note in advance."

When the case was finished, Lincoln did not delay in claiming his retainer. To one lawyer in 1851 he sent this note: "I have news from Ottawa that we *win* our Gallatin and Saline county case. As the Dutch justice said when he married folks, 'Now vere ish my hundred tollars?' " To one client, George P. Floyd of Quincy, for whom he had drawn a lease for a hotel, Lincoln in 1856 wrote: "I have just received yours of the 16th, with check on Flagg & Savage for twenty-five dollars. You must think I am a high-priced man. You are too liberal with your money. Fifteen dollars is enough for the job. I send you a receipt for fifteen dollars, and return you a ten-dollar bill."

IV

"I am not an accomplished lawyer. I find quite as much material for a lecture in those points wherein I have failed, as in those wherein I have been successful." That was Lincoln's own estimate of himself in his professional practice in words which he jotted down sometime during the 1850's.

Nonetheless the senior partner of Lincoln & Herndon rose to the foremost position at the Illinois bar during that decade preceding his election as President. Both from the standpoint of the number and importance of his cases, as counsel for either plaintiff or defendant, and in the percentage of those cases won, Lincoln emerged as one of the State's legal luminaries.

During 1850, when the Lincoln & Herndon firm was just getting reestablished, it handled one out of every five cases in the Circuit Court of important Sangamon County. That proved a record exceeded only by the redoubtable Stephen T. Logan, Lincoln's former partner. Five years later Lincoln's firm led the Springfield bar in the number of cases argued, and appeared for its client in the person of Lincoln or Herndon in every fourth case on that court's docket. When Lincoln returned more actively to politics after late 1854, however, the firm's activity fluctuated.

Lincoln demonstrated himself as especially active, and often successful, in the state Illinois Supreme Court at Springfield. In all, as far as available Illinois court records indicate, he appeared as counsel for the plaintiff or the defense in 243 cases there during his entire legal career, winning most of them. Some of these litigations helped to establish points of law that are standards in Illinois today.

In *Barrett v. The Alton & Sangamon Railroad Company,* a case handled by Lincoln in the state Supreme Court during 1851, he devoted a huge amount of time and effort in preparation of his argument. It concerned the right of railroads to enforce prior pledges for subscriptions of stock after change in the direction of the road, pursuant to an act of the Legislature.

Lincoln, appearing as counsel for the Alton & Sangamon Railroad in the Supreme Court, drove home the argument that the benefit which accrues to individual property, by the location of a public road, does not, in contemplation of law, enter into the consideration of the contract of subscription to stock of the railroad, and that subscriptions are made subject to the power of the Legislature to change the location of the right of way.

The Supreme Court adopted Lincoln's argument in its entirety. The decision proved of major significance, not only to Lincoln's client, the Alton & Sangamon line, but, in its long-range impact, to all other projected railroads.

Another significant case argued by Lincoln in his State's Supreme Court, concerned with the Democrat-Republican party fight for political power, was that of *People ex rel. Lanphier and Walker v. Hatch,* the defendant being the Republican-elected Secretary of State of Illinois, Ozias M. Hatch, a friend and party ally of Lincoln.

Governor William H. Bissell, a Republican, friend and political associate of Lincoln, in 1857 vetoed a state apportionment bill passed by the Democrat-controlled Legislature, a measure by which the Democrats sought to "gerrymander" the State's electoral districts in order to give their party an undemocratic advantage over their Republican foes in future elections.

Governor Bissell, in an unthinking moment, had unintentionally approved this Democrat-passed apportionment bill which would work to the election disadvantage of his own Republican Party!

When Republican leaders learned of Governor Bissell's unwitting blunder in signing an apportionment bill that would discriminate against their party in the conduct of elections, they vigorously protested to him and set him "right" on the issue. Thereupon the Governor, as a loyal Republican, sought to correct his political error by sending a message to the Speaker of the Assembly, informing him that the measure had been signed by him through inadvertence. On that same day the Governor not only crossed out his signature to the bill, but returned it to the Democrat-controlled Assembly with a veto message. The Democrats then through their party lawyers brought a *mandamus* proceeding to compel Hatch, the Secretary of State, to certify the Governor's act in having signed the apportionment bill.

Lincoln and Jackson Grimshaw, as good Republicans, represented Governor Bissell and Secretary of State Hatch. John A. McClernand argued the case for the Democratic plaintiffs in the state Supreme Court in February, 1858. Lincoln and Grimshaw forcefully contended that the Governor possessed the inherent power to rectify his error, especially where, as here, the act of the Legislature had not passed from his control by the customary modes of legislation.

The Springfield correspondent of the St. Louis *Republican* (a Democratic daily despite its name) had a favorable comment on Lincoln's legal argument. That reporter declared about the Lincoln & Herndon senior partner's presentation: "He made one of the best arguments he ever made, and, although at the time, we differed with him in his position, yet candor compels us to admit that he presented his case in a strong light and with much force."

Lincoln's argument, essentially a clear exposition of the law despite the political partisanship involved in it, removed all doubt as to the validity of Governor Bissell's veto.

The Court on February 6, 1858, found in favor of Lincoln's and Grimshaw's client, the Republican Governor of Illinois. The Court held that, while a bill is in possession and control of the executive (the Governor), within the period limited by the state Constitution, it has not the force of law, and the Governor may exercise a veto power and so return the measure to that house of the state Legislature where it originated, with his name erased, notwithstanding he had once announced his approval of it.

Lincoln had a mighty personal and Republican political party stake in having Governor Bissell upheld in court on his second-thought decision to veto the Democrat-passed apportionment bill. For in the coming autumn state elections, he planned to run against the Democrat, Stephen A. Douglas, for Douglas's United States Senate seat during that era when federal Senators were, by United States constitutional provision, chosen by state legislatures, not directly elected by the qualified voters. If the Democrat-enacted Illinois apportionment bill "gerry-mandering" the election districts were allowed to become law by Governor Bissell's unintended approval of it, Lincoln, or any other Republican candidate for United States Senator, would be placed at grossly unfair disadvantage in combatting Senator Douglas, the Democratic incumbent.

V

The Lincoln & Herndon firm also actively engaged in the United States courts at Springfield. Lincoln, even before he went to Congress, had been a prime favorite of Judge Nathaniel Pope of the United States District Court at Springfield, who served until his death in 1850. Judge Anson S. Miller of Rockford, Illinois, later reminisced: "Judge Pope loved Lincoln. His affection for Lincoln was very marked. He would snub Logan. He didn't like Baker." There are those who later contended that when Lincoln, as President more than a decade hence, appointed Judge Pope's son, Major-General John Pope, to head the newly created Army of Virginia, he was partly motivated by his personal feeling for the late Judge and the Pope family. General Pope was to lead his vast army to humiliating and costly defeat at Second Bull Run in 1862.

Thomas Drummond succeeded Judge Pope as federal jurist for Illinois in 1850, then was transferred to Chicago when the State was divided into two federal judicial districts. Samuel H. Treat sat for the Southern District, at Springfield. With both Judge Drummond and Judge Treat Lincoln was on the most favorable of terms.

One of Lincoln's criminal cases in the United States District Court during 1852 was his defense of William Williamson, former Postmaster of Lacon, a one-legged veteran of the Mexican War, who was indicted for stealing a package containing $15,000 from the mail. Assisting Lincoln in his defense of Williamson was his old friend from Quincy, Orville H. Browning. So overwhelming was the evidence against their client, that Browning grew discouraged. Noted Browning in his famous diary on July 13: "The evidence was very strong. Almost conclusive. I was so discouraged that I wished to decline a speech, but at the persuasion of Lincoln addressed the jury for something over two hours." But the jury found Williamson guilty. He was sentenced to ten years in prison.

Those preserved federal court records for the Southern District of Illinois reveal that, from 1855 to 1860, Lincoln was the counsel in at least eighty-five of the thousand cases tried in that United States court during those five years. More than a hundred papers on cases there, in his handwriting, have been unearthed over the decades. Occasionally Lincoln had a case alone, or in association with attorneys other than Herndon, but the papers were nearly always in Lincoln's handwriting.

One case in the federal court at Springfield, which gave Lincoln deep displeasure toward his own client, was *Ambos v. Barrett et al.* Lincoln represented the plaintiff, Charles Ambos, really the Columbus Machine Manufacturing Company of Columbus, Ohio, who was suing James A. Barrett for a debt of $15,000. Lincoln early in 1859 succeeded in collecting $1,000 from the defendant, Barrett, and continued the case. But this was not speedy enough for Lincoln's client, Ambos, who constantly complained about Lincoln's dawdling. "I would now," Lincoln answered Ambos irritably in July, 1859, "very gladly surrender the charge of the case to anyone you would designate, without charging anything for the much trouble I have already had."

This troublesome case was again continued in the federal court at Springfield in the following month. Things were still not moving fast enough for the impatient Ambos. This aroused in Lincoln more wrath, since he had concluded that the plaintiff, Barrett, was an honest man and would pay off in time when previous judgments against him were satisfied. Lincoln sent off a message to Ambos's Columbus attorney, Samuel Galloway, with whom he was then corresponding, about possible Republican candidates for President the following year. "My chief annoyance with the case now," he informed Galloway, "is that the parties at Columbus seem to think it is by my neglect that they do not get their money. There is an older mortgage on the real estate [of Barrett] though not on the machinery. I got a decree of foreclosure in this present month; but I consented to delay advertising for sale till September, on a reasonable prospect that something will then be paid on a collateral Barrett has put in my hands." Lincoln assured Galloway: "My impression is that the whole of the money cannot be got very soon, anyway; but that it all will be ultimately collected, and that it could be got faster by turning in every little parcel we can, than by trying to force it through by the law in a lump."

One of Lincoln's most lucrative cases in the federal court, *Beaver v. Taylor and Gilbert,* involved possession of sixty-five acres of land adjoining the city of Cairo, Illinois, near the Kentucky line. This case was tried in 1859. Lincoln, along with Herndon, Logan, and Stuart & Edwards, represented the defendants, who were being sued by the plaintiff for recovery of the land. The case was submitted without argument on June 20 and taken under advisement by Judge Samuel H. Treat. Finally Treat decided in favor of the defendants, whereupon the plaintiff entered a motion for a new trial. This motion, argued before the court in January, 1860, was later denied. The Lincoln & Herndon firm received half of the $3,000 retainer.

VI

Lincoln's career as an attorney is indissolubly associated with the Eighth Judicial Circuit of Illinois, where he did the bulk of his legal work, although not always the most successful part of it.

When the former Whig Congressman of the Seventh District returned nearly full time to the law in 1849, the State was then divided into nine judicial districts, over each of which an elected Judge presided. His

Honor traveled from one county-seat town to another within his jurisdiction, hearing civil and criminal cases and acting as an appelate tribunal for minor cases decided by justices of the peace. During the spring and fall of the year the Judge of each of these districts went continually on his rounds, conducting court, with circuit lawyers, such as Lincoln, as his "equestrian retinue," accompanying him or closely following on his trail.

The Eighth Judicial Circuit in 1849 included no less than fourteen counties: Lincoln's own Sangamon, Tazewell, Woodford, McLean, Logan, De Witt, Piatt, Champaign, Vermilion, Edgar, Shelby, Moultrie, Macon, and Christian. The district's vast dimensions were 100 by 140 miles. The State Legislature in 1853, however, organized several new circuits, reducing the Eighth to eight counties, Sangamon, Logan, McLean, Woodford, Tazewell, De Witt, Champaign, and Vermilion. Four years later further reduction of the Eighth was found necessary owing to population increase and more litigations. In the last reapportionment Lincoln's home county, Sangamon, was detached from the Eighth, but he continued to ride that circuit until the very eve of his nomination for President in 1860.

Whereas Lincoln, before his congressional service, usually rode the Eighth on horseback, after his return to active practice in 1849 he often traveled by railroad. By 1853 a train route connected Springfield with other county seats where courts were held on that circuit.

Lincoln, as in his pre-congressional days on the circuit, relished this migratory life, jogging over the prairies on horseback, in a rickety buggy drawn by a rawboned nag, or by train at times; meeting other lawyers and the Judge; and joining others as they made taverns resound with their hilarity, swapped stories, tried moot cases, and lodged together in overcrowded, unsanitary hotels and boarding houses.

During Lincoln's years on the Eighth, lawyers held more intimate social relations with the Judge than prevailed in later decades. When the court had adjourned for the day, at times it was the Judge's custom to cast aside his judicial dignity and aloofness, and join his professional brethren, the lawyers, in only partially restrained efforts to contribute his share toward the impromptu joviality and informality of those assembled at the same inn, boarding house, or hotel.

The Judge of the Eighth Judicial Circuit was Maryland-born David Davis of Bloomington, McLean County. He was a conservative Whig elected in 1848, of pachydermic portliness in weight under whom chairs groaned, stern on the bench but jovial enough after court adjourned. A fast friendship sprang up between Lincoln and Davis which was to prove of the most colossal importance to both. The Judge would be one of the two (Norman B. Judd of Chicago being the other) of the Illinois Republican leaders most responsible for Lincoln's nomination for President in

1860, and Lincoln as President would elevate Davis to the United States Supreme Court bench.

A selected few attorneys on the circuit were sometimes invited by Judge Davis to share his room at night. But since Davis, a three-hundred-pounder, was almost as wide as the four-poster bed, His Honor's offer was merely a graceful gesture which few lawyers ever dared to accept.

When Judge Davis was forced to be temporarily absent from his bench, he arranged with one of the more favored lawyers, sometimes Lincoln, to hold court in his stead. That procedure had no sanction in law and was quite irregular. But the Illinois frontier of the pre-Civil War period was full of informality. Lawyers, litigants, or jurors seldom voiced objections to an attorney sitting in the absent Judge's place.

Lincoln presided over Circuit Court sessions on the Eighth at least seven different times during that decade of the '50's. In order to prevent reversal on appeal, the clerk's official record, again irregularly enough, would show the real Judge as presiding and would not mention the substitute jurist. Lincoln possessed the tact called for by the unofficial character of this very temporary judicial position as well as caution and judgment in exercising his authority.

Courts on the Eighth Circuit were usually overcrowded with spectators when cases were being tried. To go to their sessions and listen to lawyers and witnesses talk constantly was among the frontier's free amusements, the court room substituting for the theatre, concert hall, church, and "opry" house. The Judge and the lawyers were the stellar attractions, and some stood aghast at the long, lank Lawyer Lincoln in contrast to the overweight Judge Davis. Audiences drank in the eloquence, pathos, and humor displayed in a judicial atmosphere where cases were often not won or lost on strict adherence to the letter of the law. At times local newspapers would chide the courts about their inconsequential cases, one Urbana, Champaign County, newspaper in 1857 disapprovingly mentioning a docket with "a dog-suit, a wood-stealing Irishman, a half-crazy horse thief, and other small business."

Lincoln appeared as unfastidious in dress on the circuit as anywhere else. He wore a faded hat, sometimes a top one, with the nap usually worn or rubbed off. His coat and vest hung loosely on his gaunt frame, and his trousers were considerably too short. He carried in one hand a faded green umbrella, with "A. Lincoln" in cotton letters sewed on the inside; the knob was gone from the handle, and when closed a piece of cord was often tied around it in the middle to keep it from flying open. In his other hand he carried a carpet bag, in which were stored the papers he used in court.

Judge Davis, after Lincoln's death, confidentially asserted to another that Lincoln spent so much time on the circuit partly because he wanted to avoid home and the temper of his wife.

VII

The well-known trio who constantly rode the Eighth during the 1850's were Lincoln, Judge Davis, and Davis's firm friend and fellow townsman of Bloomington, the Maine-born Leonard Swett.

Lincoln attended every April and every September term of the McLean County Circuit Court from the fall of 1849 through the spring of 1860, with the two exceptions of April, 1851, and September, 1859. To a degree Lincoln had cases in other courts of the circuit quite as regularly.

Lincoln, in his itinerant professional practice, followed the common custom of having local lawyers act as associate counsel, or they had him do so, at the various county courts of the Eighth. The resident attorney would "get the business," prepare the case, file the necessary papers, and perform other preliminaries for presentation in court. One of these local lawyers with whom Lincoln was most often and closely associated on the circuit as co-counsel was the Virginia-born Ward Hill Lamon of Danville, Vermilion County, who several years later moved to Bloomington, McLean County. Among the junior lawyers of Illinois, Lamon was by all odds held in highest esteem by Lincoln, who was to refer to him as "my particular friend." Lamon grew deeply attached to Lincoln.

Few friends seemed more unlike each other than Lincoln and Lamon, one the quiet teller of stories and anecdotes, the other a boisterous singer of lewd ballads and "comic" songs; one a teetotaler, the other an excessively thirsty guzzler of any whiskey in sight; one the conciliator always trying to spread harmony and prevent fist fights on the rough frontier, the other a belligerent bruiser ever ready for a bar-room brawl; one a family man with wife and sons, the other having his law office over a saloon on the same floor with a house of assignation in Danville. But theirs was a friendship destined to last until Lincoln's death, for Lamon would accompany his friend to Washington in 1861, become Lincoln's bodyguard and United States Marshal for the District of Columbia, and would be entrusted with numerous confidential missions for the President throughout the war.

Lamon in Vermilion County and elsewhere advertised himself as Lincoln's law partner, with Lincoln's agreement. Such a notice appeared in a rural Illinois newspaper in November, 1852:

> *LINCOLN AND LAMON, Attorneys-At-Law, having formed a co-partnership, will practice in the courts of the Eighth Judicial Circuit and the Superior Court, and all business entrusted to them will be attended to with promptness and fidelity. Office on the second floor of the "Barnum Building" over Whitcomb's Store.*

LINCOLN'S CELEBRATED LAW CASES

11

I

DURING Lincoln's years of practice, attorney's retainers were usually modest, especially low by present-day standards, even considering the then vastly greater value of the dollar. Few lawyers in Illinois or elsewhere throughout the United States grew tremendously wealthy through their cases in those days before the rise of numberless colossal corporations, giant manufacturing companies, big banks, transportation monopolies, unlimited numbers of millionaire private clients, and huge estate litigations. Those advocates who accumulated fabulous private fortunes of their own did so during that pre-Civil War era, not from the law, but from speculation in lands and shrewd investments in rapidly developing business enterprises.

During the 1850's only a handful of lawyers earned as much as $20,000 or more a year, and did not do this every year. At that time America's leading lawyer, Rufus Choate, took in $22,000 in a twelve-month period. In 1859 the firm of Butler, Evarts and Southmayd, considered at the head of the New York bar, netted $20,000. In Chicago, Isaac N. Arnold, Lincoln's friend, future congressman, and later his biographer, realized $22,000 in his practice during 1860. Such instances were the few exceptions to the generally niggardly fees then earned by most attorneys.

Lincoln, considering the fees of his era, could be considered a highly prosperous advocate. He had some money-laden clients. Among them were Nicholas H. Ridgely, Springfield banker interested in the Gas Light Works then laying pipe in Sangamon County. Lincoln also had among his clients such financial institutions as the Bank of Illinois, Tinkham & Company's Bank, the Bank of the Republic in McLeansboro, McLean County Bank, Bank of Missouri, Morgan County Bank, Bank of Commerce, Lafayette Bank, Bank of Indiana, and the banking firm of Page & Bacon in St. Louis. Insurance companies, too, retained the future President of the United States as their counsel, including the Delaware Mutual Safety Insurance Company, and the North American Insurance Company. Included among his manufacturing and commercial clients were the Columbus Machine Manufacturing Company and the St. Louis merchants, S. C. Davis & Company. The railroads for which he handled cases were the Ohio & Mississippi, the Rock Island, the Chicago, Alton & St. Louis, the Tonica & Petersburg, the Alton & Sangamon, and that biggest transportation interest, the Illinois Central.

II

Lincoln's most lucrative client was the Illinois Central Railroad. He collected his biggest retainer, with difficulty, after he had served as its counsel in *Illinois Central Railroad v. the County of McLean*.

McLean County in August, 1853, started proceedings to force the Illinois Central to pay taxes on the property it owned within that county. A county tax, in addition to the payment of five per cent of its gross earnings which it was forced to pay to the State of Illinois by its charter terms, would have endangered the financial stability of the railroad, which now refused to pay the tax levied by the county. The railroad, too, brought suit against the county in the McLean County Circuit Court to enjoin that county from collecting the taxes levied on it.

Lincoln was determined to get into this litigation as counsel, either on the side of the railroad or for the county, whichever paid him an adequate retainer. For a time he seriously thought that he would go on the side of McLean County and another county, Champaign, which was also contemplating taxing the railroad. He approached by mail the Clerk of the Champaign County Circuit Court, Thompson R. Webber. Lincoln's idea was to have McLean and Champaign counties make common cause against the Illinois Central with him as their counsel, or else, to have Champaign County release him from a prior commitment to serve them, so that he could go on the side of the railroad. Writing Webber, spokesman for Champaign County, he told how the Illinois Central had approached him for his services although he was bound to Champaign County. His note to Webber in September, 1853, reads:

> I am somewhat trammelled by what has passed between you and me; feeling that you have the prior right to my services; if you choose to secure me a fee something near such as I can get from the other side. The question, in its magnitude, to the Co. [company] on the one hand, and the counties in which the Co. [company] has land, on the other, is the largest law question that can be got up in the State; and therefore, in justice to myself, I can not afford, if I can help it, to miss a fee altogether. If you choose to release me; say so by return mail, and there an end. If you wish to retain me, you better get authority from your [Campaign County] court, come directly over [to Bloomington] in the Stage, and make common cause with this county [McLean].

Lincoln ended by joining the side of the Illinois Central against McLean County, explaining to one of the railroad's attorneys, Mason Brayman: "Neither the county of McLean, nor any one on its behalf, has yet made any engagement with me in relation to its suit with the Illinois Central Railroad, on the subject of taxation. I am now free to make an engagement for the Road; and if you think fit you may 'count me in.'"

Lincoln in 1854 argued the railroad's case in the McLean Circuit Court. The case was decided against him, and he and associate counsel appealed the decision to the state Supreme Court. It was stipulated that "the only question to be made in the Supreme Court" was whether the railroad could be taxed by the county. Lincoln and his associate, James F. Joy, orally argued their case in the Supreme Court, opposed by both of Lincoln's former law partners, John T. Stuart, who had started him in law, and Stephen T. Logan, from whom he learned so much. The case was continued and re-argued. It was heard again in January, 1856, with Lincoln making the opening argument for the railroad and Joy concluding it.

The Supreme Court unanimously held that, under the state constitution, the Legislature of Illinois could make exceptions from the rule of uniformity in taxation and that the provision in the railroad's charter, requiring payment to the State of a percentage of its gross earnings, was such an exception. Therefore counties could not tax the Illinois Central. Accordingly the anti-railroad McLean County Court decision was reversed. Lincoln, Joy, and their associate counsel had won for the Illinois Central.

Lincoln submitted a big bill for his legal services—$5,000. This steep statement shocked the railroad's officials and they held up payment. Although the amount of money saved to the railroad by its victory in court as argued by Lincoln and Joy was considerable, the size of Lincoln's fee was mostly unheard of in the West. The angry Illinois Central management continued to be delinquent in their satisfaction of Lincoln's $5,000 retainer for nearly a year. Lincoln sued the railroad to collect it. Thus a new suit emerged, *Abraham Lincoln v. the Illinois Central Railroad,* in the McLean County Circuit Court.

Lincoln's collection suit was called in court on June 18, 1857. No one appearing for the railroad, the court awarded Lincoln $5,000 by default. Five days later, however, on motion of the railroad's attorney, John M. Douglass, the verdict was set aside, and another jury was called. The new jury found for Lincoln in the amount of $4,800, since Lincoln had previously been paid an initial part retainer of $200.

But Lincoln found more delay in collecting on his judgment. On August 1 an execution was issued to the McLean County sheriff to seize enough of the Illinois Central's property to satisfy Lincoln's judgment. On the 12th he deposited $4,800 in his bank, the Springfield Marine and Fire Insurance Company.

Highly significant in Lincoln's life, more than a minor event in American history, was this large fee from the Illinois Central. For it aided in enabling Lincoln to take time out from his law practice to campaign for United States Senator against Stephen A. Douglas during the next year—a campaign that paved his way to the White House.

III

Next to his retainer in the great Illinois Central case, Lincoln's most lucrative fee was received in 1855 from Manny and Company of Rockford, Illinois, a reaper manufacturer, from whom he received probably $1,000 for his hard but futile work as a minor associate counsel against Cyrus H. McCormick of Chicago, who was suing Manny for infringement of patent. It was a litigation in which he labored long and went to terrific trouble but was not appreciated by the nationally known and more distinguished associate counsel with whom he was allied for the defense of Manny. This case, *McCormick v. Manny et al,* was subsequently called Lincoln's "Reaper Case."

American farmers' demands for improved reaping and harvesting machinery, with resulting attractive profits to be earned by inventors, manufacturers, promoters, and infringers of patents, led to fierce competition among the inventors, makers, and entrepeneurs of such labor-saving agricultural equipment. Soon incessant law suits were filed against business rivals for infringement of patents. Too, a law suit was recognized as a cheap and excellent method of advertising one's reaper or harvester, since such litigations filled newspaper columns.

Head and shoulders above all other reaper inventors and manufacturers was Cyrus H. McCormick, who sued John H. Manny and his associates of Rockford for infringement of patents. McCormick's rivals in the East joined Manny and his group in their defense against McCormick, although they did not appear on record in the litigation. Huge sums of money were raised for attorney's retainers on both sides, with nationally known counsel opposing each other. "I should not be willing to pay the costs in this case for one of the best patents in the country," wrote one McCormick employee in 1855. McCormick retained as his counsel Edward M. Dickerson, celebrated New York patent lawyer, and Reverdy Johnson, one of the leaders of the American bar. George Harding of Philadelphia, who was partly responsible for the establishment of some fundamental doctrines of United States patent law, was retained by the heavily-financed Manny. Harding chose as his associate counsel Peter H. Watson of Washington, a good legal "fixer" and influence peddler, and Edwin M. Stanton of Pittsburgh, destined to be Lincoln's Secretary of War. Harding, Watson, and Stanton, believing that the suit would be tried at Springfield, believed that it would be wise to employ a popular, influential local lawyer. They brought in Lincoln. "Since Lincoln," writes Professor Hutchinson, biographer of McCormick, "was known to be a friend of Judge Drummond, in whose court the case would be heard, he was retained."

Lincoln labored diligently and long on his brief for Manny, even going to Rockford, near Chicago, to study Manny's reaper and its intricate parts. Then he wrote his associate counsel Watson in Washington, who was apparently ignoring Lincoln and seeking to have him withdrawn from the case, since they were working to have the coming trial moved from Springfield, Illinois, to Cincinnati, Ohio. On July 23 Lincoln's letter stated:

"At our interview here [in Springfield] in June, I understood you to say you would send me copies of the Bill and Answer in the case of McCormick vs. Manny and Co. and also of depositions, as fast as they could be taken and printed. I have had nothing from you since. However, I attended the U. S. Court at Chicago, and while there, got copies of the Bill and Answer. I write this particularly to urge you to forward on to me the additional evidence as fast as you can. During August, and the remainder of this month, I can devote some time to the case, and, of course, I want all the material that can be had.

"During my stay at Chicago, I went out to Rockford, and spent half a day, examining and studying Manny's Machine."

The coming trial was soon transferred from Chicago to Cincinnati, by agreement of both sides. September came, and still Lincoln had heard not the slightest word from Watson or his other associate counsel about the case. On the first of that month he sent off an inquiry to Manny and Company, the defendant:

"Since I left Chicago about the 18th of July, I have heard nothing concerning the Reaper suit. I addressed a letter to Mr. Watson, at Washington, requesting him to forward me the evidence, from time to time, as it should be taken, but I have received no answer from him.

"Is it still the understanding that the case is to be heard at Cincinnati on the 20th inst.?

"Please write me on receipt of this."

Lincoln's associate counsel for Manny continued to pay no attention to him, leaving him completely ignorant of how they proposed to handle the defense against McCormick. After all, since the trial was to be held in Cincinnati, instead of at Springfield as at first planned, they no longer needed Lincoln. Too, they considered him not worth too much attention, or even common courtesy, since he was then not too greatly known, and would not be for another three years, when he would cross verbal swords with Senator Douglas in the great debates.

Lincoln nonetheless turned up at Cincinnati in late September, 1855, armed with briefs which he had prepared after long study in the technical fields of reaper mechanics and patent law. He particularly wanted to have a legal duel in court with Reverdy Johnson, one of McCormick's cousel, a nationally feared pleader, and future United States Senator from Maryland. One Cincinnati lawyer, W. M. Dickson, later recounted: "Mr. Lincoln had prepared himself with the greatest care; his ambition was to speak in the case and measure words with the renowned lawyer from Baltimore . . . He came with the fond hope of making fame in a forensic contest with Reverdy Johnson. He was pushed aside, humiliated and mortified."

Lincoln was given no active part in the trial, for Harding, Watson, and Stanton decided that he would not only not be needed but that his mere appearance might jeopardize the case. Whatever their motives, they effectively side-tracked him. Stanton acted particularly rudely toward the man into whose presidential Cabinet he was to enter within seven years. The irascible Pittsburgh attorney is quoted as insultingly describing the Springfield lawyer as: "A long, lank creature from Illinois, wearing a dirty linen duster for a coat, on the back of which the perspiration had splotched wide stains that resembled a map of the continent."

Lincoln, after his rejection from the *McCormick v. Manny* trial in Cincinnati, returned to Springfield deeply hurt. Watson sent him a check for his services. But Lincoln returned it. Watson mailed it back to him, so Lincoln decided to keep it, since Watson insisted that he had earned it. The amount is not definitely known; but today Rockford citizens, in stories handed down from their ancestors, maintain that Watson's check to Lincoln was for $600. This, added to $400 which had previously been advanced, would make his total retainer from Manny $1,000.

IV

One celebrated case handled by Lincoln was part and parcel of the commercial rivalry between Chicago and St. Louis. Tried at the United States District Court at Chicago in long drawn-out proceedings, this was the so-called "bridge" litigation. Sometimes it was called the "Effie Afton" case. Officially on the Court docket it was *Hurd v. Rock Island Bridge Company.*

This legal fight was provoked by a Mississippi River steamboat, the *Effie Afton,* which crashed into a privately owned bridge and destroyed a span. The bridge located at Rock Island, Illinois, was owned by the Rock Island Bridge Company. Back of that resulting law suit was the struggle between Missouri water transportation interests and Illinois railroad groups, all part of the incessant economic and legal fights that helped to make St. Louis a secondary transportation center to Chicago.

The Rock Island bridge was the first across the Mississippi, completed in the spring of 1856. In May the *Effie Afton* crashed against the bridge, destroying part of it, and then the ship's owner, Jacob S. Hurd, and his associates brought suit against the bridge's owners, the Rock Island Bridge Company, for damages. Hurd and his backers were supported by steamboat interests up and down the river. The St. Louis Chamber of Commerce, dismally foreseeing the adverse effect on their city of railroad bridges across the Mississippi—St. Louis was the center of steamboat transportation—promoted the cause of Hurd against the bridge company.

Lincoln, along with Norman B. Judd of Chicago and Joseph Knox of Rock Island, represented the bridge company, defendants. Within three years Judd, as Chairman of the Republican State Central Committee of Illinois, would skilfully and successfully take the lead in securing the party's presidential nomination for Lincoln.

The long trial was held during September, 1857, in the United States District Court at Chicago, presided over by Mr. Justice John McLean of the United States Supreme Court, sitting on circuit.

The *Effie Afton* owners, in demanding damages from the bridge company, alleged that the bridge was an obstruction to navigation. The company, with Lincoln, Judd, and Knox as its counsel, maintained that the accident, so called, was in fact an intentional and premeditated act.

The questions involved proved extremely complicated, embracing mechanical engineering, bridge construction, river currents and their varying velocity, the size and navigation of vessels, and other problems bewilderingly technical to the layman.

Lincoln went into court adequately prepared. He had a mechanical turn of mind, as evidenced by his invention for aiding ships over shoals, patented eight years before. Too, he had previously argued two cases in the federal district court involving the question of the obstruction of navigable rivers by the construction of bridges.

During fourteen days witnesses for both sides testified. Eye-witnesses to the accident of the *Effie Afton,* shipowners and shipbuilders, river men, civil and government engineers passed through the grilling and cross-examination of contending counsel. The opponents of the bridge endeavored to convince the jury that the river could not legally be obstructed by a bridge, and that this particular Rock Island bridge, defended by Lincoln, was so situated as to constitute a constant peril to all boats sailing on the river.

At long last both sides rested their cases and began their addresses to the jury. Lincoln, in closing the arguments for the defense on September 22 and 23, 1857, rose to answer the contentions of the plaintiff's lawyers. He opened his argument by stressing that he would not "assail anybody" and would be "not ill natured." But he contended: "There is some conflict of testimony in the case, but one quarter of such a number of witnesses seldom agree, and even if all had been on one side some discrepancy might have been expected. We are to try to reconcile them, and to believe that they are not intentionally erroneous, as long as we can." He told the jury that he had "no prejudice against steamboats or steamboat men, nor any against St. Louis." But he pointed out: "St. Louis as a commercial place may desire that this bridge should not stand, as it is adverse to her commerce, diverting a portion of it from the river."

Lincoln then assured the jurors that it would not be pleasing to him to have the Mississippi River blocked up, then emphasized: "But there is a travel from East to West, whose demands are not less important than that of the river," and he mentioned railroad travel which needed bridges to cross the river. This East-West rail travel, he argued, "has its rights," just as the North-South water transportation.

Lincoln went into technical details to show his own version of why the *Effie Afton* met her tragic fate. He read from the testimony of various witnesses to support his contention that the boat's starboard wheel was not working while she steamed through the stream; and he recited testimony of other witnesses to show that the captain knew that the wheel was not functioning. He explained to the jurors about the currents of the river at that point where it was crossed by the Rock Island Bridge.

He contended that the captain had failed to use reasonable care in piloting the *Effie Afton* past that point.

Lincoln talked from Tuesday afternoon through Wednesday morning. But he knew when to stop. "Gentlemen," he addressed the jury in conclusion, "I have not exhausted my stock of information and there are more things I could suggest regarding the case, but as I have doubtless used up my time, I presume I had better close."

Following a lengthy argument by one of the opposing counsel, Justice McLean charged the jury. After several hours of deliberation the jurors divided nine to three in favor of the bridge. They reported that they could not agree. McLean dismissed the jury.

Lincoln collected a $400 fee from the Rock Island Bridge Company.

After the jury disagreement, Hurd abandoned any further attempt to secure remuneration for his loss. The river interests, however, started new proceedings, though not in the Chicago district, which they decided was not the happiest forum for their cause. They began another action, this time in the United States District Court for the Southern District of Iowa. James Ward, a St. Louis steamboat owner, charged that the bridge was a nuisance. The bridge was declared by the Court to be "a common and public nuisance," and the bridge company was ordered to restore that part of the bridge within the State of Iowa. An appeal was taken to the United States Supreme Court, which reversed the lower court. This proved the final chapter in the celebrated *"Effie Afton"* litigation concerning the Rock Island bridge.

V

Lincoln also handled criminal cases in his diverse law practice, including those involving murder, the first being his successful defense of the killer, Henry B. Truett, in 1838. After profound research on Lincoln's legal career, Reverend William E. Barton concluded that Lincoln did not work up his criminal cases in law libraries but emphasized an appeal to the jurors. Barton has declared: "Lincoln was not given to careful preparation of his criminal cases. He took them as they came, and depended far more upon his ability to influence a jury."

By far the best known criminal case which Lincoln handled was his defense of William ("Duff") Armstrong, son of his late New Salem crony, Jack Armstrong (leader of the Clary's Grove boys back in the early 1830's). Duff Armstrong and another man were charged with murdering James Metzker. This case, tried at Beardstown, in Cass County, during May, 1858 ended in Armstrong's acquittal presumably by the use of an almanac.

Armstrong's troubles actually started one Saturday night, often a time of disorder, rowdyism, and drunken violence on the frontier, in August, 1857, at a camp meeting in Mason County. Some rough, alcohol-crazed men, among them "Duff" Armstrong, James H. Norris, and Metzker engaged in a brawl using fists and other weapons. Metzker was badly beaten by Armstrong and Norris. The injured Metzker then rode off to his home on his horse but supposedly fell from the mount at least twice. He died at his house three days later. Armstrong and Norris were arrested and charged with Metzker's murder. Norris had already killed a man in Havana, Illinois, but had been acquitted. Now he was tried for Metzker's death, found guilty, and sentenced to the penitentiary for eight years, though the Governor later pardoned him.

Armstrong was tried separately for Metzker's murder. His local attorneys secured a change of venue for his trial from Mason County to Beardstown, Cass County.

Lincoln, in the midst of political maneuvers to have himself named Republican candidate for the Senate, acted as Armstrong's counsel. He supposedly offered his services to Armstrong's mother in a letter, the original of which has never been found, which was published and republished throughout the country after Lincoln's death. It read:

> Dear Mrs. Armstrong: I have just heard of your deep affliction, and the arrest of your son for murder. I can hardly believe that he can be capable of the crime alleged against him. It does not seem possible. I am anxious that he should be given a fair trial at any rate; and gratitude for your long-continued kindness to me in adverse circumstances prompts me to offer my humble services gratuitously in his behalf.
>
> It will afford me an opportunity to requite, in a small degree, the favors I received at your hand, and that of your lamented husband, when your roof afforded me a grateful shelter, without money and without price.

Whether or not this letter from Lincoln to Hannah Armstrong is a forgery penned after Lincoln was buried—this author considers it a spurious document, lacking Lincoln's phrasing and style—he turned up at Beardstown to defend "Duff." At that precise time Lincoln also had a divorce case that he was handling, *Ruth Gill v. Jonathan Gill,* pending in the court there.

One young Cass County attorney, Abram Bergen, later a Judge in Kansas, claims to have attended Armstrong's trial, and describes Lincoln there: "While waiting for the Armstrong case to be called . . . Lincoln sat with his head thrown back, his steady gaze apparently fixed upon one spot of the blank ceiling, entirely oblivious to what was happening about him. . . . But when he began to talk his eyes brightened perceptibly, and every facial movement seemed to emphasize his feeling and add expression to his thoughts."

The prosecution's principal witness was Charles Allen. He had sworn in Norris's trial that, by the aid of a brightly shining moon, he had seen "Duff" Armstrong hit Metzker with a sling shot. Metzker, as the post mortem showed, had suffered two wounds on the head, one in the back of the brain alleged to have been inflicted by Norris using the neck-yoke of a wagon and the other in front, alleged to have been caused by a blow from Armstrong's sling shot. Either one of the blows, the presecution contended, had caused Metzker's death.

Lincoln found Allen a crafty and nimble witness. Allen testified that, though it was eleven o'clock at night when the fight occurred, and he stood 150 feet away from the combatants, he could see everything clearly because the moon was shining directly overhead at the time. When the State's Attorney, Hugh Fullerton, had finished questioning Allen, his star witness, the outlook for Lincoln's client looked bleak.

Then Lincoln cross-examined Allen. He adroitly led the witness to commit himself repetitiously to the statement that he could not be mistaken. Then Lincoln went after the witness. He riddled Allen's testimony by confronting him with an almanac for the year 1857, which showed that, at the precise hour of Armstrong's fight with Metzker, the moon was not in the position stated by Allen. On the contrary, the moon then lay low in the sky, within an hour of setting.

Lincoln, as an experienced trial lawyer, knew how to build the foundations for the complete repudiation of Allen as a witness. By a deft performance of cross-examination, in a courteous manner more seductive than antagonistic, Lincoln finished off Allen as a reliable witness.

In behalf of Armstrong, Lincoln called Nelson Watkins as a witness. Watkins testified that the sling shot found near the scene of the alleged crime and produced by the State as the weapon with which Armstrong had struck Metzker, was in fact Watkins's own property, that he, Watkins, had it in his home on the night of the supposed murder, and that he had thrown it away, at the exact spot where it had been found, on the day following the alleged murder. Lincoln later expressed the opinion that Watkins's testimony proved as helpful to his defense of Armstrong as did the refutation of Allen's testimony by use of the almanac.

Lincoln also put on the stand a physician, Dr. Charles Parker, as a defense witness. Parker testified, in reply to a hypothetical question propounded by Lincoln, about the possibility of Metzker meeting his death when he fell from his horse. Dr. Parker apparently made an influential impression on the Court, for Judge James Harriott, who presided at the trial, maintained that the physician had given the most persuasive testimony in the defendant's behalf.

Lincoln, in his summation to the jury, pleaded for an hour for Armstrong's life. He made effective use of his almanac from all accounts, pointing out to the jurors that, if the chief prosecution witness, Allen, had been so badly mistaken as to the position of the moon, he could be in gross error on other relevant points.

Lincoln made certain to preserve his defendant's rights on appeal, in the event that the jury should find him guilty. Lincoln did this by his requests to Judge Harriott for instructions to the jury. The Judge's charge to the jurors declared:

"The Court instructs the jury that if they have any reasonable doubt as to whether Metzker came to his death by the blow on the eye or the blow on the back of the head, they are to find the defendant not guilty, unless they further believe from the evidence, beyond all reasonable doubt, that Armstrong and Norris acted on concert against Metzker and that Norris struck the blow on the back of the head.

"That if they believe from the evidence that Norris killed Metzker, they are to acquit Armstrong unless they also believe from the evidence, beyond a reasonable doubt, that Armstrong acted with Norris in the killing on purpose to kill or hurt Metzker."

The jury, after one hour's deliberation, found Lincoln's client, "Duff" Armstrong, not guilty.

After the trial a rumor was circulated that, in discrediting Allen as a witness, Lincoln had deliberately used the wrong almanac—one for a year other than 1857. It was a charge that was to be levelled at him when he ran for President two years later.

Lincoln, as President, performed another extraordinarily significant service for "Duff" Armstrong. The young man was serving in the Eighty-fifth Illinois Volunteers in the war, stationed in Kentucky, and his mother, Hannah, appealed to Lincoln to have him discharged from the army because he suffered from sciatic rheumatism. The President had him mustered out, and in September, 1863, assured Mrs. Armstrong in a note: "I have just ordered the discharge of your boy, William, as you say, now at Louisville, Ky."

VI

Lincoln acted as counsel, sometimes for the defense, occasionally for the prosecution, in other murder cases and many sundry cases involving lesser crimes.

In 1850 he defended Samuel Short, a farmer from Taylorville, in the Christian County Circuit Court on a charge of shooting and wounding with intent to kill. Short had fired his shotgun at a group of boys who were raiding his melon patch, seriously wounding one of them. Short was indicted and tried for this offense. Lincoln succeeded in securing his acquittal.

The exonerated Farmer Short showed his lack of appreciation by refusing to pay Lincoln's attorney's fee of $10. Lincoln promptly sued him for it in a Justice of the Peace court.

Lincoln, in 1859, served as one of the counsel for Quinn Harrison, known as "Peachy," who with a knife had mortally wounded Greek Crafton, a fellow villager from Pleasant Plains in Sangamon County. Harrison was the grandson of Reverend Peter Cartwright, Lincoln's now aged Democratic opponent in the race for Congress thirteen years before. The murdered man, Crafton, was a student in Lincoln's law office. Associated with Lincoln in "Peachy" Harrison's defense were his law partner, Herndon; his former law partner, Logan; and Shelby M. Cullom, future Governor of Illinois and United States Senator, best known today as Senate sponsor of the federal Interstate Commerce Act.

Harrison's trial for Crafton's murder was held at the Court House in Springfield during September, 1859. After the prosecution finished its case against Harrison, it looked like wilful, premeditated murder.

Cartwright was called to give evidence about his nephew. The white-haired evangelist told of his visit to the dying Crafton, avowing that the latter had freely begged that his assaulter, Harrison, be forgiven since it was his (Crafton's) fault. Lincoln and Logan, for the defense, argued for the admission of Cartwright's testimony as evidence.

Lincoln closed the argument for Harrison's defense. One Illinois old-timer subsequently told of Lincoln's "moving power and pathos of that appeal to the jury." More dramatically than he had ever acted in any previous pleading in court, Lincoln brought forward the dying scene of Crafton, who as a last request asked that his assaulter, Harrison, be forgiven. In the words of John M. Zane, a student of Lincoln's law career and an Illinois attorney himself: "His listeners were moved to tears, as he described the repentant sinner on his deathbed, stretching out his hands with the hope of a farther shore, seeking to right his life with his salvation and imploring that he should have no part in bringing even his slayer to the scaffold."

Lincoln persuaded the jury that they ought not to wrench from the dead man, Crafton, his best claim to Divine mercy. The jurors acquitted Harrison.

In 1853 Lincoln was appointed by the Tazewell County Circuit Court, held in Pekin, to serve as special prosecutor in a rape case, *The People v. Thomas Delny*. Charged with raping a seven-year-old girl, Delny stood trial on an indictment drawn by Lincoln. Lincoln's paper recited: "That Thomas Delny, a male person above the age of fourteen years . . . with force of arms . . . in and upon Jane Ann Rupert, a female child under the age of ten years, to wit of the age of seven years, ... feloniously did make an assault, and her the said Jane Ann Ruppert, then and there feloniously did unlawfully and carnally know; contrary to the form of the statute in such case made and provided."

Lincoln secured Delny's conviction. He was sentenced to eighteen years in the penitentiary. Feeling ran riot against the child's convicted raper, one Illinois paper reporting: "A mob came very near getting possession of the base wretch and hanging him."

Lincoln, early in 1857, was retained by his young friend and circuit law-partner, Ward H. Lamon, who had moved to Bloomington and been elected Prosecuting Attorney of the Eighth Judicial Circuit, to aid him in the prosecution of Isaac Wyant for murder.

Wyant had, in the presence of witnesses in De Witt County, ended the life of Anson Rusk with four bullets two years previous, after Rusk had shot him in the arm, necessitating amputation of Wyant's arm. The murder indictment against Wyant was transferred to Bloomington, McLean County, on a change of venue. With Lincoln and Lamon prosecuting Wyant, and Leonard Swett of Bloomington and others defending him, the trial was held in March, 1857.

Lincoln opened and closed the case against Wyant. The next morning Defense Counsel Swett, over Lincoln's objection, proceeded to establish through testimony of neighbors, that for some time prior to the feud between Wyant and the murdered Rusk, Wyant had acted in an irrational manner; that Wyant, brooding over the loss of his arm from Rusk's bullet, had his mind unhinged. Swett produced the defendant's sister, who testified to a tendency toward insanity in the Wyant family, citing the case of an uncle who had become completely mentally deranged because he had lost a "girl he had sparked." Lincoln, in rebuttal, called sixteen witnesses to contradict those of the defense. One eye-witness later quoted prosecutor Lincoln, cross-examining a physician called by the defense. Lincoln presumably said to the physician: "You say, doctor, that this man picks his head, and by that you infer that he is insane. Now, I sometimes pick my head, and those joking fellows at Springfield tell me that there may be a living, moving cause for it, and that the trouble isn't at all on the inside. It's only a case for fine-tooth combs."

Lincoln failed to secure conviction of Wyant. The jury found the defendant not guilty by reason of insanity and recommended that he be committed to the State asylum at Jacksonville.

VII

Lincoln's last important case before he was nominated for President in 1860 was that popularly known as the "sandbar" litigation. It concerned ownership of title to extensive and valuable lake-front property created by the accretion on the shores of Lake Michigan in or near Chicago. It was tried in the United States Circuit Court for the Northern District of Illinois at Chicago.

Prior to 1833 the Chicago River, through what later became the old part of Chicago, running from the west toward the east, just before entering Lake Michigan, turned to the south and had formed between the River and the Lake a "sandbar." But in 1833 the United States Government made, from the turn to the south, straight out into the Lake, a channel between two piers, called the North pier and the South pier. This left the "sandbar" south of the new channel. Thereupon the Lake waters washed in sand along the north side of the North pier, making very valuable land out of what had heretofore been water of the Lake. The case, *Johnston v. Jones and Marsh,* in which Lincoln acted as one of the defense counsel, was concerned with the land formed alongside the North pier thus formed by the accretion from the Lake. Since the Lake shore on the north side of the new channel had receded, the legal point at issue concerned the ownership of this newly formed land, north of the new channel.

This case was first tried in 1855, and was reversed by the United States Supreme Court early the following year for a misdirection of the court, in *Jones v. Johnston.* The litigation was remanded for a new trial and was tried a second time, but the jury disagreed. The third trial was held early in 1860, and it was then that Lincoln appeared in the case.

Lincoln's reputation as a lawyer and powerful Republican state leader, his political reputation catapulted by his showing against Douglas in the Senate campaign almost two years earlier, and his name now being circulated as a possible presidential candidate, persuaded William Jones and Sylvester Marsh to retain him to argue their interests over the disputed "accretion" land. A formidable interest behind Jones and Marsh was a railroad operating in Illinois.

The "sandbar" case was tried in the federal court at Chicago during March, before Judge Thomas Drummond. Among the opposing counsel for the plaintiff was the high-priced Isaac N. Arnold of Chicago, Lincoln's fast friend personally, who was soon to be a Republican congressman, a strong supporter of Lincoln's administration in the House of Representatives, and a future biographer of Lincoln.

Judge Drummond handed down a decision upholding Lincoln's contention.

On May 25, one week following his nomination as Republican candidate for President, Lincoln deposited $500 in his account and a like amount in Herndon's account at a Springfield bank. Probably these sums included some of the fee received from his clients in the "sandbar" case.

Lincoln's very last appearance as attorney in any court was in the case of *Dawson v. Ennis and Ennis,* which involved infringement of a patent right in a double plow. That was on June 20, 1860, when he stood before the nation as his party's presidential standard-bearer.

In that litigation Lincoln and two other lawyers represented the plaintiff, who sought to recover damages of $10,000 because the defendant had violated an agreement not to sell a certain patented plow. Lincoln lost that case, but the verdict was not to be announced until five days after his inauguration as President of the United States in March, 1861.

VIII

From the law Lincoln learned more than mere technical knowledge of rules of practice, of demurrers, of pleas in abatement and pleas at the bar. His practice from 1837 until 1860, interrupted only by his single term in Congress during 1847-49, taught him about men and their possible inner motives. Also he became an intimate friend of many lawyers who were influential in Whig and Republican politics in Illinois, who later aided his rise to State and national power. Particularly effective in securing him the presidential nomination were his old friends of the Eighth Judicial Circuit, Judge David Davis of Bloomington and Norman B. Judd of Chicago, with whom he was associated as defense counsel in the *"Effie Afton"* bridge case. By 1860 Judd was Chairman of the Republican State Central Committee of Illinois. Judge Davis and Judd were destined to be Lincoln's principal "Warwicks."

The law, too, prepared Lincoln for the presidency. Since the war between North and South in 1861 was to be grounded more on the constitutional question of whether the Southern states possessed the legal right to secede, rather than on the moral and economic issue of Negro slavery, Lincoln's pre-presidential law practice carries major significance.

While Lincoln was practicing law, this North-South controversy over slavery was gradually growing toward the ultimate disruption of the Union, precipitated by, more than any other single incident, the passage of Senator Stephen A. Douglas's Kansas-Nebraska Act of 1854.

ANTI-SLAVERY MODERATE

12

I

LAWYER Lincoln participated only casually in politics for five years after his service in Congress, but he returned to the political arena almost full time in 1854, following passage of Stephen A. Douglas's Anti-Nebraska Act.

The fruits of the Mexican War, ended in 1848, proved bitter to the United States because the ceded territories raised again the old slavery issue in a more explosive form. When California, ceded by Mexico, petitioned Congress for admission into the Union as a free State, with slavery prohibited, a sectional controversy of almost fatal proportions engulfed the nation. Throughout most of 1850 the halls of the United States Senate and House of Representatives resounded with angry oratory and threats to break up the Union. Northern and Southern sectionalists threatened disunion and civil war over the status of slavery in California and New Mexico.

This mid-century crisis, so pregnant with danger for the survival of the nation, did not unduly ruffle the Former Congressman from Springfield. Though it appeared that the Republic might be split over the controversy on slavery, Lincoln showed scant interest in the important debates in Congress and throughout the country. His main concern with politics at the turn of the half century centered on his persistent efforts to persuade President Zachary Taylor's administration to award federal jobs to his friends and associates among Illinois Whigs. But hardly any of his recommendations for patronage were heeded by Whig officials in Washington. He was treated in 1850 as inconsiderately as in the previous year, when he had unsuccessfully tried to have himself appointed Commissioner of the General Land Office.

Busy with the law and his family affairs, Lincoln discouraged a movement to make him a candidate for Congress once more. In June, 1850, he sent a public letter to the Whig *Illinois State Journal:* "I neither seek, expect, or desire a nomination for a seat in the next Congress. . . . I prefer my name should not be brought forward in that connection."

After President Taylor, weakened by the infirmities of age, burdens of his office, and the importunities of office-seekers, died in July, Lincoln journeyed to Chicago, where he delivered a eulogy to the dead Chief Executive. He ended his speech on a morbidly philosophical note: "The death of the late President may not be without its use, in reminding us, that *we,* too, must die." And he recited parts of his favorite poem, "Oh, why should the spirit of mortal be proud."

Lincoln approached the administration of Taylor's successor, President Millard Fillmore, for federal patronage for his party associates. But during 1850-51 he met as little success with Fillmore's followers in Washington as he had with Taylor's administration. At the end of 1851 Lincoln signed an appeal, with others, for a Whig convention at Springfield in order "to secure a more thorough organization of the Whig party at an early day." Clearly, Whig prospects in Lincoln's State and the nation did not look optimistic.

Lincoln in the following year, 1852, joined other citizens in publicly appealing for the freedom of Hungary from the Austrian Hapsburg yoke, and he called for a meeting endorsing the visiting Hungarian nationalist leader, Louis Kossuth. Later in the year he made two addresses for the Whig presidential candidate, General Winfield Scott, but they were uninspired speeches and not among his best. His eulogy on the death of Henry Clay, the political idol of his younger years, in that same year, was his best effort of that period. In his oration commemorating Clay he revealed his own views of the slavery question. They were similar to those of Clay, a very moderately anti-slavery man who believed in permanence of the Union as the paramount object.

In his eulogy Lincoln said of the venerable Kentuckian: "He knew no North, no South, no East, no West, but only the Union, which held them all in its sacred circle." The sectional dispute of 1820, adjusted by the Missouri Compromise, Lincoln noted, "sprang from that unfortunate source of discord—negro slavery. . . . A fearful and angry struggle instantly followed. This alarmed thinking men, more than any other question, because, unlike all the former, it divided the country by geographical lines." But thanks to Clay's magnificent "inventive genius, and his devotion to his country in the day of her extreme peril," Clay had found a way out in 1820. Thereafter the Kentucky statesman "seems constantly to have been regarded by all, as *the* man for a crisis." So it was in the Nullification crisis of 1832-33, when South Carolina rebelled, and also in that of 1850 "the task of devising a mode of adjustment seems to have been cast upon Mr. Clay, by common consent."

Although "Mr. Clay was the owner of slaves," Lincoln pointed out, he stood for something greater: "He ever was, on principle and in feeling, opposed to slavery. The very earliest, and one of the last public efforts of his life, separated by a period of more than fifty years, were both made in favor of gradual emancipation of the slaves in Kentucky." But, Lincoln declared, "he did not perceive, as I think no wise man has perceived, how it [slavery] could be at *once* eradicated, without producing a greater evil, even to the cause of human liberty itself. His feeling and his judgment, therefore, ever led him to oppose both extremes of opinion on the subject."

Two years later, in 1854, the most distinguished of all Democrats, Senator Stephen A. Douglas of Lincoln's own Illinois, succeeded, with President Franklin Pierce's support, in persuading both houses of Congress to pass his Kansas-Nebraska Act. That measure, whose main intent was to provide territorial government for the wild Nebraska lands, contained in it the explosive sectional clause repealing the slavery-restriction line above the 36°, 30′ line provided in the Missouri Compromise of 1820.

During that fall of 1854, Abraham Lincoln, inspired by the fight against Douglas's law, devoted more time to politics than he had since he had left Congress more than five years before. He would continue in politics until Booth's bullet brought him down in 1865.

II

Lincoln, six years later, wrote of himself in the third person: "In 1854, his profession [of law] had almost superseded the thought of politics in his mind, when the repeal of the Missouri compromise aroused him as he had never been before.

"In the autumn of that year he took the stump with no broader practical aim or object than to secure, if possible, the re-election of Hon. Richard Yates to congress. His speeches at once attracted a more marked attention than they had ever before done. As the canvass proceeded, he was drawn to different parts of the state, outside of Mr. Yates' district. He did not abandon the law, but gave his attention, by turns, to that and politics. The State agricultural fair was at Springfield that year, and Douglas was announced to speak there."

It was the big Democratic game that Lincoln was hunting: Douglas, the Little Giant himself, the nation's most distinguished Democrat, President Pierce not excepted. Seemingly everywhere Douglas went to defend his Kansas-Nebraska Act, Lincoln went on his trail to answer him, first at Chicago, then downstate to various places, and finally at the Agricultural Fair in Lincoln's own home town.

The Illinois State Fair opened at Springfield on October 3, 1854. Amidst prize cattle, hogs and horses, exhibitions of corn, and displays of bread, jellies, jams, and cakes, the squatty, self-esteemed Senator Douglas, despite his low height, shown above all, vigorously explaining the righteousness of his Kansas-Nebraska legislation and hurling invectice at his foes who, he charged, deliberately misrepresented him on the slavery question. He spoke at the Hall of Representatives, greeted by hurrahs of approval, for his repeal of the slavery-restriction clause of the Missouri Compromise.

While Douglas was speaking, one of his friends, Samuel S. Gilbert of Carlinville, noticed Lincoln walking back and forth in the lobby of the hall, all of the while listening intently to Douglas's every word. When the meeting broke up and the crowd was passing out of the hall, Lincoln's tall, gaunt figure appeared on the landing of a stairway and he announced that, on the next afternoon, Congressman Lyman Trumbull, an "Anti-Nebraska" or anti-Douglas Democrat, would address the people in that same hall, replying to the Illinois Senator. But if anything happened to prevent Trumbull from coming, Lincoln added, he himself would make reply to Douglas.

On that afternoon of October 4, 1854, Lincoln mounted the platform in the Hall of Representatives, clad in shirt sleeves, without collar or tie. His ill-fitting trousers, too short for his lanky legs, added to his untidiness. There Lincoln made his first important speech as an anti-slavery leader. He came well prepared. As the opposition Democratic *State Register* revealed: "He had been nosing for weeks in the State Library, pumping his brain and imagination for points and arguments." Lincoln, not unfamiliar in the art of self-advertising, had asked that Douglas be present and make reply if he wished to do so, and the celebrated Senator was there.

In his speech Lincoln first cracked a few jokes, or what then were recognized as jokes, in the words of the *State Register,* "the character of which will be understood by all who know him, by simply saying they were *Lincolnisms.*"

Lincoln did not assume strongly Northern sectional ground. He knew of the conservative sentiment in his part of Illinois and in the southern counties. Nor did he assail the Kansas-Nebraska Act as a "plot" of the "Slave Power," as so many rabid anti-slavery men were doing in their oratorical and editorial "open season" on Douglas. Lincoln's words were free from abuse and vituperation, which made them more effective. The crux of his argument lay in the paraphrase as reported by the Whig *Illinois State Journal:*

"It is vain, said Mr. Lincoln, for any advocate of the repeal of the Missouri Compromise to contend that it gives no sanction or encouragement to slavery. . . . The Missouri Compromise forbade slavery to go north of 36°-30′. Our government breaks down that restriction and opens the door for slavery to enter where it could not go. This is practically legislating for slavery, recognising it, extending it. . . .

"It is said that the slave holder has the same political right to take his negroes to Kansas that a freeman has to take his hogs or his horses. This would be true if negroes were property in the same sense that hogs and horses are. But is this the case? It is notoriously not so."

Lincoln repeated his Springfield oration of October 4 twelve days later at Peoria. Some have even called this first major anti-slavery address by Lincoln his "Peoria Speech."

III

But while he was basking in the glory of his Springfield oration, Lincoln revealed that he was actually a moderate on the slavery issue.

Immediately after the speech, abolition-minded men, such as Owen Lovejoy and Ichabod Codding, tried to lure him into an embryo anti-slavery "Republican Party" which they were organizing on that very day. But Lincoln would have no part of that militantly abolitionist group and left Springfield to elude both Lovejoy and Codding.

When, four years later at Ottawa, Douglas in his joint debate with Lincoln accused him of "abolitionism" and referred to that October day when Lovejoy used Lincoln's name on the new Republican Party's resolutions adopted while Lincoln was purposely out of town, Lincoln answered Douglas. He explained:

"I say I never had anything to do with them [the resolutions]. . . . There was a call for a convention to form a Republican party at Springfield, and I think that my friend Mr. Lovejoy . . . had a hand in it. He tried to get me into it, and I would not go in. I believe it is also true, that I went away from Springfield when the convention was in session, to attend court in Tazewell County. It is true that they did place my name, though without my authority, upon that committee, and afterwards wrote me to attend the meeting of the committee, but I refused to do so, and I never had anything to do with that organization."

Herndon in later years always insisted that he persuaded Lincoln to get out of town in order to elude Lovejoy and Codding, declaring: "On learning that Lovejoy intended to approach him with an invitation, I hunted up Lincoln and urged him to avoid meeting the enthusiastic champion of Abolitionism," and Herndon told about how Lincoln took his son, Bob, and hurried out of town, on the pretext of having law business in Tazewell County.

While Lincoln hid out in Tazewell, Lovejoy, Codding, and their radically anti-slavery apostles held their "abolitionist" Republican meeting in Springfield, adopted fiery anti-slavery resolutions, and formed a party state central committee, on which they took the liberty of placing Lincoln's name!

Lincoln waxed furious when he belatedly learned that he had been placed on a Republican committee. He wrote a sharp letter rebuking Codding. "I have been perplexed some to understand," he told Codding, "why my name was placed on that committee. I was not consulted on the subject; nor was I apprized of the appointment until I discovered it by accident two or three weeks afterwards. I suppose that my opposition to the principle of slavery is as strong as that of any member of the Republican party; but I had also supposed that the *extent* to which I feel authorized to carry that opposition practically was not at all satisfactory to that party. The leading men who organized that party were present, on the 4th. of Oct. at the discussion between Douglas and myself at Springfield, and had full opportunity to not misunderstand my position. Do I misunderstand theirs? Please write, and inform me."

By that time, late 1854, Lincoln was out for a United States Senate seat.

The extent to which Lincoln was distrusted by advanced anti-slavery men in Illinois was manifest in contemporary correspondence. One citizen of Rockford in December, 1854, unburdened his mind to Congressman Elihu B. Washburne: "I have spoken to our Senator and Representative [in the Legislature] as to Lincoln for U.S. Senator. They are not committed but one thinks L. is not enough anti-slavery. He wishes him—L—to take the ground of 'no further extension of slavery'—'No more slave territory.'" The anti-slavery editor of the Galena *Jeffersonian,* Charles H. Ray, later of the Chicago *Press & Tribune,* in that same month confided to Washburne: "I must confess I am afraid of 'Abe.' . . . I have thought that he would not come up to the mark in a hand to hand fight with Southern influence and dictation;" and Ray mentioned Mrs. Lincoln's pro-slavery Kentucky family.

During those closing weeks of 1854 the ambitious Lincoln sent numerous letters to Whig leaders throughout Illinois, appealing for support in persuading their state senators and assemblymen in the Legislature to vote for him for United States Senator. To one leading citizen he sent this plea: "I have a suspicion that a Whig has been elected to the Legislature from Edgar. . . . Could you not make a mark with him for me, for U.S. Senator?—I really have some chance. . . . Let this be confidential." To one legislator: "You are a member of the Legislature, and have a vote to give. Think it over, and see whether you can do better than go for me." To another citizen: "I have got it into my head to be U.S. Senator, and I wish somehow to get at your Whig member, Mr. Babcock. I am not acquainted with him—could you not make or cause to be made, a mark with him for me? Would not Judge Kellogg lend a helping hand?" To Joseph Gillespie, his old colleague in the Legislature: "I should like to be remembered affectionately by you; and also, to have you make a mark for me with the Anti-Nebraska members, down your way. . . . We [Whigs] have the Legislature clearly enough on joint ballot; but the Senate is very close."

As Whig condidate for federal Senator when the Illinois Legislature voted on February 8, 1855, Lincoln led his opponents with 44 votes. Senator James Shields, the incumbent (the same State Auditor of 1842 with whom Lincoln had once almost fought a duel) drew 41 votes. Congressman Lyman Trumbull, insurgent "Anti-Nebraska" or anti-Douglas Democrat, had only 5. Other votes were scattered. Five more ballots were taken, with the result substantially the same. On the seventh ballot the Democrats switched their votes from Shields to Governor Joel A. Matteson.

Then on the succeeding eighth ballot Lincoln saw his votes transferred from himself to Trumbull, nominally a Democrat but an "Anti-Nebraska" leader and opponent of Douglas. Whigs and anti-slavery, anti-Douglas Democrats had agreed to unite on Trumbull, thus eliminating Lincoln as a candidate. Lincoln's vote on that eighth toboganned down to 15. Lincoln, out of the running, gave the word to his remaining supporters to go for Trumbull. From Lincoln's viewpoint, if he could not be elected United States Senator, an Anti-Nebraska Democrat like Trumbull was to be vastly more preferred than a Nebraska, or pro-Douglas, Democrat like Matteson. And so Lyman Trumbull, with Lincoln's aid, would be Douglas's Illinois colleague in the Senate at Washington, a development galling to the Little Giant.

The day following Trumbull's election Lincoln told Elihu B. Washburne about it. "The agony is over; and the result you doubtless know," he wrote Washburne. "I began with 44 votes, Shields 41, and Trumbull 5—yet Trumbull was elected. In fact 47 different members voted for me—getting three new ones on the second ballot, and losing four old ones."

But why was Lincoln defeated, then? He continued his story to Washburne: "How come my 47 to yield to T's 5? It was Govr. Matteson's work. He has been secretly a candidate ever since (even before) the fall election." That was Lincoln's own explanation of how he was beaten. He took his defeat philosophically, although he was deeply disappointed. Too, Lincoln drew consolation in reflecting on how distasteful Trumbull's election was to Douglas and his "Nebraska" Democrats. He concluded his letter to Washburne: "On the whole, it is perhaps as well for our general cause that Trumbull is elected. The Neb. men confess that they hate it worse than any thing that could have happened."

By "our general cause," Lincoln did not specify to Washburne, also a Whig, whether that meant Whig party advancement or the anti-slavery cause. Gleefully Lincoln could reflect that Douglas, at Washington, would have a colleague from his own Democratic Party and his own state constantly sniping at him. Democrats were working up to a terrible party split which was to Lincoln's ultimate advantage.

IV

The Illinois political landscape throughout 1855 was changing and confused, like that in the rest of the North. Veteran leaders were passing from the scene. Old combinations were declining, and new issues and slogans were crowding out the time-worn ones about banks, the tariff, and internal improvements. Senator Douglas's Democratic Party was now fractured into his own dominant faction, the "Nebraska" men, and Senator Trumbull's "Anti-Nebraska" advocates. Illinois Whigs were themselves split into Lincoln's own "Anti-Nebraska" followers, mildly anti-slavery, and those who had gone into the new anti-Catholic, anti-immigrant "American" or Know-Nothing third party.

Throughout 1855 Lincoln remained in his ever declining Whig Party. He feared to enter the new anti-slavery Republican Party, which had been organized in embryonic form in Illinois and other Northern states. Ever moderate in his views against slavery, and cautious to the point of opportunism where his future political career figured, he preferred to ride with the conservative sentiment of the central and lower counties, inhabited largely by descendants of Southern families, rather than go with the more radically anti-slavery sentiment of the northern counties, settled by moralistic New Englanders, upstate New Yorkers, and abolition-tinged German immigrants. The bulk of the State's Republican Party strength was then, and would remain, in Northern Illinois, not in Lincoln's home bailiwick downstate.

For the entire year of 1855, Lincoln clung tenaciously to Whiggery, resisting strenuous efforts to attract him into the nativistic Know-Nothing or "American" Party or into the radical anti-slavery "fusion" Republican Party. To Owen Lovejoy, still relentless in endeavoring to lure Lincoln into the Republican ranks, he wrote on August 11, 1855 that "not even *you* are more anxious to prevent the extension of slavery than I." But the time was not ripe for him to "fuse" with the Republican Party because Know-Nothingism had not yet entirely tumbled to pieces. "Until we can get the elements of this organization," he told Lovejoy about the American Party, "there is not sufficient materials to combat the Nebraska democracy with." He also expressed to Lovejoy his disapproval of the Know-Nothings' doctrines. He concluded: "I have no objection to 'fuse' with any body provided I can fuse on ground which I think is right; and I believe the opponents of slavery extension could now do this, if it were not for this K.N. ism."

From Lincoln's viewpoint the fight against the Douglas-dominated Democracy had to be waged on "Anti-Nebraska," or anti-slavery, grounds, not on anti-Catholic and anti-immigrant principles. One Ohio Republican politician put it this way: "Take care of the Dutch and Irish after the nigger question is settled."

Lincoln felt confused about where he stood, party-wise, at this precise time, with State and National Whiggery declining as an organization. Only two weeks after he wrote Lovejoy, he sent thoughts about politics and slavery to his close Kentucky crony, Joshua F. Speed: "I confess I hate to see the poor creatures hunted down, and caught, and carried back to their stripes, and unrewarded toil; but I bite my lip and keep quiet. . . . You enquire where I now stand. That is a disputed point. I think I am a whig; but others say there are no whigs, and that I am an abolitionist. . . . I am not a Know-Nothing. That is certain. How could I be? How can any one who abhors the oppression of negroes, be in favor of degrading classes of white people?"

The year 1855 closed with Lincoln still a Whig. He could not be swayed into the Republican Party ranks. He called himself a Whig—but an "Anti-Nebraska" Whig. And that was that.

V

In February, 1856, Lincoln, veering cautiously from Whiggery toward ideas of a new "Anti-Nebraska" party, had a confidential conference with Paul Selby, Whig editor of the *Morgan Journal* of Jacksonville, Illinois. Selby told Congressman Richard Yates about it in a note: "I have had an interview with Mr. Lincoln to-day, and some conversation in reference to matters we were talking about last evening. I wish you would endeavor to see him soon, at least before the Editorial Convention. He tells me he thinks he will try and have some business at Decatur at the time of the Convention."

Lincoln managed to "have some business at Decatur" on February 22. That Washington's Birthday, 1856, proved a decisive date in Republican Party annals. Not only was the party organized on a national basis at Pittsburgh, Pennsylvania, on that day, but Lincoln put in an appearance at the Anti-Nebraska Editorial Convention at Decatur, which laid ground work for a thriving Republican Party in Lincoln's own state. It was the first time that Lincoln ever sat down with leaders at a convention which was planning a new anti-slavery party. He aided in the drafting of resolutions and making arrangements for a state Republican convention to be held at Bloomington in three months, on May 29. But as yet he had not publicly cast his lot with the Republicans. He was still a Whig.

Soon the Whig *Illinois State Journal* of Springfield, which some called "Lincoln's paper," was printing kind words about Republicans—a curious and sudden turn of events.

When in early May a Sangamon County convention met at Springfield to select delegates to the coming Illinois state Republican Convention at Bloomington, Lincoln was riding the circuit in his law practice. But Herndon always claimed that he put Lincoln's name at the head of a list of citizens who signed the call for the anti-slavery "Anti-Nebraska" conclave at Bloomington. Actually Lincoln's name did appear at the top of that "call." According to Herndon, when Lincoln learned about his unauthorized action in placing the name, "A. Lincoln," to the call, he acquiesced, telling his law partner forgivingly: "All right; go ahead. Will meet you, radicals and all."

When May 20 arrived, Herndon, watching Lincoln, delightedly reported to Senator Trumbull that he had never seen Lincoln "so sanguine of success. . . . He is warm."

May turned out grim and bloodthirsty, but the events of that month provided new strength for the Republican Party. Kansas Territory again captured national notoriety when a sheriff's posse of pro-slavery men sacked the town of Lawrence. In Kansas, too, the crazed abolitionist, John Brown, scourged Pottawatomie with his cold-blooded murders. On the Senate floor Congressman Preston Brooks of South Carolina maimed with a cane the Republican Senator Charles Sumner of Massachusetts, providing a martyr for the new political party.

On the 29th Lincoln turned up at Bloomington, Illinois, for the state Republican convention. He was garbed in his long, sweat-stained linen duster and tall battered hat, in hand his old umbrella tied with a string.

Those who attended that convention at Major's Hall in Bloomington indicated that the new Illinois Republican Party, composed of more practical politicians than that started by Owen Lovejoy and Ichabod Codding almost two years previous, would be a latitudinarian creed—seemingly everybody in it except Douglas Democrats, slave-holders, Mormons, and Irish Roman Catholics. Seen in attendance were Anti-Nebraska Whigs, such as Lincoln, a few Old-Line Whigs such as Orville H. Browning, anti-German Know-Nothings, anti-Know-Nothing Germans, disgruntled Democrats, Anti-Nebraska Democrats, and numberless groups who detested Douglas, President Pierce, or the national and state Democratic Party doctrines and leadership.

On the state ticket nominated at that Bloomington conclave the various more potent factions were represented. William H. Bissell, for Governor, had been an Anti-Nebraska Democrat. Francis A. Hoffman, born in Germany, was nominated for Lieutenant-Governor; although he was later forced off the ticket because he failed to meet legal citizenship qualifications. Jesse K. Dubois, for State Auditor, had been an Anti-Nebraska Whig, like Lincoln. Ozias M. Hatch, for Secretary of State, and James Miller, for State Treasurer, were erstwhile Know-Nothings. "It was a coalition," commented two nineteenth-century historians, "which the Republicans were content to support with the hope of future reward."

The resolutions adopted at Bloomington proved most moderate in their expression of anti-slavery views, since Central and Southern Illinois, settled originally by Southerners, had to be considered. The resolutions were drafted by Orville H. Browning, proof enough that they would not be too radical. Browning had confided to Senator Trumbull only ten days previous: "We wish if possible to keep the state under the control of moderate men, and conservative influences, and if we do so the future destiny of the State is in our hands and victory will inevitably crown our exertions. On the other hand if rash and ultra counsels prevail all is lost."

"Rash and ultra counsels" did not prevail at Bloomington, with Browning in control of platform-making.

Abraham Lincoln formally let Illinois know that he was now a Republican when he gave the main address at Bloomington. They were crowd-compelling words which have since become known as his "Lost Speech" because no authentic copy of it has been located.

The Bloomington convention represented a body blow to Illinois Whiggery, for a robust Republican Party, with radicalism toned down, would henceforth be the Democrats' main opposition. And Lincoln was at long last a Republican. He had remained with the Clay's conservative party for more than twenty years. He could well write one Kentuckian: "I belonged to the whig party from it's origin to it's close."

VI

1856 was a presidential election year, too. The new Republican leader of Illinois, popular Springfield citizen, and Eighth Judicial Circuit lawyer revealed his own extreme moderation on the anti-slavery political front when he supported the aged, ultra conservative Whig, United States Supreme Court Justice John McLean, for the Republican presidential nomination. Of that perennially presidential-bug-bitten Jurist, the late John Quincy Adams had recorded that he thought "of nothing but the Presidency by day and dreamed of nothing else at night." Lincoln insisted that McLean was "the man to effect that object" of beating James Buchanan, who would be the Democratic candidate for President. He ended his plea for McLean's nomination with the request: "Let this be confidential."

But the Republican National Convention at Philadelphia in June, 1856, which Lincoln did not attend, passed over Justice McLean and nominated for President the colorful Colonel John C. Frémont, famed explorer of fierce physical courage but modest mentality, on a strong anti-slavery platform.

In the balloting for a Vice-Presidential candidate on Frémont's Republican ticket, Lincoln's name was presented for that second place. He polled 110 votes on the first ballot. But the convention designated William L. Dayton of New Jersey as Frémont's running mate.

Lincoln's name for Vice-President had been brought forward by William B. Archer, an Illinois congressman, who conceived the idea of proposing his name only a short time before balloting began, and secured the co-operation of one Allison, a Pennsylvania McLean supporter, to have Lincoln's name presented for the Vice-Presidency. Archer soon wrote Lincoln that, if this bright idea had occurred to him a little earlier, he could have obtained a majority of delegates for the Illinois lawyer-politician. Two days later Archer apologized to Lincoln: "I think you will pardon me for the move. I had a strong hope and felt disposed to make the move."

Lincoln presented congratulations to Dayton of New Jersey, who had beat him for the Vice-Presidency, through a letter to John Van Dyke of that state, with whom he had served in Congress. Lincoln requested Van Dyke: "When you meet Judge Dayton present my respects, and tell him I think him a far better man than I for the position he is in, and that I shall support both him and Colonel Fremont most cordially."

And so Lincoln took the stump for Frémont and Dayton.

VII

Why did Lincoln, a moderate man himself, support the then militantly anti-slavery Republican platform in 1856? Two explanations suggest themselves. Either it was his own political opportunism, or, he failed to realize the importance the Republican Party would have in brewing disunion sentiment in the South.

The Republicans were, after all, almost an entirely sectional party, made up principally of Northerners and in angry Southern minds out to destroy the Southern way of life. An inflammable reaction engulfed Dixie when they realized that the sectional Republicans were displacing the nationally minded Whigs as the main opposition to the dominant Democrats.

Lincoln, in an address at Galena, Illinois, weeks following Frémont's nomination, denied that his new Republican Party was a threat to the Union. He assured his hearers, addressing people of the South from a distance: "You further charge us with being Disunionists. If you mean that it is our aim to dissolve the Union, for myself I answer, that it is untrue; for those who act with me I answer that it is untrue. Have you ever heard us assert that as our aim? Do you really believe that such is our aim? Do you find it in our platform, our speeches, our conversation, or anywhere? If not, withdraw the charge."

Lincoln, always excessively frugal, found himself accepting financial support from the wealthy former Mayor Alexander Campbell of La Salle to defray the expenses of his stumping for Frémont. Campbell offered him $500, but Lincoln accepted only from $200 to $300.

Not all of those Republicans of 1856, of course, were simon-pure anti-slavery idealists concerned with eliminating black human bondage. They concerned themselves with such mundane matters as campaign funds, although a "bleeding" Kansas and an injured Senator Sumner were the emotional stimulus in generating votes among the Northern populace. They chose the fabulously rich merchant prince and shipping tycoon, Edward D. Morgan of New York, as Chairman of the Republican National Committee and chief party fund-raiser. Untold thousands of dollars were raised and expended in the efforts to elect Frémont.

Lincoln in August accepted an invitation to take to the hustings for Frémont in Michigan, before the "Young Men's Republican Rally" at Kalamazoo on the 27th. There he experienced more of the noise and carnival-like support for Frémont and Republicanism than existed in his own downstate section of Illinois. Michigan, more northern in sentiment than Illinois and filled with settlers from New England, upstate New York, and German immigrants rather than people from the South was more rabidly anti-slavery and, of course, more Republican.

Returning home to Springfield, Lincoln then traveled some twenty miles away to speak at Petersburg. The politicians and editors of that strongly anti-Republican and conservative community now called him "that high priest of abolitionism, Abram (sic) Lincoln . . . the *post-mortem* candidate for the vice-presidency of the political cock-boat, the depot master of the underground railroad, the great Abram (sic) Lincoln."

Only a corporal's guard of Republicans, with blaring band, met the electioneering Lincoln as he stepped from the stage coach at Petersburg, his old home community. In the crowd hurrahs went up for Buchanan, the Democratic standard-bearer, and for Millard Fillmore, former President, running on a third-party Whig-"American" Know-Nothing ticket, who was influential among Illinois conservatives. Scant cheers were given for Frémont. It was observed that Lincoln might just as well have entered Charleston, South Carolina, for all the enthusiasm there was for Frémont in Petersburg. The little band of Republicans escorted Lincoln to a platform in a courthouse yard, and unfurled a banner reading: *Free Speech, Free Soil, Free Kansas, and Fremont.* The crowd rushed forward to tear down that "Abolition" standard, let out cat-calls, and yelled threateningly, "Black Republicans!" More huzzas went up for Buchanan and Fillmore. Lincoln weathered the ordeal with difficulty.

Lincoln's hard stumping for Frémont proved futile. The Pathfinder lost both Illinois, and the presidency, to Buchanan.

If the third-party "American Party" candidate, an arch conservative, Former President Fillmore, had not been in the national race, Frémont would have won Illinois and Pennsylvania, and with them the presidency.

DUELING WITH DOUGLAS

13

I

"TWENTY-TWO years ago Judge Douglas and I first became acquainted. We were both young then; he a trifle younger than I. Even then, we were both ambitious; I, perhaps, quite as much so as he. With *me,* the race of ambition has been a failure—a flat failure; with *him* it has been one of splendid success. His name fills the nation; and is not unknown, even, in foreign lands."

Lincoln jotted down these thoughts about Senator Stephen A. Douglas in 1856. He had first known Douglas as a fellow legislator at Vandalia, he then a Whig, Douglas a Jacksonite. But as he noted, the years had dealt considerably more generously with the Democratic Little Giant, now of Chicago, than with him.

In the public image Douglas was the nation's dominant Democrat, greater even than President Pierce and the incoming President Buchanan. The public's anxiety to hear Douglas on the Senate floor in Washington and on the Illinois hustings was equalled only by its impatient desire to read newspaper accounts of his speeches. And these speeches had made him internationally famous.

And Lincoln? For years he had drunk the galling dregs of defeat. All of his public life had been spent in the minority Whig Party, now all but collapsed. Over the years his lot had been numerous reverses, only temporarily sweetened by a few victories. Whigs of his home Sangamon County had been strong enough to send him to the state Legislature in the past generation as often as he might choose to go—but that was all. He and his Whig coterie had been uninterruptedly unsuccessful in efforts to carry Illinois for the Party's presidential candidates. He had been elected to Congress for a single term, but only after fierce rivalry with Edward D. Baker and John J. Hardin over the nomination. In Congress his anti-Mexican War stand did not prove popular back home, and he did not run again. His seat was filled by a Democrat, thus losing the only dependable Whig district in the State. President Taylor's Whig administration had declined to give him the job of Commissioner of the General Land Office, no matter how hard he had fought to secure it. Only the governorship of wild, remote Oregon Territory was tendered him, and he had declined it. Then six years later, in 1855, the state Legislature had defeated him for United States Senator after he had led on the opening ballots. Now, in 1856, after forsaking Whiggery and joining the Republican Party, he and his new associates had been unable to carry Illinois for Frémont.

II

But only one month after the Republican Frémont's defeat by Buchanan, Lincoln was again plunging himself into politics. He spoke at a Republican banquet in Chicago on December 10.

His main theme was that President-elect Buchanan was merely a "minority" Chief Executive, not elected by a majority popular vote of the nation. Denouncing the Democratic President Pierce's annual message because it hailed Buchanan's victory over Frémont, Lincoln told his cheering Republican party brethren:

"We have another Presidential Message. . . . The President felicitates hugely over the late Presidential election. . . . He says the people did it. He forgets that the 'people,' as he complacently calls only those who voted for Buchanan, are in a minority of the whole people, by about four hundred thousand votes—one full tenth of the voters. . . . All of us who did not vote for Mr. Buchanan, taken together, are a majority of four hundred thousand. But, in the late contest we were divided between Fremont and Fillmore. Can we not come together, for the future. . . . Let bygones be bygones. Let past differences as nothing be. . . . We *can* do it."

Lincoln had his eye already on Douglas's Senate seat. He watched, hawk-like, the Little Giant's political moves, and he was given an opportunity when, in June, 1857, Douglas held forth at Springfield in defense of the Dred Scott decision handed down by the United States Supreme Court.

The sectional passions aroused by the presidential campaign of 1856 were a deep concern to President-elect Buchanan, who felt that the Republicans were doing the nation irreparable harm by agitating the slavery problem. He looked to a decision from the United States Supreme Court that might settle the status of the South's "peculiar institution" in the territories. While Buchanan prepared for his inauguration, the case of a slave, Dred Scott, which had begun in the Missouri courts, lay on the Supreme Court docket. A majority of the Court had agreed to dispose of this litigation without raising the delicate questions of the lower courts' jurisdiction, of Dred Scott's citizenship, or of the Missouri Compromise of 1820. Justice John McLean and Justice Benjamin R. Curtis, however, anxious to demonstrate their anti-slavery views for personal and political reasons, declared their intention of filing dissenting opinions. Their insistence on reviewing the status of slaves in the territories forced the other judges to review the whole question of the constitutionality of the Missouri Compromise.

Meanwhile Buchanan, anxious for a decision that would settle the controversy in the territories, wrote one of the judges, Justice John Catron, to ascertain whether a decision on the Dred Scott case might be expected before March 4, 1857, Inauguration Day. The President-elect emphasized the need for strong language (without, of course, advising what the decision should be). In his Inaugural Address on the 4th Buchanan referred to the forthcoming decision and expressed his intention to submit to the Court's ruling, "whatever this may be." Two days later Chief Justice Roger B. Taney delivered a majority opinion of the Court: that a Negro was not a citizen, and that the Missouri Compromise was unconstitutional.

In short, the Court ruled on two significant and fiercely controversial points. First, a Negro had no status as a citizen. Second, Congress had no constitutional authority to exclude slavery from national territory, and the national legislators had only "the power coupled with the duty of . . . protecting the owner in his rights." Thus was the provision of the Missouri Compromise of 1820, by which Congress had forbidden slavery north of the 36° 30′ line, together with similar laws, declared unconstitutional and void.

Pro-Douglas Democrats found themselves in a deep dilemma. For if the nation's highest court decreed that slavery could not be excluded from the national domain, how could a territorial legislature choose between freedom and slavery? What, then, became of "popular sovereignty," Senator Douglas's own favorite doctrine, which declared that the inhabitants of a territory possessed a right to forbid or sanction slavery in their own domain?

So the Grand Jury of the federal court at Springfield invited Douglas to speak on the Dred Scott decision, and he accepted. Abraham Lincoln sat in Douglas's audience.

With Lincoln listening intently, Douglas on June 12, 1857, held forth in the Hall of the House of Representatives at Springfield. Upholding the Dred Scott decision, the Senator insisted that the right of the master to his slave, affirmed in the Court's decision, was "a barren and worthless right, unless sustained, protected, and enforced by appropriate police regulations and local legislation, prescribing adequate remedies for its violation. These regulations and remedies must necessarily depend entirely upon the will and wishes of the people of the Territory, as they can only be prescribed by the local legislatures." In those words Douglas expressed the doctrine that "unfriendly legislation" could effectively exclude slavery. That was the same position that he would take against Lincoln at Freeport in the next year.

Lincoln, with his arm full of books, on June 26 took the same platform that Douglas had occupied. He said nothing about Douglas's assertion that slavery could not last anywhere without friendly legislation. He elaborated on several points. He dwelt on the Declaration of Independence and found slavery inconsistent with its principles. He denounced Douglas because the Senator had charged that Republicans, by insisting that Negroes have rights in the Declaration, were taking that view because they wanted to "vote, and eat, and sleep, and marry with negroes." Continued Lincoln: "Now I protest against that counterfeit logic which concludes that, because I do not want a black woman for a *slave* I must necessarily want her for a *wife.* I need not have her for either. I can just leave her alone. In some respects she certainly is not my equal; but her natural right to eat the bread she earns with her own hands without asking leave of any one else, she is my equal, and the equal of all others."

The sectional struggle over slavery raged throughout the nation. By the close of 1857 Douglas's personal and political split with President Buchanan over the "Bleeding" Kansas imbroglio, filled the headlines. It divided the Democratic Party right down the middle, much to Lincoln's ultimate advantage.

III

Lincoln's Republican Party in Illinois and throughout the North grew into a formidable political organization partly because of the "family" troubles of its Democratic foes—troubles caused not entirely by the wrangle over slavery.

Within Andrew Jackson's historic party following Old Hickory's death there festered feuds over personal power, political patronage, and the sectional clash over slavery. But amidst the wilderness of political thistles and thorns of the fractured Democratic Party the break between the nation's two most powerful men of that party, Senator Douglas and President Buchanan, loomed largest.

Douglas was annoyed at Buchanan for not having consulted with him about the distribution of federal patronage in the Northwest, his own bailiwick. Then the Kansas problem burst forth again to drive another wedge between the Democratic President and the most powerful Democratic Senator. The Southern-minded Buchanan recommended to Congress that it pass legislation for the admission of Kansas Territory as a State of the Union under a pro-slavery constitution adopted at Lecompton, Kansas. Douglas flared up, for the Lecompton document would practically nullify the Senator's favorite doctrine of popular sovereignty by making it impossible for the people of Kansas, in adopting it, to vote separately on the question of whether the proposed new state should be admitted "free" or "slave" into the Union. Douglas had a showdown with the President, who threatened him: "Mr. Douglas, I desire you to remember that no Democrat ever differed from the administration of his own [party] choice without being crushed." The Little Giant, already at odds with Buchanan because of the patronage policy, moved by a sense of honor about his popular sovereignty doctrine, and concerned for public opinion in anti-slavery Northern Illinois, stood his ground.

On December 7, 1857, Douglas held the United States Senate floor, assailing the Lecompton Constitution as a pro-slavery document and berating the Chief Executive for his proposal to have Congress admit Kansas into the Union under it. Buchanan retaliated by wielding the patronage axe on pro-Douglas office-holders in Illinois and elsewhere. Hotly irate, Douglas complained to Judge Samuel Treat on February 28, 1858: "The administration is more anxious for my destruction than they are for the harmony & unity of the Democratic party. You have doubtless seen that they are removing all my friends from office. . . . If the party is divided by this course, it will not be my fault."

But tens of thousands of Democrats by 1858 were fighting not only over Kansas, slavery, federal patronage, and respective loyalties to Douglas and Buchanan, but also because of resentments over what had happened after Andrew Jackson had retired to his Hermitage in Tennessee. In the no-holds-barred Democratic Party family quarrel of 1858, the ancient deal by which Martin Van Buren of New York had been dumped by a coalition of anti-Van Buren Democrats was uncovered. Anti-Polk Democrats joined the Douglas-Buchanan battle. Other past personal and political feuds between dead leaders, such as the vendetta between pro-Jacksonian Thomas Hart Benton of Missouri and anti-Jacksonian John C. Calhoun of South Carolina, were resurrected. And when Stephen A. Douglas returned to Illinois to fight for re-election to his Senate seat in 1858, the Democrats in the State and the nation were hopelessly divided into pro-Buchanan "Lecomptonites" and pro-Douglas "Anti-Lecomptonites."

IV

At this time a discordant note was suddenly injected by Easterners into Lincoln's plans to secure the Republican nomination for United States Senator.

Horace Greeley, editor of the Republicans' most widely circulated daily and weekly, the New York *Tribune,* decided that Douglas, although a Democrat, should be offered the Republican nomination to succeed himself. It was all good strategy, from the New York editor's viewpoint. Other Eastern men thought so, too. These reports came to Lincoln's attention.

Lincoln feared that Illinois Republicans, listening to Greeley and others like him, might adopt Douglas. Herndon related how Lincoln told him in hurt feeling: "Greeley is not doing me right. His conduct, I believe, savors a little of injustice. I am a true Republican . . . and yet I find him taking up Douglas."

Lincoln, determined not to be ditched in favor of a Democrat, who was his worst political foe at that, sent a stern note to Senator Trumbull, then in Washington: "What does the 'New York Tribune' mean by its constant eulogizing, and magnifying Douglas? Have they concluded that the Republican cause, generally, can be best promoted by sacrificing us here in Illinois?" He added: "But if the 'Tribune' continues to din his praises into the ears of its five or ten thousand Republican readers in Illinois, it is more than can be hoped that all will stand firm."

Norman B. Judd of Chicago, Chairman of the Republican State Central Committee, and a close friend of Lincoln and Senator Trumbull, hurried to Washington to find out what the Eastern leaders had in mind by their meddling in Illinois affairs. The State Chairman, on his return to Illinois in February, 1858, gave out glad tidings. The Eastern leaders for the most part did not take Greeley too seriously; and President Buchanan planned to have his federal office-holders organize Illinois against the Little Giant. "Douglas is dead," reported Judd. Not even Republicans could save him. Lincoln was relieved by the end of that foolish talk about Douglas running as a Republican. And, in the end, the Illinois Republicans resented the attempted Eastern meddling in their party affairs. Too, Lincoln was the State's most distinguished Republican, unless Senator Trumbull could be considered that.

Republicans, jubilant over Democratic dissension, assembled in a state convention at the House of Representatives Hall in Springfield on June 16, 1858. Waving Lincoln banners, they yelled for him, then unanimously nominated him as "the first and only choice of the Republicans of Illinois for the United States Senate."

That same evening the Convention reassembled and heard its senatorial candidate give his acceptance oration. What they heard was his since oft-quoted "House Divided" speech, the most radical address on anti-slavery he was ever to utter in his life. Slowly, gravely, Lincoln began: "If we could first know *where* we are, and *whither* we are tending, we could better judge *what* to do, and *how* to do it. A house divided against itself cannot stand. . . . Either the *opponents* of slavery will arrest the further spread of it, and place it where the public mind shall rest in the belief that it is in the course of ultimate extinction; or its *advocates* will push it forward, till it shall become alike lawful in *all* the States, *old* as well as *new—North* as well as *South.*"

All evidence, continued Lincoln in his speech, pointed to a design to make slavery national. The Kansas-Nebraska Act of Douglas's authorship, the popular endorsement of Buchanan, and the Dred Scott decision were so many parts of a plot. Particularly partisan—even unfair—of Lincoln was his absurd insinuation that there had existed an understanding between Douglas, Former President Franklin Pierce, Chief Justice Roger B. Taney, and President James Buchanan to have a pro-slavery decision rendered by the Supreme Court in the Dred Scott case. Lincoln declared that a lot of framed timbers were gotten out in different portions at different times and places by different workmen: "Stephen, Franklin, Roger, and James, for instance." When those timbers were joined together to make an exact frame of a house or a mill, he continued, "we find it impossible not to *believe* that Stephen and Franklin and Roger and James all understand one another from the beginning." Lincoln denounced Douglas's "popular sovereignty" doctrine as if the Senator supported it as part of a designed conspiracy to foist slavery on the territories.

Lincoln had done the thing which fans a leader's fame without clarifying his position: he had coined a quotable phrase. Henceforth Illinois people and other Americans might know almost nothing about

Lincoln's views, yet know that he had used the words, "house divided" and "half slave, half free." In reality, Lincoln was basically conservative on the slavery question but such slogans sounded radical. Never again was he ever to utter such an extreme doctrine as that of presenting the nation with the two alternatives: all slave or all free. In the weeks ahead he would be at pains to persuade his listeners, particularly in the central and lower counties, that he had been misunderstood and misinterpreted by opponents.

Douglas, from the Tremont House balcony in Chicago on July 9, answered Lincoln's "House Divided" speech. He was heard by thousands of his cheering cohorts. Just behind the Senator as he spoke, but within the hotel, Lincoln listened. Herndon had confided to Senator Trumbull: "Douglas is to be in Chicago on the 9th inst., and Lincoln told me he should be on hand to hear what the giant had to say."

Douglas, from that hotel balcony, courteously termed Lincoln a "kind, amiable, and intelligent gentleman, a good citizen and an honorable opponent" and then verbally charged into that kind, amiable, intelligent, and honorable gentleman's House Divided address. He accused Lincoln of encouraging a Northern war against the South for the extermination of slavery, until each state should become all free or all slave.

Senatorial Candidate Lincoln on the following evening, the 10th, answered Douglas from that same Tremont House balcony. He found the flaw in his opponent's armor. "Popular sovereignty! everlasting popular sovereignty! . . . What is popular sovereignty?" Calling it "Squatter Sovereignty," "another name for this same thing," Lincoln demanded to know how there could be such a doctrine, in the original sense, since the Supreme Court in the Dred Scott decision had decided that the people in their territorial status could not prohibit slavery. Lincoln was troubled by Douglas's charges that "House Divided" doctrines would lead to a war between North and South. He fell back on the defensive and sought to explain it away. He insisted that he did not favor such a war between the sections for the extinction of slavery. "I only said," he protested, "what I expected would take place. I made a prediction only—it may have been a foolish one perhaps. I did not even say that I desired that slavery should be put in course of ultimate extinction. I do say so now, however." In affirming that the opponents of slavery would arrest its further spread, he only meant that they would put it where the fathers had originally placed it. He did not favor interfering with slavery where it existed in the states. As to the charge that he was inviting people to resist the Dred Scott decision, Lincoln responded rather weakly: "We will try to reverse that decision. . . . We mean to reverse it, and we mean to do it peaceably."

Lincoln several days later admitted to the German-born Former

Lieutenant-Governor Gustave Koerner that Douglas's Chicago reception looked large and imposing. But he maintained: "It is all as bombastic and hollow as Napoleon's bulletins sent back from his campaign in Russia. . . . We could have voted him down in that very crowd. Our meeting, twenty-four hours after, called only twelve hours before it came together and got up without trumpery, was nearly as large and five times as enthusiastic."

From Chicago the Lincoln-Douglas senatorial campaign moved downstate, the lesser known Lincoln following the more distinguished Douglas. For more than four months, until early November, 1858, they stumped Illinois, each trying to persuade the people to elect a majority of their respective parties to seats in the Senate and House of Representatives of the state Legislature, which would determine who would be the next United States Senator. Each candidate spoke one hundred times at his own party rallies and engaged in seven face-to-face formal debates with each other.

Lincoln's strategy was to stay on Douglas's trail and answer him to audiences in the same places. The well-tailored Senator traveled in a gaudily bannered private railroad car, accompanied by his attractive wife and busy secretarial staff. The lone Lincoln, with his wife Mary at home with the boys, followed closely behind in another car. He wore a weather-beaten "stove pipe" hat and dusty coat and carried a carpet bag and a cane made from the wood of Henry Clay's house. Hitched to Douglas's train was a flat car on which was mounted a brass cannon. As the Senator's car approached a town, the cannon would be fired to inform the townspeople that the Little Giant was coming. "Wherever the Little Giant happens to be," came one report, "Abe is sure to turn up and be a thorn in his side."

V

Douglas, hoping to divert attention from Lincoln, engaged himself in loud and excitable verbal warfare with his Republican colleague, Senator Trumbull. But Lincoln had no intention of being overshadowed by this Douglas-Trumbull duel. The Republican candidate for United States Senator realized that he was likely to be ignored if Trumbull were permitted to monopolize Douglas's attention. His only course, then, was to challenge the Little Giant to a series of debates on the same platform at the same time.

So in late July Lincoln consulted with Republican State Chairman Norman B. Judd and other party strategists. Judd, acting as intermediary, visited Douglas and proposed that he and Lincoln, "divide time and address the same audiences." After profuse dickering and exchanges of correspondence, Lincoln and Douglas met in conference and came to terms. They agreed to share the same platform in seven formal joint debates, beginning at Ottawa on August 21. The individual electioneering of neither was to be interfered with.

As they faced each other in those seven forensic duels Lincoln's ill-fitting clothes contrasted with Douglas's well-groomed appearance. More striking were the candidates' physical differences. Next to Lincoln's gaunt, tall form, the Senator looked like a broad-chested corpulent dwarf, his massive head upon a strong, bulldog-like neck. Lincoln spoke in a thin tenor voice verging on a falsetto, whereas Douglas's baritone voice boomed across the crowd, reminding some of verbal artillery. Audiences found themselves fascinated by the big lean man with the little voice and the little fat man with the big voice. Carl Schurz, who saw and heard them at the Quincy debate, noted Lincoln's mannerisms. The Republican candidate's gestures appeared awkward. He swung his arms clumsily and, to give emphasis to a point, he would bend his knees and body with a sudden downward jerk and then shoot up again with a vehemence that raised him to his tiptoes, making him seem even taller. Douglas would excitedly shake his lengthy black locks and walk back and forth across the platform, as if steamingly angry.

Too much attention has been given in books over the decades to the physical and sartorial differences between the two candidates. And all too few pages have been devoted to their ideological differences as expressed in this most famous of Senatorial campaigns. Apparently it has always been easier and vastly less onerous to relate the picturesque features of both candidates than to read and analyze the debates containing their actual views on the difficult slavery problem.

Traditional accounts of that famous senatorial contest of 1858 have usually portrayed Lincoln as an indignant, even radical, anti-slavery crusader, tackling Douglas, a Democratic pro-slavery defender completely under the South's domination because of his presidential ambitions. Certainly it was not that simplified. Actually Lincoln held only mild anti-slavery views—during the campaign he had constantly to explain away his "House Divided" speech—while Douglas favored popular sovereignty, the right of people in the Territories to decide whether to permit or exclude slavery within their domain. Lincoln, although opposed to slavery extension to the Territories, constantly repeated that he would never interfere with Negro bondage in the States where it already existed. Lincoln was also sympathetic to the South, and would always remain so. As for Douglas being controlled by the South, that simply was not the case, for in breaking with President Buchanan on the slavery issue and denouncing the pro-slavery Lecompton Constitution adopted in Kansas, the Little Giant was jeopardizing his own support in the South. Without the South, a Democrat could never be elected President—a curious situation that still exists today.

In reading the Lincoln-Douglas debates sentence by sentence it is apparent that both candidates, like the practical politicians they were, misrepresented the other to the public. To the crowds Lincoln painted Douglas in pro-slavery colors, while Douglas assailed Lincoln as an abolitionist. In their vote-garnering efforts for their candidates to the state Legislature, both went in for twitting and banter, maneuvering for party advantage, and shaping their ideas for local effect. Different appeals were used, depending on whether they were in Northern, Central, or Southern Illinois. Both talked endlessly on slavery, without clarifying their position so that it could be understood by even the more intelligent citizens.

To this day the Lincoln-Douglas debates are vastly more admired than read.

VI

The opening joint debate took place on August 21 in Northern Illinois, at Ottawa, seventy miles southwest of Chicago.

Douglas accused Lincoln of having conspired with Senator Trumbull, a former "Anti-Nebraska" Democrat, to bring Old-Line Whigs and Democrats into an Abolitionist "Republican" Party in 1854. He also reminded his listeners that Lincoln, "Whilst in Congress . . . distinguished himself by his opposition to the Mexican War, taking the side of the common enemy against his own country." Referring to his and Lincoln's early days Douglas stated: "I was a schoolteacher in the town of Winchester, and he a flourishing grocery-keeper in the town of [New] Salem." The term, "grocery-keeper," was another name for tavern-keeper.

Lincoln, answering Douglas on that Ottawa platform with him, protested that he had not been in Springfield when that original Republican convention, composed mostly of abolitionists like Lovejoy, met to form a Republican Party four years before. He denied any compact with Trumbull and challenged Douglas to prove his charge. To demonstrate how moderate his views were in 1854, Lincoln quoted parts of his Peoria speech. He did not answer other questions put to him by the Democrat. "I do not mean to allow him to catechise me," he declared, "unless he pays back for it in kind." The Peoria quotation gave his position on the fugitive slave law. He had no purpose of interfering with slavery in states where it existed. He did not favor political and social equality between the white and colored races; he insisted that his own race should have what he called "the superior position." He only believed that the Negro *"is my equal and the equal of Judge Douglas, and the equal of every living man."* He told of his votes for appropriations to supply the soldiers fighting in Mexico while he served in Congress. Popular sovereignty he called a plan which allowed the people of a Territory to have slavery if they wanted to, "but does not allow them *not* to have it if they do *not* want it." In replying to Douglas's reference to himself as a former "flourishing grocery-keeper" in New Salem, Lincoln denied this. He stated: "The Judge is woefully at fault about his early friend Lincoln being a 'Grocery keeper.' I don't know as it would be a great sin, if I had been, but he is mistaken. Lincoln never kept a grocery anywhere in the world." That was the only instance in which Lincoln deliberately misstated the truth to the public. The liquor-sale license to the Berry & Lincoln store in New Salem is a matter of record.

The second Lincoln-Douglas joint debate occurred at Freeport, also in Northern Illinois, on August 27. Here Lincoln took the offensive. After answering several questions put to him by Douglas, he propounded four questions of his own, which he demanded that the Senator answer. His second question proved a crucial one: "Can the people of a United States Territory, in any lawful way, against the wish of any citizen of the United States, exclude slavery from its limits prior to the formation of a state constitution?" Some have since maintained that this was Lincoln's biggest trap for Douglas.

Lincoln's query put Douglas in an uncomfortable spot. For the Dred Scott decision, which the Senator had defended, decided that Congress possessed no constitutional power to exclude slavery in the Territories and also had the duty to protect slavery there. Douglas made the best of a painful necessity. In his reply, which became known as the "Freeport Doctrine," Douglas proclaimed the theory that unfriendly legislation could exclude slavery, whatever the implications to the contrary in the Dred Scott decision. The Senator stated:

"In my opinion the people of a territory can, by lawful means, exclude slavery from their limits prior to the formation of a state constitution. Mr. Lincoln knew that I had answered that question over and over again. . . . It matters not what way the Supreme Court may hereafter decide as to the abstract question whether slavery may or may not go into a territory under the Constitution, the people have the lawful means to introduce it or exclude it as they please, for the reason that slavery cannot exist a day or an hour anywhere, unless it is supported by local police regulations. . . . I hope Mr. Lincoln deems my answer satisfactory on that point."

Lincoln was *not* sure whether his opponent's answer was satisfactory. Certainly it was not satisfactory in the deep South. Partisan Republican newspapers seized upon the Freeport Doctrine to convince Southern

Democrats and pro-Buchanan Democrats that Douglas was false to their creed. Papers in the lower south let loose a fiery editorial barrage at the Little Giant for considering slave-property rights an "abstract question" and maintaining that people could destroy slavery by passing unfriendly legislation. Within three months United States Senator Jefferson Davis presented Dixie's position before the Mississippi legislature and in straight language opposed Douglas's views recorded at Freeport. Howell Cobb, Georgia's influential congressman, vowed to Alexander H. Stephens that the Illinois Senator would be restored to the confidence of Cracker State Democrats over his dead body.

So by his "loaded" question, Lincoln made Douglas anathema to the angry Southern Democrats. With his query the little-known man from Springfield had brought himself national attention. And by causing a split between Douglas and the Southern Democrats he had destroyed the Little Giant as a presidential possibility for 1860.

After Freeport, Lincoln and Douglas stumped their separate ways through various counties until they met in their third forensic encounter on September 15 at Jonesboro, in the Southern part of Illinois near the Kentucky border.

At Jonesboro, Lincoln, to further embarrass Douglas in that region of Southern sympathizers, reminded them of the Freeport Doctrine. He brought up the point that members of a territorial legislature were bound to protect slavery under the Dred Scott decision, that they could not, by withholding necessary protective laws, or by passing laws hostile to slavery, nullify that constitutional right. He pointed up Douglas's inconsistencies by emphasizing that the idea of a state outlawing slavery by the passage of "unfriendly legislation" directly violated the Supreme Court decision.

VII

In their fourth formal joint debate Lincoln and Douglas met at Charleston on September 18, in politically enigmatic central Illinois, where conservative Old-Line Whigs, who still worshipped their dead chieftain, Henry Clay, were thick in numbers. Lincoln's supporters made political capital of his Whig past and long devotion to Clay by hiring young girls to parade in a float carrying a large banner reading:

> Westward, the star of Empire makes it way,
> The girls *link-on* to Lincoln, as their mothers did for Clay.

Lincoln correctly judged the sentiment of this old Whig region. In his verbal exchange with Douglas, he adopted an expedient line. He reversed the "all men are created equal" doctrine contained in his

Chicago speech and told his Charleston audience that he was not "nor ever have been, in favor of bringing about in any way the social and political equality of the white and black races." He added:

"I am not nor ever have been in favor of making voters or jurors of negroes, nor of qualifying them to hold office, nor to intermarry with white people; and I will say in addition to this that there is a physical difference between the white and black races which I believe will for ever forbid the two races living together on terms of social and political equality. And inasmuch as they cannot so live, while they do remain together there must be the position of superior and inferior, and I as much as any other man am in favor of having the superior position assigned to the white race. I say upon this occasion I do not perceive that because the white man is to have the superior position the negro should be denied everything. I do not understand that because I do not want a negro woman for a slave I must necessarily want her for a wife. My understanding is that I can just let her alone."

Douglas, in reply, stated: "I am glad that I have at last succeeded in getting an answer out of him upon this question of negro citizenship and eligibility to office." The Little Giant virtually accused Lincoln of being a political chameleon, able at will to change his colors to suit the climate of opinion in the region in which he happened to be speaking. In describing his Republican opponent and his fellow party men, the Senator noted: "Their principles in the north are jet black, in the center they are in color a decent mulatto, and in lower Egypt they are almost white."

On October 7 at Knox College, Galesburg, in the Republican county of Knox, Lincoln and Douglas met in their fifth forensic duel.

Douglas led off in that northern anti-slavery community with his "chameleon" theme again. "Abolitionists up north are expected and required to vote for Mr. Lincoln because he goes for the equality of the races . . . and down south [in central and lower Illinois] he tells the old Whigs, the Kentuckians, Virginians, and Tennesseeans, that . . . he is in favor of maintaining the superiority of the white race over the negro. . . . Now, how can you reconcile these two positions, Mr. Lincoln?" Lincoln's political meetings, reminded the Senator, were called by different names in different counties, in Knox, "Republican," in Tazewell County, where Old-Line Whigs and Democrats were numerous, "a grand rally of the *Lincoln men,*" in Monroe County, in "Egypt," the "Free Democracy," and in Springfield they were termed meetings for "all opposed to the Democracy." Lincoln's creed, observed the Senator, changed its hue and became lighter as it traveled from upper to lower counties, "until it [was] nearly white when it [reached] the extreme south of the State." Douglas declared, also, that the Founding Fathers never dreamed of the Negro when drafting the Declaration of Independence.

Lincoln, among his Republican friends and supporters in Galesburg, replied that Negroes *were* included in the Declaration of 1776, and he parried Douglas's questions about the various titles of Republican meetings in other parts of the State. To the Little Giant's charges that Republicans were a sectional party, Lincoln pointed out: "He is himself fast becoming sectional. . . . His speeches would not go as current now south of the Ohio River as they have formerly gone there." Slavery was a "moral, social and political evil," contended Lincoln to his anti-slavery Knox County audience. He accused Douglas of rejecting the idea that slavery was wrong.

VIII

Lincoln's remaining two debates with Douglas were held at Quincy on Oct. 13, and at Alton on the 15th. For the remaining time until Election Day Lincoln and Douglas continued separately on the hustings. Traveling due north from Alton, the scene of the last of their debates, Lincoln encountered at Naples "about fifteen Celtic gentlemen, with black carpet sacks," who worried him, lest they be colonizers brought in by the Democrats. Lincoln anxiously wrote to State Chairman Judd that the opposition might secure enough fraudulent Irish votes to swing the doubtful districts. On the following day he heard rumors at Mt. Sterling, where he spoke, that 400 Irish would be brought into neighboring Schuyler County before the election, to work on the railroads—and to vote Democrat. Continuing north, Lincoln spoke in Hancock County. There he suspected that the pro-Douglas Democrats and pro-Buchanan Democrats, mutual enemies, would bury the hatchet until after the election. He warned the Republicans: "Beware of a deal between the Douglas and National Democrats in Hancock County."

Lincoln closed his campaign at Springfield on October 30 in a speech distinguished for humility and friendliness to the South.

Election Day, 2nd of November, 1858, dawned dreary and rainy in Illinois. The result would determine whether Republicans or Democrats would control the state Legislature. But the stake was whether Lincoln or Douglas would be the next Senator.

Lincoln voted early. In the evening he spent an unhappy time listening to the incoming returns in the telegraph office. The final figures came over the wire. The Republicans elected their State ticket and polled more of the total popular vote than the Democrats in the race for offices in the Legislature. But the Democrats won control of the Legislature!

Lincoln would not be chosen Senator!

Lincoln's Republican legislative candidates had polled 190,000 votes to 176,000 for Douglas's Democrats. But an unfair apportionment law nullified this Republican advantage. The Republican organ of Lincoln's town, the *State Journal,* bemoaned that an apportionment of legislative seats according to population would have given Lincoln's supporters forty-one members in the lower house and fourteen in the upper, enough of a majority to elect him Senator. As the election for the lower house turned out, though, thirty-five seats were held by Lincoln men and forty by Douglas disciples. In the Upper House only eleven senators were Lincolnites, while the Douglasites numbered fourteen.

Lincoln, hurt to the quick, was despondent and depressed for days.

His law partner, Herndon, gave the best explanation of why Lincoln was beaten by Douglas. In a letter to Theodore Parker he explained gloomily: "We are beaten in Illinois, as you are aware; but you may want to know the causes of our defeat . . . the extreme north, the middle, and the extreme south. . . . If a man spoke to suit the north—for freedom, justice—this killed him in the center, and the south. So in the center, it killed him in north and south. So in the south, it surely killed him north. Lincoln tried to stand high and elevated, so he fell deep."

Came February 5, 1859. The Legislature at Springfield, in joint session of both houses, elected Douglas over Lincoln, 54 to 46.

Henry C. Whitney, the circuit-riding Eighth Judicial Circuit lawyer, dropped into the Lincoln & Herndon office and found Lincoln dejected that day. "I never saw a man so depressed," reminisced Whitney. "I tried to rally his drooping spirits. He was simply steeped in gloom."

PURSUING THE PRESIDENCY

14

I

"YOU have sprung at once from the position of a capital fellow, and a leading lawyer in Illinois, to a national reputation" remarked Charles H. Ray of the Chicago *Press & Tribune* to Lincoln at the beginning of the campaign against Douglas. And hardly had the outcome of the Illinois senatorial contest become known in November, 1858, than small-town Republican newspapers in Illinois and outside the State ran the masthead: LINCOLN FOR PRESIDENT, 1860!!! Other sheets proposed that he might be nominated for Vice-President on a ticket headed by the celebrated Senator William H. Seward of New York.

Though pleased by mention of his name for a national position, Lincoln appeared indifferent. He was mainly interested in building the Republican Party in Illinois and trying again for Douglas's Senate seat in 1864. Toward those twin ends he advised Republican leaders on strategy, assured Republican Senator Lyman Trumbull that he would not put himself in his way for re-election in 1860, and counselled Illinois and out-of-state party chieftains, by mail, to tone down radical and unpopular doctrines and not to bait the Democrat-voting immigrants.

Lincoln counselled expediency in preparation for the hard national fight with the Democrats in 1860. Ambitious Republicans, unlike four years before when they had lost, now were adopting as their theme the three "c's": conservatism, caution, and conciliation. Lincoln's views, temperament, and practicality were well adapted to this safe policy.

II

"For the future my view is that the fight must go on," the defeated Republican candidate for Senator from Illinois in mid-November, 1858, assured the party's State Chairman, Norman B. Judd. He assured Judd that, in 1860, he would not go after Senator Trumbull's Senate seat, for Judd was Trumbull's best friend. "In that day I shall fight in the ranks. . . . I am especially for Trumbull's re-election."

To a Winnebago County Republican state legislator four days later Lincoln encouragingly advised: "The fight must go on. . . . Another explosion will come before a great while." Three weeks later he confided to another party man: "I have an abiding faith that we shall beat them in the long run. . . . I write merely to let you know that I am neither dead nor dying."

Early in the new year, 1859, Lincoln sent off a note to Senator Trumbull in Washington, asking him to keep a vigilant eye on Senator Douglas: "Write me your present impressions of Douglas' movements." He followed this with another one, assuring Trumbull: "Any effort to put enmity between you and me, is as idle as the wind. . . . You can scarcely be more anxious to be sustained two years hence than I am that you shall be so sustained."

During those early 1859 weeks Lincoln revealed his view that the Republicans must fight the presidential battle in the following year on moderate doctrines. Anti-slavery extremism was out. In late January he sent word to Congressman Elihu B. Washburne of the Galena, Illinois, district, disapproving of part of the speech of Washburne's brother, a Maine congressman, which advocated suffrage for the few freed Negroes in Oregon, a territory then petitioning for statehood.

But in other parts of Illinois and out of state where he spoke, Lincoln toned down any strong tendencies toward anti-slavery doctrines. His speech at Council Bluffs, Iowa, in August, 1859, in which he muffled the slavery issue, was typical. The Council Bluffs *Bugle* reported: "He carefully avoided coming directly to the extreme ground occupied by him in his canvass against Douglas."

Lincoln was well aware of the so-called "German" vote. He redoubled efforts to attract more of the German-born citizens into the Republican ranks. He grew alarmed in 1859, when Massachusetts Republicans, to curb the Democrat-voting Irish, adopted an anti-alien "Two-Year" amendment to their state constitution, providing for a longer residence requirement for immigrants before they were permitted to vote. "Massachusetts republicans," Lincoln wrote impatiently to Congressman Schuyler Colfax of Indiana, "should have looked beyond their noses; and then they could not have failed to see that tilting against foreigners would ruin us in the whole North-West."

Lincoln set himself right with the Teutonic voters. To the Springfield German-born editor, Dr. Theodore Canisius, formerly of the Alton *Freie Presse,* he wrote a public letter on May 17, disapproving of the Massachusetts anti-alien amendment. "I am against its adoption in Illinois, or in any other place, where I have a right to oppose it." His letter was given wide reprinting in the German-language press in and out of Illinois, and made him acceptable to them as a presidential possibility. During that same month Lincoln entered into a written contract with Canisius, providing that he would turn over to that German editor a printing press and German types for establishment of a German-language Republican Party newspaper in Springfield. By early 1860 the *Baltimore Turn-Zeitung,* the main spokesman for the United States Turner Bund, declared: "If on the score of expediency we pass Mr. Seward by, then will Mr. Lincoln be the man."

Being "second choice" among delegates at the national convention might well be a good spot in which to be placed, with so many better known presidential contenders in the field. Lincoln fully realized this and encouraged the movement to make him an alternative choice to more distinguished candidates than himself. "My name is new in the field; and I suppose I am not the *first* choice of a very great many," he advised an Ohio leader, Samuel Galloway, early in 1860. "Our policy, then, is to give no offense to others—leave them in a mood to come to us, if they shall be compelled to give up their first love."

Twice during 1859 Lincoln had mentioned himself as unqualified for highest national honors. He wrote the Rock Island *Register* editor: "I must, in candor, say I do not think myself fit for the Presidency." And to Galloway he had sent word: "I must say I do not think myself fit for the Presidency."

By early 1860, however, he was admitting in a message to Senator Trumbull: "As you request, I will be entirely frank. The taste *is* in my mouth a little."

It was not merely a little taste in his mouth. It was actually a sharp hunger for this greatest of American distinctions.

III

Lincoln's conservative course was proving wise strategy.

Four conservative Northern states, Lincoln's own Illinois, his boyhood home of Indiana, pivotal Pennsylvania, and, to a lesser degree, New Jersey, would hold the key to Republican success in the presidential election of 1860. Had the Republicans carried these states in 1856, Frémont rather than Buchanan would have been elected. Even vote-rich Pennsylvania alone would have tipped the scales in his favor if the conservative "third party" candidate, Millard Fillmore, had not split that state's anti-Democratic vote. But, instead, Pennsylvania had put its favorite son, Buchanan, into the White House. Republicans bitterly remembered that appalling situation in 1856 and were intent that it should not happen again. They felt that they would carry Pennsylvania, Illinois, Indiana, and New Jersey in 1860 by nominating a conservative candidate rather than a radical abolitionist like Frémont. But, nevertheless, they were faced with a difficult political problem.

If during 1859-60 an imaginary line had been drawn from the Atlantic coast to the Mississippi River at the forty-first degree of north latitude, those portions of the free states of Illinois, Indiana, Ohio, Pennsylvania, and New Jersey lying below that line would have differed in their politics, particularly their views on slavery, from the portions of their own states above that forty-first parallel line. The geographically lower parts of those states sympathized with their respective conservative Southern neighbors in border slaveholding Kentucky, Delaware, Maryland, and upper Virginia more than with the northern regions of their own free states. Lower Illinois, Indiana, and Ohio had strong affinity with upper Kentucky, lower New Jersey with Delaware, and lower Pennsylvania with upper Delaware and Maryland. Significantly, Frémont, as an anti-slavery candidate, had carried the northern counties of Illinois, Indiana, Ohio, and Pennsylvania, but had lost the southern counties of those states to Buchanan. Also in all these states except Ohio, the conservative "third party" candidate, Millard Fillmore, had polled a huge popular vote. It could be easily seen that Illinois, Indiana, Pennsylvania, and New Jersey would spell victory or defeat for Republicans in the national election of 1860.

Republican strategists were well aware of the necessity of satisfying the conservative elements of Illinois, Indiana, Pennsylvania and New Jersey. Therein lay the basic weakness of such advanced anti-slavery presidential hopefuls as Senator Seward of New York and Governor Salmon P. Chase of Ohio. In the last analysis, too, Republicans did not have to worry about carrying Seward's Empire State and Chase's Buckeye State. They had done so back in 1856. So Lincoln, who had grown up in Indiana, lived in Illinois, and was sound on the tariff, an important issue in both Pennsylvania and New Jersey, became a stronger candidate. Too, Lincoln was vastly more moderate on the slavery question than was Seward or Chase.

Lincoln's King-makers, his prairie Warwicks, knew his potential acceptability to the doubtful states. Joseph Medill, boss of the Chicago *Press & Tribune,* most influential Republican paper in Lincoln's state, put it this way when he privately enlisted support from a western Virginia leader late in 1859: "If the doubtful states of Pa. Ind. and Ill, are to name the candidate the west will settle down upon the tall son of this State. He can carry the entire Northwest—Ind. included. He is Kentuckian by birth, lived 10 years in Indiana—stumped it for Henry Clay in 44,—and 25 (sic) in Illinois, was an old Clay Whig, is right on the tariff and he is exactly right on all other issues. Is there any man who could suit Pennsylvania better [?]. The West is entitled to the president and he lives in the very heart of it."

The tariff, a major issue in pivotal, protectionist-minded Pennsylvania and smaller New Jersey, two of the doubtful states, proved a source of supreme strength to Lincoln. He had a long record as a disciple of Henry Clay, whose cardinal principles had included demands that Congress enact higher import rates in order to protect American industry.

Lincoln made known his high-tariff past to at least one Pennsylvanian, but cautioned him not to agitate the issue, lest it drive away the former "free trade" Democratic element of the Republican Party. To Edward Wallace, of Philadelphia, Lincoln in October, 1859, wrote: "I was an old Henry Clay Tariff Whig. In old times I made more speeches on that subject than on any other. I have not changed my views. . . . Still, it is my opinion that, just now, the revival of that question will not advance the cause itself, or the man who revives it."

Shortly after that letter to Wallace, Lincoln sent word to a lieutenant of United States Senator Simon Cameron of Pennsylvania, answering a query about a possible Cameron-Lincoln Republican national ticket for 1860: "It certainly is important to secure Pennsylvania for the Republicans in the next presidential contest, and not unimportant to also secure Illinois. As to the [Cameron-Lincoln] ticket you name, I shall be heartily for it after it shall have been fairly nominated by a Republican national convention; and I cannot be committed to it before."

Lincoln demonstrated his interest in the delegate-rich Keystone commonwealth, second only to New York State in voting strength, when in answer to a request in December (1859) he prepared an autobiographical account of himself which Jesse W. Fell, Secretary of the Illinois Republican State Central Committee, wanted for a West Chester, Pennsylvania, newspaper. This autobiography emphasized that Lincoln had some Pennsylvania Quaker ancestors in Berks County and that he had been a high tariff man in the Clay tradition.

Illinois Republican State Chairman Norman B. Judd fully realized the importance in 1860 of Pennsylvania and the other three "doubtfuls," Illinois, Indiana, and New Jersey, all of which had been lost to the Democrats four years before. And he recognized that Lincoln had powerful qualifications as a presidential possibility. Thus this adroit Chicago political promoter became the main managing force in Lincoln's pre-convention campaign. In December, Judd had gone East and successfully persuaded the national Republican leadership to hold the party's national nominating convention at Chicago. That rising Illinois city on Lake Michigan prevailed over St. Louis as the convention site by a lone vote of members of the party's national committee.

Lincoln constantly concerned himself over the strength of the conservative Judge Edward Bates of Missouri as a presidential possibility in southern Illinois and of the power of the radically anti-slavery Senator Seward of New York in northern Illinois. Anxiously Lincoln on February 9, 1860, sent word to Judd: "I am not in a position where it would hurt much for me not to be nominated on the national ticket; but I am where it would hurt some for me not to get the Illinois delegates." He told how some of his opponents within the party "will, for revenge upon me, lay the Bates egg in the South and the Seward egg in the North, and go far towards squeezing me out in the middle with nothing. Can you not help in your end of the vineyard? I mean this to be private."

Judd during the next weeks stepped up his organizing activities to assure a solid Illinois delegation to the national convention pledged to Lincoln. He grew more than ever convinced that a combination of the four doubtful states could be effected and that all could unite on Lincoln if he had his own state solidly behind him at the national convention. On April 2 Judd sent confidential word to Senator Trumbull:

"Cannot a quiet combination between the delegates from New Jersey, Indiana, and Illinois be brought about—including Pennsylvania? United action by those delegates will probably control the convention. Nothing but a positive position will prevent Seward's nomination. The movement for Lincoln has neutralized to some extent the Bates movement in our State. It will not do to make a fight for delegates distinctly Lincoln. But state pride will carry a resolution of instruction through our state convention. This suggestion has been made to Mr. L."

Judd's strategy and that of the other Lincoln backers, with his acquiescence, was to refrain from making an active bid for delegates in states presumably loyal to Seward, Bates, Chase, or other presidential aspirants on the Republican ticket. Thus those delegates would be in a friendly mood for Lincoln after the leading candidates for the nomination deadlocked each other, and they would be persuaded that the Illinois entry, Lincoln, was really the only Republican who could carry the four doubtful states and defeat the Democratic standard-bearer in November. The plans of these Judd-led politicians involved having the state Republican convention endorse Lincoln as the favorite son of Illinois Republicanism.

IV

The most formidable Republican presidential contender in 1860 was Seward of New York. Numberless political professionals and his legions of admirers convinced themselves that nothing could stop him. New York's former two-term Governor would be backed for the presidential nomination at the party's national convention by his home state's vote-heavy delegation, by Massachusetts and Maine Republicans, and by such Northwestern states as Michigan, Minnesota, and Wisconsin, so many of whose settlers had migrated from upstate New York and New England.

The supremely confident Seward, however, was confronted with a minority of Republicans in his own state who opposed him and his friend Thurlow Weed, Albany editor and ingenious electioneering engineer. Especially antagonistic to the Seward-Weed machine in New York City were such former Free Soil Democrats as William Cullen Bryant, New York *Evening Post* editor, and future Mayor George Opdyke, both of whom were working with James A. Briggs, Eastern pre-convention campaign manager for Governor Chase of Ohio. The sixty-six-year-old Bryant was a member of the Advisory Board of "The Young Men's Republican Union," which also included such youthful anti-Seward ex-Whigs as fifty-five-year-old William Curtis Noyes, fifty-two-year-old Hamilton Fish, and forty-nine-year-old Horace Greeley of the New York *Tribune*. Together these Seward-despising Republicans arranged with The Young Men's Republican Union to have Briggs invite Abraham Lincoln of Illinois to New York for a speech under their society's auspices in February, 1860.

Lincoln accepted the invitation. At first it was decided that he would speak at Reverend Henry Ward Beecher's Plymouth Church in Brooklyn. When he left Springfield on February 23 the Democratic *State Register* sarcastically commented:

> *Significant:* The Hon. Abraham Lincoln departs to-day for Brooklyn under an engagement to deliver a lecture before the Young Men's Association in that city in Beecher's church. Subject: not known, Consideration: $200 and expenses. Object: presidential capital. Effect: disappointment.

Lincoln, *en route,* stopped off in Philadelphia. Perhaps Senator Cameron of Pennsylvania, still an active Republican presidential contender, wanted to see him—or Lincoln might have wanted a conference with

Cameron. But they did not meet. Arriving at New York City, Lincoln sent on February 26 a note of explanation to the Pennsylvania Senator "I write this to say the card of yourself, and Hon. David Wilmot, was handed me yesterday at Philadelphia, just as I was leaving for this city. I barely had time to step over to the Girard, where I learned that you and he were not in your rooms. I regret that being so near, we did not meet; but hope we may yet meet before a great while."

Lincoln learned that he was scheduled to speak, not at Beecher's Brooklyn church, but in Cooper Institute in Manhattan. With Bryant presiding and Horace Greeley conspicuously present, the anti-Sewardites' motive for inviting the phrase-turning, clever Illinoisan to New York looked obvious. Also, the man who carried on correspondence with Lincoln for his appearance was Briggs, Chase's manager in the East.

Lincoln, hewing closely to his conservative course at Cooper Institute on that February 27, stood on most moderate ground in the slavery controversy, and spoke conciliatory words to be re-echoed in the South. He condemned the abolitionist John Brown's Harper's Ferry insurrection, terming it "so absurd" and emphasized that not a single Republican was involved in Brown's bloody deed. Lincoln denied that the Republican Party was sectional or revolutionary. It would stick to American ways that were old and reliable. And he harked back to the Founding Fathers. "Wrong as we think slavery is," Lincoln urged, "we can yet afford to let it alone where it is." He ended his address to his Cooper Institute audience on a noble note: "Let us have faith that right makes might, and in that faith, let us, to the end, dare to do our duty as we understand it."

The Cooper Institute oration was the Springfield lawyer-politician's introduction to the East as a presidential possibility. From New York he visited New England, partly to see his son, Bob, at Phillips Exeter Academy in New Hampshire, partly to perform more politicking.

Lincoln calculated the states to visit and the states to avoid in New England, determined not to ruffle the sensitivities of supporters of other presidential contenders. Republican leaders in Massachusetts and Maine were nearly solid for Seward, and Vermont had its favorite son, Senator Jacob Collamer. So Lincoln did not enter these states. That left New Hampshire, Connecticut, and Rhode Island, whose Republican leaders were still uncommitted. The visiting Illinoisan spoke at various places in those three states in between Cooper Union and his stay with his son at Exeter. He also cultivated acquaintances in all of those New England states, including James F. Babcock of the New Haven, Connecticut, *Palladium*.

Lincoln's New England speeches continued to strike the note of conservatism, caution, and conciliation. Though not mere repetitions of his Cooper Union Speech, they pointed out that slavery was wrong, and also they expressed a hope for an abatement of sectional strife and controversy.

He arrived home in Springfield on March 14.

V

Lincoln, back in Illinois, set about capitalizing on his Eastern tour. He made arrangements to have his Cooper Institute speech printed for mass circulation in his home state. On April 6 he informed one Edwards County party man: "Pamphlet copies of my late speech at Cooper Institute, N. Y., can be had at the office of the N. Y. Tribune; at the Republican Club Room at Washington, and at the Illinois Journal at this place." He kept in touch with the ensuing hard-fought elections in Connecticut and Rhode Island and requested Senator Trumbull, who had been born in the former state, to rush there and make political addresses "as a son of their soil."

After the Republican candidate for Governor had achieved only a narrow victory in Connecticut and the Party's gubernatorial choice was beaten in Rhode Island, Lincoln took opportunity to show that those two New England states wanted none of anti-slavery extremism as symbolized by Seward. On April 14 he pointed out in a letter to the unsavory Mark Delahay, a supporter in otherwise pro-Seward Kansas Territory:

"You know I was in New-England. Some of the acquaintances I made while there, write me since the elections that the close vote in Conn. & the quasi defeat in R.I. are a drawback upon the prospects of Gov. Seward; and Trumbull writes Dubois to the same effect. Do not mention this as coming from me. . . . I see by the despatches that since you wrote, Kansas has appointed Delegates and instructed them for Seward. Don't stir them up to anger, but come along to the convention, & I will do as I said about expenses." Lincoln apparently had thoughts that he might secure the delegates from Kansas after they learned that Seward could not be nominated at the national convention. It was Lincoln's firm policy not to antagonize the delegates pledged to his rival presidential aspirants. He had outlined that course to Samuel Galloway of Ohio, in his advice: "Our policy, then, is to give no offense to others—leave them in a mood to come to us, if they shall be compelled to give up their first love."

To his acquaintance in Connecticut, Babcock of the New Haven *Palladium,* who had asked him for the names of prominent Republicans "who are your confidential friends, to whom I can write," Lincoln replied by sending Babcock the names and addresses of supporters in Illinois, Iowa, and Ohio. Lincoln also congratulated Babcock on the close Republican victory in Connecticut, "much gratified that it is all safe."

To one of those Iowans he mentioned, Hawkins Taylor, a delegate from the Hawkeye State to the national convention, Lincoln on April 21 sent word: "I am glad there is a prospect of your party passing this way to Chicago. Wishing to make your visit here as pleasant as we can, we wish you to notify us as soon as possible, whether you come this way, how many, and when you will arrive."

On May 1, two weeks before the national convention assembled at Chicago, Lincoln sent a letter to a party politician and lawyer of Vincennes, Indiana, Cyrus M. Allen: "Our friend Dubois, and Judge David Davis, of Bloomington, one or both, will meet you at Chicago on the 12th."

And so State Auditor Jesse K. Dubois left his desk at Springfield and Judge Davis laid aside his Eighth Judicial Circuit robe and hurried up to Chicago fully four days before the national convention convened. They opened Lincoln-for-President headquarters at the Tremont House.

But first there was the Republican convention at Decatur, Illinois, at which Lincoln hoped to be named his home State's first choice for President.

VI

"State pride will carry a resolution of instruction through our state convention. This suggestion has been made to Mr. L." So Republican State Chairman Judd had confided to Senator Trumbull on April 2. Lincoln would be designated as the choice of Illinois Republicans at the state party convention, and that convention was to meet at Decatur on May 9-10, only one week before the great national conclave opened at Chicago, where the party's candidate for President would be selected. The date for the Decatur party gathering was well "timed," late enough so that its full impact for Lincoln would be felt spontaneously at Chicago.

Republicans of Lincoln's home county, Sangamon, met on April 28 at Springfield and chose delegates to the Decatur state assemblage. During the week that followed, other county conventions throughout Illinois followed suit by picking representatives to Decatur. Controlling each of these county conclaves were avid pro-Lincoln professionals, dedicated to his presidential cause. Supporters of Seward and Bates seemed to have gone into hiding, or were effectively quashed by the Lincoln majority.

When the state convention convened at Decatur on May 9, Lincoln's supporters, some taking the role of crusaders, held unchallenged control, led by Judge David Davis and State Chairman Judd. A few pro-Seward supporters made some noise but were quickly drowned out and "steam-rollered" into insignificant spots on minor committees.

Lincoln himself stood outside the convention hall, on hand to respond to the expected call. Inside, Richard J. Oglesby, one of his Decatur friends and a future Governor, announced that "a distinguished citizen of Illinois and one whom Illinois will ever delight to honor, is present; and I wish to move that this body invite him to a seat on the stand." A roar of applause rent the hall as Oglesby announced the name: Abraham Lincoln.

A madly happy and hilarious rush was made for Lincoln as he entered the hall. He was "troosted," lifted up bodily, as the delegates ecstatically yelled themselves hoarse. Lincoln lay wriggling for a few seconds, sprawling and kicking upon the heads and shoulders of the noisy throng. They carried him to the rostrum and planted him there. Then Lincoln rose, smiled, bowed and blushed.

Lincoln addressed the wildly shouting convention. Before he had half finished his speech, Oglesby interrupted, announcing that an "Old-time Democrat of Macon County" wanted to make a contribution to this Republican convention. At a signal John Hanks, one of Lincoln's cousins, marched into the hall, carrying two time-stained fence rails. Supported between these rails, festooned with flags and streamers, was held a banner, reading:

ABRAHAM LINCOLN FOR PRESIDENT
The Rail Candidate For
President in 1860

Two rails from a Lot of 3,000 Made
in 1830 by Thos. Hanks and Abe Lincoln—
Whose Father was the First
Pioneer of Macon County.

Thos. Hanks should have read "John" Hanks. More cheers burst forth in the humid air of the convention hall. And there were yells for Lincoln to continue his speech. He admitted that he had split rails in Macon County in 1830 with John Hanks. But whether these were of his cutting, he did not know. But he had split many better ones, he assured the joyful audience.

Thus did Abraham Lincoln, by this device of political showmanship, emerge as the "Rail Splitter" candidate.

The following day the top-heavy Lincoln majority, led by Davis and Judd, succeeded in having the Decatur convention adopt the resolution,

"That Abraham Lincoln is the choice of the Republican party of Illinois for the Presidency, and the delegates from this state are instructed to use all honorable means to secure his nomination by the Chicago Convention, and to vote as a unit for him."

Only two days later Judge Davis, Judd, and their aides left for Chicago. Lincoln remained in Springfield, knowing that his future fortunes lay in skilful hands.

VII

Into the vast wooden tabernacle, or "Wigwam," erected for their purpose on Lake and Market streets, Chicago, 466 Republican delegates and hordes of party hangers-on, newspapermen, and observers assembled in national convention on May 16.

Some delegates submerged into a festive mood. Drinking and "singing songs not found in hymn books" had started on the trains, and now, in the growing city on Lake Michigan, it was observed that "the Republicans are imbibing the spirit as well as the substance of the old Democratic party." One delegate was awakened by boisterous roommates in a "sardine-packed" hotel: "I was aroused by a vehement debate among them, and rubbing my eyes, discovered that they were sitting in bed playing cards to see who should pay for gin cock-tails all around, and the cocktails being an indispensable preliminary to breakfast." When "Long John" Wetworth, Mayor of Chicago, made a police raid on assignation resorts, he discovered several delegates.

Most delegates, however, were steeped in their electioneering profession. "Victory in November!" sounded the clarion call to close ranks behind any Republican candidate who could collect the greatest number of votes against the Democratic standard-bearer.

That partially national conclave in the Wigwam at Chicago—all Northern states and border regions were represented, as well as a bogus "Texas" delegation recruited in Michigan—comprised a curious agglomeration of political opinion and lack of opinion, causing interest today as to why some historians have maintained that the presidential election of 1860 was purely a public mandate on slavery. One Massachusetts observer critically commented about the convention:

"Probably no deliberative body ever came together, even in France during the old revolutionary period, composed of such miscellaneous elements. There were Free Soil Whigs in the largest proportion, and with them Free Soil Democrats, Native Americans [Know-Nothings], foreign [German] adventurers; abolitionists, and their lifelong opponents; those for saving the Union, and those for dividing it; professed conservatives and the most thoroughgoing radicals; sentimentalists; ideologists; 'economists and calculators;' a sprinkling of delegates pretending to represent some sort of constituency in two or three of the border States; and, to crown all, Mr. Horace Greeley of the *New York Tribune,* as an accredited deputy from the somewhat distant regions of Oregon."

This diversity indicates that the Republican Party was then a catch-all-votes organization rather than a group totally dedicated to anti-slavery idealism. This was further demonstrated by the resolutions, or "platform," adopted by the convention. Greeley, holding the proxy of an absent Oregon delegate who never arrived in Chicago, was active on the resolutions committee. He had previously written privately: "I don't believe the time ever has been, or soon will be, when on a square slavery issue the Republicans could or can poll one hundred electoral votes." To another associate, the New York *Tribune* editor, supporting the conservative Judge Bates of Missouri, confided: "An Anti-slavery man *per se* can not be elected; but a tariff, River and Harbor, Pacific Railroad, Free Homestead man may succeed. I wish the country were more anti-slavery than it is." The issue of anti-slavery was one that must not be overemphasized, if victory were to come in November. Frémont in 1856 had demonstrated that a Republican candidate could not be elected President by giving prominence to the slavery question. The Pathfinder had offended sentiment in conservative Illinois, Indiana, Pennsylvania, and New Jersey. Opposition to slavery extension, by itself, was too weak a reed on which to base hope of victory at the nationwide polls.

The platform adopted at Chicago identified the Republican Party with all that was right in the nation, paid glowing tribute to the Declaration of Independence, uttered other noble phrases, looked with alarm on any continued Democratic Party power, and de-emphasized the slavery issue by fewer words and milder language than four years previous. This platform also appealed to special regional and economic interests.

This latitudinarian platform, broad enough to attract most groups above Mason and Dixon's line, softened the slavery issue by merely opposing the recent re-opening of the African slave trade, called for admission of Kansas Territory as a free State, and denied that Congress or a territorial legislature could "give legal existence to Slavery in any Territory of the United States."

The platform also commended a tariff policy that was ambiguously presented but was supposed to favor protection—for the benefit of Pennsylvania and New Jersey. The old Democratic "free trade" element of Republicans did not relish this plank sympathizing with some protectionist principle, but went along with it in the interests of party harmony and the necessity for carrying Pennsylvania, although one of the ex-Democrats later growled about the Keystone Staters: "Damn their iron and coal."

A "free homestead policy," gift of government-owned land to actual settlers, was called for in another plank, to satisfy the Northwest. The Great Lakes area was courted with the fifteenth plank, demanding "appropriations for Congress for River and Harbor improvements;" this satisfied Old-Line Whigs who fondly remembered their former Clay credo of internal-improvements at federal government expense. Distant California and Oregon were attracted by "a Railroad to the Pacific Ocean" and "a daily Overland Mail."

Even the conservative States' Rights doctrinaires were not forgotten by the Republicans at Chicago, although many were of the belief that all foes of federal government encroachments were in the Democratic Party lured by the Jeffersonian tradition. The Republican platform made a promise that sounded like a courting of Southern conservative votes: the promise of "the maintenance inviolate of the rights of the States, and especially the right of each State to order and control its own domestic institutions according to its own judgment exclusively." And the Germans were given the homestead plank and another, the fourteenth, which demanded no change in the existing federal Naturalization laws and also denied the right of any State to "abridge or impair" the rights of immigrants—a provision which ran counter to the principles of States' Rights.

And so the Republicans, like the Democrats, followed the standard electioneering strategy of appealing to diverse groups with the intention of garnering votes from men of different and even diametrically opposite views. In that Republic platform of 1860 there could be read so many things for almost everybody, except the Southern slaveholders, Northern town Irish, and those who were umbilically tied to Douglas or Buchanan.

Overshadowing the platform, of course, was the nomination of a candidate for President.

VIII

As Lincoln agonizingly waited in downstate Springfield for word about his candidacy, his supporters in Chicago operated feverishly in his behalf. Men in hotel lobbies and bars, on street corners, behind closed doors in private rooms, gathered in knots, sometimes in a huddle with arms about each other, chatting and whispering, in the words of one newshawk, "as if the fate of the country depended upon their immediate delivery of the mighty secrets with which their imaginations are big." Rumors ran riot, and "matters of incalculable moment were communicated confidentially at intervals of five minutes."

Behind the scenes, the floor managers, aided by their skilled emissaries and "leg men" assistants, worked tirelessly night and day, Judge David

Davis and State Chairman Judd leading the Lincoln forces. Thurlow Weed of Albany, generalissimo of the party in New York State, directed strategy for the candidacy of his friend and political partner, the celebrated Seward, who would go into the balloting with the most delegates. The Blairs of Maryland and Missouri, aided by the irascibly anti-Seward Horace Greeley "of Oregon," mapped the fight for Judge Edward Bates's nomination. Managers for Governor Chase of Ohio, for United States Supreme Court Justice John McLean (perennial presidential aspirant), and for other hopeful White House aspirants, were seen everywhere. With ceaseless activity these modern Warwicks conducted backstage operations. They received floor managers and other aides with their reports, thought what should be their next move, gave new instructions, "buttonholed" uncommitted (and committed) delegates, and now and then took a delegate or political lieutenant into the corner of a room for secret talk, or disappeared with another through a side door for transactions still more secret.

Lincoln's Illinois workers performed highly adroit services in attracting key delegations to their favorite. Judge Davis promised the supporters of Senator Simon Cameron that their favorite, the unsavory Pennsylvanian, would be tendered a Cabinet post if Lincoln were nominated and elected President, should the Cameron delegates go for Lincoln in the balloting. The Lincoln men gave a similar pledge to Caleb B. Smith of Indiana, head of the Hoosier delegation, if that State's delegates would go into Lincoln's camp.

Two days following the Convention Dr. William Jayne of Springfield, brother-in-law of Senator Trumbull and an observer at Chicago, sent private word to Trumbull: "Logan & Davis, Butler & Dubois, Judd, Cook & Palmer, & Jack Grimshaw worked like Turks for Lincoln's nomination." They labored incessantly, scarcely sleeping. Lincoln's former law partner, Stephen T. Logan of Springfield; David Davis of Bloomington, Judge of the Eighth Judicial Circuit; William Butler of Chicago, State Treasurer; Jesse K. Dubois of Lawrence County, State Auditor; Norman B. Judd, Republican State Chairman; Burton C. Cook of Ottawa, State Senator; John M. Palmer of Carlinville, future Civil War general, Governor, and United States Senator; and Jackson Grimshaw of Quincy, lawyer and politician. To these men mentioned by Dr. Jayne, Ozias M. Hatch of Springfield, Secretary of State of Illinois, Leonard Swett of Bloomington, Judge Davis's closest crony, Charles H. Ray and Joseph Medill, both of the Chicago *Press & Tribune,* and Gustave Koerner of Belleville, German-born former Lieutenant-Governor of Illinois should be added. Chief leadership, however, was wielded by Davis and Judd. As Palmer correctly noted in his reminiscences: "Undoubtedly Judge David Davis and Norman B. Judd contributed most to the nomination of Lincoln."

But why were the strategy and labors of Davis, Judd, and the others successful in persuading the Convention to nominate Lincoln?

In choosing a presidential candidate, the Republican professionals, who controlled the Chicago Convention, finally cast aside better known but more controversial figures, the radical Seward, the even more radical Chase, the conservative, Know-Nothing Bates, and the unsavory Cameron, to unite behind a lesser known but middleground "available" candidate, Lincoln.

Seward proved too anti-slavery to suit conservatives. He had acted too friendly toward parochial Catholic schools and European immigrants generally to satisfy Know-Nothings. He was too tainted with Thurlow Weed's "Albany Institute" of applied politics to please moralists and reformers and too long in national politics not to have made numerous enemies. Chase, even more than Seward, was too radically anti-slavery to suit conservatives and too much associated with old Democratic "Free trade" tariff ideas to please Pennsylvania. Bates proved too conservative to satisfy radicals and extreme anti-slavery advocates. "Fossil of the Silurian era," the white-bearded Bates was dubbed. Besides, his having presided over a national Know-Nothing convention only four years previous and his support of Millard Fillmore, the nativistic "American Party" presidential candidate at that time, made him *persona non grata* to the German-born element, who actively opposed his nomination. Cameron had too stained a reputation for sharp practices in public life to be even considered. His arch rival, Andrew G. Curtin, Pennsylvania gubernatorial candidate on the Republican ticket, worked until all hours of the evening to remove Cameron from consideration at Chicago.

So there remained only Lincoln, who had only a measure of national fame from his debates against Douglas in 1858 and his short tour of New York City and New England in 1860. He was the first choice of very few delegates outside Illinois. But he was disliked by none, so unknown a quantity was he and so little had he done in public life. He became the second choice of a formidable number of party leaders and delegates. Most significant, he was acceptable to Republican leaders of the four "doubtful" states which Republicans had lost to the Democrats in 1856. Lincoln was Illinois's favorite son. He had lived in Indiana fourteen years of his youth and knew party leaders of that State's western counties because his Eighth Judicial Circuit bordered on that region. He was acceptable to Pennsylvania because of his past protectionist tariff record as an old Henry Clay Whig. And New Jersey took him for that same reason. Too, in each of those four states which had to be carried in November, there were great numbers of old Whig conservatives, to whom Lincoln was vastly more acceptable than was Seward or Bates. The large German immigrant faction that had been responsible for knocking Bates out of consideration held Lincoln second only to Seward because of his longtime friendliness to Germans and because of his public flattery of them.

Illinois, Indiana, Pennsylvania, and New Jersey bulked largest in assigning any single reason for the nomination. As Congressman Schuyler Colfax of Indiana wrote to Lincoln on the day of his nomination: "Your name was the most hopeful, around which to rally in the doubtful states."

The selection of Lincoln as Republican standard-bearer was a story of practical politics, the familiar one unfolded in so many national and state nominating conventions of all parties before and since. Seward, the most prominent and powerful contender, had strongest delegate support, but his leading position lasted only as long as his opponents failed to unite. When they combined against him, the Senator from New York was dropped and a rather obscure but considerably less controversial figure was chosen.

IX

Lincoln on the momentous mid-May day of his nomination had gone to his office during the morning. He was speaking with two law students when an *Illinois State Journal* editor ran in, a despatch clutched in hand. It was news of the result of the first ballot taken at the convention in Chicago. Seward was leading him, 173½ to 102. 233 votes, a majority of the total 465 of the convention, were required to nominate. Lincoln rushed out of his office, with the editor trailing in his long steps. On the way to the *State Journal* building, they stopped at the telegraph office. No further news had come from Chicago.

A crowd awaited Lincoln at the *State Journal* office. News of the second ballot ticked over the wire and was brought to him. He grew tense. The vote stood: Seward, 184½, Lincoln, 181. Pennsylvanians had switched to Lincoln and other delegates had joined the band-wagon.

The next hour was tense. Finally news of the third ballot came over the wire. A telegram was handed him. It read: "Vote just announced—whole no 466—necessary to choice 234—Lincoln 354 votes—on motion of Mr Evarts of NY the nomination made unanimous amid intense excitement."

The boy who delivered the telegram to Lincoln recalled that "Mr. Lincoln opened it and a sudden pallor came over his features. He gazed upon it intently nearly three minutes." Then he rose from his chair, saying that he would go home and tell the news to Mrs. Lincoln.

REPUBLICAN STANDARD-BEARER

15

I

ABRAHAM LINCOLN made his way from the *State Journal* office to his home on Eighth Street, half dazed, half exhilarated by the announcement of his nomination. A hundred-gun salute was sounded by proud Springfielders and bells clanged as cheering throngs followed him to his house. Within a few hours flags fluttered from Republican headquarters and atop the *State Journal* building.

The night of Lincoln's nomination throughout Illinois was the most deliriously and noisily exuberant evening that the state had ever experienced. In nearly every county, except those down in Southern-oriented "Egypt" near the Kentucky line, cannons boomed, tar barrels were set afire, and happily semi-hysterical citizens marched along carrying rails, symbolic of their presidential candidate. "The cry is already 'Rails, Rails, Rails,'" wrote J. H. Burnham to his father the next morning. Lincoln's son, Bob, was dubbed "The Prince of Rails." Soon Springfield did a brisk business in wooden souvenirs made from an "identical rail" split by the standard-bearer in his youth. The city's streets, noted one Indianapolis newsman, "resemble a Hindoo bazaar."

All the joyful clamor for Lincoln reflected a militant sectional pride. For years the Northwest had been demanding the presidency. The region had only once been represented in the White House—by General Harrison of Ohio, and he had lived but one month following his inauguration. Lewis Cass of Michigan had run as Democratic standard-bearer in 1848 but had lost to the Whig, General Taylor of Louisiana. Illinois' own Stephen A. Douglas had already been twice by-passed for his party's nomination in 1852 and 1856. Now Lincoln, the Illinois Republican, was running, with excellent prospects of being elected.

II

On Saturday, May 19, the committee of notification from the Republican National Convention arrived in Springfield, headed by George Ashmun of Massachusetts, who had presided at the convention. Ashmun had also served as a fellow Whig member with Lincoln in Congress.

The Springfield Lincoln Club, the official greeter, had organized crowds of cheering citizens, who yelled festively, sang, and marched to music dispensed by the Young American and the German Saxe Horn bands. Bonfires blazed, rockets were shot in the air and cannons were fired to commemorate the unprecedented occasion.

The committee of notification proceeded to the Lincoln home, a prim looking, light chocolate-colored dwelling with green shutters, where Lincoln had now recovered from the first shocks of his nomination. Mrs. Lincoln, even prouder than her proud Kentucky heritage warranted, had ideas of serving champagne to the committee. But Gustave Koerner and Ebenezer Peck advised that alcoholic beverages would not do, since some of the committee men might be temperance disciples. Lincoln agreed, and so the committee was served ice water.

Lincoln three weeks later, in a note marked with his customary "Private & Confidential" restriction of his candidacy days, explained to J. Mason Haight, a Wisconsin temperance leader: "Having kept house sixteen years, and having never held the 'cup' to the lips of my friends then, my judgment was that I should not, in my new position, change my habits in this respect. What actually occurred upon the occasion of the Committee visiting me, I think it would be better for others to say."

No notification committee member had ever seen Lincoln, except Ashmun, who had known him in Congress, and Carl Schurz, who had heard him debate against Douglas two years previous. As the members gathered in the little Lincoln parlor, they found themselves non-plussed by their new national leader's ill-fitting clothes and melancholic expression. Ashmun formally notified him that he had been nominated for President. Lincoln thanked Ashmun and his associates, and then somewhat startled them by remarking that his nomination was "a responsibility which I could almost wish had fallen upon some one of the far more eminent men and experienced statesmen whose distinguished names were before the Convention." He added: "I shall, by your leave, consider more fully the resolutions of the Convention, denominated the platform, and without unreasonable delay, respond to you, Mr. Chairman, in writing—not doubting now, that the platform will be found satisfactory, and the nomination accepted."

Later, Senator Hannibal Hamlin of Maine, Vice-Presidential candidate on Lincoln's slate, was officially notified that he had been nominated. In that second-place selection at Chicago, the political rules of geography and past party antecedents were followed. Hamlin, whose Senate achievements had never reached weighty proportions, was named as Lincoln's running mate because the national ticket must be "balanced." Since Lincoln was of the Northwest and an ex-Whig, Hamlin qualified since he was of New England and an ex-Democrat.

Lincoln sent his formal letter of acceptance to Ashmun on May 23, officially accepting the party designation and agreeing with the platform adopted. "It shall be my care not to violate, or disregard it, in any part."

Ashmun proceeded to release a copy of Lincoln's letter to the nationwide press, but the printer had spelled Lincoln's first name "Abram." Fortunately, the error was caught in time to be corrected before the letter was sent out to other newspapers.

So many newspapers were calling the Republican candidate "Abram" Lincoln, that Lincoln on June 4 sent a message to Ashmun: "It seems as if the question whether my first name is 'Abraham' or 'Abram' will never be settled. It is *'Abraham'* and if the letter of acceptance is not yet in print, you may, if you think fit, have my signature thereto printed *'Abraham Lincoln.'* Exercise your own judgment about this."

Ashmun's printing of Lincoln's acceptance letter was being held up, but only because Vice-Presidential candidate Hamlin delayed in sending his acceptance letter to Ashmun. Lincoln's note to Ashmun, telling about the confusion over his first name, reached Ashmun before Lincoln's acceptance letter was printed, and so Ashmun had time in which to correct the error and change Lincoln's Christian name to its proper spelling. Ashmun two weeks later explained to Lincoln: "When your note arrived the official letter had been in type some days, awaiting the arrival of Mr. Hamlin's reply. I called on one of the Editors of the *Republican* [newspaper in Springfield, Massachusetts], & authorized a change in the full Christian name. The official letters appeared the next day in proper form."

Thus was avoided the embarrassing predicament (to Lincoln) of having himself introduced to the nation as "Abram" Lincoln.

III

Some party leaders grew disturbed over the general unfamiliarity with Lincoln outside Illinois. Greeley of the New York *Tribune* complained about Lincoln's anonymity to the public: "There should be at least one million copies of some cheap Life of Lincoln. There are thousands who do not yet know Abraham Lincoln."

Greeley's call for biographies of the standard-bearer was answered with a bountiful vengeance. The electioneering Boswells and assorted hack writers, some authorized by the Republican high command and others on their own initiative, hastily ground out short-order booklets on the little-known Lincoln. Their published products, quickly fashioned, cheap, paper-backed pamphlets and glued pages, followed a then familiar format. They were hodge-podges of sketchy details of the careers of Lincoln and Hamlin, with extracts from their stump speeches, "humanized" with homely family lore, profusely padded with party propaganda. The authors' main equipment were scissors, paste, and brush. These crude literary productions were the first books on the man destined to have more works, excellent, good, bad, and terrible, published about him than any other American before or since.

The "Wigwam Edition," anonymously written but published by Rudd & Carleton of Canal Street, New York, with Lincoln's first name spelled "Abram," was probably the first of these campaign biographies, published June 2, only two weeks following Lincoln's nomination, the first trickle of a vast flood of Lincolniana which still cascades from presses after an entire century. Twelve thousand copies of the "Wigwam Edition" were sold within a week.

Joseph Medill, editor, chief stock holder, and big power of the Chicago *Press & Tribune,* main Republican journal of Illinois, had aided in Lincoln's pre-convention campaign and done yeoman work at the national convention to secure his nomination. Now Medill decided that his newspaper should sponsor the writing of a life of Lincoln. He assigned his senior editor, John L. Scripps.

Lincoln received Scripps at his Springfield office, in early June. Together the two talked of Lincoln's life, with Scripps taking notes and persuading the standard-bearer to prepare an autobiographical sketch. Scripps later recalled: "The chief difficulty I had to encounter was to induce him to communicate the homely facts" of his youth. Scripps quoted Lincoln as telling him: "It is a great piece of folly to attempt to make anything out of my life. It can be all condensed into a simple sentence, and that sentence you will find in Gray's Elegy—'The short and simple annals of the poor.' That's my life, and that's all you or any one else can make of it."

The autobiographical sketch, written by Lincoln for Scripps's guidance in June, 1860, proved more lengthy than the one he had done of himself for Jesse W. Fell seven months previous. Writing in the third person, Lincoln detailed for Scripps the fullest and most fact-filled narrative of himself that he was ever to compose for anyone during his lifetime. He detailed incidents from his Kentucky birth through his stump-speaking for Frémont four years before. The book which Scripps completed on Lincoln was closer to Lincoln and more truly a biography than any other campaign *Life* of 1860.

Among other partisan biographies of Lincoln, produced during that election season, was that written by William Dean Howells. Then a twenty-three-year-old staff member of the Republican *Ohio State Journal* of Columbus, the future "Dean" of American letters did his work for Follett, Foster & Co, of that city. Only a few hours after Lincoln was nominated, a representative of that publishing firm, which was putting out a Lincoln-Douglas Debates volume, had telegraphed Lincoln: "We have announced your biography. Please designate your pleasure if any as to who the writer shall be." Lincoln made no reply, so Foster, Follett & Co. selected Howells.

Howells, however, did not even go to Springfield for a visit with Lincoln. Instead, he sent a young law student of Columbus, James Quay Howard, to interview Lincoln and collect material. "When he [Howard] brought it back," Howells subsequently revealed, "I felt the charm of the material, the wild poetry of its reality was not unknown to me; I was at home with it, for I had known the belated backwoods of a certain region of Ohio; I had almost lived the pioneer." And so the Columbus publishing house put out *Lives and Speeches of Abraham Lincoln and Hannibal Hamlin*. Another writer did the part on Hamlin.

Howard, however, having done the research in Springfield and having interviewed Lincoln, decided that he, too, would become a Lincoln biographer. Almost simultaneously with Howell's work, Follett, Foster & Co. published James Quay Howard's *Life of Abraham Lincoln, with extracts from his speeches*.

Lincoln received a shock when that Columbus publisher advertised one of its coming books—Howells or Howard's, it is not certain—as having been authorized by him.

The Republican presidential candidate sent a sharp letter of protest to Samuel Galloway, a prominent Columbus Republican, who wanted Lincoln to look over proof sheets. In his stinging note to Galloway, marked *"Especially Confidential,"* on June 19, Lincoln reminded him: "Messrs. Follett, Foster & Co's Life of me is *not* by my authority; and I have scarcely been so much astounded by anything, as by their public announcement that it is authorized by me." He had not objected to the firm's publishing the work "*upon their own responsibility*. I even took pains to facilitate them. But, at the same time, I made myself tiresome, if not hoarse, with repeating to Mr. Howard, their only agent seen by me, my protest that I *authorized nothing*—would be *responsible for nothing*. How, they could misunderstand me, passes comprehension." He explained: "As a matter, *wholly my own,* I would authorize no biography, without *time,* and *opertunity* (sic) to carefully examine and consider every word of it." Lincoln requested Galloway: "I barely suggest that you, or any of the friends there, on the party account, look it over, & exclude what you may think would embarrass the party—bearing in mind, at all times, that I *authorize nothing*." The candidate closed his letter, "Your friend, as ever, A. Lincoln."

Besides the campaign biographies of Scripps, Howells, and Howard, scores of others appeared, including one by Joseph H. Barrett of the Cincinnati *Gazette,* who wrote the 216-page *Life of Abraham Lincoln . . . With a Condensed View of His Most Important Speeches.* Several German-language *Lives* also were circulated.

After election most copies of those first of all Lincoln books were consigned to the rubbish heap, though Lincoln was to care for some of the authors after he assumed the presidency. He selected Scripps as Postmaster at Chicago, appointed Howells as United States Consul at Venice, Italy, and chose Barrett as Commissioner of Pensions.

IV

All the while, the opposition Democratic Party, a bulwark of the Union, was fracturing itself into factions. Intraparty struggles over slavery, States' Rights, and other sectional issues, disputes concerning complex constitutional controversies, divisions caused by devotion to dead leaders (such as Jackson and Calhoun), disappointments about federal and state patronage, relentless rivalries for personal and party power were among the disruptive forces which lead to the partition of the party of Jefferson and Jackson.

At the Democratic National Convention in Charleston, South Carolina, during April, 1860, a month before the Republicans nominated Lincoln at Chicago, the intraparty discord crashed to a fatal crisis. This crisis was precipitated by, among other factors, the determination of Senator Douglas's supporters to have him nominated for President, by the equal insistence of anti-Douglas Democrats (aided by President Buchanan's men) that he must not be chosen the party's standard-bearer, and by the "Southern Rights" fire-eaters, led by Robert Barnwell Rhett of South Carolina and William L. Yancey of Alabama, who vowed that the slave states must have a showdown with the Northern Democrats at the convention, even if it meant destroying the national Democratic Party and dissolving the Union.

The selection of Charleston in the secession-fevered Palmetto State as the convention site could not possibly contribute to Democratic Party peace or stifle sectionalism. But the anti-Douglas Democratic National Committee, controlled by a union of Buchanan's backers and Southerners, had settled on the metropolis of the future state of "Secessia" because its very atmosphere would not favor Douglas's nomination. The Little Giant had offended Dixie because of his opposition to Buchanan on Kansas in the Senate and by his enunciation of the "Freeport Doctrine," wrung out of him by Lincoln almost two years previous.

The Democratic conclave at Charleston wrangled for two days over whether Mayor Fernando Wood's delegation or Dean Richmond's "Albany Regency-Tammany Hall" delegation should be seated as the official New York State representatives. Tempers became irritated as that party fight for power in the Empire State forced discordant groups to take sides, adding more disharmony to the national gathering. Then Yancey of Alabama, leading his "Southern Rights" ultras to a rule-or-ruin result, demanded that the platform, which they insisted must contain guarantees of Congressional protection for slavery in the territories, be adopted before the balloting for a presidential candidate. They cared not whether they would sabotage the convention and wreck the Democratic Party as a national body. The Douglasites, for their part, determined that Douglas must be nominated, were willing enough that the Southern Righters should bolt the convention, in which event they would have a delegate two-thirds majority necessary to nominate the Senator from Illinois. Thus Douglasites, opportunistically, joined with their foes, the Yanceyites, in agreeing that the convention should act on the party platform first, then proceed to presidential balloting. The Douglas disciples made an "unholy" agreement with Yancey's followers to vote on the platform. Scant statesmanship was shown on either side.

The Convention adopted a "minority" report on the platform, which did not protect slavery in the territories but left that matter to future Supreme Court decisions. The slave-state fire-eaters yelled angrily. Then, headed by Yancey, the deep-Dixie delegates marched out of the convention hall. The Charleston convention had blown up. The Douglasites would reassemble in two months.

The Republicans, in great glee over the Democratic division, nominated Lincoln at Chicago in May. Then in June the Douglas Democrats reconvened at Baltimore and named their leader as the party's candidate for President. But that did not end Democratic discord. Subsequent conventions of Southern "bolters," along with dissident anti-Douglas men, met in conventions and nominated the Vice-President of the United States, John C. Breckinridge of Kentucky, on a conservative platform appealing to a majority of Southern Democrats and a minority of Northern Democrats.

As if three presidential candidates, Lincoln, the Republican, and Douglas and Breckinridge, Democrats, were not enough, elderly conservatives of Whig background, Unionists opposed to perilous sectionalism in both North and South, had formed a new party, the "Constitutional Unionists." They named for President the old Clay Whig, Senator John Bell of Tennessee. The Bell party's platform simply called for "The Constitution of the Country, the Union of the States, and the Enforcement of the Laws." The Constitutional Unionists' integrity belonged to that era of American politics before Jackson. They became the butt of ridicule by their foes. Since the able Edward Everett was Bell's Vice-Presidential running-mate, they called the slate the "Kangaroo Ticket" because all of its strength was in the hind quarters.

V

Lincoln, from his nomination until after election, remained in Springfield, traditionally agreeing with the custom that a presidential candidate should not gallivant about the country talking, or even seeing and being seen. This practice of standard-bearers remaining quiet suited him well. For throughout the canvass he had no intention of committing himself publicly on any question, major or minor.

So heavily did Lincoln's mail mount, that he retained John G. Nicolay, a German-born resident of Pike County, Illinois, who worked in Secretary of State Ozias M. Hatch's office, to assist him. Lincoln had known Nicolay intimately, since he was also custodian of Illinois state election records in Hatch's office; and, as Nicolay observed, Lincoln was constantly visiting his office, "an assiduous student of election tables."

Lincoln's queues of callers included harassing hopefuls, who assured him of their past titanic labors to secure him the presidential nomination and now pointed to their present gruelling efforts to elect him—harbingers of his future office-hunting problems. Visiting and talking with Lincoln, too, were politicians big and little and those who wanted to be big by giving him advice; portrait painters, photographers, and sculptors who implored him to pose for them; autograph seekers; and numberless newspaper reporters.

Those gentlemen of the fourth estate received no statements of consequence from Lincoln. He simply was not talking, except to express pleasantries and utter a few words on strictly non-political subjects. He wrote only a score of private letters during the canvass, always marking them "Confidential," not to be divulged to anyone but the receiver. He also kept sharp watch on his three-fold opposition by mail and received personal reports from visiting key politicians, advising on stumping tours and the states and localities to be visited by his campaigners. He wrote on electioneering tactics to Chairman Edwin D. Morgan (Governor of New York) and Secretary George G. Fogg of New Hampshire of the Republican National Committee.

By mail Lincoln asked Secretary Fogg for counsel: *"How does it look now?* I am invited to a horse-show, at Springfield, Mass. beginning, I believe, on the 4th. of September. Would it *help,* or *hurt,* our cause, if I were to go? I am not itching to go, and seek to be advised thereto." Lincoln did not travel from Springfield, Illinois, to Springfield, Massachusetts, nor did he even set foot outside of his town until after election. In another letter to Fogg toward the campaign's end Lincoln gave assurances that he would be vigilant about talking: "Allow me to beg that you will not live in much apprehension of my precipitating a letter upon the public."

Aside from some brief non-committal remarks at his home in August, when he was merely being seen by a group of citizens, Candidate Lincoln made no speeches. This determination not to touch on issues he rationalized privately on the ground that "writing for the public" would "do no good." People, he thought, would not be persuaded. His confidential letter to one Tennessean, William S. Speer, on October 23, 1860, is typical of his view:

"Yours of the 13th was duly received. I appreciate your motive when you suggest the propriety of my writing for the public something disclaiming all intention to interfere with slaves or slavery in the States; but in my judgment, it would do no good. I have already done this many —many times; and it is in print, and open to all who will read. Those who will not read, or heed, what I have already publicly said, would not read, or heed, a repetition of it.

" 'If they hear not Moses and the prophets, neither will they be persuaded though one rose from the dead.' "

And so the candidate maintained his Sphinx-like silence.

If Lincoln remained quiet, the campaigners of all four parties did not.

The American love of showmanship and susceptibility to homely hokum in political campaigns, and the professional vote-gatherers' ready response to give the public pageantry and fanfare, in exchange for support at the polls, were conspicuous in that fight for the White House. In retrospect that national election appears grotesquely incongruous, tragically ominous, a spectacle of electioneering marching clubs such as the "Wide-Awakes," carnival-like maneuvers for the masses' votes reminiscent of the "log cabin" and "cider" campaign of two decades before. All the while, Lincoln, the probable winner, maintained silence on the bedeviling problem of slavery, as the Union reeled in the balance. The showmanship and popular entertainment at times crowded out discussion of weighty issues in all parties, except the Constitutional Unionist.

Republicans vied with each other in noisy praise of their candidate's simplicity, homely virtues, and humble background. For this almost demagogic approach to ballot-collecting by his working campaigners Lincoln was admirably adapted. Around him clustered the pioneer tradition, and emphasis was oratorically and editorially placed on his log-cabin birth and rail-splitting youth.

Those tactics of popular political warfare were proving handsomely rewarding. One Republican worker later exulted, "It has also afforded me sincere pleasure to think of Mr. Lincoln taking possession of the White House; he, who was once the inmate of a log cabin—were he the pampered, effeminated child of fortune, no such pleasing emotions would be inspired."

The "rail-splitter" motif was worth untold thousands of votes to Lincoln. The spark that had been ignited at the Republican state convention in Decatur, the week preceding the national convention, caught fire and spread when Medill of the Chicago *Press & Tribune* prominently exhibited two rails in his building. Lincoln himself added to the idea when, to a New York *Herald* reporter in Springfield, he showed a rail and explained: "Yes, sir, here is a stick I received a day or two since from Josiah Gentry, of Gentryville, Indiana. He writes me that it is one of the rails that I cut for him in 1825." A campaign newspaper, The *Rail Splitter,* was established at Chicago and also at Cincinnati and became the Northwest's outstanding electioneering sheet.

All of that manufactured noise, simulated enthusiasm, and fanfare cost money. Speakers had to be paid, too, and newspapers subsidized. It was not surprising that the crinkling of campaign dollars was audible behind the scenes. Judge David Davis appealed to Thurlow Weed to raise more, and ever more, funds, commenting in underscored words: *"Men work better with money in hand."*

That task of collecting the currency sinews of party warfare was undertaken mainly by Governor Edwin D. Morgan of New York, Republican National Chairman and a money-laden merchant, and Fogg. The affluent Morgan borrowed $20,000 for the campaign on his own collateral.

Seward's banker-friend, Richard M. Blatchford of New York, generously opened his checkbook, reminding the party powers after the election, "Mr. Weed tells me the $3,000 which I advanced in one sum last October was sent by him to Mr. Lincoln's relative Mr. Smith at Mr. Lincoln's suggestion for the purpose of carrying the Legislature of Illinois which was deemed in danger." In Illinois Lincoln's former law-partner, Logan, took leadership in raising electioneering funds. In Lincoln's home county, Sangamon, an estimated $12,000 was raised.

The Douglasites found hard sledding in efforts to collect campaign currency. Douglas's National Chairman, August Belmont of New York, in July complained to Douglas about *"those lukewarm and selfish money-bags,"* explaining: "Unless we can give to our merchants and politicians some *assurance of success,* I fear that it will be impossible to raise the necessary funds for our campaign."

Breckinridge's candidacy did not require too much cash, since it was supported by the anti-Douglas federal office-holders under President Buchanan, who would have been fired from their jobs if they had worked for the Little Giant's election. Bell's cause received substantial contributions from conservative merchants in New York City and New England and big slaveholders in the border states, who feared that Lincoln's election would cause disruption of the Union. One Republican worker reported in alarm: "The Bell men have raised considerable money."

It seemed apparent that the campaigns of all four candidates for President were being handled by practical politicians.

VI

In the race for the White House waged by the forces of Lincoln, Douglas, Breckinridge, and Bell, there could be no clearcut mandate on what should have been—and what later writers alleged was—the paramount issue: slavery. For there existed no consistent grouping of voters, to start with. The South's "peculiar institution" simply could not be made a defined issue on which to vote in November. The nation reeled from the heady spirit of party and sectionalism. There was not produced a like-minded opinion, pro or con, but rather organized pressure from the professionals in the four parties, Republican, "Douglas" Democrat, "Breckinridge" Democrat, and Constitutional Union, to win the election merely for the sake of winning, with scant regard for the future of the Union. Bell's party, however, was more free from this crass opportunism than were the three others.

Matters were made more complex, and more bewildering to the voters, when Lincoln, a moderate himself, appealed to radical anti-slaveryites, middle-of-the-roaders, and conservative Old-Line Whigs, in addition to German immigrants and special interest groups wanting a higher tariff, or homestead, or other material benefit for their section. This confusion grew even greater when Douglas held his personal following in the North, including Irish-born Catholics because he had married into that faith. He also had followers in the South, his Vice-Presidential running-mate being Herschel V. Johnson, a Georgian. Breckinridge, holding most of the Southern voters, had support in the North, in New York City which had commercial ties with the South, and "Breckinridge" state tickets were run in the Empire State, Massachusetts and other presumably surprising places. Breckinridge drew strength from conservative border men as well as from the most hidebound slaveocrats and fire-eating fanatics in deep Dixie. And Breckinridge had an Oregonian, Senator Joe Lane, as his running-mate, so the Breckinridge-Lane slate would run a close second to Lincoln in Oregon. John Bell appealed to Old-Line Whigs, particularly in the border states, yet some of those old disciples of Henry Clay would go for Lincoln because he had been a Whig and they knew him to be moderate. It was an unrecognizably scrambled picture, that election of 1860, and it could not be discovered just where slavery figured.

Any intent to make that national election a drawn fight between opponents and defenders of slavery was further complicated by the Republicans' appeals to voters on issues other than slavery: the tariff, homestead, immigrant-catering, a Pacific railroad, and river-and-harbor improvements.

Lincoln learned how wisely, from the viewpoint of victory, the platform makers at Chicago had drafted the Republican party platform, with "subsidiary" issues besides slavery in it.

The tariff plank, sympathetic to higher import rates, particularly pleased Pennsylvania and parts of New Jersey. Philadelphia's main Republican mouthpiece, the *North American and United States Gazette,* printed only six editorials relating to slavery between early September and national election day in November; whereas it ran sixteen lengthy editorials lauding the party's tariff-protectionist plank between September 3 and October 11. On October 2 Lincoln privately answered one query about his tariff views by pointing to his acceptance of the party platform. To the correspondent of the Philadelphia *North American,* James E. Harvey, Lincoln sent "private and confidential" word: "In 1844 I was on the Clay electoral ticket in this State (i.e. Illinois) and, to the best of my ability, sustained, together, the tariff of 1842 and the tariff plank of the Clay platform. This could be proven by hundreds —perhaps thousands—of living witnesses."

Homestead was proving a winner in the West. Samuel C. Pomeroy of Atchison, future United States Senator from Kansas, on July 17 reported to Lincoln that the defeat of the Homestead Bill in the Senate by Democratic votes "has sufficiently damned the Democratic Party for the present." The Germans liked the pro-immigrant plank, and the Indianapolis *Journal* editor, John D. Defrees, in a May 26 letter to Lincoln, called it a wisely devised "Dutch" plank.

Out in California, Republicans were making effective use of the party's promise of a railroad to the Pacific. William Rabé, Secretary of that State's Republican State Central Committee, in early July sent news to Lincoln: "The People of this State look for a Pacific Rail Road as their greatest desideratum, and I have as you will perceive by the heading of this letter taken good care." On Rabé's letterhead was an immense lithograph of a steam locomotive chugging along, labeled "LINCOLN." Slavery was not even mentioned. In the Great Lakes region the party orators and editors pounded away at the theme that the congressional Democrats had not voted sufficient government money for river-and-harbor improvement.

There appeared something for many people in that Republican platform of 1860. If there was a disposition for any one not to cast his ballot in the Republican column, it surely was no fault of the platform-makers at Chicago.

This same electioneering technique of diverse appeals in different states and localities was seen even on the presumably paramount slavery question in Lincoln's own state. The Illinois of that day comprised at least two distinct political communities—the upper part, settled by people from New England and upstate New York and immigrants, many of them anti-slavery; and the lower counties, inhabited primarily by people from the Southern states. In both regions the Republicans went after votes, and suited their appeals on an opportunistic basis of presenting themselves as "all things to all men." One Republican party strategist in late May outlined tactics to candidate for Governor: Richard Yates "I believe the most effective Document for all the region North of the Rock River will be Lovejoy's last speech—then for the whole state prepare a Document composed of choice selections from Lincoln's. I think Jeff Davis' last speech would be good to distribute down in Egypt—vs. Douglas Democracy."

And so the time-tested, vote-catching strategy of using different issues and arguments in different sections went on as the stability of the Union hung in the balance.

VII

Lincoln, by early August, brimmed with confidence, sure that he would win all Northern states, both those won and lost by Frémont, as well as Minnesota and Oregon, each admitted into the Union since 1856. On August 4 Lincoln wrote his old Springfield friend, Simeon Francis, former editor of the *Illinois State Journal,* now living in Oregon. To Francis, the Republican standard-bearer, he confided his happy thoughts. It appears, he told Francis, that Republican victory was "inevitable." He added:

"We have no reason to doubt any of the states which voted for Fremont. Add to these, Minnesota, Pennsylvania, and New-Jersey, and the thing is done. Minnesota is as sure as such a thing can be; while the democracy are so divided between Douglas and Breckinridge (sic) in

Penn. & N.J. that they are scarcely less sure. Our friends are also confident in Indiana and Illinois. I should expect the same division would give us a fair chance in Oregon. Write me what you think on this point."

The first major tests to indicate how the presidential contest would result came in October, when state elections were held in Pennsylvania, Ohio, and Indiana, the second, third, and fifth most populous states in the nation. Pennsylvania and Indiana had been lost by Frémont four years before and had tipped the scales in favor of Buchanan's election.

Lincoln vigilantly watched developments in Indiana and Pennsylvania through his private correspondence and talks with visiting politicians. He advised Governor Morgan, Republican National Chairman:

"No one thing will do us so much good in *Illinois* as the carrying of *Indiana* at the October election. The whole surplus energy of the party throughout the nation, should be bent upon that object up to the close of that election. I should say the same of Pennsylvania, were it not that our assurances seem so abundant of Curtin's election there.

"If I might advise, I would say, bend all your energies upon Indiana now."

The election of the Republican gubernatorial candidate, Andrew G. Curtin, seemed sure in Pennsylvania because of the wide division among the Democrats as well as the Republicans' agitation for higher tariff rates. "The Republicans, in their speeches," gloomily reported one Pennsylvania Democratic chieftain to Douglas, "say nothing of the nigger question, but all is made to turn on the tariff."

Lincoln's spirits jumped happily when the state election returns from the Keystone and Hoosier commonwealths came over the wires. To Herndon, who was campaigning in Petersburg, Lincoln sent a joyful note: "I cannot give you details, but it is entirely certain that Pennsylvania and Indiana have gone Republican very largely, Penn 25,000 & Indiana 5 to 10. Ohio of course is safe."

VIII

With four presidential candidates in the race, what did election prospects portend?

Hostility among Lincoln's opposition, still split three ways into Douglasites, Breckinridgers, and Bellites, was pointing ever closer to Lincoln's triumph.

The Democratic division opened wider in some sections, making impossible any co-operation between disciples of Douglas and Breckinridge until the October election results in Pennsylvania, Indiana, and Ohio threw a scare into them, after which it was too late. The Illinois Senator's supporters berated Breckinridge as a pro-slavery secessionist, while Breckinridge's backers denounced Douglas as a party traitor to the South and to President Buchanan.

And John Bell? His Constitutional Union candidacy fizzled. Trying to maintain a moderate course between anti-slavery Northern Republican zealots and pro-slavery Democratic fire-eaters, Bell's backers were attempting the same thing as the Douglasites: to combat sectionalism above and below Mason and Dixon's line. The Tennessean's supporters, conservative Old-Line Whigs still devoted to the dead Henry Clay's compromising, Union-loving doctrines, found themselves out of tune with those 1860 days of rampant sectionalism and political madness. The Constitutional Unionists were attracting support in the border slave states, but little more.

Breckinridge was conceded to carry most of the South, although Douglas and Bell had minority support there. The Constitutional Unionists could not get together in a "fusion" coalition with Douglas Democrats or Breckinridge Democrats against Lincoln in most Northern regions. Bell's backers were still hard-shelled Whigs, devoted to the late Clay, and Democrats still revered the memory of Clay's old foe, the late Andrew Jackson.

Senator Jefferson Davis of Mississippi sought to have Douglas, Breckinridge, and Bell withdraw from the presidential race, in favor of a single anti-Lincoln candidate: Horatio Seymour of New York. Breckinridge and Bell agreed. Not so Douglas. He termed the plan "impracticable." Were he to withdraw, the Illinois Senator explained, his Northern Democratic supporters "would join in the support of Lincoln rather than of anyone who should supplant him," a rather egotistical, unstatesmanlike view. Soon it was announced that the Little Giant and his loyal legions were against fusion "all the way from Maine to California."

Douglas tried to offset the deficit in campaign funds and weakness in organization through the effect of his dynamic presence before the voters. He now destroyed the precedent which dictated that presidential candidates should not go on the hustings. "We must make war boldly against the Northern Abolitionists and the Southern Disunionists," he told the *Illinois State Register* editor. Douglas hoped against hope that, by hard campaigning and persuasive, relentless speaking, he could persuade the voters not to give Lincoln an electoral majority, thus throwing the national election into the popularly chosen House of Representatives.

In July and August Douglas went on the stump in New England, sadly learned that Lincoln would carry that section, returned to Washington to reflect, and then set out for Virginia and North Carolina. He found those two Upper Southern states divided in sympathy between Breckinridge and Bell, with himself squeezed out. In low spirits, Douglas took to the hustings in Maryland, oratorically thundering against Lincoln and Breckinridge alike. But that State thought like the Old

Dominion and the Tar Heel State. It was partly for Breckinridge, partly for Bell. He hurried to populous New York City in September and shouted: "I wish to God we had an Old Hickory now alive in order that he might hang Northern and Southern traitors on the same gallows."

Into doubtful Indiana and Pennsylvania Douglas rushed. He found the situation discouraging there, too. His own supporters and those of Bell could not get together on an anti-Lincoln coalition. Some Old-Line Whigs in both states were even forsaking Bell as a hopeless cause and going for Lincoln, who had once been a Whig. In Pennsylvania, the Republicans were using the tariff issue against the Little Giant, a lifelong low-tariff man.

Douglas next paid a brief visit to his own Illinois, where the Republicans were using a variety of charges against him not connected with slavery. In order to collect erstwhile Know-Nothing votes, they accused Douglas, married to a Catholic woman and having his children raised in that faith, of having "received the sacraments from the hands of the Pope" while in Rome. To ruin him with conservative Old-Line Whigs, they alleged that he had once called the revered Henry Clay a "rascal." To destroy him with moralistic "Maine-Law" men and assorted temperance advocates, they accused him of being a "habitual drunkard." Republicans also engaged in such demagoguery as the charge: "The Rothschilds want to elect him President." That sounded credible, since Douglas's National Chairman, August Belmont, was a European-born Jew who had worked for the Rothschild international banking combine in Germany, Italy, and Cuba, and was even then the Rothschilds' American representative.

October found Douglas in Iowa when he received the dreadful news that the Republicans had carried the Ohio, Pennsylvania, and Indiana state elections. "Mr. Lincoln is the next President," he dejectedly declared. "We must try to save the Union. I will go South."

After a few more Northwestern speaking engagements, hammering away against Abolitionists and Disunionists, Douglas hurried down to deep Dixie, for a last-ditch stand against Lincoln's looming triumph.

But Douglas's Southern crusade proved hopeless. The lower slave States viewed him hostilely as a traitor to the South because of his Freeport Doctrine which Lincoln had wrung out of him two years previously and because of his opposition to Buchanan's Kansas policy.

IX

Only one state, New York, cast sufficient electoral votes to deprive Lincoln of the presidency by itself. If his three-fold opposition could coalesce and keep the Empire State's big bloc of thirty-five electoral votes out of his column in November, the Republican standard-bearer would be deprived of an electoral majority, even if he carried every other Northern state, for it was conceded that most of the South would go to Breckinridge, the border slave states would divide between Breckinridge and Bell, and Douglas would receive some electoral votes in the North but not sufficient to crowd out Lincoln above Mason and Dixon's line. Should Lincoln fail to poll a majority in the electoral college, as provided in the United States Constitution, the national election would be decided by the House of Representatives, in which case Lincoln's opponents would have a chance of beating him for President. Thus Lincoln's foes paid close attention to New York State, as did Lincoln and his followers, managed by Thurlow Weed.

Lincoln in August grew concerned about the great vote-laden state along the Atlantic seaboard. "I think," he wrote Weed anxiously, "there will be the most extraordinary effort ever made, to carry New-York for Douglas. You, and all others who write me from your state, think the effort can not succeed; and I hope you are right; still it will require close watching, and great effort on the other side."

Later that month, Republican National Chairman Morgan reported to Carl Schurz about New York: "The friends of Douglas are raising considerable money and will yet try various expedients to accomplish something in this state."

Among other expedients, the New York State anti-Lincoln forces in October succeeded in forming a "fusion" electoral ticket to place on the November ballot, which gave Douglas 18 presidential electors; Bell, 10; and Breckinridge, 7.

Lincoln's opposition, however, had fused into union too late to accomplish much. Chairman Morgan on November 1, five days before election, was able to report to Lincoln: "All eyes and thoughts seem to be turned on New York. New York will not disappoint us. Her electoral ticket will have not less than 40,000 majority."

X

The 1860 presidential contest was a national election like no other in all American annals. It causes bewilderment today when its complexity, chaos, and confusion of thought are reconsidered. The four candidates representing the various splits in national thought, the intricate anti-Lincoln "fusion" electoral slates in some states, the raucous discord among Democrats, hating each other more than they did the common Republican foe, the many complex attitudes toward slavery, and the economic and special-interest appeals, such as the tariff, homestead, a Pacific railroad, daily overland mail, and river-and-harbor improvements made this one of the most complex of all American elections.

In such an emotionally charged atmosphere of abnormal intensity, the American men voted in that grimly crazy-quilt election on Tuesday, November 6, 1860.

Lincoln, in previous elections, had cast his own vote for himself. He now decided not to vote, for he held that a presidential candidate should not mark a ballot for his own electors. So he went into the polling place at the Court House in Springfield, tore off that part of his ballot listing the presidential electors, discarded it, and then voted for the Republican state ticket. His secretary, John G. Nicolay, jotted down these thoughts: "This is election day. The Hon. A. Lincoln has just been over to vote. The Courthouse steps were thronged with people who welcomed him with immense cheering. From the time he entered the room until he cast his vote and left it, wild huzzahing, the waving of hats and all sorts of demonstrations of applause rendered all other noises insignificant and futile."

That election night in Springfield crowds mobbed the telegraph offices as the returns were ticked in from state and nation. Republicans packed themselves into the state House of Representatives to hear the results. Shouts went up as returns indicated that Lincoln had carried the Northwest and New England. It was noted: "News from New York was anxiously awaited."

Republican presidential standard-bearer Lincoln himself was at the House of Representatives, along with State Auditor Jesse K. Dubois, Senator Trumbull, Baker of the *Illinois State Journal,* and other intimates.

Then word came from New York! Lincoln's electors had won that indispensable, vote-rich State! Trumbull's friend, Henry McPike, described the scene when Lincoln and party received the despatch about the glad tidings from the Empire State:

"Dubois jumped to his feet. 'Hey,' he shouted, and they began singing as loud as they could a campaign song, 'Ain't You Glad You Jined the Republicans?'

"Lincoln got up and Trumbull and the rest of us. We were all excited. There were hurried congratulations. Suddenly old Jesse grabbed the despatch out of Ed Baker's hand and started for the door. We followed . . . Lincoln last. The staircase was narrow and steep. We went down it still on the run. Dubois rushed across the street toward the meeting, so out of breath he couldn't speak plain. All he could say was, 'Spetch. Spetch.' Lincoln, coolest of the lot, went home to tell his wife the news."

PRESIDENT-ELECT: *Crisis and Cabinet*

16

I

ABRAHAM LINCOLN found himself a "minority" President, precisely what he had criticized Buchanan for four years previously. Although he polled a majority of electoral votes—he drew 180 to Breckinridge's 72, Bell's 39, and Douglas's 12—and was thus constitutionally and legally elected, Lincoln received a popular vote vastly smaller than the combined total of his three opponents. The "head" votes of more than 4,500,000 American men who went to the polls, stood: Lincoln, 1,866,452; Douglas, 1,376,957; Breckinridge, 849,781; and Bell, 588,879. Lincoln, with less than 1,900,000 popular votes, received 180 electoral votes, whereas Douglas, with more than 1,300,000, received a mere twelve electoral votes!

Broken down further, those election figures of 1860 demonstrated by what a curious "Electoral College" accident Lincoln emerged victor. His Republican Party won 39 per cent of the vote, no great increase over that polled by Frémont four years before. The combined Douglas-

Breckinridge tickets actually raised the popular Democratic vote from 45 per cent of the total (or 1,800,000) in 1856 to 47 per cent (or 2,200,000) in 1860. The Democrats, all told, cast 400,000 more votes than the Republicans in the 1860 election. Bell, another anti-Lincoln candidate and arch-conservative of border-slave state Tennessee, received more than half a million votes, nearly one-third of Lincoln's total. Yet Lincoln, by the constitutional electoral-college system of choosing presidents, was legally and properly elected, with no cloud to dim his title as Chief Executive.

Lincoln's election, however, could not be considered an anti-slavery triumph. Not all of his winning votes were cast for him because of the anti-slavery platform on which he stood. The infusion of factors other than slavery also prevented that campaign for President from being a referendum on the South's "peculiar institution." Lincoln was aided in carrying New York, with its thumping 35 electoral votes, by virtue of the Democratic split between the "Albany Regency"-Tammany Hall alliance and Mayor Fernando Wood's "Mozart Hall" machine over party power, with slavery a minor issue. Too, Lincoln polled the votes from untold thousands of erstwhile anti-Catholic, anti-immigrant Know-Nothings in the upstate counties. Pennsylvania, with 27 electoral votes, second only to New York in determining the election, went into Lincoln's column partly because of the split between the State's own son, President Buchanan, and Douglas over party power and patronage, partly because the Republicans emphasized a protective tariff, rather than the Negro question.

In Lincoln's own Northwest, homestead combined with anti-slavery influences to win for him. After election, Illinois's abolitionist Republican congressman, Owen Lovejoy, insisted to the House of Representatives that, if free land had not been pledged, "the Republicans never could have elected their President." Out on the West coast, the Democratic Party partition, plus Republican promises of a government-subsidized railroad to the Pacific and a daily overland mail, combined to give Lincoln the electoral votes of California and Oregon. The popular votes in those two Pacific coast states, indifferent to slavery, giving Lincoln a total of seven electoral votes, are instructive when examined. In California, Lincoln polled less than 40,000 to Douglas's more than 38,000 and Breckinridge's more than 34,000. In Oregon, Lincoln received less than 5,500 to Douglas's more than 3,900 and Breckinridge's 5,000.

The foreign-born did not always base their votes on their attitude toward slavery, either. The Germans were primarily attracted to the Republicans because of homestead promises and the plank guaranteeing naturalized citizenship rights to be the same as those of native-born. The Germans' sworn foes, the Know-Nothings, went for Lincoln because the Irish, whom they hated more than they did the Germans, were voting

Democratic. The sons of Erin, for their part, went for Douglas because of the Jacksonian tradition, "saloon" politics, and because Douglas was married to a Roman Catholic and was rearing his children in that faith.

In view of those foregoing non-slavery factors and mixed-up election figures, it seems beyond belief that Lincoln's elevation to the Presidency in November was a voters' mandate against slavery extension.

Yet, ironically, Lincoln's election, in which he polled not a single electoral vote in a Southern or border-slave state, was the signal for South Carolina to secede from the Union in the following month, December, 1860. Early in the new year, 1861, Mississippi, Florida, Alabama, Georgia and Louisiana followed the Palmetto commonwealth into secession, and Texas joined the secession on February 1. On their own avowal, these states comprised a separate American nation of their own.

So Lincoln's first problem as President-elect was perplexing: How should the secession be met?

II

Lincoln sent his first post-election letter to Vice-President-elect Hannibal Hamlin on November 8, 1860, requesting Hamlin to meet him at Chicago.

The President-elect on the 21st boarded a train at Springfield in the presence of a huge crowd and rode up to Chicago for his conference with Hamlin. En route he avoided speechmaking on vital issues, as he had during the recent campaign. His train stopped briefly at Lincoln, a town previously named for him in Logan County. His silence on the looming secession crisis was evident in his few words spoken there from his train platform: "I am not in the habit of making speeches now, and I would therefore ask to be excused from entering upon any discussion of the political topics of the day. I am glad to see so many happy faces, and listen to so many pleasant expressions."

The President-elect's Chicago conference with the Vice-President-elect centered, not on the obvious preparation of South Carolina to leave the Union, but on pure politics, especially the formation of his Cabinet and parceling of federal patronage. Thenceforward, until his inauguration in early March, 1861, Lincoln's handling, or rather lack of handling of the bedevilling secession crisis, might be termed "calculated inactivity." For he was to do nothing about it nor was he to provide much leadership, with the Republic tottering in balance.

Today it seems incredible that Lincoln, confronted with one Southern state after another departing from the Union to form their own Confederate States of America, from his election to his inauguration, should have paid so little attention to that secession crisis and devoted such surplus energy and precious time to Cabinet-formation and job-distribution, as he waited in Springfield for President Buchanan's administration to expire.

Even after Lincoln took the presidential oath in March, 1861, Charles Francis Adams, son of one President and grandson of another, who was to serve as Lincoln's Minister to England, was amazed in that month to find Lincoln "more intent on the distribution of offices than on the gravity of the crisis." Lincoln's Secretary of the Navy, Gideon Welles, privately explained it away in this wise:

"In striving to reconcile and bring into united action opposing views he [Lincoln] was accused of wasting his time in a great emergency on mere party appointments. Under the pressure and influence that were brought to bear upon him, some things were doubtless done, which, under other circumstances and left to himself, he would have ordered differently. . . . This crowd of active friends with their importunities at such a crisis was of course extremely embarrassing to the new administration, which commenced its labors with a demoralized government and crumbling Union that needed the vigilant attention and most considerate statesmanship."

Lincoln, however, had not yet developed qualities of statesmanship, and was not to do so until after the war against the Confederacy had started. Too, during his period as President-elect he did not fully realize the secession strength below Mason and Dixon's line and considerably overestimated the amount of pro-Union feeling in the Upper South and border slave states.

III

Lincoln's victorious Republican Party of 1860, comprising heterogeneous factions and diverse viewpoints, hitherto only an opposition whose only bond of union was denunciation of Democrats, and recently elected to national power in a four-cornered presidential contest by a minority of popular votes, lacked a common, united policy toward slavery and the whole sectional controversy. The party's spectrum ranged "leftward" as represented by the abolitionist, Congressman Lovejoy of Lincoln's own state, through Seward's and Chase's long-held, strongly anti-slavery stand, to Lincoln's own moderate anti-slavery views, all of the way "rightward" to the conservative Unionism of the Blairs of Maryland and Missouri and of the Old-Line Whiggery of Edward Bates of Missouri.

President-elect Lincoln had long believed that the South would not secede. Back in 1856 he had confidently stated in his Galena, Illinois, speech: "All this talk about the dissolution of the Union is humbug." In his recent successful campaign for President, he in August had written in a "private" letter to John B. Fry about "the many assurances I receive from the South that in no probable event will there be any very formidable effort to break up the Union. The people of the South have too much of good sense, and good temper, to attempt the ruin of the government. . . . At least, so I hope and believe."

Up to that time, Lincoln had demonstrated few, if any, signs of the great qualities that he was to reveal in future years. Essentially a prairie politician, he had shown no promise until his debates with Douglas, and even those celebrated exchanges had revealed him as more the crass oratorical maneuverer for votes than the statesman. He had drifted with the tide, and up to his election as President in 1860 he had left no record of achievement, except the quest for office.

Underestimating secessionist sentiment and overestimating the amount of militant pro-Union strength in the Upper South and border-slave regions, Lincoln rejected the "Crittenden Compromise," the proposal of the conservative Old-Line Whig Senator John J. Crittenden of Kentucky, which would have Congress extend the old "Missouri Compromise" line, separating slave states from free states, all the way to the Pacific. He marshalled his party against all other compromises with the South.

The President-elect rejected compromise as likely to inflate the prestige and strengthen the hands of secessionists, who might go to even farther extremes. On December 10 he sent "Private & confidential" word to Senator Trumbull at Washington: "Let there be no compromise on the question of *extending* slavery. If there be, all our labor is lost, and, ere long must be done again. The dangerous ground—that into which some of our friends have a hankering to run—is Pop. Sov. [Popular Sovereignty]. Have none of it. Stand firm. The tug has to come, & better now, than any time hereafter."

Lincoln at this same time urgently insisted on that same anti-compromising stand in letters to Illinois Republican Congressmen William P. Kellogg and Elihu B. Washburne. On December 11 he dispatched a "Private & confidential" message to Kellogg: "Entertain no proposition for a compromise in regard to the *extension* of slavery. The instant you do, they have us under again; all our labor is lost, and sooner or later must be done over. Douglas is sure to be again trying to bring in his 'Pop. Sov.' Have none of it. The tug has to come & better now than later." Two days later Lincoln strongly suggested to Washburne: "Prevent, as far as possible, any of our friends from demoralizing themselves, and our cause, by entertaining propositions for compromise of any sort, on '*slavery extension*.' There is no possible compromise upon it, but which puts us under again, and leaves all our work to do over again. . . . Hold firm, as with a chain of steel."

And so Lincoln "steeled" himself to preserve the *status quo* by instructing his legislative spokesmen from Illinois at Washington to resist compromise with the South, at the same time maintaining his muteness so far as public statements were concerned. He hoped that excitement would subside in the meantime and that those whom he thought comprised a Southern majority of pro-Union men, particularly in the border states, would be given time and opportunity with which to assert themselves over secessionist elements, and thus bring back the lower slave states to the Union. But always he believed that there existed more pro-Union sentiment than there actually was, or greater secessionist strength than he thought possible.

Concluding that he could not act openly while President-elect, he used the device of employing his incoming Secretary of State, Senator Seward of New York, as his undercover deputy at Washington. Seward skilfully moved among the Southern leaders at the national capital in carrying out Lincoln's plans to attract Southern Unionists by stifling secessionist activity. Soon Seward was in close touch with leaders from the seceded states, as well as with powerful men of the as yet loyal Upper Southern and border states.

From his election until his inauguration four months later Lincoln was constantly implored to move to allay the angry outbursts with which the South had reacted to his election. In view of the nature of his political party, sectional and with an anti-slavery basis, containing in it men like Senators Seward, Sumner, and Wade of Ohio, as well as Governor Chase of Ohio and the abolitionist Congressman Lovejoy, the states below Mason and Dixon's line could scarcely have been expected to be delighted with his election. South Carolina had then led the cotton states out of the nation as a result of his victory. From all sides came pleas and demands that he issue a statement, present a program, make a great gesture, release a list of Cabinet appointments, or do something that would demonstrate his moderation on the slavery issue, to explain his future course. But he continued his Sphinx-like silence until Inauguration Day in March, 1861, except to write a few letters, marked "confidential," to intimates or old acquaintances, which were not to be revealed to the public.

Tragically enough, Lincoln, who underrated secessionists strength and overrated Union sentiment in the South, was not known sufficiently below the Mason and Dixon's line. If in those weeks as President-elect, Lincoln had familiarized the South with his own fundamental reverence for law, his peaceful intent, and lack of sectional bitterness, perhaps much provocation for civil war might have been avoided.

The real Lincoln, whom Southerners should have known but did not largely because of his silence, intended to be fair to the Southern people and, as he vowed in his Cooper Institute address months before his election, "do nothing through passion and ill temper" and to "calmly consider their demands and yield to them" where possible. He was antislavery but was also thinking of a continuing Union and of the ultimate, non-violent, evolutionary outmoding of slavery. Oppression of the South found no place in his mind. He even favored enforcement of the federal fugitive-slave law.

Lincoln's colossal mistake, and it proved a fatal one, was his policy of "inaction," deferring a full statement of his views and future intentions as President, till his inauguration on March 4, 1861. He had miscalculated the full force of the secession movement until it had passed the point where reason could prevail.

Meanwhile, in Springfield the President-elect went about the formation of his Cabinet and pondered over patronage.

IV

Political pundits and newspaper correspondents furnished lists of Lincoln's Cabinet, claiming to have the "best authority" for what proved mere rumor and conjecture. Only Lincoln himself knew who would comprise a majority of his inner council of ministers, and not until he reached Washington early in 1861, did he really know for certain.

The very nature of his Republican Party, unrepresentative of the whole nation and never before victorious in a presidential election, brewed complications, problems, and dilemmas.

There was no dearth of contenders for the seven places in Lincoln's Cabinet. By late January, 1861, the President-elect had definitely decided on Seward as Secretary of State and Judge Edward Bates of Missouri as Attorney General. The New York *Herald's* Springfield correspondent, in the issue of January 23, sarcastically reported: "The number of able, enlightened, patriotic, and deserving statesmen who are willing to take place in Old Abe's Cabinet is perfectly astonishing, and somewhat bothers the veteran railsplitter. Out of all the timber offered to him he has accepted only two sticks—Mr. Seward and Mr. Bates—the latter a fine antique. Between the various factions, Old Abe is in danger of being torn to pieces."

Especially vexsome to Lincoln were those promises in his behalf made by Judge David Davis, his *generalissimo* at the Republican National Convention, promises of Cabinet positions to Caleb B. Smith of Indiana and Senator Simon Cameron of Pennsylvania in return for indispensable delegate support from the Hoosier and Keystone states. Smith felt sure less than one month after election: "I should not decline a seat in Mr. Lincoln's Cabinet. I am *very confident* that if a place is offered to any person from Ind. it will be offered to me. I do not wish to be P.M. Genl. but if I go into the Cabinet, would much prefer the Interior Department."

Now that Lincoln had been elected, would he fulfill the Cabinet pledges for Smith and Cameron made by Davis at Chicago? Davis insisted that the promises be kept, though it annoyed Lincoln to do so.

Caleb Smith had a rival for a Cabinet post from his own state—Congressman Schuyler Colfax of South Bend who now waged a fierce fight to have Lincoln choose him rather than Smith as the Hoosier member of his inner council. Colfax accused Smith of double-dealing, dishonesty, and paucity of business capacity. Smith's supporters besieged Lincoln, converging on Springfield in their dedicated efforts. One of Smith's lieutenants in Indianapolis confided to his brother in January, 1861: "Conner [Republican State Chairman Alexander H. Conner] went last evening on a pilgrimage to the *Republican Mecca,* where Old Abe is now dispensing favors. There was a determination and promise on the part of Mr. Lincoln to give Mr. C. M. Smith a place in his *Cabinet* . . . [There is] the quarrel between the friends of *Colfax & Smith."*

Out of the Hoosier wrangle Lincoln finally chose the fifty-two-year old Smith, who had once served with him as a fellow Whig in Congress, as Secretary of the Interior. But the incoming Chief Executive smoothed the thirty-seven-year-old Colfax's feelings with written balm: "I had partly made up my mind in favor of Mr. Smith—not conclusively of course—before your name was mentioned in that connection. When you were brought forward I said 'Colfax is a young man—is running a brilliant career, and is sure of a bright future in any event. With Smith, it is now or never.' " Lincoln assured Colfax that he bore no "malice" toward him, considering him "abundantly competent."

Lincoln proved correct about Colfax's "bright future." The South Bend congressman was to rise to Speaker of Congress and then Vice-President of the United States.

In appointing Smith to his Cabinet, Lincoln disappointed not only Colfax of Indiana but also Norman B. Judd, Republican State Chairman of Illinois, who had done so much to secure the presidential nomination for Lincoln. Lincoln's wife, Mary, disliked Judd. Judd's party rival, Judge Davis enlisted Mrs. Lincoln's support in trying to persuade Lincoln not to choose Judd for his Cabinet. After all, the Northwestern member who should sit in the presidential council was Caleb Smith of Indiana, in Davis's thinking. Judd, dejected about his losing fight to become a Cabinet member, referred to this "female influence" in a letter to Senator Trumbull on January 3: "As for myself I am substantially played out. I have no word from Lincoln since my return [to Chicago]. He never had a truer friend than myself—and there was no one in whom he placed greater confidence till circumstances embarrassed him about a Cabinet appointment. Or in my own language he is trimming and wants to get rid of me. The truth is that every appliance that the [pro-Davis] band could control have been brought against me even including female influence for the last month."

Lincoln finally cared for Judd by making him Minister to Prussia, then not a first-class mission.

V

To Lincoln, Senator Cameron posed an even more painfully perplexing Cabinet problem than did Caleb B. Smith.

The Pennsylvania politician had rolled up a malodorous record in public life—corrupt, contaminating Cameron, he was considered—and to know him was to detest him. For some time he had carried on a feud for party power in the Keystone commonwealth with Andrew G. Curtin, the recently elected Governor. Lincoln grew fearfully embarrassed when Cameron set his sights on the money-managing Cabinet post of Secretary of the Treasury. Some shuddered at the mere hint that he would head the Treasury, comparing Lincoln's possible selection of him for that post as akin to the appointment of a bank robber to be a bank's president. They recalled his shady dealings in his own Harrisburg bank, and some even resurrected his defrauding of the Winnebago Indians in the West some twenty-two years before when President Van Buren had appointed him to a government commission to deal with those redmen. Since then the Senator had been derisively dubbed "The Great Winnebago Chief."

Governor Salmon P. Chase of Ohio, another of Lincoln's recent rivals for the Republican presidential nomination, also wanted to be Secretary of the Treasury.

The Buckeye State Governor, anti-slavery pioneer, perennial presidential aspirant, but a man of sterling personal honesty, had been a "Free Soil" Democrat before joining the Republicans, and was now being backed for the Treasury post by the former Democratic element of the Republican Party, including Senator Trumbull and Republican State Chairman Judd of Illinois, the anti-Caleb Smith faction of Indiana, the anti-Seward wing of the party in New York, and Horace Greeley of the New York *Tribune,* who disapproved of Seward. Cameron found himself supported by Judd's Illinois rival, Judge David Davis, by Seward, and various former Whigs. Thus Lincoln was confronted with the Cameron-Chase competition for the Treasury position in his Cabinet.

Chase's friends and supporters bombarded Lincoln with visits and letters, urging that the Pennsylvania Senator not be chosen for the

Treasury or any other Cabinet post. Senator Trumbull, who knew Cameron in Washington, appealed to the President-elect: "Cameron is generally regarded as a trading, unscrupulous politician. He has not the confidence of our best men." Another Cameron critic maintained that, if Cameron had his just deserts, he would not be serving in the United States Senate but in the Pennsylvania state penitentiary. Reformers shuddered to think of him administering the nation's finances.

But Lincoln was also engulfed by Cameron's friends and supporters, who with petitions and personal calls on the President-elect, pointed to the Pennsylvania Senator's talents and even statesmanship.

On the last day of 1860, Cameron himself turned up in Springfield and had at least one conference with Lincoln. He was there to collect the political debt for services that his lieutenants had rendered Lincoln's candidacy at the national convention seven months before. He came away from Lincoln with a letter, definitely offering him a Cabinet position. Lincoln's letter to him read: "I think fit to notify you now, that by your permission, I shall, at the proper time, nominate you to the U.S. Senate, for confirmation as Secretary of the Treasury, or as Secretary of War—which of the two, I have not definitely decided. Please answer at your earliest convenience."

Chase was rudely shaken when news of Lincoln's promise to Cameron leaked out. It precipitated a violent political storm in and out of Pennsylvania. Non-political reformers and the better element of the Republican Party were shocked. They protested against Cameron's appointment to Lincoln by a flood of mail, telegrams, and personal visits to Springfield. The pro-Curtin faction of the party in Pennsylvania, led by Republican State Chairman Alexander K. McClure, hurried to see the President-elect and endeavored to persuade him to withdraw his offer to Cameron, for the sake of the integrity of the party and the nation. Newspapers filled their columns with reports of Cameron's past unsavory acts.

Such anti-Cameron protests moved Lincoln to reconsider his action in giving Cameron a written offer of a Cabinet post. On January 3 he sent a letter, marked "Private," to the Pennsylvania Senator, withdrawing the offer:

"Since seeing you things have developed which make it impossible for me to take you into the cabinet. . . . And now I suggest that you write me declining the appointment, in which case I do not object to its being known that it was tendered to you. Better do this at once, before things so change, that you can not honorably decline, and I be compelled to openly recall the tender. No person living knows, or has any intimation that I write this letter."

Lincoln received from Cameron no answer. The Senator had shown to his lieutenants Lincoln's letter offering the Cabinet position. Now, having been tossed out of the proposed Cabinet by Lincoln, Cameron kept the letter and showed it about. In the words of the New York *Herald's* Springfield correspondent: "Lincoln sticks fast upon the rock where Cameron has landed him. Cameron has enough of the Highland blood in him not to give up Old Abe's letter offering the Cabinet appointment, and so things are stuck fast."

Lincoln's law-partner, Herndon, in late January reported Lincoln's dilemma to Senator Trumbull: "Lincoln is in a fix, Cameron's appointment to an office in his Cabinet bothers him. If he do (sic) appoint Cameron, he gets a fight on his hands, and if he do (sic) not, he gets a quarrel deep-abiding, & lasting. . . . Poor Lincoln! God help him!"

And on February 6, one Pennsylvania politician reported to Cameron: "Mr. Lincoln said that Pennsylvania had given him more trouble than the balance of the Union, not excepting Secession."

VI

Maryland also presented a perplexing problem in Cabinet-building for Lincoln. That State's Republican leader, Montgomery Blair, of Silver Spring, one of the powerful political clan, wanted a Cabinet seat, and so did his arch rival for Maryland supremacy, Congressman Henry Winter Davis of the Baltimore district. Davis was the cousin of Lincoln's friend, Judge David Davis.

Lincoln had almost settled on Blair in late December, informing Senator Trumbull: "I expect to be able to offer Mr. Blair a place in the cabinet; but I can not, as yet, be committed on the matter, to any extent whatever."

One month later, Blair's brother, Francis P. ("Frank") Blair, Jr., Missouri's Republican leader, hurried to Springfield and had a long interview with Lincoln. On Blair's brother's heels came the opposition, the disciples of Congressman Davis, who insisted that Davis, not Montgomery Blair, held most power in Maryland and should go into the Cabinet as Postmaster-General.

Lincoln pondered, and on the eve of his departure for Washington he felt strongly inclined toward Blair, not Davis.

What about the Navy post? Lincoln decided that it should go to maritime New England.

A real parade of New Englanders wanted a Cabinet position: Gideon Welles of Connecticut, Governor John A. Andrew of Massachusetts, Former Governor Nathaniel P. Banks of Massachusetts, and Charles Francis Adams, also of the Bay State, and Amos Tuck and United States Senator John P. Hale, both of New Hampshire.

Finally Lincoln decided on Gideon Welles for Secretary of the Navy. The honest, long-bearded, gossipy Hartford politician and newspaper editor, who had never been to sea, was to record in his diary gems of inner history of the Lincoln administration.

In late January one of Governor Chase's friends visited Lincoln in Springfield, and very accurately reported to William Cullen Bryant, of the New York *Evening Post,* the make-up of the Cabinet as Lincoln had decided it up to that time:

> Mr. Lincoln has invited to his Cabinet only three persons to wit—Mr. Bates, Mr. Seward & Mr. Cameron. All these have accepted. In regard to the latter named however Mr. Lincoln became satisfied that he had made a mistake and wrote him requesting him to withdraw his acceptance or decline. Mr. C. refused to answer the letter. . . . Mr. Lincoln has thus a quarrel on his hands which he is anxious to adjust satisfactorily before he proceeds further in the formation of his Cabinet. He is advised from Washington not to conclude further upon the members of his Cabinet until he reaches Washington. . . . He has not offered a place to Mr. Chase. He wants and expects to invite him to the treasury department. But he fears this will offend Pennsylvania & he wants to reconcile the Republicans of that state.
>
> Wells (sic) of Connecticut is his preference for New England—Blair of Maryland is favorably considered. Caleb B. Smith of Indiana is urged upon him.

Toward the end of January, 1861, Lincoln designated February as the day of his departure for Washington, and made known his desire for the "utmost privacy."

VII

Lincoln's remaining days in Springfield were occupied with a short visit to his stepmother, Sarah Lincoln, in Coles County, and with official cares, social obligations including a farewell reception at his home, the renting of his Eighth Street house to Lucius Tilton, president of the Great Western Railroad for $350 a year, and work on his Inaugural Address.

Two days before leaving for Washington, the President-elect was visited by his old conservative Whig friend of Quincy, Orville Hickman Browning. After his visit, Browning noted in his diary: *"Sunday, Feby 9.* We discussed the state of the Country expressing our opinions fully and freely. . . . He agreed with me no concession by the free States short of surrender of everything worth preserving, and contending for, would satisfy the South. . . . I found him firmer than I had expected."

At that hour when Lincoln started for Washington on February 11, 1861, the sky was overcast, and a light rain fell. Nonetheless numerous friends and neighbors gathered at the Great Western railroad station to see him off.

On the rear platform of his train the President-elect paused to speak a few words, a brief farewell address which has since been recognized as belonging to his finest speeches. He told his fellow-townsmen:

> Friends,
>
> No one who has never been placed in a like position, can understand my feelings at this hour, nor the oppressive sadness I feel at this parting. For more than a quarter of a century I have lived among you, and during all that time I have received nothing but kindness at your hands. Here I have lived from my youth until now I am an old man. Here the most sacred ties of earth were assumed; here all my children were born; and here one of them lies buried. To you, dear friends, I owe all that I have, all that I am. All the strange, chequered past seems to crowd now upon my mind. To-day I leave you; I go to assume a task more difficult than that which devolved upon General Washington. Unless the great God who assisted him, shall be with and aid me, I must fail. But if the same omniscient mind, and Almighty arm that directed and protected him, shall guide and support me, I shall not fail, I shall succeed. Let us all pray that the God of our fathers may not forsake us now. To him I commend you all—permit me to ask that with equal security and faith, you all will invoke His wisdom and guidance for me. With these few words I must leave you—for how long I know not. Friends, one and all, I must now bid you an affectionate farewell.

The train started eastward, and Lincoln was gone from Springfield.

THE INAUGURATION

17

I

PRESIDENT-ELECT Lincoln's circuitous train trip from Springfield to Washington provided masses of Americans, outside of Illinois, with their first opportunity to see him and hear him speak. Almost entirely an Illinois state figure, he was the only American chief executive before or since who had not been a nationally known army general, minister to a foreign nation, Governor of a State, United States Senator, Cabinet officer, or a Vice-President of the United States, before assuming the presidency.

Although critical comments, both personal and political, came from anti-Lincoln citizens and press on Lincoln's journey to Washington in February, 1861, he pleased the average Northerner over whose route his train passed. In him they discerned someone like themselves, an embodiment of middle-class American spirit, the exponent of their own cherished convictions. The incoming Sixteenth President of the United States, he was only the fifth one to come from west of the Appalachians,

Of the other four Westerners who had been President, three of them, Jackson, Polk, and Zachary Taylor, had been Southern slave-holders, and Harrison, a native Virginian elected from Ohio, had lived only one month after his inauguration. One small-town Ohio newspaper man, who viewed the Lincolns as their train stopped at Columbus, commented that they were the perfect "representatives of the bourgoise (sic) or citizen class of people. If the idea represented by these people can only be allowed to prevail in this government, all will be well."

Lincoln spoke often and very briefly in non-committal phrases in various cities and towns, and occasional whistle-stops, on the trip from Illinois to Washington. From Cleveland, Lincoln's secretary, John G. Nicolay of Pike County, Illinois, sent word to his fiancée: "Mr. Lincoln has received an immense reception at every place yet visited—so large that it has been a serious task for us of his escort to prevent his being killed with kindness."

At Westfield, New York, on Lake Erie, Lincoln mentioned that he had conducted correspondence during the recent campaign with a young girl of that village, who had suggested that he grow whiskers, and he had done so. Now he "would be glad to welcome his fair correspondent, if she was among the crowd."

The little girl, Grace Bedell, had written Candidate Lincoln when he was standing for President, inquiring whether he had any little daughters like herself and had made the suggestion that he grow a beard. She had told Lincoln: "I have got 4 brothers and part of them will vote for you anyway and if you will let your whiskers grow I will try and get the rest of them to vote for you you would look a great deal better for your face is so thin. All the ladies like whiskers and they would tease their husband's to vote for you and then you would be President." Lincoln had answered her, stating that he had a wife and three sons but no daughters, adding, "As to the whiskers, having never worn any, do you not think people would call it a piece of silly affectation if I were to begin it now?"

Now, in Westfield, the bearded President-elect mentioned the little girl but not by name, and she made her way through the crowd, was helped to the platform and was kissed by the incoming Chief Executive of the nation. Grace's reply to him was drowned out in the crowd's noise.

Some later Lincoln authors grew somewhat ecstatic over the darling little Bedell girl at whose casual suggestion Lincoln had started raising a beard. Not so Lincoln's able British biographer, Lord Charnwood, who commented: "To this dreadful young person was due the ill-designed hairy ornamentation which during his Presidency hid the really beautiful modelling of his jaw and chin."

The President-elect's party continued its train trip, arriving at Albany.

II

When Lincoln and his party reached the New York capital on February 18, they heard grim news from Montgomery, Alabama, that the erstwhile United States Senator from Mississippi, the West-Point educated Jefferson Davis, Secretary of War in Pierce's Cabinet, had been inaugurated President of the Confederate States of America.

One man who saw Lincoln in Albany, A. J. Blakely, sent word to his father: "Mr. Lincoln looks much wearied & care worn."

From the Empire State capital town Lincoln and his party traveled along the Hudson River shoreline down to New York City, reaching there on the 19th. In this metropolis he was confronted with Republican opponents of Seward, who had set afoot plans to persuade him to exclude the Senator from his Cabinet. It was a repetition of situations in other states—Republican factions combatting each other, jockeying for party supremacy—all determined that this man, or that man, must be appointed to or excluded from, the President-elect's as yet uncompleted Cabinet.

At Philadelphia Lincoln's spirits rose at the news that something was being done about the Pennsylvania party's arguments over the appointment of Senator Cameron to his Cabinet. Cameron's fiercest foe in his own state, Governor Andrew G. Curtin, had by now reluctantly accepted Cameron's selection as a Cabinet officer. While the Curtinites might be powerful enough to persuade Lincoln not to take Cameron into his inner council of ministers, they were not strong enough to assure themselves that another Pennsylvanian would go into the Cabinet. The Governor and his chief lieutenant, Alexander K. McClure, were suddenly overtaken by fear that their own great Keystone State would go unrepresented in the incoming President's Cabinet, if they ruined Cameron's chances, even though they still nursed their pathological hatred. No Pennsylvanian would be "at court" to protect the State's interests and secure jobs and favors for the state's patronage-starved politicians. By the time the President-elect reached Philadelphia, the Curtin-led anti-Cameronians had performed an about-face and discarded their opposition to the slippery Senator. Their new *rapprochement* with Cameron and his faction was a mere political marriage of convenience, which could terminate in divorce at the least provocation.

Lincoln met with emissaries of both Senator Cameron and Governor Curtin at the same time at the Continental Hotel in Philadelphia. After that peace conference, one of Curtin's aides reported to Cameron about the temporary hatchet-burying: "I addressed Mr. Lincoln frankly and candidly. I pointed out our political position . . . that I was now authorized to speak for the Governor [Curtin] and say that all opposition to your [Cameron's] appointment had been withdrawn and your appointment desired. . . . Mr. Lincoln thanked us for the interview and said *that it relieved him* greatly. . . . He was not however prepared to decide the matter until he reached Washington."

At Philadelphia, too, Lincoln spoke at Independence Hall on Washington's Birthday. He paid tribute to the Declaration of Independence. "I have never," he stated to the assembled crowd, "had a feeling politically that did not spring from the sentiments embodied in the Declaration of Independence." He referred casually to the possibility of his assassination when he eulogized the idea implicit in the Declaration. "If this country can not be saved without giving up that principle," he intoned, "I was about to say that I would rather be assassinated on this spot than to surrender it."

III

It had been publicly announced that the President-elect would, on Saturday, February 23, pass through Baltimore, arriving in Washington that evening. Suddenly Allan Pinkerton appeared with startling reports.

Pinkerton, Scotch-born former deputy sheriff of Chicago and partner in a private detective agency, had aided in solving several sensational Adams Express robberies and had achieved a national reputation as a sleuth. In January, 1861, Pinkerton had been hired by Samuel M. Felton, president of the Philadelphia, Wilmington & Baltimore Railroad, to investigate threats by Southern sympathizers against the railroad's property. While Pinkerton's hired operatives were working on such cases in secession-steeped Baltimore, they made some jolting discoveries. Certain secessionist followers had hatched a plot to assassinate Lincoln as he rode in a carriage from one railroad station to another in Baltimore!

Pinkerton and his men narrowed their suspects down to three pro-Southern hotbloods of Baltimore: The city's Chief of Police, George P. Kane, who was already on record as declaring that he would provide no protection for the President-elect as he went through Baltimore; O. K. Hillard, a lieutenant in the secret secessionist Palmetto Guards; and Cypriano Ferrandini, captain of the self-styled "National Volunteers," a barber whose shop under Barnum's Hotel in Baltimore served as a rendezvous for Confederate compatriots.

Almost simultaneously, further alarming word came from Senator Seward, Lincoln's Secretary of State-designate, telling of a plot to kill Lincoln as he passed through Baltimore.

Seward secretly sent his son, Frederick, to Philadelphia with a letter to Lincoln, warning the President-elect that Colonel Charles P. Stone had heard news, based on reliable reports and independent investigation, that the President-elect would be assassinated at Baltimore, en route to Washington, that it was Seward's and Chief of Staff General Winfield Scott's urgent advice that Lincoln's announced traveling arrangements be changed.

With the aid of Lincoln's friend and bodyguard, Ward H. Lamon of Illinois, who was in the President-elect's party, Frederick W. Seward secured an interview with Lincoln. Seward related his talk with Lincoln: "I asserted my strong belief that the two investigations [Pinkerton's and Colonel Stone's] had been conducted independently of each other. . . . Shortly after breakfast, Lamon met me in the hall, and taking me aside, said that Mr. Lincoln had concluded to do as he had been advised. He would change his plan so as to pass through Baltimore at a different hour from that announced."

Felton, the railroad president, and Norman J. Judd, who was also in the Lincoln traveling party, worked out a plan for getting Lincoln secretly and unseen through the Maryland metropolis to Washington.

Was Lincoln really in danger of being murdered, or was the alleged plot simply the febrile creation of jittery advisers? The question remains a question, since the evidence is still inconclusive. That unbalanced Confederate sympathizers in Baltimore talked about killing the President-elect as he rode from one railroad station to another through that city, is certain; but that there had been formed a well-laid plot behind their bombast is yet far from clear. But Lincoln's friends and counsellors followed a wise course in taking precautions—particularly considering that the pro-Southern Baltimore Chief of Police was on record that he would give no protection to the President-elect of the United States. Events would soon demonstrate that certain Baltimoreans were capable of violence against those who were actively resisting secessionist influences. Secret service men were not in the President-elect's party as escort, and he had to depend on young friends, such as Ward H. Lamon and Colonel Elmer E. Ellsworth, to guard him against possible assassins in Baltimore's emotionally charged atmosphere.

Lincoln's young friend and bodyguard, Lamon, well-armed with bowie knife and revolver, and a man able to take care of any three men his size in physical combat, was selected, along with Allan Pinkerton, to accompany Lincoln secretly through Baltimore on the way to the national capital. Subsequently Lamon stated about Lincoln: "It was with great difficulty that he could be persuaded to make that 'clandestine escape' from Harrisburg to Washington. He protested that it was cowardly and most humiliating to him; but as General Scott and Mr. Seward had so earnestly advised it, he yielded to it under protest."

And so the President-elect, accompanied only by Lamon and Pinkerton, was taken *incognito* through Baltimore under darkness of night, ahead of his family and the rest of his party.

At six o'clock on Saturday morning, February 23, 1861, he reached the national capital without previous public announcement.

Mrs. Lincoln, still at Philadelphia with her sons, was relieved when she received news of her husband's safe arrival in Washington by receipt of Pinkerton's code telegram: "Plums arrived here with Nuts this morning —all right."

IV

Certain citizens took unkindly to what they considered the President-elect's "sneak" into the capital city. Some accused him of cowardice. *Harper's Weekly* ran a cartoon called "The Flight of Abraham." *Vanity Fair* published one caricature, entitling it, "The New President—A Fugitive Sketch."

Lincoln's opponents were given adequate ammunition by the "Scotch hat" hoax perpetrated on the public by an unscrupulous New York *Times* correspondent, Joseph Howard, Jr., who deliberately sent a concocted story to his paper about Lincoln's dress: "He wore a Scotch plaid cap and a very long military cloak, so that he was entirely unrecognizable." The pro-Lincoln *Times* unwittingly printed Howard's false report.

Lincoln's opponents in ridicule put Howard's fictitious story about Lincoln's dress to doggerel lyrics, sung to the tune of "Yankee Doodle Dandy:"

> Uncle Abe had gone to bed,
> The night was dark and rainy,
> A laurelled night-cap on his head
> 'Way down in Pennsylvany.
>
> They went and got a special train
> At midnight's solemn hour,
> And in a cloak and Scotch plaid shawl,
> He dodged from the Slave Power.
>
> *Refrain*
> Lanky Lincoln came to town
> In night and wind, and rain, sir,
> Wrapped in a military cloak,
> Upon a special train, sir.

Harper's Weekly now ran a cartoon, "The Mac Lincoln Harrisburg Highland Fling," showing the President dancing in Scotch kilts, in a grotesque drawing. In Montgomery, Alabama, the Confederate capital, a Southern society lady put in her diary: "Mr. Browne told me that Lincoln flew through Baltimore, locked up in an express car. He wore a Scotch cap."

When Lincoln arrived in Washington, his prestige was not at high tide. His studied silence on secession had not indicated that he could cope with that most baffling crisis. One publication ran a cartoon, showing the President-elect's face with a huge padlock holding his lips shut. Critical newspapers pointed up his follies and printed absurdly untrue stories about him, one fantastic tale telling how he had avoided one train *en route* because he feared a wreck but had advised his wife and sons to take it. Other stories circulated about how he wasted his time in kissing little girls even as the Union tottered. All was climaxed by his unmanly "escape" through Baltimore.

The nine days between Lincoln's arrival at Washington and his inauguration proved difficult. Members of Congress, the city's Mayor, serenaders, and the ubiquitous and surging office-seekers crowded about Willard's Hotel, where he, his wife and their sons, Bob, Willie, and Tad, were quartered.

The job-hunters proved the biggest nuisances. Congressman Henry Waldron of Michigan on March 2 sent word home: "The City is overwhelmed with a crowd of rabid, persistent office-seekers—the like never was experienced in the history of the Government." Congressman George W. Julian of Indiana recalled: "I met at every turn a swarm of miscellaneous people, many of them looking as hungry and fierce as wolves." One Washington correspondent reported on February 28, how Judge David Davis, was considered the important man to see: "Judge Davis, of Illinois, is already recognized as a power behind the throne, and is almost as sought after as Mr. Lincoln himself. His apartments are steadily crowded with place-seekers, high and low. Papers bearing his endorsement are considered gilt-edged in the place market."

Lincoln's two most immediate problems were the completion of his Cabinet and finishing his Inaugural Address.

V

About the President-elect, in reaching final decisions on his Cabinet, swirled deep and murky currents of intrigue, party factionalism, and avaricious self-seeking.

He had definitely selected only two Cabinet members when he arrived at Washington—Seward for Secretary of State and Bates for Attorney General. He had almost decided on Caleb B. Smith of Indiana and Gideon Welles of Connecticut, and he definitely wanted Governor Chase of Ohio, despite opposition from Seward and others to Chase's appointment. The Postmaster-Generalship lay between those two relentless Maryland rivals, Montgomery Blair and Congressman Henry Winter Davis. The President-elect still remained uncertain about Cameron, although he now felt less hostile to him since Pennsylvania's Governor Curtin withdrew his opposition to him. By this time Congressman Colfax's Indiana followers and Judd's Illinois faction had lost all hope of blocking Caleb B. Smith's appointment as Secretary of the Interior.

With Lincoln, Gideon Welles's stock suddenly dropped, but only temporarily, when a strenuous last-hour boom for former Governor Nathaniel P. Banks of Massachusetts was started. Banks' backers turned powerful pressure on the President-elect to have Welles dropped and Banks chosen as New England's representative in the Cabinet. Lincoln listened and wavered over Welles for a while. Then Vice-President-elect Hamlin, from down-east Maine and a New England arbiter, insisted that Lincoln turn down Banks, declaring that the former Bay State Governor was a "trimmer" of the first order and could not be trusted. Hamlin pleaded with the President-elect for Welles's selection and won his point. The white-bearded Connecticut editor and party leader was assured a Cabinet post.

But the vexing problem of Maryland's representative to the Cabinet remained. Who should it be: Montgomery Blair of Silver Spring, or Congressman Henry Winter Davis of Baltimore? The correct choice between these two quarreling Unionist leaders of strategic and neighboring Maryland was imperative.

The powerful Blair clan, so potent in influence in the vital border slave regions, followed hawk-like the activities of Lincoln's friend, Judge David Davis, whose cousin Henry Winter Davis wanted to be Secretary of the Navy. On Lincoln's first day in Washington Montgomery Blair's father and brother, Francis P. Blair, Sr., and Frank Blair, closeted themselves with him. They argued for Montgomery's appointment to the Cabinet and Davis's rejection. They also enlisted the aid of the anti-Seward Republicans, since Seward was reported as aiding Judge Davis in inducing Lincoln to choose Congressman Davis, instead of Blair.

Lincoln, with pacification of the border slave regions his main concern, chose Montgomery Blair as Postmaster General, for the Blairs were a Kentucky family with important political influence in Maryland and Missouri. Davis now nursed an almost homicidal hatred toward Lincoln, which would reach its horrifying peak in three years. And finally there was the problem of Cameron *versus* Chase for Secretary of the Treasury.

Lincoln wanted the Ohio Governor for the Treasury, knowing full well about Chase's presidential ambitions but recognizing his impeccable honesty in money matters. Yet it was necessary to pacify Pennsylvania and also to satisfy Seward, who was strongly anti-Chase. Ohio's United States Senator Benjamin F. Wade was also working against Chase.

Now the anti-Seward New York Republican leaders, headed by David Dudley Field and other former Democrats, as well as Horace Greeley, who detested Seward, worked in Washington, organizing support for Chase. They predicted dire consequences if the corrupt Cameron was made head of the "money" department. The New York *Herald's* Washington correspondent reported on February 28: "The fight between the friends of Chase and Cameron is most terrific."

As the clock ticked ever closer to Inauguration Day, Lincoln finally acted. By the close of February he decided that he would take both: Chase for the Treasury and Cameron for Secretary of War. With this idea in mind, he sent for Cameron.

The Senator from Pennsylvania told the President-elect that he could consider no other position than the Treasury. Lincoln suggested the Interior, which he had already decided to give to Smith, but Cameron did not want to head that department. It was unacceptable, he said. By now Lincoln's patience with the pernicious Pennsylvanian was nearly exhausted. He made another try. Would Cameron agree to become Secretary of War? This appeased him for he feared that it would be Lincoln's last offer. He accepted the War Department.

With his Cabinet complete, except for a last-minute resignation by Seward followed by his reconsideration and final acceptance, the President-elect breathed more easily.

The final Cabinet that Lincoln sent to the Senate for consideration was made up of:

William H. Seward, of New York, for Secretary of State.
Salmon P. Chase, of Ohio, for Secretary of the Treasury.
Simon Cameron, of Pennsylvania, for Secretary of War.
Gideon Welles, of Connecticut, for Secretary of the Navy.
Edward Bates, of Missouri, for Attorney General.
Caleb B. Smith, of Indiana, for Secretary of the Interior.
Montgomery Blair, of Maryland, for Postmaster-General.

VI

Lincoln, on the day before his inauguration, completed revision of his Inaugural Address, which he had begun at Springfield. There he had allowed Carl Schurz to look at it in confidence. Lincoln had asked Orville H. Browning, his old friend from Quincy, Illinois, to criticize it on the train from Springfield to Indianapolis. In Washington the President-elect had given a copy to Seward to examine, and the erstwhile strongly anti-slavery Secretary of State, having suddenly become more conservative and conciliatory after the secession of lower Southern states, wanted more concessions made to the South. Seward objected to a passage which announced: "All the power at my disposal will be used to reclaim the public property and places which have fallen." Seward urged Lincoln to drop that sentence, and he did so when Browning concurred. This address was causing more anxiety than had the inaugural of any previous President.

Preparations were completed for Lincoln's induction as Chief Executive. Tension permeated the air. Ezra Cornell of the Western Union Telegraph Company on the day before Inauguration sent word home to his wife: "Gen. Scott still felt some apprehension as he had received over 300 letters of a hostile and threatening character; but he got the Military so posted that he will probably chill any hostile spirit into submission before it breaks out in acts of violence and disorder."

VII

March 4, 1861: Inauguration Day.

With seven states in the Southern Confederacy, the atmosphere at Washington was filled with grim meaning. What did signs for the future promise? Hair-raising rumors of secessionist plots to seize the capital city and prevent Lincoln's installation as President, perhaps his assassination, inspired the mighty military display that Cornell had described to his wife. General Winfield Scott, long-time Chief of Staff, remained in his War Department headquarters, prepared to suppress any disturbance. Armed sentinels stood on building roofs. Artillery was brought out. Sounds of drum and fife were heard as soldiers lined the street from Willard's Hotel, where Lincoln was staying, up to the Capitol, where he would be inaugurated as the Sixteenth President of the United States. For the first time an American Chief Executive would take the oath of office and deliver his Inaugural surrounded by masses of armed troops.

By nine in the morning, crowds filled downtown Washington streets, gazing at the soldiery and listening to bands playing martial music. The throngs thickened in numbers as the mounted marshals, led by Chief Marshal Benjamin B. French, maneuvered the procession in line. By noon double columns of troops flanked Willard's Hotel.

One half hour after noon an open barouche drove up to the hotel. Out stepped a huge, heavy, awkward-appearing man with full face plentifully seamed and wrinkled, dressed in swallow-tail coat, immense cravat like a poultice, and broadbrimmed silk hat. President James Buchanan was calling to escort his successor to the inauguration ceremonies at the Capitol.

In a few minutes Buchanan reappeared with the tall, gaunt Abraham

Lincoln at his side. Outgoing and incoming Presidents took seats in the barouche, and the horse-drawn vehicle rolled up Pennsylvania Avenue, escorted by armed guards seemingly everywhere.

Up the hill the presidential carriage climbed. Arriving at the Capitol, the dome of which lay still unfinished like the Union it symbolized, Buchanan and Lincoln, arm in arm, entered the Senate chamber, where Congress, Supreme Court justices, and the Diplomatic Corps awaited them. Attendants beat the dust from the clothes of Buchanan and Lincoln. Then the outgoing and incoming Chief Executives marched to the flag-festooned platform projecting from the Capitol's east portico.

The President-elect rose from his seat on the portico platform. He was introduced to assembled crowds on the lawn by his old friend, Edward D. Baker. His old Illinois foe, Stephen Douglas, looked on. Did Douglas hold Lincoln's hat? It is one of those trivial and human interest points frozen into history, about which some people were more concerned than about the secession crisis. Latest research indicates that Douglas held the President-elect's hat.

Lincoln carried a little roll of paper—his Inaugural Address. He lay down the manuscript, pulled from his pocket steel-bowed spectacles. As he put them on, it proved the occasion for merriment among some listeners. An impertinent lusty hawk-eyed fellow roared from the crowd: "Take off them spectacles. We want to see your eyes." Another remarked, "I didn't know he wore glasses. They ain't in the picters."

Lincoln, adjusting his glasses and unrolling the manuscript, read his address in a clear, shrill voice. They were the words so anxiously awaited by the entire nation, a message which might spell peace or war between the sections.

VIII

Of what did Lincoln's words to the nation, his first public speech to the country at large, consist?

To the Southern fear that their property, peace, and personal security were endangered by the accession of a national Republican Party administration, Lincoln repeated from one of his former speeches: "I have no purpose, directly or indirectly, to interfere with the institution of slavery in the States where it exists. I believe I have no lawful right to do so, and I have no inclination to do so." Those who nominated and elected him, he added, did so with full knowledge that he had made that and many other similar declarations and that he had never recanted. He continued: "I now reiterate . . . that the property, peace and security of no section are to be in anywise endangered by the now incoming Administration."

Treating guardedly the clause for the reclaiming of fugitive slaves, contained in the federal Constitution, he declared that members of Congress should "keep good" their "unanimous oath" to support the Constitution, though he wanted safeguards so that "a free man be not, in any case, surrendered as a slave." He referred to the "fifteen different and greatly distinguished citizens" who had preceded him in the presidency during the past seventy-two years—men who had conducted the government "through many perils; and generally with great success." He pointed out that now "a disruption of the Federal Union heretofore only menaced, is now formidably attempted." He served notice: "I hold, that in contemplation of universal law, and of the Constitution, the Union of these States is perpetual. Perpetuity is implied, if not expressed, in the fundamental law of all national government. . . . No State, upon its own mere motion, can lawfully get out of the Union."

Lincoln insisted that he would maintain the Federal authority in Southern states where it was defined. He told the nation:

"I therefore consider that, in view of the Constitution and the laws, the Union is unbroken; and, to the extent of my ability, I shall take care, as the Constitution itself enjoins upon me, that the laws of the Union be faithfully executed in all the States. Doing this I deem to be only a simple duty on my part; and I shall perform it, so far as practicable, unless my rightful masters, the American people, shall withhold the requisite means, or, in some authoritative manner, direct the contrary. I trust this will not be regarded as a menace, but only as the declared purpose of the Union that it *will* constitutionally defend, and maintain itself.

"In doing this there needs to be no bloodshed or violence; and there shall be none, unless it be forced upon the national authority. The power confided to me will be used to hold, occupy, and possess the property, and places belonging to the government, and to collect the duties and imposts; but beyond what may be necessary for these objects, there will be no using of force against, or among the people anywhere."

The very source of his authority, the Constitution of the United States, enjoined Lincoln to enforce the federal laws and protect the federal property in all of the States. Yet Lincoln offered conciliatory promises toward the seceded states:

"Where hostility to the United States, in any interior locality, shall be so great and so universal, as to prevent competent resident citizens from holding the Federal offices, there will be no attempt to force obnoxious strangers among the people for that object. While the strict legal right may exist in government to enforce the exercise of these offices, the attempt to do so would be so irritating, and so nearly impracticable with all, that I deem it better to forego, for the time, the use of such offices . . .

"So far as possible, the people everywhere shall have that sense of perfect security which is most favorable to calm thought and reflection. The course here indicated will be followed, unless current events, and experience, shall show a modification, or change, to be proper; and . . . my best discretion will be exercised, according to circumstances actually existing, and with a view and a hope of a peaceful solution of the national troubles, and the restoration of fraternal sympathies and affections."

In a word, Lincoln, while serving notice that he would uphold the federal government's authority, was promising that this would not be done practically in certain troubled areas, even to the extent of suspending federal functions in some inland regions for the time being. Thus he went far toward extending the olive branch to the seceded states. A bad situation must not be made worse by aggressive blunders from his administration. Lincoln's policy was shaped as much in terms of suspension as of enforcement. Where collections of customs duties were to be made, it was to be offshore. That brought up the question of Fort Pickens, near the Florida coast, and Fort Sumter, in the harbor of Charleston, South Carolina.

For grievances Lincoln recommended the peaceful and legal processes of amending the Constitution. He made reference to an amendment then pending in Congress, which provided that the Federal Government "shall never interfere with the domestic institutions of the States, including that of persons held to service" and declared: "I have no objection to its being made express, and irrevocable."

Toward the end of his inaugural speech Lincoln stated: "In *your* hands, my dissatisfied fellow countrymen, and not in *mine,* is the momentous issue of civil war. The government will not assail *you.* You can have no conflict, without being yourselves the aggressors. *You* have no oath registered in Heaven to destroy the government, while *I* shall have the most solemn one to 'preserve, protect and defend' it."

Lincoln's concluding words, his only attempt at rhetorical display, based upon a paragraph composed by Seward but revised by himself, were lofty: "I am loth (sic) to close. We are not enemies, but friends. We must not be enemies. Though passion may have strained, it must not break our bonds of affection. The mystic chords of memory, stretching from every battle-field, and patriot grave, to every living heart and hearthstone, all over the broad land, will yet swell the chorus of the Union, when again touched, as surely they will be, by the better angels of our nature."

Lincoln's Inaugural Address, one of his notable state papers, breathed a spirit of fraternalism both appealing and pathetic as he called on his countrymen to turn from discord and separation to union. He sought to give assurances that the Federal Government under him would respect the rights of States and individuals in regard to slavery and that no interest or section would be disturbed in any constitutional right by his administration.

But this oration of conciliation, Lincoln's first official words to the entire nation, his first public expression on the secession crisis, was to be differently interpreted by the varying citizenship, sections, and political complexions that made up the American Republic.

IX

Lincoln, at the conclusion of his address, was administered the presidential oath by Chief Justice Roger B. Taney of the United States Supreme Court. The crowd's cheers burst in the air.

President Lincoln was escorted to the Senate chamber, then to his carriage, still accompanied by the now Former President Buchanan.

Troops formed in double column on Marine Avenue, and the barouche containing the presidential party passed through to the White House.

The ex-President accompanied the President to the main hall of the Executive Mansion. Before Buchanan took his leave, he cordially expressed to the new Chief Executive the hope that his "administration might prove happy and prosperous."

WAR WITH SECESSION

18

I

THE turbulence that gripped the country over slavery and secession was coming to a head around Lincoln. Complex and tortuous events were leading the Union and the Confederacy inexorably to war. And it was the new President's responsibility to prevent this war and bring the seceded states back into the Union.

Lincoln's Inaugural Address, the first indication since his election that he fully understood the seriousness of the Southerners' secession, was received with mixed reactions. He had offered the South conciliatory terms, but, at the same time, he had implied that if his terms were not accepted he would use force to protect the interests of the Union. This, however, satisfied neither the Southerners nor the majority of Lincoln's own Republican party.

Historians have found it difficult to evaluate the nation's confusing reaction to this important statement of Lincoln's intentions, but it is obvious that the various opinions expressed at the time in the press and private letters and diaries reflected mainly the prejudices and partisan passions that ruled the different parts of the country. Sectional loyalties and violently subjective opinions about the President and his policies prevented coolly detached judgments of Lincoln's ideas.

The reasons for the South's dissatisfaction with Lincoln were obvious. It saw only that he had been elected by a Northern sectional party whose only real unifying principle was opposition to slavery in the territories. In his cabinet Southerners saw men like Chase who hated them as people and who had stated that he wanted to see the slaves freed merely because he disliked their masters. So, despite Lincoln's moderate overtures in his Inaugural Address, the South saw the new President as the representative of radicals and abolitionists who threatened their very existence. It was the "House Divided" speech of three years before rather than the conciliatory inaugural that the South remembered. So the nation plunged toward war.

II

In retrospect, the great tragedy lay in the circumstance that most of the South's leaders in the secession winter of 1860-61 did not realize how moderate a man Lincoln actually was; nor did influential Southern leaders fully understand that the new President, as a native Kentuckian, intermarried into a slave-state, pro-slavery family, with his closest intimates in downstate Illinois from the Southern states, was sympathetic to their cause.

So in March, 1861, the new President faced the most bedeviling dilemma ever faced by any American Chief Executive. He had not overstated the situation when, on his departure from Springfield the previous month, he had told his neighbors and the assembled throng: "I now leave . . . with a task before me greater than that which rested on Washington."

III

During his first three days in office, Lincoln consumed considerable priceless time and energy in greeting delegations who wished him well and jockeyed for federal jobs. Office-seekers and their sponsoring senators, representatives, and governors, lay in wait for the President in every nook and cranny inside and outside of the White House, all endeavoring to obtain a secret interview.

During his first three weeks as President, he sent such notes to Attorney General Bates as, "Please let Senator Wade name the man to be District

Attorney for the Northern District of Ohio." Or, to Secretary of State Seward about that seeker after a diplomatic mission, Carl Schurz: "I wish you would give Mr. Schurz a full interview." To Postmaster-General Blair: "I understand that the outgoing and incoming Representatives for the Cleveland District unite in recommending Edwin Cowles for P.M. in that city. . . . I think Mr. Cowles better be appointed." Also he instructed Secretary of the Interior Smith: "Please make out and send blank appointments for all Indian places, to serve in Wisconsin, in favor of the persons unitedly recommended by the Wisconsin Congressional delegation."

Thus at the start of his administration Lincoln followed patronage practices in keeping with American political tradition and practical application of statecraft. He consulted with United States Senators of his own party in making appointments for or from their respective states. Less important offices were generally parceled out to those sponsored by or approved by members of the House of Representatives. Lincoln also listened to governors of states who were of his own party, and even to Democrats when the coming of war made it necessary to enlist supporters from the opposition party. Cabinet officers were also usually consulted by Lincoln in the selection of employees under their jurisdiction. Republican National Chairman Edwin D. Morgan, then Governor of New York, was given a strong voice in appointments, as were the various state chairmen and national committeemen of the Republican organization.

But secession was crowding out patronage parceling.

IV

Lincoln's predecessor, President Buchanan, had permitted the Confederates to occupy most of the federal forts, arsenals, and navy yards and to appropriate United States Government property within the seceded states because, as he later explained, he had inadequate military forces and personnel to prevent it. Some army officers and enlisted men, Southerners, had seceded with their states. Great numbers of regiments and companies were stationed on the far Western frontier. The secession caldron had been boiling over when Lincoln assumed the presidential office.

The thorniest single problem confronting Lincoln was whether Fort Sumter, in the harbor of Charleston, metropolis of secession-crazed South Carolina, and Fort Pickens, off the coast of seceded Florida, should be held or surrendered to Confederate authorities. If held, those two forts must be reinforced with supplies.

Fort Sumter faced Lincoln at a difficult time. Inexperienced himself in national problems, beset by office-seekers, and absorbed in trying to organize his administration, this most perplexing of all problems, Sumter, reared itself for decision when he had not yet learned which of his officials, civil and military, were loyal to the Union. He inquired of Joseph Holt, an anti-secession Kentuckian and Secretary of War in Buchanan's Cabinet, whether Fort Sumter's commander, Kentucky-born Major Robert Anderson, could be trusted. Yet the situation in Confederate-surrounded Sumter would not wait for Lincoln's investigation.

The President, five days after his inauguration, on March 9, held a Cabinet meeting at which Fort Sumter was discussed with his council members and military commanders. General Scott, aged Chief of Staff, voiced opinion that the fort should be evacuated. It had only a twenty-eight-day supply of provisions left and, if relieved at all, it must be by that time. In view of the Confederate shore batteries, twenty-thousand troops might be required to do it and probably a bloody battle would have to be fought with General Beauregard's Southern soldiers based at Charleston.

If his Cabinet and military advisers should have aided Lincoln in reaching a decision, they showed themselves helpless. They could not reach an agreement. Instead, they were divided as to what should be done, showing themselves a quarreling coterie. The army and navy commanders disagreed among themselves on strategy. And so the dilemma about Charleston harbor plagued the President like Banquo's ghost.

In mid-March Lincoln again submitted to his Cabinet a question as to the wisdom of provisioning Sumter. The answers were preponderantly in favor of evacuating it. Secretary of the Treasury Chase favored provisioning, but he qualified this opinion by stipulating that the supplies should be sent only if it would not cause war. If it entailed fighting by soldiers, he did not favor reinforcing the fort. Chase's advice was essentially useless, since no one could predict whether the sending of an expedition to Sumter would set guns firing on both sides. Postmaster-General Blair, alone among Lincoln's Cabinet, advocated the dispatch of supplies to Sumter, regardless of consequences.

Lincoln, on March 15 and 16, received replies to his query, and with dismay learned that all of his Cabinet members, except Blair, opposed reinforcement of the Charleston harbor fort. If he had been required to make a decision then and there, the President might well have decided to evacuate it. To Secretary of the Navy Welles it appeared that Lincoln had now made the painful decision to uphold the majority of opinion. Blair, in disgust, prepared to resign from the Cabinet. Welles later gave credit to Blair, and to Blair's father, the venerable old Francis P. Blair, Sr., who had once been Andrew Jackson's "right arm," for Lincoln's decision to overrule the Cabinet majority and to reinforce Sumter. Wrote Welles subsequently:

"Mr. [Montgomery] Blair . . . observing that the President, with the acquiescence of the Cabinet, was about adopting the Seward and Scott policy, wrote out his resignation, determined not to continue in the Cabinet if no attempt were made to relieve Fort Sumter. Before handing in his resignation, a delay was made at the request of his father. The elder Blair sought an interview with the President, to whom he entered his protest against non-action, which he denounced as the offspring of intrigue. His earnestness and indignation aroused and electrified the President; and touched a chord that responded. The President decided from that moment that an attempt should be made to convey supplies to Major Anderson, and that he would reinforce Sumter."

On March 19, however, Lincoln took a step which indicated that he had not fully made up his mind. He sent to Fort Sumter, as his emissary, the able Assistant Secretary of the Navy, Gustavus V. Fox, Postmaster-General Blair's brother-in-law, to look over the scene. Fox had the idea that Sumter could be relieved by United States steamers running past the Confederate shore batteries at night. The President agreed that Fox should visit Sumter and confer with its commander, Major Robert Anderson.

The Assistant Navy head reached Charleston on March 21, met the secessionist Governor Andrew W. Pickens of South Carolina, and then went over to the fort for a conference with Anderson. Fox found that South Carolina expected evacuation of the fort. He studied conditions without making any arrangements with the Major, who doubted the success of any relief expedition; whereas Fox remained certain that it would have a fair chance.

Lincoln sent two other emissaries to Charleston, both Southern-born citizens of Illinois: his burly, bibulous Virginia-born bodyguard, Ward H. Lamon, and the South Carolina-born Stephen A. Hurlbut. Probably the President's motives in sending those two agents lay in the circumstance that each, having Southern origins, might not be so suspect by the Confederate authorities. Hurlbut reported to Lincoln that Union sentiment was extinct in the Palmetto State.

And Lamon? His only effect was a dubious one. He left the impression that the President had decided to evacuate Sumter. This intimate crony of Lincoln, who later called him "my particular friend," had an interview with Governor Pickens and, with exaggerated authority, told the Governor that he had come to arrange for the removal of the United States garrison from Fort Sumter. Lamon, from Charleston, sent news to Secretary Seward: "From the best lights that I can judge, from casting around, *I am satisfied of the policy and propriety of immediately evacuating Fort Sumter.*" And South Carolina's Governor Pickens confided to another: "I know the fact from Mr. Lincoln's most intimate friend and accredited agent, Mr. Lamon, that the President of the United States professed a desire to evacuate Fort Sumter, and he [Lamon] would be back in a few days to aid in that purpose."

Lincoln, on March 28, suddenly suffered a severe blow when General Scott, for whose ability he had always held high regard, informed him that Fort Sumter should not be reinforced and also that Fort Pickens, off Florida, for which reinforcements had already been ordered, should be abandoned. It was Lincoln's first great personal disillusionment as President. "Lincoln had persuaded himself that the old general was a great military man," revealed Postmaster-General Blair. "I shall never forget the President's excitement when, after a Cabinet dinner at the White House, he called the Cabinet into a separate room, and informed us that General Scott had told him it would be necessary *to evacuate Fort Pickens and Fort Sumter.* A very oppressive silence succeeded the President's statement of what General Scott had said." Lincoln's secretaries, Nicolay and Hay, declared: "That night Lincoln's eyes did not close in sleep. It was apparent that the time had come when he must meet the nation's crisis."

That unnerving month of March closed with the Chief Executive still pondering what should be done. The only positive move was his order that an expedition be held in readiness for the relief of Sumter.

V

April, month of enforced decision, opened.

Soldiers and uniformed volunteers filled Washington streets, determined to defend the capital in case of possible Confederate invasion. "Thousands of soldiers are guarding us," wrote Mrs. Lincoln on April 2, exaggerating the number, "and if there is safety in numbers we have every reason to feel secure. We can only hope for peace."

General Scott feared for the safety of Washington. On April 6, he privately complained that he had only 700 to 800 regular troops to protect the city and the Navy Yard, and only two field batteries, commanded by a Southern officer of doubtful attachment to the Union. The Navy Yard commander was openly accused of secession sympathies.

In those early April days Lincoln finally issued orders to send an expedition to Fort Pickens and to be prepared to dispatch one to Sumter. Assistant Secretary of the Navy Fox was to prepare the voyage to Sumter. Lincoln still remained in dilemma, yet was reluctant to forsake Sumter unless federal authority could not somehow be upheld in terms of his Inaugural Address.

Lincoln now had another trouble with which to deal—his Secretary of State, who was acting in a strange and bellicose manner, had suddenly concocted an extraordinary "foreign war" method of ending the secession crisis and welding the states together again.

Since the cosmopolitan, European-traveled, Washington-seasoned Seward considered Lincoln too inexperienced to wield power on national and international scenes, he believed that he, as chief Cabinet officer, should lend a controlling hand in the administration; act as a sort of government-directing Prime Minister to Lincoln, a republican version of the constitutional monarch.

Secretary Seward had expressed publicly ideas that the threat of a foreign war against the United States might serve as an immediate cementing force between North and South. In the preceding December he had told the New England Society in New York City that the Empire State would leap to the defense of Charleston, in case of being attacked by a foreign power. He added that secessionists could not "humbug" him. Seward's unique proposal for a war with European nations as a means of stifling secession at home formed the central theme in Seward's written memorandum to Lincoln, entitled "Some Thoughts for the President's Consideration."

In that uncommon paper to the President, appropriately dated April 1, the Secretary of State assumed for himself the function of saving the United States from disunion.

In his "Thoughts for the President's Consideration," Seward indicated to the Chief that the administration had no policy. He proceeded to supply one. He would evacuate Fort Sumter but keep and defend the Gulf ports. Then he would demand explanations from Spain and France, who were then intervening with their troops in Santo Domingo and Mexico. If the explanations were not satisfactory, Seward would convene Congress and have war declared! He would also seek explanations from Great Britain and Russia, and would marshal a "vigorous continental *spirit of independence* on this continent against European intervention." Seward, in this memorandum to the President, insisted that, whatever policy were adopted, it must be "somebody's business" to pursue and direct incessantly. Seward added: "Either the President must do it himself, and be all the while active in it; or devolve it on some member of his Cabinet. Once adopted, debates on it must end, and all agree and abide." He concluded: "But I neither seek to evade nor assume responsibility."

Quite aside from the jocular observation that Seward's foreign-war proposal might have been a Fool's Day abberration, Lincoln's reaction to it revealed him as a leader willing to assume responsibility for the conduct of his own administration. He answered Seward tactfully but denied the wisdom of the suggestions. On Seward's appeal that, once the policy was adopted, "debates on it must end, and all agree and abide,"

Lincoln replied to his Secretary of State: "I remark that if this must be done [directing a policy], *I* must do it."

While painfully occupied with Sumter and Pickens, Lincoln was troubled by a dispute between Seward and Secretary of the Navy Welles over the proposed expeditions to those forts.

The Secretary of State induced the President to order Lieutenant David D. Porter, U.S.N., to take command of the *Powhatan*, flagship of the contemplated expedition to Sumter, and attach it to the expedition going to Pickens, far down the Florida coast—all of this over the head of the Secretary of the Navy! Seward wanted Pickens reinforced but Sumter evacuated.

Lincoln suffered some anxious hours over the Seward-Welles feud. The complications rising from the orders to the *Powhatan* to join the Pickens expedition frustrated Lincoln temporarily and made the decision to supply the two forts even more tangled and incomprehensible to those naval men in charge of the relief ships being sent there.

Meanwhile, ominous events were see-sawing, first for the Union, then for secession, in that most strategic and influential slave state, Virginia. The indispensability of holding the Old Dominion loyal to the Union was obvious.

VI

What would Lincoln do about Virginia, still not a member of the Confederate States of America? Or, what would Virginia do for or against itself?

Governor John Letcher in January had called into special session the Legislature of Virginia, which then passed a bill providing for a convention to consider the State's course of action, in view of Lincoln's election and consequent secession of her sister slave states.

As the do-nothing President-elect had sat in Springfield, building his Cabinet, pondering over patronage and urging Illinois congressmen not to compromise with the South, Senator Seward had exerted Republican leadership at Washington. Lincoln had allowed Seward, his Secretary of State-designate, to handle relations with Virginia's leaders. Seward attempted to forestall secession by maintaining constant communication and conducting private interviews with noted Virginia Unionists. On January 27 Seward had reported to the then President-elect: "Recent events have opened access for me to Union men in Virginia and other Southern states."

The Virginia situation looked more cheerful for the Union when, on February 4, by that State's legislature's proviso, a "Peace Convention" of all states met at Washington. But hopes were dashed when the Convention's work proved ineffectual. Northern delegates there thwarted any compromise measures until a few days before Lincoln assumed the presidency. Then the plan they adopted and sent to the House of Representatives was promptly rejected by that body. The Washington Peace Convention, however, provided more time in which Seward could continue negotiations with Southern Unionists.

Optimism now reigned. From early February to early April, secessionists in Virginia were decisively defeated by Unionists in a convention and a popular vote.

Lincoln relied implicitly on the great strength of Union sentiment in Virginia. For a time he seriously considered sacrificing Fort Sumter to encourage the Unionists who did not like Federal interference in any community. "A State for a fort," he is reported to have stated, "is no bad business." By the opening days of April, however, the President felt less sure, and on the 4th he gave orders that the fort must be reinforced. In the last analysis, for the Chief Executive to withdraw Major Anderson's garrison of United States troops would not have been an easy solution to the crisis, since seven Southern states were already in the new Confederacy. Such a surrender of federal rights to the secessionist South would have been angrily heralded as evidence of weakness and deliberate evasion of presidential duty.

Lincoln sought to reassure himself of Virginia's continued loyalty by trying to arrange a conference with one Unionist leader from that State, George W. Summers of Kanawha. If Summers, sitting in the convention at Richmond, could not come to Washington, the President stipulated that another representative should be sent to see him. Summers sent his emissary, John B. Baldwin of Staunton.

Lincoln's conference with Baldwin occurred on April 4 behind locked doors in a White House back room. The prime topic at this super-secret meeting was the President's urgent wish that the Virginia convention, still in session at Richmond, must adjourn without passing an ordinance of secession. The States'-Rights-steeped Virginians were insisting that Lincoln promise not to supply Fort Sumter by armed force. They would tolerate none of Lincoln's "coercion."

At that conference with Lincoln, Baldwin later insisted that the President made no offer of any sort but kept repeating to him: "I am afraid you have come too late." When Baldwin suggested that the President call a national convention which would urge all citizens to come together and settle the sectional and secession controversy, Lincoln replied, "Oh, sir, that is impossible," according to Baldwin.

On the same day of his fruitless interview with Baldwin, Lincoln issued a definite order for the relief expedition to sail for Fort Sumter.

On that day, too, Secretary of War Cameron informed Major Anderson, "The expedition will go forward; and, finding your flag flying, will attempt to provision you, and, in case the effort is resisted, will endeavor also to reinforce you." Two days later, April 6, Assistant Secretary of the Navy Fox set sail with his expedition of ships, crews, and supplies from New York to Charleston harbor. And on the 8th Lincoln sent a private messenger to Governor Pickens of South Carolina, notifying him that *provisions,* and not men, arms, or ammunition, would be landed at the fort, unless the provisions or the fort were fired upon.

This decision by Lincoln to reinforce Sumter jeopardized the period of delay for which Seward had played so skilfully with Southern Unionist leaders. It nullified all his efforts for time.

Lincoln's letter informing the South Carolina Governor of his administration's determination to supply Fort Sumter, as a piece of United States Government property, was received by Pickens, who promptly forwarded this decision by telegraph to the officials of the Confederate States of America, then sitting at Montgomery, Alabama.

The crisis had come to a head.

VII

To the Southern mind Lincoln's plan to relieve Sumter seemed a threat, a challenge, and a breach of faith. So President Jefferson Davis and his Cabinet held anxious consultation at Montgomery.

If the Confederate government leaders allowed Lincoln's expedition to proceed peaceably to Sumter, the fort would be provisioned and could hold out for months, thus publicly demonstrating a mockery of the new Confederate States of America in their claims to sovereignty within their own borders. But if the authorities acted to stop the expedition, they would be compelled to use military force against the fort or the ships, thus placing the Confederacy in the position of firing the first shot. The decision was a grave one, full of the dangers of civil war. But after discussion, President Davis and his Cabinet decided on resistance to the expedition and for the capture of Sumter.

On April 10 Confederate Secretary of War Leroy P. Walker sent orders to General P. G. T. Beauregard, in command at Charleston, to demand of Major Anderson the evacuation of Fort Sumter and, if Anderson should refuse this demand, to "reduce it." Ironically enough, Beauregard had once been a pupil of Anderson at West Point, where Anderson had served as instructor in artillery.

Beauregard obeyed his orders. On the afternoon of April 11, a boat carrying three of his emissaries, Colonel James Chesnut, Jr. (recently resigned as United States Senator from South Carolina), Captain Stephen

D. Lee, and Lieutenant Alexander R. Chisolm, visited Fort Sumter under flag of truce and presented to Major Anderson the demand that he surrender the fort. Anderson refused, but remarked to the three Confederate officers that he would "await the first shot," and that his United States garrison would be "starved out in a few days."

General Beauregard wired the Secretary of War at Montgomery for further instructions, and they came. During the night of April 11-12 the three Confederate officers, with Colonel Roger A. Pryor, visited Fort Sumter again. Anderson directed a reply to Beauregard. But without waiting to transmit this answer, the four aides at 3:30 A.M., April 12, served notice, by Beauregard's authority, that the siege of Fort Sumter would open in one hour. The Confederacy was demanding evacuation of a fort which President Lincoln had determined not to evacuate.

At half past four on that April 12th morning, firing on the fort began.

As the Confederate officers rowed back to their headquarters in their boat, after giving the order at Confederate-held Fort Johnson to open fire on Sumter, Lieutenant Chisolm recorded: "We delayed for a few minutes to see the first Mortar fired at 4:30 A.M. We heard the report and saw the red ball scribe a semi-circle and explode immediately over the Fort."

That "red ball" over Fort Sumter was the opening shot of the Civil War.

VIII

All during the day of the twelfth, a dull drizzle fell on Charleston city and harbor. At night it turned into a cold, driving rain, with strong winds.

The morning of the 13th dawned bright, sunny, and cool, and Confederate batteries renewed their siege of Sumter. After hours upon hours of bombardment, Major Anderson, his ramparts wrecked, ammunition nearly exhausted, and fierce damage done by fire, formally surrendered his fort to the Confederates on April 14.

President Lincoln's relief expedition, commanded by Assistant Secretary of the Navy Fox, arrived and found itself powerless to do more than carry off Anderson and his men, after the surrender.

The firing on Fort Sumter and its capture by Confederate troops brought matters to a boil in Washington. The President was forced to render a decision.

On that grim Sunday afternoon, April 14, as Lincoln pondered, everything in the national capital became feverish excitement. At the White House and the government departments there appeared no end of plans to be discussed, messages to be sent to all parts of the country, orders to military and civil authorities to be prepared and signed.

Lincoln assembled his Cabinet and announced his decision. The states of the Union were to provide 75,000 militia for three months' service, and a special session of Congress was to meet on July 4. In this decision he acted on the authority of a United States militia law of 1795, under which provision was made for the summoning of militia of the States into Federal service whenever the national laws should be resisted "by combinations too powerful to be suppressed by the ordinary course of judicial proceedings."

The war was begun.

If the leading men of politics, on both sides of Mason and Dixon's line, had worked toward harmony with each other and stifled agitation and abuse, and had Lincoln not unwittingly contributed to national disunity by joining the northern sectional Republican Party five years before—who can doubt that this greatest of American tragedies might have been averted? It is a hypothetical question, but a germane one.

FROM FORT SUMTER TO FIRST BULL RUN

19

I

WAR fever started to infect the North and loyal border regions as soon as the horrifying news of the first shot on Sumter flashed over telegraph wires. As further tidings came concerning the Confederates' continued bombardment of Major Anderson and his garrison, intense patriotism was displayed from the Great Lakes south to the Ohio River and from the Atlantic Ocean west to beyond the Mississippi River. Men wore badges of loyalty, housewives hung out the stars-and-stripes from their windows, children pinned on red-white-and-blue bunting buttons, and clergymen inveighed from their pulpits against the rebels.

Washington, D. C., was thrown into confusion, for the national capital was known as a "Southern" town filled with secessionist sympathizers; the army, navy, and government departments were believed to be controlled by Southerners whose loyalty to the Union was questionable.

Outraged patriotism, uncontrolled anger, and even blood-chilling fear blended into emotionalism throughout the North when word arrived that Major Anderson had been compelled to surrender the fort.

When Lincoln, on that unnerving Sunday, April 14, 1861, drafted his call for 75,000 state militia men and for the convening of Congress, he found his office packed with people, as if a general reception were being held—patriotic men and women offering their aid in the crisis that had just enfolded the nation. Senators and representatives tendered the President their support, although Congress was not in session. Most Southern members of both houses had already resigned their seats to follow their states into secession. Of all congressmen who offered cheer and aid to Lincoln, none proved more personally and politically more welcome than his long-time Illinois rival, Senator Stephen A. Douglas.

George Ashmun of Massachusetts arranged for a meeting between Lincoln and Douglas, the two old political foes now bound together by concern for the Union. The President and the Little Giant met with outstretched hands at the White House on that Sunday evening after Lincoln had completed the draft of his call for troops. Together they went over Lincoln's as yet unreleased paper. Douglas suggested that 200,000, not 75,000, should be called. Bent over a map with Lincoln, the Senator marked strategic points to be protected from Confederate capture—not only Washington, but also Fortress Monroe, Harper's Ferry, and Cairo in southern Illinois. Lincoln asked Douglas to repeat these views to General Scott. Douglas also cautioned that trouble lay ahead in bringing federal troops to Washington through then secession-crazed Baltimore and suggested to Lincoln an alternative Maryland route by Perryville, Havre de Grace, and Annapolis.

After his conference with the President, Douglas authorized a release to the press, declaring that "while Mr. Douglas was unalterably opposed to the administration on all its political issues, he was prepared to sustain the President in the exercise of all his constitutional functions to preserve the Union, and maintain the government and defend the federal capital."

From this time on, Douglas consulted frequently with the President. It was with Lincoln's strong approval that the Senator, recognized leader of Union Democrats, left Washington to rouse his supporters in the Northwest to the seriousness of the secession crisis. He spoke three times on his way back to Illinois, at Wheeling, Virginia, Columbus, Ohio, and Indianapolis, Indiana, on each occasion with sincere emotion, denouncing disunion and pleading for support of Lincoln's national administration and the President's efforts to save the Republic from disruption.

On April 25 he held forth in a remarkable oration in the Capitol at Springfield. His booming voice reverberated throughout the lawmakers' chamber in defense of the Union cause, stirring his audience to a frenzy of patriotic fervor. To the legislators of his home state Douglas appealed: "Lay aside, for the time being, your party creeds and party platforms. . . . Dispense with your party organizations and party appeals.

. . . Forget that you were ever divided, until you have rescued the Government and the country from their assailants."

In several weeks Douglas's great voice for the Union would be still forever. Stricken with a sickness, probably typhoid fever, soon after his mighty Springfield speech, this celebrated Democratic chieftain, the Little Giant of national and international renown, battled his dread illness as resolutely as he had ever fought his Whig and Republican political foes. He succumbed to death on June 3. His last words to his sons cautioned them to obey the laws and support the Constitution.

Douglas's death shocked most of the nation, and Lincoln deeply mourned the passing of his former political foe. The White House was somberly festooned with black drapes. The War Department ordered that all regimental colors be draped in mourning, honoring this deceased patriot "who nobly discarded party for his country."

Lincoln's Secretary of State, Seward, insisted that the illustrious dead man belonged to the nation and should be buried in Washington. But Illinois would not hear of it, and Illinois had its way. The Little Giant's remains were interred at Chicago, attended by thousands in grief-stricken respect, as the rest of Union-lovers throughout the United States mourned him justifiably.

II

President Lincoln's prime purpose late in April, 1861, was the defense of Washington. Suddenly he received a jolting blow. Virginia seceded!

The guns of Fort Sumter had been unhappily heard in Virginia. But Old Dominion leaders heard even louder Lincoln's call for 75,000 militiamen to suppress the Confederacy. On April 17 the Convention at Richmond passed an Ordinance of Secession. This most influential of Southern states, the home of Washington, Jefferson, Patrick Henry, Madison, and other immortal Founding Fathers of the Republic, with the step of a proud Queen, walked out of the Union.

In another month a popular vote would be held on secession, but for all practical purposes Virginia had already lined up with the Confederate States of America.

Lincoln at the same time received gratifying news from the governors of the Northern states in his appeal for three-months' service volunteers.

Maine's Governor Israel Washburn, Jr., wired his assurances that "the people of Maine of all parties will rally with alacrity to the maintenance of the government." New Hampshire's Ichabod Goodwin replied that he would take "vigorous measures to form companies." Vermont's Erastus Fairbanks promised that he would raise a regiment. Massachusetts' John

A. Andrew telegraphed: "Dispatch received. By what route should I send?" Rhode Island's William Sprague offered to lead personally one thousand men. Connecticut's William A. Buckingham answered: "Your request will receive immediate attention." New York's Edwin D. Morgan replied enthusiastically in behalf of the Empire State, as did Governor Charles S. Olden of New Jersey. Pennsylvania's Andrew G. Curtin asked: "Could you accept Ringgold's Artillery of Reading? They are ready to start." Ohio's William Dennison pledged that his state "will furnish the largest number you will receive." Indiana's Oliver P. Morton offered 10,000 men "for the defense of the nation and to uphold the authority of the Government." Iowa's Samuel J. Kirkwood offered his co-operation in raising troops in his state, as did Michigan's Austin Blair and Wisconsin's Alexander W. Randell. Minnesota's Alexander Ramsey, in Washington looking for patronage for his supporters, offered 1,000 volunteers. Illinois' Richard Yates promised that the President's home state would send soldiers to uphold the Union.

Within several days some hastily recruited regiments started on their way to Washington to defend the national capital, some Pennsylvania units and the Sixth Massachusetts Militia. How would they pass through sensitive pro-Southern Baltimore without untoward incident?

The nation's eyes turned toward Maryland, corridor from New England, New York, New Jersey, Pennsylvania, and Delaware to Washington.

III

In Maryland, a border slave state, there existed genuine Southernism, not only on the Eastern Shore but all around Chesapeake Bay through Baltimore and to the south. What was of concern to Lincoln, the historic Calvert commonwealth held extreme strategic importance. With Virginia out of the Union, if Maryland should secede, the capital of the United States would lie in Confederate-held territory. Governor Thomas H. Hicks, believing neither in Jefferson Davis's "secession" nor in Lincoln's "coercion," was playing with the idea of state neutrality.

Of immediate urgency, Pennsylvania units and the Sixth Massachusetts Volunteers, en route to Washington, reached Baltimore on April 19. That Massachusetts contingent, commanded by Colonel Edward F. Jones, was the first fully organized and equipped regiment to answer Lincoln's call. It numbered 700 men.

As Colonel Jones's men marched from one station to another in Baltimore, secession-crazed citizens in surging crowds fired at them. The Colonel, in retaliation, ordered his troops: "Fire!" A street brawl resulted, and blood was spilled on both sides. When Jones counted his casualties, he found that three of his men were killed, eight wounded, and 130 missing. Some of the latter had deserted.

The Sixth Massachusetts continued by train to Washington.

Near panic gripped the national capital at news of the bloody and unseemly demonstration at Baltimore. Lincoln's assistant secretary, John Hay, noted on the 20th in his diary: "The streets were full of the talk of Baltimore. The town is full to-night of feverish rumours about a meditated assault upon this town."

Lincoln, confronted with the Maryland problem, sought to avoid extreme measures. He was working for two objectives: to assert the Federal authority and to conciliate the State temporarily in order to avert further bloodshed.

On the day after the Baltimoreans had fired on the Massachusetts troops, Lincoln sent a joint letter to Governor Hicks and Mayor George W. Brown. He thanked them for their efforts in behalf of peace, insisted that troops must move across Maryland, but they need not necessarily pass through Baltimore. He told Hicks and Brown: "For the future, troops *must* be brought here, but I make no point of bringing them *through* Baltimore. . . . By this, a collision of the people of Baltimore with the troops will be avoided, unless they go out of their way to seek it. I hope you will exert your influence to prevent this.

"Now, and ever, I shall do all in my power for peace, consistently with the maintenance of government."

On that same day, the 20th, Lincoln sent another message to Governor Hicks and Mayor Brown, requesting to consult with them. Hicks did not accept, but Brown did. The Mayor left an account of his talk, along with three Maryland associates, with the President at the White House. Lincoln declared that he appreciated the Baltimore public's excited feeling and told of his desire to "avoid the fatal consequences of a collision with the people." He insisted on right of transit through Maryland for troops on their way to defend the national capital. Brown noted: "He protested that none of the troops brought through Maryland were intended for any purposes hostile to the State, or aggressive as against the Southern States." The President then called on General Scott, who was present, for his opinion. Two other Maryland routes, by-passing Baltimore, were suggested. Happily the Mayor related: "The President . . . said no more troops should be ordered through Baltimore if they were permitted to go uninterruptedly by either of the other routes suggested." Thus the Chief Executive came to agreement with the Baltimore Mayor.

Lincoln had not heard the last of complaints from Baltimoreans. One delegation from the city's Young Men's Christian Associations visited him on the day after he had spoken to Mayor Brown. He told this latest group of visitors from the Maryland metropolis bluntly that they were using no words of condemnation of Union-wreckers and those citizens who had attacked the Massachusetts soldiers. Troops had to cross the State to get to Washington, for the captial's defense, he emphasized, adding to them: "Our men are not moles, and can't dig under the earth; they are not birds, and can't fly through the air. There is no way but to march across, and that they must do. But in doing this there is no need of collision. Keep your rowdies in Baltimore, and there will be no bloodshed."

Finally Lincoln found an end to his Maryland troop-transit difficulties in the selection of routes through the State which avoided Baltimore and other populous, turbulent centers.

IV

Particularly painful to the President were the delays encountered by troops who traveled through these circuitous routes to Washington, merely to by-pass Baltimore during that fortnight following his call for militia men.

The Seventh New York Regiment and some Rhode Island companies were held up at Annapolis by various traveling difficulties. Lincoln grew impatient to the point of fearing that a Confederate force might descend on Washington before the New Yorkers and Rhode Islanders arrived. In his address to the Sixth Massachusetts troops on April 24, he semi-gloomily told them: "I don't believe there is any North. The Seventh Regiment is a myth. R. Island is not known in our geography any longer. *You* are the only Northern realities."

Not until the New York and Rhode Island soldiers arrived two days later did Lincoln emerge from his despondency.

More trouble soon lay ahead: those Southern states which had not yet seceded.

The withdrawal of Virginia from the Union was heeded in other parts of Dixie. On May 6 Arkansas joined the Confederate States of America, followed by North Carolina on the 20th. Tennessee joined them in early June. These four new seceded states, Virginia, Arkansas, North Carolina, and Tennessee, added to the original seven, made eleven stars in the Confederate flag. Would there be other stars? How far north would the Confederacy spread? Would secessionism enclose the border slave states, Kentucky, Missouri, Maryland, and Delaware?

Constant concern plagued Lincoln that his native Kentucky could not be held in the Union. He bent every energy toward fostering Unionist sentiment there, for, as he confided to his Illinois friend, Orville H. Browning, several months later: "Kentucky gone, we can not hold Missouri, nor, as I think, Maryland. These all against us, and the job on our hands is too large for us."

Lincoln gave thought to the army command. General Scott, Chief of Staff, was obviously too aged and infirm to actively take the field. Besides, he wanted to have Scott in Washington for over-all military decisions. The 75-year-old Chief of Staff found that his excruciatingly painful gout prevented him from even mounting the White House steps to the President's office, and at least once Lincoln had to come down to talk to him.

With Lincoln's permission, Francis P. Blair, Sr., father of his Postmaster-General, on April 18 offered Colonel Robert E. Lee, commanding the First United States Cavalry, a high place in the Army, perhaps commander in the field. But Lee, heart wrapped in his Virginia people, would not consider it. Lee then called on General Scott and recounted what he had told the senior Blair about his decision not to cast his lot with the Union until he learned the course of his native State. Soon, without waiting for the popular vote on secession in Virginia, he cast his lot with the Confederacy.

Later Secretary Seward, with Lincoln's concurrence, offered a high-ranking commission in the United States Army to—of all people!—Giuseppe Garibaldi. This offer to the Italian patriot-warrior was made through the American Minister at Brussels. But the matter was bungled. It was misunderstood, and Garibaldi himself set up impossible conditions. It was probably just as well. It is difficult to conceive of the famous Italian liberator successfully commanding American troops in 1861. It might well have added another military headache to Lincoln's accumulation.

The last effort to effect a compromise between the warring sections was undertaken in late April, one week following Lincoln's call for troops. The intermediary, self-constituted, was Rudolf Schleiden, Minister of the German Hanseatic States at Washington.

Schleiden offered his services as a third party intermediary to Secretary of State Seward, proposing to journey to Richmond, where he planned to confer with Confederate Vice-President Alexander H. Stephens. Seward encouraged the Hanseatic envoy to make the trip, but he insisted: "Neither the President nor the entire Cabinet could expressly authorize such *pourparlers* or draw up conditions under which it would be willing to entertain an armistice."

Lincoln gave the Hanseatic representative the impression, or so the representative interpreted it, that he desired Schleiden to attempt negotiations with Vice-President Stephens without any special authorization.

"I therefore tried," reported Schleiden to his Government, "to cause the gentlemen [Lincoln and Seward] to state whether the suspension of all hostilities for the term of three months would be accepted under a simultaneous revocation of the two opposing proclamations [of Presidents Lincoln and Davis], the one referring to the issues of mark and reprisal, the other to the blockade of the southern ports." Lincoln declined to make any definite statement, declared Schleiden.

Schleiden reached Richmond on April 25 and consulted with Vice-President Stephens. He failed in his mission of conciliation of the views of Lincoln and Stephens. On May 2 the Hanseatic envoy reported his failure to his superiors in Europe.

The last effort to prevent a long war of American brothers was ended.

V

Lincoln had decided that he would make no attempt to retake the forts and other federal property, which he considered unlawfully seized by the insurrectionists. Instead, he would leave the then existing condition to be considered by Congress, which he had called into special session for July 4. Meanwhile, his administration's work of raising an army went forward.

Throughout the North, Lincoln's call for militia men to serve for three months seemed to imply that the "insurrection," or the "rebellion," as many were now disdainfully terming it, would be suppressed in that short quarter of a year. In the South, the Confederates felt confident that they would be left unmolested by Lincoln in their efforts to maintain a separate nation of their own, or else they would capture Washington, drive out Lincoln and the Republican regime, and save the nation in their own way.

During the several weeks that followed Lincoln's appeal for volunteers, drilling, recruiting, parading, and camps of military instruction were evident throughout the North, except in distant and apparently oblivious California and Oregon. Volunteers were signed up at rallies and mass-meetings. Also, any one who wished would advertise his purpose to "raise a company" and in that way become its commanding captain, regardless of his ignorance of profession of arms and warfare. Appeals went out to "all willing to join to come on a certain morning to some saloon, hotel, or public hall." Recruitment became a most informal and personal activity, and an amazing variety of military companies and regiments, some with colorful, racial, or geographically descriptive names came into being: The "Excelsior Brigade" of New York, the "Buena Vista Guards" of Philadelphia, the "Plainfield Light Artillery" of New Jersey, the "Springfield Zouaves," the "St. Patrick Brigade," the "Irish

Volunteers," the "Steuben Volunteers," the "German Rifles," and even the "Polish Legion," although immigration from Poland was then negligible.

Bloody battles in the field between Federals and Confederates were deferred throughout the rest of April, through May and June, and for a part of July because neither side judged itself in fighting fettle. During those first weeks of war only a few Union officers and men were killed or wounded in isolated regions. The first mortally wounded Union officer who fell in Confederate-held territory was Lincoln's own devoted young friend, Colonel Elmer E. Ellsworth.

The twenty-four-year-old Ellsworth had become known throughout the North for the precision drill of his Zouaves. A man of ability and magnetic personality, Lincoln in Illinois had taken a fancy to him and given him a place in his Springfield law office. He accompanied the President-elect on the train to Washington, serving as an adjutant of sorts and a bodyguard. He became a favorite of the entire Lincoln family and lived at the White House.

The day after his inauguration the President requested Secretary of War Cameron to appoint Ellsworth to a clerkship in the War Department. Upon the outbreak of hostilities against the Confederates in mid-April, Lincoln wrote Ellsworth: "Ever since the beginning of our acquaintance, I have valued you highly as a personal friend, and at the same time (without much capacity for judging) have had a very high estimate of your military talent. Accordingly I have been, and still am anxious for you to have the best position in the military which can be given you, consistently with justice and proper courtesy towards the older officers of the army. I can not incur the risk of doing them injustice, or a discourtesy; but I do say they would personally oblige me if they could, and would place you in some position, or in some service, satisfactory to yourself."

Ellsworth organized the New York Fire Zouaves in the metropolis, composed of members of that city's fire department, and drilled them into fairly good fighting condition in the next several weeks. On May 23 he was ordered with his men to cross the Potomac River to Alexandria, Virginia, into Confederate-occupied territory, and capture that town. Early the following morning, the 24th, he and some of his units invaded Alexandria, captured a small detachment of Confederate cavalry, and occupied the town.

Suddenly the youthful Colonel noticed a Confederate flag flying over the town's principal hotel, the Marshall House. He rushed there, followed by his men, demanded to know whose flag was hoisted and, receiving an evasive answer, dashed upstairs with several of his soldiers at his heels. Mounting to the roof, Ellsworth cut the halyards and started down the stairs with the stars-and-bars under his arm.

As he reached the second landing, the hotel's owner, James Jackson, a pro-secession Kentuckian, sprang at him, discharging both barrels of a shot gun. Ellsworth dropped dead. Immediately Ellsworth's men opened fire on Jackson, and he, too, fell.

Ellsworth's death was the first Federal blood shed in the Civil War, if the few casualties at Sumter and the small number of dead and wounded among the Sixth Massachusetts by the Baltimore mob can be excepted.

A few hours after Ellsworth's death, a New York *Herald* reporter called at the White House on a news assignment, accompanied by Senator Henry Wilson of Massachusetts. "We observed Mr. Lincoln before a window, looking out across the Potomac," reported the *Herald* correspondent. "He did not move until we approached very closely, when he turned abruptly, and advanced toward us, extending his hand." He told them, "Excuse me but I cannot talk." Visibly affected, the President explained to him and Senator Wilson: "I will make no apology, gentlemen, for my weakness; but I knew Ellsworth well, and held him in great regard. Just as you entered the room, Captain Fox [Assistant Secretary of the Navy] left me, after giving me the principal details of his unfortunate death. The event was so unexpected, and the recital so touching, that it quite unnerved me. . . . Poor fellow!"

Both Lincoln and Mrs. Lincoln went to the Navy Yard, where Ellsworth's body lay temporarily, and gazed on the stilled youthful face with deep emotion. The Confederate flag which the dead Colonel had pulled down from the Marshall House mast and which he held when he was killed—a banner stained with blood—was given to Mrs. Lincoln. But that stars-and-bars banner proved such a tragic reminder of the Lincolns' young friend, that she could not bear to have it around, and she put it away in a bureau drawer.

The passing of Ellsworth, Lincoln's first real personal loss as President, inspired him to write to Ellsworth's parents one of his really memorable letters.

> My dear Sir and Madam: In the untimely loss of your noble son, our affliction here is scarcely less than your own. So much of promised usefulness to one's country, and of bright hopes for one's self and friends, have rarely been so suddenly dashed, as in his fall. In size, in years, and in youthful appearance, a boy only, his power to command men was surpassingly great. This power, combined with a fine intellect, an indomitable energy, and a taste altogether military, constituted in him, as seemed to me, the best natural talent, in that department, I ever knew. And yet he was singularly modest and deferential in social intercourse. My acquaintance with him began less than two years ago; yet through the latter half of the intervening period, it was as intimate as the disparity in our ages, and my engrossing engagements would permit. To me, he appeared to have no indulgences or pastimes; and I never heard him utter a profane, or an intemperate word. What was conclusive of his good heart, he never forgot his parents. The

honors he labored for so laudably and, in the sad end, so gallantly gave his life, he meant for them, no less than for himself.

In the hope that it may be no intrusion upon the sacredness of your sorrow, I have ventured to address you this tribute to the memory of my young friend and your brave and early fallen child.

May God give you that consolation which is beyond all earthly power. Sincerely your friend in a common affliction—

A. Lincoln.

Ellsworth was buried from the East Room of the White House. The President and Mrs. Lincoln attended the funeral, and it was noted that they were visibly affected.

VI

Lincoln assumed oppressive responsibilities with the social and "protocol" demands of his position.

The President was uninstructed in the rules of greeting official dignitaries and ignorant of the picayunish necessities of protocol. Except for an inconspicuous two-year service in Congress more than a decade previous, he had never moved in official Washington, high, intermediate, or low.

For the information of Lincoln and Mrs. Lincoln, the protocol-steeped Department of State furnished a detailed memorandum on social functions, the order of precedence, and the use of calling cards. The President and the First Lady were cautioned not to address a titled foreigner as "Sir" and advised that state dinners should take place at seven o'clock, although the family might dine privately at six. There were pointed admonitions that gentlemen, for evening affairs, should never wear frock coats. In matters of protocol the Secretary of State acted as the President's guide and guardian, to the intense irritation of Mrs. Lincoln, who heartily hated Seward.

One of Lincoln's earliest duties was to receive the Italian Minister, the Chevalier Bertinatti. The President from Illinois prairies did the honors with bows and a proper ceremonial speech to the Chevalier in his cocked hat, fancy silver lace, and polished sword.

A few days following the Inauguration, the President and Mrs. Lincoln held their first levee at the Executive Mansion, where American army and navy officers, the Diplomatic Corps, and other guests presented themselves. From 8:00 until 10:30 in the evening Lincoln, wearing white gloves and his black inauguration suit, shook hands, sometimes using his left hand to pass the guests along. "Mr. Lincoln wore white kid gloves," wrote one of those present, William H. L. Wallace, to his wife in Ottawa,

Illinois, "& worked away at shaking hands with the multitude, with much the same air & movement as if he were mauling rails."

Office-seekers were thick in numbers at those crowded presidential receptions. John Bigelow of the New York *Evening Post,* slated for appointment by Lincoln as United States Consul-General at Paris, confided to his diary about his meeting with one gorgeous woman, seeking a consulate for her husband at one of those White House levees, in early summer of 1861. Wrote Bigelow to himself: "Walked around the grand salon once, twice or thrice with Mrs. O'Sullivan who was the handsomest and the best dressed lady there. She is still solicitous for her husband's appointment as consul in the East. . . . Nicolay [the President's secretary] came to me and asked who that lady was. I availed myself of the occasion to say what I could in favor of her application for a new consulate." The lady's husband, John P. O'Sullivan, received the Consulate at Singapore.

Ever closing in on Lincoln were place-seekers, intent on a full feeding at the taxpayers' trough, ravenous for big jobs as well as post offices and Indian agencies for themselves, relatives, and political allies. They still crowded the White House halls and loitered in the anterooms of the President's office. Lincoln found his Cabinet members bickering about jobs. Attorney General Bates in late March privately sent news home: "They are squabbling around me, in a quasi-Cabinet council, about the distribution of loaves and fishes."

Lincoln, hard pressed by the office-hunters, was learning that it was ever more difficult to live up to his previously announced job policy to Seward: "In regard to the patronage, sought with so much eagerness and jealousy, I have prescribed for myself the maxim, 'Justice to all.' "

In parceling out patronage Lincoln followed practices in keeping with American political tradition in its grossest form dating from Jackson's day. Lincoln consulted Senators in making major federal appointments for or from their states, not being one to defy "senatorial courtesy." Minor jobs, especially post offices in their districts, were generally given to those Representatives in Congress. Lincoln also gave heed to the voices of Governors in the loyal states. Cabinet officers and also certain powerful party chieftains, such as Seward's political partner, Thurlow Weed, the Albany editor and New York State Republican boss, were influential with the President on some appointments.

Lincoln gave out the federal offices as wisely as any human could in his harrowing predicament. Not only did he face the task of keeping together his Republican Party, comprising diverse and complex elements, but he found it indispensable to hold the allegiance of those outside his own party who loyally supported the Union.

In the last analysis, a politician of Lincoln's ability was highly qualified to deal with such a mundane matter as patronage.

The opposition Democrats realistically accepted Lincoln's wholesale dismissals of their party brethren as part of the great game of politics, a part of the professional game they had played with no holds barred, and had lost to the Republicans in 1860.

VII

In answer to Lincoln's call, Congress met in a special session on July 4, 1861.

The President's prime purpose was to save the Union, which meant, of course, crushing the Confederate States of America. In his message to Congress, carefully prepared by himself and previously read privately by his friend, Orville Browning, Lincoln presented a history of events, a report of his stewardship, a constitutional argument, and commented on fundamentals. "This is essentially a people's contest," he insisted. For the first time Lincoln underlined democracy as a world goal. The issue, he told Congress, "embraces more than the fate of these United States. It presents to the whole family of man the question whether a constitutional republic, or democracy—a government of the people by the same people—can or can not maintain its territorial integrity against its own domestic foes."

In that congressional message to this specially called session Lincoln apologetically explained: "It was with the deepest regret that the Executive found the duty of employing the war power in defense of the Government forced upon him. He could but perform this duty or surrender the existence of Government." He closed his message: "And having thus chosen our course, without guile and with pure purpose, let us renew our trust in God and go forward without fear and with manly hearts."

All of those weeks since the firing on Fort Sumter the public, press, and crowd-catering politicians were yelling: "On To Richmond!" In June, Lincoln's Secretary of the Interior, Smith, had sent word home to Indiana: "Matters are approaching a crisis & we will very probably soon have to fight."

In the Virginia theatre of war during early July were stationed 50,000 untrained Federal troops and 30,000 untrained Confederates. Slightly over 20,000 Confederates were at Manassas, the rest in the Shenandoah Valley facing a bigger Federal force. If the blue-clad troops in the Valley could neutralize the gray-garbed foe, Major-General Irvin McDowell, the Union field commander, could move his men against Manassas with a superior force. If he crushed the Confederates, McDowell could disperse the remaining Southern soldiers in Virginia, take the Confederate capital, Richmond—and that would be the end of Jefferson Davis and his rebels. So figured McDowell.

McDowell brought his plan to General Scott. The two pondered it.

On June 29 they discussed it with Lincoln, the Cabinet, and the senior generals. The President favored an immediate advance, although Scott pleaded for another plan. But the aged Chief of Staff yielded when he saw how anxious Lincoln was for a quick drive on Manassas. McDowell pleaded for more time in which to organize, drill, and discipline his army. Lincoln answered McDowell: "You are green, it is true; but they [the Confederates] are green, also; you are green alike."

McDowell moved his men toward Manassas in mid-July. Northern newspapers, voracious for circulation, published accounts of McDowell's numbers and line of march. Crowds of civilian spectators, including United States Senators and Representatives, some carrying their lunches, trailed after the army and made for no great order or discipline. The Confederacy was about to be conquered! That was sure. The entire North, except a minority of anti-war citizens, fell almost delirious with joy and their hearts throbbed with martial thoughts.

McDowell, on that hot Sunday, July 21, led his army across Bull Run, near Manassas, twenty miles southwest of Washington. Here they struck the Southern forces.

McDowell and his strategists had miscalculated! They had not anticipated that General Joseph E. Johnston and his army, thought to be in the Winchester-Harper's Ferry region facing the Federals under Major-General Robert Patterson, had been permitted to slip away and unite with the main Confederate units under General Beauregard at Manassas, ready to greet McDowell's men with withering fire.

The Federals, after a few initial successes, were turned back with profuse bloodshed. The Federal line was broken, part of the army disintegrated into a disorganized mass, and the officers lost control over their men in a melee of soldiers, spectators, and congressmen.

VIII

As the Manassas, or Bull Run, battle raged, Lincoln in Washington was constantly on the alert for the smallest scrap of news about the fighting a score of miles distant. Telegrams came to the White House at intervals about the progress of McDowell's men—broken reports from Bull Run. Though fragmentary, these pieces of news sounded encouraging at first. The President studied them, reflected, and appeared optimistic. Then he hastened to see General Scott at the War Department, and listened to more wires from the front. By 5:30 Lincoln felt so confident of victory, that he went for a drive in his carriage.

While the Chief Executive went on his drive, Secretary Seward rushed breathlessly into the White House. He gave to Nicolay and Hay the latest news from Bull Run: McDowell's army was in full disorderly retreat!

Lincoln returned from his carriage trip. He was told the nerve-shattering news. His two secretaries stated subsequently: "He listened in silence, without the slightest change of feature or expression, and walked away to army headquarters."

By dawn of the next day the President could dishearteningly view from a White House window hordes of demoralized, tattered blue-uniformed troops hurrying back from the front as fast as their bruised bodies allowed.

FROM BULL RUN TO BALL'S BLUFF

20

I

LINCOLN, on that night following Bull Run, did not sleep. "The President," noted his secretaries, "did not go to bed that night; morning found him still in the executive office, hearing repetitions of those recitals [about the battle] and making memoranda of his own conclusions."

The President put the results of his own reflections in a paper entitled, "Memorandum of Military Policy Suggested By the Bull Run Defeat," dated July 23, with additional notes on the 27th. These were executed as orders, in his constitutional capacity as commander-in-chief of the nation's army and navy.

This "Memorandum" directed the strengthening of the blockade of Southern ports by the navy, the continuance of drilling and disciplining of Union military forces at Fort Monroe and vicinity under Major-General Benjamin F. Butler, the holding of Baltimore "with a gentle, but firm, and certain hand;" strengthening of the Federal forces under Major-Generals Robert Patterson and Nathaniel P. Banks in the Winchester,

Virginia, area, door to the Shenandoah Valley; the Western Virginia forces to receive all orders from Major-General George B. McClellan; and pushing forward military operations in the West, "giving rather special attention to Missouri" under Major-General Frémont.

The President's Memorandum, translated into orders, also called for reorganization of the main Federal armies in and near Washington; the mustering out of those three-month-enlistment men who declined to enter longer military service "as rapidly as circumstances will permit;" the establishment into camps, on both sides of the Potomac River, of the new volunteer forces.

When all those instructions were carried out, Lincoln directed, Manassas Junction or some point near it, as well as Strasburg, in the Shenandoah Valley, were to be seized and permanently held. Also, there must be established open Union lines from Washington to Manassas and from Strasburg to Harper's Ferry, "the military men to find the way of doing these," the President in his capacity as commander-in-chief of the armed forces, ordered. "This done," he concluded, "a joint movement from Cairo on Memphis; and from Cincinnati on East Tennessee."

The loyal-state populations, from Maine to Minnesota, from Maryland to Missouri, even over the plains and mountains to remote and rather indifferent California and Oregon, fell into despair. They sought to blame someone for Bull Run, particularly the President. Doubts about him as leader were angrily voiced. Inadequacy, weakness, even "imbecility," were attributed to him.

Elderly and infirm General Scott, even though he had agreed reluctantly to the advance on Manassas against his own better judgment, quixotically took responsibility for the disaster on himself, in the presence of the President, Cabinet members, and members of Congress at an Executive Mansion conference held on July 23.

Even though major responsibility for Manassas might be justifiably lodged against any number of leaders, particularly General Patterson for allowing General Johnston and his troops to escape from Winchester and join General Beauregard's battalions at Bull Run to combine against McDowell's main army, the aged Chief of Staff insisted that he alone was to blame. He told the President and those present: "I am the greatest coward in America. I have fought this battle, sir, against my judgment; as God is my judge, after my superiors had determined to fight it, I did all in my power to make the Army efficient. I deserve removal because I did not stand up when my Army was not in condition for fighting, and resist it to the last."

Lincoln replied to Scott: "Your conversation seems to imply that I forced you to fight this battle."

Gloom engulfed the North and loyal border states for months after Manassas.

II

Lincoln felt that a new Federal field commander was indispensable.

Two days after Bull Run he rode out to Arlington to visit General McDowell. Supposedly he assured the beaten commander: "General, I have not lost a particle of confidence in you," to which McDowell is alleged to have replied: "I don't see why you should, Mr. President."

That story might be true or partially true. It sounds characteristically Lincolnian to say something kind. Yet McDowell could not remain in field command, for he too glaringly symbolized defeat. Lincoln decided on Major-General George Brinton McClellan, then in Western Virginia clearing Confederates out of the mountains, as ranking field general under Chief of Staff Scott in succession to McDowell.

What became of General Irvin McDowell? He served as corps commander in the Army of the Potomac under McClellan, later in the Army of Virginia under General John Pope, was finally relieved after the Second Bull Run disaster, and was not used again until 1864, when he was given the exile Pacific Coast command.

George B. McClellan, the new field commander, had graduated from West Point, had served in the Mexican War, had acted as United States War Department observer in the Crimean War, had demonstrated great talents as an army engineer, and was a $10,000-a-year railroad president, at the age of thirty-five, when the war against secession broke out. Probably he had no peer among the Federal generals as an organizer of troops. The Governor of Ohio gave McClellan command of that State's volunteers after Fort Sumter and Lincoln's call for militia. He had performed notable work in getting the Ohio soldiers fed, clad, trained, and mustered into fighting shape. When the Confederates sent troops into mountainous western Virginia, across the river from Ohio, McClellan found himself, by late May, 1861, leading to victory regiments of Ohioans, Hoosiers from Indiana, and some anti-secession Virginians. McClellan's was the first victorious feat of arms enjoyed by the Federals, and Unionists rejoiced at the news of his triumphs.

Lincoln summoned McClellan to Washington, and he arrived on July 26. The President asked him to attend a Cabinet meeting but did not ask General Scott. The feeble Chief of Staff was enraged, and McClellan felt superior. Everyone seemed to defer to him, President, Cabinet, and others. "By some strange operations of magic, I seem to have become the power of the land," he confided to his wife with no surplus of modesty. And at thirty-five McClellan was appointed by Lincoln commander of the Division of the Potomac. But McClellan, despite his egotism, had genuine military qualities. On July 27 he formally assumed command, with headquarters at Washington. Scott was still Chief of Staff.

Lincoln was now bothered by almost immediate friction between Scott and McClellan. Behind the scenes the President endeavored to ease the strained relations between the ancient warrior and the youthful new field commander. Scott was in his way, McClellan insisted, and he communicated directly with the President and Cabinet members, bypassing the Chief of Staff. Scott complained to Lincoln about McClellan's lack of courtesy and insubordination.

Despite Lincoln's unobtrusive efforts to achieve harmony between his Chief of Staff and commanding general, the Scott-McClellan irritations continued, and seemed to grow worse and more bitter.

When in October Scott finally asked to be retired, Lincoln agreed. He brought before his Cabinet the Chief of Staff's retirement request, assuring all that he would do right by Scott and his family.

Lincoln and his Cabinet members repaired to Scott's home. There the Chief Executive read an affecting eulogy to the feeble retiring patriot. The Chief of Staff was retired with full pay and allowances.

In his first Annual Message to Congress, Lincoln lauded the General's fifty-year service to his country. "In calling to mind," he told Congress, "how faithfully, ably, and brilliantly he has served his country, from a time way back in our history, when few of the now living had been born, and thenceforward continually, I can not but think we are still his debtors."

On November 1 Lincoln directed McClellan to "assume the command of the Army of the United States." That did not mean that McClellan was given Scott's lofty Lieutenant-General's grade. Yet Lincoln appointed him in Scott's stead and soon referred to him officially as "General in Chief of the Army."

III

A bedevilling problem to Lincoln during that late summer of 1861 was Major-General John C. Frémont, whom he had appointed to command the Department of the West, with headquarters at St. Louis.

The picturesque Pathfinder, whose explorations in the West, romantic elopement with Senator Thomas Hart Benton's energetic daughter, Jessie, and Mexican War exploits had endeared him to thousands, was as attractive a hero as the Northern masses then had to worship. His near-victory at the election polls, as Republican candidate for President in 1856, had won him support from strongly anti-slavery agitators and whetted his appetite for high public office. The problem of the Pathfinder became more acute to Lincoln because he was a popular idol and the darling of anti-slavery extremists commanding in a vital but sensitive border slave state, Missouri.

By August Lincoln had grown convinced that Missouri would remain loyal to the Union, particularly because of the great military work done by Colonel Nathaniel Lyon and other Union commanders there. Governor Hamilton Gamble, brother-in-law of Lincoln's Attorney General, and Frank Blair of St. Louis, brother of his Postmaster-General, Montgomery Blair, also had proven themselves formidable political warriors in the struggle to keep Missouri in the Union.

But although Lincoln's concern over Missouri's loyalty was ended, new worries, centering around a flare-up between General Frémont and Frank Blair, entered the scene.

This Frémont-Blair feud was created by their quarrels over State political power and military administration, along with rivalries of party factions over federal patronage and army contracts, and a contest among pro-slavery, moderate, and anti-slavery groups about Negro emancipation.

Frank Blair, brother of Lincoln's Postmaster-General, regarded Missouri as his own particular preserve and waxed irate at the erratic, impetuous Frémont. Especially irritating to Blair was the General's anti-slavery appeal to the St. Louis German-Americans, hitherto Blair's "vest pocket" ethnic vote, and he concluded that Frémont intended to build a political machine and challenge the Blair bossdom. In August Blair was interfering in military matters, for he imagined himself a prospective war hero and wanted to accommodate his followers with army contracts and officer's commissions. Frémont, for his part, fervently hoped that Lincoln would give Blair an army post in the East that would take him out of Missouri. The situation worsened when Blair insistently reported to his brother, the Postmaster-General, by urgent letters and telegrams, that something be done about Frémont. According to Frank Blair the Pathfinder was carelessly awarding contracts to the most corrupt operators at highwaymen's prices. St. Louis, indeed all of Missouri, had become too small to hold both Blair and Frémont.

Lincoln, concerned over this feud, sent Postmaster-General Blair, and the able Quartermaster General Montgomery C. Meigs, to St. Louis in early September, 1861, to look into the Missouri mess. Lincoln had always thought that the Blairs and the Frémonts were the closest of friends. The Blairs had been original Frémont-for-President workers in 1856 and had warmly supported the idea that the Pathfinder should be given the Western army command.

In all probability the President was acting unwisely in dispatching Frank Blair's own brother, and General Meigs, a Blair brother-in-law, to the personal and political combat zone of St. Louis, for, in the last analysis, Montgomery Blair and Meigs could not give an objective opinion on their relative Frank's controversy with Frémont. But Lincoln was deeply sincere and acting in full good faith when he sent Montgomery Blair to try to iron out the differences. As he explained to Frémont's wife, Jessie, in a note shortly after: "Post-Master General Blair did go, with my approbation, to see and converse with Gen. Fremont as a friend."

Lincoln gave to Montgomery Blair and Meigs, before they left for St. Louis, a letter to be delivered to West-Point-educated Major-General David Hunter, then in Chicago. "General Fremont needs assistance which it is difficult to give him," the President informed Hunter. "He is losing the confidence of men near him, whose support any man in his position must have to be successful. His cardinal mistake is that he isolates himself, & allows nobody to see him; and by which he does not know what is going on in the very matter he is dealing with. He needs to have, by his side, a man of large experience." Lincoln tactfully requested Hunter: "Will you not, for me, take that place? Your rank is one grade too high to be ordered to it; but will you not serve the country, and oblige me, by taking it voluntarily?"

Postmaster-General Blair and Quartermaster General Meigs reached St. Louis on September 12. Their friends gave out the story that their business concerned the overland mail. But Meigs was Army Quartermaster! They deceived nobody, least of all the newspaper reporters. All remembered the Blair family maxim: "When the Blairs go in for a fight, they go in for a funeral." This time they were after Frémont's official military scalp. Frémont, understandably enough, did not regard Frank Blair's brother "as a friend," which Lincoln had intended. As the General declared later: "Early in September, I began to feel the withdrawal of the confidence and support of the administration."

Meanwhile, Frémont's wife, with the pugnacity of her late father, had plunged herself into the stormy struggle. She left for Washington the week before Montgomery Blair and Meigs departed for St. Louis, and their trains passed each other going in opposite directions. She was intent on seeing the President personally and having a showdown with him about the Blairs. Mrs. Frémont arrived in Washington on September 10, two days before Montgomery Blair and Meigs reached St. Louis. Immediately she sought an interview with Lincoln.

The President's conference with Frémont's fiery wife proved unsatisfactory to both. It upset him and made her convinced that he was bossed by the Blairs. John Hay jotted down Lincoln's comments two years later about his private ordeal with Jessie: "She sought an audience with me at midnight and taxed me so violently with many things that I had to exercise all the awkward tact I have to avoid quarreling with her. She surprised me by asking why their enemy, Monty Blair, had been sent to Missouri. She more than once intimated that if Gen. Fremont should conclude to try conclusions with me, he could set up for himself."

Lincoln had not heard the last from Mrs. Frémont in Washington. She had gone to see the Blairs' father, old Francis P. Blair, Sr., and he told her about some letters that his son, Frank, had sent to Lincoln, charging Frémont with corruption. That threw Jessie into renewed rage. She now was more convinced than ever that Lincoln had sent Postmaster-General Blair solely to investigate her husband with full intentions of firing him from his military command. Now Jessie sent at least two letters to Lincoln, demanding to see copies of Frank Blair's written charges against her husband.

Lincoln on September 12 answered Mrs. Frémont:

> It is not exactly correct, as you say you were told by the elder Mr. Blair, to say that I sent Post-Master-General Blair to St. Louis to examine into that Department, and report. Post-Master-General Blair did go, with my approbation, to see and converse with Gen. Fremont as a friend.
>
> I do not feel authorized to furnish you with copies of letters in my possession without the consent of the writers.
>
> No impression has been made on my mind against the honor or integrity of Gen. Fremont; and I now enter my protest against being understood as acting in any hostility towards him.

When Montgomery Blair returned to Washington, he handed Lincoln a severely worded report against Frémont. This report, added to Mrs. Frémont's display of temper and threats, deepened the President's feeling that, however intrepid an explorer of dangerous mountains and trails Frémont had shown himself to be, and however popular he was in the public imagination, he had been a poor choice with whom to entrust the vital Western command. Still, with Job-like patience, Lincoln kept Frémont at his military post, until he went completely out of bounds with his arbitrary action in issuing military edicts and by-passing civil law.

IV

Tightly intertwined with Lincoln's ultimate action on General Frémont in Missouri was the delicate situation in his own and Mrs. Lincoln's native Kentucky, a border slave state which, in some regions, still seesawed between Unionism and secession, with the vast majority of its people endeavoring to remain neutral.

Kentucky, with its conservative, conciliatory, Union-loving tradition, had found it difficult to make up its mind following the firing on Fort Sumter and the President's call for volunteers. Governor Beriah Magoffin, a staunch secessionist, had angrily replied to Lincoln's request for soldiers: "I say, emphatically, Kentucky will furnish no troops for the wicked purpose of subduing her sister Southern states." The antagonistic Union and secession forces finally agreed on a policy of neutrality, and on May 20 Magoffin had issued a proclamation warning both Federal and Confederate troops not to enter the State.

The Blue Grass commonwealth, most central of the American states in 1861, held such strategic position on the Middle Western frontier that Lincoln was reputed to have remarked that he wanted both God and Kentucky on his side.

Though Kentucky neutrality might be as unconstitutional as secession, Lincoln for a time respected the State's decision. A Kentucky Unionist, Garrett Davis, one week following the Fort Sumter firing, had rushed to Washington and had had a conference with the President. Lincoln reassured Davis that he would not "force" the State, and that he had in mind no military movement requiring troops to cross its soil. "If Kentucky made no demonstration of force against the United States," the Chief Executive emphasized to Davis, he "would not molest her."

Lincoln's rival President in Richmond, Jefferson Davis, also realized the necessity of keeping Kentucky on his secession side. Davis accepted all troops leaving that State to join the Confederacy, and the Confederate military command set up recruiting stations on the Kentucky-Tennessee state line. In late August, 1861, the Congress of the Confederate States of America appropriated $1,000,000 to be expended in aiding Kentucky and luring her into the new Southern nation.

Both President Lincoln and President Davis felt that Kentucky's neutrality could not endure permanently. Each side, Federal and Confederate, was soon sufficiently violating the official neutrality to lead the other to poise for seizing the Blue Grass prize.

Lincoln, from then until his dying day, refrained from interfering with slavery by proclamation in those border states still in the Union: Delaware, Maryland, Missouri, and Kentucky. He determined to build and maintain strong Unionist sentiment in those border regions among slaveholders and non-slaveholders alike. On the idea of keeping the border regions loyal, or making them loyal where secession influences were strong, he based his course of action toward Frémont, when that impetuous, abolitionist commander, by proclamation, freed the slaves of secessionists in officially loyal Missouri.

V

General Frémont broke into the newspaper headlines before the month of August was out—even before Lincoln sent Postmaster-General Blair, "as a friend," to see him.

The General, still commanding the Department of the West, issued a proclamation taking over administrative powers in Missouri, invoking martial law, and decreeing the confiscation of the property of all persons who had taken up arms against the United States Government and declaring their slaves emancipated.

Lincoln was crestfallen. Frémont's arbitrary action placed him in a tight position. The President knew that, even aside from Frémont's lack of authority to emancipate slaves, anti-secession slaveholders must not be antagonized or alienated in the border regions, especially Missouri and Kentucky. The Blue Grass State was then in a delicate and critical phase in its transition from neutrality to unqualified support of the Union.

Lincoln delayed three days in taking action against Frémont. Then he sent a tactful but disapproving note to the General, marked "Private and confidential." "Your proclamation of August 30th gave me some anxiety," he began. First, the President instructed, do not shoot any rebel because the rebels would retaliate by killing the best Federal men in their hands. "It is therefore my order that you allow no man to be shot, under the proclamation, without first having my approbation or consent." Secondly, Lincoln informed Frémont, "I think there is great danger that the closing paragraph, in relation to the confiscation of property, and the liberating slaves of traitorous owners, will alarm our Southern Union friends, and turn them against us—perhaps ruin our rather fair prospect for Kentucky." He then asked the General to modify that paragraph about the seizure of property so that it conformed to the existing confiscation act passed by Congress only the month previous.

Lincoln worded this message to Frémont in conciliatory phrases. "This letter is written in a spirit of caution and not of censure," he concluded. Yet it amounted to orders to Frémont.

Lincoln sent his communication to Frémont by special messenger. But the General did not follow Lincoln's orders. In reply, he requested the President to issue an open order to modify the clause liberating the slaves. And on September 11 Lincoln accommodated him. He instructed Frémont: "It is therefore ordered that the said clause of said proclamation be so modified, held, and construed" as to conform strictly to the Congress-enacted federal law for confiscation of insurrectionists' property.

Mrs. Frémont was still in Washington on her husband's behalf when Lincoln sent orders to Frémont to modify that slavery-emancipation section of his proclamation.

Orville Browning, now the late Stephen A. Douglas's successor in the Senate, took issue with the President for his action in overruling Frémont, and wrote Lincoln about it. Lincoln's answer gave his reasons for opposing the General's proclamation. After telling the Illinois Senator about his protest—"coming from you, I confess it astonishes me," he told Browning—the President informed him that the property-confiscation and slavery-emancipation parts of the Pathfinder's proclamation were *"purely political,* and not within the range of *military* law, or necessity. . . . That must be settled according to laws made by law-makers, and not by military proclamations. The proclamation in the point in question, is simply 'dictatorship'. . . But I can not assume this reckless position; nor allow others to assume it on my responsibility." About the probable adverse effect of Frémont's Missouri edict on Kentucky, another border slave state, Lincoln reminded Senator Browning: "The Kentucky Legislature would not budge till that proclamation was modified. . . . I think to lose Kentucky is nearly the same as to lose the whole game. Kentucky gone, we can not hold Missouri, nor, as I think, Maryland."

All of the while the Blairs were insisting to Lincoln and Lincoln's advisers that something should be done about Frémont as military commander in the West. They wanted him removed. That was all. So did other conservatives who were motivated less by personal motives than the ubiquitous Blair clan.

But Lincoln delayed about relieving Frémont of his command. Only when the Missouri mix-up needed unscrambling and could wait no longer, and after carefully weighing the factors, pro and con, did Lincoln reach his reluctant decision that Frémont must go.

On October 24 the President approved an order that Major-General David Hunter should "temporarily" relieve Frémont of the command of the Department of the West.

VI

Lincoln's removal of Frémont from his command aroused tremendous storms of protest throughout the North, and partially ruptured his party from that time onward.

The colorful explorer, soldier, romantic, and radical Republican politician had for years captivated mass imagination. His presidential candidacy of five years before, and his countermanded slavery emancipation had endeared him to extreme anti-slavery and abolitionist groups, who chafed at Lincoln's reluctance to take action against slavery, lest it alienate pro-Union slaveholders in the border states. When Frémont noisily took his leave of St. Louis after turning over his command to his successor, a monster meeting of German-Americans (hitherto Blair's strong supporters) shouted praises in the Pathfinder's honor and paraded for him to show their loyalty to him. Such demonstrations of acclaim were imitated in other cities through which he passed, so that his journey from St. Louis to the Eastern seaboard seemed one continual tour of triumph.

For weeks thereafter mail poured into the offices of Northern congressmen from strongly anti-slavery constituents and pathological Lincoln-haters, praising the Pathfinder and assailing Lincoln. There were thousands of these letters such as one to Senator Lyman Trumbull, ridiculing Lincoln's "silly desire to conciliate *loyal slaveholders.*" The view was taken that the Chief Executive had removed Frémont only because of his radically anti-slavery views, a gross over-simplification indeed. Little was said in these letters to senators and congressmen about the General's incompetence as a commander and the corruption that thrived under him at St. Louis.

The immediate reaction to Lincoln's removal of Frémont was to split Missouri's already ruptured Republican-Union ranks into more fragments. To quarrels over patronage spoils and party rivalries was now added the disrupting issue of Negro emancipation.

Division or no division in his party over Frémont, Lincoln in the long view demonstrated excellent judgment and courage in his constant concern for Kentucky, against the fuming opposition of the radically anti-slavery groups of his political ranks.

The Blue Grass State proved a determining factor in the salvation of the Union. By its decision to remain loyal, it lent aid and encouragement to Union men in neighboring western Virginia, east Tennessee, and Missouri. Kentucky's decision to reject the Confederacy consolidated the cause of the United States in the lower part of what would become the State of West Virginia. Kentucky's adherence to the Union opened the way for the Federals into the heart of the Confederacy, making possible the later military campaigns against Confederates in Tennessee. The Blue Grass commonwealth served as one of the major bases of army operations against Southern forces in the West. Any President other than Lincoln might well have blundered in the delicate Kentucky situation. But he knew the temper of those people.

Lincoln realized that he could not force the issue with proud Kentuckians but must give them time and opportunity with which to make their own decision and fix their own course. In the meantime, the President would muffle abolitionist agitation and stifle any attempt to liberate the slaves which might offend Kentucky.

Frémont's removal was gleefully received in Kentucky.

VII

As Lincoln was reaching his reluctant decision to remove Frémont from command, a minor military engagement, with major political consequences, was fought between Federal and Confederate forces at Ball's Bluff on October 21.

Brigadier-General Charles P. Stone was chosen to lead a division of Federals to occupy the valley of the Potomac above Washington. One regiment under Stone was commanded by Colonel Edward D. Baker, Republican Senator from Oregon and Lincoln's old Illinois Whig friend.

Colonel Baker, with a recklessness prevalent in brave but inexperienced officers, led his regiment in a foolhardy unprepared assault against the Confederate position at Ball's Bluff, a high wooded region near

Leesburg. A withering fire from the Southern batteries cut down Baker's men. Baker was hit and died instantly.

Lincoln grieved over Baker's death more deeply than he had over any personal loss since his young friend, Colonel Ellsworth, had been fatally shot at Alexandria five months before.

Only two days before Ball's Bluff, Lincoln had seen and talked with Baker at the White House, and both had talked about old Whig times in Sangamon County. Baker had then kissed Willie Lincoln, the President's son, Mrs. Lincoln had presented him with flowers, and he had mounted his horse for the battle front. Lincoln's eyes had followed Baker as he rode off toward Ball's Bluff.

When Lincoln received the news of Baker's death at the telegraph office, the Boston *Journal's* Washington correspondent related, he watched the President. The Boston reporter noted: "His hands were clasped upon his breast, his head bowed, his body bent as if he was carrying a great burden. He took no notice of anyone, but with downcast eyes and faltering steps passed into the street and towards the Executive Mansion." In speaking of Baker's tragic passing, Lincoln confessed that it "smote him like a whirlwind."

Baker's death cut deeply into the hearts of all the Lincolns. The son, Willie, penned a poem about the fallen hero and family intimate, which appeared shortly after in a Washington daily:

There was no patriot like Baker,
So noble and so true:
He fell as a soldier on the field,
His face to the sky of blue.

His voice is silent in the hall,
Which oft his presence grac'd
No more he'll hear the loud acclaim,
Which rang from place to place.

No squeamish notions filled his breast,
The Union was his theme,
"No surrender and no compromise,"
His day thought and night's dream.

His country has *her* part to play,
To'rds those he left behind,
His widow and his children all—
She must always keep in mind.

VIII

The Ball's Bluff defeat and Baker's death proved more than personal ordeals to Lincoln and his family. They produced a thunderous political tempest that shook the North and loyal border regions.

Mass admiration for the dead Colonel and Senator reached unbounded emotionalism, and the suspicion that his life had been needlessly destroyed by General Stone's alleged incompetence brewed an atmosphere which demanded a scapegoat. Popular wrath, fed by politicians, was turned against Stone without regard for truth or facts. Rumors and exaggerations filled Northern newspapers. Portions of the public, in a condition of naïve credulity that accepted almost every conjecture and whisper as authentic, demanded revenge. And the radically minded Republicans of the Senate and House, in an ugly mood since the removal of Frémont, and angry at Bull Run and Ball's Bluff, obliged them. Since the late Colonel Baker had been a Senator, numerous members of that exclusive legislative "club" sought to avenge his death.

During the first week of the new session of Congress in December, 1861 Senator Charles Sumner of Massachusetts, darling of the abolitionists and an extraordinarily self-righteous moralist, delivered a eulogy on Baker, whom the strongly anti-slavery men dogmatically charged had been sacrificed at Ball's Bluff by the supposedly pro-Southern General Stone. Nothing was said about Baker's own unauthorized rashness in charging the enemy.

Lincoln sat in the Senate galleries as the embittered Senator from Massachusetts attacked slavery as the war's cause and called on Lincoln's administration to cease protecting the very institution of black bondage and its pro-Southern defenders who had created the rebellion. Dramatically—as only Sumner could—he told the spine-chilling story of Baker's death, a tragedy vastly more painful to Lincoln than it could ever have been to Sumner. Looking straight up at the President in the galleries, Sumner charged that slavery had been "the murderer of our dead Senator." And the observing correspondent of the *National Anti-Slavery Standard* reported with satisfaction that, as the Bay State Senator pronounced these words, Lincoln started violently.

Out of the melange of radical Republican anger over Bull Run and Ball's Bluff, with the late Baker's ubiquitous ghost haunting all and serving as rallying symbol of almost mystical proportions, there developed the radical Republicans' most formidable challenge to Lincoln's conservative war policy. The "Jacobins," as John Hay liked to call the radicals, were convinced that General Stone was responsible for Baker's needless death—and, incredibly enough, that even the ranking General, McClellan, had been in back of the whole affair.

Prophetically Lincoln's old friend, Joshua F. Speed, during a Washington visit, on December 8 confided to another Kentuckian, Former Secretary of War Joseph Holt: "I am fully persuaded that there is mischief brewing here. A large and powerful party of ultra men is being formed to make war upon the President and his conservative policy."

The Jacobins' chief target would be Lincoln's highest general, McClellan.

LINCOLN AND HIS LIEUTENANTS

21

I

"THIS evening," noted the President's assistant secretary, John Hay, on October 26, 1861, only five days following the Ball's Bluff defeat, "the Jacobin club, represented by [Senators] Trumbull, Chandler and Wade, came up to worry the administration into a battle. The wildest howl of the summer is to be renewed. The President stood up for McClellan's deliberateness."

After the departure of the three Western radical senators, Lyman Trumbull from Illinois, Zachariah Chandler from Michigan, and Benjamin F. Wade from Ohio, who demanded more and immediate action at the battle front, Lincoln and Hay then visited General McClellan's headquarters. The General "talked about the Jacobins. McC. said that Wade preferred an unsuccessful battle to delay." Lincoln talked about the public's impatience for a victory over Confederates but assured McClellan: "At the same time, General, you must not fight till you are ready."

Senators Chandler and Wade, after their call on Lincoln, visited McClellan at his Army of the Potomac camp, urging him to fight. Wade, in a later speech to his Ohio constituents, exaggeratedly told of that meeting: "We had an interview with Gen. McClellan, and remonstrated with him. We exhorted him, for God's sake, to at least push back the defiant traitors. Why can't you? 'Oh, I have not enough men. . . . They are at least 220,000 or more, and they are behind fortifications stronger than those of Sebastopol.' "

Lincoln, during that autumn of 1861, was assured by McClellan that he would take the offensive as soon as he was ready, which would be soon. And on November 1 he had made "Little Mac" commander-in-chief immediately following General Scott's retirement. That evening Lincoln called on him. He reminded the General: "In addition to your present command, the supreme command of the Army will entail a vast labor on you," to which McClellan replied to the President: "I can do it all."

All through November, Lincoln conferred almost every day with McClellan. Some times he summoned his commander to White House meetings, but more frequently he went to McClellan's headquarters. From the first, however, the General had scant respect for Lincoln's suggestions about military operations, as was perhaps natural in the view of any professional toward an amateur.

On November 11 Major-General Samuel P. Heintzelman came into headquarters when the President was examining a map of Virginia and making suggestions about military movements. Heintzelman noted that McClellan pretended to take the Chief Executive's ideas seriously. When Lincoln had left, McClellan confided to Heintzelman: "Isn't he a rare bird?"

McClellan several days later resented Lincoln's elaboration of a proposed land-river expedition to capture New Orleans in collaboration with the Navy in a conference in which Secretary of the Navy Welles and Lieutenant David D. Porter participated. On one occasion, when the President and Secretary of State Seward went to the General's quarters at night, he did not even greet Lincoln and Seward but went straight to bed.

II

McClellan was a conservative Democrat in party politics, and therein lay much of the radical Republicans' opposition to him.

Lincoln had appointed McClellan supreme commander, along with other Democrats, since he realized the indispensability of giving members of the opposition party high command, particularly West Point-educated professional army officers. In a non-partisan appointments policy the

President braved the ire of some of his more narrow fellow-Republicans. In the following year Lincoln defended his course in answer to complaints from Carl Schurz. "It so happened that very few of our [Republican] friends had a military education or were of the profession of arms," he explained to Schurz. "It would have been a question whether a war should be conducted on military knowledge, or on political affinity." He pointed out that McClellan was a Democrat urged by Republicans. "He was first brought forward by the Republican Governor of Ohio, & claimed, and contended for at the same time by the Republican Governor of Pennsylvania."

The angry Jacobins in Congress placed the stigma of the administration's slow military movements against the Confederates and the President's inaction on slavery emancipation upon the Democratic generals like McClellan. Radical Republicans, in and out of Congress, charged that Lincoln's military and civilian governmental bureaucracy was shot through with pro-Southern Northern Democrats, some of them lukewarm toward the Union, or even treasonable. Among these Democratic commanders were snobbish West Pointers symbolized by McClellan himself. Their main weapon was the congressional Committee on the Conduct of the War.

The movement for such an "overseer" group of Congressmen had begun with the resolution of Roscoe Conkling of New York, on December 2, 1861, calling for an investigation of the disasters at Bull Run and Ball's Bluff. Grieved at the death of Baker at Ball's Bluff and furiously annoyed at McClellan's seeming inactivity in getting started against the Confederates, both houses of Congress in December passed a measure creating a standing two-house "Joint Committee on the Conduct of the War." Its members were Senators Wade of Ohio, Chandler of Michigan, and a War Democrat, Andrew Johnson of Tennessee, and Representatives Daniel Gooch of Massachusetts, George W. Julian of Indiana, John Covode of Pennsylvania, and Moses F. Odell of New York. The most militant Committee members was its chairman, Senator Wade, and Senator Chandler, who had demanded that McClellan fight at once and who viewed the war as an opportunity to punish the South and build up Republican party power below the Mason-Dixon line after the Rebellion. It is noteworthy to reflect that none of the Committee members ever had military experience of any kind. The Committee's powers were broad, since it was difficult to discover any activity of Lincoln's administration that did not concern conduct of the war.

The Committee held its first meeting on December 20. It set out to probe the causes for the Bull Run and Ball's Bluff defeats and also restore the reputation of General Frémont. But the main target of the radical Republicans was Lincoln's commanding general, McClellan. Some committee members, with distorted imaginations, concluded that Mc-

Clellan was really pro-Southern and pro-slavery and did not want to conquer the Confederates. They swallowed the lurid accusations of disgruntled army officers out of McClellan's favor, who were ready to tell the inquisitorial senators and representatives anything that would damage the General-in-Chief. One member, Congressman Julian of Indiana, subsequently confessed that the Committee was "practically incapable" of treating McClellan justly. They gave McClellan's subordinate officers a thorough grilling in a futile attempt to make them reveal the nature of the military movements he proposed to launch against the Southern armies.

Just at this time General McClellan was stricken with typhoid fever.

On New Year's Day, 1862, Lincoln sought to soothe the sick McClellan in his irritation over the Committee's actions. He sent this message to the General: "I hear that the doings of an Investigating Committee give you some uneasiness. You may be entirely relieved on this point. The gentlemen of the Committee were with me an hour and a half last night; and I found them in a perfectly good mood."

The Committee on the Conduct of the War, however, was far from being in "a perfectly good mood." To the members things were too excessively quiet on the Potomac, with McClellan ill but doing nothing when he was well. Within a few days they collected sufficient testimony to give them justification, in their own estimation, to appeal to Lincoln about the General-in-Chief's incompetence.

Lincoln was determined to give McClellan time in which to organize his offensive for a drive on Richmond. Above all, he was eager to keep the lid on the slavery issue, lest anti-slavery agitation or loud abolitionism alienate the border region Unionists. With a feeling of dread the President met members of the Committee on the Conduct of the War on January 6, 1862, while McClellan lay in bed with typhoid.

At that conference Lincoln was told by Chairman Wade and his Congressional colleagues that, according to testimony submitted, the army was in splendid shape, the weather and roads ideal for an invasion of Virginia, and the Confederate foe outnumbered by the Federal forces. Wade asked Lincoln what he knew about McClellan's proposed plans. The President replied that he had no knowledge of the General's contemplated operations or his reasons for not attempting an immediate forward movement. It was all McClellan's business as commander, Lincoln emphasized, and he had no intention of interfering. Wade spoke harsh words about McClellan's unfitness and inaction. In uncouth Western speech the Senator from Ohio urged a radical change in the policy of the war at once. Lincoln overlooked Wade's unseemly demonstration and rejected his demands. He would not interfere with his commanding General.

Still, Lincoln, always the conciliator, sought to pacify the Committee by having McClellan co-operate fully with them. Three days after his conference with them, on the 9th, he sent a note to the still sick McClellan: "I think you better go before the Congressional Committee the earliest moment your health will permit—to-day, if possible."

In any appraisals of Lincoln's future transition from straight conservatism to anti-slavery moderation and in any consideration of Lincoln's political interference in McClellan's military operations, the Committee on the Conduct of the War must constantly be taken into account.

III

With McClellan still bedded down with typhoid fever, Lincoln projected himself more into the military picture.

He telegraphed orders to Major-General Don C. Buell in the West: "General McClellan should not yet be disturbed with business. I think you better get in touch with General Halleck at once. I write you to-night. I also telegraph and write Halleck." The President sent identical orders to Major-General Henry W. Halleck. Buell commanded the Army of the Ohio, stationed in Tennessee and parts of Kentucky. Halleck headed Frémont's old Department of the West and also troops in western Kentucky.

Lincoln soon received unsatisfactory news from Buell, who wanted to assault Nashville in Middle Tennessee. Lincoln wanted him to drive on Knoxville, in East Tennessee, of major importance because of the hard pressed Union-loving, anti-slaveholder mountaineers there who were calling for help to combat Confederates. Buell's idea of going after Nashville, instead of Knoxville, did not please Lincoln. "It disappoints and distresses me," he wrote General Buell. He conceded, "I am not competent to criticise your views," but he would rather liberate east Tennessee, in preference to Nashville. He pointed out to that western commander that "our friends in East Tennessee are being hanged and driven to despair" and, if they were not aided, "we lose the most valuable stake we have in the South." He urged Buell to march on both Nashville and Knoxville, a rather impossible undertaking in view of Buell's limited number of troops and supplies and the territorial width of the seceded state of Tennessee. Lincoln ended the letter to his Army of the Ohio commander with an expression that, in varied forms, would appear in numberless despatches to his lieutenants: "I do not intend this to be an order in any sense, but merely, as intimated before, to show you the ground of my anxiety."

Lincoln showed to the ill McClellan his letter to Buell. And the General-in-Chief, from his sick bed, sent orders to Buell that the Army of the Potomac's coming advance on Richmond depended upon Buell occupying east Tennessee.

Lincoln received an upsetting letter from General Halleck. The western commander in Missouri and western Kentucky informed the President that his force was too small for him to help Buell in the Tennessee drive and, besides, Buell's plan of a co-operative movement with him was not much good, anyhow. On January 10, only four days after the Committee on the Conduct of the War had met and hectored him because of McClellan's inactivity, Lincoln wrote this endorsement on Halleck's letter: "It is exceedingly discouraging. As everywhere else, nothing can be done."

Despondent, Lincoln then went to see Quartermaster General Montgomery C. Meigs on that same January 10. He seated himself before the fire in Meigs's office and lamented: "General, what shall I do? The people are impatient; Chase has no money and he tells me he can raise no more; the General of the Army has typhoid fever. The bottom is out of the tub. What shall I do?" He was given scant encouragement by Meigs's reminder that typhoid fever meant an illness of six weeks, by which time the Confederates might launch an offensive against the Army of the Potomac. Lincoln was advised by Meigs to call a conference of the Army's ranking officers, consult with them, and perhaps from their numbers a new top commander might be selected.

Lincoln followed Meigs's counsel at once. He invited Major-General McDowell, now a subordinate commander, Major-General William B. Franklin, Secretary of State Seward, Secretary of the Treasury Chase, and Assistant Secretary of War Thomas A. Scott. To them Lincoln told his problems. McClellan was sick, and out West Buell and Halleck were not in agreement. He must talk to somebody. If something were not done, "the bottom would be out of the whole affair," and if McClellan did not want to use the army, he would like to "borrow" it. McDowell recommended a drive on Manassas, a word that should have been nightmarish to him. Franklin, a follower of McClellan, favored an operation against Richmond via one of the water routes on which McClellan had been insisting. Lincoln asked that this conference be continued the next night.

When the participants returned to the White House the following evening, Lincoln happily announced that McClellan was feeling better and would meet with them the following day. McClellan, however, later gave this version: He had heard that a conference was on at the Executive Mansion—really a plot to have him deposed, he strongly suspected. He later explained: "The difficulties of my position commenced when I was first confined to my bed with typhoid fever." One politician friendly to him revealed: "They are counting on your death, and are already dividing among themselves your military goods and chattels."

McClellan, in a rage and suspecting that he was being undermined, rose from his sick bed and hurried over to the White House conference. He remained convinced that McDowell, now his subordinate, was the secret spearhead of a movement to have him ousted as General-in-Chief. At that conference McClellan insisted that he would not reveal his own plans to the group unless the President ordered him to do so. He assured all that he meant to have Buell move his army from Kentucky into Tennessee, which appeased Lincoln. The President ended the conference with these words: "Well, on the assurance of the General that he will press the advance in Kentucky, I will be satisfied, and will adjourn this council."

IV

In those conferences during early January, 1862, a conspicuous absentee was Lincoln's Secretary of War. Filling in for Secretary Cameron was Assistant Secretary of War Scott. And for good reason. Cameron was well on his way out of the Cabinet.

Ever since the administration's start, complaints against Cameron's unsatisfactory conduct of the War Department, his fraudulent contracts and gross mismanagement owing to appointment of his Pennsylvania spoilsmen as subordinates, had poured into Washington and filled the loyal state press. "Public good requires another man in his place." Cameron was "more interested in fat contracts than in the speedy and successful termination of the war." "Mr. Lincoln should rise to the dignity of his position, and remove him."

The President realized the mounting opposition to his Secretary of War and pondered over the maladministration of that now indispensable department's functions. Against his own better judgment and purely because of political considerations Lincoln had tendered the War portfolio to this unsavory party operator. The best that can be said of Lincoln's appointment was that he had not chosen Cameron as Secretary of the Treasury, which he had demanded.

Cameron felt his own plague-like unpopularity and sought to neutralize it by switching over to the radical anti-slavery side. In his abrupt about-face on the question, this life-long opportunist, always indifferent to slavery, authorized in December, 1861, the use of Negro soldiers and recommended in his annual report creation of an army of freed slaves. Lincoln was not even consulted on this point, and the report was hurried to the newspapers, unknown to the President. Lincoln ordered the report to be recalled, and the slave-army proposal was deleted.

Those who knew Cameron best were agreed that the Secretary of War had seized on the slavery issue expediently in order to gain support of the radical faction in and out of Congress. A. B. Ely confided to Senator Sumner of Massachusetts that he should beware of falling into a trap: "Cameron's report which contained the suppressed part about contrabands was got up by him and put out by him not because he cared anything about the slaves, but merely as a tub to the popular whale, so as to turn away inquiry from the corruptions of his department."

By the end of 1861 Cameron was made aware that Lincoln's axe might fall on him. Half-heartedly he indicated to the President that he was willing to resign but did not want to leave under fire. Fortune suddenly played into Lincoln's hands when Cassius M. Clay, tempestuous Kentucky abolitionist, who held the post of Minister to Russia, expressed desire to return home and enter army service.

Lincoln on January 11, 1862, sent a curt letter to Cameron indicating that he could gratify the latter's "desire for a change of position" and informing him that he was about to nominate him as Minister to Russia. Cameron did not want to go to St. Petersburg, which his critics insisted was a good place for him for the welfare of the United States. Cameron "wept bitterly" over what he considered this "personal affront from Lincoln," and grieved that it would mean his personal and political destruction. Because of Cameron's attitude, Lincoln arranged for him to send a letter of resignation, pre-dated January 11, 1862, whereupon Lincoln sent him a similarly pre-dated answer, expressing, as he had not done originally, his "personal esteem" and "my personal regard for you, and my confidence in your ability, patriotism, and fidelity to public trust." Lincoln also assured Cameron that, at the Court of Tsar Alexander II, "you will be able to render services to your country, not less important than those you could render at home."

Thus did Lincoln, partly motivated by his own tender consideration, partly to preserve peace within his Republican party ranks at this critical period, conceal the true situation about his Secretary of War.

The specific reasons for Lincoln's action in easing Cameron out of his Cabinet were given by the Cincinnati *Commercial's* Washington correspondent. He "divided his efforts between Pennsylvania contractors and Massachusetts abolitionists." *Vanity Fair* ran a caricature of Cameron in which he was sprawled on the floor, covered with contracts, entitled, "A Fall Not Contracted For."

Lincoln's old Kentucky friend, Speed, still in Washington, was shocked when Lincoln confirmed the truth of the report that Cassius M. Clay, on relinquishing his Russian post for Cameron, would be given a General's commission. Speed wrote home to a fellow-Kentuckian, who knew Clay well: "I asked him [Lincoln] if it was true that Cash M. Clay was to be made a Major General—he said it was—I protested very earnestly against it—asking that we should not be troubled with him, remarking that he was now in great hopes that the rebelion (sic) would be pretty much ended before he would get here." Speed considered that Clay as a Federal commander would pump new confidence into the Confederate ranks.

As Cameron's successor as the indispensable Secretary of War the President chose a vigorous "War" Democrat, Edwin M. Stanton, who had served as Attorney General under President Buchanan.

Though Stanton proved arbitrary, bullying, and often vengeful, he brought to the War Department a needed efficiency and personal honesty unknown under Cameron.

Meanwhile, the military situation was not going well in the West. But in the East General McClellan was finally ready to take the field against Richmond.

V

Lincoln persisted in efforts to persuade Generals Buell and Halleck to do something in the West. He proposed that Buell menace Confederates in east Tennessee and eastern Kentucky while Halleck simultaneously should go after the secession forces in western Kentucky and on the Mississippi River. The Confederates would then be compelled to weaken one or another point in their line, and the Federals could thus break through the weakened point. Lincoln on January 13 urged Buell: "My idea is that Halleck shall menace Columbus [in Kentucky], and 'down river' generally; while you menace Bowling-Green [in Kentucky], and East Tennessee. If the enemy shall concentrate at Bowling-Green, do not retire from his front; yet do not fight him there, either, but seize Columbus and East Tennessee, one or both, left exposed by the [Confederate] concentration at Bowling-Green." He reminded Buell: "We have the *greater* numbers, and the enemy has the *greater* facility of concentrating forces upon the points of collision." Lincoln sent Halleck a copy of his letter to Buell. But Buell and Halleck were not in a mood to co-operate with each other.

Buell attempted an advance of part of his army in eastern Kentucky. He beat the Confederates at Mill Springs (otherwise known as Logan's Crossroads) on January 17, but mired roads prevented further progress toward east Tennessee.

Halleck himself did little except to try to persuade Buell to go under his command, an idea most repulsive to Buell. Halleck's subordinate generals, however, registered some victories early in 1862. Ulysses S. Grant, with the aid of Commodore Andrew H. Foote's gunboat flotilla, won Fort Henry and Fort Donelson. Samuel R. Curtis was successful at Pea Ridge, Arkansas; and John Pope took New Madrid, Missouri, and

Island No. 10 in the Mississippi River. So well did these subordinates do that much prestige passed to Halleck, who was now held in high estimation by Lincoln.

Then, in April, came Shiloh. More than anything thus far, this battle emphasized the tragedy of the war, for the losses on both sides were appalling. The Confederacy gained the field but lost over 10,000 men, including one of its finest generals, Albert S. Johnston. And the Union, whose troops had been defeated but not routed, severly criticized its commander for the seemingly senseless slaughter. This was the same commander who not long before had been the hero at Fort Donelson: Ulysses S. Grant.

Lincoln, contrary to present-day popular belief, was slow to perceive Grant's qualities as commander. Anti-Grant generals, such as Halleck and William A. Richardson, plus unfavorable reports about Grant's faulty strategy at Shiloh and complaints about his excessive whiskey drinking, cast doubt on his competence for more than a year afterward.

The Navy gave an excellent account of itself early in 1862. "Uncle Sam's web-feet," as Lincoln called the naval units later, enforced the blockade comparatively well and had co-operated with the land forces in exploiting the break-through into the North Carolina sounds, hammering Confederate shore batteries into submission, seizing New Bern and Roanoke Island, and opening the way for a seaborne invasion. Farther south, the Navy had broken its way into Port Royal, South Carolina, securing possession of a southern deep-water base for its blockading squadrons and raising a threat to Charleston. Another amphibious operation would be hitting the Georgia coast and would soon be controlling the approaches to Savannah.

In March the Union ironclad, *Monitor,* commanded by Lieutenant John L. Worden, fought a duel at sea with the Confederate ironclad, *Merrimack,* now rechristened the *Virginia.* Neither destroyed the other, but the *Monitor* had eased Northern minds from their fright over the appearance of the *Virginia.*

In the Gulf, a fleet of Union warships under that fighting salt, Flag Officer David G. Farragut, was steaming toward the grand prize, the port of New Orleans. On May 1 Major-General Benjamin F. Butler led his forces into New Orleans, which lay under Farragut's guns.

But most Northern eyes were not focused on Generals Buell, Halleck, or Grant in the West, or on Butler in New Orleans, or on Flag Officer Farragut, but on McClellan in the eastern theatre. This was the significant area of warfare. The war, everyone felt, would be won in the small area between the Federal capital Washington, and the Confederate capital, Richmond. Here the Union armies were not moving fast enough to satisfy Lincoln, members of Congress, and great masses of the public in the North.

VI

As if to make Lincoln's relations with McClellan more difficult, the two differed on the choice of a route to Richmond.

The President strongly held the belief that the Confederate capital should be captured by a direct land operation, via Manassas. But the General-in-Chief firmly stood for his own "peninsula" plan, a drive by the Army of the Potomac, partly by sea, reaching Richmond by way of the peninsula between the York and James rivers. McClellan would move his men by ship down Chesapeake Bay, up the Rappahannock River to Urbana, Virginia, thence across land to a railroad terminus below Richmond on the York River. From there he would lay siege to the Confederate capital.

Lincoln, consulting no one, issued his General War Order No. 1, prescribing an advance of all military and naval forces on February 22, and then gave his Special Order No. 1, requiring that the Army of the Potomac should move on Manassas.

It seemed unwise of Lincoln. It bore the mark of the amateur in military matters to order an advance four weeks hence without considering what the weather might be on the 22nd or what the Confederates might do in the interim. Lincoln's defenders have pointed out, however, that he did not intend his order to be taken too seriously as a program of action, that his prime purpose was to stir up some action by McClellan. Demands for a march against Richmond were being made loudly in Congress and by the arm-chair strategists at home. Newspapers throughout the North wanted some movements by McClellan. And the congressional Committee on the Conduct of the War was the most vociferous of all bodies.

Those orders by Lincoln, however, brought matters to a head with McClellan. Lincoln had ordered an advance on Manassas. McClellan, however, still insisted that Richmond be assaulted, not via Manassas, but by his own planned "peninsula" route. Ever present in Lincoln's mind was the indispensability of having the main Army of the Potomac units on land between Washington and Richmond, lest the Confederates take it into their heads to invade the national capital. McClellan, insisting on his peninsula plan, would not give up. He knew that his strategy had the support of a majority of his subordinate commanders.

On February 3 Lincoln sent word to McClellan, telling of their differences of opinion on the route to Richmond. He asked his General-in-Chief to present in writing his objections to the President's plan to capture the Confederate capital by a direct land operation via Manassas and to explain why he thought the peninsula plan better. "If you will give me satisfactory answers to the following questions," Lincoln promised, "I shall gladly yield my plan to yours."

McClellan gave written answers to Lincoln's questions to his own satisfaction. The General-in-Chief pointed out that, even if the Federals won over Confederates at Manassas, there would not be a decisive victory. The rebels would be defeated only by a bold stroke at Richmond, their very heart, rather than by a meaningless success a short distance from Washington.

Lincoln, not fully convinced of the wisdom of a peninsula campaign, yielded his "via Manassas" route to McClellan's plan. But he did not give up until he had the judgment of McClellan's twelve subordinate generals in a vote taken when McClellan was not present. The generals favored McClellan's peninsula campaign over Lincoln's Manassas plan by a vote of eight to four. "The President stated," confided Senator Browning of Illinois to his diary several months later, "that his opinion always had been the great fight should have been at Manassas—that McClellan was opposed to fighting at Manassas, and he, the President, then called a Council of twelve generals . . . and that eight of them decided against him. . . . The majority being so great . . . he yielded."

Ominously enough, the four generals, McDowell, Heintzelman, Barnard, and Sumner, who voted against McClellan's proposed peninsula route, were all in sympathy with the radical anti-slavery Republicans. Three of them, Heintzelman, Barnard, and Sumner, would in the future testify against McClellan before the congressional Committee on the Conduct of the War.

By March, 1862, McClellan considered his army ready to march. Abandoning his Urbana route to Richmond, the General-in-Chief launched what came to be known as his "Peninsular Campaign," with Fort Monroe as a base.

At long last McClellan was on his way to Richmond.

THE LINCOLN–McCLELLAN MUDDLE

22

I

WHILE Lincoln, concerned with the defense of Washington, and McClellan, planning a spectacular conquest of the Confederacy, were debating over strategy for the Army of the Potomac, political intrigue, hostile to the General, was developing. This anti-McClellan plot was brewed from numerous ingredients, among them some narrow Republican partisanship, personal ambitions, vindictiveness toward the South, distrust of West Point generals, and sincere if not always wise agitation for abolition of slavery. And the North's growing impatience at McClellan's agonizing delays in advancing against the Confederate capital catalyzed these ingredients.

Lincoln's commanding General, a Pennsylvania-born West Point graduate and a Democrat in politics, had proven himself a fighting Unionist against the Confederates in western Virginia, and certainly could not be considered an instrument of the South, as his foes contended. He did not believe that abolition of slavery, the desire of the radical factions of

Lincoln's Republican-Union party, should be mixed with the prime purpose of the war: preservation of the Union. McClellan was the highest ranking military commander of the constitutionally elected President of the entire nation—the pro-slavery South and the conservative border-slave regions, as well as of the North—and he considered himself such. He declined to ally himself with political groups, in or out of Congress, who would interfere with slavery or any other legalized institutions within the states. As an American nationalist and professional soldier, McClellan looked forward to an harmonious rather than a vengeful restoration of the Union after the secessionist government and armies were suppressed. All the while, the General-in-Chief felt that the radical Republican congressional clique, aggressively abolitionist, was under mining him. He was correct in this diagnosis.

He was contemptuously accused by his radical political enemies, and by those who grew impatient at his delay in getting on to Richmond, of timidity, tardiness (he had "the slows," to use Lincoln's later expression about him), insubordination, and even pro-Confederate sympathies. They even charged him with seeking a stalemate with the South, rather than a military victory.

So the radicals sought to turn the President against his General-in-Chief. They circulated falsehoods about McClellan and used the congressional Committee on the Conduct of the War to defame him. Working in close co-operation with them was McClellan's civilian superior, Secretary of War Stanton.

Part of the radicals' strategy, motivated by their hatred of McClellan, and their impatience with his presumably snail-like slowness in taking the field, was their demand that his immediate command, the Army of the Potomac, be reorganized on an "army corps" basis.

This army-corps proposal, which they clothed in impressive-sounding French phrases (*corps d'armee* and the like) with emphasis on its success in European military operations, was essentially a device of the radical leaders and McClellan's rivals among his subordinate generals to take authority and his huge command from him. It provided that the several corps commanders, to be created by this reorganization, must take orders directly from the Secretary of War, the radicals' favorite, thus by-passing McClellan.

On February 25 the radical congressional Committee on the Conduct of the War met with Lincoln. The minutes of that Committee told what occurred at that White House conference: "The President observed that he had never considered the organization of this army into army corps so essential as the committee represent it to be; still he had long been in favor of such an organization."

The Committee members were determined to downgrade McClellan, and Lincoln still felt that there must be more troops to guard Washington in case of Southern attack. The most effective way of assuring these troops for the Capital seemed to be to follow the Radicals' suggestion. So Lincoln gave way to their demands, and just as McClellan was starting his expedition down the Chesapeake Bay, the army was reorganized into corps.

On March 18, Lincoln issued an order, followed by another three days later, directing that the Army of the Potomac be formed into five corps, to be commanded, by Major-Generals McDowell, Samuel P. Heintzelman, Edwin V. Sumner, Erasmus D. Keyes, and Nathaniel P. Banks. Three of the five, McDowell, Heintzelman, and Sumner, were rabidly opposed to McClellan. Only Keyes had agreed with him on fundamental strategy and supported him in councils of war, and Banks was a political general, former Republican Speaker of Congress and ex-Governor of Massachusetts. Lincoln did not even consult McClellan before he ordered the "army corps" reorganization, and this reorganization impaired McClellan's plans for his campaign.

Lincoln retained McClellan as Army of the Potomac commander. But he had relieved the General-in-Chief of authority over other departments on the eve of his expedition against Richmond. Political influences, added to his own distrust of McClellan's sea route to the Confederate capital and the necessity for keeping more troops near Washington, had persuaded the President.

II

Because of Lincoln's corps-reorganization orders, McClellan found himself in the painful predicament of having to work with corps commanders who for the most part distrusted him and his peninsula plan of operation. McClellan, abandoning his Urbana-West Point plan, decided upon what came to be called his "Peninsular Campaign," with Fortress Monroe as a base. Beginning in March, the sailing of his troops carried over into April. But before he embarked, the Confederates had forsaken their positions at Manassas, leaving wooden guns in their fortifications near Centerville! The Confederates, pioneers of what later was known as *camouflage,* had installed black-painted logs to resemble artillery.

The "wooden guns" situation made both the President and McClellan targets of ridicule. Snorted Senator William Pitt Fessenden of Maine in a letter to his wife on March 15: "You will have heard of the wooden guns at Centerville? It is all true, and we are smarting under the disgrace which this discovery has brought upon us. We shall be the scorn of the world. It is no longer doubtful that General McClellan is utterly unfit for his position. . . . Every movement has been a failure. And yet the President keeps him in command, and leaves our destiny in his hands, I am at times almost in despair. Well it cannot be helped. We went in for a railsplitter, and we have got one."

Lincoln's faith in McClellan was strained further by the "wooden guns" fiasco. There had been an opportunity by the General-in-Chief to end the war in one blow, and he had muffed it!

The congressional radicals and Secretary Stanton agitated for McClellan's removal. In characteristic fashion, Lincoln, usually a moderate, yielded to them part of the way. On March 11 he issued the "President's Special War Order No. 3," which provided that McClellan was to retain the Army of the Potomac command but "he is relieved from the command of the other Military departments," whose respective commanders must "report severally and directly to the Secretary of War." Unfortunately, Stanton was a lawyer then unfamiliar with military administration and was politically hand-in-glove with such congressional radicals as Senators Wade of Ohio and Chandler of Michigan, controlling members of the Committee on the Conduct of the War.

Lincoln believed that he was being fair to McClellan in allowing him to keep the major Potomac command. It was a painful decision to take away part of the army and transfer it to other commanders, the President explained to his Cabinet, but McClellan was still left with "opportunity to retrieve his errors."

In that same Order No. 3 Lincoln tendered the Western command to the conservative Major-General Henry W. Halleck, and gave concession to the radicals by giving command of the newly created Mountain Department to the radicals' prime favorite, Major-General John C. Frémont, whom he had deposed five months before. The Mountain Department comprised parts of Kentucky, east Tennessee, and western Virginia.

III

The farther McClellan advanced on his Peninsular Campaign, the more the President restricted his authority and reduced the number of his available forces.

In late March Lincoln called on McClellan at Alexandria, Virginia, and talked about naval co-operation. But little of that sea support was to come. In that meeting Lincoln confided that pressure was being exerted on him to detach Major-General Louis Blenker's crack German division from McClellan's command and give it to Frémont's Mountain Department. According to McClellan, the President assured him that he was personally opposed to taking away Blenker's units, but a few days later, on March 21, bad news came to McClellan from the President: "This morning I felt constrained to order Blenker's Division to Frémont, and I write this to assure you that I did so with great pain, understanding that you would wish it otherwise. If you could know the full pressure of the case, I am confident you would justify it—even beyond a mere acknowledgment that the Commander-in-Chief may order what he pleases."

Lincoln's withdrawal of Blenker's division from McClellan did not end his denuding of McClellan's Army of the Potomac at the very start of his Peninsular Campaign. Concerned for the defense of Washington, the President detained General McDowell's corps near the capital city.

Commanding Fortress Monroe, McClellan's base, was the Department of Virginia head, seventy-eight-year-old Brigadier-General John E. Wool. Lincoln at first believed that McClellan should not be hampered by Wool, and directed Stanton: "In going to Fortress Monroe, Gen. McClellan gets into Gen. Wool's Department. He must not be interfered with by Gen. Wool. Yet I do not wish Gen. Wool's feelings hurt, and I am ready to make him a Major Genl. if it will do any good." Eight days later the President placed McClellan in command of Fort Monroe and of Wool's troops. But two weeks later he experienced a change of heart, and on April 3 ordered the moribund Wool to "continue in command of Fort Monroe and the troops heretofore assigned to the Department of Virginia."

The President on the 6th telegraphed McClellan: "You now have one hundred thousand troops with you independent of Gen. Wool's command. I think you better break the enemies' line from York-town to Warwick River, at once." McClellan's reply to the President on the following day was pointed: "I have the honor to state that my entire force for duty, only amounts to about eighty-five thousand. . . . Genl. Wool's command . . . has been taken out of my control. . . . The only use that can be made of his command is to protect my communication in rear."

Lincoln answered that reply by sending McClellan a long letter of explanation and advice, dated April 9. He was not offended but pained, Lincoln told the General, by his despatches complaining that he was not being properly sustained. "Blenker's Division was withdrawn from you before you left here; and you know the pressure under which I did it, and, as I thought, acquiesced in it—certainly not without reluctance." About his detachment of General McDowell's troops from the Peninsular Campaign, Lincoln pointed out to McClellan: "My explicit order that Washington should, by the judgment of *all* the commanders of Army corps, be left entirely secure, had been neglected. It was precisely this that drove me to detain McDowell." Lincoln explained further: "As to Gen. Wool's command, I understand it is doing for you precisely what a like number of your own would have to do, if that command was away." Then the President gave counsel to McClellan: "And, once more let me tell you, it is indispensable to *you* that you strike a blow. *I* am powerless to help this. . . . I always insisted, that going down the Bay in search of a field, instead of fighting at or near Manassas, was only shifting, and not surmounting a difficulty. . . . *But you must act.*"

So McClellan, stripped of the sorely needed troops of Blenker, McDowell, and Wool, faced enemy forces of slightly fewer numbers but superbly commanded and fighting on their own soil.

After almost four weeks of siege, McClellan captured Yorktown, Virginia, from the Confederates on May 4. But they were checked by General James Longstreet, commanding the Confederate rear guard, at Williamsburg on the following day. That dislocated McClellan's plan to fall upon the main Southern force under General Joseph E. Johnston. And the Federal fleet had been halted at Drewry's Bluff.

Lincoln, meanwhile, personally took actual military command and launched a movement to capture Norfolk, Virginia. The President, accompanied by Secretary of War Stanton and Secretary of the Treasury Chase, visited Fort Monroe, where he conferred with military and naval officers. He expressed disapproval over what was being done under Wool's direction, questioned subordinate officers, tossed his stovepipe hat on the floor, and issued military orders. Here he discussed plans to take Norfolk with General Wool. He, Wool, Stanton, and Chase steamed around the coast in a boat looking for a landing place for the troops to be sent against Norfolk. The President stayed at the Fort when Wool made his attack, which turned out to be unnecessary. The Confederate army units had evacuated that seaport city on news of McClellan's capture of Yorktown. Lincoln returned to Washington highly pleased.

But his hopes for the capture of Richmond were soon dashed. With the fall of Norfolk into Union hands it seemed that the James River was now open to the type of land-and-water operations with which the Federals had been successful in the West. But the halting of the Federal naval units at Drewry's Bluff, near Richmond, and subsequent events rendered useless its whole effort on the line of the James.

IV

General McClellan set up his base and headquarters at White House Landing and planned a cautious drive on Richmond—excessively cautious, in the estimation of political forces at Washington and among large groups of the Northern public. Still the General called for more reinforcements. Co-operation in Washington was withheld. Lincoln convinced himself that the way to "cover" Washington from Southern attack was to keep General McDowell's corps directly between the two capitals, while McClellan hammered his way up the peninsula to Richmond. But McClellan, thinking in terms of strategy, urged that the Confederates were not attacking Washington by way of Fredericksburg, that Washington was really being defended on the peninsula. Take Richmond by a mass troop movement, said the General, and the Confederates would collapse. As things happened, McDowell, with his 40,000, was finally ordered to advance on Richmond—but by direct land route and too late. McDowell's effective co-operation with McClellan never materialized.

Meanwhile, as McClellan was challenging the Southern armies under Generals Robert E. Lee and Joe Johnston on the peninsula, General Thomas J. ("Stonewall") Jackson and his men were shifting, feinting, and striking in the Shenandoah Valley. Jackson defeated part of General Frémont's Mountain Department forces and then, at Winchester on May 23-25, drove back General Banks's Federals across the Potomac.

Lincoln and his advisers grew ever more alarmed for Washington's safety, though Jackson's forces were woefully inadequate for an assault on the national capital. McDowell must be kept in and around Washington.

On May 24 Lincoln telegraphed McClellan: "In consequence of Gen. Banks' critical position I have been compelled to suspend Gen. McDowell's movement to join you. The enemy are making a desperate push upon Harper's Ferry, and we are trying to throw Fremont's force & part of McDowell's in their rear."

On the following day, the President telegraphed McClellan that "the time is near when you must either attack Richmond or give up the job and come to the defense of Washington"—on the erroneous supposition that the Confederates were planning a "general and concerted" movement against the national capital.

So McClellan, at the most critical stage of his assault on Richmond, had no help from McDowell's huge corps. In the estimate of America's distinguished military analyst, Colonel Emory Upton, who was serving under McDowell, "McClellan might have had 40,000 [additional men], had not McDowell's orders to join him been countermanded and his troops sent on a hopeless chase after Jackson in the valley."

Major-Generals McDowell, Frémont, Banks, and James Shields could not whip the elusive Jackson in the Shenandoah, and in another month Jackson and his men were back in Richmond, joining Lee's army against McClellan.

V

McClellan's line was attacked on May 31-June 1 by Johnston's army south of the Chickahominy, at Seven Pines (Fair Oaks), only several miles from Richmond. Johnston struck at the precise time that McDowell, on Lincoln's orders, was marching with his men in the wrong direction, into the Valley. But McClellan nonetheless repulsed the Confederates, and Johnston himself was twice wounded.

As the Battle of Seven Pines raged, Lincoln telegraphed advice to McClellan, at the same time guessing that it must be the Rebels, not McClellan, who were on the defensive. He told McClellan: "You are probably engaged with the enemy. I suppose he made the attack. Stand well on your guard—hold all your ground, or yield any only, inch by inch and in good order." The President also sent glad tidings that old General Wool's Department of Virginia was being added to McClellan's Army of the Potomac, with Wool sent off to command Fort McHenry, where he would not be in McClellan's way.

McClellan, quite correctly, renewed his demands for reinforcements. Lincoln sent him more troops under Major-General George A. McCall. The Chief Executive on June 15 pointed out to McClellan in a letter: "This, with what you get from Gen. Wool's old command, and the new regiments sent you, must give you an increase since the last battle of over twenty thousand."

Lincoln now also offered McClellan McDowell's force—but only as a separate command under McDowell. This arrangement was unsatisfactory to McClellan, and he wrote Lincoln so. "If I can not fully control all his [McDowell's] troops," McClellan replied to Secretary Stanton on the 14th, "I want none of them, but would prefer to fight the battle with what I have, and let others be responsible for the results." That answer was an extraordinary statement for an American field commander to address to his civilian superior, the Secretary of War, who was the President's deputy in military administration. But the General found himself subjected to irritating political interference and unwise military decisions from Washington.

While McClellan carried on controversy with Washington officials and his soldiers sweated and swore through the peninsula marshes, Robert E. Lee had assumed command of the Confederate columns defending Richmond, following the wounding of Johnston. McClellan was now facing one of the most formidable of military tacticians. Lee conceived an audacious plan to annihilate McClellan, part of which called for "Stonewall" Jackson to march back from the Valley speedily and secretly join him in a combined assault on McClellan. In late June, Lee carried through his concentration of forces, and on the 26th attacked McClellan's army at Mechanicsville. But McClellan beat him.

While McClellan was defeating Lee's army at Mechanicsville, Lincoln was issuing an order for the creation of a new "Army of Virginia," to be commanded by Major-General John Pope, son of the late federal judge in Springfield. The President's purposes were better protection for

Washington and to relieve pressure on McClellan in the Peninsula. Pope's new army, to be distinguished from McClellan's Army of the Potomac, was made up of the scattered forces of Frémont, Banks, and McDowell, together with minor units near Alexandria and in the intrenchments that guarded Washington.

Pope was a handsome, dashing, soldierly looking general but a pretentious person of military mediocrity who was constantly egotistical. He impressed the President and dazzled the victory-starved Northern public, who did not seem to appreciate that McClellan had chalked up the first major Federal triumph on the Eastern front. There spread exaggerated accounts of Pope's victories in the West, for Pope knew how to write official reports that were sparkling and quotable, while rendering lavish praise on himself. It was said of him that, if he had possessed a coat of arms, it should have been bombast rampant upon an expansive field of incompetence. Pope's most powerful recommendation came from Senator Wade's ubiquitous anti-McClellan Committee on the Conduct of the War. Professor T. Harry Williams has noted: "The Committee, constantly on the look-out for a general with the right political ideas whom it could push into McClellan's place, saw in Pope a chance to accomplish its design. The members pelted Lincoln with praise of the new military luminary and urged that he should have an important command in the East." And so, with Pope as its leader, the new Army of Virginia was created to protect Washington and to relieve the pressure on McClellan, while Lincoln's critics accused him of repaying Pope's dead father for past favors in the courts over which he had presided in Illinois.

Lincoln's creation of the new army was notice to McClellan that he could not then re-inforce him on the Peninsula. Unfortunately, the President gave orders for the new Army of Virginia at a time when the main business of the Peninsular Campaign was well under way.

VI

McClellan's repulse of Lee at Mechanicsville, occurring on the same day that Lincoln issued orders for the formation of the Army of Virginia under Pope, was followed by the Seven Days' Battle. McClellan fell back, inflicting heavy losses on the Southerners at Gaines' Mill, shifted his base to the James River for better protection, and on July 1 badly beat Lee's men at Malvern Hill. After Malvern Hill, Lee's biographer, Freeman, relates, "Lee's brigades were still hopelessly confused. Commanders did not know where their men were; men could not find their officers."

McClellan found rough going after Malvern Hill and awaited Lincoln's reply to his request for additional troops; he wanted 50,000 more. Lincoln, waxing impatient, answered that, outside of McClellan's own Army of the Potomac, there were not 75,000 soldiers in the entire Eastern theatre. "Thus, the idea of sending you fifty thousand, or any other considerable force promptly," the President telegraphed on July 2, "is simply absurd." But he did not expect McClellan to do the impossible: "If you think you are not strong enough to take Richmond just now, I do not ask you to try just now. Save the Army, material and personal (sic); and I will strengthen it for the offensive again, as fast as I can."

McClellan retreated again to Harrison's Landing, where he stopped to lick his wounds. He managed the withdrawal with skill. Lincoln had told him to save the Army, material, and men. He did so. McClellan's retreat was an orderly one, not the rout that Lee had planned. He brought back an army, not a rabble, and on July 4 he could report to the President: "We have preserved our trains, our guns, our material, and above all, our honor."

Lincoln grew more disturbed by the stalled condition of McClellan's great Army. His fears were increased when Quartermaster General Montgomery C. Meigs visited him, woke him up at night, and pleaded with him to order the army away from the Peninsula—otherwise the Confederates might slaughter it.

Lincoln hastened to McClellan's headquarters at Harrison's Landing, and there asked questions of him and the subordinate generals. His main query was: "If it were desired to get the army away from here, could it be safely effected?" Only two of McClellan's generals would agree to a removal.

McClellan felt desperately fearful that Lincoln would order his army from the Peninsula. While honestly serving Lincoln's administration, he had little faith in it or in the President himself. The day following Lincoln's visit to McClellan, the General sent word to his wife that he did not like Lincoln's manner and that Lincoln was an old stick and pretty poor timber at that. But he continued to send requests to Lincoln for troop re-enforcements with arguments why the army should not be withdrawn. Soon McClellan had thoughts of resigning.

Into this muddling and complex military situation, worsened by political pressure from Congress for McClellan's removal, the bewildered Lincoln added another complication. On July 1 he called Major-General Henry W. Halleck to Washington from the West to "command the whole land forces of the United States, as General-in-Chief."

A desk general rather than a field commander, and author of textbooks on military tactics, Halleck was known as "Old Brains." He would direct army operations from his War Department office.

General-in-Chief Halleck had been in Washington only a few weeks when, on August 3, with Lincoln's approval, he issued a startling order to McClellan. He instructed McClellan to embark his sick and wounded, move his entire army, then before Richmond, to Aquia Creek, south of Bull Run and close to Washington. McClellan's men were to join Pope's Army of Virginia!

And this at a time when McClellan's Army of the Potomac was strongly intrenched only twenty-five miles from the Confederate capital!

In vain did McClellan protest against movement of his soldiers from the Peninsula to join Pope. His army was in a good position and he was planning a drive on Richmond by way of Petersburg, thus anticipating the successful plan of General Grant more than two years later. Ironically enough, Grant was destined to hammer away at Petersburg for nine full months before taking Richmond early in 1865.

"Here," declared McClellan about his Peninsular Campaign, "is the true defense of Washington." In front of this army is the "heart of the rebellion." Withdrawal, in his opinion, would be disastrous. His advice, however, went unheeded. Halleck, as Lincoln would say in numerous communications, "commands."

VII

As August ended the commander of the newly created Army of Virginia, Major-General John Pope found himself beset by the South's three most cunning military strategists, Generals Lee, "Stonewall" Jackson, and J.E.B. ("Jeb") Stuart.

Jackson, by a daring march on Pope's right flank, swept north (away from Lee) through Thoroughfare Gap in the Bull Run mountains, reached Pope's rear, and assailed his communications. At this time "Jeb" Stuart's gray-garbed cavalry raided the Federal base at Manassas. This apparently left Jackson's detached forces open to attack by Pope. But he failed to accomplish it. The Federals made a shift which Lee anticipated, and Jackson slipped back to the precise point where Lee needed him for the following assault on the Federals.

In that two-day battle, known as Second Bull Run, or Second Manassas, on August 29-30, the rebels repulsed the fierce Federal attacks with terrible losses. Pope launched a furious offensive on the 30th and failed because of his strategic errors in the very uncertain game of warfare. The battle closed with Lee's counter-stroke against Pope's fast-retreating Union forces.

At 8:50 on the morning of September 1 General Pope advised General-in-Chief Halleck that he should order the army to fall back to the entrenchments in front of Washington.

VIII

"What news? Do you hear firing this morning?" so President Lincoln telegraphed Colonel Herman Haupt, chief of military railroads at Alexandria at ten o'clock on that melancholy morning of September 1.

But firing had mostly ceased. An hour and a half before, Lincoln's General-in-Chief, Halleck, had received an urgent wire from General Pope, advising that the army should be ordered to fall back to the entrenchments in front of Washington for reorganization. And soon the depressed President told Hay, his assistant secretary: "Well, John, we are whipped again." Gloom shrouded the Executive Mansion.

From his White House window Lincoln could view the chaos, confusion, and fright in the capital city following Second Manassas. Disorder reigned unchecked. Crowds of straggling soldiers, in tattered and mud-splashed blue uniforms, some wounded, accompanied seemingly endless streams of army wagons and ambulances as they all poured into Washington at break-neck speed. Government clerks were recruited as nurses and formed into battalions of defense. A Navy gunboat, with steam up, lay in the Potomac River off the White House. Some over-excited citizens feared that the Chief Executive and his Cabinet were about to flee the city and set up the capital at Baltimore or Philadelphia.

General-in-Chief Halleck sank into demoralization, then rose to desperation. Swallowing his pride, this head of Lincoln's lieutenants, who had ordered McClellan's Peninsular Campaign halted and his Army of the Potomac withdrawn to Aquia Creek less than one month previous, now turned to McClellan for help. Late on August 31 Halleck telegraphed the demoted General, asking for his "ability and experience." "I am almost entirely tired out," confessed "Old Brains" to McClellan. In reply "Little Mac" advised him to order Pope to fall back to the capital defenses and asked for an appointment with him in Washington on the next day. McClellan saw Halleck, who gave him verbal orders to assume command of the Washington defenses, and later in the day McClellan conferred with Lincoln.

The President took a hard look at the critical situation. All he needed to do was to look at the military map and compare the Federal front now with what it had been three months before, to realize that he had committed gross, almost fatal blunders in demoting McClellan, elevating Pope, and agreeing to Halleck's order to abandon the Peninsular Campaign. This was stark and grim reality, looking back over the three months: On June 2 McClellan had been hammering at Richmond's gates, the Federal forces under Frémont, Banks, and McDowell had been occupying "Stonewall" Jackson in the Shenandoah Valley, and most of western Virginia lay in Union hands. By September 1, the Federals had evacuated most of western Virginia and Pope's men were racing in disorderly retreat from Bull Run to Washington. Except for Federal forces at Norfolk and Fort Monroe, the only Union troops closer than 80 miles to Richmond were the prisoners of war held by the Confederates and the regiments busily preparing to abandon their base at Aquia Creek.

At this super-critical hour on September 1, 1862, described by Secretary of the Treasury Chase in his diary in vast understatement as an "anxious day," Lincoln verbally ordered McClellan to take command of Pope's forces as they retreated to their fortifications. Later a formal order was issued, placing McClellan in command of troops defending Washington. Lincoln, too, had heard reports that Lee was preparing a Northern invasion.

When on the following day, the 2nd, Lincoln walked into a Cabinet meeting and startled all by announcing that he had ordered McClellan to take command of Pope's lamented Army of Virginia, the two radical members, Stanton and Chase, angrily protested. But Lincoln had made up his mind. According to Chase, "The President said it distressed him exceedingly to find himself differing on such a point from the Secretary of War and Secretary of the Treasury . . . but he could not see who could do the work wanted as well as McClellan." Secretary of the Navy Welles noted that at that Cabinet session the President, backed only by Postmaster-General Blair, insisted that McClellan "had beyond any officer the confidence of the army. Though deficient in the positive qualities which are necessary for an energetic commander, his organizing powers could be made temporarily available till the troops were rallied."

The infuriated Chase went home from that Cabinet meeting and angrily jotted down in his diary: "I could not but feel that giving the command to him [McClellan] was equivalent to giving Washington to the rebels." Stanton was equally inflamed at Lincoln's renewed confidence in McClellan, and felt so disgusted that for a while he thought of resigning as Secretary of War.

Lincoln's restoration of McClellan to high command—next to Halleck, he was the ranking general—meant the demotion of Pope. That beaten commander had to go, not only because he and McClellan could not work together but because he bore the imprimatur of defeat at Manassas. Pope has been succinctly summed up by Blair as "a braggart, with some courage, perhaps, but not much capacity."

McClellan rode out to meet Pope, took over command from him, and went on to join the retreating troops who received him with boisterous enthusiasm. They partially forgot their defeat at Bull Run as they joyously tossed their blue caps in the air, frolicked like school boys, and gave loud vent to their relief that McClellan was back. Soon the beloved "Little Mac" was whipping the disorganized soldiers into battle shape again.

The West Point-educated Major-General Oliver O. Howard, who had lost an arm in the Peninsular Campaign and had commanded the rear guard of Pope's retreating army after Bull Run, and who formerly had been critical of McClellan, breathed easier when he returned. "I am heartily glad," Howard wrote his wife on September 6, "we are back with McClellan. He will not throw us away through sheer incompetency. He is the only man yet who has the love & confidence of this entire army." Howard four days later sent word to Mrs. Howard: "Gen. McClellan is now back with the army in the field. We cannot help feeling well about the matter. His fortifications saved Washington & his system gives us something to hope for, and for some indescribable reason the army loves him. Pope's reckless course has brought McClellan's caution into good repute."

IX

It was highly fortunate that Lincoln had restored McClellan to top field command. For within one week Lee led his formidable Army of Northern Virginia in an invasion of Maryland. The entire North grew fearful.

Lee's legions occupied Frederick, Maryland, on September 7, only six days after Lincoln restored "Little Mac." Confederate attacks on Baltimore, then Wilmington, and finally Philadelphia were fearfully expected. Or, maybe Lee would turn about and lay siege to Washington! The Confederate commander's own purpose in his advance north was to liberate "sister State" Maryland from this "foreign yoke" of Yankeedom.

McClellan, to check Lee, with the reaction of a professional soldier, slowly and thoroughly interposed his army between Washington and the invading secession troops. Then Lee took a risk. He sent 25,000 of his men, under "Stonewall' Jackson, to capture Harper's Ferry, the gateway to Maryland from the Shenandoah Valley. McClellan came into possession of a Confederate document showing that Lee's forces were not concentrated but widely separated. A Confederate officer had dropped this document, wrapped around three cigars, and it had been picked up by a Federal private.

On September 15 the Confederates captured more than 11,000 Federals and small arms and took the garrisons at Winchester and Martinsburg. But Lee nonetheless found himself in a perilous predicament. Although he was able to delay a Federal advance by a stiff engagement at South Mountain, his force was far inferior in numbers to McClellan's. The Southern general faced a battle with the river at his rear and with the danger of losing his whole force in case of defeat. Having pushed his plans for a victorious invasion of the North, Lee now realized his danger and was preparing to withdraw across the Potomac into Virginia.

At this very time McClellan attacked at Sharpsburg on September 17. That day has sometimes been called "the bloodiest day of the war." The wholesale slaughter there made this Battle of Antietam Creek the most gory military engagement America had ever suffered up to that time.

McClellan stopped Lee's invasion cold.

But McClellan had also allowed Lee and his men to escape across the Potomac into Virginia.

X

Although he had beaten Lee at Antietam, a factor that settled once and for all any British idea of intervening in the War, the fact that McClellan had not crushed the Confederate army and had not even given chase, badly shook Lincoln. The President considered McClellan's failure to pursue Lee more important than the prevention of the Rebels' further invasion into the North. With appreciation for McClellan's ability and achievements, Lincoln, like numerous other impatient amateur strategists in time of war, concluded that the General simply was not fast enough. Some weeks later the Chief Executive told his old friend, Senator Browning of Illinois, that McClellan "could better organize, provide for and discipline an army, and handle it with more ability in a fight than any general we had, but that he was too slow." Certainly, up to that time, McClellan, with the careful and cautious planning of a true professional soldier, had demonstrated that he was the only Federal commander who could win major battles in the East; the only one who had thus far whipped Lee.

On the first day of October, two weeks after Antietam, Lincoln paid an unannounced visit to McClellan's headquarters in order to persuade him to take the offensive at once. He treated the General kindly and told him of his confidence in him. But within himself McClellan resented the President's attempts to hurry him into battle before the troops were ready and his own plans perfected. On the day following Lincoln's visit, the General wrote home to Mrs. McClellan: "His ostensible purpose is to see the troops and the battle-field. I incline to think that the real purpose of his visit is to push me into a premature advance into Virginia."

Lincoln now persisted, through General-in-Chief Halleck, to get McClellan on the march immediately. "The President," telegraphed "Old Brains" to "Little Mac" on October 6, "directs that you cross the Potomac and give battle to the enemy or drive him south. Your army must now move while the roads are good." Halleck offered him more men.

The first two weeks of October had almost passed, and still McClellan lingered, not yet ready to go on the advance. On the 13th Lincoln sent the General a lengthy letter:

> Are you not over-cautious when you assume that you can not do what the enemy is constantly doing? . . . Change positions with the enemy, and think you not he would break your communication with Richmond within the next twenty-four hours? . . . If he should . . . move towards Richmond, I would press closely toward him, fight him if a favorable opportunity should present, and, at least, try to beat him to Richmond on the inside track. I say 'try;' if we never try, we shall never succeed. . . . If we can not beat the enemy where he now is, we never can, he again being within the intrenchments of Richmond.

McClellan, professional military strategist and veteran field commander, better than Lincoln, who, besides being an amateur strategist, was subject to political pressures, knew the tremendous preparations required for another mass offensive that would not be perilously premature. Inadequately planned drives, from McClellan's viewpoint, were vastly more dangerous to the Federal army and the Union cause than any delay in striking at Lee. The hastily prepared assaults of his predecessor, McDowell, at First Bull Run, and then Pope at Second Bull Run, had proved costly and had led to humiliating Federal defeat. But Lincoln was, understandably enough, impatient. The off-year elections were raging at this precise time, October, 1862, and bad reports for the administration candidates in State and congressional elections were already coming in.

As McClellan, for the remainder of October, painfully rebuilt his army and determined that he must choose his own hour for advance against the rebel hosts, the patience of Lincoln and other political figures at Washington was wearing threadbare. When McClellan referred to his ill and tired horses, the President curtly telegraphed in answer: "I have just read your despatch about sore tongued and fatigued horses. Will you pardon me for asking what the horses of your army have done since the battle of Antietam that fatigue anything?"

Two days later, on October 26th, McClellan, with 116,000 men, crossed the Potomac. By the first week of November he had massed his army around Warrenton, Virginia. At last he was advancing.

Meanwhile, Lee was ordering Lieutenant-General James Longstreet's First Corps over the Blue Ridge into Culpepper County. Longstreet's army reached Culpepper on November 5, interposing itself between Richmond and McClellan's army.

Lincoln had previously decided that, if McClellan allowed the Confederates to cross the Blue Ridge and take a position between Richmond and the Army of the Potomac, he would remove him from command.

The President, hearing of Longstreet's arrival at Culpepper with his forces, took action. Two days later, shortly after the off-year election returns had come in, Lincoln had a messenger dispatched to McClellan, with orders removing him from the Army of the Potomac command and directing him to turn his forces over to Major-General Ambrose E. Burnside.

Thus did Lincoln break the Federal general most feared by Lee.

The following year, 1863, Lee's daughter declared: "Genl. McClellan was the only Genl. Father dreaded." And after the war Lee himself, when asked who was the ablest Federal general he had fought, answered emphatically: "McClellan, by all odds."

Late in 1862, however, Lincoln relegated McClellan to the inactive list.

FACING THE SLAVERY ORDEAL

23

I

DURING that agonizing year, 1862, Lincoln found himself faced with the most perplexing and provocative problem which had ever agitated the American Republic; the explosive, turbulence-brewing, and complex question of Negro slavery.

This issue of black bondage, so tightly interlaced with the sectionalism that spawned secession and consequent civil war, presented to the President throughout that dreadful blood-letting conflict a many-faceted dilemma, with its sharp military and political points that threatened to cut down his administration. This convulsive slavery controversy, waged by advanced anti-slavery men, moderates, and purely pro-slavery adherents, finally produced in the world image a fixed stereotype of Lincoln as the Emancipator.

II

Lincoln, destined as the most immortalized emancipator in world annals, paradoxically enough, continued to be moderate when dealing with slavery during his presidency. It could hardly have been otherwise, considering his heritage, background, family associations by marriage, friendships of earlier years, and the very moderate anti-slavery platform on which he was elected.

Although making his public career in Illinois, a Northern free state, Lincoln was bound to the conservative South by ties that were fundamental and experiences that were underlined. Of Kentucky birth himself, the son of Virginia parents, he was reared in a region of lower Indiana populated almost entirely by Southerners, a community directly across the Ohio River from slaveholding Kentucky and startlingly similar to the poorer parts of upper Dixie. He had lived for one year, 1829-30, in Macon County, Illinois, before settling in New Salem, Sangamon County. Both of those Southern-settled Central Illinois regions then retained numberless characteristics of a slave state, as did Springfield, also in Sangamon County, where he resided from 1837 until his assumption of the presidency in 1861. From Springfield south to Cairo, near the Kentucky-Illinois line, the cultural types and mannerisms were those of the South. Most of Lincoln's closest cronies of his early and late Illinois years were originally from the South. His three law partners, Stuart, Logan, and Herndon, were all from Kentucky, as were Joshua F. Speed and Orville H. Browning. On the Eighth Judicial Circuit his most intimate friends, the two conservatives, Maryland-born Judge David Davis and Virginia-born Ward H. Lamon, had come from slave states. Leonard Swett, from Maine, was perhaps Lincoln's only fast friend who had come from a Northern state. Also, Lincoln had married Mary Todd, of the slaveholding Kentucky Todds, and Lincoln's first great political idol, Henry Clay, was at best a most moderate anti-slavery advocate, and owned slaves himself.

As member of Congress during 1847-49 Lincoln's closest associates among his Whig colleagues were from the South, especially Alexander H. Stephens of Georgia, now the Confederate Vice-President. Lincoln showed his lack of ultraism by clinging doggedly to the conservative Whig Party until it nearly ceased to exist, entering the new anti-slavery Republican Party only when there remained no other political organization to oppose the Democrats. In 1856 he had wanted to see the conservative Whig-minded Supreme Court Justice John McLean named Republican national standard-bearer and supported the more radical Frémont for President only after he had been nominated. Mrs. Lincoln, who knew him best of all, had assured her Kentucky half-sister: "Although Mr. L. is, or was, a *Frémont* man, you must not include him with so many of those who belong *to that party*, an *Abolitionist*. In principle he is far from it. All he desires is that slavery shall not be extended, let it remain where it is."

Lincoln in 1858 delivered his lone radically anti-slavery address, his celebrated and oft-reprinted "House Divided" speech. It was the most extreme oration he was ever to make in his life and as such was unique among his state papers. He spent a good deal of time after he delivered that speech in explaining it away to his audiences, particularly in lower Illinois. Repeated by his foes in his famed debates with Douglas, he vigorously denied that he was an abolitionist, and on several occasions he spoke against the social equality of the white and black races. He even claimed that he wanted to see his own white race maintain its superior position.

In his Cooper Institute address during February, 1860, Lincoln stood on conservative ground toward slavery. He denied that his Republican Party favored interference with slavery in the Southern states, and he condemned John Brown's Harper's Ferry raid. It was only because he was less radical than Seward on the slavery issue that he was nominated as Republican presidential candidate in the following May. And in November he was elected President of a nation nearly half of whose states had legalized Negro slavery.

In his Inaugural Address of March 4, 1861, Lincoln spoke conciliatory words to the South, even with some slave states out of the Union and in the Confederacy. He told the nation that he would not interfere with slavery in states where it already existed: "I believe I have no lawful right to do so, and I have no inclination to do so."

Constantly the President justified his war against the South as a struggle against secession, not a crusade against slavery. To him the all-embracing issue was precisely the same, salvation or division of the Union, as it would have been if not a single slave existed in the United States. And he would pin together the two sections, North and South, with bayonets if that were the only way of keeping the Republic together —slaves or no slaves.

III

By the summer of 1861 Lincoln's Republican Party was splitting into moderate and radical factions over slavery. The President was among the moderates, those men who, although hating slavery, wanted it eradicated by legal and gradual means, with compensation to slaveowners, and colonization of the freed blacks in Central America or the West Indies. Opposed to them were radical abolitionists, who demanded immediate emancipation, with no payment to slaveowners—freedom for the bonded blacks by presidential or military edict if necessary.

Lincoln distrusted the radicals' revolutionary ardor, and their spirit of fanaticism grated on his own sensitivities. Too, as a lawyer wedded to a system of rule by law, he frowned on the flaunting of legal rights in property. Also, he feared that any arbitrary freeing of slaves would alienate Union-lovers in the border slave states, as well as East Tennessee and western Virginia. He felt that any program for liberating slaves should be merely incidental to the vastly larger problem of preserving the Union.

The Chief Executive's first major test of strength against the radicals had come in the summer of 1861, when Major-General Frémont, commanding the Department of the West, had issued his military proclamation freeing the slaves of secessionists in Missouri. Lincoln promptly countermanded Frémont's emancipation edict, to the irritation of abolitionists, advanced anti-slavery advocates, and his assorted critics. Lincoln, in overruling Frémont, was concerned for the illegality of the proclamation and also for fear that such a pronunciamento would antagonize the border slave regions, especially Kentucky. "How many times," irritably demanded the anti-slavery James Russell Lowell about Lincoln's cancelling of Frémont's freedom edict, "are we to save Kentucky and lose our self-respect?"

During the late fall of 1861 radical Republicans grew obsessed with fear that Lincoln would do little or nothing about emancipation. The only reference to the subject in his First Annual Message to Congress on December 3 was his recommendation that already freed Negroes, as well as those to be liberated by their masters by the Congress-enacted Confiscation Act of four months previous, be colonized in foreign tropical nations—"at some place or places in a climate congenial to them," to quote his own phrase. In that Congressional message, too, the President laid emphasis on "suppressing the insurrection" and recommended that the war with the Confederacy should "not degenerate into a violent and remorseless revolutionary struggle." He pointedly suggested to the radicals who wanted to emancipate all slaves immediately: "The Union must be preserved, and hence all indispensable means must be employed. We should not be in haste to determine that radical and extreme measures, which may reach the loyal as well as the disloyal, are indispensable."

Lincoln's message provoked contempt in radical circles, in and out of Congress. The anti-slavery press attacked it with unrestrained invective. "What a wishy-washy message from the President," complained the abolitionist, William Lloyd Garrison. "He has evidently not a drop of anti-slavery blood in his veins"—a "man of very small calibre." The celebrated slavery-hating preacher, Wendell Phillips, thundered from his pulpit: "I demand of the government a policy." The powers-that-be of the Chicago *Tribune,* main Republican organ in Lincoln's home state, on December 6 addressed some harsh words to Senator Trumbull of Illinois about the President's pandering to the border states. Lincoln was now bothered by the verbose activities of his about-to-be-fired Secretary of War Cameron. That hitherto non-committal political opportunist, concluding that his future lay with the radicals, so powerful in Congress, had instructed the commanding General at occupied Port Royal, South Carolina, to employ fugitive slaves and to organize them into "squads" and "companies" in his armed forces. Now Cameron publicly advocated the use of Negro soldiers in the Federal Army. In his annual report he inserted a previously mentioned recommendation for the creation of an army of freed slaves. Cameron hurried his report to the newspapers, without even consulting Lincoln about it.

The President acted against Cameron's anti-slavery action immediately. As soon as he learned of the proposal to arm slaves, he ordered the report recalled, and compelled Cameron to delete that section.

Out of the welter of radical anger at Lincoln for his conservative war policy, his do-nothing policy on emancipation, and the lost battles of Bull Run and Ball's Bluff developed the radical-dominated Joint Committee on the Conduct of the War.

Lincoln ended that year, 1861, with his troubles over slavery mounting and the radicals pressing him for action on freedom for Negroes.

IV

Major-General Frémont was one of the main stumbling-blocks in Lincoln's efforts to muffle anti-slavery agitation.

The President had overruled Frémont's Missouri slave-emancipation edict, and soon had found it necessary to remove him from the Western command. Now, early in 1862, the picturesque Pathfinder became a rallying point for abolitionists and the darling of radical Republicans. For through his edict he had become a symbol of their feelings that the war was a sacred crusade against slavery in addition to a national struggle for survival against secession.

The anti-slavery leaders set about refurbishing Frémont's tarnished reputation. He was then still the greatest of popular heroes, hailed as a martyr to the cause of freedom when Lincoln removed him as Western commander, rather than disdained as an incompetent general and military administrator. He met with the Committee on the Conduct of the War members, who soon hectored Lincoln to give him a new high army assignment in the field. Startlingly enough, some of them even wanted the Chief Executive to remove McClellan and replace him with Frémont as General-in-Chief early in 1862—a frightening thought in retrospect. Lincoln would have none of that preposterous proposal.

Lincoln, ever hoping to quiet the radicals, yielded some to them on Frémont. As Allan Nevins, biographer of Frémont, has pointed out: "The pressure for Frémont's reappointment to a military command was becoming irresistible. Many radicals and many even of the moderate German-Americans were implacable in their anger over his treatment. Early in 1862 Frémont had appeared before the Committee on the Conduct of the War. . . . Lincoln saw that it was best to yield to the storm, and give Frémont another opportunity in the field."

The President thus on March 11 issued an order creating the Mountain Department of the Army in western Virginia, and chose Frémont as its commander. Three weeks later Lincoln instructed that General Louis Blenker's German division be detached from McClellan's Army of the Potomac and be assigned to Frémont's new Mountain Department. Lincoln apologized to McClellan for taking Blencker's units from him and giving them to Frémont: "If you could know the full pressure of the case, I am confident you would justify it."

Lincoln paid a high price to the anti-slavery zealots in giving this popular but inept General the Mountain Department command. He not only partly sapped some of McClellan's military strength at a critical hour of the Peninsular Campaign, but he found that Frémont would not even obey presidential orders in the campaign against "Stonewall" Jackson in the Shenandoah Valley. On May 24 Lincoln ordered Frémont to move against Jackson at Harrisonburg in order to relieve General Banks's hard-pressed troops. But Frémont did not heed this, and three days later the President sent him a curt telegram: "I see you are at Moorefield. You were expressly ordered to march to Harrisonburg. What does this mean?" Frémont replied the next day that his troops were in no condition to heed Lincoln's order; he would use his own discretion about the best way to help Banks.

In that Valley campaign of early 1862 "Stonewall" Jackson successfully outgeneraled Frémont, as well as Generals Banks, Shields, and Milroy.

By late June, only little more than three months after he had created Frémont's Mountain Department, Lincoln reduced it to the First Corps of General Pope's new Army of Virginia. The President's demotion of the Pathfinder to a mere corps commander under Pope, whom he detested, proved galling to him. Frémont requested Lincoln to be relieved of his command. The President with reluctance accommodated him. Thus ended Frémont's disappointing Civil War battle service. His appointment to the Mountain Department command had been a huge price for Lincoln to pay in return for time in keeping the lid on the boiling abolitionist plot, thus reassuring border-state conservative Unionists.

Frémont, however, proved not the only anti-slavery Union general who gave Lincoln trouble by arbitrarily, via military power, interfering with slavery. Among others were Generals David Hunter, commanding the Department of the South, and James S. Wadsworth, military Governor of Washington.

In May, General Hunter, taking a page from Frémont's record on slavery in Missouri the previous year, issued a proclamation for emancipation of slaves in occupied Federal parts of South Carolina, Georgia, and Florida. The slaves were proclaimed by Hunter "forever free."

Lincoln acted on Hunter only ten days later. Although the anti-slavery Secretary of the Treasury Chase had advised him that the General's order be "not revoked," the President publicly revoked Hunter's proclamation, just as he had done to Frémont's proclamation in Missouri. "Whereas the same," the President said of Hunter's order, "is producing some excitement, and misunderstanding," he declared that slavery-emancipation matters "are questions which, under my responsibility, I reserve to myself, and which I can not feel justified in leaving to the decision of commanders in the field."

Then there was Wadsworth involving himself in the slavery problem. That General had his own little private "war" over runaway slaves in the District of Columbia. Pro-slavery groups insisted that the federal Fugitive Slave Law of 1850, providing for capture and return of runaway bonded blacks, applied to the capital District. But General Wadsworth denied this, and pursued such an anti-slavery policy that some Unionist Maryland slaveholders presented complaints to Lincoln against Wadsworth—on May 19, the same day as the President was publicly overriding General Hunter's slave-emancipation order. "The President," reported the New York *Tribune's* Washington correspondent, assured the Marylanders that he had confidence in Wadsworth but he himself would "see that no injustice was done."

So concerned was Lincoln about catering to anti-abolitionist sentiment in the loyal border slave states, that it irritated his more anti-slavery Cabinet members. Secretary of the Treasury Chase in early September, 1862, lamented to his diary: "The President with the most honest intentions in the world, and a naturally clear judgment and a true, unselfish patriotism, has yielded so much to Border State and negrophobic counsels."

V

Lincoln was confronted with the problem of whether or not he should enforce Congress-enacted laws, which he had signed into law, which freed slaves for use for labor in the Union Army. Border-state sentiment opposed this idea, United States Senator Garrett Davis of Kentucky insisting: "Congress has neither the expressly delegated nor implied power to liberate these slaves."

Under the first Confiscation Act, passed in the previous August (1861) it was inferred that slaves should be liberated if their masters used them against the United States federal authority. But Lincoln did not enforce this—at least, not very effectively. He was to be criticized later by Senator Trumbull of his own State, who declared sharply: "That act, however, has not been executed. So far as I am advised, not a single slave has been freed under it."

The question of using Negroes in the Union Army grew into a fierce snarl in Congress during the summer of 1862. Senate and House floors fairly seethed with grim maneuvers and angry words hurled by moderate Republicans, radical Republicans, border-state "Old-Line" Whig conservatives, Northern "War" Democrats and pro-Southern "Copperhead" Democrats—all in a hot and angry cross-fire of charges and counter-charges. Out of it all came the passage of the second Confiscation Act and the Militia Act, both of July 17. The former measure provided that any one thereafter committing treason should "suffer death, and all his slaves, if any, be declared and made free." The latter law, provided that when any slave belonging to an enemy of the United States should render military service, he should be forever thereafter free; and his mother, wife, and children (unless belonging to loyal owners) should be forever free.

Passage of the Second Confiscation and Militia acts in July placed Lincoln in a painful predicament. Congress was forcing his hand on slavery.

Horace Greeley, editor of the New York *Tribune,* most widely circulated of all Republican newspapers, was typical of radical men who were rebuking Lincoln for not utilizing the Second Confiscation Act for the freeing of slaves. "We think you are strangely and disastrously remiss with regard to the emancipation provisions of the new Confiscation Act," Greeley told the President in his public letter, "The Prayer of Twenty Millions," of August 19, 1862, which he printed in his *Tribune* on the following day. Greeley continued in this public letter to Lincoln: "We think you are unduly influenced by the counsels . . . of certain fossil politicians from the Border Slave States." Too, "the Confiscation Act which you approved is habitually disregarded by your Generals." Greeley demanded that the President enforce the law and free the slaves of secessionists.

Greeley's letter, reprinted in the Northern press, brought from Lincoln that well-known reply, in which he announced that slavery emancipation was strictly secondary to the preservation of the Union. Wrote Lincoln to the *Tribune* editor:

> My paramount object in this struggle *is* to save the Union, and is *not* either to save or destroy slavery. If I could save the Union without freeing

> *any* slave I would do it, and if I could save it by freeing *all* the slaves, I would do it; and if I could save it by freeing some and leaving others alone I would also do that. What I do about slavery, and the colored race, I do because I believe it helps to save the Union; and what I forbear, I forbear because I do *not* believe it would help save the Union.

Those words succinctly summed up Lincoln's attitude toward emancipation of slaves.

VI

Closest to Lincoln's heart as possible permanent solution of the slavery problem was gradual "compensated emancipation"—the bonded blacks to be freed, for which their owners would be financially remunerated by public tax money—and then the settlement of those liberated slaves in overseas tropical lands. It was the same proposal of the President's first political idol, Henry Clay, except that Harry of the West had wanted the freed Negroes transplanted in Africa, whereas Lincoln thought of Central America and the West Indies as their possible places of colonization.

In 1852 Lincoln had said of Clay, "His views and measures were always the wisest" and "His judgment was excellent" and had lauded him for his "deep devotion to the cause of liberty" and for having emancipated his own slaves. Of Clay's moderate anti-slavery views, Lincoln had told his fellow-Springfielders at that time: "Clay did not perceive, as I think no wise man has perceived, how it [slavery] could be at *once* eradicated, without producing a greater evil, even to the cause of human liberty itself."

Lincoln had praised the great Kentuckian's long years of activity in the American Colonization Society, which had aimed to find homes for freed slaves in Africa, and he had quoted an earlier oration by Clay which declared that colonization on the Dark Continent for liberated black humans was "one of the great designs of the Ruler of the universe." Lincoln had ended his tribute to Clay by expressing his own approval of such a back-to-Africa movement for emancipated Negroes. "May it indeed be realized!" he had hopefully stated. If, "in restoring a captive people to their long-lost fatherland," Lincoln had concluded, "neither races nor individuals shall have suffered by the change, it will be a glorious consummation."

In his debates against Douglas for Senator in 1858, Lincoln had again revealed interest in Negro migration to Africa.

Lincoln's First Annual Message to Congress on December 3, 1861, recommended that slaves (presumably freed by the First Confiscation Act but actually not freed) be colonized—in his words, "at some place or places in a climate congenial to them." If any of the States should adopt emancipation measures, Lincoln believed that their ex-slaves might be accepted by the United States in lieu of taxes—a rather extraordinary proposal—and that they might be included in a general colonizing project in a foreign land. He would also extend the process of overseas colonization to those Negroes already freed who might desire a foreign home.

No attention being paid by the border slave states, which had not seceded, to his recommendation for gradual emancipation, the President in April, 1862, sent a special message, asking that Congress pass a resolution for the United States Government's co-operation with any state of the Union which might adopt gradual abolishment of slavery, giving in return to such a state some federal financial aid. He told Congress that "very soon the current expenditures of this war would purchase, at fair valuation, all the slaves in any named State."

Lincoln wrote both Henry J. Raymond, New York *Times* editor, and Senator James A. McDougall of California about the infinitesimally small cost of compensation for slaves freed, in contrast to the astronomically high cost of waging war. To Raymond the President pointed out: "Have you noticed the facts that less than one half-day's cost of this war would pay for all the slaves in Delaware, at four hundred dollars per head?—that eighty-seven days cost of this war would pay for all in Delaware, Maryland, District of Columbia, Kentucky, and Missouri at the same price?" To Senator McDougall, Lincoln sent a tabulated list of the costs of war and an estimate of the cost of emancipated slaves in the border states: $174,000,000 for every eighty-seven days of war but only slightly less than that for the cost of all emancipated slaves in the border states at $400 a head. Emancipation would shorten the war, the Chief Executive insisted. So he held conferences with members of Congress from the border-state districts, requesting them to use their influence to have their respective states adopt gradual emancipation.

Congress responded by passing a bill providing for gradual, compensated emancipation in the District of Columbia, with voluntary colonization of freed Negroes in Haiti and Liberia. The niggardly sum of $1,000,000 was appropriated for such colonization. When Lincoln happily signed this bill, he announced: "I have never doubted the constitutional authority of Congress to abolish slavery in this District, and I have ever desired to see the national capital freed from the institution in some satisfactory way. . . . I am gratified that the two principles of compensation and colonization are both recognized and practically applied to this act."

Three months later, on July 17, an act freed slaves in the hands of the United States Army and granted $500,000 for colonization. Less than one month later, August 14, Lincoln granted an interview to a committee of free Negroes, headed by Edward M. Thomas, who were interested in colonizing colored people in Chiriqui, Colombia (later the Republic of Panama).

That interview between the President and the Negro delegation is today disillusioning to many who have always looked upon Lincoln as a militant champion of Negro rights in the United States. Actually Lincoln wanted the colored people out of the country because he believed that both black and white races could not conveniently and comfortably live side by side.

The two races, Lincoln told that Negro delegation on August 14, 1862, both suffer from the presence of each other. He informed them:

"You and I are different races. We have between us a broader difference than exists between almost any other two races. Whether it is right or wrong I need not discuss, but this physical difference is a great disadvantage to us both, as I think your race suffer very greatly, many of them by living among us, while ours suffer from your presence. In a word, we suffer on each side. If this is admitted, it affords a reason at least why we should be separated."

"But even when you cease to be slaves," the Chief Executive continued to those sponsors of colonization in Colombia, "you are yet far removed from being placed on equality with the white race. . . . I cannot alter it if I would. It is a fact. . . . But for your race among us there could be no war, although many men engaged on either side do not care for you one way or another. Nevertheless, I repeat, without the institution of slavery and the colored race as a basis, the war could not have an existence. It is far better for us both, therefore, to be separated." And the President strongly and unflatteringly recommended overseas settlement for all freed Negroes and those to be freed in future.

Lincoln was never to accomplish anything with his plans for compensated emancipation. The border states did not co-operate with the federal Government on the proposal.

Nor did success crown two private projects for colonization in foreign lands, one at Chiriqui, Colombia, and the other at *Isle a'Vache,* off the Haitian coast, which the President backed strongly. Both the Chiriqui and Haitian enterprises were handicapped by unscrupulous promoters, lack of natural resources in those tropical lands, and reluctance of Negroes to settle outside the United States.

VII

The summer of 1862 was proving a critical season for the Union.

To Lincoln, or to anyone else who studied it at that time, the Eastern military front did not look promising. In the Shenandoah Valley "Stonewall" Jackson had just outmaneuvered Generals Shields, Milroy, Banks, and Frémont in June, and the President had formed their forces into the Army of Virginia, commanded by Pope. Before Richmond the Seven Days Battle had ended at Malvern Hill on July 1, with McClellan's victory over Lee. But then McClellan fell back to Harrison's Landing to regroup and recondition his Army of the Potomac, and Lee was solidly entrenched again in Richmond. Lincoln, in desperation and painfully impatient over McClellan's delay in capturing the Confederate capital, called Halleck from the West to become General-in-Chief. Such a discouraging view of Union prospects at the battle front moved Lincoln into a great act that would weaken the Confederacy and impress England: preliminary moves for the emancipation of slaves by presidential edict. It was something that the radicals of his own Republican Party had been long nagging him to do.

With McClellan still inactive on the Virginia front but preparing another drive on Lee before Richmond, Lincoln on July 13 brought up the subject of presidential emancipation before Secretary Seward and Secretary of the Navy Welles as the three rode in a carriage after attending the funeral of Secretary Stanton's infant child. It was the first time he had spoken on the subject to anyone. Welles in his diary told how the President emphasized its gravity and delicacy, and that the President said he "had given it much thought and had about come to the conclusion that it was a military necessity absolutely essential to the salvation of the Union, that we must free the slaves or be ourselves subdued." Welles observed: "It was a new departure for the President, for until this time, in all our previous interviews, whenever the question of emancipation or the mitigation of slavery had been in any way alluded to, he had been prompt and emphatic in denouncing any interference by the General Government with the subject."

But now the military front looked especially unpromising to Lincoln. "It had got to be mid-summer of 1862," explained Lincoln to the artist, Francis B. Carpenter, one and a half years later. "Things had gone . . . from bad to worse, until I felt that we had reached the end of our rope on the plan . . . we had been pursuing; that we must change our tactics or lose the game. I now determined upon the adoption of the emancipation policy; and without consultation with, or the knowledge of, the Cabinet, I prepared the original draft of the proclamation, and, after much anxious thought, called a Cabinet meeting upon the subject."

It was on July 22, only nine days after he had spoken to Secretary Seward and Secretary Welles about presidential emancipation of slaves by proclamation, that Lincoln brought up the subject in Cabinet council.

He told his Cabinet that he would proclaim "the emancipation of all slaves within States remaining in insurrection on the first of January, 1863."

All of the Cabinet members agreed to his proposed proclamation except Seward. The Secretary of State doubted the expediency of such action at a time of public pessimism over the stalled condition of the Union armies. Seward advised: "I suggest, sir, that you postpone its issue until you can give it to the country supported by military success." This counsel impressed the President, who put away his proclamation until a victory in the field would crown Union arms. Thus presidential emancipation was decided on by Lincoln and his Cabinet—but postponed until better news came from the battle front.

In the following month, August, only dismal tidings arrived from the war theatre—especially General Pope's calamitous collapse at Manassas. That Second Bull Run battle prevented Lincoln from issuing his proclamation.

The next month brought better news from the fighting front. McClellan had turned back Lee at Antietam on the 17th.

Lincoln, less than one week after Antietam, acted against slavery in the disloyal regions. Immediately he prepared a second draft of his preliminary Proclamation of Emancipation and summoned a Cabinet meeting for two days hence.

Lincoln indicated that the Proclamation of September 22, 1862, was a military measure by designating himself (as he rarely did in presidential proclamations) as "commander-in-chief of the army and navy." He decreed that, on January 1 of the new year, 1863, "all persons held as slaves" in areas in rebellion against the United States, were to be "then, thenceforward, and forever free." Lincoln clearly pointed out that, in States and regions which had returned to the Union by that New Year's Day, the freedom-for-slaves proclamation did not apply. Those states and regions covered by his edict would be designated on January 1, 1863. Actually, what the President in effect was offering the secessionists was one of two alternatives: return to the Union by the first of the year, or have your slaves freed. In this preliminary Emancipation Proclamation, Lincoln promised that, upon restoration of the Union, he would recommend that loyal citizens "be compensated for all losses by acts of the United States, including the loss of slaves."

Lincoln, eight days after he issued his New Year's Day Emancipation Proclamation, pointed out to Major-General John A. McClernand, an old Douglas Democrat of Illinois, that he had given fair warning—100 days, from September 22 to January 1—to secessionists to return to the Union, or lose their slaves. Wrote the President to McClernand: "I gave a hundred days fair notice of my purpose, to all the States and people, within which time they could have turned it wholly aside, by simply again becoming good citizens of the United States. They chose to disregard it, and I made the peremptory proclamation [of January 1, 1863] on what appeared to be a military necessity."

And so the slaves in regions and States in rebellion against the Union were emancipated on the first of the year, 1863, by presidential proclamation, essentially out of military necessity.

Before that dreadful year, 1862, was ended, Lincoln found himself beset by the mid-term State and congressional elections, Cabinet dissensions, McClellan's case of "the slows," General Buell's lack of progress in the West, and the nightmare of Fredericksburg.

POLITICAL PROBLEMS AND MILITARY MISTAKES

24

I

THE near unanimous support for Lincoln throughout the North in his struggle to subdue the secession insurrection, a popular determination to back him to the end, which he had enjoyed for months following Fort Sumter's fall, had by late 1862 declined appallingly. Military reverses, such as First Bull Run and Ball's Bluff in 1861, and McClellan's stalled Peninsular Campaign, Buell's stalemate in Tennessee, and then Second Bull Run during this year, 1862, had all vastly lessened Lincoln's prestige. In September, many Northerners and loyal border-state citizens were less impressed by the mauling that McClellan's men had given to Lee's legions at Antietam than they were by McClellan's failure to pursue and capture the Confederates' main Army of Northern Virginia.

So, during the last quarter of 1862, the President was forced to fight politically for the survival of his administration, while simultaneously struggling with military matters—all to save the life of the Republic. Party feuds and losing or stalemated fights on battlefields seemed the usual order of developments for Lincoln's administration, and this order grew more grim with each step that the President took in the political and military arenas.

Public anxiety during those closing months of the year was focused on the State and congressional elections and, as always, on reports from the battle front.

II

Even as Lincoln pondered over and then finally issued his preliminary Proclamation of Emancipation in September, 1862, the loyal states were enduring the speechmaking strife and talkative turmoil of the off-year elections.

Not only did the unpromising Federal military front make prospects look glum for his Republican-Union Party candidates at the polls, but the President's party was fractured into at least two fighting factions in the most populous Northern states. Some Republican-Unionists resented each other, personally and politically, nearly as deeply as they detested the common Democratic foe. Administration candidates for State office and Congress were handicapped in their vote appeals by Lincoln's Proclamation. For that edict offended conservatives in the Union-Republican ranks, who insisted that the Chief Executive held no legal power to liberate slaves. It even displeased thousands of radical Republican-Unionists, who regarded it as too "wishy-washy," diluted in provisions and wordage in order to conciliate loyal slaveholders in the Union border states.

In fabulously vote-rich New York State, the Seward-Weed organization of Republican-Unionists had exerted efforts and pulled strings in backstage operations to have the conservative Major-General John A. Dix nominated for Governor; but the opposing radical faction of the party had succeeded in persuading the state convention to name Brigadier-General James S. Wadsworth as Republican-Union state standard-bearer. Too, Horace Greeley of the New York *Tribune* was making trouble.

In Pennsylvania, second only to the Empire State in voting power, the old feud between Governor Curtin and Simon Cameron still flared, although Cameron himself was still frozenly ensconsed in St. Petersburg as United States Minister. In Ohio, casting the third largest number of votes among the states, the "Copperheads," or "Peace" Democrats, sympathetic to the South, were demonstrating surprising strength, with Congressman Clement L. Vallandigham magnetically drawing war-weary crowds. In Indiana, the especially energetic Governor Oliver P. Morton, who publicly insisted that the war against secession must be made "instant and terrible," was encountering strong opposition from such peace-at-any-price societies as the Knights of the Golden Circle, the Order of American Knights, and the Sons of Liberty, who retarded Union enlistments, freed Confederate prisoners, and even tried to form a new and independent Northwestern confederacy.

In the President's own Illinois, Copperheads were powerfully active in the lower counties bordering on Kentucky and Missouri. And in Lincoln's home Springfield district his friend, Leonard Swett of Bloomington, was having an uphill, discouraging fight for Congress against John T. Stuart, Lincoln's first political mentor and law partner, now running as a Democrat.

When the votes were all counted, Lincoln learned with dismay that these five most populous states, all of which he had carried two years before, were sending Democratic-majority delegations to Congress. A sixth state, Wisconsin, which had gone for him in 1860, was evenly divided, with three Republican-Union and three Democratic congressmen. His friend, Swett, went down before Stuart, the Democrat, in the Sangamon-McLean County district, where Lincoln had lived for a quarter of a century.

It was only by the thinnest of margins that the President's party, in coalition with border-state conservative Unionists, retained control of the incoming Thirty-eighth Congress. For that unsubstantial margin of eighteen votes in the House of Representatives which Lincoln's supporters retained, the border-states were partly responsible. In the estimate of James G. Blaine, just elected to Congress from Maine: "But for the aid of the Border slave States the anti-slavery position of Mr. Lincoln might have been overthrown by a hostile House of Representatives."

In all-powerful New York, Wadsworth, the Republican-Union administration candidate for Governor, was whipped by his Democratic opponent, Horatio Seymour. And the new Empire State Governor was soon to torment Lincoln about conscription. New Jersey, too, elected a Democratic Governor, Joel Parker.

Lincoln, in analyzing the melancholy election results, saw several reasons for the public repudiation of his party. "We have lost the elections;" he wrote Carl Schurz, now a Brigadier-General stationed in Virginia. "I think I know what it is, but I may be mistaken. Three main causes told the whole story. 1. The democrats were left in a majority by our friends going to war. 2. The democrats observed this & determined to re-instate themselves in power, and 3. Our newspapers, by vilifying and disparaging the administration, furnished them all the weapons to do it with. Certainly the ill-success of the war had much to do with this."

In the following month of December, however, Lincoln added another contributing cause of Republican-Union defeat at the polls—his issuance of the preliminary Proclamation of Emancipation. He received a delegation of anti-slavery clergymen, who insisted that much stronger action must be taken for Negro liberation. They had argued some months earlier, that if he issued such an emancipation edict, the whole nation would rally around him. And he had issued it in September, when the election was raging. Now in December at the White House, they wanted Lincoln to go farther on abolition of slavery. He answered them briefly, referring to the lost election: "The proclamation was issued, and see what the result was in the elections, the opposing party gaining strength and carrying the majority against us. Instead of the proclamation having brought support to the administration, it has done the reverse."

III

Lincoln, even before those elections ended, was tormented by another cautious West Point-trained professional, Major-General Don Carlos Buell.

Buell commanded Union troops in eastern Kentucky and Tennessee, charged with quieting the troubled border region while U. S. Grant, farther west and south, groped down the Mississippi Valley toward Vicksburg. Buell, a friend of McClellan and soldier of considerable ability, had been having his own agonizing problems with politicians, not the least of which was his inability to work with the tempestuous and arrogantly tyrannical Governor Morton of Indiana. Since Buell had Indiana troops under his command, some of whom had been recruited and equipped by the State, the Governor tried to retain some control over them even after they had gone on active service outside of Indiana. Since Buell also commanded troops from Ohio and Illinois, he found himself involved in controversy with Governors David Tod and Richard Yates of those states. Cynics queried whether Buell and the Midwestern governors fought each other more vigorously than they combatted the Confederates.

Buell's troubles with the governors were abruptly interrupted in late September, as the mid-term 1862 elections raged, when Confederate armies, led by Generals Braxton Bragg and Edmund Kirby-Smith, slipped through the Federal cordons and marched through Kentucky toward the Ohio River, raising Midwestern temperatures to a fever pitch.

Buell, in order to protect Kentucky and his base of supplies at Louisville, found himself forced to leave Tennessee and march back to the Ohio River. His retrograde movement, coming after a previous perilously slow advance on Chattanooga and his failure to take that city, irritated both Lincoln and Secretary of War Stanton. To make matters worse for

Buell, Governor Morton was inundating the President with complaints. The Hoosier Chief Executive, detesting West Pointers, argued to the President that "the cold professional leader, whose heart is not in the cause," should be removed from army command, and the fight against the secession forces be put into "the hands of men who are greatly in earnest, and who are profoundly convinced of the justice of our cause." This politician's distrust of graduates from the government military academy was expressed also by Gustave Koerner to Senator Trumbull: "Most of the West Pointers are of very little account. Most of them are dissipated and tyrannical; and they hate everybody not of their caste."

General Buell was of the McClellan circle, a product of that damnable aristocratic war school on the Hudson. "Truly a West Point diploma can cover more sins than charity," growled one anti-slavery editor who convinced himself that officers of the regular army were all pro-Southern and therefore pro-slavery. Governor Yates of Illinois added his voice to that of Governor Morton that the President should break Buell.

Lincoln pondered the problem of Buell. Like McClellan, that Western commander organized and led troops superbly, but was afflicted, the President concluded, with "the slows." Buell stopped Bragg's Confederate invasion of Kentucky but, like McClellan only some weeks previous at Antietam, he had not pursued his foe. He had not caught Bragg or destroyed his army.

The President sent Buell an order, through Halleck, that his Federal forces must enter east Tennessee, center of anti-secession sentiment in a seceded state, before the end of autumn, while the roads were still passable. Expressing Lincoln's thoughts, the General-in-Chief on October 19 pointed out by telegraph to Buell about the anxious Chief Executive: "He does not understand why we can not march as the enemy marches, live as he lives, and fight as he fights, unless we admit the inferiority of our troops and our generals." That was the precise question which Lincoln had asked McClellan about the Eastern front: Why can we not do what the foe does?

But Buell, a professional soldier and careful planner to the core, insisted on preparing his army before he engaged the Confederates. Lincoln concluded, however, that he and the Union cause could not afford to wait until Buell considered himself ready. On October 23, 1862, only two weeks before election day, orders were prepared at the War Department, relieving Buell of command of the Department of the Ohio, whose organization and fighting and fire power he had worked for so many months to develop.

Buell's command, involving also the Department of the Cumberland, was turned over to Major-General William S. Rosecrans—"Old Rosy," as his troops dubbed him.

Within a month the broken Buell asked the Secretary of War, Stanton, for a court of inquiry to determine the truth of charges that he had been inefficient. Stanton and his radical supporters feared that Buell was out to undermine his successor, Rosecrans, and have himself restored to command and that he wanted a public hearing in order to publicize himself before the nation. They were determined to block Buell in these plans. Stanton refused the deposed General's request for a court of inquiry but granted a "military commission," which turned out to be a court-martial under another name. There were no official, only implied charges, against Buell; but there was a prosecutor, Donn Piatt. By the questions he asked, the witnesses he introduced, and his final report, Piatt managed to reduce Buell's record and prestige effectively and even cast doubts on his loyalty.

Thus did Buell, then second only to McClellan in the number of Federal troops he led in the field, end his Civil War military service.

IV

"The heaviest load which the friends of the Government have been compelled to carry through the [election] canvass has been the inactivity and inefficiency of this Administration," noted the normally pro-Lincoln New York *Times* on the day when men voted and shortly before Buell was removed. The *Times* added: "The fate of the nation must no longer be committed to Generals who, like Essex in the English Revolution, 'next to a great defeat, *dread a great victory.*'"

That was the editorial voice of the President's most important New York City journalistic supporter, Henry J. Raymond, speaking, with implied demands that McClellan, too, be removed. And three days later Lincoln had deposed McClellan.

The President several weeks later informed Carl Schurz by letter: "I certainly have been dissatisfied with the slowness of Buell and McClellan."

During that same season when he removed both Buell and McClellan, Lincoln changed commanders in another vital theatre of warfare, the Department of the Gulf, where New Orleans citizens nurtured homicidal tendencies toward the Federal commander, Major-General Benjamin F. Butler, whom they dubbed "Beast" Butler.

Efficient to the point of semi-sadism in his military administration of captured New Orleans, General Butler, a former Democratic politician in Massachusetts, destined to turn into one of America's most successful rabble-rousing demagogues and radical politician *par excellence,* had fought bravely enough, but his oppressive rule and the corruptions of his brother irritated Crescent City citizens to high emotion. Sensational was his "Order No. 28," inspired by the Southern ladies' unpleasant attitude toward the occupying Federal troops, an order which decreed: "When any female shall, by word, or gesture, or movement, insult or show contempt for any officer or soldier of the United States, she shall be regarded as a woman of the town plying her vocation." A storm of indignation fell on Butler and also on Lincoln's Administration for keeping such a character in responsible command. Suspicion of Butler's honesty was heard all over Louisiana. Presumably he stole silver spoons from the house he occupied, so Southerners to this day insist, and he was then given another derisive sobriquet besides "Beast"—"Spoons" Butler. The General also quarreled with foreign consuls, embarrassing Secretary Seward's conduct of diplomatic affairs. He had one man summarily shot for allegedly insulting the United States flag. Of major significance, Butler was proving too radically anti-slavery for such a sensitive Southern city as New Orleans.

Lincoln had no intention of permitting the military Department of the Gulf, headed by General Butler, to be turned into a laboratory for anti-slavery extremism or a recruiting ground for a slave army, as was planned by Butler. The President was determined to reconstruct Federal-occupied portions of Louisiana by executive action and along his own moderate lines of restoration of the Southern states to the Union. There was no room for a General who would use his military power to tear apart the social system of a secession area which Lincoln was attempting to take back into the family of American states. In December, 1862, the President removed Butler from command of the Gulf Department, replacing him with the more moderate Major-General Nathaniel P. Banks, another politician-warrior from Massachusetts. Banks had been Speaker of Congress and Governor of the Bay State.

The radical Republicans in Congress, with the Committee on the Conduct of the War still their spearhead, at first thought that Lincoln had removed Butler, one of their favorite generals and a strong anti-slaveryite and South-hater, in order to give him a more important post. The General arrived at Washington, held a conference with the President, and rumors soon floated that he would even replace Stanton as Secretary of War, a rumor most painful to Stanton. Lincoln confided to Secretary of the Navy Welles that he had Butler in mind for a command in the Shenandoah Valley.

Lincoln's removal of Butler from the Gulf leadership further infuriated the radicals in and out of Congress. They talked about using their influence with the Chief Executive to give Butler a new major command. Within two months they had him testify before the Committee on the Conduct of the War in a session that suggested deep mutual admiration for each other.

Finally the President gave Butler a command in eastern Virginia and North Carolina.

V

Lincoln in early November appointed Major-General Ambrose E. Burnside, perhaps remembered best today as the man after whom his brand of side whiskers were named, as McClellan's successor as commander of the Army of the Potomac.

To the President his decision to make Burnside head of the greatest Federal military force seemed a logical move at the time. Burnside had a good record and came highly recommended. West Point graduate, pre-war veteran commanding officer on the frontier, inventor of a breech-loading rifle, former commanding Major-General of the Rhode Island state militia, then treasurer of the Illinois Central Railroad, Burnside as Colonel had led the First Rhode Island Regiment into Washington to defend the capital shortly after Lincoln's call for troops following Fort Sumter's fall. Burnside had fought bravely at First Bull Run, conducted successful Federal operations against the Confederates on the North Carolina coast, and had commanded McClellan's right wing at Antietam.

Not long after he had chosen Burnside to succeed McClellan, however, Lincoln felt doubts, a certain misgiving. Only two weeks later, on November 24, in a letter to Carl Schurz, he referred to his removal of both Buell and McClellan, adding: "Before I relieved them I had great fears I should not find successors to them, who would do better; and I am sorry to add, that I have seen little since to relieve these fears. I do not clearly see the prospect of any more rapid movements."

Buell's successor in the West, Rosecrans, with his Army of the Cumberland, comprising three corps, had advanced to Nashville, only to remain there a month accumulating supplies against probable enemy interruption of his communications and transport system. Now Lincoln feared that Burnside, in the East, was dawdling as much as Rosecrans in the West.

Lincoln's appointment of Burnside did not elate the Army of the Potomac officers and men, nor did it make Burnside himself supremely happy.

Major-General Oliver O. Howard, the commander of the Army of the Potomac's Second Corps, who had differed with McClellan on occasions, grew worried about the President's action in changing commanders. In a letter of November 8 to his brother, Howard expressed the melancholy feeling of his fellow-officers and soldiers:

> Gen. McClellan was relieved to-day & ordered to Trenton, N.J. We are frightened. Here we are in the midst of a rapid march—the enemy on one side of the Blue Ridge and we [on] the other; running for 'gaps' & positions. Burnside feels dreadfully—without a staff—and without sufficient statistical & topographical knowledge to be put over an army that he hardly

could have commanded under the best of circumstances, all this creates uneasiness. I should feel safer with McClellan to finish what he had planned & was executing so well. I now feel sorry for McClellan. I feel we haven't a better man.

When McClellan turned over the mighty Army of the Potomac command to Burnside, General Howard wrote to his wife: "This morning we turned out our troops and drew them up along the road to give a parting salute to Gen'l McClellan. He rode along and the tattered colors were lowered, and the drums beat, and men cheered him. Gen. Burnside rode up by his side. . . . After visiting McClellan I went to pay my respects to Gen'l Burnside. He looked very tired as he undoubtedly was. He had concluded to take command but did not regard it as a fit subject for congratulation."

VI

Burnside, despite his reluctance to assume command, went ahead with his preparations for an attack on Lee's Army of Northern Virginia. To those who saw him at this time, he looked apprehensive. But he conscientiously worked out his plans for a crushing blow against the Confederate hosts.

By the end of November (1862) Burnside finally got his army on the march toward Richmond. He reached the Rappahannock River. Across it lay the town of Fredericksburg, Virginia. This was the time to strike the decisive blow which Lincoln and nearly the whole North were demanding. His success was dependent upon his ability to get his men and supplies across the river and on to Richmond before the Confederate army, part of it in the Shenandoah Valley and part east of the Blue Ridge, could shift east to stop him. This called for break-neck speed in moving a massive army.

Burnside started promptly enough, marching down the north side of the Rappahannock to Falmouth, reaching there on November 19. But he decided not to cross that river to take Fredericksburg until he had brought up pontoon bridges to establish a secure connection between his troops who would soon be on both sides of the river.

The Army of the Potomac commander expected to find such pontoon bridges waiting for him at Falmouth. He had told General-in-Chief Halleck that he would require them, and Halleck had issued orders to send huge numbers of them to Falmouth. But they were not there when Burnside and his men arrived, and they would not be delivered until eight days later!

This delay provided General Lee with sufficient time in which to move his main army to Fredericksburg—ready to welcome Burnside from behind formidable elevated and entrenched positions. Something had been snarled in the Union supply system and chain of command. Too, there must be considered the strategy of Lee and his lieutenants, who by mid-November interpreted certain Federal troop movements to indicate that Burnside was marching toward Fredericksburg.

Perhaps Burnside's biggest blunder was that he missed a chance to strike "Stonewall" Jackson and James Longstreet, Lee's corps commanders, separately with the advantage of position but went on to Fredericksburg, where he found himself confronted with united Confederate forces. Numberless complex strategic and tactical factors figured in what followed, the details of which are still debated spiritedly by present-day armchair strategists.

So great was Burnside's disadvantage of position at Fredericksburg that his superiority of numbers over his secession foes was neutralized. The Southern commanders had established part of their forces in an almost impregnable position on Marye's Heights west of the city, while the brigade of General T. R. R. Cobb, together with some of Brigadier-General Joseph B. Kershaw's South Carolina brigade and General John R. Cooke's North Carolinians, maintained an unassailable defense behind a stone wall in the "sunken road" at the base of the hill.

Part of the fearful Fredericksburg fracas resolved itself into forlorn, desperate Union charges, which proved to be self-inflicted murder. The bewildered, bewhiskered Burnside stubbornly threw in fresh troops, who were mowed down by withering Confederate artillery and infantry fire. Still another gruesome part of the Fredericksburg slaughter occurred on the Confederate right, where futile Federal attacks were launched against "Stonewall" Jackson's strongly entrenched columns in an effort to turn that side of Lee's line. Southern batteries rained incessant shells on charging blue-uniformed men, leaving piles of dead and wounded.

In Washington, President Lincoln sent for Henry Villard, war correspondent for the New York *Tribune,* who had witnessed that spine-chilling charge against Marye's Heights, the Falmouth mud still on his campaign clothes. "We are very anxious and have heard very little," Lincoln told Villard. The *Tribune* correspondent informed him of the worst, sparing nothing. The President questioned him for half an hour. Every general officer to whom he had spoken, Villard revealed, held that the Army of the Potomac must be withdrawn; but Burnside, up to that previous night, had no intention of calling for a retreat. The President should order the withdrawal, the officers under Burnside believed fervently. Lincoln looked at Villard and sadly answered: "I hope it is not as bad as all that."

But Villard had not overstated the seriousness of this by far the worst Federal defeat of the war up to that time.

VII

General Burnside at last had his army on his own side of the Rappahannock.

For a time Burnside nurtured a wild notion of making another monster assault on the stone wall behind which the Confederates entrenched themselves. He planned to lead his own Ninth Corps, which was said to love him still, on that advance; but his subordinate commanders persuaded him that such a charge could not possibly succeed. Perhaps Burnside inwardly felt the same way about the futility of another major charge just then. Major-General Darius N. Couch, commanding the Second Corps under Burnside, talking to him that melancholy evening, "could see that he wished his body was also lying in front of Marye's Heights." The whole project might have been an unreasoned groping by Burnside for a dramatic and honorable exit from the gross military debacle that he had led.

The Federal casualties at Fredericksburg, when counted, were appallingly high. Over 12,000 were killed, wounded, or missing out of the entire force of 114,000. More than 1,200 were dead and almost 10,000 maimed, and some disappeared or deserted. Lee lost 5,300 of his army of 72,000, of whom 600 were killed.

Grief and gloom engulfed the North and loyal border regions, followed by anger and then the customary search for a scapegoat on whom to lay the responsibility for the slaughter.

Incompetent leadership, both military and political, was freely blamed for the Fredericksburg disaster. Some victims were needed as atonement, and they were quickly found by opposition politicians and carpingly critical editors. Burnside came in for his abuse and invective. But it was agreed in so many circles and by numberless thousands of private citizens, from Maine to Missouri, that Lincoln, Stanton, and Halleck were the satanic triumvirate who "sent to death thousands on thousands of our brothers and friends"; the flower of Northern manhood sent tumbling over the Rappahannock into the furnace of Fredericksburg. Confidence in Lincoln's administration was shaken to its very foundations.

It seemed scant wonder that the President sank into melancholic gloom for days following Fredericksburg.

A few days after that ever haunting battle on the Rappahannock Lincoln was threatened with the wreck of his Cabinet.

VIII

The Fredericksburg defeat afforded opportunity for radical Republicans in Congress to present the President with their latest demand: Seward must go!

Lincoln's able Secretary of State and loyal supporter, once a vigilant struggler against slavery in and out of the United States Senate in pre-war years, had grown more conservative since joining the Cabinet and confronting the realities of war. Seward was now muffling anti-slavery agitation, like Lincoln considering Union salvation the exclusive issue of the fight against the South. He lent a moderating influence against such radical Cabinet colleagues as Secretary of the Treasury Chase.

The newly conservative Seward infuriated radicals in and out of Congress. "Seward must be got out of the Cabinet," insisted the Chicago *Tribune's* editor, Joseph Medill, to Congressman Schuyler Colfax of Indiana. "He has been *President de facto,* and has kept a sponge saturated with chloroform to Uncle Abe's nose all the while." The President must also oust other conservatives from his Cabinet, insisted Medill: "Smith is a cipher on the right hand of the Seward integer—by himself nothing but a doughface [a pro-Southerner]. Bates is a fossil of the Silurian era—red sandstone at least. Seward, Smith, and Bates must go out!"

Radicals in and out of Congress had been ceaselessly endeavoring to persuade the President to reorganize his Cabinet with a view to increasing Secretary Chase's power and downgrading Seward. Lincoln's old friend, the conservative Senator Orville H. Browning of Illinois, told his diary: "Chase was at the bottom of all mischief, and was setting the radicals on to assail Seward."

The radical Republicans on December 16 and 17 held caucuses and mapped strategy against Seward, deciding to call upon the President and persuade him to "reorganize" his Cabinet.

Thus did senators of the Chief Executive's own political party, immediately following Fredericksburg, in a week of dire national peril and gloom, promote factional attacks on him and the head of his Cabinet.

Seward, hearing of the Republican Senators' caucuses, submitted his resignation as Secretary of State, along with that of his son, Assistant Secretary of State Frederick W. Seward, and prepared to leave Washington. Lincoln saw the Senators' anti-Seward move as aimed at him, and he confided to Senator Browning: "They wish to get rid of me, and I am sometimes half disposed to gratify them." Browning replied that, while some senators wanted to see Lincoln go, the nation's fortunes were bound up with the President's fate. Lincoln then told Browning: "We are now on the brink of destruction. I can hardly see a ray of hope. The Committee [of Senators] is to be up to see me at 7 o'clock. Since I heard last night of the proceedings of the caucus I have been more distressed than by any event in my life."

Lincoln met the delegation of nine senators, including Wade of Ohio, on Thursday evening, December 18. They stated their demands and presented their case against Seward. Lincoln listened to the Senators cordially. But he gave them no hoped-for galvanizing of resolve. Instead, he invited the Senators to call again the next morning. He needed more time.

That day Lincoln sank into the most depressed mood into which he had fallen since assuming the presidential office. The Cabinet crisis had come on the very heels of the bad news from Fredericksburg. "Lincoln said yesterday," wrote Sam Wilkeson, of the New York *Tribune* Washington staff, to his managing editor, "that if there was any worse Hell than he had been in for two days, he would like to know it. He is awfully shaken."

On Friday morning, December 19, shortly before he was to meet the complaining senators for a second session, the President held a momentous Cabinet meeting. All were present except Seward. Lincoln informed the surprised members that Seward and his son had tendered their resignations, and he requestd secrecy on that startling development. He told them that the Senators had demanded the removal of no other Cabinet member except Seward, whom they had charged "with indifference, with want of sympathy with the country in this great struggle" and desire to secure "control of the President and measures of administration." Lincoln told the Senators that their demand for Seward's ouster "shocked and grieved" him. He suggested that the Cabinet join him in the conference with the senators that evening. Tactfully Lincoln, by inference, gave his Cabinet members their directions: co-operation with him and agreement among themselves.

Thus when the senatorial committee again visited the President that evening, they found themselves confronted by a presumably united Cabinet. Chase, the Senators' favorite among them, was even in the unique position of feigning harmony with his colleagues. When the President questioned the Senators, only four spoke up in favor of Seward's removal.

The following day rumors were rife in Washington that the entire Cabinet had resigned. But it was largely wishful thinking. When Chase reluctantly handed in his resignation, Lincoln accepted it. "This cuts the Gordian knot. I can dispose of this subject without difficulty. I see my way clear."

Lincoln's next move, on December 20, was to address to both his resigned Cabinet members, the conservative Seward and the radical Chase, identical notes, in which he asked each to remain in his Cabinet. His note ended: "After most anxious consideration, my deliberate judgment is, that the public interest does not admit of it. I therefore have to request that you resume the duties of your Departments respectively."

Seward and Chase reconsidered their resignations, and remained at their posts. And so Lincoln weathered that Cabinet crisis of the depressing December of 1862, while the entire North and loyal border regions were angrily clamoring against him because of Fredericksburg.

IX

Lincoln at this time was faced with another Cabinet problem, although a minor one: Secretary of the Interior Caleb B. Smith.

While grim news from Fredericksburg was still shocking and angering the North, and as radical Republicans had just failed to persuade the President to drop Seward, Lincoln was mulling over the idea of dispensing with the services of his corrupt Secretary of the Interior.

An old Indiana Whig wheelhorse with whom Lincoln had served in Congress, Caleb Smith had headed the Hoosier delegation at the Republican National Convention which had nominated Lincoln for President. His labors in steering the Indiana delegates into Lincoln's column there had been decisive, and on reliable evidence Judge David Davis had assured Smith that he would go into the Cabinet if Lincoln were nominated and elected President. Lincoln, after hesitation, had finally selected Smith in preference to Colfax of Indiana and Judd of Illinois as the Northwestern member of his inner council. He had written the disappointed younger Colfax soothingly: "With Smith, it is now or never."

But Smith had not excelled as an administrator of the vast Interior Department. Too, he had been involved in shady deals for promoting private colonization schemes for Negroes in tropical America. Mrs. Lincoln, on December 14, told Senator Browning how "the President was anxious to get Secretary Smith out of the Cabinet." The First Lady, who always liked Browning, assured him that the President would like to put him, Browning, in Smith's place.

Smith, for his own part, felt dreadfully unhappy handling the Interior Department details, with its work stretching out to the wild Indian lands, all the way to Washington Territory. Essentially a spellbinding party orator and jobbing politician, always indolent and now actually in poor health, Smith had little taste for his Cabinet job. He hoped that Lincoln would elevate him to the United States Supreme Court, since geographically he was eligible, he thought.

Secretary Smith inspired his friends in Congress to work for a law that would so "gerrymander" the federal judicial circuits so as to make him eligible for the nation's highest tribunal (United States Supreme Court justices also sat on circuit) without interfering with the ambitions of Senator Browning of Illinois, who also wanted Lincoln to appoint him to that most elevated of American benches.

Lincoln, meanwhile, was being subjected to pressure to make Judge David Davis, his long time friend of the old Eighth Judicial Circuit of Illinois, a Justice of the United States Supreme Court. Davis had performed effective work in having Lincoln nominated for President, along with Norman B. Judd, whom Lincoln had appointed Minister to Prussia. Davis's friends did not permit the President to forget how greatly indebted he was to Davis. A Bloomington, Illinois, friend of Davis reminded Lincoln's friend, Ward H. Lamon, about Davis: "He was so instrumental in giving position to him who now holds the matter in the hollow of his hand. If justice and gratitude are to be respected, Lincoln can do nothing less than to tender the position to Judge Davis. I want you to suggest it to Lincoln." In the summer just passed, Hawkins Taylor, who had been an Iowa delegate to the convention that nominated Lincoln, had bluntly written the President: "With every opportunity for knowing, that but for the *extraordinary* effort of Judge Davis, you would not have received the nomination at the Chicago Convention. . . . I feel that it is due to yourself as well as to Judge Davis that you should tender him the appointment of Supreme [Court] Judge."

No one worked harder to line up party support for Davis than did his staunch friend and fellow-townsman of Bloomington, Leonard Swett. In Washington, Swett saw Lincoln about the matter, and Lincoln requested that recommendations in favor of Davis should be forwarded to him.

Lincoln had already, during 1862, made two Supreme Court appointments: Noah Swayne of Ohio and Samuel F. Miller of Iowa. Now, who should be chosen for this third vacancy? Secretary of the Interior Smith was out of the running, since the appointment must go to one of the federal Eighth Circuit, comprising Michigan, Wisconsin, and Illinois—and Smith was of Indiana. The choice narrowed down to one of two from Illinois, Judge Davis or Senator Browning.

In recent months Lincoln and Browning, fast friends in Illinois, had drifted apart. As Lincoln moved in the direction of emancipation, their personal and political relationship cooled. This Senator from the President's own State had opposed the Second Confiscation Act in the Senate during July, and made no secret of the fact that he regarded Lincoln's Proclamation of Emancipation in September as a calamity. Browning's backward attitude in the elections of 1862 was partly responsible for the election of a Democratic-controlled Legislature in Illinois.

When Lincoln sent his nomination for Associate Justice of the United States Supreme Court to the Senate on December 1, 1862, it was not the name of Orville H. Browning—but David Davis.

But what of Secretary of the Interior Smith? Lincoln made him a federal District Judge for Indiana. He lived for one year more.

As Smith's successor to head the Interior Department Lincoln chose another Hoosier, John P. Usher of Terre Haute, then Assistant Secretary of the Interior under Smith. Usher had once known Lincoln as a circuit-riding lawyer near the Indiana-Illinois state line.

X

As the year, 1862, closed, the President's face betrayed his inner feelings to those who saw and talked with him. Joshua F. Speed, on a Washington visit, following Fredericksburg and the Cabinet crisis over Seward, alarmingly commented on how "haggard and care worn" Lincoln looked. On Christmas Day, one citizen who saw Lincoln described him in a note to Congressman Washburne of Illinois as "perplexed to death nearly."

FALLING FORTUNES

25

I

LINCOLN, as the new year, 1863, opened, was confronted with the dilemma of the beaten General Burnside. Of greater gravity, but another aspect of the same problem, was what and when should be the next movement of the Army of the Potomac following its Fredericksburg failure?

The President received Burnside on New Year's morning. He told the General that some officers under him, whose names he would not divulge, had told him that Burnside's new proposed move over the Rappahannock River would end in another disaster and that none of the subordinate commanders had any faith in its probable success. Burnside, feeling the nightmarish strain of his defeat and painfully aware of the lack of confidence in him felt by most of his officers, explained his plan to Lincoln. He wanted merely to cross the river at some point below Fredericksburg. Lincoln expressed misgivings about this strategy and sent for Secretary Stanton and General-in-Chief Halleck.

So the President, Burnside, Stanton, and Halleck discussed Burnside's new plans. Halleck revealed himself to be of scant help. Lincoln wanted the General-in-Chief, "Old Brains" himself, to examine the places where Burnside contemplated crossing the river and then to give his opinion as to whether he approved or disapproved of Burnside's plan. Lincoln, impatient, sent sharp words to Halleck:

"Gen. Burnside wishes to cross the Rappahannock with his army but his Grand Division commanders all oppose the movement. If in such a difficulty as this you do not help, you fail me precisely in the point for which I sought your assistance. You know what Gen. Burnside's plan is; and it is my wish that you go with him to the ground, examine it as far as practicable, confer with the officers, getting their judgment, and ascertaining their temper, in a word, gather all the elements for forming a judgment of your own; and then tell Gen. Burnside that you *do* approve, or that you do *not* approve his plan. Your military skill is useless to me, if you will not do this."

Lincoln, however, reconsidered these irritating words to Halleck on New Year's Day. On the back of his letter he jotted down the words: "Withdrawn, because considered harsh by Gen. Halleck."

On that same afternoon the President received callers at his New Year's reception. His countenance betrayed his concern to those who saw him. "As I watched his face," related Noah Brooks, "I could see that he often looked over the heads of the multitudinous strangers who shook his hand with fervor and affection. 'His eyes were with his thoughts'—and they were far away on the bloody field of Fredericksburg, or with the defeated and worn Burnside, with whom he had that very day had a long and most depressing interview."

II

The next few days were devoted to more agonizing conferences between Lincoln, Burnside, Stanton, and Halleck. But no decision was reached as to what Burnside should try next.

Burnside fluttered between a desire to rid himself of the Army of the Potomac command responsibility (which he had really never wanted) and an ambition to recoup his completely deflated post-Fredericksburg reputation by striking at the enemy again. On January 5 he decided to quit and sent the President his resignation as Major-General of Volunteers. In that letter he sorrowfully informed Lincoln: "Since my return to the Army I have become more than ever convinced that the General Officers of this command are almost unanimously opposed to another crossing of the river; but I am still of the opinion that the crossing should be attempted, & I have accordingly issued orders to the Engineers and Artillery to prepare for it."

Lincoln declined to accept Burnside's resignation. He replied: "I deplore the want of concurrence with you, in opinion of your general officers, but I do not see the remedy. Be cautious, and do not understand that the government, or country, is driving you. I do not see how I could profit by changing the command of the A.P. [Army of the Potomac] & if I did, I should not wish to do it by accepting the resignation of your commission." And so the Chief Executive approved another attempt by Burnside to cross the Rappahannock River.

Burnside's new effort resulted in nothing more than a wretched "mud march" which began January 21, the best of Burnside's units foundering in floods of rain and seas of sticky clay without progressing far in its chase after Lee.

With Burnside bogged down and unable to go much farther, Lincoln concluded that a change of commanders was now imperative.

In the West three competent field generals, Ullyses S. Grant, William T. Sherman, and George H. Thomas, were beginning to demonstrate ability to take the measure of Confederates. But each of them lacked General-in-Chief Halleck's favor. The previous year Halleck had clashed temperamentally with Grant and had a difference of opinion on tactics in the West. Grant, too, was under a cloud because of rumors of his excessive heavy drinking and spotty pre-war record. Sherman had not outlived an early accusation of being "insane." Thomas, a native Virginian, would wait for numerous months longer for the opportunity to demonstrate his undiluted loyalty to the Union and his military ability at Chickamauga.

Thus early in 1863 Lincoln did not look westward for a new Army of the Potomac commander to succeed Burnside. He decided instead on Major-General Joseph Hooker, affectionately known as "Fighting Joe."

III

Joseph Hooker, Massachusetts-born and West Point educated, had served against the Indians in Florida, along the Canadian border, and in the Mexican War, going through part of General Zachary Taylor's campaigns against Santa Anna and through General Scott's advance on Mexico City. Then he had farmed in California, where he also served in the State Militia. On the outbreak of war in 1861 he had come East and aided in the defenses of Washington and was chosen Brigadier-General of Volunteers. At Williamsburg in May, 1862, in McClellan's Peninsular Campaign, Hooker's division bore the brunt of the fighting.

Facing rain and bullets, he inspired his men and directed his artillery fire even after he had fallen in the mud with his dying horse. His courageous conduct at Williamsburg earned him a Major-Generalship of Volunteers and the nickname, "Fighting Joe." His further engagements at Fair Oaks, Williamsburg Road, Glendale, Malvern Hill, Bristoe Station, and Second Bull Run were strongly flavored with his daring. He commanded McClellan's First Corps against Lee in Maryland and distinguished himself at South Mountain. Then he was wounded at Antietam and was elevated to Brigadier-General in the regular Army.

Hooker fought at Fredericksburg under Burnside, and was outspoken against his superior's strategy in that appalling defeat. Burnside tried to have Hooker relieved of his command, the name "Hooker" standing at the very top of the list of men whom the bewhiskered Army of the Potomac head insisted must go.

Hooker's personality and appearance exuded confidence. His physical attractiveness lent prestige. His frank, affable manners made him popular. Too, he always fought dauntlessly under the heaviest enemy fire. But Lincoln had a certain misgiving about him, although he had been impressed by Hooker's record. Hooker had talked blatantly to reporters about the new military regime that would prevail if he himself were chosen to replace Burnside. He had co-operated with anti-Lincoln senators at Washington. To a New York *Times* war correspondent Hooker had denounced Burnside as "incompetent," which seemed true enough, and had referred to Lincoln as a "played out imbecile," and suggested that a dictator for the nation might be desirable.

Lincoln, in his celebrated and remarkable letter to Hooker of January 26, 1863, appointing him Burnside's successor, revealed some uneasiness about the brave, rash, and loose-talking General. The President sent these words of admonishment and friendly advice to him:

> I have placed you at the head of the Army of the Potomac. Of course I have done this upon what appear to me to be sufficient reasons. And yet I think it best for you to know that there are some things in regard to which, I am not quite satisfied with you. I believe you to be a brave and skilful soldier, which, of course, I like. I also believe you do not mix politics with your profession, in which you are right. You have confidence in yourself, which is a valuable, if not an indispensable quality. You are ambitious, which, within reasonable bounds, does good rather than harm. But I think that during Gen. Burnside's command of the Army, you have taken counsel of your ambition, and thwarted him as much as you could, in which you did a great wrong to the country, and to a meritorious and honorable brother officer.
>
> I have heard, in such a way as to believe it, of your recently saying that both the Army and the Government needed a Dictator. Of course it was not *for* this, but in spite of it, that I have given you the command. Only those generals who gain success, can set up dictators. What I now ask of you is military success, and I will risk the dictatorship.

Lincoln ended this letter to Hooker: "And now, beware of rashness. Beware of rashness, but with energy, and sleepless vigilance, go forward, and give us victories."

IV

Lincoln, while pondering the Army of the Potomac's fate, all of the while anxiously watched, through War Department telegrams, personal correspondence and conversations with returning officers, developments on the Western front. How was General Rosecrans, leading the Army of the Cumberland, progressing in Tennessee?

At the turn of the year, 1862-63, Rosecrans's army clashed in bloody combat with General Braxton Bragg's battalions at Murfreesboro (Stone's River) in Tennessee. On January 2 Bragg resumed his attack, tried to hit Rosecrans's left. The ground proved unfavorable and the Federal artillery caught Bragg's charging gray-garbed brigades in flank and broke them apart, crushing the Southerners' assault almost before it got started. Bragg had had enough. At night he ordered a retreat, drawing his army miles to the rear and leaving Rosecrans in possession of the field.

Rosecrans overestimated the magnitude of his victory. He telegraphed Halleck: "We have fought one of the greatest battles of the war, and are victorious." Lincoln, delighted, by wire on January 5 congratulated the Army of the Cumberland commander: "Your despatch announcing retreat of enemy has just reached here. God bless you, and all with you. Please tender to all, and accept for yourself, the Nation's gratitude for yours, and their, skill, endurance, and dantless (sic) courage."

Rosecrans was soon complaining about lack of adequate support from Washington. Secretary Stanton had assured him after the Stone's River victory: "Anything you and your command want you can have." Now the General, in mid-March, wrote Lincoln, protesting that his request for paymasters to serve with his troops in the field had not been granted; that his plea that his own commission as Major-General be dated from December, 1861, had not been heeded; that a hopeless drunkard had been chosen his chief paymaster. Those were among Rosecrans's gripes.

Lincoln replied to Rosecrans. He tactfully smoothed over the matter of paymasters. As to Rosecrans's request that his army commission as Major-General be pre-dated, the President answered sharply:

> Now, as to your request that your Commission should date from December 1861. Of course you expected to *gain* something by this; but you should remember that precisely so much as you should gain by it others would lose by it. If the thing you sought had been exclusively ours, we would have given it cheerfully; but being the right of other men, we having a merely

> arbitrary power over it, the taking it from them and giving it to you, became a more delicate matter, and more deserving of consideration. Truth to speak, I do not appreciate this matter of rank on paper, as you officers do. The world will not forget that you fought the battle of 'Stone River' and it will never care a fig whether you rank Gen. Grant on paper, or he so, ranks you. And now be assured, you wrong both yourself and us, when you even suspect there is not the best disposition on the part of us all here to oblige you.

By April, Rosecrans had another irritation to air before the President. He telegraphed Lincoln that, on three occasions, news had come to him that complaints were being sent to high Washington officials against his "army policy." "I want to know it," he asked the President, "& appeal to you to please order the complaints to be communicated to me fully. If the Fox is unearthed I will promise to skin him or pay for his hide." Lincoln replied to Rosecrans: "I really *can not* say that I have heard of any complaints of you."

All of these weeks of early 1863 Lincoln wanted military action from Rosecrans, insisting that he go after Bragg. The Confederate commander, following his repulse at Stone's River at the start of the year, had withdrawn his army to the Shelbyville-Tullahoma region, south of Murfreesboro. But during all those weeks, running into months, Rosecrans had determined that he would not go after Bragg until his army had plenty of rest and further preparations were completed. Like McClellan in the East and his own predecessor, Buell, before him, "Old Rosy" concluded that it was vastly easier for political chiefs and desk generals at Washington to order an advance, than it was for a field commander to whip his men into fighting condition, accumulate arms and supplies, and perfect a communications system.

May, 1863, ended with the armies of Rosecrans and Bragg facing each other, engaging only in occasional minor skirmishes in Tennessee—five months after Stone's River.

V

Lincoln found irritations among other Western commanders, some of whom hated each other nearly as deeply as they detested the Confederates. There was that gross nuisance, Major-General John A. McClernand, a powerful Democratic politician from Lincoln's own Illinois, a former lieutenant of the late Stephen A. Douglas. McClernand was carrying on a long feud with General-in-Chief Halleck by long distance and a controversy with General Grant along the Mississippi.

The year, 1863, was only seven days old when General McClernand, from his command along the Mississippi, sent Lincoln a letter of major complaint about Halleck because Halleck had replaced him with Grant. McClernand also resurrected some old chestnuts from the previous year: "I charge him [Halleck] with incompetency on many grounds. . . .Without ever having fought a battle, he curtailed the success of our arms at Fort Henry. Before Corinth . . . he permitted the enemy to escape. . . . Since he assumed the functions of General-in-Chief, scarcely anything but disaster has marked the experiences of our arms."

Lincoln, if for no other reason than the fact that McClernand led the "War" Democrats of Illinois, found himself smoothing McClernand's feelings, at the same time retaining Halleck as his General-in-Chief. The President on January 22 answered McClernand:

> I have too many *family* controversies, (so to speak) already on my hands, to voluntarily, or so long as I can avoid it, take up another. You are now doing well—well for the country, and well for yourself—much better than you could possibly be, if engaged in open war with Gen. Halleck. Allow me to beg, that for your sake, for my sake, & for the country's sake, you give your whole attention to the better work.
>
> Your success upon the Arkansas, was both brilliant and valuable, and is fully appreciated by the country and government.

McClernand now turned his attention to feuding with Grant, who was near him, not in distant Washington.

Grant, late in 1862, had devised an assault on Vicksburg, Mississippi, the capture of which would give the Union army control, not only of the Mississippi River, but also the Confederates' main railroad in that region. In November he had, with 30,000 men, marched south from Memphis in his first effort to take Vicksburg. Sherman's force was to co-operate by moving down the Mississippi. Sherman was defeated. Grant's movement was halted when the Confederates cut his railroad line of communications and burned his supply depot at Holly Springs, Mississippi. Back again in Memphis, Grant began on January 20, 1863, the formation of the second expedition. In this latest movement, several projects were attempted, all of which contemplated the cutting of waterways—building of canals—for placing the troops by boats, south of Vicksburg, without encountering the Confederate river batteries. Mud, mosquitoes, and swamp fever plagued his soldiers.

By March Grant's engineers were still digging canals. Lincoln was growing impatient. On the 29th he visited Captain John A. Dahlgren, U.S.N., at the Navy Department and complained about the long delay in capturing Vicksburg. They were "doing nothing" down there, he told Dahlgren. After the President left, Dahlgren noted in his day-book: "He said the canal at Vicksburg was of no account, and wondered that a sensible man would do it."

VI

The Navy, too, suffered its worst reverse in April, 1863, bringing more political predicaments to Lincoln, since it found its way into Congress.

Captain Samuel F. DuPont, U.S.N., had distinguished himself by his command of the flotilla against Port Royal, South Carolina, late in 1861. Early the following year the President requested Congress: "I cordially recommend that Captain Samuel F. DuPont receive a vote of thanks for his services and gallantry, displayed in the capture of Forts Walker and Beauregard, commanding the entrance of Port Royal Harbor." Both houses passed such a resolution and Lincoln signed it. Then DuPont had led successful naval operations against the South Carolina, Georgia, and Florida coasts, and again Lincoln requested Congress to thank him formally, and both houses did so. The Chief Executive then elevated DuPont to Rear-Admiral's rank. It appeared that DuPont was on his way to a career as the war's outstanding Union naval hero.

Meanwhile, the success of the Federal *Monitor* over the Confederate *Merrimack* had focused attention on the possibilities of ironclad warships. The capture of Charleston, South Carolina, formidably defended by Confederate land batteries and Fort Sumter and other works, appeared feasible. A fleet of monitors was assembled under DuPont with the view of capturing the South Carolina metropolis. DuPont tested his monitors in an engagement with Fort McAllister and reported the ships deficient "in aggression or destructiveness as against forts," and believed that, in order to secure success in such operations, great bodies of supporting troops were also necessary. But DuPont and his officers were of opinion that Fort Sumter could be reduced.

On April 7, 1863, Rear-Admiral DuPont led his squadron against the defenses of Charleston. He had seven monitors, the ironclad *New Ironsides* (his flagship), and an armored gunboat. The battle lasted from afternoon until near dawn the next day. DuPont was repulsed. He signalled his ships to withdraw from action, intending to resume the attack the following morning. The armored gunboat was so badly damaged that she sank the next day. Five of the monitors were temporarily put out of action. His squadron fired 139 projectiles and was hit 411 times. Fifty of his men were lost. When in the evening DuPont learned from his captains the extent of the damage, he declined to renew the attack.

Lincoln on April 13 sent orders to Admiral DuPont to stand fast:

> Hold your position inside the bar near Charleston; or if you shall have to leave it, return to it, and hold it till further orders. Do not allow the enemy to erect new batteries or defences, on Morris Island. If he has begun it, drive him out. I do not, herein, order you to renew the general attack. That is to depend on your own discretion, or a further order.

Lincoln continued his concern over the attempted capture of Charleston. More particularly, there seemed a lack of co-operation between Admiral DuPont and Major-General David Hunter, commanding the Department of the South. On the 14th, Lincoln sent joint instructions to DuPont and Hunter:

> This is to clear up an apparent inconsistency between the recent order to continue operations before Charleston and the former one to move to another point in a certain contingency. No censure upon you, or either of you, is intended. We still hope that by cordial and judicious co-operation, you can take the batteries on Morris Island and Sullivan's Island, and Fort Sumpter (sic). But whether you can or not we wish the demonstration kept up for a time, for a collateral and very important object. We wish the attempt to be a real one, (though not a desperate one) if it affords any considerable chance of success. But if prossecuted (sic) as a *demonstration* only, this must not become public, or the whole effect will be lost. Once again before Charleston, do not leave until further orders from here. Of course this is not intended to force you to leave unduly exposed, Hilton Head, or other near points in your charge.
>
> Yours truly,
> A. Lincoln.
>
> P.S. Whoever receives this first, please send a copy to the other immediately.
>
> A.L.

Admiral DuPont, rendered super-sensitive by his failure and fancying that the President's order implied a censure, wrote Secretary of the Navy Welles not to hesitate to relieve him by an officer more able to execute the service in which he had not succeeded; the capture of Charleston.

Dupont's defeat cast more gloom over the Northern public and produced political repercussions for Lincoln. The Admiral continued an acrimonious correspondence with Secretary Welles. He believed that Welles and Assistant Secretary of the Navy Gustavus V. Fox (a brother-in-law of Lincoln's Postmaster General, Montgomery Blair) were trying to shift to him the blame for the Charleston defeat that should really go to the civilian Navy Department chiefs. And DuPont found a congressional ally in Blair's fierce foe for Maryland political supremacy, Congressman Henry Winter Davis of the Baltimore district. Soon Lincoln found himself faced with the worsening of the ever smouldering Davis-Blair feud within the Republican-Union Party of that neighboring border slave state.

Davis was more than eager to take up DuPont's quarrel with the administration, since Secretary Welles was an ally of his foe, Blair, in the Cabinet; and many suspected that the man who made decisions in the Navy Department was not Welles, but Fox, the Assistant Secretary, who was also Blair's brother-in-law! The whole situation was made more bitter since Davis was Chairman of the House Naval Affairs Committee. Later in the season matters came to a head on the floor of the House of Representatives when Davis, defending Admiral DuPont and assailing Fox, clashed with another Blair over the issue—Congressman Frank Blair of Missouri, brother-in-law of Fox and brother of Lincoln's Postmaster General.

VII

Lincoln had "Blair Trouble" not only in Maryland but also in another border slave state, Missouri. During that spring of 1863 he was tormented by the complex and ever boiling Missouri muddle, of which Frank Blair was a part.

As in Maryland, the Unionists were split into conservative and radical factions over Negro emancipation and federal patronage, among other vexations.

Missouri had been a political powder keg ever since General Fremont and Frank Blair had crossed swords in their power struggle there in 1861. This situation was made worse when Lincoln removed the Pathfinder from the Western command. It grew more impossible, too, because Missouri was a slave state, brewing the slavery-emancipation controversy between conservative gradual emancipationists and radical "immediate" emancipationists. Factional party feuds over power and federal patronage, controversy over the relative powers of civilian and military authorities, problems of martial law, and clashes between anti-slavery and old-line pro-slavery groups made Missouri a center of turbulence, chaos, and often violence. Continual written complaints about almost every fight, major and minor, poured in on Lincoln from that pivotal border State. "Tattle-tale" visitors from Missouri, too, were constantly calling at the White House.

Lincoln had originally parcelled out the State's share of federal patronage by consultation with his Attorney General, Edward Bates, and Frank Blair, his Postmaster General's brother, both conservatives from St. Louis. Soon Governor Hamilton R. Gamble, also a conservative and the brother-in-law of Attorney General Bates, was given strong voice in patronage matters by Lincoln. Soon after the President removed General Fremont from his command, the Missouri Unionists split down the middle on the mundane question of patronage and the moral issue of slavery emancipation. Governor Gamble and Frank Blair headed the conservatives, called "Claybanks," who favored gradual compensation of the Negro, whereas Blair's own cousin, B. Gratz Brown, editor of the St. Louis *Missouri Democrat,* led the radicals, the "Charcoals," who demanded immediate emancipation with no compensation to slave-owners.

Brown's radical newspaper had kept up a running editorial barrage against the conservatives, advising Lincoln that he should remove Blair's brother, the Postmaster General, from his Cabinet, and also accusing the President of appointing only "the pets and partisans of Governor Gamble."

By mid-May, 1863, the President was sending sharp messages to leaders of the "Charcoal," or radical faction, including Henry T. Blow, former Minister to Venezuela who had returned home to Missouri to be elected to Congress as a "Charcoal." To Congressman Blow and his associates Lincoln sent a message of rebuke: "It is very painful to me that you in Missouri can not, or will not, settle your factional quarrel among yourselves. I have been tormented with it beyond endurance for months, by both sides. Neither side pays the least respect to my appeals to your reason, I am now compelled to take hold of the case."

Lincoln "took hold" of that particular source of complaint by removing Major-General Samuel R. Curtis as commander of the Department of the Missouri, a favorite of Congressman Blow and other radical "Charcoals," because of that General's constant controversy with Governor Gamble. Lincoln in late May explained to Major-General John M. Schofield, whom he chose as Curtis's successor, why he removed General Curtis: "I did it because of a conviction in my mind that the Union men of Missouri, constituting, when united, a vast majority of the whole people, have entered into a pestilent factional quarrel among themselves, Gen. Curtis, perhaps not of choice, being the head of one faction, and Gov. Gamble that of the other. . . . As I could not remove Gov. Gamble, I had to remove Gen. Curtis."

The displaced General Curtis felt hurt about his removal but invited the President to use his services again. Lincoln, in reply, explained that his change of commanders had become "almost a matter of personal self-defence to somehow break up the state of things in Missouri." He assured General Curtis: "I did not mean to cast any censure upon you, nor to endorse any of the charges made against you by others. With me the presumption is still in your favor that you are honest, capable, faithful and patriotic."

Early the next year Lincoln made Curtis commander of the Department of Kansas.

VIII

Early in 1863, too, political troubles engulfed Lincoln from the opposition Democratic Party—more particularly, the pro-Southern faction whom Unionists contemptuously called "Copperheads."

The end of the first year and a half of the apparently futile bloody struggle against the South had inspired an anti-war movement, organized and unorganized, operating within the Democratic Party in both the Northwest and such teeming Eastern centers as New York City. The President's Republican-Unionists had lost the state and congressional elections in the Northwest, as well as New York State, in the autumn of 1862. His Proclamation of Emancipation, issued in September and taking effect on January 1, 1863, strengthened this anti-Lincoln, sometimes disloyal, faction in the Democratic Party. People in the lower regions of Illinois, in Iowa, in Indiana, and Ohio, as well as in the nation's metropolis, with its huge population of Irish, feared that freed Negroes would engulf their sections, crowding them out. Some even angrily viewed the war against the South as a Lincoln fight to bring equality between the races.

These peace-without-victory Democrats also received support from citizens who sincerely were apprehensive of a Lincoln dictatorship, with consequent ruin to their country, if the conflict with their fellow-Americans in the South were to continue. Thus the anti-Lincoln anti-war groups within the Democratic Party were motivated by various forces, ranging all the way from patriotic concern for preservation of American liberties, through strong sympathy for Southerners, down to hatred of Negroes and narrow partisan hostility to Lincoln and all things Republican. Loosely these opposition groups were castigated as "Copperheads," suggesting a snake which strikes without warning.

As 1863 opened Lincoln grew alarmed about Copperhead sentiment in the Northwest. He spoke to Senator Charles Sumner of Massachusetts about it in January. And Sumner confided about it to his friend, Professor Francis Lieber, in a letter: "These are dark hours. The President tells me that he now fears 'the fire in the rear'—meaning the Democracy especially at the Northwest—more than our military chances."

The Copperheads were suddenly dramatized in April, 1863, by the arbitrary action of Lincoln's commander of the Department of the Ohio—Major-General Burnside, the loser of the ill-fated Fredericksburg battle. That General gave the Copperheads a martyr in the person of the "lame duck" Congressman Clement L. Vallandigham of Ohio.

On April 13, the very day the worried Lincoln was advising Admiral DuPont about operations against Charleston, General Burnside, with headquarters at Cincinnati, issued General Order No 38. That military edict directed: "All persons found within our lines who commit acts for the benefit of the enemies of our country will be tried as spies or traitors, and if convicted, will suffer death." To this Burnside added: "The habit of declaring sympathy for the enemy will not be allowed in this department. Persons committing such offenses will be at once arrested, with a view to being tried as above stated, or sent beyond our lines into the lines of their friends."

Burnside's order was defied by the "lame duck" Copperhead Democratic Representative in Congress from the Dayton district, Vallandigham. He delivered a fiery political speech at Mount Vernon, Ohio, in which he denounced the "wicked and cruel" war as a diabolical attempt to destroy slavery and establish a Republican despotism. Burnside caused Vallandigham to be arrested and tried before a military commission, on a charge of publicly expressing sympathy for those in arms against the United States, "declaring disloyal sentiments," and violating Order No. 38. Vallandigham was condemned to confinement in Fort Warren.

Lincoln was embarrassed by Burnside's action. It was not merely an Ohio matter, or a Burnside matter, but a national one on which the President was pressed for a decision. Burnside offered to resign. Lincoln on May 29 answered the arbitrary General by telegraph: "When I shall wish to supersede you I will let you know. All the cabinet regretted the necessity of arresting, for instance, Vallandigham, some perhaps, doubting that there was real necessity for it—but being done, all were for seeing you through it."

Lincoln, under those circumstances, concluded that he could not release Vallandigham, whose arrest he inwardly could not approve; nor did he want the sentence of the convicting military court enforced. The Chief Executive solved the dilemma by directing, through Secretary Stanton, that the imprisoned Copperhead Congressman be transferred "beyond our military lines."

When Vallandigham was escorted by Federal troops to the Confederate lines, the Southerners treated him hospitably. Then he went to Canada by running past the Union blockade, and thence to Halifax, and on to Windsor.

Soon the "Peace" faction of Democrats in Ohio secured control of their party, and nominated Vallandigham for Governor of Ohio. Vallandigham accepted the nomination, in absentia, hoping to ride the wave of war-weariness into the State House at Columbus.

IX

Anti-Lincoln Copperheads were thick not only in the Northwest. They operated actively also in New York City, where Fernando Wood alternated between jobs as Mayor and Congressman.

Philip Hone had once declared of Fernando Wood: "Instead of occupying the Mayor's seat, he ought to be on the rolls of the State prison." He was one of a long line of corrupt Democratic mayors who have cursed the American metropolis ever since, with a few notable exceptions. Prosperous in business, legitimate and otherwise, Wood had achieved influence in Tammany Hall, controlling the Democratic Party of New

York City, before he broke with the regular organization to build his own rival Democratic organization, "Mozart Hall." He had risen to various terms in the City Hall via the roaring factionalism and saloon politics of Manhattan in those days of the "Bowery b'shops." He had supported the "Southern" Democratic candidate for President, John C. Breckinridge, in 1860, and then had accepted the secession of the slave states as inevitable. He even proposed a preposterous plan to have New York City secede from the United States and set itself up as a "free city." Wood became Lincoln's most annoying "Copperhead" problem in the East, for Governor Seymour of New York State was at heart a staunch Unionist, although strongly anti-Lincoln.

Late in 1862 Lincoln had entered correspondence with Wood, now once more Mayor of the metropolis. His Honor insisted that he had good reason to believe that the South wanted a restoration of the Union. On December 12 the President replied to Wood that he had no confidence in that impression but that he would receive any proposition on the subject of a cessation of hostilities with the Confederacy. All of those letters that passed between the President and the Mayor were confidential. But in February, 1863, the Mayor insisted to the Chief Executive, by telegraph, that the time had arrived when the Lincoln-Wood correspondence should be published. But the President rightly viewed Wood's demand as a political maneuver for Wood's own party advantage in New York City, where he was catering to crowds of anti-war, anti-Lincoln Irish immigrants, who viewed the war against the Confederacy as a struggle for freedom of the Negro, with whom the Celt workingmen competed in the labor market.

By April, 1863, the demagogic Mayor Wood, who had, shortly before, publicly called himself a staunch Unionist supporter of the war, was delivering an incendiary anti-war harangue to a mob of workingmen at a mass meeting advertised as one "opposed to the war for the negro and in favor of the rights of the poor."

X

Meanwhile, on the north bank of the Rappahannock in Virginia, the Army of the Potomac was preparing for another great battle, this time under its new commander, "Fighting Joe" Hooker.

While Hooker was whipping his men into battle shape, Lincoln found himself troubled by the ambitions of various Republican politicians in uniform who wanted themselves and their commands shifted from one Union army to another, to suit themselves personally. One of the biggest nuisances of this type in the spring of 1863 was Carl Schurz.

With inflated opinion of his political power among his fellow German-

Americans and convinced of his own great military talents, this celebrated German-born Wisconsin Republican leader had remained at his post as United States Minister to Spain less than one year after Lincoln appointed him. Then the President had made him a Brigadier-General in Frémont's now disbanded Mountain Department. Schurz had distinguished himself at Second Bull Run. When Hooker took over as head of the Army of the Potomac, Schurz commanded the Third Division of the Eleventh Corps, a unit containing numerous German-born troops. After the Eleventh's commander, Major-General Franz Sigel, received a leave of absence in those very informal days of army discipline, Hooker had chosen Major-General Oliver O. Howard as Sigel's successor, and Schurz felt slighted, believing that he should have been picked.

Schurz now proposed that his own Third Division be detached from the Army of the Potomac and transferred to one of the Western armies. "I do not want to interfere with the arrangements already made," Schurz informed the President by letter, "but should be happy to be assigned to another Department, but I cannot go without my old troops. . . . I should be glad to be ordered off to Gen. Burnside or Gen. Rosecrans, and I am very sure every man in my command would hail the order with enthusiasm."

Lincoln's answer to Schurz on April 11 was direct and courteous: "I can not comply with your request to take your Division from the Army of the Potomac. Gen. Hooker does not wish it done. I do not myself see a good reason why it should be done. The Division will do itself, and its officers, more honor; and the country more service, where it is. Besides these general reasons, as I understand, the Army of the Potomac will move, before these proposed changes could be conveniently made. I always wish to oblige you, but I can not in this case."

XI

As Lincoln wrote Schurz, "The Army of the Potomac will move. . . ."

In his letter appointing Hooker to the then greatest of all Union commands in January, Lincoln had frankly pointed out that General's shortcomings to him, but complimented him on his bravery, skill, ambition, and self-reliance.

Hooker was an excellent organizer and could instill morale into his soldiers. The Army of the Potomac that he took over from Burnside in January, 1863, was a demoralized unit but formidable in numbers despite the Fredericksburg defeat. Hooker reported in February that 25 per cent of his men were absent and that desertions averaged several hundred a day. Around camp fires criticism of the replaced Burnside and of Lincoln and his administration was rife, some profane words being uttered about the military leadership in Washington. Hooker set about abolishing the grand divisions and consolidated the cavalry into a corps. He improved the food situation, ordering the erection of bakeries. He tackled the problem of supply with a vigor that soon unchoked subsistence lines and brought the hungry soldiers an unprecedented quantity and variety of food. But he seemed insufferably conceited in expressing what he would do to the Confederates when he clashed with them. In late March he announced to his officers: "My plans are perfect. May God have mercy on General Lee, for I will have none."

Lincoln permitted Hooker an unusual freedom of control from General-in-Chief Halleck. Hooker and Halleck held mutual distrust of each other, ever since their pre-war days together in California. From the time of his assumption of the main Federal field command Hooker reported directly to the President and received all his orders from him. Halleck was not kept informed of what movements Hooker was devising against Lee or what had occurred in those that he had executed. Halleck, essentially a desk general interested in the theory of army movements and the author of textbooks on the art of warfare, was himself mostly to blame for his own lack of authority over this new field commander of the largest Federal army. Ever since Second Manassas, "Old Brains" had increasingly refused to exercise his entire functions as Lincoln's General-in-Chief.

Hooker had assured his subordinate officers: "My plans are perfect." They might have been, but Lincoln still had his misgivings. The President felt uneasy.

Early in April, before Hooker had decided on definite plans of operations to bag Lee's Army of Northern Virginia, the President, in company with his family, Noah Brooks, Dr. Anson G. Henry, and others, visited Hooker at his headquarters in Falmouth, Virginia. The Chief Executive, on horseback, reviewed the troops, with his son, "Tad," riding beside him. But one thing disturbed Lincoln: Hooker, a courageous fighter indeed, sounded too boastful. Brooks noted that the President felt that Hooker was using too often such phrases as, "When I get to Richmond. . . ." The President uncomfortably confided to a friend: "That is the most depressing thing about Hooker. It seems to me that he is overconfident."

Hooker's talk made a deep impression on one of Lincoln's party, Dr. Henry, Lincoln's old Springfield friend and physician, whom the President had appointed to a federal job in Washington Territory, and who was then a temporary White House guest. Henry waxed enthusiastic over Hooker's army. "I feel very sure that we have got the right man at last, and one that will take his army into Richmond before the end of 90 days," he wrote home to Mrs. Henry on April 12, 1863. "He [Hooker] has the finest army ever marshaled upon one field in the world. . . . Handled as I am confident they will be by Gen. Hooker, they will be able to march, not only to Richmond, but to New Orleans if necessary."

XII

The President and General Hooker at Falmouth had apparently not decided on any specific strategy against Lee's army. Later, on April 27, Hooker submitted a plan to the Chief Executive—superior to the ones he had previously considered, he avowed. He would entrap the entire Confederate Army of Northern Virginia in a vise.

Hooker enjoyed a vast advantage over Lee in manpower. The top Confederate commander, after Fredericksburg, divided his army, sending Longstreet on a minor enterprise against Suffolk. Thus he gave a great superiority of men to Hooker: 130,000 Federals facing 60,000 Confederates. Hooker's men were in fine physical trim, too, and morale appeared to be running high when they struck the enemy at Chancellorsville. The battle raged from May 1 through May 5.

Hooker divided his forces, which he pridefully termed "the finest army on the planet." Major-General John Sedgwick's corps was to threaten Lee's right below Fredericksburg. Hooker's own forces were to strike at Lee from the direction of Chancellorsville, west of Fredericksburg. Major-General George Stoneman's cavalry was to execute a sweep to the rear of the Confederates and destroy their communications with Richmond. Hooker had divided his army into two wings, and the Southern battalions lay between them. It was a "vise."

Lee learned of Hooker's positions and designs, and now further divided his forces by sending "Stonewall" Jackson on a wide flanking movement to strike Hooker's detached right under Major-General Oliver O. Howard, while Lee himself, with a small force of 15,000, was to hold Hooker.

Jackson's crack troops succeeded in surprising Howard's Eleventh Corps, inflicting severe losses. Lee, meanwhile, with his thin line, farther to the east, had deterred Hooker from sending troops against Jackson. All was lost for the Federals.

Lee congratulated "Stonewall" Jackson, who was then accidentally wounded fatally by his own men, as the real victor of Chancellorsville.

XIII

Lincoln went through an agonizing ordeal as the Battle of Chancellorsville raged. News from the front sounded fragmentary. The President knew not where Hooker and his chief commanders were with their forces. On May 3, main day of the fighting, he telegraphed Major-General Daniel Butterfield, Hooker's Chief of Staff: "Where is Gen. Hooker? Where is Sedgwick? Where is Stoneman?"

Late in the day, Butterfield replied to the President: "General Hooker is at Chancellorsville. General Sedgwick, with 15,000 to 20,000 men, at a point 3 or 4 miles out from Fredericksburg, on the road to Chancellorsville. Lee is between. Stoneman has not been heard from. This is the situation at this hour from latest reports, 4:30 p.m."

The disturbed Lincoln on the following day, the 4th, sent Hooker a telegram, through Butterfield: "We have news here that the enemy has re-occupied heights above Fredericksburg. Is that so?" Hooker answered with distressing news: "I am informed that this is so, but attach no importance to it."

Lincoln was described by his young California friend, Noah Brooks, Washington correspondent of a California newspaper, as the final bad news came in a telegram from General Butterfield about the Federal defeat at Chancellorsville. "I shall never forget that picture of despair. . . . His face was ashen in hue," declared Brooks. "Never, so long as I knew him, did he seem so broken, so dispirited, and so ghostlike." The President muttered, "What will the country say!"—and he appeared incapable of uttering further words.

Then the President, accompanied by General-in-Chief Halleck, gravely rode off in a carriage to Hooker's Army of the Potomac headquarters.

PORTRAIT OF THE PRESIDENT

26

I

"THERE are not two of the whole numbers who agree in their estimate of him," commented Lincoln's first serious biographer, Reverend Josiah G. Holland, late in 1865, after he had interviewed scores of people who had known Lincoln intimately. And in 1866 his closest crony, Joshua F. Speed, remarked: "Mr. Lincoln was so unlike all the men I had ever known before or seen or known since that there is no one to whom I can compare him."

Any pen portrait of the President as a personality must of necessity be pieced together not only from his own correspondence but especially from the observations of men and women to whom he revealed one aspect of his nature during his White House tenure.

II

Upon his nomination for President in 1860 Lincoln appeared to Easterners as a Western rustic professional man and politician, but they recognized that he was superior in his unpretentiousness, honesty, and mental capacities. In describing him during that summer the New York *Evening Post's* John Bigelow, destined to be Lincoln's Consul-General at Paris, then Minister to France, gave his private estimate to a friend: "Mr. Lincoln is not precisely the sort of man who would be regarded as entirely *a la mode* at splendid European courts, nor indeed is his general style and appearance beyond the reach of criticism in our Atlantic drawing rooms. He is essentially a Western man . . . self-made man. With great simplicity of manners and perhaps ignorant of the trans-Atlantic world, he has a clear and eminently logical mind, a nice sense of truth and justice."

What did Lincoln look like?

Lincoln's visage depended upon his moods, and he was a man of varying moods. The huge framework of his facial features was modified by the emotions which controlled them. The merest delicate touch of those artists who painted him and those men of the camera who photographed him often wholly changed the expression of their portraits and pictures. In a countenance of strong lines and rugged masses like Lincoln's, the lift of an eyebrow, the curve of a lip, the flash of an eye, the momentary movement of prominent muscles created a vast facial play. His features from the top of his tousled hair to the bottom of his beard proved the despair of more than one painter or photographer.

Those who knew Lincoln intimately and saw him continually between 1861 and 1865, such as his main secretary, John G. Nicolay, gave their opinion of a dozen oils or camera shots of him, and could not agree on which resembled Lincoln most closely. Some of the artists put into their creations the large, rugged features and strong, prominent lines unduly conspicuously, others less so; they made measurements to obtain exact proportions, each to his own satisfaction; they "petrified" some single expression. But the resultant art creation did not convince Lincoln's very personal associates that they looked exactly like the Chief Executive. "Even before these paintings were finished," related Nicolay, "it was plain to see that they were unsatisfactory to the artists themselves, and much more so to the intimate friends of the man." For their efforts were handicapped before a face that moved through various delicate gradations of line and contour, light and shade, sparkles of the eye and circle of the lip, in the gamut from grave to gay, and back again. There were numerous pictures of Lincoln but no portrait.

When Richard C. McCormick in 1861 told Lincoln, then President-elect, that none of his pictures did him justice, he jocularly suggested that it might not be so desirable to have justice done to such forbidding features as his.

Lincoln, five months before he was nominated for President, in his autobiography for Jesse W. Fell of late 1859, described himself: "If any personal description of me is thought desirable, it may be said, I am, in height, six feet, four inches, nearly; lean in flesh, weighing one hundred and eighty pounds; dark complexion, with coarse, black hair, and grey eyes—no other marks or brands recollected."

Following his election as President late in 1860, however, Lincoln acquired his most conspicuous facial "mark" or "brand"—he grew his beard.

Substantial agreement exists among those who viewed Lincoln, as President, closely about his general physical appearance—toweringly tall, with long legs and gangling arms, powerful in his hand clasp; especially unhandsome of looks, with coarse and rugged features but kindly visage when examined closely; tangled, black hair, fine chiseled features covered with the strikingly familiar beard; swarthy skin of dark complexion; and, in dress, far from sartorially elegant.

The Washington correspondent of *Macmillan's Magazine,* of London, in 1862 described the American President:

"To say that he is ugly, is nothing; to add that his figure is grotesque, is to convey no adequate impression. Fancy a man six foot high, and thin *out* of proportion; with long bony arms and legs, which somehow seem to be always in the way; with great rugged furrowed hands . . . a long, scraggly neck, and a chest too narrow for the great arms at its side . . . rough, uncombed and uncombable hair . . . a face furrowed, wrinkled and indented . . . a close-set-thin-lipped, stern mouth, with two rows of large white teeth, and a nose and ears which have been taken by mistake from a head of twice the size."

The *Macmillan's Magazine* observer had equally unflattering remarks about Lincoln's dress:

"Clothe this figure, then, in a long, tight, badly-fitting suit of black, creased, soiled, and puckered up at every salient point of the figure (and every point of this figure *is* salient); put on large ill-fitting boots, gloves too long for the long bony fingers, and a fluffy hat, covered with dusty puffy crape; and then add to all this an air of strength, physical as well as moral, and a strange look of dignity coupled with all this grotesqueness; and you will have the impression left upon me by Abraham Lincoln."

Another visiting British journalist, George Augustus Sala, in his day-book described the President as having "that lengthy face, those bushy locks, that shovel beard, that ungainly form, those long, muscular, attenuated limbs, those bony and wide extremities. Mr. Lincoln is so tall that, looking up in his face, you might, did not your respect forbid you, ask, 'How cold was the weather up there?'. . . When he rose there did not seem the slightest likelihood of his getting up ever coming to an end. He seemed to be drawing himself out like a telescope." Sala added, "He is exceptionally dark—not so dark as Mr. Hannibal Hamlin [the Vice-President]. . . . His dark face, strongly marked, tanned and crows-footed, and fringed with coarse and tangled hair, is so uncouth and rugged that it narrowly escapes being either terrible or grotesque."

Lincoln was publicly described by his friend, Congressman Henry C. Deming of Connecticut, only two months after the assassination: "Conceive a tall and gaunt figure, more than six feet in height, not only unencumbered with superfluous flesh, but reduced to the minimum working standard of cord and sinew and muscles, strong and indurated by exposure and toil, with arms long and attenuated. . . . His dress is uniformly of black throughout and would attract but little attention in a well dressed circle. . . . The face that surmounts this figure is half Roman and half Indian, bronzed by climate, furrowed by life's struggles, seamed with humor; the head is massive and covered with dark, thick and unmanageable hair, the brow is wide and well developed, the nose large and fleshy, the lips full, cheeks thin, and drawn in strong corded lines which, but for the wiry whiskers, would disclose the machinery which moves the broad jaw."

III

Despite Lincoln's unattractive looks, general agreement prevailed that he was not so displeasing to the eye when seen at very close range; that underneath his physically unhandsome features lay signs of kindly qualities.

Donn Piatt, who knew Lincoln well, noted that "Mr. Lincoln was the homeliest man I ever saw;" but added that his face, when animated, brightened like a lantern. "His dull eyes would fairly sparkle with fun, or express as kindly a look as I ever saw, when moved by some matter of human interest."

One Britisher, Professor Goldwin Smith, who was granted an interview by Lincoln late in 1864, described him: "The large-boned and sinewy frame, six feet four inches in height, is probably that of the yeoman of the north of England—the district from which Lincoln's name suggests that his forefathers came—made spare and gaunt by the climate of America." The face, added Smith, is "one of kindness" and "denotes an English yeoman's solidity of character and good sense, with something added from the enterprising life and sharp habits of the Western Yankee."

During the four years of war Lincoln was watched by tens of thousands of Union troops and officers in the field when he visited the battle front. Some recorded their impressions, among them Private Flavius J. Bellamy of the Second Regiment, Indiana Volunteers. From a camp near Washington in 1861 Bellamy sent word home: "The Pres. is not half so ugly as he is generally represented—his nose is rather long but he is rather *long* himself so it is Necessary to keep the proportion complete." Three years later, when Lincoln visited City Point, Virginia, Colonel Theodore Lyman, of General Meade's staff, told about him in a letter to his family: "The President is, I think, the ugliest man I ever put my eyes on; there is also an expression of plebeian vulgarity in his face that is offensive. On the other hand, he has the look of sense and wonderful shrewdness, while the heavy eyelids give him a mark almost of genius. He strikes me, too, as a very honest and kindly man; and with all his vulgarity, I see no trace of low passion in his face. . . . As humanity runs, I am well content to have him at the head of affairs."

Lincoln was described by Walt Whitman, who saw him in Washington, in a private note to friends in 1863—"a face like a Hoosier Michelangelo, so awfully ugly it becomes beautiful, with its strange mouth, its deep cut, criss-cross lines, and doughnut complexion."

Another eminent American man of letters, the famed Nathaniel Hawthorne, on a White House visit, perceived that same blend of ugliness of looks and finer basic qualities in Lincoln. Hawthorne jotted down: "The whole physiognomy is as coarse as you would meet anywhere in the length and breadth of the States; but withal, it is redeemed, illumined, softened and brightened by a kindly though serious look of his eyes, and an expression of homely sagacity, that seems weighted with rich results of village experience. A great deal of native sense; no bookish cultivation, no refinement; honest at heart, and thoroughly so."

Lincoln possessed mighty physical endurance and strength, in keeping with his long, muscular, and bony frame. His secretary, Nicolay, accompanied the President and Secretary of War Cameron on a visit to the Army of the Potomac in 1861, and noted how Cameron grew tired and had to dismount from his horse after two hours in the saddle in the inspection of troops. But, Nicolay observed, "the President went through the whole without the least symptom of fatigue." The visiting Britisher, Sala, always remembered what he called "the cast-iron grip of Abraham Lincoln" when he shook hands with him. Sala, in descriptively exaggerated phrase, wrote: "I shall never forget that memorable handshaking without tears coming into my eyes . . . reducing my own hand nearly to the consistency of pulp. . . . He merely takes it, and quietly and silently squeezes it into dough."

Lincoln's Assistant Secretary of War, Charles A. Dana, remarked about the Chief Executive's thin arms and strong, active muscles—"nothing flabby or feeble about Mr. Lincoln," he commented. Dana was astonished to perceive the President's habit of working late night after night, made possible by his "immense physical endurance." Dana noted: "He always seemed as ready for the next day's work as though he had done nothing the day before."

The nephew of Lincoln's stepmother, R. Y. Bush, put it this way in a letter back to Illinois after he had called at the White House: "Tell

Aunt [Lincoln's stepmother] that they are working him very hard at Washington & if he had not been raised to *maul rails,* he could never stand the hard labor at the White House."

IV

Lincoln's formidable physical constitution served him well for the tremendous load of the presidential office during war time. Too, his labors were made more time-consuming and back-breaking by his habit of receiving so many people of every kind who called on him. He saw and spoke with more men and women privately than any preceding President.

Secretary Seward in 1863 commented on Lincoln's habit of receiving so many people, in a conversation with Henry W. Bellows, head of the United States Sanitary Commission. And Bellows told about it in a note home to his wife: "Mr. Seward had a great deal to say about the President. . . . He rec'd any & every body, as long as time held out—selecting from the hundreds applying those he thot (sic) best entitled to come—and except on Cabinet days Tuesday & Friday, he spent his day morning & evening till 11 in this way. The actual work thrown on him by his ministers was small. He had a notion he was a servant of the people & that he was there to hear their complaints & he spent his time at it."

No one but Lincoln himself ever appreciated how heavily this onrush of callers exhausted his otherwise bountiful energy. He confided to Noah Brooks: "I some times fancy that every one of the numerous grist ground through here daily, from a Senator seeking a war with France down to a poor woman after a place in the Treasury Department, darted at me with thumb and finger, picked out their special piece of my vitality, and carried it off. When I get through such a day's work there is only one word which can express my condition—*flabbiness.*"

The cares of a war-time administration and the energy expended in attending to office-seekers and listening to scores of callers nearly every day made themselves apparent in Lincoln's face. His old friend of the Illinois Eighth Judicial Circuit, Judge David Davis, in 1862 sent sad news home: "The President looks weary & care worn."

When Lincoln entered upon his second administration early in 1865, he still possessed a sturdy and resilient constitution, but by this time those who saw him remarked how badly he looked.

V

If Lincoln's physical capacity was sufficiently sturdy to withstand the strength-sapping cares and duties of the presidency during America's most critical ordeal, his mental resources were just as adequate to meet the ever recurring problems and crises of four harrowing years of attrition.

Behind the President's furrowed countenance lay an inquisitive mind. It ranged over the abstract and the infinite, the absolute and the immediate. His mental processes were philosophical, but at the same time practical, although he was not a prolific reader of books, except poetry, and he lacked the advantages of formal schooling. Herndon has commented that Lincoln read less and thought more than any man imaginable.

Especially impressed with Lincoln's mentality was the world-renowned historian, John Lothrop Motley, who saw and observed Lincoln closely in 1861, and studied his administration minutely for four years through private correspondence with party men. Shortly after Lincoln's assassination in 1865 Motley gave his opinion to his friend, the Duchess of Argyll. Declaring, "I can not trust myself yet to speak of President Lincoln, for I am afraid of possible exaggeration," Motley wrote the Duchess: "His mental abilities were large, and they became the more robust as the more weight was imposed upon them, and his faculty of divining the right amid a conflict of dogmas, theories, and of weighing other men's opinions while retaining his own judgment, almost amounted to political genius."

Lincoln possessed a retentive memory. Another immortal American historian, George Bancroft, was struck by Lincoln's remarkable recollections of names and faces. "Last night I went to the President's reception," Bancroft sent home word to his wife in 1864. "He took me by one of his hands, and trying to recall my name, he waved the other a foot and a half above his head, and cried out, greatly to the amusement of the by-standers: 'Hold on—I know you; you are—History, History of the United States—Mr.—Mr. Bancroft,' and seemed disposed to give me a hearty welcome—expressing a wish to see me some day apart from the crowd."

Lincoln was measured by Horace Greeley, who recorded: "His mental processes were slow, but true; if he did not acquire swiftly, he retained all that he had once learned."

Lincoln, for a man whose two main interests had been law and politics, had a mind which understood elementary mechanics and technical details well.

Lincoln's early self-education in mathematics, his youthful experience in surveying roads, bounding farms, and platting town sites as one of his New Salem jobs, had given him an appreciation of exactness in measuring and precision. His taste for mechanics had carried over into his law practice in Illinois, making him proficient in handling patent cases. Besides having taken out a United States patent of his own on a device for lifting vessels over shoals, he also prepared and delivered a few lectures on "Discoveries and Inventions" to groups. Living on the periphery of the machine age in America, he was familiar in a non-professional way with the technological advances that were in their infancy taking place about him.

Lincoln, as President, turned his mechanical bent to the improvement of the tools of war. Eager to utilize to the fullest the North's superiority over the South in the mechanical and technical arts as a factor in crushing the Confederacy, he made ordnance one of his special concerns during his first two years in the White House. When inventors beset him in his office, often bringing their contraptions along, Lincoln listened to them patiently, sometimes amused by their eccentricities but always alert to new ideas about a new machine or weapon. If he thought one of their devices showed promise, he would arrange for it to be tried by the proper officials in the War or Navy departments. Occasionally he witnessed the test himself.

Lincoln in August, 1862, saw successfully tested in Washington the "Rafael Repeater" gun, produced by a New York inventor, James R. Haskell, and a Frenchman named Rafael. The day following the President sent word to Secretary of War Stanton:

"I have examined, and seen tried, the 'Rafael Repeater' and consider it a decided improvement upon what was called the 'Coffee Mill gun' in these particulars, that it dispenses with the great cost, and liability to loss, of the steel cartridges, and that it is better arranged to prevent the escape of gas. Other advantages are claimed for it upon which I can not so well speak. While I do not order it into service, I think it well worthy the attention of the Ordnance Bureaus, and should be rather pleased, if it should be decided to put it into service."

The War Department, however, showed no interest in the Rafael Repeater so far as adopting that weapon for the Army.

Old-line ordnance officers showed little enthusiasm for what they regarded as the President's amateur suggestions about new weapons. Although his ideas on technical war instruments were more often than not rejected, Lincoln played a major but hitherto unnoticed part in bringing about the introduction of the breech-loading rifle and the machine gun, as well as a few less significant innovations of weapons in the Union Army.

VI

Lincoln, like numerous other men of practical bent of mind veering toward the mechanical, was no prolific reader, except the Bible, poetry, and pamphlets on humor.

Lincoln was essentially not a literary-minded man, aside from his fondness for poetry. Nathaniel Hawthorne in 1863 pronounced him as having "no bookish inclination." "I never read an entire novel in my life," he told Senator Ira Harris of New York and the artist, Francis B. Carpenter. "I once commenced 'Ivanhoe,' but never finished it." Lincoln indeed had doubts as to whether his fellow-Americans had produced great literature. In 1862 he wrote George Robertson of Kentucky: "I believe you are acquainted with the American Classics, (if there be such)."

For published history and biography Lincoln, as in his Illinois years, continued to have scant respect, distrusting the reliability of such books. He particularly was averse to authors making saints of their subjects.

Among the poets Lincoln chose Shakespeare as his first choice. John Hay revealed that Lincoln read more of the works of the Bard of Avon than all others combined. Perhaps this was because Shakespeare dealt in severe realism, rather than romanticism. The President declared: "It matters not to me whether Shakespeare be well or ill acted; with him the thought suffices." One of his favorite scenes in *Hamlet,* he told Carpenter, the artist, was the King's soliloquy after the murder. And he repeated stanzas from it.

Lincoln became acquainted with the then famed Shakespearan actor, James H. Hackett. That performer in 1863 wrote a book, *Notes and Comments on Certain Plays and Actors of Shakespeare,* and he presented a copy of it to Lincoln. In acknowledging this gift, Lincoln wrote Hackett:

> The first presentation of Falstaff I ever saw was yours here, last winter or spring. Perhaps the best compliment I can pay is to say, as I truly can, I am very anxious to see it again. Some of Shakespeare's plays I have never read; while others I have gone over perhaps as frequently as any professional reader. Among the latter are Lear, Richard Third, Hamlet, and especially Macbeth. I think nothing equals Macbeth. It is wonderful. Unlike you gentlemen of the profession, I think the soliloquy in Hamlet commencing 'O, my offence is rank' surpasses that commencing 'To be, or not to be.' But pardon this small attempt at criticism. I should like to hear you pronounce the opening speech of Richard the Third. Will you not soon visit Washington again? If you do, please call and let me make your personal acquaintance.

Hackett, not averse to self-advertising, proceeded to issue a broadside printing of his letter from the President of the United States, which bore the notice, "Printed not for publication but for private distribution only, and its convenient perusal by personal friends." Lincoln's political opponents proceeded to use this semi-publicly circulated letter from Lincoln to Hackett, and they made it the occasion for sarcastic and ridiculing comments in the New York *Herald* and other newspapers critical of the President.

Lincoln was provoked by Hackett's circularization of his letter. The actor sent him a note of apology. The President, characteristically, overlooked the matter, and assured Hackett: "Give yourself no uneasiness on the subject." But he added to Hackett: "My note to you I certainly did not expect to see in print; yet I have not been much shocked by the newspaper comments upon it. These comments constitute a fair specimen of what has occurred to me through life. I have endured a great deal of ridicule without much malice; and have received a great deal of kindness, not quite free from ridicule." Several weeks later, on December 13, the President had Hackett as his guest at the White House.

On his trip to City Point, Virginia, shortly before his death in 1865, Lincoln took along a copy of Shakespeare's poems, and read it avidly. On the way home to Washington on April 9, the day of Lee's surrender and less than a week before his own murder, the Marquis de Chambrun, a young French nobleman intermarried into the Lafayette family, accompanied Lincoln, Mrs. Lincoln and the presidential party. Chambrun has related about that occasion: "We were steaming up the Potomac. That whole day the conversation dwelt upon literary subjects. Mr. Lincoln read to us for several hours passages taken from Shakespeare. Most of these were from 'Macbeth,' and, in particular, the verses which follow *Duncan's* assassination. . . . He read over again the same scene."

Another favorite poet of Lincoln was Robert Burns. The President's friend and early biographer, Congressman Isaac N. Arnold of the Chicago district, has pointed out: "Next to Shakespeare among the poets, his favorite was Burns." One visitor who called on Lincoln as President-elect during 1860-61 suggested that there was something in the lowly origins of Burns and his checkered life, no less than his verses, that attracted Lincoln.

Still another poet read by Lincoln was Alexander Pope. A visiting scholar from Cambridge University, England, George Tuthill Borrett, told about his talk with Lincoln on the subject: "The conversation turned on English poetry, the President saying that when we disturbed him he was deep in Pope. He seemed to be a great admirer of Pope, especially of his 'Essay on Man;' going so far as to say that it contained all the religious instruction which it was necessary for a man to know. Then he mused for a moment or two, and asked us if we could show him any finer lines than those ending, as he quoted them without hesitation—

> " '*All nature is but art, unknown to thee;*
> *All chance, direction, which thou canst not see;*
> *All discord, harmony not understood;*
> *All partial evil, universal good;*
> *And, spite of pride, in erring treason's spite,*
> *One truth is clear, whatever is, is right.*' "

On Lincoln's general reading, his friend, Congressman Deming of Connecticut, said several weeks after his death: "The books which he chiefly read, in his leisure hours, were the Bible, Shakespeare, the peasant poet of Scotland [Burns], with whom his sympathies were very acute, and those peculiar off-shoots of American wit, of which Orpheus C. Kerr, Artemus Ward, and Doesticks are types."

VII

One of Lincoln's favorite relaxations was the theatre. Few of his earlier nineteenth-century biographers, however, gave space to this partiality of the President, perhaps because it spontaneously suggested his visit to Ford's on April 14, 1865.

Lincoln's preference for play-going had seized him back in Illinois. "Brought up in a provincial way, in the days when theatres were unknown outside the larger cities, the beautiful art of the actor was fresh and delightful to him," observed Herndon.

Although Lincoln acquired a critical sense where Shakespeare was concerned, his usual standards did not reach high. Riding the Judicial Circuit in his county-to-county law practice, he had attended by himself various little shows, variety acts, and concerts in the larger towns on the law trail. In Springfield he had seen and heard an abundance of diverse theatrical fare: poetry readings, Swiss bell ringers, Negro singers, P.T. Barnum's Grand Colossal Museum and Menagerie, along with the Illinois Theatrical Company in plays such as *Richelieu* and *The Denouncer, or The Miser of Marseilles.* He had also seen a performance given by Lola Montez, celebrated actress and once mistress of a Bavarian king.

Lincoln during his presidency attended Shakespearean performances by such celebrated interpreters of the Bard of Avon as Hackett, Edwin Forrest, and Edwin Booth.

On November 9, 1863, Lincoln, accompanied by Mrs. Lincoln, John Hay, and others, saw a performance by Edwin Booth's younger brother, John, then only twenty-five years old, in *The Marble Heart; or, The Sculptor's Dream.*

From his box on that autumn night of 1863 Lincoln looked down on John Wilkes Booth playing the role of a passionate and ultimately frustrated sculptor, "Raphael," in *The Marble Heart,* a laboriously allegorical play whose moral was that a beautiful girl often prefers a rich old man to an impoverished young one. With its scene laid in ancient Greece, this play featured action in which statues of Phidias come to life and desert him for greener pastures, and ended in contemporary times, when a real-life beauty, but one with a "marble heart," turns her back on the sculptor, flamboyantly played by John Wilkes Booth, and chooses a wealthy ancient aristocrat instead. There is no record of what Lincoln thought of Booth's performance, but John Hay noted in his diary that the play was "rather tame than otherwise."

Lincoln's habit of attending the theatre without adequate guards for personal protection became a source of annoyance to his young friend and former Illinois law associate, Ward Hill Lamon, now holding the federal job of United States Marshal for the District of Columbia. In December, 1864, only four months before Lincoln met his tragic end by Booth's bullet, Lamon grew impatient at Lincoln for going out to the theatre without a bodyguard. He rebuked the President:

"I regret that you do not appreciate what I have repeatedly said to you with regard to the proper police arrangements connected with your household and your personal safety. You are in danger. . . . To-night, as you have done on several previous occasions, you went unattended to the theatre. When I say unattended I mean you went alone with Charles Sumner and a foreign minister, neither of whom could defend himself against an assault from any able-bodied woman in this city. And you know or ought to know that your life is sought after and will be taken unless you and your friends are cautious, for you have many enemies within our lines."

VIII

Humor, however, was Lincoln's main form of relaxation.

The President's deputy assistant secretary, Reverend Edward D. Neill, later pointed out: "He had from youth indulged in pleasantry, by telling to farmers at the country store, and to fellow-lawyers going to court, amusing, if not always classic stories, not to raise a laugh, but to illustrate his views. This habit remained through life."

Secretary Seward in 1863 privately stated to another that the President "had no notion of recreation as such . . . found his only recreation in telling or hearing stories in the ordinary way of business—often stopped a cabinet council at a grave juncture, to jest a half hour with the members before going to work; joked with every body, on light & grave occasions. This is what saved him."

Illinois people who knew Lincoln intimately and saw and heard him on White House visits, noted his jocular manner and propensity for spouting humorous stories. Mrs. Milton Hay wrote home to her husband at Springfield in 1862: "The President looks much as he did when he left Springfield—and tells jokes yet." Judge David Davis in the same year sent word to a friend in Bloomington: "It is a good thing that he is fond of anecdotes & telling them, for it relieves his spirits very much." The Minnesota feminist, Mrs. Jane Grey Swisshelm, in 1863 reported from Washington that "when committees wait upon the President to urge strong measures he tells them a story," that he told one committee four anecdotes, and that when one visitor told him one, Lincoln requested: "Wait a minute! I want you to give me the notes to that story." And he filed such notes about jokes in his desk.

John Hay related how the chuckling President came into his and Nicolay's room, with a copy of a book by the British humorist, Thomas Hood, in hand during the middle of the night. Hood's character, "An unfortunate Bee-ing," especially tickled Lincoln. Hay recorded: "He with his short shirt hanging over his long legs & setting out behind like the tail feathers of an enormous ostrich was infinitely funnier than anything in the book he was laughing at." Admiringly Hay added: "What a man it is! Occupied all day with matters of vast moment; deeply anxious about the fate of the greatest army of the world, with his own fame and future hanging on the events of the passing hour, he yet has such a wealth of simple bonhomie & good fellowship that he gets out of bed & perambulates the house in shirt to find us that we may share with him the fun of poor Hood's queer little conceits."

More than the British humorist Hood, however, Lincoln relished three American writers of wit, Robert H. Newell, who published under the *nom de plume,* "Orpheus C. Kerr;" Charles Farrar Browne, whose pseudonym was "Artemus Ward;" and an Ohio newspaperman, David R. Locke, whose pen name was "Petroleum V. Nasby."

Lincoln habitually told anecdotes in order to illustrate a point. When three clergymen called on him the last day of 1862, urging him to issue a proclamation freeing all of the slaves in the United States, the Chief Executive gave them a story about a calf in order to illustrate his contention that such an act did not necessarily make them free. Said he: "As an illustration, there is an anecdote, rather a homely one. In one of our western courts there had been an attempt made to show that a calf had five legs—the way the point was to be established was by calling the tail a leg, but the decision of the judge was that *calling* the tail a leg did not make it a leg, and the calf had four legs after all."

Another of the President's anecdotes concerned diplomatic relations with Spain over the status of the Dominican Republic, in which Spain was vitally involved. Secretary of the Navy Welles in 1864 related it: "Seward was embarrassed about the Dominican question. To move either way threatened difficulty. On one side Spain, on the other side the negro. The President remarked that the dilemma reminded him of the interview between two negroes, one of whom was a preacher endeavoring to admonish and enlighten the other. 'There are,' said Josh, the preacher, 'two roads for you, Joe. Be careful which you take. One of dem leads straight to hell, de odder go right to damnation.' Joe opened his eyes under the impressive eloquence and awful future and exclaimed, 'Josh, take which road you please. I go troo de wood.' 'I am not disposed to take any new trouble,' said the President, 'just at this time, and shall neither go for Spain nor the negro in this matter, but shall take to the woods.' "

Lincoln made one of his most hilarious quips to John Hay when he was considering the case of Captain James Madison Cutts, Jr., the late Senator Stephen A. Douglas's young brother-in-law. Cutts, a "Peeping Tom," had been found guilty by army court martial of various charges, one of which concerned his looking through a door transom in a Cincinnati hotel, watching a lady undress. Cutts's case came before Lincoln for pardon. The President remarked to Hay that Cutts should be elevated to the peerage—with the title, "Count Peeper!" The Swedish Minister at Washington was then Count Pieper.

Another of Lincoln's humorous replies was made in 1863, shortly after the Chancellorsville defeat, when a citizen appealed to him for a pass so that he could go through the Union lines in order to reach Richmond, where he had legitimate business. Lincoln, having in mind the Federal Army's long delay in capturing the Confederate capital, answered the seeker after the pass: "I would be most obliged if my passes were respected; but the fact is I have within the last two years given passes to more than two hundred and fifty thousand men to go to Richmond, and not one of them has got there in any legitimate way."

Lincoln was visited late in 1862 by a Sanitary Commission worker, Horace H. Furness, along with others. The President lamented that "the great difficulty was that our army couldn't be got together . . . One half of our army was either sick or skulking & the trains carried away from Washington as many soldiers as they brought to it." The President illustrated to Furness and the others his point: "Just like trying to shovel fleas,—before the shovel load fell the fleas were all gone." He then "wrinkled up his nose, showed his front teeth, gave a wheezy, catching laugh, and fell to scratching his elbows."

Lincoln's distribution of jobs gave him opportunity to indulge in humorous or whimsical expressions.

When in 1861 Christopher Adams of New York was recommended by both Thurlow Weed and Horace Greeley, those mortal party enemies, for a Treasury Department architect's position, the President queried Secretary Chase: "Ought Mr. Young to be removed, and if yea, ought Mr. Adams to be appointed? Mr. Adams is magnificently recommended; but the great point in his favor is that Thurlow Weed and Horace Greeley join in recommending him. I suppose the like never happened before, and never will again; so that it is now or never. What say you?"

When, in the following year, Governor Yates of Illinois and William

Butler recommended John Pope of their State for a Major-Generalship in the regular Army, Lincoln answered: "I fully appreciate Gen. Pope's splendid achievements with their invaluable results; but you must know that Major-Generalships in the Regular Army are not as plenty as blackberries."

Came an urgent request to Lincoln from his old Illinois political friends, State Secretary of State Ozias M. Hatch and State Auditor Jesse K. Dubois, asking that Brigadier-General Robert Allen be appointed Quartermaster General of the Army, a post held by Montgomery C. Meigs, who was erroneously reported to have resigned. Lincoln by wire answered Hatch and Dubois: "What nation do you desire Gen. Allen to be made Quartermaster-General of? This nation already has a Quartermaster-General."

Hatch and Dubois thought that the President's reply was not humorous, and answered him: "We confess your despatch read harshly to us." Lincoln responded by sending them a tactful note of apology and explanation: "Your letter is just received. The particular form of my despatch was jocular, which I supposed you gentlemen knew me well enough to understand. Gen. Allen is considered here as a very faithful and capable officer; and one who would be at least thought of for Quartermaster-General if that office were vacant."

IX

Counterbalancing Lincoln's humorous disposition was quite another one which he had in abundance—melancholia.

Lincoln's friends, political and military associates, and casual White House visitors observed this abysmal sadness. His face often reflected his quickly alternating switch from gaiety to despondency. His secretary, Nicolay, spoke of Lincoln's "long gamut from grave to gay, and back again from the rollicking jollity of laughter to that serious, faraway look." The British journalist, Sala, commented: "The melancholy look struck me most forcibly, when I remembered that I was in the presence of the great joker of jokes."

The historian, George Bancroft, who saw Lincoln often, publicly stated in 1865: "He was of the temperament called melancholic, scarcely concealed by an exterior of lightness of humor." David R. Locke, the humorist who wrote under the *nom de plume,* "Petroleum V. Nasby," told another: "I never saw so sad a face."

Lincoln's disposition was reflected in his choice of music. He liked plaintive Scotch songs best. "Annie Laurie," "Mary of Argyle," and especially "Auld Robin Gray," never lost their attraction to him. Songs which had for their theme the rapid flight of time, decay, the more morbid recollections of early days, were certain to make a deep impression on him. One song which he liked deeply was "Twenty Years Ago," with its lyrics the words uttered by a man who visited the playground of his youth. Lincoln himself had once composed a morbid poem, "My Childhood Home I See Again," after a visit to his youthful Indiana home.

As further sign of his melancholia, Lincoln's favorite poem remained "O, why should the spirit of mortal be proud."

Lincoln in his gloomier moments privately confessed that he did not expect to serve out his presidential term.

X

Lincoln as President still refrained from affiliating with a church or sect, although on occasions he accompanied Mrs. Lincoln to services at the New York Avenue Presbyterian Church, whose pastor was the Reverend Phineas Gurley. But as the war years dragged on, Lincoln's underlying consciousness of Deity grew steadily.

When Lincoln had run for Congress in 1846, he had been accused of agnosticism and infidelity to Christianity by his Democratic opponent. In the only public statement of his life about his religious views, he had then confessed to the voters that, in early life, he had believed in what was called the "Doctrine of Necessity," the belief that the human mind was moved by some power over which it had no control. Then he had "entirely left off" his habit of arguing it, he told them in a circulated handbill, but he did not say that he had abandoned that belief.

By the time of his departure for Washington as President-elect early in 1861, however, Lincoln began to think that God foreordained events. With Southern states already out of the Union and the Confederacy formed, he told his fellow Springfielders as he left for Washington that he was assuming a task more difficult than that forced on George Washington. He declared: "Unless the great God who assisted him, shall be with and aid me, I must fail. But if the same omniscient mind, and Almighty arm that directed and protected him, shall guide and support me, I shall not fail, I shall succeed. Let us all pray that the God of our fathers may not forsake us now. To Him I commend you all—permit me to ask that with equal security and faith, you all will invoke His wisdom and guidance for me."

Evidence of Lincoln's growing faith in the Almighty is plentiful during the war years, usually from his own speeches and private letters.

To a committee seeking a Proclamation of Emancipation on religious grounds in 1862, the President replied: "I hope it will not be irreverent for me to say that if it is probable that God would reveal His will to others, on a point so connected with my duty, it might be supposed he would reveal it directly to me; for, unless I am deceived in myself than I often am, it is my earnest desire to know the will of Providence in this matter. *And if I can learn what it is I will do it!*"

In September, 1863, Lincoln proclaimed a day of Thanksgiving and thanks to the Almighty, to be observed on the coming last Thursday of November. And in October he spoke significant words to members of the Baltimore (old school) Presbyterian Synod. The Reverend Phineas Gurley, pastor of the New York Avenue Presbyterian Church in Washington, introduced them to the President. Lincoln assured them that he was "profoundly grateful" for any form of support from the nation's religious bodies. When he assumed the presidency, he told them, "I was brought to a living reflection that nothing in my power whatever would succeed without the direct assistance of the Almighty." He added, "I have often wished that I was a more devout man than I am. Nevertheless, amid the greatest difficulties of my Administration, when I could not see any other resort, I would place my whole reliance on God, knowing that all would go well, and that He would decide for the right."

To the editor of a Kentucky newspaper, Albert G. Hodges, Lincoln early in 1864 wrote about possible abolition of slavery, invoking God's name. "If God now wills the removal of a great wrong," he informed Hodges, "and wills also that we of the North as well as you of the South, shall pay fairly for your complicity in that wrong, impartial history will find therein new cause to attest and revere the justice and goodness of God."

Lincoln publicly expressed gratitude to God for his re-election victory in 1864. Several days after that verdict at the polls, he told serenaders: "I am thankful to God for this approval of the people. . . . I give thanks to the Almighty for this evidence of the people's resolution to stand by free government and the rights of humanity."

Lincoln's clearest expression of his religious predestinarian interpretation of the war is found in his Second Inaugural six weeks before his death. He told the nation: "The Almighty has His own purposes. . . . If we shall suppose that American slavery is one of those offenses which, in the providence of God, must needs come, but which, having continued through His Appointed time, He now wills to remove, and that He gives to both North and South this terrible war as the woe due to those by whom the offense came, shall we discern therein any departure from those divine attributes which the believers in a living God always ascribe to Him?"

Lincoln, years after his death, was referred to by his son, Robert, as a person "like many other men; he did not take any interest in church matters." And Lincoln was described by his wife, Mary, as "not a technical Christian."

Reverend Henry A. Nelson, visiting preacher at the Presbyterian church in Springfield, Illinois, declared in his sermon on the Sunday following Lincoln's burial in May, 1865: "He had never here been known as a professor of religion. But that he was an honest believer is generally understood. . . . During the last two or three years, if not since his elevation to office, his published language and his public deportment have increasingly, and very decidedly, impressed us as altogether becoming to a Christian."

Two months following Lincoln's death his friend, Congressman Deming of Connecticut, publicly declared: "He said, he had never united himself to any church because he found difficulty in giving his assent, without mental reservations, to the long and complicated statements of Christian doctrine." And Phebe A. Hanaford, in her 1865 biography (the first *Life* of Lincoln to appear after the assassination) declared: "Abraham Lincoln was a Christian; but no particular branch of Zion can claim him. He belongs to that universal Church of which Christ alone is head, and all whose members are imbued with their Master's spirit."

Ever since Lincoln's death certain occult-minded writers have maintained that Lincoln was a Spiritualist. Few decades have passed between Appomattox and the present years without some esoteric and usually privately printed account of seances held in the White House during Civil War times, detailing how the President was supernaturally ruled by forces from the spirit world. Involved in such accounts were table rappings, unseen hands, materializations of ghosts, and other practices and paraphernalia of those who professionally communicated with the dead. Lincoln scholars have effectively demolished ideas of Lincoln being a Spiritualist, and have exposed such books for what they were.

One of Lincoln's law students of the Springfield days, Henry B. Rankin, has said of Lincoln: "He was not of the cast of mind attracted by occult things."

XI

Uniquely enough in view of his scant formal schooling, Lincoln emerged as a mighty master of English prose. His private letters, public utterances, and handwritten state papers, for his presidential years, are plentifully studded with literary gems, human interests extraordinarily expressed, and alluringly worded doctrines of supreme historical significance, in addition to Western "cracker barrel" philosophy.

"The source and development of language" attracted him strongly,

Lincoln had once confided to an Illinois Whig party colleague, Joseph Gillespie.

Lincoln in his Illinois years had not been the great technician and architect of rheortic that he was now demonstrating himself to be. During his pre-presidential period he was essentially the professional party pleader and political partisan, ever gearing his expressions to the voters' moods. Before 1861 he was author of only a few impressionable utterances, the most conspicuous being, "A house divided against itself can not stand," spoken when he accepted the Republican senatorial nomination to run against Stephen A. Douglas in 1858. And in his campaign against the Little Giant that followed, he expended much time and many words explaining that was really not what he intended to say, when those radically anti-slavery sentiments proved unpopular in Central and Southern Illinois.

To indicate how miraculously Lincoln improved his word power and made less partisan and more inspiringly elevated speeches after he was inducted as President, it is sufficient to compare those debates with Douglas in 1858 (seldom read but always over-praised) with the verbal power, lofty idealism, and high statesmanship of his Second Inaugural of 1865.

It is quite impossible to speak of Lincoln's "style" of writing and use of words, for he had numerous styles. Through the scores of printed speeches and hundreds of personal letters and state papers of his four presidential years there runs a wider variety of styles than in those of perhaps any other major American statesman. The range of his personality ran far, identifying itself with the tumults and follies of mankind, keeping touch with multitudes and solitudes. The free-going and friendly companion, as well as a man of intense seclusion, is evident in Lincoln's privately and publicly spoken and written phrases.

The President remained till his dying day, by use of tongue and pen, a formidable political protagonist, as he had demonstrated during his Illinois career. By logical reasoning or whimsical anecdote he reduced or overcame his opponents' position. Some of the figures of speech, which tremendously strengthened his viewpoint, have come down through the decades as the folk wisdom of the presumably sturdy and wise American pioneer and frontiersman. An example was his remark to the Republican-Union political delegation which officially informed him in 1864 that he had just been renominated for a second term by the national convention. He said: "I have not permitted myself, gentlemen, to conclude that I am the best man in the country; but I am reminded, in this connection, of a story of an old Dutch farmer, who remarked to a companion once that 'it was not best to swap horses when crossing streams.' "

Lincoln has nonetheless been credited with originating hundreds of anecdotes that he never actually told. He has been the victim for an entire century of writers who "improved" his messages, or even concocted phrases he never said. His words often have been revised, paraphrased, or deliberately manufactured from some one's fertile imagination in order to put made-to-order sentiments in his mouth. So universal did the fame and presumably superior wisdom of the Prairie President grow, that frequently whenever supporters, or opponents, of a controversial issue could support his view with a pointed saying by Lincoln, he considered his case formidably strengthened. Lincoln's words and phrases have been quoted to prove or disprove seemingly every political, social, economic, or moral issue. This process began with his death and continues to the present day. The only difficulty lies in the fact that many of these quotations, presented to the public as the Civil War President's, were not always his.

Perhaps the best known Lincoln quotation of doubtful authenticity—at best, based on hearsay after Lincoln's death—is the one concerning deceiving the people. Alexander K. McClure, prominent Republican leader of Pennsylvania during Civil War times, in 1901 published a book, *Abe Lincoln's Yarns and Stories,* and first quoted Lincoln as declaring: "It is true that you may fool all the people some of the time; you can even fool some of the people all the time; but you can't fool all of the people all the time."

XII

Lincoln's Gettysburg Address of 1863 and his Second Inaugural of 1865 remain the finest and most familiar of his public orations.

Lincoln's Special Message to Congress of July 4, 1861, not nearly as well known as it deserves to be, illustrates several of his superior traits as a thinker, literary composer, and philosopher of democracy. In words antedating the Gettysburg Address by more than two years, the President told the law-makers and the public on that Independence Day: "This issue embraces more than the fate of the United States. It presents to the whole family of man the question whether a constitutional republic, or democracy—a government of the people by the same people—can or can not maintain its territorial integrity against its own domestic foes." On the question of votes versus guns, alliteratively Lincoln called them ballots against bullets; he appealed to the nation in that Fourth-of-July congressional message: "It is now for them [the American people] to demonstrate to the world that those who can fairly carry an election can also repress a rebellion; that ballots are the rightful and peaceful successors of bullets, and that when ballots have fairly and constitutionally decided there can be no successful appeal back to bullets; that there can be no successful appeal except to ballots themselves at succeeding elections. Such will be a great lesson of peace, teaching men that what they can not take by an election neither can they take by a war."

Among Lincoln's private letters none is more famous, nor more magnificently composed, than his celebrated words to Mrs. Lydia Bixby of Boston.

Lincoln had received the partly inaccurate information from the Massachusetts Adjutant General's Office that Mrs. Bixby had five sons in the army, all of whom had been killed in battle. Later investigations revealed that actually two of the Bixby boys had been killed. A third was captured by Confederates or perhaps deserted. A fourth was honorably discharged. And the fifth definitely deserted his regiment.

Lincoln in November, 1864, wrote to Mrs. Bixby this famous message of condolence, which appeared in a Boston newspaper four days later:

> Dear Madam,—I have been shown in the files of the War Department a statement of the Adjutant General of Massachusetts, that you are the mother of five sons who have died gloriously on the field of battle.
>
> I feel how weak and fruitless must be any words of mine which should attempt to beguile you from the grief of a loss so overwhelming. But I can not refrain from tendering to you the consolation that may be found in the thanks of the Republic they died to save.
>
> I pray that our Heavenly Father may assuage the anguish of your bereavement, and leave you only the cherished memory of the loved and lost, and the solemn pride that must be yours, to have laid so costly a sacrifice upon the altar of Freedom.

A lesser known but exquisitely phrased letter was sent by Lincoln to Fanny McCullough in 1862. Fanny was the daughter of the former McLean County Court Clerk of Bloomington, Lieutenant-Colonel William McCullough of the Fourth Illinois Cavalry, who had fallen on a battlefield in Mississippi. The President sent these words:

> Dear Fanny
>
> It is with deep grief that I learn of the death of your kind and brave Father; and, especially, that it is affecting your young heart beyond what is common in such cases. In this sad world of ours, sorrow comes to all; and, to the young it comes with bitterest agony, because it takes them unawares. The older have learned to ever expect it. I am anxious to afford some alleviation of your present distress. Perfect relief is not possible, except with time. You can not now realize that you will ever feel better. Is not this so? And yet it is a mistake. You are sure to be happy again. To know this, which is certainly true, will make you less miserable now. I have had experience enough to know what I say; and you need only to believe it, to feel better at once. The memory of your dear Father, instead of an agony, will yet be a sad sweet feeling in your heart, of a purer, and holier sort than you have known before.
>
> Please present my kind regards to your afflicted mother.
>
> Your sincere friend
>
> A. Lincoln.

Lincoln's best friend, Joshua F. Speed, would in 1866 prophetically comment privately: "While no set speech of his (save the Gettysburg Address) will be considered as entirely artistic and complete, yet, when the gems of American literature come to be selected, as many will be culled from Lincoln's speeches as from any American orator."

XIII

"The waggoners (sic) and train rabble have committed great outrages in the rear of this army. . . . All this proceeds from one thing—the uncertainty of the death penalty through the false merciful policy of the President." So privately complained Colonel Theodore Lyman of General Meade's Army of the Potomac staff in 1864.

Colonel Lyman's irritation at Lincoln's lenient pardon policy for offenders in the military was shared by numberless other Union commanding officers.

Countless cases involving soldiers and officers, convicted by courts martial for offenses, came before Lincoln for pardons, submitted sometimes by commanding officers, sometimes by the convicted men's family or friends, or by members of Congress.

Study of Lincoln's pardon policy reveals a rather well defined pattern. In purely military offenses, such as sleeping while on sentry duty, insubordination, and desertion, where either a commanding General or the Judge Advocate of the Army recommended clemency, the President almost invariably accepted the recommendation. In death sentences he frequently ordered mitigation or pardon on his own authority. In February, 1864, by Lincoln's direction, the War Department issued a blanket order requiring mitigation of all pending sentences of death for desertion to imprisonment on Dry Tortugas for the rest of the war. This order also empowered Army and department commanders to restore to duty deserters under sentence when in their judgment the service would be benefited by the restoration. In pursuance of this order, sixty-two death sentences were commuted at one stroke in 1864.

In instances of crimes against civilians or those which civil courts treated as heinous, however, Lincoln was consistently inclined to severity. When clear cases of rape, robbery, arson, and the like came before him with the death penalty prescribed, the President usually approved them. But when all types of cases passed on by him are considered, it becomes apparent that his influence was a softening one.

Lincoln's correspondence is filled with orders to his Cabinet members and Union commanders to release convicted soldiers. It would require many pages to list all of such instances. Among the Chief Executive's notes are numerous ones such as the order he sent to Attorney General Bates about a Private in the 25th New York Volunteers, sentenced to hard labor for desertion: "Let Calvin Beckwith, named within, be pardoned for so much of his punishment as remains unexecuted."

Lincoln also granted pardons to civilians imprisoned, indicted, or convicted for federal offenses, on requests of members of Congress. To Secretary of War Cameron he would order: "This man William Martin, it seems, has been imprisoned on some charge of kidnapping and as Senator Pomeroy [of Kansas] and Hon. Green Adams ask his release, let him be released." To Attorney General Bates about a man held for larceny: "If Mr. Anconia, Rep. of the Reading District & Mr. [Thaddeus] Stevens, Rep. of Lancaster District will investigate this case and say in writing they wish the young man pardoned, I will do it." Again to Bates, in the case of James Ranking, convicted by federal court of robbery, for whom Senator Zachariah Chandler of Michigan interceded: "The Attorney General will please make out a pardon in this case." Still another order to Bates, which affected Herman Franks, indicted for treason: "I said yesterday if the Kentucky delegation or a majority of them, would ask in writing, for the pardon of Franks, I would grant it. Having so asked, then the Attorney General will please make out the pardon."

An insight into Lincoln's forgiving qualities is contained in his order to the Attorney General concerning one man who had served a good deal of his sentence for a federal offense: "On examination of George Krager's case, I think he was properly convicted; but as he was young, was of good character before the offence, and has behaved well in the prison, and has already suffered more than four years, I have concluded to direct his pardon for the remainder of his punishment."

One of Lincoln's remarkable acts of clemency—to a Confederate—has recently come to light. It involved Lieutenant John A. Stephens, C.S.A., a nephew of Confederate Vice-President Alexander H. Stephens. Lincoln and the Southern Vice-President had once served in Congress together and had been the fastest of friends during 1847-49. When the two met again, after sixteen years, one the leader of the Union, the other the second ranking Confederate official, at the Hampton Roads "Peace Conference" in February, 1865, Stephens told Lincoln that he had a nephew who, when last heard from, was a prisoner of the Federal Army at Johnson's Island, in Lake Erie. Stephens hoped that Lincoln would learn something about the young man and to have him told that all was well back home in Georgia. When Lincoln returned to Washington, he sent an order to Colonel Charles W. Hill, in command of Johnson's Island, ordering the parole of the Southern prisoner of war, Lieutenant Stephens. Lincoln's communique to Colonel Hill read: "Parole Lieut. John A. Stephens, prisoner of War, to report to me here [in Washington] in person, and send him to me. It is in pursuance of an arrangement I made yesterday with his uncle, Hon. A. H. Stephens."

Lieutenant Stephens was paroled, and Lincoln several days later sent him back to his uncle, the Confederate Vice-President, with a note to Stephens:

> According to our agreement, your nephew, Lieut. Stephens, goes to you, bearing this note. Please, in return, to select and send to me, that officer of the same rank, imprisoned at Richmond, whose physical condition most urgently requires his release.
>
> Respectfully, A. Lincoln.

Lincoln's Secretary of the Interior, John P. Usher, revealed after the war about the President: "His great effort seemed to be to find some excuse, some palliation for offenses charged. He strove at all times to relieve the citizens on both sides of the inconveniences and hardships resulting from war."

WHITE HOUSE FAMILY

27

I

THE national capital city, Washington, to which Abraham Lincoln as President-elect went with his family in February, 1861, was then still an easy-going Southern community, whose social life was largely dominated by slave-state men and women. But by the time that Lincoln had assumed the presidential office, nearly all the Southerners had left their seats in the Senate and the House, their commissions in the United States Army and Navy, and their jobs in the government departments to follow their states into the Confederacy. Lincoln led the Republican invasion of Washington, engulfing the federal bureaucracy from every direction. From the viewpoint of the subjected Southerners, the whole place was inundated by dangerous abolitionist Yankees and uncouth frontier Westerners.

The vaunted buildings of Washington then were the Capitol (with its dome still unfinished), the General Post Office, the Treasury, the Smithsonian Institution, and the White House. There, in the stately white-columned mansion on Pennsylvania Avenue, Lincoln went to live after inauguration in March, 1861, with his family, his wife, Mary, and their three sons, Bob, Willie, and Tad. Bob, though, was absent attending Harvard most of the time.

Willard's, the city's principal hotel, had its lobby, bar, and six stories of rooms crowded with members of Congress and office-seekers, from the hour that Lincoln reached Washington late in February, 1861, until his stilled body was borne back to Illinois more than four years later. That hotel, noted the London *Times* Washington correspondent, William H. Russell, during the first days of Lincoln's administration, contained "more scheming, plotting, planning heads and joyful hearts, than any building of the same type in the world. . . . Up and down the long passages doors were opening and shutting for men with papers bulging out of their pockets, who hurried as if for their life in and out, and the building almost shook with the tread of candidates." Those testimonials, which each and every aspiring feeder at the federal trough carried, assured the President and his department heads that John Smith, or some other name, of Hartford, Connecticut, or some other town, was the ablest, cleverest, most honest, and finest man the testifier had ever known. It was little wonder that Lincoln, following his re-election in 1864, complained to one of the Senators from New Hampshire: "Can't you and others start a public sentiment in favor of making no changes in office except for good and sufficient cause? It seems as though the bare thought of going through again what I did the first year here, would *crush* me." But patronage is a weapon of American political warfare that has not yet been outmoded.

With the start of war with the South in April, 1861, Washington turned into an armed camp, a city of barracks and hospitals. From his White House windows Lincoln could, for the next four agonizing years, view and hear long lines of army wagons and horse-drawn artillery rumbling through the streets. He saw field fortifications and the dirty tents of soldiers beyond the hills as he looked toward Virginia from an elevated position. The clatter of galloping squads of cavalrymen pounded his ears night and day as he pondered the problems of war, politics, and the complaints and importunities of private citizens.

By 1864 another Britisher, George Tuthill Borrett, Fellow of Cambridge University, on a visit described the American capital. "Washington now," observed Borrett, "is nothing more or less than a gigantic military depot. The pavement is crowded with uniforms. Paris cannot show half as many. Every open piece of ground is converted into a camp; every square is built over with Aldershot huts; every other house is a military storehouse, or a hospital, or a recruiting office. . . . The center of the chief streets is occupied with an interminable chain of ambulances and military wagons, carrying down supplies to the front. . . . Hear the dull, distant rumbling of the eternal ambulances, and the everlasting tramp of horses' feet!"

II

The Executive Mansion on Pennsylvania Avenue, where Lincoln lived and worked for more than four years (except for summer evenings spent at the Soldiers' Home on the outskirts), had arrangements that would not have met approval of modern efficiency experts and professional office managers. The President's secretaries, Nicolay and Hay, slept in the northeast room on the second floor. Directly across the broad corridor, on the southeast corner, was their office. Adjoining the latter was Lincoln's office, which some called "the President's room," while beyond it lay the reception room. The secretaries were thus placed, not in the line of the callers' advance, but in the rear, where they could cover only the President's retreat. Lincoln had a bell cord at his desk with which to summon Nicolay or Hay, or their assistant, William O. Stoddard. During the last months of war, 1864-65, an Amherst-educated clergyman, Reverend Edward D. Neill, was employed to aid with the ever mounting mail.

Throughout the war Lincoln's burdens mounted with each month: ever graver military decisions to make, constant endeavors to patch up party factionalism, the never absent patronage problems, numberless delicate details associated with the relations of Congress, and meetings with hundreds of casual callers, as well as favor-seekers who looked upon him as a blend of father confessor, Mr. Fix-it, and Santa Claus.

Besides his back-breaking load at the White House, Lincoln spent considerable time at the battle front and in army camps, partly to talk military strategy and tactics with commanders, partly to review troops and to visit with some of them.

No President before or since, except Andrew Jackson who had been a General, was more beloved by the troops than was Lincoln. A study of hundreds of letters and scores of diaries written by Union soldiers and officers indicates that the President's popularity among the rank and file of men was enormous. The warmth with which they received him when he visited their camps and regiments is suggested by the affectionate nicknames which they dubbed him. A few called him, behind his back, "President Lincoln," "the President," or "Mr. Lincoln," but to the overwhelming number of Federal troops in the field who saw him he was "Old Abe," "Honest Abe," or "Father Abraham." Their confidence in him rarely wavered, except temporarily when he removed General McClellan as Army of the Potomac commander.

Even so, when Lincoln visited McClellan's headquarters at Harrison's Landing, Virginia, in the summer of 1862 when the Federals were stalled on the Peninsula, Sergeant Felix Brannigan, of the 74th New York Regiment, expressed a prevailing viewpoint among his comrades when he sent word home: "Old Abe was here a few days ago and saw for himself the state of things. He, we are all convinced, is the soldier's friend. We feel he takes an interest in us. . . . He came and saw for himself. Talk of McClellan's popularity among the soldiers. It will never measure a hundredth part of Honest Abe's. Such cheers as greeted him never tickled the ears of Napoleon in his palmiest days."

Another New Yorker, Private A. Davenport of the 5th Regiment of that State, in that same year sent a note home: "President Lincoln Reviewed the whole Army in a flying visit. The men were all glad to see him & like him & have full confidence in him to a man. They feel he is not to be fooled & that he wants to see with his own eyes how matters are."

The Shakespearean scholar, Horace H. Furness, serving as a Sanitary Commission worker with McClellan's army, saw Lincoln as he departed from a visit to McClellan's headquarters near Frederick, Maryland, in October, 1862, the month after Antietam. Furness wrote his wife: "The soldiers crowded round his wagon, an open chaise, shaking both his hands with such enthusiasm as to almost tumble his hat over his eyes."

When in 1864 Lincoln ran for re-election against the soldier's favorite, McClellan, the men in uniform mostly favored the President.

De Haven Norton, of the 4th Wisconsin Cavalry, in his letter to his father following Lincoln's renomination, declared: "I Voted for him in 1860, and have fought for him three years. I shall vote for him in 1864 and fight for him three years more, that's fair." Luther Short, of the 43rd Indiana Regiment, at the same time informed his father: "I want Abraham to handle the rains (sic) until this rebellion is crushed and the old Flag waves proudly over this land again. I think to elect any other man than Old Abraham will only prolong the war." An Illinois soldier, Cornelius Johnson, communicated to his sister by mail: "I think that President Lincoln is the Only man at the present time that is fit for A President. If Old Ab (sic) is Realeced (sic) Again the war will not last long."

III

Mary Todd Lincoln reigned as First Lady.

Mrs. Lincoln had come to Washington in the flush of gratified ambition. Her husband's elevation to America's highest office had justified the marriage of this proud, well-born former Kentucky belle to the rather uncouth, self-educated lawyer and aspiring Illinois frontier politician of backwoods beginnings.

As Madam President, she attained power of many kinds. She intervened with her husband in some appointments on several occasions, she had him distribute federal jobs to those members of her Todd family who had not gone into the Confederacy, and used her influence in securing favors for friends, and for even those who flattered her adroitly.

Quite aside from her tempestuous nature and occasionally waspish tongue (and later her mentally unbalanced actions), Mrs. Lincoln was highly qualified as a White House hostess. She had grown up among proud and hospitable people in Lexington, in the Blue Grass region, and had lived in the stately mansion of her half-sister and brother-in-law, Ninian W. Edwards, in Springfield. By the standards of her day, she had enjoyed a superior education, having learned a smattering of French, and being able to turn a graceful phrase in conversation or letter. After the then prevailing custom of the South, she addressed men as "Sir," using the word to punctuate her conversation like a comma. Her manners were genteel and she struck most who encountered her as basically a lady of grace and culture.

Mary's position at Washington proved always a trying one. As the wife of the Republican President, she incurred the hostility of those Southern sympathizers who still hung about Washington. Being a Southern woman, with the speech and manners of her native Kentucky —and with all four of her half-brothers in the Confederate Army—she was caustically criticized by the more intemperate Unionists. The anti-slavery zealots constantly berated her behind her back because her family held slaves in Kentucky.

Although Mrs. Lincoln's familiar tantrums were some times vented on her husband, she was an indulgent mother. She had borne four sons, the second of whom, Eddie, had died eleven years before.

Willie, ten years old in 1861, and Thomas (or "Tad"), then nearly eight, were lively boys whom their parents, or anyone else, did not take pains to correct or reprimand in the slightest. Willie was the brightest of the three living Lincoln sons, Tad the most backward mentally, and Bob the most aloof and aristocratic. Bob was at Harvard during most of the war years.

The President was a doting father, blind to the antics and pranks of Willie and Tad. Lincoln was oblivious to their noise and intrusions on important conferences, and some times he was ready to throw himself full length on the floor with them.

IV

Before Lincoln had ended his first year as President, death came to the White House in a deeply personal way on three occasions: in May, 1861, the death of the Lincolns' young protegé, Colonel Elmer E. Ellsworth; in the following October, the mortal wounding of their old

Illinois friend, Colonel (and Senator) Edward D. Baker, in the Ball's Bluff battle; and in February, 1862, the death of their son, Willie Lincoln.

Willie, the most mentally promising of the Lincolns' sons, appeared alert and especially intellectual for his young years in an age of few precocious children. Willie liked to compose poetry, and had contributed some verses of memoriam on the death of Colonel Baker, which had appeared in a Washington newspaper. Too, he had a sympathetic nature, unlike his older brother, Bob. Willie felt grieved over the death of the mother of a playmate in Illinois, and was particularly saddened when the Lincoln family's friend, Colonel Ellsworth, had been shot dead. Willie wrote a young Illinois crony, Henry Remann, a note:

> Washington, D.C., May 25/61.
>
> Dear Henry
>
> You request a letter, & here it is. I want you to give my respects to Edward McClernand, and tell him that I feel very sorry about his mother, and one more thing. Colonel E.E. Ellsworth went over to Alexandria, Va. and determined to take the secession flag down of the Marshall house. So he rushed up the steps untill (sic) he reached the pole, took down the flag, wrapped it around him (eight men with him), and coming down the steps (his comrade, Brownell, being in front of him) & Jackson (a secessionist) behind him, shot him, immediately his (ellsworth's comrades) went & killed Jackson.
>
> Your truly,
> Willie Lincoln.

Willie was suddenly taken ill in February, 1862. For days the President and the First Lady worried over their son's malady, diagnosed as a certain fever, and stood vigil over his sick bed for the greater part of entire nights. The newspapers kept the public informed about the boy's condition day by day. He was often apparently improved, but there would come a relapse, followed by another rally, and then definite sinking. On February 20, after one of these periodic rallies, the worst relapse set in, and Willie Lincoln died.

The President, his features distorted with grief, pulled back the cover of his dead son and looked on the lifeless face. Mrs. Lincoln, after days of agonizing watching and constant prayer, fell exhausted. Growing semi-mad in her agony, she went into strange convulsions. Her defective nervous mental equipment lacked sufficient resources of strength, balance, and maturity required to meet this most destructive of all shocks up to that time.

The wholesomeness and attractiveness of life for Mrs. Lincoln dulled from that time.

They buried Willie Lincoln on an extremely windy day. Roofs were torn off houses and flags were slashed to fragments. The father drove, unseeing, through this wreckage in a carriage with his eldest son, Bob, and the two Senators from Illinois, Orville H. Browning and Lyman Trumbull. Mrs. Lincoln felt too gravely ill from shock to attend her son's funeral services.

V

Willie's death darkened the White House for months thereafter, and elaborate social functions were temporarily discontinued. Worst still, the Lincoln boy's passing produced devastating effects on the First Lady, both physically and mentally.

Coming from a family with more than a normal number of people with abnormalities in it, Mary Todd Lincoln had her powers of rationalism unhinged from the time of her son's death. And she grew increasingly worse with each additional shock.

Her associations and dealings with the White House staff and other government officials involved in the management of the mansion became more strained. She is "like no other human being I ever saw," noted Commissioner of Public Buildings Benjamin B. French to a relative one month following Willie's passing. French added, "She is not easy to get along with although I succeed pretty well with her."

She tormented John Hay, who found her exasperating in the management of White House details. In his eyes she was a diabolical woman always bent on mischief. To Nicolay, who was then temporarily absent from the city, Hay reported: "My Dear Nico: The devil is abroad, having great wrath. His daughter, the Hell-Cat, sent Stackpole in to blackguard me about the feed of her horses. She thinks there is cheating round the board. . . . I declined opening communications on the subject." Hay added: "She is in a state of mind about the Steward's salary. There is no Steward."

Hay was still too young and immature to understand Mrs. Lincoln's plight. He could not comprehend that acute mental illness was setting in. Her condition grew more terrible when she received news (in that same month of April, when Hay was complaining to Nicolay) that her half-brother, Sam Todd, had been killed leading his Confederate command at Shiloh. In another few months even worse tidings arrived: her favorite half-brother, Alec Todd, fell in the fighting against the Federals at Baton Rouge. In another year still a third Confederate brother, David Todd, would be killed at Vicksburg. Only one of her brothers, George, would survive the war. And in the autumn of 1863 the husband of her favorite half-sister, Brigadier-General Ben Hardin Helm, C.S.A., would be trampled to death as he led his Kentucky and Mississippi troops against the Unionists in the slaughter at Chickamauga.

During the summer of 1862, after the death of her son and two of her brothers, Mrs. Lincoln sought the services of a Spiritualist medium, who called himself "Colchester," in the hope that he could put her in communication with Willie. She even permitted Colchester, who was known by responsible parties to be a charlatan, to hold a séance at the Lincolns' summer residence in the Soldiers' Home. There this medium had the distraught First Lady "receive messages" from her dead son.

President Lincoln, learning of Colchester's exploitation of his wife, called on Professor Joseph Henry, an eminent scientist and Director of the Smithsonian Institution, for aid in determining the integrity of that medium. A meeting was arranged with Colchester at Henry's office at the Smithsonian, where the medium tried to impress Henry by creating various sounds which, he insisted, sprang from different indicated corners of the room. Henry remained skeptical and brought that private séance to a close by informing Colchester: "I do not know how you make these sounds, but this I perceive very clearly—they do not come from the room but from your person."

Henry later was confirmed in his conclusion about Colchester when he met a manufacturer of electrical instruments used by Colchester and other professional communers with the dead in the performance of their supernatural tricks.

VI

With the advent of 1863 Mrs. Lincoln ceased her heavy mourning. She wore diamonds and pearls, and garlanded her hair with white flowers, draped her handsome black shawl around her new dresses of purple, lilac, white, and silver-colored silk. At the big public receptions of the new year, people once more saw the same richly gowned and gracious plump lady who had first appeared at the White House two years previous.

But the First Lady, despite her surface of fine decorum and exquisite manners, inwardly felt excruciating pain gnawing at her mind and system. Snide remarks about her alleged secession sympathies, with her brothers in the Confederate Army, the snubs of her own Todd family in Kentucky because she was the wife of the "Black" Republican President who was presumably subjugating the South with Federal bayonets, unfounded but always persistent rumors that she was using her husband's position to favor her friends by interceding for them in the award of government contracts, and, above all, her never fading memories of Willie, were proving too great burdens for her to withstand.

Mrs. Lincoln was described in her distress by Commissioner of Public Buildings French, who stayed near her during that New Year's reception of 1863: "I stood at Mrs. Lincoln's side during the reception. It was the first one since we placed little Willie in the tomb. She remarked with a sad, sad look, 'Oh, Mr. French, how much we have passed through since last we stood here.' She seemed much affected through the first part of the reception and was too much overcome by her feelings to remain until it ended." That was the same New Year's Day reception at which Lincoln steeped himself in gloom over the Federal defeat at Fredericksburg, which had occurred a few weeks earlier.

That New Year's Day Mrs. Lincoln rode in a carriage with Senator Orville H. Browning of Illinois. After the ride Browning noted in his day-book:

"*Thursday, Jany 1, 1863.* Mrs. Lincoln told me she had been, the night before, with old Isaac Newton [United States Commissioner of Agriculture], out to Georgetown, to see a Mrs. Laury, a spiritualist, and she made wonderful revelations to her about her little son Willy (sic) who died last winter, and also about things on earth. Among other things she revealed that the cabinet were all the enemies of the President, working for themselves, and that they would have to be dismissed, and others called to his aid before he had success."

Her dead son continued to crowd out all other visions from Mary Lincoln's mind. Only several weeks following that New Year's Day, she wrote the wife of her husband's Secretary of the Navy, Mrs. Gideon Welles, when Willie had been dead exactly one year: "Only those who have passed through such bereavements, can realize, how the heart bleeds at the return, of these anniversaries."

Later in the year, in September, the Confederate husband of Mary's younger half-sister Emilie, Brigadier-General Ben Hardin Helm, was killed at Chickamauga. It is quite impossible to read Mrs. Lincoln's story, as told by her niece, Katherine Todd Helm, without realizing that on no one did civil war bear more crushingly heavy than on the First Lady. The agonies of bloody fighting had come to the very White House.

Mary's half-sister, Emilie, who had always been her favorite, at Atlanta, Georgia, attended the last rites of her husband, General Helm. "Mrs. Helm is crushed by the blow—almost broken hearted—and desires to return to her Mother and friends in Kentucky" wrote a friend of Mrs. Helm in Georgia to President Lincoln, and he requested that Lincoln issue a pass through the Union lines so that Mrs. Helm could return to her parent in Kentucky. This ended by Lincoln sending orders to the Federal commanding officer at a location where Mrs. Helm arrived: "Send her to me."

Thus Lincoln and his wife in 1863 had as their White House guest her Confederate half-sister.

Criticism ran riot when it was learned that the President and the First Lady were harboring a rebel woman in the Executive Mansion—even though that rebel was blood kin to Mrs. Lincoln. Major-General Daniel E. Sickles, having left a leg at Gettysburg, visited the President, pounded the table angrily, and raised his voice to the President: "You should not have that rebel in your house." Lincoln was quoted as having retorted: "Excuse me, General Sickles, my wife and I are in the habit of choosing our own guests. We do not need from our friends either advice or assistance in the matter. Besides, the little 'rebel' came because I ordered her to come, it was not of her own volition." Lincoln might, or might not have, said those words to Sickles. But his Confederate sister-in-law remained at the Executive Mansion a while longer. Senator Browning of Illinois recorded in mid-December, 1863: "The President told me his sister-in-law, Mrs. Helm, was in the house, but he did not wish it known."

While Mrs. Emilie Todd Helm was staying at the Executive Mansion, she had occasion to watch closely the strange conduct of her half-sister, Mrs. Lincoln. One evening Mary, with tear-stained face and quivering smile, came to Emilie's room and frightened her by her talk of having received a visit from her dead sons, Willie and Eddie, and her brother, Alec, who had been killed one year and a half before fighting the Federals in Louisiana. According to Mrs. Helm, Mary strangely told her: "If Willie did not come to comfort me I would still be drowned in tears, and while I long inexpressibly to touch him, to hold him in my arms, and still grieve that he has no future in this world that I might watch with a proud mother's heart—he lives, Emilie!" Mrs. Lincoln thrillingly confided to Emilie: "He comes to me every night, and stands at the foot of my bed with the same sweet, adorable smile he has always had; he does not always come alone; little Eddie is sometimes with him and twice he has come with our brother Alec. . . . You can not dream of the comfort this gives me." Mrs. Helm, in alarm, noted in her diary: "It *is* unnatural and abnormal, it frightens me. It does not seem like Sister Mary to be so nervous and wrought up. She is on a terrible strain and her smiles seem forced."

By autumn of the following year, 1864, Mrs. Lincoln was still pining over Willie. "Since we were so heavily visited by affliction, almost three years since, in the loss of our darling, idolized Willie, with the sensitiveness of a heavy sorrow," she told a former Springfield neighbor in a letter, "I have shrank (sic), from all communication, with those, who would most forcibly recall, my sorrows to my mind." She added to this former neighbor, Mrs. John Henry Shearer: "Since I last saw you, I have sometimes feared, that the *deep waters,* through which we passed would overwhelm me. Willie, darling Boy! was always the idolized child, of the household. So gentle, so meek, for a more Heavenly Home." She told of her now lack of interest in social affairs: "My position, requires my presence, where my heart, is *so far* from being."

VII

Mary Lincoln, in her ever weakening mental condition, on at least two occasions, flared into jealousy in front of others at the presumably harmless attention that the President publicly received from two women. One of them was the former Agnes Leclerque of Baltimore, later Princess Salm-Salm, and it happened in 1863. The other scene involved Mrs. Mary Ord, wife of Major-General Edward O. C. Ord, Commander of the Army of the James, early in 1865.

Princess Salm-Salm was the wife of a Prince who had left Europe for some mysterious reason and had maneuvered Governor Edwin D. Morgan of New York into giving him a commission as Colonel of the Eighth New York Regiment in the heavily German Eleventh Corps.

Lincoln, along with Mrs. Lincoln and son Tad, visited General Sickles's headquarters. A line of officers' wives waited to be presented to the President. Sickles playfully suggested that they encircle Lincoln in a bevy and kiss him. Mrs. Lincoln was not there at that time, but Tad was, and he told his mother that which had happened. All of the women declined Sickles's half-serious, half-joking idea of the lady folks kissing Lincoln—all but the adventurous Princess Salm-Salm. On tiptoes she pulled Lincoln's head down and kissed him fondly on the cheek.

Lincoln took this nonsense in his stride. Not so Mrs. Lincoln, who, when she learned about it, flew into a short-lived rage and remained permanently cool toward General Sickles. The following day, when he lunched with the Lincolns, Sickles recalled later: "Seated at the table in a private cabin, face to face with Mrs. Lincoln, I at once saw how much I was out of favor. I was not recognized. The President tried his best to put his wife in better humor, but in vain."

While at City Point in late March or early April, 1865, only days before the war ended and the President was shot, Mrs. Lincoln put on an unseemly demonstration when she publicly took offense at Major-General Ord's wife for riding directly beside the President and his staff. The First Lady brusquely left City Point, departed for Washington, and remained angry for several days. Then she returned just in time to accompany the President and his party on the return trip to Washington.

VIII

Willie Lincoln's death had proved nearly as shattering a blow to the President as it had to Mrs. Lincoln.

The Chief Executive, not of a temperament to mention often subjects that affected him deeply, maintained his outward pleasant self following his son's passing. But his intimates continued to note his bright face assuming an even more melancholic aspect after Willie had gone. "Some of us know," related his young California newspaper correspondent friend, Noah Brooks, "that, in the long nights when Lincoln sat alone in his chamber, oppressed with unspeakable anxieties for the whole country, the darkness of his own personal grief came over him to deepen his loneliness and gloom." To Colonel Cannon, on General Wool's staff at Fortress Monroe, Lincoln read morbid passages from Shakespeare about one character who bewailed the loss of his son, and then confided to Cannon, "Just so, I dream of my boy Willie."

After Willie's death, Lincoln found ever more consolation in Tad, his youngest son. He was never known to punish the boy or rebuke him in any manner for misbehavior, and the boy was constantly misbehaving. Whenever the son was guilty of misconduct, it was always the father who sought to make excuses for him or to present some extenuating circumstances to account for his major and minor misdeeds. The President's office was usually the sanctuary to which Master Thomas Lincoln would hurriedly retreat after committing some childish misdemeanor.

Lincoln's letters and telegrams to Mrs. Lincoln, when she was absent from Washington with Tad, are filled with concern for the boy. One wire to his wife would read: "Think you better put 'Tad's' pistol away. I had an ugly dream about him." Another telegram would request Mrs. Lincoln: "Tell dear Tad, poor 'Nanny Goat' is lost; and Mrs. Cuthbert [Mary Ann Cuthbert, White House housekeeper] & I are in distress about it. The day you left Nanny was found resting herself, and chewing her little cud, on the middle of Tad's bed. But now, she's gone!" Again: "Tell Tad the goats and father are very well—especially the goats." The President, four days before he was shot, requested Secretary of War Stanton: "Tad wants some flags. Can he be accomodated?" And on the same day, Lincoln asked Secretary of the Navy Welles: "Let Master Tad have a Navy sword."

Tad was taken along by the President and Mrs. Lincoln on that last trip Lincoln was ever to make alive out of Washington—to City Point aboard the *River Queen,* in late March, 1865. Tad, too, stood at his father's feet on that evening of April 11, a few weeks later, when from the White House portico Lincoln made his last of all public speeches to an assembled crowd below.

Tad Lincoln was destined to outlive his immortal father by six years. In 1871 the youth died in Chicago.

Alone of Lincoln's four sons, only Robert was to live to ripe maturity.

IX

The eldest of the Lincolns' sons, Robert Todd Lincoln, had reached seventeen years of age and was attending Phillips Exeter Academy in New Hampshire when his father was running for President in 1860. Then he was enrolled at Harvard College, and remained there studying throughout most of the war, except for vacation periods and brief visits home to Washington.

The President's very rare written statements about Robert are characterized by a curious restraint most unusual from a man who gave out all-embracing parental affection to other young people. In 1860 Lincoln confided in a note to his old Illinois friend and physician, Dr. Anson G. Henry, then of Washington Territory, about his eldest son: "He promises very well, considering we never controlled him much." His references to his eldest offspring usually lacked warmth.

As the nation burst into unfathomable war, the junior Lincoln led a not insufferable life at Harvard while untold thousands of youths of his age were combatting Confederates under shot and shell on the battlefields. Bob was inducted into the Institute of 1770, joined a secret campus society, and was elected Vice-President of the Hasty Pudding Club in that celebrated college.

The harried President could find little time for correspondence with his son in Cambridge. But during 1863 and 1864 he sent Bob some telegrams which are still preserved: "Don't be uneasy. Your mother very slightly hurt by her fall;" or, when Bob was in New York: "Come to Washington;" followed three days later by another urgent wire: "Why do I hear no more of you?" Early in 1864 Lincoln sent another telegram to his son at Cambridge: "I send you draft to-day. How are you? Answer by telegraph at once." Later in that year: "Your letter makes us a little uneasy about your health. Telegraph us how you are. If you think it would help you make us a visit."

Lincoln had not as many talks with his eldest son as the usual father had with his offspring, partly because of the President's overcrowded hours, partly because Bob never felt as close to his father as toward his mother. Herndon, Lincoln's law partner, always insisted with abundant truth, "Bob is a Todd, not a Lincoln." After the war Bob testified before a Board of Inquiry about his not too numerous talks with his father: "I was not accustomed to have conversations with him, when I could find him alone in his office, on subjects that were then current. Sometimes the conversation would arise from a remark of his own, and sometimes by a question of mine."

Bob acted like a distant relative in later years when he was questioned about his father's love for the theatre. He answered: "Personally I never attended a play with my father . . . as I was very little in Washington while he was there. I have a general understanding that he frequently visited the theatre there as a matter of recreation, but I know nothing of the particulars."

On one visit home Bob was accidentally pushed off a railroad platform at the Jersey City station, and momentarily faced grave danger, perhaps missing death—when miraculously enough, a man rushed forward and pulled him away from danger by yanking him from the tracks. Bob told about his narrow escape from harm in later years: "The platform was about the height of the car floor, and there was of course a narrow space between the platform and the car body. There was some crowding, and I happened to be pressed by it against the car body while waiting my turn. In this situation the train began to move, and by the motion I was twisted off my feet, and had dropped somewhat, with feet downward, into the open space, and was personally helpless, when my coat collar was vigorously seized and I was quickly pulled up and out to a more secure footing on the platform. Upon turning to thank my rescuer I saw it was Edwin Booth, whose face was of course well known to me, and I expressed my gratitude to him."

On visits or vacations home in Washington, Bob Lincoln renewed his less than strong intimacy with his father, struck up a lasting friendship with John Hay, talked with and even lectured his younger brother, Tad, sternly, drove the White House horses, escorted and danced with girls in the city, and went on trips and vacations with his mother.

Bob accompanied two of his Harvard classmates and his mother to the vacation resort of Long Branch, New Jersey, during the summer of 1861, along with John Hay. There Bob was lionized by the debutantes who buzzed about him and awaited his invitations to dance; he was the President's son. The society "gossip" reporter for the New York *Herald* sent word from Long Branch: "Mr. Lincoln, and after him Messrs. Hay, McConkey, and Forbes, were admired, followed and sought for by every lady . . . not one belle at the National but was all aflutter to be introduced to, to dance and talk with Mr. Lincoln; but not one beau but was outrageously jealous of the whole party." The *Herald* correspondent found the President's son merely wanting to be left alone: "He doesn't talk much, Though we christened him the 'Prince of Rails' during that memorable tour from Springfield, he is only Mr. Robert Lincoln of Cambridge, and I believe he desires to be only that."

Bob became infatuated with an attractive German girl, Fräulein von Gerolt, daughter of the Minister from Prussia, Baron von Gerolt. John Hay called her "the *Teutonne.*" But suddenly in 1863 the girl married a British officer, and Bob sank into temporary depression. Hay in a note to Nicolay gave the gossip: "Bob and his mother have gone to the white mountains. Bob was so shattered by the wedding of the idol of all of us, the bright particular *Teutonne,* that he rushed madly off to sympathize with nature in her sternest aspects."

President Lincoln's oldest son in short order forgot about Baron von Gerolt's daughter. Soon he was seeing frequently Miss Mary Harlan of Mount Pleasant, Iowa, daughter of United States Senator James Harlan from that State.

X

Bob Lincoln, following his graduation from Harvard College in 1864 —after the war had been raging for more than three years—came home to the White House. That fall he was back at Harvard, in the law school.

All of the while critical comments and innuendoes of citizens posed a pertinent question: When was Lincoln's son going into uniform?

Mrs. Lincoln was the main reason why Lincoln's son was not in the army, like the sons of hundreds of thousands of other Northern parents. Of abnormally nervous temperament, Mrs. Lincoln found herself on the verge of mental breakdown. She opposed Bob going into military service, and the President feared to press the point further. According to her half-sister, Mrs. Emilie Todd Helm, Mrs. Lincoln pleaded with the President: "I know that Robert's plea to go into the Army is manly and noble, and I want him to go, but oh, I am so frightened he may never come back to us!"

One day Senator Ira Harris of New York called at the White House. Brusquely he asked: "Why isn't Robert in the Army? He is old enough to serve his country. He should have gone to the front some time ago." Mrs. Lincoln's face blanched, and she sought to control herself. Biting her lip, she snapped back: "Robert is making his preparations now to enter the Army, Senator Harris; he is not a shirker as you seem to imply, for he had been anxious to go for a long time. If fault there be, it is mine. I have insisted that he should stay in college a little longer as I think an educated man can serve his country with more intelligent purpose than an ignoramus." The Senator from New York retorted coldly: "I have only one son and he is fighting for his country."

Finally Lincoln, on January 19, 1865, less than three months before the war ended, wrote an embarrassing letter to General Grant about Bob's joining the Army. The President wrote the General of the Armies:

> Please read and answer this letter as though I was not President, but only a friend. My son, now in his twenty second year, having graduated at Harvard, wishes to see something of the war before it ends. I do not wish to put him in the ranks, nor yet to give him a commission, to which those who have already served long, are better entitled, and better qualified to hold. Could he, without embarrassment to you, or detriment to the service, go into your Military family with some nominal rank, I, and not the public, furnishing the necessary means? If no, say so without the least hesitation, because I am as anxious, and as deeply interested, that you shall not be encumbered as you can be yourself.

Lincoln received this answer from Grant: "Your favor of this date in relation to your son serving in some Military capacity is received. I will be most happy to have him in my Military family in the manner you propose. The nominal rank given him is immaterial but I would suggest that of Capt. as I have three staff officers now, of considerable service, in no higher grade. Indeed I have one officer with only the rank of Lieut. who has been in the service from the beginning of the war. This however will make no difference and I would still say give the rank of Capt."

Lincoln and Secretary of War Stanton signed Bob's commission as "Assistant Adjutant General of Volunteers with the rank of Captain" on February 17, 1865. Seven weeks more remained of the war.

Captain Lincoln's military career was necessarily short-lived. He participated in the Federal operations which led to the Confederates' evacuation of Petersburg. He accompanied his father on the visit to the scenes of military combat, and was shortly after present at Appomattox when General Lee surrendered to General Grant.

The next day, Bob started for Washington. But because of the destruction of railroads and unforeseen travel difficulties, he did not reach the White House until Friday morning, the 14th—just in time to have breakfast with his father on the President's last full day alive.

After his father's burial Bob Lincoln studied law in Chicago, was admitted to the bar in 1867, and in the following year married Mary Harlan, daughter of the Senator from Iowa and Abraham Lincoln's Secretary of the Interior-designate, Senator James Harlan. In his law practice at Chicago Abraham Lincoln's blood heir gained profitable clients, among them railroads and corporations. Bob showed no inclination for politics, and never ran for elective office of any kind. President Garfield made him Secretary of War and he accepted the post of Minister to England from President Benjamin Harrison. He acted as counsel, then President, of the Pullman Company, a position he resigned in 1911. Then he moved to

Washington, and in 1926, at the ripened age of eighty-three, passed away at his Vermont estate.

When, toward the end of the nineteenth century, Abraham Lincoln's famed biographer, Ida M. Tarbell, talked and had tea with Mr. Robert Todd Lincoln, she was deeply disappointed. Expecting to see and hear so much qualitatively, she was confronted essentially by quantity and excessive dignity. Miss Tarbell commented in her autobiography of Lincoln's eldest son: "I searched his face and manners for resemblances. There was nothing. He was all Todd, a big plump man perhaps fifty years old, perfectly groomed."

Today the story of Robert Todd Lincoln remains obscure. Having led a life of aloofness, accumulating wealth, and having served in the Cabinets of Presidents Garfield and Chester A. Arthur and in the mission at London, he never fit into what Americans set up as the "Lincoln legend." Whenever Robert is mentioned, he is usually called by his full name, Robert Todd Lincoln, with emphasis on his mother's name, as if to underscore Herndon's and Ida M. Tarbell's discerning observation that he was "all Todd."

XI

Despite their drastically different family backgrounds and social strata, President and Mrs. Lincoln held some interests in common. Each supplied qualities which the other lacked. Lincoln felt his deficiency of educational and other advantages in early life. Mary brought to him from her own "well born" Kentucky heritage and way of life, a social decorum which also contributed so vastly to her qualifications as the nation's First Lady, quite aside from the breakdown of her reasoning faculties, which was not to grow intolerably acute until after his assassination.

Whereas in public Lincoln was abstracted and melancholy, she usually acted animated and cheerful; whereas he was concerned with justice and welfare for the public, she was interested in justice and welfare for herself, her husband, her sons.

Mrs. Lincoln worried constantly about the President's waning strength during the ordeal of war. The First Lady's worry ran through her letters. Her dread of losing her husband, combined with her disintegrating rationalism and her unrestrained urge to shop in stores, strangely led her to purchase mourning clothes in anticipation of his death.

Mary Lincoln watched agonizingly at the back-breaking load under which the President worked in war time. "I consider myself fortunate," she confided in a letter to her girlhood chum, Mercy Levering, now Mrs. James L. Conkling, after nearly four years of war, "if at eleven o'clock, I once more find myself, in my pleasant room & very especially, if my tired & weary Husband, is *there,* resting in the lounge to receive me—to chat over the occurrences of the day."

Lincoln planned to travel after his second administration ended—but that would not be until March, 1869. "My husband intended, when he was through with his Presidential term," she revealed one year after his assassination, "to take me and our boys with him to Europe. After his return from Europe he intended to cross the Rocky Mountains and go to California, where soldiers were to be digging out gold to pay the national debt."

The President, at the time of his death, had not yet decided where his permanent residence would be. When Booth's bullet struck him down, he still had nearly his entire four-year presidential term to serve.

For the Lincolns in the White House, the avalanche of war grimly engulfed them in four seemingly unending and nearly unendurable years. But daily existence for America's first family during 1861-65 differed in no vital heart-rupturing degree from those of millions of other Americans, in the North, the border regions, and the South.

UPWARD SWING: *Gettysburg and Vicksburg*

28

I

TO return to those depressing days following Chancellorsville.

After that disastrous Federal defeat in early May, 1863, any possible reborn confidence in Lincoln and his administration would be entirely dependent upon the battlefront situation.

Lincoln had a lengthy talk with the beaten General Hooker on May 7, after the grim returns from Chancellorsville were in. Major-General George G. Meade, commanding the Fifth Corps under Hooker, on the day following the President's conversation with Hooker, wrote his wife about it. Lincoln had said that he had come down to Hooker's headquarters to enquire for himself and spoke with Hooker about "all sorts of things," General Meade informed Mrs. Meade. The President, too, had told Hooker that "the result was in his judgment most unfortunate; but he did not blame any one—he believed every one had done all in his power;" but the Chief Executive also concluded that the horrible effect of Chancellorsville "both at home and abroad, would be more serious and injurious than any previous act of the war."

Hooker's prestige declined to rock-bottom depths. At New York bars they served a mixed drink, guaranteed to put the imbiber under, called "Hooker's Retreat." Even his subordinate generals scorned him. Several of them proposed sending a delegation to Lincoln to request his removal as Army of the Potomac commander, suggesting Meade as his successor. Major-General Darius N. Couch, heading the Second Corps, actually called on the President and avowed that he would serve under Hooker no longer.

Lincoln gave Hooker a letter, dated May 7, expressing his own thoughts on what should be done next against Lee. In gross understatement the President wrote the defeated General: "The recent movement of your army is ended without effecting its object, except perhaps some important breakings of the enemies' communications." Lincoln then asked, "What next?" He suggested that the Confederates' communications were stretched west of Fredericksburg and were vulnerable to attack, adding: "An early movement would also help to supersede the bad moral effect of the recent one." But he cautioned Hooker that nothing should be "done in desperation or rashness." Lincoln queried: "Have you already in your mind a plan wholly, or partially formed? If you have, prossecute (sic) it without interference from me. If you have not, please inform me, so that I, incompetent as I may be, can try [to] assist in the formation of some plan for the Army."

Lincoln received reply from Hooker, declaring that he wanted to continue operations on the Rappahannock line and would launch a movement as soon as he judged his men in condition to fight. Lincoln again heard from Hooker one week later. The General informed him that, although the Southerners had received reinforcements and now outnumbered him (an exaggeration), he hoped to start an offensive across the Rappahannock the next day. He requested Lincoln not to speak of his proposed move.

There occurred another conference between Lincoln and Hooker. On May 14 the President wrote him again, expressing doubt about another crossing of that river whose name had by now become a bad nightmare to him. The Confederates had re-established their deranged communications, Lincoln told Hooker. He also pointed out: "It does not now appear probable to me that you can gain any thing by an early renewal of the attempt to cross the Rappahannock. I therefore shall not complain, if you do no more, for a time, than to keep the enemy at bay, and out of other mischief, by menaces and occasional cavalry raids, if practicable; and to put your own army in good condition again. Still, if in your own clear judgment, you can renew the attack successfully, I do not mean to restrain you. Bearing upon this last point, I must tell you I have some painful intimations that some of your corps and Division Commanders are not giving you their entire confidence. This would be ruinous, if true; and you should therefore, first of all, ascertain the real facts beyond all possibility of doubt."

Rankling in Lincoln's mind was that image of Hooker being distrusted by his own subordinate commanders. Some of them had seen or written him at the White House, expounding on Hooker's shortcomings in detail. Third parties had informed him, too, of the Generals' and the Colonels' lack of faith in their top commander in the field. Charles F. Benjamin of the War Department staff later insisted that Lincoln had already made up his mind about Hooker immediately after Chancellorsville, that he and General-in-Chief Halleck termed the defeat "inexcusable" and that Hooker must not be entrusted with the conduct of another battle.

Early in June, Major-General John F. Reynolds, one of Hooker's corps commanders with a fighting record in the field, who had vainly tried to persuade Hooker to attack the enemy's left flank at Chancellorsville, held a lengthy conference with the President in the Executive Mansion. Reynolds's colleagues always insisted henceforth that Lincoln offered Reynolds the Army of the Potomac command then, but that Reynolds insisted on absolute control, with no dictation from Washington.

Suddenly, the North was thrown into fright by news that General Lee was about to invade Pennsylvania!

II

General Robert E. Lee, with the Fredericksburg, Chancellorsville, and lesser victories over the Federal forces chalked up, felt depressed about the loss of his best subordinate general, "Stonewall" Jackson, accidentally shot mortally by his own men after defeating the Union's Eleventh Corps at Chancellorsville. In grief Lee wrote: "I know not how to replace him." Lee had lost his "right arm."

In reorganization of his Army of Northern Virginia, necessitated by Jackson's death and other circumstances, Lee increased the number of his corps from the two, commanded by the late Jackson and by Longstreet, to three, and reduced their size, because he considered the two old-corps commands too huge for one General to handle to fullest advantage in a wooded country. Lee retained Lieutenant-General Longstreet in command of the First Corps, made Lieutenant-General Richard S. Ewell head of the reorganized Second Corps, and selected Lieutenant-General Ambrose P. Hill to lead the Third Corps—with himself in over-all command.

Lee's choice of Ewell for Jackson's old command was dictated by sentiment partially, for Ewell had been associated with the late Jackson's most illustrious battles; but Ewell's selection as head of the Second placed one-third of Lee's entire army under an officer who had served only a few weeks directly under Lee and was unaccustomed to exercise the discretion that Lee usually gave his corps generals. The Confederate staff, of course, was reorganized at the same time in May and June, 1863, and numberless new officers were assigned to direct troops of whom they knew little. All of this created a new machinery of command for two-thirds of Lee's Army of Northern Virginia, the Confederates' main force in the field. Lee did not fully appreciate the dangers that this change of command involved. His decision to resume immediately the offensive after Chancellorsville, driving north to the enemy's country—into Pennsylvania!—before the officers familiarized themselves with their troops, was to prove one of Lee's major military mistakes.

But Lee concluded that he must invade Pennsylvania shortly after his Chancellorsville victory, in order to supply his army, to strengthen peace sentiment in the North by showing the futility of trying to subdue the South, and to compel Lincoln to detach Federal troops from the far South, thereby relieving the Confederates at Vicksburg from some of the pressure of Grant's advance. Surely, the Federals would have to take soldiers and supplies from Grant to meet this Southern threat by Lee in Pennsylvania!

Lee, leaving Hill with 20,000 to hold the line of the Rappahannock temporarily, skilfully moved into Maryland, with Harrisburg, Pennsylvania's capital, as his objective. On June 23 General J.E.B. ("Jeb") Stuart's fondness for cavalry raids around the Federal enemy led him to exceed his orders and to separate the most proficient part of the Confederate cavalry from the rest of Lee's army at a time when Lee most needed the reconnoitering horsemen to watch Hooker, who was now between Lee and Stuart.

Finding that Hooker and his army had crossed into Maryland three days before, Lee quickly concentrated his columns, which had been widely scattered, for the collection of supplies. As June ended, Hill's men discovered a Federal force of unknown strength near Gettysburg, Pennsylvania.

III

At Washington and throughout the North, panic reigned during that frightful June of Lee's Northern invasion.

On June 10 General Ewell's Second Corps of Lee's army set off for the Shenandoah Valley, Virginia, crossed by Chester Gap, and swept the Valley free of Federal troops as far as the Potomac. Brigadier-General

Albert G. Jenkins's Confederate cavalry crossed the Potomac at Williamsport, Maryland, forced the Federals out of Hagerstown, entered it on the fifteenth. Then Jenkins led his horsemen into Chambersburg—in Pennsylvania!

Lincoln sprang to action. On June 15 he called for 100,000 troops from Maryland, West Virginia, Pennsylvania, and Ohio, to serve six months. He justified this proclamation on the basis of the "armed insurrectionary combinations" who were "threatening to make inroads into the States of Maryland, Western Virginia, Pennsylvania and Ohio."

Governor Andrew G. Curtin of Pennsylvania appealed to Governor Parker of New Jersey, and called upon his fellow-Pennsylvanians: "A people who want the heart to defend their soil, their families, and their firesides are not worthy to be accounted men." Other states were not overready to answer Lincoln's latest call for troops, even with Lee's men in Pennsylvania. Governor Tod of Ohio pleaded with his fellow Buckeye Staters to "meet the horde of rebels" and to "remember that our own sacred homes are threatened with pillage and destruction and our wives and daughters with insults." Governor Augustus W. Bradford of Maryland threatened a State draft. In New England, Governor James Y. Smith of Rhode Island dallied while he argued over the worth of a six-months' militiaman on the State's draft quota. One Massachusetts regiment, just home and still unpaid, mutinied. The Western governors, Morton of Indiana and Yates of Lincoln's own Illinois, were even slow in responding to the President's call for more men with which to combat Lee's Northern drive.

The President at this precise time of peril, as Lee's legions advanced northward, was desperately endeavoring to smooth out fresh difficulties between Hooker and General-in-Chief Halleck.

"You have long been aware, Mr. President," complained Hooker in a telegram on June 16, day following Lincoln's new call for troops, "that I have not enjoyed the confidence of the Major General Commanding the Army [Halleck] & I can assure you so long as this continues we may look in vain for success. . . . It may be possible now to prevent a junction of A. P. Hill's Corps with those of Ewell & Longstreet. If so, please let instructions to that effect be given me." Hooker was indirectly asking Lincoln for assurance that Halleck would have no power to order his movements.

Lincoln, in answer to Hooker, upheld Halleck. He directed the Army of the Potomac commander: "To remove all misunderstanding, I now place you in the strict military relation to Gen. Halleck, of a commander of one of the armies, to the General-in-Chief of all the armies. I have not intended differently; but as it seems to be differently understood, I shall direct him to give you orders, and you to obey them."

On that same day, the 16th of June, Lincoln sent a lengthy letter to Hooker, marked "Private." He cautioned the General:

> I believe Halleck is dissatisfied with you to this extent only, that he knows that you write and telegraph ('report,' as he calls it) to me. I think he is wrong to find fault with this; but I do not think he withholds any support from you on account of it. If you and he would use the same frankness to one another, and to me, that I use to both of you, there would be no difficulty. I need and must have the professional skill of both, and yet these suspicions tend to deprive me of both.

All of the while, as Lee's army drove through town after town in lower Pennsylvania, Hooker was not quite certain of the exact whereabouts of the Confederate invaders. On June 18 one Washington observer communicated to the now long-retired General McClellan: "Hooker does not know Lee's position. Halleck does not know what Schenck [in command at Baltimore], or Hooker, is doing, or where Hooker is. We are adrift."

As precious days passed—days before the Federals' Army of the Potomac would clash head-on with the Confederates' Army of Northern Virginia, somewhere in Pennsylvania—Lincoln came to his long-delayed decision about Hooker's future; more particularly, the identity of the General who would lead the grand Union army in driving back Lee. The President chose to replace Hooker with Major-General George G. Meade.

Meade, a grizzled, bad-tempered Pennsylvanian, with goggle eyes and straggly beard, one of Hooker's corps commanders, was a self-effacing man, excellent soldier, competent commander, devoted to military duty and disdaining army feuds and politicking in Washington, was truly one of the most underrated of Federal generals—a man who today is still unsung when praise is lavished on Union heroes.

A personal representative of Lincoln, Colonel James A. Hardie of the War Department staff, was sent to deliver carefully prepared and authenticated duplicate orders, dated June 27, 1863, to Generals Hooker and Meade, removing Hooker and appointing Meade as commanding officer of the Army of the Potomac.

General-in-Chief Halleck was delighted, and two weeks later wrote his old foe, General Grant: "Meade seems the right man for the right place. Hooker was worse than a failure. Had he remained in command he would have lost the army & the capital."

No sooner was news out about the change in commanders from Hooker to Meade, than some of General McClellan's admirers let up a cry that "Little Mac" should be called back to stop Lee's Pennsylvania invasion, just as he had checked Lee's Maryland drive at Antietam less than one year before. Alexander K. McClure, Republican Chairman of Pennsylvania, and Governor Parker of New Jersey both implored Lincoln to make McClellan the Army of the Potomac head once more. Lincoln on June 30 (three days after he had approved the order appointing Meade) answered McClure: "Do we gain any thing by opening one leak to stop another? Do we gain any thing by quieting one clamor, merely to open another, and probably a larger one?" On that same day the President replied to the Governor of New Jersey: "I beg you will not see the foe in New-Jersey. I beg you to be assured that no one out of my position can know so well as if he were in it, the difficulties and involvements of re-placing Gen. McClellan in command—and this aside from any imputations upon him." And he thanked Governor Parker for his efforts in raising New Jersey troops.

While Lincoln was still resisting political pressure to bring back McClellan to command, the Army of the Potomac, now under Meade, clashed head on with Lee's Army of Northern Virginia at Gettysburg.

IV

Gettysburg, a dot on the map where numerous roads crossed, was a pleasant Pennsylvania town lying amid rolling hills and broad shallow valleys, a blue mountain wall rising miles to the west. The biggest Federal and Confederate armies moved toward Gettysburg.

Lee went into that three-day battle of July 1, 2, and 3, 1863, handicapped by lack of the most proficient part of his cavalry. His greatest mounted leader, "Jeb" Stuart, had slipped the leash and gone off with his men on a wild, meaningless raid that took him out of the play, leaving Lee to fight a battle in which he could not maneuver. Lee's reorganization of his army after "Stonewall" Jackson's death added little efficiency to his fighting forces—a regrouping of commanders and staff officers which Lee's great modern biographer, Douglas Southall Freeman, calls "the reorganization that explains Gettysburg."

Lee reached Gettysburg on the afternoon of July 1, after his Second Corps, under Ewell, and his Third Corps, under Hill, had defeated the Federals under Major-General John F. Reynolds, with Reynolds himself falling as he led the Second Wisconsin Regiment. That first day's battle proved a fierce fight, but only a preliminary one.

Lee suggested to Ewell that the Confederate advantage be pushed south of Gettysburg. But Ewell delayed the attack and provided the Federals with time in which to strengthen their forces on Cemetery Hill and Culp's Hill. To present-day students who deal in hypothetical strategy, Lee's best chance of victory would have been to strike before the Federals could concentrate formidable forces on the strong ground of Cemetery Hill.

July 2 dawned in Gettysburg and its vicinity with the Union line reinforced by more men and artillery on Cemetery Hill. Lee now found himself faced with an unexpected difficulty. Before his army had left Virginia, the commander of his First Corps, Longstreet, had urged him to employ offensive strategy but defensive tactics in Pennsylvania, and he had persuaded himself that Lee had promised to do this. When Longstreet discovered that Lee was determined to attack Meade, he believed that he was courting ruin. Longstreet was chagrined and humiliated at the rejection of his plan. If at Gettysburg Longstreet did not intentionally delay in the hope of keeping Lee from plunging into what he believed would be a slaughter of troops, he at least acted so slowly and unwillingly, that Cemetery Hill was heavily-manned by Federals when his First Corps assaulted it on that grim blood-letting afternoon of July 2. Lee, in his later official report, merely stated: "Longstreet's dispositions were not completed as early as was expected."

Yet Longstreet's men in their advance did remarkably well in face of hopeless odds. They all but took Little Round Top, the commanding position, whose capture would have unhinged Meade's line. Fortunately for the Federals, however, Major-General Gouverneur K. Warren perceived that Little Round Top was then too weakly-manned and hurried infantry and artillery into position just in time to repulse the advancing troops in gray. Had this critical position been taken by Longstreet's legions, the Union army might have been driven back in disorder.

On the Union right, the late "Stonewall" Jackson's old division, commanded by Major-General Edward Johnson, in Ewell's Second Corps, attacked the Federal position at Culp's Hill, east of Cemetery Hill, and captured it—only to lose it the next day. A further Confederate assault on Cemetery Hill, under Major-General Jubal A. Early, was repulsed.

And so the second horrible day at Gettysburg ended.

That evening, General Meade held a council of war with his subordinate commanders, and it was decided to have the existing Union line remain on the defensive, and await Lee's expected attack. As for Lee, he considered the Confederate showing sufficiently satisfactory to renew his assault on Federal positions.

On that next day, the third, Lee's main attack was directed against the Union center in the afternoon. Again Longstreet urged that the frontal assault be avoided and that an attempt be made to turn the Federal position by a maneuver on Meade's left. Longstreet was overruled once more. The attack by Major-General George E. Pickett's Virginia division, advancing over half a mile of broken ground against withering Federal artillery and musket fire, was ordered in the vain hope that, by a supreme effort, the Federal center could be broken and put to rout. Scarcely one-fourth of Pickett's men returned from that memorable charge, which was a ghastly slaughter. Meade had anticipated the Southern attack on his center and had concentrated there his First and Second Corps, under Major-General Winfield S. Hancock.

So the third and last day of the Gettysburg carnage ended, with the Union and Confederate armies facing each other like exhausted lions licking their wounds.

Meade did not follow up his advantage, and on July 4 Lee began his orderly retreat back to Virginia.

It had been a three-day battle the likes of which had never been suffered by Americans up to that time. It had been the most thundering cannonading and grimly appalling loss of lives on both sides that had ever occurred in the Western hemisphere.

V

While the guns of Gettysburg roared and men fell dead or maimed on the field, Lincoln in Washington was subjected to double strain. Not only did he lie awake at night, unable to sleep, and spend hours during the day at the War Department telegraph office, but on the second day of the Gettysburg battle Mrs. Lincoln was injured in a carriage accident.

On the morning of July 2, while driving in from the Soldiers' Home, where the Lincolns spent summer nights, the First Lady was violently thrown from her carriage to the ground, her head striking a sharp rock. In agonizing pain, Mary Lincoln was carried to the nearest hospital, where her wound was dressed. She was then removed to her private quarters in the Soldiers' Home.

It was learned that the driver's seat had become detached from the rest of Mrs. Lincoln's carriage, with the result that the driver was thrown out, the frightened horses ran away, and the First Lady was tossed out upon the ground. It was suspected, but never proved, that most of the screws which held the driver's seat had been deliberately removed by hostile hands in an attempt to injure the President by harming his wife.

As he worried over his wife's condition—a physical as well as mental one now—Lincoln set about learning the latest news from Gettysburg.

By the end of the third day of battle, July 3, the President had received the definite news that the Federals had driven the Confederates away and could register a triumph of the Union. But he still hoped that General Meade would give chase to the fleeing Lee and capture him and his army.

On the following morning, Independence Day, Lincoln authorized the issuance by the War Department of an announcement that he had prepared for the public: "The President announces to the country that news from the Army of the Potomac, up to 10 P.M. of the 3rd. is such as to cover that Army with the highest honor, to promise a great success to the cause of the Union, and to claim the condolence of all for the many gallant fallen. And that for this, he especially desires that on this day, He whose will, not ours, shall ever be done, be everywhere remembered and reverenced with profoundest gratitude."

That Fourth-of-July proved the most joyful of hours that the Union-lovers had exuberantly enjoyed since the war had begun. For on that same day, as Northerners and loyal border state citizens celebrated alike the eighty-seventh anniversary of the Declaration of Independence and news of the Gettysburg battle of the three preceding days, General U. S. Grant was performing at Vicksburg, Mississippi, some significant work which would raise Union hopes even higher.

VI

Lincoln, contrary to later legend, was slow to recognize the fighting qualities of Ulysses S. Grant.

That failure of Grant to impress the President and others with his war-making abilities appears understandable, in view of Grant's none too good reputation as a pre-war soldier, made worse by reports of his excessive whiskey-drinking, and the opposition of such army rivals as General-in-Chief Halleck and Major-General John A. McClernand, the Illinois Democratic politician-warrior.

The President for a while lent a willing ear to the attractive but hollow promises of McClernand, who proposed to raise a new corps to be used in trying to capture the Confederate bastion of Vicksburg. Lincoln authorized McClernand, a veteran but still influential political lieutenant of the late Senator Stephen A. Douglas, to approach the governors of Western states with his proposal for recruiting the troops for a new army corps with McClernand at its head, of course. The Chief Executive almost gave that Illinois political leader an independent commission for an expedition in Grant's bailiwick. That contemplated McClernand-led military expedition was kept a secret from Grant, who did not learn of it until Admiral Porter, commanding the Mississippi naval squadron, told him what was in the air.

The alarming news that McClernand was coming down to take a hand in the assault on Vicksburg galvanized Grant into action. With a West Point professional's distrust of Generals whose military reputation had been acquired mostly on the electioneering stump and in party caucuses, Grant decided to forestall McClernand by stepping up his drive on Vicksburg.

From the last months of 1862 Grant's whole effort was directed against this greatest of enemy fortresses in the West. The capture of Vicksburg, on a high bluff commanding a hairpin bend in the Mississippi River, would give the Federal forces control of that mighty waterway, the "Father of Waters," all of the way down to New Orleans. But the surrounding topography was cruel and uninviting, making it seem unapproachable except from the south and east. On the west the river approach was blocked by Confederate batteries, while on the north the region of Yazoo delta constituted an intricate and seemingly hopeless tangle of back-water areas, lakes, swamps, creeks, bayous, and wooded bluffs.

For months during early 1863 Grant found himself enmeshed in events that retarded him, quite aside from the impossibility of the terrain. His campaign against Vicksburg appeared an object lesson in frustration. While being spied on by Secretary of War Stanton's agents, maligned in the nation's press, his personal reputation spattered by reports of his over consumption of liquor, and embarrassed by a curious situation which allowed McClernand, a politician in a Major-General's uniform, to vie with him for command, Grant made repeated attempts to take Vicksburg, all ending in failure.

At a time when Hooker was about to lead his Army of the Potomac to the Chancellorsville defeat in the east, Grant in the west was edging closer to Vicksburg. By the end of April, he had his force of 20,000 ready for transportation to the Mississippi side of the river by Commodore Andrew H. Foote's gunboats. Within the next month Grant led his men across difficult terrain, scoring a series of victories over the Southern troops encountered. And he pushed on. It was the sort of dogged persistency that later inspired Lincoln to say that Grant went after things as if he had inherited them.

Grant closed in on the enemy forces, under Major-General John Pemberton, defending Vicksburg. On May 19 and 22 he assaulted Pemberton's works without let-up. Failing in this, he laid siege to the great bastion.

By this time Lincoln in Washington was immensely impressed by Grant. On May 26 the President expressed his appreciation of the General in a note to his Chicago friend, Congressman Isaac N. Arnold: "Whether Gen. Grant shall or shall not consummate the capture of Vicksburg, his campaign from the beginning of this month up to the twenty-second day of it, is one of the most brilliant in the world."

Grant, hammering away at Vicksburg, soon found opportunity to rid himself of his most painful Federal irritant, General McClernand. McClernand, a politician with General's stars on his shoulders, published in a Memphis newspaper an army order in which he praised his own Thirteenth Corps and insinuated that, in an unsuccessful assault on Vicksburg, he was not supported by General Sherman and another Federal commander. McClernand failed to submit that order to Grant before issuing it to the press, as required by army regulations. Grant removed McClernand from his command on June 18, and sent him back to Illinois. "I should have relieved him long since for general unfitness for position," Grant reported to General-in-Chief Halleck.

Pemberton, defending Vicksburg against Grant's pounding, found himself handicapped by dissensions behind his own lines—Confederate politics and military rivalries and feuds. General "Joe" Johnston, in chief command along the Mississippi, tried to bring troops from Arkansas to strengthen Pemberton. But General Theophilus H. Holmes, at the head of Southern forces west of the Mississippi, a friend, West Point classmate and favorite of President Jefferson Davis, evaded, delayed, and sent no troops. President Davis could have enforced Holmes's compliance but, instead, suggested that Pemberton secure reinforcements by gathering convalescents, home guards, and coast defense units from Georgia, Florida, and Alabama, and by transferring fighting brigades from General Bragg in Tennessee. The net of the effort to reinforce Pemberton was an inadequate force of 10,000 men. As if to aid Grant more, Pemberton found himself at odds with Johnston, who was not then in good condition, physically or mentally. Pemberton and Johnston never got to the point of joining their forces against Grant.

So on July 2, as Lee was being repulsed by Meade at Gettysburg, Pemberton sent up a flag of truce.

The next day the surrender terms were agreed to by the two Generals and on July 4 Grant received the surrender of Pemberton's army of 30,000.

VII

Lincoln's spirits, like those of the millions of other Union-loving Americans, rose further at the news from Vicksburg of Grant's victory, coming only a day after the glad tidings from Gettysburg.

On July 7 the President greeted serenaders before the White House with hopeful words. "We have," he happily pointed out to them, "the surrender of a most powerful position and army" and "a succession of battles in Pennsylvania" which portended well for the Union.

A week later, on the 13th, the President sent Grant warm thanks for the Vicksburg victory. In that humility-filled letter Lincoln informed the General:

> I do not remember that you and I ever met personally. I write this now as a grateful acknowledgment for the almost inestimable service you have done the country. I wish to say a word further. When you first reached the

> vicinity of Vicksburg, I thought you should do, what you finally did—march the troops across the neck, run the batteries with the transports, and thus go below; and I never had any faith, except a general hope that you knew better than I, that the Yazoo Pass expedition, and the like, could succeed. When you got below, and took Port-Gibson, Grand Gulf, and vicinity, I thought you should go down the river and join Gen. Banks; and when you turned Northward East of the Big Black, I feared it was a mistake. I now wish to make the personal acknowledgment that you were right, and I was wrong.

The war had definitely turned for the better with the Gettysburg and Vicksburg victories. But the conflict with the Confederates was far from won. Since war was a continuing game, there were other ways of scoring the results than at the end of one, or even two, spectacular triumphs in the field.

SUMMER STORM CLOUDS—1863

29

I

NO sooner had Lincoln elatedly announced the glad news from Gettysburg and Vicksburg, and tendered heartfelt thanks to General Grant, during that summer of 1863, than varieties of disappointments depressed him. Merely to mention some of them is a task. His irritation over General Meade's failure to pursue Lee's army after Gettysburg, his concern about placating Major-General McClernand when Grant removed that politically powerful Illinois Democrat from his command, his worry over the New York City "draft riots," followed by Governor Horatio Seymour's insistence on suspension of conscription in the populous Empire State, his anxiety over the coming state elections in Pennsylvania and Ohio, worry over French military intervention in Mexico, and the awful fate of General Rosecrans's Army of the Cumberland at Chickamauga as the summer closed—all tended to offset the optimism created by the victories at Gettysburg and Vicksburg.

II

"These are trying occasions, not only in success, but for want of success," Lincoln had told those serenaders before the White House after

Gettysburg and Vicksburg. He had in mind the distressing thought that, although General Meade had beaten Lee, he had not captured or destroyed Lee's Army of Northern Virginia.

Meade showed indecision in contemplating whether to pursue the Southern army. He displayed little aggressiveness, perhaps because he feared the same heckling that had beset his predecessors. Meade had been given the Army of the Potomac command only three days before that bitterly contested Pennsylvania battle. He now found his troops exhausted after that three-day blood-letting struggle, and the topography of the country favored an orderly retreat by the master of maneuver, Lee.

Lee's defeated infantry, after Gettysburg, reached Hagerstown, Maryland, on July 6 and 7 and there formed a line to cover the crossing of the Potomac River by their retreating comrades between Falling Waters, Pennsylvania, and Williamsport, Maryland. Until the 12th no battle action occurred between Federals and Confederates except cavalry clashes and skirmishes. Lee's ragged veterans steeled themselves for a defensive fight, but Meade's men did not attack. All the while, Confederate detachments were building pontoons. The 13th of July found the Potomac still swollen high, but passable. At Falling Waters a satisfactory pontoon bridge was completed. During July 13-14 Lee's warriors passed back into Virginia.

Lincoln's elation over Meade's great Gettysburg triumph was neutralized when he learned of the General's failure to capture Lee and his army, or even to go in pursuit of them. Lincoln became downcast.

On July 14, the day on which the Confederates found themselves safe again behind their Virginia defenses, John Hay noted the President's sunken spirits over Meade's lack of aggressiveness. "Every day," wrote Hay in his diary about the Chief Executive, "he has watched the progress of the Army with agonizing impatience, hope struggling with fear." Hay quoted Lincoln as dismally remarking: "This is a dreadful reminiscence of McClellan. The same spirit that moved McC. to claim a great victory [at Antietam] because Pa. and Md. were safe."

On that same day, the 14th, Lincoln penned a lengthy letter to Meade, which he decided not to send after he had reflected on it. Marking it, "To Gen. Meade, never sent, or signed," these written words revealed Lincoln's innermost thoughts about the victor of Gettysburg, who in a dispatch to General-in-Chief Halleck had wanted to resign because of the President's lack of confidence in him. Lincoln wrote Meade in that unsent letter: "I am very–*very*–grateful to you for the magnificent success you gave the cause of the country at Gettysburg; and I am sorry now to be the author of the slightest pain to you. But I was in such deep distress myself that I could not restrain some expression of it." He went on to confess to Meade that Meade and two subordinate commanders, Generals Couch and William F. Smith, were "not seeking a collision with the enemy, but were trying to get him across the river without another battle." Lincoln continued: "You fought and beat the enemy at Gettysburg . . . and yet you stood and let the flood run down, bridges to be built, and the enemy move away at his leisure, without attacking him." Toward the letter's end the President pointed out to Meade: "Again, my dear General, I do not believe you appreciate the magnitude in Lee's escape. He was within your easy grasp, and to have closed upon him would, in connection with our other late successes, have ended the war. As it is, the war will be prolonged indefinitely."

Within a week Lincoln's feelings toward Meade had softened, and he told Hay: "Still, I am very grateful to Meade for the great service he did at Gettysburg."

III

"I should have relieved him long since for general unfitness for position," General Grant had reported to General-in-Chief Halleck in June, when he had removed Major-General John A. McClernand from his command.

The bad blood brewed between Grant and McClernand proved distressing to Lincoln, who realized the necessity of granting high military recognition to influential "War" Democrats, and McClernand, who had been the late Stephen A. Douglas's "right arm" in politics, still wielded strong influence in the opposition party of Lincoln's own State. Lincoln told Congressman Josiah B. Grinnell of Iowa confidentially why he appointed McClernand to a Major-Generalship: "I have to do with those whom I despise, for we are at war. Democratic aid we must have if possible, and I conciliate to avoid friction. There is General McClernand from my own state. . . . The devotees of Douglas I honor and praise often, as I would have promoted their chief had he lived."

When, back in January (1863) Lincoln had congratulated McClernand and his forces for their "both brilliant and valuable work" at Arkansas Post, Lincoln had tactfully answered McClernand about his complaints against both Halleck and Grant.

After Grant had removed McClernand from his command in June and ordered him back home to Illinois, Governor Richard Yates of Illinois had pleaded with Lincoln to give McClernand the Army of the Potomac command when it was decided that Hooker had to go—a frightening thought, in retrospect! But Lincoln had given that big eastern command to Meade, and Meade had turned in the Gettysburg victory.

By August the press was rife with rumors that the War Department would prefer charges against McClernand, who now complained to Lincoln about the foul treatment by Grant and demanded another command.

Lincoln's answer to McClernand on August 12 revealed the political pressures to which he was subjected, all in the face of the necessity of not offending Grant, the victor of Vicksburg. Tactfully the President expressed his sympathy to the militarily deposed politician General: "I doubt whether your present position is more painful to you than to myself. Grateful for the patriotic stand so early taken by you in this life-and-death struggle of the nation, I have done whatever has appeared practicable to advance you and the public interest together. No charge, with a view to a trial, have been preferred against you by any one; nor do I suppose any will be." The President sought to smooth over McClernand's poor relations with Grant by a mixture of flattery and common sense: "It is a case, as appears to me, in which I could do nothing without doing harm. Gen. Grant and yourself have been conspicuous in our most important successes; and for me to interfere, and thus magnify a breach between you, could but be of evil effect." He signed this letter, "Your friend as ever, A. Lincoln."

Early the following year Lincoln, to heal McClernand's sensitivities, agreed to the restoration of his command of the old Thirteenth Corps. It was in a remote theatre of warfare, scattered from New Orleans to the Rio Grande, where he could do as little harm as possible, and where he was sufficiently far enough removed from Grant.

Still Lincoln's attempts to heal the breach with McClernand did not succeed. The General would be opposing Lincoln for re-election, actively on the stump.

IV

In mid-summer, 1863, there descended on Lincoln and his administration a crisis in the enforcement of the Conscription Act.

The volunteer and State militia systems had proved woefully inadequate in satisfying the constant demands of the War Department and Federal commanders for men, and still more men, to fill the armies. Congress, to meet that call, had in March, 1863, passed a federal Conscription Bill which Lincoln signed into law. It provided that all able-bodied male citizens, between ages of twenty-five and forty-five, were to "constitute the national forces," and declared liable to military service. Exemptions were extended to the mentally and physically unfit, certain high federal and State officials, and the only son of a dependent widow or of infirm parents. Federal machinery for enforcement of this compulsory draft of men for military service was elaborately provided, including enrollment officers organized by congressional districts, a board of enrollment, provost marshals, and, over all, a Provost Marshal General in Washington.

To Lincoln this conscription legislation enforcement, along with the War Department's demands for more troops, brought numberless difficulties and vexations, the most trying of which were his relations with Governor Horatio Seymour of New York, a Democrat.

The reality of a member of the opposition political party as chief executive of the Empire State in itself seemed to spell discord between Washington and Albany at a time when this richest and most populous of all the States was sorely needed to bolster the Union cause.

The preceding gubernatorial campaign of 1862 in New York State had been viciously fought on national issues relating to the war. The pro-Lincoln Republican-Union candidate, General James S. Wadsworth, had approved publicly Lincoln's then recently issued preliminary Proclamation of Emancipation, commending it as an effectual, speedy, and humane way of repelling the rebellion. But Seymour, the Democratic candidate for Governor, a conservative trying to adhere to Jeffersonian concepts, assailed the President's slave-liberating Proclamation as a "proposal for the butchering of women and children," denounced arbitrary arrests by Lincoln's administration, and maintained in his electioneering speeches that the war's only purpose must be suppression of the secessionist insurrection, not to effect a change of the American social system. Some of Seymour's supporters had arraigned the war as an abolitionist attempt to elevate the Negro. Seymour won the governorship over Wadsworth.

In his first annual message Governor Seymour pledged himself to a prompt response to "all constitutional demands" of Lincoln's national government. But he was soon quarreling with the President and the federal authorities over what demands were "constitutional." He could find no constitutional warrant for the Proclamation of Emancipation, suppression of civil liberties in war time—or conscription of men into the army. The Governor, lacking a sense of realities but motivated by his sincere convictions, could not comprehend that, if Lincoln kept too sharp an eye on the Constitution during the war, there might not be any nation left to be governed by that Constitution. Seymour boldly challenged the President's policy in the drafting of New York troops.

Lincoln's first letter to Seymour had been sent in March, 1863, only three weeks after Congress passed and Lincoln signed the Conscription Bill into law. Lincoln in that message sought to introduce himself to the Empire State's Democratic Governor, which he thought might lead to co-operation. "You and I," the Republican-Union President communicated to the Democratic Governor of New York, "are substantially strangers; and I write this chiefly that we many become better acquainted. I, for the time being, am at the head of a nation which is in great peril;

and you are at the head of the greatest State of that nation." There could "not be a difference of *purpose*" between the two of them in the maintenance of the united nation, he pointed out to Seymour. He continued: "If we should differ as to the *means,* it is important that such difference should be as small as possible—that it should not be enhanced by unjust suspicions on one side or the other. In the performance of my duty, the co-operation of your State, as that of others, is needed—in fact, is indispensable. This alone is a sufficient reason why I should wish to be at a good understanding with you."

Seymour waited three weeks, then replied to Lincoln in cordial tone, explaining that "pressure of official duties" prevented his giving his official views sooner. He assured Lincoln: "For the preservation of this Union I am ready to make every sacrifice." Significantly, the Governor used the words, "a just and generous support in all measures they may adopt within the scope of their constitutional powers."

Lincoln's relations with Seymour remained peaceful until the New York City "draft riots" put the Governor in a thankless predicament.

V

As Lincoln was besieged by Secretary of War Stanton and various Federal field commanders to send more soldiers to the front in early summer of 1863, he authorized the execution of the draft under the Conscription Act. Provost Marshal General James B. Fry set the draft machinery in operation.

On July 7 the draft began in Rhode Island, the next day in Massachusetts, and then proceeded in other states. Then came Saturday, July 11—the day appointed for the drawing of selectees in New York City. Within two days the uprising had been set off.

General antipathy to compulsory army service, density of population making for fertile field in which anti-war agitators operated with fruitful results, the class-dictated $300 commutation clause in the federal law that permitted wealthier men to buy a substitute draftee to send in their places, irritations felt by belligerent anti-Negro Irish immigrants, all were among mixed forces that inspired the grisly draft riots of July 13-16 in the nation's metropolis. Those days of deliberately set fires, sadistic skull-cracking, mob violence, and even murder of a still uncalculated number of innocent people, proved the most shameful civic uprising in American municipal annals up to that time.

Those New York City draft riots fully convinced Governor Seymour that the Conscription Act was an unwise measure. He persuaded himself that such Congress-enacted legislation was contrary to the Constitution of the United States. Less than three weeks later, on August 3, he dispatched a request to the President, asking that the draft be suspended in New York State. In that lengthy message to Lincoln, the Governor gave a resumé of the riots in New York City. He protested: "The quotas now demanded from the Congressional districts in New York and Kings County are glaringly unjust. . . . I ask that the draft may be suspended in this State, as has been done elsewhere, until we shall learn the results of recruiting which is now actively going on." The Governor also proposed that the constitutionality of the draft law should be judged by the courts before the law was executed.

Lincoln could not consider Seymour's proposal for draft suspension favorably. If one section of the nation were exempted from contributing man power to the Federal armies by legal compulsion, the whole conscription system would collapse throughout the loyal states, with consequent draining of the armies which were trying to crush the Confederacy. In late July Lincoln already had replied to Governor Parker of New Jersey, whose State had been running thousands of men behind in supplying her levied quotas of troops. Lincoln informed the New Jersey Governor: "It is a very delicate matter to postpone the draft in one State, because of the argument it furnishes others to have postponements also."

Lincoln on August 7 sent the only possible reply to Governor Seymour. "I can not," he told the Empire State's Chief Executive, "consent to suspend the draft in New York, as you request, because, among other reasons, *time* is too important." He pointed out to Seymour: "We are contending with an enemy who, as I understand, drives every able bodied man he can reach, into his ranks, very much as a butcher drives bullocks into a slaughter-pen. No time is wasted, no argument is used. This produces an army which will soon turn upon our now victorious soldiers . . . with a rapidity not to be matched on our side, if we first waste time to re-experiment with the volunteer system . . . , and then more time to obtain a court decision as to whether a law is constitutional."

Lincoln revealed abundant logic and common sense in that reply to Seymour.

The President might well have felt more cheerful if he had known fully the troubles that his opposite number, President Jefferson Davis, was having with some of the Southern Governors, particularly with Governor Joseph E. Brown of Georgia and Governor Zebulon B. Vance of North Carolina, about drafting troops. Davis was finding conscription one of his most vexing problems. The Confederate Secretary of War had written imploringly to Governor Brown: "I think we might as well drive out the common enemy before we make war on each other."

More correspondence passed between Lincoln and Seymour on the enforcement of the federal draft law. The Governor, through his state Judge Advocate General, complained that unjustifiably heavy quotas of conscripts were demanded of the metropolitan districts, New York City and vicinity, where Democratic voters predominated. Other disputes between the President and the Governor bristled in their correspondence before the controversy died down and normal recruiting was resumed in New York.

VI

In the summer of 1863, too, came preliminaries of the autumn elections in Pennsylvania and Ohio, crucial states. If both or either of those states were carried by the Democrats in the coming gubernatorial contests for Governor in October, it might spell defeat for Lincoln's re-election candidacy in the following year. Next to New York, Pennsylvania and Ohio were the most populous states and cast the greatest bulks of electoral votes in a national presidential election.

In Pennsylvania, the early months of the campaign brought forth the old party vendetta between the strongly pro-Lincoln Governor Andrew G. Curtin and Former Secretary of War Simon Cameron, who had returned from his inept diplomatic labors in Tsarist Russia. As the war wore on, Curtin had grown more conservative, whereas Cameron had veered more toward radicalism.

Curtin, for reasons of health, felt reluctant to try for a second term in the State House at Harrisburg, and even sent an emissary to Lincoln, requesting that he be given a foreign mission. The President told Cameron about Curtin's decision not to run for Governor again, and Cameron grew deliriously happy. The Former Secretary of War showed his opinion of Curtin by suggesting that a second-class diplomatic post, not a first-class one, would be ideal for the retiring Governor. Cameron was made even happier when Curtin informed the State Legislature that he would not stand for a second term.

Cameron and his party cronies—the "Harrisburg Gang"—agreed on a suitable radical as their candidate for Governor. But they suddenly found themselves faced with the awful truth that their fierce foe, Governor Curtin, was the strongest Republican-Union vote-getter in the whole Keystone commonwealth. The Governor had tremendous support among voters in the rural districts, voters who looked disapprovingly on Cameron's machine type of politics. The Cameronians, in desperation, appealed to the radical Secretary of the Treasury Chase, who took the matter up with the President. Lincoln only stated that he would support any Union man nominated for Governor.

The Pennsylvania Democrats nominated as their gubernatorial candidate Judge George W. Woodward of the state Superior Court. Woodward had once spoken pro-Southern sympathies: "If the Union is to be divided,

I want the line of separation run north of Pennsylvania." This politically steeped Judge, in his decision on the *Kneedler v. Lane* case, had declared the Federal Conscription Act unconstitutional. The deposed General McClellan, a Pennsylvanian, lent more strong anti-Lincoln tinge to Woodward's candidacy by endorsing him: "I regard his election as Governor of Pennsylvania called for by the interests of the nation."

Woodward's nomination by the Democrats meant that, regardless of Governor Curtin's illness and Cameron's opposition to him, the Republican-Unionists would simply have to run the Governor again, since he was the strongest man in the party, against the wily Woodward. Cameron was irritated, and the press friendly to him sniped editorially at Curtin. In August the Republican-Union state convention renominated Curtin for Governor, "though Cameron fumed in frustration and his cohorts hissed in the galleries."

Then there loomed an ugly situation in Ohio because of strong anti-war sentiment in the lower counties and General Burnside's recent rash move in arbitrarily arresting the "Copperhead" Congressman Clement L. Vallandigham. That anti-war "lame duck" legislator had finally been escorted behind the Confederate lines by Lincoln's order, as the best way out of the predicament caused by Burnside. But Vallandigham had escaped to Canada by a roundabout way, and the Democrats were now nominating that Copperhead martyr as their candidate (in absentia) for Governor of Ohio.

Governor David Tod of Ohio, a Republican-Unionist and friend of Lincoln, had planned to run for re-election, but he was beaten for renomination by a Cleveland railroad president, John Brough, also a staunch Union supporter. President Lincoln tactfully telegraphed Tod: "I deeply regret that you were not re-nominated—not that I have aught against Mr. Brough. On the contrary, I say, hurrah for him."

Soon Ohio's fiercely fought gubernatorial race was in full swing, with Vallandigham in Canada. But it would be a showdown, on significant state level, between continuation of the war and peace at any price. Lincoln anxiously watched developments in the Buckeye State.

VII

Not as huge in population and votes as Pennsylvania or Ohio, but highly strategic because of its location on the border, was Missouri. No election was being waged there in 1863, but the political situation was constantly deteriorating.

The Missouri muddle became more mixed up, and feuds still festered. Radical "Charcoals" still fought conservative "Claybanks" over the moral slavery-emancipation issue and the mundane question of federal patronage.

When, in late May, the President had removed the Charcoals' favorite, Major-General Samuel R. Curtis, and replaced him with Major-General John A. Schofield, as Department of the Missouri commander in order to appease Governor Hamilton R. Gamble and other Claybank leaders, Lincoln had given Schofield some sage advice. He cautioned the new commanding General in St. Louis to do what was "right" in the public interest but to beware of factionalism. He wrote Schofield on July 13: "Now that you are in the position, I wish you to undo nothing merely because Gen. Curtis or Gov. Gamble did it; but to exercise your own judgment, and do *right* for the public interest. Let your military measures be strong enough to repel the invader and keep the peace, and not so strong as to unnecessarily harrass (sic) and persecute the people. It is a difficult *role,* and so much greater will be the honor if you perform it well. If both factions, or neither, shall abuse you, you will probably be about right. Beware of being assailed by one, and praised by the other."

General Schofield in July arrested William McKee, an editor of the radical Charcoal daily, the St. Louis *Missouri Democrat,* because McKee had printed a confidential letter from Lincoln to Schofield. Congressman Henry T. Blow, a Charcoal leader, angrily protested to Lincoln. Tactfully the President answered Blow: "The publication of a letter without the leave of the writer or the receiver I think cannot be justified, but in this case I do not think it of sufficient consequence to justify an arrest; and again, the arrest being, through a parole, merely nominal, does not deserve the importance sought to be attached to it. Cannot this small matter be dropped on both sides without further difficulty?"

To General Schofield, however, the President sent sharp words: "I regret to learn of the arrest of the *Democrat* editor. I fear this loses you the middle position I desired you to occupy;" adding, "Please spare me the trouble this is likely to bring."

General Schofield, in the midst of the Missouri caldron, continued to fail in practicing Lincoln's dictum to him: "Beware of being assailed by one, and praised by the other."

By the beginning of autumn, a delegation of Charcoal leaders journeyed to Washington and protested to the President against Schofield's unneutral conduct. By the end of the year Lincoln, in efforts for political peace in Missouri, was to remove Schofield—his second change in the Department of the Missouri command within seven months.

VIII

Then there festered during the summer of 1863 the problem of Mexico—more especially, the French military invasion of that neighboring Latin nation.

The second French Empire's slippery dictator, Napoleon III, having trampled on republicanism in France, was now having his troops do the same three thousand miles away in the land of the Montezumas. Although President Benito Juarez of Mexico had led his armed followers against the French soldiers, his men were reduced to guerilla bands, and Juarez fled north. The French forces occupied Mexico City, the capital, on June 7, 1863. Within a matter of weeks the French commander brought together a hand-picked Assembly of Notables, comprising native Mexican collaborationists who offered the throne of Mexico to Napoleon III's puppet, Archduke Ferdinand Maximilian of Austria.

Lincoln grew deeply concerned over the French aggression in Mexico, but he let Secretary of State Seward handle the delicate situation. Emperor Napoleon III had for two years shown himself highly hostile to the Union, and for a time his Government at Paris toyed with the thought of diplomatically recognizing the Confederacy as a sovereign nation.

Lincoln decided that, as a counter stroke to the French in Mexico, Federal army movements must be pushed in Texas, to demonstrate the Union's military might and seal off the Lone Star State from any possible French-dictated aid to the Confederates. "Recent events in Mexico, I think, render early action in Texas more important than ever," Lincoln directed Major-General Nathaniel P. Banks, commander in New Orleans, on August 5. He added to Banks in his wire: "The General-in-Chief will address you more fully upon this subject."

On the following day General-in-Chief Halleck telegraphed orders to Banks: "There are important reasons why our flag should be restored in some point of Texas without the least possible delay. Do this by land at Galveston, at Indianola, or at any other point you may deem preferable."

But Banks needed more troops, a constant cry of all commanders. At that precise time General Grant was planning an advance on Mobile, Alabama, by which he hoped to cut the Confederate forces there—this only one month following his Vicksburg victory. The President now concluded to have Grant's movement on Mobile deferred, so that some of his troops could be sent to Banks for the advance into Texas. "He is very anxious," noted John Hay about the Tycoon on August 9, "that Texas should be occupied and firmly held in view of French possibilities. He thinks it just now more important than Mobile. He would prefer that Grant should not throw his army into the Mobile business before the Texas matter is safe."

Lincoln on that same day, the 9th, sent word to Grant: "I see by a despatch of yours that you incline quite strong towards an expedition against Mobile. This would appear tempting to me also, were it not that in view of recent events in Mexico, I am greatly impressed with the importance of re-establishing the national authority in Western Texas as soon as possible. I am not making an order, however. That I leave to the General-in-Chief."

Grant two weeks later assured Lincoln that he had not forgotten the Mobile offensive but assured the President on sending aid to Banks: "I see however the importance of a movement into Texas just at this time. I have reinforced Gen. Banks with the 13th Army Corps."

Inwardly Grant distrusted Banks and held scant respect for this political General's military ability. Grant's decision to send the Thirteenth Corps to Banks, however, indicated his determination to agree with Lincoln. In his post-war *Memoirs* Grant was to give vent to his own irritation at having to send soldiers to Banks instead of marching with his own forces on Mobile. And then Banks never did get really started on his advance deep into the heart of Texas.

IX

After Grant's victory at Vicksburg, Mississippi, in early July, the strategic focus in the West had shifted east to the Chattanooga, Tennessee, theatre. That city, goal of contending Federal and Confederate armies since the early war months, was the key to eastern Tennessee, as well as a valuable river location and vital highway between East and West.

In late June General Rosecrans had moved his mighty Army of the Cumberland out of Murfreesboro, Tennessee, and had maneuvered General Bragg's forces out of Tullahoma into Chattanooga. Rosecrans' task was now to get the Confederates out of there. But after that, the two opposing armies faced each other in another stalemate. Lincoln was growing ever more impatient with "Old Rosy's" seemingly snail-crawling speed.

Rosecrans had for months convinced himself that Secretary of War Stanton and General-in-Chief Halleck were his enemies, seeking to undermine him, and he criticized them both openly to newspaper reporters at his headquarters. The General manifested kind feelings toward the President, who insisted that the Army of the Cumberland must hurry its advance against Bragg's battalions.

During most of July, 1863, Rosecrans remained inactive, preparing his final drive on Chattanooga. But he did not give his Washington superiors, civilian or military, any indication of when he would take the offensive. Lincoln now feared that Rosecrans might be stalled for the rest of the summer. Soon Rosecrans was conducting a long-distance argument with Halleck by telegram and letter.

At Lincoln's insistence, Halleck in late July telegraphed Rosecrans to move ahead. By the first of August the General had gone not even a mile on his advance, and Halleck ordered him to go ahead immediately. Rosecrans asked if that order removed his discretion as to the time and manner of moving his troops. The General-in-Chief replied that the order was peremptory. Rosecrans then said that he was ready to move but, if he had no discretion as to where he would cross the Tennessee River, he wanted to be relieved. Halleck authorized him to choose what routes of march he pleased but to get ahead without further quibbling.

Now, in early August, Rosecrans took his troubles directly to Lincoln. He complained to the President that, from Halleck's dispatches, he became depressed by the impression that Lincoln was dissatisfied with his supposed inactivity. The General explained why he had not moved against Bragg faster: he had a long supply line to maintain and he lacked sufficient cavalry. He told the Chief Executive that he failed to advance before Vicksburg fell to Grant because, if he had gone forward then, he would only have driven the Confederates in his front closer to Mississippi, and thus he would have made it easier for them to attack Grant.

Lincoln answered Rosecrans in a lengthy letter on August 10, in which he endeavored to calm the General's troubled mind. "I have not abated in my kind feeling for you and confidence in you," he assured his Army of the Cumberland commander. The President admitted that he had not liked the General's failure to take the offensive against Bragg during Grant's long siege of Vicksburg. When part of Bragg's force had been detached in order to aid the enemy in their defense of that great bastion, Lincoln pointed out, "it did seem to me, it was the exactly proper time for you to attack Bragg. . . . In all kindness, let me say, it so seems to me yet." The President announced that he was leaving the decision, as to what should be done next, to Rosecrans and Halleck. Lincoln ended his letter to "Old Rosy" in tender vein: "And now, be assured once more, that I think of you in all kindness and confidence: and that I am not watching you with an evil eye."

Rosecrans finally pushed ahead, Bragg evacuated Chattanooga. On September 9 Rosecrans' Twenty-first Corps, commanded by Major-General Thomas L. Crittenden, marched into the coveted city.

But the worst lay ahead for the Federals.

X

General Bragg, strongly re-enforced, on September 19 attacked General Rosecrans' army, opening the Battle of Chickamauga.

Lincoln agonizingly heard reports of Rosecrans' danger. He telegraphed Major-General Burnside in east Tennessee: "Go to Rosecrans with your force, without a moments delay." Burnside and his army, having captured Knoxville two weeks previously, were still in the eastern Tennessee counties, on their way to take Jonesboro, near present-day Johnson City. The President persisted with another wire to Burnside: "If you are to do any good to Rosecrans it will not do to waste time with Jonesboro. It is already too late to do the most good that might have been done, but I hope it will still do some good. Please do not lose a moment."

But Burnside could not reach Rosecrans, with hundreds of miles of treacherous mountains and bad terrain separating him. Bragg, reinforced by Longstreet, thoroughly thrashed Rosecrans' Army of the Cumberland on September 19-20.

Only the Union left, under Virginia-born Major-General George H. Thomas, bent into a horsehoe shape but not broken, was able to hold off the Confederates, earning Thomas his subsequent sobriquet, "The Rock of Chickamauga."

As a carnage ground Chickamauga was grimly comparable to Antietam and Gettysburg.

General Rosecrans reported the dismal news to Halleck by wire on the late afternoon of September 20, last day of that stormy summer: "We have met with a serious disaster. . . . Enemy overwhelmed us. . . . It seems that every available man was thrown against us."

XI

After the joy of the Gettysburg and Vicksburg victories in early July, it had proved a stormy summer for Lincoln. A succession of irritations and gnawing troubles and "family" fights—Meade's failure to capture Lee's army after Gettysburg, the disgruntlement of General McClernand following his removal by Grant, the violence of the New York draft riots followed by Governor Seymour's anti-conscription policy, uncertainties over the coming autumn elections in Pennsylvania and Ohio, the ever-simmering Missouri feuds and factionlism over patronage, emancipation, and party power, the French occupation of Mexico with peril to Texas, and, above all, General Rosecrans' dilatory advances in Tennessee, ending in the frightful defeat at Chickamauga on the last day of summer.

BRIGHT AUTUMN—1863

30

I

CHICKAMAUGA had proved a grisly blood bath, with appalling losses on both sides. The Confederates suffered the greater casualties, although they won the battle. Whereas the Federals lost over 16,000 in missing, dead, and wounded, of whom more than 1,600 were killed, the secession forces suffered 18,000 casualties, of whom more than 2,300 died. Southern papers called Chickamauga Creek "the river of death."

The Confederates at Chickamauga lost heavily in high ranking commanders, including one of Mrs. Lincoln's Kentucky brothers-in-law, the youthful thirty-three-year old Brigadier-General Ben Hardin Helm, married to her favorite young half-sister, Emilie. Helm, leading his Second Brigade of Kentucky, Alabama, and Mississippi troops, fell from his horse and was mortally wounded.

The President sent the horrible news to his wife, then out of town: "We lost, in general officers, one killed, and three or four wounded, all Brigadiers; while according to rebel accounts . . . they lost six killed, and eight wounded. Of the killed, one Major-Genl. and five Brigadiers, including your brother-in-law, Helm; and of the wounded, three Major Generals, and five Brigadiers."

Lincoln was grieved over the death of his Confederate brother-in-law by marriage, General Helm. Back in 1861 he had offered Helm a paymastership in the United States Army, but Helm had declined it and joined the Southern cause. Judge David Davis told how deeply affected the Chief Executive was at Helm's death. Lincoln always had to watch the effect of any sorrowful shock on his wife, who by 1863 was declining mentally.

One bright spot for Lincoln, after the Chickamauga defeat, was the emergence of another talented Federal commander—Major-General George H. Thomas.

A Virginia-born West Point graduate, classmate of Sherman, Thomas had served in the Mexican War—under the Confederate commander he opposed at Chickamauga: Bragg! After the war he had taught artillery and cavalry tactics at the government military academy. He had served in pre-war times in California and then under Robert E. Lee in Missouri. When war came in 1861, Thomas was one of the very few Southerners of the regular army who did not go with the Confederacy. He fought bravely as a Federal corps commander in the West against his fellow-Southerners. He courageously led the Fourteenth Corps of Rosecrans' Army of the Cumberland. Leading Rosecrans' left wing at the ill-fated battle, he earned his nickname, "The Rock of Chickamauga." Only the stand of Thomas' men, who under fierce Confederate shelling covered the Federal retreat, saved Rosecrans's army.

Lincoln was highly pleased with Thomas' performance at Chickamauga and quickly emphasized it to a Philadelphia citizen, Robert A. Maxwell, who like others had cast suspicions of disloyalty on Thomas because of his Southern birth and connections. Three days after the battle, on September 23, the President wired Maxwell: "I hasten to say that in the state of information we have here, nothing could be more ungracious than to indulge any suspicion towards Gen. Thomas. It is doubtful whether his heroism and skill exhibited last Sunday afternoon, has ever been surpassed in the world."

II

Lincoln, on that night of September 23, 1863, was suddenly awakened from his sleep at the Soldiers' Home by his assistant secretary, John Hay, who had come with an emergency message to start back for Washington, at the very urgent request of Secretary Stanton. Lincoln feared the worst. Rosecrans was in dire peril at Chattanooga!

Lincoln hastily dressed and drove quickly into the city with Hay. An emergency conference was held, lasting well past midnight. At that meeting were the President, Stanton, Seward, Chase, General-in-Chief Halleck, General Daniel C. McCallum, Military Director of Railroads, and others. The main work of their deliberations was the decision to detach the Eleventh and Twelfth Corps from Meade's Army of the Potomac and dispatch them speedily, under General Hooker's command, to aid Rosecrans in the Chattanooga vicinity.

Hooker, still smarting over his great Chancellorsville defeat less than five months previous, left the Washington vicinity with the Eleventh Corps, comprising two divisions under Generals Carl Schurz and Adolph von Steinwehr, and the Twelfth Corps, consisting of two divisions under Generals Alpheus S. Williams and John Geary, in all totaling 15,000 men, two days later, on September 25. In what was regarded as the most successful swift movement of so huge a body of troops during the entire war, Hooker and his corps reached Tennessee and Alabama in time to bolster Rosecrans' beleagured army.

But Lincoln, as the days passed agonizingly, realized that Rosecrans' position at Chattanooga was still perilous. Bragg might be secretly reenforced any day and then be able to strike the Army of the Cumberland in a massive surprise attack!

For long the President had been displeased with Rosecrans. His performance at Chickamauga had detracted even more from his luster. As he pondered over Rosecrans during early and middle October he grew ever more convinced that "Old Rosy" should be removed from the Army of the Cumberland command. On the 19th the President told John Hay: "Rosecrans has seemed to lose spirit since the battle of Chickamauga." Lincoln announced that he would have Rosecrans relieved of his command and agreed to General Thomas as his successor.

Lincoln felt grieved at what he considered his duty to relieve Rosecrans. "No man in the nation," wrote Noah Brooks, Washington correspondent, Lincoln's young friend, for his California newspaper several days later, "was more pained at the necessity of the removal . . . than was the President himself."

Lincoln did considerably more than agree to Thomas' promotion as Rosecrans' replacement. He made a complete change in the top command system of the West. In mid-October he and Stanton turned to the Vicksburg victor, General Grant, and appointed him to lead all Federal troops from the Alleghanies to the Mississippi, except in the southwestern sector which would still be entrusted to the inept political General, Banks.

And so Ulysses S. Grant proceeded to Chattanooga, where he found the Federal troops hungry and without adequate clothing for the coming winter. With the aid of Generals Thomas and Sherman and other subordinate commanders, Grant would very soon be mapping grand strategy against Bragg's Army of Tennessee.

III

While Lincoln was contemplating the reshuffling of the Western military command in October, the state elections were raging in Pennsylvania and Ohio. The President confessed to Secretary of the Navy Welles that he "had more anxiety in regard to the election results than he had in 1860 when he was chosen."

In the Keystone commonwealth prospects looked dismal for Lincoln's Republican-Union Party, particularly when the deposed General McClellan, a Pennsylvania Democrat, endorsed his party's gubernatorial candidate, the pathologically anti-Lincoln Judge George W. Woodward against Governor Curtin. Woodward had declared the federal Conscription Act unconstitutional in his state court and had previously voiced secessionist sentiments. "I regard his election as Governor of Pennsylvania called for by the interests of the nation," announced Major-General George B. McClellan, U.S.A., retired.

In Ohio the canvass for Governor was not to be closely contested but it was filled with turbulence, since the Democrats were running for Governor Former Congressman Vallandigham, the Copperhead's martyr, still "exiled" up in Canada. Because Vallandigham was the symbolism of opposition to subjecting the South militarily and the Republican-Union candidate for Governor was John Brough, a vigorous pro-Lincoln Unionist, the gubernatorial contest was watched by the nation as a pitched battle between pro-peace and pro-war forces.

Brough conducted a fierce fight against the absent Vallandigham, using every electioneering device that he and his campaign command could conjure up. When he campaigned among Germans in Cleveland, Teutonic leaders assured Brough: "Johnny, if you ain't elected, it won't be de fault of Schenkenheimer's brewery."

Lincoln, still worried over the Pennsylvania and Ohio situations, authorized a fifteen-day leave for federal government clerks from those states, so that they could go home to electioneer and vote. He authorized the protesting, wry-faced Secretary Stanton to grant furloughs home to Pennsylvanians in the army. Secretary of the Treasury Chase, an Ohioan, rushed home to stump for Brough.

Lincoln, on election night, October 13, went over to the War Department telegraph room to listen to the returns.

Curtin was carrying Pennsylvania in a neck-and-neck, see-sawing race against Woodward. He finally emerged winner by a razor-thin margin.

In more than half a million votes cast, Curtin polled 269,000 to Woodward's 254,000.

Bending over the War Department wireless apparatus that election night, Lincoln absorbed himself in the Ohio returns ticking in. A Copperhead in absentia, Vallandigham, whom Lincoln had ordered banished behind the Confederate lines once, was challenging the Union cause at the polls, and it seemed indispensable that Brough should win,—and by a top-heavy majority.

The President at ten o'clock that night wired parties in the Ohio state capital town, Columbus: "Where is John Brough?" Back came word that Brough, too, was in a telegraph office, eagerly listening to figures coming in from the Buckeye counties. The President telegraphed the Republican-Union candidate: "Brough, what is your majority now?" Brough wired back: "Over 30,000." At midnight Brough made Lincoln more elated by sending word: "Over 50,000." At five in the morning the next Governor of Ohio sent even better news: "Over 100,000." The President, exuberant, telegraphed Brough: "Glory to God in the highest. Ohio has saved the nation. A. Lincoln."

Brough's majority mounted to 101,000.

The Pennsylvania election, although carried by Lincoln's party by a breath-taking thin margin, had good results for the Union. Not the least beneficial was the newly-elected Republican State Chief Justice David Agnew. In short order Agnew proceeded to reverse his predecessor Woodward's adverse decision on the constitutionality of the Federal Conscription Act.

IV

Local and state elections were held in other Northern states during the following month, November.

1863 was an off-year in vote-rich New York State. No Governor was to be elected, for Seymour had been chosen only the year before. But candidates for the Legislature fought it out that year. This campaign, with only minor offices involved, was nonetheless viewed as a preliminary test for the big national campaign the next year, when Lincoln would undoubtedly run for re-election.

A noteworthy feature about that Empire State canvass of 1863 was the Lincolnites' substitution of the name, "Union," for the old party title, "Republican." The state convention at Utica in September was summoned under the call, "Union," and that label was so called by the stump orators, editors, and electioneering pamphleteers carrying Lincoln's banner on a statewide level against the Democrats.

With Lincoln's approval a galaxy of Union luminaries were sent into New York State to pour forth oratory in that seemingly unimportant election. But the power of the State was recognized. Among the big-name orators who gave their verbose talents to the New York electorate were Vice-President Hannibal Hamlin, Governors Curtin of Pennsylvania, Andrew of Massachusetts, and Yates of Illinois, former Governors Boutwell of Massachusetts and Randall of Wisconsin, United States Senators Henry Wilson of Massachusetts, Chandler of Michigan, Trumbull of Illinois, and Hale of New Hampshire; hosts of members of Congress; and Major-General Franz Sigel, who whipped up the "German" vote. Just before election day Secretary of State Seward rushed to his upstate New York home in Auburn to hold forth against the Democrats.

The Lincoln Administration provided New York soldiers with furloughs shortly before election day, which inspired the Democrats to yell protests of foul play by their opponents.

The Republican-Union efforts were well rewarded in November. Their "Union" tickets carried overwhelmingly in the various precincts. The Empire State as a whole, compared with the results at the polls of the previous year, showed a Unionist gain of more than 18,000 and a Democratic loss of over 21,000. Governor Seymour did not feel quite happy.

Elsewhere throughout the North, it was good news for Lincoln, state after state rolling up Republican-Union majorities, or else putting "War" Democrats, rather than "Copperheads," in office. The careers of most of the prominent "Copperheads" appeared ended, a refreshing reverse to the terrifying anti-Lincoln returns of the year before.

In late November Lincoln expressed his satisfaction with the results at the polls in a letter to Senator Zachariah Chandler of Michigan:

"I am very glad the elections this autumn have gone favorably, and that I have not, by native depravity, or under evil influences, done anything bad enough to prevent the good result.

"I hope to 'stand firm' enough not to go backward, and yet not go forward fast enough to wreck the country's cause."

Those last words expressed Lincoln's characteristic of steering clear of extremism without being a complete starchy conservative.

V

The joy of the autumn elections lay still fresh in Lincoln's mind when, later in that same month of November, he reached a high peak in his career with a "few appropriate remarks" spoken to a crowd at the dedication of the military cemetery at Gettysburg.

Since early July, when that memorable three-day carnage had been wrought, thousands of blue-clad and gray-garbed men, who had fallen at Gettsburg, had lain there openly, or only hastily half-buried. Public demands for a fitting burial of the dead heroes, together with expressions of state pride, led to a movement for a "national cemetery" at Gettysburg. Arrangements were in charge of David Wills of that town, who acted as Governor Curtin's agent. As chief orator for the dedication the committee in charge chose Edward Everett, who had held numerous distinguished positions—Unitarian minister, Harvard professor of Greek literature, *North American Review* editor, orator, poet, five-term Representative in Congress, four-term Governor of Massachusetts, United States Minister to England, President of Harvard College, United States Secretary of State, United States Senator, and unsuccessful candidate for Vice-President in 1860.

The invitation to President Lincoln to speak at the dedication was an after-thought in the minds of the Gettysburg Cemetery Commission. Everett had asked that the date be postponed until November 19, and this was agreed to. Everett would deliver the main speech. Lincoln would make a "few appropriate remarks" after the distinguished Bay State citizen had held forth.

Lincoln was to leave Washington at six o'clock on the morning of the 19th, reach Gettysburg via Baltimore, deliver his short speech there, and return to Washington at six in the evening. But the President vetoed this proposed schedule, answering Stanton, who had prepared it: "I do not like this arrangement. I do not wish to so go that by the slightest accident we fail entirely, and, at the best, the whole to be a mere breathless running of the gauntlet. But, any way." So Lincoln and his party left Washington for Gettysburg on November 18th, the day before the cemetery dedication.

En route the presidential party stopped momentarily at a few towns, including Hanover, Pennsylvania. There Lincoln, from the rear train platform, addressed his greeters in a quaint phrase: "Well, you have seen me, and according to general experience, you have seen less than you expected to see." The crowd cheered, having heard about his peculiar brand of humor.

On arrival at Gettysburg that evening, Lincoln stayed at David Wills' home, where he had dinner with Everett. Everett, less than two years later, told of this first social occasion on which he was in Lincoln's company. "In gentlemanly appearance, manners and conversation," related Everett, "he was the peer of any man at the table." That company included, besides Lincoln and Everett, various European diplomats and American dignitaries who had come to Gettysburg for the occasion.

After dinner a crowd gathered about the Wills house, and the Fifth New York Artillery unit serenaded the President. He addressed them briefly in non-committal terms. He thanked them for the compliment, told them that he had no speech to make, adding, "In my position it is somewhat important that I should not say foolish things." An impertinent voice roared, "Not if you can help it." The President retorted: "It very often happens that the only way to help it is to say nothing at all. Believing that is my present condition this evening, I must beg you to excuse me from addressing you further."

And on the following day he gave forth truly one of the masterful brief addresses in all of the English language.

VI

"Early on the morning of the 19th," wrote Harvey Sweney to his brother ten days later, "everything was bustle and commotion. At daylight the streets were a dense mass of living beings. Crowds were moving to Cemetery Hill and wending their way over the bloody grounds of the 1st, 2nd and 3rd of July. . . . About 9 o'clock the roll of the drum and the heavy rumble of cannon announced the preparations of the day, when the loud booming of the minute guns on Cemetery Heights gave warning of the solemn occasion. At 10 o'clock the procession was formed and began to move."

Lincoln's Illinois friend, bodyguard, and United States Marshal for the District of Columbia, Ward Hill Lamon, served as Chief Marshal of the procession. It was a long formal line of marching or mounted dignitaries, led by President Lincoln on horseback, which included diplomatic representatives, Vice-President Hamlin, governors of states, United States senators and representatives, military companies, Sanitary Commission officials and corps, and distinguished citizens. Thousands who had poured into that little town, straining its facilities and accommodations, followed.

Lincoln, Everett, Secretary Seward, and others were escorted to the platform. A dirge was played. Then a clergyman pronounced a prayer, the crowd standing with men bareheaded. Everett, who had two months previously cautioned David Wills, "The occasion is . . . not to be dismissed with a few sentimental or patriotic commonplaces," gave the best in him, physically, intellectually, and oratorically, as he held forth for two hours in a lengthy and learned address, studded with historical and classical allusions. The Philadelphia *Press* reporter, John Russell Young, subsequently called the Massachusetts orator's speech "like a bit of Greek sculpture—beautiful but cold as ice," but nonetheless "resonant, clear, splendid rhetoric."

When Everett finally concluded and sat down, the nation's Chief Executive was introduced. "The tall form of the President," wrote Robert

Miller, an Ohio state legislator, who was present, one week later, "appeared on the stand, and never before have I seen a crowd so vast and restless, after standing so long, so soon stilled and quieted. Hats were removed and all stood motionless to catch the first words he should utter."

Lincoln's words were, perhaps, best and most accurately reported by Charles Hale, the Boston *Daily Advertiser's* correspondent at Gettysburg that day. Hale, intelligent, educated at Harvard and trained by difficult journalistic experience, sent these words to his Boston paper as he heard Lincoln speak them:

"Four score and seven years ago our fathers brought forth upon this continent a new nation, conceived in liberty and dedicated to the proposition that all men are created equal. (Applause.) Now we are engaged in a great civil war, testing whether that nation, or any nation so conceived and so dedicated, can long endure. We are met on a great battle-field of that war; we are met to dedicate a portion of it as a final resting place of those who have given their lives that that nation might live. It is altogether fitting and proper that we should do this, but in a larger sense we cannot dedicate, we cannot consecrate, we cannot hallow this ground. The brave men living and dead who struggled here have consecrated it far above our power to add or detract. (Applause.)

"The world will note (sic) nor long remember what we say here, but it can never forbid [forget?] what the did here. (Applause.) It is for us, the living, rather, to be dedicated here to the unfinished work that they have thus so far nobly carried on. (Applause.) It is rather for us to be here dedicated to the great task remaining before us, that from these honored dead we take increased devotion to that cause for which they here gave their last full measure of devotion that we here highly resolve that the dead shall not have died in vain; (applause) that the nation shall, under God, have a new birth of freedom, and that government of people by the people and for the people shall not perish from the earth. (Long continued applause.)"

VII

Lincoln sounded emotional as he spoke those noblest of thoughts reduced to a few phrases. The Washington *Daily Morning Chronicle* correspondent reported: "It seemed to us that the President sensibly felt the solemnity of the occasion and controlled himself by an effort. This might have been fancy but it was our impression, and as such we record it."

Actually Lincoln's immortal words made deep impact on most of the thousands who heard them. The special committee from Boston, in charge of the burial of the long-uninterred Massachusetts soldiers, stated in its report: "Perhaps nothing in the whole proceedings made so deep an impression on the vast assemblage in so concise a form the lesson of the hour, as the remarks of the President. Their simplicity and force made them worthy of a prominence among the utterances from high places."

Lincoln returned from Gettysburg to Washington, taken ill with what his physician diagnosed as "varioloid," or a mild case of small-pox. Gossips around Washington now speculated on the qualifications of Vice-President Hamlin. As if to depress Lincoln more deeply, his favorite son, Tad, was also sick and had been for more than a week.

The President was cheered by a letter from Everett about his Gettysburg effort: "I should be glad, if I could flatter myself that I came as near to the central idea of the occasion, in two hours, as you did in two minutes. . . . I hope your anxiety for your child was relieved on your arrival."

Lincoln, though ill, immediately sent a reply to Everett's gracious letter: "In our respective parts yesterday, you could not have been excused to make a short address, nor I a long one. I am pleased to know that, in your judgment, the little I did was not entirely a failure. Of course I knew Mr. Everett could not fail. . . . Our sick boy, for whom you kindly inquire, we hope is past the worst." Lincoln did not tell Everett, or anyone else except his doctor and the more intimate members of the White House staff, about his own illness.

Three days later, in the Chattanooga area of Tennessee, the Federal cannons were about to thunder at the Confederates in an important battle.

VIII

The pivot of the Federal-Confederate fight in the West, the ground for which each side was prepared to commit all its human resources, was still the region in and around Chattanooga, Tennessee.

Next to the yet uncaptured Confederate capital, Richmond, Virginia, the greatest prize that the Federals sought for their undisputed possession was Chattanooga, held by them but constantly menaced by Bragg's Army of Tennessee, which might be reinforced and attack shortly.

The center of great railroad lines radiating in every direction to the Mississippi and Ohio Rivers, the Atlantic Ocean, and the Gulf of Mexico, Chattanooga lay at the lower end of that monstrous mountain defile known as East Tennessee, guarding the only avenue by which

Virginia could then be approached by land from the Southwestern states. Its possession by a Federal army, with Southern forces cleared from the region, would do much to isolate all-important Virginia and North Carolina, and lop off the Confederate states of Mississippi and Alabama in the West. If the western Federal armies, now under the over-all command of Grant, could secure undisputed occupation of the Chattanooga neighborhood and crush the Confederate columns there, it would largely open the way into the interior of Georgia and thus throw what was left of the war into the Atlantic region. A union of Meade's great Army of the Potomac with Grant's western forces would surely be too much for Lee to withstand, and Richmond would be certain to fall. On the other hand, if the Confederates under Bragg could oust Grant and his armies from the Chattanooga area and decisively defeat them, the rebels would control much of East Tennessee and thus could move troops, arms, supplies, and food between the West and Virginia.

Chattanooga, besides its invaluable strategic military and economic importance, also held potent political value. It was situated near East Tennessee, where non-slaveholding mountaineer people had maintained strict adherence to the Union—a Unionism made less effective because of their land's isolation and sometime occupation by Confederate forces. Those East Tennessee mountain settlers, geographically living in a seceded state and nominally in Confederate territory, were in no sense associated by bonds of interest and personal ties with the slaveholding-controlled low lands. Lincoln, one month after the Federal reverse at Chickamauga, wired two importunate citizens of Knoxville, in East Tennessee: "You do not estimate the holding of East Tennessee more highly than I do."

Thus military, economic, and political considerations made Chattanooga and its surrounding country the great objective point in the West late in 1863.

Grant, with his subordinate generals, Thomas, Sherman, Sheridan, and Hooker, had facing him in the Chattanooga-Lookout Mountain-Missionary Ridge theatre of warfare in November one of the least talented Confederate supreme commanders.

Braxton Bragg did not enjoy the confidence of his generals, intermediate officers, or men. He lacked the resourcefulness, dash, and craftiness of Lee, and he found it difficult to work in harmony with his military associates. Bragg tolerated no opposition from subordinates, and sometimes he was wrong about it. James Longstreet, Nathan B. Forrest, Leonidas Polk, D. H. Hill, Frank Cheatham, and Simon Buckner were among those gray-uniformed generals who differed with Bragg and found it impossible to work effectively with him. But Bragg remained an extra special favorite of President Jefferson Davis. The Confederate Secretary of War, James A. Seddon, held a poor opinion of Bragg's military ability and advised that he be removed. But Davis continued to maintain Bragg in the Army of Tennessee command. "The President," noted J. B. Jones of the War Department at Richmond in his diary on November 3, 1863, "is resolved to sustain Gen. Bragg at the head of the army in Tennessee in spite of tremendous prejudice against him in and out of the army."

IX

"All preparations should be made for attacking the enemy's position on Missionary Ridge by Saturday at daylight," General Grant, Lincoln's supreme commander in the West, ordered General Thomas on November 18, the day on which the President left Washington for Gettysburg.

Grant went on to explain in his order to Thomas that the general plan against Bragg's Army of Tennessee was for General Sherman, with his forces strengthened by a division from Thomas' command, to cross the Tennessee River just below the mouth of the Chickamauga. That crossing was to be protected by artillery from the heights on the north bank of the river (to be located by Thomas' chief of artillery) and to secure the heights on the northern extremity to about the railroad tunnel before the enemy could concentrate. "You will co-operate with Sherman," Grant emphasized to the "Rock of Chickamauga." Thomas' forces were to form a junction with Sherman's men, advancing toward the northern end of Missionary Ridge, and the armies of the two Generals were to move as near simultaneously with each other as possible. Grant enumerated other technical details of military combat to be followed.

Thus Grant's orders for battle were all prepared when, on that same day, Sherman arrived at Chattanooga.

Within a week there was fought the bloody three-day battle of Lookout Mountain—Missionary Ridge on November 23-25. Grant had assembled about 60,000 troops to Bragg's 40,000.

That three-day carnage had three main phases. Sherman, having crossed the Tennessee River at Brown's Ferry and marched east of Chattanooga, assaulted the Confederate right at the north end of Missionary Ridge. Hooker struck the opposite extreme flank of the Southerners on Lookout Mountain and repulsed the enemy skirmishers, carrying that high position. Bragg's army was now concentrated on Missionary Ridge. The main engagement developed at 3:30 on the afternoon of November 25. Two of Thomas' divisions, commanded by Major-Generals Philip H. Sheridan and Thomas J. Wood, moved out for what was intended to be a "demonstration" to aid Sherman by relieving the pressure in that area.

The orders to Sheridan's and Wood's men, and to Major-General Absalom Baird's division, were to carry the rifle pits at the foot of the ridge. Having done this, however, the three divisions pushed on—exceeding their orders!—to the surprise of their generals. When the Federal divisions recklessly stormed their way over rough ground up the ridge, the Confederates retreated en masse.

Never before in the war had Federal commanders seen anything like the divisions of Sheridan, Wood, and Baird charging up Missionary Ridge. The Chicago *Journal's* war correspondent, Benjamin F. Taylor, dumbfoundedly reported: "I can not render it in words; dictionaries are beggerly things. They seemed to be spurning the dull earth under their feet, and going up to do Homeric battle with the greater gods."

The Union losses for that three-day battle numbered twice as many as those of the Confederates. During November 23-25 more than 750 Federals were killed and over 4,700 wounded; whereas the Southerners lost less than 375 in dead and fewer than 2,200 maimed. But Bragg's army was in disorderly retreat.

In the red-hazed moonlight on that November 25 evening there could be heard the agonizing shrieks and groans and the pitiful appeals of the wounded and the dying on that blood-spattered field of Missionary Ridge.

X

"Well done. Many thanks to all." So telegraphed Lincoln to Grant on November 25, upon completion of the Lookout Mountain-Missionary Ridge-Chattanooga victory.

The next day, Thursday, November 26, Thanksgiving was celebrated.

Lincoln had, two months previously, issued a Proclamation designating the last Thursday of November as a national day of thanksgiving and praise to God, at the urging of Sarah Josepha Hale, editress of *Godey's Lady's Book*. Hitherto, Thanksgiving had been commemorated in various states at different times.

In his Proclamation Lincoln had noted: "The year that is drawing to its close has been filled with the blessings of fruitful fields and healthful skies." Pointing to continued peaceful industry amid war, he had declared: "No human counsel hath devised, nor hath any mortal hand worked out these great things. They are the gifts of the . . . Most High God." He requested all Americans: "I do, therefore, invite my fellow citizens in every part of the United States, and also those who are at sea and those who are sojourning in foreign lands, to set apart and observe the last Thursday of November next, as a day of Thanksgiving and Praise to our beneficient Father who dwelleth in the Heavens."

So this first of national Thanksgivings fell on the day following Grant's victory at Chattanooga. Cabinet members, members of Congress, the Diplomatic Corps, Army and Navy officers, and a few intimate friends of the President called on him at the White House. Congratulations on Grant's triumph for the Union and good wishes for Thanksgiving were simultaneously passed all around.

Lincoln appeared in more festive a mood than at any time since his inauguration nearly three years before, all were agreed. He made merry and seemed jocular with all who came and talked with him, and there was not the slightest look of the familiar Lincolnian melancholia. The New York *Herald's* Washington correspondent, who was present at that private reception, quoted the President as asking John Hay, a most infrequent request: "Col. Hay, let Burgdorf, my messenger, send us up the decanters." Lincoln continued in a happy vein: "I have French wines, sent me from Paris by Secretary of Legation Pennington, who is so completely occupied in the business of tasting vintages that he has never had time to teach it French, though a resident in Paris many years. If you prefer whiskey, I have some that can be relied upon—a present from Mr. Leslie Coombs. I call it 'Grant's Particular,' and Halleck is about issuing an order that all his generals shall drink it."

General-in-Chief Halleck answered, addressed the President and assembled guests: "With the news we have to-day from Chattanooga I think the country will endorse the order to which Mr. Lincoln has referred."

The teetotalling President's reference to "Grant's Particular" brand inspired all sorts of versions of his words that have come down through the decades. The aprocryphal statement most frequently credited to Lincoln runs similar to this request: "I wish you would find out what kind of whiskey Grant guzzles. I want to send a barrel of it to each of my other Generals, so they might win some battles from the rebels for a change."

Only three days after Thanksgiving, in East Tennessee, Major-General Burnside, hitherto stigmatized as the commander who had led the Union army to one of its worst defeats at Fredericksburg the previous year, turned in another victory for the Union.

Burnside's men, on November 29, defeated the Confederate assault on Knoxville led by General Longstreet, Lee's "war horse." The Federals held Knoxville, inflicted heavy losses on the Southerners, and sustained remarkably small casualties themselves. General Sherman, arriving with reinforcements for Burnside in that East Tennessee town one week later, was highly elated over Burnside's performance.

XI

Before 1863 ended, Lincoln was again pleased and the rest of the North, overjoyed by the sudden, unannounced visit of two Russian naval squadrons, one commanded by Rear-Admiral Lissovskii, dropping anchor in New York harbor in late September, followed by another in San Francisco bay.

Those two Russian fleets had taken refuge in American ports temporarily partly to escape possible capture or destruction by the British fleet, in event of war between England and Russia, a conflict then imminent because of Russian expansion into British spheres of influence in Asia and the Pacific Ocean and the suppression of the Poles by the Tsar's Government. Less than a decade before, England and France had fought Russia in the Crimean War over control of the Turkish Straits and Dardanelles region.

Lincoln previously had never held any admiration for the Tsar and his Imperial Government. During his pre-presidential years in Illinois he had denounced Russian interference in Hungary's struggle for independence against Austria, and in 1855, in private correspondence, he referred to the then Tsar as the "Autocrat of all the Russias;" that year, too, he disapprovingly called Russia a country "where despotism can be taken pure." The measure of his scant respect for Russia lay in the circumstance that he had sent two of his Republican Party's biggest problems, Cassius M. Clay of Kentucky, then Secretary of War Cameron, and finally Clay again, as United States Minister to St. Petersburg.

Practical reasons existed for a rapprochement between the New World's biggest and most advanced republic and the Old World's biggest and most backward autocracy. Both nations distrusted Britain, the United States, irritated at their Anglo cousins overseas because of their sympathy for the Southern Confederacy, and Russia combatting Britain because of rival imperialist and expansionist ambitions. The Americans and the Russians too, paradoxically enough, had certain basic similarities, both nations being huge, self-sufficient areas, energetic and expanding. Both maintained gigantic "melting pots" of population with the task of fusing different races. Each country had almost simultaneously freed millions of subject people: Negro slaves in America, feudal serfs in the Tsar's domains. In 1863, moreover, no friction points existed to brew bad blood between republican American and autocratic Russia, for they were sufficiently separated to remove reasons for colliding with each other.

Lincoln and his administration recognized Russia as a counterweight against Great Britain and France, in view of those two nations' threats to intervene in the American civil war on the Confederacy's side. At this time France was especially obnoxious with her military invasion of

Mexico and efforts to set up the Austrian Archduke as her puppet on a Mexican throne. Russia, for her part, was still smarting from her defeat by Anglo-French forces in the Crimean War.

Lincoln left nearly all foreign affairs to Secretary of State Seward, rarely intervening. Seward had indicated the Lincoln Administration's friendly attitude toward Russia, with whose social system Lincoln was not in sympathy, when he sent a dispatch the previous year to the Tsar's Minister at Washington, Baron Eduard de Stoeckl—a message filled with diplomatic unctiousness: "The relations of mutual confidence and friendship between a republican power in the west and a great and enterprising and beneficent monarchy in the east will afford new and important guarantees of peace, order and freedom to the nations."

"God bless the Russians!" exclaimed Lincoln's Secretary of the Navy, Gideon Welles, to his diary when Admiral Lissovskii's squadron landed in New York harbor. And Welles, with Lincoln's approval, gave the Tsar's warships the facilities of the United States Navy Yard in Brooklyn. Dances and banquets were given in honor of the visiting naval officers by "high society" in various American cities. Alexander II's royal imperial name was lustily cheered as America's ally and as the emancipator of serfs. The disciplined Russians toasted Lincoln as the great leader of a great republic and as the emancipator of slaves.

The colossal banquet and ball tendered to the Muscovite officers was held at the Academy of Music and neighboring Irving Hall in New York in November, one week before the bloody Battle of Chattanooga. The cuisine was provided by Delmonico's. Tables upon tables of carved meats arranged on platters amid jellies, sugar roses, winged doves, and pyramided canapés, were devoured by the 3,000 who attended. *Pièces montées* of confectionary represented President Lincoln and Tsar Alexander II, as well as the long-departed George Washington and Peter the Great. One New York newspaperman reported the gormandizingly gigantic quantities of food and drink under which the tables rocked: 12,000 oysters (10,000 poulette and 2,000 pickled), 12 monster salmon—30 pounds each, 1,200 game birds, 250 turkeys, 400 chickens, 1,000 pounds of tenderloin beef, 100 pyramids of pastry, 1,000 large loaves of bread, and 3,500 bottles of wine.

In London, numerous eyebrows were raised at the exaggerated diplomatic *affaire d'amour* between the screeching American eagle and the grasping Russian bear, and it was reported that the British lion "was growling." *Punch* satirically reported Lincoln as saying to the Tsar:

> Imperial son of Nicholas the Great,
> We air in the same fix, I calculate,
> You with your Poles, with Southern rebels I,
> Who spurn my rule and my revenge defy.

When in early December Admiral Lissovskii's squadron sailed into Chesapeake Bay and up the Potomac River, Secretary of State Seward himself entertained the Admiral and his officers, as did Secretary of the Navy Welles. Lincoln still lay ill, suffering from the sickness he had contracted after he had returned from Gettysburg. Seward represented him. "The President," wrote Seward to Minister Clay in St. Petersburg, "earnestly desired that their reception at the Capital might reflect the cordiality and friendship which the nation cherishes toward Russia. Indisposition of the President has, until now, prevented him from giving them a formal audience."

Welles' reception for the Russian naval officers and their wives on December 9, 1863, was attended by Lincoln's assistant secretary, John Hay. That observant young man was astonished by the visitors' capacity for food and drink and their unhandsome looks: "They have vast absorbent powers and are fiendishly ugly. I grieve to say that Mme. Lissovskii is not an exception."

Lincoln grew impressed with the possibility of using the Tsar's recent serf-emancipation ukase to bolster the cause of freedom and the Union in America. He mentioned to the intellectual Bayard Taylor, just returned home from his post as Secretary of Legation at St. Petersburg: "I think a good lecture or two on 'Serfs, Serfdom, and Emancipation in Russia' would be both interesting and valuable. Could you not get up such a thing?"

Taylor promised to prepare such a lecture but also informed the President in reply: "There are only slight resemblances between Russian serfdom and slavery in the southern states, although they rest on the same basis—property in Man—but the complete success of the schemes of emancipation in Russia has much significance for this nation at the present time."

XII

While the Russian naval men were being fêted in Washington during December the great dome of the Capitol was finished and its crowning statue fastened into place. To those who hoped for the Union's survival the completed Capitol appeared as a heartening symbol forecasting the triumph of the national cause.

Lincoln had been criticized by some for not having work stopped on the Capitol building when men, materials, and money were so desperately needed for the war. But he had grown convinced that continued construction of the official home of Congress would exert beneficial effects on the public. "If the people see the Capitol going on," the President told one caller, "it is a sign we intend the Union shall go on."

By the end of 1863 Lincoln could see gratifying results, an indication that the Union would continue. By the Gettysburg and Vicksburg victories in July the Confederacy had been pressed back and shut in by a wall of Federal warships and military forces. It's borders had been narrowed and its territories divided by Union control of the Mississippi River. In the President's public statement of August: "The signs look better. The Father of Waters again goes unvexed to the sea." The autumn state elections had been won, followed by the important Chattanooga victory in November and the emergence of four talented Union commanders—Grant, Sherman, Thomas, and Sheridan. Even Burnside had won in East Tennessee. Then those strange diplomatic bedfellows, the Russians, had arrived, providing an intangible warning to the French, who were destroying republican institutions in Mexico.

With the Chattanooga triumph by the Federal forces, the Confederacy was more deeply cut in parts than it ever had been. The rebel Government at Richmond, earlier in the year, had set up a Trans-Mississippi Department of their army, consisting of Texas, Louisiana, Arkansas, and the "Indian Territory" which would become Oklahoma nearly a half century later. In command of this new far-flung western military division of the Confederacy was placed General Edmund Kirby-Smith, a West Point-educated Floridian. But, late in 1863, Kirby-Smith found himself cut off from Richmond, being able to communicate with the Confederate authorities only by running his agents and messengers through the dangerous Union blockade. He developed into the virtual civil and military ruler of the Confederacy in the West, and wags called this vast, isolated region "Kirby-Smithdom." But the General and his scattered forces in that huge territory henceforth were of little help to the Confederate war effort, except when his forces beat the incompetent General Banks and his army in the foolhardy and futile Red River campaign early the following year.

XIII

Lincoln might have felt even more optimistic, when 1863 closed, if he had known fully and in detail the difficulties and dissensions which the highest Confederate civilian and military authorities were experiencing angrily among themselves.

After General Bragg was beaten at Chattanooga, President Davis held a Cabinet meeting to decide on a new commander for the Army of Tennessee. Secretary of War James A. Seddon proposed General "Joe" Johnston, but Secretary of State Judah P. Benjamin objected on the ground that, while Johnston was a good strategist in defense, he lacked the initiative requisite in a commander. President Davis agreed with Benjamin, but most of the Cabinet, however, favored Johnston as Bragg's replacement. Davis yielded, and reluctantly chose Johnston as head of the Confederacy's biggest western army, the largest Southern force next to Lee's Army of Northern Virginia. In mid-December, the Cabinet ordered Johnston to take command of the Army of Tennessee, and, discouraged and resentful because of Davis' and Benjamin's lack of faith in his abilities, old "Joe" dejectedly went into the field to assume the impossible responsibility of defending the Deep South against the vastly superior Federal forces of Grant, Sherman, Thomas, and Sheridan.

The choice of Bragg's successor, however, was only one of the insidious controversies that were undermining Davis' government. More important was the Confederate President's festering feud with his Vice-President, Alexander H. Stephens. By 1863 this feud had become so significant that a split in the Confederacy's war policy developed.

Davis and Stephens had never been particularly compatible personally or politically. Before the Secession, Davis had been a Democrat, and Stephens had been a Whig turned Democrat. Each had been a power in his respective state, Davis in Mississippi and Stephens in Georgia. And they had always had some basic ideological differences. When, at General Lee's urging, Davis authorized a Conscription act in 1862, Stephens opposed him, allying himself rather with Governors Brown and Vance of Georgia and North Carolina, who were jealously guarding their power in their states under the excuse of "States Rights."

In 1863, a letter written by the Vice-President found its way into the Southern press, stating that: "All that is wanting with us . . . is the brains to manage and mould our recourses." This stunned Davis. And his animosity toward Stephens intensified. In reaction Stephens revolted from the President's policy of pursuing the war to its bitter end, and from 1863 until the end of the war, he constantly worked for a negotiated peace with his old Whig colleague from the Thirtieth Congress, Abraham Lincoln.

With quarreling in the Cabinet, resistance from the state governors, and opposition from his Vice-President, Davis was experiencing difficulties as great as any of those which had been depressing Lincoln. It has never been determined whether the North or the South, Lincoln or Davis, the Army of the Potomac or the Army of Northern Virginia, were more impaired by the constant feuds, quarrels, and conspiracies that occured in the governments and armies of both sides throughout the war. But by the end of 1863, the South could least afford these impairments, for, despite the carnage that had been wrought in the first years of the war, the sternest fighting and the bloodiest battles still lay ahead.

XIV

In the last month of 1863, Lincoln sent his annual message to Congress. In it he suggested a plan for the restoration to the Union of those Southern states which the Federal armies had detached from Confederate control. Simultaneously he issued a proclamation, offering general terms of pardon, amnesty, resumption of allegiance, and reconstruction of loyal State governments.

To this indispensable subject, "Reconstruction"—the President, conservative as he was, always called it "restoration"—it would be well to turn.

PLANS FOR REUNION: *Restoring the Recovered States*

31

I

LINCOLN, besides using the United States armies to suppress the secession, was soon using Union troops to set up civil State governments in Confederate regions recovered by the Federal forces. He started putting into effect his plans for reunion, restoring the Southern states to what he considered their proper places in the Union, early in 1862.

"What will be most wanted by the South after they have been starved and whipped handsomely," Governor Edwin D. Morgan of New York confided to Thurlow Weed in February, 1862, "will be an excuse for returning to the old flag. Mr. Lincoln has endeavored to furnish such an excuse when on so many occasions and in so many ways he has caused it to be made known that there is no disposition to subjugate the South."

Morgan accurately expressed the President's attitude toward the South. Lincoln's plans were free from vindictiveness. He wanted to reconstruct those states on the basis of that part of their populations, even a small minority, that had remained loyal to the Union or could be induced to break from the Confederacy and reassert its adherence to the Union. Lincoln wanted no revenge on the South; bygones were to be bygones. All he desired was that the seceded states should return to their former allegiance to the United States Government. Since his idea was to persuade the Southerners to come back to the family of states where he thought they belonged, without any radical changes from conditions existing before the war, his policy for the return of the seceded states should, more accurately, be termed not "reconstruction" but "restoration." Rarely did Lincoln use the word, "reconstruction." In his own conservative way, he usually spoke of "restoring."

But "reconstruction," or "restoration," whatever it was called, the President found a painful but necessary problem, and handled it with Job-like patience and rare delicacy.

II

To understand Lincoln's restoration policy, it is helpful to understand his genuine affinity to the South through his past Southern associations, personal, professional, and political.

Although Lincoln had made his career of law and public life in Illinois and was of the North, he was bound to the South by ties that were fundamental. A native Kentuckian of Virginia-born parents, he had spent one quarter of his life growing up in a Southern-populated region of lower Indiana, across the Ohio River from slaveholding Kentucky and then lived in a region of Illinois settled mostly by Southerners.

Lincoln had married into a Kentucky family, owners of slaves and largely pro-slavery, and his ties to the Blue Grass State held strong and sure. His very speech was of the Kentuckian idiom. His partner, Herndon, in 1858 had referred to Lincoln as a "Kentucky gentleman." All three of Lincoln's law partners, Stuart, Logan, and Herndon, were Kentucky-born, with only Herndon an anti-slavery advocate. Lincoln's earliest close cronies, Joshua F. Speed and Orville H. Browning, were from that State. His first and most impression-making political idol was Henry Clay, the Blue Grass's nationally-famed conservative and compromiser. Traveling on the Eighth Judicial Circuit, Lincoln had hosts of intimates from below Mason and Dixon's line, especially the Virginia-born Ward Hill Lamon and the Maryland-born Judge David Davis. His most intimate Whig congressional associates at Washington during 1847-49 had been Southerners, particularly Alexander H. Stephens. Of Lincoln's original Cabinet members, two were slave-state conservatives, the Kentucky-born Marylander, Postmaster General Blair, and the Virginia-born Missourian, Attorney-General Bates. In 1861 Seward had advised one of the Southern peace-makers: "See Montgomery Blair, see Mr. Bates, see Mr. Lincoln himself. I wish you would. They are all Southern men."

With such a background, Lincoln knew actual conditions in the slave states better than most top-ranking Northern Unionists. He appreciated the wisdom of having civilian Southern leaders take charge of restoring the Confederate states to the Union. And his system was completely lacking in gall, for he had no intention of inflicting punishment on the Southern people, against whose troops he felt it his duty to use Federal military force. No vengeful peace was to be extracted from a defeated South, he was determined. The President in 1862 had told Army of the Potomac troops that "our opponents were our brothers in error, & that our descendants for a thousand generations must live under that glorious Union established by Washington & his compeers."

III

Tennessee was the first seceded state which Lincoln endeavored to restore to the Union.

While East Tennessee was still in the Confederacy's grip, its central and western regions were conquered by Federal armies. Lincoln, in March, 1862, appointed as the State's Military Governor the unassailable Unionist, United States Senator Andrew Johnson of Tennessee, the only member of the national Upper House at Washington from a seceded State who refused to join the Confederacy. Lincoln gave Johnson the rank of Brigadier-General of Volunteers. Johnson's duties were to effect a reorganization of Tennessee politically, creating a State government on the basis of that portion of the population (a minority) that had remained, or could be induced to become, loyal to the United States.

Governor Johnson, in his March 18 appeal to Tennesseeans, stated that "the Government of the United States could not be unmindful of its high constitutional obligation to guarantee to every State . . . a republican form of government," adding that his purpose was, "as speedily as may be, to restore her government to the same condition as before the existing rebellion."

Governor Johnson's task proved trying and also premature. He faced the bitterness, hatred, violence, and lawlessness of emotionally charged war times in usually tempestuous Tennessee besides having to contend with the political feuds, and feuds within feuds, that converged on Nashville in countless controversies over party power, slavery, and personal dislikes. Too, the inactivity of General Rosecrans' Army of the Cumberland for the first five months of the following year, 1863, left in the interior counties strong Confederate forces under Bragg and others, which discouraged Union men from activity.

Lincoln encouraged Johnson to continue his efforts to form a loyal State civilian government. He cited the "guarantee" clause of the United States Constitution as his authority for maintaining Federal military occupation of the State. That fourth section of the Fourth Amendment of the federal Constitution reads: "The United States shall guarantee to every State in this Union a Republican Form of Government, and shall protect each of them against Invasion; and on Application of the Legislature, or of the Executive (when the Legislature cannot be convened) against domestic Violence."

Lincoln on September 19, 1863, sent directions to Johnson: "You are hereby authorized to exercise such powers as may be necessary and proper to enable the loyal people of Tennessee to present such a republican form of State government, as will entitle the State to the guarantee of the United States therefore, and to be protected under such State government, by the United States against invasion and domestic violence, all according to the fourth Section of the fourth Article of the constitution of the United States."

Only one week before, the President had ordered Johnson: "All Tennessee is now cleared of all armed insurrectionists. You need not to be reminded that it is the nick of time for re-inaugurating a loyal State government. Not a moment should be lost."

Lincoln spoke prematurely. Only ten days after he sent that letter to his Military Governor about Tennessee being "cleared of all armed insurrectionists," General Bragg's Army of Tennessee thoroughly thrashed Rosecrans' Army of the Cumberland at Chickamauga.

Governor Andrew Johnson's efforts to form a loyal civil government in the Volunteer State had to wait another two months until Grant's victory over Bragg at Lookout Mountain-Missionary-Ridge-Chattanooga in November, 1863.

IV

"Broken eggs cannot be mended; but Louisiana has nothing to do now but to take her place in the Union as it was, barring the already broken eggs," Lincoln informed August Belmont, New York banker and "money bags" for the Democrats. Lincoln added: "The sooner she does so, the smaller will be the amount of that which will be passed mending."

Louisiana, most of which had been taken from Southern armies in 1862, was given major attention by Lincoln—perhaps because of its strategic location on the Gulf, the turbulence of the Latin people there, the racial tensions between white and huge percentages of Negroes, and the oppressive rule under General Benjamin F. ("Beast") Butler. He devoted more time and energy to that State than to any other region of regained territories of the Confederacy. In Louisiana the President saw, in terms of military occupation, an early opportunity to make reconstruction, or restoration, a war-time reality handled by Southern civilians, not Northern "invaders."

The State Department had sent Reverdy Johnson, recently elected United States Senator from Maryland, and a conservative, to captured New Orleans to investigate and report on complaints by foreign consuls against the oppressive and high-handed rule of General Butler. Brigadier-General John S. Phelps, Military Governor of Louisiana and Arkansas, had allegedly tried to emancipate slaves on his own authority, or so it was reliably reported. Reverdy Johnson reported to the President by mail: "Depend upon it, my Dear Sir, that unless this is at once corrected, this State [Louisiana] cannot be, for years, if ever, reinstated in the Union."

The President, in answer to Johnson, did not believe that Union feeling was being crushed by General Phelp's conduct. In this reply, however, he expressed his wish not to interfere with the way of life of that State's inhabitants: "The people of Louisiana—all intelligent people every where—know full well, that I never had a wish to touch the foundations of their society, or any right of theirs." The way for Louisianians to persuade him to remove General Phelps, Lincoln informed Johnson, was "simply to take their places in the Union upon the old terms."

Lincoln in August, 1862, appointed Major-General George F. Shepley Military Governor of Louisiana, with General Butler still heading the army forces there. Unsatisfactory as this Shepley-Butler administration in New Orleans was, the President used it as best he could, hundreds of miles from Washington, to push ahead civil reconstruction.

In Washington Lincoln, always wanting natives and residents to undertake the job of aiding in creating loyal governments, turned to former Congressman John E. Bouligny of Louisiana, one of the few members of the lower house of Congress from the seceded states who had not joined the Confederacy. Bouligny was then living in the national capital.

Bouligny returned to Louisiana in October (1862) with a letter from Lincoln to Generals Shepley and Butler and other Federal officers in New Orleans. In that letter the President directed Shepley, Butler, and others holding office under him to help Bouligny in efforts to secure "peace again upon the old terms under the Constitution of the United States." Such a desirable end, the President strongly urged, was to be attained by "elections of members to the Congress of the United States particularly, and perhaps a legislature, State officers, and United States Senators friendly to their object." Lincoln further directed: "Follow forms of law, as far as convenient, but at all events get the expression of the largest number of people possible." He cautioned about the candidates: "Of course the men elected should be gentlemen of character, willing to swear support to the Constitution, as of old, and known to be above reasonable suspicion of duplicity."

In accordance with Lincoln's orders, December 3 was set as the election date behind the Union Lines in Louisiana. Before that day, however, certain suspicious Louisianians feared that avaricious out-of-staters, particularly opportunistic Northerners, holding civil or military offices in the State, would set themselves up as candidates—forerunners of the detested "carpetbaggers" of post-war years. Dr. Hugh Kennedy, a New Orleans dentist, in November went to Washington and protested to Lincoln about such a danger of non-Louisianians running for office in Louisiana.

The President, realizing the evil consequences that might ensue if the Louisiana ballot were filled with Northern candidates, perhaps backed by Federal occupation troops, gave Dr. Kennedy a letter to carry back to Military Governor Shepley in New Orleans. It is the best statement ever made by Lincoln concerning his own opinion of that type of politician who, after the President's death and the coming of peace, would become derisively known to Southerners as "carpetbaggers." "Dr. Kennedy, bearer of this," Lincoln told Shepley in that letter of November 21, 1862, "has some apprehension that Federal officers, not citizens of Louisiana, may be set up as candidates for Congress in that State." That must not be allowed, Lincoln directed the Governor. He ended his letter to Shepley:

> What we do want is the conclusive evidence that respectable citizens of Louisiana are willing to be members of congress & to swear support to the constitution; and that other respectable citizens there are willing to vote for them and send them. To send a parcel of Northern men here, as representatives, elected as would be understood, (and perhaps really so,) at the point of the bayonet, would be disgusting and outrageous; and were I a member of congress here I would vote against admitting any such man to a seat.

Lincoln on that same day sent Governor Shepley a private note: "I wish elections for Congress to take place in Louisiana; but I wish it to be a movement of the people of the Districts, and not a movement of our military and quasi-military authorities there. . . . Fix a day for an election in all the Districts, and have it held in as many places as you can."

In those Louisiana elections on December 3, B. F. Flanders, from New Hampshire, and Michael Hahn, a German-born citizen of Louisiana, were chosen congressmen. Flanders was of the radical faction, Hahn more moderate and closer in tune with Lincoln's views.

During that same month, December, 1862, Lincoln removed the controversial and radically anti-slavery General Butler from the Department of the Gulf command and replaced him with the more moderate Major-General Nathaniel P. Banks.

Military Governor Shepley, however, grew enormously ambitious politically. During 1863 Shepley had his faction, including strongly anti-slavery men, try to control Louisiana politics in a purely personal way. Shepley commissioned one of his followers, Thomas J. Durant, as Commissioner of Registration, in charge of compiling lists of qualified voters and certifying them for the suffrage. Shepley and Durant were enabled to perform this work well because Lincoln's trusted military commander, General Banks, was occupied with operations against the Confederate forces at Alexandria and Port Hudson and in Texas. Lincoln approved the Shepley-Durant registration as the best obtainable under the circumstances. "Gov. Shepley has informed me," the President sent word to General Banks on August 5, 1863, "that Mr. Durant is now taking a registry, with a view to the election of a Constitutional convention in Louisiana. This, to me, appears proper. . . . I think the thing should be pushed forward."

There followed delay upon delay. Shepley was making little or no progress in the election of a constitutional convention of loyal Louisianians who might bring their State back into the Union in a legal manner. Durant never seemed to finish his registry list. On November 5, 1863, the President, impatient, expressed his dissatisfaction in a letter to General Banks: "This disappoints me bitterly; yet I do not throw blame on you or on them. I do, however, urge both you and them, to lose no time . . . I wish him [Shepley] . . . to go to work and give me a tangible nucleus which the remainder of the State may rally around as fast as it can, and which I can at once recognize and sustain as the true State government. . . . Time is important."

Thus Lincoln patiently waited for a "Louisiana movement" to return the State to the Union.

V

Lincoln tried his hand at reconstruction also in Arkansas.

Arkansas, hesitant about seceding, had finally taken the plunge into the Confederacy. Remote from Richmond, the mountainous Ozark commonwealth received scant support from the Confederate Government. In March, 1862, heterogeneous Confederate forces, only partially organized and trained, with the dubious help of Indians, all under Major-

General Earl Van Dorn, had been badly beaten by the Federals at Pea Ridge, Arkansas. Two months later the terrible-tempered Governor Henry M. Rector was threatening to have the State secede from secession "if the arteries of the Confederate heart do not permeate the west bank of the Mississippi."

When in July, 1862, Helena, Arkansas, fell to the Federal forces, Lincoln considered the time ripe to appoint Major-General John S. Phelps Military Governor of both Louisiana and Arkansas. The President's prime purpose was, of course, to strengthen Union feeling in that State.

The War Department, by Lincoln's direction, assured Phelps of its cooperation and support, and ordered General Butler, then in command at New Orleans, to detail army forces to serve under Phelps. It was all toward the end of bringing Arkansas back into the Union.

Lincoln in November (1862) sent a lawyer with Arkansas connections, William M. McPherson, to arrange for elections for members of Congress and State officers there. Lincoln gave McPherson a letter to Governor Phelps and General Frederick Steele, commanding in Arkansas, in which he urged:

> I shall be glad for you and each of you to aid him [McPherson] and all others acting for this object, as much as possible. In all available ways give the people a chance to express their wishes at these elections. Follow law & forms of law as far as convenient, but at all events get the expression of the largest number of people possible. . . . Of course the men elected should be gentlemen of character, willing to swear support to the Constitution, as old, and known to be above reasonable suspicion of duplicity.

Lincoln found his Arkansas reconstruction efforts premature, but he kept at it doggedly. In July, 1863, he learned that one of the former United States Senators from Arkansas, William K. Sebastian, then living in Memphis, nurtured ideas (right after the fall of Vicksburg) about going to Washington and reclaiming his Senate seat. Immediately the President manifested interest, and instructed General Hurlbut, then commanding in Memphis:

> I understand that Senator Sebastian of Arkansas thinks of offering to resume his place in the Senate. Of course the Senate, and not I, would decide whether to admit or reject him. Still I should feel great interest in the question. It may be so presented as to be one of the very greatest national importance. . . . If Senator Sebastian could come with something of this sort [a plan for gradual emancipation, since the Proclamation of Emancipation had freed slaves in secession territory] from Arkansas, I at least should take great interest in his case; and I believe a single individual will have scarcely done the world so great a service. See him, if you can, and read this to him; but charge him not to make it public for the present. Write me again.

Sebastian apparently feared repercussions, or at least social ostracism, by his fellow-Southerners if he tried to reclaim his United States Senate seat and became an emancipationist. General Hurlbut, after discussing the matter with the former Arkansas Senator in Memphis, replied to the President: "I have seen Mr. Sebastian and shown him your letter. I doubt if Sebastian has nerve enough."

Lincoln was aided in his Arkansas efforts when at this time, September, 1863, the Federals captured the state capital, Little Rock. Soon movements, looking to the establishment of loyal state government and ultimate return to the Union, sprang up. It was by no means spontaneous, however, but pushed along by Lincoln's political and military office holders. The historian of Arkansas reconstruction, Dr. Staples, concluded: "It was originated and carried through by the politicians and soldiers, with the sympathy of the loyal masses. There is no doubt as to the irregularity of their procedure, but the encouragement they received was such as to warrant the leaders in believing that their work would be endorsed by those in authority at Washington."

VI

Lincoln, too, turned his attention to restoration of Florida to the Union. That southernmost Confederate outpost held special strategic value because of its location along the Atlantic coast and on the Gulf—an indispensable region for effective enforcement of the Federal blockade of the Confederacy.

Florida, never a State of great plantations, had seceded with high hopes for its future. If the logic of her geographical unity with Georgia and Alabama had been sound when she flew the Spanish flag, it was still sound in 1861, it was persuasively argued by the disunionists. So she had seceded. Lincoln's later Attorney-General, James Speed, referred to "the so-called secession of Florida."

With the outbreak of war, Key West, Tortugas, and Fort Pickens (which guarded the entrance to Pensacola bay) had remained in Union hands. By the spring of 1862 Federal forces had also captured Pensacola and Apalachicola on the West coast and St. John's Bluff, below Jacksonville, and Fernandina on the East coast. The Unionists' military operations were part of their strategy requiring the possession of Confederate ports for making the blockade more effective.

No sooner did the Federals seize huge slices of Florida than Major-General David Hunter, commanding the Department of the South, which included the State, in May, 1862, ordered emancipation of slaves by military proclamation there and in South Carolina and Georgia. It took Lincoln only a little more than a week to revoke Hunter's arbitrary action because it had no legal basis. Of special gravity, if Hunter's

Negro-liberation edict had been allowed to stand, it would have alienated Unionists in those three states. On May 19 the President issued his countermanding order which, declaring that Hunter's proclamation "is producing some excitement and misunderstanding," declared: "Neither General Hunter, nor any other commander, or person, has been authorized by the Government of the United States, to make proclamations declaring the slaves of any State free; and that the supposed proclamation, whether genuine or false, is altogether void." Lincoln emphasized that such matters as emancipation "are questions which, under my responsibility, I reserve to myself, and which I can not feel justified in leaving to the decision of commanders in the field."

Meanwhile, enterprising Yankees, as in later post-war years and the still later modern periods, were soon scurrying down to Florida in pursuit of fortune. "Carpetbag Imperialism" was the description given to this business and promotional endeavor by a later Southern historian. It began in 1862, close on the heels of the Union military victories. The carpetbaggers, according to that historian, writing on war-time and reconstruction-period Florida, brought "nothing with them except a carpetbag and empty but yearning pockets." Most militant of these non-military money-maddened Northern entrepeneurs, who looked over the possibilities in the Sunshine State, was Massachusetts-born Eli Thayer, former member of Congress from the Worcester district, veteran promoter of the "humanitarian" (and land-speculating) New England Emigrant Aid Society, who had operated successfully in "Bleeding Kansas" with colonization a few years before the war. Now, in 1862, Thayer envisioned lucrative exploitation in Federal-occupied Florida by setting up a plan for a "free labor" colonization project for soldiers. That would bring Florida back to loyalty to the Union! It was the sort of plan—Northern invasion of a "recovered" seceded state—that would never be approved by Lincoln.

Thayer went to Washington late in 1862 and put pressure on Lincoln and his Cabinet for his "military colonization" scheme. "Hon. Eli Thayer's schemes for the colonization, by armed men, of the Southern states, meets with much favor from the President, Secretary of War, and the other Secretaries, has been discussed several times in the Cabinet meetings and will probably soon receive official action"—so reported the New York *Tribune's* grossly misinformed Washington correspondent in late September, 1862. Thayer's plan was discussed, but Lincoln gave it no support. The *Tribune* reporter told of the miracle that Thayer would perform: "Mr. Thayer promises, if allowed to carry out his plan in its entirety, to bring Florida into the Union as a Free State by the 1st of February."

Thayer enlisted the aid of Lincoln's radical Secretary of the Treasury, Chase, and of Brigadier-General James A. Garfield, an Ohio politician during peace time (and subsequently President of the United States). Thayer was soon appealing to Lincoln to create a military "Department of Florida," with Garfield as commanding General and himself, Thayer, as Military Governor of the State—all with a view to bringing that Confederate member back into the Union through an extraordinary "armed colonization" program.

It is needless to emphasize that Lincoln gave Thayer no satisfaction or support. By October General Garfield was writing home to his wife: "I had a conference with Thayer. The only thing now needed is the action of the government, and we seem as far from that as ever."

Thayer would not give up so easily. Early in February, 1863, his supporters, a motley group containing New York business men, expecting trade in Florida, humanitarians, anti-slavery zealots, and the New York *Evening Post* editor, William Cullen Bryant, held a meeting at Cooper Institute, and drew up resolutions calling for "armed free labor colonies" in Florida. A "committee of citizens" was chosen to consult with Lincoln on the subject. On February 17 the President granted the committee an interview but gave no support to their novel ideas of regaining Florida's loyalty by antagonizing its natives and residents. Thus did Lincoln discourage Thayer's Florida "reconstruction" enterprise.

By the turn of the year 1863-64, after he had issued his Amnesty Proclamation of December 8, Lincoln was finally ready to do something about restoration of Florida.

Unknown to Secretary of the Navy Welles and Secretary of War Stanton, Lincoln sent a naval-military expedition to Florida. "The Florida expedition," bitterly commented Welles in his diary, "has been one of the secret movements that have been projected, I know not by whom, but suspect the President has been trying a game himself. . . . Admiral Dahlgren went off on it without orders from me, and had only time to advise me he was going."

Along with that expedition, commanded by Major-General Quincy A. Gillmore, Lincoln sent his young assistant secretary, John Hay, to Florida to aid in reconstruction. He gave Hay a letter to General Gillmore, which read:

> I understand an effort is being made by some worthy gentlemen to reconstruct a loyal government in Florida. Florida is in your department, and it is not unlikely that you may be there in person. I had given Mr. Hay a commission as Major, and sent him to you with some blank books and other blanks, to aid in reconstruction. He will explain, as to the manner of using the blanks, and also my general views on the subject. It is desirable for all to co-operate; but if irreconcileable (sic) differences of opinion shall arise, you are master. I wish the thing done in the most speedy way possible, so that, when done, it lie within the range of the late [Amnesty] proclamation on that subject.

Hay, as Lincoln's personal representative, reached Jacksonville in February, 1864. But he failed in trying to inaugurate the President's measures for a "loyal" government. The minority of Union men in East Florida showed that they were not in accord. One group even sent to Lincoln a formal condemnation of those whom Hay had seen fit to call about him as advisers.

Hay, too, was handicapped by the Federal defeat by the Confederate foe at Olustee in February. He remained in Florida until early March, then gave up his reconstruction efforts and returned to the White House as Lincoln's secretary.

The anti-Lincoln New York *Herald* gave a sinister explanation for Lincoln's action in sending Hay to Florida. General Gillmore's military expedition had been undertaken only to trump up a State party organization to send pro-Lincoln delegates to the coming Republican-Union National Convention some months hence. The "Copperhead" New York *World* made a similar observation. After saying that a conquest of Florida could have no more effect on the winning of the war than "the occupation of Yucatan or Coney Island," the *World* insisted: "The object is political. Florida has been marked out as one of the 'rotten borough' states which are to help make Mr. Lincoln President."

As a matter of record, it was not Lincoln, but his own Secretary of the Treasury, Chase, whose men were trying to organize Florida delegates to the national convention for a Chase-for-President, movement who was responsible for Hay's Florida expedition.

VII

North Carolina's possible return to the Union also occupied Lincoln's time and attention during 1862.

This state had left the Union less wholeheartedly than other Southerners, and it had been the last to pass an ordinance of secession in 1861. Union feeling ran high in this conservative and comparatively democratic commonwealth wedged between aristocratic, proud Virginia and secession-crazy South Carolina. North Carolinians, a heterogeneous people consisting of a few big planters, numerous small land owners, tenant farmers, petty merchants, artisans, budding manufacturers, self-sustaining mountaineers, and poverty pinched hillbillies, had gone into the Confederacy after deciding that the Union was broken up and they must remain with the South or go with the North.

Open disloyalty to the Confederacy manifested itself after the Federals' capture of Fort Hatteras in 1861, when a local convention in November declared secession null and void and "elected" Marble Nash Taylor "Governor." But Lincoln did not recognize this farcical government.

The President, however, was ready for action early in 1862, when much of the State's eastern region fell to the Federal forces. He appointed Edward Stanly Military Governor of North Carolina.

Stanly, born at New Bern, North Carolina, son of a die-hard Federalist member of Congress from whom he acquired his national opinions and hot hatred of the "States Rights" Democratic Party, had in pre-war years been a prominent Whig, serving in Congress and in the Legislature as state Attorney General. His temper was passionate, and his unrestrained tongue inspired John Quincy Adams to call him "the terror of the Lucifer party." A Unionist to the core, Stanly had supported in Congress the Compromise of 1850, and later he had run for re-election to Congress on the promise to vote men and money to whip any seceding state back into the Union. After his defeat for re-election, he had moved to California.

In the spring of 1862 Stanly, in Washington, expressed to the President his ideas on how his native and former home state could be brought back into the United States, and he even had offered to undertake such a thankless mission. Lincoln thereupon, in May, chose him as Military Governor, charged with fostering Unionist sentiment there and promoting a loyal State government.

Stanly established headquarters in his native town, New Bern, on May 26. In behalf of Lincoln, Secretary of War Stanton ordered General Burnside, then in command in the State, to co-operate with him. But Lincoln's Military Governor soon learned that he was confronted with an impossible situation. He was distrusted as a traitor and renegade by his fellow North Carolinians, while at Washington the radically anti-slavery Republicans, especially Senator Charles Sumner of Massachusetts, opposed him because he did not favor Negro schools and was apprehending fugitive slaves.

One Northerner, Vincent Colyer, was around New Bern, establishing a school for Negro children. Stanly announced that, while he approved of kindness to the destitute, black or white, he had been sent by the President to restore the old order of things. Thus he could not approve of Colyer's school for the colored, since it would injure the Union cause. He pointed out that North Carolina state laws forbade the teaching of slaves to read or write. He could not succeed in restoring the State if he encouraged violation of its laws, Stanly insisted, and demanded the closing of Colyer's school. In respect to fugitive slaves, Stanly took a similar position. Slaves were constantly leaving their masters and coming into the Union lines and often were taken away by the Northern soldiers and notified that they were free. Whenever the owners would take the oath of allegiance to the United States, Stanly had their slaves restored to them.

Colyer, owner of the Negro school at New Bern, hastened to Washington and invoked the ready aid of Sumner against Stanly. Sumner's biographer, Edward L. Pierce, states that when the Senator went to protest to the President about Stanly's school policy, Sumner "discovered an impatience in Mr. Lincoln which he had not encountered before." Lincoln snapped at Sumner: "Do you take me for a school-committee man?" This offended the Senator, who proceeded to raise a verbose rumpus against Stanly in the Senate.

In the lower house of Congress, Representative John Hickman, of Pennsylvania, in early June sponsored a resolution, calling on the President to forward information on the powers that he had conferred on Stanly. He wanted to know whether Stanly had tried to "prevent the education of children, white or black, in said State" and whether Stanly had been instructed to prevent it. Hickman's resolution passed the House, and a similar resolution was passed in the Senate.

But the President retained confidence in Stanly's ability to accomplish something. The Governor spent considerable time at Washington during the late summer of 1862, deciding on his fate. When he finally returned to his military gubernatorial duties in his native State, Lincoln sent him this message of confidence and good wishes: "Your note informing me that you will leave for North Carolina soon, is received. Your conduct as Military Governor of that State, as reported to me by Gen. Burnside, and as I have heard it personally from yourself, has my entire approbation." Lincoln added: "I shall be much gratified if you can find it practicable to have congressional elections held in that State before January. It is my sincere wish that North Carolina may again govern herself conformably to the constitution of the United States."

Lincoln was disappointed when Stanly, returning to North Carolina, found matters there too much for him. Distrust of him by the natives, for holding office under a "Black" Republican President, and disgust at him for once having left North Carolina for California. Stanly for his own part grew cool when Lincoln's final Proclamation of Emancipation took effect on New Year's Day, 1863. Two weeks later he resigned his military governorship and returned to California.

It was unfortunate that Stanly, tactless and explosive in temperament, was confronted with so many obstacles from native North Carolinians and from radically anti-slavery Republicans at Washington. For if he remained at New Bern for another half year, he might have had favorable Unionist sentiment with which to work.

During 1863, as Confederate casualty rolls were reported and as Jefferson Davis' government passed unpopular laws, especially conscription of men for the Southern armies and tax increases, an ever growing number of North Carolinians became less devoted to the secession cause. The States-Rights people were no more ready to tolerate encroachments on them by a regime at Richmond than by one at Washington. Secret "peace" societies sprang up.

By early 1864 Former Military Governor Stanly, back in California, wanted to return to North Carolina. He had received an urgent wire from a friend in New Bern: "Important movements on foot in interior. Your friends want you to come home." Immediately Stanly telegraphed Lincoln about it, declaring: "When the Country needs my service not as Governor, I am ready to come." But the President concluded that Stanly had outlived his usefulness down in New Bern and to send him back might be more harmful to the Union cause than beneficial. Also, the occupation of North Carolina had not progressed sufficiently for appointment of another Military Governor. Tactfully Lincoln on January 28, 1864, answered Stanly:

> Yours of yesterday received. We have rumors similar to the dispatch received by you, but nothing very definite from North Carolina. Knowing Mr. Stanley (sic) to be an able man, and not doubting that he is a patriot, I should be glad for him to be with his old acquaintances South of Virginia, but I am unable to suggest anything definite upon the subject.

VIII

Restoration of North Carolina's great neighbor, Virginia, received constant attention from Lincoln.

Virginia's strategic location adjacent to and extending from Washington; its prestige as the illustrious State of George Washington, Jefferson, Patrick Henry, Madison, and other Founding Fathers; its then huge boundary (until 1863) stretching from the Atlantic Ocean to southeastern Ohio; the site of the Confederate capital, Richmond, within its borders; its mighty contribution of troops, including the greatest Generals of the South, Lee, "Stonewall" Jackson, "Joe" Johnston, Jubal Early, and J.E.B. ("Jeb") Stuart—all these circumstances had given the proud Old Dominion the strongest influence in the Confederacy. Without Virginia, there probably would have been no Southern nation of formidable power and proportions.

Institutions, traditions, mountainous topography to the west, and differences in economy and national origins drove wedges of separation between eastern and western counties of the Old Dominion.

The white people of the western counties, a mixture of English, Scotch-Irish, and Germans, had come largely from New Jersey, Pennsylvania, and Maryland. The leveling tendencies of the frontier had moulded tastes and outlook toward democracy. The eastern Virginia white people, in contrast, were presumably "better born," and were partial to the aristocratic, slave-holding life, even though only a small minority owned the Negro bondsmen. This schism between western and eastern Virginians was aggravated by an unfair system of representation in the state capital, which discriminated in favor of the East.

Slavery drove another wedge of division between the two Virginia sections. Slavery thrived in the eastern party, whereas the western region had no mighty stake in preserving the South's "peculiar institution" if it meant dissolution of the Union. One of the main troubles lay in the fact that eastern politicians held the principal offices and the westerners had little chance of securing them under the eastern oligarchy.

Francis H. Pierpont, a former Whig politician in western Virginia, who had supported Lincoln for President in 1860, had organized a pro-Union mass meeting at Wheeling shortly after Lincoln's call for troops following Fort Sumter's fall. The meeting arranged for a convention, which met in that town, and decided that the secessionist officials of Virginia had vacated their offices. It elected Pierpont (at times his name was spelled "Pierpoint" and even "Peirpont" or "Peirpoint") as Provisional Governor of Virginia. He thereupon organized the Unionist members of the state Legislature from the western counties into a rump legislature. A constitution was framed, and the name, "West Virginia," adopted.

Congress passed the bill admitting West Virginia as a State of the Union. Lincoln inwardly opposed the bill, doubting its constitutionality in view of the highly irregular manner in which the State had been formed. "We have great fears," wrote Senator Whitman T. Willey of "Loyal" Virginia, to Governor Pierpont in December, 1862, "that the President will veto the new State bill." The President feared that, if he signed the West Virginia statehood bill into law, it might alienate the Unionist element in eastern secession-held Virginia. After a Cabinet meeting at which the spikey issue was discussed, Secretary of the Navy Welles noted: "The President thinks creation of this new State at this time of doubtful expediency." Lincoln's Attorney-General, Bates, viewed the admission of West Virginia as a State as nothing more than a radically anti-slavery conspiracy. It was conceived, in Bates' opinion, as "a fraudulent party trick, by a few unprincipled Radicals, and the prurient ambition of a few meritless aspirants urged it, with indecent haste, into premature birth."

Lincoln searched his soul before he decided to sign the West Virginia bill. But concern for the Union—a new State on loyal principles would aid in crippling secession—turned the balance in favor of the creation of a new state. Was it expedient to carve Virginia into two states? he asked himself repeatedly. And he answered privately in these words which he jotted down:

"More than anything else, it depends on whether the admission or rejection of the new state would under all circumstances tend the more strongly to the restoration of the national authority throughout the Union. That which helps most in this direction is the most expedient at this time. . . . The division of a State is dreaded as a precedent. But a measure made expedient by a war, is no precedent for times of peace." Could the creation of West Virginia as a State be considered "secession" from the remainder of Virginia? The President noted: "Well, if we call it by that name, there is still difference enough between secession against the constitution, and secession in favor of the constitution." He concluded: "I believe the admission of West-Virginia into the Union is expedient." And he signed the Statehood bill.

The admission of the Old Dominion's western mountain counties into the Union as the State of West Virginia placed Governor Pierpont in a peculiar predicament. How could he continue as Governor of two States, "Loyal Virginia" and West Virginia?

Pierpont solved his extraordinary problems by moving his capital from western Virginia to Alexandria, Virginia, adjacent to Washington, D.C., only a carriage ride from the White House, calling his new government the "Restored" State of Virginia. Presumably this Pierpont-ruled State comprised a few Virginia counties and communities under Federal military occupation but was not part of the legal, Congress-sanctioned State of West Virginia. Pierpont's radical foes sneered at his administration. Senator Sumner disparaged it by calling it "little more than the Common Council of Alexandria." General Ben Butler disrespectfully termed Pierpont "the *soi disant* Governor of Virginia." Soon Governor Pierpont and General Butler were quarreling over jurisdiction in Norfolk and other Union-held regions, since they lay in Butler's military department.

Governor Pierpont, besides having four different spellings to his name, had even more titles by which he was addressed, according to letters in his preserved papers. Among such nomenclatures were Governor of Virginia; Governor of West Virginia; Governor, State West-Virginia; Governor of Loyal Virginia; His Excellency, the Governor of East Virginia; and Governor of New Virginia.

Lincoln aided Pierpont's efforts to create a formidable loyal Government within Virginia as the Federal armies continue to occupy more of it, giving him ample federal patronage to sustain his rule and military support, although Butler was not cooperative.

But restoration efforts were not to give promise of success until Lee's surrender early in 1865, and Lincoln was to be brought down by Booth's bullet five days after Appomattox.

IX

Toward the end of 1863 Lincoln thought in terms of a huge program of amnesty and pardon for secessionists, and in early December proclaimed his plan of reconstruction and amnesty to Congress and the nation.

The besieged General Rosecrans, defending Chattanooga after his defeat at Chickamauga, made a suggestion to Lincoln by mail while the autumn elections were raging in Pennsylvania, Ohio, and less important Northern states in early October. Rosecrans wrote the President: "If we can maintain this position in such strength that the enemy are obliged to abandon their position, and the Elections in the great States go favorably, would it not be well to offer a general amnesty to all officers and soldiers in the Rebellion? It would give us moral strength and weaken them very much."

Lincoln, in replying to Rosecrans, revealed: "I intend doing something like what you suggest, whenever the case shall appear ripe enough to have it accepted in the true understanding, rather than as a confession of weakness and fear."

One week following Lincoln's answer to Rosecrans the significant state elections in Pennsylvania and Ohio were won by the Republican-Union candidates. And six weeks after that, in late November, Grant achieved his great military victory at Chattanooga-Lookout-Mountain-Missionary Ridge. The time was "ripe." Lincoln could now present his amnesty proclamation without having it appear "as a confession of weakness and fear."

On December 8, only two weeks after Grant's mighty military victory in Tennessee, Lincoln issued his Amnesty Proclamation. Using his constitutional "power to grant reprieves and pardons for offences against the United States, except in cases of impeachment," Lincoln offered pardon, with certain exceptions, to any adherents of the Confederacy who would take the oath to support "the Constitution of the United States and the Union of the States thereunder." Whenever in any State a loyal nucleus, equal to one-tenth of the votes cast at the presidential election of 1860, should qualify by such oath-taking and establish a state government with abolition of slavery, Lincoln promised executive recognition of such a state government. This has been called the President's "ten per cent plan" of reconstruction.

Lincoln was convinced that reconstruction, or restoration, was a presidential or executive function, not one for Congress. Herein lay the fierce fight between him and the radical majority in the Senate and House of Representatives.

No more than several months had elapsed following his Amnesty Proclamation of December, 1863, than the demon of political partisan controversy emerged, led in the Senate by Senator Benjamin F. Wade of Ohio and in the House by Representative Henry Winter Davis of Maryland.

X

The anti-Lincoln activities of Senator Wade and Congressman Davis, both Republican-Unionists, over reconstruction and other matters in 1864 demonstrated anew that the President continually conducted a three-front war, against the Confederacy, against the opposition Democrats, and against radicals within his own Republican-Union ranks. Lincoln's troubles with Henry Winter Davis, the irascible and unforgiving Baltimore congressman, had started when he passed Davis over for a Cabinet post in 1861 and chose Davis' arch rival, Montgomery Blair, as Postmaster General. The Chief Executive had tried valiantly for three years to preserve peace between Davis and the Postmaster General. But this Davis-Blair battle grew rougher when the followers of each fought over their shares of federal patronage. Lincoln's Proclamation of Emancipation provoked further fights over slavery, with Davis, a radical, demanding uncompensated emancipation of the bonded blacks immediately, whereas Blair, a conservative, wanted the slaveholders to be compensated and the slaves to be freed only very gradually. All through the winter, spring, and summer of 1864 Davisites and Blairites went after each other's political blood. Davis grew increasingly anti-Lincoln, partly because Blair was kept in the Cabinet, and partly because the President was pursuing too moderate a course on Negro emancipation and reconstruction of the "recovered" Southern states.

In early summer, 1864, Davis joined hands with the equally radical Senator Wade of Ohio, Chairman of the anti-Lincoln congressional Joint Committee on the Conduct of the War, in steering through both houses of Congress the drastic Wade-Davis reconstruction bill, which provided for a harsh Congressionally dictated program for the return of the Southern states to the Union, the antithesis to Lincoln's lenient, conciliatory "ten per cent" plan of reconstruction.

The Wade-Davis measure, designed to thwart the President's plan of easy reconstruction, made the work of restoring the seceded states more difficult and more punitive by entrusting the Confederates' return to the Union not to a minority ready for future loyalty but to those whose Unionism was a matter of past record. The bill of Wade and Davis stipulated that, under authority of a provisional governor, an enrollment of white male citizens was to be made. If the persons taking the oath to support the United States Constitution should number a majority of those enrolled, the loyal people of the "recovered" secession state were to be invited to choose a constitutional convention for the launching of a new state government. But no one who had held office, State or Confederate, "under the rebel usurpation," or who had voluntarily borne arms against the United States, should be permitted to vote or serve as a delegate at such an election. In the new government to be set up in a militarily

Federal-occupied Confederate state, slavery was to be prohibited, the rebel debt repudiated, and no office-holder under the "usurping power" (with minor exceptions) could "vote for or be a member of the legislature or governor."

President Lincoln applied the pocket veto to that drastic Wade-Davis reconstruction bill. But he had not heard the last of Wade, Davis, and their radical followers who made life miserable for him during his campaign for re-election.

PRESIDENTIAL RIVALS AND MILITARY REVERSES

32

I

"A second term," confided President Lincoln to his Illinois supporter, Congressman Elihu B. Washburne, before 1864 opened, "would be a great honor and a great labor, which together, perhaps I would not decline if tendered."

Thus did the President send private word down the party line that he would run for re-election.

Throughout most of 1864 professional politicians and public alike divided their attention between the battle of bullets against Confederates and the battle of ballots against Democrats.

Lincoln, in testing himself before the voters for a second term, was destined to be bedevilled by depressing political and military developments: the attempts of members of his own Republican-Union Party to displace him with another presidential candidate, and a deteriorating situation at the war front after the three great victories at Gettysburg, Vicksburg, and Chattanooga of the previous year.

II

As the grim military conflict wore on, Lincoln continued to bolster his administration with shrewd distribution of the federal patronage—"Justice to all" was still his attempted policy—and by cultivating Congress with what has cynically been called "the cohesive power of the public plunder."

At times he found the awards of government jobs, big and little, a bitter bone of contention between two senators from the same state. "I did not doubt yesterday that you desired to see me about the appointment of assessor in Kansas," the President communicated to Senator Samuel C. Pomeroy of the Sunflower State, who was belligerently at odds with his colleague, Senator James H. Lane. "I wish you and Lane would make a sincere effort to get out of the mood you are in. It does neither of you any good. It gives you the means of tormenting the life out of me, and nothing else."

This ever-festering feud between the two Kansas senators, both of the President's own Republican-Union Party, grew more acute when the 1864 national election year opened. Lane, an opportunist and haranguing frontier demagogue intent on feasting further at the federal job trough, favored Lincoln's re-election. Pomeroy, a grasping land speculator who had come up in Kansas politics via the New England-sponsored Emigrant Aid Society to do something for "Bleeding" Kansas in pre-war years, felt himself abused by Lincoln and convinced himself that the President was neither prosecuting the war vigorously enough nor moving sufficiently fast on Negro emancipation. Pomeroy favored a more radical presidential candidate as the party's standard-bearer to run against the Democrat in November. His favorite candidate was Lincoln's own Secretary of the Treasury, Chase.

In February, 1864, there appeared in a Washington newspaper a copy of a pamphlet, worded "strictly private" and bearing Senator Pomeroy's signature, although it was later revealed to have been "ghost" written by another, J. M. Winchell of Hyde Park, New York.

This Winchell-written so-called "Pomeroy Circular," declared that it would be well for friends of the Union to do everything possible to repress the rebellion. But now that "party machinery and official influence" were being used to perpetuate the administration, "friends of the Union and of freedom" must assert themselves. The Circular stated that Lincoln's re-election was an impossibility and, even if it were possible, it was undesirable because of the President's tendency toward "compromise and temporary expediency." Also, the patronage had been so abused under Lincoln as to render the one-term principle essential to the preservation of republican institutions. The Pomeroy Circular demanded a more vigorous prosecution of the war and insisted that Secretary of the Treasury Chase was the man for the task.

White House hopes still fevered Chase's imagination in 1864, just as they had in 1856 and 1860 and were to do in 1868 and 1872. Letters from his Treasury subordinates and radically anti-slavery supporters poured in on Chase, assuring him that he was the only qualified leader. In his appointment of "Special Treasury Agents" throughout the North and in Federal-occupied Southern regions Chase chose those politicos who sympathized with his ambitions to succeed Lincoln. Typical among Chase's preserved papers is the letter from the Collector of the Federal-occupied Port of New Orleans, George S. Denison: "We are forming a Chase Club and meet for organization next Monday. I believe we can control the election of delegates to the National Convention."

Lincoln's other Cabinet members were aware that Chase was allowing his Treasury office-holders to build his presidential boom and to hunt for delegates to the coming Republican-Union National Convention four months off. Attorney-General Bates confided to his diary: "I am afraid Mr. Chase's head is turned by his eagerness in pursuit of the presidency. For a long time back he has been filling all the offices in his own vast patronage with extreme partisans, and contrives also to fill many vacancies, properly belonging to other departments." Secretary of the Navy Welles jotted down in his day book: "Chase intends to press his pretensions as a candidate, and much of the Treasury machinery and the special agencies have that end in view." John W. Forney, Washington and Philadelphia newspaper publisher and Secretary of the United States Senate, a recipient of lucrative printing contracts from Lincoln's administration, in early March angrily charged in his Philadelphia daily, the *Press:* "The enormous catalogue of offices (almost a Blue Book in itself) attached to the Treasury Department is crowded with personal adherents of the distinguished Secretary"—and Treasury agents everywhere who, with Chase's sanction, were launching attacks, undercover, on President Lincoln, so charged Forney.

III

"Have his head in the basket if he does not take heed. . . ."

So the President's old party crony of Illinois, State Auditor Jesse K. Dubois, advised the President, using French guillotine language, as he recommended that Chase be fired from the Cabinet. Dubois sent a copy of the Pomeroy Circular for Lincoln's enlightenment.

But Lincoln was not the man to act hastily in such delicate matters. He did not rid his Cabinet of his undermining Secretary of the Treasury, as some Chief Executives before and since did to subordinates who coveted their chief's position.

The preserved correspondence that passed between the President and his Treasury head reveals embarrassment on both sides, especially by Chase.

The ambitious Cabinet member, in a letter on February 22, protested to Lincoln that he had no previous knowledge of the Pomeroy Circular until he had read it in a Washington newspaper. He told Lincoln in that letter that, when friends approached him with the proposal that he allow his name to be used in connection with the coming national election, he had told them that he could "render them no help" and had instructed them to withdraw his name whenever the "public interest" would require it. He assured the President: "I do not wish to administer the Treasury Department one day without your entire confidence;" and also told Lincoln: "For yourself I cherish sincere respect and esteem. . . . Great numbers now desire your re-election."

Chase was handling the truth carelessly when he avowed to Lincoln that he had no knowledge of the Pomeroy Circular until it had appeared in print, according to J. M. Winchell later. Winchell, one decade later, after Chase's death, gave the lie to the late Chase in a letter to the New York *Times: "Mr. Chase was informed of this proposed action and approved it fully*. He told me himself that the arraignment of the Administration . . . was one which he thoroughly indorsed and would sustain. The Circular was, therefore, sent out." Winchell did the actual writing of the Pomeroy Circular.

Lincoln replied to Chase's letter of explanation on February 29, 1864. He told his Treasury chief: "On consideration, I find there is very little to say. My knowledge of Mr. Pomeroy's letter having been made *public* came to me only the day you wrote; but I had, in spite of myself, known of its *existence* several days before. I have not yet read it, and I think I shall not." He knew as "little of these things" as his friends allowed him to know, he added to Chase. He assured Chase that neither could be "justly held responsible for what our respective friends may do without our instigation or countenance." Whether Chase should remain as Secretary of the Treasury, the President concluded, would be decided only on the basis of the President's own judgment of the public's service. He informed Chase: "I do not perceive occasion for change."

The President several days later expressed to Chase his own preference that their correspondence on the Pomeroy Circular be not published; but added, "yet you are at liberty, without in the least offending me, to allow the publication, if you choose."

Chase chose to have the correspondence made public, and the letters that passed between him and the Chief Executive on the embarrassing subject appeared in the New York *Herald* on March 7.

IV

Chase was not the only figure in the national focus who covetously cast eyes at Lincoln's place in the White House. Several others operated, intent on capturing the glittering bauble at the polls in November. In particular were those two spectacular politician warriors, Generals John C. Frémont and Benjamin F. Butler, both rich in popular acclaim but poor in military achievements. Lincoln had found it necessary to remove each from his command—Frémont from the Department of the West at St. Louis in 1861, then from the Mountain Department in the Shenandoah Valley in 1862; and Butler from the Department of the Gulf at New Orleans in 1862.

Despite Frémont's and Butler's hollow military records, undiscriminating portions of the Northern public curiously hailed both as admirable war heroes, perhaps because of their bizarre crowd-capturing talents. Each had distinguished himself more at currying popular favor on the home front than at conquering Confederates on battle fields. Thus in turn certain radical Republican-Union anti-Lincoln politicians joined forces with extreme anti-slavery advocates to take up the Pathfinder and the "Beast" as possible presidential candidates to succeed Lincoln.

To great masses Frémont's name sounded a magical ring. His slavery-emancipation proclamation as commander in Missouri, which Lincoln had overruled, followed by his removal from command there and then from his Mountain command by Lincoln—all had endeared the picturesque explorer to advanced anti-slavery groups and other ultras in Lincoln's Republican-Union Party, who now took him up as Lincoln's replacement.

Radicals and old-school abolitionists, fondly remembering Frémont's Missouri emancipation edict, assembled on March 19 in a "Fremont meeting" at Cooper Union in New York. The sponsors were obscure and uninfluential politicians and the well-known eccentric, Horace Greeley. The *Tribune* editor spoke, pointing out that it would be well to postpone all nominations and campaigning until people could see what General Grant could do against the Confederates in the coming summer. Greeley also called for only a single term for a President and he eulogized Frémont as an apostle of freedom.

Thus Frémont was being kept "on ice" until the time was opportune for bringing him forward as a presidential candidate against Lincoln.

General Ben Butler for a while took his presidential boom seriously. This politician in general's dress, pompously wearing two stars on each shoulder of his blue uniform, was kept informed by his political manipulators. "Gen. B. is more dreaded as a presidential candidate than any one spoken of," one party worker reported to "Gen. B.;" and on March 25 he assured "Gen. B." confidentially: "The Pres. to a very particular friend of mine a week or ten days ago spoke of Gen. B. in connection with the presidency, showing his fears."

Lincoln actually grew troubled by persistent rumors that Chase, Butler, Frémont, and others might make common cause against him. The Chief Executive recognized the mass support of Butler, whose popularity catapulted because he directed his demagogic talents at masses of people swayed by appeals to emotion and excessive flag-waving. Butler's blunt and forceful treatment of the Southerners under his control in Federal-occupied territory, his disinclination to be troubled with accepted niceties, his refusal to remain on the defensive in any arguments which might be provoked had all struck responsive chords among the Northern populace. Newspapers praised this political General for his "energetic and able" record.

To this politician General, who had captured Northern civilian imaginations rather than Southern military strongholds, Lincoln sent Senator Cameron of Pennsylvania, his former Secretary of War and ex-Minister to Russia, as an emissary. Supposedly, Cameron, presumably in the President's behalf, offered Butler the Vice-Presidential nomination, but he declined second place. This, however, is still an unproved story.

More responsible opinion prevailed. Butler's presidential candidacy soon inspired more derision than enthusiasm. Then, too, certain influential citizens began mentioning General Grant as a prospective successor to Lincoln, overlooking the fact that Grant had a war to fight against the rebels in the field. James Gordon Bennett, publisher of the nation's most widely circulated daily, the New York *Herald,* was printing such conspicuous articles as "Why Grant Is the Best Candidate For the Presidency."

V

While billowing storm clouds, such as the candidacies of Secretary Chase and Generals Frémont and Butler, for a while darkened his renomination prospects early in 1864, Lincoln devoted his attention to the crucial question of an over-all supreme commander of the Federal armies in the field. It proved not a perplexing problem, since only one name was in his, the politicians', and the public's minds throughout the North: General Grant.

Grant came along as a victorious commander precisely at the right time to be accepted as the Union's great military hero. Ever since Fort Sumter, the North had longed for a war hero. Major Robert Anderson, Sumter's commander, was idolized for a few months, serving as a rallying cry to recruit soldiers and unite the North against the secessionists, but

Anderson's exalted reputation was somewhat tarnished by the growing feeling that he had surrendered the fort too soon. Then Lincoln's youthful friend, Colonel Elmer E. Ellsworth, briefly captivated the public imagination when he was shot dead cutting down a stars-and-bars flag in Alexandria, but he also was soon forgotten. It was the same with Lincoln's old friend, Colonel Edward D. Baker, who was lauded as a hero for months after he fell at Ball's Bluff. Captain John Wilkes had been semi-hysterically acclaimed by the crowd above Mason and Dixon's line when he humbled Great Britain by taking two Confederate commissioners from the British ship, *Trent,* on the high seas. Wilkes found his name leading all the rest in the Northern section of a nation which needed a hero. But soon the people realized that Wilkes had done nothing more than what the British, themselves, had been doing for a few centuries.

None of the Federal generals in the field had become idols among the populace, although General McClellan was loved and admired by most of his Army of the Potomac. McClellan might have fought his way to victory and Northern acclaim, but Lincoln had removed him shortly after his Antietam triumph because he lacked aggressiveness. McClellan's successor, Burnside, was disgraced by his Fredericksburg failure. Then early in 1863, Hooker, Burnside's replacement went the terrible way of his predecessors at Chancellorsville. Meade, victor of Gettysburg, moved too slowly after that triumph and lacked a spectacular personality. In the West, General Buell had been removed by Lincoln. And Buell's replacement, Rosecrans, disgraced himself in the Chickamauga defeat. There remained Grant, who registered two major Federal triumphs in five months: Vicksburg in July, Chattanooga in November. Clearly he was the great man of the hour.

When news of Grant's Chattanooga triumph reached Washington in late November, 1863, Congress was just about to assemble for its long session. Grant's chief political sponsor, Congressman Elihu B. Washburne of Grant's home Galena, Illinois, district, introduced a bill to revive the grade of Lieutenant-General, which had been held by the retired Winfield Scott.

Washburne, lauding Grant on the floors of Congress in support of his bill to revive the three-star General's rank, contributed to the rapidly growing legend of Grant's simple and democratic bearing. "He fared like the commonest soldier in his command, partaking of his rations, and sleeping upon the ground with no covering except the canopy of heaven," intoned Congressman Washburne. Congress passed a resolution of thanks to Grant and authorized the President to have a gold medal struck to be presented to the hero of Vicksburg and Chattanooga, in the name of the American people.

When in February, 1864, Washburne's bill, reviving the Lieutenant-

Generalship of the army, passed both houses of Congress, Lincoln signed it and then nominated Grant to this then highest of all American military grades.

Lincoln called Grant to Washington, and he arrived there in early March.

The U. S. Grant who was greeted by Lincoln and the rest of Washington was a short, round-shouldered, rather scrubbly-looking man, untidily garbed in a tarnished Major-General's uniform, a figure with a brownish-skinned, inscrutable face adorned with rough, light-brown short whiskers. From his mouth protruded an unlighted cigar.

Grant attended a White House levée. The President, towering above the crowd, observed his entrance. "Why, here is General Grant!" he exclaimed. Eager to lionize the hero, the vast throng pressed close as the victor of Vicksburg and Chattanooga mumbled an embarrassed reply to Lincoln's greeting. He was presented to Mrs. Lincoln and various notables and then turned over to the throng. Immediately there formed the worst "coat-tearing, button-bursting jam" that the Executive Mansion had seen since Andrew Jackson's day. Secretary Seward persuaded the General to stand on a sofa so that the people might see him. All of it, complained Secretary of the Navy Welles, appeared "rowdy and unseemly."

At long last the hero-hungry North had a real live epauletted idol who had won great battles.

VI

Lieutenant-General Grant, no reader of military textbooks like Halleck, but a field commander who insisted on fighting the foe, whatever the cost in manpower or materials, rejected suggestions that he rent a house in Washington and direct military operations from the War Department. He set up headquarters with the Army of the Potomac and traveled with it wherever it went, maintaining General Meade as head of that most formidable of all Federal forces, with himself as supreme head of all armies except General Banks' unit in Louisiana.

For two months Grant studied the situation on all fronts, consulted with his commanders, mapped future strategy, pondered over varying tactics to be followed, switched units about, and was ready to move against the Confederates on most fronts by early May.

Sherman, whom Grant had made commander of the Division of the Mississippi, was to move against "Joe" Johnston's Southern Army, with Atlanta, Georgia, as his objective. General Franz Sigel, who had just been placed in command of the Department of West Virginia, was to move up the Shenandoah Valley. General Ben Butler was to bring the Army of the James up the James River, and take Petersburg and Richmond. The Army of the Potomac, under Meade, was, if possible, to destroy Lee's Army of Northern Virginia, the Southerner's biggest unit. Sheridan was ordered to bring his cavalry from Chattanooga and was assigned to the command of two cavalry corps. Units under Burnside, at Annapolis, were to act as reinforcements and were to go wherever needed.

Before the Union armies had acted separately. Grant changed this and made all Federal forces one great army under him, except those headed by that politically privileged former Speaker of Congress and former Governor of Massachusetts, General Banks, who still headed his independent command in Louisiana. In Grant's inauguration of his chain of command lay his military constructiveness. The Army of the Potomac was the center, the Army of the James the left wing, and all the troops between the Mississippi River and the eastern Tennessee mountains and as far south as Memphis and Chattanooga, the right wing. Soldiers further south became a force at the Southern enemy's rear. As one grand army, under Grant's supreme command, it was to move against the Confederates on May 4.

Lincoln on April 30 described to Grant the command relationship that should exist between the two of them:

"Not expecting to see you again before the Spring campaign opens, I wish to express, in this way, my entire satisfaction with what you have done up to this time, so far as I understand it. The particulars of your plans I neither know, or seek to know. You are vigilant and self-reliant; and, pleased with this, I wish not to protrude any constraints or restraints upon you. While I am very anxious that any great disaster, or the capture of our men in great numbers, shall be avoided, I know these points are less likely to escape your attention than they would be mine. If there is any thing wanting which is within my power to give, do not fail to let me know it."

It was not long before Grant was troubled by quarrels between General Meade and General Sheridan. The Army of the Potomac commander disagreed with Grant's celebrated cavalry leader on the use and significance of mounted troops. Sheridan's proposal for a concentration of his cavalry seemed to stagger Meade, who deemed a commander of horse troops only "an adjunct at army headquarters," a sort of chief of cavalry rather than the leader of an integrated fighting force. The terrible-tempered Sheridan threatened to resign his command, which was quite all right with the victor of Gettysburg. Grant had to bring his good offices to bear, and very tactfully, to preserve the peace between Meade and Sheridan.

By early May Grant gave his orders to move ahead.

VII

On May 4 Grant, after sending his army across the Rapidan River in its drive on Richmond, encamped in "the Wilderness," an aptly named treacherous, wooded hell region of Virginia, filled with low ridges and swamps, covered with a dense second growth of small trees and thick, matted underbrush. A diabolical battlefield for both Federals and Confederates, "the Wilderness" served as the profusely blood-letting site for a fierce fight that "no man saw or could see," never knowing when he was accidentally killing or maiming an unseen comrade. In that constant exchange of infantry and artillery fire between May 5 and 7, 1864, thousands on both sides were killed or wounded, and an unknown number were missing, never to be heard from again.

Lincoln endured mental torture during the Wilderness battle. "He scarcely slept at all," declared the artist, Francis B. Carpenter, who was staying at the White House then, painting his famous picture of the drafting of the Proclamation of Emancipation. Carpenter saw the President late at night, "pacing back and forth . . . his hands behind him, great black rings under his eyes, his head bent forward upon his breast."

On the Virginia front Grant, between early May and early June, traveling with the Army of the Potomac under Meade, fought a series of battles with Lee and his Army of Northern Virginia, still the Confederates' biggest force, ending at Cold Harbor on June 3. In that one month the Federals suffered more than 50,000 casualties, nearly as many killed, wounded or missing as the total number of men in Lee's entire army. Grant would confess in his *Memoirs,* not long before his death: "I have always regretted that the last assault at Cold Harbor was ever made. No advantage whatever was gained to compensate for the heavy loss we sustained."

Grant, during the week after his colossally costly Cold Harbor attack, marched his baffled, depressed, and tattered men southward by the left and on June 14 crossed the James River at City Point.

With his drive against Lee's army unsuccessful, and Lee and his men safely back behind their Petersburg-Richmond line of defenses, Grant settled down to a siege of Petersburg which would last for the best part of nine months.

VIII

Elsewhere on the Virginia front, too, Federal commanders were leading their men to defeat at precisely the same time that Grant was having his terrible ordeal in May. On the 15th of that month, General Ben Butler got himself bottled up in Bermuda Hundred and General Franz Sigel was defeated in the Shenandoah Valley.

Butler, leading two corps from south of the James River up toward Richmond, which he hoped to capture, had been attacked by the Confederates, an inferior force in numbers, under Beauregard, on May 15. Butler found himself being driven into a peninsula jutting out into the James. The Southerners promptly dug across the neck of the peninsula, leaving Butler and his army locked up at Bermuda Hundred as securely as if they had been incarcerated, arms and all, in one vast prison. And, to make matters worse, the tempestuous Butler quarreled with his two corps commanders. General Grant gloomily reported that this Massachusetts politician-warrior was "as completely shut off from further operations against Richmond as if he had been in a bottle strongly corked." One contemporary phrased it slightly differently: Butler had bottled himself up in Bermuda Hundred by his stupidity, and Beauregard was ready there to put in the stopper.

At precisely the same time that Butler was being "locked up" by Beauregard in Bermuda Hundred, General Franz Sigel was meeting a bad fate at the hands of Major-General John C. Breckinridge, former Vice-President of the United States and now a fighting Confederate commander.

Grant's plan for a general advance of all armies required Sigel, Baden-born and graduate of the Karlsruhe military academy in Germany, and a power in German-American politics, to lead his forces up the Shenandoah Valley and capture Lynchburg. But by May 15 Sigel and his men encountered the rebels under Breckinridge at New Market and were badly beaten.

Lincoln had given Sigel command of the Department of West Virginia less than three months before at the urging of the West Virginia Legislature and of certain German-born leaders, such as Sigismunde Kaufman of New York. Carl Schurz had also congratulated the President on his appointment of Sigel: "I am very glad you gave Sigel the Dept. of West-Virginia. It was a very judicious measure in every respect."

Although Sigel had fought bravely at New Market and continually exposed himself to the heaviest Confederate fire, he was defeated. That finished him as a Union commander, and Lincoln found it necessary to replace him with General David Hunter. But the Northern press assailed the administration for Sigel's appointment in the first place, accusing Lincoln, with large measure of truth, of cultivating the "foreign" Germans.

IX

The failures of Grant, Butler, and Sigel in Virginia did not end the number of Federal reverses at the front during that nightmarish month of May, 1864. There was also Major-General Nathaniel P. Banks and his Red River expedition, in the Louisiana-Texas theatre.

Lincoln had been concerned with establishing a strong loyal government in Louisiana. The Department of State, headed by Seward, wanted the American flag quickly restored in Confederate-occupied Texas as a counter move to the French military maneuvers in Mexico. And United States agents, as well as avaricious speculators, were lured by great stores of cotton in the Red River region of Louisiana and Texas. These considerations inspired Lincoln and his advisers to agree to General Banks's Red River drive.

Banks's operation, begun in March, intended to open up the way to Texas through the Red River valley of Louisiana. With aid of troops from General Sherman in Mississippi and from the Federal commander in Arkansas, and with river support from United States Navy gunboats under Rear-Admiral David D. Porter, Bank's big force comprised nearly 30,000 men, ranging all the way from seasoned veterans to nondescript "persons" who could hardly be classified as soldiers. Opposing Banks were the Confederates under General Richard ("Dick") Taylor, son of the late President Zachary Taylor. On April 8-9 at Sabine Crossroads, near Mansfield, Louisiana, the two armies clashed. The Federals were roundly thrashed.

General Grant, who had opposed Banks's campaign from the first but had finally acquiesced to it reluctantly because it was a decision from his superiors at Washington, now clamored for Banks' removal. On May 3 Chief of Staff Halleck in a note explained to the irritated Grant why Banks was still tolerated in independent command and was not relieved even after his defeat at Mansfield:

> The Secretary of War has copies of all your telegrams [of protest], and I believe they have all been read by the President. . . . General Banks is a personal friend of the President, and has strong political supporters in and out of Congress. There will undoubtedly be a very strong opposition to his being removed or superseded, and I think the President will hesitate to act unless he has a definite request from you to do so. . . . I expressed to the President months ago my own opinion of General Banks's want of military capacity."

Banks, ten days later, May 13, evacuated Alexandria, Louisiana, and before the month ended abandoned his whole futile Red River campaign because of its dismal failure.

The Red River fiasco angered Admiral Porter, commanding Banks' naval support, until his dying day. In his post-war reminiscence Porter held back no words in describing the whole campaign in choice phrases: "It was an army of cotton speculators, commanded by General Greed, General Avarice, General Speculation, and General Breach of Trust, with all their attendant staff of harpies, who were using the army and navy for the vilest purposes."

For Lincoln that month of May proved excessively trying. From the viewpoint of actual number of battles lost by the Federals it was among the worst months of the entire war. And the month of May was the eve of the Republican-Union National Convention for the nomination of the President for a second term.

X

As if that maddening May were not unkind enough to Lincoln, he was placed in an embarrassing public predicament by an unscrupulous "hack" newspaper writer, who issued a fake draft call for 400,000 troops, forging Lincoln's name.

Joseph Howard, Jr., deficient in scruples and looking for sensationalism, had circulated a bogus story in 1861 about the then President-elect Lincoln's disguising himself in a "Scotch cap" and military cloak as he passed through Baltimore on his way to Washington. Now in May, 1864, this same Howard distributed to New York newspapers copies of a proclamation, allegedly by Lincoln, signed by the President and countersigned by Secretary of State Seward, calling for 400,000 men for the Union Army! Howard worded it gloomily, making Lincoln urge "fasting, humiliation, and prayer" as he conscripted that huge number of men, the quotas of each state to be filled by June 15. It mentioned, in words that were true enough, that Grant's Virginia campaign had terminated with only partial success and referred to "the disaster at Red River."

Most of the metropolitan newspapers, to which Howard had copies of his concocted and forged presidential proclamation delivered, wisely hesitated to print it before obtaining further verification of its authenticity. But the New York *World, Journal of Commerce,* and *Herald,* all usually hostile to Lincoln's Administration, on May 18 printed the proclamation in full and without explanation, at the very time when Grant was sustaining his heavy casualties, Butler was locked up in Bermuda Hundred, Sigel had just lost to Breckinridge at New Market, and Banks was abandoning his Red River campaign. The *Herald* discovered this forgery by Howard after its first edition had been put through the press and destroyed that edition. But the *World* and the *Journal of Commerce* printed it.

All might have died down right then and there, had not Secretary of War Stanton, without waiting for an investigation, issued an order, which he persuaded the President to sign. This order, declaring that Howard's counterfeit conscription call in Lincoln's name had been traitorously published in order to "give aid and comfort to the enemies of the United States," instructed Major-General John A. Dix, commanding the Department of the East at New York City, to "arrest and imprison" the editors and to hold them "in close custody until they can be brought to trial before a military commission." Dix was also ordered by this Lincoln-signed, Stanton-issued communication to take forcible military possession of the printing establishments of the papers which had printed the spurious presidential proclamation and to "prohibit any further publication thereof."

Fortunately for Lincoln and the Union cause and for the future of freedom of the press in the United States, General Dix did not demonstrate hysteria or indulge in emotional pseudo-patriotism as a General Ben Butler might have done in his place. Reluctantly, as a soldier obeying his superior, Dix executed the order of Lincoln and Stanton. But on discovering that the *World* and *Journal of Commerce* editors were innocent—only victims of Howard's hoax—General Dix released them.

Dix's course of action was creditable. Of him it was truly said by Thurlow Weed: "General Dix was firm, but temperate and moderate. He was decided, but not a man of passion and excitement."

XI

Before May was ended, another irritation loomed for Lincoln: the nomination of General Frémont on a "third party" radical anti-slavery ticket.

This splinter "stop Lincoln" launching of minor proportions, which, in the unpredictable condition of politics and the deteriorating Federal position at the front, might become a major threat, jelled at Cleveland on May 30. Heterogeneous groups met in convention at the Ohio city and nominated the Pathfinder for President. These diverse anti-Lincoln delegates, and those who attended as delegates without credentials, comprised extremist Republican-Unionists dissatisfied with Lincoln's moderation, German-American leaders who thought that Frémont was a supreme statesman, disgruntled "War" Democrats who wanted more personal and political power, abolitionists, and motley assortments of cranks and chronic complainants, as well as those patriots who were convinced that Lincoln could not bring the war to a beneficial conclusion in favor of the Union and freedom. As Frémont's Vice-Presidential running mate they named a "War" Democrat, General John Cochrane of New York, a former Tammanyite who had been elected State Attorney General on the Republican-Union ticket, and who had served as Brigadier-General in the Union Army.

The Cleveland Convention adopted a radical platform, demanding a drastically accelerated prosecution of the war, constitutional prohibition of slavery, free speech and a free press, and a one-term-only administration for Presidents.

What were the reasons of those who put the Pathfinder, a proven bad administrator of unbalanced temperament, into the presidential race in opposition to Lincoln? They had not the slightest chance of electing him. But some delegates at Cleveland were anti-slavery idealists who firmly believed that Frémont was the answer to Lincoln's dawdling on Negro emancipation. Others, with more sordid motives, hoped that Frémont would take sufficient number of Union votes from Lincoln to throw the national election into Congress. Others merely wanted to vent their spleen on the President. Some party-loyal Democrats at Cleveland, too, were of hopeful opinion that, with Frémont in the canvass, the Democratic presidential candidate might be elected President because Lincoln and Frémont might divide the Republican-Union vote.

XII

During those early months of 1864 Lincoln was vexed by opposition to the admission of the Territory of Nevada as a State of the Union.

The President wanted Nevada brought in as a full-fledged member of the United States, despite its infinitesimally small population, although it contained immense territory. Lincoln wanted this great desert, underpopulated with miners, gamblers, Indians, half-breeds, and stranded people whom life had passed by, made a State because it would increase the power of the loyal states, providing two new Senators and a member of the House to add to the Union forces in the national legislative body. He had for long opposed the admission of West Virginia as a state in the previous year because it was a matter of detaching part of a State, Virginia, to make another state, thus setting a dangerous precedent. But Nevada was another story. It was an organized Territory, belonging to no other State. Also, the potential wealth of the Comstock Lode, and of other mining districts in Nevada, was becoming recognized throughout the world. Congressmen in some states were even running on platforms with promises to sell mineral lands on the public domain as a means of paying the astronomical costs of war.

Opposition to the admission of Nevada flared in both branches of Congress, based partly on the argument that its sparse population, no matter how vast its land size, did not justify statehood. Three members from New York and New Jersey resisted Nevada more vigorously in both the Senate and the House than any other. Lincoln grew concerned as the vote in Congress approached in March, 1864. "I am very anxious about this vote," he told his Assistant Secretary of War, Charles A. Dana, influential in New York City politics. "It has got to be taken next week. The time is very short. It is going to be a great deal closer than I wish it was." What would those opposing New York and New Jersey members be likely to want, asked Dana. Lincoln replied: "I don't know. It makes no difference, though, what they want. Here is the alternative: that we carry this vote, or be compelled to raise another million, and I don't know how many more men, and fight no one knows how long. It is a question of three votes or new armies."

Dana, acting for Lincoln, promised lucrative federal patronage in that bountiful storehouse of government jobs, the New York Custom House, to the New York and New Jersey members of Congress.

The Nevada statehood bill was passed. The President signed it into law on March 21, 1864. Seven months later he signed the proclamation admitting Nevada into the Union as a State.

Dana, in subsequent years, philosophized: "People complain of Nevada as superfluous and petty, not big enough to be a State, but when I hear that complaint, I always hear Abraham Lincoln saying, 'It is easier to admit Nevada than to raise another million of soldiers.' "

And with June 1864, came the convention at Baltimore of the Republican-Union party to renominate Lincoln for President.

RENOMINATED FOR PRESIDENT

33

I

LINCOLN, as the incumbent President, in the last analysis, wielded the most potent persuader in assuring himself renomination as Republican-Union standard-bearer in 1864, a weapon which Secretary Chase, General Frémont, General Butler, or any other White House aspirant did not possess—federal jobs and favors to distribute among the party professionals who decide nominations. "President Lincoln," noted the Washington correspondent of an Indianapolis daily in March, 1864, "can now so wield the patronage as to secure his election for a second term."

The use of patronage as an all-compelling weapon in party warfare, an irresistible force with which to steer the party nominating and election machinery, had been accepted as standard political practice by Presidents, Governors, and Mayors on a national, state, and local level in the United States ever since Andrew Jackson's day, the start of the "Common Man's" America.

II

Those Republican-Unionist politicians of 1864, for months active in assuring selection of an overwhelming pro-Lincoln majority of delegates to the coming national nominating convention in June, were the President's officeholders, or those who had been given jobs or favors by him at one time, or who hoped to receive them.

New Hampshire, where Secretary Chase, an Ohioan, had been born, was the first State to express a party choice for President. Meeting at Concord on January 7, the Republican state convention was steered by Lincoln's Navy Agent at Portsmouth, Thomas L. Tullock, by George G. Fogg, who had been Lincoln's Minister to Switzerland, and William E. Chandler, who was to be given the post of Solicitor and Judge Advocate of the Navy Department. They arranged for that Granite State convention to pass resolutions which complimented Secretary Chase but declared Lincoln "the people's choice for re-election to the Presidency."

A few days later the Republican members of the Pennsylvania Legislature, with Lincoln's former Secretary of War and ex-Minister to Russia, operating among them, asked Lincoln to run again.

February 17 saw Connecticut Republicans assembled in convention at Hartford, led by Lincoln's Collector of the Port of New Haven, James F. Babcock. A slate of Connecticut delegates-at-large to the national convention were hand-picked, pledged to give "united support" to Lincoln's renomination.

Five days later, Washington's Birthday, was an important day in Lincoln's pre-convention campaign. Seventeen members of the Republican (now called the "Union") National Committee met privately in the Washington home of its Chairman, Senator (former Governor) Edwin D. Morgan, of New York, and chose June 7 as the date for the national nominating convention at Baltimore. Of the seventeen, one each from that number of Northern states, four had held, or were holding, high federal office under Lincoln, including the Connecticut member, Secretary of the Navy Welles.

The preliminaries for Lincoln's renomination had thus been set in motion. As the critical New York *Herald* subsequently observed: "Came the New Hampshire Convention, where Mr. Fogg [Lincoln's former envoy to Switzerland] figured, and, through postmasters, provost marshals and other government officials getting elected to the Convention, the endorsement of Lincoln for another term was obtained. Then came the resolution of the Pennsylvania Legislature, which Cameron pocketed and took to Washington."

III

Throughout February, March, April, and May, state after state held conventions of the Republican-Union Party and selected pro-Lincoln delegations to the national convention for early June.

The briefest manner to show the extent of the labors of Lincoln's officeholders, former officeholders, and future officeholders, in the choosing of handpicked delegations, is to glance into the proceedings of the conventions in the most populous loyal states. Of the 516 convention votes destined to be cast for the nomination of the party's presidential candidate at Baltimore, a clear majority, 264, came from seven states: New York, 66; Pennsylvania, 52; Ohio, 42; Illinois, 32; Indiana, 26; Massachusetts, 24; and Kentucky, 22.

The New York state Republican-Union convention met on May 25 at Syracuse, in command of Seward's *alter ego,* Thurlow Weed of the Albany *Evening Journal,* recipient of bountiful patronage from the President. Weed's chief lieutenants at Syracuse were Postmaster Abram Wakeman of New York City and Postmaster George Dawson of Albany, a co-editor of Weed's paper. "A glance at the list of delegates to the Republican state convention," angrily observed the Democratic *Atlas & Argus* of Albany, "will satisfy anyone that the people have had nothing to do with their selection, and that they represent only the great army of office-holders in our state. From every county come the internal revenue collector, the assessor, the sub-collectors, the provost marshal or his deputy, and the city and village postmasters."

The Syracuse convention expressed its "preference for his [Lincoln's] renomination." Among the delegates and alternates to the Baltimore convention, picked by Weed and Postmasters Wakeman and Dawson, were Wakeman himself, the Surveyor of Customs of the Port of New York, a Lincoln-appointed Brigadier-General soon to be made a federal judge in occupied Alabama, and various sub-collectors of internal revenue from districts of upstate New York.

Second to New York in delegate strength in nominating a presidential candidate was Pennsylvania, whose Republican-Union convention met at Harrisburg in late April. Cameron operated conspicuously there, aided by Lincoln's Postmaster of that capital town, George Bergner. Among the four delegates-at-large chosen to the national convention were Alexander K. McClure, Republican State Chairman, holding the post of Assistant Adjutant-General under Lincoln; and W. W. Ketcham, whom Lincoln had made a federal judge in Nebraska Territory. Lincoln's assistant secretary, John Hay, happily noted in his diary: "A dispatch just rec'd from Cameron stating that the Harrisburg [convention] had elected Lincoln delegates to Baltimore properly instructed."

In choosing the other Pennsylvania delegates, by districts, the full force of the federal patronage was exerted. Among those delegates hand-picked for Baltimore were Postmaster Bergner of Harrisburg, Postmaster Cornelius A. Walborn of Philadelphia, and various other job-holders under Lincoln.

Third state in number of delegates was Ohio, Secretary Chase's home. Presiding at the Republican-Union state convention at Columbus was former Governor William Dennison, to be appointed Lincoln's Postmaster General in succession to Blair. The chief strategist there was former Congressman John A. Bingham, whom Lincoln had made a Judge-Advocate, with the rank of Major, four months before and soon to be elevated to Solicitor of the federal Court of Claims. The Columbus correspondent of the Cincinnati *Commercial* reported: "There is a shoal of office-seekers hereabouts to-day, who are watching for the crumbs from the master's table, who will tag at the White House with unwearing importunity for consulships, postmasterships, and Heaven only knows what."

A rabidly pro-Lincoln Ohio delegation to Baltimore was chosen, and Chase had to be content with a resolution complimenting him but not mentioning his name, "in the Cabinet and in the councils of the nation the ability, fidelity and patriotism of Ohio has been manifested." That was the requiem for the Treasury head's presidential boom.

Following Ohio in number of delegates to the national convention was Lincoln's own Illinois. There much of the pre-convention labor was performed by Ebenezer Peck of Chicago, whom Lincoln had appointed Judge of the United States Court of Claims. The President's Marshal for the Southern District of Illinois, David L. Phillips, with headquarters at Springfield, took the lead in issuing the "call" for the Republican-Union convention which met on May 25 in Lincoln's home town and the Illinois capital. An emphatic resolution was adopted, in which the Illinois delegates were "instructed" to vote as a unit for the President's renomination. Burton C. Cook of Ottawa, who had a voice in distributing the federal patronage, was chosen a delegate-at-large to Baltimore. Among other delegates was John H. Bryant, Lincoln's Collector of Internal Revenue for the Fifth Illinois District.

After Illinois came neighboring Indiana, casting 26 votes at the national convention. John D. Defrees, Lincoln's Superintendent of Public Printing at Washington and a Hoosier party leader, made the trip to Indianapolis, his home town, for the meeting of the Republican-Union convention held there in late February. Also active at that Indianapolis conclave was Richard W. Thompson of Terre Haute, holding a Provost-Marshalship under Lincoln.

The Lincolnites steamrollered over Chase's supporters at Indiana. One of Chase's men there, B. F. Tuttle, gloomily sent word to Chase: "The late efforts made by the appointees and agents sent here by Mr. Lincoln succeeded yesterday in convention." Among the Hoosier delegates to Baltimore were James L. Yater, Collector of Internal Revenue for the Fourth Indiana District, and William M. Dunn, Judge-Advocate with the rank of Major.

Then came Massachusetts, which would cast 24 votes at Baltimore. The party state convention met at Boston on May 19. The abolitionist, Wendell Phillips, staged a noisy and unseemly demonstration there when one Lincolnite presented a resolution instructing the Bay State delegates to the national convention to support Lincoln for a second term. But Phillips was quelled. The dominating figure at the Boston delegate-picking conclave was John Z. Goodrich, Lincoln's Collector of Customs of the Port of Boston.

The Massachusetts delegates chosen to the national convention included United States Commissioner of Internal Revenue George S. Boutwell; William Whiting, Solicitor of the War Department; the Collector of Customs of the Barnstable district; and other Lincoln appointees.

Kentucky followed Massachusetts in delegate strength, tied with Missouri with 22 votes each; but Missouri proved to be the only anti-Lincoln state at the national convention.

Meeting at Louisville in late May, the Union state convention selected a unanimous pro-Lincoln delegation to go to Baltimore. Among them were George D. Blakey, Collector of Internal Revenue for the First Kentucky district; two others, an Assistant Adjutant-General and a Brigadier-General by Lincoln's appointment; and also Joshua F. Speed's brother, James Speed, whom Lincoln would take into his Cabinet as Attorney-General in succession to Bates.

In the smaller populated states in the North and loyal border regions, it was substantially the same story. Lincoln's present, past and future officeholders chose in state Republican-Union conventions only Lincoln-pledged delegates. Before May was ended, one of Chase's aides, B. F. Mullett, dejectedly told him: "The Baltimore Convention has been packed in favor of Mr. Lincoln and he has used the power and patronage of his office."

IV

As the Baltimore convention approached, the scene shifted to Washington, where delegates, on their way to the convention city, stopped for secret conferences, last-minute instructions from administration leaders, and general frolicking. From the national capital one Midwestern correspondent sent home word about "the unprincipled wire-working now going on here, by the office-holders, for the purpose of securing the election of the President for a second term."

The quadrennial Republican National Convention assembled at the Front Street Theatre in Baltimore on June 7. More than 500 delegates, not counting alternates, appeared, along with newspapermen and thousands of spectators, most of whom could not crowd into the theatre. Former Governor Dennison of Ohio, Lincoln's future Postmaster-General, presided. For two days delegates talked, raised points of order, considered and reconsidered, argued over delegations claiming to represent this or that state, and considered the ever-boiling feud among Missouri delegates. The real power at Baltimore was Henry J. Raymond, editor of the pro-Lincoln New York *Times,* who would succeed Senator Morgan of New York as the party's National Chairman.

Lincoln's renomination was, of course, a foregone conclusion, since it was a "closed" convention fully controlled by Lincoln's officeholders, expectant officeholders, and their allies. His main rivals, Chase, Frémont, and Butler, had long before spent themselves, having no patronage to dispense by which they could attract delegate support. Even Chase's indefatigable Treasury agents scattered throughout the nation had been effectively curbed. They had not been able to enlist substantial support from influential professional party men. Nor could the colossally ambitious Secretary of the Treasury, or the "Beast" of New Orleans, or the Pathfinder arouse sufficient popular non-professional support. They could not match the popularity of the President, no matter how often his prestige might tumble, rise, and tumble again according to the news from the battle front. In the words of John D. Defrees, Lincoln's Superintendent of Public Printing and an Indiana leader: "Mr. Lincoln can get more votes than any other man."

At Baltimore Lincoln's power of patronage and his personal popularity in some sections, plus his radical opponents' failure to unite on any single candidate, made for a Lincoln-dominated closed convention, except for the Missouri delegation, which cast its convention votes for General Grant. In that State the anti-Lincoln radicals outmaneuvered the pro-Lincoln conservatives and secured control of the delegation at Baltimore.

Lincoln's secretary, John G. Nicolay, appeared at Baltimore, as a sort of liaison between the President and the party leaders. Aside from the ever-quarreling Missouri delegation, which went for Grant, all States cast their votes for the renomination of Lincoln. But maneuvering and rivalry broke out among delegates for the well-publicized privilege of being the first to present the President's name for renomination. "The struggle between several of the delegates to be recognized as the mover of the nomination of Lincoln," reported the New York *Herald's* Baltimore correspondent, "was ridiculous in the extreme. Charges were made that others were trying to cheat others out of the motion. The whole affair looked like a struggle of delegates to obtain capital upon which they could lay claim upon Old Abe for a fat office."

Lincoln was thus named for a second term by his party.

Of grave significance at the Baltimore convention, especially in view of the coming unforeseen tragic event of April 14, 1865, was the choice of Lincoln's running mate on the "Union" ticket.

One thing was certain. Since a leading "War" Democrat had to be nominated for second place in order to make Lincoln's candidacy truly a "Union" one, Vice-President Hannibal Hamlin, a Republican, had to be shelved and a prominent Union Democrat selected as Lincoln's partner on the national ticket.

New York, with its delegation top-heavy in voting strength, might have been honored with a New Yorker for Vice-President. Governor Seymour, of course, was not considered. He was too much the Democratic party man and had given Lincoln trouble in the matter of enforcing the draft act the year previous. There were two strong "War" Democrats of the Empire State, though, former Senator Daniel S. Dickinson and former Governor John A. Dix, then a Union general. But New York delegates, feuding, could not decide on either. The convention thereupon named for Vice-President that staunchest of Southern Unionist Democrats, Military Governor of Tennessee, the only secession-state United States Senator who had remained with the Union, Andrew Johnson.

A controversy still rages today over whether Lincoln worked to shelve Hamlin as his running mate and requested that Johnson be on his ticket.

Raymond of the New York *Times* drafted much of the party platform adopted at Baltimore, on which Lincoln would stand for a second term. At the request of Senator Edwin D. Morgan of New York, a plank was put into the platform calling for an amendment to the United States Constitution abolishing slavery. The third plank adopted at Baltimore thus demanded the "utter and complete extirpation from the soil of the Republic" of slavery, the cause and present strength of the rebellion. Also there was demanded a constitutional amendment to "terminate and forever prohibit the existence of slavery" in the United States.

The fifth plank in the platform approved Lincoln's Proclamation of Emancipation and "the employment as Union soldiers of men heretofore held in slavery." To appease the radicals' hatred of Postmaster General Blair and other conservatives in Lincoln's Cabinet, the sixth plank declared that "harmony should prevail in the national councils" and stated that confidence should be placed only in those who "cordially indorse the principles proclaimed in these resolutions." Blair was known as the ultra-conservative on the slavery issue, and he harbored only the mildest of views toward emancipation.

In that platform, on which Lincoln would run for re-election, the soldiers and sailors of the Union were thanked; immigrants' votes were courted by an advocacy of admitting still more immigrants, with the United States lauded as "the asylum of the oppressed of all nations;" and California and Oregon were remembered by the ninth plank, which promised "the speedy construction of the railroad to the Pacific."

V

President Lincoln, renominated for another term by his "Union" Party, received citizens' committees and delegates returning from the Baltimore convention. "It seemed," noted one Washington journalistic observer as he watched constant arrivals at and departures from the White House, "that every man who was in the Convention was anxious to convey the idea that he was particularly instrumental in procuring the nomination at Baltimore. Everybody had something pleasant to say, and Mr. Lincoln endeavored to say something pleasant to everybody."

In one response of thanks the renominated Chief Executive spoke words which, in slightly altered phrasing, have come down through the decades as homely, homespun advice of wisdom. Declaring that he did not consider himself the nation's best man, Lincoln nonetheless told the visitors: "I am reminded of a story of an old Dutch farmer, who remarked to a companion once that 'it was not best to swap horses when crossing streams.' "

Lincoln had been renominated only a month when the beginning of what was to prove a tortuous summer time set in.

THE TORTUROUS SUMMER TIME

34

I

"THE very darkest hours of our contest—those in which our loyal people most profoundly despaired of a successful issue," according to Horace Greeley, speaking three years later, "were those of July and August, 1864." So it seemed to numberless thousands of Unionists who lived through those torturous summer months as Lincoln stood for a second presidential term.

II

While Lincoln's political lieutenants were privately and publicly performing skilled professional party work in backstage caucuses, closed conventions, and open newspaper columns for his renomination, his military captains were being defeated at the battle front.

The eloquently lauded Lieutenant-General Grant had led his armies into wholesale butchery between early May and early June. Masses of Northern men had been mowed down by the Confederates in the Wilderness, at Spottsylvania, on the North Anna, and finally in the slaughter at Cold Harbor. General Meade commented: "Grant has had his eyes opened, and is willing to admit now that Virginia and Lee's army is not Tennessee and Bragg's army." Secretary of the Navy Welles phrased it another way: "Grant has not great regard for human life."

Grant, after Cold Harbor, had called off the attack on Lee three days following Lincoln's renomination in early June. For the next nine months he would besiege Petersburg, waging a campaign of attrition. In Northern opinion the victor of Vicksburg and Chattanooga was not quite living up to expectations.

Some weeks before on two other Virginia fronts, the Federals had been stopped or defeated. And in the Southwest General Banks had now completely given up his ridiculous and costly Red River expedition.

Sherman, in Georgia, had occupied the Allatoona Pass on June 1 but then had found progress slow, to the impatience of the Northern public. Then Sherman's violent drive on Kenesaw Mountain at the end of June failed. The Confederate commander, General "Joe" Johnston, was demonstrating skilled defensive strategy. By July, Sherman, finding the Southern fortifications at Atlanta too formidable for an assault, laid siege to that Georgia town, with no decisive results.

III

Following Lincoln's renomination in June it was grimly demonstrated that the political warfare at home, behind the lines, could grow almost as intense and merciless as the fighting at the battle front. This became obvious in the fight for party power within the President's Republican-Union ranks in vote-loaded New York, immediately after he had been named at Baltimore for another term.

Henry J. Raymond of the New York *Times* had been chosen the new party National Chairman, charged with management of Lincoln's campaign. Raymond's selection was considered a victory for the faction headed by Secretary of State Seward and Thurlow Weed, since Raymond was of the Seward-Weed wing of the party. Opposing them were the radicals, who looked upon Seward's Cabinet foe, Secretary of the Treasury Chase, although an Ohioan, as their national leader. This anti-Seward-Weed element found strong support in the pro-Chase Hiram Barney, Collector of Customs of the Port of New York, a position yielding more money and influence than any other federal spot in the nation below

Cabinet rank. This anti-Seward-Weed faction found its newspaper mouthpieces in Horace Greeley's New York *Tribune,* and William Cullen Bryant's New York *Evening Post.*

When Bryant's radically anti-slavery *Post* editorially stated that the sixth plank of the national platform, recently adopted at the Baltimore convention, really was an invitation to Lincoln to toss Secretary Seward and Postmaster General Blair, conservatives, out of his Cabinet, Weed came to Seward's rescue and unleashed a fierce editorial barrage in the Albany *Evening Journal* at Bryant and his *Post.* Bryant countered by branding Weed the corrupt "Father of the Lobby" in the State capital. Weed then fired a wordy broadside in the *Evening Journal's* columns at Greeley's New York *Tribune,* charging that paper's correspondents and associates with making money out of government contracts and even of supplying the Confederates with materials through the New York Custom House. The deeply disturbed Greeley in his June 25 issue indignantly avowed: "I have been a partner in *no* contract, job, or undertaking of the sort since Lincoln became President." Now National Chairman Raymond, having rather homicidal tendencies toward Greeley as a political rival and newspaper competitor, joined Weed's Albany *Evening Journal* in flinging insults at Greeley. Soon Raymond's New York *Times* teemed with pointed gibes at Greeley and his *Tribune.*

Lincoln endeavored to preserve peace between the Empire State's Republican-Union factions, who had plunged into an unseemly newspaper war. Suddenly a vacancy occurred in the federal position of Assistant Treasurer at New York City. This set the State factions quarreling more than ever. It also brewed a crisis in the already lacerated relations between the President and his Secretary of the Treasury, Chase.

IV

Secretary Chase was determined that his supporter, Maunsell B. Field, should be appointed by Lincoln as Assistant Treasurer in the metropolis. But the President, striving for party harmony to preserve the Union and strengthen his own chances for re-election, wanted no man who would be obnoxious to the Seward-Weed wing of the party in New York State. Too, Lincoln always was a firm advocate of what later became known as "Senatorial courtesy" in the matter of appointments. He consulted with the two United States Senators from New York, Senators Morgan (affiliated with the Seward-Weed group) and Ira Harris. Morgan found Chase's man, Field, personally obnoxious, and advised Lincoln against the appointment. Morgan submitted three names to Lincoln, any one of whom he said would be acceptable to him as Assistant Treasurer at New York

City. The President then got in touch with Secretary Chase on June 28, writing him: "It will really oblige me if you will make choice among these three, or any other man that Senators Morgan and Harris will be satisfied with, and send me a nomination for him."

Lincoln followed this brief note to Chase with another letter, marked "Private," that same day. He indicated his displeasure at the pro-Chase activities, explaining to his Treasury chief:

"As the proverb goes, no man knows so well where the shoe pinches as he who wears it. I do not think Mr. Field a very proper man for the place, but I would trust your judgment, and forego this, were the greater difficulty out of the way. Much as I personally like Mr. Barney [pro-Chase Collector at New York], it has been a great burden to me to retain him in his place, when nearly all our friends in New York, were directly or indirectly urging his removal. Then the appointment of Judge Hogeboom to be general Appraiser, brought me to and has ever kept me at, the verge of open revolt. Now, the appointment of Mr. Field would precipitate me in it, unless Senator Morgan and those feeling as he does, could be brought to concur in it. Strained as I always am at this point I do not think I can make the appointment [of Field] in the direction of still greater strain."

Chase refused to consider anyone for New York Assistant Treasurer except Field. But rather than disrupt relations with the President then and there, he persuaded the incumbent of the office to withdraw his resignation temporarily. But after receiving Lincoln's letter, intimating that Field's appointment might necessitate removing the strongly pro-Chase Barney from the powerful and lucrative New York Collectorship, Chase sent Lincoln his own resignation as Secretary of the Treasury.

On that same evening, June 29th, Lincoln, with Chase's proffered resignation at hand, called in for consultation Governor John Brough of Ohio, then visiting Washington. Brough expressed the opinion that he could persuade Ohio's Republican-Union congressmen to prevail upon Chase to reconsider his resignation and remain in the Cabinet. But Lincoln had finally had enough of his Treasury head. Chase had more than once threatened to resign the Treasury post. Now Lincoln answered Governor Brough about Chase: "But this is the third time he has thrown this at me, and I do not think I am called on to continue to beg him to take it back, especially when the country would not go to destruction in consequence."

And so the President, on the next day, answered Chase: "Your resignation of the office of Secretary of the Treasury, sent me yesterday, is accepted."

Lincoln added in that letter to Chase: "Of all I have said in commendation of your ability and fidelity, I have nothing to unsay; and yet you and I have reached a point of mutual embarrassment in our official relations which it seems can not be overcome, or longer sustained, consistently with the public service."

Chase was out of the Cabinet. He had meant his letter of resignation to the President to be, as on previous occasions, the beginning of a correspondence which would happily terminate in a soothing letter from Lincoln, asking him to stay and giving him further concessions in his long feud with Seward.

Lincoln chose as Chase's successor United States Senator William Pitt Fessenden of Maine, Chairman of the Senate Finance Committee. Fessenden accepted the Treasury portfolio only on Lincoln's appeal and with his own understanding that he would be relieved as soon as the situation permitted. Fessenden always felt unhappy about leaving the Senate and looked forward to returning to his seat there.

In the back of Lincoln's mind was the hope that his shelved Vice-President, Hannibal Hamlin, a former member of the Senate from Maine, would be chosen by the Legislature of Maine to fill Fessenden's vacated Senate seat. That would take care of Hamlin with a job. But Fessenden was determined that Hamlin should not go to the Senate.

Lincoln's problem as to what to do about the soon to be unemployed Vice-President would remain on the crowded agenda.

Lincoln had ended his unsatisfactory relations with Chase in the Cabinet. But even now he already had in mind the thought of appointing Chase Chief Justice of the United States Supreme Court, whenever the eighty-seven-year-old incumbent, Roger B. Taney, should decide to depart from the earth.

V

July opened with Lincoln antagonizing radical members of Congress of his own Republican-Union Party, particularly Senator Benjamin F. Wade of Ohio and Representative Henry Winter Davis of Maryland.

Lincoln's acceptance of Chase's resignation as Secretary of the Treasury rekindled the anger of his fellow radicals in and out of Congress, as Lincoln stood for re-election. The "Jacobins," as John Hay called them, stepped up their venomous vendetta against Lincoln's conservative Cabinet members, Seward, Postmaster General Blair, and Blair's friend and ally, Secretary of the Navy Welles.

Only one day after Chase's resignation the radicals released to the anti-Lincoln press a blistering blast at the Blairs' interference and control in Welles' Navy Department, since one of the Blair's brothers-in-law, Assistant Secretary of the Navy Gustavus V. Fox, was really the power behind Secretary Welles. It was all ominous enough, since Postmaster General Blair's Maryland political rival, Congressman Davis, was Chairman of the House Naval Affairs Committee. This article, anonymously appearing in the New York *Herald,* entitled "The Blair Family And The Navy Department," charged that the Blair clan, with its multitudinous relatives and in-laws, "have their broad feet upon the Navy Department" and "keep the fossilized stick, Gideon Welles, in office." "Welles is too far gone to do anything except what the Blairs tell him."

Underneath the radicals' fight against Lincoln's Postmaster General, Montgomery Blair, could be seen Blair's continuing controversy with Congressman Henry Winter Davis for Maryland political control. Blairites and Davisites went at each other over the problems of federal patronage, the speed of Negro emancipation, and a reconstruction policy toward the South.

Lincoln, only five days after he accepted Secretary Chase's resignation, found on his desk, for his signature or his veto, the drastic reconstruction bill sponsored in the House by Davis and in the Senate by Senator Wade of Ohio.

Excitable speculation reigned in Washington as to whether Lincoln would sign the Wade-Davis bill into law or veto it. Congressman Davis himself, suspecting that the President would veto it, grew more bellicose and ugly.

On Independence Day morning of 1864, when Congress had just adjourned, Lincoln (who had been renominated as Republican-Union standard-bearer a month before) pored over the bills for approval or rejection in a room of the Senate wing of the Capitol. Radical senators and representatives advised him to sign the Wade-Davis bill into law. Some even demanded that he do so. Most belligerent was Senator Wade's fellow extremist, Senator Zachariah Chandler of Michigan. Lincoln answered him: "Mr. Chandler, this bill was placed before me a few minutes before Congress adjourns. It is a matter of too much importance to be swallowed in that way." The Senator from Michigan impatiently pointed out that a presidential veto would damage the party in his State and Ohio and emphasized: "The important point is that one prohibiting slavery in the reconstructed States." Lincoln replied: "That is the point on which I doubt the authority of Congress to act." Chandler retaliated by telling the Chief Executive: "It is no more than you have done yourself." Lincoln answered the Michigan Senator: "I conceive that I may in an emergency do things on military grounds which can not be done constitutionally by Congress."

The President, after Chandler had departed in a huff, told John Hay: "I do not see how any of us now can deny and contradict all we have always said, that Congress has no constitutional power over slavery in the States. If they choose to make a point upon this I do not doubt that they can do harm, They have never been friendly to me & I don't know that this will make any special difference as to that."

Lincoln firmly believed that there was only one way to abolish slavery: by an amendment to the United States Constitution which would abolish the South's "peculiar institution." And he was now running for re-election on a platform which, at his suggestion, had a plank in it favoring such a constitutional amendment to be passed by Congress and submitted to the states for ratification or rejection.

Lincoln pocket-vetoed the Wade-Davis reconstruction bill.

VI

"Early's army is marching on Washington!"

That frightening cry threw Washington into a panic only several days after Lincoln had his unsatisfactory interview with the radical members of Congress over the Wade-Davis bill.

General Robert E. Lee, hard pressed by Grant's interminable siege of Petersburg, sent a force under General Jubal A. Early into Maryland to threaten Washington, by such strategy hoping to compel Grant to detach huge numbers from the Army of the Potomac to rush to the defense of the Federal capital.

Early, on July 6, crossed the Potomac River. While part of his army marched on to Maryland Heights, others destroyed the Baltimore and Ohio Railroad, the aqueduct over Antietam Creek, and the canal locks and boats; and a unit of crack cavalrymen entered Hagerstown, Maryland. All roads northward were choked with fugitives.

While some of Early's men entered Frederick, the rest of his army encountered a small Federal force under General Lew Wallace (perhaps best remembered today as the author of "Ben Hur") which was posted on the east bank of the Monocacy River, near Frederick. The outnumbered Wallace was beaten back and retreated toward Baltimore. Early, with part of his force advancing on Baltimore, took the others and moved ahead toward Washington. He bivouacked on July 10 near Rockville, Maryland.

From Rockville, the next day, Early took the pike which led to Seventh Street, Washington, burned Postmaster General Blair's home at Silver Spring, and by noon was before Fort Stevens, within the District of Columbia!

For three days, July 10, 11, 12, 1864, it was touch and go whether the national capital city would be invaded by enemy forces. Nearby Fort Stevens and other defenses were poorly manned by raw troops and semi-invalids. Many of the regular garrisons had been sent to Grant as replacements for his heavy losses suffered some weeks before from the Wilderness to Cold Harbor. Nicolay and Hay later pointed out: "Washington had been left nearly unguarded. The confidence felt by the President in the prudence of Grant had permitted almost all the effective force to be sent to the Army of the Potomac." Lincoln was giving Grant an all-out support that he had never extended to McClellan two years before, protection of Washington or not.

Grant had learned of Early's advance from the officials at Washington and his own intelligence service. On July 9 he telegraphed General Halleck that the Federal forces in the Shenandoah Valley should be able to get in Early's rear and trap him. The supreme Union commander telegraphed that he saw no danger to the capital city, but if the President thought it advisable, he would come with reinforcements to Washington, leaving operations at Petersburg to stand on the defensive.

Grant's telegram reached Washington at one o'clock on the afternoon of July 10. Lincoln answered it one hour later. The President expressed to Grant his anxiety, telling him that they had no force fit or large enough to take the field against Early. Washington could probably be held against an attack but Baltimore could not, Lincoln believed. He told Grant in that wire: "Now what I think is that you should provide to retain your hold [at Petersburg] where you are certainly, and bring the rest with you personally, and make a vigorous effort to destroy the enemie's (sic) force in this vicinity. I think there is a fair chance to do this if the movement is prompt. This is what I think, upon your suggestion, and is not an order."

Lincoln, on the previous day, had received a frightening appeal from Thomas Swann, future Governor of Maryland, and from other citizens of that state, reading frantically: "Baltimore is in great peril. We have been appointed by the mayor a committee to confer with you on the absolute necessity of sending large re-inforcements." Lincoln on the 10th replied to the Maryland committee: "I have not a single soldier but whom is being disposed by the Military for the best protection of all. By latest account the enemy is moving on Washington. They cannot fly to either place. Let us be vigilant but keep cool. I hope neither Baltimore or Washington will be sacked."

VII

General Grant, after reflection and a conference with his Chief of Staff, decided to send two corps to Washington but not to go himself. If he left Petersburg, he wired Halleck, Northern people would consider it a sign of weakness in the Union cause. The reinforcements he was sending, he pointed out, should be able to cope with General Early's threat. Grant's telegram arrived on the morning of the day that the Confederates were approaching the national capital city, July 11. Lincoln replied, accepting Grant's decision. "Very satisfactory," he telegraphed his supreme commander, adding: "Some firing between Rockville and here now."

As Early's men drove down the Seventh Street pike in clouds of dust, to within sight of the recently completed Capitol dome, masses of refugees swarmed into Washington. They told blood-chilling tales. Thirty to forty thousand Confederates were sweeping toward them! The whole Maryland countryside was colored with gray uniforms! Momentarily terror gripped the United States capital. The soldier supply was drained low. Lincoln ordered ten companies of District of Columbia militiamen to aid the green and semi-fit forces defending Washington, pending the arrival of reinforcements from Grant.

Early's real threat to Washington proved exaggerated, for he had woefully inadequate forces with which to take it. Early had told his troops that he would lead them into the Yankee capital on the 11th, and they had joyously let out the loud rebel yell. But Early's officers soon observed that the heat was exhausting the men, some of whom were falling out of the ranks. When one of his divisions came within sight of the Soldiers' Home, Lincoln's summer home, Early took stock of his chances for a full-scale attack on Washington. Before he could decide, he learned that the Federals' Sixth Corps had arrived from Petersburg. During that night of the 11th-12th the Confederate commander received word from his subordinate General near Baltimore that two Federal corps from Grant's army had arrived to defend Washington. This unpromising prospect of being overwhelmingly outnumbered compelled Early to hesitate. The whole Army of the Potomac might even be advancing northward to thrash him! He would assuredly be captured and his forces destroyed or taken prisoners. Contemplating such heavy odds against him, Early halted his drive, with the Capitol dome looming in the near distance.

As Early drew deep satisfaction from escaping the heavily superior numbers of the Federal foe he took delight in telling his officers: "We haven't taken Washington, but we've scared Abe Lincoln like hell!"

Lincoln had indeed been "scared" about the safety of Washington. But during the crisis the President demonstrated incredible personal physical courage in exposing himself to Confederate gun fire.

Making a tour of the Washington defenses as Early's army approached Washington, in company with Mrs. Lincoln, Lincoln visited Fort Stevens, beyond the Soldiers' Home, near the northern corner of the District of Columbia, on the Seventh Street road. Actually the President stood on the parapet when the Southern soldiers, advancing through heat and dust from Silver Spring, first opened fire on Fort Stevens.

"The President evinced a remarkable coolness and disregard of danger," declared Major-General Horatio G. Wright, commanding the Sixth

Corps at the fort. "He took his position at my side on the parapet, and all my entreaties failed to move him, though in addition to the stray shots that were passing over, the spot was a favorite mark for sharp shooters."

One Union soldier stationed at Fort Stevens, David Bull, sent word home to his wife two days after Lincoln exposed himself to rebel fire. "Old Abe and his wife was (sic) in the Fort at the time," Bull related to Mrs. Bull on July 14, "and Old Abe and his doctor was (sic) standing up on the parapets and the sharp shooter that I speak of shot the doctor through the left thigh."

Lincoln thought not of the danger to which he and Mrs. Lincoln were exposed. He had in mind primarily the alarming fact that Early and his men had been allowed to escape. A few days after his Fort Stevens experience he met Senator Browning of Illinois and expressed his disappointment. He told Browning that he was "in the dumps—the rebels who had besieged us were all escaped."

VIII

During that same jittery July of Early's threat to Washington the President found himself confronted with Horace Greeley's "peace" follies. The unpredictable New York *Tribune* editor's attitude toward Lincoln and the war, it was jocularly quipped, varied with the condition of his liver. Greeley had first favored peaceful separation of the South from the Union without war in 1861, and had later reversed himself by hectoring Lincoln in his *Tribune* columns and private correspondence for not prosecuting the war against Southerners vigorously enough. Then he waxed irate at the Chief Executive for being partial to his ancient foes, Secretary Seward and Thurlow Weed, and grew indignant at Lincoln's acceptance of Secretary Chase's resignation from the Treasury. By July, 1864, Greeley concluded that Lincoln was incompetent and that the war would fail, a viewpoint bolstered by Grant's severe loss at Cold Harbor, followed recently by Early's near approach to Washington. Why not make a try for peace with the Confederates, questioned the *Tribune* sage.

Any weakening of Lincoln during that uncertain summer would have been fraught with dire consequences for the Union cause. Yet this was the precise time when Greeley, whether naïvely or malevolently, selected to place the President in a predicament where he appeared to be willing to make peace with the South and call off hostilities with the secessionists, at any price.

Greeley had been in correspondence with William Cornell Jewett, New York City-born former resident of Pike's Peak, known as "Colorado" Jewett, a fabulously unsavory character who had returned from France on idealistic fire for the crafty Emperor Napoleon III's possible mediation in the American civil war.

Greeley, justifiably enough in view of the French royal adventurer's designs on Mexico, distrusted the good faith of French "feelers" for peace in the American war, but he continued in correspondence with "Colorado" Jewett. At that time Canada harbored a heterogeneous group of bizarre Americans from Northern, border, and Southern states, who had taken refuge there for different motives. Those unique types of Americans in Canada were described by Professor Edward C. Kirkland, in his volume, *Peacemakers of 1864:* "Northern traitors and politicians, Southern gentlemen and representatives, intriguers and conspirators of unknown allegiance, Confederate soldiers escaped from Northern prisons, spies, adventurers, and an imbecile from Europe and Colorado"—the latter referring unflatteringly to "Colorado" Jewett.

Jewett, by the summer of 1864, fell into the hands of George N. Sanders, Kentucky-born long-time New York resident, former business promoter, real-estate and wheat speculator, and pre-war revolutionary "Young America" agent in Europe to bring the blessings of republicanism to monarchy-ridden countries. Sanders was now a go-between for Canadian-based Confederate agents whose undercover work was to encourage the machinations of the "Peace" Democrats (the "Copperheads"), foster a Northwestern confederacy, and sabotage the Union war effort. "Colorado" Jewett and Sanders now approached Greeley for the promotion of "peace" efforts with President Lincoln.

IX

Greeley, having heard from Jewett and Sanders about the readiness of Confederate "ambassadors" in Canada (as Jewett extravagantly titled them) to talk peace with Lincoln's administration, now appealed to the President. The *Tribune* editor on July 7 dispatched to Lincoln a note from Jewett and sent a letter of his own: "Our bleeding, bankrupt, almost dying country also longs for peace; shudders at the prospect of fresh conscriptions, of further wholesale devastations, and new rivers of human blood."

Lincoln, from long experience, realized that Greeley was often buried in a maze of inconsistencies and contradictions, and at times liable to be "taken in." He had serious doubts as to the accuracy of the *Tribune* editor's representations and skepticism about Greeley's contacts. The proposed Confederate commissioners, whom Greeley grandiosely called "ambassadors," had no credentials from the Government at Richmond authorizing them to negotiate. Their former titles sounded most impressive: former Secretary of the Interior Jacob Thompson, a Mississippian; former United States Senator C. C. Clay, Jr., of Alabama; and Professor James P. Holcombe of Virginia.

At this time, however, Lincoln could not overlook the fact that Greeley, despite his eccentricities, ever-changing opinions, and oft-demonstrated naïvete and unreliability, wielded power in party journalism and exerted a force on public opinion. His New York *Tribune* was still the nation's most widely circulated Republican newspaper, its weekly edition even going out as far as Minnesota and Iowa.

The President, in reply to Greeley, agreed to confer with accredited Confederate representatives. He told the peace-minded Greeley on July 9, as General Early's men marched toward Washington:

"If you can find, any person anywhere professing to have any proposition of Jefferson Davis in writing, for peace, embracing the restoration of the Union and abandonment of slavery, what ever else it embraces, say to him he may come to me with you, and that if he really brings such proposition, he shall, at the least, have safe conduct, with the paper (and without publicity, if he choose) to the point where you shall have met him. The same, if there be two or more persons."

News of "peace" negotiations between President Lincoln's administration and President Davis's emissaries filled the press. But it soon developed that the Confederate negotiators lacked credentials from Davis. Lincoln found himself in an embarrassing position, and more so when Greeley tried to pass the whole business to him. But the President was not to allow Greeley to extricate himself from the abortive negotiations which he had started.

On July 15, when he had not yet recovered from the shock of General Early's approach to Washington, Lincoln sent John Hay to see Greeley, arming him with a letter to the *Tribune* editor, telling him: "I not only intend a sincere effort for peace, but I intend that you shall be a personal witness that it is made."

Greeley grew irritated. But he proceeded up to the Canadian side of Niagara Falls. Acting through "Colorado" Jewett, he sent a note to the Confederate commissioners, Thompson, Clay, and Holcombe, informing them that, as "duly accredited from Richmond as bearers of propositions" for peace, they were offered safe conduct to Washington with him, on President Lincoln's authority. But Greeley did not tell the three Southern "peace-makers" about Lincoln's prime condition—"the restoration of the Union and the abandonment of slavery."

Thompson, Clay, and Holcombe deliberately dawdled. They were, after all, actually Confederate secret service agents intent, not on peace, but determined to cause confusion in Federal councils and doubts in mass Northern minds. Clay and Holcombe now confessed to Greeley that Lincoln's safe-conduct promises had been offered them under a misapprehension, since they had not been accredited by the Government at Richmond to treat with Lincoln for peace.

Greeley, perplexed and beside himself, wired to Washington for new instructions. The President's answer was to entrust John Hay with a paper for delivery to appropriate persons. That presidential paper read:

Executive Mansion,
Washington, July 18, 1864.

TO WHOM IT MAY CONCERN:

> Any proposition which embraces the restoration of peace, the integrity of the Union, and the abandonment of slavery, and which comes by and with an authority that can control the armies now at war against the United States will be received and considered by the Executive government of the United States, and will be met by liberal terms on other substantial and collateral points; and the bearer, or bearers thereof shall have safe-conduct both ways.
>
> Abraham Lincoln.

Hay and Greeley, on behalf of Lincoln, met Holcombe, one Confederate commissioner, in conference at the Cataract House on the Canadian side of Niagara Falls. Nothing resulted from the meeting. All possible fruitful negotiations had turned into seed.

Other such peace plans continued to be presented to Lincoln, in behalf of the Confederate Government, but all lacked responsible Southern backing or did not contain Lincoln's two basic war aims, restoration of the Union and abolition of slavery.

X

Before July was out, Lincoln grieved to hear of the loss of one of the best Federal commanders, Major-General James B. McPherson, head of the vital Department and Army of the Tennessee under Sherman.

McPherson had graduated first in his West Point class and performed skillfully in battle in Mississippi, Tennessee, and Georgia. Lincoln in the previous year had named him, in a private letter to Carl Schurz, as one of Grant's finest corps commanders before Vicksburg. Sherman had lauded him as among the best Union generals. But now, on July 22, 1864, McPherson was brought down and killed by a hidden Confederate sharpshooter in a wooded area near Atlanta.

"Who should succeed General McPherson?" was Sherman's thorniest problem as he maneuvered his armies in attempting to take Atlanta. Major-General (and former Congressman) John A. Logan, Illinois politician and a courageous warrior under fire, by virtue of his seniority took over McPherson's command and expected to remain there. But Sherman declared to himself about Logan: "I did not consider him equal to the command of three corps." General Thomas was also opposed to tendering such an important command to such a non-professional soldier as Logan, and told Sherman so emphatically. To make matters more complicated, Major-General Frank Blair, Congressman from Missouri and brother of Lincoln's Postmaster General, also wanted to succeed the late McPherson—and Blair loathed Logan. But from Sherman's viewpoint, both Blair and Logan were "men of great courage and talent, but were politicians by nature and experience" whose military activities, said Sherman, were "secondary to their political ambition . . . Not professional soldiers." Sherman recommended for McPherson's place a fellow-West Pointer of proved battle bravery, Major-General Oliver O. Howard, to head the Department and Army of the Tennessee. "It was promptly ratified by the President," declared Sherman, satisfied.

Logan grew disgruntled at being passed over in favor of Howard. He sent home word to his wife: "West Point must have all under Sherman who is an infernal brute. As soon as this campaign is over I think I shall come home, at least I will not serve longer under Sherman." Two months later found Logan back in Illinois, stumping for Lincoln's re-election. But he finally returned to his service under Sherman.

General "Fighting Joe" Hooker, former Army of the Potomac head, was grieved at both Lincoln and Sherman for giving McPherson's command to Howard. He, too, wanted that top post. Despite his costly Chancellorsville defeat of more than a year before Hooker had fought well in Tennessee, and was conspicuous in the Chattanooga victory. Now inflamed at being rejected in favor of Howard, Hooker resigned his own command, explaining, "Justice and self respect alike require my removal from an army in which rank and service are ignored." Yet Howard's military service and battle record compared favorably with Hooker's. Sherman later admitted about Hooker: "I did feel a sense of relief when he left."

So ended Hooker's services at the front. The ghastly image of Chancellorsville haunted him forever, never being erased from the Northern public mind. "Fighting Joe" ended the war as commander of the non-combatant, behind-the-lines Northern Department at Cincinnati.

July ended with Sherman still having difficulty in trying to capture Atlanta. Grant kept hammering away at Petersburg, with no apparent results.

XI

If July had turned into a torturous month for Lincoln, August proved just as bad.

While General Early's near invasion of the national capital and the abortive "peace" feelers, Greeley's and others, remained grimly green in the Northern mind, with Sherman stalled in Georgia and Grant stalemated before Richmond, the congressional radical Republicans in August issued to the press their "Wade-Davis Manifesto."

This scorching personal and political indictment of the President, over the signatures of the Ohio Senator and Maryland Representative who had grown pathological in their hatred of Lincoln because he had pocket-vetoed their reconstruction bill the previous month, was the most abusive public document denouncing an American President ever given to the voters by members of his own political party during a campaign for re-election up to that time. Addressed to "the Supporters of the Government," the Manifesto appeared in Greeley's widely circulated New York *Tribune* on August 5 and was widely reprinted in other dailies and weeklies. An incendiary-like essay of invective, this Wade-Davis Manifesto assailed Lincoln for embarking on his own presidential reconstruction plan for the Federal-occupied Confederate states, in disregard of the aims of Congress. By vetoing their bill, Senator Wade and Congressman Henry Winter Davis, in this denunciatory document, charged that the President "holds the electoral votes of the rebel States at the dictation of his personal ambition." They also charged Lincoln with "grave Executive usurpation" and of perpetrating a "studied outrage on the legislative authority." They scored what they called his "shadows of governments" in Arkansas and Louisiana as "mere oligarchies" and "mere creatures of will." They insinuated that the Chief Executive had ulterior motives: his real reason for setting up governments in restored secessionist states was to grab their electoral votes for his own re-election. His veto of their reconstruction bill, wrote the Senator from Ohio and Representative from Maryland in their articles of abuse, was a "rash and fatal act," a "blow at the friends of the Administration," and a repudiation of "the rights of humanity" and the principles of republican government. The President was warned to confine himself to his executive functions and "leave political organization to Congress."

Lincoln listened to the Wade-Davis Manifesto as it was read to him by Seward. He reflected, then posed a question about Wade and Davis: "I would like to know whether these men intend openly to oppose my election—the document looks that way." To his young newspaper correspondent friend from California, Noah Brooks, the President commented: "To be wounded in the house of one's friends is perhaps the most grievous affliction that can befall man."

Henry Winter Davis' motives in blasting Lincoln in so public and blistering manner were not alone owing to the pocket-veto applied to his reconstruction bill. Davis waxed furious against the President because he kept his arch rival, Montgomery Blair, in his Cabinet, and because he was not given control of the Maryland patronage, as befitted a congressman of the President's own party. This patronage factor is prominent in the preserved private papers of Davis's lieutenant, Congressman John A. J. Cresseell of Maryland. There were a few newspapers who looked beneath the surface for Davis's irate feeling toward Lincoln. Commented one paper of Buffalo, New York: "If Mr. Lincoln had granted Winter Davis what he modestly asked a year ago—the control of all the military and civil appointments for Maryland—Winter wouldn't have issued his protest."

As the Wade-Davis Manifesto stirred sensationalism throughout the North and elated Lincoln's foes, and further fractured the President's Republican-Union Party while Lincoln stood for a second term, Davis started a search for a new presidential candidate with whom to replace Lincoln.

In mid-August, only nine days after publication of the Manifesto, Davis met with Horace Greeley, the New York lawyer, David Dudley Field, and other radicals in Field's home in the metropolis. There they drew up plans to concentrate Republican-Union strength on a candidate, other than Lincoln, for President. They also arranged to call a convention in late September for the nomination of such a radical candidate with whom to replace Lincoln in the November election against the as yet unnamed Democratic standard-bearer. Then Davis hied himself to Long Branch, New Jersey, for conferences with other anti-Lincoln politicians. The Maryland extremist had in mind, for a candidate, Lincoln's own Minister to England of distinguished historical name, Charles Francis Adams, son of John Quincy Adams and grandson of John Adams.

XII

"The people," lamented Lincoln to Major-General Schuyler Hamilton on August 11, "promised themselves when Gen. Grant started out, that he would take Richmond in June—but he didn't take it, and they blame me, but I promised them no such thing, & yet they hold me responsible." Lincoln also confessed to Alexander Hamilton's grandson: "You think I don't know I am going to be beaten *but I do* and unless some great change takes place *badly beaten.*"

Lincoln's fear of defeat was a reflection of news from pivotal, vote-rich states reaching him and his closest advisers. One observer on August 14 reported to Congressman Washburne of Illinois: "Things in a political way do not look so favorable as they did some time ago. Pennsylvania, New York, and all the New England States are getting down on *Old Abe* as they call him."

Lincoln's fears of being beaten in November by the still unnominated

Democratic candidate were shared by his campaign manager, Union Republican National Chairman Henry J. Raymond in late August. Raymond sent confidential word to Senator Cameron of Pennsylvania that the President would be defeated. And on the 22nd such a skilled engineer of the electioneering crafts as Thurlow Weed of New York dispatched very unnerving news to Seward: "Mr. Raymond thinks commissioners should be immediately sent to Richmond offering to treat for peace on the basis of Union. That something should be done and promptly done to give the Administration a chance for its life is certain."

Again on that same day, August 22, Lincoln received agonizing word from National Chairman Raymond: "From all I hear but one report. The tide is setting strongly against us. Hon. E. B. Washburne writes that 'were an election to be held now in Illinois we should be beaten.' Mr. Cameron writes that Pennsylvania is against us. Gov. Morton writes that nothing but the most strenuous efforts can carry Indiana. This State [New York], according to the best information I can get, would go 50,000 against us to-morrow. And so of the rest."

Lincoln was informed by Raymond that two prime reasons accounted for this coming probable defeat—"the want of military successes, and the impression in some minds, the fear and suspicion in others, that we are not to have peace *in any event* under this administration until Slavery is abandoned." Raymond advised Lincoln to appoint a commission to negotiate peace with Jefferson Davis on the basis of acknowledging the supremacy of the United States Constitution.

Lincoln found himself in deepest dilemma, and prepared for the worst at the polls in November. On August 23, day after Raymond had sent that gloomy message, the President penned a most extraordinary and highly statesmanlike memorandum, which he folded, pasted, and gave to each of his Cabinet members to endorse, sight unseen. In that memorandum Lincoln pledged his own and his Cabinet's support to his successor:

"This morning, as for some days past, it seems exceedingly probable that this Administration will not be re-elected. Then it will be my duty to so cooperate with the President-elect, as to save the Union between the election and the inauguration; as he will have secured his election on such ground that he can not possibly save it afterwards."

RUNNING FOR RE-ELECTION

35

I

LINCOLN, lacking confidence about his re-election prospects, penned a pessimistic but supremely statesmanlike memorandum, committing himself and his Cabinet to cooperation with his probable successor for the salvation of the Union. And a week later the Democrats convened to nominate this possible next President.

That convention at Chicago of the traditional Jeffersonians and Jacksonites culminated an expedient political reconciliation between "War" Democrats and "Peace" Democrats in a party remarriage that was expected to last only during the campaign against Lincoln and his Republican-Unionists.

With unabashed opportunism the Democrats nominated a "war" candidate for President, General McClellan, who symbolized anti-Lincolnism. At the same time they adopted a "peace" platform, partly drafted by the guiding light of Copperheadism, former Congressman Clement L. Vallandigham of Ohio. One plank, written by Vallandigham, returned from "exile" in Canada, disapproved of Lincoln's "four years of failure to restore the Union by the experiment of war" and demanded cessation of hostilities "to the end that at the earliest possible moment peace may be restored on the basis of the Federal Union of the States."

McClellan's candidacy appeared contradictory. He, a retired West Pointer who had fought the Confederates as Lincoln's commanding field General, was now running against Lincoln on what looked like a peace-at-any-price platform! It sounded incongruous.

Embarrassed by the anti-war plank, McClellan repudiated it in his letter accepting the Democratic presidential nomination. He sought to counteract that peace platform by stating: "I could not look into the face of my gallant comrades of the army and navy who have survived so many bloody battles and tell them that their labors . . . were in vain; that we have abandoned the Union for which we have so often periled our lives."

The Lincoln-McClellan contest for the White House went into full swing with the opening of September.

II

"Hold on with a bull-dog grip, and chew & choke, as much as possible," Lincoln had ordered General Grant in mid-August.

The Lieutenant-General was holding on, still besieging Petersburg for more than two months. But he had not yet captured Richmond.

Admiral Farragut had just turned in a Union naval success by closing Mobile Bay, one of the last Gulf ports left to the Confederates, after growling his since oft-quoted command: "Damn the torpedoes!" But Farragut's victory had not yet made the impact on the public imagination that a land victory would have.

As August closed, with McClellan nominated as Democratic standard-bearer with the intention of drawing anti-war votes from Lincoln, with Frémont still in the presidential race on a "third party" ticket to take radical and anti-slavery votes from Lincoln, and with Congressman Henry Winter Davis of Maryland and his group trying to organize a convention for nominating another Republican candidate, Lincoln sank into deep despondency. He gloomily confided to his former Minister to Mexico, Tom Corwin of Ohio: "I am a beaten man, unless we can have some great victory."

The President would have felt more optimistic if he had known that, at this precise time in Atlanta, Georgia, a combination of General Sherman's aggressive military tactics, overwhelming army might, and Confederate dissension was about to bring heart-warming news to the North.

III

For more than three years the Confederate leaders, civic and military, had been quarreling and bickering among themselves, adding personal dissensions and policy disagreements to their already weighty manpower, food, and war-material handicaps.

Contrary to present-day belief, the Confederate States of America had never been blessed with a "one for all and all for one" patriotism. The new Southern nation had never been a complete emotional reality for all the Southern people, and it did not become so until the political excesses of radical-dictated military Reconstruction. The seceded states had been formed as a nation in 1861 on the inaccurate assumption that Dixie would present a united front. The border slaves states, Delaware, Maryland, Missouri, and Kentucky, had not joined the Confederacy; eastern Tennessee and western Virginia had remained mostly loyal to the Union when their states seceded; and parts of seceded "deep Southern" states, Georgia, South Carolina, Alabama, Mississippi, Louisiana, and Arkansas, and the Western State of Texas, contained sizeable minorities who inwardly felt no allegiance to the Richmond regime. Remote Confederate states, Florida, Arkansas, and Texas, were too far distant to be close to the Confederacy, and so there was considerable sentiment for secession from the Secession.

Relentless rivalries and deep disappointments came to surface as the costly conflict against Yankees grimly continued into its fourth blood-letting year, and war weariness increased with each incoming Confederate casualty list. By 1864 the South's political and military chieftains were bickering among themselves more than previously. And as Sherman advanced on Atlanta, the Confederates changed commanders.

General Joe Johnston had made a sturdy stand against the Federals at Kenesaw Mountain. Sherman had lost 30,000 men. But meanwhile, in Richmond, President Jefferson Davis, himself a West Pointer but a politician by profession, had grown alarmed at Johnston's constant retreating, and he also disliked Johnston personally. Although a competent commander—some Southern historians rate him only below Lee and Stonewall Jackson—Johnston had acquired a reputation of having a dread of losing a battle, making him a defensive rather than an offensive fighter. Davis sought to learn what Johnston's plans against Sherman were, but the General had as little use for the President as the President had for him. Johnston did not confide in Davis, which infuriated Davis even more. All the while, panic-stricken Georgians were demanding Johnston's dismissal and the appointment of a commander who would drive Sherman back.

Davis, mindful of the fact that Johnston had allowed Sherman to approach Atlanta and had not pushed the Yankees back into Tennessee, with concurrence of his Cabinet, eagerly removed Johnston from command of the Army of Tennessee. In Johnston's place was appointed the dashing, thirty-three-year-old Lieutenant-General John B. Hood, an offensive fighter. That occurred in July.

Hood, a Kentuckian who had graduated forty-fourth in his class of fifty-two at West Point, had started his war career as a bold, likeable man, demonstrating bravery in battle and excelling as an aggressive leader of regiments, brigades, and divisions. But the plaudits of worshipping women and the acclaim of political leaders turned his head. Hood sank to unseemly criticism of his superior, Johnston, and poured forth designing flattery of politicians. Now he found himself ill-equipped to lead the hard fighting but hapless Army of Tennessee against Sherman. He had never before exercised independent command. This rash young General was distrusted by his subordinate commanders, who failed to cooperate with him. When Lee's troops in Virginia learned of Hood's appointment, they were crestfallen.

Hood's perilous predicament was grounded not entirely on his own inadequacies. The youthful rebel commander found his outnumbered and poorly provisioned men confronting Sherman's numerically greater, better fed, and more amply armed Federals. Too, Hood was forced to face numberless troubles behind his own Confederate lines—especially from Governor Joseph E. Brown of Georgia.

Governor Joe Brown had set up for a long time strong constitutional "States' Rights" stumbling blocks against President Davis and the War Department at Richmond in their efforts to conscript Georgia troops for the Confederate armies. So, as Sherman marched on Atlanta in August, 1864, General Hood received scant support in troops from the strongly pro-Brown Governor Brown, a demagogue delicately tuned to the see-sawing Southern victories and defeats. Southern historians have since maintained that the opportunistic Georgia Chief Executive's war career verged on treason to the Confederacy. Brown's post-war career revealed him as an artful political chameleon, and he even became a Republican.

Hood, defending Atlanta against Sherman's huge forces, committed a major blunder on August 10, when he sent "Fightin' " Joe Wheeler, with 4,000 cavalry, to smash Sherman's communications. Without the eyes of his army, Hood was deceived into thinking that the Federals were leaving their retrenchments north of the city because of a shortage of food. Actually Sherman was shifting around Atlanta. When Hood finally learned the true state of affairs on August 31, he sent General Hardee to drive back the superior Federal flanking force. Hardee and General Stephen D. Lee attempted to smash the Federal flank attack at Jonesboro, south of Atlanta. When this effort failed, Hood started evacuating Atlanta on September 1.

Sherman's troops marched into Atlanta the following day.

IV

To Lincoln, long at bay in his re-election campaign and losing hope for both his own victory in November and the Union's ultimately, Sherman's capture of Atlanta on September 2 proved a Providence-provided gift, the type of major field victory that could captivate imagination and catapult public morale. With these joyful tidings from Georgia, too, Admiral Farragut's earlier Mobile Bay triumph was given greater acclaim than it had been previously.

On the day after Sherman marched into Atlanta, Lincoln issued an order that a salute of one hundred guns should be fired at every arsenal and navy yard in recognition of "the recent brilliant achievements of the fleet and land forces of the United States in the harbor of Mobile" and in recognition of the "brilliant achievements of the army under command of Major-General Sherman in the State of Georgia and the capture of Atlanta." Coupled with these orders Lincoln requested that, on the following Sunday at all churches, "thanksgiving be offered to Him and His Mercy in preserving our national existence against the insurgent rebels." And finally the President issued an order for public thanks to Admiral Farragut and his sailors and to General Sherman and his soldiers.

Before the month of September was out, Lincoln, was made familiar with the fracturing dissensions, political and military, that were tearing the Confederacy apart from within, and which had been of aid to Sherman in the capture of Atlanta. The President on the 27th telegraphed Sherman: "You say Jeff. Davis is on a visit to Hood. I judge that [Governor] Brown and [Vice-President] Stephens are objects of his visit." And Sherman replied to Lincoln: "Jeff Davis made a speech at Macon. . . . It was bitter against [General] Johnston & Gov. Brown."

V

Although Atlanta and Mobile Bay bolstered Northern morale and drove a body blow to McClellan's presidential candidacy—Seward exulted, "Sherman and Farragut have knocked the bottom out of the Chicago nominations"—Lincoln's re-election fight was not yet won, from the viewpoint of the professional politicians. Two more months were to elapse before Election Day, time enough for any unforeseen circumstance which might damage the President's re-election chances to occur. McClellan and Frémont, both Unionists, were still in the race and were likely to siphon off enough votes from Lincoln to deprive him of an electoral majority, thus throwing the national election into Congress with unpredictable results.

In populous, vote-rich New York City, which often determined how the Empire State's big bloc of electoral votes went in November, the Democrats were still dominant, and they were convinced that General McClellan had been a brave General who had been treated shabbily by Lincoln. Tammany Hall and the "Copperhead" Fernando Wood's Mozart Hall, the main metropolitan Democratic organizations, told the Irish how to cast their ballots, leading Erin's sons to the polls, Pied Piper-like. The rancors from the Draft Riots of the preceding year remained belligerently fresh. Anti-Negro feeling in New York City was strong. Freed colored men had irritated Irish by invading the pick-and-shovel field, hitherto monopolized by them, and the Celts often denounced Lincoln's war against secession as a bloody fight to give the blacks equality. The Democratic Party was made even more powerful in the nation's most crowded city, too, because wealthy merchants opened their checkbooks for the party's campaign chest. The traders and merchants had never fully approved of the war, for they had always enjoyed harmonious and profitable business relations with the South.

In September Lincoln turned his attention to his campaign against McClellan and the Democrats in New York City. As usual, factions of the President's party were fighting each other quite as furiously as they were battling the Democrats, especially over the Customs House patronage.

Seward's political partner and most personal friend, Thurlow Weed, had in July indignantly sounded off in his Albany *Evening Journal:* "The organization of the New York Custom House is a living, burning disgrace," which meant that the pro-Chase, anti-Seward, anti-Weed Hiram Barney was still Collector of the Port of New York. "Time and again during the present year," reported one New York politico to Senator Trumbull of Illinois on September 1, "have his [Barney's] enemies gone to Washington, and told Mr. Lincoln that he [Barney] was opposed to the election of the Baltimore nominees [Lincoln and Andrew Johnson]. . . . It now seems that these men have succeeded in inducing the President to give credence to their stories, and promise the appointment of either Mr. Wakeman or Mr. Draper. Both of these men are personal and political friends of Secretary Seward."

When Lincoln was offered the resignation of the embattled Collector Barney, he happily accepted it as a way to appease Seward, Weed, and their faction and to eliminate the long anti-Lincoln activity of Chase's followers in the party. Then the President removed the anti-Weed Surveyor of the Port of New York, Rufus F. Andrews, the Custom House's second-ranking officer. In those vacant places wielding great political power and patronage Lincoln appointed Seward-Weed adherents. Simeon

Draper was given Barney's place as Collector, Postmaster Abram Wakeman was appointed to Andrews's job of Surveyor, and James Kelley was chosen for Wakeman's vacated Postmastership. In the words of Dr. Brummer, political historian of war-time New York: "Draper, Wakeman and Kelly were all good Weed men; and thus this important patronage, which Weed and his followers had so long coveted, was at last captured from his adversaries."

Lincoln's reshuffling of the chief New York City patronage proved a strengthening force to his campaign in the metropolis, which was important because the State would be nip and tuck between the two parties.

Lincoln lost little time in utilizing the New York Custom House. On September 8, the day after he appointed Draper Collector, he wrote him a note in behalf of a former Governor of evenly contested New Jersey: "Allow me to introduce Gov. W. A. Newell of New Jersey. You know him by reputation. He and I were in congress together sixteen years ago. He is a true friend of the Union, and every way a reliable gentleman. Please hear him whenever he calls."

Democrats, in their efforts to defeat Lincoln and other Republican-Union candidates, realized how handicapped they were by their opponents' control of the federal war-time patronage. "The Democrats," bemoaned the Democratic New York *World* on August 25, "will enter the coming canvass under the great disadvantage of having to contend against the greatest patronage and the greatest money-power ever wielded in a presidential election."

The aristocratic Old-Line Whig, Robert C. Winthrop of the Massachusetts Winthrops, for whom Lincoln as a congressman two decades before had voted for Speaker of the House, took the stump for McClellan. Unused to rough politics, the gentlemanly Winthrop waxed bitter as he told Connecticut voters: "The Republican Party have so thriven and fattened on this rebellion, and it has brought them such an overflowing harvest of power, patronage, offices, contracts, and spoils that they are in danger of forgetting that their country is bleeding and dying on their hands."

Managing Lincoln's fight for re-election was National Chairman Henry J. Raymond, otherwise New York *Times* editor. Raymond at the start of the canvass let it be known that those holding positions under Lincoln must contribute to the campaign coffers. He queried Senator Simon Cameron of Pennsylvania, an old hand in such mundane matters: "Does your State Committee expect to make *exclusive* assessments upon Federal office-holders within the state for purposes of the canvass, or is our [national] Committee to go over the same ground?" By October, observed the New York *Herald,* "Raymond walks into the Post Office and Custom House and collects his bills like one having authority."

Here is a copy of one form letter, sent out by Raymond:

Rooms of the National Union
Executive Committee,
Astor House, September 15.

(Private)
Dear Sir:

Your name, with others, has been handed me as having been employed by the government in furnishing supplies to the medical department of the army during the past year. I take it for granted you appreciate the necessity of sustaining the government in its contest with the rebellion, and of electing the Union candidates in November, the only mode of carrying the war to a successful close, and of restoring a peace which shall also restore the Union.

I trust you will have anticipated the application now made for a contribution to the fund which we need for organizing and carrying on the presidential canvass. The amount of this contribution I of course leave to yourself. Please remit whatever you feel inclined to give in a check, payable to my order as treasurer of the national executive committee. I respectfully ask your immediate attention to this matter, as the need of funds is pressing and the time for using them is short.

H. J. Raymond,
Chairman.

The preserved papers of Raymond, as found in the collection of his New York *Times* partner, George Jones, are filled with evidence of untold thousands of dollars contributed to Lincoln's campaign by federal office-holders and merchants who received government war contracts.

Lincoln personally saw to it that his office-holders did not oppose Republican-Union candidates for Congress. One Democratic daily phrased it this way: "Mr. Lincoln is determined to have a Congress elected in his personal interest, and has been using his power and patronage unsparingly to that end."

Lincoln received a complaint from Congressman George W. Julian, Republican-Unionist of Indiana, that Commissioner of Patents David P. Holloway, a newspaper owner in Julian's district, was refusing to recognize him, Julian, as the party's candidate for re-election. Lincoln assured Julian: "Your nomination is as binding on Republicans as mine, and you can rest assured that Mr. Holloway shall support you, openly and unconditionally, or lose his head."

The President learned that Cornelius Walborn, his Postmaster at Philadelphia, was endeavoring to induce his subordinates to defeat Congressman William D. Kelley, of that city's district, for renomination. Lincoln told Walborn that he could do what he wanted with his own vote, but added sternly: "My wish, therefore, is that you will . . . not constrain any of your subordinates." But when Postmaster Walborn persisted in his anti-Kelley campaign, Lincoln told Morton McMichael, the Philadelphia editor: "I am now told that, of the two or three hundred employees in the Post-Office, not one of them is for Judge Kelley. This, if true, is not accidental. . . . Please tell the Post-Master he must find a way to relieve me from the suspicion that he is not keeping his promise to me in good faith."

The same situation existed in Chicago, where Lincoln's Postmaster, John L. Scripps, was using his employees to oppose the re-election of Congressman Isaac N. Arnold, known as "the President's man" in Congress. Lincoln sent the same orders to Scripps of Chicago as he had to Walborn.

Before the campaign ended in November the President, fully aware of the power of the press, tendered the post of Minister to France to that enigma, James Gordon Bennett, editor of the widely circulated New York *Herald*. Bennett, who more often than not roasted Lincoln and his administration on his invective-infused editorial grill, had for years wanted to be American envoy at Paris. Earlier in the year, 1864, he had printed an editorial, "Why Grant Is The Best Candidate For The Presidency." Lincoln, through a third party, offered the French mission to Bennett.

As Election Day drew ever nearer, Lincoln learned that his most pressing patronage problem was the continued presence in his Cabinet of Postmaster-General Montgomery Blair.

VI

"We have Lee & his _______s on one side, and Henry Winter Davis & Wade and all such Hell cats on the other" irately growled Lincoln's Postmaster-General when he read the intemperately worded anti-Lincoln Wade-Davis Manifesto.

The hostility between the terrible-tempered Blair and the equally terrible-tempered Congressman Henry Winter Davis had degenerated to almost homicidal proportions, after more than three years of personal animosities and rival political maneuvers for control of the Republican-Union party in Maryland. Their respective followers in the precincts were often actually engaged in fisticuffs. By 1864 Blairites and Davisites were still scrambling for job spoils from Lincoln; their never-ceasing arguments still flared over the speed of Negro emancipation; and their no-holds-barred differences made for party turmoil over the President's conciliatory reconstruction policy. All such fracturing forces had piled high, pyramiding into an uncompromising controversy between Lincoln's Postmaster-General and the Congressman from Baltimore.

From the viewpoint of Davis and other congressional radicals, Blair (not Seward) was now the primary conservative enemy to be ousted from the President's Cabinet. Blair was mainly in the radicals' minds when they insisted on the inclusion of the sixth plank of the platform adopted at the Baltimore convention. That sixth plank declared that "harmony should prevail in the national councils" and that "only those who cordially indorse" the platform, which demanded Negro emancipation, should "characterize the administration of the Government." Stripped of this indirect wordage, it meant one thing: Conservatives must go.

To most of the radicals, then, Montgomery Blair remained the eyesore symbol of the Blair influence, of Frank Blair's personal and political warfare against General Frémont in 1861 in Missouri, of his congressional attacks on the radical Cabinet favorite, the now-ousted Secretary of the Treasury Chase, and of Old Man Blair's constant counseling of Lincoln. But, above all, the radicals resented the Postmaster-General's attack on Davis's political power in Maryland and his extreme conservatism on the Negro-freedom issue, for Blair wanted the blacks shipped back to Africa, or deported to Central America.

Lincoln listened to the radicals' clamor against his conservative and highly controversial Postmaster-General, just as he had done to the conservative complaints against his now deposed radical Secretary of the Treasury, Chase, several months before. Lincoln had held on to Blair, however, and had even told the radical Congressman Thaddeus Stevens of Pennsylvania: "What right have I to promise you to remove Mr. Blair, and not make a similar promise to any other gentleman of influence to remove any other members of my cabinet whom he does not happen to like?"

Some time in September, Republican United States Senator Zachariah Chandler of Michigan, a politician more interested in winning November elections than in his radical principles, decided to support Lincoln. So Chandler then turned peacemaker between the radical faction of the party and the conservatives. If General Frémont were allowed to remain in the presidential race as a "third party" anit-slavery candidate, he might take sufficient votes from Lincoln to throw the election into Congress, and Chandler recognized this danger. Leaving Frémont on the ballot in some states might conceivably even result in the election of the conservative Democrat, General McClellan, one of the radical Republicans' worst foes. With a Democrat in the White House, patronage would be withdrawn from Republicans, and Chandler saw his own re-election as Senator endangered in the future.

Chandler, as party harmonizer for the campaign's duration, first visited his radical colleague, Senator Ben Wade of Ohio, at his Ashtabula home. Wade, co-author of the Wade-Davis reconstruction bill and of the anti-Lincoln Wade-Davis Manifesto, was then also thinking of party success in November. So he agreed to withdraw his opposition to Lincoln's re-election, but only if the President would drop Blair as Postmaster-General. Chandler, on his return East, obtained similar assurances of support for Lincoln from other radical leaders, on condition that Lincoln would withdraw Blair from his Cabinet.

Chandler then turned up at the White House. There he had a prolonged conference with Lincoln. In the end, the President with misgivings agreed to ask the conservative Postmaster-General for his resignation if Frémont, still in the national contest, would withdraw.

After his meeting with the President, the Senator from Michigan called on Congressman Henry Winter Davis at Baltimore. Dangling the bait of Lincoln's promise to remove Blair, a wish dearest to Davis's heart, Davis agreed to support Lincoln for re-election and forget about trying to find a new Republican-Union presidential candidate. Also, Davis was by now less certain about a new candidate since Sherman's capture of Atlanta on September 2 had boosted Lincoln's re-election prospects meteorically. Davis insisted to Senator Chandler that Lincoln must call for the resignation of his arch Maryland rival, Blair.

Chandler's last stop was at New York, where he saw General Frémont, who still nursed his grievance against the Blairs for their presumably shabby treatment of him in St. Louis in 1861. The Pathfinder had always blamed the Blairs for prejudicing Lincoln against him—with great justification. After hours of persuasion by the Michigan Senator, Frémont agreed to withdraw as a presidential candidate. Historians are still in controversy over whether Frémont agreed to take himself out of the campaign for President in a "bargain" by which Lincoln would discharge Blair as Postmaster-General. Frémont's few defenders insist that the Pathfinder had no sordid motives but merely did not want to see McClellan win—in the name of pure patriotism.

Frémont's letter, publicly withdrawing himself as a candidate, was published on September 22, three days after General Sheridan's great victory over General Early at Winchester. On the 23rd Lincoln sent a written request to Blair for his resignation:

> You have generously said to me, more than once, that whenever your resignation could be a relief to me, it was at my disposal. The time has come.

The President softened the blow on Blair by adding:

> You very well know that this proceeds from no dissatisfaction of mine with you personally or officially. Your uniform kindness has been unsurpassed by that of any friend. . . . In the three years and a half during which you have administered the General Post-Office, I remember no single complaint against you in connection therewith.

Blair briefly replied to the President on that same day, formally resigning the Postmaster-Generalship. Like a Southern gentleman, Blair told Lincoln: "I can not take leave of you without renewing the expressions of my gratitude for the uniform kindness which has marked your course towards, Yours very truly, M. Blair."

Lincoln's re-election chances were now vastly strengthened by the radicals' approval of Lincoln's action in disposing of Blair. "When I saw it announced in the papers that he [Blair] was to leave," Senator Wade wrote Senator Chandler, "I knew it was brought about by your labor. I don't see how you effected it, except it was by working on Old Abe's fears, for I know him too well to know that he would not have done it because all his political friends desired it; he was governed by a fear that Blair's continuing might affect his re-election. . . . But he is gone and I thank God for it. I only wish Seward was with him. It *is* a great victory and you may well be proud of it." Chandler celebrated by getting drunk.

Lincoln chose former Governor William Dennison of Ohio to succeed Blair as Postmaster-General. A loyal Lincoln man, Dennison had responded readily to the President's call for troops at the war's start, had presided over the Ohio state Republican-Union convention which had selected pro-Lincoln delegates to the national convention, and had wielded the gavel as Permanent Chairman of that Baltimore conclave which had renominated Lincoln.

VII

Just as General Frémont was about to withdraw from the presidential race, and the radicals were partially appeased by Postmaster-General Blair's departure from the Cabinet, more good news came to Lincoln, his campaign managers, and all who hoped for the Union's triumph. Major-General Philip H. Sheridan had won a great victory in the Shenandoah Valley.

Grant had made Sheridan, his most competent cavalry commander, head of the Army of the Shenandoah, with orders to dispose of General Jubal A. Early's forces and devastate the Valley's fertile farmland, the Confederates' bountiful "bread basket." On September 19 Sheridan's men defeated Early's army at Winchester.

Lincoln's spirits rose at the news of Sheridan's performance. On the following day he telegraphed that swift, talented head of Grant's horsemen: "Have just heard of your great victory. God bless you all, officers and men. Strongly inclined to come up and see you."

Sheridan was not finished with Early. Two days later he whipped the Rebels' former raider of Washington at Fisher's Hill. "Little Phil" then proceeded to lay waste the Valley, driving out its herds of livestock and nearly reducing its non-combatants to starvation, a precursor of General Sherman's tactics two months later in Georgia.

Lincoln remained concerned about Sheridan's position. He feared that Early might be reinforced by Lee for an attack on him, since he was then half way up the Valley and in an exposed spot if assaulted by numerically superior Confederate units. The President in late September expressed his anxiety about Sheridan in a wire to Grant: "I hope it will lay no restraint on you, nor do harm any way, for me to say I am a little afraid lest Lee sends re-enforcements to Early, and thus enables him to turn upon Sheridan."

Grant reassured Lincoln that steps were being taken to prevent Lee from sending aid to Early. But in another three weeks Early's forces did "turn upon" a unit of Sheridan's army at Cedar Creek on October 19, forcing back the Federals.

Sheridan himself, resting at Winchester en route with his main army, was then twenty miles from Cedar Creek. Immediately upon being told of the attack "Little Phil" rushed with his men in a celebrated horseback gallop to the battlefield and rallied his demoralized troops. He re-formed his retreating lines and snatched victory from defeat. And Early retired up the Valley.

Lincoln grew almost ecstatic about Sheridan's performance of October 19. To serenaders two days later the President requested: "Give three hearty cheers for Sheridan!" He added, "How fortunate it was for Secesh that Sheridan was a very little man. If he had been a large man, there is no knowing what he would have done with them."

To Sheridan the President sent congratulations: "With great pleasure I tender you and your brave army, the thanks of the Nation, and my own personal admiration and gratitude, for the month's operations in the Shenandoah; and especially for the splendid work of October 19, 1864."

Northern Democrats now found themselves in a rather ridiculous predicament. Their national platform had called the war a failure. But Admiral Farragut, even before the Democrats had adopted their "peace" plank, had closed Mobile Bay. Then, no sooner did their national convention adjourn, than General Sherman took Atlanta. And then by late September, Sheridan had badly beaten Early in the Shenandoah, the feared rebel invader of Washington of less than three months before.

Democrats in the West conducted their campaign against Lincoln and his party on a qualified "peace" basis, whereas Democrats in the East did so on a qualified "war" basis. It made for confusion and a lack of unity of the anti-Lincoln effort as western Democrats pointed out that McClellan's vice-presidential running-mate, George H. Pendleton of Ohio, was a moderate peace man, while eastern Democrats lauded McClellan's war record and maintained silence on the "Copperhead" Clement L. Vallandigham's anti-war doctrines.

VIII

Lincoln, following the then usual custom for presidential candidates to refrain from stumping, did not take to the hustings. He remained in Washington (except for a speech at the Sanitary Commission Fair in Philadelphia), attending to critical military administration, facing the burdens of patronage, and, by word or letter, privately advising on electioneering strategy. But on several occasions, as his contest against McClellan was actively conducted by his party managers, orators, and editors, he mentioned the election to callers at the White House, especially to soldiers.

Lincoln addressed troops of the 148th Ohio Regiment on the last day of August, just after McClellan was nominated by Democrats. It was a unit comprising militia men called up for one hundred days' service, who were now returning home. The President emphasized to those soldiers from the Buckeye State, where Copperheads and anti-war agitators were still thick in numbers, the necessity of upholding the Union at home as well as at the front. "To do this," he told the Ohioans, "the constitutional administration of our government must be sustained, and I beg of you not to allow your minds or your hearts to be diverted from the support of all necessary measures for that purpose, by any miserable picayune arguments addressed to your pockets, or inflammatory appeals made to your passions or your prejudices." He concluded: "Again I admonish you not to be turned from your stern purpose of defending your beloved country and its free institutions by any arguments urged by ambitious and designing men."

The two opposing parties had come to regard the soldiers and mustered-out soldiers as a separate group, and developed special appeals by which they courted their votes—standard American political practice before and since. To attract the servicemen and former servicemen, as well as to impress the vote-casting civilians, the professionals among both Republican-Unionists and Democrats nominated soldiers or former soldiers as candidates. McClellan himself was the prime showpiece on the ballot in this connection. There were now organized by both sides temporary veterans' political societies, the pro-Lincoln "Veteran Union Club," the "McClellan Legion," and the like with their pageantries, parades, meetings, mass conventions, popular demonstrations, and spread-eagle oratory, much of it of rank demagogic quality.

Republican-Union electioneering belittled McClellan's military record, denounced Democrats for opposing state soldier-voting bills, and insisted that the professed political heirs of Jefferson and Jackson favored the rebel cause—a precursor to the "bloody shirt" haranguing of the post-war period. Democrats, for their activity, capitalized on McClellan's well-known past popularity with the Army of the Potomac troops.

Lincoln insisted that the Union troops be permitted to vote at the front, if their states had legally provided them with the franchise. To General Rosecrans, now commanding in Missouri, the President sent orders: "Wherever the law allows soldiers to vote, their officers must allow it."

IX

Coming up in early October were state elections in Pennsylvania, Ohio, and Indiana. Those contests were considered harbingers of what might happen to Lincoln at the polls against McClellan in November.

The Keystone and Buckeye states were considered safe enough for Lincoln and his Republicans, since both had been won the previous year in the governorship contests. Indiana, however, appeared a different story.

The arbitrary, dictatorial but uncompromisingly pro-Unionist Governor Oliver P. Morton was waging an uphill fight for re-election in the Hoosier State, whose lower counties were filled with Southern-born and Southern-descended settlers. In a few Southern Indiana regions domestic violence threatened between Unionists and Copperheads. It was an ugly situation worsened by Morton's iron-fisted harshness.

Morton turned panicky about his chances for re-election against his Democratic opponent, Joseph E. McDonald. The Governor in early September, with Election Day only one month off, implored Secretary of War Stanton and General Halleck to postpone Lincoln's new conscription call in Indiana until after election. He rushed to Washington and saw the President on the dire necessity of delaying the draft in the Hoosier State. He would be surely beaten by McDonald at the polls if more Indiana troops were called up, he pleaded with Lincoln. But the Chief Executive could not accommodate Morton because General Sherman, now about to prepare his march to the sea and wondering about the Confederate General Hood's next move, sternly advised that, if the draft were not executed, the army would turn against the administration.

Since the Indiana legislature had not passed a law permitting its men in uniform to vote in the army camps, Lincoln did the next best thing for Morton. He wrote Sherman, requesting him to furlough his Indiana soldiers so that they could go home and vote. On September 19 the President communicated to the conqueror of Atlanta:

> The State election of Indiana occurs on the 11th of October, and the loss of it to the friends of the Government would go far towards losing the whole Union cause. The bad effect upon the November election, and especially the giving the State Government to those who will oppose the war in every possible way, are too much to risk, if it can possibly be avoided. The

> draft proceeds, notwithstanding its strong tendency to lose us the State. Indiana is the only important State, voting in October, whose soldiers cannot vote in the field. Any thing you can safely do to let her soldiers, or any part of them, go home and vote at the State election, will be greatly in point. They need not remain for the Presidential election, but may return to you at once. This is, in no sense, an order, but is merely intended to impress you with the importance, to the army itself, of your doing all you safely can, yourself being the judge of what you can safely do.

Sherman showed himself impervious to Lincoln's urging that the Hoosier warriors be permitted to go home for the election. Governor Morton now turned to other expedients. Morton had already received promises that all the hundred-day men would be back in Indiana by October. These he welcomed officially at carefully planned receptions. Too, he postponed the moving of recruits from the State by his own administrative machinery—delay, delay, and still more delay! Morton finally won a general furlough for Indiana sick and wounded. One Hoosier soldier would soon observe: "A great many Indiana troops went home . . . on an order from the War Department . . . that the sick shall be furloughed. Indiana soldiers seem to be rather sickly."

Lincoln on that "October election" night listened eagerly to the incoming returns from Pennsylvania, Ohio, and Indiana in the War Department telegraph office. When a lull set in over the wires, he relieved the agonizing wait by reading pages from the humorist, "Petroleum V. Nasby."

Pennsylvania was running dangerously close between the two parties. When Lincoln left the telegraph office after midnight, Indiana was reported safe for the Republican-Unionists. Morton was re-elected. But Pennsylvania see-sawed between the two sides. Lincoln wired Senator Cameron, the State's party chairman: "Am leaving to go home. How does it stand now?"

The next day the Keystone commonwealth still remained in doubt. The President telegraphed General Grant: "Pennsylvania very close, and still in doubt on home vote. Ohio largely for us, with all the members of congress but two or three. Indiana largely for us. Governor, it is said by 15,000, and 8 of the eleven members of congress."

Returns finally came in from Pennsylvania. Republican-Unionists carried that pivotal state by a mere 13,000 votes over the Democrats. The soldier vote was decisive there for Lincoln's party.

X

The closeness of the Pennsylvania and Indiana state elections in October, plus the ever threatening circumstance that vote-rich New York

State might be pushed into McClellan's column in November by populous, immigrant-filled, anti-draft Democratic New York City under the Copperhead Fernando Wood, plus Governor Seymour's popularity, indicated that Lincoln's re-election was not completely assured in the unpredictable game of politics. This despite the success of Farragut at Mobile Bay, Sherman at Atlanta, and Sheridan in the Shenandoah. Some Democrats were remaining hopeful of Lincoln's defeat.

It was natural that Republican-Unionists should not relax in their electioneering efforts for the Lincoln-Johnson ticket. They continued to pour money into Pennsylvania. They exerted special efforts in New York State. Democratic workmen were discharged from the Brooklyn Navy Yard, and the pro-Lincoln Brooklyn *Daily Union* on October 15 frankly explained: "Some men had to be discharged. It was desirable that none but loyal men should receive the preference of retention. The only questions asked were, whether they were loyal men or not, and whether they were Union men or Democrats, which amounted to the same thing."

In view of Lincoln's paltry majority over McClellan in the crowded Empire State—only 7,000—it was good that the Lincolnites used the federal patronage weapon until the very close of the contest.

XI

Lincoln and his Republican-Unionists need not have feared about the November verdict at the polls. Lincoln's prestige, aided by his patronage and party organization, and above all, the victories of Farragut, Sherman, and Sheridan, proved too much for the Democrats to overcome.

Lincoln carried nearly every loyal state, polling 212 electoral votes to McClellan's 21. The Democrat won only New Jersey, Delaware, and Kentucky. In a single huge state, New York, the contest was close. Lincoln in the whole nation polled a majority of nearly 500,000 popular votes over McClellan.

Exulted Ralph Waldo Emerson to a friend a few days later: "Seldom in history was so much staked on a popular vote. I suppose never in history."

Lincoln now had a second term—time and the public mandate to finish his Union-saving task.

PATRONAGE PROBLEMS AND MILITARY VICTORIES

36

I

WITH Lincoln overwhelmingly re-elected, it was certain that the war against secession would be fought to a finish.

Exactly what would have happened in relations with the Confederacy if Lincoln had lost and McClellan had won at the polls, no one could have predicted, since McClellan said one thing and the Democratic platform said another.

Post-election problems, political and military, now urgently clamored for Lincoln's immediate attention: redistribution of patronage, especially the appointment of a new Chief Justice of the Supreme Court and changes in the Cabinet, and the ever present battle front. Grant was still pounding the Confederates on the Petersburg-Richmond line, General Thomas was facing Hood in Tennessee; General Sherman was preparing his torchlit march to the sea in Georgia, and General Benjamin F. Butler was gumming up matters as Army of the James commander.

II

"Can't you and others start a public sentiment in favor of making no changes in office except for good and sufficient cause? It seems as though the bare thought of going through again what I did the first year here, would *crush* me." Lincoln spoke those exasperated words to Senator John B. Clark of New Hampshire following his re-election as he found himself besieged by office-seekers who insisted that he reshuffle his administration and give them a feeding at the public job trough.

The significant position now to be filled was that of Chief Justice of the United States Supreme Court, left vacant by the recent death of nearly ninety-years-old Roger B. Taney.

Most formidable contenders for Chief Justice were Lincoln's two former Cabinet members, ex-Secretary of the Treasury Salmon Chase, and ex-Postmaster General Montgomery Blair. Two of Lincoln's then present Cabinet members, Attorney-General Bates and Secretary of War Stanton, were also enlisting support for themselves among their political partisans, each wanting this highest of judicial positions.

Secretary Seward's friend, William M. Evarts of New York, exceptionally distinguished member of the nation's bar, was also being pressed on Lincoln for the Chief Justiceship. "Evarts," admitted Chase to one friend, "is a man of sterling abilities and excellent learning and a much greater lawyer than I ever pretended to be;" but Chase added, "And yet I think I have more judgment than Evarts." It was reported that the Supreme Court justices unanimously favored Evarts's appointment. "What I want is to have Chase and Stanton, the Kilkenny cats, kill off each other in the scramble for Chief Justice," confided E. Rockwood Hoar to Evarts, "and have you come in as an innocent third person—on the grounds aside from politics." But Lincoln's choice would be dictated by politics, not considerations of a man's legal learnedness.

To the surprise of no one who knew them, the Blair family united once more for another fight—this time to persuade Lincoln to choose their fellow clansman, Montgomery Blair, as Chief Justice. "The Blairs," Lincoln remarked to John Hay, "have to an unusual degree the spirit of the clan. They have a way of going with a rush for anything they undertake, especially Montgomery and the Old Gentleman."

Now the "Old Gentleman," Francis P. Blair, Sr., went "with a rush" in enlisting support for his son against Chase, who was recognized as the chief contender for this most coveted of judicial honors. The senior Blair, only two weeks after Taney's death, even as the election campaign raged, reminded the President: "I think Montgomery's unswerving support of your administration in all its aspects, coupled with his unfaltering attachment to you personally, fits him to be your representative man at the head of the Bench." Lincoln remained non-committal.

Galling as wormwood to the elderly Blair was to watch the radicals exert efforts in Chase's behalf for Chief Justice. "Chase & his friends," Blair complained in an appeal to Senator Simon Cameron of Pennsylvania on November 20, 1864, "are moving all the powers of darkness to put him at the Head of the Supreme Court, and I have intimated to the President that if he was (sic) (& as I hoped might be disposed to remember the service rendered him by the members of his Cabinet) I would be glad if his choice would fall on Montgomery." Blair, Senior, further requested Cameron: "If you would write me a letter of reply to this, which I could show to Lincoln as a manifestation of your opinion in favor of it, I would be extremely gratified—and if you could get some of your influential friends in Pa. also to back me, it would increase the many obligations I owe you personally."

But the radicals of the Republican-Union Party were putting powerful pressure on the President to appoint Chase. To them the conservative Blair was still anathema, and during the recent campaign they had successfully persuaded Lincoln to have Blair leave the Cabinet. Blair's relentless radical Maryland rival, "lame duck" Congressman Henry Winter Davis, added his voice to the clamor against Blair and demanded that Chase be made Chief Justice.

Lincoln made his choice for Chief Justice in early December: Chase.

The President decided on his former Secretary of the Treasury and erstwhile presidential rival reluctantly, confiding to one Senator that he "would rather have swallowed his buckhorn chair than to have nominated Chase." Lincoln's Commissioner of Internal Revenue, George S. Boutwell, former Governor of Massachusetts, quoted Lincoln as telling him about his decision for Chase: "There are three reasons in favor of the appointment, and one very strong reason against it. First, he occupies the largest place in the public mind in connection with the office, then we wish for a Chief Justice who will sustain what has been done in regard to emancipation and legal tenders. . . . We must take a man whose opinions are known." Lincoln listed as his strong reason against Chase's selection: "He is a candidate for the Presidency, and if he does not give up that idea it will be very bad for him and very bad for me."

III

Lincoln's decision to make Chase Chief Justice added new fuel to the ever-flaming party fight between radicals and conservatives, especially in Maryland, where the feud between the disappointed Montgomery Blair and the extremist Congressman Henry Winter Davis still festered.

Blair, four days after Lincoln sent to the Senate Chase's nomination as Chief Justice, in sour mood called on his friend and former Cabinet colleague, the conservative Secretary of the Navy Gideon Welles, "in somewhat of a disturbed state of mind," recorded Welles in understatement. Blair told the Navy head how he had just had an interview with the President about his own future, with no favorable commitments from Lincoln. The lucrative Baltimore collectorship of customs, held by Henry W. Hoffman, a follower of Henry Winter Davis in the Maryland political caldron, was discussed. Blair now told Welles: "The appointment of Chase has brought the Maryland malcontents [radicals] into position." Blair wanted to be United States Senator, which could be arranged (according to Blair's idea) if only Lincoln would remove Hoffman from the Baltimore collectorship, give the vacant collectorship to Senator Thomas H. Hicks, leaving a Senate vacancy from the Calvert commonwealth which Blair could fill. Welles noted in his diary: "Blair feels the President is flinching and will succumb [to the radicals], and thought it advisable that he, or some one, should have an explicit conversation with the President."

At this point another turbulent radical Republican politician appeared on the scene to inject himself into the Blair-Davis brawl, United States Senator John P. Hale of New Hampshire, Chairman of the Senate Naval Affairs Committee.

Hale, in a disgruntled mood ever since 1861 when Lincoln chose Welles, instead of him, as the New Englander to head the Navy Department, had for sometime started to pick a quarrel with the Navy Department, and had begun a vendetta against Welles. He joined Henry Winter Davis in assailing the Blairs, since the chief aide of Welles was Gustavus V. Fox, a brother-in-law of the Blairs. Hale also waxed furious at Fox because he angrily accused Fox of having him "spied on" when he endeavored to obtain naval war contracts for his New Hampshire constituents.

Secretary Welles had seen trouble ahead as far back as a year earlier, when he noted in his day-book:

> I am informed the Senators are unanimously opposed to placing John P. Hale on the Naval Committee, where he has been Chairman, but persistently hostile to the Department. The sentiments of Senators, I am told, confounded Hale, who alternately blusters and begs. Some, very likely a majority, want the moral courage to maintain and carry out their honest convictions, for there is not a Senator of any party who does not know he is a nuisance and discredit to the Naval Committee, and that he studies to thwart and embarrass the Department and never tries to aid it.

Senator Hale joined hands with Congressman Davis, now Chairman of the House Naval Affairs Committee, in fierce political warfare even while the conflict with the Confederacy had some months more to run. As the New York *Herald's* correspondent early in 1865 noted, Davis's activities comprised "a cooperative movement with Senator Hale, each of these gentlemen availing themselves of the opportunity to avenge their grievances and annihilate Secretary Welles and Captain Fox by a simultaneous discharge of their rhetorical batteries."

Following Lincoln's re-election in November, 1864, Assistant Secretary Fox, feeling the force of Hale's and Davis's opposition in congressional circles and concerned for the bleak future of his brother-in-law, Montgomery Blair, visited the President. Fox complained about Hale and Davis, "two fellows that have been especially malignant to us," Fox told Lincoln. But Lincoln, so free from vindictiveness and anxious to heal any wounds in his Republican-Union Party, announced that he would take no measures against either the Senator from New Hampshire or the Representative from Maryland. With regard to Henry Winter Davis, who had authored the violently anti-Lincoln Wade-Davis Manifesto during the recent campaign and who had tried to find a rival Republican-Union presidential candidate, Lincoln told the Assistant Secretary of the Navy:

> You have more of that feeling of personal resentment than I. Perhaps I may have too little of it, but I never thought it paid. A man has not time to spend half his life in quarrels. If any man ceases to attack me, I never remember the past against him. It has seemed to me recently that Winter Davis was growing more sensible to his own true interests and has ceased wasting his time by attacking me. I hope for his own good he has. He has been very malicious against me but has only injured himself by it. His conduct has been very strange to me. I came here, his friend, wishing to continue so. I had heard nothing but good of him; he was the cousin of my intimate friend Judge Davis [David Davis]. But he had scarcely been elected when I began to learn of his attacking me on all possible occasions.

IV

With the opening of the new year, 1865, Senator Hale and Congressman Davis created annoying trouble in Congress for Lincoln and his two Navy heads, Secretary Welles and Assistant Secretary Fox. From the viewpoint of Hale and Davis, the President was still maintaining an obnoxiously "Blairish" Navy Department.

When on January 30 the annual Naval Appropriation Bill came up for consideration, Senator Hale on the Senate floor attacked the Blair kinsman, Assistant Secretary of the Navy Fox. The New Hampshire solon held forth verbosely on the allegedly shabby treatment that Lincoln's Navy Department, under Welles and Fox, had accorded Congressman Davis's friend, Admiral Dupont, more than one year before. Hale's oratory in the Senate sounded much like Davis's refrain in the House of Representatives the previous year.

In the House, Davis moved amendments creating a "Board of Admiralty," consisting of high-ranking naval officers whose all-embracing duties would be to "deliberate in common and advise the Secretary [of the Navy] on . . . the direction, employment, and disposition of the naval forces in time of war." This proposal was purely to shear the power of Welles and Fox. A few weeks later, February 17, Davis's co-sponsor of the radical Wade-Davis reconstruction bill of the previous year, Senator Benjamin F. Wade of Ohio, introduced in the Senate legislation creating a "Board of Admiralty," similar to Davis's motion in the House. In the debate that followed Senator Hale took the floor and blisteringly accused Fox: "It was the Assistant Secretary of the Navy who sent . . . spies to Boston and Portsmouth, instructing them to inquire especially into any connection that I might have had with any contracts for the Navy Department." Thus the fight against the Navy under Lincoln's administration raged in both houses of Congress.

Secretary Welles and Assistant Secretary Fox, through their supports in the Senate and the House, retaliated against Senators Hale and Wade and Congressman Davis by requesting Congress to provide for the creation of a law officer of the Navy Department, a "Solicitor and Naval Judge-Advocate General." Congress approved this request.

With legislation passed creating the post of Solicitor and Naval Judge-Advocate General, the burning question was posed: Who would Lincoln appoint to this power-wielding civilian naval post?

Here Lincoln upheld Welles and Fox with positive action. He appointed to the newly-created legal post in the Navy the youthful and talented political maneuverer, William E. Chandler of New Hampshire—Senator Hale's most bitter political foe.

Chairman of the New Hampshire Republican State Central Committee, the twenty-nine-year-old Chandler, state legislator, Speaker of the New Hampshire Assembly, and as skilled a political strategist as ever came out of New England in his day, had recently led the successful fight in the New Hampshire legislature against Hale's re-election to the Senate. In later years Chandler was to serve as Secretary of the Navy under President Arthur, as a United States Senator, and as a mighty power in the Republican National Committee. Lincoln's selection of Chandler as the first naval Judge-Advocate General proved a crushing blow to Senator Hale.

In that same month, February, 1865, the Davis-Wade proposal for the creation of a Board of Admiralty was overwhelmingly defeated in both houses of Congress. Assistant Secretary Fox could now gleefully write Chandler on February 23: "Hale and Davis and Wade have given us a very small trouble. They were easily beaten. The Admiralty bill was aimed at me. It got one vote—John P. Hale! I don't think there is the slightest chance of these fellows to get Mr. Welles out. I told the Prest. that. We both went together. Blair will not get the U.S. Senate."

When Lincoln was assassinated less than two months later, he had not healed the bad Blair-Davis party split in Maryland. On the afternoon of April 14, the day on which Booth's bullet felled him, he was still reshuffling the patronage for that State, on a paper listing appointments evenly divided between the followers of Montgomery Blair and Henry Winter Davis.

V

Lincoln made three Cabinet changes after his re-election. He acquired a new Attorney-General to succeed Bates, a new Secretary of the Treasury to fill the resigned Fessenden's place, and a new Secretary of the Interior to take Usher's post.

Lincoln's white-bearded, retiring, Old-Line Whig conservative Attorney-General, Edward Bates, had never felt comfortable in intrigue-infested war-time Washington. The turbulent course of anti-slavery Republican politics and the confusion and factionalism of the parties grated on the sensitivities of this aging jurist and gentleman of antebellum society. During the heat of Lincoln's re-election campaign he had confided to the President that he wanted permanent relief to retire to his more peaceful Missouri home. And on November 24, two weeks after election day, he tendered his resignation as United States Attorney-General to Lincoln. The President accepted it.

One week later Lincoln sent a wire to Joshua F. Speed's lawyer brother, James, in Kentucky: "I appoint you to be Attorney-General. Please come on at once." James Speed, delighted, answered that same day: "Will leave tomorrow for Washington."

Personal, and to a lesser extent political, reasons, accounted for Lincoln's selection of his new Attorney-General. James Speed was the brother of his closest of all friends. Politically, he came from a pivotal border state, Kentucky, and had adhered to the Union loyally during the war. Since the outgoing Bates was of a border state, Missouri, his replacement must come from such a region, Lincoln decided. All of the other members of the Cabinet were Northerners. Of James Speed the President said: "He is an honest man and a gentleman, and one of those well-poised men, not too common here, who are not spoiled by a big office."

Lincoln's second change in his Cabinet was the Secretary of the Treasury. Senator Edwin D. Morgan of New York, former Governor and ex-Chairman of the Republican National Committee, and a fabulously rich merchant, was Lincoln's immediate first choice to succeed the resigned Secretary Fessenden, who wanted to return to his Senate seat.

The President, after consulting with New York's Republican boss, Thurlow Weed, about Senator Morgan, sent Morgan's name to the Senate for confirmation as Secretary of the Treasury—with Morgan himself not even being notified. Revealed the Senator from New York later: "No one was more surprised than myself to hear the appointment read when it was sent to the Senate for approval. I asked them to lay the matter over until I should return, and then drove to the White House and represented to Mr. Lincoln, that for many reasons, I could not accept the position, and the appointment was withdrawn."

Morgan remained silent about his reasons for declining Lincoln's offer of the Treasury post. Morgan's biographer, Dr. James A. Rawley, has given the most logical reason for the Senator's lack of interest in heading the Treasury Department. It was this: Morgan's party foe, Reuben Fenton, a radical Republican, had just been elected Governor of New York, thus increasing the strength of the party's extremists in the Empire State. If Morgan left the Senate to become Secretary of the Treasury, Fenton might succeed him in the Senate and be given a powerful voice in national affairs.

Lincoln, following Morgan's refusal of the Treasury post, decided on Hugh McCulloch, conservative Indiana banker and then Comptroller of the Currency, a competent man well-versed in national finances. "If you do not object to it," the President told McCulloch upon summoning him to the White House, "I shall send your name to the Senate." When the Indiana banker told Lincoln of his inadequacies in the management of the entire nation's finances, the President (according to McCulloch) replied: "I will be responsible for that, and so I reckon we will consider the matter settled." McCulloch, Lincoln's new Secretary of the Treasury, took his leave, subsequently describing his state of mind: "I could not say which feeling predominated—gratification or dread."

The third and last change that Lincoln made in his Cabinet was in the Interior Department. He had long been dissatisfied with Secretary of the Interior John P. Usher, and Usher was prepared for the worst.

Lincoln's old Whig and later Republican friend and associate of Illinois, State Auditor Jesse K. Dubois, was in Washington working to secure the Secretaryship of the Interior for himself. This veteran political manager had gone largely unrewarded for his invaluable work in aiding Judge David Davis, Norman B. Judd and others in securing Lincoln the Republican presidential nomination in 1860. Lincoln's Illinois supporters were out in force to persuade him to appoint "Uncle Jesse" to head the farflung Interior Department, traditionally a post for a Western man. The recently-elected Republican congressman from Lincoln's Springfield district, Shelby M. Cullom, strongly presented Dubois's case to Lincoln.

Lincoln soon let it be known that Dubois stood no chance, since he had promised the Interior portfolio to Senator James Harlan of Iowa. The President told Congressman Cullom about Dubois: "I can not appoint him. I must appoint Senator Harlan. I promised Bishop Simpson to do so. The Methodist Church has been standing by me very generally. I agreed with Bishop Simpson to give Senator Harlan this place, and I must keep my agreement. I would like to take care of Uncle Jesse, but I do not see that I can as a member of my cabinet." Cullom noted at that time: "President Lincoln seemed much affected. He followed me to the door, repeating that he would like to take care of Uncle Jesse, but could not do so."

Lincoln, besides trying to please Bishop Matthew Simpson and the Methodists by choosing Harlan, formerly President of the Iowa Conference University (later Iowa Wesleyan), had other reasons, political and personal, for wanting the Senator from the Hawkeye State for his new Secretary of the Interior. Harlan had been Lincoln's loyal lieutenant in the Senate, had headed the Union Congressional Campaign Committee in the recent election, and was a firm friend of President and Mrs. Lincoln. Harlan escorted Mrs. Lincoln to the Second Inaugural, and Harlan's daughter, Mary, became the favorite girl and later the wife of the Lincolns' eldest son, Bob.

When Usher submitted his resignation as Secretary of the Interior, to take effect on May 15, 1865, Lincoln named Senator Harlan as his successor on March 9. But Lincoln was to be killed before Harlan assumed his Interior duties.

VI

"I think him a very ordinary affair, at best, and he should not have the place any how." So in late November, 1864, wrote Lincoln's then Secretary of the Treasury, William Pitt Fessenden, to a Maine politician about Vice-President Hannibal Hamlin's desire to return to the United States Senate after his term as the nation's second highest elective officer expired. Fessenden himself was determined to return to his Senate seat from Maine, too. So when the Legislature of Maine met, a furious, no-holds-barred fight was waged between the forces of Fessenden and Hamlin over election to the United States Senate, with Fessenden winning it. Now this posed a patronage problem for Lincoln: What should now be done with the "lame duck" Vice-President of the United States, who had been shelved for renomination at the party's national convention in favor of Andrew Johnson of Tennessee?

With the assembling of Congress in December, 1864, Hamlin was back in Washington, as presiding officer of the Senate in his capacity as the nation's Vice-President. Lincoln, sympathetic with Hamlin's plights told him: "You have not been treated right. It is too bad, too bad. But what can I do? I am tied hands and feet." When it was suggested that he might make Hamlin Secretary of the Treasury in succession to Fessenden,

Lincoln told Thurlow Weed: "Hamlin has the Senate on the brain, and nothing more or less will cure him." Fessenden, indeed, was threatening to block Hamlin's appointment to the Treasury post if Lincoln should send his name to the Senate.

In early March, 1865, several days after Lincoln was inaugurated for a second term and Andrew Johnson was inducted as Vice-President in succession to Hamlin, Hamlin returned to Maine, disenchanted about politics, sour about all with whom he had come in contact in Washington. One Washington correspondent reported: *"Mr. Hamlin Going Home Disgusted:* Ex-Vice-President Hamlin departed for his home in Maine this morning, thoroughly disgusted with everything and almost everybody in public life, excepting the President. He complains that almost every one with whom he has had anything to do has played him false."

Lincoln grew ever more bothered about the ungracious treatment accorded the man who had served for four years as Vice-President with him. Now the President thought that he might persuade Collector John Z. Goodrich of the Port of Boston to relinquish his highly lucrative federal job, which paid between $20,000 and $30,000 yearly in salary and "pickings," in which event he, Lincoln, could make Hamlin the Boston Collector. Only three days after Hamlin left Washington for his Maine home, Lincoln sent a note to Collector Goodrich, sounding him out about his quitting his job. The President wrote Goodrich: "Your official term expires about this time. I know not whether you desire re-appointment; and I am not aware of any objection to you personal, political, or official. Yet if it be true, as I have been informed, that the office is of no pecuniary consequence to you, it would be quite a relief to me to have it at my disposal."

Lincoln's kind suggestion to Goodrich, a wealthy Massachusetts factory owner, that he resign the Boston collectorship was received coldly but politely by Goodrich. But he wanted to hold on to the job. In answer, Goodrich told the President: "I do so desire re-appointment;" and the office really was of "pecuniary" consequence to him; he concluded: "But of this you will judge. There is no man living I would sooner relieve from embarrassment than yourself."

Before further developments occurred in the special case of Hamlin, Lincoln was assassinated. Later, however, President Andrew Johnson was to take care of Hamlin by giving him the Boston collectorship.

VII

Lincoln, besides attending to mundane patronage problems, Cabinet changes, and other such time-consuming and often irritating political details, kept close watch on the most important facet of the American scene at this time—the battle fronts.

He managed to keep himself excellently informed, quite unlike his first years of the war. He did this through written reports from Stanton, Halleck, Grant, and others and by conversations with officers and newspaper correspondents returning from the battle fields. So, in those closing weeks of 1864 and early days of 1865, he intervened in the military management of the war only on rare occasions. He felt essentially satisfied with the new chain of command. He was particularly pleased with Grant, his over-all field commander, even though he had been constantly hammering at Petersburg since June without reducing it. The President revealed a patience with the aggressive, extravagant, manpower-spending Lieutenant-General that he had not shown toward the cautious McClellan more than two years earlier. And on all other fronts everything appeared promising for the Federals.

Before General Sherman, victor of Atlanta, set out from there on his destructive and ravaging march to the sea, General John B. Hood had presented to President Jefferson Davis his plan for a campaign into Tennessee to cut Sherman's communications with Nashville, defeat General Thomas at that Federal-held city, and march to the Ohio River. Davis gave his consent, for both he and Hood believed that Sherman would follow the Southern army in order to preserve his communications. General Beauregard, whom Davis placed in command of the Confederates' Military Division of the West (including the departments headed by Generals Hood and Richard, "Dick," Taylor) also consented to Hood's risky plan. But they urged Hood to execute it with utmost speed.

Hood, with 40,000 troops, moved north toward the Tennessee River. Sherman followed him briefly but, unable to force the Southerners into battle, returned to Atlanta. From there Sherman put into execution a bold plan of abandoning his line of communications and marching to the sea—all the way to Savannah. Before Sherman left the ruined town of Atlanta, he dispatched large forces, under General John A. Schofield, to reinforce General Thomas in Tennessee.

Hood, heading his Army of Tennessee, did not heed Beauregard's advice to make speed. Instead, the Confederate commander was dilatory and moved toward his objective in a roundabout way, crossing the Tennessee River at Tuscumbia, Alabama. Hood found himself handicapped by the hunger of his badly equipped and ill-fed troops. One of General Sherman's subordinate generals in late October had reported to Sherman: "I omitted to mention another reason why Hood will go to Tuscumbia before crossing the Tennessee River. He was evidently out of supplies. His men were grumbling; the first thing the prisoners asked for was something to eat."

Not until mid-November did Hood's men, having found food, complete the crossing of the Tennessee River. Then on November 30, at Franklin, eighteen miles from Nashville, Hood rashly ordered an attack on the entrenched Federals under General Schofield, without waiting for his artillery to arrive. This resulted in appalling losses in Confederate lives. The Federal brigades were strongly armed with deadly Spencer breech-loading rifles.

The secession forces under Hood in that Battle of Franklin lost twelve generals and fifty-three regimental commanders by death, wounds, or capture. The charge of the Army of Tennessee at Franklin was quite as brave and tragic as Pickett's charge at Gettysburg.

Hood, after his defeat at Franklin, marched his hungry, depleted, and war-weary men to the environs of Nashville, formidably held by General Thomas and his Federals. For the entire first half of December, 1864, the Confederate commander and his forces waited for Thomas to order his men into the fight against them. Although Thomas had more than 60,000 to Hood's 30,000 and was better equipped and armed than were the Southerners, Thomas decided that he would wait for reinforcements for his cavalry, under the very competent General James H. Wilson, for the protection of his infantry's flanks, before going out to fight Hood.

Lincoln, in Washington, grew alarmed at Thomas's delay. Was it the same snail-paced tactics of wait, wait, and wait, which McClellan, Rosecrans, and other Federal commanders had pursued, he wondered.

Lincoln spoke to Secretary Stanton about Thomas's "indecision." And Stanton on December 2 relayed the President's fears by wire to General Grant at City Point, Virginia: "The President feels solicitous about the disposition of General Thomas to lay in fortifications for an indefinite period 'until [General] Wilson gets equipments.' This looks like the McClellan and Rosecrans strategy to do nothing and let the rebels raid the country. The President wishes you to consider the matter."

Grant "considered the matter" and through the first week of December bombarded Thomas with wires ordering him to fight Hood at once. Still Thomas delayed.

Nashville, held by Thomas' big Federal army, was tremendously important, particularly since Hood had a plan which, by its very audaciousness, might have had a chance of success in that ever uncertain chess-like game of military strategy. Grant, after the war, confessed: "I was never so anxious during the war as at that time. I urged Thomas again and again to move. So long as Hood was loose the West was in danger."

Hood, despite the depleted condition of his Army of Tennessee, was of confident belief that, if by a desperate attempt he could manage to capture Nashville from Thomas and reinforce his army from there, he could move into Kentucky and recruit and bolster his forces there, and he could threaten Cincinnati while General Sherman lost himself in Georgia, many hundreds of miles away. If Sherman should return to Tennessee, Hood hoped by that time to have his army in condition to offer battle and, if blessed with victory, to send reinforcements to General Lee in Virginia through the Cumberland Mountains gaps of East Tennessee and attack Grant from the rear.

The Federal commanders feared Hood second only to Lee at this time. When that one-armed, one-legged Southern general had taken command of the Army of Tennessee, General Sherman had consulted with his subordinate commanders who had been Hood's classmates at West Point, and in his later *Memoirs* Sherman revealed: "We agreed that we ought to be unusually cautious and prepared for hard fighting, because Hood, though not deemed much of a scholar, or of great mental capacity, was undoubtedly a brave, determined, and rash man."

VIII

At Lincoln's urging, Grant continued sending insistent telegrams to Thomas at Nashville, ordering him to strike Hood immediately without another day's delay. On December 5 the supreme Union commander wired "Old Pap" Thomas: "Hood should be attacked where he is." On the next day, another telegram to Thomas: "Attack Hood at once, and wait no longer for a remnant of your cavalry." On the 8th Grant angrily wired: "Why not attack at once?"

Thomas sent replies to Grant that Grant considered highly unsatisfactory. At that precise time, however, Thomas was organizing against Hood what was the best planned and efficiently executed battle of the war, the strategy and tactics of which would in future be long and intensely studied in the best European military academies as a perfect exemplification of the art of offensive warfare.

But Grant's patience with Thomas's delay wore threadbare. He waited no longer for "Old Pap" to attack Hood. On December 9 the supreme Union commander issued an order, relieving the Rock of Chickamauga from command of his big army at Nashville and replacing him with General Schofield.

Lincoln, hitherto so impatient at Thomas's slowness, now grew crestfallen over Grant's decision to remove Thomas. The President suggested that, since Thomas was one of the most cautious and prudent of generals, was it possible that his judgment, on the ground at Nashville, was better than that of others in and around Washington five hundred miles away? Grant replied that the consequences of a Federal defeat at Nashville would be really serious, terrifically perilous, and that Thomas was "habitually slow, and this time was slower than ever." Lincoln replied: "But has he not always 'got there' in time? Some generals have been in such haste that they have had to move in the wrong direction." But the

President allowed Grant to have his way, and Grant prepared to go down to Nashville in person.

Suddenly, before the order relieving him of his command could be served on him, General Thomas struck at Hood, letting loose the full force of his army's power in a brilliantly planned operation.

On December 15 Thomas ordered his men into action. With thundering power they crashed into Hood's left wing and by dusk had turned it. The whole Confederate line fell back in the dark to a new position on the Overton Hills in Nashville. There the Southerners threw up sketchy entrenchments during the night. Major-General J. C. Van Duzer, of Thomas' staff cabled to the War Department: "Our line advanced . . . driving enemy from his entrenchments . . . about 1,500 prisoners. . . . From our new line General Thomas expects to be able to drive the enemy at daylight."

When word reached Washington of Thomas' advance, all ideas of relieving him from command were dropped, even as Grant personally prepared to board the train to Nashville. The elated Lincoln, after learning of Thomas' first day of offensive against Hood, telegraphed Thomas congratulations and words of advice: "Please accept for yourself, officers, and men, the nation's thanks for your good work of yesterday. You made a magnificent beginning. A grand summation is within your easy reach. Do not let it slip."

Thomas did not "let it slip." On the second day of his drive against Hood, December 16, he launched another massive attack on the Army of Tennessee seemingly with every detail worked out in advance. Thomas' tactics were nearly a duplicate of those of the preceding day: a strong feint by the Federal left, with a powerful attack delivered by his particularly strong right wing. Again Hood's left crumbled. The coming of night saw the Confederates in full flight.

Hood retreated with his broken army to Tupelo, Mississippi. When Hood's superior, General Beauregard, reached there the following month, he was shocked to see the shattered ranks of the once-proud and formidable Army of Tennessee. Only one corps was left fit for action.

Hood, as broken as his army, asked to be relieved. Beauregard gave the remnants of the command to General "Dick" Taylor, son of the late President Zachary Taylor.

When the year, 1864, went out, the great Confederate army of the West virtually expired with it.

IX

"If the people raise a howl against my barbarity and cruelty, I will answer that war is war, and not popularity-seeking. If they want peace, they and their relatives must stop this war."

General William Tecumseh Sherman, in those words to General Halleck in early September, 1864, two days after he marched his army into Atlanta, Georgia, had succinctly hinted what his future operations against the Confederates would be like.

This spectacular yet calculating Union general, reputed to have stated in conversation, "War is hell," held a most modern concept of how military conflicts should be conducted: success was to be achieved not merely by defeating hostile armies but also by breaking the morale of the civilian population, no matter the cost in human misery for the noncombatants, in enemy territory. Sherman declared to Halleck: "We are not only fighting hostile armies, but a hostile people, and must make old and young, rich and poor, feel the hard hand of war, as well as their organized armies."

Sherman had in mind from the first a further movement across Georgia from Atlanta to some point on the Atlantic seacoast. After correspondence with General Grant, his superior, Sherman put his plan into operation. He sent Generals Thomas and Schofield back to hold Hood and to protect Tennessee and made preparations to march across the Cracker State in truly devastating style.

In early November Sherman started his men on their trek from Atlanta. His troops were shrouded in a pall of black smoke from that embers-blanketed, cinders-scented town.

Sherman's force, 62,000 men, most of them seasoned veterans, moved in four parallel columns, carrying pontoon bridges in sections with which to cross the countless rivers ahead of them. He was able to deceive the Confederate commanders as to his objective, whether it was Macon or Augusta, so that he was practically unopposed. "As to the 'lion' in our path, we never met him," Sherman declared later.

Sherman's troops did not need to be told twice to obey his orders: "The army will forage liberally on the country during the march." One principal object was to destroy Georgia's railroads, and his men went at this with soldierly efficiency. In their torchlit advance to Savannah Sherman's forces captured thousands of cattle and other livestock, tore up railroad tracks and telegraph poles, and all too many went in for wanton vandalism. They had a lark marching through Georgia, some of them singing, "John Brown's soul goes marching on!" Feasting royally on the fat of the Cracker land, they were in superb physical condition, so that when they reached Milledgeville, then the State capital, they held a mock assembly and repealed Georgia's ordinance of secession. Huge numbers of Negroes, with Sherman's disapproval, followed his army.

General Oliver O. Howard, commanding Sherman's right wing, reported to Sherman: "I regret to say that quite a number of private dwellings which the inhabitants have left, have been destroyed by fire, but without official sanction; also many instances of the most inexcusable and wanton acts, such as the breaking open of trunks, taking of silver plate, etc."

Some of Sherman's officers and men wrote home revealing accounts of their march. O. M. Poe sent word to his wife on December 16: "We have left nothing but desolation behind us. Every railroad is destroyed, and everything eatable is carried away. The rebel state of Georgia will long have cause to remember the march of Sherman's army. For forty miles in width, the country throughout our whole line of march is a desert." Rufus Meade, Jr., wrote home: "We had a glorious old tramp right through the heart of the State, rioted and feasted on the country, and destroyed all the R.R. Left a barren waste for miles either side of the road, burnt millions of dollars worth of property, wasted & destroyed all the eatables we couldn't carry off. They will long remember the Yankee raid."

Colonel Samuel Merrill of the Seventeenth Regiment, Indiana Volunteers, wrote these melancholy thoughts to his daughter: *"Four Miles From Savannah. Dec. 15, 1864:* As the region through which we passed was a wealthy one, we obtained all the meal, flour, pork, beef, chickens, turkies (sic), honey, preserves, sweet potatoes, rice. . . . Well, I've almost had enough. . . . In many of the houses the ladies sat amid the ruins of their furniture and tattered contents of drawers and trunks. . . . Vast amounts of silverware hid away in the ground, thro. information derived from the negroes fell into the hands of the men. Now and then stragglers were guilty of outrages, such as hanging a citizen until he would confess where his silver was, or rifling trunks in the presence of the dying."

X

Lincoln, in his Annual Message to Congress on December 6, referred laudably but cautiously to Sherman's presumably perilous action in detaching his army from the rest of his forces and going off on an invasion of Georgia. "The most remarkable feature in the military operations of the year is General Sherman's attempted march of 300 miles directly through the insurgent region," the President told Congress. He added: "It tends to show a great increase of our relative strength that our General in Chief [Grant] should feel able to hold in check every active force of the enemy, and yet to detach a well-appointed large army to move on such an expedition. The result not yet being known, conjecture in regard to it is not here indulged."

The President privately told two Senators: "We all know where Sherman went in, but none of us know where he would come out."

Sherman marched into Savannah on the Atlantic coast, his forage through Georgia nearly ended, in mid-December, in time to give it to

Lincoln as a "Christmas present," to use Sherman's own words. On the day following Christmas, Lincoln sent his thanks to Sherman and his men, at the same time confessing his own hitherto held fears:

"When you were about leaving Atlanta for the Atlantic coast, I was *anxious,* if not fearful; but feeling that you were the better judge, and remembering that 'nothing risked, nothing gained' I did not interfere. Now, the undertaking being a success, the honor is all yours; for I believe none of us went farther than to acquiesce. And, taking the work of General Thomas into the account, as it should be taken, it is indeed a great success."

Although Sherman's defenders have pointed out that his shambles-inflicting Georgia march was conceived as a substitute for further human slaughter because it would bring the civil war to a conclusion sooner, it nevertheless was characterized by unjustifiable excesses of near barbaric proportions.

XI

Before December brought 1864 to a close, Lincoln was pained by another problem: more trouble with that politician-warrior, General Benjamin F. Butler, who continued to clash with almost everybody about him.

For months Butler, commanding the Army of the James, had been conducting a vendetta against Francis H. Pierpont, Governor of "the Restored Government" of Virginia, a regime set up with Lincoln's approval containing those counties of the Old Dominion under Federal army occupation. Pierpont had set up his State capital at Alexandria, adjacent to Washington, but had sought to administer civilian affairs in Norfolk and other regions of Virginia.

Butler sneered publicly at Pierpont as a counterfeit. "The *soi disant* Governor of Virginia," he called him contemptuously, and Pierpont retaliated by branding Butler "the Beast" and other sobriquets that would not read appropriately in print. Pierpont had published a pamphlet describing the "abuses of military power" in Virginia and North Carolina, Butler's army district. He charged the belligerent Butler with imposing illegal arbitrary orders, such as levying taxes on oyster boats in Chesapeake Bay and on vessels using the port of Norfolk. Butler's provost marshal's courts, too, were in competition with the civilian tribunals of Pierpont's government. The *"soi disant* Governor" also accused Butler of setting up a big money-making liquor monopoly and giving it to promoter friends from Boston.

Now, in December, 1864, General Butler called for elections. Lincoln sternly warned him in a letter of the 21st: "I now learn, correctly I suppose, that you have ordered an election . . . to take place on the Eastern Shore. Let this be suspended, at least until conference with me, and obtaining my approval." Butler wired back, denying that he, or any officer under his command, had ordered an election on the Eastern Shore. But Lincoln learned otherwise, and on December 27 telegraphed Butler: "I think you will find that the Provost-Marshal on the Eastern Shore has, as by your authority, issued an order, not for a *meeting*, but for an *election*. The order printed in due form was shown to me."

Butler, during that last month of 1864, conceived a rather extraordinary plan of capturing Confederate-held Fort Fisher, guarding the approaches to Wilmington, North Carolina, in conjunction with Admiral Porter's naval forces. He thought that if a steamer loaded heavily with dynamite could be run up near the shore of that Southern-occupied fort, and was touched off for an explosion, such havoc would be created that the Federal troops would have an easy task of taking the fort.

Butler, still aching for the glorious military success that had eluded him since the start of the war, chose to command personally the expedition to take Fort Fisher. The movement proved a complete failure. General Grant described this Fort Fisher fiasco: "At two o'clock in the morning the explosion took place—and produced no more effect on the fort, or anything else on land, than the bursting of a boiler anywhere on the Atlantic Ocean would have done." Admiral Porter disgustedly noted that the dynamite-exploding barge did nothing except awaken "everybody in Fort Fisher."

Lincoln grew concerned about Butler's progress against Fort Fisher. "Please tell me," the President wired General Grant on December 28, "what you now understand of the Wilmington expedition, present & prospective." And the General-in-Chief answered the Chief Executive: "The Wilmington expedition has proven a gross and culpable failure;" adding (with Butler irritatingly in his mind): "Who is to blame I hope will be known."

The Fort Fisher folly, the culminating act of a long series of military incompetencies by Butler, inspired Grant to blast Butler out of his command considerably more effectively than the dynamite-laden ship had blasted Fort Fisher. The new year, 1865, was only four days old when Grant requested Secretary of War Stanton to remove Butler, explaining: "I do this with reluctance, but the good of the service requires it. In my absence General Butler necessarily commands, and there is a lack of confidence in his military ability, making him an unsafe commander for a large army. His administration of the affairs of his Department is also objectionable."

Three days later Butler was relieved of command of the Army of the James, and ordered to "repair to Lowell," his Massachusetts home town.

Butler's ire at being sent home caused an ugly, unseemly scene at his headquarters, in which he fumed and ranted against the machinations of West Point-trained Regular Army officers, and explosively detailed their jealous and malign interference as responsible for his downfall. In his rage, this Bay State politician in General's uniform, whose name is even today an epithet in Louisiana and a anathema to the better class of New Englanders, tried to take Grant down with him as well. In his farewell address to his troops, he growled to them his insinuating disrespect to Grant: "I have refused to order the useless sacrifice of the lives of such soldiers, and I am relieved from your command. The wasted blood of my men does not stain my garments. I am responsible to God and my country."

Butler's departure from high Union command could be considered a major Federal victory in the field. With him out of the way, operations could now proceed more intelligently with a new combined naval-military expedition to capture Fort Fisher, key to the last of the major Confederate-held seaports, Wilmington, North Carolina. On January 15, 1865, that fort was taken from the Southerners. And nine days later Lincoln, elated, wrote one Kentuckian: "Wilmington, N.C., is ours, of right and in fact."

Actually the Federals captured Wilmington one month later, on Washington's Birthday.

By the opening of 1865 the Confederate military might was fast draining away.

SLAVERY ABOLITION AND RECONSTRUCTION

37

I

LINCOLN, as the war approached its end between late 1864 and early 1865, found himself still inundated by those two seemingly perpetual problems: slavery and reconstruction.

What should be the status of slavery? Also, what should be the method of bringing back into the Union those militarily defeated states of the crumbling Confederacy? On those bedevilling twin dilemmas a constant no-holds-barred political controversy flared in and out of Congress. It was a fight waged by Old-Line border-state pro-slavery Whigs, Southern-sympathizing moderates of both the Republican and the Democratic parties who wanted a minimum of governmental interference in the South's social problems, and, above all, by South-hating, zealous anti-slavery radical Republicans, extremists who demanded racial equality immediately, punishment of white Southerners for starting the war, and the creation of a robust Negro-voting Republican Party below Mason and Dixon's line.

II

Lincoln was personally opposed to slavery, and had been since early manhood. But he believed that he held no legal power to abolish it. As he had stated in his First Inaugural four years earlier: "I have no purpose, directly or indirectly, to interfere with the institution of slavery in the States where it exists. I believe I have no lawful right to do so, and I have no inclination to do so."

Continually the President had tried to persuade Congress to enact an adequate program of compensated emancipation, slaveholders to be paid for freeing their bonded blacks, and he had supported plans for colonization of the liberated Negroes in Central America and the West Indies. It was Henry Clay's old program, except that Clay thought in terms of Africa as the final settlement site for freed American Negroes. Lincoln only a few months before his death told a Missouri congressman, Representative James S. Rollins, about Clay's influence on him: "I never had an opinion on slavery that I did not get from him." But support in Congress and the border-slave states, Missouri, Kentucky, Maryland, and Delaware, was lacking for the President's ideas.

"I am naturally anti-slavery. If slavery is not wrong, nothing is wrong. I can not remember when I did not so think, and feel," Lincoln had written a Kentucky editor, Albert G. Hodges, in April, 1864. But he added: "And yet I have never understood that the Presidency conferred upon me an unrestricted right to act officially upon this judgment and feeling. . . . To this day, I have done no official act in mere deference to my abstract judgment and feeling on slavery."

The President in that letter told Hodges that, when he countermanded the arbitrary military Negro-emancipation proclamations of Generals Frémont and Hunter earlier in the war, he did so because he did not consider them "indispensable necessities" to his work of preserving the Republic. He pointed out to Hodges that, after the border states had rejected his appeals for compensated emancipation, he had been "driven to the alternative of either surrendering the Union, and with it, the Constitution, or of laying strong hand upon the colored element. I chose the latter." His Proclamation of Emancipation resulted in "no loss by it in our foreign relations, none on our home popular sentiment, none in our white military force. . . . On the contrary, it shows a gain of quite a hundred and thirty thousand [Negro] soldiers, seamen, and laborers. . . . We have the men; and we could not have them without the [Proclamation of Emancipation] measure."

Thousands of Negroes, particularly in those Federal-occupied Southern regions, were assuming roles in the cast of the grim drama of combatting the Confederacy, which was Lincoln's prime concern. Black men were serving in labor battalions which hauled supplies, dug trenches, and built fortifications for the Federals. Tens of thousands of colored men would serve in the Union armies between 1861 and 1865.

Yet Lincoln had in no way settled the spikey slavery issue by his final Emancipation Proclamation. That Negro-liberation presidential edict had freed the bonded blacks only in secession-held territory. Too, Lincoln himself felt that it was of dubious legality, since the United States Constitution had not given the Federal Government, either the President or Congress, power to emancipate slaves. Lincoln had issued his world-renowned Proclamation of Emancipation upon assumed war powers only, and it did not rest on any constitutional authorization. Lincoln as a lawyer knew that all too well.

Just before he vetoed the drastic Wade-Davis reconstruction bill in 1864, Lincoln disapproved of its provision prohibiting slavery in the "recovered" Southern states, explaining to the radical Senator Zachariah Chandler of Michigan: "That is the point on which I doubt the authority of Congress to act." When Chandler answered by telling him, "It is no more than you have done yourself," the President replied: "I conceive that I may in an emergency do things on military grounds which can not be done constitutionally by Congress." A few minutes later he told his Secretary of the Treasury, Fessenden, that he favored an amendment to the United States Constitution abolishing slavery in the nation.

Members of the President's own Republican-Union Party in Congress were as well aware as Lincoln that his Proclamation of Emancipation rested on dubious legality. Senator Sumner, in pushing for federal legislation on that explosive subject in 1864, told the Senate: "I wish to see emancipation in the rebel States placed under the guarantee of an act of Congress. I do not wish to see it left to float on a presidential proclamation."

Senator John B. Henderson, Unionist of Missouri, in the previous January (1864) had sponsored in the Senate a resolution to amend the Federal Constitution by a provision prohibiting slavery or involuntary servitude in the United States, except as a punishment for crime. The resolution was referred to the Senate Judiciary Committee. One month later, in February, Senator Lyman Trumbull, of Lincoln's own Illinois, reported to the Senate from that committee an amended version of Henderson's motion which became the Thirteenth Amendment to the Constitution of the United States:

> Section 1. Neither slavery nor involuntarily servitude, except as a punishment for crime whereof the party shall have been duly convicted, shall exist within the United States, or any place subject to their jurisdiction.
>
> Section 2. Congress shall have power to enforce this article by appropriate legislation.

Such phraseology followed closely that in the Ordinance of 1787, which had applied to the Northwest Territory. "Trumbull adopted it," revealed his biographer, "because it was among the household words of the nation."

The Henderson-Trumbull amendment was passed by the Senate in April, 1864, but it was stalled in the House of Representatives. Lincoln, on July 4, 1864, told Secretary of the Treasury Fessenden: "I earnestly favored the movement for an amendment to the Constitution abolishing slavery, which passed the Senate and failed in the House."

III

Lincoln stood for re-election on a slavery abolition platform in 1864.

He had urged Senator Edwin D. Morgan, of New York, Republican National Chairman, before Morgan departed for the party's National Convention: "I want you to mention in your speech when you call the convention to order, as its key note, and to put it into the platform, the amendment to the Constitution abolishing and prohibiting slavery forever."

After Morgan had pounded the gavel, calling to order the convention at Baltimore, he told the assembled delegates that the terrible war "has all been caused by slavery." Morgan exhorted them: "The party of which you, gentlemen, are the delegates and only representatives, will fall short of accomplishing its great mission, unless among its other resolves it shall declare for such an amendment of the Constitution as will positively prohibit African slavery in the United States." Ear-drum-piercing cheers and applause greeted National Chairman Morgan's recommendation, for the leaders who would dictate to the delegates how to vote knew that Morgan's remarks represented the wishes of the President, whom they were about to renominate. It should be remembered that the national convention was nearly completely controlled by Lincoln's federal office-holders.

Thus into the national platform, on which Lincoln would run for a second term, went a plank which demanded "an amendment to the Constitution. . . . as shall terminate and forever prohibit the existence of slavery within the limits or jurisdiction of the United States."

Lincoln, the day following his renomination in early June, took pains to assure the Convention's official notification committee:

"I approve the declaration in favor of so amending the Constitution as to prohibit slavery throughout the nation. When the people in revolt, with the hundred days of explicit notice [September 22, 1862, to January 1, 1863], that they could, within those days, resume their allegiance, without the overthrow of their institution, and that could not so resume it afterwards, elected to stand out, such an amendment of the Constitution as is now proposed, became a fitting, and necessary conclusion to the final success of the Union cause. Such alone can meet and cover all cavils."

As Lincoln's re-election race against McClellan raged, late in 1864, one Democratic congressman from Ohio, Representative Samuel S. ("Sunset") Cox, noted about the pending Thirteenth Amendment: "Mr. Seward and the President considered this amendment worth an army." Cox added that it was "a part of the programme for strengthening the Federal cause."

IV

The re-elected President Lincoln, in his Annual Message to Congress on December 6, 1864, recommended favorable action on the proposed Thirteenth Amendment, which in the previous session had been passed by the Senate but rejected by the House of Representatives. Lincoln appealed to the law-makers of the lower chamber:

"Without questioning the wisdom or patriotism of those who stood in opposition, I venture to recommend the reconsideration and passage of the measure at the present session. Of course the abstract question is not changed; but an intervening election [of the previous month] shows almost certainly that the next Congress will pass the measure if this does not. Hence there is only a question of *time* as to when the proposed amendment will go to the States for their action. And as it is to go at all events, may we not agree that the sooner the better."

Lincoln entrusted the task of securing the passage of the Thirteenth Amendment in the House to the leadership of Congressman James M. Ashley, Republican of Ohio. On January 6 of the new year, 1865, Ashley called up the amendment in the House. He moved to reconsider the vote by which it had been rejected at the preceding session. This unloosed an explosive debate, demonstrating the deep division of opinion.

By mid-January the President had grown alarmed about the coming vote on the Thirteenth Amendment. He summoned to the White House his friend, Congressman Rollins of Missouri. "He was doubtful about its passage," revealed Rollins in later years. Rollins quoted Lincoln as appealing to Henry Clay's memory to have old Whigs support the amendment. The President pleaded with Rollins: "You and I were old Whigs, both of us followers of Henry Clay. This is my chief hope and reliance to bring the war to a speedy close, and I have sent for you, as an old Whig friend, to make an appeal to you to vote for this amendment." Rollins assured Lincoln that he would vote for it. Then the Chief Executive asked the Representative from Missouri about the other members from his state—a slave state! He implored Rollins to work among his Missouri colleagues in support of the amendment.

Representative Ashley of Ohio, still leading the fight for the Thirteenth Amendment in the House, found himself several votes short of the constitutional two-thirds required for passage of an amendment to the Federal Constitution. Two or more Democrats still would be needed to aid the Republican-Union majority in having the amendment approved. "Finally we were told, in confidence of course," subsequently revealed Ashley's Republican colleague, Representative Albert G. Riddle of the Cleveland district, "that Mr. Ashley could report the acquisition [of two new Democratic supporters]. A New Yorker greatly desired a federal place in New York; he had a brother, a Democrat, in the House, who was assured that his vote for the abolishing amendment would largely augment his brother's chances."

Of the means—i.e., federal patronage from Lincoln—employed to attract more House votes for passage of the Thirteenth Amendment, Congressman George W. Julian, Republican of Indiana, in later years merely stated: "The success of the measure had been considered very doubtful, and depended upon certain negotiations, the result of which was not fully assured, and the particulars of which never reached the public."

Pandemonium, followed by tenseness, reigned in the House of Representatives on January 31, 1865, when the Thirteenth Amendment came up for a final vote. From his House desk Congressman Cornelius Cole, of California, on that last day of the first month of the new year wrote home: "We are voting at last on the great question and it will just pass."

The name of each member of the House was called for his vote. Representatives and spectators in the galleries strained their necks, eyes, and ears, as every congressman cast his vote. The House was hushed as it feverishly waited for the end. All who had followed the balloting, with pencil and paper, knew what the verdict would be, but nevertheless the suspense was intense.

Finally the clerk announced: For passage, 119; against passage, 58. Eleven members abstained from voting.

It was an uncomfortably close victory for the abolitionists—only three more House votes than the necessary two-thirds.

When the result was announced, Congressman James G. Blaine of Maine related, "the Speaker became powerless to preserve order. The members upon the Republican side sprang upon their seats, cheering, shouting, and waving hands, hats, and canes, while the spectators upon the floor and in the galleries joined heartily in the demonstrations."

The abolitionist, William Lloyd Garrison, gave Lincoln full credit for persuading the House of Representatives to pass the Thirteenth Amendment. Said that dour but now happy incendiary to a Boston meeting on

February 4: "And to whom is the country indebted more immediately for this vital and saving amendment of the Constitution than, perhaps, to any other man? I believe I may confidently answer—to the humble railsplitter of Illinois, to the Presidential chain-breaker for millions of the oppressed—to Abraham Lincoln!"

In view of the narrowness of the vote in the House on the amendment, it is probable that it could not have been approved at that time, if the President, with his prestige and power of the patronage, had not actively supported it.

V

Lincoln and Seward, on February 3, three days following the House's approval of the Thirteenth Amendment for submission to the states for ratification or rejection, met Lincoln's old colleague of the Thirtieth Congress, Alexander H. Stephens, now Vice-President of the Confederate States of America, and other Southern officials, in an abortive "peace" conference aboard a Union ship at Hampton Roads.

There at Hampton Roads the President repeated his support of a fair indemnity to Southern slaveholders if they would liberate their bonded Negroes. With remarkable objectivity, he informed Vice-President Stephens and the two other Confederate commissioners that Northern people were not blameless for slavery in America. Stephens revealed about Lincoln at Hampton Roads: "He went on to say that he would be willing to be taxed to remunerate the Southern people for their slaves. He believed the people of the North were as responsible as the people of the South, and if the war should cease, with the voluntary abolition of slavery by the States, he should be in favor, individually, of the Government paying a fair indemnity for the loss to the owners."

Abraham Lincoln, throughout the world, is today acclaimed as the Great Emancipator, and universally inspires, as an historic and spiritual beacon, freedom movements among the globe's teeming masses. But he has been portrayed to posterity as a stronger and more enthusiastic anti-slavery advocate than he actually was. Always during the war his prime purpose was to save the Union, with emancipation of slaves a subsidiary by-product. His famous letter to Horace Greeley of 1862 still remains the most succinct and accurate summary of his views on slavery. That letter warrants reiteration:

"My paramount object in this struggle *is* to save the Union, and is *not* either to save or to destroy slavery. If I could save the Union without freeing *any* slave I would do it, and if I could save it by freeing *all* the slaves I would do it; and if I could save it by freeing some and leaving others alone I would also do that. What I do about slavery, and the colored race, I do because I believe it helps to save the Union; and what I forbear, I forbear because I do *not* believe it would help save the Union."

As Democratic Congressman "Sunset" Cox of Ohio said, the Thirteenth Amendment was "a part of the programme for strengthening the Federal cause."

Ratification of the Thirteenth Amendment by the three-fourths of the states, required to incorporate it into the United States Constitution, was not completed until the following December, eight months after Lincoln's assassination.

When in that month Secretary of State Seward officially announced adoption of the slavery-abolishing amendment, he counted among the required three-fourths of the states ratifying it eight militarily Federal-occupied former Confederate states, thus achieving the three-fourths majority necessary. Those eight erstwhile rebel members were Virginia, Tennessee, Arkansas, South Carolina, Alabama, North Carolina, Georgia, and Louisiana.

Thus ludicrously enough, as Lincoln lay in his grave, radical Republican senators and congressmen, who at that precise time were vehemently insisting that those eight Southern states (except Tennessee, which had elected a radical Republican governor) had forfeited their privileges in the Union by their record of secession and armed strife against the United States, approved Seward's action in counting those states as having "ratified" the Thirteenth Amendment. It was another of those contradictions and bewildering anomalies of post-Lincolnian reconstruction.

VI

As soon as the Thirteenth Amendment should be ratified by the requisite three-fourths of the states, Negroes would be freed throughout the United States. Slavery would be legally outlawed. But in early 1865, while Lincoln still lived, the question loomed: "Would the freed slaves be given the vote in Southern states?" This issue of Negro suffrage below Mason and Dixon's line is still an explosive question, after almost a century. Today it still plagues the Republic and threatens at times possible disruption of the Democratic Party along North-South sectional lines.

Franchise for the colored freedmen in Dixie was a proposal on which Lincoln was determined to move exceedingly slowly and cautiously during 1864-65. It was an issue which had to be left to decisions by each individual state, he concluded. For the United States Constitution had left to the states the power of fixing qualifications of voters within their respective borders. Lincoln, as a lawyer, recognized this completely. As a staunch supporter of the Federal Constitution (aside from his own flaunting of it in assuming what he considered "war" powers), Lincoln would not attempt to circumvent it for the sake of giving voting privileges to Negroes in the South.

Although not inclined to force Negro suffrage upon Southern states, Lincoln hoped personally that the states of the crumbling Confederacy would give colored men suffrage in an extremely limited way to those Negroes who were, as he said, "very intelligent" and also those who had served in the Union army. This view the President expressed in a letter of 1864 to the then recently elected Governor Michael Hahn of Louisiana. He wrote Hahn:

"Now you are about to have a Convention which, among other things, will probably define the elective franchise. I barely suggest for your private consideration, whether some of the colored people may not be let in—as, for instance, the very intelligent, and especially those who have fought gallantly in our ranks. They would probably help, in some trying time to come, to keep the jewel of liberty within the family of freedom. But this is only a suggestion, not to the public, but to you alone."

Lincoln repeated that same view to the great throng gathered on the White House lawn one year later, on April 11, 1865, in the last speech he was ever to make. On that occasion, three days before he was shot, Lincoln called for extremely limited suffrage for Louisiana Negroes: "It is also unsatisfactory to some that the elective franchise is not given to the colored man. I would myself prefer that it were now conferred on the very intelligent, and on those who serve our cause as soldiers."

One generation later Lincoln's one-time Secretary of the Interior, John P. Usher, authentically explained Lincoln's view on votes for colored men. Usher pointed out that the Civil War President did not intend "to force negro suffrage upon the people of the slaveholding States. Doubtless he contemplated that, sometime in the future, suffrage would be voluntarily yielded to the blacks by the people of those States."

Lincoln's contemporary, George Ticknor Curtis, one of the great constitutional lawyers of his day and a scholarly historian of the United States Constitution, has pointed out about Lincoln: "He would leave the question of suffrage entirely in the hands of the people of each state, to be regulated as they should see fit. He knew well that it could only be after a training for freedom and for the exercise of citizenship that the Negroes of the South could be safely entrusted with the ballot." Curtis, who knew so many of Lincoln's intimate associates well and questioned them about his views on suffrage for colored men down South, emphasized that Lincoln did not contemplate "the use of force" to compel white Southerners to adopt a system of voting for Negroes.

VII

Quite as persistent a problem as slavery and political rights for Southern Negroes, with which it was tightly intertwined, was reconstruction—or, as Lincoln preferred to term it, "restoration." The future status of the seceded states grew more urgent as final military victory over the Confederacy approached.

Lincoln, not a theorist but a practical and humane man sobered by years of harrowing war and heavy responsibility, fully comprehended the precarious reconstruction situation during 1864-65. He had tried, since 1862, to secure an early restoration of solidarity with as little political friction and as few social collisions as possible. Better than most Union leaders, he knew and understood conditions in the South as they actually existed, not as the radicals believed them to exist. He was conservative, conciliatory, and considerate. He wanted no executions or imprisonments. He even wanted the Confederate leaders to escape. And he was anxious that the mass of Southerners be welcomed back into the Union without loss of citizen rights. For constantly he envisioned an enduring Union, a future permanence of the American Republic.

Lincoln had already based his "ten per cent" plan of reconstruction, for bringing back the erstwhile Confederate states, on his belief that in the South there existed potentially strong Union sentiment even in its hour of military defeat. He intended to nourish that anti-secession feeling in the nearly collapsed Confederacy, rather than take it for granted. But the more radical members of his Republican-Unionist Party in Congress, ever so many of them vindictively seeking vengeance on Southerners, did not share the President's moderate and statesmanlike views.

Lincoln tried to conciliate the recent rebels and to adapt his own unvindictive plan of "presidential" reconstruction, to meet conditions that might vary from state to state. He did not want to inflict a hard and fast severe reconstruction policy as embodied in the radical Wade-Davis bill that he had killed by veto in July, 1864. When he disapproved of that Congress-enacted plan of reconstruction, he declared publicly that he was not prepared "to be inflexibly committed to any single plan of restoration" and he was not in favor of seeing the free-state constitutions of Arkansas and Louisiana (formed under his sponsorship) set aside because it would have the baneful effect of "repelling and discouraging the loyal citizens" in those states. As his Secretary of the Interior, John P. Usher, pointed out after the war: "Mr. Lincoln had no thought of restoring State governments in seceded States, through any other instrumentality than by the qualified voters of those States before secession was inaugurated."

With a mass movement of "War" Democrats from Lincoln's "Union" Party back to their traditional loyalties to the party of Jefferson and

Jackson, as the war neared its end, Lincoln's Republicans were left under the control of radical influences—reconstruction extremists. It was these Radical Republicans who were controlling Congress as the new session convened in early December, 1864. Their leaders demanded more drastic, even punitive, treatment to be meted out to the secessionist South. These radicals distrusted Lincoln because he did not admit the right of Congress to dictate reconstruction terms, because of his generous, humane attitude toward former Confederates, and because he was only lukewarm on the Negro-suffrage question. Some Radical Republicans were motivated by their sincere concern to give the Southern colored men their just political rights. Others, more crassly opportunistic and vote-avaricious, looked forward to a future robust Republican Party in the South, with Negroes marching obediently to the polls to cast ballots for Republican candidates and measures.

Lincoln's conciliatory plans of "presidential" reconstruction had been in operation in Arkansas, Tennessee, and Louisiana in some embryonic form since 1862. But now, by late 1864 and early 1865, the President and the majority in Congress found themselves deadlocked, sadly stalemated over the manner in which the Southern states should be brought back into the Union.

Since the Confederacy was correctly considered to be rattling in its death throes when Congress assembled in the last month of 1864, the reconstruction problem grew ever more pressing. The Radical Republicans, who dominated both houses, were insistent that they, not the re-elected President, would decide on how the seceded states would be welcomed to the Union again.

The Russian Minister at Washington, Baron Eduard de Stoeckl, reported to his St. Petersburg superiors by February 13, 1865: "Already a certain coldness exists between the President and the ultras of his party who fear that Mr. Lincoln, now that he has been re-elected, will try to free himself from their influence." The Tsar's envoy quoted one radical Senator as telling him about the President: "He must accept our views, whatever they are, or we will find means to ruin him. . . . We want to subjugate the South completely, and reduce it to a territory governed by the North."

By February, Louisiana and Arkansas had complied with the terms of the President's proclamation of restoration and had applied for readmission into the Union. A resolution was introduced in Congress to effect that readmission. It might well have passed, probably making Lincoln's moderate and more intelligent presidential plan of reconstruction successful, except for a group of Radical Republican Senators.

Led by those two ultras, Senator Benjamin F. Wade of Ohio and Senator Charles Sumner of Massachusetts, this anti-slavery extremist group succeeded in blocking the resolution by an adroit series of parliamentary maneuvers, by threat of filibuster or by forcing the measure to be postponed so that it would never come up again under the same comparatively favorable circumstances while Lincoln lived.

Congress adjourned on March 4, 1865, Lincoln's Second Inauguration Day, leaving the President an open field for his lenient policy of "restoration," only six weeks before his assassination.

VIII

The re-elected Lincoln, regardless of Radical Republican sentiment against him in Congress on the issue, continued to display a decided preference for his own moderate "presidential" plan for restoring the recovered states.

Lincoln's program encountered harrowing difficulties and seemingly never-ending obstacles, especially in Louisiana, where sometimes trouble was caused by his own civil and military appointees.

Especially irritating to the President about Louisiana in 1864 was the action of his own military commanders in opposing the loyal State government created in that sensitive State. Major-General Canby, who headed the Military Department of West Mississippi, had ordered Major-General Hurlbut, his assistant in command of the Department of the Gulf, to consider that "all attempts at civil government, within the territory declared to be in insurrection, are the creation of military power, and of course, subject to military revision and control." General Hurlbut had arrested the New Orleans *Times* editor for publishing a description of the Louisiana constitutional convention, in which he charged that some delegates were drunk.

Lincoln on November 14, one week following his re-election, sent General Hurlbut a sharp lengthy letter, marked "Private." "Few things since I have been here," he told Hurlbut with some impatience, "have impressed me more painfully than what, for four or five months past, has appeared as bitter military opposition to the new State Government of Louisiana. I still indulge the hope that I was mistaken in the fact; but copies of a correspondence on the subject, between Gen. Canby and yourself, and shown me to-day, dispel that hope." Sternly the President ordered Hurlbut to support the new civil government in Louisiana, pointing out: "Every Unionist ought to wish the new government to succeed; and every disunionist must desire it to fail. Its failure would gladden the heart of Slidell [John Slidell of Louisiana, Confederate commissioner in France], and of every enemy of the old flag in the world. . . . But why Gen. Canby and Gen. Hurlbut should join on the same side is to me incomprehensible." Lincoln disapproved of Hurlbut's action—it "is difficult to perceive," he told the General.

Lincoln received a reply from Hurlbut, in which the General promised to "recognize as thoroughly as any man" the new Louisiana constitution, which provided for abolition of slavery.

The President also sent orders to Hurlbut's superior, General Canby, the other disrupting force. He directed Canby: "As to the new State Government of Louisiana. . . . it is a worthy object to again get Louisiana into proper practical relations with the nation; and we can never finish this, if we never begin it." Lincoln also sent this wish to Canby, who had been shot by Confederate guerillas and was still recuperating: "I am happy in the hope that you are almost well of your late and severe wound."

IX

There pressed on Lincoln the case of vital Virginia, most influential of Confederate states, site of the secession capital and bordering on Washington.

When he visited Richmond on April 4, 1865, following its fall to the Federals, Lincoln consulted with John A. Campbell, Assistant Secretary of War of the all but collapsed Confederacy (whom he had met at the Hampton Roads "peace" conference two months previous) and with an attorney of that city, Gustavus A. Myers, about methods of returning the Old Dominion to the Republic. Also present at that meeting between Lincoln, Campbell, and Myers was Major-General Godfrey Weitzel, commanding the Federal occupation troops in the captured Confederate capital. Campbell, an Alabamian and former Justice of the United States Supreme Court, was one of the few high-ranking Confederate officials who had not fled Richmond when it was evacuated two days before.

At this conference Lincoln gave Campbell his terms of peace: restoration of the national authority throughout all of the states, no receding on slavery-emancipation, and the disbanding of all forces hostile to the United States. Lincoln promised that confiscations of property, except for slaves and except where the interests of third parties intervened, would be remitted to the people of any state which promptly should withdraw its troops and other support from resistance to the Federal Government.

Lincoln, Campbell, Myers, and General Weitzel discussed oaths of allegiance, pardons, amnesty, and also plans to have the Legislature of Virginia called into session.

Exactly what occurred, after Lincoln left Richmond, about these embryonic steps toward restoration of Virginia is still argued by historians, the true facts being smothered under a welter of conflicting testimony, claims and counter claims, reiterations and denials by those who participated in two conferences with Lincoln at Richmond.

Lincoln, however, on April 6 sent written authorization to General Weitzel to permit the assembly of the Legislature with a view to taking steps to bring Virginia back to the Union. Weitzel carried out Lincoln's request. But it turned out that Campbell was recognizing these lawmakers as the legal Legislature, whereas Lincoln wanted them accepted only as individuals.

The President, upon returning to Washington, found confusion over the possible restoration of Virginia. He had not been satisfied with the quantity or quality of information that he had obtained during his all too brief stay in Richmond. He decided to consult with Governor Francis H. Pierpont on the long-since Union-sponsored "Restored" Government of Virginia. On April 10, 1865, Lincoln wired Pierpoint: "Please come up and see me at once."

At his conference with Governor Pierpont in the White House on that day Lincoln went over details of what he had tried to learn, but did not, about Unionism in the Old Dominion. He could get no accurate information while in Richmond—"it was all a sealed book," he told Pierpoint discouragingly. Pierpont promised to do what he could.

Soon Lincoln learned, through a letter that Campbell had written to General Weitzel, that Campbell was misunderstanding him about the status and powers of the Legislature which had held office under the late Confederate regime, which was now being convened. And on April 12, two days before he was shot, Lincoln sent a letter to General Weitzel saying:

> I have just seen Judge Campbell's letter to you of the 7th. He assumes as appears to me that I have called the insurgent Confederate Legislature of Virginia together, as the rightful Legislature of that State, to settle all differences with the United States. I have done no such thing. I spoke of them not as a Legislature, but as 'the gentlemen who have *acted* as the Legislature of Virginia in support of the rebellion.' I did this on purpose to exclude the assumption that I was recognizing them as a *rightful* body. I dealt with them as men having power *de facto* to do a specific thing, to wit, 'to withdraw the Virginia troops, and other support from resistance to the General Government,' . . .

Campbell was misconstruing his intent, the President pointed out in his letter to Weitzel, by pressing for an armistice. Besides, Grant had since (three days before) captured the Virginia troops in Lee's surrender. And Lincoln ordered the General to have his (Lincoln's) paper, empowering Weitzel and Campbell, withdrawn. Of the Virginia legislators about to assemble in Richmond, the President instructed Weitzel: "Do not allow them to assemble; but if any have come, allow them safe-return to their homes."

Two days later, General Weitzel's successor as Federal commander in Richmond, General Edward O. C. Ord, telegraphed to Lincoln that Campbell and another Confederate commissioner, Hunter (both of whom had met the President at the Hampton Roads "peace" conference) two months before, wished to visit Lincoln in Washington. Ord's telegram reached Washington at half-past nine in the evening. But Lincoln never received Ord's wire about Campbell's and Hunter's desire to see him. Lincoln was not in when the wire arrived. He, Mrs. Lincoln, and two guests were watching "Our American Cousin" at Ford's Theatre.

X

As Lincoln's and Grant's personal friend, Congressman Elihu B. Washburne of Illinois, present as Grant's guest at Lee's surrender at Appomattox on April 9, rode away in company with his recent foe, Lieutenant-General John B. Gordon, C.S.A., Washburne gave assurances that the South would receive "generous treatment." When the General from Georgia, a future Governor of his State and United States Senator, asked the Congressman from Illinois (who had intimately known Lincoln since the old days of Whig politics on the prairies), why he knew that the South would be generously treated by the Federal Government, Washburne told the apprehensive Gordon: "Because Abraham Lincoln is at its head."

Others in high places at Washington, however, were determined that the Southerners must pay for their sins of secession. As soon as news came of General Lee's surrender, Radical Republican reconstructionists went into private consultations and behind-doors party caucuses. Conspicuous among them was one who, by the very nature of his position, should not have been in partisan politics so blatantly, Chief Justice Salmon P. Chase of the United States Supreme Court. This perennial presidential aspirant (since 1856) was personally honest but could not remove the White House from his brilliant but at times sordidly political mind. In 1865 he was still plunged deeply into party politics, this time looking forward to 1868, when Lincoln would be out of the way and he could float into the presidency on a fanned-up wave of radical reconstruction inflicted on the South with the aid of Negro votes below Mason and Dixon's line.

Two days after Appomattox, on April 11, 1865, Chase dined at Baltimore with Maryland's "lame duck" radical congressman, Henry Winter Davis, and other politicians intent on battling Lincoln's plans for restoring seceded states to the Republic. Chase left a short record of that Baltimore dinner meeting: "Dined in the evening (at 6 p.m.) with

Henry Winter Davis . . . mostly the radicals. . . . Wrote a letter to Prest. Lincoln."

In that letter to Lincoln of April 11, the Chief Justice vigorously pointed out to him: "I am very anxious about the future; and most about the principles which are to govern reconstruction. . . . It will be, hereafter, counted equally a crime & a folly if the colored loyalists of the rebel states shall be left to the control of restored rebels, not likely, in that case, to be either wise or just, until taught both wisdom and justice by new calamities."

That same evening Lincoln himself spoke on reconstruction, particularly as it applied to Louisiana. In that speech, delivered to an assembled crowd on the White House lawn, Lincoln lauded Grant and his men and also the Navy, and then he dealt with "restoration." The program as he saw it, he told his listeners, was essentially one of reestablishing the national authority throughout the South. This problem was complicated by the fact that there was "no authorized organ" there with which to treat. He pointed out: "Nor is it a small additional embarrassment that we, the loyal people, differ among ourselves as to the mode, manner, and means of reconstruction." He told the crowd: "We all agree that the seceded States, so called, are out of their proper practical relation with the Union; and that the sole object of the government, civil and military, in regard to those States is to again get them into that proper practical relation."

He acknowledged that he had been criticized for setting up and sustaining the new state government of Louisiana, which rested on the support of only ten per cent of the voters and did not give the franchise to the colored man. He conceded that the Louisiana government would be better if it rested on a larger electorate, including the votes of those Negroes who were "the very intelligent" or who had served as soldiers. "Concede that the new government of Louisiana is only to what it should be as the egg is to the fowl, we should sooner have the fowl by hatching the egg than by smashing it."

To the nation at large Lincoln's speech inspired widespread speculation about his undisclosed future intentions. But the radicals fumed unhappily. "The radicals are by no means pleased with the President's speech made to-night," reported one Washington correspondent. "To judge from the general tone of their conversation they almost regret that Lee has surrendered."

Senator Sumner was grieved and partially irate at Lincoln's speech. The celebrated Massachusetts anti-slaveryite confided to his friend, Professor Francis Lieber: "The President's speech and other things augur confusion and uncertainty in the future, with hot controversy. Alas! Alas!"

Chief Justice Chase saw nothing but doom ahead as a result of the President's views expressed in that speech. Three days later he sent some alarming words to an Ohio political aide, Stanley Matthews, future United States Senator and Justice of the United States Supreme Court:

"Reconstruction has been made almost wholly a military job; with no good results so far. Louisiana is the only result as yet; and there the old secession element is rapidly gaining ascendancy in consequence of the disfranchisement of the colored loyalists.

"And now the President has given a sort of sanction, and a pretty strong one too, to the meeting of the rebel Legislature with a view to its putting itself right by a simple declaration of submission and acquiescence in Emancipation."

But Lincoln, on that same 14th of April, the last full day of his life, felt satisfied that his moderate restoration policy was receiving support from conservative circles. On that day he wrote James H. Van Alen: "I thank you for the assurance you give me that I shall be supported by conservative men like yourself, in the efforts I may make to restore the Union, so as to make it, to use your language, a Union of hearts and hands as well as of States."

TRIUMPH OF THE UNION

I

1865 opened in Washington with New Year's Day merrymakers still singing, "When This Cruel War Is Over."

The New Year's White House reception was held on Monday, January 2, and proved a surging crush of people. Ladies and children were lifted in the arms of their escorts to escape the suffocating pressure of milling crowds. One lady reached the door of the Blue Room with her bonnet so smashed and her shawl so torn that she was ashamed to enter.

When the President's ordeal of handshaking ended, he rallied his physical forces to welcome a throng of colored folk who had lingered around the Executive Mansion in the hope of being admitted. For a little time the trampled reception room knew laughter and tears and cries of "God bless Abraham Lincoln!"

There followed a series of other White House receptions and entertainments during those opening weeks of 1865. The newspapers extended themselves in describing the brilliance of these social functions and the illustriousness of such guests as Cabinet members, gold-braided diplomats from England, the European continent, and more exotic lands, epauletted generals, colonels, and their expensively gowned wives. The extravagant Mrs. Abraham Lincoln's costumes were described in minute detail: "heavy brocade purple silk, very richly trimmed with black velvet, over which was thrown a rich and exquisitely wrought black lace shawl;" or, "rich dress of pearl color, heavily trimmed with the richest black lace, with neat head-dress composed of a coronet of exquisite flowers."

The President, in his physical chores of handshaking, remained his usual unaffected self. At times he revealed boyishness. He was overheard on one of these occasions telling his old friend Judge Davis: "I never knew until the other day how to spell the word, 'maintenance.' " And syllable by syllable he spelled it to Justice Davis between greetings to the long line of guests who passed by to speak with him and shake his hand.

The rejoicing in Washington during war time seemed understandable at this precise time. For when 1865 opened, the boundaries of the Confederacy had shrunk so small, and its secession-held territory was so divided by invading Federal forces, that it appeared certain that the Southern armies and the Government at Richmond would soon be doomed. The Mississippi River, water jugular vein of Western economic life, was completely open, its land on both sides under Federal occupation. Louisiana was completely ruled by Union military government. Missouri, Kentucky, and the seceded state of Tennessee were now so cleared of Confederate troops that they again produced good crops. The southern Atlantic ports of Norfolk, Virginia, Savannah, Georgia, and Fernandina, Florida, as well as the gulf ports of New Orleans, Louisiana, Mobile, Alabama, and Pensacola, Florida, were in Union hands and were reopened to commerce. General Grant, still battering at Petersburg in a campaign of attrition, kept General Lee's Army of Northern Virginia, the main Confederate force, pinned down in Richmond, and General Thomas had knocked out Hood's Army of Tennessee. General Sherman was about to lay waste to South Carolina, pursuing the other remaining big Southern army under General "Joe" Johnston. Confederate units remained in the field, fighting bravely, but it was apparent to careful observers that they no longer posed a major threat. General Kirby-Smith's Far Western Confederate command found itself completely cut off from Richmond. The Confederate Navy, too, had by this time been largely destroyed or captured.

II

When the new year, 1865, opened, Fort Fisher, guarding the approaches to Wilmington, North Carolina, the Confederates' last important seaport, still lay in Southern hands. The foolish plan of the now removed General Ben Butler to capture the fort had failed, and Grant had been instrumental in having Lincoln and Stanton remove Butler from the Army of the James command. So a new naval-military operation was launched against Fort Fisher, and the fort fell to the Unionists on January 15, 1865.

Fort Fisher's fall proved a major blow to the Southerners. "Its capture," later lamented its Confederate defender, "with the resulting loss of all Cape Fear River defenses, and of Wilmington, the great importing depot of the South, effectually ended all blockade-running. Lee sent me word that Fort Fisher must be held, or he could not subsist his army."

Congress nine days later formally thanked Admiral Porter in joint resolution. Lincoln signed it, forwarded it to the Admiral, and added his own congratulatory message to "the officers and men under your command, for their gallantry and good conduct in the capture of Fort Fisher, and through you to all who participated in that brilliant and decisive victory under your command."

III

Although the war's end was obviously happily near, the courage of the Southern men and women was such that Lincoln did not relax his efforts. Nonetheless the advocates of peace conferences hectored him about the necessity of meeting with President Davis or any other authorized Confederate commissioner for the discussion of the cessation of military hostilities between Union and Confederate armies. Among the avid peace makers was old Francis P. Blair, Sr.

Following an unofficial visit of Blair to Richmond, Lincoln consented to receive secession representatives within the Union lines and talk of peace between the sections. The President had already made vigorously clear his principal peace terms with the Southern government—reunion and abolition of slavery.

President Davis had already written Blair expressing his willingness to enter into conference "with a view to secure peace between our two countries."

What "two countries?" was what Lincoln wanted to know when he saw Davis's letter to Blair. Lincoln replied to Blair that he would be willing to see Confederate representatives with a view to secure peace—"to the people of our one common country," the President emphasized.

Lincoln was talking about one thing: "our one common country." His Confederate counterpart, Davis, was speaking of another: "our two countries." Despite this deadlock of purpose, Lincoln, accompanied by Secretary of State Seward, on February 3, 1865, participated in a meeting with three Confederate commissioners, Vice-President Alexander H. Stephens, Senator Robert M. T. Hunter, and Assistant Secretary of War John A. Campbell. The scene of their conference was aboard the Union transport, *River Queen,* lying in Hampton Roads.

Lincoln at that Hampton Roads Conference had opportunity to meet again Secession's second top-ranking official, Vice-President Stephens, for the first time since they had been fellow-Whig members of Congress together more than fifteen years before. Then, in 1848, Congressman Lincoln had eulogistically written home to Herndon, his law partner, "Mr. Stephens of Georgia, a slim, pale-faced, consumptive man, with a voice like Logan's, has just concluded the very best speech of an hour's length, I ever heard. My old, withered, dry eyes are full of tears yet."

That peace conference aboard the *River Queen* in early February, 1865, was opened by the revival of reminiscences and associations of former happier years. The President of the United States of America and the Vice-President of the Confederate States of America inquired of each other about their old fellow Whig colleagues, Truman Smith of Connecticut and William Ballard Preston and Thomas Flournoy, both of Virginia, the little Whig coterie who, along with Lincoln and Stephens, were known as the "Young Indians," promoting General Zachary Taylor's presidential candidacy.

Lincoln and Seward, and the three Confederates, then plunged into business. Lincoln's terms for peace were set in writing before the conference: restoration of the Union, no receding on emancipation, no cessation of hostilities short of an end of the war and the disbanding of all military forces hostile to the United States Government.

Various matters were discussed by the five statesmen. Among the topics they went into were the possibility of an armistice, the postponement of the question of separation, the possible diversion of attention to some intrinsic policy for a period so that passions might subside, the antislavery policy, Southern representation in Congress, and the attitude to be taken toward punitive measures. On collateral issues, Lincoln showed generosity, assuring Stephens, Hunter, and Campbell that executive policy would be lenient and remarking that he would, for himself, be willing to consider compensation for slaveholders.

But the President emphatically insisted that the re-establishment of the Union was indispensable and that the Confederate armies must be disbanded. Thus the Hampton Roads Conference adjourned without agreement of views.

Its failure to bring about peace meant that the war would go on until the secession armies were destroyed or captured.

IV

General Sherman, after more than a month in Savannah, on February 1, struck north for his continued devastating march, this time through South Carolina, the cradle of secession.

General Halleck had written to Sherman: "Should you capture Charleston, I hope that by *some* accident the place may be destroyed; and if a little salt should be sown upon its site, it may prevent the growth of future crops of nullification and secession." Sherman answered: "I will bear in mind your hint as to Charleston, and don't think salt will be necessary. . . . The truth is the whole army is burning with an insatiable desire to wreak vengeance upon South Carolina."

It turned out, however, that Charleston, being off the main line of march northward, happily escaped the ravages and figurative rape of Sherman's men. They took it out, however, on South Carolina's state capital town, Columbia. As they approached there some Union soldiers sang in parody:

> Hail, Columbia, happy land,
> If I don't burn you, I'll be damned.

The worst destruction was caused to Columbia by a ferocious fire there in mid-February. Sherman in his *Memoirs* explained that the conflagration was accidental; that the flames started with the cotton which Confederates under General Wade Hampton had set afire on fleeing the town. Sherman then made the damaging admission in his *Memoirs* that in his official report he deliberately charged the fire to Hampton in order "to shake the faith of his people" in that adored Southern commander. Numerous other towns in the Palmetto commonwealth, too, had the torch applied to them by Sherman's incendiary-crazed, anti-secession troops.

General Hampton for the remainder of his life always vigorously denied that any cotton had been burned at his order. Undoubtedly lax military discipline and drunkenness, combined with the memory of South Carolina having done so much to touch off the war, were contributing factors to the Federal troops' destruction of Columbia and other towns in the State.

South Carolinians for generations remembered the devastations of Sherman's marauders as long and bitterly as did the Georgians.

V

Inauguration Day. Saturday, March 4, 1865.

That black and appalling cloud of secession, which four years earlier had hung frighteningly and oppressively over the Republic, had poured forth its fury and carnage and was finally passing away.

Lincoln was beset by a new anxiety: the disturbing indication that the North, bitter over the deaths and maiming of so many tens of thousands of its best men and sour over the secessionists' struggles to disrupt the Union, would vengefully harden itself into a vindictive temper and deal harshly with the militarily conquered South, thus perpetuating sectional antagonisms. It was a Northern extremist reaction which had been displayed in the Federal troops' wanton destruction of South Carolina towns and which, at that precise time, was grimly obvious in the aggressive activities of radical Republican leaders in Congress insistent on a drastic, punitive reconstruction policy toward the crumbling Confederate states.

From Lincoln's sane and humane viewpoint, mere conquest and punishment of the South could not be a proper and intelligent culmination of the difficult work of restoring the Republic. His own plans were best actively expressed in his lenient reconstruction measures toward the "recovered" Southern states. Appropriately and consistently enough, he now prepared to deliver a supremely statesmanlike Inaugural Address filled with generosity and lacking revenge toward the South which, he hoped, would put a damper on sectional passions and also heal the wounds and sores of four years of blood-spilling and name-calling civil war.

The capital city of Washington had for days been grooming itself for its monster Inaugural pageant. The triumph of the Union was close at hand. Once more the platform was erected on the east front of the Capitol and crowds assembled to see Lincoln sworn in for a second term and hear his Inaugural Address. But whereas four years earlier an unfinished truncated dome rose back of the platform, there now towered the majestic curves of the completed structure.

Into the Senate Chamber on that very late morning of March 4, 1865, packed with Senators, Representatives, Army and Navy officers whose uniforms could not vie with the colorful, braided ornateness of those worn by the foreign Diplomatic Corps, as well as countless well-dressed women, the black-robed Chief Justice, Salmon P. Chase, wishing he were going to receive the presidential oath instead of merely administering it, led his eight judicial colleagues, including Lincoln's friend, Mr. Justice David Davis. Lincoln's Cabinet members took their places. Mrs. Lincoln was escorted to a seat in the diplomatic gallery, and she was pleased by both her husband's elevation to another White House term and her presence among the courtly Ministers, *Chargés d'Affaires,* and Military *Attachés* of the foreign legations.

Shortly before noon, the outgoing Vice-President Hannibal Hamlin entered the Senate chamber, arm in arm with his incoming successor,

Andrew Johnson, a one-time Tennessee tailor. Johnson should have been thankful for Hamlin's arm as he walked to the dais of the presiding officer on the greatest day of his life up to that time. For Johnson had attended a party the night before, was in poor health, and had taken some whiskey that morning to reinvigorate his nerves.

Johnson launched into the speech which preceded his taking of the oath as Vice-President of the United States.

A rough-hewn Tennessee mountaineer who usually could take his liquor or leave it, Johnson on that momentous occasion had apparently consumed a bit too much. His words rambled and at times he was rantingly incoherent. The audience was partly angry, partly mortified. The Marquis de Chambrun wrote to his wife in France about this incident: "Johnson was still wearying the assembling with desultory discourse when President Lincoln entered through a side door directly facing the Speaker. The Chief Executive was respectfully saluted. . . . During Mr. Johnson's continued ramblings, the President closed his eyes and seemed to retire within himself as though beset by melancholy reflections."

After Chief Justice Chase had administered the vice-presidential oath to Johnson, and following the swearing in of newly-elected Senators, the dignitaries lined up for the procession to the East front of the Capitol, where Abraham Lincoln was to be inaugurated President for a second four-year term.

Crowds packed themselves on the lawn and street before the Capitol's East wing, awaiting Lincoln's appearance. Spontaneously they filled the air with thunderous cheers, as the tall gaunt form, dressed in dignified black, walked out on the portico and advanced toward the table with its lonely tumbler of water and glass. Abruptly the last clouds in the sky rolled away, and the scene was flooded with sudden sunshine, as if symbolic that bright days lay ahead for the Union and its mightiest living advocate. Lincoln had at that point attained higher prestige and popularity than he had ever enjoyed before.

The multitude hushed to hear the President's short address. It was the briefest induction speech that any President had ever yet offered, but it proved the loftiest, most supremely statesmanlike speech of all his orations, along with his Gettysburg Address. It pleaded for perpetual peace between his country's sections. He cautioned his fellow-Americans: "Let us judge not that we be not judged." He ended with the immortal appeal:

"With malice toward none; with charity for all; with firmness in the right, as God gives us [power] to see the right, let us strive on to finish the work we are in; to bind up the nation's wounds; to care for him who shall have borne the battle, and for his widow, and his orphan—to do all which may achieve and cherish a just, and a lasting peace, among ourselves, and with all nations."

Lincoln then pronounced the presidential oath to Chief Justice Chase.

Lincoln kissed the open Bible held out to him by Chase on the page containing the twenty-seventh and twenty-eighth verses of the fifth chapter of Isaiah, beginning: "None shall be weary nor stumble among them; none shall slumber nor sleep. . . ."

Artillery mingled with the shouts of thousands of voices, as Lincoln, now beginning his second presidential term, bowed and retired. The sea of humanity below stirred, milled about, and began to disintegrate into twos, threes, and small throngs.

As Lincoln returned to the White House, accompanied by his son, Tad, he was viewed by Walt Whitman, who observed:

"March 4th: I saw him on his return, at three o'clock, after the performance was over. He was in his plain two-horse barouche, and look'd very much worn and tired; the lines, indeed, of vast responsibilities, intricate questions, and demands of life and death, cut deeper than ever upon his brown face; yet all the old goodness, tenderness, sadness, and canny shrewdness, underneath the furrows. (I never see that man without feeling, that he is one to become personally attach'd to, for his combination of purest, heartiest tenderness, and native western form of manliness). By his side sat his little boy of ten years. There were no soldiers, only a lot of civilians on horseback, with huge yellow scarfs over their shoulders, riding around the carriage. (At the inauguration four years ago, he rode down and back again surrounded by a dense mass of arm'd cavalrymen eight deep, with drawn sabres; and there were sharpshooters station'd at every corner on the route)."

VI

How was Lincoln's Second Inaugural Address received?

While this immortal classic, like his Gettysburg Address, was not hailed unanimously at that time as a world-renowned masterpiece, there were those who noted its mighty and inspiring message so free from tawdry partisanship and lack of vindictiveness.

In England, usually reserved in its reaction to Americans' orations, Lincoln's Second Inaugural was recognized as a statement of future policy elevatingly out of the ordinary. The *Spectator* of London went so far as to comment: "No statesman ever uttered words stamped at once with the seal of so deep a wisdom and so true a simplicity." The famed London *Times,* with a four-year pro-Confederate editorial record, reported Lincoln's address favorably. And the Duke of Argyll congratulated his friend, Senator Sumner, by mail, "on the *remarkable speech* of your President," adding: "It was a noble speech, just, and true, and solemn. I think it has produced great effect in England."

Lincoln himself felt confident that his Second Inaugural would endure. Eleven days after he delivered it, on March 15, the President informed Thurlow Weed by letter:

> Every one likes a compliment. Thank you for yours on my little notification speech, and on the recent Inaugural Address. I expect the latter to wear well—as perhaps better than—anything I have produced; but I believe it is not immediately popular. Men are not flattered by being shown that there has been a difference of purpose between the Almighty and them. To deny it, however, in this case, is to deny that there is a God governing the world. It is a truth which I thought needed to be told; and as whatever of humiliation there is in it, falls directly on myself, I thought others might afford for me to tell it.

Following his re-inauguration in March, Lincoln was not a well man. When Walt Whitman noted that the President "look'd very much worn and tired" returning from the induction ceremonies on the 4th, he was expressing what others were also observing. The Cincinnati *Gazette's* Washington correspondent reported that the President had been stricken with "no serious illness" but was "suffering from the exhausting attentions of the office hunters."

Horace Greeley later revealed about the Chief Executive: "When I last saw him, a few weeks before his death, I was struck by his haggard, care-fraught face, so different from the sunny, gladsome countenance he first brought from Illinois."

Lincoln himself confided about this time to his good friend, Joshua F. Speed: "I am very unwell now; my feet and hands of late seem to be always cold, and I ought perhaps to be in bed." The President, in one of his more melancholy moods, remarked to Mrs. Harriet Beecher Stowe: "I shall never live to see peace; this war is killing me."

VII

By mid-March, 1865, the Confederacy's remaining days could be counted on the fingers of five hands.

Lincoln, throughout the four years of war, had deeply grieved over the possible Confederate triumph and consequent end of the Union. Yet the danger of Secession's victory was overestimated, if it be considered how fundamentally weak the Confederate States of America actually were internally. The inadequacies, disadvantages, and blunders of the United States Government at Washington under Lincoln were equally matched, and perhaps surpassed, by those disrupting forces within Jefferson Davis' regime at Richmond.

Since the war's beginning, there had really never been any such thing as the "Solid South" about which so much has been written and spoken since those days. Leaders in the government and within the Southern states fought each other with intensity, some detesting the other almost as deeply as they did the common Yankee foe.

In Georgia a powerful core of citizens regarded President Davis as a despicable despot and opposed laws of the Confederate Congress, particularly conscription, and also taxation and suspension of *habeas corpus.* Robert Toombs, who served in Davis' Cabinet, had grown embittered because he had not been chosen President of the new nation and then failed as a General. Toombs constantly opposed Davis. Vice-President Stephens, Toomb's erstwhile friend and fellow Georgian, lent his brains to the anti-Davis movement in his State. Stephens served as the abettor of Governor Joseph E. Brown in his States-Rights policies, and instead of attending to his vice-presidential duties at Richmond, spent much of his time in Georgia. The feud between the South's President and Vice-President was only one of the numberless vendettas within the Confederacy in the highest political circles. Among the military hierarchy, too, Generals and Colonels in gray fought each other just as if they were combatting the men in blue.

In addition to these political and military rivalries, the Confederates were perplexed by problems beyond human control. They had inadequate man-power compared with the more thickly populated North. By early 1865, to fill the Southern armies, they set about drafting Negro slaves for combat service. Too, as essentially agrarian and non-manufacturing people, Southerners found themselves unhappily hard put to produce guns, munitions, and other sinews of warfare. Food ran alarmingly low, and Confederate desertions rose to huge figures.

The Confederates had reached their high tide of power, victory, and confidence at the half-way point of the war, when Lee thoroughly thrashed Hooker at Chancellorsville in May, 1863. But Southern hopes were abruptly dashed only two months later, in early July, when simultaneously Meade bested Lee at Gettysburg, and Grant scored his victory over Pemberton at Vicksburg. These Federal triumphs had been partially cancelled out two months later, in September, when Rosecrans' Army of the Cumberland had been badly beaten by Bragg's Army of Tennessee at Chickamauga. But Southern elation over Chickamauga proved especially short-lived, for two months later, in November, Grant's armies routed Bragg's forces at Chattanooga-Lookout Mountain-Missionary Ridge.

Hopes of the more optimistic Southerners revived in the spring of 1864, when Grant's armies suffered horribly high casualties in the Wilderness, on the North Ana, and at Cold Harbor, when General Butler was bottled up at Bermuda Hundred by Beauregard, when General Franz

Sigel was stopped by Breckinridge at New Market in the Shenandoah Valley, and when General Banks' ambitious and cumbersome Red River campaign in the Southwest was stopped by Confederates.

But Southerners in ever greater numbers lost hope in the late summer and early autumn of 1864, when Admiral Farragut triumphed at Mobile Bay, Sherman took Atlanta, Sheridan scored victories over Early in the Valley, and Lincoln was decisively re-elected.

The last month of 1864 proved a galling one for the Confederacy. Simultaneously in mid-December Thomas put out of action Hood's Army of Tennessee, and Sherman completed his march across Georgia and entered Savannah. In February, 1865, the Federals, by amphibious operation of land and sea forces, captured Wilmington, North Carolina, the only remaining major Confederate-held Atlantic port!

In the West, the Confederate armies were nearly annihilated and were disintegrating in organization, with desertions running high. In the far Southwest, General Kirby-Smith, commanding the Southerners' detached Trans-Mississippi Department, so-called "Kirby-Smithdom," saw the end at hand. Economic as well as military problems and feuds among Kirby-Smith's subordinate commanders were bringing that chivalrous General to defeat.

In the East, the vital theatre of warfare because it was the center of both the Federal and Confederate capitals, General Sherman's army by mid-March had reached North Carolina after devastating portions of South Carolina. Sherman's men began a three-day battle with General "Joe" Johnston's disintegrating forces at Bentonville, near Goldsboro. Then Sherman pushed on to Goldsboro, a strategic railroad point, where he formed a juncture with Federal forces of General Alfred H. Terry from Wilmington and of General Schofield from New Bern.

The final military operations on the vital Virginia front was what General Lee's masterful biographer, Douglas Southall Freeman, has called a "study in attenuation," the process of Grant's anaconda of an army, by constant bombardment, reducing and making ever more slender and thinner Lee's Petersburg-Richmond line of defenses still held by his once great Army of Northern Virginia, now composed of hungry, war-weary, and vastly outnumbered men. Soon Grant was even more strengthened by the arrival of General Sheridan and his crack cavalrymen.

Grant on March 19, the same day that Sherman was thrashing Joe Johnston in North Carolina, penned a letter to his father: "We are now having fine weather and I think will be able to wind up matters about Richmond soon. I am anxious to have Lee hold on where he is a short time longer so that I can get him in a position where he must lose a great portion of his army. The rebellion has lost its vitality and if I am not much mistaken there will be no rebel army of any great dimensions in a few weeks hence."

On that same day, Grant sent a letter to President Lincoln, inviting him to visit his headquarters at City Point, Virginia.

The President accepted Grant's invitation. In company with Mrs. Lincoln, his son Tad, and a small party, he departed from Washington four days later.

"We cannot but fervently hope," Mrs. Lincoln wrote Senator Sumner on March 23, "that change of air & rest, may have a beneficial effect on my good Husband's health."

VIII

Boarding the *River Queen,* the same boat on which the abortive Hampton Roads "peace" conference had been held some weeks before, the President, his wife, son Tad, and party of intimates sailed down to City Point, where they were General Grant's guests as his army hammered away at Petersburg. Here Lincoln could not be easily reached by office-seekers and other annoyances. Here, too, he could witness some of the final military operations against the Confederates from a distance.

Grant's City Point headquarters lay in a group of cottages on a high bluff at the juncture of the Appomattox and James rivers. It was a point which commanded a view of a wide and active war theatre, including numerous sites made grimly historic by the military operations of years just passed; today, they are "hallowed ground."

To the north lay the flats of Bermuda Hundred, with its conspicuous look-out tower, with tents, barracks and wharves. Beyond were the wooded slopes of Malvern Hill, where McClellan had beaten Lee three years before. Looking eastward across the great bay, there could be seen Harrison's Landing. On every side wharves ran out from the shore. Here night and day, steamers, transports, gun boats came and went, unloading well-fed and fully equipped blue-uniformed men and tons of supplies, and also carrying away wounded and half-starved gray-garbed prisoners who had for seasons gone down the line for Lee and the "Lost Cause."

The President's little river steamer anchored before the foot of the bluff at City Point. Here he lived, saw, and reviewed troops, shook their hands, and heard the roar of guns in the distance. It had been intended that on the day of his arrival, March 25, Lincoln should review a portion of the troops on the Petersburg line. But an engagement between the Federal besiegers and the Confedrate besieged was begun by Lieutenant-General John B. Gordon's surprise attack on Federal-held Fort Stedman. A bloody battle raged, interrupting Lincoln's review.

Gordon had brought to Lee his audacious plan. At a point he believed vulnerable to the Federals, he would assault the enemy line, break through, take a position in the rear, sweep down the Union works and force Grant to abandon the left of his line. Lee would then have a shorter front and thus could have a greater density of force. Gordon would strike the Federals at Fort Stedman, situated on the high ground known as Hare's Hill, near the crossing of Grant's line and the Prince George Court House road, southeast of the Appomattox River.

Fort Stedman was protected by obstructions made of rails with the lower ends deeply buried in ground, and the upper ends sharpened and resting upon poles fastened by strong wires. After initial successes, Gordon and his valorous men were decisively defeated. Lee's biographer, Freeman, concludes about General Gordon: "His repulse was due, in part, to his failure to appreciate the severity of the artillery fire he had to encounter while developing his attack or while retiring in the event of repulse."

Again Lee's fast disintegrating armies had suffered a reverse.

IX

Lincoln made the *River Queen* his home. He conferred with Grant frequently on the Union armies' progress during those closing days of March. He visited various camps, chatted with the troops and was cheered lustily by them.

General Sherman, still down in North Carolina pursuing "Joe" Johnston's retreating forces, made a hasty trip up to City Point to talk with Lincoln in two conferences, in company with General Grant and Admiral David D. Porter.

Of those two conferences on the *River Queen* both Sherman and Porter later told how Lincoln asked if it were possible to avoid another fight. Grant and Sherman replied that they feared that it would "take one more desperate and bloody battle." Sherman emphasized: "We can not control that event; this necessarily rests with our enemy." Lincoln replied depressed, "Can't you spare more effusions of blood? We have had so much of it." Lincoln also told the General that, when the Confederates were finally defeated, he was expected to get the Southern soldiers back to work on their farms. As for Jefferson Davis, Lincoln expressed the confidential wish that the Confederate President would clear out, "escape the country," but that it would not do for himself, Lincoln, to express this publicly. The President also authorized Sherman to assure the now anti-secession Governor Zebulon B. Vance of North Carolina that, as soon as the rebel soldiers laid down their arms, they would have their United States citizenship rights restored. Lincoln, in addition, authorized Sherman to recognize Vance's administration as a government *de facto* in the Tar Heel State.

At City Point during those closing days of March Lincoln sat in the telegraph office, hour after hour, receiving reports from Grant and sending them on to Secretary of War Stanton at Washington, with his own summaries and comments. On March 30 he wired Stanton: "I begin to feel that I ought to be at home, and yet I dislike to leave without seeing nearer to the end of General Grant's present movement. . . . Last night at 10:15, when it was dark as a rainy night without a moon could be, a furious cannonade, soon joined by a heavy musketry fire, opened near Petersburg and lasted about two hours. The sound was very distinct here, as also were the flashes of the guns up the clouds."

Grant did not fully confide to Lincoln his plans, which were to capture Richmond and Petersburg and dispose of Lee's Army of Northern Virginia without waiting for Sherman's men, still in North Carolina, to join in a final assault. Grant intended to send General Sheridan with his cavalry around to the southwest of Petersburg to take Five Forks and thus cut off Lee's lifeline, the railroad leading to Danville and the south. Lee, in an effort to save his communications and protect his flank and rear, could be expected to weaken his defenses before Petersburg—the bastion barring the Yankees from Richmond—and leave them vulnerable to a Federal break-through.

Lee's long line of Petersburg and Richmond defenses was now so thinly manned that a Federal break-through seemed certain. The Confederates were at the end of their resources in manpower, materials, food, and will to fight. As if to hasten the end for Lee and his army, General Sheridan shifted his forces southward from Winchester in the Shenandoah Valley and effected a juncture with the Army of the Potomac.

On April 1 the Federals under Sheridan decisively defeated the enemy under Pickett at Five Forks. Sheridan took 6,000 prisoners—an indication of the Southerners' fatigue and hunger.

Lincoln at City Point on that day elatedly telegraphed Secretaries Stanton and Seward: "Sheridan, aided by Warren, had, at 2 p.m., pushed the enemy back so as to retake Five Forks."

Now there seemed nothing left for Lee but to withdraw from Petersburg, abandon the Confederate capital, Richmond, and hastily fall back to the southwest in hope of joining with General "Joe" Johnston's army to make some vaguely considered united stand against the Federals. So Lee began his last retreat—a retreat which was soon to end at Appomattox.

Coming thick and fast to Lincoln at City Point on April 2 were batches of dispatches, all filled with glad tidings. "Dispatches frequently coming in. All going finely," the President happily wired Stanton. The Federal forces had broken through the enemy's Petersburg defenses, and Sheridan's cavalrymen were industriously tearing up the tracks of the Danville railroad.

X

Dateline: Richmond, Virginia, April 2, 1865.

Sunday dawned a magnificent spring day. Recent rains had brought out the yellow and pale green flowers, and the trees were bright. Only an occasional rumbling of Grant's guns in the distance disturbed the otherwise quiet Confederate capital town. Underneath the apparent serenity, however, all was not happy—at least not with the top-ranking Confederate officials, military and civil.

The heads of the Confederate States of America had been told the preceding night the bad news by General Lee himself! The Southerners' supreme commander could not hold his weakened lines against the ceaseless assaults of Grant's formidable armies.

President Jefferson Davis attended St. Paul's church for his last Sabbath in Richmond. As the clergyman was delivering his sermon, an official messenger came down the aisle to Davis's pew and handed him a message. Calmly the Confederate Chief Executive read it, then hurriedly followed the messenger out of the church.

Davis met with his Cabinet in the most critical of all its sessions. Present were the Governor of Virginia, the Mayor of Richmond, and other secession dignitaries. They discussed the disposition of the Government's records and archives, and the more significant documents were prepared for shipment out of the city. The Confederate seat of government had to be abandoned and they hoped that they might set it up again farther south, for continuance of the war. Last minute orders were given.

By nightfall Davis, his Cabinet, and nearly all high-ranking officials of the secession regime were in flight which, some of the more optimistic vainly hoped, would be only a temporary strategic retreat.

XI

President Lincoln on April 3 left City Point and visited General Grant in captured Petersburg.

That town lay nearly deserted of troops, since Grant had immediately sent nearly all of them in pursuit of Lee's army, instead of waiting for General Sherman to come up from North Carolina to join him for a concerted Federal knockout blow on the Army of Northern Virginia.

Lincoln was somewhat surprised that he saw so few Federal troops in Petersburg, for up to that time Grant had not confided to the President that he would not wait for Sherman's men before chasing Lee. Later Grant explained: "I would have let him [Lincoln] know what I contemplated doing, only, while I felt a strong conviction that the move was going to be successful, yet it might not prove so; and then I would have only added another to the many disappointments he had been suffering for the past three years."

Lincoln felt so elated at the fall of Petersburg and Richmond that he was not hurt by not being informed of Grant's plans. According to Grant, among the first words that the President said on greeting him in Petersburg were: "Do you know, general, that I have had a sort of sneaking idea for some days that you intended to do something like this?"

The two parted, the President to return to City Point, the General-in-Chief to join his armies in pursuing Lee.

Lincoln found a telegram from Secretary Stanton awaiting him, advising him against visiting Petersburg. Lincoln replied to Stanton: "Yours received. Thanks for your caution; but I have already been to Petersburg, staid (sic) with Gen. Grant an hour & a half and returned here. It is certain now that Richmond is in our hands, and I think I will go there to-morrow. I will take care of myself."

And on to Richmond the President went the following day.

XII

On that April 3 morning Major-General Godfrey Weitzel, commanding the Federal line between the James and Appomattox rivers, rode into Richmond with a detachment. Soon Colonel Charles Francis Adams, Jr., great-grandson of one President and grandson of another, led his Negro regiment, the Fifth Massachusetts Cavalry, into the fallen Confederate capital.

The next day, the 4th, President Lincoln reached Richmond.

Accompanied by his son, Tad, Lincoln traveled by a Navy gunboat, the *Malvern,* up the James River to a point where it was obstructed, from which he was rowed by twelve sailors in a small boat to Rockett's wharf. Negroes shouted their praises of him as he landed in Richmond. Some fell on their knees kissing his feet, and others shouted: "Glory, Hallelujah!" "Mr. Lincoln was surrounded by these people," related Admiral David D. Porter, who accompanied the President. The Negroes had treasured up the image of him caught from a photograph, declared Porter, "and had looked up to him as the one who was to lead them out of captivity." It was with difficulty that Porter and his aides could rescue Lincoln from the Negroes' adulation.

While in Richmond, Lincoln sanctioned the assembling of the Virginia legislature and consulted with General Weitzel about cooperating with erstwhile secession leaders in the work of restoring the Old Dominion to the Union. He held conversations with Assistant Secretary of War John A. Campbell, of the recently deceased Confederacy, whom he had met at the unsuccessful Hampton Roads "peace" conference two months earlier. The President discussed reconstruction with Campbell, and gave him authorization to perform work toward that end which was soon misunderstood. In the Confederate capital the towering, gaunt Chief Executive of the Union, in a long black coat and a high silk hat, stood out above the throngs surrounding him, and blacks and whites followed him through the streets. A clerk in the Southern War Department, J. B. Jones, noted in his diary: "The cheers that greeted President Lincoln were mostly from the negroes and Federals comprising the great mass of humanity. The white citizens felt annoyed that the city should be held mostly by negro troops."

Lincoln went to the former home of the now fleeing President Davis. And there he sat in Davis's chair. Some Federal troops, feeling that this was symbolic, cheered loudly.

XIII

Lincoln returned from Richmond to City Point, and before he went on to Washington he made a few more inspection tours.

One hospital where he visited was that in which a Quakeress, Cornelia Hancock, was nursing the wounded. Miss Hancock told about his visit in a letter to her sister: "President Lincoln visited our hospital a few days since. When the medical directors wanted to call his attention to the appointments of the hospital, he said: 'Gentlemen, you know better than I *how to conduct* these hospitals, but I came here to take by the hand the men who have achieved our glorious victories.' After that the men who were able stood in line and he shook hands with them—and the others, he went to their bedsides and spoke to *them*. He assured us the war would be over in six weeks."

Suddenly Lincoln received bad news from Washington: Seward had been thrown from his carriage and had sustained serious damage to his shoulder bone! That accident hastened Lincoln back to Washington. He explained to General Grant by letter: "Secretary Seward was thrown from his carriage yesterday and seriously injured. This, with other matters, will take me to Washington soon."

April 7 was Lincoln's last full day at City Point. General Sheridan, smashing victoriously at the Confederates, telegraphed Grant: "If the thing is pressed I think that Lee will surrender." Grant sent Sheridan's dispatch to Lincoln. The President replied to Grant: "Let the *thing* be pressed."

Lincoln on the following day, the 8th, accompanied by Mrs. Lincoln, son Tad, and several guests, started on the return trip to Washington aboard the *River Queen*. Among his guests was the young French lawyer and journalist, the Marquis Adolphe de Chambrun, who had married Lafayette's granddaughter and had witnessed Lincoln's Second Inauguration.

Lincoln suggested that the Army band play the "Marseillaise," in Chambrun's honor. Then he asked the Marquis if he had ever heard of the song, "Dixie." The Frenchman admitted that he had not. Lincoln explained: "The tune is Federal property. It belongs to us, and, at any rate, it is good to show the rebels that with us they will be free to hear it again." The President then asked the surprised musicians to play "Dixie."

Lincoln was described by Chambrun as the *River Queen* left the City Point wharf: "At ten o'clock our boat steamed off. Mr. Lincoln stood a long while looking at the spot we were leaving. Mr. Lincoln's mind seemed absorbed in the many thoughts suggested by this scene, and we saw him still pursue his meditation long after the quickened speed of the steamer had removed it forever from him."

The President and his party reached Washington on Palm Sunday, April 9, 1865. As he, the First Lady, Tad, and Chambrun rode toward the White House in their carriage, Mrs. Lincoln felt fearful and remarked to the Marquis: "That city is filled with our enemies." When the President heard this, he raised his arm and somewhat impatiently retorted: "Enemies! We must never speak of that."

XIV

As Lincoln and his party approached Washington from City Point, the most exhilaratingly pleasant of all developments for the Union cause was transpiring in the village of Appomattox Court House, Virginia.

The situation of General Robert E. Lee's Army of Northern Virginia had grown both hopeless and helpless. General Grant's overwhelming columns, so well manned, provisioned and armed, had effectively cut off the Confederates' escape. Not only were the Southern soldiers trapped but their food was nearly exhausted and their spirits had sagged into defeatism. Notes had already passed between Lee and Grant, looking to a cessation of hostilities. The Union commander-in-chief had made known his desire to avoid further effusion of blood on battlefields. Lee two days before had asked Grant for terms of surrender. And on Palm Sunday, the 9th, the two opposing commanders met at a house owned by Major Wilmer McLean.

Terms of surrender were discussed by Grant and Lee and their respective aides. Officers and men of Lee's command, it was agreed, were to be released on giving their paroles not to take up arms against the United States until exchanged. Confederate arms, artillery, and public property were to be turned over to the Federal forces. Then Grant added: "This will not embrace the side arms of the officers, nor their private horses and baggage." Lee was reportedly visibly touched by this concession which he declared would have a happy effect upon his still proud army. Lee also inquired whether his private soldiers in cavalry and artillery could retain their horses. Grant graciously replied that he would issue orders that all men of the Confederate army who claimed to own a horse or mule would be permitted to take them home "to work their little farms." Lee did not offer his sword, nor did Grant ask for it. All portended a harmonious reconciliation between North and South in future.

Lee, after surrendering his depleted and defeated army to Grant, rode back to his own lines. He spoke to some of his idolizing troops who had followed him through the fierce fire of the Peninsula, Malvern Hill, Second Manassas, Antietam, Fredericksburg, Chancellorsville, Gettysburg, the Wilderness, Cold Harbor, Petersburg, and lesser theaters of warfare. Filled with emotion, "Marse Robert" could only tell them: "Men, we have fought through the war together. I have done the best I could for you. My heart is too full to say more." And soon, mounted on his horse, "Traveller," he headed back to Richmond.

The Confederate star had set. The Union had emerged triumphant.

XV

Lincoln, immediately upon reaching Washington on the 9th, rushed to see the invalided Seward.

The President gave to his Secretary of State, all bandaged up, an account of his Richmond visit and Grant's victory over Lee—"throwing himself, in his almost boyish exultation, at full length across the bed, supporting his head upon one hand." He told Seward: "And now for a day of Thanksgiving!" But Seward, with characteristic caution even in his illness, mumbled through his bandages and gauze that Sherman had not yet captured Johnston's army in North Carolina. The Secretary urged that the President postpone a national day of celebration "until the result of Sherman's combinations was known." Lincoln agreed and there gave up his intention of proclaiming a day of thanksgiving at once. Then he tiptoed out of Seward's room as the Secretary drowsed off into sleep.

Lincoln that night told his wife the felicitous news of Lee's surrender. And the First Lady wrote Senator Sumner the following morning:

"Mr. L. told me the news, last night at ten o'clock, that Lee & his Army were in our hands. The crowds around the house have been immense, in the midst of the bands playing, they break forth into singing."

Washington, like the rest of the North and loyal border regions, went wild with ecstatic joy and boisterous celebrations. Capital newspaper correspondents wrote their stories about Lee's surrender, put the exhilarating tidings on the wires, and embarked on a drunken spree; or, as Lincoln's young California friend, Noah Brooks, scheduled to succeed Nicolay as the President's secretary, phrased it, "unbent themselves in a private and exclusive jollification." Cannon boomed all over Washington on the 10th, exuberant crowds ran happily through the streets, toasted Lincoln and the Union, and serenaded the White House.

On that evening of April 10, Lincoln was serenaded by a particularly victory-crazed and joyful crowd who packed into the Executive Mansion grounds, cheering lustily and calling for the President. He came to a huge open window. He addressed them a few words, and requested the band to play—of all songs!—"Dixie." "I see you have a band of music with you," Lincoln observed. And he told them: "I have always thought 'Dixie' one of the best tunes I have ever heard. Our adversaries over the way attempted to appropriate it, but I insisted yesterday that we fairly captured it. I presented the question to the Attorney-General, and he gave as his legal opinion that it is our lawful prize. I now request the band to favor me with its performance."

The band played "Dixie."

Then the President told the crowd that he would address them formally from the same place on the following evening, the 11th.

XVI

Tuesday, April 11, 1865, proved busy, with all of the President's hours crowded.

He was sending on a mission to Richmond his young Illinois friend, former part time law partner on the Illinois Eighth judicial circuit, and sometime bodyguard, United States Marshal Ward H. Lamon of the District of Columbia. Lincoln made out a pass: "Allow the bearer, W. H. Lamon & friend, with ordinary baggage, to pass from Washington to Richmond and return."

Also, there was for Lincoln deep concentration about reconstruction in Louisiana, Tennessee, Arkansas, and Virginia. Only the day before he had held a lengthy conversation about the restoration of the Old Dominion with Governor Francis H. Pierpont of the "Restored" State of Virginia.

Also there loomed matters of vastly lesser significance than reconstruction, such as the case of a half-breed Quawpaw Indian, Robert P. Lombard, under court martial sentence on a conviction for stealing cattle from Federal-occupied Indian Territory. Lincoln's agent for the Seminole Indians had written the President that Lombard had a family and was useful in controlling his tribe. Lincoln's order to Attorney-General Speed about Lombard read: "Pardon & send to tribe."

That evening of the 11th, when Lincoln would deliver his promised speech from a White House window, was misty in Washington. But the illuminated dome of the Capitol could be seen miles away through the moist air. Arlington House, General Lee's old home across the Potomac, blazed brilliantly, lighted with exploding rockets and colored candles on its lawn, where the ex-slaves sang "The Year of Jubilee."

Immense throngs, carrying flags and banners, with victory slogans in bold type, accompanied by blaring bands, surged boisterously and exuberantly into the semi-circular avenue in front of the White House. After repeated calls, loud and enthusiastic, the President appeared at the window, spontaneously touching off outbursts of acclaim and expressed hero-worshipping. Lincoln addressed them, chiefly on reconstruction as it applied particularly to Louisiana.

From a point of concealment behind the window drapery, Noah Brooks, scheduled to succeed Nicolay as Lincoln's secretary, held a candle as the President read his words. Little Tad, scrambling on the floor at his father's feet, caught each page of manuscript as the President finished reading it and dropped it, the boy imploring his parent to send down "another." The vast throngs outside, their faces illuminated by lights that burned in festive array in the misty darkness, listened to each word of the President.

In that speech Lincoln expressed the wish to welcome the South back into the Union. The restoration of Louisiana to the Union, as recorded in the previous chapter, occupied most of Lincoln's sentences. And at one point he called for very limited voting rights for Louisiana Negroes.

Among those thousands on the White House lawn who heard Lincoln speak, stood a rather theatrical and surly appearing, slim man of perhaps thirty years old, who spoke in an undertone to his companion, a brawny, low-bowed, moronic-looking giant.

Those words which John Wilkes Booth whispered to Lewis Thornton Powell (alias "Paine"), were: "That is the last speech he will ever make."

ENTER BOOTH

39

I

ENTER on stage, in the final tragic act of the great Lincoln drama, the actor in his most diabolical real-life role—John Wilkes Booth.

II

This grim perpetrator of the most significant of all American murder crimes was born near Bel Air, Maryland, in 1838, the son of the celebrated London-born actor, Junius Brutus Booth, and was distantly descended from the late eighteenth-century English exhibitionist and demagogic politician, John Wilkes, for whom he was named.

John Wilkes Booth was raised on the family farm near Bel Air. He received irregularly spaced and interrupted formal education at academies near Baltimore—at a Quaker school in Cockeysville, then at St. Timothy's Hall, an Episcopal institution in Catonsville. He grew up into a good-looking boy, spoiled by his mother and neglected by his strongly erratic actor father, who was often on tour.

During our present modern times, when a tendency to insanity is often interpreted medically as being associated with mentally defective heredity, it is revealing to glance at the temperament and conduct of Booth's famous father.

In England, theatres competed for Junius Brutus Booth's acting services when he was only twenty-one. In 1821 he came to America, and scored a series of spectacular successes as tragedian. In time he fell increasingly subject to temporary fits of insanity. On one occasion in the South in 1838 he attempted to drown himself, and one night he attacked his manager with an andiron, receiving in that fight a broken nose, which permanently marred his handsome countenance and somewhat nasalized his melodious voice. From that time he performed in the theatre less frequently.

Owing to his attacks of madness, his intemperance, and his irresponsibility, this famous father of John Wilkes Booth broke his theatrical engagements with reckless frequency, and on more than one occasion, when irritated or enraged, he rushed forward to the footlights and spewed forth epithets of contempt and invective at the audience. But his public, a huge one, usually forgave him because of his unquestioned acting artistry. The senior Booth constantly dominated the stage over the other players by the passion and fire of his performances. His best roles were those of villains and rogues, and his talents showed exceptionally well when, on stage, he depicted unrestrained ambition, jealousy, hatred, fear, and revenge. Junius Brutus Booth died in 1852, when his son, John, was fourteen.

John, as a boy, demonstrated traces of his father's paucity of mental balance. Once he drove a sleigh in July across the hot Maryland dirt roads. He revealed sadistic traits, and once exterminated all the cats on his father's farm for sheer pleasure.

III

Early attracted to the stage, John made his debut at nineteen at the St. Charles Theatre, Baltimore. During that 1857-58 season he played minor roles in Philadelphia and was frequently hissed by the audience for failure to learn his lines adequately. He developed into an actor of average ability and portrayed Shakespearan roles and others, as did his older brothers, Edwin and Junius Brutus, Jr.

John engaged an "agent" who was described by a contemporary as "a trumpeter who goes on before, writing the notices which you see in the editorial columns of country papers and counting noses at the theatre doors." Booth's agent was Matthew Canning, who succeeded in contracting for good parts for John in Alabama and other parts of the South.

One of his most frequent roles was that of Richard III, which had been so perfectly performed by his late father.

Booth enjoyed handsome looks. He possessed a dark, romantic physical attractiveness. He had skin of ivory color, very silky black hair, a mustache of the same hue, and lustrous, heavy-lidded eyes, an appearance that proved fatal to more than one of the feminine sex—so the famed actress, Clara Morris, has enlightened posterity. He resembled Poe, but was considered vastly better looking. In dress he seemed the picture of nonchalant dandyism. He wore a claret-colored coat with velvet lapels, a pale buff waistcoat and dove-gray trousers strapped down under his boots, and a wide-brimmed tropical-straw hat. At times he wore a long, flowing cape, hiding his bowlegs in his theatrical vanity.

John Wilkes Booth attracted women more magnetically than his more theatrically talented brother, Edwin. "For every woman who ran after Edwin Booth," concludes Eleanor Ruggles, biographer of Edwin, "there were two running after John's elegant figure in its stylish accoutrements." Hotel maids tore his bed apart continuously for the ecstacy of making it up again. Clara Morris felt John's technique applied to her as, with sweeping bow characteristic of continental Europe, he gallantly kissed her fingers. Miss Ruggles gives assurances on a still bewildering point: "He never seduced a girl he knew was pure." He had at least one close escape when, in an Indiana town in 1861, Henrietta Irving, an actress, attacked him with a dirk and then stabbed herself almost fatally.

John was rich in thespian-inspired "ham," and he was often prone to give impassioned gestures on stage. He rendered the death of Richard III in such spectacularly dramatic portrayal as to astound other actors, who considered his performances marked more by vigor than artistic polish. He wielded a dirk so realistically at Albany that he slightly stabbed himself accidentally, the dispatch from that city reporting: "*Albany, Tuesday, Feb. 12, 1861:* J. Wilkes Booth, a tragedian, met with an accident at the Gayety Theatre this evening by falling on his dagger, and inflicting a muscular wound under his right arm between one and two inches in depth. It is not serious in character, however." That was on President-elect Lincoln's fifty-second birthday, and he would pass through the New York state capital town six days later, en route to Washington for his First Inauguration. Fort Sumter's fall was another two months off.

Booth was appraised by Kate Reignolds, who played opposite him. She called him a "sad-faced handsome, passionate boy" who had "more of the native fire and fury of his great father than any of his family" but was "undisciplined on the stage as off." Miss Reignolds noted: "When he fought, it was no stage fight." She told about some of her own acting experiences opposite him: "In *Othello,* when, in fiery remorse, he rushed to the bed of Desdemona after the murder, I used to gather myself together and hold my breath, lest the bang his scimitar gave when he threw himself at me should force me back to life with a shriek." Of her encounter with Booth, when she played Juliet to his Romeo, Miss Reignolds revealed: "The curtain fell on Romeo with a sprained thumb, a good deal of hair on his sleeve, Juliet in rags and two white satin shoes lying in the corner of the stage." She also noted about John: "The stage door was always blocked with silly women waiting to catch a glimpse, as he passed, of his superb face and figure."

Of Booth's exhibitionism on stage, his great leaps impressed John T. Ford, part owner of Ford's Theatre in Washington, more than any of his acting techniques. Ford told how Booth introduced the most spectacular and highest of his leaps in the "witch" scene of *Macbeth.* In that portrayal Booth jumped from a rock higher than any box in his theatre, Ford revealed, making the landing on stage with ease. Such jumps inspired the Baltimore *Sun's* dramatic critic to refer to him as a "gymnastic actor."

Booth in mid-March, 1862, made his New York City debut at Mary Provost's Theatre (formerly Wallack's), where he portrayed Richard III. The New York *Herald* gave him an excellent notice:

"Mr. Booth undertook no small task when he attempted to act a character in which his father was famous, and which his brother, Edwin, plays so well; but the result justifies the undertaking. . . . He reads the play capitally, and makes all the well known points with ample effect. But in the last act he created a veritable sensation. His face blackened and smeared with blood, he seemed Richard himself; and his combat with Richmond [played by E. L. Tilton] was a masterpiece. An audience packed and crammed beyond the usual limits of the theatre applauded him to the echo. Mr. Booth has much experience in the provinces, and his conception and rendition are most mature, his self-possession extraordinary."

The following year, 1863, in a blaze of newspaper publicity, Booth opened at Grover's Theatre in Washington, portraying Richard III. The Washington *Evening Star,* in its advertising announcement, sounded the call in bold print letters with theatrical trumpetry:

GROVER'S THEATRE

Saturday Evening, April 11, 1863

J. WILKES BOOTH

THE PRIDE OF THE AMERICAN PEOPLE

THE YOUNGEST TRAGEDIAN IN THE WORLD

Son of the great
Junius Brutus Booth
and brother and artistic rival of
Edwin Booth
Who is engaged to commence this evening
ONLY SEVEN NIGHTS

Later that season, on November 9, Booth acted the role of an erratic, love-disillusioned sculptor in *The Marble Heart* at Ford's Theatre in Washington. In the audience sat President Lincoln.

IV

Booth, early in 1864, contracted slight bronchial trouble—a frightening ailment for an actor. He went to Federal-occupied New Orleans in March, when he opened at the St. Charles Theatre with a performance as Richard III again. "It is a matter of regret," noted the New Orleans *Times,* "that he is at present laboring under a severe hoarseness, in consequence of which his efforts have been much less satisfactory to himself than to his friends." Later issues were more critical of his acting and voice in the Louisiana metropolis. By the end of that month, he ended his presentations at the St. Charles, the theatre management publicly announcing its regret that he was forced to cancel future performances "at the suggestion of his medical adviser."

After his ill-fated New Orleans tour, Booth played less often after returning North. The Booth family's critical biographer, Kimmel, concluded: "The day of reckoning had arrived. Wilkes' 'hoarseness' was not due to a bronchial infection resulting from a severe cold but was the reprisal from the lack of study and training in voice control. He knew his future as a star was doomed."

It seemed tragic enough: His career jeopardized at the immature age of twenty-six in 1864! But he had parsimoniously saved most of his money, unlike average actors of his day. He spent only on his personal and theatrical wardrobe and traveling expenses. He was still a bachelor, with neither wife nor family to support, and it is not of record that he sent funds home to his mother, living in New York. One estimate is that in one year of his brief career as a star he earned nearly $20,000, a colossal sum for his day.

So he bought shares in oil lands at Franklin, in western Pennsylvania. In that region five years earlier Edwin L. Drake, a former railroad conductor, had struck oil, which some called "grease," by successfully drilling a well near Titusville. During 1864 Booth spent considerable time in that Pennsylvania oil vicinity. But as with nearly every actor, he could not dismiss the theatre from his mind, and he played roles when he could obtain them.

V

Booth, not unlike his celebrated father, acted not quite mentally normal, on stage or off. Nor were his sympathies and abnormally militant love for the South of rational proportions.

The pending war of brothers had caused a breach among the Booths, as it had to thousands of other American families. Most of the Booth clan remained ostensibly neutral, but Edwin supported the Union. John openly, belligerently, and vociferously defended the Confederacy.

John's sister, Mrs. Asia Booth Clarke, left a memoir—not published until 1938, numerous years after her death—in which she maintained that her brother, whom she and the rest of the family called "Wilkes," had served as a blockade runner for the South, smuggling quinine into the Confederacy in his theatre luggage. Mrs. Clarke also gave credence to rumors that he had acted as a Southern spy for a while. But this is not otherwise verified.

John's more talented brother, Edwin, subsequently wrote privately in one of his rare letters about his defective-minded kin: "My brother John was a rattle-pated fellow, filled with Quixotic notions. . . . We used to laugh at his patriotic froth whenever secession was discussed. That he was insane on that one point, no one who knew him well can doubt. . . . He declared that Lincoln would be made king of America. I asked him once why he did not join the Confederate army. To which he replied: 'I promised mother I would keep out of the quarrel, if possible, and I am sorry I said so.' . . . All of his theatrical friends speak of him as a poor, crazy boy, and such his family think of him."

Booth, in 1863 playing at Ben De Bar's Theatre in St. Louis, and a member of the stock company, T. L. Conner, were arrested for utterances against Lincoln's administration. Conner was committed to a military prison, while Booth was hailed before Colonel H. L. McConnell and accused of having said that he "wished the whole damn government would go to hell." Wilkes was released when he paid a fine and took an oath of allegiance to the Union. The theatre owner, De Bar, a British subject and a strong secessionist sympathizer, had his establishment frequented largely by pro-Southern zealots.

Booth, sometime in 1864, penned a lengthy letter, addressed "To Whom It May Concern," which he sealed in an envelope and gave to his brother-in-law, John Sleeper Clarke.

That letter by Booth, apparently not revealed to the public until immediately after he had performed his evil deed in April, 1865, began, "*My Dear Sir:* You may use this as you think best." He spewed forth written words expressing his "lasting condemnation of the North," and added, "I have ever held that the South were right. The very nomination of Abraham Lincoln, four years ago, spoke plainly of war upon Southern rights and institutions. . . . This country was formed for the *white,* not for the black man." He condemned Lincoln's war policy as one of "total annihilation" of the South. He declared fervently, "My love (as things stand to-day) is for the South alone." He ended this rambling anti-Lincoln epistle, "*A Confederate doing his duty upon his own responsibility,* J. Wilkes Booth."

Booth always acted off stage as a man of extreme reticence, rarely revealing his inner thoughts to anyone about what he proposed to do, despite his outspoken condemnation of the Union fight against the South. His brother-in-law, Clarke, deplored what he called "the secretiveness of the whole Booth race."

In his secretive and infected imagination, Booth in the autumn of 1864, when Lincoln was running for re-election, started forming plans to abduct the President.

In his mind ran a stupendous scheme to seize Lincoln, spirit him out of Washington at the point of gun and dagger, down through the disloyal southern Maryland counties to the Potomac River, ferry him across to Virginia, carry him to Richmond, and there turn him over to the Confederate authorities. There in the secession capital the President would be detained until the war was ended, or until all Confederate prisoners held by the Federals were freed. General Grant had previously put a stop to the exchange of prisoners of war.

Aside from his unbridled, fanatically extreme Southern bias, what were Booth's motives, particularly in his later decision to murder Lincoln?

An abnormally distorted ambition to be never forgotten after he himself was dead and also a diseased mentality, perhaps inherited from his father, are the prime explanations given by men who knew Booth well. One of his classmates at St. Timothy's Hall maintained: "It was a 'name in history' he sought. A glorious career he thought of by day and dreamed of by night. He always said he would 'make his name remembered by succeeding generations.' " And he did, in the grimmest of styles. Another close Booth associate, Charles Warwick, presented this explanation; "The whole proceeding can be accounted for in no other way than on the score of insanity."

VI

Booth, in September, 1864, enrolled his first two recruits. Samuel Bland Arnold and Michael O'Laughlin.

Arnold, a native Marylander like Booth and his fellow student at St. Timothy's Hall in Catonsville a dozen years before, had served in the Confederate army, then "left" that service, although retaining his strong secession sympathies. O'Laughlin, also a born Marylander and former Confederate soldier, had got out of the Southern army, too, and then had engaged in the feed and produce business at Baltimore. O'Laughlin was described as a small, quiet, delicate-appearing young man with black hair and heavy mustache.

During that September, Booth met Arnold and O'Laughlin in confidential conclave at Barnum's Hotel in Baltimore.

The following month, October, found Booth in Canada, registering at the swank St. Lawrence Hall in Montreal. He recorded his name and his address as Baltimore. That hostelry was known as a favorite rendezvous of Confederate agents then operating in Canada—a circumstance which inspired a few later writers hastily and erroneously to conclude that Jefferson Davis' regime at Richmond was in close conspiracy with Booth to kidnap or kill Lincoln.

In Montreal the prospective kidnapper of the President placed his theatrical wardrobe in safe custody and deposited $700 in a bank. By this time he was supposed to have sold out his western Pennsylvania oil holdings.

Booth was back in the United States by late October. Early the next month he sank into deeper despair when Lincoln was overwhelmingly re-elected President. "When I told him," later recalled his brother, Edwin, "that I had voted for Lincoln's re-election, he expressed deep regret."

John, although absorbed in details of how the President could best be abducted, did not completely forget the theatre. On November 25 he appeared with his two brothers, Edwin and Junius Brutus, Jr., in Shakespeare's *Julius Caesar* at the Winter Garden in New York. It was presented for the benefit of the fund with which to erect a statue of the Bard of Avon in Central Park. Edwin played Brutus, Junius Brutus portrayed Cassius, and John himself was seen in Marc Antony's role. The *Herald's* dramatic critic reviewed it: "The audience was fairly carried from the first entrance of the three brothers side by side. Brutus was individualized with great force and distinctness—Cassius was brought out equally well—and if there was less of real personality given to Mark Anthony (sic), the fault was rather in the part than the actor."

That audience who saw John and his two brothers perform together was "fairly carried" by something besides the three portrayals on stage. The brothers' acting was horribly interrupted by a necessary invasion of the theatre by firemen dragging hose and other flame-fighting apparatus. A fire in the Lefarge House, a hotel next door, forced them to break into the Winter Garden as John, Edwin, and Junius Brutus Booth were spouting Shakespeare's stanzas. That evening, Friday the 25th, an attempt was being made in various parts of New York City to set fire to at least six hotels, Barnum's Museum, and other buildings almost simultaneously by deliberately setting torches to inflammatory material. The press blamed this wholesale arson activity on incendiary Southern sympathizers.

It was a coincidence that John Wilkes Booth should have been there at that time. Another arresting coincidence lay in the circumstance that in the play, *Julius Caesar,* selected for that performance by the three brothers, *"Filii Patri Digniores,"* as the playbill advertised them, John should have enacted Marc Antony, friend of law and order as well as the friend of the Roman nation's murdered ruler, Caesar.

VII

Booth spent considerable time going into and out of Washington during December.

In that last month of 1864 he formed a friendship with John H. Surratt, son of a widow, Mrs. Mary H. Surratt, who had kept a tavern in Surrattsville, Maryland, but was now conducting a boarding house in Washington.

John Surratt two years before had left a Catholic seminary, where he had been studying for the priesthood, a coincidence that inspired bigoted anti-Roman zealots later to write trashy, lie-studded pamphlets inferring that somehow the Vatican was implicated in the assassination of Lincoln! Surratt had served as a Confederate dispatch-rider between the North and Richmond.

Surratt eagerly entered into Booth's plans to abduct the President. "In the fall of 1864 I was introduced to John Wilkes Booth," he revealed six years later. Booth whispered to him: "It is to kidnap President Lincoln and carry him off to Richmond." Surratt confessed in that later account: "I believed it practical at the time. . . . I was led by a desire to assist the South in gaining her independence. Such a thing as the assassination of Mr. Lincoln I never heard spoken by any of the parties—never!"

Surratt gained for Booth two other accomplices, the middle-aged George E. Atzerodt and the youthful David Herold.

The German-born Atzerodt, a coach painter in Port Tobacco, Maryland, had been secretly ferrying Confederate sympathizers back and forth across the Potomac River. He was described as "a short, thick-set, round-shouldered, brawny-armed man, with a stupid expression, high cheek bones, a sallow complexion, small grayish-blue eyes, tangled light brown hair, and straggling sandy whiskers and mustache." Herold, only nineteen years old, feeble-minded and reckless son of a government naval-stores clerk, had worked in a Washington drug store. Herold fell mesmerized under Booth's spell, and he admiringly told another: "Booth is a good fellow."

Not until two months later, on March 1, 1865, did Booth add the last and most brutal conspirator to his band—big, brawny, mentally subnormal twenty-year-old Lewis Thornton Powell, who used the alias, "Paine." This young giant, son of a Florida clergyman, had served in the Confederate army, been wounded at Gettysburg, was captured by Federals, then escaped, and was now wandering, friendless, penniless, and without food, through Baltimore.

Powell's lawyer based part of his later defense of Powell on the thorough poisoning of his mind against Lincoln in the South: "This is what he [Powell] heard in Florida, among the village politicians. This is what he read in the Richmond papers, in the orders of the [Confederate] generals, in the gossip of the camp fire, in the letters he got from home. . . . Every Southern lass that waved her handkerchief toward him repeated it; every prisoner returned from Northern prisons told it. Lincoln, the oppressor, was in the air."

Powell's father, the Reverend Powell of Live Oak, Florida, within a year wrote about his son to another clergyman: "Lewis left home to enlist in the war against the wish of the whole family. Previous and up to the time of his leaving home he was very pious and consistent, was much respected by all of his associates, and took great interest in the young men's prayer meeting and all other religious services."

Booth supplied Powell with funds, though just how much is impossible to determine. Also, according to the clergyman who later spiritually administered to Powell in his death cell before he was hanged, Powell confided that Booth had appealed to him "with dreams of glory and the lasting gratitude of the Southern people."

Thus by the start of March, 1865, Booth had his kidnapping crew organized, ready for action—himself, Samuel B. Arnold, Michael O'Laughlin, John H. Surratt, George E. Atzerodt, David Herold, and Lewis Thornton Powell. Except for the middle-aged Atzerodt, all were young in years, still younger in mentality, like the twenty-seven-year-old Booth himself.

VIII

Booth, on Lincoln's Second Inauguration Day, March 4, mixed among the crowds who besieged the Capitol, inside and outside, just before Lincoln took the presidential oath.

An obstreperous man, later positively identified as John Wilkes Booth by a Capitol Police detective, John W. Westfall, on duty there, broke through the police line and dashed toward the inauguration platform. He was seized by Westfall. A scuffle followed, and police and other Inauguration guards hustled him away, throwing him back into the crowd with an angry warning, according to Westfall, who identified Booth in later weeks, from pictures. The story rests on not unimpeachable evidence.

On that Inauguration Day, a fellow actor and friend of Booth, John McCullough, who later became a stage favorite, visited Booth at his room in the National Hotel. McCullough entered without knocking. "At the first wink," McCullough alleged in later years, "I saw Booth sitting behind a table, on which was a map, a knife, and a pistol. He had gauntlets on his hands, spurs on his boots, and a military hat of a slouch character on his head." When McCullough asked, "John, what in the name of sense is the matter with you?" Booth arrested himself and answered: "Why, how are you?"

Booth's sister declared: "Wilkes had a great and sincere affection for John McCullough as a man and an unbounded admiration for him as an actor."

One month later Booth was in New York, drinking with an actor acquaintance, Samuel K. Chester. According to Chester, who testified two months later, under oath, Booth pounded the table and told him: "What an excellent chance I had to kill the President, if I had wished, on inauguration day!"

Two weeks following Inauguration Day, on March 17, Booth and his conspiratorial dupes made an attempt to kidnap Lincoln. All were armed, and they lay in wait for the President, ready to seize him, when he was expected to drive near the Soldiers' Home.

But Lincoln did not put in an appearance!

As disclosed by John Surratt nearly six years later in a public lecture at Rockville, Maryland, the plan was to abduct the President when he attended an entertainment at the army hospital on Seventh Street. Booth, Surratt, and the others were to seize Lincoln's carriage, have one of them mount the box and drive fast with the captured Chief Executive for southern Maryland via Benning's bridge, over the eastern branch of the Potomac. They felt confident that, given this head start, the Federal cavalry could not overtake them, since they would be mounted on fast horses and they knew the country well. They planned to abandon the carriage after leaving the Washington city limits. But their plan failed when Lincoln did not ride through the vicinity at that time.

Arnold also told about that abortive abduction attempt in his reminiscences:

"On the 17th day of March, 1865, about two o'clock Booth and Herold met O'Laughlin and myself. Booth stated that he was told the President was going to attend a Theatrical performance out on 7th street, at a soldiers encampment or Hospital at the outer edge of the city. Booth had previously sent a small black box (containing 2 carbines, a monkey wrench, amunition (sic) & piece of rope) by the Porter of the National Hotel to our room at Mrs. Van Tynes. . . . The understanding was that Herold was to take the box with Booth's horse and buggy to Surrattsville or T. B. and there meet us in case the abduction was successful. . . . O'Laughlin returned and we took our dinner at the Franklin Hotel as usual.

"After dinner we met Booth and accompanied him to a livery stable near the Patent Office at which place Booth obtained horses for us. O'Laughlin and myself rode to our room on D. Street and made all our necessary arrangements. Each arming himself—O'Laughlin and myself rode out to where the performance was to take place. . . . We stopped at a resteraunt (sic). Whilst in there Atzerodt came in who had just arrived with Payne [Powell]. A short time after Booth and Surratt came in and we drank together. Booth made enquires (sic) at the encampment at which place the performance was to be held, and learned he, the President, was not there. After telling us this we separated . . .

"O'Laughlin and myself left Washington on the 20th day of March and went to Baltimore. Booth went to New York and thus I thought the whole affair abandoned. I then told my family I had ceased business in Washington and severed my connections with Booth."

Booth, frustrated in his effort to kidnap Lincoln, played a performance, the role of "Pescara" in *The Apostate,* at Ford's Theatre on the following day, the 18th. It was his last performance on stage—except for the grim real-life roles he would enact within a month.

Booth and his fellow conspirators, fearing that their plans would be now suspected, separated. Arnold and O'Laughlin returned to Maryland. Surratt went, first to Richmond, then up to Canada. Booth checked out of his National Hotel room on March 21, left Washington, and returned four days later.

Soon Booth received a letter, addressed to him as "Dear John," dated March 27, 1865—from Arnold. It was bad news to him. Arnold was not returning to Washington to continue in this kidnapping game! At least, Arnold was not going to continue as a party to it at that time. Grown frightened at possible consequences and now frigid toward Booth's macabre schemes, Arnold advised Booth in that letter:

> I told my parents I had ceased with you. Can I, then, under the existing circumstances, come as you request? You know full well that the G———t [Government] suspicions that something is going on there; therefore, the undertaking is becoming more complicated. Why not, for the present, desist, for various reasons, which, if you look into, you can readily see, without my making any mention thereof. You, nor any one, can censure me for my present course. You have been its cause, for how can I now come after telling them I had left you? Suspicion rests upon me now from my whole family, and even parties in the county [Baltimore County]. None, no not one, were more in favor of the enterprise than myself, and to-day would be there, had you not done as you have—by this I mean, manner of proceeding . . . Time more propitious will arrive. Do not act rashly or in haste. I would prefer your first query, 'go see how it will be taken at R———d [Richmond], and ere long I shall be better prepared to again be with you.

Arnold signed this discouraging message to Booth: "Your friend, Sam.

Soon Arnold's friend, Michael O'Laughlin, also abandoned Booth's abduction aberration.

Booth departed from Washington again on April 1. The following day he was jolted by crushing news: Richmond fell to the Federals!

His sister, Mrs. Asia Booth Clarke, subsequently insisted: "If Wilkes was mad, his mind lost its balance between the fall of Richmond and the terrific end."

By now, the opening days of April, Booth had lost the loyalty of Arnold, O'Laughlin, and John Surratt—all three had left Washington and had no intention of rejoining him. But he still held the dogmatic devotion of his other dupes, Powell, Atzerodt, and Herold.

IX

Booth was soon back in Washington after more trips—"arrived April 8th, room 228," testified the National Hotel clerk, G. W. Bunker.

The following day General Lee surrendered to General Grant. That threw Booth into an access of unbridled malice and unrestrained rage, akin to sheer madness. Returned to the national capital on this day, the 9th, was also President Lincoln, after his stay at City Point.

Two days after Lincoln's April 11 speech on the White House lawn concerning Louisiana reconstruction, as most of Washington prepared to celebrate Lee's surrender in spectacular style, drinking, shouting, cheering, shooting off Roman candles, and watching the illumination of buildings, Booth dropped in to see C. D. Hess, manager of Grover's Theatre. A story had circulated that President Lincoln would attend a performance at Grover's on the following night, Friday the fourteenth. But as Hess himself told later about Booth's visit to him:

"He came into the office [of Grover's Theatre] some time during the afternoon, I think, of Thursday, interrupted me and the prompter of the theatre in reading a manuscript, seated himself in a chair, and entered upon the subject of the illumination. . . . The next night [Friday] would be a great night of illumination, that being the celebration of the fall of Sumter. He asked me the question,—my impression is his words were, 'Do you intend,' or 'Are you going to invite the President?' I think my reply was, 'Yes; that reminds me I must send that invitation.' I had had it in my mind for several days to invite the Presidential party down on that night—on the night of the 14th."

Booth left Grover's Theatre. Within a matter of hours, after visiting Hess on that Thursday the 13th, he made an entry into his diary. Under dateline, "April 13, 14, Friday the Ides," Booth confided to his private day-book: "Until to-day nothing was ever thought of sacrificing to our country's wrongs. For six months we had worked to capture. But our cause being almost lost, something decisive & great must be done."

FATEFUL FRIDAY

40

I

"I INTEND to adopt the advice of my friends and use due precaution."

President Lincoln sent those words of assurance to the anxious James H. Van Alen on Friday, April 14, 1865. It was in reply to Van Alen's plea that the President provide himself with adequate guards and not expose himself to possible assailants, as he had recklessly done during his recent visit to Richmond.

Lincoln, nonetheless, was negligent about his own personal protection and certainly did not "use due precaution" on that day, as he had just promised Van Alen.

On that Friday Lincoln had no regular full-time bodyguard assigned to him. Three days earlier he had even sent on a special mission to Virginia his loyal Illinois friend and United States Marshal for the District of Columbia, big, burly, well-armed Ward Hill Lamon, who often constituted himself Lincoln's bodyguard.

II

Friday the 14th in mid-April, 1865, dawned balmy and fair in the national capital city—good pre-summer Washington weather. One of Lincoln's military escorts, Smith Stimmel of the Union Light Guard, phrased it: "The fourteenth of April was warm, calm and beautiful, an ideal spring day. All nature seemed to bask in the warm sunlight of assured peace, and the general public had settled down to dream of a glorious future for our reunited country."

Throughout the North and border regions, too, an exhilarating Friday was forecast, and not alone because of the salubrious spring climate. The four-year fratricidal fight had passed. The harrowing holocaust, when hundreds of thousands of blue-clad and gray-garbed Americans had shed each others' blood on battlefields, had happily ended. Lee had surrendered the ragged remnants of his once mighty Army of Northern Virginia to Grant less than one week before, and the capitulation of General "Joe" Johnston's remaining Confederate force to General Sherman in North Carolina was expected in only a matter of days. Secretary of War Stanton, the day before, had sent out orders to cease the drafting of men for the Union armies.

Lincoln had selected the 14th as a seemly day for the re-raising on the Fort Sumter ruins of the identical stars-and-stripes flag that Major (now General) Robert Anderson had been forced to haul down in surrender exactly four years before.

That day, too, was Good Friday on the Christian church calendar, and as such was solemnly observed by masses of Americans in prayer, fasting, and serious meditation.

On that Friday morning the Washington newspapers carried an announcement: "Lieutenant General Grant, President and Mrs. Lincoln and ladies will occupy the state box at Ford's Theatre to-night to witness Laura Keene's Company in Tom Taylor's *Our American Cousin.*"

III

President Lincoln rose early that Friday morning, according to his custom. He went to his office about seven o'clock and requested, by note, that Secretary Seward's son, Acting Secretary of State Frederick W. Seward, have the Cabinet assembled for an eleven o'clock meeting.

The President then had breakfast with his son, Captain Robert Todd Lincoln, just returned from the Virginia front.

Bob showed his father a picture of General Lee. "It is a good face, it is the face of a noble man. I am glad that the war is over at last," remarked Lincoln, according to the mulatto White House seamstress, Mrs. Elizabeth Keckley, in words spoken to a "ghost" writer three years later. Lincoln then addressed Bob, and according to Mrs. Keckley, told him: "You must lay aside your uniform, and return to college. I wish you to read law for three years, and at the end of that time I hope that we will be able to tell whether you will make a lawyer or not."

That morning Lincoln was visited by Schuyler Colfax of Indiana, Speaker of Congress. The President spoke to him about "the policy to be adopted by the Administration" toward the South and also mentioned his recent visit to Richmond. He expressed a wish to accompany Colfax on his Western trip—all the way to California. But he regretted that his work in the presidency did not allow that time away from Washington. Colfax quoted the President as telling him:

"I have very large ideas of the mineral wealth of our Nation. I believe it practically inexhaustable. It abounds all over our Western country from the Rocky Mountains to the Pacific; and its development has scarcely commenced. During the war, when we were adding a couple of millions of dollars every day to our National Debt, I did not care about encouraging the increase in the volume of our precious metals. We had the country to save first. But, now that the Rebellion is overthrown, and we know pretty nearly the amount of our Debt, the more gold and silver we mine makes the payment of that Debt so much easier.

"Now I am going to encourage that in every possible way. We shall have hundreds of thousands of disbanded soldiers; and many have feared that their return home in such great numbers might paralyze industry, furnishing suddenly a greater supply of labor than there will be demand for. I am going to try to attract them to this hidden wealth of our mountain ranges, where there is room enough for all.

"Immigration, which even the War has not stopped, will land upon our shores hundreds of thousands more per year from overcrowded Europe. I intend to point them to the gold & silver that waits for them in the West. Tell the miners for me that I shall promote their interests to the utmost of my ability; because their prosperity is the prosperity of the Nation. We shall prove in a very few years that we are indeed the Treasury of the World."

Those were Lincoln's words to him, Colfax insisted, as he could recall them, explaining that he wrote them out the following day.

Lincoln, following his conference with Colfax, hastily tripped over to the War Department to his favorite spot, the telegraph office. He wanted news from General Sherman, whose army was still chasing General Johnston's exhausted forces in North Carolina. But no wire had come in from Sherman.

Lincoln returned to the White House office, where at eleven o'clock he met his Cabinet, along with General Grant, for a session.

IV

Lincoln, at that late morning Cabinet meeting, looked relaxed and free from anxiety. "I never saw Mr. Lincoln so cheerful and happy," related Secretary of the Treasury McCulloch. "The burden which had been weighing upon him for four long years had been lifted. The weary look which his face had so long worn, and which could be observed by those who knew him well, even when he was telling stories, had disappeared. It was bright and cheerful." Attorney General James Speed later recollected how well the President appeared with "shaved face, well brushed clothing and neatly combed hair and whiskers."

At that Cabinet session Lincoln confessed that he had had a peculiar dream the previous night, one which had recurred to him several times since the war had begun, a vague sense of floating toward an unknown shore. His dream meant good news from General Sherman, still pursuing General Johnston's remaining Confederate forces, the President declared, because on those previous occasions the dream had been followed in a few hours by news of a great occasion. He told his Cabinet members: "I had this strange dream again last night, and we shall, judging from the past, have great news very soon. I think it must be from Sherman. My thoughts are in that direction, as are most of yours."

Lincoln expressed his own opinion on what should happen to the fleeing and captured Confederate leaders, when Postmaster General Dennison brought up that subject. The President answered: "I should not be sorry to have them out of the country; but I should be for following them up pretty close to make sure of their going."

The spikey issue of reconstruction was discussed. There Lincoln learned that his Cabinet was divided. Stanton had a project calling for military occupation of the South as a preliminary step toward restoration of the recent Confederate states to the Union—a horrible harbinger of what was to come in post-Lincolnian years below Mason and Dixon's line. Virginia and North Carolina could be combined in a single army district. Secretary of the Navy Welles, a conservative, objected to Stanton's punitive proposal to be inflicted on the prostrate South, and favored the idea that Lincoln's administration should recognize Governor Pierpont's regime for Virginia. The President showed that, despite Stanton's radical reconstruction views, he was standing by his own moderate policy when he supported Welles's viewpoint. But to keep peace within his inner council family, Lincoln did not reject Stanton's proposal fully. He suggested that Virginia and North Carolina be dealt with separately, not ruling out the necessity for Federal occupation troops.

Lincoln was quoted by Acting Secretary of State Frederick Seward, sitting in on the meeting in absence of his injured father, as declaring: "We can't undertake to run State Governments in all these Southern

States. Their people must do that, though I reckon that, at first, they may do it badly."

Before that meeting ended, Lincoln expressed satisfaction that Congress was not in session; it had adjourned on Inauguration Day, six weeks before. He did not intend to call a special session of Congress, he had just informed Speaker Colfax. Thus it can be inferred that the President had misgivings about the Senate and the House, both of the chambers controlled by the radically dominated wing of his Republican Party. They might undo or scrap his moderate reconstruction plans as represented in the state governments that he had sponsored in Louisiana, Tennessee, and Arkansas.

"It must have been about two o'clock, when the Cabinet meeting broke up," recorded Acting Secretary Seward.

V

After the Cabinet session General Grant lingered for a while to inform the President that he and Mrs. Grant would be unable to accept his and Mrs. Lincoln's invitation to accompany them to Ford's Theatre the coming evening. The General and his wife were going to New Jersey to see their son.

Lincoln had a light lunch and returned to his office—then more of those everlasting patronage problems!

He requested his Commissioner of Indian Affairs, William P. Dole: "Please do not send off the commission of W. T. Howell, as Indian agent until the return of Mr. Harlan, and hearing from me again." The President wanted no appointments made until they were approved by his new Secretary of the Interior, James Harlan, who had not yet taken office.

Worse still, the Montgomery Blair-Henry Winter Davis party fight still flared in Maryland, with rivalries over federal jobs. Lincoln now made out a memorandum, "Concerning Maryland Appointments," shuffling the positions of Collector, Surveyor, and Naval Officer at the Port of Baltimore, the Postmaster there, the United States Marshal for that state, and other political plums over which the belligerent factions feuded.

Then Lincoln sent a note to Attorney General Speed: "Send me a Commission for William Kellogg, to be Judge in Nebraska in place of W. P. Kellogg resigned." On the previous day William P. Kellogg, an Illinois politician, had been appointed Collector of the Port of New Orleans, after resigning as Nebraska Territory judge. Still more job requests piled up on that Friday afternoon. Milton Kelley of Idaho wanted to succeed Samuel C. Parks as Associate Justice of that Territory's Supreme Court. Lincoln approved in a message to the Attorney General: "If it is definitely concluded to accept Judge Parks' resignation, as I understand it is, let the within appointment [Kelley's] be made." For a new federal Marshal of Idaho Territory the President then approved one James H. Avord in one word to Speed: "Appoint."

Next Lincoln saw a favor-hunting New Hampshire Congressman, Edward H. Rollins, and gave him a note to Stanton: "The Hon. Secretary of War, please see and hear Hon. Mr. Rollins, & oblige him if you consistently can."

On that afternoon there were pardons, reprieves, and amnesties that came before the President, involving both soldiers and civilians. There was the case of seventeen-year-old Thomas Geary of Maine, who had collected $300 in bounty from a legally draft-shunning citizen, in return for which Geary would serve in his place. The boy's mother, perhaps through her Senator or Congressman, appealed to Lincoln for his release from the army. The President signed an order: "Let Thomas Geary be discharged from the service on refunding any bounty received." Then a Senator from Maryland, John A. J. Creswell, wanted a constituent, Benjamin F. Twilley, a Confederate prisoner of the Federals at Point Lookout, in his state, released. Lincoln endorsed Senator Creswell's appeal: "Let it be done."

And so Lincoln's anteroom continued packed with people most of that afternoon, some crowding into the corridors. When Lincoln's Register of the Treasury, Lucius E. Chittenden of Vermont, called at the White House at one of those hours, he recalled subsequently: "So many were waiting, the President seemed so much occupied with pressing business, that I came away without sending in my card."

But the callers were finally disposed of, taken care of by the Chief Executive or requested to return the following day. He had an engagement to go carriage riding with Mrs. Lincoln.

Starting down the corridor, Lincoln noticed two ladies, one was Mrs. C. D. Hess, wife of the manager of Grover's Theatre, sometimes called the National Theatre. The other woman was Mrs. Hess's sister. (Only the previous day, Hess had been visited in his theatre by the actor, John Wilkes Booth, who had inquired of Hess whether Lincoln would be invited to Grover's on Friday evening).

Lincoln recognized the identity of Mrs. Hess when her name was mentioned to him, and in the White House corridor he told her how sorry he felt that he had been unable to accept her husband's invitation to attend Grover's that coming evening. Playing there would be a performance of *Aladdin! Or, The Wonderful Lamp*. It is improbable that Lincoln would have enjoyed such theatrical fare from the *Arabian Nights*. He preferred comedy and humor, and the play he would see in the evening at Ford's Theatre would be *Our American Cousin*, from the pen of Tom Taylor, editor of the British humor magazine, *Punch*. It was advertised on its playbill as the "celebrated eccentric comedy."

When Mrs. Hess and her sister informed the President that the White House conservatory was their object that afternoon, he led them to it. Lincoln also showed them a lemon tree that someone had sent him, and he gave each woman a lemon.

About three o'clock Lincoln went for the carriage ride with his wife. That occasion lingered in Mrs. Lincoln's memory. She told about it to the artist, Francis B. Carpenter, in a letter seven months later. *"The Friday,* I never saw him so supremely cheerful—his manner was even playful," she confided to Carpenter. "At three o'clock in the afternoon, he drove out with me in open carriage. . . . During the drive, he was so gay." She laughingly said to him in the carriage: "You almost startle me, by your great cheerfulness." And the First Lady quoted him as answering her: "And well may I feel so, Mary, I consider *this day,* the war has come to a close. We must *both,* be more cheerful in the future—between the war & the loss of our darling Willie—we have both been very miserable."

Plans for their future were discussed—a time still nearly four full years off, when Lincoln's second administration would expire. "My husband intended when he was through with his Presidential term, to take me and our boys to Europe," she revealed a year later. After their return from abroad, added Mary Lincoln, they "intended to go across the Rocky Mountains and go to California, where the soldiers were to be digging out gold to pay the national debt."

The President and Mrs. Lincoln returned to the White House at five o'clock.

VI

And what were John Wilkes Booth's morning and afternoon like?

Booth apparently lay awake in his National Hotel room at Washington as the clock struck midnight, proclaiming Friday, April 14. Two hours later he penned a letter to his mother in New York:

April 14—2 a.m.

Dearest Mother—I know you expect a letter from me, and am sure you will hardly forgive me. But indeed I have had nothing to write about. Everything is dull; that is, has been till last night. Everything was bright [in the illumination] and splendid. More so in my eyes if it had been a display in a nobler cause. But so goes the world. Might makes right. I only drop you these few lines to let you know I am well, and to say I have not heard from you. Excuse brevity; am in haste. Had one from Rose. With best love to you all,

I am your affectionate son ever,

John.

At that precise time or thereabouts, the "affectionate son" really found himself "in haste," as he said. He had a grotesque, fiendish thought which he now confided to his diary: "Something decisive must be done." A full diabolical day's work lay ahead. And for the next twenty and a half hours his every move was alert and energetic, each thought concentrating on human destruction in a distorted view of what must be done to save the country, especially the South. Constantly, and all day long, he mulled over details of the devilish deed. Throughout that day he and his dupes, Powell ("Paine"), Atzerodt, and Herold, were seen on foot or on horseback in various parts of Washington.

Booth, some time after sunrise, was seen by a Negro woman, Mrs. Mary J. Anderson, loitering about Ford's Theatre. She lived in the public alley behind the theatre, and she noticed the actor "by the stable" nearby. One hour later Booth went into the theatre lobby. He engaged the man at the ticket window in conversation. The ticket-seller told Booth that a box in the dress circle was being reserved for Lincoln, General Grant, and their wives for that evening's performance. Booth thanked him, then sauntered down the street.

H. Clay ("Harry") Ford, one of the theatre-owning brothers, subsequently insisted that it was he who on that morning informed Booth that Lincoln and Grant would be present at the evening performance: "About 12 M., Booth came down Tenth Street to the theatre, and stopped there to read a letter. I told him that President Lincoln and General Grant were coming to the theatre that night." Harry Ford, with the aid of one of his employees, prepared the reserved presidential box for the evening, draping the outside of the box, facing the audience, with American flags and a banner of the Treasury Department-recruited regiment and also furnishing the interior of the box with a couch and some chairs, including Ford's own horsehair rocker, in which Lincoln would sit as he watched the play.

Booth, after learning about Lincoln's intention to be present at the performance of *Our American Cousin*—a play whose plot, acts, scenes, lines, and stage timing he knew nearly from memory—walked down the street. He went into James W. Pumphrey's livery stable on C Street, and hired a high strung horse capable of swift speed. Pumphrey recorded: "He came to my stable about twelve o'clock on that day, and engaged a saddle horse . . . a small bay mare."

Booth, according to his most murderous accomplice, Powell, until that morning had expressed no intention to kill Lincoln. But by this Friday morning Booth was fully decided that the President of the United States must be removed.

VII

Booth arranged his whole plan of assassination and escape during that afternoon and early evening.

He felt at home in Ford's Theatre. He had cultivated the acquaintance of its stage employees, and had become their drinking companion at times. He entered and left the theatre at will and often had his mail sent there. The scene-shifter, Edman (known as "Edward") Spangler, who years before had worked at chores for Booth's late father, said about John: "Booth had free access to the theatre at all times, and made himself familiar with all persons connected with it."

This humble admirer of Booth was a middle-aged, hard drinking fellow, who had worked for Booth's father, and had often looked after Booth's horse. But it is said that the actor did not pay him for his hostler's work. Booth and Spangler at times drank together, like cronies. No evidence yet uncovered links him with Booth in the plot to kill Lincoln. But the actor capitalized on Spangler's devotion and counted on him to hold his horse at the rear of the theatre, ready for him when he should rush out after murdering the President.

Booth depended for success of his deadly deed on his audacity, on his familiarity with the theatre's architectural and physical layout, with its various passages and exits; and on his "timing." This last factor appeared all-important for the success of his lethal act, for he had to choose the precise minute when *Our American Cousin* would reach a suspenseful moment so that the audience's eyes would be away from the President's box and fixed on the stage, and the stage would not be crowded with actors and actresses. Preferably it would be best if only one player were on stage, for Booth's purposes, as future events were to demonstrate.

Booth counted on his own daring and his close familiarity with the theatre employees, the door-keeper and the stage hands, to gain access to Lincoln's box that evening.

During that Friday afternoon Booth unobtrusively visited Ford's Theatre. He made his way toward the box reserved and furnished for Lincoln and his party. It is presumed that he bored a tiny hole in the door of the box from the outside, scraping it clean with a pen knife so that he could peer in from the outside and observe the sitting positions of Lincoln and other occupants of the box that evening. He also cut a mortise in the wall plaster. A pine bar about three and a half feet long was provided, apparently intended to brace the outer door to the box (which had no lock) from the inside, when one end was placed in the mortise, thus protecting the assassin from possible interference from anyone who might try to apprehend him. Thus, once he entered the box to shoot Lincoln, the door could not easily be opened from without. That would not handicap him, as would be grimly seen within a matter of hours, with any pursuit from the rear as he made his contemplated jump to the stage.

No one actually saw Booth performing this preparatory simple carpentry work for his coming crime; but an iron-handled gimlet was found in his trunk at his National Hotel room after, and the tiny hole was there to be used by him that night, as was the wooden bar inserted into the mortise.

After Booth had apparently contemplated this preliminary work at the box, he left Ford's and then visited Grover's Theatre. He wrote a letter, explaining how he had long tried to capture President Lincoln but must now change his plans, that he felt certain that posterity would justify him. He signed this letter: "Men who love their country better than gold or life, J. W. Booth,–Payne,–Atzerodt,–Herold." He addressed it to the *Washington National Intelligencer* editor and put it into his pocket.

A little later Booth encountered his fellow actor and boyhood friend, John Matthews. The two walked together down Pennsylvania Avenue. He grew disturbed, then humiliated and shocked to anger, when he watched some of General Lee's surrendered officers being marched down the street, as prisoners under Federal guard. He dramatically slapped a hand to his forehead in simulated disbelief at what he saw, and exclaimed to Matthews: "Great God! I have no longer a country!" Then he requested Matthews to deliver his sealed letter to the *National Intelligencer* editor, but to do so the next morning!

Shortly after four that afternoon, while President and Mrs. Lincoln were driving in their carriage, Booth returned to Pumphrey's livery stable to get the mare that he had hired in the morning. Jim Pumphrey disclosed, under oath: "About four or half-past four . . . he came for the saddle-horse, he asked me to give him a tie-in to hitch the horse."

Booth, after securing the bay mare from Pumphrey, went into Ford's Theatre and talked to Spangler, who later related:

"Between five and six o'clock, Booth came into the theatre and asked me for a halter. I was very busy at work at the time on the stage preparatory to the evening performance. . . . I went out to the stable and put the halter upon the horse. I commenced to take off the saddle when Booth said, 'Never mind, I do not want it off, but let it and the bridle remain.' He afterward took the saddle off himself, locked the stable, and went back to the theatre.

"Booth, Maddox [theatre property man], 'Peanut John' [the stable boy], and myself immediately went out of the theatre to the adjoining restaurant next door, and took a drink at Booth's expense. . . . I did not see Booth again until between nine and ten o'clock." Then Spangler performed a service for Booth by agreeing to hold his horse in the rear of the theatre.

Between six and nine Booth would be completing arrangements for the night's carefully calculated work, in conference with his accomplices, Powell, Atzerodt, and Herold.

VIII

President Lincoln, returning from his carriage ride with Mrs. Lincoln shortly after five o'clock, found Governor Richard J. Oglesby of Illinois and Isham N. Haynie, that state's Adjutant General, leaving the White House. Lincoln shouted after them to return and have a visit. Those two leading citizens from Springfield then had a prolonged conversation with the President.

General Haynie recorded in his diary: "April 14, 1865. . . . The President called us back. We went up to his reception-room and had a pleasant, humorous hour with him. He read four chapters of Petroleum V. Nasby's book (recently published) to us, and continued reading until he was called to dinner at about six o'clock." Governor Oglesby recalled: "Lincoln got to reading some humorous book. They kept sending for him to come to dinner. He promised each time to go, but would continue reading the book. Finally he got a sort of peremptory order that he must come to dinner at once."

There were other visitors before Lincoln finally arrived at the dinner table, among them the Illinois politician, William Pitt Kellogg, recently resigned Chief Justice of Nebraska Territory, whom Lincoln had only the preceding day appointed Collector of the Port of New Orleans. Kellogg had come to pick up his new commission for his new lucrative job and to bid goodbye to the President. Kellogg told about his departure from Lincoln: "With a few words, to be careful and discreet in the discharge of my duties, he bade me good-bye." Kellogg was destined to make a malodorous record as the "carpet bag" Governor of Louisiana.

Finally Lincoln sat down to dinner with Mrs. Lincoln (and perhaps with their son, Robert). The President looked cheerful, felt happy over the war's end, but spoke of a fatigued feeling. He believed that the theatre might do him some good. "Mrs. Lincoln says he was more cheerful and joyous that day and evening than he had been for years," revealed the Lincolns' old friend and physician of the Springfield years, Dr. Anson G. Henry, to his wife five days later, after speaking privately with Mary Todd Lincoln. Henry continued telling Mrs. Henry what Mrs. Lincoln had just told him: "When at dinner he complained of being worn out with the incessant toils of the day, and proposed to go to the theatre and have a laugh over the Country Cousin (sic). She says she discouraged going, on account of a bad headache, but he insisted that he must go, for if he stayed at home he would have no rest for he would be obliged to see company all the evening as usual. Finding that he had decided to go, she could not think of having him go without her, never having felt so unwilling to be away from him."

Since General and Mrs. Grant were unable to be their theatre guests, the Lincolns invited in their place a younger couple, Miss Clara Harris, daughter of the Senator from New York, and her fiance and stepbrother, Major Henry R. Rathbone, an officer with an outstanding war record. The two accepted.

Lincoln, following dinner, went over to the War Department. He had a talk with Stanton. The Secretary of War had something critical to say about a decision of the President not to have a Confederate commissioner, Jacob Thompson, arrested. Thompson in his flight was expected to reach Portland, Maine, that evening, so the undercover Federal government sources learned. But Lincoln had declined to approve an order for Thompson's apprehension, explaining to Assistant Secretary of War Charles A. Dana: "No. I rather guess not. When you have got an elephant by the hind leg, and he is trying to run away, it's best to let him run."

Before leaving Stanton, however, Lincoln exchanged congratulations on the success of the Federal armies and the triumph of the Union. Provost-Marshal-General James B. Fry commented about the parting of the President and his Secretary of War: "Lincoln, from his greater height, dropped his long arm upon Stanton's shoulders, and a hearty embrace terminated their rejoicings over the close of the mighty struggle. Stanton went home happy."

It was now past the time when Lincoln should have started for the theatre.

IX

Who would guard the President, his wife, and their two guests at Ford's Theatre that evening?

No one had emphasized unduly the question of bodyguards for the President that fateful Friday. Earlier that day Lincoln had assured James H. Van Alen by mail that he would "use due precaution" about his personal protection. But his own attitude toward guards for himself had been expressed the previous July 4 when he sent this answer to Major-General Christopher C. Augur, commanding the military Department of Washington: "I believe I need no escort, and unless the Sec. of War directs, none need attend me."

Seward shared his Chief's belief in the improbability of attacks by assailants or assassins. Nearly three years earlier the Secretary of State had written his friend, John Bigelow, now Consul-General at Paris, concerning reports of rumors that Bigelow had heard about a plot to kill Lincoln and his Cabinet: "Assassination is not an American practice or habit, and one so vicious and desperate cannot be engrafted into our political system. This conviction of mine has steadily gained strength since the Civil War began. Every day's experience confirms it. The President, during the heated season, occupies a country-house near the Soldiers' Home, two or three miles from the city. He goes to and from that place on horseback, night and morning, unguarded. I go there unattended at all hours."

In the previous November (1864) the Superintendent of the Metropolitan Police in Washington, William B. Webb, had detailed four men as special guards for the President, Alfonso Dunn, Alexander Smith, Thomas F. Pendel (the then White House doorkeeper), and, more recently, John F. Parker. Upon Pendel being appointed doorkeeper, that vacancy as personal presidential protector was filled by William H. Crook.

In the usual routine, according to Crook later, two of those four police officers stood duty from eight in the morning to four in the afternoon, guarding the approach to Lincoln's office or whatever room in which he happened, supposedly accompanying him on any walks that he might take. At four in the afternoon another man went on duty till midnight, or later if the President ventured outside the White House and did not return. At midnight the second night guard went on duty and stayed until relieved at eight in the morning. "We were all armed with revolvers," noted Crook. "The night guards were expected to protect the President on his expeditions to and from the War Department, or while he was at any place of amusement, and to patrol the corridor outside his room while he slept."

Sometimes big, belligerent Ward Hill Lamon, always anxious about Lincoln's safety, would appoint himself the President's personal protector. He had served as the Chief Executive's guard at the Gettysburg dedication ceremonies and on numberless other occasions. John Hay, in the preceding November, had noted about Lamon: "W.H.L. took a glass of whiskey and then, refusing my offer of a bed, went out &, rolling himself up in his cloak, lay down at the President's door; passing the night in that attitude of touching and dumb fidelity, with a small arsenal of pistols and bowie knives around him. In the morning he went away leaving my blankets at my door, before I or the President were awake."

But, on Friday evening, April 14, not even Lamon was around to shield the President from possible physical attack.

The only guard assigned to Lincoln and his party for their Ford's Theatre visit was one of these four men detailed by the Metropolitan Police—John F. Parker. And the worst one imaginable!

Parker was new on the job as a Lincoln guard, having been detailed to that post only a few weeks before. Mrs. Lincoln had dismissed the veteran White House doorkeeper, Edward McManus. Thomas Pendel, one of the original detail of special presidential guards, took McManus' doorkeeping job. The vacant post of guard to the President was given to Parker, a grossly irresponsible and negligent man whose record of inefficiency, insubordination, habitual drunkenness, use of disrespectful language, and wholesale absences from the force was such that it might well have pleased John Wilkes Booth exceedingly. But Parker had always been reinstated by Superintendent Webb's police regime. So Parker was to serve as Lincoln's guard at Ford's Theatre!

Meanwhile, as Lincoln saw last-minute visitors at the White House before departing for the theatre, ominous events were occurring some blocks away.

At seven o'clock John Wilkes Booth left his National Hotel room—"I last saw him about seven o'clock . . . when he passed out of the hotel for the last time," declared the hotel's clerk, G. W. Bunker. About one hour later just after the curtain raising at Ford's Theatre and a few minutes before President and Mrs. Lincoln left the White House for that theatre, Booth met in final conference on his strategy of murder at the Herndon House with his homicidal minded dupes. The Herndon House, where Powell had a room at Booth's expense, was on Ninth and F Streets, lying diagonally across from the Patent Office, in the same "square" as Ford's Theatre.

To himself and each of his instruments Booth assigned tasks. He himself would attend to Lincoln. Atzerodt, the middle-aged coach painter from Port Tobacco, Maryland, a sort of comic villain in this frightfully real melodrama, was to repair to the Kirkwood House (where Atzerodt already had hired a room) and kill Vice-President Andrew Johnson at his quarters there. Powell, the murderous young brute, was to gain entrance to the home of Seward on a manufactured pretext, and stab to death the Secretary of State (who already lay recuperating from his carriage accident). The youthful Herold was to guide Powell out of the city after he had disposed of Seward.

All seemed perfectly planned to the last diabolical detail.

X

The President and Mrs. Lincoln found themselves late in leaving the White House for the theatre. He had more callers—Speaker Schuyler Colfax again, and also George Ashmun of Massachusetts, accompanied by Chief Justice Charles Patrick Daly of the Court of Common Pleas of

New York City. Ashmun was an old friend. He and Lincoln had served together as fellow Whig members in Congress more than fifteen years before. In 1860 Ashmun had wielded the gavel as Chairman of the Republican National Committee which had nominated Lincoln for President.

In his conversation with Colfax, Ashmun, and Daly, Lincoln appeared in exuberant spirits. They talked about his recent visit to Richmond, and he sportively replied that he "supposed he should have been uneasy also, had any other man been President and gone there; but as it was, he felt no apprehension of danger whatever." He told Speaker Colfax, who presided over the House of Representatives when in session: "Sumner has the 'gavel' of the Confederate Congress, which he got at Richmond, and intended to give it to the Secretary of War, but I insisted he must give it to you."

Colfax, scheduled to leave for California on the morrow, spoke to the President about the Pacific coast, and Lincoln requested him: "Don't forget, Colfax, to tell those miners that that is my speech to them, by you"—he expected them to dig sufficient gold with which to pay the war debt. Colfax bid goodbye and departed.

Lincoln, his coat on and his stovepipe hat in hand, as Mrs. Lincoln awaited him, attended to Ashmun, accompanied by Judge Daly.

George Ashmun's call concerned a cotton claim of one of his law clients. He wanted the President to grant him a "commission" to pass upon the merits of that case. "With considerable warmth of manner," Lincoln answered Ashmun: "I have done with 'commissions.' I believe they are contrivances to *cheat* the Government out of every pound of cotton they can lay their hands on."

Ashmun's face flushed. He trusted that the President did not mean any personal imputation. Lincoln perceived that he had deeply offended his old congressional crony. "You did not understand me, Ashmun. I did not mean what you inferred. I take it all back."

They were interrupted by more callers. But Lincoln could not attend to their wants just then. Mrs. Lincoln was waiting, her irritation somewhat up at the delay in starting for the theatre. Hurriedly the President scribbled on a card for Ashmun and Judge Daly:

Allow Mr. Ashmun
& friend to come in
at 9 A.M. to-mor-
row.

A. Lincoln
April 14, 1865.

Those words were Lincoln's last bit of handwriting.

President and Mrs. Lincoln bid goodbye to the White House door-keeper as the footman, Charles Forbes, helped Mrs. Lincoln and the President into the carriage driven by Francis Burke. Forbes climbed to the box.

The Lincolns were driven over to the residence of Senator Ira Harris of New York, where they met their two guests, Major Henry R. Rathbone and Miss Clara Harris, who entered the carriage—and all rode off to Ford's Theatre.

Not an armed guard for them was in sight as they rode to see the play.

XI

At about 8:30 o'clock the Lincolns' coachman, Francis Burke, reined in his horses and stopped before Ford's Theatre on Tenth Street, between E and F Streets. The footman, Charley Forbes, swung down and opened the carriage door. The President, Mrs. Lincoln, Major Rathbone and Miss Harris alighted upon a wooden platform, or horse block, on the curb.

The four in the presidential party were escorted by Forbes and the special police guard, John F. Parker, past the dress circle in the back of the theatre, to the accompaniment of loud applause from the audience, excited murmurs, craning of necks, and turning of eyes from the stage. The orchestra leader, William Withers, tapped his director's stick in signal to his musicians, and they struck up "Hail The Chief!"

One woman in the audience, Mrs. Helen A. Du Barry, sitting next to her husband, an Army major, sent word to her mother about the President's entrance two days later: "In the mid'st of the 2nd scene there was a great applause & cheering and our attention was directed from the stage to the Dress circle—close to the wall—walked Miss Harris—Mrs. Lincoln—Major Rathbun (sic)—a gentleman, the President & another gentleman behind him. These two gentlemen were *watchmen* in citizens dress who have *always* accompanied the President since the War commenced. We followed him with our eyes until he entered the box." The two *"watchmen"* mentioned by Mrs. Du Barry were Forbes, Lincoln's footman, and Parker, the guard who was not guarding effectively.

Another of the audience, the youthful James Suydam Knox, Princeton graduate and former soldier of the Twenty-First Infantry, New Jersey Volunteers (and a future physician and professor at the Rutgers Medical School) wrote to his father about Lincoln's arrival: "My room mate and I were seated on the second row of orchestra seats, just beneath the President's box," Knox informed his parent. "The President entered the theatre at 8½ oc'k, amid deafening cheers and the rising of all. Everything was cheerful, and never was our Magistrate more enthusiastically welcomed, or more happy. Many pleasant allusions were made to him in the play, to which the audience gave deafening responses, while Mr. Lincoln laughed heartily and bowed frequently to the gratified people."

Among those "pleasant allusions" to the President in the dialogue on stage was one spoken by the actor, Harry Hawk, portraying the role of an exaggeratedly homespun American in England, "Asa Trenchard." Hawk "ad libbed" a line: "This reminds me of a story, as Mr. Lincoln would say." The audience roared its approval and clapped hands, as if calling for more. Lincoln, seated in Harry Ford's horsehair rocking chair in the box, turned smilingly to Mrs. Lincoln and uttered something.

Our American Cousin had been a mediocre melodrama, which, when brought to the United States, was transformed into a popular comedy by its actors' adoption of ridiculous mannerisms, excessive gestures, and absurd lines. The playbill advertised it as "an eccentric comedy."

Walt Whitman (not in the audience that evening) held no high opinion of Tom Taylor's play: "One of those singularly written compositions which . . . makes not the slightest call on either the moral, emotional, esthetic or spiritual nature—a piece in which, among other characters, so call'd, a Yankee, certainly such a one as was never seen, or the least like it ever seen in North America, is introduced with a varied fol-de-rol of talk, plot scenery, and such phantasmagoria as goes to make up a couple of its acts. . . . There is a scene in which two unprecedented English ladies are inform'd by the impossible Yankee that he is not a man of fortune, and therefore undesirable for marriage-catching purposes."

Our American Cousin, starring Laura Keene with President and Mrs. Lincoln looking down from the box, concerned a money-minded English matron, "Mrs. Mountchessington," who worked indefatigably in luring the reputedly rich Yankee, "Asa Trenchard," portrayed by Hawk, into marrying her daughter, "Augusta."

Lincoln watched the performance in apparent enjoyment. It seemed strange that he, who had just been the leading player in the grimmest real-life drama ever known to America, could sit in the horsehair rocker, looking at and listening to those thespians on stage moving about with their exaggerated gestures, simulated speech, and unreal lines. But it was understandable. The theatre was a relief from the drudgery and worry of the presidential office in war time. Ahead lay the thorny dilemma of reconstruction for the South, and his disagreement with Congress. He had always enjoyed comedy on stage. His Secretary of the Treasury, Hugh McCulloch, subsequently commented correctly: "The theatre had great attractions for him, but it was comedy, not tragedy, he wanted to hear. He had great enjoyment of the plays that made him laugh, no matter how absurd or grotesque."

Mrs. Lincoln pointed out this or that bright spot in the idiocy of the play, noted Dr. Charles Sabin Taft, an Army physician in the audience. Taft commented in his note book: "Only his left profile was visible to most in the audience; but from where I sat, almost under the box, I could see him plainly. Mrs. Lincoln rested her hand on his knee much of the time, and often called his attention to some humorous situation on the stage. She seemed to take great pleasure in witnessing his enjoyment."

The actress who played the role of "Miss Augusta Mountchessington," Helen Coleman, whose stage name was Helen Truman (but the program had her down as Helen "Trueman"), noted that Mrs. Lincoln was dressed in a dark gray silk dress, with flowers in hair, and clapped her hands in applause; while the President "never applauded with his hands, but he laughed heartily on occasion, and his face spoke plainly of his approval."

As Lincoln watched the performance, the door of his box remained closed—but unlocked. Worse still, his guard, Parker, had left his post there—perhaps to watch the play from a seat among the audience, perhaps to go next door for a drink. Not until decades later did one of the President's police guards, William H. Crook (off duty at the time; it was not his shift) reveal a startling circumstance:

"It was the custom of the guard who accompanied the President to the theatre to remain in the little passageway outside the box. . . . Whether Parker occupied it at all I do not know. . . . If he did, he left it almost immediately; for he confessed to me the next day that he went to a seat at the front of the first gallery, so that he could see the play. The door of the President's box was shut; probably Mr. Lincoln never knew that the guard had left his post."

The clock was reaching the hour of ten. The second scene of the third act was approaching, with Mrs. Lincoln nestled somewhat closely against the President and looking up into his face. Suddenly she realized that she was in partial view of some in the audience, and with Major Rathbone and Clara Harris right there beside them in the box. The First Lady queried her husband: "What will Miss Harris think of my hanging on to you so?" Lincoln answered his wife: "She won't think anything about it."

Those were Lincoln's last words as they were recorded contemporaneously for posterity. Mrs. Lincoln repeated them to her friend, Dr. Anson G. Henry, five days later.

XII

"I should judge it was about ten o'clock that he came there to the theatre, walked in, and walked out again," later testified Ford's Theatre doorman, John E. Buckingham, about Booth's movements that Friday night.

On stage, the fortune-chasing "Mrs. Mountchessington" was about to make the appallingly disheartening discovery that her hoped-for prospective American son-in-law, "Asa Trenchard," was "church mouse" poor and not the fabulously wealthy suitor for her daughter, "Augusta," whom she has fondly imagined him. "Trenchard" had a rather unelevated opinion of the English matron, calling her (to himself when she is not on the stage) the "old gay." The unreal lines drew unreal laughter from the audience, including a mild smile from the President, looking down from his box only nine feet above the stage.

Where did Booth go after he unobtrusively left Ford's Theatre?

The owner of *The Star* saloon a few doors away, Peter Taltavull, said later: "He was there [in my place], I judge, a little after ten o'clock. . . . He just walked into the bar, called for some whiskey. I gave him the whiskey; put the bottle on the counter; and he called for some water. . . . He put the money on the counter, and went right off."

Booth was confident that all preparations had been made. All details had been attended to; nothing could go wrong. He had arranged with his dupe and idol, Edman Spangler, the scene-shifter, to tend to his horse in the alley outside of the rear stage exit of the theatre. Actually Spangler had just called on a minor theatre employee, Joseph Burroughs (known as "Peanut John") to hold Booth's hired bay mare. And Peanut John testified afterwards: "He [Spangler] told me to hold it . . . so I held the horse."

From Taltavull's bar Booth hurriedly and nonchalantly went back into the theatre. The doorkeeper, Buckingham, revealed under oath: "He returned, I judge, in about two or three minutes. He came to me, and asked me what time it was. I told him to step out into the lobby that leads out into the street, and he could see. He stepped out, and walked in again, and stepped into the door that leads to the parquette and dress circle, and returned immediately; came out, and went up the stairway to the dress circle."

The dress circle led to the "State" box, where the President, Mrs. Lincoln, Major Rathbone, and Miss Harris looked down at the performance, a mere nine feet below.

One of the theater-owning Ford brothers (it is not certain which of the three) saw Booth go toward the dress circle. Booth's biographer, George A. Townsend, who covered those days minutely in fine-comb detail, reported to his newspaper, the New York *World,* three days later: "Ascending the dress circle, he [Booth] stood for a little time gazing upon the audience and occasionally upon the stage in his usual graceful manner. He was observed by Mr. Ford, the proprietor of the theatre, to be slowly elbowing his way through the crowd that packed the rear of the dress circle toward the right side, at the extremity of which was the box where Mr. and Mrs. Lincoln and their companions were seated. Mr. Ford casually noticed this as a slightly extraordinary sympton of interest on the part of an actor so familiar with the routine of the theatre and the play."

Booth a few hours later jotted down in his diary: "I walked with a firm step through a thousand of his friends, was stopped but pushed on. A colonel [Major Rathbone] was at his side."

By whom was Booth "stopped" as he made his way toward the presidential box? Probably it will never be known for certain. At this precise point the historical evidence turns into a maze.

Back of the dress circle, not far from the door of the passageway to Lincoln's box, sat Captain Theodore McGowan, a Pennsylvanian serving as Assistant Adjutant General to the commander of the military Department of Washington, General Augur. Beside Captain McGowan was another Pennsylvanian, Lieutenant A. M. S. Crawford of the Veteran Reserve Corps.

McGowan told the New York *Tribune's* Washington correspondent within an hour, after it was too late:

"Lieut. Crawford and I . . . took seats in the passage above the seats of the dress circle, and about five feet from the door of the box occupied by President Lincoln. During the performance, the attendant of the President [Parker, the guard, or perhaps Forbes, the coachman?] came out and took the chair nearest the door. I sat, and had been sitting, about four feet to his left and rear, for some time.

"I remember that a man, whose face I do not distinctly recollect, passed me and inquired of one sitting near who the President's messenger was, and learning, exhibited to him an envelope, apparently official, having a printed heading and superscribed in a bold hand. I could not read the address and did not try. . . . That man went away.

"Some time after I was disturbed in my seat by the approach of a man who desired to pass up on the side of the aisle in which I was sitting. Giving him room by bending my chair forward, he passed me, and stepped one step down upon the level below me. Standing there, he was almost in my line of sight, and I saw him while watching the play. He stood, as I remember, one step above the messenger, and remained perhaps one minute apparently looking at the stage and orchestra below. Then he drew a number of visiting cards from his pocket, from which, with some attention, he drew or selected one. These things I saw distinctly. I saw him stoop, and I think, descend to the level with the messenger, and by his right side. He showed the card to the messenger, and as my attention was then more closely fixed upon the play, I do not know whether the card was carried in by the messenger, or his consent given to the entrance [to the President's box] of the man who presented it. I saw, a few moments later, the same man entering the lobby [passageway] leading to the box and the door closing behind him."

In a few minutes, Captain McGowan partially identified the man who had entered Lincoln's box as the same one who so spectacularly jumped to the stage: "I did not see his face as he leaped or ran, but I am convinced that it was the man I saw enter." The Captain described him: "His face was smooth, with the exception of a mustache of moderate size, but of this I am not positive. He was dressed in a black coat, approximating to a dress frock, dark pants, and wore a stiff-rimmed, flat-topped, round-crowned black hat of felt, I think. He seemed for a moment or two to survey the house with the deliberation of an habitue of the theatre."

Booth's biographer, Townsend, also revealed in another three days that Booth was stopped on his way by a "servant" of the President, without naming that servant:

"A young man, so precisely resembling the one described as J. Wilkes Booth that he is asserted to be the same, appeared before the open door of the President's box, and prepared to enter.

"The servant who attended Mr. Lincoln [Forbes, the coachman?] said politely, 'this is the President's box, sir, no one is permitted to enter.' 'I am a senator,' responded the person. 'Mr. Lincoln has sent for me.' The attendant gave way, and the young man passed into the box."

XIII

As Booth entered the President's box, "Mrs. Mountchessington" on stage had just learned, with excruciatingly painful shock, that "Trenchard" is not rich, therefore not eligible to wed her daughter. She ordered her daughter: "Augusta, dear, to your room!" Helen Truman, as "Augusta," answered: "Yes, ma. The nasty beast!" and exited.

Only two players were left on stage, Mrs. H. Muzzy as "Mrs. Mountchessington" and Harry Hawk as "Asa Trenchard."

Booth, having "timed" his movements and speed with precision, and knowing that in another minute there would be not two, but only a single actor, remaining on stage, and listening to the dialogue from Mrs. Muzzy and Hawk, tiptoed at that point into Lincoln's box and closed the door quietly behind him. He paused a few seconds, until "Mrs. Mountchessington" had told off "Trenchard," and had made her exit, leaving Hawk on stage. His Deringer pistol and dagger were concealed.

Booth picked up a wooden plank which he knew exactly where to find. He slipped one end of it into the mortise in the door casing that someone (apparently he himself) had cut that afternoon. The plank made a crude but temporarily effective bolt, barring the door from the inside. From behind he surveyed Lincoln, Mrs. Lincoln, Rathbone, and Clara Harris.

On stage during these few moments "Mrs. Mountchessington," with frigid British anger in exaggerated "silly ass" English stage accent, rebuked the now financially ineligible suitor: "I am aware, Mr. Trenchard, you are not used to the manners of good society, and that alone will excuse the impertinence of which you have been guilty." She brusquely and haughtily, in total repudiation of him, walked from the boards into the wings. "Trenchard," played by Harry Hawk, was left alone on stage.

Inside the President's box, directly above, Major Rathbone turned around. He saw the invading Booth and confronted the wild-eyed actor playing a real-life role of villainy. Clara Harris, shocked, told about it the next day: "Upon his entering the box Major Rathbone arose and asked the intruder his business. He rushed past the Major without making a reply. . . ."

On stage Harry Hawk, as "Trenchard," called after the excited "Mrs. Mountchessington" loudly, so that the audience listened and watched intently: "Don't know the manner of good society, eh? Wal, I guess I know enough to turn you inside out, old gal—you sockdologizing old man trap. . . ."

Hawk spoke not an epithet farther in shouting after the departed "Mrs. Mountchessington," when from directly above, from the President's box, a pistol shot cracked the air.

XIV

Clara Harris the next day recounted what had happened in Lincoln's box: "Placing his pistol close to the President's head, actually in contact with it, [Booth] fired, and instantly sprang upon the cushioned baluster of the box, when he made a backward plunge with his knife, aimed at the face or breast of Mr. Lincoln. Major Rathbone, springing forward to protect the President, received a stab in his arm. The murderer then jumped upon the stage."

Some in the audience heard the shot, and looked up toward the President's box. They saw a wild-looking, black-mustached young man emerge atop the balustrade of the box, the Nottingham curtains encircling him. Roaring out, *"Sic semper tyrannis,"* the State of Virginia's motto, he leapt over the box toward the stage. A spur of his boot ripped a flag draping the box. He plunged forward, crashed on to the stage, and fell on one knee. Instantly he recovered, and limped with athletic agility across the stage, brandishing a dagger theatrically and menacingly.

"Asa Trenchard," or rather Harry Hawk, was panic stricken. The wild man who had jumped from the box was after him with a knife, he thought. He ran offstage and upstairs, lest Booth should catch him. Hawk wrote later to his father about his blood-chilling half-minute:

> The "old lady" [Mrs. Mountchessington] had just gone off the stage, and I was answering her exit speech when I heard the shot fired. I turned, looked up at the President's box, heard the man exclaim *'sic semper tyrannis,'* saw him jump from the box, seize the flag on the staff, and drop to the stage. He slipped when he gained the stage, but got upon his feet in a moment, brandished a large knife, saying, 'The South shall be free!' turned his face in the direction I stood. I recognized him as John Wilkes Booth. He ran towards me and I, seeing the knife, thought I was the one he was after, ran off the stage and up a flight of stairs.

For two full minutes nearly all actors, actresses, and the audience were paralyzed with a certain bewilderment and shock. Some even thought that Booth's leap was part of the play, or some new twist of play-acting. And almost everyone in the theatre turned to his neighbor to find out what had happened.

One man, the six-foot-six Washington lawyer-lobbyist, Joseph B. Stewart, however, realized instantly what had just occurred. Stewart jumped from his second row seat, as did the former soldier and Princeton graduate James Suydam Knox, and his companion. Stewart vaulted to the stage, chased Booth out of the rear exit of the theatre and almost caught the assassin. But Booth was able to throw Stewart off as he rode off on his waiting horse into the black night.

Inside the President's box, the First Lady was shrieking hysterically. Clara Harris was valiantly attempting to console her and yelling frantically for help. Major Rathbone, his arm bleeding from Booth's knife plunge, tried to unbar the box door to let in the men who were hollering and banging on it from the outside.

And the President of the United States sat limply in his rocking chair, his eyes closed and his unmoving head on chest, drooped to one side.

A NIGHT OF HORROR—AND DEATH

41

I

TO an occasion of violence, when the natives struck at them in darkness, the old *conquistadores* of Mexico gave the name, *Noche Triste,* or sorrowful night. That Good Friday of 1865, merging into Easter Saturday, proved the *Noche Triste* of Washington, the worst hours since the British set the torch to the national capital during the War of 1812-15. To the rest of the nation it seemed like a complete reign of death and terror as the grim news, some true, other stories mere pernicious rumor, ticked over telegraph wires.

Those hours from almost half-past ten in the evening until nearly half-past seven in the morning were filled with mass fear, sadness, anger, and hysteria, at the end of which the President passed away—truly a night of horror.

II

What happened immediately after Booth pulled the trigger?

Inside the President's box, Major Rathbone grappled with the assassin, only to receive a deep stab in the arm before Booth plunged to the stage. "I instantly sprang toward him and seized him," Rathbone related three days later. "He wrested himself from the grasp and made a violent thrust at [my] breast with a large knife. I parried the blow by striking it up, and received a wound several inches deep in the left arm, between the elbow and shoulder. . . . As he went over the stage, I cried out with a loud voice, 'Stop that man!' "

A hush of some moments followed. Then through the ornamental Nottingham curtains that encircled the President's box, a figure, a black-haired man with mustache of the same hue, suggesting the villain of future macabre fiction tales, raised himself with hands and feet, and stood for a partial minute atop the flag-draped box. From the balustrade he leaped down, ripping one flag, and landed on the stage, angrily shouting, *"Sic semper tyrannis."* This was to become one of the most familiar scenes in all of American historical illustrations.

As the shot from the "state" box resounded throughout the theatre, followed by the sight of the knife-brandishing Booth crashing to the stage and frightening the actor, Harry Hawk, into the wings, some in the audience spontaneously concluded that the pistol report had come from an irresponsible individual, a practical joker, or perhaps a drunk, and that Booth's gymnastic feat was something added to *Our American Cousin.*

"I at first thought it was accidentally discharged by some soldier or drunken men & looked around," narrated one of the audience, a government Paymaster, Charles A. Sanford, in a note to a friend in Michigan the next day. Sanford added: "As I turned my head to the stage I saw a man thrust aside the flags that decorated the box which the President & family occupied & leap out of the box down upon the stage with knife in his hand &, if I mistake not, a revolver in the other. He rushed across the stage. . . . Many, with myself, at first took it to be part of the play. Everybody was confounded & paralyzed."

Captain Theodore McGowan, who from his seat in back of the dress circle had seen Booth enter the box (and had thought nothing unusual about it) within one hour after Booth's shooting of Lincoln, declared about the pistol report: "While it startled all, it was evidently accepted by everyone as an introduction to some new passage, several of which had been interpolated in the early part of the play."

But one quick-witted, alert lawyer-lobbyist of Washington in the audience instantly had sensed that the man who jumped from the box after the report of a fired revolver might have shot Lincoln or someone else there. With incredible agility for a man of his size, the six-foot-six Stewart vaulted to the stage, running after Booth. On Stewart's heels rushed young James Knox. Two days later Knox told about his thrilling experience in a letter home to his father: "But two men sprang to the stage, a Mr. Stewart and myself. Both of us were familiar with the play, and suspected the fearful tragedy. We rushed after the murderer, and Mr. Stewart being familiar with the passages reached the rear door in time to see him spring on his horse and ride off. I became lost amid the scenery and was obliged to return. My room mate had followed me and secured the murderer's hat."

Booth, madly dashing out of the rear exit into the alley, where "Peanut John" Burroughs was holding the hired horse, was able to shake off Stewart. The assassin seized the reins of the bay mare from the waiting "Peanut John," and rode off into the night toward F Street. "Peanut John," in his sworn testimony, told this story: "I heard the report of the pistol. I was still out by the bench, and had got off when Booth came out. He told me to give him his horse. He struck me with the butt of a knife, and knocked me down. He did this as he was mounting his horse, with one foot in the stirrup; he also kicked me, and rode off immediately."

Stewart, one month later under oath, told of his attempt to catch Booth:

"At about near half-past ten . . . the report of a pistol, which was evidently a discharged pistol, a sharp report, startled me. . . . At the same time an exclamation was made, and simultaneously a man leaped from the President's box, exclaiming, as he came out, some words. . . .

"I jumped to the stage to the right of the foot-lights from where I sat. . . . I followed the direction he took. I exclaimed, 'Stop that man!' . . . Some one said, 'He is getting on a horse'; and at the door, almost as soon as the words reached my ears, I heard the tramping of a horse. . . . I perceived a man mounting a horse. He was at that instant imperfectly mounted. . . . I ran in the same direction, where the horse was heading. . . . I crossed in the same direction, aiming at the rein, and was now on the right flank of the horse. . . . The horse went forward then, and soon swept to the left up towards F Street. I still ran after the horse some forty or fifty yards. . . . It all occupied a space of a few seconds from the time I reached the stage until this occurred."

Stewart's law-partner, Congressman Albert G. Riddle of Ohio, maintained: "Stewart would certainly have captured Booth had not the stage carpenter closed a door in his face," although Stewart testified that he pursued the assassin out to the alley and actually got near the right flank of Booth's mare. But Stewart, in retrospect, could breathe easily in future years when he reflected that he might have been killed himself in the confused, chaotic melee by other pursuers of Booth. A dozen years later he publicly declared: "It was fortunate that I did not catch him. The theatre was filled with soldiers. If Booth had been there he would have been shot into small pieces. Many of themselves would have accidentally fallen victims to their reckless fury. If I had stood there holding him when they came out, my virtues would now be proclaimed on a piece of marble."

All of the while the President of the United States lay slumped, unconscious with blood dripping from the back of his head, in his rocking chair in the box.

III

As Booth, brandishing his dagger, ran across the stage and then fled out the rear exit to jump on his horse, with Stewart pursuing him, all was hysteria and confusion. President Lincoln lay slumped in the rocking chair, as if dead. Mrs. Lincoln was shrieking madly while bending over him. Clara Harris was endeavoring to pacify the First Lady. Major Rathbone, his arm dripping with blood, was trying to find out why the door to the box would not open. And then Clara ran to the front of the box, and shouted out: "The President is shot!"

Actors, audience, and theatre employees now grasped the grim meaning of the turbulent, confused scene. Within a few minutes the stage filled with actors and actresses in their grease paint and costumes, scrambling about; musicians with their instruments rushed excitedly about; and civilian men and army officers tried to climb to the stage or the box. Aimlessly most rushed out of the theatre, and it looked for a while as their scramble for the exit would end in near panic or the trampling of many people. It all suggested a spontaneous mob reaction to a fire in an overcrowded auditorium, as if flames were enveloping them.

Men stretched out inarticulate arms, as if struggling to tear themselves from the ghastly, grotesque real-life nightmare which held them. Women shrieked and cried hysterically. When their strength returned, some plunged over seats, bruising themselves, forgetting the companions and relatives with whom they had come to the theatre. Some were intent on rushing out into the street to tell the terrible news, and others were trying to find room on the overcrowded stage; many tried to shinny up the balustrade of the box to get a look at the President or to try to help him and Mrs. Lincoln. Some ran to the box door and banged furiously on it, but Major Rathbone inside was having difficulty unbarring it, so secure was Booth's makeshift bolt. Throughout the theatre the walls resounded to demands that the assailants or assassins be captured.

Among those in the audience on that harrowing night was Captain Oliver C. Gatch, commander of a company in the 89th Ohio Regiment, whose brother, Dr. Charles D. Gatch, who had come with him, was trying to get into the box to render medical aid to Lincoln. Captain Gatch reminisced about that night: "The crowd went mad. A wilder sight I never saw in battle, even. Stunned at first, the people awoke and blazed with fierce passion against the murderer, yelling, 'Hang him! Hang him!'

They shouted and screamed and shrieked hysterically in every conceivable tone and key. While this bedlam was going on, there began the mad, terror-stricken clambering of the people toward the exits."

The star of *Our American Cousin,* Laura Keene, who had played "Florence Trenchard," like a trouper of stern stuff, yelled from the stage in frantic efforts to prevent panic: "For God's sake, have presence of mind and keep your places, and all will be well!"

Inside the box, Major Rathbone, with a big wet crimson stain on the left sleeve of his uniform, set about trying to unbar the door as men pounded on it from outside and yelled profanely, demanding admission instantly, or they would break it down. Testified Rathbone under oath the following month:

"As he [Booth] went over the stage, I cried out, 'Stop that man.' I then turned to the President; his position was not changed; his head was slightly bent forward, and his eyes were closed. I saw that he was unconscious, and, supposing him mortally wounded, rushed to the door for the purpose of calling medical aid.

"On reaching the outer door of the passageway, I found it barred by a heavy piece of plank, one end of which was secured in the wall, and the other resting against the door. It had been so securely fastened that it required considerable force to remove it. This wedge or bar was about four feet from the floor. Persons upon the outside were beating against the door for the purpose of entering. I removed the bar, and the door was opened. Several persons, who represented themselves as surgeons, were allowed to enter."

IV

The first physician from the audience to reach the wounded unconscious President in the box was a twenty-three-year-old New Yorker, Dr. Charles A. Leale, a recent graduate of Bellevue Hospital Medical School, then serving as an Assistant Surgeon in the army.

Lincoln appeared to be dead. His eyes were closed and his head fallen forward. Leale felt his pulseless wrist and immediately laid him out on the floor. Since Leale saw a clot of blood on the Chief Executive's stilled shoulder, he looked for a knife wound, for fresh in his mind was his image of Booth jumping from the box and crossing the stage with dagger in hand. Dr. Leale slit open the coat and shirt sleeve with a borrowed knife; but found no injury. On lifting the eyelids, he saw evidence of brain injury. Then he discovered the clotted wound in the back of Lincoln's head. When he removed the clot, the intracranial pressure was eased, and shallow breathing and a weak pulse followed.

Leale's emergency treatment of Lincoln was perhaps best told by himself. Two years later, when the incidents were still fairly fresh in his mind, this first physician to reach the unconscious Lincoln in the theatre box wrote about it privately to General Benjamin F. Butler, then a member of Congress from Massachusetts. Leale told Butler:

> I saw a man with dark hair, and bright black eyes, leap from the box to the stage below. While descending he threw himself a little forward and raised his shining dagger in the air, which reflected the light as though it had been a diamond. . . . I then heard cries that the President had been murdered which were followed by those of "Kill the murderer" and "Shoot him" etc. which came from different parts of the audience.
>
> I remained in my seat not believing it, until I saw some one [Major Rathbone] open the door of the box, and heard the call for a surgeon and help.
>
> I arrived at the door of the box. Mr. Lincoln was sitting in a high backed arm chair with his head, leaning towards his right side, and which was supported by Mrs. Lincoln who was weeping bitterly, Miss Harris was at her left side and behind the President. Major Rathbone was at the door of the box.
>
> While approaching the President I was told that he had been murdered, and I sent for some brandy and water.
>
> Upon Mrs. Lincoln being told that I was a surgeon, she said, "Oh, Doctor, do what you can for my dear husband—do what you can for him" and "send for Dr. Stone."

The Lincoln's family physician, Dr. Robert King Stone, requested by the First Lady, was summoned immediately, but he did not arrive at the President's side until after he was carried out of the theatre.

Dr. Leale continued his account of how he administered aid to Lincoln, in this letter to Butler:

> When I reached the President he was almost dead. His eyes were closed, he was paralysed. I placed my finger on his right radial pulse, but could feel no movement of the artery.
>
> His breathing was exceedingly stertorous, there being intervals between each inspiration and he was in a most profoundly comatized condition.
>
> With the assistance of two gentlemen I immediately placed him in a recumbent position. While doing this and holding his head and shoulders my hand came in contact with blood in his left shoulder. The thought of the dagger then recurred to me, and I supposed he might have been stabbed in the subclavian artery or some of its branches. I asked a gentleman near by [William Kent?] to cut his coat and shirt off that shoulder to enable me if possible to check the supposed hemorrhage.
>
> As soon as his arm was bared to a distance below the shoulder, and I saw that there was no wound there, I lifted his eyelids, the pupils of one of which was dilated. I then examined his head and soon discovered a large firm clot of blood situated about one inch below the superior curved line and an inch and a half to the left of the median line of the occipital bone, the coagula which was firmly matted with the hair, I removed, and passed the little finger of my left hand directly through the perfectly smooth opening made by the ball. He was then apparently dead.

When I removed my finger which I used as a probe, an oozing of the blood followed and he soon commenced to show signs of improvement.

I believe he would not have lived five minutes longer, if the pressure on the brain had not been relieved and if he had been left that much longer in the sitting position.

Dr. Leale's confident belief in his method of treating Lincoln in the emergency was soon justified by other physicians. When Dr. Charles Sabin Taft and Dr. Albert F. A. King rushed into the box shortly afterward and examined Lincoln, both agreed to the correctness of Leale's treatment. Taft gave Leale full credit for keeping the President alive at that precise time. Another physician who joined Leale, Taft, and King was Dr. Charles D. Gatch.

The doctors decided that it would be best to move Lincoln from the box; he surely could not remain there. With the aid of onlookers, they carried him out of the theatre.

The onlooker who had loaned Dr. Leale his knife, with which to cut Lincoln's clothes open, William Kent, returned to the box, looking for keys that he had lost in the excitement. His foot kicked something on the floor of the box. It was Booth's Deringer pistol! Kent gave the weapon, which had wounded Lincoln, to the Associated Press correspondent, Lawrence A. Gobright, who turned it over to the Washington police. Kent, under oath the following month, told about it:

"About three minutes after the President was shot, I went into his box; there were two other persons there and a surgeon [Leale], who asked me for a knife to cut open the President's clothes. On leaving the theatre I missed my night-key, and thinking I had dropped it in pulling out my knife, I hurried back, and on searching around the floor of the box I knocked my foot against a pistol, which I picked up, and holding it up, I cried out, 'I have found the pistol.' I gave it up to Mr. Gobright, the agent of the Associated Press. The next morning I went around to the police station and identified it there."

That weapon was a Deringer make, six inches long and weighing a half-pound, easily concealable on a person. On its butt was the lettering, *Deringer, Philad.* That Philadelphia gun-maker, Henry Deringer, Jr. (his name sometimes erroneously spelled with three "r's") had a huge sale of his lethal products in the South and California.

V

The crowd outside Ford's Theatre parted to let through the doctors and volunteers carrying out the President.

A young soldier, Private William T. Clark of the Thirteenth Massachusetts Regiment, who had rented a room across the street in a house owned by a Swedish tailor, William Petersen, motioned to the doctors and other bearers of Lincoln to carry him up to his place. The doctors, somewhat in a quandary as to where to take the President, agreed to Clark's offer. Other stories insisted that the doctors simply had him carried to the Petersen house without saying anything to Clark. But finally they brought him up the winding steps of that lodging house across the street from the theatre and then down a hall into the room rented a few days previously by Private Clark.

Clark's back room, one flight up, into which Lincoln was brought, was only fifteen feet square. It was covered with a worn Brussels carpet (bits of which were appropriated not long after by souvenir-hunters), and had walls papered in brown. From those walls hung an engraved copy of Rosa Bonheur's "Horse Fair," and also an engraved copy of J. H. Herring's "Village Blacksmith" and two smaller ones by the same artist, titled "The Stable" and "The Barnyard." A table and bureau spread with crochet work, chairs and a bed comprised the furniture. Upon this bed, a walnut four-poster, they laid Lincoln.

Soon the Surgeon-General of the United States Army, Dr. Joseph K. Barnes, and the Lincolns' family physician, Dr. Stone, arrived. Dr. Taft narrated: "About twenty-five minutes after the President was laid upon the bed, Surgeon-General Barnes and Dr. Robert King Stone, the family physician, arrived and took charge of the case. . . . At Dr. Stone's suggestion, I placed another teaspoonful of diluted brandy between the President's lips, to determine whether it could be swallowed, but as it was not, no further attempt was made."

During that horrible night Dr. Neal Hall, with whom Dr. Stone had consulted during the last illness of Lincoln's son, Willie, more than three years before, came in, as did other prominent Washington physicians, including Dr. J. F. May and Dr. C. H. Lieberman. A cousin of Mrs. Lincoln, Dr. Beecher Todd of Lexington, Kentucky, was present most of the night. Other medical men there were Acting Surgeon Ford and Dr. E. W. Abbott. Abbott kept a detailed record of the President's pulse and respirations, which was released to the press nearly hourly, as a grief-stricken nation waited for the latest "extra" edition of their town newspapers.

Lincoln's upper eyelid was dark and swollen after he was put to bed. Thirty minutes later the inner angle of the right eye grew dark and swollen, and soon there appeared what Dr. Milton H. Shutes, modern Lincoln scholar and physician, calls "a double exophthalmus." At half-past eleven, a twitching of Lincoln's left side developed, which continued for fifteen to twenty minutes, with the mouth pulled slightly to the left side. The intracranial pressure, causing strain on the heart and lung centers, was frequently relieved by removing blood clots from the wound.

At one A.M., spasmodic contractions of the forearms occurred, and the muscles of the chest became fixed, causing the breath to be held during the spasm, which in turn was relieved by a sudden expulsive respiration.

One hour later, at two, Dr. Barnes attempted to find the bullet with an ordinary silver probe which met obstruction in the path of the bullet about two inches deep.

Booth had pulled his trigger aiming at the back of the left side of Lincoln's head, and the bullet had shot obliquely toward his right eye. In his autopsy report, written by another but approved by him, Surgeon-General Barnes stated:

> The fatal wound was on the left side of the head, behind and in a line with and three inches from the left ear. The course of the ball was obliquely forward toward the right eye, crossing the brain in an oblique manner and lodging a few inches behind that eye. In the track of the wound were found fragments of bone, which had been driven forward by the ball, which was embedded in the anterior lobe of the left hemisphere of the brain. The plates of both eyes were the seat of communicated fracture, and the eyes were filled with extravasated blood. The serious injury of the orbit plates was due to the centre-coup, the result of the intense shock of so large a projectile fired so closely to the head. The ball was evidently a Derringer (sic), hand-cast, and from which the neck had been clipped. A shaving of lead had been removed from the ball in its passage through the bones of the skull and was found in the orifice of the wound. The first fragment of bone was found two and one-half inches within the brain; the second and larger fragment about four inches from the orifice of the wound. The ball lay still further in advance. The wound was about one-half inch in diameter.

VI

When Lincoln was carried into the Petersen house, Mrs. Lincoln, near collapse, was helped through the narrow hall into that back bedroom, escorted by Major Rathbone, his arm still bleeding, and Clara Harris.

In the crowding and confusion the First Lady momentarily lost sight of him and shrieked, "Where is my husband? Where is my husband?" She was tenderly guided into the room, where the President lay breathing heavily. The constant sound of her husband's labored efforts at respiration drove her into such convulsions of grief that at intervals she had to be led away from the bedroom and be taken to a front room, from which her heart-broken sobs and exclamations could be heard.

Rushing to console Mrs. Lincoln was Mrs. Elizabeth Cogswell Dixon, wife of Senator James Dixon of Connecticut, accompanied by her relative, a Mrs. Kinney. They arrived at midnight. Mrs. Dixon, two weeks later, sent an account of those hours to her sister:

"Miss Harris's dress was spattered with blood as was Mrs. Lincoln's who was frantic with grief beside him calling on him to take her with him, to speak one word to her—but her agonizing appeals were of no avail! I led her & supported her as well as I could & twice persuaded her to go into another room."

The Lincolns' son, Robert, came rushing into the Petersen house, flew up the stairs and in to see his sinking father, with whom he had never been on the closest of personal terms. Never before had this naturally cold-natured eldest son of the President been so broken. And he cried on Senator Sumner's shoulder. Then Major Rathbone fainted from loss of the blood seeping from his arm and was carried home. This made Miss Harris weep even more. The President dying, her good friend, Mrs. Lincoln, hysterical, and her fiance bleeding and unconscious!

The diabolical news of Lincoln's shooting spread with nearly lightning-like speed. A mad rush was made for the Petersen house on Tenth Street. Adjutant-General Isham N. Haynie of Illinois arrived early accompanied by Governor Richard J. Oglesby, the two Springfielders to whom Lincoln had read pages from "Petroleum V. Nasby" only before dinner that same evening. Haynie noted in his diary: *"April 14, 1865.* . . . At 11 P.M. Governor Oglesby and myself were admitted to the room. Remained. . . . The cabinet all surrounded the dying chief. . . . Surgeon-General Barnes, holding the President's arm, feeling his pulse; the cabinet seated around, and some standing; Governor Oglesby at the head of the bed, and myself near the door. The President lay with his feet to the west; his head to the east; insensible; in comatose state; never spoke."

Secretary of the Navy Welles, in understatement, jotted down in his diary: "The room was small and overcrowded. The surgeons and members of the Cabinet were as many as should have been in the room, but there were many more, and the hall and other rooms in the front or main house were full. . . . The excitement and bad atmosphere from the crowded rooms oppressed me physically."

Soon Secretary of War Stanton arrived and took charge of everything. He set up an office in an adjoining room. He sent for his Assistant Secretary of War, Charles A. Dana, and started sending scores of communiques, orders to army commanders and civil officers of the federal Government, and had subpoenaes served on seemingly everyone who had even the remotest association with the crime or suspected assassins. He determined who should be arrested.

Some of Stanton's orders were intelligent. Others were foolish and bordered on hysteria and sheer emotionalism.

VII

While doctors struggled hopelessly to save Lincoln's life, news spread through Washington, and over the wires by telegraph to all parts of the country, about the shooting of the President. It all burst like a black thunderbolt out of a calm sky, made so calm only five days before by General Lee's surrender and the end of the war.

Men and women had dashed out of Ford's Theatre, yelling to all within ear shot: "The President is shot!" "Lincoln's murdered!"

As the news circulated and was retold time after time in the space of an hour, even more gruesome details were added, so that rumor was rife for a while, and in some crowded regions of the city, the American national capital, like Paris in 1789, was held vice-like in a reign of veritable terror.

Anger and threats of revenge against the unknown assassins and assailants alternated among the Washington crowds who darkened the streets with sorrow and sympathy for Lincoln. Some who waited in vigil outside of Petersen's house on Tenth Street looked across and growled irately: "Burn the theatre!" Men, women and children were out on seemingly every street for miles around, throbbing with alternate anger, sorrow, and fear. Men let forth vile epithets, some of them profane, against the still unknown assassin of Lincoln. They feared that other killers might be lurking in the dark, and their faces looked fearfully distressed as they tearfully made inquiries about the President's condition. He still lived, they were assured. But for how long they asked agonizingly.

Then again anger asserted itself. All over Washington crowds gathered aimlessly all night long, while the military and civilian police searched for the assassins still at large, patrolling and weaving cordons of armed guards around the approaches and exits of the city and in its outskirts.

Weird tales about more impending disaster were given credence by the news that, simultaneously with Booth's shooting of Lincoln, an assassin had stabbed Secretary Seward, Seward's son (the Acting Secretary of State), and two other men at the Seward home in Lafayette Square, opposite the White House. The Seward mansion was turned into a bloody field that night—at the same time that Booth was murdering Lincoln!

Booth's accomplice and instrument, Powell, had appeared at Seward's home and asked the servant to see the Secretary of State, who was convalescing from his carriage accident of the previous week. Powell's pretext was that he was bringing Seward medicine from the doctor. When he was refused admission by Seward's son, Frederick, the Acting Secretary of State, Powell pushed his giant frame inside. He grappled with Frederick Seward in an effort to fire his pistol, and then savagely beat the junior Seward over the head until the weapon broke. Frederick went down, unconscious.

Instantly Powell dashed up stairs to Secretary Seward's bedroom. He plunged a bowie knife into Seward several times, cutting his throat on both sides and nearly severing the Secretary's right cheek from his face.

Powell, however, had not yet finished his homicidal rampage.

When the male army nurse attending Seward, George T. Robinson, tried to protect the Secretary of State, Powell went after him with his knife, stabbing Robinson several times. Another of the Secretary's sons, Major Augustus Seward of the Army, rushed in, garbed only in underwear and was knocked down and almost cut by Powell, who now flew down the stairs. On the way he wounded another man, a Department of State messenger coming in.

Then Powell rode off madly on his waiting horse. The steed was found within two hours, abandoned, drenched in perspiration with the bridle cloth stained with blood.

When Quartermaster-General Montgomery C. Meigs was summoned to Seward's home by news of the dreadful happenings there, he found some rooms in partial shambles with Lincoln's Secretary of State on the floor, groaning and bleeding, gashed with knife wounds. Seward's son, Acting Secretary of State Frederick W. Seward, was in a coma, deeply stabbed. The Department of State messenger was gagging with blood from a stab by Powell. And on the white coat of the male army nurse, Robinson, the damp red spot was spreading. Seward's daughter, Fanny, lay unconscious on the floor, the result of terror.

And how was George Atzerodt, another Booth dupe, doing in his assigned task of killing Vice-President Andrew Johnson?

Occupying room 126 at the Kirkwood House, near the Vice-President's quarters there, the Port Tobacco coach painter had his lethal tools all in readiness for the murder job. But he spent his time, while Booth was shooting Lincoln and Powell was stabbing Seward, going from bar to bar, in company with young David Herold, who had been assigned by Booth to guide Powell out of the city after Powell visited the Secretary of State. When it came time for Atzerodt to end the Vice-President's life, he could not find it within himself to do it.

After more visits to saloons, Atzerodt and Herold parted on their separate ways of flight. The coach painter hurried into western Maryland, and the young simpleton, Herold, started on his way to join his mentor and idol, Booth.

All of the while Lincoln's assassin was at large.

VIII

Booth, in his flight from Ford's Theatre after shooting the President at about 10:30 o'clock, had jumped on his horse, galloped madly along F Street, around the Capitol to Pennsylvania Avenue, and had come to the Navy Yard Bridge, his straightest, shortest, and quickest route into southern Maryland.

But he was halted at the bridge by a Sergeant on guard duty there!

Sergeant Silas T. Cobb stopped Booth at the bridge between 10:30 and 11 o'clock. He detained the fast-riding horseman, asked his name, residence, and destination. Booth gave his correct name and answered Cobb's questions to Cobb's satisfaction and was allowed to continue on his way. The Sergeant later testified under oath:

"He said, 'My name is Booth.' I asked him where he was from. He made answer, 'From the city . . . I am going home [to Charles County, Maryland] . . . I live close to Beantown' . . . I asked him why he was out so late. . . . He said . . . it was a dark night, and he thought he would have the moon to ride home by. . . . I thought he was a proper person to pass, and I passed him." Sergeant Cobb further related: "In perhaps five or seven minutes another person came along. . . . I asked who he was, and he said that his name was Smith, and that he was going home; that he lived at the White Plains . . . said that he had been in bad company . . . I allowed him to pass."

It turned out that "Smith" was David Herold! And he caught up with Booth shortly.

Booth and Herold, now together, stopped at Lloyd's Tavern in Surrattsville (present-day Clinton) in Maryland at midnight to obtain whiskey and a carbine secreted there.

From Surrattsville the two fugitives galloped off on the road to the village of T. B. There they stopped long enough to mend a broken saddle girth. Booth's left leg was paining him excruciatingly. The two raced their horses to the home of a Southern-sympathizing physician, Dr. Samuel A. Mudd, near Bryantown. Booth had damaged his leg as he went flying down from Lincoln's box to the stage. Booth shortly entered in his diary: "In jumping broke my leg. I passed all his [Lincoln's] pickets, rode sixty miles that night with the bone of my leg tearing the flesh at every jump. I can never repent it though we hated to kill. Our country owed all her troubles to him and God simply made me the instrument of his punishment."

Booth and Herold reached Dr. Mudd's house at four in the morning. That physician told his story afterwards under oath:

> On opening the door I found two men, one on a horse led by the other man who had tied his horse to a tree near by. I aided the man in getting off his horse and into the house, and laid him on a sofa in my parlor.
>
> After getting a light, I assisted him in getting up-stairs where there were two beds, one of which he took. He seemed to be very much injured in the back, and complained very much of it. I did not see his face at all. He seemed to be tremulous and not inclined to talk, and had his cloak thrown around his head and seemed inclined to sleep, as I thought, in order to ease himself; and every now and then he would groan pretty heavily.

The younger man, who really was Herold, gave his name to Dr. Mudd as "Huston" and called his older companion, who of course was Booth, "Tyson" or "Tyser," according to Mudd.

Today a controversy rages among historians and Lincoln scholars concerning the guilt of Mudd, who was to be convicted as a party to the murder conspiracy and then sentenced to the army prison on Dry Tortugas Island, Florida, a sort of American "Devil's Island," not to be freed until President Johnson pardoned him.

Dr. Mudd and his wife had once had Booth as an overnight guest some months before, it is alleged. It is certain that Booth had once been introduced to the physician. The modern scholarly biographer of the Booth family, Stanley Kimmel, interprets Mudd as vastly more guilty than the physician's defenders have portrayed him. Mudd's role still continues as one of the scores of moot questions in the never-ending controversies among historians and scholars with which the Lincoln story is filled. Today there is an ever-increasing number who accept as true Dr. Mudd's protest that he did not recognize Booth as Booth.

"Tyson," rather Booth, told Mudd that he wanted to have his leg fixed up roughly, until he could get home and consult with his regular physician, or Mudd declared that Booth told him. Mudd made a splint for the assassin's leg by doubling a piece of an old bandbox. The Doctor testified:

"On examination I found there was a straight fracture of the tibia above the ankle. My examination was quite short, and I did not find the adjoining bone fractured in any way. I do not regard it a peculiarly painful wound; there was nothing resembling a compound fracture. . . ."

Mudd slit "Tyson's" left boot across the instep and removed it. Written inside was the name, "J. Wilkes." This lettering proved the means of later identifying "Tyson" as Booth, Lincoln's assassin.

Dr. Mudd and his odd-jobs man, an Englishman named John Best, made a pair of rude crutches for the injured murderer's use. Late that Saturday afternoon, April 15, between four and five, Booth and Herold departed from Mudd's place. The two fugitives from Lincoln's murder hurried on their flight, with swarms of soldiers and detectives pursuing them.

IX

The assassins were still at large!

A form of mania, verging on partial hysteria and near panic, seized the multitude in Washington from the very few minutes after Booth shot Lincoln, and continued all night long.

Mingled with unrestrained grief over Lincoln's now ebbing life were fears that the Southern rebellion, so confidently and happily believed to have been suppressed by Lee's surrender, could still strike another blow at the Union. When terror-stricken citizens heard the further appalling news of the stabbing of Seward and his son, perpetrated at the same hour as that in which Booth committed his mad act, this public feeling swelled into blatant emotionalism and hysteria. The wildest tales found quick belief and easy credence.

Seward was not merely wounded but had been knifed to death instantly; Vice-President Johnson was killed; and General Grant, on his train to New Jersey, was already murdered—these were among the stories spread throughout Washington and by telegraph to all parts of the nation. It was highly emotionally suspected that this was all part and parcel of the resurgence of a newly infused formidable Southern conspiracy. The Confederacy was still grimly alive, with terror injected into it, even political assassination! Maybe the rebels, supposed to have been crushed for good at Appomattox, would soon seize Washington!

With the federal Government's functioning at a standstill, the nation with a dying President and no directing head, Secretary of War Stanton took full charge. There was indeed no one else to assume responsibility. Vice-President Johnson, in the harrowing novelty of his new position, was awed to passive docility. Besides, there had never been any such thing as an "Acting President of the United States," with the President still alive. The Cabinet's first officer, the Secretary of State, was badly wounded by Powell's knife wounds, some people gravely reporting that he could not live. Secretary of the Treasury McCulloch knew little except banking and financial affairs. Stanton, as Secretary of War, was truly the next ranking Cabinet officer.

Stanton, convinced that the shooting of Lincoln and stabbing of Seward were parts of a grand, organized, elaborate Southern plot to kill all other heads of departments, including himself, placed all War Department resources, soldiers, civilian personnel, secret-service men, material, money, and military transportation and communication systems into his relentless drive to arrest all persons connected, or even remotely suspected of association with attacks on Lincoln, the administration, or the Union cause. It was all an unfinished Confederate conspiracy against the Republic, concluded the Secretary of War grimly, and he was acting against the guilty and taking precautions to thwart future violence. Prisons, army and civil, were being filled in Washington and vicinity even before the dawn of Saturday, April 15, rose in the sky.

Stanton caused to be sent out emotion-infused telegrams to army commanders and civil government officials, revealing that "the murderer of the President has been discovered" and erroneously stating that it was nothing but a Southern plot, a conspiracy "deliberately planned and set afoot by rebels." And some of Stanton's hysteria was reflected in the enforcement conduct of army commanders and police officials.

Soon a sullen dawn was breaking out of the black skies after this night of horror.

X

At the Petersen house crowds had stood all night long outside on Tenth Street and surrounding thoroughfares; they appeared partially broken with sadness, partially inflamed by the assassins still being at large, partially frightened lest other killers be roaming about.

Inside the house, in Private Clark's rented room, the torturous early morning hours had passed without change in the President's condition. But only occasionally the well known personalities packed around Lincoln's bedside in the humid, cramped atmosphere, had changed to make space for others.

At frequent intervals Mrs. Lincoln, still semi-hysterically sobbing and near physical and mental collapse, had come into the room, then had grown more grief-stricken and had let out more shrieks of fright as she watched her husband laboriously trying to breathe, stretched on the bed diagonally. The First Lady, after gentle persuasion by women friends, including Mrs. Dixon, had allowed herself to be led out into a front room where she was shielded from onlookers who had packed the narrow hallway.

After those dark hours of horror, a gray dawn broke through the sky. It was soon to rain heavily. That dawn dimmed the bleak gaslight in the overcrowded bedroom.

Mrs. Lincoln's anguish increased and grew more audible with each view of her sinking husband. One War Department clerk, James Tanner, who knew shorthand and lived next door to the Petersen house, had been called into service by Assistant Secretary of War Dana to take down the testimony of witnesses. Tanner, a former Corporal of the 87th New York Volunteer Infantry from upstate Schoharie County, whose legs had been amputated following wounds suffered at Second Bull Run, walked on artificial limbs. In shorthand he sent a description of Mrs. Lincoln during her hours of tremendous ordeal at the Petersen house. Tanner wrote his friend, Henry F. Walch, two days later:

> In the front room Mrs. Lincoln was uttering the most heart broken exclamations all the night long. As she passed through the hall to the parlor after she had taken leave of the President for the last time—as she went by my door, I heard her moan, 'Oh, my God, and have I given my husband to die?' and I tell you, I never heard so much agony in so few words. The President was still alive, but sinking fast.

At 6:45 Saturday morning I finished my notes and passed into the back room where the President lay. It was very evident that he could not last long. There was quite a crowd in the room, which was small, but I approached quite near the bed on which so much greatness lay, fast loosing its hold on this world. The head of the bed was near the door. At the head stood Captain Robert Lincoln, weeping on the shoulder of Senator Sumner. General Halleck stood just behind Robert Lincoln and I stood just between him and General Meiggs (sic). Stanton was there, trying every way to be calm and yet he was very much moved. The utmost silence pervaded, broken only by the sounds of strong men's tears. It was a solemn time, I assure you.

Secretary of the Navy Welles, at Lincoln's bedside since before midnight, had gone out for a short walk, and had seen the crowds of people outside. He noted in his diary: "I took a short walk in the open air. It was a dark and gloomy morning, and rain set in. Large groups of people were gathered every few rods, all anxious and solicitous. Intense grief was on every countenance when I replied that the President could survive but a short time."

At six the President's right eye, behind which was lodged Booth's bullet, had become ever more swollen and discolored. At that hour the doctors' bulletin of his condition had read, "Pulse failing;" that at half-past six, "Still failing." Now the reading at seven grimly said: "Symptoms of immediate dissolution."

Reverend Dr. Phineas D. Gurley, pastor of the New-York Avenue Presbyterian Church in Washington, where Mrs. Lincoln worshipped and had a pew, came in at seven. "All present," related Dr. Gurley shortly after, "were gathered anxiously around him, waiting to catch his last breath. The physician with one hand upon the pulse of the dying man, and the other hand laid upon his heart, was intently watching for the moment when life should cease." Then the clergyman offered some prayers.

As Lincoln's life ebbed to expiration during that last twenty minutes, around his bed, or outside in the hall trying to look in, were gathered, in addition to the battery of doctors and all his Cabinet members except the sick and unconscious Seward, various government officials, military and civilian, personal friends, and a few miscellaneous people. Among them were Assistant Secretary of the Treasury Maunsell B. Field, Assistant Secretary of the Interior William T. Otto, Robert Lincoln, Senator Sumner, Congressman (and Brigadier-General) John F. Farnsworth of Illinois, General Halleck, Quartermaster-General Meigs, John Hay, Governor Oglesby of Illinois, Rufus F. Andrews, Surveyor of the Port of New York, General John B. S. Todd of Dakota Territory, a cousin of Mrs. Lincoln, Clara Harris, and others whom it is difficult to identify today.

Lincoln's last moments are perhaps best described by that talented young physician who had first treated him in the Ford's Theatre box,

Dr. Charles A. Leale, who in later years was to have a distinguished career in New York City medicine. In that previously quoted letter to Congressman Ben Butler, which he wrote two years later, Leale also described Lincoln's very last minutes alive:

> As morning dawned it became quite evident that he was gradually sinking, and at several times his pulse could not be counted, two or three feeble pulsations being felt and followed by an intermission when not the slightest movement of the artery could be felt. The inspiration now became very prolonged, accompanied by a gutteral sound. At 6:50 A.M. the respirations ceased for some time and all eagerly looked at their watches until the prolonged silence was disturbed by a prolonged inspiration which was soon followed by a corrorous expiration.
>
> During his dying moment the Surgeon-General held his finger to the carotial artery.
>
> Col. Crane [Assistant Surgeon-General] held his head. Dr. Stone who was sitting on the bed held his left pulse, and his right pulse was held by myself. . . .
>
> We arose to witness the struggles between life and death. At 7:20 he breathed his last.

Lincoln was dead. But most authorities placed his passing at 7:22.

Secretary Stanton broke the tomb-like stillness by asking Reverend Curley: "Doctor, will you say something?"

The clergyman answered quietly: "I will speak to God" and then said a prayer, while all in the room bowed heads. When he had finished, they spontaneously intoned: "Amen."

Surgeon-General Barnes tenderly drew a sheet over the dead President's face.

At this point Stanton uttered that enduring phrase: "Now he belongs to the ages."

TO THE AGES

42

I

UNPRECEDENTED public interest in Abraham Lincoln's funeral throughout the North, stimulated by extreme coverage in the press, served to dampen excitement and temporarily soften angry demands for vengeful action and relentless retaliation against the South.

Under Surgeon-General Joseph K. Barnes' supervision, an autopsy was performed on Lincoln before he was embalmed on the Saturday on which he died. The bullet from Booth's pistol was removed from the President's body. The Lincolns' family physician, Dr. Robert King Stone, who was present, testified the next month:

"Previous to the process of embalment, an examination was made in the presence of Surgeon-General Barnes, Dr. Curtis, and Dr. Woodward, of the army. We traced the wound through the brain, and the ball was found in the anterior part of the same side of the brain, the left side; it was a large ball, resembling those which are shot from the pistol known as the Derringer [Deringer]; an unusually large ball—that is, larger than those found in ordinary pocket revolvers. It was a leaden hand made ball, and was flattened somewhat in its passage through the skull, and a portion had been cut off in going through the bone."

After the autopsy, Lincoln's body was turned over to Brown & Alexander, undertakers, one of whose employees, Harry P. Cattell, embalmed it. Cattell had prepared the Lincolns' son, Willie, for burial more than three years previous. Cattell did his work at the President's own room in the White House west wing, in the presence of President Johnson and (representing Secretary Stanton) Generals Augur and Rucker. Cattell drained the dead Chief Executive of his blood and removed those parts of his body that might produce decay in near future. A strong chemical preparation, of undetermined identification, was injected which hardened the corpse to an almost stone-like consistency, giving the body firmness and the solid immobility of a statue.

The embalmer and undertakers reputedly were not permitted to remove a discoloration on Lincoln's face by chemical means, by Stanton's stern order. And so the President would go to his grave with Booth's mark plainly visible, to be seen by hundreds of thousands who would view his face as his body lay in state in cities on the way back to Springfield.

Government officials wanted to have Lincoln interred in the unused Capitol niche which had been prepared for Washington's remains but had never been used. A delegation from Springfield, however, persuaded Mrs. Lincoln, who had first considered Chicago as a final resting place, that Lincoln's home town was best. Springfield had not taken any chances on losing Lincoln's body to another city and had hurried this committee of persuasive townsmen on its way to Washington to see the First Lady and the son, Robert, to expedite the return of the lifeless Lincoln to Springfield. Springfielders and other Sangamon Countyites had immediately purchased a plot of ground in the center of the town (site of the present-day Illinois Capitol building) from the Mather family, where they planned to bury Lincoln and erect an elaborate monument to his hallowed memory. But soon Mrs. Lincoln, who agreed to Springfield as the burial place for her husband, was heard from, in dissenting vein.

Stanton, still calling many of the tunes, decided that Lincoln's funeral must be military. He also immediately set about arranging an itinerary and schedule for special trains with various railroads required to transport Lincoln's body home to Springfield. Some felt that the funeral cortege should follow in reverse the identical route over which Lincoln, as President-elect, had traveled from Springfield to Washington more than four years before. But Stanton now altered the itinerary of 1861 slightly. He omitted Pittsburgh and Cincinnati. He included Chicago, instead of having the funeral train go directly from Indianapolis to Springfield.

II

Lincoln on Monday, April 17, was laid out in his Second Inauguration black suit in the White House guest room, preparatory to being brought down to the East Room for public view. Officials and close friends came to bow and pray before the four-poster bed, whose pillow was strewn with flowers.

Mrs. Lincoln hardly left that room all day long. Comforting her for a while was the Lincolns' old, beloved family friend and physician, Dr. Anson G. Henry, who had always neglected medical practice to plunge into Whig politics with Lincoln in the early Illinois years. In 1841 Lincoln had tried to persuade President Harrison's administration to give the Springfield postmastership to Henry, even writing his then law partner, Congressman John T. Stuart, in Washington: "Dr. Henry is necessary to my existence."

Now Dr. Henry was comforting Mary Todd Lincoln, the widow, before the lifeless form of Lincoln. "I sought the presence of poor heartbroken Mrs. Lincoln," Henry wrote home to his wife in Washington Territory.

> I found her in bed more composed than I had anticipated, but the moment I came within her reach she threw her arms around my neck and wept most hysterically for several minutes, and this completely unmanned me again, but my sympathy was to her most consoling, and for a half hour she talked most composedly about what had transpired between her and her Husband the day and evening of his death.

The widowed First Lady told the old family physician and friend how she had not wanted to go to Ford's Theatre that night, but the President concluded that a comedy on stage would do him good.

The distraught, even half mentally unhinged Mary Todd Lincoln grew worse as she overheard workmen mounting the mourning framework in the East Room in preparation for the laying out of Lincoln in state. In a few days, the son of Secretary of the Navy and Mrs. Gideon Welles, Edgar, after talking with his mother, Mary Lincoln's best friend in Washington, privately wrote a friend that "every plank that dropped gave her a spasm and every nail that was driven seemed to her like a pistol shot." In another three weeks, after Lincoln had been buried in Springfield, the First Lady still was staying, aimlessly, at the Executive Mansion. Noah Brooks, Lincoln's young California newspaper friend, slated to have been Nicolay's successor as presidential secretary, on May 10 sent word to one clergyman: "Mrs. Lincoln still remains at the White House, shattered and broken by the horrors of that dreadful night, as well as worn down by bodily sickness." All that time the new President, Johnson, still lived at the Kirkwood House, and used space in the Treasury building for his offices.

Most places of business were mournfully closed on Saturday, the 15th, the day of Lincoln's death. The next day was Easter, when clergymen throughout the nation had the assassination as their sermon themes, and on Monday people from seemingly all over the North flocked into Washington. Dry goods stores and dealers in "Yankee notions" advertised their readiness to make up black mourning dresses, bonnets, and veils for women, and tailors hawked their wares of crepe bands for men's hats and sable sashes. Huge supplies of jet-colored draperies were immediately rushed to the national capital on order from New York.

Every over-crowded train, with all standing room occupied, coming into Washington now disgorged its load of passengers, influential and obscure.

Tenth Street swarmed with sight-seers. By devious means they tried to gain entrance to Ford's Theatre and look into the room of the Petersen house across the street, where Lincoln had breathed his last. That room was still rented to Private Clark of the Tenth Massachusetts Regiment, and in another two days Clark wrote home to his sister in Boston:

> Hundreds daily call at the house to gain admission to my room. . . . Everybody has a great desire to obtain some memento from my room, so that whoever comes in has to be closely watched for fear they will steal something. I have a lock of Mr. Lincoln's hair, which I have had neatly framed; also a piece of linen with a portion of his brain. The pillow and case upon which he lay when he died, and nearly all his wearing apparel, I intend to send to Robert Lincoln as soon as the funeral is over, as I consider him the mostly justly entitled to them. The same mattress is on my bed, and the same coverlid covers me nightly that covered him while dying. Enclosed you will find a piece of lace that Mrs. Lincoln wore on her head during the evening and was dropped by her while entering my room to see her dying husband; it is worth keeping for its historical value. The cushion worked by Clara, and the cushion by you, you little dreamed would be so historically connected with such an event.

Not only Private Clark acquired a bit of Lincoln's hair. So, too, did Dr. Robert King Stone, the Lincolns' family physician, who gave it to an army officer, George D. Wise. Another of Lincoln's attending physicians, Dr. Charles Sabin Taft, cut off a piece of Lincoln's locks, left it to his son, who sold it to John Hay, Lincoln's assistant secretary. Years later, in 1905, Hay, then Secretary of State in President Theodore Roosevelt's Cabinet, gave it to Roosevelt, who proudly and delightedly carried it during his presidential inauguration ceremony.

Thus was inaugurated, even before Lincoln was interred, that thriving hobby, growing into a commercial enterprise, of collecting very intimate pieces of Lincoln's property, or presumably Lincoln's property, pieces of rail allegedly split by Lincoln as a youth in Indiana and Macon County, Illinois, opera glasses supposedly used by the Lincolns at Ford's Theatre that night, and countless other objects actually or, more often, merely allegedly used by Lincoln.

III

The deceased Lincoln was allowed to remain in the White House guest room from the Saturday of his death, the 15th, until Tuesday, the 18th, when he was laid in an open casket, costing $1,500, under a giant catafalque in the East Room, to be viewed by the public.

The East Room had been prepared in mourning furnishings under supervision of one of the undertakers, John Alexander. Windows and chandeliers were draped with black barege. Pictures were enshrouded, mirrors covered with white crape. The central chandelier was removed to make room for the colossal catafalque which would support the coffin. On top of that casket a silver plate bore the simple engraved inscription:

ABRAHAM LINCOLN
16th President of the United States
Born February 12, 1809
Died April 15, 1865

George Alfred Townsend, the New York *World's* competent Washington correspondent, acclaimed for his minute and accurate details of Lincoln's funeral, and shortly to be the first biographer of John Wilkes Booth, on April 19 described the President in his casket. Townsend pictured Lincoln as deeply ensconsed in white satin stuffing, with a cross of lilies at his head, an anchor of roses at his foot. The lid was drawn back to show his face and bosom. Atop the coffin rested heather, flowers, and sprigs of green. "Death has fastened into his frozen face all the character and idiosyncrasy of life," noted Townsend. "He has not changed one line of his grave, grotesque countenance, nor smothered out a single feature. The hue is rather bloodless and leaden; but he was always sallow. The dark eyebrows seem abruptly arched; the beard, which will grow no more, is shaved close, save the tuft at the short small chin. The mouth is shut, like that of one who had put the foot down firm, and so are the eyes, which look as calm as slumber."

Practically all of Washington's population filed into the East Room, many abreast, causing a problem for the guards and White House attendants; and also thousands of others from Virginia, Maryland, Delaware,

Pennsylvania, and farther regions of the nation. All day long they surged steadily past the President's bier. The Paymaster's clerk, Charles A. Sanford, who had been in the audience at Ford's Theatre four days before on that night, now sent word to his friend in Michigan: "The rush & jam to see him is indescribable. It is with the utmost difficulty that the guard can restrain the crowd which extends up the street 50 or 60 rods. They are not allowed to pass in faster than they pass out. No one is allowed to loiter but must pass by the catafalco (sic) under which the President lies without stopping."

When the White House gates closed late that Tuesday night, April 18, Lafayette Park and adjoining streets were still packed with people of all ages clamoring for admission.

IV

As Lincoln's funeral was being prepared, the search for his assassins was pushed feverishly.

As that horrible night of April 14-15 wore away, overwhelming evidence pointed to John Wilkes Booth as the dark, mustached man seen entering Lincoln's theatre box and then, after the pistol shot was heard from inside there, leaping down from the box to the stage, in full view of nearly all the audience. By daylight the actors's guilt was reasonably certain. The search for him and his accomplices was harrowingly and turbulently evidenced throughout Washington and vicinities in Virginia and Maryland. And a monster manhunt it was, the likes of which had never been seen anywhere in the United States. Since lucrative rewards were offered for the apprehension of the wanted assassins—a total of $100,000—the chase after them grew into something of a treasure hunt, quite aside from the eager determination to capture the men who had ended Lincoln's life.

Next to the biggest criminal was caught early. On April 17 Powell, who had cut up Secretary Seward and his son and two other men, was arrested when he returned to Mrs. Surratt's house after hiding out in the woods for more than two days. On the same day Booth's original conspirators, Samuel B. Arnold and Michael O'Laughlin, who had participated in the kidnapping, but not the murder plot, were roughly taken into custody, Arnold at Fort Munroe and O'Laughlin in Baltimore. Three days later, the 20th, Atzerodt, drunk, was captured in western Maryland. Those four, along with Booth's dupe, Edman Spangler, were locked in double irons and thrown into the hold of a monitor anchored off the Navy Yard. Mrs. Mary E. Surratt, John Surratt's mother and owner of the boarding house where the conspirators sometimes met, was arrested early, only hours after Booth shot Lincoln.

Still at large, however, were Booth and Herold, who together were hiding out in southern Maryland and soon escaped into Virginia. John Surratt, in Elmira, New York, at the hour when Booth shot Lincoln, was also in flight and ultimately escaped to Italy, where he joined the Papal Zouaves, and was not tried as an accomplice to Lincoln's murder until two years later, when he was acquitted.

The accused conspirators (all except Booth who was killed and John Surratt who was still at large) during the weeks after Lincoln's burial were, irregularly, tried for the President's murder by a military commission, when the ordinary civil criminal courts were open and fuctioning. Lawyers, concerned for the American constitutional processes, protested—and have been protesting ever since in legal articles—that the military commission held no jurisdiction over Booth's fellow conspirators, since such army tribunals were not courts within the meaning of the United States Constitution. Legal authorities maintained then, and today, that the accused murderers of Lincoln, in being tried by a military commission, were deprived of the right of trial by jury. But in those emotion-charged days of May, June, and July, 1865, no one successfully contradicted the Johnson Administration's contention that a military tribunal held jurisdiction over civilians by virtue of "war powers"—even though the nation was not at war!

Powell, who had knifed Seward and his son; Atzerodt, who reneged at the decisive hour on his Booth assignment to kill Vice-President Johnson; Herold; and Mrs. Surratt, mother of John Surratt, were to be found guilty and hung. Also found guilty, but given prison sentences, were Dr. Mudd, who had set Booth's injured leg, Edman Spangler, and the two Marylanders, Samuel B. Arnold and Michael O'Laughlin, who had participated in Booth's plot to kidnap Lincoln but were not involved in Lincoln's murder.

Meanwhile, as Lincoln's funeral was about to be held at the White House, preparatory to having the President's body brought back to Springfield for burial, two of the wanted assassins were still at large: Booth himself and his youthful instrument, David Herold.

V

Abraham Lincoln's official funeral ceremony took place at the White House on April 19. On each side of the metal casket were four silver handles, with stars between and a vein of silver winding around the whole case in serpentine form. This rested upon a canopied catafalque and was decorated with wreaths of evergreen and moss, with white flowers and lilies intermingled.

Around the catafalque, at noon, were gathered Robert Lincoln (Mrs. Lincoln was too weak to attend and Tad could not bear to be present), the officiating clergymen, delegations representing various Northern states and Kentucky, representatives of the Sanitary Commission and the Christian Commission, Cabinet members and their Assistant Secretaries, Senators and Representatives in Congress, the nine United States Supreme Court justices, among whom Judge David Davis, with his obese form, was conspicuous, the Diplomatic Corps, and others who managed to secure an admission ticket.

Reverend Charles H. Hall of the Church of the Epiphany in Washington opened the services by reading from the Episcopal burial service the passage beginning with, "I am the resurrection and the life," and then, opening the Bible, he intoned the sonorous sentences of the fifteenth chapter of First Corinthians. This was followed by a prayer from Bishop Matthew Simpson of the Methodist church. Reverend Phineas D. Gurley of the New-York Avenue Presbyterian Church, which Mrs. Lincoln attended, and who had been at the Petersen house when Lincoln died, preached the funeral discourse. The service was closed with prayer by Reverend Edgar H. Gray, Chaplain of the United States Senate, a Baptist.

Among those attending the White House funeral service was the prominent New Yorker, George Templeton Strong, member of the Sanitary Commission. Strong confided to his diary about the new President, Andrew Johnson, taking a last glance at his deceased predecessor: "President Johnson, stepping quietly up to the side of the coffin, looking down a few minutes solemnly and thoughtfully upon the dead face—a subject for some future Delaroche."

At two in the afternoon, booming cannon and tolling bells announced that the funeral services were terminated. Then Lincoln's casket was carried out of the White House, his home for more than four years, and placed in a huge hearse. That somber black vehicle, specially built for the journey down Pennsylvania Avenue and up Capitol hill, measured fourteen feet long, seven feet wide, with a towering canopy "surmounted by a gilt eagle, covered with crepe." Numerous regimental bands, playing in muffled tone mournful dirges, preceded the hearse. More guns boomed, and horse-drawn artillery, covered with black crepe, moved ahead of the hearse. Then followed the pall-bearers on either side. Directly behind followed Lincoln's horse, riderless.

After the hearse and Lincoln's horse, came his son Robert. President Johnson, closely escorted by Former Senator Preston King of New York, his close friend, Cabinet members, the nine Supreme Court justices including portly Judge David Davis, the Diplomatic Corps, and numberless government officials, down to departmental bookbinders. Bringing up the rear marched members of lodges, clubs, organizations, and delegations of one sort or another. In all, an estimated 50,000 followed Lincoln's remains from the White House up to the Capitol.

During that hour the wounded Colonel Selden Connor, a future Governor of Maine, recuperating in Douglas Hospital, heard the mournful music and shots accompanying the funeral. He sent his sister these thoughts:

> While I write, the sound of minute guns booming a hoarse requiem for the nation's highest, most loved and honored man, now cold in death, comes in at my open window. . . . President Lincoln was a great and good man, and not even the great and good Washington deserved more of the country; but from all I hear the impression prevails, and it is certainly my own, the nation will benefit by the martyrdom of her greatest son. Ah! how unruffy (sic) boom the guns and toll the bells as I write! Flags wave listlessly and a solemn hush seems to rest on the city.

Connor had only the day before written his father: "The survived republic is his most fitting monument."

Lincoln's funeral procession met head-on with a Negro regiment on Pennsylvania Avenue, whereupon the colored troops did a prompt "to the rear" march and headed the procession up to the Capitol. Thousands lined curbstones on either side of the avenue, most of them weeping or endeavoring to restrain tears.

Lincoln's casket was placed in the rotunda of the Capitol, and the public was permitted to file past and glance at Lincoln's face for the last time in the national capital. Over 25,000 managed to catch a fleeting farewell glimpse at the body before the casket was closed and prepared for its next show place.

At six o'clock on the morning of Friday, April 21, there gathered in the Capitol rotunda the Cabinet members, General Grant and his staff, Senators and Representatives, high Army and Navy officers, and other dignitaries. After a prayer by Reverend Gurley, the party followed the coffin to the railroad station, from which a special train was to convey the President's remains to Springfield.

Crowds waited in silence as the casket was placed in the car. Men stood with bared heads, women in bowed bonnets, and children fidgeted, in tomb-like silence.

At the foot of Lincoln's coffin was placed a smaller one, containing the remains of Lincoln's son, Willie, who had passed away more than three years before. Following Mrs. Lincoln's directions, Willie's body was disinterred from its Washington burial site, and father and son were to make together this last earthly journey.

VI

On that Friday, the 21st, when Lincoln's funeral train started circuitously and slowly from the Potomac to the prairies along its 1,600-mile route, the President's slayer, Booth, was still at large in southern Maryland, with his young accomplice, David Herold. On that day, just one week following his murder of the President, Booth made an entry in his diary as he and Herold hid out in the thickets and swamps:

> *Friday, 21*—After being hunted like a dog through swamps and woods, and last night being chased by gunboats till I was forced to return, wet, cold, and starving, with every man's hand against me, I am here in despair. And why? For doing what Brutus was honored for—what made William Tell a hero; and yet I, for striking down an even greater tyrant than they ever knew, am looked upon as a common cut throat. My act was purer than any of theirs. One hoped to be great himself; the other had not only his country's, but his own, wrongs to avenge. I hoped for no gain; I knew no private wrong. I struck for my country, and her alone. A people ground beneath this tyranny prayed for this end, and yet now see what cold hands they extend to me! God can not pardon me if I have done wrong; yet I can not see any wrong, except in serving a degenerate people. The little, the very little, I left behind to clear my name the Government will not allow to be printed. So ends all! For my country I have given up all that makes life sweet and holy—to-night misfortune upon my family, and am sure there is no pardon for me in the heavens, since man condemns me so. I have only heard of what has been done (except what I did myself), and it fills me with horror. God, try and forgive me and bless my mother. To-night I will once more try the river, with the intention to cross; though I have a greater desire and almost a mind to return to Washington, and in a measure clear my name, which I feel I can do.
>
> I do not repent the blow I struck. I think I have done well, though I am abandoned, with the curse of Cain upon me, when, if the world knew my heart, that one blow would have made me great, though I did no greatness. To-night I try once more to escape these bloodhounds. Who, who, can read his fate! God's will be done. I have too great a care to die like a criminal. Oh! may He spare me that, and let me die bravely. I bless the entire world. I have never hated nor wronged anyone. This last was not wrong, unless God deems it so, and it is with Him to damn or bless me. And for this brave boy, Herold, here with me, who often prays (yes, before and since) with a true and sincere heart, was it crime in him? If so, why can he pray the same? I do not wish to shed a drop of blood, but I must fight the course. 'Tis all that's left me.

Booth, hiding out in lower Maryland, accompanied by Herold, ever since Dr. Mudd of Bryantown had treated his injured leg six days before, was virtually enclosed by pursuing Federal soldiers, Stanton's civilian secret-service men, and Washington Police Department detectives. Once the troops rushed by so closely that the two fugitives from Lincoln's murder could hear the rattling of the officers' sabres. Heavy rewards were on their heads, resulting in a vastly enlarged search. Stealthily fleeing from one hiding place in the wooded country to another, trying to get over the Potomac River into Virginia, and finding concealment difficult and escape nearly impossible, Booth and Herold were secretly fed and supplied by Southern sympathizers, especially a farmer and former Confederate underground-mail runner, Thomas A. Jones.

Jones awaited his chance to spirit Booth and Herold across the river secretly. He risked his life, and at least dared imprisonment, when instead he might have obtained a portion of the $100,000 reward money for the assassins' capture, not so much, Jones testified, through loyalty to the crushed Confederacy as through sympathy for Booth, who even in his despair retained his old theatrical charm and fascination.

On the early morning of April 26, while President Lincoln was lying in state in New York's City Hall, en route back to Springfield, United States troops and the War Department's secret-service detectives tracked Booth and Herold to a tobacco barn on the farm of Richard H. Garrett near Port Royal, Virginia.

Owing to the fact that the three officers in charge of the pursuers, Lieutenant Edward P. Doherty of the Regular Army, Lieutenant-Colonel Everton J. Conger of the Secret Service, and Lieutenant Luther Baker, also of the Secret Service, gave conflicting testimony in a subsequent avaricious quarrel over the reward for Booth's capture, the exact details are difficult to re-enact exactly. But the main outlines are clear.

Booth and Herold, hiding in the tobacco barn on Garrett's farm, were summoned to surrender. Herold did so and came out of the barn and threw himself into the custody of his captors. But Booth dramatically maintained an undaunted attitude. Theatrical to the end, he called out from the barn through the pre-dawn darkness: "Captain, give a lame man a chance. Draw up your men before the door, and I'll come out and fight the whole command!" This request being refused by the besiegers, Booth's voice rang out in thespian-like vein: "Well, my brave boys, you can prepare a stretcher for me!"

The pursuers set the barn afire to burn or smoke Booth out. The assassin of Lincoln was dimly seen for a moment in the blaze, erect on the crutch that Dr. Mudd's hired man had made for him.

Suddenly a shot was heard. It came apparently from the gun of one of the pursuing soldiers, Sergeant Boston Corbett of the Sixteenth New York Cavalry. Corbett's act was completely unauthorized by his superior officers. Some students contend, however, that it was Lieutenant-Colonel Conger's shot that went into Booth. But most scholars have concluded that Corbett was the man who fatally wounded the man who fatally wounded President Lincoln.

Corbett had seen Booth through a crack in the barn. Leveling his cavalry six-shooter, Corbett aimed, fired, and Booth fell. Lieutenant

Doherty and detectives Conger and Baker, aided by Corbett and others, rushed into the burning barn, and brought out Lincoln's wounded assassin. Booth breathed for two hours more. Found on his dead body were guns, a pocket knife, a compass, and his diary.

They sewed Booth's body into a sack and brought it to the Navy Yard in Washington. With Secretary of War Stanton's approval, or perhaps by his order, it was taken aboard the Navy monitor, *Montauk,* where it was identified by Dr. John F. May, a distinguished Washington surgeon who had operated on Booth's neck for a tumor the previous year. The corpse of Lincoln's murderer was then, on April 27, 1865, secretely buried under the floor of a warehouse in the Arsenal Grounds on Greenleaf's Point, where at that time it was customary for dead felons to be buried.

Not until four years after he had shot Lincoln, in 1869, was Booth released to his family for re-burial. President Johnson, in signing an order for the War Department to turn Booth's body over to the Booth family, stipulated that no monument or mound would be permitted to mark the actual location of Booth's grave.

With some fellow actors serving as pallbearers, Booth in 1869 was reinterred in an unmarked grave of the Booth family's burial plot at Greenmount Cemetery in Baltimore.

For years thereafter tales persisted that the corpse brought back from Garrett's farm was not Booth's body. These were the stories of rumormongers and elaborated by authors with ghoulish imaginations, who contributed sensational "Sunday supplement" features about how Lincoln's assassin had really escaped and was prowling here, there, or somewhere above ground.

But it can reasonably be concluded, on unimpeachable historical evidence, that Boston Corbett mortally shot Booth (if it was not Lieutenant-Colonel Conger) and that Booth's remains were positively identified by Dr. May and others in a position to know. Plethoras of post-Lincolnian stories about the "real Booth" still living in Oklahoma and various other unlikely places for the next few decades belong in the realm of fantasy and mystery fiction.

Such writers of tales of the "escaped" Booth still make a gross story of alleged authenticity, and their odd conclusions are given a semblance of credulity by the mystery which Secretary Stanton chose to throw around the capture, death, identification, and burial of Booth.

VII

"The funeral of Abraham Lincoln! How can justice be done to the theme? The obsequies continued through sixteen days and sixteen nights.

. . . History has no parallel to the outpouring of sorrow which followed the funeral *cortége* on its route from Washington to Springfield." So commented Brigadier-General E. D. Townsend, who accompanied the funeral train from the Potomac to the prairies.

Lincoln's elaborate funeral train procession started from Washington on April 21. It was a veritable mass pageant of exaltation to the dead, as untold hundreds of thousands, estimated at more than 2,000,000, thronged the tracks over which the special train traveled at a crawl on its 1,600-mile roundabout route to Springfield. The mourners, who looked on his face, as he lay in state in principal cities of the nation, were the most numerous ever to view any American in death.

Springfield was finally reached at nine o'clock in the morning twelve days later, on May 3. Bishop Simpson would soon observe in his funeral oration: "Far more eyes have gazed upon the face of the departed than ever looked upon the face of any other departed man. More eyes have looked upon the procession than ever before watched the progress of a procession."

In not too distant St. Louis, Missouri, Lincoln's former Attorney-General, Edward Bates, had attended services at his church some days before. The preacher's tone was "harsh, vindictive, and out of keeping with his usually bland and amicable character." Bates confided to his diary about that clergyman's sermon on Lincoln's assassination: "This cry for vengeance is not his natural temper, and I can not help fearing that his ardent temperament has been worked upon by crafty partizans, to make him seem to be one of them. For I know that it is the present scheme of the extreme radicals, who never were Lincoln's friends, to make party capital out of his flagitious murder."

After Lincoln's burial, his assassination would indeed be made a major pretext for meting out punishment to the "rebel" South for partisan political reasons.

For days before Lincoln's funeral train had reached Springfield, thousands had poured into town from seemingly everywhere in Illinois and outside of the State. Crowds visited the Lincoln brown-painted house on Eighth and Jackson Streets, Abraham and Mary Lincoln's home for seventeen years before his inauguration—a dwelling rented since 1861 to Lucian A. Tilton, head of the Great Western Railroad. The Tilton family was now kept busy and exhausted in showing rooms to strangers, rooms which had now turned into hallowed ground. Crowds around the house grew so thick that it was found necessary to prevent depredations and dismantling of it by souvenir hunters. A few of these chipped off pieces of the fence, and one man was caught carrying away a brick from the wall.

Lincoln's body was transferred from the draped railroad car and placed in a large black hearse from St. Louis, which had been used for the late

Senator Thomas Hart Benton seven years before. Drawn by six superb black horses, this hearse carried Lincoln's remains to the Doric-columned yellowish brown state Capitol and to the House of Representatives Hall, followed by a long procession of the 146th Illinois Volunteer Infantry, a Wisconsin detachment of troops, a guard of honor, and thousands of grief-bent citizens.

How drastically different had been the circumstances of Lincoln's departure from Springfield back in February, 1861, from those which were now witnessing his return after more than four years of warfare and turbulent politics, followed by his own murder. This thought gnawed agonizingly at the minds of all. From the moment that Lincoln's casket was opened to the public at 10 o'clock on that May 3 morning, a never-ending stream of Illinoisans and out-of-staters filed past reverently.

Hardly any one in all of Springfield grieved more deeply than Lincoln's law-partner, William H. Herndon. Before he had departed for Washington in February, 1861, Lincoln had glanced up at the battered shingle, LINCOLN & HERNDON, and had told "Billy" Herndon: "Let it hang there undisturbed. Give our clients to understand that the election of a President makes no change in the firm of Lincoln and Herndon." The junior partner had remained in Springfield, carrying on the firm's practice during the President's harrowing war years and had never been asked advice on any governmental point by Lincoln.

Now with Lincoln dead, Herndon confessed that "I did not feel like doing any business." Three weeks later he would confide in a letter to a Massachusetts friend:

> My good friend—*is* gone—yet is with us in *Spirit,* The news of his going struck me dumb, the deed being so infernally wicked—so monstrous—so huge in consequences, that it was too large to enter my brain. Hence it was incomprehensible, leaving a misty doubt of its truth. . . . It is . . . grievously sad to think of—one so good—so kind—so loving—so honest—so manly, & so *great,* taken off by the murderous hand of an assassin.

Suddenly an unpleasant controversy over Lincoln's burial place in Springfield flared briefly. One group there, without consulting Mrs. Lincoln who had remained in Washington under a doctor's care, had already bought six acres of what was called the Mather grounds in the heart of Springfield (on the site of the present day Illinois State House) and were planning to bury the President there. When the widowed First Lady found out about it, she angrily refused her consent, presumably for two good reasons: Lincoln had supposedly requested that he be interred in a quiet country cemetery when he died, and also, Mrs. Lincoln feared that she could not be buried beside him in a public location in town. Others claimed that she did not like the Mather family, from whom the planned burial site had been bought. Mrs. Lincoln, through her son,

Robert, demanded that Lincoln be buried in Oak Ridge Cemetery, on the town's outskirts.

Local Springfield interests, which might have been financially involved, were furious over Mrs. Lincoln's refusal to have her husband interred in the Mather location and criticized her unsparingly.

A Republican lawyer and politician of Charleston, Illinois, Henry P. H. Bromwell, future Congressman, watched the funeral arrangements in Springfield. On April 30, three days before Lincoln's remains reached there, he wrote a letter to his parents, telling about Mary Todd Lincoln's veto of the Mather grounds and the town's reaction to it: "The people have bought the Mather grounds in the heart of the city six acres for a burial place. . . . They got it for 5300.00 and have a vault nearly finished, but last night Mrs. Lincoln telegraphed that she would not let him be buried there. The people are in a rage about it and all the hard stories that were ever told about her are told over again. She has no friends here."

Lincoln's son, Bob, supported his mother in the controversy over the location of the final resting place. On May 1, two days before his father's remains reached Springfield, he sent a tart telegram to Governor Richard J. Oglesby of Illinois: "There seems to be a disposition at Springfield to disregard my mother's wishes in regard to the interment. Both the temporary and final interment must take place in the Oak Ridge Cemetery. We have reasons for not wishing to use the Mather place for either purpose and we expect and demand that our wishes should be consulted."

And so the Mather location in town was abandoned, and certain groups in town were inflamed over Mrs. Lincoln's decision. Lincoln would be buried in Oak Ridge Cemetery, two miles out of town.

VIII

Near noon on Thursday, May 4, Lincoln's coffin was sealed—nineteen days after he died. The funeral procession to Oak Ridge Cemetery started.

A twenty-one-gun salute was fired, followed by single shots at intervals. Lincoln's bier was brought from the Doric-pillared State House, placed in the hearse surmounted with profuse flowers and evergreens. From the portico a chorus solemnly sang:

> Children of the Heavenly King,
> As we journey let us sing,
> Sing our Saviour's worthy praise,
> Glorious in his works and ways.

Lord, obediently we'll go,
Gladly leaving all below;
Only thou our leader be,
And we still will follow thee.

General "Fighting Joe" Hooker led the long funeral procession to the cemetery. The Guard of Honor was the 146th Illinois Volunteers, the most complete unit available. The march played by the band, heading the procession, was "O Wrap The Flag Around Me, Boys," purportedly the words of a dying Union soldier. The lyrics ended:

Then wrap the flag around me, boys,
To die were far more sweet,
With Freedom's starry emblem, boys,
To be my winding sheet.

The cemetery reached, the choir chanted again. Lincoln's body was placed in a temporary vault. Nearby was laid the body of Willie.

Prayer was offered by Reverend Albert Hale, followed by a dirge composed for the occasion by G. W. Root of Chicago. Reverend N. W. Miner read selections from the first chapter of John's Gospel, after which a choral was sung. Reverend A. C. Hubbard read Lincoln's Second Inaugural: "With malice toward none; with charity for all. . . ."

Then Bishop Matthew Simpson of the Methodist Church pronounced the funeral oration—an extraordinarily political one, with appeals to take retribution against the South. After praising the dead President, his mental talents and his genius, the Bishop praised him for giving freedom to a race. The "High Priest of Radical Republicans," as his biographer called him, Simpson, a friend of both Secretary Stanton and Chief Justice Chase, praised the administration of the War Department and the Treasury Department under the late Lincoln and then spoke some vindictive words toward the conquered Confederacy—quite out of keeping with Lincoln's views—directly after quoting Lincoln's words, "With malice toward none. . . ." To the deluded masses, Simpson would extend his "arms of forgiveness" down South, but every man, who as Senator or Representative, had aided in the Rebellion, was to be "brought to speedy and to certain punishment;" and every secession military leader, educated at public expense, must be "doomed to a traitor's death." Men might attempt to compromise and to restore these "traitors and murderers" to society again. But the American people would "rise in their majesty and sweep all such compromise and compromisers away."

From this bitter mood Bishop Simpson returned to words of praise for his country, the flag, and Lincoln: "Chieftain, farewell! The nation mourns thee. Mothers shall teach thy name to their lisping children. The youth of our land shall emulate thy virtues. Statesmen shall study thy record, and from it learn the lessons of wisdom. . . . We crown thee as our martyr, and humanity enthrones thee as her triumphant son. Hero, Martyr, Friend, farewell."

The final funeral services closed with the choir singing the doxology and the benediction by Reverend Gurley of Washington.

Then the vast multitude melted away and sought the railroad depots, from which the special trains would transport them to their homes—to the north, east, west, and south.

BIBLIOGRAPHY AND NOTES

GENERAL NOTE ON BIBLIOGRAPHY AND SOURCES FOR ABRAHAM LINCOLN

Paul M. Angle, *A Shelf of Lincoln Books: A Critical, Selective Bibliography of Lincolniana* (New Brunswick, N.J., 1946) lists less than 100 books on Lincoln, of the thousands that appeared from 1860 to 1945, which he considers the only works essentially accurate and of enduring value published up to that latter year. Mr. Angle's guide remains the most discriminating, intelligent appraisal of the unnumbered thousands of books on Lincoln, and it is hoped that he will bring his *A Shelf of Lincoln Books* up to date. Strongly recommended by the present author is James G. Randall, "Has the Lincoln Theme Been Exhausted?" *The American Historical Review*, January, 1936, pp. 270-294, in which the late Professor Randall, incontestably the greatest of all twentieth-century Lincoln scholars, analysed the then present condition of Lincoln publications.

A list of books, published during the past three decades and a half, most of them the work of historians, which add to our knowledge of Lincoln's life and career, follows:

Papers of the Abraham Lincoln Association, 1929-1939, successively edited by Paul M. Angle, Benjamin P. Thomas, and Harry E. Pratt; *The Abraham Lincoln Quarterly*, 1940-1952, edited successively by Harry E. Pratt, William E. Baringer, and Roy P. Basler.

Paul M. Angle (ed.), *Created Equal? The Complete Lincoln-Douglas Debates of 1858* (Chicago, 1958), the most accurate edition of the debates; Paul M. Angle, *"Here I Have Lived:" A History of Lincoln's Springfield, 1821-1865* (Springfield, Ill., 1935), the best account of Lincoln's home town while he lived there; Paul M. Angle (ed.), *Herndon's Life of Lincoln* (Cleveland, Ohio, 1949), with valuable footnotes by Angle; Paul M. Angle, *Lincoln, 1854-1861* (Springfield, Ill., 1933), listing Lincoln's day-by-day activities from the beginning of 1854 until his presidential inauguration in 1861. Companion volumes by Harry E. Pratt, Benjamin P. Thomas (see below) cover other periods. See also Paul M. Angle (ed.), *The Lincoln Reader* (New Brunswick, N.J., 1947), the most judicious of all Lincoln anthologies.

William E. Baringer, *A House Dividing: Lincoln As President-Elect* (Springfield, Ill., 1945), in scholarly fashion treating Lincoln from his presidential election in November, 1860, to his inauguration in March, 1861; William E. Baringer, *Lincoln's Rise to Power* (Boston, 1937), a lively written and accurate account of Lincoln's nomination for President in 1860; William E. Baringer, *Lincoln's Vandalia: A Pioneer Portrait* (New Brunswick, N.J., 1949), the definitive treatment of Lincoln's earlier years in the Legislature of Illinois.

William E. Barton, *The Life of Abraham Lincoln* (Indianapolis, 1925), 2 vols., written by one of the better early twentieth-century Lincoln students; William E. Barton, *The Lineage of Lincoln* (Indianapolis, 1929), ranking high as an authority on Lincoln's ancestry; Roy P. Basler, *The Lincoln Legend: A Study of Changing Conceptions* (Boston, 1936), a scholarly and readable study of American opinion of the post-assassination Lincoln; Roy P. Basler, Marion D. Pratt, and Lloyd A. Dunlap (ed.), *The Collected Works of Abraham Lincoln* (New Brunswick, N.J., 1953), 8 vols., and *Index* (1955), the definitive edition of Lincoln's letters, state papers, and other writings, a monumental work faultlessly researched and judiciously edited, which has superseded the previous *Works* edited by John G. Nicolay and John Hay, Lincoln's presidential secretaries; Maurice G. Baxter, *Orville H. Browning, Lincoln's Friend and Critic* (Bloomington, Ind., 1957), a monographic study revealing Lincoln's associations with his old conservative Whig friend from Quincy, Illinois; Howard K. Beale, *The Critical Year: A Study of Andrew Johnson and Reconstruction* (New York, 1930), indispensable for the radical Republican attack on President Johnson following Lincoln's death; Howard K. Beale (ed.), *Diary of Edward Bates, 1859-1866* (Washington, 1933), Bates being Lincoln's Attorney General. Also the same editor's *The Diary of Gideon Welles* (New York, 1960), 3 vols.

Albert J. Beveridge, *Abraham Lincoln, 1809-1858* (Boston, 1928), 2 vols., still the most distinguished and detailed scholarly biography of Lincoln from his birth to the Lincoln-Douglas debates, despite Beveridge's over-dependence on Herndon's collected material, inadequacy of the treatment of Lincoln's law career, and the author's acceptance of such legends as the Ann Rutledge "romance"; Jim Bishop, *The Day Lincoln Was Shot* (New York, 1956), the most lively and readable account of the assassination; Robert V. Bruce, *Lincoln and the Tools of War* (Indianapolis, 1956), detailing Lincoln's interest in ordnance and new weapons for the Union Army; George S. Bryan, *The Great American Myth* (New York, 1940), a little known and poorly circulated book, with an unfortunate title, but nonetheless the most accurate account of Lincoln's assassination; it is strongly recommended as the most carefully researched and reliable volume on the assassination.

Harry J. Carman and Reinhard H. Luthin, *Lincoln and the Patronage* (New York, 1943), a detailed account of President Lincoln's distribution of the federal jobs and favors; Olive Carruthers and R. Gerald McMurtry, *Lincoln's Other Mary* (Chicago, 1946), concerned with Lincoln's abortive romance with Mary Owens; Bruce Catton's works on the campaigns of the Union Army, particularly in the West: *Glory Road: The Bloody Route From Fredericksburg to Gettysburg* (Garden City, N.Y., 1952); *Grant Moves South* (Boston, 1960); *Mr. Lincoln's Army* (Garden City, N.Y., 1951); *A Stillness At Appomattox* (Garden City, N.Y., 1956); *This Hallowed Ground* (Garden City, N.Y., 1956); *U.S. Grant and the American Military Tradition* (Boston, 1954);

Marquis Adolphe de Chambrun, *Impressions of Lincoln and the Civil War: A Foreigner's Account,* translated by Gen. Aldebert de Chambrun (New York, 1952), the impressions of Chambrun, a French visitor who had married into the Lafayette family and who was on close terms with President and Mrs. Lincoln in the months preceding Lincoln's death; Charles H. Coleman, *Lincoln and Coles County, Illinois* (New Brunswick, N.J., 1955), containing hitherto little known facts about Lincoln's father, stepmother, and stepbrother; Ollinger Crenshaw, *The Slave States in the Presidential Election of 1860* (Baltimore, 1945), a brilliant and scholarly treatise on the conduct of that vital campaign in the South; Richard N. Current, *The Lincoln Nobody Knows* (New York, 1958), a stimulating book on the various disagreements among Lincoln authors, written by one of the premier Lincoln scholars; Norma B. Cuthbert (ed.), *Lincoln and the Baltimore Plot, 1861: From Pinkerton Records and Related Papers* (Henry E. Huntington Library, San Marino, Calif., 1949), containing hitherto unpublished material on the presumed plot to assassinate President-elect Lincoln as he passed through Baltimore in February, 1861.

Tyler Dennett (ed.), *Lincoln and the Civil War in the Diaries and Letters of John Hay* (New York, 1939), the day-book and correspondence of Lincoln's presidential assistant secretary, invaluable for a knowledge of events transpiring at the White House during 1861-1865; also the same author's *John Hay: From Poetry to Politics* (New York, 1934); David Donald, *Lincoln's Herndon* (New York, 1948), a superb treatment of Herndon as Lincoln's law-partner and later biographer; David Donald, *Lincoln Reconsidered* (New York, 1956), containing essays interpreting various aspects of Lincoln; David Donald (ed.), *Inside Lincoln's Cabinet: The Civil War Diaries of Salmon P. Chase* (New York, 1954), Chase being Lincoln's Secretary of the Treasury; Jonathan T. Dorris, *Pardon and Amnesty Under Lincoln and Johnson* (Chapel Hill, N.C., 1953), the definitive book on that complex subject; John J. Duff, *A. Lincoln, Prairie Lawyer* (New York, 1960), the all-embracing scholarly work on Lincoln's legal career, well-written and superseding all previous accounts of Lincoln as an attorney.

William A. Evans, M.D., *Mrs. Abraham Lincoln: A Study of Her Influence on Lincoln* (New York, 1932), a brilliant interpretation of Lincoln's wife, written by a physician and Lincoln authority, ranking high as an analysis of her; Douglas Southall Freeman, *R. E. Lee: A Biography* (New York, 1935), 4 vols., and the same author's *Lee's Lieutenants* (New York, 1942-1944), 3 vols., extremely helpful for a knowledge of the great Union-Confederate military campaigns; Norman A. Graebner (ed.), *The Enduring Lincoln* (Urbana, Ill., 1959), containing essays by Roy P. Basler, T. Harry Williams, David Donald, and Dr. Graebner; Wood Gray, *The Hidden Civil War: The Story of the Copperheads* (New York, 1942), the narrative of the disloyal Democratic Party opposition to Lincoln in the West.

David J. Harkness and R. Gerald McMurtry, *Lincoln's Favorite Poets* (Knoxville, Tenn., 1959), excellently treating Lincoln's main literary interest, poetry; Robert S. Harper, *Lincoln and the Press* (New York, 1951), the best account of Lincoln's relations with newspapers and journalists; Katherine Helm, *The True Story of Mary, Wife of Lincoln* (New York, 1928), useful for the diary extracts, letters, and reminiscences of Miss Helm's mother, Mrs. Emilie Todd Helm, one of Mrs. Lincoln's half-sisters; Burton J. Hendrick, *Lincoln's War Cabinet* (New York, 1948), concerning details of Lincoln's chief inner council advisers; William B. Hesseltine, *Lincoln and the War Governors* (New York, 1948), a scholarly account of the President's difficult relations with the Northern governors and those State Executives' indispensable aid in the war effort; Harlan Hoyt Horner, *Lincoln and Greeley* (Urbana, Ill., 1953), concerning the President's see-sawing relations with the celebrated and eccentric New York *Tribune* editor; Marie Hochmuth, "Lincoln's First Inaugural," in Wayland M. Parrish and Marie Hochmuth (ed.), *American Speeches* (New York, 1954), pp. 21-71.

Edgar DeWitt Jones, *Lincoln and the Preachers* (New York, 1948), which tells of various clergymen's relations with Lincoln; Robert Lee Kincaid, *Joshua Fry Speed: Lincoln's Most Intimate Friend* (Lincoln Memorial University, Harrogate, Tenn., 1943), containing illuminating and very personal correspondence between Lincoln and this closest of all cronies; Willard L. King, *Lincoln's Manager:* David Davis (Cambridge, Mass., 1960); Edward C. Kirkland, *The Peacemakers of 1864* (New York, 1927), the story of efforts to persuade President Lincoln to negotiate peace with the Confederacy; Henry B. Kranz (ed.), *Abraham Lincoln: A New Portrait* (New York, 1959), consisting of essays by twenty-two Lincoln authorities; Otto R. Kyle, *Abraham Lincoln in Decatur* (New York, 1957), detailing Lincoln's associations with Macon County, Illinois.

Margaret Leech, *Reveille in Washington, 1860-1865* (New York, 1941), the best narrative of Washington during Lincoln's presidency; Lloyd Lewis, *Myths After Lincoln* (New York, 1929), the title of which describes its contents, concerning the dead Lincoln in the American imagination; *Lincoln Herald,* an excellent quarterly published by Lincoln Memorial University, Harrogate, Tennessee, February, 1938, to date, edited successively by R. Gerald McMurtry and Wayne C. Temple; *Lincoln Lore,* April 15, 1929, to date, published periodically by the Lincoln National Life Foundation, Fort Wayne, Indiana, edited successively by Louis A. Warren and R. Gerald McMurtry; Reinhard H. Luthin, *The First Lincoln Campaign* (Cambridge, Mass., 1944), a detailed account of Lincoln's nomination for President in 1860 and the conduct of the campaign in the Northern states.

Edgar Lee Masters, *Lincoln the Man* (New York, 1931), the best known of the few anti-Lincoln books; William Q. Maxwell, *Lincoln's Fifth Wheel* (New York, 1956), the complete story of the United States Sanitary Commission; R. Gerald McMurtry, *Ben Hardin Helm* (Chicago, 1943), a short biography of Lincoln's Confederate brother-in-law; Jay Monoghan, *Diplomat in Carpet Slippers: Abraham Lincoln Deals With Foreign Affairs* (Indianapolis, 1945), a well-written book, which perhaps overemphasizes Lincoln's role in conducting diplomatic relations, for the President left most of that difficult field of foreign affairs to Secretary of State Seward; Guy W. Moore, *The Case of Mrs. Surratt* (Norman, Okla., 1954), the most thorough and analytical treatment of the allegedly guilty Mary Surratt in the conspiracy to kill Lincoln.

Allan Nevins's five notable volumes: *Ordeal of the Union* (New York, 1947), 2 vols., *The Emergence of Lincoln* (New York, 1950), 2 vols., and *The War For the Union: The Improvised War* (New York, 1959), Vol. I—embracing a comprehensive history of the United States from the end of the War with Mexico in 1848 and continuing through the Civil War in 1862, each volume containing abundant valuable material on Lincoln; Helen Nicolay, *Lincoln's Secretary: A Biography of John G. Nicolay* (New York, 1949), a life of Lincoln's main secretary, written by his daughter, based partly on Nicolay's private papers; Theodore C. Pease and James G. Randall (ed.), *The Diary of Orville Hickman Browning, 1850-1864* (Springfield, Ill., 1925), Vol. I, containing revealing material on Lincoln as recorded by Lincoln's then friend in Illinois, Browning. For Vol. II of Browning's diary, see under "James G. Randall;" David M. Potter, *Lincoln and His Party in the Secession Crisis* (New Haven, Conn., 1942), which deals intelligently and in critically scholarly fashion with Lincoln's handling, or perhaps lack of handling, of the secession of the Southern states between his election and his inauguration.

Harry E. Pratt, *The Personal Finances of Abraham Lincoln* (Springfield, Ill., 1943), one of the great specialized works on Lincoln, appraising him as business man, investor, saver of money, and collector of legal retainers, written by one of the truly learned Lincoln scholars of the twentieth century; Harry E. Pratt, "David Davis, 1815-1886," *Transactions of the Illinois State Historical Society,* 1930, pp. 157-183, short biography of Judge Davis of the Eighth Judicial Circuit and Lincoln-appointed Justice of the United States Supreme Court, Lincoln's personal friend and "King-maker" in 1860; Harry E. Pratt, *Lincoln, 1809-1839* (Springfield, Ill., 1941) and also the same author's *Lincoln, 1840-1846* (Springfield, Ill., 1939), listing Lincoln's day-by-day activities for those years; Harry E. Pratt (ed.), *Concerning Mr. Lincoln* (Springfield, Ill., 1944), a compilation of illuminating letters about Lincoln, written by contemporaries who saw and heard him, and recorded their impressions at that time. The late Dr. Pratt, Illinois State Historian, was one of this century's truly eminent Lincoln authorities.

James G. Randall, *Lincoln, the President* (New York, 1945-1955), 4 vols., the last volume co-authored by Richard N. Current, a uniquely distinguished work, based on years of research, with evidence carefully appraised and sifted, containing sound conclusions, making it far and away the most authentic account of Lincoln during his presidency. Among Randall's other notable works are the following: *Constitutional Problems Under Lincoln* (New York, 1926); *The Civil War and Reconstruction* (New York, 1937) and future revised editions, the best survey of that critical period; *Lincoln, the Liberal Statesman* (New York, 1947), containing profound essays in Lincolniana; and *Lincoln and the South* (Baton Rouge, La., 1946); also his edition of *Diary of Orville Hickman Browning, 1865-1881* (Springfield, Ill., 1933), Vol. II. For Vol. I of this work, see under Theodore C. Pease. Indispensable for an understanding of Lincoln's personal, marital, and private life are the works of Mrs. James G. Randall: Ruth Painter Randall, *Mary Lincoln; biography of a marriage* (Boston, 1953), the most complete life of Mrs. Lincoln, especially favorable to her and condemnatory of Herndon as a vindictive critic of her; *Lincoln's Sons* (Boston, 1955), with revealing data on the Lincolns' offspring, Robert, Eddie, Willie, and "Tad"; and *The Courtship of Mr. Lincoln* (Boston, 1957), which narrates the uneven romance of Lincoln and Mary Todd, culminating in marriage.

James A. Rawley, *Edwin D. Morgan, 1811-1883: Merchant in Politics* (New York, 1955), an excellent treatment of Morgan, Republican National Chairman, war-time Governor of New York and U.S. Senator, in his relations with Lincoln; Donald W. Riddle's two monographs on Lincoln's successful campaign for Congress in 1846 and his service in the national House of Representatives: *Lincoln Runs For Congress* (New Brunswick, N.J., 1948) and *Congressman Abraham Lincoln* (Urbana, Ill., 1957).

Carl Sandburg, *Abraham Lincoln: The Prairie Years* (New York, 1926), 2 vols., and *Abraham Lincoln: The War Years* (New York, 1939), 4 vols., also the same author's one-volume condensation of that title (New York, 1954)—a massive work impressively performed, the lengthiest and most famous of all Lincoln biographies, brilliantly written, suffering only from this eminent poet and folklorist's inadequate knowledge of history, excessive number of errors in the 1926 and 1939 editions, and lack of documentation; Carl Sandburg, *The Lincoln Collector* (New York, 1950), a detailed and interesting story of Oliver R. Barrett and his then famous Lincoln collection; Carl Sandburg and Paul M. Angle, *Mary Lincoln, Wife and Widow* (New York, 1932), especially useful for the letters by Mrs. Lincoln edited by Angle.

Fred A. Shannon, *The Organization and Administration of the Union Army, 1861-1865* (New York, 1928), 2 vols., the most detailed and profound work on the subject; Milton H. Shutes, *Lincoln and the Doctors: A Medical Narrative of the Life of Abraham Lincoln* (New York, 1933), written by a physician and Lincoln authority, narrating facts about Lincoln's illnesses and his various doctors; David M. Silver, *Lincoln's Supreme Court* (Urbana, Ill., 1956), a well-written account of the highest court during the Civil War, treating also the Lincoln-appointed Justices, Swayne, Miller, David Davis, Field, and Chase, and also presenting the differences between Lincoln and Chief Justice Taney; Donnal V. Smith, *Chase and Civil War Politics* (Columbus, Ohio, 1931), useful for the role of Lincoln's ambitious Secretary of the Treasury in trying to supplant Lincoln as Republican-Union presidential candidate in 1864.

William E. Smith, *The Francis Preston Blair Family in Politics* (New York, 1933), Vol. II, containing good material on Lincoln's Postmaster General, Montgomery Blair, and his relations with Lincoln; Zarel C. Spears and Robert S. Barton, *Berry and Lincoln, Frontier Merchants* (New York, 1947), the story of Lincoln's New Salem store, in which he had William F. Berry as partner; Kenneth M. Stampp, *And the War Came* (Baton Rouge, La., 1950), treating the attitude of portions of the North toward the secession movement in 1860-61, Wayne C. Temple's two works: *Mrs. Frances Jane Todd Describes Lincoln's Wedding and Mrs. Mary Edwards Brown Tells Story of Lincoln's Wedding* (Harrogate, Tenn., 1960).

Benjamin P. Thomas, *Abraham Lincoln, A Biography* (New York, 1952), an accurate, extremely well-written one-volume life of Lincoln, done by one of the twentieth century's eminent Lincoln scholars; Benjamin P. Thomas, *Portrait For Posterity: Lincoln and His Biographers* (New Brunswick, N.J., 1947), interesting for the quarrels and disagreements between Lincoln authors; Benjamin P. Thomas, *Lincoln's New Salem* (Springfield, Ill., 1935) and Revised Edition of same (New York, 1948), best treatment of Lincoln's residence in that village between 1831 and 1837; Benjamin P. Thomas, *Lincoln, 1847-1853* (Springfield, Ill., 1936), listing Lincoln's day-by-day activities for those years.

William H. Townsend's two works on Lincoln's relations with Kentucky and Kentuckians: *Lincoln and His Wife's Home Town* (Indianapolis, 1929) and *Lincoln and the Blue Grass* (Lexington, Ky., 1955); and the same author's *Lincoln and Liquor* (New York, 1934), analyzing Lincoln's attitude toward the alcoholic problem and that issue in politics.

Charles G. Vannest, *Lincoln the Hoosier: Abraham Lincoln's Life in Indiana* (St. Louis, Mo., 1928), an early account of Lincoln's residence in Spencer County, Indiana, which has been superseded recently by Louis A. Warren's volume, listed below; Harold G. Villard and Oswald Garrison Villard (ed.), *Lincoln on the Eve of '61: A Journalist's Story* (New York, 1941), the compiled New York *Herald* dispatches about President-elect Lincoln, written by that newspaper's correspondent, Henry Villard, who "covered" Lincoln at Springfield and on his trip to Washington for his inauguration.

Louis A. Warren, *Lincoln's Parentage and Childhood* (New York, 1926), the standard work on Lincoln's earliest years in Kentucky, with much revealing material on Lincoln's father, written by a great Lincoln scholar of thirty years' standing and distinguished scholarship, the Director Emeritus of that great repository of Lincoln research materials, the Lincoln National Life Foundation, Fort Wayne, Indiana; Louis A. Warren, *Lincoln's Youth: Indiana Years, Seven to Twenty-one, 1816-1830,* published in 1959 by both the Indiana Historical Society, Indianapolis, Indiana, and Appleton, Century, Crofts, the definitive work on Lincoln's residence in Spencer County, Indiana.

John W. Wayland, *The Lincolns in Virginia* (Staunton, Va., 1946), concerning Abraham Lincoln's Virginia ancestry; Richard S. West's works on Lincoln's Secretary of the Navy and the administration and conduct of that department under President Lincoln: *Gideon Welles, Lincoln's Navy Department* (Indianapolis, 1943) and *Mr. Lincoln's Navy* (New York, 1957).

Kenneth P. Williams, *Lincoln Finds a General* (New York, 1949-1959), 5 vols., a history of the Union Army's military campaigns; T. Harry Williams, *Lincoln and the Radicals* (Madison, Wis., 1941), in scholarly fashion telling the story of the split between radicals and conservatives within Lincoln's Republican Party, and how it affected Lincoln; T. Harry Williams, *Lincoln and His Generals* (New York, 1952), an excellent analytical and narrative account concerning Lincoln's relations with the main Union commanders, emphasizing Lincoln's role as military strategist.

Albert A. Woldman, *Lawyer Lincoln* (Boston, 1936), a good but not definitive account of Lincoln's legal career; William F. Zornow, *Lincoln and the Party Divided* (Norman, Okla., 1954), the most complete account of Lincoln's successful re-election campaign in 1864.

NOTES TO CHAPTERS

Chapter 1—BACKWOODS BEGINNINGS

The best one-volume survey of Kentucky history from its beginnings is Thomas D. Clark, *A History of Kentucky* (New York, 1937). For accounts of the pioneer, frontier, and backwoods history of the State, consult the titles in J. Winston Coleman, Jr., *A Bibliography of Kentucky History* (Lexington, Ky., 1949), pp. 234-245.

The basic works on Lincoln's paternal ancestry are William E. Barton, *The Lineage of Lincoln* (Indianapolis, 1929); Marion Dexter Learned, *Abraham Lincoln: An American Migration* (Philadelphia, 1909), Waldo Lincoln, *History of the Lincoln Family* (Worcester, Mass., 1923); Louis A. Warren, *Lincoln's Parentage and Childhood* (New York, 1926), containing valuable data on Lincoln's father; John W. Wayland, *The Lincolns of Virginia* (Staunon, Va., 1946). See also Louis A. Warren, "The Lincolns—Frontiersmen All," *Lincoln Lore,* March 22, 1937. Lincoln's words about his paternal ancestry and his grandfather's death by Indians are quoted in his autobiography for Jesse W. Fell, 1859, which appeared in West Chester (Pa.), *Chester County Times,* February 11, 1860, and was widely recopied in the Republican press of that time.

Abraham Lincoln's reference to his father, Thomas Lincoln, as a "wandering labor boy" is contained in his autobiography for John L. Scripps of the Chicago *Press & Tribune,* June, 1860, a copy of which is in the Robert Todd Lincoln Collection, Library of Congress. Thomas Lincoln's later years, 1830-1851, are accurately followed in Charles H. Coleman, *Abraham Lincoln and Coles County, Illinois* (New Brunswick, N.J., 1955).

The wedding of Lincoln's parents is described in Louis A. Warren, "The Romance of Thomas Lincoln and Nancy Hanks," *Indiana Magazine of History,* September, 1934, pp. 213-222, based partly on Washington County, Kentucky, court records. For Reverend Head: J. Winston Coleman, Jr., "A Preacher and a Shrine: Rev. Jesse Head and the Lincoln Marriage Temple," *Lincoln Herald,* December, 1944, pp. 2-9; L. C. Pence, "Life of Rev. Jesse Head," Lebanon (Ky.) *Enterprise,* April, 1921–June, 1922. Dr. Drake's description of Kentucky frontier weddings of that era is in Emmet Field Horine, M.D. (ed.), *Pioneer Life in Kentucky, 1785-1800* (New York, 1948), p. 184. Graham's account of the "infare" following the Hanks-Lincoln wedding, dictated in 1882, is in Durrett Collection, University of Chicago Library.

Herndon's claim that Lincoln told him that his mother was illegitimately born is in William H. Herndon and Jesse W. Weik, *Herndon's Lincoln: The True Story of a Great Life* (Chicago, 1889), I, 3; Herndon to T. H. Bartlett, September 22, 1887, MS., Massachusetts Historical Society, Boston. Lincoln's letter to Haycraft, May 28, 1860, is in Roy P. Basler, Marion D. Pratt, and Lloyd A. Dunlap (ed.), *The Collected Works of Abraham Lincoln* (New Brunswick, N.J., 1953), IV, 56. This work will hereafter be cited as *Lincoln's Collected Works.* Dr. Louis A. Warren, who believes that Nancy Hanks was not born out of wedlock, makes a strong statement in her behalf in *The Lincoln Kinsman,* No. 33.

The description of "the Barrens," where Thomas Lincoln had his cabin, is taken from Francois Andre Michaux's *Travels into Kentucky,* in Reuben G. Thwaites (ed.), *Early Western Travels* (Cleveland, Ohio, 1904), III, 215ff. For an account of Elizabethtown: Samuel Haycraft, *History of Elizabethtown* (Elizabethtown, Ky., 1921). Lincoln's statement of his birth on Nolin Creek, not Knob Creek, is in his letter to Haycraft, June 4, 1860, Huntington Library, San Marino, California. For an account of Hodgen's mill, later Hodgenville, see Otis M. Mather, "History of Hodgenville," *Larue County* (Ky.) *News,* April 22, 1920. Consult also the same author's "Explorers and Early Settlers South of Muldraugh Hill," *Register of the Kentucky State Historical Society* (1924), Vol. 22, pp. 21-39.

Lincoln's earliest years in Kentucky are most accurately followed in Albert J. Beveridge, *Abraham Lincoln, 1809-1858* (Boston, 1928), Vol. I, Chapter 1, still the best treatment of Lincoln's life up to the Lincoln-Douglas debates; Harry E. Pratt, *Lincoln, 1809-1858: Being the Day-By-Day Activities of Abraham Lincoln From February 12, 1809, to December 31, 1839* (Springfield, Ill., 1941), pp. xii-xvii, 1-3; Warren, *Lincoln's Parentage and Childhood.* Herndon's statement about the paucity of information concerning Lincoln's Kentucky youth and Lincoln's reluctance to talk about that period of his life, plus the comments of John L. Scripps, are in Herndon and Weik, *Herndon's Lincoln,* 1889 edition, I, 1-2, 17; Scripps to Herndon, June 24, 1865, Herndon-Weik Collection, Library of Congress. Lincoln's quotation about his gift of a fish to a soldier is in John G. Nicolay and John Hay, *Abraham Lincoln: A History* (New York,

1890), I, 27. Lincoln's reference to his attendance at "A.B.C. schools," taught by Riney and Hazel, is in his autobiography for Scripps, June, 1860.

For the birth and death of the Lincolns' third child, presumed to have been named Thomas Lincoln, Jr., see R. Gerald McMurtry, "Rediscovering the Supposed Grave of Lincoln's Brother," *Lincoln Herald,* February, 1946, pp. 12-19; Warren, *Lincoln's Parentage and Childhood,* pp. 81, 136, 154-155; Josiah G. Holland, *The Life of Abraham Lincoln* (Springfield, Mass., 1866), p. 22, William L. Kent, "Tommy Lincoln's Grave Marked," *Lincoln Herald,* Summer 1960, pp. 51-53.

The legal difficulties of Lincoln's father over his Kentucky land titles are revealed in Harry E. Pratt, *The Personal Finances of Abraham Lincoln* (Springfield, Ill., 1943), p. 4. Lincoln's statement about land title difficulties being the main reason for his father's removal from Kentucky to Indiana is in his autobiography for Scripps. The Lincoln family's migration from Kentucky to Indiana in 1816 is described in Joseph H. Barrett, *The Life of Abraham Lincoln* (Cincinnati, 1860), p. 22. Lincoln's remarks about the difficulties of the last part of the trip from Kentucky to Indiana, told years later to Raymond, are quoted in Henry J. Raymond, *The Life and Public Services of Abraham Lincoln* (New York, 1865), p. 19.

Lincoln's life in Indiana is exhaustively and accurately treated in Louis A. Warren, *Lincoln's Youth: Indiana Years, Seven to Twenty-one, 1816-1830* (New York, 1959), a work of distinguished scholarship. See also Beveridge, *Abraham Lincoln, 1809-1858,* Vol. I, Chapter 2; Bess V. Ehrmann, *The Missing Chapter in the Life of Abraham Lincoln* (Chicago, 1938); *Pratt, Lincoln, 1809-1839,* pp. xvii-xxi, 4-7. Accounts of Lincoln's Indiana community include Thomas J. De La Hunt, *Perry County* (Indianapolis, 1916); William H. Cockrum, *Pioneer History of Indiana* (Oakland City, Indiana, 1907); (No author), *History of Warrick, Perry and Spencer Counties* (Chicago, 1885).

Lincoln's description of Indiana as a "wild" region and his work with the axe there during his first weeks there are in his autobiography for Scripps. Oliver Johnson's description of cabin building in southern Indiana is in "A Home in the Woods: Reminiscences of Early Marion County," *Indiana Historical Publications* (Indianapolis, 1951), Vol. 16, p. 149. For a controversy about the Lincoln cabin in Indiana: Charles H. Coleman, "The Half-Faced Camp in Indiana—Fact or Myth?" *The Abraham Lincoln Quarterly,* September, 1952, pp. 138-146. For social customs in Lincoln's Indiana home community, consult Ward H. Lamon, *The Life of Abraham Lincoln* (Boston, 1872), pp. 42ff. Lincoln's reference to having been kicked by a horse is in his autobiography for Scripps.

The passing of Lincoln's mother is detailed in Philip D. Jordan, "The Death of Nancy Hanks Lincoln," *Indiana Magazine of History,* June, 1944, pp. 103-110. A good sketch of Lincoln's stepmother is Louis A. Warren, "Sarah Bush Lincoln," *Transactions of the Illinois State Historical Society,* 1926, pp. 84ff. Thomas Lincoln's anecdote about his two wives, from Nancy Hall's scrap-book, is quoted in Carl Sandburg, *The Lincoln Collector* (New York, 1949), pp. 108-109.

Lincoln's reference to the poor quality of schools in Indiana is in his autobiography for Jesse W. Fell in 1859. For Lincoln's limited education in Indiana: Louis A. Warren, "Lincoln's Hoosier Schoolmasters," *Indiana Magazine of History* (1931), Vol. 27, pp. 104-118. Lincoln's childish doggerel is in *Lincoln's Collected Works,* I, 1. For Lincoln's written exercises in arithmetic: Lloyd A. Dunlap, "Lincoln's Sum Book," *Lincoln Herald,* Spring, 1959, pp. 16-19; M. L. Houser, *Young Abraham Lincoln, Mathematician* (Peoria, Ill., 1943). Dennis Hanks' remarks about Lincoln's informal education are quoted in Lamon, *Life of Abraham Lincoln,* p. 66. Lincoln's speech at Trenton in 1861, referring to Weems' biography of Washington, is printed in New York *Tribune,* February 22, 1861. Rev. Gulliver's remarks about Lincoln's early self-education are in "Mr. Lincoln's Early Life," New York *Times,* September 4, 1864.

John Romaine's remarks about Lincoln's indolence and aversion to hard labor are in the Herndon-Weik Collection, Library of Congress. For Lincoln's views on a farm, expressed to Speed in 1842, see *Lincoln's Collected Works,* I, 282. Lincoln's Wisconsin agricultural speech in 1859 is in Milwaukee *Sentinel,* October 1, 1859; Chicago *Press & Tribune,* October 1, 1859. Lincoln's reminiscence about earning his first dollar in one day is told in Francis B. Carpenter, *Six Months At the White House With Abraham Lincoln* (New York, 1867), pp. 96-97. Lincoln's litigation with the Dill brothers is described in William H. Townsend, *Lincoln the Litigant* (Boston, 1925) and John J. Duff, *A. Lincoln: Prairie Lawyer* (New York, 1960), pp. 4-5.

Lincoln's description of his flatboat trip to New Orleans with Gentry is in his autobiography for Scripps. Lincoln's strained relations with the Grigsbys because of his sister's death is mentioned in Jonathan T. Hobson, *Footprints of Abraham Lincoln* (Dayton, Ohio, 1909), p. 24. The indelicate doggerel, supposedly written by Lincoln and recited by Mrs. Crawford years later, is printed in Herndon and Weik, *Herndon's Lincoln,* 1889 edition, I, 55. Lincoln's doggerel about his Indiana home community, penned in 1844, is in *Lincoln's Collected Works,* I, 378. Lincoln's account of the trip from Indiana to Macon County, Illinois, in 1830 is in his autobiography for Scripps.

The Lincolns' year in Macon County, Illinois, is best followed in Edwin Davis, "Lincoln in Macon County, 1830-1831," *Journal of the Illinois State Historical Society,* April-July, 1932, pp. 63-107; Otto R. Kyle, *Abraham Lincoln in Decatur* (New York, 1957), Chapters 1-3. See also Mabel E. Richmond, *Centennial History of Decatur and Macon County* (Decatur, Ill., 1930); R. Gerald McMurtry, "The Lincoln Cabin on Boston Common," *Lincoln Lore,* November, 1958, pp. 1-3, describing the alleged Macon County Lincoln cabin, exhibited for admission fees at Boston in 1865. George Close's description of Lincoln's first political speech is taken from Roy P. Basler (ed.), "James Quay Howard's Notes on Lincoln," *The Abraham Lincoln Quarterly,* December, 1947, p. 391.

John Hanks' account of Offutt's offer is in the Herndon-Weik Collection, Library of Congress. Lincoln's written reminiscence about his employment by Offutt and the building of a boat for the New Orleans trip is in his autobiography for Scripps. For Offutt: William H. Townsend, *Lincoln and the Blue Grass* (Lexington, Ky., 1955), Chapter 4, and Harry E. Pratt, "Dr. Denton Offutt: Horse Tamer," *The Abraham Lincoln Quarterly,* September, 1943, pp. 330-333.

Chapter 2—NEW SALEM LIFE

Edgar Lee Masters, *The Sangamon* (New York, 1942), a blend of history, legend, and folklore, concerns the life and customs in Lincoln's region of Illinois through which flows the narrow, rather unnavigable Sangamon River, written by an eminent American man of letters, Masters, who had been born and raised in that part of Illinois. For Sangamon County history: Paul M. Angle, *"Here I Have Lived:" A History of Lincoln's Springfield,* (Springfield, Ill., 1935), pp. 1ff; John Carroll Power, *History of the Early Settlers of Sangamon County, Illinois* (Springfield, Ill., 1876); [No author], *History of Sangamon County, Illinois* (Chicago, 1881); [No author], *Portrait Biographical Album of Sangamon County, Illinois* (Chicago, 1891).

The meeting of Lincoln, Johnston, and Hanks with Offutt at Springfield in 1831, and their building of the flatboat at Sangamo Town for Offutt, are followed in William H. Townsend, *Lincoln and the Blue Grass* (Lexington, Ky., 1955), pp. 34-35. Caleb Carman's description of Lincoln in 1831 is in his letter to Herndon, November 30, 1866, Herndon-Weik Collection, Library of Congress. Erastrus Wright's description of Lincoln as he helped to build the boat is in "Lincoln in 1831," *Bulletin of the Abraham Lincoln Association,* December, 1937, p. 9. Lincoln's account of the hogs' sewed eyes and the flatboat trip down to New Orleans is in his autobiography for

Scripps, June, 1860. Lincoln's words to the voters in 1832 about the flatboat's mishap at the New Salem mill dam in April, 1831, are in Springfield (Ill.) *Sangamo Journal*, March 15, 1832. Lincoln's account of how Offutt hired him to be his clerk at the proposed New Salem store is told by him in his autobiography for Scripps. A copy of Lincoln's letter to Morris, March 26, 1843, about his being a penniless flatboat worker in 1831 is in the Herndon-Weik Collection.

Lincoln's residence of nearly six years in New Salem is most accurately detailed in Albert J. Beveridge, *Abraham Lincoln, 1809-1858* (Boston, 1928), Vol. I, Chapter 3. Excellent specialized treatments include William E. Barton, "Abraham Lincoln and New Salem," *Journal of the Illinois State Historical Society* (1926-1927), Vol. 19, pp. 74-101; Benjamin P. Thomas, *Lincoln's New Salem* (Springfield, Ill., 1934); Thomas P. Reep, *Lincoln At New Salem* (Petersburg, Ill., 1927); Harry E. Pratt, *Lincoln, 1809-1839: Being the Day-by-Day Activities of Abraham Lincoln From February 12, 1809, to December 31, 1839* (Springfield, Ill., 1941), pp. 10ff.

The typical early nineteenth-century western frontier store, such as that of Offutt, is described in Lewis E. Atherton, *The Pioneer Merchant in Mid-America* (Columbia, Mo., 1939), Chaptr 2. The turbulence and pugnacity of some New Salem settlers is mentioned in Ward H. Lamon, *The Life of Abraham Lincoln* (Boston, 1872), pp. 91-93. Lincoln's fight with Armstrong is treated in Ida M. Tarbell, *In the Footsteps of the Lincolns* (New York, 1924), p. 174.

Kunigunde Duncan and D. F. Nickols, *Mentor Graham, the Man Who Taught Lincoln* (Chicago, 1944) should be used with caution. There exists no contemporary evidence that Lincoln attended Graham's classes; indeed Lincoln in his autobiographies for Fell and Scripps declared that he only attended "A.B.C. schools" in Kentucky and Indiana, and that what he learned he picked up by himself. Lincoln's draft of the ferry bill-of-sale for Ferguson is in the Illinois State Historical Library, Springfield. Logan's comment about Lincoln's paucity of reading is in "Stephen T. Logan Talks About Lincoln," *Bulletin of the Abraham Lincoln Association,* September 1, 1928, pp. 3, 5. Herndon's estimate of Lincoln as a newspaper reader rather than a book reader is printed in George Alfred Townsend, "Abraham Lincoln: A Talk With the Late President's Law Partner," New York *Tribune,* February 15, 1867.

Lincoln's attraction to Knox's poem is treated in Maurice Boyd, "Lincoln and the Influence of William Knox," *Lincoln Herald,* Spring, 1958, pp. 12-15; M. L. Hauser, *Abraham Lincoln's Favorite Poem: Its Author and His Book* (Peoria, Ill., 1935). Lincoln's letter to Johnston about the poem in 1846 is in *Lincoln's Collected Works,* I, 377-378. Lincoln's eulogy of President Taylor on Taylor's death, quoting the poem, is in Chicago *Weekly Journal,* August 5, 1850; Chicago *Daily Journal,* July 27, 1850.

R. B. Rutledge's reminiscences about Lincoln's first public speech at New Salem, early in 1832, is in Lamon, *Life of Abraham Lincoln,* p. 121. For Denton Offutt's fate in the years following failure of the store, see Offutt to Lincoln, September 7, 1859, February 11, 1861, Robert Todd Lincoln Collection, Library of Congress; Harry E. Pratt, "Dr. Denton Offutt: Horse Tamer," *The Abraham Lincoln Quarterly,* September, 1943, pp. 330-333. For the *Talisman's* voyage: Harry E. Pratt, "Lincoln Pilots the *Talisman,*" *The Abraham Lincoln Quarterly,* September, 1943, pp. 319-329. The doggerel about Captain Bogue is from William H. Townsend, *Lincoln the Litigant* (Boston, 1925), p. 50.

On the Black Hawk War consult William T. Hagan, "The Black War," MS., Ph. D. Dissertation, University of Wisconsin, 1950; Frank E. Stevens, *The Black Hawk War* (Chicago, 1903). The source material on this conflict against the Indians, in which Lincoln served, is the rich Black Hawk Collection in the Illinois State Historical Library, Springfield, gathered by Lieutenant (later Major and General) Robert Anderson, who commanded Fort Sumter when he surrendered it in 1861. The best work on Lincoln's participation in that conflict is Harry E. Pratt, "Abraham Lincoln in the Black Hawk War," in O. Fritiof Ander (ed.), *The John H. Hauberg Historical Essays* (Augustana College, Rock Island, Ill., 1954), pp. 18-24. See also "Earliest Known

Lincoln-Black Hawk War Discharge," *Journal of the Illinois State Historical Society,* Winter, 1959, pp. 544-545.

Lincoln's pre-war election as Captain in the Thirty-first Regiment of Illinois Militia is treated in Harry E. Pratt, "Lincoln Was First a Militia Captain," *Journal of the Illinois State Historical Society,* Summer, 1953, pp. 188ff. Dr. John Allen's recollections are in Robert Todd Lincoln Collection, Library of Congress, Vol. I. Lincoln's later joshing reference to his Black War service, in Congress in 1848, is printed in *Congressional Globe,* 30th Cong., 1st., Appendix, p. 1042. Lincoln's reference to the Black Hawk War in 1858 is in his speech of August 16, 1858, at Bath, Illinois, reported in Chicago *Daily Press & Tribune,* August 21, 1858. For Lincoln's land warrant in Iowa: E. R. Harlan, "Lincoln's Iowa Lands," *Annals of Iowa,* April, 1927, pp. 621-623; Jonathan T. Hobson, *Footprints of Abraham Lincoln* (Dayton, Ohio, 1909), p. 101.

The Berry & Lincoln store is treated in Zarel C. Spears and Robert S. Barton, *Berry and Lincoln, Frontier Merchants* (New York, 1947). The store's liquor license is printed in William H. Townsend, *Lincoln and Liquor* (New York, 1934), p. 33. The New Salem old-timer's reminiscence about liquor in frontier stores is from Petersburg (Ill.) *Menard Axis,* quoted in Springfield *Illinois State Journal,* June 2, 1860. Douglas's reference to Lincoln as a "flourishing grocery-keeper" is in Paul M. Angle (ed.) *Created Equal? The Complete Lincoln-Douglas Debates of 1858* (Chicago, 1958), p. 107. The "grog-shop keeper" charge against Lincoln in 1860 is in Reinhard H. Luthin, *The First Lincoln Campaign* (Cambridge, Mass., 1944), p. 199. See also Charles H. Coleman, "The 'Grocery Keeper' and His Customer," *Journal of the Illinois State Historical Society,* Winter, 1959, pp. 547-551.

Lincoln's postmastership is followed in Benjamin P. Thomas, "Lincoln the Postmaster," *Bulletin of the Abraham Lincoln Association,* June, 1933, pp. 3-9; Harvey Lee Ross, *Lincoln's First Years in Illinois* (Reprint of *Early Pioneers and Pioneer Events*) (Elmira, N.Y., 1946), pp. 37-38. Marsh's letter to his relative in New England, September 17, 1835, is in *Journal of the Illinois State Historical Society* (1926-1927), Vol. 19, p. 88. Lincoln's letter to Spears is in *Lincoln's Collected Works,* I, 25. Harry E. Pratt has revealed Lincoln's compensation as Postmaster in his *The Personal Finances of Abraham Lincoln* (Springfield, Ill., 1943), pp. 16-17.

For Lincoln as deputy surveyor: Pratt, *The Personal Finances of Abraham Lincoln,* p. 18; Fern Nance Pond, "Two Early Lincoln Surveys," *The Abraham Lincoln Quarterly,* June, 1950, pp. 121-125. Lincoln's reference to his surveying of Bath, Illinois, is in his speech at that town in 1858, reported in Chicago *Daily Press & Tribune,* August 21, 1858.

Chapter 3—PRAIRIE POLITICIAN AND LEGISLATOR

Politics in Illinois during the second quarter of the nineteenth century is treated in Thomas Ford, *A History of Illinois . . . To 1847* (Chicago, 1854); Henry C. Hubbart, *The Older Middle West, 1840-1880* (New York, 1936); Theodore C. Pease, *The Frontier State* (Springfield, Ill., 1915); E. B. Washburne (ed.), *The Edwards Papers . . . Papers and Manuscripts . . . of Ninian Edwards* (Chicago, 1884).

Lincoln's references to himself as a politician are in Vandalia (Ill.) *Free Press,* in Springfield (Ill.) *Sangamo Journal,* January 28, 1837; *Lincoln's Collected Works,* II, 482; Milwaukee *Sentinel,* October 1, 1859; Chicago *Press & Tribune,* October 1, 1859. For his campaign for Representative in 1832 and 1834 see James A. Herndon to William H. Herndon, May 29, 1865; J. R. Herndon to William H. Herndon, May 28, 1865, Herndon-Weik Collection, Library of Congress; William H. Herndon and Jesse W. Weik, *Abraham Lincoln: The True Story of a Great Life* (New York, 1892), I, 94-96, 117. The election results in the 1832 and 1834 campaigns are in Theodore C. Pease (comp.), *Illinois Election Returns, 1818-1848* (Springfield, Ill., 1923), pp. 262, 275. Logan's recollection about Lincoln's vote is in "Stephen T. Logan Talks About Lincoln," *Bulletin of the Abraham Lincoln Association,* September 1, 1928, p. 2. For Lincoln's opinion of politicians: William B. Hesseltine, "Abraham Lincoln and the Politicians," *Civil War History,* March, 1960, pp. 43-55.

Lincoln's legislative service at Vandalia is excellently followed in William E. Baringer, *Lincoln's Vandalia: A Pioneer Portrait* (New Brunswick, N.J., 1949).

Smoot's reference to Lincoln's tailor-made suit is in Smoot to Herndon, May 7, 1866, Herndon-Weik Collection. For Mrs. Stuart's description of Lincoln, see Mrs. John T. Stuart, "Recollections of Lincoln," MS., Illinois State Historical Library, Springfield. For Lincoln's affiliation with the Whig Party see Edgar DeWitt Jones, *The Influence of Henry Clay Upon Abraham Lincoln* (Lexington, Ky., 1955). For the observations of Governors Reynolds and Ford on the state legislature, consult John Reynolds, *Reynolds's History of Illinois* (Chicago, 1879), p. 200; Ford, A *History of Illinois . . . To 1847,* p. 88. Lincoln's comment on Douglas is printed in *Lincoln's Collected Works,* II, 382-383. For Douglas's electioneering and oratorical histrionics see Frank E. Stevens, *Life of Stephen Arnold Douglas* (Springfield, Ill., 1923), pp. 328ff; *Memoirs of John Quincy Adams* (Philadelphia, 1876), XI, 510.

Lincoln in his first legislative session is presented in Baringer, *Lincoln's Vandalia,* and *Journal of the House of Representatives of the Ninth General Assembly of the State of Illinois* (Vandalia, Ill., 1835). See also Lincoln's remarks in the House on January 6, 1835, in Springfield (Ill.) *Sangamo Journal,* January 17, 1835. Governor Ford's comment is quoted from his *A History of Illinois . . . To 1847,* p. 32. For Lincoln's law study: Paul M. Angle, "The Record of a Friendship," *Journal of the Illinois State Historical Society,* June, 1938, p. 127. For Lincoln's letter supporting Levi Davis for Auditor see *Lincoln's Collected Works,* I, 38.

Lincoln's 1836 campaign for re-election, followed by the successful passage of the capital-removal bill, may be followed in Ford, *A History of Illinois . . . To 1847,* p. 182; *Illinois House Journal, Tenth General Assembly,* pp. 752-759; John H. Krekel, "Internal Improvements in Illinois Politics, 1837-1842," *Mid-America,* April, 1949, pp. 67ff; "Stephen T. Logan Talks about Lincoln," *op. cit.,* p. 3; Harry E. Pratt, "Lincoln and the Division of Sangamon County," *Journal of the Illinois State Historical Society,* Winter, 1954, pp. 398ff; letter of Dr. John Allen in Springfield (Ill.) *Sangamo Journal,* July 14, 1838. The banquet bill rendered by Capps is in Walter B. Stevens, *A Reporter's Lincoln* (St. Louis, 1916), p. 74.

Albert S. Edwards is quoted on Lincoln's move to Springfield in Stevens, *A Reporter's Lincoln,* p. 72. Lincoln's meeting with Speed is told in Robert L. Kincaid, *Joshua Fry Speed: Lincoln's Most Intimate Friend* (Harrogate, Tenn., 1943); and Speed's lecture at Louisville, Kentucky, in New York *Times,* December 3, 1877.

Chapter 4—EARLY SPRINGFIELD YEARS

The best account of early Springfield is Paul M. Angle, *"Here I Have Lived:" A History of Lincoln's Springfield, 1821-1865* (Springfield, Ill., 1935). Lincoln's letter to Mary Owens is in *Lincoln's Collected Works,* I, 78-79. For Speed's store see Robert L. Kincaid, *Joshua Fry Speed: Lincoln's Most Intimate Friend* (Harrogate, Tenn., 1943). For Stuart: C. C. Brown, "Major John T. Stuart," *Transactions of the Illinois State Historical Society,* 1902, pp. 109-114; Frank E. Stevens, "Life of Stephen A. Douglas," *Journal of the Illinois State Historical Society* (1923-1924), Vol. 16, pp. 317.

Lincoln's association with the *Sangamo Journal* is followed in Robert S. Harper, *Lincoln and the Press* (New York, 1951), pp. 2ff. "Sampson's Ghost" letters are printed in Springfield (Ill.) *Sangamo Journal,* June 24, July 8, 1837. Lincoln's Lyceum speech is in Springfield (Ill.) *Sangamo Journal,* February 3, 1838.

The county-division issue and Lincoln's action in it are treated in Harry E. Pratt, "Lincoln and the Division of Sangamo County," *Journal of the Illinois State Historical Society,* Winter, 1954, pp. 404ff. For the efforts of pro-Vandalia legislators to keep the capital in Vandalia, consult William E. Baringer, *Lincoln's Vandalia* (New Brunswick, N.J., 1949), pp. 111ff. Ewing's personal insult to Lincoln is mentioned in Usher F. Linder, *Reminiscences of the Early Bench and Bar of Illinois* (Chicago, 1879), p. 63.

The national election of 1840 is exhaustively treated in Robert G. Gunderson, *The Log-Cabin Campaign* (Lexington, Ky., 1957). Lincoln's activity in it is narrated in Logan Hay, "Lincoln One Hundred Years Ago," *The Abraham Lincoln Quarterly* (1940), I, 82-93; *Lincoln's Collected Works,* I, 157-210; Springfield *Illinois State Register,* February 21, 1840; Springfield (Ill.) *Sangamo Journal,* January 3, February 28, March 6, May 15, 1840; Louis A. Warren, "Lincoln—Presidential Elector, 1840," *Lincoln Lore,* December 5, 1955.

Washburne's description of Lincoln's stumping in 1840 is in his "Abraham Lincoln: His Personal History and Public Record," May 29, 1860, in *Congressional Globe,* 36th Cong., 1st sess., *Appendix,* p. 377; and also in his "Abraham Lincoln in Illinois," *The North American Review,* October, 1885, pp. 309-310. For Lincoln as an orator in 1840 consult Mildred Berry, "Abraham Lincoln: His Development in the Skills of the Platform," in William N. Brigance (ed.), *A History and Criticism of American Public Address* (New York, 1943), II, 849ff. Lincoln's vote for re-election in 1840 is listed in Pease, *Illinois Election Returns, 1818-1848,* p. 344.

Lincoln's letter to Stuart about Dr. Henry is in *Lincoln's Collected Works,* I, 221. For Dr. Henry: Harry E. Pratt, "Dr. Anson G. Henry, Lincoln's Physician and Friend," *Lincoln Herald* (1943), Vol. 45, pp. 3-17, 31-40. Lincoln's jump from a window is told in Harry E. Pratt "Lincoln's 'Jump' From the Window," *Journal of the Illinois State Historical Society,* Winter, 1955, pp. 457ff.

Chapter 5—LAW OFFICE, COURT, AND CIRCUIT

John J. Duff, *A. Lincoln: Prairie Lawyer* (New York, 1960) is the recently published definitive book on Lincoln's legal career. A work of distinguished scholarship written by an eminent New York attorney and profound student of Lincoln, who has dug deeply into Illinois court records, Lincoln's personal papers, the press of that day, and other basic sources, the author combines the talents of professional law study and practice, critical approach to Lincoln scholarship, and a fine readable literary style. Little, if anything, remains to be written on Lincoln's hitherto poorly known law practice. Albert J. Beveridge, *Abraham Lincoln, 1809-1858* (Boston, 1928), 2 vols., best of the pre-presidential accounts of Lincoln, nonetheless treats Lincoln's law career only briefly, inadequately, and haphazardly.

Among other accounts of Lincoln as an attorney are Frederick T. Hill, *Lincoln the Lawyer* (New York, 1906); John T. Richards, *Abraham Lincoln, the Lawyer-Statesman* (Boston, 1916); Albert A. Woldman, *Lawyer Lincoln* (Boston, 1936); John M. Zane, *Lincoln the Constitutional Lawyer* (Chicago, 1932). Lincoln as a plaintiff or defendant is excellently done in William H. Townsend, *Lincoln the Litigant* (Boston, 1925). Consult Carl W. Schaefer, "Lincoln the Lawyer," *Lincoln Herald,* June, 1949, pp. 10-16; Benjamin P. Thomas, "Abe Lincoln, Country Lawyer," *The Atlantic,* February, 1954, pp. 57-61. Recommended are the works of two Illinois lawyers who knew Lincoln intimately: Isaac N. Arnold, "Reminiscences of the Illinois Bar Forty Years Ago: Lincoln and Douglas As Orators and Lawyers," *Fergus Historical Series* (1881), No. 14, pp. 132-154; Usher F. Linder, *Reminiscences of the Early Bench and Bar of Illinois* (Chicago, 1879). Lincoln's income from law practice is detailed in Harry E. Pratt, *The Personal Finances of Abraham Lincoln* (Springfield, Ill., 1943), Chapter 2, "Income From the Law."

Lincoln's first interest in the law is followed in Harry E. Pratt, "The Genesis of Lincoln the Lawyer," *Bulletin of the Abraham Lincoln Association,* September, 1939, pp. 3-9. His first reading in the law is treated in William H. Townsend, "Lincoln's Law Books," *The American Bar Association Journal,* March, 1929, pp. 125-126. Conant's account of Lincoln's acquisition of the Blackstone volume is in Allan J. Conant, "A Portrait Painter's Reminiscences of Lincoln," *McClure's Magazine* (1909), Vol. 32, pp. 514ff. Legal documents drafted by Lincoln in New Salem are printed in *Lincoln's Collected Works,* I, 3-4, 15-19. Stuart's encouragement of Lincoln in law study, and Lincoln's association with Stuart's partner, Dummer, are detailed in Paul M. Angle, "The Record of a Friendship," *Journal of the Illinois State Historical Society,* June, 1938, pp. 125-137. For Stuart: R. Gerald McMurtry, "Centre College, John Todd Stuart, and Abraham Lincoln," *The Filson Club History Quarterly,* April, 1959, pp. 117-124. Lincoln's later letters to students about law study are in *Lincoln's Collected Works,* II, 327; III, 344. Lincoln's certification as a "person of good moral character," in preparation for admission to the bar, March 24, 1836, is in Record C, Circuit Court of Sangamo County, quoted in Hill, *Lincoln the Lawyer,* p. 60.

The description of the first Stuart & Lincoln office is from William H. Herndon and Jesse W. Weik, *Abraham Lincoln: The True Story of a Great Life* (New York, 1892), I, 175; statement of James H. Matheny, May 3, 1866, Herndon-Weik Collection, Library of Congress; Harry E. Pratt, *Lincoln's Springfield: A Guide Book and Brief History* (Illinois State Historical Library, Springfield, Ill., 1955), p. 9. An excellent record of the Stuart & Lincoln firm is Paul M. Angle, *One Hundred Years of Law: An Account of the Law Office Which John T. Stuart Founded in Springfield, Illinois, a Century Ago* (Springfield, Ill., 1928). Lincoln's first case, *Hawthorne v. Wooldridge,* is followed in Jesse W. Weik, *The Real Lincoln* (Boston, 1922), pp. 134-138.

Lincoln's work as co-counsel for Mary and Richard Adams, and the political factors involved in it, are followed in Duff, *A. Lincoln: Prairie Lawyer,* pp. 46-49. See also Beveridge, *Abraham Lincoln, 1809-1858,* I, 212-218. The original of Lincoln's contract, in behalf of himself, Stuart, and Logan, with Anderson's widow and son, in the case against Adams, is in Illinois State Historical Library, Springfield. The handbill attacking Adams, of Lincoln's anonymous authorship, is printed in Springfield *Sangamo Journal,* August 19, 1837. The "Sampson's Ghost" letters appeared in that same Whig newspaper on June 17, 24, July 8, 15, 22, 29, 1837.

Lincoln's work as associate counsel in defense of Truett is followed in Duff, *A. Lincoln: Prairie Lawyer,* Chapter 4; Harry E. Pratt, "Abraham Lincoln's First Murder Trial," *Journal of the Illinois State Historical Society,* September, 1944, pp. 242-249.

For Lincoln's first Illinois Supreme Court cases: Harry E. Pratt, "Lincoln's Supreme Court Cases," *Illinois Bar Journal,* January, 1943, pp. 23-25. *Scammon v. Cline* is followed in Richard V. Carpenter, "Lincoln's First Supreme Court Case," *Journal of the Illinois State Historical Society* (1911-1912), IV, 317-323; 3 *Illinois* 456. Carpenter was of erroneous opinion that this case, *Scammon v. Cline,* was Lincoln's first state Supreme Court case; it was actually his third in that tribunal. Lincoln's letters to Stuart are in *Lincoln's Collected Works,* I, 158-159, 228-230.

The three Illinois cases in which Lincoln beat Logan were *Cannon v. Kinney; Bailey v. Cromwell;* and *Elkin et al v. The People of the State of Illinois,* cited in 4 *Illinois* 9, 71, 207. Logan's quotation about Lincoln as a lawyer is in "Stephen T. Logan Talks About Lincoln," *Bulletin of the Abraham Lincoln Association,* June 1, 1928, pp. 3, 5. A good summary of the Logan & Lincoln partnership is Duff, *A. Lincoln: Prairie Lawyer,* Chapter 6. The Logan & Lincoln bankruptcy cases are treated in Harry E. Pratt, "Lincoln and the Bankruptcy Law," *Illinois Bar Journal,* January, 1943, pp. 201-208. Lincoln's letter to another attorney, Shelledy, on bankruptcy case procedure, is in *Lincoln's Collected Works,* I, 270-271. Lincoln's argument for Margrave in September, 1841, is in 4 *Illinois* 372.

The Trailor case of 1841 was detailed anonymously five years later in the Quincy (Ill.) *Whig*, April 15, 1846. For Lincoln's authorship of this article about the Trailor affair see Ward H. Lamon, *Life of Abraham Lincoln* (Boston, 1872), p. 318. Lincoln's letter to Speed about this case is in *Lincoln's Collected Works*, I, 254ff. For Lincoln's suit to collect his retainer in that case, consult *Illinois Bar Journal*, September, 1943, p. 23. For the Wren divorce and alimony suit: Pratt, *Personal Finances of Abraham Lincoln*, pp. 32-33.

Herndon's life is best followed in David Donald, *Lincoln's Herndon* (New York, 1948). The Lincoln & Herndon law office is described by William H. Townsend in *The American Bar Association Journal*, March, 1929, p. 126; Beveridge, *Abraham Lincoln, 1809-1858*, I, 498-499. Bledsoe's comments about Herndon's hard work are in *The Southern Review*, April, 1873, p. 332.

Lincoln's prosecution of the Denton brothers for murder is detailed in John J. Duff, "This Was a Lawyer," *Journal of the Illinois State Historical Society*, Spring, 1959, p. 151; also St. Louis *Missouri Republican*, January 3, 1846. Lincoln's defense of Lester and his public appeal to Governor French for clemency for Lester is treated in Harry E. Pratt, "Lincoln's Petitions For Pardon," *Illinois Bar Journal*, February, 1942, p. 238.

Lincoln's services as co-counsel for Matson in the "fugitive" slave case is best detailed and analyzed in Duff, *A. Lincoln: Prairie Lawyer*, Chapter 9. See also Beveridge, *Abraham Lincoln, 1809-1858*, I, 392-397; Charles H. Coleman, *Abraham Lincoln and Coles County, Illinois* (New Brunswick, N.J., 1955), pp. 104-111; Duncan T. McIntyre, "Lincoln and the Matson Slave Case," *Illinois Law Review*, January, 1907, pp. 386-391; Jesse W. Weik, "Lincoln and the Matson Negroes," *Arena Magazine*, April, 1897, p. 757. For a defense of Lincoln for arguing Matson's case, see Woldman, *Lawyer Lincoln*, p. 64. See especially O. B. Ficklin, "A Pioneer Lawyer," *Tuscola* (Illinois) *Review*, September 7, 1922.

For Baddeley's unfavorable reaction to Lincoln: Harry E. Pratt, "Abraham Lincoln in Bloomington, Illinois," *Journal of the Illinois State Historical Society*, April, 1936, pp. 42-43. The Eighth Judicial Circuit of Illinois and description of life and practice of law on it are well told in Paul M. Angle, "Abraham Lincoln: Circuit Lawyer," *Lincoln Centennial Association Papers*, 1928, pp. 19-41; Harry E. Pratt, "A Beginner on the Old Eighth Judicial Circuit," *Journal of the Illinois State Historical Society* (1951), Vol. 44, pp. 241-248, which deals with Leonard Swett; Benjamin P. Thomas, "The Eighth Judicial Circuit," *Abraham Lincoln Association Bulletin*, September, 1935, pp. 1-9.

Chapter 6—LINCOLN'S ROMANCES

Ward H. Lamon's comment on Lincoln is from his *Life of Abraham Lincoln* (Boston, 1872), p. 482.

The standard works on Lincoln's courtship of and marriage to Mary Todd are Ruth Painter Randall's *The Courtship of Lincoln* (Boston, 1956) and her Mary Lincoln, *Biography of a Marriage* (Boston, 1953), Chapters 1-6. See also Mary L. Miles, "The Fatal First of January, 1841," *Journal of the Illinois State Historical Society*, April, 1927, pp. 13-48. Lincoln's contemplated marriage to Mary Owens is well-treated in Olive Carruthers and R. Gerald McMurtry, *Lincoln's Other Mary* (Chicago, 1946).

The first part of this chapter is based on William E. Barton, *Life of Abraham Lincoln* (Indianapolis, 1925), II, 211; William H. Herndon and Jesse W. Weik, *Abraham Lincoln: The True Story of a Great Life* (New York, 1892), I, 36; Lincoln's letter to Mrs. M. J. Green, September 22, 1860, Huntington Library, San Marino, California;

Louis A. Warren, "Sixteen Traditional Lincoln Sweethearts," *Lincoln Lore,* December 1, 1941.

John Hill's *Menard Axis* article of 1862 about Lincoln and presumably Ann Rutledge is printed in Jay Monaghan, "New Light on the Lincoln-Rutledge Romance," *The Abraham Lincoln Quarterly,* September, 1944, p. 138ff. On Herndon's propagation of the Lincoln-Rutledge "romance," see David Donald, *Lincoln's Herndon* (New York, 1948), pp. 185-187, 223ff; Randall, *Mary Lincoln,* pp. 395-407; Ward H. Lamon, *Life of Abraham Lincoln* (Boston, 1872), pp. 159-165; William H. Herndon and Jesse W. Weik, *Herndon's Lincoln* (Chicago, 1889), I, 139-140. The authenticity of the Lincoln-Rutledge "romance" is demolished in James G. Randall, *Lincoln the President* (New York, 1945), Vol. II, Appendix, "Sifting the Ann Rutledge Evidence;" Paul M. Angle, "Lincoln's First Love?" *Bulletin of the Abraham Lincoln Association,* December, 1929, pp. 1-8; letter of Robert Todd Lincoln to Judge Davis in Ruth Painter Randall, *Lincoln's Sons* (Boston, 1955), p. 242; letter of Mary Todd Lincoln to Judge Davis, March 4, 1867, in Louis A. Warren, "The Ann Rutledge Myth," *Lincoln Lore,* May 19, 1952.

For Lincoln's temporary romance with Mary Owens and its aftermath, consult Carruthers and McMurtry, *Lincoln's Other Mary,* and Lincoln's letters to her and Mrs. Browning in *Lincoln's Collected Works,* I, 54-55, 78-79, 94-95, 117-119. Also Browning's letter to Isaac N. Arnold in Maurice G. Baxter, "Orville H. Browning: Lincoln's Colleague and Critic," *Journal of the Illinois State Historical Society,* Winter, 1955, p. 455.

The letter of Lincoln and others to Mrs. Browning, requesting feminine company, is in *Lincoln's Collected Works,* I, 156. His comment about himself as a "Long Nine" member is in *Lincoln Lore,* November 30, 1931. His letter to Speed is in *Lincoln's Collected Works,* I, 289.

Mary Todd's early Lexington years are followed in William H. Townsend's two excellent works: *Lincoln and His Wife's Home Town* (Indianapolis, 1929) and *Lincoln and the Blue Grass* (Lexington, Ky., 1955). Dr. Merryman's jingle about the "dumping" of Mary is printed in *Journal of the Illinois State Historical Society,* April-July, 1923, p. 146. For Mary's comment about her plumpness: Her letter to Mercy Levering, in Carl Sandburg and Paul M. Angle, *Mary Lincoln, Wife and Widow* (New York, 1932), p. 178. For comments on Mary Todd by Conkling and Albert S. Edwards: Conkling to Mercy Levering, September 21, 1840, Illinois State Historical Library, Springfield; Edwards quoted in Frank E. Stevens, *A Reporter's Lincoln* (St. Louis, 1916), p. 75. Mary's letter to Mrs. Gideon Welles is in Gideon Welles Papers, Library of Congress (December 6, 1865).

For Mary's visit to Missouri, her interest in the 1840 campaign, and her doubts about matrimony see her letters to Mercy Levering, July, 23, 1840, and December (no day), 1840, in Sandburg and Angle, *Mary Lincoln,* pp. 168-169, 171, 176; North Todd Gentry, "David Todd," *The Missouri Historical Review,* July, 1927, pp. 527-537; also *Ibid.,* July, 1925, p. 728. For the Todd family's disapproval of Lincoln, as expressed by Katherine Helm and Albert Edwards, see Katherine Helm, *The True Story of Mary, Wife of Lincoln* (New York, 1928), p. 82; Stevens, *A Reporter's Lincoln,* pp. 75-76. For Lincoln's illness, "the ague," consult Elihu B. Washburne, "Abraham Lincoln: His Personal History and Public Record," *Congressional Globe,* 36th Cong., 1st sess., *Appendix,* p. 377 (May 29, 1860). Lincoln's words to Speed about the 1st of January, 1841, are in *Lincoln's Collected Works,* I, 282.

Lincoln's letters to Stuart are in *Lincoln's Collected Works,* I, 228-230. For Stuart's plan to have Lincoln appointed to the Colombian mission: Claude G. Fuess, *Daniel Webster* (Boston, 1930), II, 94; F. Lauriston Bullard, "When John T. Stuart Sought to Send Lincoln to South America," *Lincoln Herald,* October-December, 1945, p. 21. Letters about Lincoln's poor physical and mental condition include Martin Kane to Hardin, January 22, 1841, John J. Hardin Papers, Chicago Historical Society; Conkling to Mercy Levering, January 24, March 7, 1841; Mercy Levering to Conkling, February 7, 1841, in Sandburg and Angle, *Mary Lincoln,* pp. 179-180. Lincoln's improvement in health is mentioned in Speed to Butler, May 18, 1841, William Butler Papers, Chicago Historical Society. Lincoln's allusion to Sarah Rickard is in his letters to Speed in *Lincoln's Collected Works,* I, 258, 268, 282. Sarah Rickard's letter to Herndon is in Herndon and Weik, *Abraham Lincoln,* 1892 edition, I, 216n. Mary Lincoln's letter to Mercy Levering about Lincoln is from Sandburg and Angle, *Mary Lincoln,* pp. 182-184.

Lincoln's letters to Speed and Mary Speed are in *Lincoln's Collected Works,* I, 260-261, 265-266, 266-267, 269-270, 280, 282-283, 288-290, 303. On the "Rebecca Letters," and Lincoln's near duel with Shields, and the reconciliation with Mary Todd: Roy P. Basler, "The Authorship of the 'Rebecca' Letters," *The Abraham Lincoln Quarterly,* June, 1942, pp. 80-90; Mrs. Lincoln's letter to Mrs. Welles, December 6, 1865, Gideon Welles Papers, Library of Congress; Randall, *The Courtship of Lincoln* and the same author's *Mary Lincoln,* Chapter 6; Louis A. Warren, "The Lincoln-Shields Duel," *Lincoln Lore,* September 21, 1942.

For accounts of Lincoln's wedding ceremony: Matheny's statement, May 3, 1866, and Matheny's letter to Jesse W. Weik, August 21, 1888, both manuscripts in the Herndon-Weik Collection, Library of Congress; Katherine Helm, *The True Story of Mary, Wife of Lincoln* (New York, 1928), p. 95, Mrs. Helm being Mary Todd Lincoln's half-sister; Eugenia Jones Hunt, "The Wedding of Lincoln and Mary Todd," *The Abraham Lincoln Quarterly,* March, 1945, pp. 236-237; Mrs. Frances (Todd) Wallace, *Lincoln's Marriage: Newspaper Interview . . . Springfield, Ill., September 2, 1895* (Privately printed, 1917), Mrs. Wallace being another of Mary Todd Lincoln's half-sisters. See especially Wayne C. Temple's two works: *Mrs. Frances J. Todd Wallace Describes Lincoln's Wedding and Mrs. Mary Edwards Brown Tells the Story of Lincoln's Wedding.* Lincoln's letter to Marshall about his recent marriage, November 11, 1842, is in Chicago Historical Society.

Chapter 7—THE LONE WHIG FROM ILLINOIS

The best work on Lincoln's congressional service is Donald W. Riddle, *Congressman Abraham Lincoln* (Urbana, Ill., 1957). See also Beveridge, *Abraham Lincoln* (Boston, 1928), Vol. I, Chapters 7, 8; Roy D. Packard, *The Lincoln of the Thirtieth Congress* (Boston, 1950); Charles O. Paullin, "Abraham Lincoln in Congress," *Journal of the Illinois State Historical Society* (1921), Vol. 14, pp. 85-89.

For Lincoln's political activity in 1843: Lincoln to John J. Bennett, March 7, 1843, Illinois State Historical Library, Springfield; Quincy (Ill.) *Whig,* March 15, 22, 1843; *North Western Gazette and Galena Advertiser,* March 17, 1843; Springfield (Ill.) *Sangamo Journal,* May 11, June 15, 1843; Burlington (Iowa) *Hawk Eye,* October 10, 1843.

Judge Davis's comment on Lincoln as speaker is in Davis to Walker, *Journal of the Illinois State Historical Society,* April, 1936, p. 45. Lincoln's stumping for Clay in Indiana is detailed in Rockport (Ind.) *Herald,* November 1, 1844, in Bess V. Ehrmann, *The Missing Chapter in the Life of Abraham Lincoln* (Chicago, 1938), facsimile opposite page 104. Mrs. Robert S. Todd's letter to Mrs. Lincoln is in William H. Townsend, *Lincoln and His Wife's Home Town* (Indianapolis, 1929), pp 109-110.

The Lincoln-Baker-Hardin rivalry for Congress and Lincoln's successful campaign for Congress is treated in Donald W. Riddle, *Lincoln Runs For Congress* (New Brunswick, N.J., 1948). Lincoln's public views on his religion are printed in Lacon (Ill.) *Illinois Gazette,* August 15, 1846; *Tazewell Whig,* August 22, 1846.

Greeley's comment about Lincoln at Chicago is in New York *Tribune,* June 17, 1847. The Boston reporter Buckingham's account of Lincoln is quoted by Harry E.

Pratt in Paul M. Angle (ed.), *Papers in Illinois History, 1937* (Springfield, Ill., 1938), pp. 139-140. Lincoln's stay in Lexington and his listening to Clay's speech is in Townsend, *Lincoln and His Wife's Home Town,* pp. 142ff.

Lincoln's service in Congress is followed in Riddle, *Congressman Abraham Lincoln* and Packard, *The Lincoln of the Thirtieth Congress;* also the *Congressional Globe* for both sessions of the Thirtieth Congress, 1847-49. See also *Lincoln's Collected Works,* I, 416-519; II, 1-30. Dr. Busey's recollections of Lincoln are in his *Reminiscences and Recollections of Samuel Clagett Busey* (Washington, 1895), pp. 25-28.

Lincoln's support of Taylor for President in 1848 and his Massachusetts tour are followed in George R. Poage, *Henry Clay and the Whig Party* (Chapel Hill, N.C., 1936); Reinhard H. Luthin, "Abraham Lincoln and the Massachusetts Whigs in 1848," *The New England Quarterly,* December, 1941, pp. 619-632.

The efforts of Lincoln to secure patronage for his friends and the Land Office commissionership for himself are mentioned in unpublished letters, between December, 1848 and April, 1849, in the Robert Todd Lincoln Collection, Library of Congress; also letters in Thomas Ewing Papers, Library of Congress. See also Thomas Ewing, "Lincoln and the General Land Office," *Journal of the Illinois State Historical Society* (1932), Vol. 25, pp. 139-153; Holman Hamilton, *Zachary Taylor: Soldier in the White House* (Indianapolis, 1951), p. 211; Paul I. Miller, "Lincoln and the Governorship of Oregon," *The Mississippi Valley Historical Review,* (1936), Vol. 23, pp. 391-394.

Chapter 8—THE PERSONAL LINCOLN

Holland's, Bledsoe's, Herndon's, and Reeves's comments on Lincoln are in J. G. Holland, *Life of Abraham Lincoln* (Springfield, Mass., 1866), p. 241; Bledsoe in *The Southern Review,* April, 1873, p. 328; Herndon to Bartlett, September 22, 1887, MS., Massachusetts Historical Society, Boston; Reeves in Bloomington (Ill.) *Pantagraph,* March 13, 1909.

Physical descriptions of Lincoln are from Louis A. Warren quoting the English visitor in *Lincoln Lore,* March 30, 1931; Lillian Foster, *Way-Side Glimpses* (New York, 1860), p. 221; Logan Hay to John Hay, February 8, 1887, in *Bulletin of the Abraham Lincoln Association,* December, 1931, p. 8; Samuel C. Parks's comments in Harry E. Pratt, *Lincoln, 1840-1846* (Springfield, Ill., 1939), p. ix; *Reminiscences of Carl Schurz* (New York, 1907-08), II, 90; Joshua F. Speed, *Reminiscences of Abraham Lincoln and Notes of a Visit to California* (Louisville, Ky., 1884), p. 34.

Bledsoe's comment about Lincoln's paucity of reading is from *The Southern Review,* April, 1873, p. 332. On Lincoln's opinion of history and biography: Albert J. Beveridge, *Abraham Lincoln, 1809-1858* (Boston, 1928), I, 520. Lincoln at the reading of "Flora McFlimsey" is described in Harry E. Pratt, "Lincoln Liked 'Nothing To Wear,'" *The Abraham Lincoln Quarterly* (1942), II, 67. Henry C. Whitney's account of Lincoln at the minstrel is in his *Life on the Circuit With Lincoln* (Boston, 1892), pp. 87-88. The New York *Times's* account of Lincoln's chess playing is quoted from *Journal of the Illinois State Historical Society,* Summer, 1953, p. 184.

For Lincoln's melancholia: Paul M. Angle (ed.), *Herndon's Life of Lincoln* (New York, 1930), p. 473; Louis A. Warren, "Abraham Lincoln—A Melancholy Man," *Lincoln Lore,* September 24, 1934; Henry B. Whitney, *Life on the Circuit With Lincoln.* Lincoln's poems are printed in *Lincoln's Collected Works,* I, 378-379, 385-386. His eulogy of Taylor is in Chicago *Weekly Journal,* August 5, 1850. For conjectures about the causes of Lincoln's melancholia: Whitney, *Life on the Circuit With Lincoln,* p. 139; William F. Petersen, *Lincoln-Douglas: The Weather As Destiny* (Springfield, Ill., 1943).

For Lincoln's liking of plaintive Scotch airs, consult Noah Brooks, "Personal Reminiscences of Abraham Lincoln," *Harper's Magazine,* July, 1865, p. 229.

Lincoln's letter about his superstition is in Lincoln's *Collected Works,* II, 348. For Lincoln's belief in the "mad stone," see Ward H. Lamon, *Life of Abraham Lincoln* (Boston, 1872), pp. 44-45; Edgar Lee Masters, *Lincoln the Man* (New York, 1931). Lincoln's "visions" in the mirror in 1860 are told in Noah Brooks, *Washington in Lincoln's Time* (New York, 1895), pp. 220-221. The claims of Spiritualists that Lincoln believed in Spiritualism are demolished in Jay Monaghan, "Was Abraham Lincoln a Spiritualist?" *Journal of the Illinois State Historical Society* (1941), Vol. 34, pp. 209-232; Louis A. Warren, "The Lincolns and Spiritualism," *Lincoln Lore,* April 15, 1946.

Comments of Herndon, Davis, and Villard on Lincoln's alternate sadness and cheerfulness include Herndon to Bartlett, July 8, 1887, MS., Massachusetts Historical Society, Boston; Davis' statement in Whitney, *Life on the Circuit With Lincoln,* p. 171; *Memoirs of Henry Villard* (Boston, 1904), I, 143. Lincoln's letters, whimsically expressing himself, are in *Lincoln's Collected Works,* I, 391, 450, 495; James G. Randall, *Lincoln and the South* (Baton Rouge, La., 1948), p. 221. Lincoln's "chalked hat" letter is in *Lincoln's Collected Works,* II, 330. The two contemporary anecdotes told by Lincoln about his own ugliness are in Benjamin F. Shaw Papers, 1856, quoted in *The Abraham Lincoln Quarterly,* March, 1948, pp. 36-37; Journal of William L. Gross, October 19, 1858, in Harry E. Pratt (ed.), *Concerning Mr. Lincoln* (Springfield, Ill., 1944), pp. 18-19.

Lincoln's speech on internal improvements is in *Congressional Globe,* 30th Cong., 1st sess., *Appendix,* pp. 709-711. Lincoln's reference to Pierce as a rejected lover is in Chicago *Democratic Press,* December 11, 1856. Lillian Foster's comment is in her *Way-Side Glimpses* p. 221. Remarks from the Lincoln-Douglas debates are in Paul M. Angle (ed.), *Created Equal? The Complete Lincoln-Douglas Debates of 1858* (Chicago, 1958), pp. 327, 356. Dr. Bailhache's comment on Lincoln's "clean" humor is from Bailhache's "Recollections of a Springfield Doctor," *Journal of the Illinois State Historical Society,* Spring, 1954, p. 61. Lincoln's "fig-leaf apron" story is told in *Lincoln's Collected Works,* III, 359-360. Mrs. Bailhache's letter is in Pratt (ed.), *Concerning Mr. Lincoln,* p. 332.

The pages on Lincoln's religious views in this chapter are summarized from William E. Barton, *The Soul of Abraham Lincoln* (New York), 1920, pp. 73-75, 87ff, 156, 227-231, 255-256; Logan Hay's letter to John Hay, February 8, 1887, in *Bulletin of the Abraham Lincoln Association,* December, 1931, p. 9; William H. Herndon and Jesse W. Weik, *Abraham Lincoln: The True Story of a Great Life* (New York, 1892), II, 150-151; John Hill in Petersburg (Ill.) *Menard Axis,* February 15, 1862, in *The Abraham Lincoln Quarterly,* September, 1944, p. 143; Lamon, *Life of Abraham Lincoln,* pp. 487, 489; Lincoln's own statement about his religion is in Lacon (Ill.) *Illinois Gazette,* August 15, 1846, and *Tazewell Whig,* August 22, 1846; Madison J. Peters, *Abraham Lincoln's Religion* (Boston, 1909), pp. 54-55; William H. Townsend, *Lincoln and Liquor* (New York, 1934), pp. 227-236. Louis A. Warren contradicts Herndon's story about Lincoln's authorship of an atheistic essay. See Warren, "The Burnt Book Myth," *Lincoln Lore,* September 27, 1954. Consult Martin L. Houser, *Some Religious Influences Which Surrounded Lincoln* (Peoria, Ill., 1941); Ralph G. Lindstrom, *Lincoln Finds God* (New York, 1958); William J. Wolf, *The Almost Chosen People: A Study of the Religion of Abraham Lincoln* (Garden City, N.Y., 1959).

The "American Party" in Lincoln's state is covered in John P. Senning, "The Know-Nothing Movement in Illinois," *Journal of the Illinois State Historical Society,* April, 1914, pp. 19ff. Lincoln's attitude toward Know-Nothings is mentioned in Harry J. Carman and Reinhard H. Luthin, "Some Aspects of the Know-Nothing Movement Reconsidered," *The South Atlantic Quarterly,* April, 1940, pp. 222ff; F. I. Herriott, "The Premises and Significance of Abraham Lincoln's Letter to Theodore Canisius," *Deutsch-Amerikanische Geschichtsblätter* (1915), Vol. 15, pp. 184ff, 249-254. For Lincoln's political cooperation with the nativists see Charles G. Hamilton, *Lincoln and the Know-Nothing Movement* (Washington, 1954). Herndon's comment about Lincoln's tolerance for immigrants is in New York *Tribune,* February 15, 1867. Herndon's anti-Irish remarks are in David Donald, *Lincoln's Herndon* (New York, 1948), pp. 124-125.

Lincoln's reply to the visitor who quoted from Caesar is in Harold G. Villard and Oswald Garrison Villard (ed.), *Lincoln on the Eve of '61* (New York, 1941), pp. 63-64. Judge Davis' remarks about Lincoln's silence are from Herndon and Weik, *Abraham Lincoln,* 1892 edition, II, 151. Herndon's comment about Lincoln is in Alfred A. North to Truman H. Bartlett, MS., Massachusetts Historical Society, Boston.

A revealing treatment of Lincoln's financial and business affairs is Harry E. Pratt, *The Personal Finances of Abraham Lincoln* (Springfield, Ill., 1943). See also Pratt's "Lincoln's Memorandum of His Savings," *Bulletin of the Abraham Lincoln Association,* September, 1938, pp. 3-6. For Lincoln's dealing in lands see Julia A. Drake, "Lincoln Land Buying," *Lincoln Herald,* December, 1948-February, 1949, pp. 32-35; Raymond N. Dooley, "Lincoln and His Namesake Town," *Journal of the Illinois State Historical Society,* Spring, 1959, pp. 137-138. Lincoln's remarks about his 1858 Senatorial campaign expenditures are from Isaac N. Arnold, quoted in Francis B. Carpenter, *Six Months At the White House With Abraham Lincoln* (New York, 1867), p. 237. Lincoln's application for his patent for lifting vessels over shoals is in *Lincoln's Collected Works,* II, 32-36. For his patent case see Charles S. Zane, "Abraham Lincoln As I Knew Him," *Journal of the Illinois State Historical Society* (1921), Vol. 14, pp. 75ff.

For the origin of the "Honest Abe" nickname: Louis A. Warren, "The Sobriquet—'Honest Abe,'" *Lincoln Lore,* August 17, 1942. On Lincoln's dignity and quotations of Illinois men about practice of not calling Lincoln "Abe," consult Isaac N. Phillips, *Abraham Lincoln, By Some Men Who Knew Him* (1910); Whitney, *Life on the Circuit With Lincoln,* p. 53; Herndon to Bartlett, July 19, 1887, MS., Massachusetts Historical Society, Boston; Lamon to Lincoln, August 17, 25, 1860, Robert Todd Lincoln Collection, Library of Congress.

This account of Lincoln's conciliatory qualities and aversion to physical combat is summarized from J. H. Buckingham's statement of 1848, quoted by Harry E. Pratt in Paul M. Angle (ed.), *Papers in Illinois History, 1937* (Springfield, Ill., 1938), p. 136; Lincoln's speech in *Congressional Globe,* 30th Cong., 1st sess., *Appendix,* p. 709; letter of Enoch Huggins, July 26, 1858, in Pratt (ed.), *Concerning Mr. Lincoln,* p. 18; Lincoln's words opposing fisticuffs with Douglas in Edwin E. Sparks (ed.), *The Lincoln-Douglas Debates of 1858* (Springfield, Ill., 1908), p. 547.

Lincoln's letter to Speed about the farm is in *Lincoln's Collected Works,* I, 282. His speech before the Wisconsin society is in Milwaukee *Sentinel,* and Chicago *Press & Tribune,* both for October 1, 1859. Herndon's and Davis' references about Lincoln's indifference to food are in Herndon to Bartlett, August 7, 1887, MS., Massachusetts Historical Society, Boston; Davis quoted in Angle (ed.), *Herndon's Life of Lincoln,* p. 280.

The most accurate treatment of Lincoln's views toward alcohol is Townsend, *Lincoln and Liquor.* See also Lamon, *Life of Abraham Lincoln,* p. 480; "Stephen T. Logan Talks About Lincoln," *Bulletin of the Abraham Lincoln Association,* September 1, 1928, pp. 3-5; Speed to Herndon, December 6, 1866, in Townsend, *Lincoln and Liquor,* p. 93; Paul M. Angle, *Lincoln in the Year 1855* (Springfield, Ill., 1929), p. 3; *Illinois State Journal,* January 27, 1859. For the controversy over Lincoln's liquor views consult Harry M. Lydenberg, "Lincoln and Prohibition: Blazes on a Zigzag Trail," *Proceedings of the American Antiquarian Society,* April, 1952, pp. 9-62. Lincoln's favorite quip about vices and virtues is from Francis B. Carpenter, *Six Months At the White House With Abraham Lincoln* (New York, 1867), p. 248.

On Lincoln as a conservative see Stanley Pargellis, "Lincoln's Political Philosophy," *The Abraham Lincoln Quarterly* (1945), III, 275-290. Lincoln's Kalamazoo oration is printed in Detroit *Daily Advertiser,* August 29, 1856. His Cincinnati speech is in Cincinnati *Gazette,* September 19, 1859; Springfield *Illinois State Journal,* October 7, 1859, Lincoln's words to the Indianapolis audience, September 19, 1859, are reported in Indianapolis *Atlas,* September 19, 1859. His New Haven speech is in New Haven (Conn.) *Daily Palladium,* March 7, 1860. Lincoln's First Annual Address to Congress is in James D. Richardson (comp.), *Messages and Papers of the Presidents, 1789-1897* (Washington, 1897), VI, 44-58.

Lincoln's Lyceum speech is in Springfield (Ill.) *Sangamo Journal,* February 3, 1838. For commentary on this oration see Arthur L. Housman, "An Appraisal of Lincoln's Lyceum Address," *Lincoln Herald,* Spring, 1959, pp. 16-19. Lincoln's words to the Workingmen's Committee in 1864 are in *Lincoln's Collected Works,* VII, 259-260.

Chapter 9—MR. & MRS. A. LINCOLN

For Lincoln's family life in Springfield the reader is recommended to David Donald, *Lincoln's Herndon* (New York, 1948); W. A. Evans, *Mrs. Abraham Lincoln* (New York, 1932); William H. Herndon and Jesse W. Weik, *Herndon's Lincoln: The True Story of a Great Life* (Chicago, 1889), 3 vols.; Harry E. Pratt, *The Personal Finances of Abraham Lincoln* (Springfield, Ill., 1943); Ruth Painter Randall, *Mary Lincoln, Biography of a Marriage* (Boston, 1953) and the same author's *Lincoln's Sons* (Boston, 1956), *Lincoln's Animal Friends* (Boston, 1958) and "Mrs. Lincoln Revealed in a New Light," *New York Times Magazine,* February 12, 1950; Carl Sandburg and Paul M. Angle, *Mary Lincoln, Wife and Widow* (New York, 1932); William H. Townsend's two works, *Lincoln and His Wife's Home Town* (Indianapolis, 1929) and *Lincoln and the Blue Grass* (Lexington, Ky., 1955).

Fordham's contrast between Kentucky, Ohio, Indiana, and Illinois in 1818 is in his *Personal Narrative of Travels in Virginia . . . Ohio, Indiana, Kentucky and . . . Illinois, 1817-1818* (Cleveland, Ohio, 1906), p. 216. Mary Lincoln's letter to Lincoln about her stepmother, May, 1848, is in Illinois State Historical Library, Springfield. Lincoln's letter to Speed about the Globe Tavern is in *Lincoln's Collected Works,* I, 325. See also Boyd B. Stutler, "Mr. Lincoln's Landlady," *The American Legion Magazine,* February, 1944, concerning Mrs. Beck. The reminiscences of Bledsoe's daughter are quoted in Sophie Bledsoe Herrick, "Personal Recollections of My Father and Mother," *Methodist Review,* April, 1915, pp. 666ff. Lincoln's purchase of his house is in *Lincoln's Collected Works,* I, 331. Mrs. Lincoln's letter to Mrs. Shearer is in *Journal of the Illinois State Historical Society,* Spring, 1951, p. 14.

Dr. Busey's recollections of the Lincolns at Mrs. Sprigg's boarding house are in his *Personal Reminiscences. . . .* (Washington, 1895), p. 28. Lincoln's letters to Mrs. Lincoln are in *Lincoln's Collected Works,* I, 465-466, 477-478, 495-496; her letter to him is in Cleveland *Plain Dealer,* February 11, 1924.

Mrs. Lincoln's bad relations with Herndon are followed in David Donald, *Lincoln Reconsidered* (New York, 1956), Chapter 3, "Herndon and Mrs. Lincoln." Mrs. Lincoln's letter to Judge Davis in 1867 is in possession of Mr. Willard L. King of Chicago. Comments of Illinois people about the difficulties of Lincoln with his wife are from Randall, *Mary Lincoln,* p. 122. Comments of Herndon and Lamon about the few diners at Lincoln's home is in Ward H. Lamon, *Life of Abraham Lincoln* (Boston, 1872), p. 482. Isaac N. Arnold's account of Mrs. Lincoln's hospitality is in *Fergus Historical Series* (1881), No. 14, pp. 137-138. On Mrs. Lincoln's instability see Randall, *Mary Lincoln,* pp. 118ff; Evans, *Mrs. Abraham Lincoln,* pp. 45ff. Mary Owens' letter is in Olive Carruthers and R. Gerald McMurtry, *Lincoln's Other Mary* (Chicago, 1946), p. 202. Emilie Todd Helm's story about Lincoln's remark on the burned chicken is from Katherine Helm, *The True Story of Mary, Wife of Lincoln* (New York, 1928), p. 112.

Lincoln's letter to the Republican editor is in *Lincoln's Collected Works,* II, 389-390. Mrs. Lincoln's letter to her half-sister, November 23, 1856, is in possession of Colonel William H. Townsend of Lexington, Kentucky. Herndon is quoted on Mary Lincoln's pro-slavery views in Paul M. Angle (ed.), *Herndon's Life of Lincoln* (Cleveland, Ohio, 1942), p. 343; Jesse W. Weik, *The Real Lincoln* (Boston 1922), p. 99. Ray's letters, December 16, 24, 1855, are in Elihu B. Washburne Papers, Library of Congress.

On Mrs. Lincoln as a housekeeper: Pratt, *The Personal Finances of Abraham Lincoln,* pp. 145; Pratt in *Illinois Bar Journal,* May, 1952, pp. 482-483. The Utica reporter's description of the Lincoln home is in *Journal of the Illinois State Historical Society,* Spring, 1955, p. 27. Lincoln's boys are best treated in Randall, *Lincoln's Sons.* For Tad: Louis A. Warren, "Tad," *Lincoln Lore,* December 19, 1932. Julia Taft Bayne, *Tad Lincoln's Father* (Boston, 1931); F. Lauriston Bullard, *Tad and His Father* (Boston, 1915). For Robert Todd Lincoln: David C. Mearns (ed.), *The Lincoln Papers* (Garden City, N.Y., 1948), I, 5-7; Emanuel Hertz, *The Hidden Lincoln* (New York, 1938), pp. 249, 261; Herndon to Weik, February 5, 1891, Herndon-Weik Papers, Library of Congress. Dr. Bailhache's comments are in *Journal of the Illinois State Historical Society,* Spring, 1954, pp. 59-60.

On Lincoln's indifference to his own Lincoln and Hanks family, see William E. Barton, "The Lincoln's in Their Old Kentucky Home," *The Magazine of History With Notes and Queries* (1928), Vol. 49, Extra No. 193, p. 6; Charles H. Coleman, *Abraham Lincoln and Coles County, Illinois* (New Brunswick, N.J., 1955), p. 57; William A. Evans, *Mrs. Abraham Lincoln* (New York, 1932), p. 327. See Dennis Hanks' remarks in Ward H. Lamon, *Life of Abraham Lincoln* (Boston, 1872), p. 78. Herndon's reference to Lincoln's "Virginia planter" maternal grandfather and his description of the Hanks family are in Herndon to T. H. Bartlett, September 22, 1887, MS., Massachusetts Historical Society, Boston.

Lincoln's stepbrother's letter to him, May 25, 1849, is in Robert Todd Lincoln Collection, Library of Congress. Lincoln's letters to his stepbrother are in *Lincoln's Collected Works,* II, 96-97, 111-112, 113.

Chapter 10—BACK TO THE LAW

For Lincoln as a constitutional lawyer see John M. Zane, "Lincoln, the Constitutional Lawyer," *Abraham Lincoln Association Papers,* 1932, pp. 27-108. Lincoln's United States Supreme Court cases are mentioned in Benjamin P. Thomas, *Lincoln, 1847-1853* (Springfield, Ill., 1936), pp. 115, 116; Albert A. Woldman, *Lawyer Lincoln* (Boston, 1936), pp. 134, 134n; 7 *Howard* 776; 7 *Howard* 185; 15 *Howard* 3.

For Grant Goodrich's Chicago offer to Lincoln, and Lincoln's resumption of his partnership with Herndon: Albert J. Beveridge, *Abraham Lincoln, 1809-1858* (Boston, 1928), I, 497-498. A copy of Lincoln's autobiography (for John L. Scripps in June, 1860) is in Robert Todd Lincoln Collection, Library of Congress. The most important works on Lincoln's resumed partnership are David Donald, *Lincoln's Herndon* (New York, 1948), Chapter 3, "Lincoln & Herndon;" William H. Herndon and Jesse W. Weik, *Abraham Lincoln: The True Story of a Great Life* (New York, 1892), Vol. II, Chapter 1. For the removal of the Lincoln & Herndon office to South Fifth Street, see Harry E. Pratt in *Illinois Bar Journal,* May, 1952, p. 483.

The diversity of Lincoln's law practice is excellently treated in John J. Duff, "This Was a Lawyer," *Journal of the Illinois State Historical Society,* Spring, 1959, pp. 146ff. Lincoln's letter to the lawyer for his "hundred tollars," July 4, 1851, is in *Lincoln's Collected Works,* II, 106. His letter to Floyd, February 21, 1856, is in *McClure's Magazine,* January, 1908, p. 303.

Lincoln's reference to himself as "not an accomplished lawyer" is in *Lincoln's Collected Works,* II, 81. The extent of the Lincoln & Herndon practice in the Sangamon County Circuit Court is followed in Donald, *Lincoln's Herndon,* pp. 43-44. Lincoln's state Supreme Court cases are treated in Harry E. Pratt, "Lincoln's Supreme Court Cases," *Illinois Bar Journal,* September, 1943, pp. 23-35. For *Alton, St. Louis, & Chicago Railroad v. Dalby,* see 19 Illinois 353; Harry E. Pratt in *Illinois Bar Journal,* May,

1952, p. 488. Herndon's appraisal of Lincoln's legal ability and success in the Supreme Court are from Herndon & Weik, *Abraham Lincoln,* 1892 edition, II, 337-338.

Judge Pope's affection for Lincoln, as quoted by Miller, is from New York *Independent,* March 19, 1868, and Paul M. Angle, "Nathaniel Pope, 1784-1850," *Transactions of the Illinois State Historical Society,* 1936, p. 178. Lincoln's practice in the federal court at Springfield is treated in Benjamin P. Thomas, "Lincoln's Earlier Practice in the Federal Courts, 1839-1854," *Bulletin of the Abraham Lincoln Association,* June, 1935, pp. 3-9; Paul M. Angle, "Lincoln in the United States Court, 1855-1860," *Bulletin of the Lincoln Centennial Association,* September, 1927, pp. 1ff. For the defense of Williamson by Lincoln and Browning: Theodore C. Pease and James G. Randall (ed.), *Diary of Orville Hickman Browning, 1850-1864* (Springfield, Ill., 1925), I, 57-58; Springfield *Illinois State Journal,* July 16, 1852.

Lincoln's letters to Ambos and Galloway on the Columbus Machine Manufacturing Company case in 1859 are in *Lincoln's Collected Works,* III, 386-387, 393-394. The *Beaver v. Taylor and Gilbert* suit is summarized in Harry E. Pratt, *The Personal Finances of Abraham Lincoln* (Springfield, Ill., 1943), p. 57.

Life on the Eighth Judicial Circuit, Lincoln's activities there, and his friendship with Judge Davis are followed in Paul M. Angle, "Abraham Lincoln: Circuit Lawyer," *Lincoln Centennial Association Papers,* 1928, pp. 19-41; Frederick Trevor Hill, *Lincoln the Lawyer* (New York, 1906), Chapters 16, 17; Harry E. Pratt, "David Davis, 1815-1886," *Transactions of the Illinois State Historical Society,* 1930, pp. 164ff; Benjamin P. Thomas, "The Eighth Judicial Circuit," *Bulletin of the Abraham Lincoln Association,* September, 1935, pp. 3-9, and the same author's "Lincoln and the Courts, 1854-1861," *Abraham Lincoln Association Papers,* 1934, pp. 47-103. For Leonard Swett: Harry E. Pratt, "A Beginner on the Eighth Judicial Circuit," *Journal of the Illinois State Historical Society,* Autumn, 1951, pp. 241-248. The seven instances in which Lincoln presided as "Judge" in Davis' absence are treated in Harry E. Pratt, "'Judge' Abraham Lincoln," *Journal of the Illinois State Historical Society,* Spring, 1955, pp. 28-39.

For the friendship and circuit law partnership of Lincoln and Lamon, consult Lavern M. Hamand, "Ward Hill Lamon: Lincoln's 'Particular Friend,'" MS., Ph.D. Dissertation, University of Illinois, 1949; Clint Clay Tilton, "Lincoln and Lamon: Partners and Friends," *Transactions of the Illinois State Historical Society,* 1931, pp. 175-228; Woldman, *Lawyer Lincoln,* p. 95. The Lamon Papers are in the Huntington Library, San Marino, California.

Chapter 11—LINCOLN'S CELEBRATED LAW CASES

The earnings of prosperous lawyers before 1860 is followed in Harry E. Pratt, *The Personal Finances of Abraham Lincoln* (Springfield, Ill., 1943), p. 52n. A list of Lincoln's wealthy clients is contained in Albert A. Woldman, *Lawyer Lincoln* (Boston, 1936), pp. 161-162. Lincoln's letters to Webber and Brayman on the Illinois Central case are in *Lincoln's Collected Works,* II, 202, 205. On this case consult Charles Leroy Brown, "Abraham Lincoln and the Illinois Central Railroad, 1857-1860," *Journal of the Illinois State Historical Society,* June, 1943, pp. 131ff; Pratt, *The Personal Finances of Abraham Lincoln,* pp. 50-54; John W. Starr, Jr., *Lincoln and the Railroads* (New York, 1927), pp. 61ff; Edwin S. S. Sunderland, *Abraham Lincoln and the Illinois Central Railroad* (New York, 1955), pp. 18-19; William H. Townsend, *Lincoln the Litigant* (Boston, 1925), pp. 24-28. Also 17 *Illinois* 291; "Brief of Argument in Abraham Lincoln *v.* Illinois Central Railroad," in *Lincoln's Collected Works,* II, 397-398.

The best account of *McCormick v. Manny et al* is William T. Hutchinson, *Cyrus H. McCormick* (New York, 1930), I, 431ff. See also Pratt, *The Personal Finances of Abraham Lincoln,* pp. 56ff; Robert H. Parkinson, "The Patent Case That Lifted Lincoln into a Presidential Candidate," *The Abraham Lincoln Quarterly,* September, 1946, pp. 105-122. Lincoln's letters to Watson and to Manny and Company are in Gilbert A. Tracy (ed.), *Uncollected Letters of Abraham Lincoln* (Boston, 1917), pp. 58-59, 61. W. M. Dickson is quoted in William H. Herndon and Jesse W. Weik, *Abraham Lincoln: The True Story of a Great Life* (New York, 1892), II, 22-24. See also *Mr. and Mrs. Ralph Emerson's Personal Recollections of Abraham Lincoln* (Rockford, Ill., 1909), p. 5. Stanton's insulting remark is quoted in Henry C. Whitney, *Life on the Circuit With Lincoln* (Boston, 1892), p. 24.

The *"Effie Afton"* case (*Hurd v. Rock Island Bridge Company*) is followed in Jesse W. Weik, *The Real Lincoln* (Boston, 1922), pp. 177-187; Woldman, *Lawyer Lincoln,* pp. 171-173; "Lincoln and the Bridge Case," *The Palimpsest,* May, 1922, pp. 142-154. Robert Hitt, shorthand reporter for the Chicago *Democratic Press,* took down much of the testimony of this "bridge" case, and it was reprinted in that paper. See Chicago *Daily Democratic Press,* September 9-25, 1857. See especially Elwyn L. Page, the *"Effie Afton* Case," *Lincoln Herald,* Fall, 1956.

Barton's comment on Lincoln as a criminal lawyer is in William E. Barton, *Life of Abraham Lincoln* (Indianapolis, 1925), I, 314. The best account of Lincoln's defense of Armstrong is John J. Duff, *A. Lincoln: Prairie Lawyer* (New York, 1960), pp. 350-359. See also Woldman, *Lawyer Lincoln,* pp. 111-116. Other accounts of the Armstrong trial are in William H. Herndon and Jesse W. Weik, *Herndon's Lincoln* (Chicago, 1889), II, 357-359; Ward H. Lamon, *Life of Abraham Lincoln* (Boston, 1872), pp. 327-331; Abram Bergen's recollections are in James L. King, "Lincoln's Skill as a Lawyer," *The North American Review,* February, 1898, pp. 186-187, 195. For Edgar Lee Masters' accounts of the Armstrong trial, consult Edgar Lee Masters, *Lincoln the Man* (New York, 1931), pp. 129ff, and also his *Mitch Miller* (New York, 1920), p. 159. Consult also Edward Eggleston, *The Graysons: A Story of Illinois* (New York, 1888). For "Duff" Armstrong's release from the Union Army by Lincoln: *Journal of the Illinois State Historical Society* (1921-22), Vol. 14, p. 266; Lincoln to Mrs. Hannah Armstrong, September 18, 1863, in Brown University Library, Providence, R.I.

Lincoln's defense of Short is treated in Townsend, *Lincoln the Litigant,* pp. 20-21. Lincoln's defense of Harrison is followed in Woldman, *Lawyer Lincoln,* pp. 108-110; John M. Zane, "Lincoln, the Constitutional Lawyer," *Abraham Lincoln Association Papers,* 1932, pp. 108ff. A photostat of Lincoln's indictment of Delny is in the Illinois State Historical Library, Springfield; on this case see also Springfield *Illinois State Register,* May 14, 1853. Lincoln's prosecution of Wyant is followed in John J. Duff, "This Was a Lawyer," *Journal of the Illinois State Historical Society,* Spring, 1959, pp. 155-158; Bloomington (Ill.) *Pantagraph,* April 6, 10, 1857.

A good brief account of the "Sandbar" case is in Zane, "Lincoln, the Constitutional Lawyer," *op. cit.,* pp. 41n-42n. See also Chicago *Press & Tribune,* April 5, 1860; 18 *Howard* 150; Whitney, *Life on the Circuit With Lincoln,* pp. 54ff. For *Dawson v. Ennis and Ennis:* Woldman, *Lawyer Lincoln,* p. 135; Springfield *Illinois State Journal,* June 21, 1860.

Chapter 12—**ANTI-SLAVERY MODERATE**

Lincoln's letter discouraging a candidacy for Congress is in Springfield *Illinois State Journal,* June 7, 1850. Lincoln's correspondence, appealing for federal patronage from the Taylor and Fillmore administrations, plus his eulogies on Taylor and Clay, are printed in *Lincoln's Works,* II, 31-132.

Lincoln's account of his return to politics in 1854 is detailed in his autobiography for Scripps, June, 1860, in Robert Todd Lincoln Collection, Library of Congress. The comments of the *Illinois State Register* are in issue of October 6, 1854. Lincoln's speech at the Hall of Representatives is reported in Springfield *Illinois State Journal,* October

5, 1858. Avery O. Craven, *Civil War in the Making, 1815-1860* (Baton Rouge, La., 1959), is an excellent summary of the sectional struggle.

For Lincoln's conservatism, his Southern-descended Illinois friends, and sympathy for the South, see James G. Randall, *Lincoln and the South* (Baton Rouge, La., 1946), pp. 11ff. Lincoln's public reply to Douglas at Ottawa in 1858 about his hasty departure from Springfield in 1854 is in Paul M. Angle (ed.), *Created Equal? The Complete Lincoln-Douglas Debates of 1858* (Chicago, 1958), pp. 114-115. Herndon's reminiscences of this departure of Lincoln for Tazewell County are in William H. Herndon and Jesse W. Weik, *Abraham Lincoln: The True Story of a Great Life* (New York, 1892), II, 40-41. Lincoln's letter to Codding, November 27, 1854, is in Robert Todd Lincoln Collection. The two letters about Lincoln's moderation on slavery are A. S. Miller to Washburne, December 18, 1854, and C. H. Ray to Washburne, December 16, 1854, Elihu B. Washburne Papers, Library of Congress.

Lincoln's solicitation of support for election as United States Senator is followed in a series of letters in *Lincoln's Collected Works*, II, 286ff; Lincoln to Gillespie, December 1, 1854, Missouri Historical Society, St. Louis. Lincoln's letter to Washburne on his senatorial defeat, February 9, 1855, is in Illinois State Historical Library, Springfield.

For the decline of the national Whig Party, see Harry J. Carman and Reinhard H. Luthin, "The Seward-Fillmore Feud and the Disruption of the Whig Party," *New York*, July, 1943, pp. 335-357. Lincoln's slow metamorphosis from Whig to Republican, 1854-56, is followed in Reinhard H. Luthin, "Abraham Lincoln Becomes a Republican," *Political Science Quarterly*, September, 1944, pp. 420-438. See also Lincoln to Lovejoy, August 11, 1855, Huntington Library, San Marino, California; Lincoln to Speed, August 24, 1855, Massachusetts Historical Society, Boston. For the Editorial Convention: Otto R. Kyle, "Mr. Lincoln Steps Out: The Anti-Nebraska Editors' Convention," *The Abraham Lincoln Quarterly*, March, 1948, pp. 25-37; Paul Selby, "The Editorial Convention, February 22, 1856," *Transactions of the McLean County (Illinois) Historical Society* (1900), III, 30-43. Selby's letter to Yates is in Richard Yates Papers, Illinois State Historical Library, Springfield. Herndon's and Browning's letters to Trumbull are in Lyman Trumbull Papers, Library of Congress.

For Bloomington convention: *Transactions of the McLean County (Illinois) Historical Society* (1900), Vol. III; J. O. Cunningham, "Old Major's Hall," in Bloomington (Ill.) *Daily Bulletin*, February 4, 1909; Luthin, "Abraham Lincoln Becomes a Republican," *op. cit.*, pp. 436-437; Henry C. Whitney, *Life on the Circuit With Lincoln* (Boston, 1892), pp. 73ff. Lincoln's letter about his long association with the Whigs, June 4, 1860, is in Huntington Library, San Marino, California.

For Lincoln's Vice-Presidential candidacy in 1856: Horace White, *Life of Lyman Trumbull* (Boston, 1913), p. 69; Archer to Lincoln, June 21, 1856, in Jesse W. Weik, "Lincoln's Vote For Vice-President," *The Century* (1908), Vol. 76, p. 189.

Lincoln's Galena speech is in Galena (Ill.) *Weekly North-Western Gazette*, July 29, 1856, and Springfield *Illinois State Journal*, August 8, 1856. Campbell's financing of Lincoln's stumping tours is mentioned in Harry E. Pratt, *The Personal Finances of Abraham* (Springfield, Ill., 1943), p. 104; Campbell to Weik, December 12, 1888, in Herndon and Weik, *Abraham Lincoln*, 1892, II, 71n. Republican financing of the national campaign is referred to in James A. Rawley, *Edwin D. Morgan, 1811-1883* (New York, 1955), pp. 53, 69-70; Roy F. Nichols, "Some Problems of the First Republican Presidential Campaign," *The American Historical Review*, April, 1923, pp. 492-496. For Lincoln's Michigan tour: Thomas I. Starr, *Lincoln's Kalamazoo Address Against Extending Slavery* (Detroit, 1941); Detroit *Daily Advertiser*, August 29, 1856; Kalamazoo *Gazette*, quoted in *Michigan History Magazine* (1921), V, 287-288. Lincoln's appearance at Petersburg is followed in Springfield *Illinois State Register*, September 4, 1856; Henry B. Rankin, *Personal Recollections of Abraham Lincoln* (New York, 1916), pp. 206ff.

Mrs. Lincoln's letter to her step-sister is in possession of Colonel William H. Townsend of Lexington, Kentucky.

Chapter 13—DUELING WITH DOUGLAS

Lincoln's notation, comparing his own career with Douglas's in 1856, is in *Lincoln's Collected Works,* II, 382. His Chicago speech of December, 1856, is in Chicago *Democratic Press,* December 11, 1856, and Springfield *Illinois State Journal,* December 16, 1856.

The Dred Scott decision is treated in James G. Randall, *The Civil War and Reconstruction* (New York, 1937), pp. 148-156; Frank H. Hodder, "Some Phases of the Dred Scott Case," *The Mississippi Valley Historical Review,* June, 1929, pp. 3-22. Douglas' speech on the Dred Scott decision is in Allen Johnson, *Stephen A. Douglas* (New York, 1908), p. 322. Lincoln's reply is in Springfield *Illinois State Journal,* June 29, 1857. The Douglas-Buchanan split is followed in Roy F. Nichols, *The Disruption of American Democracy* (New York, 1948); Philip G. Auchampaugh, "The Buchanan-Douglas Feud," *Journal of the Illinois State Historical Society,* April, 1932, pp. 5-48; Reinhard H. Luthin, "The Democratic Split During Buchanan's Administration," *Pennsylvania History,* January, 1944, pp. 13-35. Douglas' letter to Treat is in Missouri Historical Society, St. Louis.

For efforts of Eastern Republicans to have Illinois Republicans endorse Douglas for re-election: David Donald, *Lincoln's Herndon* (New York, 1948), pp. 112ff, 123ff; Horace Greeley, *Recollections of a Busy Life* (New York, 1868, p. 357). Lincoln's "House Divided" speech is in Springfield *Illinois State Journal,* June 18, 1858. See also Harry V. Jaffa, *Crisis of the House Divided* (Garden City, N.Y., 1959). Herndon's letter to Trumbull is in Trumbull Papers. Douglas' reply to Lincoln is in Chicago *Times,* July 11, 1868, and Lincoln's rejoinder is in Chicago *Daily Democrat,* July 13, 1868. Lincoln's letter to Koerner is in *Lincoln's Collected Works,* II, 502.

Carl Schurz's description of Lincoln is in *Reminiscences of Carl Schurz* (Garden City, N.Y., 1908), II, 89ff. The best published compilation of the debates is Paul M. Angle (ed.), *Created Equal? The Complete Lincoln-Douglas Debates of 1858* (Chicago, 1958). The present author has largely followed this edition. See also Edwin E. Sparks (ed.), *The Lincoln-Douglas Debates of 1858* (Springfield, Ill., 1908) and Albert J. Beveridge, *Abraham Lincoln, 1809-1858* (Boston, 1928), Vol. II, Chapter 10. For the Lincoln-Douglas debate at Ottawa: C. C. Tisler and Aleita G. Tisler, *Lincoln Was Here* (Jackson, Tenn., 1958).

Lincoln's fears about irregular Irish votes are mentioned in Jacksonville (Ill.) *Sentinel,* October 20, 1858; Lincoln to Judd, October 20, 1858, in *Lincoln's Collected Works,* III, 329-330. Herndon's letter to Theodore Parker on the election results is in Joseph Fort Newton, *Lincoln and Herndon* (Cedar Rapids, Iowa, 1910), p. 234.

Chapter 14—PURSUING THE PRESIDENCY

Ray's letter to Lincoln, July 17, 1858, is in Roy P. Basler, *The Lincoln Legend* (Boston, 1935), p. 62.

Standard historical works on Lincoln's nomination and election as President in 1860 include William E. Baringer, *Lincoln's Rise to Power* (Boston, 1937); Ollinger Crenshaw, *The Slave States in the Election of 1860* (Baltimore, 1945); Emerson D. Fite, *The Presidential Campaign of 1860* (New York, 1911); H. Preston James, "Lincoln's Own State in the Election of 1860," MS., Ph.D. Dissertation, University of Illinois, 1943; Reinhard H. Luthin, *The First Lincoln Campaign* (Cambridge, Mass., 1944); Roy F. Nichols, *The Disruption of American Democracy* (New York, 1948), Chapter 18; Wayne C. Williams, *A Rail Splitter For President* (Denver, Col., 1951).

Lincoln's letters to Judd, Trumbull, Washburne, and others late in 1858 and early in 1859 are in *Lincoln's Collected Works,* III, 340-345, 351, 355-356; Lincoln to Judd, November 15, 1858, enclosed in Mrs. Judd to John Hay, June 24, 1882, in Robert Todd Lincoln Collection, Library of Congress. Lincoln's Chicago speech is reported in *The North American Review,* July, 1893, pp. 120-124. Lincoln's Iowa speech is in Council Bluffs (Iowa) *Bugle,* August 17, 1859. See also Harry V. Jaffa and Robert W. Johannsen (ed.), *In the Name of the People: Speeches of Lincoln and Douglas in the Ohio Campaign of 1859* (Columbus, Ohio, 1959). Lincoln's courting of the "German" vote is treated in Reinhard H. Luthin, "Lincoln Appeals to German-American Voters," *The American-German Review,* June–July, 1959, pp. 4ff. The support of Lincoln as second choice for President by the Baltimore *Turn-Zeitung* is in Chicago *Press & Tribune,* May 2, 1860. See also F. I. Herriott, "The Premises and Significance of Abraham Lincoln's Letter to Theodore Canisius," *Deutsch-Amerikanische Geschichtsblätter* (1915), XV, 181-254. Lincoln's contract with Canisius for the newspaper is in Brown University Library, Providence, R.I.

The political importance of "doubtful" Pennsylvania, Indiana, Illinois, and New Jersey and its effect in strengthening Lincoln's candidacy are treated in Reinhard H. Luthin's articles: "Pennsylvania and Lincoln's Rise to the Presidency," *The Pennsylvania Magazine of History and Biography,* January, 1943, pp. 61-82; "Indiana and Lincoln's Rise to the Presidency," *Indiana Magazine of History,* December, 1942, pp. 385-405. Lincoln's past record on the tariff and its beneficial effect on Lincoln's candidacy are followed in Reinhard H. Luthin, "Abraham Lincoln and the Tariff," *The American Historical Review,* July, 1944, pp. 609-629. Judd's letter to Trumbull, April 2, 1860, is in Lyman Trumbull Papers, Library of Congress. Lincoln's autobiographical sketch for Fell and its printing in the West Chester, Pennsylvania, newspaper are treated in Frances M. I. Morehouse, *Life of Jesse W. Fell* (Urbana, Ill., 1916), pp. 60ff.

For the anti-Seward movement in New York, the invitation to Lincoln to speak, and what followed, consult George H. Putnam, *Abraham Lincoln* (New York, 1909), pp. 223-224; James A. Briggs, *"An Authentic Account of Hon. Abraham Lincoln Being Invited to Give an Address . . . February 27, 1860,"* in New York *Evening Post,* August 16, 1867; Cephas Brainerd Broadsides, in possession of Lincoln National Life Foundation, Fort Wayne, Indiana; Louis A. Warren, "Printing the Cooper Institute Address," *Lincoln Lore,* July 22, 1940; Lincoln to Briggs, November 13, 1859, Western Reserve Historical Society, Cleveland, Ohio. Lincoln's letter to Cameron, February 26, 1860, is in Simon Cameron Papers, Library of Congress. Lincoln's Cooper Institute address is printed in New York *Tribune,* February 28, 1860. His New England tour is treated in Percy C. Eggleston, *Lincoln in New England* (New York, New York, 1922); Elwyn L. Page, *Abraham Lincoln in New Hampshire* (Boston, 1929); See also Andrew A. Freeman, *Abraham Lincoln Goes to New York* (New York, 1960).

Lincoln's correspondence with politicians between March and early May, 1860, is in *Lincoln's Collected Works,* IV, 31-49. The selection of county delegates to the Decatur convention is followed in Chicago *Press & Tribune,* April 30, May 1, 2, 3, 8, 1860. Events at the Decatur convention are narrated in Ward H. Lamon, *Life of Abraham Lincoln* (Boston, 1872), pp. 444-445; Josiah G. Holland, *Life of Abraham Lincoln* (Springfield, Mass., 1866), p. 198.

The occurrences at the Republican National Convention of 1860, resulting in nomination of Lincoln for President, are detailed in Luthin, *The First Lincoln Campaign,* Chapter 9. See especially Harry E. Pratt, "David Davis, 1815-1886," MS., Ph.D. Dissertation, University of Illinois, 1930, pp. 77ff; William Jayne to Trumbull, May 20, 1860, Trumbull Papers; Schuyler Colfax to Lincoln, May 20, 1860, Robert Todd Lincoln Collection, Library of Congress; *Personal Recollections of John M. Palmer* (Cincinnati, 1901), p. 81. The defeat of Bates at Chicago is narrated in Reinhard H. Luthin, "Organizing the Republican Party in the 'Border Slave' Regions: Edward Bates's Presidential Candidacy in 1860," *The Missouri Historical Review*, January, 1944, pp. 138-161. See especially William L. King, *Lincoln's Manager:* David Davis, Cambridge, Mass., 1960).

Lincoln's receipt of the news of his nomination is reported in Champaign (Ill.) *Central Illinois Gazette*, May 23, 1860.

Chapter 15—REPUBLICAN STANDARD-BEARER

For Illinois during the period following Lincoln's nomination and the conduct of the campaign there, consult Paul M. Angle, *Here I Have Lived: A History of Lincoln's Springfield, 1821-1865* (Springfield, Ill., 1935), pp. 236ff; William E. Baringer, "Campaign Technique in Illinois—1860," *Transactions of the Illinois State Historical Society*, 1932, pp. 203-281; H. Preston James, "Lincoln's Own State in the Election of 1860," MS., Ph.D. Dissertation, University of Illinois, 1943, and the same author's articles in *Lincoln Herald* (1947), Vol. 49; Walter E. Myer, "The Presidential Campaign of 1860 in Illinois," MS., M.A. Thesis, University of Chicago, 1913. See also J. H. Burnham to his father, May 19, 1860, photostat, Brown University Library, Providence, R.I.; Indianapolis *Daily State Sentinel*, June 16, 1860.

The notification committe's call on Lincoln is followed in William E. Baringer, *Lincoln's Rise to Power* (Boston, 1937), p. 316; *Memoirs of Gustave Koerner* (Cedar Rapids, Iowa, 1909), II, 93-94; *Reminiscences of Carl Schurz* (New York, 1908), II, 187-188; William H. Townsend, *Lincoln and Liquor* (New York, 1934), pp. 100ff. The confusion over Lincoln's first name is contained in *Lincoln's Collected Works*, IV, 68; Ashmun to Lincoln, June 18, 1860, in Robert Todd Lincoln, Library of Congress.

For Lincoln campaign biographies: William E. Barton, "The Lincoln of the Biographers," *Transactions of the Illinois State Historical Society*, 1929, pp. 90ff; Grace L. S. Dyche, "John Locke Scripps, Lincoln's Campaign Biographer," *Journal of the Illinois State Historical Society*, October, 1924, pp. 333-351; James Q. Howard quoted in *Transactions of the Illinois State Historical Society*, 1929, p. 67n; Mildred Howells (ed.), *Life and Letters of William Dean Howells* (Garden City, N.Y., 1928), I, 36; Scripps to Herndon, June 24, 1865, Herndon-Weik Collection, Library of Congress; Ernest J. Wessen, "Campaign Lives of Abraham Lincoln, 1860," in Paul M. Angle (ed.), *Papers in Illinois History, 1937*, pp. 188-220. Copy of Lincoln's autobiographical sketch for Scripps, June, 1860, is in Robert Todd Lincoln Collection. Lincoln's letter to Galloway is in Illinois State Historical Library, Springfield.

The split at the Democratic National Convention in 1860, and its repercussions, are followed in Austin L. Venable, "The Conflict Between the Douglas and Yancey Forces in the Charleston Convention," *Journal of Southern History* (1942), VIII, 226-241; James L. Murphy, "Alabama and the Charleston Convention of 1860," *Transactions of the Alabama Historical Society* (1904), V, 244ff; Reinhard H. Luthin, "The Democratic Split During Buchanan's Administration," *Pennsylvania History*, January, 1944, pp. 13-35; Dwight L. Dumond, *The Secession Movement, 1860-1861* (New York, 1931), pp. 41ff; Laura A. White, *Robert Barnwell Rhett* (New York, 1931), pp. 163ff.

The conduct of the election in various sections is followed in Ollinger Crenshaw, *The Slave States in the Presidential Election of 1860* (Baltimore, 1945); Reinhard H. Luthin, *The First Lincoln Campaign* (Cambridge, Mass., 1944). Bell's candidacy is followed in John B. Stabler, "A History of the Constitutional Union Party," MS., Ph.D. Dissertation, Columbia University, 1954.

A view of Lincoln during the campaign may be gathered from Helen Nicolay, "A Candidate in His Home Town," *The Abraham Lincoln Quarterly* (1940), I, 127-143;

Baringer, *Lincoln's Rise to Power,* pp. 137ff; H. Preston James, "Lincoln and Douglas in Their Home State," *Lincoln Herald,* October, 1947, pp. 2-7. On Nicolay's work for Lincoln: Helen Nicolay, *Lincoln's Secretary: A Biography of John G. Nicolay* (New York, 1949); John G. Nicolay Papers, Library of Congress. Lincoln's private letters from May to November, 1860, are printed in *Lincoln's Collected Works,* IV, 51ff.

For the pageantry and showmanship of the campaign, with parades, rallies, songs, and the use of log cabins and rails: J. M. Davis, "Origin of the Lincoln Rail," *The Century* (1900), Vol. 40, new series, pp. 271-275; R. Gerald McMurtry, "The Rail Splitter," *Lincoln Lore,* July, 1958, pp. 1-3; New York *Herald,* September 29, 1860, article on "The Clubs of the Campaign;" H. Preston James, "Political Pageantry in the Campaign of 1860 in Illinois," *The Abraham Lincoln Quarterly* (1947), IV, 313-347; Julius G. Rathbun, "The 'Wide Awakes:' The Great Political Organization of 1860," *The Connecticut Quarterly;* October, 1895, pp. 327-337; Wayne C. Temple, "Lincoln's Fence Rails," *Journal of the Illinois State Historical Society,* Spring 1954, pp. 20-34.

Campaign funds in the 1860 election are mentioned in Hiram R. Bennett, "Financing Mr. Lincoln's First Campaign," *Lincoln Herald* (1948), Vol. 50, pp. 11-22; Luthin, *The First Lincoln Campaign,* pp. 169, 173, 185; Harry E. Pratt, *The Personal Finances of Abraham Lincoln* (Springfield, Ill., 1943), p. 110; James A. Rawley, *Edwin D. Morgan, 1811-1883* (New York, 1955), pp. 114-116; Edwin D. Morgan Papers, July-September, 1860, New York State Library, Albany, N.Y. See also Blatchford to Seward, August 8, 1861, William H. Seward Papers, copy in possession of present author; Defrees to Weed, August 25, 1860, David Davis to Weed, September 11, 1860, Thurlow Weed Papers, University of Rochester Library; Schurz to Sanderson, December 22, 1860. Carl Schurz Papers, Library of Congress; J. Z. Goodrich to Dawes, June 8, 1860, Henry L. Dawes Papers, Library of Congress. Belmont's letter to Douglas, July 28, 1860, is in Stephen A. Douglas Papers, University of Chicago Library.

For Lincoln's private assurances on the tariff, and the use of that issue in Pennsylvania and New Jersey, see Lincoln to G. Yoke Tams, September 22, 1860, copy, Robert Todd Lincoln Collection; Lincoln to Harvey, October 2, 1860, in *Lincoln's Collected Works,* IV, 125; Edgar Cale, "Editorial Sentiment in Pennsylvania in the Campaign of 1860," *Pennsylvania History,* October, 1937, pp. 221ff; Reinhard H. Luthin, "Abraham Lincoln and the Tariff," *The American Historical Review,* July, 1944, pp. 618ff; Elwyn B. Robinson, "The North American: Advocate of Protection," *The Pennsylvania Magazine of History and Biography,* Vol. 64, pp. 345ff. The letters of Pomeroy, July 17, 1860, of Defrees, May 26, 1860, and of Rabé, July 5, 1860, are in Robert Todd Lincoln Collection.

For the homestead, Pacific railroad, and internal improvement issues: Joseph G. Rayback, "Land For the Landless," MS., M.A. Thesis, Western Reserve University, 1936; Robert R. Russell, "The Pacific Railroad Issue in Politics Prior to the Civil War," *The Mississippi Valley Historical Review,* September, 1925, pp. 187-201; Thomas D. Odle, "The Commercial Interests of the Great Lakes and the Campaign Issues of 1860," *Michigan History,* March, 1956, pp. 1-23. The letter to future Governor Yates on document distribution, May 23, 1860, is in Richard Yates Papers, Illinois State Historical Library, Springfield.

Lincoln's letter to Francis is in Oregon Historical Society, Portland. The October state elections in doubtful states are detailed in Reinhard H. Luthin, "Pennsylvania and Lincoln's Rise to the Presidency," *The Pennsylvania Magazine of History and Biography,* January, 1943, pp. 61-82, and the same author's "Indiana and Lincoln's Rise to the Presidency," *Indiana Magazine of History,* December, 1942, pp. 385-405. Lincoln's letter to Morgan is in New York State Library, Albany, N.Y. Copy of Lincoln's letter to Herndon is in Herndon-Weik Collection, Library of Congress. Douglas's stumping is followed in George Fort Milton, *The Eve of Conflict: Stephen A. Douglas and the Needless War* (Boston, 1934), Chapter 29.

Lincoln's letter to Weed is in Thurlow Weed Papers, University of Rochester Library. Morgan's letter to Schurz is in Rawley, *Edwin D. Morgan,* p. 118. Morgan's letter to Lincoln is in Robert Todd Lincoln Collection. New York City newspaper reaction to Lincoln's nomination is followed in Kenneth Scott, "Candidate Lincoln in the New York Press," *The New-York Historical Society Quarterly,* January, 1959, pp. 5-36. Nicolay's remarks about Lincoln voting are in *The Abraham Lincoln Quarterly* (1940), I, 139. McPike's description of the reaction of Lincoln to his election is quoted from *Transactions of the Illinois State Historical Society,* 1932, pp. 275-276.

Chapter 16—**PRESIDENT-ELECT: Crisis and Cabinet**

The electoral and popular votes of 1860 are from Edward Stanwood, *A History of the Presidency* (Boston, 1898), p. 297; *New York Tribune Almanac, 1861,* p. 64. The election in New York is followed in Milledge L. Bonham, Jr., "New York and the Election of 1860," *New York History,* April, 1934, pp. 124-143; Louis M. Sears, "New York and the Fusion Movement of 1860," *Journal of the Illinois State Historical Society,* 1923, pp. 58-62. For the tariff issue in the campaign: Thomas M. Pitkin, "The Tariff and the Early Republican Party," MS., Ph.D. Dissertation, Western Reserve University, 1935, pp. 221ff. For homestead: Joseph G. Rayback, "Land For the Landless," MS., M.A. Thesis, Western Reserve University, 1936; the speech of Lovejoy about the importance of homestead in the election of Lincoln is in *Congressional Globe,* 37th Cong., 2nd sess., p. 39. For rivers and harbors as an issue, consult Thomas D. Odle, "The Commercial Interests of the Great Lakes and the Campaign Issues of 1860," *Michigan History,* March, 1956, pp. 1-23. See Nichols's analysis of the 1860 vote in Roy F. Nichols, *The Disruption of American Democracy* (New York, 1948), pp. 370-371.

Lincoln's speech in Lincoln, Illinois, is quoted in Raymond N. Dooley, "Lincoln and His Namesake Town," *Journal of the Illinois State Historical Society,* Spring, 1959, p. 140. Keith Sutherland, a Ph.D. candidate, is preparing a biography of Vice-President Hamlin at Columbia University. For Adams' and Welles' comments: Charles Francis Adams, *Charles Francis Adams, By His Son, Charles Francis Adams* (Boston, 1900), p. 126; Muriel Burnitt (ed.), "Two Manuscripts of Gideon Welles," *The New England Quarterly,* September, 1938, p. 594.

Lincoln's Galena speech of 1856 is printed in Galena (Ill.) *Weekly North-Western Gazette,* July 29, 1856; Springfield *Illinois State Journal,* August 8, 1856. Copy of his letter to Fry, August 15, 1860, is in Jeremiah S. Black Papers, Library of Congress. Lincoln's stand against compromise with the South is treated in David M. Potter, *Lincoln and His Party in the Secession Crisis* (New Haven, Conn., 1942), Chapter 7. Lincoln's letters to Trumbull, Kellogg, and Washburne are in *Lincoln's Collected Works,* IV, 149-151.

Lincoln's selection of his Cabinet is detailed in Harry J. Carman and Reinhard H. Luthin, *Lincoln and the Patronage* (New York, 1943), Chapter 2, "Lincoln Forms His Cabinet." Cameron's appointment is followed in Harry E. Pratt, "David Davis, 1815-1886," MS., Ph.D. Dissertation, University of Illinois, 1930, pp. 82ff., and the same author's "Simon Cameron's Fight For a Place in Lincoln's Cabinet," *Bulletin of the Abraham Lincoln Association,* September, 1937, pp. 5ff. The Blair-Davis rivalry is treated in Reinhard H. Luthin, "A Discordant Chapter in Lincoln's Administration; The Blair-Davis Controversy," *The Maryland Historical Magazine,* March, 1944, pp. 25ff. See also the following collections for period from November, 1860, to March, 1861: Bryant-Godwin Papers, New York Public Library; Simon Cameron Papers, Library of Congress; Colfax-Orth Papers, Indiana State Library, Indianapolis; Robert Todd Lincoln Collection, Library of Congress; Fishback to his brother, January 19, 1861, photostat, Indiana State Library, Indianapolis; William H. Seward Papers, University of Rochester Library; Lyman Trumbull Papers, Library of Congress; Caleb B. Smith to Schouler, December 1, 1860, William Schouler Papers, Massachusetts Historical Society, Boston; Thurlow Weed Papers, University of Rochester Library. See also Willard H. Smith, *Schuyler Colfax* (Indianapolis, 1952); Horace White, *Life of Lyman Trumbull* (New York, 1913).

For Lincoln's Attorney-General, Bates: Floyd A. McNeil, "Lincoln's Attorney General: Edward Bates," MS., Ph.D. Dissertation, State University of Iowa, 1934. Marvin Cain is also preparing a study of Bates as a Ph.D. dissertation at the University of Missouri. Professor William E. Baringer of the University of Florida has compeleted a lengthy scholarly biography of Salmon P. Chase. Harry J. Carman and Reinhard H. Luthin are completing a biography of William H. Seward.

Browning's interview with Lincoln is recorded in Theodore C. Pease and James G. Randall (ed.), *Diary of Orville Hickman Browning* (Springfield, Ill., 1925), I, 453. Lincoln's farewell address is in Springfield *Illinois State Journal,* February 12, 1861.

Chapter 17—THE INAUGURATION

Lincoln's journey to Washington is followed in William E. Baringer, *A House Dividing: Lincoln As President-Elect* (Springfield, Ill., 1945); Harold G. Villard and Oswald Garrison (ed.), *Lincoln On the Eve of '61, By Henry Villard* (New York, 1941). The small-town newspaperman's comments are in Jefferson (Ohio) *Ashtabula Sentinel,* February 20, 1861, in Kenneth M. Stampp, *And the War Came* (Baton Rouge, La., 1950), p. 179. Nicolay's letter is in Helen Nicolay, *Lincoln's Secretary: A Biography of John G. Nicolay* (New York, 1949), p. 66. Lincoln's reference to Grace Bedell and his appearance in Westfield are in Westfield (N.Y.) *Republican,* February 20, 1861; New York *Tribune,* February 18, 1861. Grace Bedell's letter to Lincoln, October 15, 1860, is in possession of Hon. George Dondero, former member of Congress from Michigan.

The onlooker at Albany was A. J. Blakely. See his letter to his father in Harry E. Pratt (ed.), *Concerning Mr. Lincoln* (Springfield, Ill., 1944), p. 53. Lincoln's Independence Hall speech is in Philadelphia *Inquirer,* February 23, 1861. Developments on the Cameron Cabinet problem are treated in Harry J. Carman and Reinhard H. Luthin, *Lincoln and the Patronage* (New York, 1943), pp. 47-49; Simon Cameron Papers, February 22-23, 1861, Library of Congress. The Baltimore "plot" to assassinate Lincoln is best followed in Norma B. Cuthbert (ed.), *Lincoln and the Baltimore Plot, 1861* (Huntington Library, San Marino, Calif., 1949). The interview of Seward's son with Lincoln is told in Frederick W. Seward, *Reminiscences of a War-Time Statesman and Diplomat* (New York, 1916), pp. 134-138. Lamon's comments are in Ward H. Lamon, "Abraham Lincoln," New York *Tribune,* July 26, 1885. Nevins concludes that the plans to murder Lincoln "may now be regarded as valid"—Allan Nevins, *The Emergence of Lincoln* (New York, 1950), II, 451n.

On the "Scotch cap" hoax, see R. Gerald McMurtry, "Scotch Cap and Military Cloak a Fabrication," *Lincoln Lore,* October, 1956; Robert S. Harper, *Lincoln and the Press* (New York, 1951), p. 91; Mary Boykin Chesnut, *A Diary From Dixie* (New York, 1905), p. 18. Lincoln's unpopularity on reaching Washington is mentioned in James G. Randall, "The Unpopular Mr. Lincoln," *The Abraham Lincoln Quarterly* (1943), II, 256ff.

For the comments of Congressmen Waldron and Julian and the Washington correspondent on the office-seekers, see Waldron to Howard, March 2, 1861, Jacob M. Howard Papers, Burton Historical Collection, Detroit Public Library; George W. Julian, *Political Recollections* (Chicago, 1884), pp. 193-194; New York *Herald,* February 28, 1861. Lincoln's completion of his Cabinet is followed in Harry J. Carman and Reinhard H. Luthin, *Lincoln and the Patronage* (New York, 1943), pp. 48-50.

Lincoln's writing of his inaugural is followed in Nevins, *The Emergence of Lincoln,* II, 460; Theodore C. Pease and James G. Randall (ed.), *Diary of Orville Hickman Browning* (Springfield, Ill., 1925), I, 455-456; Browning to Lincoln, February 17, 1861, Robert Todd Lincoln Collection, Library of Congress. The latter institution possesses the earlier printed version of Lincoln's first Inaugural Address, with secretarial reproductions of numerous handwritten changes; also a photostat of John Hay's letter to Charles Eliot Norton, March 29, 1889, explaining how the address was revised. See Marie Hochmuth, "Lincoln's First Inaugural," in Wayland M. Parrish (ed.), *American Speeches* (New York, 1954), pp. 21-71; Jay B. Hubbell, "Lincoln's First Inaugural Address," *The American Historical Review,* April, 1931, pp. 550-552. Cornell's letter, March 3, 1861, is in *Cornell University Alumni News,* February 27, 1930.

Lincoln's inauguration ceremonies are described in Charles Aldrich, "At Lincoln's First Inaugural," *Annals of Iowa,* April, 1907, pp. 43-50; R. Gerald McMurtry, "The Inauguration of Abraham Lincoln," *Lincoln Lore,* January, 1957; W. A. Janny's letter in *Lincoln Herald,* Winter, 1952, pp. 44-45; New York *Herald,* March 5, 1861. The Inaugural Address is in *Lincoln's Collected Works,* IV, 262ff. See also Allan Nevins, "He Did Hold Lincoln's Hat," *American Heritage,* February, 1959.

Chapter 18—**WAR WITH SECESSION**

Press reactions to Lincoln's First Inaugural are printed in Howard C. Perkins (ed.), *Northern Editorials on Secession* (New York, 1942), Vol. II; Dwight L. Dumond (ed.), *Southern Editorials on Secession* (New York, 1931); Louis A. Warren, "Lincoln's First Inaugural—Pro and Con," *Lincoln Lore,* February, 1953. The South's hostile reaction to Lincoln's election is analyzed in J. G. de R. Hamilton, "Lincoln's Election An Immediate Menace to Slavery in the States?" *The American Historical Review,* July, 1932, pp. 700-711.

Varying scholarly interpretations of the drift to Civil War and the Fort Sumter incident include David M. Potter, *Lincoln and His Party in the Secession Crisis* (New Haven, Conn., 1942); James G. Randall, "When War Came in 1861," *The Abraham Lincoln Quarterly* (1940), I, 3-42; Kenneth M. Stampp, *And the War Came* (Baton Rouge, La., 1950). For strongly anti-Lincoln interpretations: Charles W. Ramsdell, "Lincoln and Fort Sumter," *The Journal of Southern History* (1937), III, 259-288; John S. Tilley, *Lincoln Takes Command* (Chapel Hill, N.C., 1941); David Rankin Barbee, "The Line of Blood: Lincoln and the Coming of the War," *Tennessee Historical Quarterly,* March, 1957, pp. 3-54. Buchanan's defense of himself is contained in his own *The Administration on the Eve of Rebellion* (London, 1865), p. 169; see also Samuel W. Crawford, *The Genesis of the Civil War* (New York, 1887), pp. 167-168.

The Cabinet meeting of March 9, 1861, is detailed in Howard K. Beale (ed.), *Diary of Edward Bates, 1859-1866* (Washington, 1933), p. 177. Disagreement in the Cabinet is mentioned in Edwin M. Stanton to Buchanan, March 16, 1861, James Buchanan Papers, Historical Society of Pennsylvania, Philadelphia. For Cabinet sentiment in favor of relinquishing Fort Sumter (except for Blair's disagreement), see *Lincoln's Collected Works,* IV, 285; *Official Records of the Union and Confederate Navies,* Series I, Vol. 4, p. 247; Chase to Elihu Burritt, October 6, 1862, Salmon P. Chase Papers, Historical Society of Pennsylvania, Philadelphia; F. P. Blair, Sr., to Cameron, November 24, 1864, Simon Cameron Papers, Library of Congress; Montgomery Blair's draft of letter to Andrew Johnson, August 9, 1865, Blair Papers, Library of Congress. Welles's account of the elder Blair's intercession with Lincoln is in *Diary of Gideon Welles* (Boston, 1909), I, 13-14.

Fox's trip to Charleston and Fort Sumter is followed in *Official Records of the Union and Confederate Navies,* Series I, Vol. 4, p. 247. The missions of Lamon and Hurlbut are treated in Frederic Bancroft, *Life of William H. Seward* (New York, 1900), II, 107; Crawford, *The Genesis of the Civil War,* pp. 373-374. Pickens' letter about Lamon in the Charleston *Courier* is in James Ford Rhodes, *History of the United States From the Compromise of 1850* (New York, 1895), III, 333n. General Scott's opinion on Sumter and Pickens is printed in *Official Records of the Union and Confederate Armies,* Series I, Vol. 1, pp. 200-201. Blair's and also Nicolay and Hay's comments on Lincoln's reaction to Scott's advice are in Gideon Welles, *Lincoln and Seward* (New York, 1874), pp. 64-65; John G. Nicolay and John Hay, *Abraham Lincoln: A History* (New York, 1890), III, 395. Mrs. Lincoln's letter is in *Illinois Central Magazine,* February, 1929. Scott's estimate of his available troops is from William Howard Russell, *My Diary North and South* (Boston, 1863), p. 66.

Lincoln's reaction to Seward's "Some Thoughts For the President's Consideration" paper is treated in Frederic Bancroft, "Seward's Proposition of April 1, 1861," "For a Foreign War and a Dictatorship," *Harper's Monthly* (1899), Vol. 99, pp. 781-791; *Lincoln's Collected Works,* IV, 316-317.

Virginia's course to secession is treated in Henry T. Shanks, *The Secession Movement in Virginia, 1847-1861* (Richmond, Va., 1934). Seward's negotiations are treated in Bancroft, *Life of William H. Seward,* II, 31, 533ff; Henry Adams, "The Great Secession Winter of 1860-61," *Proceedings of the Massachusetts Historical Society* (1910), Vol. 43, pp. 660-687. Baldwin's account of his interview with Lincoln on April 4, 1861, given in 1866, is printed in *House Report* No. 30, 39th Cong., 1st sess., Part II, Serial No. 1273, p. 103. See also Allan B. Magruder, "A Piece of Secret History: President Lincoln and the Virginia Convention of 1861," *The Atlantic Monthly,* April, 1875, pp. 438-445; Wilmer L. Hall, "Lincoln's Interview With John B. Baldwin," *The South Atlantic Quarterly,* July, 1914, pp. 260-269.

The Confederate decision to capture Fort Sumter, culminating in the firing, is followed in T. Harry Williams, *P. G. T. Beauregard: Napoleon in Gray* (Baton Rouge, La., 1954), pp. 56ff; *Official Records of the Union and Confederate Armies,* Series I, Vol. 1, pp. 297ff. Chisolm's account of the first shot on Fort Sumter is detailed in his unpublished reminiscence, "Journal of Events Before and During the Bombardment of Fort Sumter, April, 1861," copy loaned to the present author by Professor T. Harry Williams of The Louisiana State University. Professor Francis B. Simkins of Farmville, Virginia, is preparing a careful biography of President Jefferson Davis. Hudson Strode, *Jefferson Davis: Confederate President* (Boston, 1959) is a sympathetic and full treatment of Davis.

The federal law on which Lincoln based his call for 75,000 state militia men is printed in *United States Statutes-At-Large,* I, 424.

Chapter 19—FROM FORT SUMTER TO FIRST BULL RUN

The spontaneous Northern support for the Union following Sumter is followed in Kenneth M. Stampp, *And the War Came* (Baton Rouge, La., 1950), pp. 287ff. For Douglas' interview with Lincoln: John G. Nicolay and John Hay, *Abraham Lincoln: A History* (New York, 1890), IV, 80; Ashmun to Isaac N. Arnold, October 15, 1864, in New York *Herald,* October 31, 1864; S. P. Hanscom's editorial in Washington *National Republican,* September 16, 1866. Douglas' dispatch to the press is printed in J. G. Holland, *Life of Abraham Lincoln* (Springfield, Mass., 1866), pp. 302-303. For Douglas' last days and death: George Fort Milton, *The Eve of Conflict: Stephen A. Douglas and the Needless War* (Boston, 1934), pp. 563-570.

The secession of Virginia is treated in Henry T. Shanks, *The Secession Movement in Virginia, 1847-1861* (Richmond, Va., 1934). Favorable response of Northern governors to Lincoln's call for troops is followed in John Bach McMaster, *A History of the People of the United States During Lincoln's Administration* (New York, 1927), pp. 32-34; William B. Hesseltine, *Lincoln and the War Governors* (New York, 1948), pp. 145-147.

For the Maryland situation in 1861 see Charles W. Clark, "Politics in Maryland During the Civil War," *The Maryland Historical Magazine,* September, 1941, pp. 239ff. For the firing on Massachusetts troops consult John W. Hanson, *Historical Sketch of the Old Sixth Regiment of Massachusetts Volunteers* (Boston, 1866); "Report of Col. Edward F. Jones, April 22, 1861," in *Official Records of the Union and Confederate Armies,* Series I, Vol. 2, p. 7; George W. Brown, *Baltimore and the 19th of April* (Baltimore, 1887), Hay's notations are in Tyler Dennett (ed.), *Lincoln and the Civil War in the Diaries and Letters of John Hay* (New York, 1939), pp. 4, 5.

Lincoln's correspondence with Hicks, Brown, and others and his reply to a Baltimore delegation are in *Lincoln's Collected Works,* IV, 340-342. Brown's account is from his own work, *Baltimore and the 19th of April,* pp. 71-72. Lincoln's words to Massachusetts troops are quoted in Dennett (ed.), *Lincoln and the Civil War in the Diaries and Letters of John Hay* (New York, 1939), p. 11. Lincoln's letter to Browning about Kentucky, September 22, 1861, is in Illinois State Historical Library, Springfield.

On Scott's condition: Nicolay and Hay, *Abraham Lincoln: A History,* IV, 126. For Lee's refusal of a high Union military command: Douglas Southall Freeman, *R. E. Lee: A Biography* (New York, 1936), I, 633ff. The Major-General's proposed commission to Garibaldi is treated in Charles Francis Adams, "President Lincoln's Offer of a Military Command to Garibaldi in 1861," *Proceedings of the Massachusetts Historical Society* (1908), Series III, Vol. 1, pp. 319-325; Charles C. Tansill, "A Secret Chapter in Civil War History," *Thought* (1940), XV, 215-224. Schleiden's abortive efforts for peace mediation is followed in Ralph H. Lutz, "Rudolf Schleiden and the Visit to Richmond, April 25, 1861," in *Annual Report, American Historical Association,* 1915, pp. 209-216.

Ellsworth's life and death is followed in Charles A. Ingraham, *Elmer E. Ellsworth and the Zouaves of '61* (Chicago, 1925). See also Julia Taft Bayne, *Tad Lincoln's Father* (Boston, 1931), p. 39; Lincoln's letter to Mr. and Mrs. Ellsworth is in *Lincoln's Collected Works,* IV, 385-386.

Lincoln's social obligations are followed in Margaret Leech, *Reveille in Washington, 1860-1865* (New York, 1941), pp. 46ff. Wallace's letter to his wife about the Lincolns' reception, March 9, 1861, is in Wallace-Dickey Papers, Illinois State Historical Library, Springfield. Bigelow's comments are in his MS diary, July 9, 1861, New York Public Library. Bates's letter, March 26, 1861, is in James O. Broadhead Papers, Missouri Historical Society, St. Louis. Copy of Lincoln's letter to Seward, "Private & Confidential," December 8, 1860, is in possession of the present author. Lincoln's patronage policy is detailed in Harry J. Carman and Reinhard H. Luthin, *Lincoln and the Patronage* (New York, 1941).

Lincoln's message to Congress is in James D. Richardson (comp), *Messages and Papers of the Presidents, 1789-1897* (Washington, 1897), VI, 20-31. See also Theodore C. Pease and James G. Randall (ed.), *Diary of Orville Hickman Browning, 1850-1864* (Springfield, Ill., 1925), I, 475-476. Secretary Smith's letter home, June 10, 1861, is in Richard W. Thompson Papers, Lincoln National Life Foundation, Fort Wayne, Indiana. The Bull Run disaster is followed in Colin R. Ballard, *The Military Genius of Abraham Lincoln* (London, 1926), pp. 49-50; Robert M. Johnston, *Bull Run* (Boston, 1913); Robert U. Johnson and Clarence C. Buel (ed.), *Battles and Leaders of the Civil War* (New York, 1887), I, 175, 230. Nicolay and Hay's account of Lincoln's reaction to the news from Bull Run is printed in their *Abraham Lincoln: A History,* IV, 353-354.

Chapter 20—FROM BULL RUN TO BALL'S BLUFF

Nicolay and Hay's account of Lincoln's failure to sleep is in their *Abraham Lincoln: A History* (New York, 1890), IV, 355. Lincoln's "Memorandum" after Bull Run, July 23 and 27, 1861, is in Robert Todd Lincoln Collection, Library of Congress. The conference at which General Scott took blame for Bull Run, and Lincoln's reply, are in Congressman William A. Richardson's speech in *Congressional Globe,* 37th Cong., 1st sess., p. 246. Lincoln's conversation with McDowell is told in William H. Russell, *My Diary North and South* (Boston, 1863), p. 507.

The best biography of McClellan is Warren W. Hassler, *General George B. McClellan: Shield of the Union* (Baton Rouge, La., 1957). For McClellan's self-esteem and letters to his wife see *George B. McClellan's Own Story* (New York, 1887), pp. 82-83; also *Official Records of the Union and Confederate Armies,* Series I, Vol. 2, pp. 753, 763, 766. McClellan's complaints are from *McClellan's Own Story,* pp. 168-170. Scott's career is followed in Charles W. Elliott, *Winfield Scott* (New York, 1937). Lincoln's Cabinet meeting concerning Scott's retirement is detailed in Howard K. Beale (ed.), *Diary of Edward Bates, 1859-1866* (Washington, 1933), pp. 196-197. Lincoln's eulogy of Scott to Congress is in James D. Richardson (comp.), *Messages and Papers of the Presidents* (Washington, 1897), VI, 56.

The Blair-Frémont feud and its repercussions are detailed in Allan Nevins, *Frémont: Pathmarker of the West* (New York, 1939), Chapter 30, "Frémont vs. Blair and Lincoln;" William E. Smith, *The Francis Preston Blair Family in Politics* (New York, 1933), Vol. II. A shorter account is in Harry J. Carman and Reinhard H. Luthin, *Lincoln and the Patronage* (New York, 1943), pp. 194-197. Turbulent politics in Missouri are treated in Sceva B. Laughlin, "Missouri Politics During the Civil War," *The Missouri Historical Review* (1929-30), Vol. 24, pp. 87ff. See also Francis P. Blair to Montgomery Blair, August 21, September 1, 1861, Lincoln to Mrs. John C. Frémont, September 12, 1861, in Robert Todd Lincoln Collection. Autographed draft of Lincoln's letter to Hunter, September 9, 1861, is in this same collection. Lincoln's words about his conference with Mrs. Frémont are quoted in Tyler Dennett (ed.), *Lincoln and the Civil War in the Diaries and Letters of John Hay* (New York, 1939), p. 133. Lincoln's letter to Mrs. Frémont is in *Lincoln's Collected Works,* IV, 519.

An extended account of Kentucky during the secession crisis and the war is E. Merton Coulter, *The Civil War and Readjustment in Kentucky* (Chapel Hill, N.C., 1926). Garrett Davis' account of his interview with Lincoln, detailed in Davis' letter to George D. Prentice, April 28, 1861, is in *Congressional Globe,* 37th Cong., 2nd sess., *Appendix,* pp. 82-83. Copies of Lincoln's letters to Frémont, September 11, 1861, in answer to Frémont's proclamation, are in Robert Todd Lincoln Collection. Copy of Lincoln's letter to Browning, September 22, 1861, in Illinois State Historical Library, Springfield. Letter to Trumbull, December 10, 1861, is in Lyman Trumbull Papers, Library of Congress. The importance of Kentucky in the salvation of the Union is emphasized in Edward Conrad Smith, *The Borderland in the Civil War* (New York, 1927), pp. 311-312.

Lincoln's last meeting with Baker is described in John J. Hay, "Edward Baker," *Harper's Magazine,* December, 1861, p. 108; Ruth Painter Randall, *Mary Lincoln* (Boston, 1953), p. 235. For Lincoln's reacton to Baker's death: Charles Carleton Coffin, *Four Years of Fighting* (Boston, 1866), p. 30; Helen Nicolay, *Lincoln's Secretary: A Biography of John G. Nicolay* (New York, 1949), p. 101. Willie Lincoln's poem on Baker's death is in Washington *National Republican,* November 4, 1861. Gayle Braden is preparing a Ph.D. dissertation on Edward D. Baker at Vanderbilt University. For the Union defeat at Ball's Bluff: Joseph D. Patch, *The Battle of Ball's Bluff* (Leesburg, Va., 1958).

Sumner's speech on Baker's death and Lincoln's reaction to it are treated in T. Harry Williams, *Lincoln and the Radicals* (Madison, Wis., 1941), p. 61. Speed's letter, December 8, 1861, is in Joseph Holt Papers, Library of Congress.

Chapter 21—**LINCOLN AND HIS LIEUTENANTS**

Conferences between Lincoln and McClellan late in 1861 are detailed in Tyler Dennett (ed.), *Lincoln and the Civil War in the Diaries and Letters of John Hay* (New York, 1939), pp. 31, 33; George B. McClellan, *McClellan's Own Story* (New York, 1887), pp. 170, 176. Heintzelman's quotation from McClellan on Lincoln is in Samuel P. Heintzelman Journal, MS., November 11, 1861, Library of Congress. Wade's account of his interview with McClellan is in *The American Historical Review,* April, 1918, pp. 551-552. For Lincoln's plan for capturing New Orleans, see David D. Porter, *Incidents and Anecdotes of the Civil War* (New York, 1885), pp. 95-96.

Lincoln's letter to Schurz, November 10, 1862, is in Carl Schurz Papers, Library of Congress. For the Jacobins' opposition to McClellan and Democratic and West Point generals, and a fine account of the Committee on the Conduct of the War, consult T. Harry Williams, *Lincoln and the Radicals* (Madison, Wis., 1941), pp. 14ff, 77ff. See also the same author's "The Committee on the Conduct of the War," *Journal of the American Military Institute* (1939), III, 139-156; William W. Pierson, Jr., "The Committee on the Conduct of the Civil War," *The American Historical Review,* April, 1918, pp. 550-576. The Committee's proceedings are printed in *Committee on the Conduct of the War* (Washington, 1863-66), 8 vols. For Julian's later view about the Committee's unfairness to McClellan: George W. Julian, *Political Recollections, 1840-1872* (Chicago, 1884), pp. 203-204.

Lincoln's letters to Generals Buell and Halleck are in *Lincoln's Collected Works,* V, 86, 87, 90-92. Lincoln's visit to Meigs, and the later conference with McDowell, Franklin, and the Cabinet members are narrated in "General M. C. Meigs on the Conduct of the War," *The American Historical Review,* January, 1921, pp. 292-293; McDowell's memorandum, January 10, 1862, in Henry J. Raymond, *Life and Public Services of Abraham Lincoln* (New York, 1865), pp. 772-774; McClellan, *McClellan's Own Story,* pp. 155ff. For Meigs: Russell F. Weigley, *Quartermaster General of the Union Army: A Biography of M. C. Meigs* (New York, 1959).

Cameron's resignation as Secretary of War is treated in Harry J. Carman and Reinhard H. Luthin, *Lincoln and the Patronage* (New York, 1943), pp. 129-132. Lincoln's two letters to Cameron, January 11, 1862, are in Simon Cameron Papers, Library of Congress. See also Alexander K. McClure, *Abraham Lincoln and Men of War-Times* (Philadelphia, 1892), p. 165. Ely's letter to Sumner is in James Ford Rhodes, *History of the United States From the Compromise of 1850,* III, 576n. Speed's letter about Clay, February 4, 1862, is in Joseph Holt Papers, Library of Congress.

A copy of Lincoln's letter to Buell is in the Edwin M. Stanton Papers, Library of Congress. Lincoln's early lack of enthusiasm for Grant is mentioned in William B. Hesseltine, *Ulysses S. Grant, Politician* (New York, 1935), p. 31. Lincoln's "Uncle Sam's Web-Feet" expression is in *Lincoln's Collected Works,* VI, 409.

Lincoln's letter to McClellan, asking him five questions, is in the above-mentioned Stanton Papers. Browning's entry in his diary is in Theodore C. Pease and James G. Randall (ed.), *Diary of Orville Hickman Browning* (Springfield, Ill., 1925), I, 552. The vote of the twelve generals is followed in Warren W. Hassler, *General George B. McClellan* (Baton Rouge, La., 1957), p. 61; Journal of Samuel P. Heintzelman, MS., March 8, 1862. For the hostility of the four opposing generals to McClellan, see Williams, *Lincoln and the Radicals,* pp. 85-86, 118, 131.

Chapter 22—THE LINCOLN-McCLELLAN MUDDLE

McClellan's fears about the radicals and evidence of his own conservative political views are in his *McClellan's Own Story* (New York, 1887), pp. 35, 150, 155. For Lincoln's Army of Potomac reorganization into corps, see T. Harry Williams, *Lincoln and the Radicals* (Madison, Wis., 1941), pp. 121ff; William Starr Myers, *A Study in Personality: General George Brinton McClellan* (New York, 1934), pp. 256ff; Journal of Samuel P. Heintzelman, MS., March 8, 1862, Library of Congress; "Journal of the Joint Committee on the Conduct of the War," *Senate Report* No. 108, 37th Cong., 3rd sess., Vol. I, pp. 86-87.

Senator Fessenden's letter to his wife is in Francis Fessenden, *Life and Public Services of William Pitt Fessenden* (Boston, 1907), I, 261. Lincoln's War Order No. 3 is in *Lincoln's Collected Works,* V, 155. Lincoln's explanation to his Cabinet is in Tyler Dennett (ed.), *Lincoln and the Civil War in the Diaries and Letters of John Hay* (New York, 1939), p. 37. Lincoln's letter to McClellan, March 31, 1862, is in George B. McClellan Papers, Library of Congress. Lincoln's telegram to McClellan, April 6, 1862, is in Brown University Library, Providence, R.I. His letter to McClellan, March 18, 1862, about General Wool is in Ethan Allen Hitchcock Papers, Library of Congress. Order to Wool on April 3, 1862, is in *Official Records of the Union and Confederate Armies,* Series I, Vol. 11, Part III, p. 65.

The relative strength of McClellan's and Lee's armies is in *Report on the . . . Army of the Potomac,* pp. 162, 191; Douglas Southall Freeman, *R. E. Lee: A Biography* (New York, 1935), II, 116. For the capture of Norfolk: William E. Baringer, "On Enemy Soil: President Lincoln's Norfolk Campaign," *The Abraham Lincoln Quarterly* (1952), Vol. 7, pp. 4-26. Emory Upton's analysis is in his *The Military Policy of the United States,* p. 312. Copy of Lincoln's letter to McClellan, June 15, 1862, is in Robert Todd Lincoln Collection, Library of Congress. McClellan's letter to Stanton is in *McClellan's Own Story,* p. 389.

The Battle of Seven Days is followed in Freeman, *R. E. Lee,* Vol. II, Chapters 12-18. Lincoln's appointment of Pope to Army of Virginia command is treated in Williams, *Lincoln and the Radicals,* pp. 140ff. Lincoln's letter to McClellan, July 2, 1862, is in Illinois State Historical Library, Springfield. Meigs' visit to Lincoln is told in Diary of M. C. Meigs, MS., July 4, 5, 1862, Library of Congress; Dennett (ed.), *Lincoln and the Civil War in the Diaries and Letters of John Hay,* p. 176.

The promotion of Halleck, demotion of McClellan, and the Second Bull Run defeat, and the restoration of McClellan to high command are treated in T. Harry Williams, *Lincoln and His Generals* (New York, 1952), Chapters 6 and 7. Williams presents an able case against McClellan, but the present author disagrees. Dr. Stephen E. Ambrose of the University of Wisconsin is completing a biography of General Halleck. The Cabinet meeting of September 2, 1862, is detailed in Diary of Salmon P. Chase, MS., Library of Congress; *Diary of Gideon Welles* (Boston, 1909), I, 104-106. The happy reaction of the troops to McClellan's restoration to command is in Clarence C. Buel and Robert U. Johnson (ed.), *Battles and Leaders of the Civil War* (New York, 1887-88), II, 551n. For the Second Manassas defeat: Edward J. Stackpole, *From Cedar Mountain to Antietam: August-September, 1862* (Harrisburg, Pa., 1960). Merlin G. Cox is preparing a dissertation on General Pope at the University of Florida.

General Howard's letters to his wife about McClellan are in John A. Carpenter, "An Account of the Civil War Career of Oliver Otis Howard Based On His Private Papers," MS., Ph.D. Dissertation, Columbia University, 1954, pp. 51, 53. For Lee's invasion of Maryland, culminating in the Battle of Antietam Creek, consult Freeman, *R. E. Lee,* Vol. II, Chapters 15-18; Capt. Isaac W. Heysinger, *Antietam and the Maryland and Virginia Campaigns of 1862* (New York, 1912); Miles C. Huyette, *The Maryland Campaign and the Battle of Antietam* (Buffalo, N.Y., 1915).

Lincoln is quoted by Browning about McClellan in Theodore C. Pease and James G. Randall (ed.), *Diary of Orville Hickman Browning, 1850-1864* (Springfield, Ill., 1925), I, 591. For the relations between Lincoln and McClellan from late September until his removal of McClellan, consult *Lincoln's Collected Works,* V, 452, 460-461, 474; *McClellan's Own Story,* pp. 627-628, 654; John G. Nicolay and John Hay, *Abraham Lincoln: A History* (New York, 1890), VI, 188. For Lee's estimate of McClellan as a general, see letter to McClellan, signed "A Friend," March 28, 1863, George B. McClellan Papers, Library of Congress, concerning Lee's daughter's revelations, and Freeman, *R. E. Lee,* IV, 475, for Lee's own view of McClellan's ability.

Chapter 23—FACING THE SLAVERY ORDEAL

For the split in the Republican Party over slavery and other considerations, see T. Harry Williams, *Lincoln and the Radicals* (Madison, Wis., 1941), pp. 5-6, 9-11. For Lincoln's countermanding of Frémont's emancipation proclamation, consult Allan Nevins, *Frémont: Pathmarker of the West* (New York, 1939), pp. 505-507; *Lincoln's Collected Works,* IV, 506, 517-518. Lincoln's First Annual Address is in James D. Richardson (ed.), *Messages and Papers of the Presidents, 1789-1897* (Washington, 1898), VI, 44-58. Garrison's comment about Lincoln is in his letter to Oliver Johnson, December 6, 1861, William Lloyd Garrison Papers, Boston Public Library. The radicals' opposition to Lincoln, Cameron's report favoring recruitment of slaves for the Army, and Lincoln's course are followed in Williams, *Lincoln and the Radicals,* pp. 58-60.

Lincoln's appointment of Frémont to the Mountain Department command and his correspondence with Frémont are followed in Nevins, *Fremont,* pp. 553ff; *Lincoln's Collected Works,* V, 230, 243, 247, 250, 270-274. Jackson's Valley campaign is treated in G. F. R. Henderson, *Stonewall Jackson and the American Civil War* (New York, n.d.), Chapters 10-12. Copy of Lincoln's overruling of Hunter's order is in Robert Todd Lincoln Collection, Library of Congress. Lincoln's meeting with Marylanders about Wadsworth is in New York *Tribune,* May 20, 1862. Chase's comments about Lincoln are in Diary of Salmon P. Chase, MS., September 12, 1862, Library of Congress.

The Confiscation Acts of 1861 and 1862 and the Militia Act of 1862 are discussed in James G. Randall, *Constitutional Problems Under Lincoln* (New York, 1926), Chapter 15. Greeley's letter to Lincoln is in New York *Tribune,* August 20, 1862. The original of Lincoln's letter to Greeley is in Wadsworth Athenaeum, Hartford, Conn. Consult Harlan Hoyt Horner, *Lincoln and Greeley* (Urbana, Ill., 1953), pp. 272-273.

Lincoln's eulogy of Clay, and reference to Clay's colonization proposals are in Springfield *Illinois Weekly Journal,* July 21, 1852. Lincoln's recommendations to Congress on emancipation and colonization are in Richardson (ed.), *Messages and Papers of the Presidents,* VI, 54, 72. Copies of Lincoln's letters to Raymond and Senator McDougall, March 9, 14, 1862, are in Robert Todd Lincoln Collection. Lincoln's words to the Negro delegation advising colonization are quoted in New York *Tribune,* August 15, 1862.

Lincoln's interest in private colonization projects is treated in Warren A. Beck, "Abraham Lincoln and Negro Colonization in Central America," *The Abraham Lincoln Quarterly,* September, 1950, pp. 162-183; Walter L. Fleming, "Deportation and Colonization: An Attempted Solution of the Race Problem," in *Studies in South-*

ern History and Politics: Inscribed to William A. Dunning (New York, 1914), pp. 3ff; Paul J. Scheips, "Ambrose W. Thompson: A Neglected Isthmian Promoter," MS., M.A. Thesis, University of Chicago, 1949; Charles H. Wesley, "Lincoln's Plans For Colonizing the Emancipated Negroes," *The Journal of Negro History,* January, 1919, pp. 7-21.

Events leading to Lincoln's issuance of the preliminary Proclamation of Emancipation have been drawn from: Lincoln's quotation, February 6, 1864, in Francis B. Carpenter, "Anecdotes and Reminiscences of President Lincoln," in Henry J. Raymond, *Life and Public Services of Abraham Lincoln* (New York, 1865), p. 761; Diary of Salmon P. Chase, MS., September 22, 1862, Library of Congress; David Davis to Leonard Swett, November 26, 1862, in Harry E. Pratt (ed.), *Concerning Mr. Lincoln* (Springfield, Ill., 1944), p. 97; John G. Nicolay and John Hay (ed.), *Complete Works of Abraham Lincoln* (New York, 1905), Tandy Edition, X, 1-3; *Diary of Gideon Welles* (New York, 1909), I, 70-71, 142-143; James C. Welling's diary, September 27, 1862, quoted in his "The Emancipation Proclamation," The *North American Review,* February, 1880, pp. 171-172. Copy of Lincoln's letter to McClernand, January 8, 1863, in Robert Todd Lincoln Collection.

Chapter 24—POLITICAL PROBLEMS AND MILITARY MISTAKES

Political conditions, including the election of 1862, in the populous Northern states, are treated in Sidney D. Brummer, *Political History of the State of New York During the Period of the Civil War* (New York, 1911); Arthur C. Cole, *The Era of the Civil War* (Springfield, Ill., 1919); Stanton L. Davis, *Pennsylvania Politics, 1860-1863* (Cleveland, Ohio, 1935); Wood Gray, *The Hidden Civil War: The Story of the Copperheads* (New York, 1942); Winfred A. Harbison, "The Opposition to President Lincoln Within the Republican Party," MS., Ph.D. Dissertation, University of Illinois, 1930, and the same author's "The Elections of 1862 as a Vote of Want of Confidence in President Lincoln," *Papers of the Michigan Academy of Science* (1931), Vol. 14, pp. 499-513; William B. Hesseltine, *Lincoln and the War Governors* (New York, 1948), pp. 265ff; George H. Porter, *Ohio Politics During the Civil War Period* (New York, 1911); Harry E. Pratt, "The Repudiation of Lincoln's War Policy in 1862 —The Stuart-Swett Congressional Campaign," *Journal of the Illinois State Historical Society* (1931), Vol. 24, pp. 129-140; Kenneth D. Raab, "The Election of 1862 in Illinois," MS., M.A. Thesis, University of Illinois, 1936; Kenneth M. Stampp, *Indiana Politics During the Civil War* (Indianapolis, 1949).

Blaine's remarks about the make-up of the new Congress is in James G. Blaine, *Twenty Years of Congress* (Norwich, Conn., 1884), I, 444. Lincoln's letter to Schurz about the reasons for the election defeat is in Carl Schurz Papers, Library of Congress. Lincoln's reply to the anti-slavery clergymen is in N. Worth Brown and Randolph C. Downes (ed.), "A Conference With Abraham Lincoln: From the Diary of Reverend Nathan Brown," *Northwest Ohio Quarterly,* Spring, 1950, pp. 58-60.

The Buell-Morton difficulties are treated in Bruce Catton, *Glory Road: The Bloody Route From Fredericksburg to Gettysburg* (New York, 1955), p. 18; Robert U. Johnson and Clarence C. Buel (ed.), *Battles and Leaders of the Civil War* (New York, 1888), III, 42-44; William D. Foulke, *Life of Oliver P. Morton* (Indianapolis, 1899), I, 187ff. For Buell's removal: T. Harry Williams, *Lincoln and the Radicals* (Madison, Wis., 1941), pp. 192-195, 226, and the same author's *Lincoln and His Generals* (New York, 1952), pp. 182-185. The inquiry into Buell is in *Official Records of the Union and Confederate Armies,* Series I, Vol. 16, Part I. For General Bragg: Grady McWhiney, "Controversy in Kentucky: Braxton Bragg's Campaign of 1862," *Civil War History,* March, 1960, pp. 5-42.

The New York *Times's* criticism of Lincoln is in its November 5, 1862, issue. The removal of Butler is treated in Williams, *Lincoln and the Radicals,* pp. 221-223. For Butler's military administration: Howard P. Johnson, "New Orleans Under General Butler," *The Louisiana Historical Quarterly,* April, 1941, pp. 434-536. Lincoln's letter to Schurz, November 24, 1862, is in Carl Schurz Papers, Library of Congress.

The Louisiana State University Press will shortly publish Warren Hassler's *Commanders of the Army of the Potomac,* in which Burnside is treated. The Battle of Fredericksburg is followed in Douglas Southall Freeman, *R. E. Lee: A Biography* (New York, 1935), Vol. II, Chapter 31, and the same author's *Lee's Lieutenants* (New York, 1943), Vol. II, Chapters 20, 21; John C. Ropes, *The Story of the Civil War: Campaigns of 1862* (New York, 1898), Part II, Chapter 6; Thomas L. Livermore, *Numbers and Losses in the Civil War in America, 1861-1865* (1901), p. 96; Edward J. Stackpole, *Drama on the Rappahannock: The Fredericksburg Campaign* (Harrisburg, Pa., 1957).

Villard's account of his interview with Lincoln following Fredericksburg is in *Memoirs of Henry Villard* (Boston, 1904), I, 389-391. General Couch's account of Burnside is told in Johnson and Buel (ed.), *Battles and Leaders of the Civil War,* III, 117, 127.

Medill's letter to Colfax is in O. J. Hollister, *Life of Schuyler Colfax* (Chicago, 1887), p. 200. For the Senators' part in the Cabinet crisis: Francis Fessenden, *Life and Public Services of William Pitt Fessenden* (Boston, 1907), I, 231-251. On the Cabinet meeting, see *Diary of Gideon Welles* (Boston, 1909), I, 194-202. See also Theodore C. Pease and James G. Randall (ed.), *Diary of Orville Hickman Browning* (Springfield, Ill., 1925), I, 597-603; Howard K. Beale (ed.), *Diary of Edward Bates, 1859-1866* (Washington, 1933), p. 598; R. Gerald McMurtry, "The Cabinet Crisis of December, 1862," *Lincoln Lore,* September, 1958; Lincoln to Seward and Chase, December 20, 1862, Robert Todd Lincoln Collection, Library of Congress; Sam Wilkeson's letter, December 19, 1862, Sidney Howard Gay Papers, Columbia University Library, New York.

Smith's departure from Lincoln's Cabinet is detailed in Harry J. Carman and Reinhard H. Luthin, *Lincoln and the Patronage* (New York, 1943), pp. 137-138. For Lincoln's appointment of Davis to the Supreme Court: Harry E. Pratt, "David Davis, 1815-1886," *Transactions of the Illinois State Historical Society,* 1930, pp. 170ff; Carman and Luthin, *Lincoln and the Patronage,* pp. 179-183. For Secretary Usher: Elmer R. Richardson, *John Palmer Usher* (Lawrence, Kansas, 1960).

Speed is quoted in T. S. Bell to Holt, December 22, 1862, Joseph Holt Papers, Library of Congress. The letter to Washburne is in Elihu B. Washburne Papers, Library of Congress.

Chapter 25—**FALLING FORTUNES**

Lincoln's interviews with Burnside following Fredericksburg are followed in T. Harry Williams, *Lincoln and His Generals* (New York, 1952), pp. 202-204. Copy of Lincoln's sharp letter to Halleck is in Robert Todd Lincoln Collection, Library of Congress. Brooks's description of Lincoln on New Year's Day, 1863, is in Noah Brooks, *Washington in Lincoln's Time* (New York, 1896), p. 42. Copies of Burnside's letter of resignation, January 5, 1863, and Lincoln's reply, declining it, January 8, 1863, are in Robert Todd Lincoln Collection. The statements about the non-recognition of the talents of Generals Grant, Sherman, and Thomas early in the war are based on Thomas Robson Hay, "President Lincoln and the Army of the Potomac," *The Georgia Historical Quarterly,* December, 1926, pp. 297-298.

The best biography of Hooker is Walter H. Hebert, *Fighting Joe Hooker* (Indianapolis, 1944). Hooker's boastfulness and remarks about Lincoln and the need for a "dictator" are mentioned in T. Harry Williams, *Lincoln and the Radicals* (Madison, Wis., 1941), pp. 265-266; "Extracts From the Journal of Henry J. Raymond," *Scribner's Monthly* (1879-1880), Vol. 19, p. 422.

Lincoln's communications to Rosecrans, of congratulation, advice, and answering complaints, include: Lincoln to Rosecrans, January 5, 1863, March 25, 1863, April 22, 1863, Brown University Library; Lincoln to Rosecrans, February 17, 1863, March 17, 1863, Robert Todd Lincoln Collection.

McClernand's letter to Lincoln, January 7, 1863, is in Robert Todd Lincoln Collection. Lincoln's answer, January 22, 1863, is in Illinois State Historical Library, Springfield. For Grant's Vicksburg campaign: Earl Schenck Miers, *The Web of Victory: Grant At Vicksburg* (New York, 1955), Lincoln is quoted about the Vicksburg canals in Madeleine Dahlgren, *Memoir of John A. Dahlgren* (New York, 1891), p. 389.

Admiral DuPont's career and his failure to take Charleston are followed in Henry A. DuPont, *Rear-Admiral Samuel Francis DuPont* (New York, 1926); Daniel Ammen, *The Atlantic Coast* (New York, 1883). The Blair-Davis Controversy and its repercussions are treated in Reinhard H. Luthin, "A Discordant Chapter in Lincoln's Administration: The Davis-Blair Controversy," *The Maryland Historical Magazine*, March, 1944, pp. 25-48. Lincoln's recommendations to Congress for thanks for DuPont are in *Lincoln's Collected Works*, V, 127-128, 166-167. Lincoln's order to DuPont, April 13, 1863, is in Brown University Library. Lincoln's instructions to DuPont and General Hunter on the following day are in Huntington Library, San Marino, California.

For Lincoln's distribution of Missouri patronage, favoring Bates and Blair, see William E. Smith, *The Francis Preston Blair Family in Politics* (New York, 1933), II, 2. The political situation in Missouri is detailed in Sceva B. Laughlin, "Missouri Politics During the Civil War," *The Missouri Historical Review* (1929-30), Vol. 24, pp. 87-113, 261-284; Harry J. Carman and Reinhard H. Luthin, *Lincoln and the Patronage* (New York, 1943), pp. 194ff. Lincoln's letter to Blow and others is in Brown University Library. Copies of Lincoln's letters to General Schofield, May 27, 1863, and to General Curtis, June 8, 1863, are in Robert Todd Lincoln Collection.

For the Vallandigham and other "Copperhead" movements in the Northwest: Elbert J. Benton, "The Movement For Peace Without Victory During the Civil War," *Collections of the Western Reserve Historical Society*, Publication No. 99, pp. 1-72; Wood Gray, *The Hidden Civil War: The Story of the Copperheads* (New York, 1942); Henry C. Hubbart, *The Older Middle West, 1840-1880* (New York, 1936), pp. 183ff, 194ff; George Fort Milton, *Abraham Lincoln and the Fifth Column* (New York, 1942). See also Mayo Fesler, "Secret Political Societies in the North During the Civil War," *Indiana Magazine of History*, September, 1918, pp. 183-286; Paul S. Smith, "First Use of the Term 'Copperhead,'" *The American Historical Review*, July, 1927, pp. 799-800. Sumner's letter to Lieber in which he quotes Lincoln is in Edward L. Pierce, *Memoir and Letters of Charles Sumner* (Boston, 1893), IV, 114.

The arrest of Vallandigham is treated in James G. Randall, *Lincoln, the President* (New York, 1952), Vol. III, Chapter 9. Lincoln's action on Vallandigham is followed in Lincoln to Burnside, May 29, 1863, telegram, in cipher, Brown University Library; Stanton to Burnside, May 19, 1863, in *Official Records of the Union and Confederate Armies*, Series II, Vol. 5, p. 657.

Fernando Wood's career is treated in Samuel A. Pleasants, *Fernando Wood of New York* (New York, 1948); Reinhard H. Luthin, "Some Demagogues in American History," *The American Historical Review*, October, 1951, p. 38. For the Lincoln-Wood correspondence, see *Diary of Gideon Welles* (New York, 1909), I, 237.

Schurz's request to be transferred to a Western army is in Schurz to Lincoln, April 11, 1863, Robert Todd Lincoln Collection. Lincoln's answer, April 11, 1863, is in

Carl Schurz Papers, Library of Congress. For Hooker's relations with Lincoln see Williams, *Lincoln and His Generals,* pp. 211-212. On Lincoln's visit to Hooker: Brooks, *Washington in Lincoln's Time,* pp. 47ff. Dr. Henry's letter to his wife, April 12, 1863, is in *The Abraham Lincoln Quarterly,* March, 1942, pp. 10-11. On Hooker's strategy before Chancellorsville: Hooker to Lincoln, April 27, 1863, Robert Todd Lincoln Collection.

For the Battle of Chancellorsville: John Bigelow, Jr., *The Campaign of Chancellorsville* (New Haven, Conn., 1910); Douglas Southall Freeman, *R. E. Lee: A Biography* (New York, 1935), Vol. II, Chapters 33-35; Augustus C. Hamlin, *The Battle of Chancellorsville* (Bangor, Me., 1896); Edward J. Stackpole, *Chancellorsville* (Harrisburg, Pa., 1958). Telegrams between Lincoln, Hooker, and Butterfield are in *Official Records of the Union and Confederate Armies,* Series I, Vol. 25, Part II, pp. 378ff, 401ff. Noah Brooks's description of Lincoln on learning about the Chancellorsville defeat is in Brooks, *Washington in Lincoln's Time,* pp. 57-58.

Chapter 26—PORTRAIT OF THE PRESIDENT

Speed's comment about Lincoln is in his letter, December 6, 1866, in William H. Herndon and Jesse W. Weik, *Abraham Lincoln: The True Story of a Great Life* (New York, 1892), II, 231. Bigelow's description of Lincoln, July 30, 1860, is in Margaret Clapp, *Forgotten First Citizen: John Bigelow* (Boston, 1947), pp. 136-137. Nicolay's remark is in John G. Nicolay, "Lincoln's Personal Appearance," *Century,* October, 1891, pp. 932-938. R. C. McCormick's account of Lincoln in 1860-61 is in *Littell's Living Age,* May 20, 1865, p. 330. Lincoln's description of himself, in his autobiography for Fell, 1859, is in *Lincoln's Collected Works,* III, 512.

For observations on Lincoln's physical appearance during the war: Washington correspondent in *Macmillan's Magazine,* May, 1862, p. 23; George Augustus Sala, *My Diary in America in the Midst of War* (London, 1865), II, 146-149; Henry C. Deming, *Eulogy of Abraham Lincoln . . . Before the General Assembly of Connecticut . . . June 8th, 1865* (Hartford, Conn., 1865), pp. 13-14; Donn Piatt in Allan Thorndike Rice (ed.), *Reminiscences of Abraham Lincoln By Distinguished Men of His Time* (New York, 1888), pp. 479-480; Goldwin Smith, "President Lincoln," *Macmillan's Magazine* (1864-1865), Vol. 11, p. 300; Flavius J. Bellamy to John Bellamy, September 6, 1861, MS., Library of Congress; George R. Agassiz (ed.), *Meade's Headquarters, 1863-1865: Letters of Colonel Theodore Lyman* (Boston, 1922), p. 323; Whitman's letter, March 19, 1863, in Emory Holloway (ed.), *Walt Whitman: Complete Poetry and Selected Prose and Letters* (London, 1938), p. 897; Nathaniel Hawthorne's description of Lincoln, 1863, in Lloyd Morris, *The Rebellious Puritan; Portrait of Mr. Hawthorne* (New York, 1927), pp. 345-346.

On Lincoln's physical strength: Nicolay's letter, November 20, 1861, in Harry E. Pratt (ed.), *Concerning Mr. Lincoln* (Springfield, Ill., 1944), pp. 89-90; Charles A. Dana, *Recollections of the Civil War* (New York, 1899), p. 173; R. Y. Bush's letter, 1865, in Charles H. Coleman, *Lincoln and Coles County, Illinois* (New Brunswick, N.J., 1954), p. 154. Bellows' letter to his wife, April 23, 1863, is in Henry W. Bellows Papers, Massachusetts Historical Society, Boston. Lincoln's comments to Brooks about his fatigue are in *Harper's Magazine,* July, 1865, pp. 226-227. Judge Davis' letter, November 26, 1862, is in Pratt (ed.), *Concerning Mr. Lincoln,* p. 95.

For contemporary estimates of Lincoln by Motley, Bancroft, and Greeley: George William Curtis (ed.), *Correspondence of John Lothrop Motley* (New York, 1899), II, 203; Bancroft to his wife, February 24, 1864, in M. A. De Wolfe Howe, *Life and Letters of George Bancroft* (New York, 1908), II, 155-156; Greeley, *Recollections of a Busy Life,* p. 409. Lincoln's ideas on ordnance are best treated in Robert V. Bruce, *Lincoln and the Tools of War* (New York, 1956). Lincoln's letter to Stanton about the Rafael Repeater, August 9, 1862, is in *Lincoln's Collected Works,* V, 365; copy also enclosed in Haskell to Weed, October 8, 1862, in Thurlow Weed Papers, University of Rochester Library, Rochester, N.Y. Justin O. Buckeridge, *Lincoln's Choice* (Harrisburg, Pa., 1956) concerns Lincoln's interest in the Spencer seven-shooter rifle.

Lincoln's remark about his not having read a novel throughout is in Francis B. Carpenter, *Six Months in the White House With Abraham Lincoln* (New York, 1867), p. 115. Copy of Lincoln's letter to Robertson, November 20, 1862, is in Robert Todd Lincoln Collection. Lincoln's opinion of history and biography, as expressed by Herndon and Gillespie, is in Albert J. Beveridge, *Abraham Lincoln, 1809-1858* (Boston, 1928), I, 520. For Lincoln's interest in Shakespeare: R. Gerald McMurtry, "Lincoln Knew Shakespeare," *Indiana Magazine of History,* December, 1935, pp. 265-277; Robert N. Reeves, "Abraham Lincoln's Knowledge of Shakespeare," *Overland Monthly,* April, 1904, pp. 336-342. Lincoln's conversation about Shakespeare with Carpenter is related in Carpenter, *Six Months in the White House With Abraham Lincoln,* pp. 49-52. Lincoln's comments to Hackett on Shakespeare, and their repercussion, are followed in Lincoln to Hackett, August 17, November 2, 1863, in *Lincoln's Collected Works,* VI, 392-393, 558-559. Chambrun's account is in *Scribner's Magazine,* January, 1893, pp. 34-35.

For Lincoln's interest in Burns' poems: R. C. McCormick's letter, April 29, 1865, in *Littell's Living Age,* May 20, 1865, p. 331. For Lincoln's interest in the poet, Pope: F. Lauriston Bullard, "Lincoln's Copy of Pope's Poems," *The Abraham Lincoln Quarterly,* March, 1946, pp. 30-35. Borrett's comments about Lincoln's conversation on Pope are in George Tuthill Borrett, *Letters From Canada and the United States* (London, 1865), pp. 254-255. Deming's summary of Lincoln's reading is in Deming, *Eulogy of Abraham Lincoln . . . June 8th, 1865,* pp. 42-43.

Lincoln's preference for the theatre is treated in Leonard Grover, "Lincoln's Interest in the Theatre," *Century,* April, 1909, pp. 943-950; Richard Hanser, "Lincoln Loved a Show," *Theatre Arts,* February, 1959, pp. 63-64. Lincoln's attendance at Booth's performance in 1863 is treated in Joseph George, Jr., "The Night John Wilkes Booth Played Before Abraham Lincoln," *Lincoln Herald,* Summer, 1957, pp. 11-15. Lamon's letter to Lincoln, December 10, 1864, is in Clint Clay Tilton, "Lincoln and Lamon: Partners and Friends," *Transactions of the Illinois State Historical Society,* 1931, p. 213.

Neill is quoted about Lincoln's humor in Edward D. Neill, "Reminiscences of the Last Years of President Lincoln's Life," in Military Order of the Loyal Legion of the U.S., Minnesota Commandery, *Glimpses of the Struggle* (St. Paul, Minn., 1887), Series I, pp. 38-39. Seward is quoted in Bellows to his wife, April 23, 1863, Henry W. Bellows Papers, Massachusetts Historical Society, Boston. The letters of Mrs. Hay and Judge Davis are in Pratt (ed.), *Concerning Mr. Lincoln,* pp. 92, 95. Mrs. Swisshelm's comments on Lincoln are in St. Cloud (Minn.) *Democrat,* February 26, 1863, in Theodore C. Blegen (ed.), *Crusader and Feminist: Letters of Jane Grey Swisshelm* (St. Paul, Minn., 1934), p. 173. John Hay's impression about Lincoln's interest in the humorist, Hood, is recorded in Tyler Dennett (ed.), *Lincoln and the Civil War in the Diaries and Letters of John Hay* (New York, 1939), p. 179.

Lincoln's devotion to the works of "Kerr," "Ward," and "Nasby" is followed in *Diary of Gideon Welles* (New York, 1909), I, 333; Diary of Salmon P. Chase, MS., September 22, 1862, Library of Congress; Don C. Seitz, *Artemus Ward (Charles Farrar Brown)* (New York, 1919), p. 115; Jack C. Ransome, "David Ross Locke," *Northwest Ohio Quarterly,* January, 1948, pp. 5-19; Francis B. Carpenter, "Anecdotes and Reminiscences of President Lincoln," in Henry J. Raymond, *Life and Public Services of Abraham Lincoln* (New York, 1865), p. 744. Lincoln's five-legged calf anecdote is quoted in N. Worth Brown and Randolph C. Downes (ed.), "A Conference With Abraham Lincoln: From the Diary of Reverend Nathan Brown," *Northwest Ohio Quarterly,* Spring, 1950, pp. 61-62. Lincoln's anecdote about the Negroes, concerning the Dominican Republic is told in *Diary of Gideon Welles,* I, 519-520. Lincoln's "Count Peeper" quip about Captain Cutts is in Dennett (ed.), *Lincoln and the Civil War in the Diaries and Letters of John Hay,* p. 53. Lincoln's humorous reply about the "pass" to Richmond is told in "A Pair of Lincoln Anecdotes," Sacramento (Calif.) *Union,* May 27, 1863.

Lincoln's story about shoveling fleas is in Furness to his wife, November 10, 1862, in *Letters of Horace H. Furness* (Boston, 1922), I, 126. Lincoln's humorous letters to Chase, to Yates and Butler, and to Dubois and Hatch on appointments are in *Lincoln's Collected Works,* IV, 361; V, 186; VI, 450, 473. See also Hatch and Dubois to Lincoln, September 16, 1863, Robert Todd Lincoln Collection.

On Lincoln's melancholia: Nicolay in *Century,* October, 1891, p. 933; Sala, *My Diary in America in the Midst of War,* II, 147ff; George Bancroft in *The Atlantic Monthly,* June, 1865, p. 763; David R. Locke in Rice (ed.), *Reminiscences of Abraham Lincoln By Distinguished Men of His Time,* p. 442. Lincoln's morbid tastes in music are followed in Noah Brooks, "Personal Reminiscences of Abraham Lincoln," *Harper's Magazine,* July, 1865, p. 229.

The best modern studies of Lincoln's religion are William E. Barton, *The Soul of Abraham Lincoln* (New York, 1920); Albert V. House, Jr., "The Genesis of the Lincoln Religious Controversy," *Proceedings of the Middle States Association of History and Social Science Teachers* (1938), Vol. 36, pp. 44-54; Edgar De Witt Jones, *Lincoln and the Preachers* (New York, 1948); Ralph G. Lindstrom, *Lincoln Finds God* (New York, 1958); Roy D. Packard, *The Riddle of Lincoln's Religion* (Midland Rare Book Co., Mansfield, Ohio, 1946); John W. Starr, Jr., "What Was Abraham Lincoln's Religion?" *Magazine of History* (Tarrytown, N.Y., 1922), Vol. 19, Extra No. 73, pp. 39-55. Orrin H. Pennell, *Religious Views of Abraham Lincoln* (Alliance, Ohio, 1899) is a good summary of Lincoln's faith.

Robert Todd Lincoln's reference to his father's lack of interest in church matters is quoted by C. F. Gunther in *Magazine of History* (Tarrytown, N.Y., 1922), Vol. 19, Extra No. 73, p. 49. Mrs. Lincoln is quoted in *Ibid.,* (1927), Vol. 34, Extra No. 133, p. 51. Reverend Nelson's sermon about Lincoln in May, 1865, is quoted in Jay Monaghan, "An Analysis of Lincoln's Funeral Sermons," *Indiana Magazine of History,* March, 1945, p. 44. For statements of Deming and Mrs. Hanaford on Lincoln's religion: Deming, *Eulogy of Abraham . . . June 8, 1865,* p. 42; Phebe A. Hanaford, *Abraham Lincoln* (Boston, 1865), p. 167.

Allegations that Lincoln was a Spiritualist are effectively demolished in Jay Monaghan, "Was Abraham Lincoln Really a Spiritualist?" *Journal of the Illinois State Historical Society,* June, 1941, pp. 209-232. Rankin's letter to John W. Starr, Jr., March 6, 1911, is in *Magazine of History* (1922), Vol. 19, Extra No. 73, p. 43.

Lincoln's literary style and use of words are treated in Paul M. Angle, "Lincoln's Power With Words," *Abraham Lincoln Association Papers,* 1934, pp. 59-87; Theodore C. Blegen, *Lincoln's Imagery: A Study in Word Power* (La Crosse, Wis., 1954); Daniel K. Dodge, *Abraham Lincoln, Master of Words* (New York, 1924); Luther E. Robinson, *Abraham Lincoln As a Man of Letters* (Chicago, 1918). Lincoln as a speaker and phrase-maker is treated in Midred F. Berry, "Abraham Lincoln: His Development in the Skills of the Platform," and Earl W. Wiley, "Abraham Lincoln: His Emergence As the Voice of the People," essays in William N. Brigance (ed.), *A History and Criticism of American Public Address* (New York, 1943), II, 828-858, 859-877.

Lincoln, as quoted by Gillespie about his interest in language is in Gillespie to Herndon, December 8, 1866, in Beveridge, *Abraham Lincoln, 1809-1858,* I, 520-521. Lincoln's words about not swapping horses when crossing streams are in New York *Tribune,* New York *Times,* and New York *Herald,* all for June 10, 1864. For exposés of apocryphal Lincoln phrases: Albert A. Woldman, "Lincoln Never Said That," *Harper's Magazine,* May, 1950, pp. 70-74; Reinhard H. Luthin, "Fakes and Frauds in Lincoln Literature," *Saturday Review,* February 9, 1959 (pp. 15ff).

The Gettysburg Address and Second Inaugural are appraised in Benjamin Barondess, *Three Lincoln Masterpieces* (Charleston, West Va., 1954). Lincoln's Special Message,

July 4, 1861, is in James D. Richardson (comp.), *Messages and Papers of the Presidents* (Washington, 1897), VI, 20-31. The best work on the Bixby letter is F. Lauriston Bullard, *Abraham Lincoln and the Widow Bixby* (New Brunswick, N.J., 1946). This famous letter, November 21, 1864, was first printed in Boston *Transcript,* November 25, 1864. The original has never been found. The purported facsimiles of this letter are considered forgeries; but there is no reason to question the authenticity of the letter as printed in the Boston *Transcript.* Sherman D. Wakefield and other Lincoln students are of opinion that the Bixby letter was really written by John Hay, not by Lincoln. See also Nicholas Murray Butler, *Across the Busy Years,* II, 390-393. Lincoln's letter to Fanny McCullough is in *Lincoln's Collected Works,* VI, 16-17. Speed's comment about Lincoln's masterpieces, December 6, 1866, is in Herndon and Weik, *Abraham Lincoln,* 1892 edition, II, 233.

Lyman's complaint about Lincoln's pardon policy is in his letter, May 23, 1864, in Agassiz (ed.), *Meade's Headquarters,* p. 117. Lincoln's military pardon policy is summarized in Belle I. Wiley, *The Life of Billy Yank: The Common Soldier of the Union* (Indianapolis, 1951), p. 216. Lincoln's orders for pardons are in *Lincoln's Collected Works,* V, 94, 202, 205, 300, 336, 347. For Lincoln's parole of Vice-President Stephens' nephew: *Lincoln's Collected Works,* VIII, 259, 287; Robert Stephens, "An Incident of Friendship," *Lincoln Herald,* June, 1943. Usher's comments about Lincoln are in "Recollections of Ex-Secretary Usher," New York *Tribune,* September 13, 1885.

Chapter 27—**WHITE HOUSE FAMILY**

The best work on war-time Washington is Margaret Leech, *Reveille in Washington, 1860-1865* (New York, 1941). The basic books on the Lincolns' family life are Ruth Painter Randall's two volumes: *Mary Lincoln* (Boston, 1953) and *Lincoln's Sons* (Boston, 1955). See also Noah Brooks, *Washington in Lincoln's Time* (New York, 1895); Francis B. Carpenter, *Six Months At the White House With Abraham Lincoln* (New York, 1867); Elizabeth Keckley, *Behind the Scenes* (New York, 1868); Reinhard H. Luthin, "The Lincolns in the White House," *Look,* February 14, 1950, pp. 74ff.

The London *Times* Washington correspondent's comments are in William H. Russell, *My Diary North and South* (Boston, 1863), p. 33. Lincoln's remark to the New Hampshire Senator, John B. Clark, is in Carpenter, *Six Months At the White House With Abraham Lincoln,* p. 276. Borrett's observation on Washington as a "gigantic military depot" is in George Tuthill Borrett, *Letters From Canada and the United States* (London, 1865), p. 214. For Lincoln's secretaries and their assistants: Helen Nicolay, *Lincoln's Secretary: A Biography of John G. Nicolay* (New York, 1948); Tyler Dennett, *John Hay* (New York, 1934); William R. Thayer, *Life and Letters of John Hay* (Boston, 1915), 2 vols.; William O. Stoddard, *Inside the White House in War Times* (New York, 1890); Solon J. Buck's sketch of Edward D. Neill in *Dictionary of American Biography* (New York, 1934), Vol. 13, pp. 408-409. For the White House Negro servants: John E. Washington, *They Knew Lincoln* (New York, 1942).

Lincoln's popularity with the Union troops is treated in Bell I. Wiley, "Billy Yank and Abraham Lincoln," *The Abraham Lincoln Quarterly,* June, 1950, pp. 103ff. For soldiers' opinion of Lincoln in their letters home and in diaries: Felix Brannigan's letter, July 16, 1862, typescript, Brannigan Papers, Library of Congress; A. Davenport's letter, July 12, 1862, Davenport Letter Book, MS., New-York Historical Society, New York. Furness' description of the soldiers' lionizing of Lincoln is told in his letter to his wife, October 5, 1862, in *Letters of Horace Howard Furness* (Boston, 1922), I, 114. The letters home of Norton, Short, and Johnson about Lincoln are quoted in Wiley, "Billy Yank and Abraham Lincoln," *op. cit.,* p. 118.

For Mrs. Lincoln as a hostess, her extravagances, travels, and other details about her: Virginia Kinnaird, "Mrs. Lincoln As a White House Hostess," in Paul M. Angle (ed.),

Papers in Illinois History, 1938, pp. 64-87; Harry E. Pratt and Ernest E. East, "Mrs. Lincoln Refurbishes the White House," *Lincoln Herald,* February, 1945, pp. 3-12; Wayne C. Temple, "Mary Todd Lincoln's Travels," *Journal of the Illinois State Historical Society,* Spring, 1959, pp. 180-194.

Willie Lincoln's letter to Henry Remann, May 25, 1861, is in *Journal of the Illinois State Historical Society,* Spring, 1956, p. 69. For Willie's fatal illness and its effect on Mrs. Lincoln: Julia Taft Bayne, *Tad Lincoln's Father* (Boston, 1931), pp. 199-200; Keckley, *Behind the Scenes,* pp. 98-100; French to H. F. French, February 27, 1862, Benjamin B. French Papers, Library of Congress.

Benjamin B. French's comment about Mrs. Lincoln being "not easy to get along with" is in his letter to H. F. French, March 23, 1862, French Papers. Hay's letter to Nicolay about Mrs. Lincoln being "the Hell-Cat," April 5, 1862, is in John Hay Papers, Brown University Library, Providence, R.I. For Mrs. Lincoln's séance with Colchester, consult Randall, *Mary Lincoln,* p. 292. Professor Henry's questioning of Colchester at Lincoln's request is recorded in Thomas Coulson, *Joseph Henry: His Life and Work* (Princeton, N.J., 1950), pp. 308-309. French's words about Mrs. Lincoln at the New Year's Day reception, 1863, are in Brown University Library. Senator Browning's revelation about Mrs. Lincoln's consultation with "Mrs. Laury," a Spiritualist, are in Theodore C. Pease and James G. Randall (ed.), *Diary of Orville Hickman Browning* (Springfield, Ill., 1925), I, 608. Mrs. Lincoln's letter to Mrs. Welles, February 21, 1863, is in Allen C. Clark, *Abraham Lincoln in the National Capital* (Washington, 1925), facsimile opposite p. 72.

For the death of General Helm: R. Gerald McMurtry, *Ben Hardin Helm* (Chicago, 1943). Mrs. Helm's story about Mrs. Lincoln's personal distress in the White House is told in Katherine Helm, *True Story of Mary, Wife of Lincoln* (New York, 1928), pp. 226ff. The letter of Mrs. Helm's Georgia friend, E. M. Bruce, to Lincoln, October 6, 1863, is in Robert Todd Lincoln Collection, Library of Congress. Mrs. Lincoln's letter to Mrs. Shearer, November 2, 1864, is in *Journal of the Illinois State Historical Society,* Spring, 1951, p. 25.

Mrs. Lincoln's irritation over Princess Salm-Salm's kissing of the President is related in Princess Salm-Salm, *Ten Years of My Life* (Detroit, 1877), Chapter 2; Brooks, *Washington in Lincoln's Time,* p. 69; Julia L. Butterfield. *A Biographical Memorial of General Daniel Butterfield* (New York, 1904), p. 161. Sickles' own account is in *Oration Delivered By Maj.-Gen. D. E. Sickles, U.S.A., Before the Society of the Army of the Potomac At Fredericksburg, Va., May 25, 1900* (1900), pp. 18-19. The best account of Mrs. Lincoln's display of temper at Mrs. Ord is in Adam Badeau, *Grant in Peace* (Hartford, Conn., 1887), pp. 358-359.

Tad Lincoln is treated in Noah Brooks, "A Boy in the White House," *St. Nicholas* (New York), November, 1882, pp. 57-65; Bayne, *Tad Lincoln's Father;* F. Lauriston Bullard, *Tad and His Father* (Boston, 1915); John Hay's article in New York *Daily Tribune,* July 17, 1871. Thomas M. Longstreth, *Tad Lincoln, the President's Son* (Philadelphia, 1944) is a part historical, part fictional account. Lincoln's letters concerning Tad are in *Lincoln's Collected Works,* VI, 256, 260, 371-372, 471; VII, 320; VIII, 395.

Lincoln's letter about Bob in 1860 and his letters to Bob in 1863 and 1864 are in *Lincoln's Collected Works,* IV, 82; VI, 314, 323, 327; VII, 121; VIII, 44. Robert Lincoln's "cold" letter about his father, to Edward Freiberger, March 1, 1910, is in Lincoln National Life Foundation, Fort Wayne, Indiana. Edwin Booth's aid to Robert Lincoln in the near railroad accident is mentioned in William Bispham, "Memories and Letters of Edwin Booth," *Century,* November, 1893, p. 133. Robert Lincoln's account of how Edwin Booth saved him is told in his own letter to Richard Watson Gilder, February 6, 1909, in *Journal of the Illinois State Historical Society,* March, 1948, p. 66. For excellent accounts of Robert Lincoln: Randall, *Lincoln's Sons;* David C. Mearns, *The Lincoln Papers* (Garden City, N.Y., 1948), Vol. I, Chapter 1; John S.

Goff, "The Riddle of Robert Todd Lincoln," *Manuscripts* (White Plains, N.Y.), Winter, 1959, pp. 2-5. Professor Goff is preparing a biography of Robert Lincoln.

The *Herald's* account of Robert Lincoln in Long Branch is in New York *Herald,* August 18, 1861. For Robert Lincoln's infatuation with Fräulein von Gerolt, see Tyler Dennett (ed.), *Lincoln and the Civil War in the Diaries and Letters of John Hay* (New York, 1939), pp. 75-76. For complaints over Robert Lincoln's failure to join the Army: Helm, *True Story of Mary, Wife of Lincoln,* pp. 227-230. Lincoln's letter to Grant, January 19, 1865, requesting a place in the Army for Robert, and Grant's reply, January 21, 1865, are in *Lincoln's Collected Works,* VIII, 223, 223n-224n. Ida M. Tarbell's description of Robert Lincoln is in her autobiography, *All in the Day's Work* (New York, 1939), p. 166.

Mrs. Lincoln's letters to Mrs. Conkling, November 19, 1864, is in *The Abraham Lincoln Quarterly,* September, 1946, p. 138. Mrs. Lincoln's quotation about Lincoln's future plans, written in 1866, is in William H. Herndon and Jesse W. Weik, *Abraham Lincoln: The True Story of a Great Life* (New York, 1892), II, 221-222.

Chapter 28—UPWARD SWING: Gettysburg and Vicksburg

Meade's letter about Lincoln and Hooker, May 8, 1863, is in George G. Meade, Jr., *Life and Letters of George Gordon Meade* (New York, 1913), I, 372. Lincoln's attitude toward Hooker after Chancellorsville is detailed in T. Harry Williams, *Lincoln and His Generals* (New York, 1952), pp. 243ff. Lincoln's letters to Hooker in May are in *Lincoln's Collected Works,* VI, 201, 215, 217. Benjamin's story about Lincoln's early decision to remove Hooker is in Robert U. Johnson and Clarence C. Buel (ed.), *Battles and Leaders of the Civil War* (New York, 1888), III, 241. For Lincoln's possible offer of the Army of the Potomac command to Reynolds: Oliver J. Keller, "Soldier General of the Army: John Fulton Reynolds," *Civil War History,* June, 1958, p. 124; Meade, *George Gordon Meade,* I, 385.

Lee's reorganization of his army, the reasons for his Pennsylvania invasion, and other incidents are fully detailed in Douglas Southall Freeman, *R. E. Lee: A Biography* (New York, 1935), Vol. III, Chapters 2, 3, 4. Lincoln's call for 100,000 volunteers is in *Lincoln's Collected Works,* VI, 277-278. The States' responses to it are followed in William B. Hesseltine, *Lincoln and the War Governors* (New York, 1948), pp. 295ff. Hooker's telegram to Lincoln, June 16, 1863, is in Robert Todd Lincoln Collection, Library of Congress. Lincoln's replies are in New York State Library, Albany, N.Y., and in *Lincoln's Collected Works,* VI, 281. The observer's letter, Richard H. Rush's, June 18, 1863, is in George B. McClellan Papers, Library of Congress, For Hooker's removal: Charles F. Benjamin, *Memoir of James Allen Hardie* (Washington, 1877), pp. 38-40. Halleck's letter to Grant is in Illinois State Historical Library, Springfield. Lincoln's letters to McClure and Governor Parker are in Brown University Library. The best work on General Meade is Freeman Cleaves, *Meade of Gettysburg* (Norman, Okla., 1960).

For accounts of the Battle of Gettysburg: H. J. Eckenrode and Bryan Conrad, *James Longstreet: Lee's War Horse* (New York, 1935); Douglas Southall Freeman, *Lee's Lieutenants* (New York, 1944), Vol. III, Chapters 6-9, and the same author's *R. E. Lee,* Vol. III, Chapters 2-9; *Official Records of the Union and Confederate Armies,* Series I, Vol. 27, Part II, James Stuart Montgomery, *The Shaping of a Battle: Gettysburg* (Philadelphia, 1959); Glenn Tucker, *High Tide At Gettysburg* (Indianapolis, 1958), from the Southern viewpoint. For Mrs. Lincoln's accident: Ruth Painter Randall, *Mary Lincoln* (Boston, 1953), p. 324. Lincoln's announcement about Gettysburg is in Brown University Library.

Grant's Vicksburg campaign is followed in Earl Schenck Miers, *Web of Victory: Grant At Vicksburg* (New York, 1955); John C. Pemberton, *Pemberton, Defender of*

Vicksburg (Chapel Hill, N.C., 1942). Miers is strongly pro-Grant, and Pemberton is sympathetic toward his grandfather. For Grant at Vicksburg: Bruce Catton, *Grant Moves South* (Boston, 1960).

Lincoln's letter to Arnold is in Chicago Historical Society. For Grant's removal of McClernand: *Official Records of the Union and Confederate Armies,* Series I, Vol. 24, Part I, pp. 43, 158-159.

Lincoln's reply to the serenaders is in New York *Tribune,* New York *Herald,* New York *Times,* issues of July 8, 1863. Lincoln's letter to Grant is in Historical Society of Pennsylvania, Philadelphia.

Chapter 29—SUMMER STORM CLOUDS—1863

For Lee's escape into Virginia after Gettysburg: Douglas Southall Freeman, *Lee's Lieutenants* (New York, 1944), III, 166-167; *Official Records of the Union and Confederate Armies,* Series I, Vol. 27, Part I, p. 118. Hay's comments about Lincoln's attitude toward Meade after Gettysburg are in Diary of John Hay, MS., July 14-19, 1863, Brown University Library, Providence, R.I.

Lincoln's remarks to Congressman Grinnell about McClernand are quoted in Josiah B. Grinnell, *Men and Events of Forty Years* (Boston, 1891), p. 174. Lincoln's letters to McClernand, January 22, 1863, and August 12, 1863, are in Illinois State Historical Library, Springfield. McClernand's letters to Lincoln, January 7, 1863, August 24, 1863, are in Robert Todd Lincoln Collection, Library of Congress. See also Arthur C. Cole, *The Era of the Civil War* (Springfield, Ill., 1919), p. 327. Robert E. Faust is preparing a Ph.D. dissertation on General McClernand at the University of Minnesota.

The Lincoln-Seymour controversy over conscription is followed in Stewart Mitchell, *Horatio Seymour of New York* (Cambridge, Mass., 1938); Alexander J. Wall, *A Sketch of the Life of Horation Seymour* (New York, 1929). Seymour's letters to Lincoln, and copies of Lincoln's letters to him in 1863 are in Robert Todd Lincoln Collection; also in this collection is a copy of Lincoln's letter to Governor Parker, July 20, 1863, about suspension of draft in New Jersey. The Conscription Act and the New York draft riots are detailed in Fred A. Shannon, *The Organization and Administration of the Union Army, 1861-1865* (Cleveland, Ohio, 1928), II, 103-243; *Irving Werstein, July, 1863* (New York, 1957).

The Confederates' difficulties with their draft, and opposition of Governors Brown and Vance are detailed in Albert B. Moore, *Conscript and Conflict in the Confederacy* (New York, 1924); Georgia L. Tatum, *Disloyalty in the Confederacy* (Chapel Hill, N.C., 1934). The Confederate Secretary of War's letter to Governor Brown is in Rembert W. Patrick, *Jefferson Davis and His Cabinet* (Baton Rouge, La., 1944), p. 125.

The elections in Pennsylvania and Ohio are followed in Stanton L. Davis, *Pennsylvania Politics, 1860-1863* (Cleveland, Ohio, 1935); George H. Porter, *Ohio Politics During the Civil War* (New York, 1911). For Judge Woodward see James G. Randall, *Constitutional Problems Under Lincoln* (New York, 1926); Horace Greeley, *The American Conflict* (Hartford, Conn., 1867), II, 508-509. The Curtin-Cameron feud and Curtin's decision to stand for re-election are treated in William B. Hesseltine, *Lincoln and the War Governors* (New York, 1948), pp. 326-329. Lincoln's telegram to Governor Tod, June 18, 1863, is in Brown University Library.

Copy of Lincoln's letter to Schofield, May 27, 1863, is in Robert Todd Lincoln Collection; that of July 13, 1863, is in Brown University Library. Lincoln's letter to Blow, July 13, 1863, is in *Official Records of the Union and Confederate Armies,* Series I, Vol. 22, Part II, p. 366.

Napoleon III's connection with the Maximilian episode is treated in Count Egon C. Corti, *Maximilian and Charlotte of Mexico* (New York, 1928), 2 vols. John Hay's comments about Lincoln's concern for Texas are in Tyler Dennett (ed.), *Lincoln and the Civil War in the Diaries of John Hay* (New York, 1939), p. 77. Lincoln's letters to Banks and Grant about the necessity for a movement in Texas are in *Lincoln's Collected Works,* VI, 364-365, 374.

Rosecrans' criticism of Stanton and Halleck to newspapermen is mentioned in *Memoirs of Henry Villard* (Boston, 1904), II, 66-68. Rosecrans' relations with Lincoln and Halleck are followed in T. Harry Williams, *Lincoln and His Generals* (New York, 1952), p. 275. Copy of Lincoln's letter to Rosecrans, August 10, 1863, is in Robert Todd Lincoln Collection. Lincoln's telegrams to Rosecrans, ordering him to go to Burnside's aid, are in Brown University Library. Rosecrans' telegram to Halleck about the Chickamauga defeat, September 20, 1863, is in Robert Todd Lincoln Collection.

Chapter 30—BRIGHT AUTUMN—1863

For the casualties at Chickamauga: Thomas L. Livermore, *Numbers and Losses in the Civil War in America, 1861-1865* (Boston, 1901), pp. 105-106; Robert U. Johnson and Clarence C. Buel (ed.), *Battles and Leaders of the Civil War* (New York, 1888), III, 673-675. Lincoln's letter to his wife about Helm's death, September 24, 1863, is in Illinois State Historical Library, Springfield. For Helm: R. Gerald McMurtry, *Ben Hardin Helm: "Rebel" Brother-in-Law of Abraham Lincoln* (Civil War Round Table, Chicago, 1943). Lincoln's offer of a paymastership to Helm in 1861 is mentioned in Lincoln to Cameron, April 16, 1861, Simon Cameron Papers, Library of Congress. The best work on Thomas is Freeman Cleaves, *The Rock of Chickamauga: The Life of General George H. Thomas* (Norman, Okla., 1948). Lincoln's letter to Maxwell, praising Thomas, September 23, 1863, is in Illinois State Historical Library, Springfield.

The midnight conference of September 23-24, 1863, is described in Tyler Dennett (ed.), *Lincoln and the Civil War in the Diaries and Letters of John Hay* (New York, 1939), p. 93. Hooker's reinforcements to Rosecrans is followed in Walter H. Hebert, *Fighting Joe Hooker* (Indianapolis, 1944), pp. 251ff. Lincoln's October 19 remarks to Hay are in Dennett (ed.), *Lincoln and the Civil War . . . ,* p. 102. Brooks' dispatch about Lincoln's sorrow over removing Rosecrans, October 24, 1863, is in Sacramento (Calif.) *Daily Union,* November 21, 1863.

Lincoln's quotation of anxiety over the Pennsylvania and Ohio elections is in *Diary of Gideon Welles* (Boston, 1909), I, 470. McClellan's support of Woodward for Governor is in Horace Greeley, *The American Conflict* (Hartford, Conn., 1867), II, 509. For the Republican campaign in Pennsylvania: Alexander K. McClure, *Abraham Lincoln and Men of War Times* (Philadelphia, 1892), p. 266. Brough's electioneering among German-born voters is recorded in Dennett (ed.), *Lincoln and the Civil War . . . ,* p. 98. Lincoln's part in the state elections is treated in William B. Hesseltine, *Lincoln and the War Governors* (New York, 1948), p. 335. The results of the Curtin-Woodward campaign are in *Annual Encyclopaedia,* 1863, p. 740. The telegrams between Lincoln and Brough on election night are quoted in Hesseltine, *Lincoln and the War Governors,* p. 335. The result of the Ohio election is in George H. Porter, *Ohio Politics During the Civil War* (New York, 1911), p. 183.

For Chief Justice Agnew's reversal of Woodward's decision on the Conscription Act, see James G. Randall, *Constitutional Problems Under Lincoln* (New York, 1926), pp. 11-12, 32-33; 45 *Pennsylvania* 310.

The election of 1863 in New York is followed in Sidney D. Brummer, *Political History of New York State During the Period of the Civil War* (New York, 1911), pp. 337ff. Lincoln's letter to Senator Chandler is in *Lincoln's Collected Works,* VII, 23-24.

The best literature on Lincoln's Gettysburg Address includes William E. Barton, *Lincoln At Gettysburg* (Indianapolis, 1930); F. Lauriston Bullard, *"A Few Appropriate Remarks:" Lincoln's Gettysburg Address* (Harrogate, Tenn., 1944); Clark E. Carr, *Lincoln At Gettysburg* (Chicago, 1906); "An Eye Witness At Gettysburg," *Journal of the Illinois State Historical Society,* Spring, 1958, pp. 104-106; Robert Fortenbaugh, "Abraham Lincoln At Gettysburg," *Pennsylvania History* (1938), V, 223-244; William Lambert, "The Gettysburg Address," *The Pennsylvania Magazine of History and Biography,* October, 1909, pp. 385-408; Henry E. Luhrs, *Lincoln At the Wills Home and the Gettysburg Address* (Shippensburg, Pa., 1938).

Lincoln's letter to Stanton about Gettysburg arrangements is in *Lincoln's Collected Works,* VII, 16. Lincoln's words at Hanover are quoted in Hanover (Pa.) *Spectator,* November 27, 1863, in Frederick S. Weiser, "Lincoln's Trip to Gettysburg," *Lincoln Herald,* Summer, 1953, pp. 4-5. Everett's quotation about Lincoln at the Wills home is in Henry C. Deming, *Eulogy of Abraham Lincoln . . . Before the General Assembly of Connecticut* (Hartford, Conn., 1865), p. 14. Lincoln's address to the Gettysburg serenaders on November 18 is in New York *Tribune,* November 20, 1863. Harvey Sweney's letter from Gettysburg to his brother, November 29, 1863, is in *Journal of the Illinois State Historical Society,* Spring, 1958, pp. 104ff. Everett's earlier letter to Wills is in *Address of Hon. Edward Everett At . . . Gettysburg* (Boston, 1864), p. 17. John Russell Young's later description of Everett's oration is in *Frank Leslie's Illustrated Newspaper,* April 10, 1886, p. 119. Robert Miller's description of Lincoln speaking at Gettysburg is taken from *Easton* (Ohio) *Register,* November 30, 1863, quoted in *The Pennsylvania Magazine of History and Biography,* October, 1909, pp. 393-394. Charles Hale's reproduction of Lincoln's words are in Boston *Daily Advertiser,* November 20, 1863. The Massachusetts committee's report, on the effect of Lincoln's words is in *Report of the Joint Committee* (Boston, 1863), quoted in Henry S. Barrage, *Gettysburg and Lincoln* (New York, 1906), pp. 124-125.

For the illness of Lincoln and his son after Gettysburg, see Ruth Painter Randall, *Mary Lincoln* (Boston, 1953), p. 329; William O. Stoddard, *Inside the White House in War-Times* (New York, 1890), pp. 189-190. Lincoln's letter to Everett, November 20, 1863, is in Massachusetts Historical Society, Boston.

Chattanooga's military importance is narrated in John Fiske, *The Mississippi Valley in the Civil War* (Boston, 1900). Lincoln's letters to the two Knoxville men about East Tennessee is in Brown University Library, Providence, R.I. For Southern estimates of Bragg as commander, consult Rembert W. Patrick. *Jefferson Davis and His Cabinet* (Baton Rouge, La., 1944), pp. 136, 140; D. H. Hill to Davis, October 30, 1886, in Dunbar Rowland (ed.), *Jefferson Davis, Constitutionalist: His Letters, Papers and Speeches* (Jackson, Miss., 1923), IX, 498-499; Howard Swiggett (ed.), *A Rebel War Clerk's Diary . . . By J. B. Jones* (New York, 1935), pp. 65-66, 74, 84, 87-88, 95-96. The present author has discussed General Bragg with his friend, Professor Grady McWhiney of Millsaps College, Jackson, Mississippi, who is completing a biography of Bragg.

Grant's orders to Thomas, November 18, 1863, are printed in *Personal Memoirs of U. S. Grant* (New York, 1895), I, 518n-519n. For the Chattanooga-Lookout Mountain-Missionary Ridge three-day battle: *Official Records of the Union and Confederate Armies,* Series I, Vol. 21, Part II; *Personal Memoirs of General William T. Sherman* (New York, 1913) Vol. I, Chapter 14. For the Union troops' action in exceeding their orders consult Johnson and Buel (ed.), *Battles and Leaders of the Civil War,* III, 726n. Taylor's description of the Federals' mad dash up Missionary Hill is found in J. Cutler Andrews, *The North Reports the Civil War* (Pittsburgh, Pa., 1955), p. 484. The casualties at Chattanooga are enumerated in Livermore, *Numbers and Losses in the Civil War in America, 1861-1865,* pp. 107-108.

Lincoln's telegram to Grant, congratulating him on the Chattanooga victory is in Brown University Library. Mrs. Hale's appeal to Lincoln for issuance of a Thanksgiving proclamation, September 28, 1863, is in Robert Todd Lincoln Collection, Library of Congress. Lincoln's Thanksgiving Proclamation, October 3, 1863, is in *Lincoln's*

Collected Works, VI, 496-497. See also James G. Randall, "Lincoln and Thanksgiving," *Lincoln Herald,* October, 1947, pp. 110-13. Lincoln is quoted about Grant and whiskey on November 26 in New York *Herald,* November 28, 1863. Burnside's victory at Knoxville on November 29 is followed in Harold S. Fink, "The East Tennessee Campaign and the Battle of Knoxville in 1863," *The East Tennessee Historical Society's Publications* (1957), No. 29, pp. 79ff.

For the Russian fleet's visits in 1863 see Thomas A. Bailey, *America Faces Russia* (Ithaca, N.Y., 1950), Chapter 8; Frank A. Golder, "The Russian Fleet and the Civil War," *The American Historical Review,* July, 1915, pp. 801-812; William E. Nagengast, "The Visit of the Russian Fleet to the United States," *The Russian Review,* January, 1949, pp. 46-55; Earl S. Pomeroy, "The Visit of the Russian Fleet in 1863," *New York History,* October, 1943, pp. 512-517. Lincoln's expressed disapproval of Tsarist Russia in 1852 and 1855 is in *Lincoln's Collected Works,* II, 115, 318, 323. Seward's dispatch to Stoeckl is in *Senate Executive Document* No. 23, 37th Cong., 2nd sess., p. 3. *Punch's* comment is in *Punch* (London), October 24, 1863, p. 169. See also *Diary of Gideon Welles* (Boston, 1909), I, 443; Dennett (ed.), *Lincoln and the Civil War . . . ,* p. 134. See also Albert A. Woldman, *Lincoln and the Russians* (Cleveland, Ohio, 1952), Chapter 9; *Harper's Weekly,* November 21, 1863, p. 746. Lincoln's letter to Bayard Taylor, December 25, 1863, is in Western Reserve Historical Society, Cleveland, Ohio. Taylor's reply, December 28, 1863, is in Robert Todd Lincoln Collection.

Lincoln's remarks about the Capitol's completion are in Margaret Leech, *Reveille in Washington, 1860-1865* (New York, 1941), p. 279. General Kirby-Smith's career is followed in Joseph H. Parks, *General Edmund Kirby-Smith, C.S.A.* (Baton Rouge, La., 1954).

For conflicts, factionalism, and dissensions among Confederate political and military leaders: Albert B. Moore, *Conscription and Conflict in the Confederacy* (New York, 1924); Frank L. Owsley, *State Rights in the Confederacy* (Chicago, 1925); Rembert W. Patrick, *Jefferson Davis and His Cabinet* (Baton Rouge, La., 1944); James Z. Rabun, "Alexander H. Stephens and Jefferson Davis," *The American Historical Review,* January, 1953, pp. 290-321.

Chapter 31—PLANS FOR REUNION: Restoring the Recovered States

Morgan's letter to Weed, February 24, 1862, is in Edward D. Morgan Papers, New York State Library, Albany, N.Y. Lincoln's Southern associations and lack of vindictiveness toward Southern people are detailed in James G. Randall, *Lincoln and the South* (Baton Rouge, La., 1946). The most complete work on Lincoln's reconstruction policy is still Charles H. McCarthy, *Lincoln's Plan of Reconstruction* (New York, 1901). A new study is badly needed. See especially Allan Nevins, "Lincoln's Plans For Reunion," *Abraham Lincoln Association Papers,* 1930, pp. 51-92; James G. Randall, "Lincoln's Peace and Wilson's," *The South Atlantic Quarterly* (1943), Vol. 42, pp. 225-242. Also Rena M. Andrews, "Johnson's Plan of Reconstruction in Relation to That of Lincoln," *Tennessee Historical Magazine,* April, 1931, pp. 165-181; Henry G. Pearson, "Lincoln's Method of Ending the War," *Proceedings of the Massachusetts Historical Society,* 1926, pp. 238-253. Lincoln's words to Army of the Potomac troops about Confederate "brothers in error" are quoted in Furness to his wife, October 5, 1862, in *Letters of Horace Howard Furness* (Boston, 1922), I, 114.

The best treatments of reconstruction in Tennessee are E. Merton Coulter, *William G. Bronlow: Fighting Parson of the Southern Highlands* (Chapel Hill, N.C., 1937) and James W. Patton, *Unionism and Reconstruction in Tennessee, 1860-1869* (Chapel Hill, N.C., 1934). Andrew Johnson's administration as Lincoln's Military Governor is followed in Clifton R. Hall, *Andrew Johnson, Military Governor of Tennessee* (Princeton, N.J., 1916); also Andrew Johnson Papers, 1862, 1863, and 1864, in Library of Congress. Copies of Lincoln's letters to Johnson, September 11, 19, 1863, are in Robert Todd

Lincoln Collection, Library of Congress. Consult also Thomas B. Alexander, *Political Reconstruction in Tennessee* (Nashville, Tenn., 1950); John W. Fertig, *Secession and Reconstruction in Tennessee* (Chicago, 1898); John R. Neal, *Disunion and Restoration in Tennessee* (New York, 1899).

Lincoln's letter about Louisiana to Belmont, July 31, 1862, is in *Lincoln's Collected Works,* V, 350. The best works on war-time reconstruction in this State are Willie M. Caskey, *Secession and Restoration in Louisiana* (Baton Rouge, La., 1938), Chapters 3-7; Fred Harvey Harrington, *Fighting Politician: Major-General N. P. Banks* (Philadelphia, 1948), Chapter 12. Copies of the following letters on reconstruction in Louisiana are in the Robert Todd Lincoln Collection: Lincoln to Reverdy Johnson, July 26, 1862; Lincoln to Butler, Shepley, and others, October 14, 1862; Lincoln to Shepley, November 21, 1862 (two separate letters); Lincoln to Banks, August 5, 1863. See also Lincoln to Banks, November 5, 1863, Huntington Library, San Marino, California.

Lincoln's efforts at reconstruction in Arkansas are best followed in Thomas S. Staples, *Reconstruction in Arkansas, 1862-1874* (New York, 1923). See also John H. Reynolds, "Presidential Reconstruction in Arkansas," *Publications of the Arkansas Historical Association* (1906), I, 352-361; Robinson V. Smith, "Loyal Government in Arkansas From Lincoln to Grant," MS., M.A. Thesis, Columbia University, 1948; David Y. Thomas, *Arkansas in War and Reconstruction, 1861-1874* (Little Rock, Ark., 1926). Lincoln's letter to Governor Phelps and General Steele, November 18, 1862, delivered by McPherson, is in Huntington Library, San Marino, California. For McPherson: *Appleton's Cyclopaedia of American Biography* (New York, 1888), IV, 159. Copy of Lincoln's letter to General Hurlbut about Sebastian, July 31, 1863, and Hurlbut's reply, September 18, are in Robert Todd Lincoln Collection.

The most adequate discussion of Florida during the war, including Lincoln's reconstruction efforts, is William W. Davis, *Civil War and Reconstruction in Florida* (New York, 1913). See also George Hendricks, "Union Army Occupation of the Southern Seaboard, 1861-1865," MS., Ph.D. Dissertation, Columbia University, 1954, Chapter 12, "Reconstruction in Florida, 1864." Florida's secession is detailed in Dorothy Dodd, "The Secession Movement in Florida, 1850-1861," *The Florida Historical Quarterly* (1933), XII, 3-24, 45-66. Speed's "so-called secession of Florida" remark is in *Lincoln's Collected Works,* VIII, 242n. Federal military operations in Florida are followed in Kathryn T. Abbey, *Florida: Land of Change* (Chapel Hill, N.C., 1941), pp. 282-285; Edward C. Bears', "Civil War Operations In and Around Pensacola," *The Florida Historical Quarterly,* October, 1957, pp. 125-165. Copy of Lincoln's countermanding proclamation, revoking Hunter's emancipation order, May 19, 1862, is in Robert Todd Lincoln Collection.

The war-time Florida invasion by Northern entrepeneurs, including Thayer, is treated in George W. Winston, "Carpetbag Imperialism in Florida, 1862-1868," *The Florida Historical Quarterly* (1848), Vol. 27, pp. 99-130, 260-299. For the activities of Thayer and his plan, and his attempted persuasion of Lincoln: Theodore C. Smith, *Life and Letters of James Abram Garfield* (New Haven, Conn., 1925), I, 239-240, 244, 248-249; Diary of Salmon P. Chase, MS., September 24, 1862, Library of Congress; New York *Tribune,* September 26, 1862.

For the military expedition to Florida and Lincoln's dispatch of Hay to that State, see Lincoln to Gillmore, January 13, 1864, copy, Robert Todd Lincoln Collection; Davis, *Civil War and Reconstruction in Florida,* pp. 254-255, 275-295; Tyler Dennett (ed.), *Lincoln and the Civil War in the Diaries and Letters of John Hay* (New York, 1939), pp. 154-166; *Diary of Gideon Welles* (New York, 1909), I, 531-532. For criticism of Hay's mission: New York *Herald,* February 23, 1864; New York *World,* February 13, 1864. For Secretary Chase's efforts to build up support for himself for President: Ovid L. Futch, "Salmon P. Chase and Civil War Politics in Florida," *The Florida Historical Quarterly,* January, 1954, pp. 163-188.

Lincoln's attempts at restoring North Carolina are well-detailed in J. G. deR. Hamilton, *Reconstruction in North Carolina* (New York, 1914). Secession of that State is treated in Joseph C. Sitterson, *Secession Movement in North Carolina* (Chapel Hill, N.C., 1939). For Edward Stanly see Hamilton's sketch in *Dictionary of American Biography* (New York, 1935), Vol. 17, pp. 515-516. For Stanly's administration: Hamilton, *Reconstruction in North Carolina,* pp. 87ff; Edward L. Pierce, *Memoir and Letters of Charles Sumner* (Boston, 1893) IV, 78; Edward Stanly, *A Military Governor Among Abolitionists* (New York, 1865). On Hickman's House resolution and Lincoln's action in forwarding information on Stanly, see *Congressional Globe,* 37th Cong., 2nd sess., p. 2495; *Lincoln's Collected Works,* V, 259-260. Copy of Lincoln's letter to Stanly, September 29, 1862, is in Robert Todd Lincoln Collection.

Anti-Confederate war-time activity is followed in A. Sellew Roberts, "The Peace Movement in North Carolina," *The Mississippi Valley Historical Review,* September, 1924, pp. 190-199; Richard E. Yates, "Governor Vance and the Peace Movement," *The North Carolina Historical Review* (1940), Vol. 17, pp. 1-25, 89-113. Stanly's telegram to Lincoln, January 27, 1864, is in Robert Todd Lincoln Collection. Lincoln's answer, January 28, 1864, is in Brown University Library.

The traditional forces of separation in Virginia are treated in Charles H. Ambler, *Sectionalism in Virginia From 1776 to 1861* (Chicago, 1910). A fresh treatment of the creation of West Virginia is the same author's *A History of West Virginia* (New York, 1933). A critical account of sources, as well as secondary accounts, pertaining to the West Virginia movement is in James G. Randall, *Constitutional Problems Under Lincoln* (New York, 1926), pp. 433-476. The best work on Pierpont is Charles H. Ambler, *Francis H. Pierpont, Union War Governor of Virginia and Father of West Virginia* (Chapel Hill, N.C., 1937).

For Lincoln's reluctant attitude about signing the West Virginia statehood bill: Willey to Pierpont, December 17, 1862, Francis H. Pierpont Papers, Virginia State Archives, Richmond, Va.; *Diary of Gideon Welles* (New York, 1909), I, 191. Bates' West Virginia criticisms are in Howard K. Beale (ed.), *Diary of Edward Bates, 1859-1866* (Washington, D.C., 1933), p. 508. Lincoln's written remarks on West Virginia statehood are in *Lincoln's Collected Works,* VI, 26-28.

General Rosecrans' letter to Lincoln, October 3, 1863, suggesting amnesty to Confederates is in Robert Todd Lincoln Collection. Lincoln's reply, October 4, 1863, is in Brown University Library. Lincoln's Proclamation of Amnesty and Reconstruction, December 8, 1863, is in *Lincoln's Collected Works,* VII, 53-56. Lincoln's troubles with Wade and Davis, his veto of the Wade-Davis bill, and the repercussions are followed in Reinhard H. Luthin, "A Discordant Chapter in Lincoln's Administration: The Davis-Blair Controversy," *The Maryland Historical Magazine,* March, 1944, pp. 35ff.

Chapter 32—PRESIDENTIAL RIVALS AND MILITARY REVERSES

Lincoln's letter to Washburne, October 26, 1863, is in *Lincoln's Collected Works,* VI, 540. Chase-for-President activity is followed in Salmon P. Chase Papers, December, 1863,–June, 1864, Library of Congress; Howard K. Beale (ed.), *Diary of Edward Bates, 1859-1866* (Washington, 1933), p. 310; David Donald (ed.), *Inside Lincoln's Cabinet: The Civil War Diaries of Salmon P. Chase* (New York, 1954), Chapter 5; Donnal V. Smith, *Chase and Civil War Politics* (Columbus, Ohio, 1931); Charles R. Wilson, *"The Original Chase Organization Meeting and The Next Presidential Election," The Mississippi Valley Historical Review* (1936), Vol. 23, pp. 64-76; William F. Zornow, "Lincoln and Chase: Presidential Rivals," *Lincoln Herald,* February–June, 1950; Philadelphia *Press* in Columbus (Ohio) *Ohio State Journal,* March 4, 1864. For Chase's pre-war presidential candidacies see Reinhard H. Luthin, "Salmon P. Chase' Political Career Before the Civil War," *The Mississippi Valley Historical Review,* March, 1943, pp. 517-540.

Dubois' letter to Lincoln, advising that Chase be discharged, is in James G. Randall and Richard N. Current, *Lincoln the President* (New York, 1955), IV, 100. Chase's letters to Lincoln, and copies of Lincoln's letters to Chase, February and March, 1864, are in Robert Todd Lincoln Collection, Library of Congress. Winchell's letter to the Editor, September 14, 1874, regarding the Pomeroy Circular, is in New York *Times*, September 15, 1874. For Winchell see Winchell to Chase, March 14, 1864, Salmon P. Chase Papers, Library of Congress.

Frémont's and Butler's presidential candidacies are followed in Allan Nevins, *Frémont: Pathmarker of the West* (New York, 1939), pp. 564ff; Louis T. Merrill, "General Benjamin F. Butler in the Presidential Campaign of 1864," *The Mississippi Valley Historical Review,* March, 1947, pp. 537-570. Reasons for Butler's popularity are discussed in Murray M. Horowitz, "Ben Butler," MS., Ph.D. Dissertation, Columbia University, 1955, pp. 195-196. For Bennett's support of Grant for President: New York *Herald,* January 6, 1864.

For the promotion of Grant to Lieutenant-General and supreme commander see William B. Hesseltine, *Ulysses S. Grant, Politician* (New York, 1935), pp. 36ff. Grant's appearance in Washington is described in Noah Brooks, *Washington in Lincoln's Time* (New York, 1896), p. 146; Charles Francis Adams, *Richard Henry Dana* (Boston, 1890), II, 271; *Diary of Gideon Welles* (New York, 1909), I, 538-539; New York *Tribune,* March 8, 1864. Lincoln's letter to Grant, April 30, 1864, is in Huntington Library, San Marino, California. For the Meade-Sheridan schism, see Richard O'Connor, *Sheridan the Inevitable* (Indianapolis, 1953), pp. 153ff; *Personal Memoirs of P. H. Sheridan* (New York, 1888), I, 355ff, 368ff.

For Grant's Wilderness and succeeding campaigns through Cold Harbor, consult "The Wilderness Campaign, May–June, 1864," *Proceedings of the Military Historical Society of Massachusetts* (Boston, 1905), Vol. IV. Carpenter's account of Lincoln during the Wilderness campaign is in Francis B. Carpenter. *Six Months At the White House With Abraham Lincoln* (New York, 1867), p. 30. For the Union losses from the Wilderness to Cold Harbor, see Thomas L. Livermore, *Numbers and Losses in the Civil War in America, 1861-1865* (New York, 1901), pp. 110-114; Robert U. Johnson and Clarence C. Buel (ed.), *Battles and Leaders of the Civil War* (New York, 1888), IV, 231. Grant's later regret about the Cold Harbor losses is expressed in *Personal Memoirs of U. S. Grant* (New York, 1895), II, 171-172.

For Butler's failure at Bermuda Hundred: *Personal Memoirs of U. S. Grant,* II, 407; Johnson and Buel (ed.), *Battles and Leaders of the Civil War,* IV, 195-200; William Swinton, *Campaigns of the Army of the Potomac* (New York, 1882), Revised Edition, pp. 460-468; George M. Wolfson, "Butler's Relations With Grant and the Army of the James in 1864," *The South Atlantic Quarterly,* October, 1911, pp. 385ff.

For Sigel's defeat at New Market: Cecil D. Eby, "With Sigel At New Market: The Diary of Colonel D. H. Strohler," *Civil War History,* March, 1960, pp. 73-83; Edward P. Turner, *The New Market Campaign, May, 1864* (Richmond, Va., 1912); *Official Records of the Union and Confederate Armies,* Series I, Vol. 37, Part I, pp. 73ff. The pressure of the West Virginia Legislature and of German-American leaders on Lincoln to give high command to Sigel is recorded in *Lincoln's Collected Works,* VII, 129, 199, 199n. See also Schurz to Lincoln, February 29, 1864, Robert Todd Lincoln Collection.

General Banks' Red River campaign is critically treated in Fred Harvey Harrington, *Fighting Politician: Major-General N. P. Banks* (Philadelphia, 1943), Chapter 13; Ludwell H. Johnson, *Red River Campaign: Politics and Cotton in the Civil War* (Baltimore, 1958); David D. Porter, *Incidents and Anecdotes of the Civil War* (New York, 1885), p. 227. General Halleck's letter to Grant, May 3, 1864, about Lincoln's reasons for keeping Banks in command, is in *Official Records of the Union and Confederate Armies,* Series I, Vol. 34, Part III, pp. 409-410.

Howard's bogus presidential proclamation, and its repercussions, are followed in Martin Lichterman, "John Adams Dix," MS., Ph.D. Dissertation, Columbia University,

1952, p. 578; James G. Randall, *Constitutional Problems Under Lincoln* (New York, 1926), pp. 496ff.

The nomination of Frémont at Cleveland is detailed in William F. Zornow, "The Cleveland Convention, 1864, and Radical Democrats," *Mid-America,* January, 1954, pp. 39-54.

The admission of Nevada as a State, and Lincoln's quotations on it, are from Effie E. Mack, *Nevada* (Glendale, Calif., 1936), pp. 255ff; Charles A. Dana, *Recollections of the Civil War* (New York, 1899), pp. 174ff.

Chapter 33—RENOMINATED FOR PRESIDENT

The substance of this chapter, detailing the activity of Lincoln's officeholders in controlling the state party conventions that chose delegates to the national convention in 1864, is taken from Harry J. Carman and Reinhard H. Luthin, *Lincoln and the Patronage* (New York, 1943), Chapter 9, "Federal Officeholders and the Renomination of Lincoln." Mullett's letter to Chase, May 16, 1864, is in Salmon P. Chase Papers, Library of Congress.

The Middle Western correspondent's report about "wire pulling" at Washington before the Baltimore convention, is in Indianapolis *Daily State Sentinel,* May 28, 1864. The New York *Herald's* Baltimore correspondent is quoted in New York *Herald,* June 9, 1864. The Union National Convention is followed in William F. Zornow, "The Union Party National Convention at Baltimore, 1864," *The Maryland Historical Magazine,* September, 1950, pp. 176-200. The anti-Lincoln Missouri delegation is treated in William F. Zornow, "The Missouri Radicals and the Election of 1864," *The Missouri Historical Review* (1951), Vol. 45, pp. 354-370. For the convention see also Francis Brown, *Raymond of the "Times"* (New York, 1951); *Proceedings of the First Three Republican National Conventions of 1856, 1860 and 1864* (Published by Charles W. Johnson, Minneapolis, 1893). The platform is in Henry Steele Commager (ed.), *Documents of American History* (New York, 1948), I, 435-436.

For the controversy over why Hamlin was dropped for renomination for Vice-President and Johnson nominated, see Noah Brooks, *Washington in Lincoln's Time* (New York, 1895), pp. 152-160; James F. Glonek, "Lincoln, Johnson, and the Baltimore Ticket," *The Abraham Lincoln Quarterly* (1951), VI, 255-271; Alexander K. McClure, *Abraham Lincoln and Men of War Times* (Philadelphia, 1892), Appendix, pp. 457ff; Helen Nicolay, *Lincoln's Secretary: A Biography of John G. Nicolay* (New York, 1949), pp. 207-208, 322-325.

The standard work on the election of 1864 is William F. Zornow, *Lincoln and the Party Divided* (Norman, Okla., 1954). See also Carman and Luthin, *Lincoln and the Patronage,* Chapter 10; Arthur C. Cole, "Lincoln and the Presidential Election of 1864," *Transactions of the Illinois State Historical Society,* 1917, pp. 130-138; Harold M. Dudley, "The Election of 1864," *The Mississippi Valley Historical Review,* March, 1932, pp. 500-518. For regional studies: Norman C. Brillhart, "The Election of 1864 in Western Pennsylvania," *Western Pennsylvania Historical Magazine* (1925), VIII, 26-36; Wilfred A. Harbison, "Indiana Republicans and the Re-Election of President Lincoln," *Indiana Magazine of History,* March, 1938, pp. 42-64; Paul G. Hubbard, "The Lincoln-McClellan Presidential Election in Illinois," MS., Ph.D. Dissertation, University of Illinois, 1949; Elizabeth F. Yager, "The Presidential Campaign of 1864," *Ohio Archaeological and Historical Quarterly,* October, 1925, pp. 548-589; William F. Zornow, "Indiana and the Election of 1864," *Indiana Magazine of History* (1949), Vol. 45, pp. 13-38.

Chapter 34—THE TORTUROUS SUMMER TIME

Greeley's comment about July and August, 1864, is in Horace Greeley, *The American Conflict* (Hartford, Conn., 1867), II, 664. Welles' remark about Grant's extravagance about manpower is in *Diary of Gideon Welles* (New York, 1909), II, 45. Conflicts within the confederacy are detailed in Albert B. Moore's, *Conscription and Conflict in the Confederacy* (New York, 1924); Rembert W. Patrick, *Jefferson Davis and His Cabinet* (Baton Rouge, La., 1944); E. Merton Coulter, *The Confederate States of America, 1861-1865* (Baton Rouge, La., 1950), Chapter 17; Clement Eaton, *A History of the Southern Confederacy* (New York, 1954), pp. 263ff.

The clash between the two New York factions following Lincoln's renomination is detailed in Sidney D. Brummer, *Political History of New York State During the Period of the Civil War* (New York, 1911), pp. 383ff; Harry J. Carman and Reinhard H. Luthin, *Lincoln and the Patronage* (New York, 1943), pp. 262ff. The account of Chase's resignation and his succession by Fessenden is based on Carman and Luthin, *Lincoln and the Patronage*, pp. 265-268; copies of Lincoln's letters to Chase, June 28, 30, 1864, is in Robert Todd Lincoln Collection, Library of Congress; see Tyler Dennett (ed.), *Lincoln and the Civil War in the Diaries and Letters of John Hay* (New York, 1939), p. 199; Chase to Cooke, July 1, 1864, in Ellis P. Oberholtzer, *Jay Cooke* (Philadelphia, 1907), I, 421; transcript of short hand records, dictated by Governor Brough, July 12, 1864; William Henry Smith Papers, Ohio Archaeological and Historical Society, Columbus.

The Blair-Davis rivalry, and the opposition of Davis to Lincoln are followed in Reinhard H. Luthin, "A Discordant Chapter in the Lincoln Administration: The Blair-Davis Controversy," *The Maryland Historical Magazine*, March, 1944, pp. 23ff; Lincoln's conversation with Senator Chandler about the Wade-Davis bill on July 4, 1864, is quoted in Dennett (ed.), *Lincoln and the Civil War in the Diaries and Letters of John Hay*, pp. 204-206.

Early's advance on Washington is treated in Douglas Southall Freeman, *Lee's Lieutenants* (New York, 1944), Vol. III, Chapter 29. Nicolay and Hay's statement about Washington's inadequate defenses is in John G. Nicolay and John Hay, *Abraham Lincoln: A History* (New York, 1890), IX, 163. Grant's telegrams to Halleck, July 9, 10, 1864, are in *Official Records of the Union and Confederate Armies*, Series I, Vol. 37, Part II, pp. 134, 155. Lincoln's telegrams to Grant, July 10, 11, 1864, are in *Lincoln's Collected Works*, VII, 437, 438. Lincoln's telegram to Swann and others, July 10, 1864, is in *Ibid.*, VII, 437-438. See also T. Harry Williams, *Lincoln and His Generals* (New York, 1952), pp. 325ff. Early's decision to stop his advance is treated in Freeman, *Lee's Lieutenants*, III, 565ff. Early's remark to his officer about scaring Lincoln is in Henry Kyd Douglas, *I Rode With Stonewall* (Chapel Hill, N.C., 1940), p. 295.

Lincoln's exposure to Confederate fire is detailed in John H. Cramer, *Lincoln Under Enemy Fire* (Baton Rouge, La., 1948). General Wright's letter, undated, is in George T. Stevens, *Three Years With the Sixth Corps* (New York, 1870), Van Nostrand Edition, p. 382n. Bull's letter to his wife, July 14, 1864, is in possession of Professor Streeter Bull of the University of Illinois. See also Dennett (ed.), *Lincoln and the Civil War in the Diaries and Letters of John Hay*, p. 208. Browning's quotation of Lincoln's remarks is in Theodore C. Pease and James G. Randall (ed.), *Diary of Orville Hickman Browning, 1850-1864* (Springfield, Ill., 1925), I, 676.

Greeley's "peace" efforts, including the roles of Jewett and Sanders, as well as the parts of the Confederate commissioners, including Lincoln's attitude, are followed in Ruth Ketring Nuermberger, *The Clays of Alabama* (Lexington, Ky., 1958), pp.

240ff; Tyler Dennett, *John Hay* (New York, 1934), pp. 45-46; Edward C. Kirkland, *The Peacemakers of 1864* (New York, 1927), Chapters 1-3; Nicolay and Hay, *Abraham Lincoln: A History,* Vol. X, Chapter 8; Frank H. Severance, "The Peace Conference At Niagara Falls," *Publications of the Buffalo Historical Society* (1914), Vol. 18; Glyndon G. Van Deusen, *Horace Greeley* (Philadelphia, 1953), Chapter 20; Lewis B. Mayhew, "The Clay-Thompson Mission Into Canada," MS., M.A. Thesis, University of Illinois, 1946. See also *Lincoln's Collected Works,* VII, 435, 440-442, 451; *Annual Cyclopaedia,* 1864, pp. 780-782.

The account of the death of General McPherson, the ambitions of Logan, Blair, and Hooker to succeed him, and Sherman's appointment of Howard is based on *Memoirs of General William T. Sherman* (New York, 1913), II, 85-86; John A. Carpenter, "An Account of the Civil War Career of Oliver O. Howard," MS., Ph.D. Dissertation, Columbia University, 1954, pp. 173; Logan's letter to his wife, August 6, 1864, John A. Logan Papers, Library of Congress. Lincoln's praise of McPherson before Vicksburg is in Lincoln to Isaac N. Arnold, May 26, 1863, Chicago Historical Society.

The Wade-Davis Manifesto is printed in New York *Tribune,* August 5, 1864. Lincoln's remarks to Seward on the Manifesto are quoted in *Private and Official Correspondence of Gen. Benjamin F. Butler* (Norwood, Mass., 1917), V, 8-9. The preoccupation of Davis with patronage is demonstrated in John A. J. Creswell Papers, Library of Congress. For the Buffalo paper's comment: Buffalo (N.Y.) *Morning Express,* August 24, 1864. The meeting of Davis with other radicals for choice of a new presidential candidate at Field's home is followed in contemporary letters later published in New York *Sun,* June 30, 1889. For Davis' anti-Lincoln intrigues at Long Branch, New Jersey, see W. J. Gordon to Tilden, August 25, 1864, Samuel J. Tilden Papers, New York Public Library.

Lincoln's conversation with General Hamilton about probable defeat for re-election is quoted in *Butler Correspondence,* V, 35. See also G. C. Rice to Washburne, August 14, 1864, Elihu B. Washburne Papers, Library of Congress. Raymond's letters to Cameron, August 19, 21, 1864, are in Simon Cameron Papers, Library of Congress. Weed's letter to Seward, and Raymond's letter to Lincoln, both of August 22, 1864, are in Robert Todd Lincoln Collection. Lincoln's Memorandum, August 23, 1864, is in *Lincoln's Collected Works,* VII, 514.

Chapter 35—**RUNNING FOR RE-ELECTION**

For McClellan's nomination, the "peace" plank, and McClellan's repudiation of it: Eugene H. Roseboom, *A History of Presidential Elections* (New York, 1957), pp. 198ff; Edward Stanwood, *A History of the Presidency* (Boston, 1912), pp. 304ff. Lincoln's telegraph to Grant, requesting a "bull-dog grip," August 17, 1864, is in *Lincoln's Collected Works,* VII, 499. Lincoln's words to Corwin are quoted in Lieber to Sumner, August 31, 1864, in Frank Freidel, *Francis Lieber* (Baton Rouge, La., 1948), p. 351.

For the Confederates' replacement of Johnston with Hood, as well as the Battle of Atlanta, see Clement Eaton, *A History of the Confederacy* (New York, 1954), pp. 288ff; Thomas R. Hay, "The Davis-Hood Controversy," *The Mississippi Valley Historical Review* (1924), Vol. 11, pp. 54-84. For the Battle of Atlanta: William Key, *The Battle of Atlanta and Georgia* (New York, 1958); Adolf A. Hoehling, *Last Train From Atlanta* (New York, 1958). For General Hardee: N. C. Hughes Jr., "William Joseph Hardee, C.S.A.," MS., Ph.D. Dissertation, University of North Carolina, 1959. For the reaction of Lee's troops to Hood's appointment, see Douglas Southall Freeman, *R. E. Lee: A Biography* (New York, 1935), III, 494. Lincoln's telegram to Sherman about Davis' visit to Hood, September 27, 1864, is in *Lincoln's Collected Works,* VIII, 27. Sherman's reply, September 28, 1864, is in Robert Todd Lincoln Collection, Library of Congress. Lincoln's proclamations on the victories of Farragut and Sherman are printed in *Lincoln's Collected Works,* VII, 532-534; James D. Richardson (ed.), *Messages and Papers of the Presidents* (Washington, 1897), VI, 238-239.

For the power of the New York Custom House, consult William J. Hartman, "Politics and Patronage: The New York Custom House, 1852-1902," MS., Ph.D. Dissertation, Columbia University, 1952. Weed's complaints against Collector Barney are in Albany *Evening Journal,* July 16, 1864. The letter to Senator Trumbull, September 1, 1864, is in Lyman Trumbull Papers, Library of Congress. The reshuffling of New York City patronage by Lincoln in September is followed in Sidney D. Brummer, *Political History of New York State During the Period of the Civil War* (New York, 1911), pp. 394-395. Lincoln's letter to Collector Draper about Governor Newell, September 8, 1864, is in *Lincoln's Collected Works,* VII, 543. Winthrop's speech, October 18, 1864, is in Edward Channing, *History of the United States* (New York, 1907), IV, 533.

Lincoln's use of patronage in his re-election campaign and Raymond's part in soliciting funds are detailed in Harry J. Carman and Reinhard H. Luthin, *Lincoln and the Patronage* (New York, 1943), pp. 282ff. Raymond's letter to Cameron, July 17, 1864, is in Simon Cameron Papers, Library of Congress. Raymond's "private" circular, soliciting funds, September 15, 1864, is in New York *World,* October 4, 1864. For Lincoln's support of Republican congressional candidates by threat of patronage, see George W. Julian's statement in Allan Thorndike Rice (ed.), *Reminiscences of Abraham Lincoln By Distinguished Men of His Time* (New York, 1886), pp. 51-52; *Lincoln's Collected Works,* VII, 402, 453, 480-481; Isaac N. Arnold, *The History of Abraham Lincoln and the Overthrow of Slavery* (Chicago, 1866), p. 506; Lincoln to Ward Hunt, August 16, 1864, in Alfred R. Conkling, *Life and Letters of Roscoe Conkling* (New York, 1889), p. 199. Lincoln's proffer of the French mission to Bennett is followed in Carman and Luthin, *Lincoln and the Patronage,* pp. 285-286; W. O. Bartlett to Bennett, November 4, 1864, in Oliver Carlson, *The Man Who Made News: James Gordon Bennett* (New York, 1942), p. 370.

Blair's angry comment about Henry Winter Davis and Senator Wade is quoted by J. K. Herbert, August 6, 1864, in *Private and Official Correspondence of Gen. Benjamin F. Butler* (Norwood, Mass., 1917), V, 8-9. For the Davis-Blair feud, see Reinhard H. Luthin, "A Discordant Chapter in Lincoln's Administration: The Blair-Davis Controversy," *Maryland Historical Magazine,* March, 1944, pp. 25-49. Lincoln's words to Stevens are quoted in Emanuel Hertz, *Abraham Lincoln: A New Portrait* (New York, 1931), II, 947. Senator Chandler's role in persuading radicals to support Lincoln for re-election, his visit to Wade, Davis, Lincoln, and others, the withdrawal of Frémont, and the resignation of Blair, with the interrelationships, are treated in Carman and Luthin, *Lincoln and the Patronage,* pp. 275ff; Winfred A. Harbison, "Zachariah Chandler's Part in the Re-Election of Abraham Lincoln," *The Mississippi Valley Historical Review,* September, 1935, pp. 267-276; Charles R. Wilson, "New Light on the Lincoln-Blair-Frémont 'Bargain' of 1864," *The American Historical Review,* October, 1936, pp. 71-78. Lincoln's letter to Blair, September 23, 1864, requesting his resignation, is in Henry J. Raymond, *Life and Public Services of Abraham Lincoln* (New York, 1865), p. 602. Blair's reply to Lincoln is in Robert Todd Lincoln Collection.

For Sheridan's Valley campaign: Major-General Wesley Merritt, U.S.V., "Sheridan in the Shenandoah Valley," in Robert U. Johnson and Clarence C. Bucl (cd.), *Battles and Leaders of the Civil War* (New York, 1888), IV, 511ff. Lincoln's congratulatory messages to Sheridan, September 20, October 22, 1864, are in *Lincoln's Collected Works,* VIII, 13, 29, 73-74. Lincoln's remarks about Sheridan to the serenaders are in Washington *Daily Morning Chronicle,* October 22, 1864.

Democratic electioneering strategy is followed in Henry C. Hubbart, *The Older Middle West* (New York, 1936), pp. 235ff. Lincoln's August 31 address to the Ohio troops is in Baltimore *Sun,* September 2, 1864. The rivalry between the parties for the "soldier" vote is treated in Mary R. Dearing, *Veterans in Politics* (Baton Rouge, La.,

1952), pp. 26-48. Copy of Lincoln's letter to Rosecrans, about soldier voting, September 26, 1864, is in Robert Todd Lincoln Collection.

Lincoln's letter to Sherman, September 19, 1864, about Indiana troops' furlough is in Lincoln National Life Foundation, Fort Wayne, Indiana. For Governor Morton's methods in making soldier voting possible: Dearing, *Veterans in Politics*, p. 36; Kenneth M. Stampp, *Indiana Politics During the Civil War* (Indianapolis, 1949), pp. 250ff. Lincoln's telegrams to Cameron and Grant on the state elections are in *Lincoln's Collected Works*, VIII, 43, 45.

Emerson's letter following Lincoln's re-election is in Ralph L. Rusk (ed.), *Letters of Ralph Waldo Emerson* (New York, 1939), V, 387.

Chapter 36—PATRONAGE PROBLEMS AND MILITARY VICTORIES

Lincoln's words of complaint to Senator Clark about patronage are quoted in Francis B. Carpenter, *Six Months At the White House With Abraham Lincoln* (New York, 1867), p. 276. Chase's appointment as Chief Justice, and the various rivalries for that position, are treated in Harry J. Carman and Reinhard H. Luthin, *Lincoln and the Patronage* (New York, 1943), pp. 315-320. See also F. P. Blair, Sr., to Cameron, November 22, 1864, Simon Cameron Papers, Library of Congress; Salmon P. Chase Papers, Library of Congress, for October-November, 1864; George S. Boutwell, *Reminiscences of Sixty Years in Public Affairs* (New York; 1902), II, 29-30.

The Blair-Davis Maryland fight over party power, patronage, and emancipation, and Davis' cooperation with Senator Hale in opposing the Navy Department, are followed in Reinhard H. Luthin, "A Discordant Chapter in Lincoln's Administration: The Davis-Blair Controversy," *The Maryland Historical Magazine*, March, 1944, pp. 25-48; Blair Papers, 1864; William E. Chandler Papers, February, 1865; John A. J. Creswell Papers, March, 1865—all in the Library of Congress; New York *Herald*, January 31, 1865. For Lincoln's shuffling of the Maryland patronage on his last day on earth: "Memorandum Concerning Maryland Appointments," April 14, 1865, in *Lincoln's Collected Works*, VIII, 411.

Lincoln's changes in his Cabinet following his re-election are detailed in Carman and Luthin, *Lincoln and the Patronage*, pp. 309-312. Bates' unhappiness in Washington is mentioned in Floyd A. McNeil, "Lincoln's Attorney General: Edward Bates," MS., Ph.D. Dissertation, State University of Iowa, 1934, p. 305. For Lincoln's appointment of Speed as Bates's successor: Helen L. Springer, "James Speed, the Attorney General," *The Filson Club History Quarterly* (1937), XI, 169-188; Lincoln to Speed, December 1, 1864, and Speed to Lincoln, same date, in *Lincoln's Collected Works*, VIII, 126, 126n.

For Lincoln's appointment of Morgan as Fessenden's successor, Morgan's refusal of the proffer, and the appointment of McCulloch as Secretary of the Treasury, consult Herbert S. Schell, "Hugh McCulloch and the Treasury Department, 1865-1869," *The Mississippi Valley Historical Review*, December, 1930, pp. 404-421; Hugh McCulloch, *Men and Measures of Half a Century* (New York, 1888), pp. 193-195; James A. Rawley, *Edwin D. Morgan, 1811-1883* (New York, 1955), pp. 201-202. For Jesse K. Dubois' efforts to be appointed Secretary of the Interior, see Dubois to Trumbull, February 2, 1865, Lyman Trumbull Papers, Library of Congress; Shelby M. Cullom, *Fifty Years of Public Service* (Chicago, 1911), p. 135. For Lincoln's appointment of Harlan as Secretary of the Interior: Johnson Brigham, *James Harlan* (Iowa City, Iowa, 1913); J. M. Davis, "Elijah Sells," *Annals of Iowa* (1895-1899), Series III, Vol. 2, pp. 520-521.

On the "lame duck" Vice-President Hamlin's predicament: Fessenden to Washburn, November 18, 1864, William P. Fessenden Papers, Library of Congress; Charles

E. Hamlin, *Life and Times of Hannibal Hamlin* (Cambridge, Mass., 1899), pp. 495ff; Francis Fessenden, *Life and Public Services of William Pitt Fessenden* (Boston, 1907), II, 1ff; *Autobiography of Thurlow Weed* (Boston, 1883), p. 622; New York *Herald*, March 10, 1865. Copy of Lincoln's letter to Collector Goodrich, March 13, 1865, and Goodrich's reply, same date, are in Robert Todd Lincoln Collection, Library of Congress. For President Johnson's appointment of Hamlin as Boston Collector, and evidence that Lincoln intended to appoint Hamlin to that job: Samuel Hooper, *Defense of the Merchants of Boston Against the Aspersions of the Hon. John Z. Goodrich, Ex-Collector of Customs* (Boston, 1866), pp. 3-4.

For Lincoln's satisfaction with Generals Grant, Sherman, and Thomas, consult T. Harry Williams, *Lincoln and His Generals* (New York, 1952), p. 336. For Hood's Tennessee operations and the Battles of Spring Hill and Franklin: Clement Eaton, *A History of the Confederacy* (New York, 1954), pp. 292-294; Thomas Robson Hay, *Hood's Tennessee Campaign* (New York, 1929) and the same author's "The Battle of Spring Hill," *Tennessee Historical Magazine,* July, 1921, pp. 74-91; W. W. Gist, "The Battle of Franklin," *Tennessee Historical Magazine,* October, 1920, pp. 213ff; *Memoirs of General William T. Sherman* (New York, 1875), II, 162ff.

Stanton's dispatch to Grant, December 2, 1864, expressing Lincoln's anxiety about Thomas' slowness, is in *Official Records of the Union and Confederate Armies,* Series I, Vol. 45, Part II, pp. 15-16. Grant's post-war words about his concern about Thomas at Nashville in December, 1864, are in John Russell Young, *Around the World With General Grant* (New York, 1879), II, 294-295. For Hood's own ideas on his proposed strategy, see John B. Hood, *Advance and Retreat* (New Orleans, 1880), p. 267.

Grant's dispatches to Thomas of early December, 1864, ordering him to fight Hood immediately, and his decision to remove Thomas from command, are in *Official Records of the Union and Confederate Armies,* Series I, Vol. 45, Part II, pp. 55, 70, 97, 114. For Lincoln's attitude toward Thomas' removal: L. E. Chittenden, *Recollections of President Lincoln and His Administration* (New York, 1891), p. 364; David H. Bates, *Lincoln in the Telegraph Office* (New York, 1907), pp. 315-317. Lincoln's telegram to Thomas, December 16, 1864, is in *Lincoln's Collected Works,* VIII, 169.

The best work of Thomas' defeat of Hood is Stanley F. Horn, *The Decisive Battle of Nashville* (Baton Rouge, La., 1956). See also Donald M. Lynne, "Wilson's Cavalry At Nashville," *Civil War History,* June, 1955, pp. 141-159; Lieut.-Col. Henry Stone, "The Battle of Nashville, Tennessee," *Papers of the Military History Society of Massachusetts* (Boston, 1908), VII, 481-542; William Swinton, *The Twelve Decisive Battles of the War* (New York, 1867), pp. 426-477. For Hood's resignation as Army of Tennessee commander see T. Harry Williams, *P. G. T. Beauregard: Napoleon in Gray* (Baton Rouge, La., 1954), p. 249.

Sherman's dispatches to Halleck on total war, September 4 and December 24, 1864, are in *Memoirs of General William T. Sherman* (New York, 1903), II, 111, 227-228. For Sherman's march: Jacob D. Cox, *The March to the Sea* (New York, 1882); Henry Hitchcock, *Marching With Sherman* (New Haven, Conn., 1927); James Ford Rhodes, "Sherman's March to the Sea," *The American Historical Review,* April, 1901, pp. 466-474; John Bennett Walters, "General William T. Sherman and Total War," *The Journal of Southern History,* November, 1948, pp. 447-480. General Howard's report to Sherman is in *Official Records of the Union and Confederate Armies,* Series 2, Vol. 44, p. 67. The letters of Poe, December 16, 1864, and Meade, December 18, 1864, are in John A. Carpenter, "An Account of the Civil War Career of Oliver Otis Howard," MS., Ph.D. Dissertation, Columbia University, 1954, p. 195n. Colonel Merrill's letter to his daughter, December 15, 1864, is in *The Mississippi Valley Historical Review,* March, 1928, pp. 523-526.

Lincoln's quotation, saying that he did not know where Sherman would "come out" is in Allan Thorndike Rice (ed.), *Reminiscences of Abraham Lincoln By Distinguished*

Men of His Time (New York, 1886), p. 71. Lincoln's letter of thanks to Sherman on occupation of Savannah, December 26, 1864, is in Edwin M. Stanton Papers, Library of Congress.

Lincoln's letter and telegram to Butler about the Virginia election are in *Lincoln's Collected Works,* VIII, 174, 186. For the Fort Fisher fiasco, consult *Personal Memoirs of U. S. Grant* (New York, 1895), II, 249, 262-267; David D. Porter, *Incidents and Anecdotes of the Civil War* (New York, 1885), p. 272. Lincoln's telegram to Grant, inquiring about the Wilmington expedition, is in *Lincoln's Collected Works,* VIII, 187. Grant's reply is in *Official Records of the Union and Confederate Armies,* Series I, Vol. 42, Part III, p. 1087. Grant's request to Stanton for the removal of Butler is in *Ibid.,* Series I, Vol. 46, Part II. Butler's rage at his removal is described in George H. Gordon, *A War Diary of Events in the War of the Great Rebellion* (Boston, 1885), p. 371. Butler's farewell to his troops, January 8, 1865, is in *Official Records of the Union and Confederate Armies,* Series I, Vol. 46, Part II, p. 71. The best works on General Butler are Hans L. Trefousse, *Ben Butler, the South Called Him Beast!* (New York, 1957); Robert S. Holzman, *Stormy Ben Butler* (New York, 1954). Lincoln's letter to the Kentuckian, William A. Menzies, January 24, 1865, is in *Lincoln's Collected Works,* VIII, 235.

Chapter 37—SLAVERY ABOLITION AND RECONSTRUCTION

Lincoln's statement to Congressman Rollins about the effect of Clay's slavery views on him is in Osborn H. Oldroyd (ed.), *The Lincoln Memorial* (Springfield, Ill., 1890), p. 492. For the failure of Lincoln's plan for compensated emancipation in Delaware, see H. Clay Reed, "Lincoln's Compensated Emancipation Plan and Its Relation to Delaware," *Delaware Notes* (University of Delaware, Newark, Delaware, 1931), 7th Series, pp. 27-28. Copy of Lincoln's letter to Hodges, April 4, 1864, is in Robert Todd Lincoln Collection, Library of Congress.

The standard work on Negro participation in the war is Benjamin Quarles, *The Negro in the Civil War* (Boston, 1953). See also Thomas Wentworth Higginson, *Army Life in a Black Regiment* (Boston, 1870); Fred A. Shannon, "The Federal Government and the Negro Soldier, 1861-1865," *Journal of Negro History,* October, 1926, pp. 563-583. For estimated number of Negroes in the Union armies: *Official Records of The Union and Confederate Armies,* Series III, Vol. 5, p. 661.

Lincoln's conversations with Chandler and Fessenden about slavery abolition, July 4, 1864, are in Tyler Dennett (ed.), *Lincoln and the Civil War in the Diaries and Letters of John Hay* (New York, 1939), pp. 204-205. Sumner's remarks are in *Congressional Globe,* 38th Cong., 1st sess., p. 3460. Trumbull's sponsorship of the Thirteenth Amendment in 1864 is detailed in Horace White, *Life of Lyman Trumbull* (Boston, 1913), pp. 223ff. Lincoln's expression of support to Fessenden for the slavery-abolition amendment, July 4, 1864, is in Dennett (ed.), *Lincoln and the Civil War in the Diaries and Letters of John Hay,* p. 205.

Lincoln's request to Morgan for a slavery-abolition plank in the national platform of 1864 is in Isaac N. Arnold, *Life of Abraham Lincoln* (Chicago, 1885), p. 358. Arnold was a friend and staunch congressional supporter of Lincoln in Congress. Morgan's speech to the national convention is in New York *Daily Tribune,* June 8, 1864. Lincoln's public endorsement of the slavery-abolition plank, June 9, 1864, is in *Lincoln's Collected Works,* VII, 380. Lincoln's July proclamation, expressing hope for passage of the Thirteenth Amendment, is in James D. Richardson (comp.), *Messages and Papers of the Presidents, 1789-1897* (Washington, 1897), VI, 223. Cox's remark about Lincoln and Seward concerning the Thirteenth Amendment is in Samuel S. Cox, *Three Decades of Federal Legislation* (Providence, R.I., 1885), p. 320.

Lincoln's recommendation to the House to pass the Thirteenth Amendment, in his Annual Message, is in Richardson (comp.), *Messages and Papers of the Presidents,* VI, 252. Lincoln's words to Congressman Rollins to support the amendment are in Oldroyd (ed.), *The Lincoln Memorial,* pp. 491-494. Congressman Riddle's revelations about the means employed to pass the amendment are in Albert G. Riddle, *Recollections of War Times* (New York, 1895), pp. 323-324. Congressman Julian's remarks are in George W. Julian, *Political Recollections From 1840 to 1872* (Chicago, 1884), p. 250. Congressman Cole's letter, January 31, 1865, is in *Memoirs of Cornelius Cole* (New York, 1908), p. 220. The Thirteenth Amendment vote in the House is recorded in *Congressional Globe,* 38th Cong., 2nd sess., p. 531. Congressman Blaine's description of the House following the amendment's passage is in James G. Blaine, *Twenty Years of Congress* (Norwich, Conn., 1884), I, 538. Garrison's credit to Lincoln in aiding the amendments passage is in *The Liberator* (Boston), February 10, 1865, quoted in John G. Nicolay and John Hay, *Abraham Lincoln: A History* (New York, 1890), X, 79n.

Vice-President Stephens' comments on Lincoln's slavery-abolition views at Hampton Roads conference are in Alexander H. Stephens, *A Constitutional View of the Late War Between the States* (Philadelphia, 1870), II, 617. Lincoln's letter to Greeley, August 22, 1862, is in Wadsworth Athenaeum, Hartford, Conn.

Lincoln's letter to Governor Hahn on Negro suffrage in Louisiana, March 13, 1864, is in *Lincoln's Collected Works,* VII, 243. Lincoln's remarks on Negro suffrage in Louisiana, April 11, 1865, are in *Lincoln's Collected Works,* VIII, 403. Usher's summary of Lincoln's views on Negro suffrage is in "Recollections of Ex-Secretary Usher," New York *Daily Tribune,* September 13, 1885. Curtis' explanation of Lincoln's attitude toward Negro suffrage is in George Ticknor Curtis, *Constitutional History of the United States* (New York, 1896), II, 347.

The best work on Lincoln's restoration policy is still Charles H. McCarthy, *Lincoln's Plan of Reconstruction* (New York, 1901). It is inadequate and a modern study is badly needed. Lincoln's proclamation, on the Wade-Davis reconstruction bill veto is in *Lincoln's Collected Works,* VII, 433-434. Usher's comment on Lincoln's reconstruction views is in "Recollections of Ex-Secretary Usher," New York *Daily Tribune,* September 13, 1885. Baron Stoeckl's dispatch, February 13, 1865, is in Benjamin P. Thomas, "A Russian Estimate of Lincoln," *Bulletin of the Abraham Lincoln Association,* June, 1931, p. 6. For debates and delaying actions on reconstruction in the Senate, consult *Congressional Globe,* 38th Cong., 2nd sess., pp. 1101-1111, 1126-1129.

Copies of Lincoln's letters to Generals Hurlbut and Canby, November 14, December 12, 1864, on Louisiana reconstruction, are in Robert Todd Lincoln Collection.

Lincoln's conferences with Campbell and Myers, along with General Weitzel, are followed in Campbell to Joseph A. Anderson and others, April 7, 1865, Edwin M. Stanton Papers, Library of Congress; *Lincoln's Collected Works,* VIII, 386-389; Gustavus A. Myers, "Abraham Lincoln in Richmond," *Virginia Magazine of History* (1933), Vol. 41, pp. 318-322; *Southern Historical Society Papers,* new series, IV, 66-74. Lincoln's telegram to Pierpoint, April 10, 1865, is in *Lincoln's Collected Works,* VIII, 392. Lincoln's conference with Pierpoint is recorded in Charles H. Ambler, *Francis H. Pierpoint* (Chapel Hill, N. C., 1937), pp. 255ff. Lincoln's letter to Weitzel, April 12, 1865 is in *Lincoln's Collected Works,* VIII, 406-407. General Ord's telegram to Lincoln, April 14, 1865, is in *Official Records of the Union and Confederate Armies,* Series I, Vol. 46, Part III, p. 748.

Washburne's words to General Gordon are quoted in John B. Gordon, *Reminiscences of the Civil War* (New York, 1904), p. 450. For Chase's dinner with Henry Winter Davis and other radicals: David Donald (ed.), *Inside Lincoln's Cabinet: The Civil War Diaries of Salmon P. Chase* (New York, 1954), p. 265. Chase's letter to Lincoln, April 11, 1865, is in Robert Todd Lincoln Collection. Lincoln's speech, April 11, 1865, is in *Lincoln's Collected Works,* VIII, 399-405.

The Washington correspondent's report on radical reaction to Lincoln's April 11 speech is in an unidentified newspaper clipping, April, 1865, in Townsend Collection,

Columbia University Library, Vol. 55, p. 192. Sumner's letter to Lieber is in Edward L. Pierce, *Memoir and Letters of Charles Sumner* (Boston, 1893), IV, 236. Chase's letter to Stanley Matthews, April 14, 1865, is in *The American Historical Review*, April, 1929, p. 555. Lincoln's letter to Van Alen, April 14, 1865, is in *Lincoln's Collected Works*, VIII, 413.

Chapter 38—TRIUMPH OF THE UNION

For White House receptions early in 1865, see Margaret Leech, *Reveille in Washington, 1860-1865* (New York, 1941), pp. 354-355; Washington *Daily Morning Chronicle*, January 3, 10, 1865. Lincoln's remark about the selling of "maintenance" is mentioned in Walter B. Stevens, *A Reporter's Lincoln* (St. Louis, 1916), p. 62.

For the capture of Fort Fisher: *Official Records of the Union and Confederate Armies*, Series I, Vol. 46, Part I, pp. 393-447; Colonel William Lamb in *Southern Historical Society's Papers*, X, 346ff; Johnson Hagood, *Memoirs of the War of Secession* (Columbia, South Carolina, 1910), pp. 320ff; Johnson and Buel (ed.), *Battles and Leaders of the Civil War*, IV, 642. Lincoln's congratulatory note to Admiral Porter is in *Official Records of the Union and Confederate Navies*, X, 459.

Copy of Lincoln's letter to Blair on a peace conference, January 18, 1865, is in Robert Todd Lincoln Collection, Library of Congress. Material on the Hampton Roads peace conference is ample: John A. Campbell, *Reminiscences and Documents Relating to the Civil War During the Year 1865* (Baltimore, 1887) and the same author's articles and memorandum on the conference in *Transactions of the Southern Historical Society* (1874), I, 187-190, 190-194; Julian S. Carr, "The Hampton Roads Conference," *The Confederate Veteran* (1917), Vol. 25, pp. 57-66; Henry H. Simms, *Life of Robert M. T. Hunter* (Richmond, Va., 1935); Alexander H. Stephens, *A Constitutional View of the Late War Between the States* (Philadelphia, 1870), II, 599-623. Stephen's account of how he and Lincoln reminisced about old days in Congress together is in *Ibid.*, II, 599. Lincoln's letter to Herndon about Stephens in 1848 is in *Lincoln's Collected Works*, I, 448.

For Halleck's words to Sherman about punishing Charleston, consult Sherman's report in Report of the Committee on the Conduct of the War, supplement to *Senate Report* No. 142, 38th Cong., 2nd sess., Vol. I, p. 287; Sherman's reply, December 24, 1864, in *Official Records of the Union and Confederate Armies*, Series I, Vol. 44, p. 799. For the burning of Columbia and other South Carolina towns: Senator Cole L. Blease, "Destruction of Property in Columbia, South Carolina, "By Sherman's Army," *Congressional Record*, 71st Cong., 2nd sess., pp. 8981-9026; Col. J. W. Davidson in *Southern Historical Society Papers*, VII, 190; James Ford Rhodes, "Who Burned Columbia?" *The American Historical Review*, April, 1902, pp. 485-493; *Memoirs of General William T. Sherman*, 1913 Edition, II, 228, 259, 274-276, 286, 287; Columbia (South Carolina) *Daily Phoenix*, cited in *Congressional Record*, 71st, Cong., 2nd sess., p. 8987.

Lincoln's inauguration, March 4, 1865, is folowed in Leech, *Reveille in Washington, 1860-1865*, pp. 365ff. For Andrew Johnson's condition at his Vice-Presidential inauguration: George Fort Milton, *The Age of Hate: Andrew Johnson and the Radicals* (New York, 1930), pp. 145ff; James G. Randall (ed.), *Diary of Orville Hickman Browning, 1865-1881* (Springfield, Ill., 1931), p. 9; William H. Townsend, *Lincoln and Liquor* (New York, 1934), pp. 125-127; *Journal of the American Temperance Union*, April, 1865, p. 57. Chambrun's letter to his wife about Johnson's drunkenness, and Lincoln's reaction, is in Marquis Adolphe de Chambrun, *Impressions of Lincoln and the Civil War: A Foreigner's Account*, translated by Gen. Aldebery de Chambrun (New York, 1952), pp. 36-37.

For the Bible used at Lincoln's second inauguration: Noah Brooks, *Washington in Lincoln's Time* (New York, 1895), p. 241; Chase to Mrs. Lincoln, March 4, 1865, Robert Todd Lincoln Collection, Library of Congress. Walt Whitman's description of Lincoln, returning from his second inauguration, is in Walt Whitman, *Complete Prose Works* (Boston, 1898), Small, Maynard & Company Edition, p. 57.

British reaction to Lincoln's Second Inaugural Address is in "English Opinion on the Inaugural," *Littell's Living Age*, April 15, 1865, pp. 86-88, Argyll's letter to Sumner is in *Proceedings of the Massachusetts Historical Society*, December, 1913, p. 87. Lincoln's letter to Weed about his Second Inaugural, March 15, 1865, is in Thurlow Weed Papers, University of Rochester Library. See especially Benjamin Barondess, *Three Lincoln Masterpieces: Cooper Institute Address, Gettysburg Address, Second Inaugural* (Charleston, West Va., 1954).

The Cincinnati reporter's comment on Lincoln's illness is in Cincinnati *Daily Gazette*, March 15, 1865. Greeley's comment is in Horace Greeley, *Recollections of a Busy Life* (New York, 1868), p. 407. Lincoln's remark to Mrs. Stowe about his bad health is in Allan Thorndike Rice (ed.), *Reminiscences of Abraham Lincoln By Distinguished Men of His Time* (New York, 1886), p. 251.

For personal, political, and military dissensions within the Confederacy: Clement Eaton, *A History of the Southern Confederacy* (New York, 1954), pp. 269ff; Thomas Robson Hay, "The Davis-Hood-Johnston Controversy of 1864," *The Mississippi Valley Historical Review*, June, 1924, pp. 54-84; Ella Lonn, *Desertion During the Civil War* (New York, 1928); Albert B. Moore, *Conscription and Conflict in the Confederacy* (New York, 1924); James Z. Rabun, "Alexander H. Stephens and Jefferson Davis," *The American Historical Review*, January, 1953, pp. 290-321; Georgia Lee Tatum, *Disloyalty in the Confederacy* (Chapel Hill, N.C., 1934). General Kirby-Smith's problems are detailed in Joseph H. Parks, *General Edmund Kirby-Smith* (Baton Rouge, La., 1954), Chapters 14, 15.

For Sherman's march through North Carolina: *Official Records of the Union and Confederate Armies*, Series I, Vol. 47, pp. 419ff, 549ff, 568ff. Grant's letter to his father, March 19, 1865, is in Jesse Grant Cramer (ed.), *Letters of Ulysses S. Grant To His Father and His Youngest Sister* (New York, 1912), pp. 106-107. Mrs. Lincoln's letter to Sumner, March 23, 1865, is in Charles Sumner Papers, Widener Library, Harvard University.

For the Fort Stedman battle: Douglas Southall Freeman, *Lee's Lieutenants* (New York, 1944), III, 645ff; Allan P. Tankersley, *John B. Gordon* (Atlanta, Ga., 1955), pp. 174-188; George L. Kilmer, "Gordon's Attack At Fort Stedman," and John F. Hartranft, "The Recapture of Fort Stedman," in Robert U. Johnson and Clarence C. Buel (ed.), *Battles and Leaders of the Civil War* (New York, 1888), IV, 579-589.

Lincoln's conversations with General Sherman at City Point are detailed in Lloyd Lewis, *Sherman: Fighting Prophet* (New York, 1932); Sherman's letter to Isaac N. Arnold, November 28, 1872, is in Chicago Historical Society. Lincoln's telegram to Stanton, March 30, 1865, is in *Official Records of the Union and Confederate Armies*, Series I, Vol. 46, Part III, p. 280.

For the Five Forks battle: *Official Records of the Union and Confederate Armies*, Series I, Vol. 46, Part III, pp. 394ff; Horace Porter, "Five Forks and the Pursuit of Lee," in Johnson and Buel (ed.), *Battles and Leaders of the Civil War*, IV, 708ff; William Swinton, *The Twelve Decisive Battles of the War* (New York, 1867), Chapter 12; Bruce Catton, "Sheridan At Five Forks," *The Journal of Southern History*, August, 1955, pp. 305-315; Richard O'Connor, *Sheridan the Inevitable* (Indianapolis, 1953), pp. 250ff. Lincoln's telegrams to Stanton and Seward are in *Official Records of the Union and Confederate Armies*, Series I, Vol. 46, Part III, pp. 392, 446.

The Confederate evacuation of Richmond is followed in Alfred J. Hanna, *Flight Into Oblivion* (Richmond, Va., 1938); Clifford Dowdey, *Experiment in Rebellion*

(Garden City, N.Y., 1946), pp. 401ff; Rembert W. Patrick, *Jefferson Davis and His Cabinet* (Baton Rouge, La., 1944), pp. 344ff; Stephen R. Mallory, "Last Days of the Confederate Government," *McClure's Magazine* (1900-1901), Vol. 16, pp. 99-107, 239-248; Rembert W. Patrick, *The Fall of Richmond* (Baton Rouge, La., 1960).

Grant's account of his failure to inform Lincoln about his final plans, and Lincoln's words to him at Petersburg, are in *Personal Memoirs of U. S. Grant* (New York, 1895), II, 317-318. Lincoln's telegram to Stanton, April 3, 1865, is in *Lincoln's Collected Works*, VIII, 385. Porter's description of the Negroes' reception of Lincoln at Richmond is in David D. Porter, *Incidents and Anecdotes of the Civil War* (New York, 1885), pp. 295-296. For Lincoln's Richmond visit: Richmond *Evening Whig* quoted in Washington *Daily Morning Chronicle*, April 8, 1865; Charles C. Coffin, "Lincoln's Visit to Richmond, April 4, 1865," *Moorsfield Antiquarian* (1937), I, 27-29, and also Coffin's *Four Years of Fighting* (Boston, 1866), pp. 510ff; Howard Swiggett (ed.), *A Rebel War Clerk's Diary . . . By J. B. Jones* (New York, 1935), p. 471; Gustavus A. Myers, "Abraham Lincoln in Richmond," *Virginia Magazine of History* (1933), Vol. 41, pp. 318-322.

Cornelia Hancock's letter to her sister about Lincoln is in Henrietta S. Jaquette (ed.), *South After Gettysburg* (New York, 1956), p. 179. Lincoln's telegram to Grant, ordering, "Let the *thing* be pressed," April 7, 1865, is in Chicago Historical Society. Chambrun's narrative about the return trip to Washington is in *Scribner's Magazine*, January, 1893, pp. 34ff. Mrs. Lincoln's letter to Sumner, "Monday noon," is in Sumner Papers, Widener Library, Harvard University.

For Lee's surrender: Freeman, *R. E. Lee: A Biography*, Vol. IV, Chapter 9; *Personal Memoirs of U. S. Grant* (New York, 1895), Vol. II, Chapter 25; Horace Porter, "The Surrender at Appomattox Court House," in Johnson and Buel (ed.), *Battles and Leaders of the Civil War*, IV, 729-746.

Lincoln's visit to the injured Seward is described in Francis B. Carpenter, *Six Months At the White House With Abraham Lincoln* (New York, 1867), p. 290. Lincoln's response to the serenaders on April 10 is in Washington *Daily National Intelligencer*, April 11, 1865. Lincoln's pass to Lamon, April 11, 1865, is in Huntington Library, San Marino, California. Lincoln's interview with Governor Pierpoint (sic) on Virginia reconstruction, April 10, 1865, is described in Charles H. Ambler, *Francis H. Pierpoint* (Chapel Hill, N.C., 1937), pp. 255ff. Lincoln's pardon of the Quawpaw Indian is in *Lincoln's Collected Works*, VIII, 398.

Brooks' description of Lincoln making his last speech, April 11, 1865, is in his *Washington in Lincoln's Time*, pp. 253-244. The speech is printed in *Lincoln's Collected Works*, VIII, 399-405. Booth's words to Powell (or "Paine") are quoted by Major Thomas T. Eckert (who cross-examined Payne after Lincoln's assassination), in *House Report* No. 7, 40th Cong., 1st sess., p. 674.

Chapter 39—ENTER BOOTH

Ever since 1865 it seems to have been impossible to prepare a satisfactory study of John Wilkes Booth. For during the hysterical reaction following his murder of Lincoln, hundreds of people who knew him intimately and had personal letters from him, hastily destroyed those papers, along with other mementoes of him, believing it dangerous to have any tangible evidence of association with him. Most of those men and women who knew Booth well, from his killing of the President until their own deaths years later, were usually silent about him, and rarely entered the prints concerning him, or permitted themselves to be quoted in writing. This attitude was inspired by shock at the very cruelty and outrageousness of his deed in removing Lincoln, who was at the height of his popularity immediately after Lee's surrender.

"Respectable" people in New York City, Maryland, Washington, and other centers, who had known the Booth family well, usually denied that they were acquainted with them; or knew them very slightly. The stigma associated with the name, "Booth," from April 14, 1865, onward, until the close of the century, was such that people, who had known John, died off before they got to the point of talking or writing about him. Too, his celebrated leap from the box to the stage, shouting *"Sic semper tyrannis,"* immediately after shooting Lincoln, is so famous and off-quoted, that it has nearly obscured other facts of his life.

The best modern work on Booth and his family is Stanley P. Kimmel, *The Mad Booths of Maryland* (Indianapolis, 1940), which sheds light on the Booths' mental quirks. Francis Wilson, *John Wilkes Booth; fact and fiction* (Boston, 1929) is the book of an actor, friend of the Booth family, and is understandable toward Lincoln's assassin. Asia Booth Clarke, "The Life of John Wilkes Booth," in Eleanor Farjeon (ed.), *The Unlocked Book* (New York, 1938), pp. 41-141, is the reminiscence of Booth by his sister. The most adequate contemporary account is George A. Townsend, *The Life, Crime and Capture of John Wilkes Booth* (New York, 1865). Townsend was the New York *World's* Washington correspondent and "covered" Lincoln's assassination from April 14 or 15, 1865, through the next few weeks.

A good critical brief summary of Booth's life is Ernest Sutherland Bates' sketch in *Dictionary of American Biography* (New York, 1929), II, 448-452. Personal material on Booth and his family is in Ella V. Mahoney, *Sketches of Tudor Hall and the Booth Family* (Bel Air, Maryland, 1925). See also Clara Morris, "Some Recollections of John Wilkes Booth," *McClure's Magazine,* February, 1901, pp. 299-304. Philip Van Doren Stern, *The Man Who Killed Lincoln* (New York, 1939) is a biography in semi-fiction form. A good modern short sketch of Booth is Margaret Leech, *Reveille in Washington, 1860-1865* (New York, 1941), pp. 359ff.

Izola L. Forrester (Mrs. Mann Page), *This One Mad Act: The Unknown Story of John Wilkes Booth and His Family* (Boston, 1937) attempts to show that Booth lived on for years after he killed Lincoln; that the author, Miss Forrester, is Booth's granddaughter. Miss Forrester's research and conclusions are unconvincing. There exists no genuine evidence that Booth was married or had a child, although the author insists that her grandmother married Booth at Cos Cob, Connecticut, in a wedding ceremony performed by Rev. Mr. Weaver.

For John Wilkes Booth's father: Ernest Sutherland Bates' sketch in *Dictionary of American Biography* (New York, 1929), II, 452-454; Asia Booth Clarke, *The Elder and the Younger Booth* (Boston, 1882); which is based largely upon an anonymous but generally accurate work, *The Actor: Passages in the Lives of Booth and Some of His Contemporaries* (1846); James Freeman Clarke, "My Odd Adventures With Junius Brutus Booth," *The Atlantic Monthly,* September, 1861, pp. 296-301; James E. Murdoch, *The Stage, Or, Recollections of Actors and Acting* (Philadelphia, 1880), pp. 174ff.

For Booth's theatrical career, see Townsend, *The Life, Crime and Capture of John Wilkes Booth,* pp. 21ff. Booth's handsome looks and attractiveness to women are followed in Eleanor Ruggles, *Prince of Players: Edwin Booth* (New York, 1953); Clara Morris, *Life on the Stage* (New York, 1902), Chapter 14 devoted to Booth. For Henrietta Irving's stabbing of Booth: Madison (Indiana) *Courier,* May 10, 1861. The Albany dispatch about Booth's knife accident to himself on stage is printed in Robert S. Harper, *Lincoln and the Press* (New York, 1951), p. 83. Kate Reignolds' appraisal of Booth is in Catherine M. Reignolds-Winslow, *Yesterdays With Actors* (Boston, 1886), pp. 140-142. Ford's description of Booth's "leaps" in performances and the Baltimore *Sun's* description of Booth as a "gymnastic actor" are in Kimmel, *The Mad Booths of Maryland,* p. 358. The New York *Herald's* favorable review of Booth is in George D. C. Odell, *Annals of the New York Stage, 1857-1865* (New York, 1931), VII, 416. For Lincoln in the Ford's Theatre audience before Booth playing in *The Marble Heart:* Joseph George, Jr., "The Night John Wilkes Booth Played Before Abraham Lincoln," *Lincoln Herald,* Summer, 1957, pp. 11-15.

Booth's appearances in New Orleans are criticized in New Orleans *Times,* March 19, 21, 27, 1864. Kimmel's explanation of Booth's "hoarseness" is in Kimmel, *The Mad Booths of Maryland,* p. 181. Booth's investments in western Pennsylvania oil shares and his frequent visits to that region in 1864 are followed in Ernest C. Miller, *John Wilkes Booth—Oilman* (New York, 1947) and the same author's "John Wilkes Booth in the Pennsylvania Oil Regions," *Western Pennsylvania Historical Magazine,* March–June, 1948, pp. 26-47.

Edwin Booth's letter, July 28, 1881, describing John, is in Edwina Booth Grossman, *Edwin Booth: Recollections By His Daughter* (New York, 1894), pp. 227-228. Booth's arrest for secession utterances in St. Louis is summarized in Kimmel, *The Mad Booths of Maryland,* p. 175. Booth's "To Whom It May Concern" letter, 1864, is Philadelphia *Press,* April 19, 1865, reprinted in Henry J. Raymond, *Life and Public Services of Abraham Lincoln* (New York, 1865), pp. 794-796. The opinions on Booth's motives, expressed by his classmate and Charles Warwick, are in Farjeol (ed.), *The Unlocked Book,* pp. 152, 173-174.

For Booth's plotting to kidnap, then assassinate, Lincoln, and his enlistment of accomplices, and what followed, consult: George S. Bryan, *The Great American Myth* (New York, 1940), the most accurate single volume on the assassination; David M. De Witt, *The Assassination of Abraham Lincoln and Its Expiation* (New York, 1909); Jim Bishop, *The Day Lincoln Was Shot* (New York, 1955); Kimmel, *The Mad Booths of Maryland.* Ben Perley Poore (comp.), *The Great Conspiracy Trial For the Murder of the President* (Boston, 1865-66), 3 vols., is the best reported proceedings of the trial. A shorter and officially expurgated edition of the trial proceedings is Benn Pitman (comp.), *The Assassination of President Lincoln and the Trial of the Conspirators* (Cincinnati, 1865); a recent edition of that work, excellently edited, is Philip Van Doren Stern (ed.), The *Assassination of President Lincoln . . . The Courtroom Testimony As Originally Compiled By Benn Pitman* (New York, 1954). See also Theodore Roscoe, *The Web of Conspiracy* (Englewood Cliffs, N.J., 1959).

Otto Eisenschiml, *Why Was Lincoln Murdered?* (Boston, 1937) should be used with caution. It is filled with sensational inuendoes and inferences, based on excessively circumstantial evidence, and hints that Secretary of War Stanton was involved in the assassination of Lincoln. This book has been discredited by more responsible Lincoln scholars.

Arnold, involved in the abduction (but not the murder) plot has told his story in Samuel B. Arnold, *Defense and Prison Experiences of a Lincoln Conspirator* (Hattiesburg, Mississippi, 1943). This account, in slightly different phrasing, originally appeared in Baltimore *American,* December 7-20, 1902, and simultaneously in the New York *Sun.* Arnold admits complicity in Booth's kidnapping plot, but denies that he was in the murder conspiracy. For O'Laughlin: Clara E. Laughlin, *The Death of Lincoln* (New York, 1909), pp. 4-5.

Facsimile of the St. Lawrence Hall hotel register, Montreal, Canada, with Booth's signature in it, October 18, 1864, is in Charles Brombach, *The Canadian Phase of Lincoln's Murder* (Philadelphia, 1953), MS., typewritten, in possession of Special Collections Department, Columbia University Library, New York. The New York *Herald* critic's review of the three Booth brothers in *Julius Caesar* is in Odell, *Annals of the New York Stage,* VII, 638-639.

The best book on Mrs. Surratt is Guy W. Moore, *The Case of Mrs. Surratt* (Norman, Okla., 1954). Recommended is David M. De Witt, *The Judicial Murder of Mary E. Surratt* (Baltimore, 1895). See also Helen J. Campbell, *The Case For Mrs. Surratt* (New York, 1943). John Surratt's story is told by him in a lecture at Rockville, Maryland, December 6, 1870, printed and paraphrased in Laughlin, *The Death of Lincoln,* pp. 224ff; Washington *Star,* December 8, 1870; New York *Daily Tribune,* December 8, 1870. For Atzerodt: Osborn H. Oldroyd, *The Assassination of Abraham Lincoln* (Washington, 1901), pp. 133-134. Herold's remark about Booth being a "good fellow" is in Washington *Star,* April 20, 1865.

The reasons for Powell's hatred of Lincoln, as presented by his defense counsel, W. E. Doster, are in Pitman (comp.), *The Assassination of President Lincoln . . .*, p. 311. The letter of Powell's father about his son, November 5, 1865, is in New York *World,* April 3, 1892, Part I, p. 17. The clergyman who consoled Powell (or Payne) before his hanging in 1865, Rev. David Gillette, quotes Powell in "Last Days of Paine," New York *World,* April 3, 1892, Part I, p. 17.

The story of Westfall, Capitol Police detective, of Booth at the Second Inaugural ceremonies, told later, is mentioned in Benjamin B. French to Benjamin F. Butler, July 25, 1867, in Hans L. Trefousse, "Belated Revelations of the Assassination Committee," *Lincoln Herald,* Spring-Summer, 1956, p. 14; "Lincoln's Assassination," New York *Daily Tribune,* August 28, 1876; Leech, *Reveille in Washington,* p. 368. McCullough's later account of his visit to see Booth on Inauguration Day is in Oldroyd, *The Assassination of Abraham Lincoln,* pp. 92-93. Booth's sister's reference to her brother's admiration for McCullough is from Asia Booth Clarke, "Life of John Wilkes Booth," in Farjeol (ed.), *The Unlocked Book,* p. 111. For McCullough: Susie C. Clark, *John McCullough As Man, Actor and Spirit* (Boston, 1905). Booth's boast to Samuel K. Chester about his opportunity to kill Lincoln at the Second Inauguration, if he had chose, is quoted by Chester in his testimony, May 12, 1865, in Pitman (comp.), *The Assassination of President Lincoln . . .*, p. 45. For Chester: Odell, *Annals of the New York Stage,* VII, 637ff.

John Surratt's account of the March 17, 1865, frustrated attempt to kidnap Lincoln is in his own Rockville, Maryland, lecture, reported in New York *Daily Tribune,* December 8, 1870. Arnold's quotation on that abortive abduction attempt is in Arnold, *Defense and Prison Experiences of a Lincoln Conspirator,* pp. 23-24. Arnold's letter to Booth, March 27, 1865, withdrawing from the abduction project, is in Pitman (comp.), *The Assassination of President Lincoln . . .*, p. 236. Asia Booth Clarke's comment about her brother's possible insanity dating from the fall of Richmond is in Farjeol (ed.), *The Unlocked Book,* p. 141.

The testimony of Bunker, National Hotel clerk, about Booth's arrival in Washington on April 8, 1865, is in Pitman (comp.), *The Assassination of President Lincoln . . .*, p. 46. Booth's words to Powell, after listening to Lincoln's April 11 speech, are quoted by Major Thomas T. Eckert (who cross-examined Powell after the assassination) in *House Report* No. 7, 40th Cong., 1st sess., p. 674. Hess's testimony about Booth's visit to him on April 13 is in Poore (comp.), *The Conspiracy Trial For the Murder of the President,* II, 539.

Booth's diary, deposited with the War Department, was taken from Booth's body after he died from shots fired by Sergeant Boston Corbett when he was tracked to the tobacco shed on the Garrett farm in late April, 1865. Two years later Colonel Lafayette C. Baker mentioned it in his *History of the United States Secret Service* (Philadelphia, 1867). Only then was the existence of the diary known. Baker's indiscreet mention of the diary in his book inspired the Congressional committee, impeaching President Johnson, to demand that Secretary of War Stanton produce Booth's diary. It was published in Washington *Daily Morning Chronicle,* May 22, 1867.

Chapter 40—FATEFUL FRIDAY

Lincoln's letter to Van Alen, April 14, 1865, opening this chapter, is in *Lincoln's Collected Works,* VIII, 413. Stimmel's description of Washington that day is in Smith Stimmel, "Experiences As a Member of President Lincoln's Body Guard," *The North Dakota Historical Quarterly,* January, 1927, p. 30. Announcement of Lincoln's planned attendance at Ford's Theatre is in Washington *National Republican,* April 14, 1865; Washington *Evening Star,* April 14, 1865.

Concerning Lincoln's activities on April 14, 1865: George S. Bryan, *The Great American Myth* (New York, 1940), the best book on the assassination, especially Chapter 7, "The Fourteenth of April." Highly recommended are Jim Bishop, *The Day Lincoln Was Shot* (New York, 1955); William H. Crook, "Lincoln's Last Day," *Harper's Magazine,* September, 1907, pp. 519-530; John W. Starr, Jr., *Lincoln's Last Day* (New York, 1922).

Mrs. Keckley's comments about Lincoln at breakfast with his son and what he said to Bob (probably "edited" by a "ghost" writer) are in Elizabeth Keckley, *Behind the Scenes* (New York, 1868), pp. 137-138. Lincoln's conversation with Speaker Colfax is contained in a manuscript, in Colfax's handwriting, which he declared that he prepared the following day, now in possession of the Indiana State Library, Indianapolis; a photostatic copy was furnished kindly by the Librarian of that institution, to the present author.

The descriptions of Lincoln at the April 14 Cabinet meeting by Secretary McCulloch and Attorney-General Speed are in Hugh McCulloch, *Men and Measures of Half a Century* (New York, 1888), p. 222; Speed's letter quoted in J. G. Randall and Richard N. Current, *Lincoln the President* (New York, 1955), IV, 365. For the happenings at that Cabinet meeting: *Diary of Gideon Welles* (Boston, 1909), II, 380-383; Gideon Welles, "Lincoln and Johnson," *The Galaxy,* April, 1872, pp. 525ff; Frederick W. Seward, *Seward At Washington, 1861-1872* (New York, 1891), pp. 273-276; Frederick W. Seward, *Reminiscences of a War-Time Statesman and Diplomat* (New York, 1916), pp. 254-257; David Donald (ed.), *Inside Lincoln's Cabinet: The Civil War Diaries of Salmon P. Chase* (New York, 1954), p. 268.

Lincoln's handling of patronage, his pardons, and other business on this April morning are followed in *Lincoln's Collected Works,* VIII, 410-412. Treasury Register Chittenden's comment about the crowd waiting for Lincoln outside his office is in L. E. Chittenden, *Personal Reminiscences* (New York, 1893), p. 241. The recollections of Mrs. Hess' sister, M. Helen Palmes Moss, about their conversation with Lincoln, and his showing them the lemon tree, are in "Lincoln and Wilkes Booth on the Day of the Assassination," *Century Magazine,* April, 1909, p. 951. Lincoln's description of her last ride with Lincoln on April 14 afternoon is in her letter to Carpenter, November 15, 1865, in *Hearst's International-Cosmopolitan,* February, 1930, p. 33. Mrs. Lincoln's remark about the Lincolns' future plans, come 1869, are quoted in William H. Herndon and Jesse W. Weik, *Abraham Lincoln: The True Story of a Great Life* (Boston, 1892), II, 221-222.

Booth's letter to his mother, April 14, 1865, is in New York *Daily Tribune,* May 1, 1865. Booth's movements from sunrise to noon on that day, his information about Lincoln's plans to attend Ford's Theatre, and Harry Ford's furnishing of the box, are traced in testimony of Mrs. Mary J. Anderson, Harry Ford, and James R. Ford, given during May and June, 1865, in Ben Perley Poore (comp.), *The Conspiracy Trial For the Murder of the President* (Boston, 1865-66), I, 236; II, 549; III, 12; George A. Townsend, *The Life, Crime, and Capture of John Wilkes Booth* (New York, 1865), p. 5; Henry Clay ("Harry") Ford, quoted in "The Lincoln Tragedy: Reminiscences of Harry Ford," Washington *Star,* clipped in New York *Evening Post,* July 8, 1884. The livery-stable owner Pumphrey's testimony about Booth's hire of a horse at noon is in Poore (ed.), *The Conspiracy Trial,* I, 174-175. Booth's decision to kill Lincoln, arrived at Friday morning, as told by Powell ("Paine") to Rev. Daniel Gillette in summer, 1865, in his death cell, is followed in "The Last Days of Payne," New York *World,* April 3, 1892. Part I, p. 17.

For Spangler, the scene shifter, and his own later story, consult his account in Nettie Mudd, *Life of Dr. Samuel A. Mudd* (New York, 1906), pp. 323ff. Spangler and Dr. Mudd, both convicted in the Lincoln murder conspiracy, were prison mates together in the army jail at Fort Jefferson, Dry Tortugas, Florida. A good summary of Booth's "work" at the Ford Theatre box that afternoon is Guy W. Moore, *The Case of Mrs. Surratt* (Norman, Okla., 1954), pp. 13-14. For testimony from witnesses about the mortise in the wall, the barred door following Booth's shooting of Lincoln, and other details, see Benn Pitman (comp.), *The Assassination of President Lincoln and the Trial of the Conspirators* (Cincinnati, 1865), pp. 77, 78, 82, 111, 112. Booth's first biographer, George A. Townsend, who "covered" Lincoln's murder in minute detail for the New York *World,* reported on April 17, 1865, three days after Booth's shooting of Lincoln: "Without this door [of the box] there was an eyehole bored it is presumed on the afternoon of the crime while the theatre was deserted by all save a few mechanics." See Townsend, *The Life, Crime, and Capture of John Wilkes Booth,* p. 8.

Matthews' account, in sworn testimony before the House committee impeaching President Johnson in 1867, detailing his meeting with Booth on April 14, 1865, and what followed, is in *House Report* No. 7, 40th Cong., 1st sess., p. 783. See also testimony in Washington *Evening Star,* December 7, 1881. For Booth's picking up his hired horse in late afternoon, see Pumphrey's testimony in Poore (comp.), *The Conspiracy Trial,* I, 174-175. Spangler's account of his association with Booth, between five and six o'clock, and Booth's borrowing of the horse's halter from Spangler, and their drinks together, is in Mudd, *Life of Dr. Samuel A. Mudd,* p. 325.

Lincoln's conversation with Governor Oglesby and General Haynie is recorded in Haynie's Diary, April 14, 1865, quoted in *The Century Magazine,* April, 1896, p. 654; Oglesby's statement in Ida M. Tarbell, *Life of Abraham Lincoln* (New York, 1917), II, 235. Kellogg's account of his parting with Lincoln is in Paul M. Angle (ed.), "The Recollections of William Pitt Kellogg," *The Abraham Lincoln Quarterly,* September, 1945, pp. 335-336. Dr. Henry's letter to his wife, April 19, 1865, is in Milton H. Shutes, *Lincoln and the Doctors* (New York, 1933), pp. 132-134.

For Lincoln's last visit to Stanton, and Thompson's case: Starr, *Lincoln's Last Day,* pp. 53-54; Charles A. Dana, *Lincoln and His Cabinet: A Lecture Delivered Before the New Haven Colony Historical Society* (Connecticut), *March 10, 1896* (Jamaica, N.Y., 1899), pp. 67-70; Dana and General Fry in Allan Thorndike Rice (ed.), *Reminiscences of Abraham Lincoln By Distinguished Men of His Time* (New York, 1888), pp. 375-376, 404.

Lincoln's endorsement on the order from General Augur, expressing desire for no escort, July 4, 1864, is in *Lincoln's Collected Works,* VII, 423. Seward's letter to Bigelow, July 15, 1862, is in Frederic Bancroft, *Life of William H. Seward* (New York, 1900), II, 418. Crook's account of police protection provided the President is in Margarita Spalding Gerry (ed.), *Through Five Administrations: Reminiscences of Colonel William H. Crook, Body-Guard to President Lincoln* (New York, 1910), pp. 1-2. Hay's account of Lamon protecting Lincoln is in Tyler Dennett (ed.), *Lincoln and the Civil War in the Diaries and Letters of John Hay* (New York, 1939), p. 236. For Parker, Lincoln's derelict guard: Bryan, *The Great American Myth,* pp. 165, 220-221; Stanley Kimmel, "Fatal Remissness of Lincoln's Guard Unpunished," Washington *Sunday Star,* February 9, 1936; Jack Kofoed, "The Man Who Helped Kill Lincoln," *Argosy,* February, 1959, pp. 40ff.

For Bunker's statement about Booth leaving the National Hotel at seven o'clock, see his testimony, June 26, 1867, in *Trial of John H. Surratt in the Criminal Court For the District of Columbia* (Washington, 1867), I, 329. For Booth's last conference with his accomplices: Moore, *The Case of Mrs. Surratt,* p. 15.

For identification of Judge Daly as Ashmun's "friend," calling on Lincoln, see Diary of Maria Lydig Daly, April 15, 19, 1865, in Harold E. Hammond, "A Commoner's Judge: The Life and Times of Charles Patrick Daly," MS., Ph.D. Dissertation, Columbia University, 1951, p. 212; J. G. Holland, *Life of Abraham Lincoln* (Springfield, Mass., 1866), p. 518. Lincoln's conversation with Colfax, Ashmun, and Daly is followed in MS., in Colfax's handwriting, original in Indiana State Library, Indianapolis, previously cited; Francis B. Carpenter, *Six Months At the White House With Abraham Lincoln* (New York, 1867), pp. 285-287; F. Lauriston Bullard, "Abraham Lincoln and George Ashmun," *The New England Quarterly,* 1946, p. 210. Facsimile of Lincoln's card to Ashmun is reproduced in Ida M. Tarbell, *Life of Abraham Lincoln* (New York, 1900), II, 237.

One unauthentic tale declares that Lincoln's last official act was to pardon George S. E. Vaughan, a Missouri Confederate prisoner held by the Federals. Actually Lincoln's pardon of Vaughan occurred one month before, on March 18, 1865. For an authentic account of this see John W. Starr, Jr., "Lincoln's Last Official Act," *The Missouri Historical Review,* July, 1929, pp. 628-629. The White House doorkeeper, Thomas F. Pendel, declared that Colfax and Ashmun were the last men to call on the President before he departed for the theatre. See Pendel's accounts in New York *Tribune,* Illustrated Supplement, November 16, 1902, p. 3; "What Tom Pendel Saw, April 14, 1865," in *Magazine of History* (Tarrytown, N.Y., 1927), Vol. 34, p. 17; Thomas F. Pendel, *Thirty-Six Years in the White House* (Washington, 1902), pp. 39-40.

The arrival of Lincoln at Ford's Theatre was described by the orchestra leader, Withers, years later in Washington *Daily Post,* quoted in New York *Daily Tribune,* November 30, 1896. Mrs. Du Barry's letter to her mother, April 16, 1865, is in *Journal of the Illinois State Historical Society,* September, 1946, pp. 366-367. James Suydam Knox's letter to his father, April 16, 1865, is in *The Princeton Alumni Weekly,* February 7, 1917, p. 407. For Knox's career: *General Catalogue of Princeton University, 1746-1906* (Princeton, N.J., 1908), p. 205. For Harry Hawk's "ad libbing" and Lincoln's pleasant reaction, see Townsend, *Life, Crime and Capture of John Wilkes Booth,* p. 7.

For the authorship and development of "Our American Cousin" and Whitman's opinion of it: Winston Tolles, *Tom Taylor and the Victorian Drama* (New York, 1940), pp. 173ff; Louis Untermeyer (ed.), *The Poetry and Prose of Walt Whitman* (New York, 1949), p. 878. Secretary McCulloch's comment about Lincoln's partiality for theatrical comedy is in "Ex-Secretary McCulloch Recalls Some Memoirs of the President," New York *Daily Tribune,* June 14, 1885. Dr. Taft's description of Lincoln and Mrs. Lincoln in the box is in Charles Sabin Taft, M.D., "Abraham Lincoln's Last Hours: From the Note-Book of an Army Surgeon Present At the Assassination," *The Century Magazine,* February, 1893, p. 634. Helen Truman's account, years later, is in "Actress in Ford's Theatre Tells of Lincoln Shooting," New York *World,* February 17, 1924, Editorial Section, p. 8. Crook's account of Parker's negligence is in Spalding (ed.), *Through Five Administrations: Reminiscences of Colonel William H. Crook,* pp. 72-73. Mrs. Lincoln "hanging on" to Lincoln in the box, and his reply to her, are described by Dr. Anson G. Henry (after he talked with Mrs. Lincoln) in a letter to his wife, April 19, 1865, in Shutes, *Lincoln and the Doctors,* p. 133.

For Booth's movements during the minutes before he shot Lincoln: Testimony of Buckingham and Taltavull in Poore (comp.), *The Conspiracy Trial,* I, 179, 188; testimony of "Peanut John" in Pitman (comp.), *The Assassination of President Lincoln and the Trial of the Conspirators,* p. 74; William H. Townsend, *Lincoln and Liquor* (New York, 1934), p. 144; testimony of James P. Ferguson (in the audience) in *Trial of John H. Surratt,* I, 130; George A. Townsend, *The Life, Crime and Capture of John Wilkes Booth* (New York, 1865), pp. 7-8. Captain McGowan's statement, April 14, 1865, about Booth talking to Lincoln's attendant and entering the box, is in New York *Daily Tribune,* April 17, 1865. For McGowan and Lieutenant Crawford: Francis B. Heitman, *Historical Register and Dictionary of the United States Army, 1789-1903* (Washington, 1903), I, 336, 667. For playbill of Ford's Theatre that evening, see John Creahan, *Life of Laura Keene* (Philadelphia, 1897), p. 26.

Clara Harris' statement on April 15, 1865, of Booth's shooting of Lincoln and stabbing of Rathbone, followed by his leap from the box, is in New York *Herald,* April 16, 1865. Harry Hawk's letter to his father, April 16, 1865, is in Chicago *Post* clipping, April 20, 1865, in Townsend Collection, Columbia University Library, Vol. 55, p. 404. Joseph B. Stewart's pursuit of Booth is detailed in his sworn testimony in Poore (comp.), *The Conspiracy Trial,* II, 70-72, and in *Princeton Alumni Weekly,* February 7, 1917, p. 407. Stewart's career is mentioned in his obituary in New York *Tribune,* August 8, 1882.

For published eye-witness accounts of Ford's Theatre on April 14, 1865, written years later:

Mrs. William A. Brown's account in Jesse W. Weik, "A New Story of Lincoln's Assassination: An Unpublished Record of an Eye-Witness," *The Century Magazine,* February, 1913, pp. 559-562; John E. Buckingham, *Reminiscences and Souvenirs of the Assassination of Abraham Lincoln* (Washington, 1894), Buckingham being the door man at Ford's Theatre; John Y. Cuyler, "The Assassination of Abraham Lincoln," *Magazine of History,* March, 1916, pp. 58-60, Cuyler being in the audience; William H. De Motte, "The Assassination of Abraham Lincoln," *Journal of the Illinois State Historical Society* (1927-28), Vol. 20, pp. 422-428, De Motte being in audience; William J. Ferguson, *I Saw Booth Shoot Lincoln* (Boston, 1930), Ferguson being call boy and bit player; Ferguson's accounts in *Theatre Magazine,* May, 1908, and New York *World,* February 12, 1926; Captain Oliver C. Gatch's account in E. R. Shaw, "The Assassination of Lincoln," *McClure's Magazine,* December, 1908, pp. 182ff, Gatch being in audience.

Harry Hawk's reminiscences in Osborn H. Oldroyd, *The Assassination of Abraham Lincoln* (Washington, 1901), pp. 27-28, and in Boston *Herald,* April 11, 1897, Hawk being the only actor on stage when Booth leaped; Charles A. Leale, "Lincoln's Last Hours," *Harper's Weekly,* February 13, 1909, pp. 7-10, Dr. Leale being the first physician in audience to reach Lincoln; Letter of James R. Morris (former Congressman from Ohio) to M. B. Archer, July 26, 1897, in *Ohio Archaeological and Historical Publications,* January, 1921, pp. 1-5, Morris being in audience; Thomas H. Sherman, "Saw Assassin From Box to Stage," New York *World,* February 12, 1926, Sherman (one-time secretary to James G. Blaine) being in audience; Joseph B. Stewart's reminiscences in New York *Sun,* November 3, 1878, Stewart being the only man in audience to pursue Booth.

Charles Sabin Taft, M.D., "Abraham Lincoln's Last Hours," *Century Magazine,* February, 1893, p. 635, and Taft's *Abraham Lincoln's Last Hours* (New York, 1934), Taft being one of the physicians in the audience who treated Lincoln; Mrs. Frank Wynkoop (Helen Truman, who played "Augusta Mountchessington"), "Actress in Ford's Theatre Tells of Lincoln Shooting," New York *World,* February 17, 1924; Annie F. F. Wright, "The Assassination of Abraham Lincoln," *Magazine of History,* February, 1909, pp. 113-114, Mrs. Wright being the wife of Ford's Theatre's stage manager.

Chapter 41—A NIGHT OF HORROR—AND DEATH

Rathbone's account is in his sworn affidavit, April 17, 1865, in Washington *Daily Morning Chronicle,* April 18, 1865. Sanford's letter to his friend, Edward P. Goodrich, April 15, 1865, is published as *Bulletin* No. 47, Clements Library, University of Michigan, Ann Arbor, Mich., February 12, 1946. For Sanford's career: *Alumni Catalogue of the University of Michigan* (Ann Arbor, Mich., 1923), p. 65; *Compendium and Biography of North Dakota* (Chicago, 1900), pp. 258ff. Captain McGowan's account, April 14, 1865 (11 p.m.), is in New York *Daily Tribune,* April 17, 1865.

Knox's letter to his father, April 16, 1865, is in *Princeton Alumni Weekly,* February 7, 1917, p. 407. "Peanut John" Burrough's testimony is in Benn Pitman (comp.), *The Assassination of the President and the Trial of the Conspirators* (Cincinnati, 1865), p. 74. Stewart's sworn testimony is in Ben Perley Poore (comp.), *The Conspiracy Trial For the Murder of the President* (Boston, 1865), II, 70-72; see also Stewart's testimony in *Trial of John H. Surratt* (Washington, 1867), I, 125-127. See also Albert G. Riddle, *Recollections of War Times* (New York, 1895), p. 331n; Stewart's recollections in New York *Sun,* November 3, 1878. For contemporary accounts of Booth's shooting of Lincoln, not previously cited: James P. Ferguson's testimony, May 15, 1865, in Pitman (comp.), *The Assassination of the President,* p. 76; Charles A. Sanford's letter to his sister, April 16, 1865, in Harry E. Pratt (ed.), *Concerning Mr. Lincoln* (Springfield, Ill., 1944), pp. 121-122; Julia Adelaide Shepard's letter to her father, April 16, 1865, in *The Century Magazine,* April, 1909, pp. 917-918.

Captain Oliver C. Gatch's description of the near panic in the theatre is in E. R. Shaw, "The Assassination of Lincoln," *McClure's Magazine,* December, 1908, p. 184. Laura Keene's appeal to the audience for order is mentioned in New York *Herald,* April 17, 1865. Rathbone's account of the wounded Lincoln's appearance in the box and his own unbarring of the door, May 15, 1865, is in Pitman (ed.), *The Assassination of President Lincoln,* p. 78.

For Dr. Leale's emergency treatment of Lincoln, consult Milton H. Shutes, M.D., *Lincoln and the Doctors* (New York, 1933), pp. 111-112. Dr. Leale's letter to Butler, July 21, 1867, (originally published by Hans L. Trefousse in *Lincoln Herald,* Summer–Spring, 1956, pp. 14-16), is in Benjamin F. Butler Papers (the "new" Butler Papers), Library of Congress. See especially Charles A. Leale, M.D., "Lincoln's Last Hours," *Harper's Weekly,* February 13, 1909, pp. 7-10. For Dr. Leale's subsequent career: *National Cyclopaedia of American Biography* (New York, 1892), II, 52-53; New York *Telegram,* April 14, 1928; New York *Times,* June 14, 1932.

There exists material on the other physicians aiding Leale in the box: For Dr. Taft: Charles Sabin Taft, M.D., "Abraham Lincoln's Last Hours," *The Century Magazine,* February, 1893, p. 635, and Taft's *Lincoln's Last Hours* (Chicago, 1934); David C. Mearns' references to Taft and Taft's son in *Journal of the Illinois State Historical Society,* Spring, 1959, pp. 46-47. For Dr. King: Washington *Evening Star* and Washington *Post,* both for December 15, 1914. For Dr. Gatch: *McClure's Magazine,* December, 1908, pp. 182-184.

For Kent's discovery of Booth's gun, and his testimony, see George S. Bryan, *The Great American Myth* (New York, 1940), p. 185; Pitman (comp.), *The Assassination of President Lincoln,* p. 82. For the type of gun with which Booth shot Lincoln: Stephen Van Rensselaer, *American Firearms* (Watkins Glen, N.Y., 1947), pp. 67-70; A. Merwyn Carey, *Ameican Firearms Makers* (New York, 1953), p. 28.

For the conveyance of Lincoln from the theatre to the Petersen house: Statement of Captain Oliver C. Gatch in E. R. Shaw, "The Assassination of Lincoln," *McClure's Magazine,* December, 1908, p. 184; letter of George Francis in Dorothy Hemenway Van Ark, "New Light on Lincoln's Death," *The Saturday Evening Post,* February 12, 1944, p. 82; Stanley W. McClure, *The Lincoln Museum and the House Where Lincoln Died* (National Park Service Historical Series, No. 3, U.S. Department of the Interior, Washington, 1949), pp. 11-12, 38. For Private William Clark, see his letter to his sister, Mrs. H. Estes Wright of Boston, April 19, 1865, in Osborn H. Oldroyd, *The Assassination of Abraham* (Washington, 1901), p. 37.

For the Petersen bedroom furnishings: George A. Townsend, *Life, Crime, and Capture of John Wilkes Booth* (New York, 1865), p. 11; McClure, *The Lincoln Museum and the House Where Lincoln Died,* pp. 38ff; Albert Berghaus' drawings in *Frank Leslie's Illustrated Weekly,* April 29–May 20, 1865. Clark, who rented the room from Petersen (as mentioned above) wrote his sister in the aforementioned letter: "I was engaged nearly all Sunday with one of Frank Leslie's special artists. . . . He succeeded in executing a fine sketch, which will appear in their paper." James Tanner, who was present in the Petersen house that evening, had a good opinion of the authenticity of Berghaus' drawings. See Tanner's letter, April 17, 1865, in *The Abraham Lincoln Quarterly,* December, 1942, p. 180.

Dr. Taft's remarks are in his article, "Lincoln's Last Hours," *The Century Magazine,* February, 1893, p. 635, and *Lincoln's Last Hours* (Chicago, 1934), pp. 12-13. A modern discussion of the physicians' treatment of Lincoln, written by a physician and Lincoln scholar, is Milton H. Shutes, *Lincoln and the Doctors* (New York, 1933), pp. 114-115. The report of the autopsy on Lincoln's body, printed thirty years later, is in New York *Daily Tribune,* December 17, 1893. See also Owen W. Parker, M.D., "The Assassination and Gunshot Wound of President Abraham Lincoln," *Minnesota Medicine,* February, 1948, pp. 147-149.

For Mrs. Lincoln at Lincoln's deathbed see Ruth Painter Randall, *Mary Lincoln* (Boston, 1953), p. 383. Mrs. Dixon's letter to her sister, May 1, 1865, describing her hours with Mrs. Lincoln at the Petersen house, is in *The Collector* (New York), March, 1950, pp. 49-50, and in New York *Times,* February 12, 1950. For the comments of Illinois Adjutant-General Haynie and Secretary Welles about the deathbed scenes: Haynie's Diary, quoted in *The Century Magazine,* April, 1896, p. 954; *Diary of Gideon Welles* (Boston, 1909), II, 287-288.

For Washington on the night of April 14-15, 1865: Noah Brooks, *Washington in Lincoln's Time* (New York, 1896), pp. 259-260; Smith Stimmel, "Experiences as a Member of President Lincoln's Body-Guard," *The North Dakota Historical Quarterly,* January, 1927, pp. 30ff; the Washington newspapers (*Daily Morning Chronicle, National Republican,* and *Star*), April 15, 16, 17, 1865.

Powell's attack on Seward, Seward's sons, the army nurse, and the fourth man is detailed in Frederic Bancroft, *Life of William H. Seward* (New York, 1900), II, 417; Frederick W. Seward, *Seward At Washington As Senator and Secretary of State, 1861-1872* (New York, 1891), pp. 276-277, and the same author's *Reminiscences of a War-Time Statesman and Diplomat* (New York, 1916), pp. 258-259; "The Last Days of Payne," New York *World,* April 3, 1892, Part I, p. 17; Russell F. Weigley, *Quartermaster-General of the Union Army: A Biography of M. C. Meigs* (New York, 1959), p. 322; Diary of M. C. Meigs, MS., April 14, 1865, Library of Congress. For the discovery of Powell's abandoned horse: New York *Herald,* April 15, 1865.

For Sergeant Cobb's testimony about stopping Booth and Herold at bridge, see Pitman (comp.), *The Assassination of President Lincoln,* pp. 84-85. For Dr. Mudd's treatment of Booth's leg: Bryan, *The Great American Myth,* pp. 247-250; Stanley Kimmel, *The Mad Booths of Maryland* (Indianapolis, 1940), pp. 227-230. See also Nettie Mudd, *Life of Dr. Samuel A. Mudd* (New York, 1906), pp. 30-33, the work by Mudd's daughter.

Tanner's letter to Walch, April 17, 1865, is in Howard H. Peckham, "James Tanner's Account of Lincoln's Death," *The Abraham Lincoln Quarterly,* December, 1942, pp. 176-183. Tanner's letter is also printed in *The American Historical Review,* April, 1924, pp. 514-517. Since Tanner's original letter is in shorthand, there are slight variations in the transcriptions. For Tanner's career: *Dictionary of American Biography* (New York, 1936), Vol. 18, pp. 297-298; Washington *Post,* October 3, 1927.

Welles' account of his walk before Lincoln's death is told in *Diary of Gideon Welles,* II, 287-288. Rev. Dr. Gurley is quoted about his visit to the dying Lincoln in Andrew Boyd (comp.), *A Memorial Lincoln Bibliography* (Albany, N.Y., 1870), pp. 21-22. See also David Rankin Barbee, "President Lincoln and Dr. Gurley," *The Abraham Lincoln Quarterly,* March, 1948, p. 20. The list of people at Lincoln's bedside, when he died, is in Townsend, *Life, Crime, and Capture of John Wilkes Booth,* p. 12.

The authenticity of Stanton's words, "Now he belongs to the ages," rests on substantial historical evidence: Gurley's account in Boyd (comp.), *A Memorial Lincoln Bibliography,* p. 22; John G. Nicolay and John Hay, *Abraham Lincoln: A History* (New York, 1890), X, 302; Frank A. Flowers, *Edwin McMasters Stanton* (New York, 1905), p. 28.

For contemporary "eye witness" accounts of Lincoln dying, not previously cited: "Exchange" (correspondent) in Washington *Daily National Intelligencer,* April 18, 1865; Letter of Maunsell B. Field in John Dawson Gilmary Shea, *The Lincoln Memorial: A Record of the Life, Assassination, and Obsequies of the Martyred President* (New York, 1865), p. 69; testimony of Dr. Robert King Stone May 16, 1865, in New York *Daily Tribune,* May 17, 1865.

For published "eye witness" descriptions of Lincoln dying, written in later years: Charles A. Dana, *Recollections of the Civil War* (New York, 1898), pp. 274-275; Maunsell B. Field, *Memories of Many Men and Some Women* (New York, 1875), pp. 324-325; John Hay's account in Nicolay and Hay, *Abraham Lincoln: A History,* X, 301-302; Hugh McCulloch, *Men and Measures of Half a Century* (New York, 1888), pp. 224-225;

Recollections of Secretary Stanton and Senator Sumner, spoken in 1868, in M. A. de Wolfe, *Portrait of an Independent: Moorfield Storey* (Boston, 1932), pp. 62-66; James Tanner's accounts in New York *Sun,* April 16, 1905, and *National Republic,* August, 1926; Brig.-Gen. Thomas M. Vincent, "Abraham Lincoln and Edwin M. Stanton: An Address . . . April 25, 1889," *Magazine of History* (1917), Extra No. 61, p. 27.

Chapter 42—TO THE AGES

Dr. Stone's testimony about the removal of Booth's bullet from Lincoln's body, May 16, 1865, is in Benn Pitman (comp.), *The Assassination of President Lincoln and the Trial of the Conspirators* (Cincinnati, 1865), p. 82. For Cattell's embalming of Lincoln: John Gilmary Shea, *The Lincoln Memorial* (New York, 1865), p. 111; Report of Lincoln's autopsy by the U.S. Surgeon, April, 1865, in New York *Daily Tribune,* December 17, 1893, Part II, p. 17. For Stanton's funeral train itinerary: R. Gerald McMurtry, "And So They Buried Lincoln," *Lincoln Lore,* May, 1958, p. 2. Dr. Henry's letter to his wife, April 19, 1865, is in Milton H. Shutes, *Lincoln and the Doctors* (New York, 1933), pp. 132-133. Edgar Welles' letter is in Ruth Painter Randall, *Mary Lincoln* (Boston, 1953), p. 385. Noah Brooks' letter to Rev. Isaac P. Langworthy, May 10, 1865, is printed in booklet, *The Character and Religion of President Lincoln,* with forward by Hugh McLellan, p. 10.

Mourning in Washington is described in Margaret Leech, *Reveille in Washington, 1860-1865* (New York, 1941), pp. 401-402. Private Clark's letter to his sister, April 19, 1865, is in Osborn H. Oldroyd, *The Assassination of Abraham Lincoln* (Washington, 1901), pp. 37-38. For collecting of Lincoln's hair by Dr. Taft, its sale by Taft's son to John Hay, Hay's gift of it to Roosevelt, and Roosevelt's use of it at his inaugural, in 1905: David C. Mearns, "Exquisite Collector, or The Scalping of Abraham Lincoln," *Journal of the Illinois State Historical Society,* Spring, 1959, pp. 45-51; Roosevelt to George O. Trevelyan, March 9, 1905, in Elting E. Morison (ed.), *The Letters of Theodore Roosevelt* (Cambridge, Mass., 1951), IV, 1133. For Dr. King's gift of hair to Brig.-Gen. George D. Wise, see E. R. Hoar to Charles Francis Adams, January 5, 1895, in *Proceedings of the Massaachusetts Historical Society,* January, 1895, p. 268. For a gift of rail, allegedly split by Lincoln, see *Ibid.,* April, 1897, p. 333.

John Alexander's mourning decoration of the East Room is described in William T. Coggeshall, *The Journeys of Abraham Lincoln* (Columbus, Ohio, 1865), pp. 110-111. The bill of Alexander, the undertaker, cost of casket, and bills for other funeral arrangements and services, paid out of the fund of the U.S. Commissioner of Buildings, are listed in Leech, *Reveille in Washington,* Appendix, pp. 422-423. Townsend's description of Lincoln in the coffin, April 19, 1865, is in George A. Townsend, *Life, Crime, and Capture of John Wilkes Booth* (New York, 1865), p. 14. Sanford's letter to his friend, April 18, 1865, was published as *Bulletin* No. 47, Clements Library, University of Michigan, February 12, 1946.

There exists abundant material on the capture, trials, and fates of Booth's accomplices and Mrs. Surratt, much of it controversial. For Powell ("Payne") and Atzerodt: William E. Doster, *Lincoln and Episodes of the Civil War* (New York, 1915), an account by the defense counsel for Powell and Atzerodt; "Last Days of Paine," New York *World,* April 3, 1892. Samuel B. Arnold, *Defence and Prison Experiences of a Lincoln Conspirator* (Hattiesburg, Mississippi, 1943), is the story by Booth's accomplice in the kidnapping plot and his classmate. Arnold admits being involved in the kidnapping attempt but not in the murder. There is no adequate study of Dr. Mudd. Nettie Mudd, *Life of Dr. Samuel Mudd* (New York, 1906) is an account by Dr. Mudd's daughter.

For Mrs. Surratt: Guy W. Moore, *The Case of Mrs. Surratt* (Norman, Okla., 1954), the standard scholarly account; Helen J. Campbell, *The Case For Mrs. Surratt* (New York, 1943); David M. DeWitt, *The Judicial Murder of Mary E. Surratt* (Baltimore,

1895). All three studies are favorable to Mrs. Surratt. For John Surratt: Alfred Isaacson, O. Carm., "John Surratt and the Assassination Plot," *Maryland Historical Magazine,* December, 1957, pp. 316-342. For disagreement between Father Isaacson and Mr. Eisenschiml, see their remarks addressed to each other in "The Final Two Chapters in the Surratt Controversy," *Journal of the Illinois State Historical Society,* Summer, 1959, pp. 279-290.

For the proceedings and events of the conspirators' and Mrs. Surratt's trials in 1865 and that of John Surratt in 1867: John A. Bingham, *Trial of the Conspirators . . . Argument of John A. Bingham, Special Judge Advocate . . . June 27 and June 28, 1865* (Washington, 1865); Henry L. Burnett, *Some Incidents in the Trial of President Lincoln's Assassins* (New York, 1891), which treats the controversy between President Johnson and Judge Advocate General Joseph Holt; John W. Curran, "The Lincoln Conspiracy Trial and Military Jurisdiction Over Civilians," *Notre Dame Lawyer* (University of Notre Dame, South Bend, Indiana), November, 1933, pp. 26-49; Thomas Ewing, "Thomas Ewing, 1829-1896, in the Lincoln Conspiracy Trials" (binder's title), comprising pamphlets, mounted clippings, copies of letters, and other material, presented to the Columbia University Libraries, New York, by Mr. Thomas Ewing, III, February 12, 1935; Edwards Pierrepont, *Argument of Hon. Edwards Pierrepont to the Jury in the Trial of John H. Surratt* (Washington, 1867); Pitman (comp.), *The Assassination of President Lincoln and Trial of the Conspirators;* Ben Perley Poore (comp.), *The Great Conspiracy Trial For the Murder of the President* (Boston, 1865-66), 3 vols.; *Trial of John H. Surratt in the Criminal Court For the District of Columbia* (Washington, 1867), 2 vols.; Judge R. A. Watts, "The Trial and Execution of the Lincoln Conspirators," *Michigan History* (1922), VI, 81-110. For the hanging of Powell, Atzerodt, Herold, and Mrs. Surratt, see John A. Gray, "Fate of the Lincoln Conspirators: The Account of the Hanging, Given By Lieutenant-Colonel Christian Rath," *McClure's Magazine* (1911), Vol. 37, pp. 626-636.

For Lincoln's White House funeral, April 19, 1865: Benjamin Franklin Morris, *Memorial Record of the Nation's Tribute to Abraham Lincoln* (Washington, 1865), p. 113-119; *Harper's Weekly,* May 6, 1865, p. 278; Shea, *The Lincoln Memorial;* Allan Nevins and Milton Halsey Thomas (ed.), *Diary of George Templeton Strong* (New York, 1952), III, 590. Selden Connor's letters to his sister and father, April 18, 19, 1865, are in Lincoln Collection, Brown University Library, Providence, R.I.

Booth's diary, April 21, 1865, is quoted in Oldroyd, *The Assassination of Abraham Lincoln,* pp. 93-94. Material on the pursuit of Booth and Herold, the shooting of Booth by Boston Corbett, and Booth's burial, is voluminous. Among the better accounts are the following: Testimony of Lieutenant Luther Baker in *Trial of John H. Surratt,* I, 320; Ray Stannard Baker, "The Capture, Death and Burial of J. Wilkes Booth," *McClure's Magazine,* May, 1897, pp. 574-585; Mrs. Belmont Billingsley, "The Man Who Avenged Lincoln," *Civil War Times,* February, 1960, p. 12, which is concerned with Boston Corbett; George S. Bryan, *The Great American Myth* (New York, 1940), pp. 249ff, 259ff; Captain R. S. Collum, U.S.M.C., "The Story of a Crime," *The United Service,* February, 1889, pp. 157-161; Lieut.-Col. Everton J. Conger's story, told half a century later, is the subject of William L. Reuter, *The King Can Do No Wrong* (New York, 1958); Boston Corbett's testimony, May 17, 1865, in New York *Herald,* May 18, 1865; Lieutenant Edward P. Doherty's narrative in *The Century Magazine,* January, 1890, pp. 446-449; G. H. Garrett, "The True Story of the Capture of John Wilkes Booth," *The Confederate Veteran,* April, 1921; Thomas A. Jones, *J. Wilkes Booth: An Account of His Sojourn in Southern Maryland After the Assassination of Abraham Lincoln* (Chicago, 1893); Stanley Kimmel, *The Mad Booths of Maryland* (Indianapolis, 1940), Chapters 3-6.

Also Nettie Mudd, *The Life of Dr. Samuel A. Mudd* (New York, 1906); Dr. Richard Mudd, "Aspects of the Assassination of Lincoln," *Records of the Columbia Historical Society* (Washington, D.C., 1948-50), Vol. 50, p. 365; Seaton Munroe, "Recollections of Lincoln's Assassination," *The North American Review,* April, 1896, pp. 424-434;

Charles O. Paullin, "The Navy and the Booth Conspirators," *Journal of the Illinois State Historical Society,* September, 1940, pp. 269-277; Philadelphia *Press,* December 15, 1881: "Booth's Capture;" Philadelphia *Press* (Sunday), April 12, 1896, Part III, pp. 29-30: "In the Track of John Wilkes Booth;" Dr. George L. Porter, "How Booth's Body Was Hidden," *Magazine of History,* Vol. 38, Extra No. 149, pp. 19-35; William Tindall, "Booth's Escape From Washington," *Records of the Columbia Historical Society* (Washington, D.C., 1915), Vol. 18, pp. 1-15; George A. Townsend, "How Booth Crossed the Potomac," *The Century Magazine,* April, 1884, pp. 822-832.

For the identification of the man shot by Boston Corbett as Booth see John F. May, "The Mark of the Scalpel," *Columbia Historical Society Records* (Washington, D.C., 1910), Vol. 13, pp. 51-87. May, a leading Washington physician who had operated upon Booth's neck the previous year, identified the body as that of Booth. May gave his lecture on this point at Washington on January 10, 1887. One dentist identified Booth by the filling in his teeth. See Ella V. Mahoney, *Sketches of Tudor Hall and the Booth Family* (Bel Air, Md., 1925), p. 48. See especially William G. Shepherd, "Shattering the Myth of John Wilkes Booth's Escape," *Harper's Magazine,* November, 1924, pp. 702-719.

Finis L. Bates, *The Escape and Suicide of John Wilkes Booth, or The First True Account of Lincoln's Assassination* (Boston, 1907) presents as sober fact the completely discredited tale that Booth lived years after he killed Lincoln. This book gives the false impression that the embalmed corpse of "John St. Helen," exhibited for admission fees at circuses and carnival side-shows actually was that of Booth. A Chicago woman later bought this corpse for $8,000. For Bates and his mummy of "Booth," see *Time,* December 28, 1931, p. 10; "'Booth Mummy' Is Forbidden To Play Broadway," New York *Herald-Tribune,* December 18, 1931. An equally unreliable book is W. P. Campbell, *The Escape and Wanderings of J. Wilkes Booth Until Ending The Trail By Suicide in Oklahoma* (Oklahoma City, Okla., circa 1922).

General Townsend's quotation about Lincoln's funeral cortege is in E. D. Townsend, *Anecdotes of the Civil War* (New York, 1884), pp. 220-221. For contemporary accounts of the funeral train, and events from Washington to Springfield: Isaac N. Arnold, *History of Abraham Lincoln and the Overthrow of Slavery* (Chicago, 1866), 668-672; Coggeshall, *The Journeys of Abraham Lincoln,* pp. 136-290; Phoebe A. Hanaford, *Abraham Lincoln: His Life and Public Services* (Boston, 1865), pp. 209-213; Benjamin Franklin Morris (comp.), *Memorial Record of the Nation's Tribute to Abraham Lincoln* (Washington, 1865); John C. Power, *Abraham Lincoln: The Great Funeral Cortege* (Springfield, Ill., 1872); John Gilmary Shea, *The Lincoln Memorial* (New York, 1865), pp. 163-222; (David B. Williamson), *Illustrated Life, Services, Martyrdom, and Funeral of Abraham Lincoln* (Philadelphia, 1865). Pictures of Lincoln's funeral and the mourning scenes in Springfield are in *The Abraham Lincoln Quarterly,* March, 1941, between pages 272 and 273.

For the controversy over the Mather grounds as the site of Lincoln's burial place and the decision to inter Lincoln in Oak Ridge Cemetery, see Ruth Painter Randall, *Mary Lincoln* (Boston, 1953), pp. 219-220. Bromwell's letter to his parents, April 30, 1865, is in Henry H. P. Bromwell Papers, Library of Congress.

For Lincoln's funeral and burial in Springfield: Paul M. Angle, *"Here I Have Lived:" A History of Lincoln's Springfield* (Springfield, Ill., 1935), pp. 290-292; Edmond Beall, "Recollections of the Assassination and Funeral of Abraham Lincoln," *Journal of the Illinois State Historical Society,* January, 1913, pp. 488-492; Robert D. Clark, *Life of Matthew Simpson* (New York, 1956), pp. 247-248; Walter H. Hebert, *Fighting Joe Hooker* (Indianapolis, 1944), p. 292; Edward L. Merritt, "Recollections of the Part Springfield Bore in the Obsequies of Abraham Lincoln," *Transactions of the Illinois State Historical Society,* 1909, pp. 179-183; New York *Herald,* May 5, 1865, correspondence from Springfield; W. W. Sweet, "Bishop Simpson and the Funeral of Abraham Lincoln," *Journal of the Illinois State Historical Society,* April, 1914, pp. 62-71; Louis A. Warren, "Lincoln's Funeral March," *Lincoln Lore,* March 2, 1931.

Index

Abbott, Dr. E. W., 649
Abell, Mrs. Bennett, 82
Abolition, of slavery, Lincoln favors in 1864-65, 570ff, 587-588
Abraham Lincoln v. The Illinois Central Railroad, case of, 160
Adams, Charles Francis, 241, 248, 520
Adams, Charles Francis, Jr., Colonel, 600
Adams, Christopher, 395
Adams, Green, Congressman, 404
Adams, James, General, 61-63
Adams, John, President, 520
Adams, John Quincy, President, 184, 483, 530
Agnew, David, Pennsylvania Chief Justice, 455
Alexander II, Tsar of Russia, 312, 466
Alexander, John, 664
Allen, Charles, 166-168
Allen, Cyrus, M., 212
Allen, Dr. John, 27, 32
Allen, Robert, 43
Allen, Robert, Brigadier-General, 396
"Almanac" murder case, see Armstrong, William ("Duff")
Ambos v. Barrett et al, case of, 152
Ambos, Charles, 152-153
Amnesty, Lincoln's Proclamation of, in 1863, 488
Anconia, Sydenham E., Congressman, 404
Anderson, Joseph, 61-62
Anderson, Mary, 61-62
Anderson, Mrs. Mary J., 626
Anderson, Richard, 61-63
Anderson, Robert, Major, and later Major-General, 28, 268, 269, 273, 273-274, 274, 275, 277, 496-497, 620
Andrew, John A., Governor, 248, 279-280, 456
Andrews, Rufus F., 537, 538, 658

Antietam, Battle of, 331, 346, 348, 367, 438, 603
Appomattox Court House, Lee's surrender at, 582, 602-604
Aquia Creek, Virginia, McClellan's retreat to, 327
Archer, William B., Congressman, 184
Argyll, Duchess, 388
Argyll, Duke of, 592
Armstrong, Mrs. Hannah, 34, 166
Armstrong, Jack, 21-22, 165
Armstrong, William ("Duff"), 165-168
Arnold, Isaac N., 119, 136, 148, 158, 171, 391, 434, 540
Arnold, Samuel Bland, 612, 615, 616-617, 617, 618, 666
Arthur, Chester A., President, 422, 554
Ashley, James M., Congressman, 572, 573
Ashmore, Gideon M., 74
Ashmun, George, Congressman, 103, 221, 221-222, 278, 632-633
Atkinson, Henry, Major-General, 26, 29
Atzerodt, George E., 614, 615, 617, 618, 626, 628, 629, 632, 665, 666
Augur, Christopher C., Major-General, 630, 638, 661
Avord, James H., 624

Babcock, James F., 210, 211-212, 508
Baddeley, John W., 76
Bailey v. Cromwell, case of; 75
Bailhache, Dr. Preston H., 118, 141
Bailhache, Mrs. William L., 119, 122
Baird, Absalom, Major-General, 463
Baker, Edward D., 48, 55, 69, 87-88, 98-100, 102, 108, 133, 188, 261, 411, 497
Baker, Edward L. (of *Illinois State Journal*), 237
Baker, Luther, Lieutenant, 670, 671
Baldwin, John B., 273
Ball's Bluff, Battle of, and effects, 302ff, 307ff, 338, 348
Bancroft, George, 388, 396
Banks, Nathaniel P., Major-General, 248, 258, 292, 319, 323, 325, 328, 339, 345, 354, 436, 447, 448, 453, 468, 477, 498, 499, 502, 516, 595. See also Red River, campaign of
Barnes, Dr. Joseph K. U.S. Surgeon-General, 649, 650, 651, 659, 660
Barnum, P. T., 392
Barney, Hiram, Collector, 516, 518, 537, 538
Barrett v. The Alton & Sangamon Railroad Company, case of, 150
Barrett, James A., 152-153
Barrett, Joseph H., 7, 225
Barrett, Richard F., 54
Barton, William E. Reverend, 79, 165
Bartlett, T. H., 142
Bates, Edward, Judge, 208, 212, 215, 217, 218, 241, 244, 249, 257, 259; as Attorney-General under Lincoln, 266, 288, 359, 373, 404, 472-473, 486, 493, 511, 550, 555, 672
Beauregard, P. G. T., Lieutenant-General, 268, 274-275, 275, 290, 293, 501, 559, 562, 594
Beaver v. Taylor and Gilbert, case of, 153
Beck, Mrs. Sarah, 132
Beckwith, Calvin, 404
Bedell, Grace, 252
Beecher, Edward, Reverend, 70
Beecher, Henry Ward, Reverend, 209, 210
Bell, John, Senator, 227, 230, 231, 233, 234, 235, 238
Bellamy, Flavius J., Private, 385
Bellows, Henry W., 387
Belmont, August, 229, 235, 474
Benjamin, Charles, 426
Benjamin, Judah P., 468-469
Bennett, James Gordon, 496, 540
Benton, Thomas Hart, Senator, 52, 192, 295, 673
Bergen, Abram, 166
Bergner, George, Postmaster, 509, 510
Bermuda Hundred, Butler "bottled up" in, 501, 503
Berry & Lincoln, New Salem store, see Berry, William F.
Berry, William F., 30-32, 122, 126, 198
Berry, Richard, Jr., 3
Bertinatti, Chevalier, 287
Best, John, 655, 670
Bigelow, John, 288, 383, 631
Bingham, John A., Former Congressman, 510
Bissell, William H., Governor, 150-151, 183
Bixby letter, see Bixby, Mrs. Lydia
Bixby, Mrs. Lydia, 402
Black Hawk, see Black Hawk War
Black Hawk War, 25-29, 104, 105
Blaine, James G., Congressman, 350, 573
Blair family, see Blair, Francis P., Sr.; Blair, Francis P., Jr. (Frank); and Blair, Montgomery
Blair, Austin, Governor, 280
Blair, Francis P., Sr., 241, 258, 268, 283, 297-298, 541, 550-551, 587
Blair, Francis P., Jr. (Frank), 241, 248, 258, 296-298, 373, 528, 541
Blair, Montgomery, 241, 248, 249, 257, 258, 259, 267, 268-270; as Postmaster General

Blair, Montgomery (*Cont.*)
under Lincoln, 283, 296-298, 299, 301, 329, 372-373, 374, 472-473, 489, 510, 513, 517, 519-520, 521, 528, 529, 540-543; as Former Postmaster General, 550, 551, 551-555, 623
Blakely, A. J., 253
Blakey, George D., 511
Blatchford, Richard M., 229
Bledsoe, Albert T., 72, 98, 111, 113, 133
Bledsoe, Sophie, 133
Blenker, Louis, Major-General, 320-322, 339
Blow, Henry T., Congressman, 374, 446
Bogue, Vincent, "Captain," 25
Bonheur, Rosa, 649
Boone, Daniel, 1
Booth, Edwin, 392, 419, 607, 608, 609, 611, 613
Booth, John Wilkes, assassin of Lincoln, 175, 392-393, 423, 487, 555, 605, 606-618, 624, 625-629, 632, 636-641, 642-647, 652, 653-655, 665-666, 669-671
Booth, Junius Brutus, Sr., 606, 607, 609, 627
Booth, Mrs. Junius Brutus, Sr., 625
Booth, Junius Brutus, Jr., 607, 613
Borrett, George Tuthill, 391, 407
Bouligny, John E., Former Congressman, 475-476
Boutwell, George S., Governor and Internal Revenue Commissioner, 456, 511, 551
Bradford, Augustus W., Governor, 428
Bragg, Braxton, Lieutenant-General, 351, 352, 368, 369, 435, 448, 449, 450, 452, 453, 454, 460, 461-463, 468, 469, 474, 594
Brannigan, Felix, Sergeant, 408
Breckinridge, John C., Vice-President of U.S., presidential candidate, 226, 230, 230-231, 232, 233-234, 234, 235, 238-239, 377; as Confederate General, 501, 503, 595
Bridges, Eloise, 113
Briggs, James A., 209, 210
Bromwell, Henry P. H., 674
Brooks, Noah, 365, 379, 381, 387, 417, 453, 529, 604, 605, 662
Brooks, Preston, Congressman, 182
Brough, John, Governor, 445, 454, 518
Brown & Alexander, undertakers, 661. See Alexander, John
Brown, B. Gratz, 373-374
Brown, Cassius, 72
Brown, George W., Mayor, 281, 282
Brown, John, abolitionist, 128, 182, 210, 336, 563
Brown, Joseph E., Governor, 443, 469, 535, 536, 594
Browne, Charles Farrar, 394
Browne, Thomas C., Justice, 96
Brownell, Private, 411
Browning, Eliza (Mrs. Orville H.), 84, 84-85
Browning, Orville H., 48, 84, 126, 152, 183, 249, 259, 260, 283, 289, 300-301, 316, 331, 335, 359, 361, 362, 412, 414, 415, 472, 524
Brummer, Dr. Sidney D., 538
Bryant, Anthony, 74
Bryant, Jane, 74, 75
Bryant, John H., Collector, 510
Bryant, William Cullen, 209, 210, 249, 481, 517
Buchanan, James, President, 118, 138, 186, 187, 188, 189, 191, 192, 193, 196, 206, 216, 225-226, 234, 235, 238, 239, 241, 260-261, 264, 267, 313
Buckingham, J. H., 101, 124
Buckingham, John E., 637
Buckingham, William A., Governor, 280
Buckner, Simon, Major-General, 461
Buell, Don C., Major-General, 309-310, 311, 313, 347, 348, 351-353, 355, 497
Bull, David, 524
Bull Run, First Battle of, 289-293, 348
Bull Run, Second Battle of, 327-328, 346, 348, 367, 603
Bunker, G. W., 618, 632
Bunn, John W., 123
Burgdorf, servant of Lincoln, 464
Burke, Francis, coachman of Lincoln, 634
Burnham, J. H., 220
Burns, Robert, 112, 391, 392
Burnside, Ambrose E., Major-General, 333, 355-358, 364-366, 366, 367, 375-376, 378, 445, 449-450, 464, 468, 483, 484, 497, 499. See also Fredericksburg, Battle of
Burroughs, Joseph ("Peanut John"), 628, 637, 644
Busey, Dr. Samuel C., 104, 134
Bush, R. Y., 387
Bush, Sarah (Sally), see Lincoln, Mrs. Sarah Bush Johnston, stepmother of Lincoln
Butler, Evarts, and Southmayd, law firm of, 157-158
Butler, Benjamin F., Major-General, 292, 314, 353-354, 475, 477, 478, 487, 495, 495-496, 496, 499, 500, 501, 502, 503, 504, 507, 512, 549, 565-567, 587, 594; as Congressman, 647, 659
Butler, Speed, 96
Butler, William (of Springfield), 48, 91, 92
Butler, Mrs. William (of Springfield), 48, 91, 92

Butler, William (of Chicago), State Treasurer, 217
Butterfield, Daniel, Major-General, 381
Butterfield, Justin, 108-109
Byron, George Gordon Byron, 6th Baron, 112

Caesar, Julius, 122
Calhoun, John (of Sangamon County), 33, 54
Calhoun, John C., Senator, 192, 225
Cameron, Simon, Senator, 207, 209-210, 217, 218, 244, 246-248, 249, 253-254, 258, 259; as Secretary of War under Lincoln, 273-274, 285, 311-312, 313, 338; as U.S. Minister to Russia, 349; as Secretary of War under Lincoln, 386, 404; as Pennsylvania politician, 444, 445; as Minister to Russia, 465; as Senator again, 496, 508, 509, 531, 538, 547, 551
Campbell, Alexander, Mayor, 185
Campbell, John A., Confederate Assistant Secretary of War, 580-582, 588, 601
Camron, John M., Reverend, 19
Canby, Edward R. S., Major-General, 579, 580
Canisius, Dr. Theodore, 205
Canning, Matthew, 607
Cannon, Colonel, 417
Capps, Ebenezer, 45, 46
Carlin, Thomas, Governor, 51
Carman, Caleb, 18
Carpenter, Francis B., artist, 22, 23, 345, 390, 500, 625
Cartwright, Peter, Reverend, 100-101, 169
Caspari, James, 104
Cass, Lewis, Senator, 105, 106, 221
Catron, John, U.S. Supreme Court Justice, 189
Cattell, Harry P., embalmer of Lincoln, 661
Cedar Creek, Battle of, 544
Chambrun, Adolphe, Marquis de, 391, 591, 602
Chancellorsville, Battle of, 380-381, 424-426, 497, 528, 594, 603
Chandler, William E., 508, 554
Chandler, Zachariah, Senator, 305-306, 307, 320, 404, 456, 520, 541-543, 570
Chapman, Augustus H., 143
Chapman, Harriett Hanks, 142
Charnwood, Godfrey Rathbone Benson, 1st Baron, 252
Charleston, South Carolina, Federal failure at, in 1863, 371-372
Chase, Salmon P., lawyer, 146; as Governor of Ohio, 206, 207, 208, 209, 217, 218, 241, 243, 246, 247, 249, 257, 258, 259; as Secretary of Treasury under Lincoln, 266, 268, 310, 322, 329, 340, 345, 359-361, 395, 444, 480, 482, 493-494, 496, 507, 508, 510, 511, 512, 516, 517-519, 524; as Former Secretary of Treasury, 537, 541, 550; as U.S. Supreme Court Chief Justice, 551, 552, 582-583, 584, 590, 591-592, 675
Chase, Salmon P. (*Cont.*)
Chattanooga-Lookout Mountain—Missionary Ridge, Battle of, 462-463, 468, 474, 488, 497
Cheatham, Frank, Major-General, 461
Chesnut, James, Jr., Colonel, 274-275
Chester, Samuel K., 616
Chickamauga, Battle of, 366, 413, 414, 474, 594
Chiriquí, Colombia, Negro colonization project in, 344
Chisolm, Alexander R., Captain, 275
Chittenden, Lucius E., Register of Treasury, 624
Choate, Rufus, 157
City Point, Virginia, Lincoln at, in March-April, 1865, 596ff
Clark, John B., Senator, 550
Clark, William T., Private, 648-649, 657, 663
Clarke, Mrs. Asia Booth (Mrs. John Sleeper Clarke), 611, 616, 617-618
Clarke, John Sleeper, 611, 612
Clary, John, 21
Clay, C. C., Jr., Senator, 526-527
Clay, Cassius M., 312, 312-313, 465, 467
Clay, Henry, Senator, 24, 30, 32, 37, 38, 39-40, 42, 52, 70, 86, 98, 102, 105, 114, 121, 127, 132, 134, 174-175, 183, 195, 199, 207, 216, 218, 231, 234, 335, 342, 472, 569, 572
Clayton, John M., Secretary of State, 109
Cline, Cornelius, 65-66
Close, George, 15
Cobb, Howell, Congressman, 199
Cobb, Silas T., Sergeant, 654
Cobb, T. R. R., Major-General, 357
Cochrane, John, Brigadier-General, 504
Codding, Ichabod, 177, 178
"Colchester," Spiritualist medium, 413
Cold Harbor, Battle of, 500, 516, 521, 524, 594, 603
Cole, Cornelius, Congressman, 573
Coleman, Helen, 636, 639
Colfax, Schuyler, Congressman, 205, 219, 245, 359, 361; as Speaker of Congress, 621, 623, 632-633
Collamer, Jacob, Senator, 210
Colyer, Vincent, 483
Committee on Conduct of the War, 307ff, 315, 316, 318, 318-319, 320, 325, 338, 339, 354, 489. See also "Jacobins"

Conant, Alban J., 61
Conger, Everton J., Lieutenant-Colonel, 670, 671
Conkling, James C., 86-87, 91, 422
Conkling, Mrs. Mercy Levering, 422-423. See also Levering, Mercy
Conkling, Roscoe, Congressman, 307
Conner, Alexander H., 245
Conner, T. L., 611
Connor, Selden, Colonel, 668
Constable, Charles H., 75
Constitutional Union Party, in 1860, 227, 230, 234
Cook, Burton C., 217, 510
Cooke, John R., Major-General, 357
Coombs, Leslie, 464
Cooper Institute address, 209-211, 244, 336
"Copperheads," 341, 350, 374-377, 454, 455, 456, 482, 525, 532-533, 537, 544, 545, 546, 548
Corbett, Boston, Sergeant, killer of Booth, 670, 670-671, 671
Corbin, Mary, 74
Corinth, Battle of, 370
Cornell, Ezra, 260
Corwin, Tom, 533
Couch, Darius N., Major-General, 358, 425, 438-439
Covode, John, Congressman, 307
Cowles, Edwin, 267
Cox, Samuel S. ("Sunset"), Congressman, 572, 575
Crafton, Greek, 169
Crane, Colonel, Assistant Surgeon-General, 659
Crawford, A. M. S., Lieutenant, 638
Crawford, Andrew, 10
Crawford, Mrs. Elizabeth, 14
Creswell, John A. J., Congressman, 530; as Senator, 624
Crittenden Compromise, 242
Crittenden, John J., Senator, 242
Crittenden, Thomas L., Major-General, 449
Crook, William H., 631, 636
Cullom, Shelby M., 169; as Congressman, 556-557
Curtin, Andrew G., Pennsylvania gubernatorial candidate, 218; as Governor, 246, 247, 253, 258, 349, 428, 444, 445, 454, 456
Curtis, Dr., physician, 660
Curtis, Benjamin R., U.S. Supreme Court Justice, 189
Curtis, George Ticknor, 576
Curtis, Samuel R., Major-General, 313, 374, 446
Cuthbert, Mary Ann, 417
Cutts, James Madison, Jr., Captain, 395
Dahlgren, John A., Captain, U.S.N., 370; as Rear Admiral, 481
Daly, Charles P., Judge, 632-633
Dana, Charles A., Assistant Secretary of War, 386, 506, 630, 651, 657
Davenport, A., Private, 409
Davis, David, Judge, 81, 98, 116, 122, 123, 126, 136, 146, 154-156, 172, 212, 212-213, 213, 214, 216-217, 217, 218, 221, 229, 229-230, 230, 244-246, 248, 257, 258, 335, 361, 362, 387, 393, 452, 472, 553, 556, 586, 590, 667
Davis, Garrett, 299; as Senator, 341
Davis, Henry Winter, Congressman, 248, 257, 258, 372-373, 488-490, 519-521, 529-530, 533, 540, 542, 551, 551-555, 582-583, 623. See also Wade-Davis Manifesto; Wade-Davis reconstruction bill
Davis, Jefferson, Senator, 199, 232, 234; as Confederate President, 280, 289, 299, 435, 443, 462, 468-469, 469, 484, 526, 531, 534-535, 535, 536, 559, 587, 587-588, 593-594, 596, 599, 601, 613
Davis, Levi, 42
Dawson, George, Postmaster, 509
Dawson v. Ennis and Ennis, case of, 171-172
Dawson, John, 44, 46, 55
Dayton, William L., 184
De Bar, Ben, 611
Defrees, John D., 231, 510, 512
Delahay, Mark, 125, 211
Delahay, Mary, 125
Delny, Thomas, see *People v. Thomas Delny,* case of
Deming, Henry C., Congressman, 385, 391-392, 399
Democratic Party, split in, 191ff, 225-226, 232-233, 233-234, 238-239
Denison, George S., Collector, 493
Dennison, William, Governor, 280; as Former Governor, 510, 512; as Postmaster General under Lincoln, 543, 622
Denton, George, 72-73
Denton, James, 72-73
Deringer, Henry, Jr., gun-maker, 648
Dickerson, Edward M., 161
Dickinson, Daniel S., Former Senator, 513
Dickson, W. M., 162
Dill, John, 12
Dill, Lin, 12
Dix, John A., Major-General, 349, 504, 513
Dixon, Mrs. Elizabeth Dixon (Mrs. James Dixon), 650-651, 657
Doherty, Edward P., Lieutenant, 670, 671
Dole, William P., Commissioner of Indian Affairs, 623
Donelson, Fort, Battle of, 313, 314

Dorsey, Azel W., 10
Douglas, Stephen A., 32, 34, 40, 48, 49, 54, 64, 87, 123, 124, 130; as Senator, 151, 160, 172ff, 187-202, 203, 204, 225-227, 229-236, 238-239, 242, 261, 278-279, 300, 342, 369, 395, 400, 433, 439
Douglass, John M., 160
"Draft" riots, in New York City, 437, 442, 450, 537
Drake, Dr. Daniel, 3
Drake, Edwin L., 610
Drake, Nathan, 29
Draper, Simeon, 537, 538
Dred Scott decision, 189ff, 193, 194, 198
Dresser, Charles, Reverend, 96, 133
Drewry's Bluff, Federal ships defeated at, 322
Drummond, Thomas, Judge, 152, 161, 171
Du Barry, Mrs. Helen A., 634
Dubois, Jesse K., Auditor of Illinois, 183, 211, 212, 217, 237, 396, 493, 556-557
Duff, John J., 74, 75, 148
Dummer, Henry E., 42, 60
Duncan, Jason, 23
Duncan, Joseph, Governor, 43
Dunn, Alphonso, 631
Dunn, William M., Judge-Advocate, 511
DuPont, Samuel F., Captain, U.S.N., 371; as Rear Admiral, 371-373, 375, 553
Durant, Thomas J., 477

Early, Jacob M., 28, 29, 64
Early, Jubal A., Major-General, 431, 485, 521-524, 528, 542, 543, 543-544, 595
Edwards, Albert S., 46, 87, 89
Edwards, Dr. B. F., 55
Edwards, Ninian, Governor, 36, 44, 48, 85
Edwards, Ninian W., 43, 44, 46, 48, 85ff, 132, 410
Edwards, Mrs. Ninian W., 48, 85ff, 132, 410
Effie Afton, case of, 163-165
Eighth Judicial Circuit, of Illinois, 76-78, 153-156
Elkin, William E., 44
Ellis, A. Y., 37
Ellsworth, Elmer E., Colonel, 255, 285-287, 303, 410, 411, 497
Ellsworth, Mr. and Mrs., 286-287
Ely, A. B., 312
Emancipation Proclamation, see Proclamation of Emancipation
Emerson, Ralph Waldo, 548
Evans, Dr. William A., 132
Evarts, William M., 219, 550
Everett, Edward, 227, 457, 458, 460
Ewell, Richard S., Lieutenant-General, 426, 426-427, 427, 428, 430
Ewing, James S., 123
Ewing, Thomas, Secretary of Interior, 108, 109
Ewing, William L. D., 15, 16, 40, 51

Fair Oaks, Battle of, 367
Fairbanks, Erastus, Governor, 279
Farnsworth, John F., Congressman and Brigadier-General, 658
Farragut, David G., Flag Officer, 314; as Rear Admiral, 533, 536, 544, 548, 595
"Father Abraham," sobriquet of Lincoln, 408
Fell, Jesse W., 4, 207, 224, 383
Felton, Samuel M., 254, 255
Fenton, Reuben E., Governor, 556
Ferguson, John, 22
Ferrandini, Cypriano, 254
Fessenden, William Pitt, Senator, 319; as Secretary of Treasury under Lincoln, 518, 555, 557; as senator again, 557-558, 570, 571
Ficklin, Orlando B., 74, 75
Field, David Dudley, 101, 259, 520
Field, Maunsell B., 517-518; as Assistant Secretary of Treasury, 658
Fillmore, Millard, Vice-Presidential candidate, 107; as President, 138-139, 174; as Former President, 186, 189, 206, 218
Fish, Hamilton, 209
Fisher, Archibald, 69-70
Fisher, Fort, Butler's foolish expedition against, 566; capture of, 586-587
Fisher's Hill, Sheridan's victory at, 543
Five Forks, Battle of, 598
Flanders, B. F., 476-477
Fletcher, Job, 44
Flournoy, Thomas, Congressman, 588
Floyd, George P., 149
Fogg, George G., 228, 229, 508
Foote, Andrew H., Commodore, 313, 434
Forbes, Bob Lincoln's friend, 419
Forbes, Charles, footman of Lincoln, 634, 638, 639
Ford, Dr., Acting Surgeon, 649
Ford, H. Clay (Harry), 626, 635
Ford, John T., 609
Ford, Thomas, Governor, 37, 40, 41, 64
Ford's Theatre, 392, 627ff, 634ff, 663
Fordham, Elias P., 132
Forney, John W., 493
Forrest, Edwin, 392
Forrest, Nathan B., Major-General, 461
Forsyth v. Reynolds, case of, 146
Foster, Lillian, 112, 118
Fox, Gustavus V., Assistant Secretary of Navy, 269, 270, 274, 275, 286, 372-373, 519, 552-554
Francis, Simeon, 49, 232
Francis, Mrs. Simeon, 96

Franklin (Tennessee), Battle of, 560
Franklin, William B., Major-General, 310
Franks, Herman, 404
Fredericksburg, Battle of, 347, 356-358, 364ff, 367, 414, 427, 497, 603
Freeman, Dr. Douglas Southall, 325, 430, 597
Freeport Doctrine, 190, 198-199, 226, 235
Frémont, Jessie Benton, 295, 297-298, 300
Frémont, John C., 138-139, 184-186, 188, 189, 206, 215, 224, 232, 233, 238, 293, 294-302, 304, 307, 320, 320-321, 323, 325, 328, 335, 337, 338-339, 345, 373, 495, 496, 504-505, 507, 512, 537, 541-543, 569
French, Augustus C., Governor, 73
French, Benjamin B., 412, 414
Fry, James B., Provost Marshal, General, 442, 630
Fry, John B., 242
Fullerton, Hugh, 167
Furness, Horace H., 395, 409

Gaines, Edmund Pendleton, Major-General, 26
Gaines Mill, Battle of, 325
Galloway, Samuel, 153, 205, 211, 224
Gamble, Hamilton, Governor, 296, 373, 374, 446
Garfield, James A., President, 421, 422; as Brigadier-General, 481
Garibaldi, Guiseppe, 283
Garrett, Richard H., 670
Garrison, William Lloyd, 337, 573-574
Gatch, Dr. Charles, 645, 648
Gatch, Oliver C., Captain, 645-646
Geary, John, Major-General, 453
Geary, Thomas, 624
Gentry, Allen, 13, 80
Gentry, James, 13
Gentry, Josiah, 229
Gentry, Matthew, 114-115
Gerolt, von, Baron, 420
Gerolt, von Fräulein, 420
Gettysburg, Battle of, 430-432, 468, 594, 603
Gettysburg Address, by Lincoln, 401, 402, 457-460, 591, 592
Gilbert, Samuel A., 176
Gill v. Gill, divorce case of, 166
Gillmore, Quincy A., Major-General, 481, 482
Gillespie, Joseph, 56-57, 113, 126, 179, 400
Gobright, Lawrence A., 648
Godbey, Russell, 34
Gooch, Daniel, Congressman, 307
Goodrich, Grant, 146
Goodrich, John Z., 511, 558
Goodwin, Ichabod, Governor, 279
Gordon, John B., Lieutenant-General, 582, 596
Grable v. Margrave, case of, 68-69
Grable, William G., 68
Graham, Christopher C., 3
Graham, Mentor, 22
Grant, Ulysses S., Major-General, 313, 314, 327, 351, 366, 369, 370, 421, 427, 429, 432-436, 437, 440, 447-448, 449, 450, 453-454, 461, 462-464, 468, 469, 488, 495-497; as Lieutenant-General and supreme Union military commander, 498-501, 502, 512, 516, 521ff, 529, 530, 533, 544, 547, 549, 559, 560, 561-562, 563, 566, 581, 582, 583, 595-601, 602-603, 612, 618, 620, 623, 626, 656, 668
Gray, Edgar H., Reverend, 667
Greeley, Horace, New York *Tribune* editor, 101, 192, 209, 210, 215, 217, 223, 246, 259, 341-342, 349, 388, 395, 495, 515, 517, 524-527, 529, 530, 574-575, 593
Green, Bowling, 31, 41, 59
Green, Mrs. M. J., 80
Gridley, Asahel, 56-57
Grigsby, Aaron, 13
Grigsby, Charles, 14
Grigsby, Reuben, 14
Grimshaw, Jackson, 151, 217
Grinnell, Josiah B., Congressman, 439
Gross, William L., 117
Gulliver, J. P., Reverend, 11
Gurley, Phineas D., Reverend, 398, 658, 659, 667, 668, 676

Hackett, James H., 390-391, 392
Hahn, Michael, 476-477; as Governor, 576
Haight, J. Mason, 221
Hale, Albert, Reverend, 675
Hale, Charles, 459
Hale, John P., Senator, 248, 456, 552-554
Hale, Sarah Josepha, 463
Hall, Charles H., 667
Hall, Nancy, 9
Hall, Dr. Neal, 649
Halleck, Henry W., Major-General, 309-310, 313, 320; as General-in-Chief, 326-327, 327, 328, 329, 331, 345, 352, 356, 364-366, 368, 369-370, 379, 381, 426, 428-429, 433, 435, 438, 439, 447, 448, 448-449, 450, 453, 464; as Chief-of-Staff following Grant's promotion to supreme commander, 502, 522, 546, 559, 563, 589, 658
Hamilton, Alexander, 530
Hamilton, Schuyler, Major-General, 530
Hamlin, Hannibal, as Lincoln's Vice-Presidential running-mate in 1860, 222, 223, 224; as Vice-President-elect, 240, 258; as Vice-President, under Lincoln, 456, 458, 460, 513, 519, 557, 557-558; as Former Vice-President, 558
Hampton, Wade, Major-General, 589

Hampton Roads "Peace" Conference, 404, 574, 587-588, 596, 601
Hanaford, Phebe, 399
Hancock, Cornelia, 601
Hancock, Winfield S., Major-General, 432
Hanks, Charles, 15
Hanks, Dennis F., 9, 10, 15, 37, 73, 141, 142
Hanks, John, 16, 17, 18, 213
Hanks, Lucy, 4
Hanks, Nancy, mother of Abraham Lincoln, see Lincoln, Nancy Hanks
Hardee, William J., Major-General, 535
Hardie, James A., Colonel, 429
Hardin, John (of Kentucky), 9
Hardin, John J. (of Illinois), 87-88, 91, 95, 98-100, 133, 188
Harding, George, 161
Harlan, James, Senator, 420, 556-557, 557; as Secretary of Interior designate under Lincoln, 623
Harlan, Mary, 420, 421, 557
Harriott, Charles, Judge, 167-168
Harris, Clara, 630, 634, 636, 637, 640, 641, 645, 647, 650, 651, 658
Harris, Ira, Senator, 390, 420, 421, 517, 518, 630, 634
Harrison, George M., 29
Harrison, Quinn ("Peachy"), 169
Harrison, Reuben, 19
Harrison, William Henry, Major-General and President, 52-55, 66, 88, 89, 91, 221, 252, 421, 662
Hart, Ellis, 70, 86
Harvey, James E., 231
Haskell, James R., 389
Hatch, Ozias M., Secretary of State of Illinois, 150-151, 183, 217, 227, 396
Haupt, Herman, Colonel, 328
Hawk, Harry, 635, 639, 640, 640-641, 643
Hawthorne v. Wooldridge, case of, 61, 67
Hawthorne, James P., 61
Hawthorne, Nathaniel, 386, 389-390
Hay, John, assistant secretary to Lincoln, 5, 120, 148, 270, 281, 290-291, 292, 297, 304, 305, 328, 390, 392, 393, 394, 408, 412, 419, 420, 438, 439, 447, 452, 453, 464, 467, 481-482, 509, 519, 521, 521-522, 526, 527, 550, 631, 658; as U.S. Secretary of State under Theodore Roosevelt, 663
Hay, Logan, 120
Hay, Milton, 48, 65, 137
Hay, Mrs. Milton, 393, 397
Haycraft, Samuel, 4
Haynie, Isham N., Adjutant-General of Illinois, 629, 651
Hazel, Caleb, 6
Head, Jesse, Reverend, 3
Heintzelman, Samuel P., Major-General, 306, 316, 318
Helm, Ben Hardin, Brigadier-General, 412-413, 414, 451, 452
Helm, Emilie Todd (Mrs. Ben Hardin Helm), 138, 335, 414-415, 420, 451
Helm, Katherine, 89, 137, 415
Henderson, John B., Senator, 570
Henning, Fanny (Mrs. Joshua F. Speed), 93, 94
Henry, Fort, Battle, 313, 370
Henry, Dr. Anson G., 54, 55, 56, 62, 90, 109, 126, 379-380, 418, 629, 636, 662
Henry, Mrs. Anson G., 379-380
Henry, Joseph, Professor, 413
Henry, Patrick, 88, 279, 485
Herndon, Archer G., 44, 70
Herndon, J. Rowan, 25, 37
Herndon, William H., 4, 5, 22, 23, 70-78, 80-81, 103, 104, 105, 106, 107, 111, 113, 115, 116, 117, 121, 122, 124, 126, 136, 141, 142, 146ff, 169, 178, 182, 192, 194, 202, 248, 335, 388, 392, 419, 422, 472, 588, 673
Herold, David, 614, 615, 616, 618, 626, 628, 629, 632, 653-655, 666, 669-670
Herring, J. H., 649
Hess, C. D., 618, 624
Hess, Mrs. C. D., 624-625
Hickman, John, Congressman, 484
Hicks, Thomas, as Governor, 280, 281; as Senator, 552
Hill, Ambrose P., Lieutenant-General, 426, 427, 428, 430
Hill, Charles W., Colonel, 404
Hill, D. H., Major-General, 461
Hill, Frederick Trevor, 66
Hill, John, 80, 119, 120
Hillard, O. K., 254
Hoar, E. Rockwood, 550
Hodges, Albert G., 398, 569
Hoffman, Francis A., 183
Hoffman, Henry W., Collector, 552
Hogeboom, John T., Judge, 518
Holcombe, James P., Professor, 526, 526-527, 527
Holland, Josiah G., 111, 119, 382
Holloway, Commissioner of Patents, 539
Holmes, Theophilus, Major-General, 435
Holt, Joseph, 268, 304
Hone, Philip, 376
"Honest Abe," sobriquet of Lincoln, 408, 409
Hood, John B., Lieutenant-General, 535, 536, 546, 549, 559-562, 563, 587, 595
Hood, Thomas, 394
Hooker, Joseph ("Fighting Joe"), Major-General, 366-368, 377-381, 424-426, 427,

Hooker, Joseph (*Cont.*)
428-429, 434, 453, 461, 462, 497, 528, 594, 675. See also Chancellorsville, Battle of
"House Divided" speech, by Lincoln, 193-194, 196, 266, 336, 400
Howard, James Quay, 224, 225
Howard, Joseph, Jr., 256, 503-504
Howard, Oliver O., Major-General, 330, 355-356, 356, 378, 380, 528, 563-564
Howell, Joseph C., 55
Howell, W. T., 623
Howells, William Dean, 59, 224, 225
Hubbard, A. C., Reverend, 675
Huggins, Enoch, 124
Hunter, David, Major-General, 297, 301, 340, 372, 479-480, 501, 569
Hunter, Robert M. T., Senator, 582, 588
Hurd v. Rock Island Bridge Company, case of, see *Effie Afton*, case of
Hurd, Jacob S., 163, 165
Hurlbut, Stephen A., 269; as Major-General, 478, 479, 580
Hutchinson, William T., Professor, 161

Iles, Elijah, Captain, 28
Illinois Central Railroad v. The County of McLean, case of, 158-160
Inaugural Address, First, by Lincoln, 259-264, 336, 401
Inaugural Address, Second, by Lincoln, 401, 590, 591, 592
Ingram v. Gibbs, case of, 65
Irving, Henrietta, 608
Island No. 10, Federal capture of, 314
Isle a'Vache, Haiti, Negro colonization project in, 344

Jackson, Andrew, President, 24, 30, 32, 38, 39, 40, 42, 52, 54, 191, 192, 225, 227, 234, 235, 240, 252, 268, 288, 408, 498, 507, 578, 545
Jackson, James, 286, 411
Jackson, "Stonewall," see Jackson, Thomas J. ("Stonewall"), Lieutenant-General
Jackson, Thomas J. ("Stonewall"), Lieutenant-General, 323, 324, 327, 328, 330, 339, 345, 357, 380, 427, 430, 431, 485, 534
"Jacobins," radical Republicans, 304ff, 519
Jayne, Julia (Mrs. Lyman Trumbull), 96
Jayne, Dr. William, 217
Jefferson, Thomas, 118, 216, 279, 485, 545, 577
Jenkins, Albert G., Brigadier-General, 427-428
Jewett, William Cornell ("Colorado"), 524-525, 526
Johnson, Andrew, Senator, 307; as Military Governor of Tennessee, 473-474, 513; as Vice-Presidential candidate in 1864, 537, 548, 557; as Vice-President, 558; as President, 558; inaugurated Vice-President, 591; as Vice-President, 632, 653, 655, 656; as President, 661, 662, 666, 667, 671
Johnson, Cornelius, 409
Johnson, Edward, Major-General, 431
Johnson, Herschel V., 230
Johnson, Oliver, 7-8
Johnson, Reverdy, 161, 162; as Senator, 475
Johnston v. Jones and Marsh, case of, see "Sandbar" case
Johnston, Albert Sidney, Major-General, 314
Johnston, Andrew, 23
Johnston, Daniel, 3
Johnston, Elizabeth, 9
Johnston, John D., stepbrother of Lincoln, 9, 16, 17, 73, 140, 141, 142-144
Johnston, Joseph E., General, 290, 293, 322, 323-324, 324, 435, 468-469, 485, 498, 516, 534-535, 586, 595, 597, 620, 621, 622
Johnston, Matilda, 9
Johnston, Mrs. Sarah (Sally) Bush, see Lincoln, Mrs. Sarah Bush Johnston, stepmother of Lincoln
Jones, Edward F., Colonel, 280-281
Jones, George, 539
Jones, J. B., 462, 601
Jones, Thomas A., 670
Joy, James F., 159, 160
Juarez, Benito, President of Mexico, 447
Judd, Norman B., 66, 154, 163, 172, 192-193, 195-196, 201, 204, 208, 208-209, 212-213, 213, 214, 217, 218, 245-246, 246, 255, 361, 362, 556
Julian, George W., Congressman, 257, 307, 308, 539, 573

Kane, George P., Baltimore Police Chief, 254, 255
Kansas, "Bleeding," as issue, 182, 190ff, 226
Kansas-Nebraska Act, 175ff, 193ff
Kaufman, Sigismunde, 501
Keckley, Elizabeth, 621
Keene, Laura, 620, 635, 646
Kelley, Milton, 623-624
Kelley, William D., Congressman, 539-540
Kelly, James, 538
Kellogg, William, 623
Kellogg, William P., as Congressman, 242; as Collector, 623, 629
Kennedy, Dr. Hugh, 476
Kent, William, 647, 648
"Kerr, Orpheus C.," see Newell, Robert H.
Kershaw, Joseph B., Brigadier-General, 357

Ketcham, W. W., 509
Keyes, Erasmus D., Major-General, 319
Kimmel, Stanley P., 610, 655
King, Dr. Albert F. A., 648
King, Preston, Former Senator, 667
Kinney, Mrs., 650
Kinzie, Robert, 66
Kirby-Smith, Edmund, Lieutenant-General, 351, 468, 586, 595
Kirkham, Samuel, 22
Kirkland, Edward C., Professor, 525
Kirkwood, Samuel J., Governor, 280
Kneedler v. Lane, case of, 445
Knox, James Suydam, 634-635, 641, 643-644
Knox, Joseph, 163
Knox, William, 23, 81
Knoxville, Battle of, 464
Koerner, Gustave, 195, 217, 221, 352
Kossuth, Louis, 174
Krager, George, 404

Lamborn, Josiah, 72
Lamon, Ward Hill, 79, 81, 97, 124, 125, 126, 127, 148, 156, 170, 255-256, 269-270, 335, 362, 393, 458, 472, 604, 619, 631
Lane, James H., Senator, 492
Lane, Joseph, Senator, 231
Langford, James R., 70
Laury, Mrs., Spiritualist medium, 414
Leale, Dr. Charles A., 646-648, 648, 658-659
Leclerque, Agnes, see Salm-Salm, Princess
Lecompton constitution, 191ff, 196
Lee, Stephen D., Captain, 274-275; as Major-General, 535
Lee, Robert E., Colonel, 283; as General of the Confederate Army, 323, 324, 325, 326, 327, 330-331, 333, 345, 356ff, 366, 379, 380, 421, 425-430, 435, 438, 452, 461, 485, 487, 499, 500, 516, 521, 534, 535, 540, 544, 561, 581, 582, 583, 586, 587, 594, 596, 599, 602-604, 605, 618, 620, 620-621, 628, 652
Lester, Sigler H., 73
Letcher, John, Governor, 272
Levering, Mercy, 86, 87, 88, 89, 91, 92-93
Lewis v. Lewis, case of, 145-146
Lieber, Francis, Professor, 375, 583
Lieberman, Dr. C. H., 649
Lincoln, Abraham, grandfather of Lincoln, 2, 3

LINCOLN, ABRAHAM, Sixteenth President of U.S., ancestry and birth, 2-5; Kentucky boyhood, 5-6; first New Orleans trip, 13; Indiana youth, 7-14; writes poem on Indiana home, 14-15;

LINCOLN, ABRAHAM (*Cont.*)
first political speech, 15; Macon County, Illinois, residence, 1830-1831, 15-16; second trip to New Orleans, flatboat worker for Offutt, 16-19; first sight of New Salem, 18; residence in New Salem, 19ff; as Offutt's store clerk, 20, 24; wrestling match with Armstrong, 21-22; interest in poetry, 23; preference for Clay, 24; works for *Talisman* enterprise, 25; service in Black Hawk War, 25-30; ridicules Cass's 1812 war service, 29-30; store partnership with Berry, 30-32; as liquor seller, 31-32; as New Salem postmaster, 32-33; as deputy county surveyor, 33-34; his odd jobs, 34; admits being politician, 36; defeated for Legislature in 1832, 37; elected to Legislature in 1834, 38; first months as state Representative at Vandalia, 39-42; his support of Clay, 39-40; compares self with Douglas in later years, 40; commences law study, wins re-election in 1836, 42; leads fight to remove state capital to Springfield, 43, 44-45, 51; moves residence from New Salem to Springfield, 46; early years in Springfield, 48ff; his Lyceum speech, 48, 49-50; as anonymous political contributor to press, 49; aids in law for dividing Sangamon County into four counties, 50-51; denounced by Ewing, 51

LINCOLN, ABRAHAM (continued), works for Harrison-Tyler Whig ticket, 53-55; re-elected to Legislature in 1840, 55; unsuccessfully seeks federal patronage for supporters, 55-56; last months as state Representative, "jump" from window, 56-57; loss of interest in legislative duties, his melancholia and "hypochrondriasm," 57-58; retirement from Legislature, 58; commences law study, admission to bar, 59-60; moves from New Salem to Springfield, 60; law partnership with Stuart, 60-67; law partnership with Logan, 67-70; law partnership with Herndon, 70-78; counsel in Matson slave case, 73-76; as circuit lawyer, 76-78; "romance" with Ann Rutledge, 80-82; abortive romance with Mary Owens, 82-84; romance with Mary Todd, 86-88; mental depression, his broken engagement to Mary Todd, 89-92; "Rebecca" letters, near duel with Shields, reconciliation with Mary Todd, his marriage to her, 94-96

LINCOLN, ABRAHAM (continued), campaigns for Clay for President in 1844,

LINCOLN, ABRAHAM (*Cont.*)
98-99; rivalry with Baker and Hardin for Whig congressional nomination, election to Congress over Cartwright, 98-101; publicly denies atheistic expressions, 100-101; attends rivers-and-harbors convention, noticed by Greeley, 101; described as politician by Boston reporter in 1847, 101; as Congressman-elect, 101-103; career in Congress, 103-108; stumps for Taylor for President in 1848, 106-107; seeks federal patronage for supporters and Land Office commissionership for himself, declines governorship and secretaryship of Oregon Territory, 108-109; personal appearance, 111-112; his reading, 112-113; taste for theatre, 113; melancholic disposition, 114-115; musical taste, 115; superstition, 116; not a Spiritualist, 115; gaiety and humor, 116-119; religious views in Illinois years, 100-101, 119-120; views toward Catholics, Irish, Germans, and Know-Nothings, 120-121; his modesty, reticence, earning and saving of money, mechanical mind, 121-123; personal honesty, sobriquet of "Honest Abe," 123; his dignity but approachability, 124; his distaste for physical violence, belief in conciliation, 124, 129; advice to young people, 124-125; aversion to farm life, indifference to food, abstention from liquor, 125-127; as a conservative, 127-128; views on capital and labor, and private property, 127-130; opposed to mob rule, champions law and order, 129; married life with Mary Todd Lincoln, 132-144; relations with sons, 140-141; attitude toward his father, stepmother, and Hanks and Johnston families, 141-144

LINCOLN, ABRAHAM (continued), his cases in U.S. Supreme Court, 145-146; resumes law partnership with Herndon in 1849, 146ff; professional law ethics, 148, 149; diversity and extent of Lincoln & Herndon firm's legal practice, 148-153, 158; on Eighth Judicial Circuit, 153-156; close friendship with Judge Davis, 154-155; friendship and circuit partnership with Lamon, 156; famous law cases of Lincoln, 157ff; defends Illinois Central Railroad, 158-160; associate counsel in "reaper" case, 160-163; associate counsel in *Effie Afton* case, 163-165; defends "Duff" Armstrong for murder in "Almanac" case, 165-168; defends Short and

LINCOLN, ABRAHAM (*Cont.*)
Harrison, 168-170; unsuccessfully prosecutes Wyant for murder, 170; as co-counsel in *Dennis v. Ennis and Ennis*, 171-172; effect of legal practice on his career, 172

LINCOLN, ABRAHAM (continued), indifferent attitude toward 1850 sectional crisis, seeks patronage from Taylor administration, delivers speech mourning President Taylor's death, seeks patronage from Fillmore administration, 173-174; supports Hungary's fight for freedom, speaks for Scott's presidential candidacy in 1852, eulogizes recently deceased Henry Clay, 174-175; participates in "Anti-Nebraska" movement against Douglas in 1854, 175ff; shuns proposed abolitionist Republican Party in 1854, 176ff; unsuccessful campaign for U.S. Senator, 1854-55, 179-180; refusal to join Republican Party in 1855, 180-181; attitude toward Know-Nothings, 181; attends "Anti-Nebraska" Editorial Convention at Decatur in February, 1856, delivers "Lost Speech" at Republican state Convention in Bloomington, May 29, 1856, joins Republican Party, 181-184; supports McLean for Republican presidential nomination in 1856, 184; Frémont nominated for President in 1856, 184; Lincoln defeated for Republican Vice-Presidential nomination on Frémont's slate, 184; Lincoln stumps for Frémont-Dayton ticket, 184-186; Frémont defeated for President by Buchanan, 186

LINCOLN, ABRAHAM (continued), compares own career with Douglas's in 1856, 187; opposes Douglas and Dred Scott decision, 190; irritated by Eastern Republicans' efforts to endorse Douglas, a Democrat, for re-election to U.S. Senate, 192; nominated by Republicans for U.S. Senator against Douglas in 1858, delivers "House Divided" speech, 193-194; campaigns for Senator against Douglas in 1858, 194ff; famous debates with Douglas, 195-201; repudiates equality of races idea, 197-198, 199-200; defeated for Senator by Douglas, 201-202; disappointed over Senate defeat, 202

LINCOLN, ABRAHAM (continued), mentioned for President or Vice-President following defeat by Douglas for Senate,

LINCOLN, ABRAHAM (*Cont.*)
desires to build Republican party power and oppose Douglas for Senator in 1864, muffles strong anti-slavery agitation, 203-204; cultivates "German" vote, disapproves of Know-Nothingism, finances German-language Republican party newspaper, 205; admits ambition to be President, 205; his "availability" in doubtful states in 1860, 206-207; concern for Illinois delegate support at Republican National Convention, 208; delivers Cooper Institute address, speaks in New England, 209-211; efforts to secure delegates to Republican National Convention, 211ff; named Illinois Republicans' choice for party presidential nomination, attends Republican state Convention in Decatur, becomes the "Railsplitter" presidential contender, 212-214; nominated candidate of Republican Party for President at party's national convention in Chicago, May 18, 1860, 217-219; receives news of presidential nomination, 219-220; official notification ceremony, 221-222; confusion over his Christian name, 222, 223; biography by Howells and Howard, 224-225; silence during 1860 campaign, May-November, 227-228; mentions railsplitter youth, 229; conduct as Republican presidential candidate, 220-225, 227-228, 232, 236-237; elected President of U.S., 37; analysis of presidential vote of 1860, 238-240

LINCOLN, ABRAHAM (continued), as President-elect, 240ff; his lack of handling of secession crisis, his time devoted to Cabinet formation and practical politics, opposes compromise with seceded states, 240-244; begins formation of Cabinet, 244-249; visits stepmother, works on Inaugural Address, rents home, departs for Washington, 249-250; farewell words to Springfield townsmen, 250; journey to Washington, 251-256; presumed plot to assassinate President-elect in Baltimore, 254-256; arrival in Washington, 256; "Scotch hat" hoax by Howard, 256; lack of prestige during pre-Inauguration days in Washington, 256-257; besieged by office-seekers, 257; completes formation of Cabinet, 257-259; completes Inaugural Address, 259-260; delivers Inaugural Address, 261-264; takes presidential oath administered by Taney, 264

LINCOLN, ABRAHAM (continued), distributes patronage, 266-267; in secession crisis, 265-266; problems of Fort Sumter and Fort Pickens, 267ff; rejects Seward's "foreign war" panacea, 270-272; negotiation with Virginia leaders, 273; orders relief of Fort Sumter, 273; surrender of Fort Sumter, 274-275; calls for 75,000 volunteers, start of Civil War, 276; accepts Douglas's pro-Union support, grieved over Douglas's death, 278-279; governors' response to his appeal for volunteers, 279-280; problem of troop transit through Baltimore, consults with Baltimore Mayor and others, solution of Maryland troop-transit impassé, 280-283; anxiety over arrival of New York and Rhode Island soldiers, 282; concern over border-slave states, 282-283; authorizes Blair to offer Union command to Robert E. Lee, 283; friendship for Ellsworth and grief over his death, 285-286; letter to Mr. and Mrs. Ellsworth, 286-287; in Washington social life, 287-288; annoyed by office-seekers, his patronage policy, 288-289; depression over First Bull Run defeat, his orders following battle, 291-293; trouble with Frémont, 296ff; concern over Kentucky's loyalty, 298-299, 302; overrules Frémont's slave-emancipation proclamation, removes Frémont from Western command, 300-301; saddened by Baker's death at Ball's Bluff, 303; his conservative slavery policy opposed, his confidence in McClellan, relations with congressional Committee on Conduct of War, 304-309; communications with Buell and Halleck, 309-310; worried over Army command during McClellan's illness, consults Meigs, calls conference of Generals, 310-311; dissatisfaction with Cameron, his maneuvering of Cameron out of Cabinet, and appointment of him as Minister to Russia, 311-312; tangled relations with McClellan, 315-327; creates Army of Virginia with Pope as Commander, 324-325; appoints Halleck General-in-Chief, 326; approves Halleck's order withdrawing McClellan's Army of Potomac to Aquia Creek, 326-327; gloom over Pope's defeat at Second Battle of Bull Run, 328; restores McClellan to top field command, 329

LINCOLN, ABRAHAM (continued), displeased by McClellan's failure to pursue Lee after Antietam, tries to per-

LINCOLN, ABRAHAM (*Cont.*) suade McClellan to take offensive immediately, 331; removes McClellan from Army of the Potomac command, 332-333; his Southern background, Southern-born friends, his extremely moderate anti-slavery sentiments, 334-336; his views on slavery late in 1861 and early in 1862, 337ff; favors compensated emancipation and overseas colonization for freed Negroes, 337ff; the problems of Generals Frémont, Hunter, and Wadsworth in slavery emancipation, 339-340; his view toward Confiscation Acts, 340-341; his letter to Greeley on Union preservation and slavery emancipation, 341-342; his slavery views in eulogy of Clay in 1852, his compensated emancipation and colonization efforts, 342-344; his belief that whites and Negroes suffer in living side by side, 344; steps leading to preliminary Proclamation of Emancipation, 345-346; issues preliminary Proclamation of Emancipation, 346-347; reaction to loss of 1862 elections, 350-351; removes Buell from command, 352; removes Butler from New Orleans command, 353-354; appoints Burnside to command of Army of the Potomac, then feels doubts, 355; dejected over Fredericksburg defeat, 357, 365; Cabinet crisis of December, 1862, 359-361; accepts Secretary Smith's resignation, appoints Usher as Smith's successor, strained relations with old friend, Browning, chooses Judge David Davis for U.S. Supreme Court, 361-363; worn look on face, 363; dilemma over Burnside, resignation of Burnside as Army of the Potomac commander, appointment of Hooker as Burnside's successor, letter to Hooker, 364-368; difficulties with Rosecrans and McClernand, 368-370; concern over Grant's Vicksburg preparations, 370; directions to Du-Pont, naval reverse off Charleston, political repercussions in Congress, 370-373; handling of Missouri factionalism and troubles, removal of Curtis and appointment of Schofield, 373-374; problem of the "Copperheads," handling of Vallandigham's arrest by Burnside, relations with Fernando Wood, 374-377; declines Schurz's request for transfer to new command, 377-378; visits Hooker, 379; reaction to Chancellorsville defeat, 381

LINCOLN, ABRAHAM (continued), personal characteristics, physical appearance, strength and mental qualities, daily routine, and type of man, 383-405; described by men who saw and heard him, 383ff; personal appearance and physical power; mental capacity, 387-390; taste in poetry, interest in Shakespeare, Burns, and Pope, 390-392; favorite humorists, 392, 394; liking for theatre, carelessness in attending theatre unguarded, 392-393; his humor and jokes, 393-396; his melancholia, partially for plaintive music, 396-397; attitude toward religion, 397-399; not a Spiritualist, 399; his mastery of English language, 399-400; anecdotes, later attributed to him, 400-401; writes Mrs. Bixby, 402; writes Fanny McCullough, 402; his pardon policy, 403; his White House offices, reception of callers, 408; popularity among Union troops, 408-409; love for sons, Willie and "Tad," 410; grief over Willie's death, 411-412, 417; concern for Mrs. Lincoln's mental instability, request to Professor Henry to investigate "Colchester," Spiritualist medium, 413; befriends wife's Confederate half-sister, 414-415; affection for son, "Tad," 417-418; reference to his last public address, 418; relations with son, Bob, 418-419; requests Grant for Army commission for son, Bob, signs Bob's commission, 421; wife's concern for his health, 422-423; intention to travel in Europe after his second presidential term, 423

LINCOLN, ABRAHAM (continued), conversations and correspondence with defeated Hooker after Chancellorsville, 424-426; his alleged offer of Army of the Potomac command to Reynolds, 426; calls for 100,000 volunteers to repel Lee's Northern invasion, tries to cure Halleck-Hooker feud, replaces Hooker with Meade in Army of the Potomac command, 428-429; refuses to reappoint McClellan to Army of the Potomac command, 429-430; announces Gettysburg victory, 432-433; attitude toward Grant and McClernand, 433; elated over Vicksburg victory by Grant, congratulates Grant, 435-436; depressed over Meade's failure to pursue Lee after Gettysburg, 438-439; reassures McClernand, 439-440; relations with Governor Seymour, refuses Seymour's request for

LINCOLN, ABRAHAM (*Cont.*)
conscription postponement, 441-444; concern over Pennsylvania and Ohio elections, 444-445; troubles with Missouri political and personal feuds and party factionalism, 445-446; worried over French intervention in Mexico, orders military action in Texas, 446-448; advises Rosecrans, 449; orders Burnside to reinforce Rosecrans, 449-450

LINCOLN, ABRAHAM (continued), informs Mrs. Lincoln of Chickamauga defeat and of death of her Confederate officer brother-in-law, Helm, 451-452; defends Thomas as brave Union general, 452; sanctions huge reinforcements to Rosecrans, 452-453; removes Rosecrans from command, appoints Thomas, makes Grant supreme commander in West, 453; continued worry over Pennsylvania and Ohio elections, listens to Ohio election returns, 454-455; comment to Chandler on 1863 election results, delivers Gettysburg Address, 457-459; reaction to Gettysburg Address, "Tad's" illness, his own illness, his letter to Everett, 459-460; proclaims national Thanksgiving Day, 463-464; overjoyed at Grant's Chattanooga victory, humorous remark about Gran't whiskey-drinking, 464; attitude toward Russians and visit of Tsar's naval squadron, his mention of emancipation of Russian serfs to Bayard Taylor, sponsorship of completion of Capitol dome, 467; favorable prospects for Union at end of 1863, 468; present author's comparison of Lincoln's troubles with those of Jefferson Davis, 468-469; Lincoln's Southern background and sympathy for South, 472-473; his reconstruction, or "restoration," efforts in Tennessee, Louisiana, Arkansas, Florida, North Carolina, and Virginia, 473-487; his Amnesty and Pardon Proclamation of December 8, 1863, his "Ten per cent" plan of reconstruction, 487-488; vetoes Wade-Davis reconstruction bill in 1864, 490

LINCOLN, ABRAHAM (continued), intimates he will run for re-election, 491; use of federal patronage, difficulties with Senators Pomeroy and Lane, 491; attitude toward Chase and publication of Pomeroy Circular, 493-494; attitude toward presidential ambitions of Chase,

LINCOLN, ABRAHAM (*Cont.*)
Frémont, and Butler, 493-496; appoints Grant Lieutenant-General, greets Grant in Washington, relations with Grant as supreme Union field commander, 498-499; his mental torture over Wilderness battle, 500; victim of Howard's forged presidential proclamation for volunteers, 502-503; sponsors admission of Nevada as State of the Union, 505-506; use of federal office-holders to assure renomination for President, accepts renomination, 507-514; bothered by Republican-Union Party factionalism and rivalry in New York City, accepts Chase's resignation as Secretary of the Treasury, appoints Fessenden as Chase's successor, 516-518; troubled by anti-slavery radicals, 520; vetoes Wade-Davis reconstruction bill, 521; action to combat Early's raid on Washington, faces Confederate military fire at Fort Stevens, disappointed over Early's escape, 521-524; handling of Greeley's "peace" efforts, 524-527; praise of General McPherson, agrees to General Howard as dead McPherson's successor, 527-528; grieved over Wade-Davis Manifesto, motives of Davis in opposing Lincoln, 529-530; fears being defeated for re-election, 531, 533; overjoyed at Farragut's victory at Mobile Bay and Sherman's capture of Atlanta, 536; reshuffling of New York Customs House and Post Office patronage, 537-538; curbs office-holders in their opposition to administration candidates, 539-540; asks for Blair's resignation as Postmaster General to pacify radicals, 541-543; appoints Dennison as Blair's successor, 543; congratulates Sheridan on victory, fears Sheridan still in danger of Confederate attack, congratulates Sheridan again, 543-544; addresses Ohio troops on campaign issue, 545; insists on soldiers' right to vote, 546; requests Sherman to furlough Indiana soldiers for election day, 546-547; concern over Pennsylvania election, 547; re-elected President over McClellan, 548

LINCOLN, ABRAHAM (continued), post-election patronage problems, appoints Chase U.S. Supreme Court Chief Justice, 550-551; attitude toward Henry Winter Davis, 553; appoints William E. Chandler to highest Navy legal position, 554; makes changes in Cabinet posts of Attorney-General, Secretary of the

LINCOLN, ABRAHAM (*Cont.*)
Treasury, and Secretary of the Interior, 555-557; problem of "lame duck" Vice-President Hamlin, 557-558; confidence in Grant as commander, 559; fears Thomas to be dawdling about attacking Hood at Nashville, 560-562; congratulates and advises Thomas on Battle of Nashville, 562; reference to Sherman's "march to the sea" in Georgia, 564; congratulates Sherman on capture of Savannah, 565; troubles with General Butler about Virginia administration and Fort Fisher expedition, 565-566; announces Federal possession of Wilmington, North Carolina, 567; attitude toward slavery inspired by late Henry Clay, comments on problem in letter to Hodges, supports Thirteenth Amendment, 569-574; attitude toward Negro voting, 575-576; continues efforts at reconstruction, or "restoration," of seceded state to the Union, 577-584; attends Hampton Roads "Peace" Conference, meets Stephens there, adamant about slavery abolition and restoration, re-inaugurated President, March 4, 1865, delivers Second Inaugural Address, 589-592; reaction to his Second Inaugural Address, his own words about it to Weed, 592-593; his declining health early in 1865, 592, 596

LINCOLN, ABRAHAM (continued), visit to City Point, Virginia, as guest of Grant, conferences with Sherman and Admiral Porter, Confederate evacuation of Richmond, Lincoln's visits to Petersburg and Richmond, visits Army hospital, return to Washington, 596-602; sees injured Seward, 603; tells wife news of Lee's surrender at Appomattox, 603-604; addresses crowd on White House grounds, calls for playing of "Dixie," 604; delivers last public address of his life on White House grounds, April 11, 1865, 605; watches Booth play in *The Marble Heart* in 1863, 610; Booth's hatred of Lincoln, 605, 611; Booth's plans to abduct Lincoln, 612ff; unsuccessful attempt to kidnap Lincoln by Booth and accomplices, 616-617

LINCOLN, ABRAHAM (continued), his last full day, April 14, 1865, 619ff; promises Van Alen to safeguard himself, 619; orders re-raising of U.S. flag over Fort Sumter, 620; talk with son,

LINCOLN, ABRAHAM (*Cont.*)
Bob, praises General Lee, visited by Speaker Colfax, visits telegraph office for news from Sherman, last Cabinet meeting, discussion of reconstruction, 620-623; attends to appointments, pardons, reprieves, 623-624; goes for carriage ride with Mrs. Lincoln, talks of war's end and his dead son, Willie, 625; his assassination plotted by Booth, Powell, Atzerodt, and Herold, 626ff; Lincoln returns from carriage ride with wife, talks with Governor Ogleby and Adjutant-General Haynie, has dinner with wife, invites Major Rathbone and Clara Harris as guests of himself and Mrs. Lincoln at Ford's Theatre, visits Stanton at War Department before going to theatre, 629-630; talks with Colfax, Ashmun, and Judge Daly before going to theatre, 632; arrival at Ford's Theatre with wife, Rathbone, and Miss Harris, acclaimed by audience, 633-635; watches *Our American Cousin,* the play, seated in box with wife, Rathbone, and Miss Harris, 635-636; shot by Booth, 639-641; medical treatment by physicians in theatre box and later at Petersen's house across street, 646-650; last hours of Lincoln, 657-658; Lincoln dies, April 15, 1865, 658

LINCOLN, ABRAHAM (continued), autopsy on him, 660-661; embalmed, 661; itinerary of funeral train, 661; victim of souvenir hunters, 663-664; lies in state at White House, 664-665; appearance of him in coffin, 664; search for his assassin, Booth, and accomplices, 665; funeral from White House, 666-668; capture and killing of assassin, Booth, 670-671; funeral train to Springfield, 671-672; sad reaction of Herndon to his death, 673; controversy over burial site, 673-674; funeral and burial in Oak Ridge cemetery, Springfield, 674-676

Lincoln, Mrs. Abraham, see Lincoln, Mary Todd
Lincoln, Bob, see Lincoln, Robert Todd
Lincoln, Eddie, see Lincoln, Edward Baker
Lincoln, Edward Baker (Eddie), son of Lincoln, 102, 104, 117, 120, 133, 134, 135, 137, 140, 410, 415
Lincoln, Enoch, 2
Lincoln & Herndon, law firm of, 70-78. See also Herndon, William H.
Lincoln, Levi, 2

Lincoln, Mary Todd (Mrs. Abraham Lincoln), arrival in Springfield, 45, 48; mentioned, 49; broken engagement to Lincoln, 58, 78; denies Lincoln's "romance" with Ann Rutledge, 81; ancestry and early life in Kentucky, 85-86; early residence in Springfield, Illinois, 86-88; uneven romance with Lincoln, 89-94; authorship of "Rebecca" letters, 95; marriage to Lincoln, 96; mentioned, 97; receives news of Clay's defeat for President in 1844, 99; accompanies Lincoln to Lexington, Kentucky, en route to Washington, 102-104; mentioned, 114; her temperament, 115; humorous letter from Lincoln, 117; religious devotion, 120; her extravagance, 122; her ancestry and early Kentucky life, 131-132; marriage to Lincoln, residence at Globe Tavern in Springfield, birth of first son, Bob, purchase of Eighth Street house by Lincoln in 1844, 132-133; birth of second son, Eddie, 133; married life with Lincoln, in Springfield, 132-144; her encouragement of Lincoln in Whig politics, 134; in Washington with Lincoln as Congressman's wife, prolonged stay at father's and stepmother's home in Lexington, Kentucky, letters from and to Lincoln, 134-135; her dislike of Herndon, 136; her mental instability, 137-138

Lincoln, Mary Todd (continued), pro-Southern sympathies, disapproval of Republicans and abolitionists, 138-139; as housewife, disapproval of Irish, 139-140; death of son, Eddie, and birth of sons, Willie and Thomas ("Tad"), 140; remains at home while Lincoln runs for U.S. Senator against Douglas in 1858, 195; told news of his presidential nomination by Republicans, 219; at notification ceremony of Lincoln's nomination, 221; her husband elected President of U.S., 237; dislikes Judd, opposes his appointment to husband's presidential Cabinet, 245, 246; overjoyed at Lincoln's safe arrival in Washington as President-elect, 256; in Washington with President-elect, 257; describes Washington during secession crisis, 270; grief over Ellsworth's death, 286-287; dislike of Seward, 287; sorrow over Baker's death, 303; her pro-slavery Todd family and her disdain of abolitionists, 335; confides to Browning that Lincoln wants him in Cabinet, 361; at City Point, Virginia, with husband, 391; with husband sees John Wilkes Booth perform on stage in 1863, 392; attends Presbyterian church in Washington, 397; refers to Lincoln's religion, 399; in White House, 407; interferes in job distribution for friends and Todd family, 409-410; as White House hostess, 410; her difficult position as a Southern woman and as wife of Republican President, 410

Lincoln, Mary Todd (continued), grief and prolonged shock over death of son, Willie, 411-412; declining mental faculties following deaths of son, Willie, and of brothers and brother-in-law, Helm, in battle, 412-413; consults Spiritualist medium, 413; veiled accusations against her, 413-414; her continued mental distress, 414-416; consults another Spiritualist medium, 414; gives half-sister, Emilie Todd Helm, shelter and hospitality in White House, 415; receives "visits" from dead sons and dead brother, 415; her persistent pining for dead Willie, 415-416; her jealousy over Princess Salm-Salm and Mrs. Ord, 416-417; opposes son, Bob, going into army, reply to Senator Harris, 420; contrasted with her husband, 422; her anxiety over husband's health, her letter to Mercy Levering Conkling, 422-423; injured in carriage accident, 432; informed by husband of brother-in-law Helm's death as Confederate commander at Chickamauga, 451-452; Grant presented to her, 498; with Lincoln under Confederate gun fire at Fort Stevens, 523; escorted to Lincoln's Second Inaguration by Senator Harlan, 557; at Ford's Theatre, 582; her elegant dress at social functions, 586; at husband's Second Inauguration, 590; concern for husband's health, 596

Lincoln, Mary Todd (continued), goes to City Point, Virginia, with Lincoln in March, 1865, 596; leaves City Point with Lincoln in early April, 1865, 602; receives news of Lee's surrender from Lincoln, 603-604; goes for carriage ride with Lincoln on April 14, 1865, 624-625; describes Lincoln at dinner in evening before going to Ford's Theatre, 628-629; leaves for theatre with Lincoln, Major Rathbone, and Clara Harris, arrival at theatre, enthusiastic reception from au-

Lincoln, Mary Todd (*Cont.*)
dience, 634-635; watches *Our American Cousin,* seated beside Lincoln, with Rathbone and Clara Harris in theatre box, 635-636; sees Booth shoot Lincoln, 640, 641; her hysteria following shooting of husband, 645, 650-651; her intense grief as Lincoln lay dying, 657

Lincoln, Mary Todd (continued), agrees to Springfield as Lincoln's burial place, opposes Mather site in town center as interment site, 661, 673-674; comforted by Dr. Henry, 662; grows mentally worse before Lincoln's funeral, remains in White House long after Lincoln's burial in Springfield, 662; too weak to attend Lincoln's White House funeral or accompany body to Springfield, 667; directs disinterment of son, Willie, for his corpse to accompany Lincoln's body on trip to Springfield, 668; has son, Bob, protest against burial of Lincoln in Mather site in town center, decision to bury Lincoln in Oak Ridge Cemetery, 673-674

Lincoln, Mordecai, 2, 3
Lincoln, Nancy Hanks, mother of Lincoln, 3-4, 8-9, 9, 141, 142
Lincoln, Robert Todd (Bob), son of Lincoln, 81, 102, 116, 117, 132-133, 133, 134, 135, 137, 140-141, 178, 210, 220, 257, 398-399, 407, 410, 411, 412, 418-422, 557, 620-621, 629, 651, 658, 661, 662, 667, 673-674, 674
Lincoln, Mrs. Robert Todd, see Harlan, Mary
Lincoln, Samuel, 2
Lincoln, Sarah, sister of Lincoln, 4, 6, 9, 13, 14
Lincoln, Mrs. Sarah (Sally) Bush Johnston, stepmother of Lincoln, 3, 9, 73, 141, 143, 249, 386-387
Lincoln, Solomon, 2
Lincoln, "Tad," see Lincoln, Thomas ("Tad"), son of Lincoln
Lincoln, Thomas ("Tad"), son of Lincoln, 141, 257, 379, 407, 410, 416, 417-418, 419, 460, 592, 596, 600, 602, 605, 667
Lincoln, Thomas, father of Lincoln, 2-9, 14-15, 73, 141-143, 144
Lincoln, Thomas, Jr., infant brother of Lincoln, 6
Lincoln, William Wallace (Willie), son of Lincoln, 140, 257, 303, 407, 410-416, 417, 625, 649, 661, 668, 675
Lincoln, Willie, see Lincoln, William Wallace (Willie), son of Lincoln
Lincoln-Douglas debates, of 1858, 195-201, 336
Linder, Usher F., 74, 75, 127
Lindsay, Vachel, 76
Lissovskii, Madame, 467
Lissovskii, Rear Admiral, commander of Russian naval squadron, 465, 466, 467
Littell's *Laws of Kentucky,* 12
Little Rock, Arkansas, Federal capture of, 479
Locke, David R., 394, 396
Lockwood, Samuel D., 33
Log cabin, as vote-catching symbol, 52-53, 229
Logan, John A., Major-General, 527-528, 528
Logan & Lincoln, law firm of, 67-70. See also Logan, Stephen T.
Logan, Stephen T., 22, 23, 38, 45, 62, 64, 67-70, 91, 98, 104, 106, 117, 120, 122, 124, 126, 127, 149, 152, 159, 169, 217, 229, 335, 472, 588
Logan's Crossroads, Battle of, see Mill Springs, Battle of
Lombard, Robert P., 605
"Long Nine," Lincoln-led Sangamon County members in Illinois Legislature, 44, 45, 70, 85
Longstreet, James, Lieutenant-General, 332, 357, 380, 427, 428, 431, 450, 461, 464
Lookout Mountain, see Chattanooga-Lookout Mountain-Missionary Ridge, Battle of
Loop, James, 66
Lovejoy, Elijah P., 49, 129
Lovejoy, Owen, 120, 177-178, 197, 232, 239, 241, 243
Lowell, James Russell, 337
Ludlum, Cornelius, 134
Lyman, Theodore, Colonel, 386, 403
Lyon, Nathaniel, Colonel, 296

McCall, George A., Major-General, 324
McCallum, Daniel C., Major-General, 453
McClellan, George B., Major-General, 293, 294ff, 304-311, 313, 315-327, 328-333, 338, 345, 347, 351, 352, 353, 355, 355-356, 366, 367, 369, 408, 409, 429, 429-430, 438, 445, 454, 497, 522, 532-533, 533, 536, 537, 541, 544, 545, 546, 548, 549, 559, 572, 596
McClellan, Mrs. George B., 294, 331
McClernand, John A., Congressman, 102; as Major-General, 346, 369, 411, 433, 434-435, 437, 439-440, 450
McClure, Alexander K., 247, 253, 401, 429-430, 509
McConkey, Bob Lincoln's friend, 419

McConnell, H. L., Colonel, 611
McCormick v. Manny et al, case of, 160-163
McCormick, Andrew, 44
McCormick, Cyrus H., 161-163
McCormick, Richard C., 383
McCulloch, Hugh, Secretary of the Treasury under Lincoln, 556, 622, 635, 656
McCullough, Fanny, 402
McCullough, John, 615-616, 616
McCullough, William, Lieutenant-Colonel, 402
McDonald, Joseph E., 546
McDougall, James A., Senator, 343
McDowell, Irvin, Major-General, 289-294, 310, 311, 316, 319, 322, 322-323, 324, 325, 328, 332
McGowan, Theodore, Captain, 638-639, 643
McHattan, Samuel, 42
McKee, William, 446
McLean, John, U.S. Supreme Court Justice, 146, 163, 184, 189, 217, 335
McLean, Wilmer, Major, 602
McManus, Edward, 632
McMichael, Morton, 539
McNamar, John, 80, 81
McPherson, John B., Major-General, 527-528
McPherson, William M., 478
McPike, Henry, 237
Maddox, James, property man at Ford's Theatre, 628
Madison, James, President, 279, 485
Magoffin, Beriah, Governor, 299
Malvern Hill, Battle of, 325, 345, 367, 596, 603
Manassas, First Battle of, see Bull Run, First Battle of
Manassas, Second Battle of, see Bull Run, Second Battle of
Manny, John H., 161-163
"March to the sea," by Sherman and his men through Georgia, 562-565
Margrave, Thomas, 68-69
Marsh, Mathew S., 32
Marshall, Samuel D., 96
Martin, William, 404
Matheny, James, 48, 96, 127
Matson, slave case, 73-76
Matson, Robert, 73-76
Matteson, Joel A., Governor, 179, 180
Matthews, John, 628
Matthews, Stanley, 584
Maximilian, Archduke Ferdinand, 447, 466
May, Dr. John F., 649, 671
May, William L., 64
Meade, George G., Major-General, 386, 403, 424, 429-432, 435, 437, 438, 439, 453, 461, 497, 498, 499, 500, 516, 594
Meade, Mrs. George G., 424
Meade, Rufus, Jr., 564
Mechanicsville, Battle of, 324, 325
Meigs, Montgomery C., Quartermaster General, 296, 297, 310, 326, 396, 653, 658
Medill, 207, 217, 223, 229, 359
Mentelle, Madame Victorie, 86
Meredith, William M., Secretary of the Treasury, 108
Merrill, Samuel, Colonel, 564
Merrimack, Battle of, with *Monitor,* 314, 371
Merryman, Dr. Elias H., 86
Metzker, James, 165-168
Mexico, French intervention in, 437, 446-448, 465-468, 502, 525
Mill Springs, Battle of, 313
Miller, Anson S., Judge, 152
Miller, James, 183
Miller, Robert, 459
Miller, Samuel F., U.S. Supreme Court Justice, 362
Milroy, Robert H., Major-General, 339, 345
Miner, N. W., Reverend, 675
Missionary Ridge, see Chattanoogo-Lookout Mountain-Missionary Ridge, Battle of
Mitchell, Sarah, 3
Mobile Bay, Farragut's victory at, 533, 595
Monitor, battle with *Merrimack,* 314, 371
Montez, Lola, 392
Morgan, Edwin D., as Republican National Chairman, 185; as Governor, 228, 229, 233, 236, 267, 280, 416, 471; as Senator, 508, 512, 513, 517-518, 555-556, 571
Morris, Clara, 608
Morris, Martin S., 18
Morton, Oliver, P., Governor, 280, 349-350, 351, 352, 428, 531, 546-547
Motley, John Lothrop, 388
Mudd, Dr. Samuel A., 654-655, 666, 669, 670
Mullett, B. F., 511
Murfreesboro, Battle of, see Stone's River, Battle of
Musick, Samuel, 42
Muzzy, Mrs. H., 639
Myers, Gustavus A., 580

Napoleon, 195, 409
Napoleon III, 447, 525
"Nasby, Petroleum V.," 547, 629, 651
Nashville, Battle of, 561-562

Neill, Edward D., Reverend, 393, 408
Nelson, Henry A., Reverend, 399
Nevada, admission of, as State of the Union, sponsored by Lincoln, 505-506
Nevins, Allan, Professor, 339
New Ironsides, Admiral DuPont's flagship, 371
New Bern, North Carolina, Federal capture of, 314
New Madris, Missouri, Federal capture of, 313
New Market, Battle of, 501, 503, 594-595
New Salem, Illinois, village of, 19ff
Newell, Robert H., 394
Newell, W. A., Former Governor, 538
Newton, Isaac, Commissioner of Agriculture, 414
Nicholas I, Tsar of Russia, 465
Nicolay, John G., 148, 227, 237, 252, 270, 290-291, 292, 383, 386, 394, 396, 408, 420, 512, 521-522, 604
Norfolk, Virginia, Federal occupation of, 322
Norris, James H., 166-168
North Anna, Battle of, 516
Norton, De Haven, 409
Noyes, William Curtis, 209

Odell, Moses F., Congressman, 307
Offutt, Denton, 16-21, 24, 143, 144
Oglesby, Richard J., 213; as Governor, 629, 651, 658, 674
O'Laughlin, Michael, 612, 615, 616-617, 617, 618, 665, 666
"Old Abe," sobriquet of Lincoln, 408, 408-409, 513, 524, 531, 543
Olden, Charles S., Governor, 280
Oliver, William, 39
Olustee, Florida, Federal defeat at, 482
Opdyke, George, Mayor, 209
Ord, Edward O. C., Major-General, 416, 582
Ord, Mary (Mrs. Edward O. C. Ord), 416-417
O'Sullivan, John P., 288
O'Sullivan, Mrs. John P., 288
Otto, William T., Assistant Secretary of the Interior, 658
Our American Cousin, play at Ford's Theatre seen by Lincoln when shot by Booth, 620, 624, 626, 627, 629-630, 635ff
Owens, Mary, 44, 48, 82-84, 138

"Paine," Lewis (alias), murder accomplice of Booth, see Powell, Lewis Thornton
Paine, Tom, 119
Palmer, John M., 217
Pardons, issued by Lincoln as President, 403-404, 624
Parker, Dr. Charles, 167
Parker, Joel, Governor, 350, 428, 429, 430, 443
Parker, John F., 631, 631-632, 634, 638
Parker, Theodore, 202
Parks, Samuel C., 623-624
Pate, Samuel, Squire, 12
Patterson, Robert, Major-General, 290, 292, 293
Pea Ridge, Arkansas, Battle of, 313, 478
"Peanut John," see Burroughs, Joseph
Peck, Ebenezer, Judge, 510
Peirpoint, Francis H., Governor, see Pierpont, Francis H., Governor
Peirpont, Francis H., Governor, see Pierpont, Francis H., Governor
Pemberton, John, Major-General, 434, 435, 594
Pendel, Thomas F., 631, 632
Pendleton, George H., 544
Peninsular Campaign, 315-327, 345, 348, 366, 603
Pennington, U.S. Secretary of Legation in Paris, 464
People ex. rel Lanphier and Walker v. Hatch, case of, 150
People v. Thomas Delny, rape case of, 169-170
Peter the Great, 466
Petersburg (Virginia), Grant's long siege of, 516, 521, 528, 533, 559, 586, 595, 596, 598, 603
Petersen, William, 649
Petersen, William F., 115
Phelps, John S., Major-General, 475, 478
Phillips, David L., U.S. Marshall in Illinois, 510
Phillips, Wendell, Reverend, 337, 511
Piatt, Donn, 353, 385
Pickens, Andrew W., Governor, 269, 274
Pickens, Fort, problem of, 267, 270, 272
Pickett, George E., Major-General, 431, 560, 598
Pieper, Count, Minister from Sweden, 395
Pierce, Edward L., 484
Pierce, Franklin, President, 118, 175, 176, 187, 188, 193
Pierpoint, Francis H., Governor, see Pierpont, Francis H., Governor
Pierpont, Francis H., Governor, 486-487, 565, 581, 604, 622
Pinkerton, Allan, 254-256
Poe, Edgar Allen, 608
Poe, O. M., 564
Polk, James K., President, 99, 101, 103, 105, 118, 192, 252

Polk, Leonidas, Major-General, 461
Pomeroy Circular, 492-494
Pomeroy, Samuel C., Kansas politician, 231; as Senator, 404, 492-494. See also Pomeroy Circular
Pope, Alexander, 391
Pope, John, Major-General, 152, 294, 313-314, 324-325, 325, 327, 328, 328-329, 330, 332, 339, 345, 346, 396
Pope, Nathaniel, Judge, 152, 324, 325
Porter, Andrew, General, 131
Porter, David D., Lieutenant, U.S.N., 272, 306; as Vice-Admiral, 443, 502, 502-503, 566, 587, 597, 600
Posey, John F., 15, 16
Powell, Lewis Thornton (alias Louis Paine), murder accomplice of Booth, 605, 614-615, 617, 618, 626, 628, 629, 632, 652-653, 656, 665, 666
Powell, Reverend, father of Lewis Thornton Powell, 615
Prentice, George D., 53
Preston, William Ballard, Congressman, 588
Proclamation of Emancipation, 345-346, 347, 350-351, 375, 489, 569, 570
Provost, Mary, 609
Pryor, Roger A., Colonel, 275
Pumphrey, James W., 626, 628

Rabé, William, 231-232
Radford, Reuben, 31
Rafael, inventor of "Rafael Repeater" gun, 389
"Railsplitter," as Lincoln campaign sobriquet, 213, 220, 229
Ramsey, Alexander, Governor, 280
Randall, Alexander W., Governor, 280, 456
Randall, Ruth Painter, biographer of Mrs. Lincoln, 137
Rankin, Henry B., 399
Ranking, James, 404
Rathbone, Henry R., Major, 630, 634, 636, 637, 638, 640, 641, 642-643, 645, 646, 650
Rawley, Dr. James A., 556
Ray, Charles H., 139, 178, 203, 217
Raymond, Henry J., 7, 343, 353, 512, 513, 516, 517, 531, 538-539
"Rebecca" letters, 95, 96
Reconstruction, Lincoln's efforts to "restore" seceded states to the Union, 470-490, 520-521, 529-530, 577-584, 590, 601, 604, 605, 622-623
Rector, Henry M., Governor, 478
Red River, campaign of, and its effects, 468, 502, 503, 516, 595
Reeves, O. T., Judge, 111
Reignolds, Kate, 608-609
Religion, Lincoln's attitude toward, 100-101, 119-120, 591, 593
Remann, Henry, friend of Willie Lincoln, 411
Republican National Convention of 1860, 214-219
Republican National Convention of 1864, 512-514
Republican Party, formed in Illinois, 177-178, 181-183, 191; Lincoln leaves Whig Party and joins Republicans, 181-184, 191
Reynolds, John, Governor, 26-27, 27, 40
Reynolds, John F., Major-General, 426, 430
Rhett, Robert Barnwell, 225
Richardson, William A., Major-General, 314
Richmond, Dean, 226
Rickard, Sarah, 92
Riddle, Albert G., Congressman, 573, 644
Ridgely, Nicholas H., 158
Riney, Zachariah, 6
Roanoke Island (North Carolina), Federal capture of, 314
Robertson, George, 390
Robinson, George T., 653
Roby, Kate, 80
Rollins, Edward H., Congressman, 624
Rollins, James S., Congressman, 569, 572
Romine, John, 11
Roosevelt, Theodore, President, 663
Root, G. W., 675
Rosecrans, William S., Major-General, 352, 353, 355, 368, 378, 437, 448-450, 450, 452, 453, 473-474, 488, 497, 540, 560, 594
Rothschilds, European banking family, 235
Rucker, Major-General, 661
Ruggles, Eleanor, biographer of Edwin Booth, 608
Rupert, Jane Ann, see *People v. Thomas Delny,* rape case of
Rusk, Anson, 170
Russell, William H., 407
Rutherford, Dr. Hiram, 74
Rutledge, Ann, 80-82, 115, 136, 137
Rutledge, James, 80
Rutledge, John M., 19
Rutledge-Lincoln "romance," see Rutledge, Ann
Rutledge, R. B., 24

Sabine Crossroads (Louisiana), Battle of, 502

Sala, George Augustus, 384-385, 386, 396,
Salm-Salm, Princess, 416
"Sampson's Ghost," anonymous political letters by Lincoln, 63
"Sandbar" case, Lincoln as counsel in, 170-171
Sanders, George N., 525
Sanford, Charles A., 643, 665
Santa Ana, General and President of Mexico, 363
Savonarola, 8
Scammon v. Cline, case of, 65-66
Scammon, Jonathan Y., 65-66
Schenck, Robert C., Major-General, 429
Schleiden, Rudolf, 283-284
Schofield, John M., Major-General, 374, 446, 559, 560, 561, 563, 595
Schurz, Carl, 112, 196, 221, 236, 259, 267, 307, 350, 353, 355, 377-378, 453, 501, 527
Scott, Thomas A., Assistant Secretary of War, 310, 311
Scott, Winfield, Lieutenant-General and Chief of Staff, of U.S. Army, 174, 255, 260, 268, 269, 270, 278, 281, 283, 289, 290, 293-295, 306, 366, 497
Scripps, John L., 4, 5, 22, 30, 38, 223-224, 540
Sebastian, William K., Former Senator, 478-479
Seddon, James A., Confederate Secretary of War, 462, 468
Sedgwick, John, Major-General, 380, 381
Selby, Paul, 181-182
Seven Days' Battle, 325, 345
Seven Pines, Battle of, 323-324, 324
Seward, Augustus, Major, 653
Seward, Frances (Fanny), 653
Seward, Frederick W., 107, 254, 255; as Assistant Secretary of State under father, 359, 620, 622-623, 623, 652-653, 656, 666
Seward, William H., 12; as Former Governor, 107; as Senator, 203, 205, 206, 207, 208, 209, 210, 211, 212, 217, 218, 219, 241, 243, 244, 246, 249, 253, 254, 255, 257, 258, 259; as Secretary of State under Lincoln, 259-260, 267, 268, 269, 270-272, 272-273, 274, 283-284, 287, 288, 290-291, 306, 345, 346, 349, 354, 358-361, 387, 393, 394, 447, 453, 456, 458, 466, 467, 472-473, 502, 503, 509, 517, 519, 524, 529, 531, 537-538, 541, 543, 550, 574, 575, 588, 598, 601, 603-604, 620, 630-631, 632, 652-653, 656, 665, 666
Seymour, Horatio, New York Democratic leader, 234, 350, 377; as Governor, 437, 441-442, 442-444, 450, 455, 456, 513, 548
Shakespeare, William, 112, 390, 391, 392, 417, 613
Sharpsburg, Battle of, 331
Shaw, Benjamin F., 117
Shearer, Mrs. John Henry, 416
Shepley, George F., Major-General, 475, 476, 477
Sheridan, Philip H., Major-General, 461, 462, 468, 469, 499, 542, 543, 543-544, 595, 598, 601
Sherman, William T., Major-General, 366, 370, 434, 452, 453-454, 461, 462, 464, 468, 469, 498, 502, 516, 527, 528, 529, 533, 534, 535, 536, 542, 544, 546, 547, 548, 559, 560-561, 562-565, 586, 589, 595, 597-600, 603, 620, 621, 622
Shields, James, Auditor of Illinois, 87-88, 95-96; as Senator, 179; as Major-General, 323, 339, 345
Shiloh, Battle of, 314
Short, Luther, 409
Short, Samuel, 168-169
Shutes, Dr. Milton, 649
Sickles, Daniel E., Major-General, 415, 416
Sigel, Franz, Major-General, 378, 456, 498-499, 500, 501, 503, 594-595
Simpson, Matthew, Bishop, 556-557, 667, 672, 675-676
Slavery, Lincoln's views on, 73-76, 102, 106, 107, 174-186, 190, 193-201, 204, 210, 211, 228, 242-243, 219, 259-260, 261, 299-302, 304, 311, 334-347, 394, 398, 479-480, 488, 520-521, 526-527, 569-576, 587-588
Slidell, John, Confederate commissioner in France, 579
Smith, Alexander, 631
Smith, Caleb B., Indiana politician, 217, 244-245, 246, 249, 257, 258, 259; as Secretary of the Interior under Lincoln, 267, 289, 359, 361-362, 362-363
Smith, Clark M., 139
Smith, Goldwin, Professor, 385
Smith, James, Reverend, 120
Smith, James Y., Governor, 428
"Smith, John," 407
Smith, Truman, Congressman, 588
Smith, William F., Major-General, 438-439
Smoot, Coleman, 39
South Mountain, Battle of, 330, 367
Spangler, Edman (Edward), 627, 628, 637, 665, 666
Speed, James, Attorney General under Lincoln and brother of Joshua F. Speed, 479, 511, 555, 604, 605, 622, 623, 624
Speed, Joshua Fry, 12, 46, 48, 54, 69, 70, 85, 88, 90, 91, 92, 93-94, 117, 121, 125, 125-126, 304, 312-313, 335, 363, 382, 403, 472, 511, 555, 593
Speed, Mary, 93

Speer, William S., 228
Spottsylvania, Battle of, 516
Sprague, William, Governor, 280
Sprigg, Mrs. Ann, 103, 104, 134
Stanly, Edward, Military Governor, 483-485
Stanton, Edwin M., counsel in *McCormick v. Manny et al* case, insults associate counsel, Lincoln, 161; as Secretary of War under Lincoln, 313, 318, 320, 321, 322, 324, 329, 345, 351, 352-353, 354, 364-365, 368, 376, 389, 417, 421, 434, 442, 448, 452, 453, 454, 456, 481, 483, 503-504, 546, 550, 559, 560, 566, 587, 598, 622, 624, 630, 651, 656-657, 658, 659, 661, 669, 671, 675
Staples, Dr. Thomas S., 479
Stedman, Fort, Battle of, 596-597
Steele, Frederick, Major-General, 478
Steinwehr, von, Adolph, Major-General, 453
Stephens, Alexander H., Congressman, 104-105, 199; as Confederate Vice-President, 283-284, 335, 404-405, 469, 472, 574, 588, 594
Stephens, John A., Lieutenant, 404-405
Stevens, Thaddeus, Pennsylvania politician, 106; as Congressman, 404, 541
Stewart, Joseph B., 641, 643-645
Stimmel, Smith, 620
Stoddard, William O., 408
Stoeckl, Baron Eduard de, Minister from Russia, 466, 578
Stone, Charles P., Colonel, 254, 255; as Brigadier-General, 302, 303, 304
Stone, Dan, 44
Stone, Dr. Robert King, 647, 649, 659, 660-661, 663
Stone's River, Battle of, 368, 369
Stoneman, George, Major-General, 380-381
Story, Joseph, U.S. Supreme Court Justice, 60
Stowe, Mrs. Harriet Beecher, 70, 593
Strong, George Templeton, 667
Stuart, J. E. B. ("Jeb"), 327, 427, 430, 485
Stuart, John T., 38, 39, 41, 42, 43, 46, 49, 50, 53, 55, 60-67, 76, 87, 90-91, 114, 115, 120, 122, 126, 137, 159, 335, 350, 472, 662
Stuart, Mrs. John T., 39
Stuart & Lincoln, law firm of, 60-67. See also Stuart, John T.
Summers, George W., 273
Sumner, Charles, Senator, 182, 243, 304, 312, 375, 393, 483-484, 487, 570, 578, 583, 592, 633, 651, 658
Sumner, Edwin V., Major-General, 316, 319
Sumter, Fort, problem of, in secession crisis, 267-276
Sumter, Fort, unsuccessful Federal attempt to capture, in 1863, 371-372
Surratt, John H., 614, 615, 616, 617, 618, 665, 666
Surratt, Mrs. Mary E., 665, 665-666
Swaney, James, 10
Swann, Thomas, Governor, 522
Swayne, Noah H., U.S. Supreme Court Justice, 362
Sweney, Harvey, 458
Swett, Leonard, 124, 126, 156, 170, 217, 335, 350, 362
Swisshelm, Mrs. Jane Grey, 393-394

Taft, Dr. Charles Sabin, 636, 648, 649, 663
Talisman, voyage of, along Sangamon River, 24-25, 70
Taltavull, Peter, 637
Taney, Roger B., U.S. Supreme Court Chief Justice, 146, 189, 193, 264, 519, 550
Tanner, James, 657-658
Tarbell, Ida M., 422
Taylor, Bayard, 467
Taylor, Benjamin F., 463
Taylor, Hawkins, 212, 362
Taylor, James, 12
Taylor, "Governor" Marble Nash, 482
Taylor, Richard (Dick), Major-General, 502, 562
Taylor, Tom, 620, 624
Taylor, Zachary, General and President, 23, 28, 102, 105-110, 115, 135, 145, 174, 188, 221, 252, 366, 502, 562, 588
Tell, William, 669
"Ten per cent plan," Lincoln's proposal on reconstruction, 488, 489, 577, 583
Terry, Alfred H., Major-General, 595
Thanksgiving Day, Lincoln's Proclamation for, in 1863, 463-464. See also Hale, Sarah Josepha
Thayer, Eli, 480-481
Thirteenth Amendment to U.S. Constitution (for abolishing slavery), Lincoln's support of, 571, 572-573, 573-574
Thomas v. Heirs of Broadwell, case of, 65
Thomas, Edward M., 344
Thomas, George H., Major-General, ("Rock of Chickamauga"), 366, 453-454, 461, 462, 468, 469, 528, 549, 559, 560-562, 563, 565, 586, 595
Thomas, Jesse B., 55
Thompson, Jacob, Confederate agent, 526, 630
Thompson, Richard W., 510
Thompson, Samuel, Colonel, 29
Tilton, E. L., 609
Tilton, Lucius, 249, 672

Tod, David, Governor, 351, 428, 445
Todd, Alec, 412, 415
Todd, Anna Maria, 139
Todd, Dr. Beecher, 649
Todd, David, 412
Todd, David, Judge, 88
Todd, Mrs. Eliza (Betsey) Parker (Mrs. Robert S. Todd), stepmother of Mary Todd Lincoln, 86, 99, 102, 132
Todd, Elizabeth, see Edwards, Mrs. Ninian W.
Todd, George, 412
Todd, John B. S., Major-General, 658
Todd, Levi, Major-General, 132
Todd, Mary Ann, see Lincoln, Mary Todd (Mrs. Abraham Lincoln)
Todd, Robert Smith, father of Mary Todd Lincoln, 86, 102, 104, 108, 133
Todd, Sam, 412
Toombs, Robert, 594
Townsend, George Alfred, 637-638, 639, 664
Trailor, Archibald, 69-70
Trailor, Henry, 69-70
Trailor, William, 69-70
Treat, Samuel, Judge, 74, 75, 152, 191
Trent, Alexander, 22
Truett, Henry B., 64, 165
Truett, murder case of, see Truett, Henry B.
Truman, Helen, see Coleman, Helen
Trumbull, Lyman, 87-88; as Congressman, 176; elected Senator, 179-180; as Senator, 182, 192, 193, 194, 195, 197, 203, 204, 205, 208, 211, 212, 217, 237, 242, 245, 246, 247, 248, 301, 305, 337, 341, 352, 412, 456, 537, 570-571
Tuck, Amos, 248
Tullock, Thomas L., 508
Tuttle, B. F., 510-511
Twilley, Benjamin F., 624
Tyler, John, President, 52, 53

Upton, Emory, Colonel, 323
Usher, John P., Secretary of the Interior under Lincoln, 363, 405, 555, 556, 557, 576, 577

Vallandigham, Clement L., "Copperhead" Congressman, 349, 375-376, 445, 454, 532; as Former Congressman, 544
Van Alen, James H., 584, 619, 630
Van Buren, Martin, President, 52, 53, 55, 89, 90, 106, 192, 246
Van Dorn, Earl, Major-General, 478
Van Duzer, J. C., Major-General, 562
Van Dyke, John, Congressman, 184
Van Tynes, Mrs., Washington landlady, 616
Vance, Zebulon B., Governor, 443, 469, 597
Vicksburg, Grant's capture of, 433-435, 468, 497, 594
Villard, Henry, 116, 357
Vineyard, Jesse, 83
Virginia, Confederate ironclad warship, see *Merrimack*
Voltaire, François Marie Arouet de, 119
Voting, by Negroes, Lincoln's views on, 575-576, 578, 583, 584. See Lincoln-Douglas debates

Wade, Benjamin F., Senator, 243, 258, 266, 305-306, 307, 308, 320, 325, 359, 488-490, 519-521, 529-530, 540, 541, 543, 554, 578. See also Wade-Davis Manifesto and Wade-Davis reconstruction bill
Wade-Davis Manifesto, 529-530, 540, 553
Wade-Davis reconstruction bill, 489-490, 520-521, 570, 577
Wadsworth, James S., Brigadier-General, 340, 349, 350, 441
Wakeman, Abram, Postmaster, 509, 537, 538
Walborn, Cornelius, Postmaster, 510, 539-540
Walch, Henry F., 657
Waldron, Henry, Congressman, 257
Walker, Cyrus, 64
Walker, Leroy P., Confederate Secretary of War, 274
Wallace, Edward, 207
Wallace, Lew, Major-General, 521
Wallace, William H. L., 287-288
Wallace, Dr. William S., 132
Wallace, Mrs. William S. (formerly Frances Todd), 140
"Ward, Artemus," see Browne, Charles Farrar
Ward, James, 165
Warren, Gouverneur K., Major-General, 431, 598
Warren, Dr. Louis A., 4
Warwick, Charles, 612
Washburn, Israel, Jr., Governor, 279
Washburne, Elihu B., 55, 178, 179, 204, 242, 363, 491, 497, 497-498, 530, 531, 582
Washington, George, General and President, 10-11, 250, 266, 279, 397, 466, 473, 485, 668
Watkins, Nelson, 167
Watson, Peter H., 161-162
Webb, Edwin B., 91, 92
Webb, William B., Washington Police Superintendent, 631, 632

Webber, Thompson R., 158-159
Webster, Daniel, 52, 91
Weed, Thurlow, 107, 218, 229, 236, 288, 349, 395, 471, 509, 516, 517, 524, 531, 537-538, 538, 555, 558, 593
Weems, Parson, 10-11
Weik, Jesse W., 81
Weitzel, Godfrey, Major-General, 580-582, 600, 601
Welles, Edgar, 662
Welles, Gideon, Secretary of the Navy under Lincoln, 241, 248-249, 257, 258, 259, 268, 272, 329, 345, 354, 372, 394, 417, 454, 466, 467, 481, 486, 493, 498, 508, 519-520, 552-554, 622, 651, 652
Welles, Mrs. Gideon, 87, 414
Wentworth, "Long John," Mayor, 214
West Virginia, Lincoln's attitude on its admission as State of the Union in 1863, 486-487, 505
Westfall, John W., 615
Wheeler, "Fightin' Joe," Major-General, 535
Whiteside, Samuel, Major-General, 27, 29
Whiting, William, War Department Solicitor, 511
Whitman, Walt, 386, 592, 593, 635
Whitney, Henry C., 113, 114, 123, 124, 126, 147, 148, 202
Wickliffe, Robert, 135
Wilderness, Battle of, 500, 516, 521, 594, 603
Wilkes, John, Captain, 497
Wilkeson, Sam, 360
Willey, Whitman T., Senator, 486
Williams, Alpheus S., Major-General, 453
Williams, T. Harry, Professor, 325
Williamson, William, 152
Wills, David, 457, 458
Wilmington, North Carolina, Federal capture of, 567, 595
Wilmot, David, Congressman, 210
Wilmot Proviso, 108
Wilson, Henry, Senator, 286, 456
Wilson, James H., Major-General, 560
Wilson, Robert L., 44
Winchell, J. M., 492, 494. See also Pomeroy Circular
Winchester, Virginia, Sheridan's victory at, 542, 543
Winthrop, Robert C., Speaker of Congress, 103, 106; as Former Congressman, 538
Wise, George D., 663
Withers, William, 634
Wood, Fernando, Mayor, 226, 239, 376-377, 537
Wood, Thomas J., Major-General, 462-463
"Wooden guns," *camouflage* of Confederates, 319-320
Woodward, George W., Judge, 454, 454-455, 455
Woodward, Dr., physician, 660
Wool, John E., Brigadier-General (later Major-General), 321, 322, 324, 417
Worden, John L., Lieutenant, U.S.N., see *Monitor*
Wren, Aquilla, 70
Wren, Clarissa, 70
Wright, Erastus, 18
Wright, Horatio G., Major-General, 523-524
Wyant, Isaac, 170

Yancey, William L., 225, 226
Yater, James L., Collector, 511
Yates, Richard, Congressman, 176, 181; as gubernatorial candidate, 232; as Governor, 280, 351, 352, 395, 428, 439, 456
Young, John Russell, 458

Zane, John M., 169